SUMMARY CONTENTS

PART ONE: CRIMINAL LAW
Keith Smith   1

PART TWO: STATUTES, SOCIAL REFORM,
AND CONTROL
Raymond Cocks   465

PART THREE: LABOUR LAW
William Cornish   621

PART FOUR: LAW OF PERSONS: FAMILY AND
OTHER RELATIONSHIPS
William Cornish   721

PART FIVE: PERSONALITY RIGHTS AND
INTELLECTUAL PROPERTY
William Cornish   845

TABLE OF CONTENTS

Abbreviations   xv
Table of Cases   xix
Table of Statutes   xlvii

PART ONE: CRIMINAL LAW   *Keith Smith*

I.   **General Introduction and Overview**   3

      Introduction   3
      Overview   18

II.   **Stumbling Towards Professionalism: The Establishment**
      of English Policing in the Nineteenth Century   21

      1. London   21
      2. The Provinces   36
      3. Accountability and Expanding Capabilities   44
      4. Conclusions   56

III. **The Trial: Adversarial Characteristics and Responsibilities;**
      Pre-trial and Trial Procedures   58

      1. Prosecution   58
      2. Defence   71
      3. Regulating the Trial: Criminal Evidence: Refining and
         Formalising its Exclusionary and Protective Emphasis   83
      4. Forms of Trial: The Rise of Summary Trial
         and Decline in Jury Trial   115

IV.   **Sentencing and Review**   122

      1. Sentencing: Curbing Judicial Discretion   122
      2. Appeals and Executive Review   128

V.   **Punishment: Death and Transfiguration**   138

      1. The Capital Question   138
      2. Prisons, Transportation, and Institutional Detention   154

VI. The Sources and Form of the Criminal Law: The Medium of Change
and Development: Consolidation or Codification? 180

1. Sources of The Criminal Law 180
2. The Criminal Law's Form: Codification: Shimmering
Vista or Threatening Spectre? 187

VII. General Principles of Criminal Law 217

1. General Principles of Criminal Fault and Defences 217
2. Punishing Preparatory Activities and Assistance:
Complicity and Inchoate Liability 282

VIII. Excluding Fault from Criminal Responsibility: Strict and
Vicarious Liability: Quasi-criminal or Regulatory Offences? 321

1. Strict Liability 322
2. Deducing Parliament's Will 328
3. Vicarious Responsibility 330
4. Overview 332

IX. Securing the State, the Institutions of Government,
and Maintaining Public Order 334

1. Offences Against the State, Government, and its Institutions:
Sedition, Treason, and Secrets 334
2. Offences Against Public Order: Unlawful Assembly and Riot 344

X. Public Morality and Social Control: Prostitution,
Gambling, and Obscenity 352

1. Prostitution 355
2. Gambling 359
3. Obscenity 363

XI. Protecting Property from Dishonesty and Harm:
Larceny and Malicious Damage 374

1. The Expanding Concept of Larceny 374
2. Malicious Damage 388

XII. Offences Against the Person 392

1. Non-Fatal Assaults and Woundings 393
2. Sexual Offences 401
3. Homicide 409

The Oxford History of the Laws of England

THE OXFORD HISTORY OF THE LAWS OF ENGLAND

General Editor: Sir John Baker, Q.C., LL.D., F.B.A., Downing Professor of the Laws of England, and Fellow of St Catharine's College, Cambridge

The Oxford History of the Laws of England will provide a detailed survey of the development of English law and its institutions from the earliest times until the twentieth century, drawing heavily upon recent research using unpublished materials.

Volume I: The Canon Law and Ecclesiastical
Jurisdiction from 597 to the 1640s   Helmholz
ISBN 0–19–825897–6

Volume II: *c.* 900–1216   Hudson
ISBN 0–19–826030–x

Volume III: 1216–1307   Brand
ISBN 0–19–826866–6

Volume IV: 1307–1377   Donahue
ISBN 0–19–926951–3

Volume V: 1399–1483
ISBN 0–19–926599–2

Volume VI: 1483–1558   Baker
ISBN 0–19–825817–8

Volume VII: 1558–1625   Ibbetson
ISBN 0–19–825802–x

Volume VIII: 1625–1689   Brooks
ISBN 0–19–826031–8

Volume IX: 1689–1760
ISBN 0–19–826100–4

Volume X: 1760–1820   Oldham
ISBN 0–19–826494–1

Volume XI: 1820–1914   English Legal System
Cornish, Anderson, Cocks, Lobban, Polden, and Smith
ISBN 978–0–19–9258819

Volume XII: 1820–1914   Private Law
Cornish, Anderson, Cocks, Lobban, Polden, and Smith
ISBN 978–0–19–9258826

Volume XIII: 1820–1914   Fields of Development
Cornish, Anderson, Cocks, Lobban, Polden, and Smith
ISBN 978–0–19–9239757

(Three volume set of Volumes XI, XII, and XIII: ISBN 978–0–19–9258833)

The Oxford History of the Laws of England

VOLUME XIII

1820–1914

Fields of Development

OXFORD

UNIVERSITY PRESS

OXFORD
UNIVERSITY PRESS

Great Clarendon Street, Oxford OX2 6DP

Oxford University Press is a department of the University of Oxford.
It furthers the University's objective of excellence in research, scholarship,
and education by publishing worldwide in

Oxford New York

Auckland Cape Town Dar es Salaam Hong Kong Karachi
Kuala Lumpur Madrid Melbourne Mexico City Nairobi
New Delhi Shanghai Taipei Toronto

With offices in

Argentina Austria Brazil Chile Czech Republic France Greece
Guatemala Hungary Italy Japan Poland Portugal Singapore
South Korea Switzerland Thailand Turkey Ukraine Vietnam

Oxford is a registered trade mark of Oxford University Press
in the UK and in certain other countries

Published in the United States
by Oxford University Press Inc., New York

First published 2010

British Library Cataloguing in Publication Data

Data available

Library of Congress Cataloging in Publication Data

Data available

Typeset by Newgen Imaging Systems Pvt Ltd., Chennai, India
Printed in Great Britain
on acid-free paper by
Antony Rowe, Chippenham, Wiltshire

ISBN 978-0-19-9239757

1 3 5 7 9 10 8 6 4 2

PART TWO: STATUTES, SOCIAL REFORM,
AND CONTROL   *Raymond Cocks*

I.   Introduction: 'Legislation the Only Remedy'   467

II.   The Poor Law   473

      1. The 'Old' Poor Law   473
      2. The Nineteenth-Century Disputes   476
      3. The Royal Commissioners   478
      4. Parliament and the Balance of Power   481
      5. A Factory for the Making of Unpopular Rules   484
      6. The Proliferation of Legal Issues   488
      7. Controlling the Machinery of the Poor Law   496
      8. Rivals to the Principles of 1834   499
      9. The Failure of the Law   502
      10. New Dimensions: Pensions and National Insurance   504

III. Charity and Education   507

      1. Charity   507
      2. The Public Scrutiny of Charitable Trusts   510
      3. Education   517
      4. 'A Sum, Not Exceeding Twenty Thousand Pounds'   520
      5. 'Parliament Should Guarantee to Every Child an Education'   525
      6. National Expectations and University Autonomy   529
      7. Secondary Education   531

IV.   Health for the Public   535

      1. Poverty, Health, and the Law   535
      2. 'The Poor Man's Measure'   542
      3. Scientific Expertise   543
      4. Incremental Reform   546
      5. Public Health Laws in Combination: Legal Sophistication
         and the Persistence of Stench   553

V.   Safety in Factories, Shops, and Ships   558

      1. The Poor in the Work-place   558
      2. 'Deforming the Limbs of Children' or 'Puffing Humanity'?   562
      3. The Extension of Controls over Working Conditions   563
      4. Beyond the Factory Gate: 'Legislation the Only Remedy'   567

5. Safety on Ships: The 'Plimsoll-Line'   571
6. '…One of the Most Difficult and Vexed Questions…'   577

VI.   **Building Houses and Planning Communities**   580

1. Private Ownership and Social Need   580
2. The Public Dimension   583
3. Planning Law   590

VII. **Conclusion**   598

1. A. V. Dicey and Reforming Statutes   598
2. O. MacDonagh and Reforming Statutes   606
3. Expertise and the Making of Statutes   610
4. Explaining the Reforming Legislation   615

PART THREE: LABOUR LAW   *William Cornish*

I.   **From Labouring to Employment: 1820–1867**   623

1. Work for oneself, Work for Others: The Traditions   625
2. Theories of Labour   629
3. Free Bargaining and Enforced Obligation   633

II.   **The Roots of Collective Action**   650

1. The Condition of Labour   650
2. Criminal Discipline   651
3. Combination Under the 1825 Act   657

III. **Law and Organised Labour 1867–1914**   667

1. Political Concessions and Constraints on Labour:
   The Erle Commission   667
2. Trade Union Legislation in the Wake of
   The Royal Commission   670
3. Collective Bargaining as the Aim of Labour Relations   679
4. Employment Without Criminal Sanctions   681
5. Politics of Employment in the 1890s   686
6. Judges vs Unions   692
7. Putting Paid to Judicial Antipathy   702
8. Governance Within the Union: Further Legal Attacks   708
9. Legislative Support for Better Conditions   715
10. Conclusion   718

PART FOUR: LAW OF PERSONS: FAMILY
AND OTHER RELATIONSHIPS *William Cornish*

I. Family Law, Family Authority 723
   1. Introduction 723
   2. Courts Used for Family Disputes 724
   3. Private and Public Obligation 726
   4. The Husband as Patriarch 729
   5. Dominance and Dutiful Submission 730
   6. Property During a Marriage and After
      the Death of One Spouse 735
   7. Male Attitudes to the Opposite Sex 744

II. Marriage 747
   1. The Values of Marriage 747
   2. Capacity to Marry and Nullification 748
   3. Familial Relationship: The Prohibited Degrees 749
   4. Pre-Contracts and Religious Ceremony 751
   5. The Established Church and the Public Record 755

III. Wives: The Quest for Civil Independence 757
   1. The Struggle for Legislation 758
   2. Partial Victory 760
   3. The Victorian Settlement 761

IV. Marital Breakdown: Separation and the Coming
    of Judicial Divorce 767
   1. Ecclesiastical Jurisdiction: Restitution and Separation 767
   2. Separation by Agreement 769
   3. Informal Arrangements to Separate: Divorce by
      Local Custom and by Wife Sales 774
   4. The Poor Law and Desertion 776
   5. Full Divorce by Private Act of Parliament 777
   6. Campaign for a Divorce Court 781
   7. Judicial Divorce *a vinculo* in Action 784
   8. Violence and Desertion among Ordinary People 796

V. Children 802
   1. The Wedlock-born and the Bastard 802

        2. Capacity in Civil Law   806
        3. Legitimate Children: The Governance of the Father   807
        4. Endangered Children: Plights and Rescues   814
        5. Jurisdiction over Children   819

VI.   **Insanity and Mental Deficiency**   823

        1. Introduction   823
        2. Legal Obligations and the Mentally Disturbed or Deficient 824
        3. Detention and Release   827

VII. **Foreign Elements in Family Disputes**   835

        1. Domicil   836
        2. Marriage and Divorce   838
        3. Family Governance: Children   842

PART FIVE: PERSONALITY RIGHTS AND
INTELLECTUAL PROPERTY   *William Cornish*

I.   **Personal Reputation, Privacy, and Intellectual Creativity**   847

        1. Defamation of Character   852
        2. Libel as Against Slander   857
        3. The Communication and 'malice'   858
        4. Secondary Liability   866
        5. Limits to Liability   868

II.   **Copyright**   879

        1. Print and its Purveyors: Demands for a 'Copy' Right   879
        2. The Legal Sources of Copyright   881
        3. Justifications and the Evolving Law   884
        4. The Victorian Debates: Of Duration and Other Basic Concepts 886
        5. New Subject-matter   889
        6. Authorship and Entitlement   893
        7. Infringing Acts   896
        8. The Overall Direction of Victorian Copyright Law   907
        9. Foreign Relations   908
       10. Implementation of the Berlin Act and the Establishment
           of Imperial Copyright   924

III. **Industrial Property: Patents for Inventions** 931

    1. Origin and Essence of a Patent System 932
    2. Terms of the Royal Grant 934
    3. Justifying the Patent System 936
    4. The Long Course to a Patent Grant 942
    5. Developing the Substantive Law 943
    6. Specifications and their Drafting 949
    7. Application and Grant: Administrative Reform 951
    8. A New Openness 953
    9. Abolition or International Solidarity? 956
    10. The Paris Industrial Property Convention of 1883 961
    11. The National System from 1883 963
    12. Patentee and Competitors: The Balancing Criteria 964
    13. Exploitations of Patented Technology 972

IV. **Industrial Property: Designs for Products** 978

    1. The Designs Register: Appearance and Function 978
    2. Cumulation of Intellectual Properties 982

V. **Trade Secrets and Other Confidences** 984

    1. The Innominate Equity Against Breach of Confidence 984
    2. Contract Express or Implied 987

VI. **Industrial Property: Trade Marks and Unfair Competition** 990

    1. Public and Private Control of Marketing Practices 990
    2. The Common Law Action Against 'Passing, Palming,
       or Putting Off' 991
    3. A Register of Trade Marks 998
    4. Trade Marks in International Trade 1007
    5. Passing Off as an Adjunct of Trade Mark Registration 1008
    6. Envoi 1013

Further Reading 1015
Index of Names 1033
Index of Subjects 1053

ABBREVIATIONS

Statutes of UK Parliament: the regnal year is included in a first citation of a statute until 1853. Then the modern series published by HM Stationery Office begins, the annual volumes having reliable indices.

Law Reports: Abbreviations of series of Law Reports are not listed here. The names of nominate series follow standard practice for the nineteenth and twentieth centuries as listed in Halsbury's *Laws of England* (4th aand 5th eds, 2009), Consolidated Tables, Cases A–L pp. xi–xlvi. Further assistance may be found in C. W. Ringrose (ed.), *Where to Look for your Law* (14th edn, 1962) and also within D. Raistrick's very thorough *Index of Legal Citations and Abbreviations* (3rd edn, 2008).

AJLH	American Journal of Legal History
Am J. Comp. Law	American Journal of Comparative Law
Am. J. Int. Law	American Journal of International Law
Am. Soc. Of Int. Law	American Society of International Law
Anglo-Am. Law Rev.	Anglo-American Law Review
App.	Appendix
Att.-Gen.	Attorney-General
B.	Baron of the Exchequer
Bt	Baronet
BIHR	Bulletin of the Institute of Historical Research
Bl. Comm.	Blackstone's Commentaries on the Laws of England
BYIL	British Yearbook of International Law
CB	Chief Baron
CCC	County Courts Chronicle
CFLQ	Child and Family Law Quarterly
Ch. Chs	Chapter, Chapters
CJCP	Chief Justice of Common Pleas
CJK(Q)B	Chief Justic of King's (Queen's) Bench
CLE	Council for Legal Education
CLJ	Cambridge Law Journal
CLP	Current Legal Problems
Con. and Ch.	Continuity and Change
Cornhill Mag.	Cornhill Magazine
Crim. Law Rev.	Criminal Law Review*JEH* *Journal of Economic History*
DC	Departmental Committee

DNB	Dictionary of National Biography
East P. C.	East, Pleas of the Crown
Econ. Hist. Rev.	Economic History Review
Edinburgh Rev.	Edinburgh Review
EHR	English Historical Review
Hale H.P.C	Hale, History of the Please of the Crown
Hawk P. C.	Hawkins, Pleas of the Crown
Hist. J.	Historical Journal
Hist. St. Ind. Rels	Historical Studies in Industrial Relations
Holdsworth, HEL	Sir W.S. Holdsworth, History of English Law
ICLQ	International and Comparative Law Review
ILS	Independent Law Society
Int. Rev. Soc. Hist.	International Review of Social History
J., JJ.	Justice, Justices
JBS	Journal of British Studies
JEH	Journal of Economic History
J. Hist. Geography	Journal of Historical Geography
J. Hist. Ideas	Journal of the History of Ideas
J. Hist. Int. L.	Journal of the History of International Law
JL & E	Journal of Law and Economics
JLH	Journal of Legal History
JLS	Journal of Legal Studies
JPOS	Journal of the Patent Office Society
JPTOS	Journal of the Patent and Trade Mark Office Society
JP	Justice of the Peace
JR	Juridical Review
J. Soc. Hist.	Journal of Social History
JSPTL	Journal of the Society of Public Teachers of Law
KC	King's Counsel
LAS	Law Amendment Society
LC	Lord Chancellor
LCO	Lord Lord Chancellor's Office
Leg. Ob.	Legal Observer
LG	Law Gazette
LJ, LJJ	Lord Justice, Lord Justices
LHR	Law and History Review
LJ	Law Journal

LM	Law Magazine
LN	Legal Notes
LQR	Law Quarterly Review
LR	Law Reporter
LS	Legal Studies
LT	Law Times (journal)
MLR	Modern Law Review
MPLA	Metropolitan and Provincial Law Association
MR	Master of the Rolls
NA	The National Archives
NILQ	Northern Ireland Legal Quarterly
19C Fict.	Nineteenth-century Fiction
ODNB	Oxford Dictionary of National Biography
OED	Oxford English Dictionary
OJLS	Oxford Journal of Legal Studies
P &P	Past and Present
para., paras	Paragraph, paragraphs
PDA	Probate, Divorce and Admiralty Division (High Court)
PRO	Public Record Office
QC	Queen's Counsel
Quart. Rev.	Quarterly Review
RC	Royal Commission
SC	Select Committee
Sjt	Serjeant
Sol.-Gen.	Solicitor-General
SJ	Solicitors Journal
SLT	Scots Law Times
SPAL	Society for Promotion of the Amendment of the Law (?)
State Tr.	State Trials
TNAPSS	Transactions of the National Association for the Promotion of Social Science
TRHS	Transactions of the Royal Historical Society
VC	Vice-Chancellor
VCH	Victoria County History
Vict. St.	Victorian Studies
West. Rev.	Westminster Review
YLJ	Yale Law Journal

TABLE OF CASES

Note: Criminal prosecutions are indexed under the defendant's name.

Abernethy v. Hutchinson (1825)..898, 899, 923
Abramovitch (1914) 110
Adam v. Ward (1917)...870, 877
Agar-Ellis (No. 1), Re (1878) 812
Agar-Ellis (No. 2), Re (1883) 812
Aguilar v. Aguilar (1820)...743
Ahler (1915)..340
Aitken v. ACJ Scotland (1885)...710
Aldred (1909)..337
Alexander (1913) 424
Allchorn v. Hopkins (1905)..332
Allen (1835)..459
Allen (1872) 408
Allen v. Flood (1898)...696, 698, 707
Allen v. Rawson (1845) 973
Almon (1770) 321
Amalgamated Society of Railway Servants v. Osborne (No. 1) (1910)................710, 713, 714
Ampthill Peerage Case (1977)...805
Anderson (1816)...431
Anderson v. Anderson (1822) 741
Anderson v. Gorrie (1894)...874
Andrews v. DPP [1937] 446
Archard v. Hornor 646
Armytage v. AG (1906)..841
Armytage v. Armytage (1898)...841
Arnold (1838) 93
Arnold's Case (1731) 235
Ashover v. Brampton (1777) 646
Ashwell..383, 384
Aslatt v. Corporation of Southampton (1880) 865
Aspdin v. Austria (1844) 639
Aspinall (1876)...416
Atcheson v. Everitt (1775)..375
Attorney General v. Birmingham Tame and Rea District Drainage Board (1908)...............556
Attorney General v. Bovill (1840) 508
Attorney General v. Clarendon (Earl) (1810) 518
Attorney General v. Council of the Borough of Birmingham (1858–1895).......................554
Attorney General v. Exeter Corp (1827) 508
Attorney General v. Exeter Corp (1828) 508
Attorney General v. Ironmongers' Co (1834)...509
Attorney General v. Lonsdale (1827) 510
Attorney General v. Whelan...279
Attorney General v. Whelan (1934)..279
Attorney General v. Whiteley (1805)...517
Attorney General v. Wilkinson (1839)..508

Attorney-General v. Lockwood (1842) 323
Atwood and Robbins (1788) 87
Australian Wine Importers' Trade Mark, Re (1889)....................................1003
Avards v. Dance (1862)...331
Ayes (1810) 423
Aylesford Peerage case (1885) 805
Ayling v. London and India Docks Committee (1893)................................. 687
Ayre v. Craven (1834) 856, 858

Bach v. Longman (1777)..882, 912
Badische Analin v. Isler (1906)..975
Badische Analin v. Usines de Rhone (1898)... 968
Bailey (1867)... 695
Bailey and Collier, Re (1854)... 640
Bailey v. Pye...698
Baldry (1852) 95, 97
Baldwin v. Society for Diffusion of Useful Knowledge (1838) 647
Balfour v. Balfour (1919)..729, 765
Ball (1808)..91
Ball (1911) 137
Ball v. Ball (1827)...810
Bank of New South Wales v. Piper (1879)..282
Banks v. Goodfellow (1870).. 824
Barnard (1823) 87
Barnardo (1889)...819
Barnardo (1891) 819
Barnardo v. Ford (1892)...819
Barnardo v. McHugh (1891) 819
Barrack v. McCulloch (1856)...757
Barrett (1846).. 443
Barronet (1852) 429
Barrow (1868)... 404
Barthelemy (1852)... 429
Barton (1848) 244
Barton v. Briscoe (1822)..741
Barwell v. Brooks (1784).. 770
Baskerville (1916) 88
Bateman v. Ross (Countess) (1813)...771
Batstone (1864)... 390
Batting v. Bristol and Exeter Railway Co (1861) 324
Batty v. Hill (1863)..1011
Bauld (1876) 678, 695
Bayer's Design, Re (1907)... 980
Baylis v. Baylis (1867)...792
Bazeley (1799)...376
Bazeley v. Forder (1868).. 808
Beach (1912) 419
Beal, Ex p (1868) 891
Beall v. Smith (1873)...825, 828
Beard...264, 265
Beard v. Webb (1800) 742
Beatty v. Gillbanks [1882] 348, 349

Bebbe v. Sales (1916) 806
Beddow v. Beddow (1878) 865
Beecham (1851) 381
Bell v. Bell and the Marquis of Anglesey (1859). 734
Bellingham (1812) 237
Bendall v. McWhirter (1952). 762
Bennett v. Deacon (1846). 869
Bennett v. NAS Housepainters (1915) 714
Bernard (1888). 290
Berriman (1852–5). 98
Besant, Re (1878). 810, 812
Besant v. Wood (1882) 773
Betts v. Armstead (1888) 328
Betts v. Willmott (1870). 974, 975
Beynon v. Jones (1846) 737
Bloxham v. Elsee (1827) 973
Bircot's case 946
Birt (1831) 347
Birtwhistle v. Vardill (1826) 837
Bishop (1880). 326
Bishop of Hereford v. Adams (1805) 509
Bishop v. Bishop (1893). 773
Blackburn (1868). 665
Blackman v. Pugh (1846) 869
Blade v. Higgs (1861) 385
Blagg v. Sturt (1846) 869
Blake v. Tilstone [1894] 327
Blampied (1875) 245
Blanchard v. Hill (1742) 991
Blatherwick (1911) 88
Bleak House (1853) 468
Blofeld v. Payne (1833) 993, 996
Blunt v. Blunt (1943) 794
Board of Education v. Rice [1911] 533
Bohn v. Bogue (1847) 903
Bolster (1909). 291
Bond v. Evans (1888). 331
Bonnard v. Perryman (1891) 866
Bonner v. Lyon (1890). 764
Bonnyman (1940–2). 458
Boosey v. Davidson (1849). 913
Boosey v. Purday (1849). 913
Boosey v. Wright (1900). 929
Booth and Jones (1910) 98
Borthwick (1779) 185
Borthwick v. Evening Post (1888). 995, 997
Boucher (1837) 77, 101
Boulter (1908) 364
Boulton (1871) 318
Boulton and Others (1871). 407
Boulton and Watt v. Bull (1795) 933, 946, 947, 949, 950
Bourne (1939). 448

Bovill v. Moore (1816)... 950
Bowden Brake v. Bowden Wire (1913)................................. 1004
Bowen (1841)... 292
Bowen v. Hall (1881).. 694
Bowers v. Lovekin (1856).. 636
Bowes v. Press (1894).. 681
Bowler (1812)... 237
Bowman v. Secular Society (1917)..................................... 364
Boyes (1861).. 87
Boyle v. Smith [1906]... 331
Bradbury Agnew v. Day (1916).. 926
Bradlaugh (1883)... 364
Bradlaugh and Besant (1877)...................................... 369, 370
Bradshaw (1878)... 437
Brailsford [1905].. 317
Brain (1834).. 446
Bramwell v. Halcomb (1836)... 903
Bramwell v. Penneck (1827).. 647
Braunstein v. Lewis (1891) 65 LT 449............................... 764
Brett (1874)... 460
Brett v. Greenwell (1838).. 744
Briant, Re (1888)... 744
Briggs v. Briggs (1880)... 840
British United Shoe Machinery v. Fussell (1908)................. 966
British Vacuum Cleaner v. New Vacuum Cleaner (1907)....... 1009
Brixey (1845)... 245
Bromage v. Prosser (1909).............................. 860, 863, 866, 868
Brook v. Brook (1861).. 751, 839
Brooke v. Clarke (1818).. 887
Brough (1856).. 244
Brown (1889).. 311, 312
Brown v. Foot (1892).. 332
Brown v. Pocock (1833).. 742
Brown v. Randall (1827).. 826
Bruce (1847).. 433
Brunton v. Hawkes (1820)... 948, 949
Bryan, Re (1880).. 737
Budd v. Lucas [1891].. 331
Bull and Schmidt (1845)... 290
Bunn (1872).. 675, 676, 694
Burdett (Sir Francis) (1821)... 335, 337
Burgess (1862)... 422
Burnard v. Haggis (1863).. 807
Burns (1886)...................................... 186, 335, 337, 348
Burrow (1823).. 260
Burton (1863)... 245
BUSM v. Somervell (1907).. 976
Butchell (1829)... 439, 440
Butler v. Butler (1885).. 765
Butt (1884).. 289
Button (1900)... 305
Button v. Thompson (1869)... 646

Byker (1823) 637

Bykerdike (1832) 657

Byron (Lord) v. Johnstone (1816) 992

C & W's Application (1916) 968

Cabbage (1815) 381

Cafferata v. Wilson (1936) 290

Caird v. Sime (1887) 899, 923

Callo v. Brouncker (1831) 645

Campbell v. Corley (1862) 768

Campbell v. MGN (2004) 900

Campbell v. Spottiswoode (1863) 871

Camplin (1845) 404

Canham v. Jones (1813) 984

Capital and Counties Bank v. Henty (1882) 853, 861, 863, 867

Carlile (1819) 875

Carnan v. Bowles (1786) 880, 902, 907

Carpenter v. Smith (1841) 969

Carr (1875) 256

Carr, Re (1871) 744

Carr v. Hood (1808) 871

Carr v. Taylor (1805) 743

Carroll (1835) 258

Carroll (No. 2), Re (1931) 813

Carter v. US Boilermakers (1915) 714

Cary v. Kearsley (1802) 902

Casement (1917) 340

Castro v. R (1883) 137

Cate v. Devon (1889) 904

Caton (1874) 292, 294

Cellular Clothing v. Moxton & Murray (1899) 1008

Chamberlain's Wharf v. Smith (1900) 710, 713

Chambers v. Caulfield (1805) 778

Chambers v. Chambers (1810) 778

Champagne Heidsieck v. Buxton (1930) 1011

Chapin (1909) 390, 419

Chapman (1849) 302

Chappell v. Purday (1841) 912

Chappell v. Purday (No. 2) (1845) 908, 912, 913

Charnock v. Court (1899) 695

Chattaway (1922) 461

Chatterton v. Cave (1878) 903

Chatterton v. Secretary of State for India (1895) 876

Cheeseman (1862) 304

Cherry's Case (1782) 297

Chesnutt v. Chesnutt (1854) 792

Chetwynd (1912) 256

Child (1871) 390

Christie (1914) 88, 91

Chubb v. Flanagan (1834) 867

Churchward v. R (1865) 639

Cindy v. Le Cocq (1884) 328, 329

Clarence (1888) 404, 732
Clark and Bagg (1842) 455
Clark v. Freeman (1842) 994
Clark v. Freeman (1848) 864
Clark v. Price (1819). 647
Clarke (1817). 403
Clarke v. Clarke (1865) 794
Clarkson (1892) 349
Clemens [1898] 389
Clement v. Chivis (1829) 858
Clementi v. Walker (1824). 881, 912
Clements v. LNWR (1894). 806
Clothmakers of Ipswich (1915) 935
Cluderay (1850) 310, 311
Clyde Nail v. Russell (1916) 948
Cobbett (1831) 336
Cochrane, Re (1840) 731
Cochrane v. Moore (1890). 762
Cockcroft (1870) 403
Cocks v. Purday (1848). 913
Cogan (1979) 289
Cohen (1858) 323
Cohen (1914) 88
Colclough (1909) 136
Cole (1810) 90
Coleman v. Coleman (1866) 794
Coleman v. Wathen (1793) 896
Collins (1839) 335, 337
Collins (1864). 310, 311, 312, 448
Collins v. Reeves (1858) 1002
Collison (1837). 292
Commissioner of Police v. Cartman [1896] 331
Commissioners of Income Tax v. Pemsel (1891) 510
Coney (1882). 285, 286, 290, 437, 461
Contra Tate (1908) 88
Conway v. Wade (1909) 707, 708
Cook & Stockwell (1915). 290
Cook v. Pearce (1844). 950
Coombes (1785) 1 Leach 388 288
Coombes (1785) 288
Cooper (1846) 291
Cooper (1846) Q.B. 533. 291
Cooper (1849). 400
Cooper v. Lawson (1838) 871
Cooper v. Wandsworth Board of Works (1863). 546, 556, 583
Coppen v. Moore [1898]. 331, 332
Corbett v. Poelnitz (1785). 770
Cornish v. Keene (1835) 969
Coulson v. Coulson (1887). 866
Cowles v. Potts (1865). 869
Cox and Coleridge (1822). 94, 112
Coxhead v. Richards (1846). 869

Crabb v. Crabb (1868)..773
Crabtree v. Hole (1879)...332
Crane v. Price (1842)...........................946, 947, 948, 949, 968, 971
Crawshay v. Thompson (1842) 994
Creuze v. Hunter (1790) 809
Crisham (1841)...295
Crisp and Homewood (1919)..343
Croft v. Day (1843)... 995
Cross v. Andrew (1598)...825
Crossfield (1796) 258
Cruise v. Hunter (1790) 809
Crump (1825) 381
Cruse (1838) 259, 263
Crutchley (1831).. 268
Crutwell v. Lye (1810) 991
Cuddy (1843) 429
Cullen v. Elwin (1903) 709
Cunninghame Graham and Burns (1888) 344
Cunnings (1861)...87
Curley (1909) 457
Curran (1931) 297
Curran v. Treleavan (1891)... 678
Curry v. Walter (1796) 875
Curtis v. Curtis (1858) 791
Curtis v. Harvey & Pape (1887).. 1002
Cuthill (1799)..337
Cutter v. Powell (1795) 645, 646

Daily Telegraph v. McLaughlin (1904) 826
Dakhyl v. Labouchere (1908)...872
Dale (1852) 310, 311
Dalloz (1908) 444
D'Almaine v. Boosey (1835)...903, 912
Dalrymple v. Dalrymple (1811)...839
Dant (1865).. 444
Darcy v. Allin (1602)...935
Davies (1912).. 111
Davies (1913)...419
Davies v. Snead (1870) 869, 870
Davis (1806).. 284
Davis (1881) 252, 253, 262, 263
Davis (1883) 456
Davison (1808).. 89
Davison v. Duncan (1857) 876
Davitt (1870)...342
Dawkins v. Lord Rokeby (1875)...875
Day (1844)...389
Day v. Bream (1837)... 867
Day v. Day (1816) 991
De Berenger (1814) 317
de Crespigny v. Wellesley (1829)... 866
De Francesco v. Barnum (1890) 806

De Manneville (1804). 809, 810
De Manneville v. De Manneville (1804). 809
Deasy (1883). 342
Deaves (1869). 383
Dee (1884). 404
Delaval (1763). 775
Dempster v. Dempster (1864). 793
Denaby and Cadeby Main Collieries v. Yorkshire Miners Association (1906). 703
Dent v. Turpin (1861). 997
Despard (1803). 340
Devonald v. Rosser (1906). 684
Dewhurst (1820). 346
Dibdin v. Swan (1793). 871
Dickens v. Lee (1844). 902
Dickenson (1820). 381
Dickenson (1843). 96
Dickinson (1844). 245
Dicks v. Brooks (1880). 903, 906
Dixon (1814). 330, 332, 416
Dixon v. Holden (1869). 864
Dodd v. Dodd (1906). 799
Doherty (1887). 260, 261, 263, 420, 443, 444
Dollond's case (1764). 933, 945
Donaldson v. Becket (1774). 883, 884, 886, 889, 896, 912, 915, 919
Doody (1854). 260
Dove (1856). 252
Dowling (1848). 342, 350
Doyley v. Roberts (1837). 852
DPP v. Beard [1920]. 415
DPP v. Smith. 229
Druitt (1867). 317, 662, 676
Drummond v. Drummond (1861). 795
Du Cros v. Lambourne (1907). 287
Duckworth [1892]. 305, 311
Dudgeon v. Thomson (1877). 949
Dudley and Stephens (1884). 275, 277, 278
Duels, The Case of (1615). 297
Duffield (1851). 319, 660, 661, 663, 676
Duffy's Trust, Re (1860). 743
Dugdale (1853). 302
Duke of Bedford v. Ellis (1901). 700
Duke v. Littleboy (1880). 710
Duncan (1872). 245
Duncan v. Thwaites (1824). 876
Duncan v. Toms (1887). 67
Dunn v. Sayles (1844). 639
Dunne v. Anderson (1825). 871
Durant v. Titley (1819). 772
Durham v. Crackles (1868). 743
Durham v. Durham (1885). 825
Durrant v. Ricketts (1881). 764
Dutt (1912). 136

Dyer, Ex p (1812) 933
Dymond (1920) 216
Dyson (1908) 454

Eagle (1862) 423, 428
Eagleton (1855). 303, 304, 305, 307
Eaton v. Lake (1888) 893
Eccles (1783) 652
Edelsten v. Edelsten (1863). 995, 996, 997
Edge v. Nicolls (1911). 982, 1009
Edgeberry v. Stephens (1697) 935
Edmeads (1828) 291, 296
Edwards v. Bell (1824) 854
Edwards v. Porter (1925). 764
Egginton (1801) 378, 381
Eldershaw (1823) 295
Eley v. Lytle (1885). 391
Elliott (1889). 443, 444
Elliott v. Cordell (1820) 743
Ellis (1826) 93
Elliston v. Reacher (1908) 581
Emery v. Nolloth (1903) 331, 332
Emmens v. Elderton (1853) 639
Emmens v. Pottle (1883). 867
Emmett v. Norton (1836) 738
Emperor of Austria v. Day (1861) 849, 864, 995
Empire Typesetting v. Linotype (1898). 859
Errington (1838) 411
Escourt v. Escourt Hop Essence (1875) 984
Evans v. Evans (1790) 791
Evans v. Evans and Elford (1906). 794
Evans v. Harlow (1844). 859
Everest (1909). 88
Exall (1866) 109
Exchange Telegraph v. Howard (1906) 989

Farina v. Silverlock (1856) 995, 1011
Farmer v. Wilson (1900) 696
Farrel's Case (1787). 297
Farrer v. Close (1869) 664, 676
Farrington (1811) 416, 418
Farrington (1812) 390
Faulder v. Rushton (1901). 1002, 1004
Faulkner (1877) 390
Fawcett v. Cash (1834) 643
Feather v. Regina (1865). 944
Fender v. St. John Midlmay (1938) 748
Fenton (1831) 432, 436
Ferguson and Edge (1819) 652
Ferguson v. R (1979) 110
Ferguson's Case (1830) 440
Fergusson v. Clayworth (1844). 737

Ferodo's Application (1945). 1010
Ferray (1839). 259
Field v. The Receiver of Metropolitan Police (1907) 348, 351
Finney (1874) 444
Firestone v. Butcher (1840) 738
Fisher (1811) 875
Fisher (1865) 391
Fisher v. Clement (1830). 861, 867
Fisher v. Fisher (1861) 787
Fitzpatrick v. Kelly (1873). 331
Flattery (1877) 404
Fletcher (1841) 454
Fletcher (1859) 404
Fletcher v. Fletcher (1788) 771
Flight v. Bolland (1828) 806
Flint v. Pike (1825). 875
Flintan (1830). 776
Flowers (1886) 383
Folkes v. Child (1782) 85
Foote (1883) 364
Forster v. NU Shop Assistants (1927). 714
Forsyth v. Riviere (1819). 933
Foster (1852). 296, 391
Foster v. Redgrave (1868). 807
Fowler v. Dowdney (1838) 858
Fowler v. Padget (1798) 321
Foxwell v. Bostock (1864) 965
Franklin (1883) 435
Franz (1861) 292
French v. Getting (1922). 762
Fretwell (1862). 290
Friend (1802) 458
Frost (1844) 245
Fryer (1915) 253
Fuller (1816) 302

Gafee, Re (1850). 742
Gallagher (1883). 342
Gambart v. Ball (1863) 906
Gandell v. Potigny (1816) 646
Gandy v. Gandy (1882). 773
Gardner and Hancox (1915) 98, 99
Gathercole v. Miall (1846) 871
Gavin (1885) 98
Gayford v. Chouler (1989) 391
Gaylor (1857) 311
Gee v. Pritchard (1818) 673, 849, 864, 898
George v. Davis (1911). 684
Giacometti v. Prodgers (1873). 743
Giblan v. National Amalgamated Labourers' Union (1903) 701, 703
Gibson v. Lawson (1891). 678
Gipps v. Gipps (1864) 793

Glide (1868) 383
Goodfellow (1845) 291
Goodfellow v. Prince (1887) 1002
Goodspead (1911) 296
Gordon (1781) 340
Gordon v. Gordon (1903) 805
Goulder v. Rook (1901) 327, 328
Gozney v. Bristol Trade Society (1909) 709
Graham (1910) 87
Graham and Burns (1888) 348
Graves v. Gorrie (1903) 894
Great Tower Street Tea v. Langford (1887) 1002
Green (1832) 93
Greenacre (1837) 111
Greenhill (1836) 810
Greening (1913) 425
Greenwood (1825) 284
Greenwood (1857) 413
Gregory..295
Grey (1666) 411
Grey (1864) 370
Griffith (1553) 284, 291
Griffiths (1838) 396
Grindley (1819) 258
Groombridge (1836) 289
Gutch (1829) 321
Guth v. Guth (1792) 771
Gyles v. Wilcox (1741) 901
Gyngall (1893) 808, 812

Hadfield (1800) 234, 235, 237
Haigh and others (1813) 89
Haines (1847) 443
Haines (1848) 459
Halford (1868) 282
Hall (1828) 382
Hall (1849) 381
Hall (1919) 461
Hall v. Barrows (1864) 996, 997
Halliday (1889) 457
Hamilton v. Wright (1842) 772
Hammond (1799) 319
Hammon's Case (1812) 377
Hancock v. Peaty (1866) 825
Handley (1874) 443, 444
Hanfstaegl v. Baines (1895) 903, 926
Hanson v. Keating (1844) 744
Hardy v. Ryle (1829) 647
Hargrave (1831) 437
Harmer v. Playne (1807) 949
Harper v. Biggs (1907) 904
Harrald (1872) 731

Harris (1836) 396
Harrison v. Anderston Foundry (1876). 965
Harrison v. Bush (1856) 869, 870
Harrison v. Leaper (1862) 332
Harrison v. Smith (1869) 861
Harrison-Owen (1951) 257
Hartley v. Cummings (1846). 640
Harvey and Caylor (1843) 292
Harvey and Chapman (1823). 335
Harvey v. Farnie (1882) 840
Hassett (1861). 98
Hatschek's Patent (1909) 976
Hawkins 295
Hay (1911) 254
Haynes (1859). 245, 247
Hayward (1833) 423
Hayward (1908). 454, 457
Hearn (1841). 94
Hearne v. Garton (1859) 327
Heath (1810) 302
Heath v. Smith. 945, 969
Heaven (1903). 389
Hebditch v. MacIlwaine (1894). 870
Hecla Foundry v. Walker (1889). 980
Hedley v. Barlow (1865) 871
Hehir (1895) 384
Hensleer (1870) 311
Hepworth (1955) 110
Herbert Morris v. Saxelby (1916) 685
Hermann v. Charlesworth (1905). 727
Herne v. Garton (1859). 323
Hewitt (1851) 659
Hewitt (1925) 92
Hezell (1844) 62
Hibbert (1869) 327
Hibbert (1875) 674, 676
Hicklin (1868) 268, 369, 416
Hickton's Patent Syndicate v. Patents and Machine
    Improvements (1909). 970
Higgins (1734) 300
Higgins (1801) 297, 298, 299, 301,
                                                                            302, 307, 317
Higgins (1829) 109
Hill (1790). 258
Hill v. Evans (1862) 969
Hill v. Thomson (1817) 944, 945, 950
Hilton v. Eckersley (1855). 663, 669, 693
Hindley v. Westmeath (1827) 772
Hinton v. Donaldson (1773). 883
Histed (1898) 98
Hoare v. Silverlock (1850) 875

Hobbs v. Young (1689) 629
Hodgkinson v. Fletcher (1814) 770
Hodgson (1811).. 403
Hodgson v. Roberts (1906) 787
Hodgson v. Scarlett (1818) 874
Hodgson v. Temple (1813)... 290
Hogg v. Kirby (1803)..991
Holbrook (1878)... 288
Holden (1892)..343
Holland (1841) 454
Holmes (1871).. 403
Holt (1920) 253
Honner v. Morton (1828)..736
Hope v. Hope (1857) 808
Hopkins, Ex p. (1732) 808
Hopwood (1913)... 420
Hornblower v. Boulton (1799)....................................... 946
Hornby v. Close (1867) 664, 670
Horsey (1862)..413
Horton v. McMurtry (1862)..645
Hotchkiss v. Greenwood (1850) 948
Hough v. Windus (1884) 615
Howe (1987) 277
Howell (1839) 284
Howells v. Wynne (1863) 288
Howes (1834) 94
Howlett (1836) 109
H's Settlement, Re (1909)...754
Hubbuck v. Wilkinson (1899)..859
Huggins (1730)..288, 458
Hughes (1857)..459
Hughes (1860) 295
Hulton v. Jones (1910) 862, 867
Humpherson v. Syer (1887) 969
Humphreys v. Thompson (1905).......................................923
Hunt (1820) 319, 346, 347
Hunt (1845).. 344
Hunt v. Hunt (1861)..773
Hunter v. Edney (1881)...749
Huntley v. Ward (1859)... 869
Husle v. Husle (No. 2) (1872) 795
Hyde v. Hyde (1866) 838
Hyman v. Hyman (1929) 773

Ibrahim v. R (1914) 98
IG Farbenindustrie's Patents (1930)................................... 948
Imperial Loan v. Stone (1891) 826
Incandescant Gas Light v Cantelo (1895) 975
Ingram v. Barnes (1858) 642
Ingram v. Lawson (1840) 859
Instan [1893]..446, 461, 463
J v. C (1969)..812

Jack v. Jack (1862) 841
Jackson (1822) 404
Jackson v. Hobhouse (1817) 741
James' Trade Mark, Re (1886) 1004
James v. Phelps (1840) 389
Jamieson v. Jamieson (1898) 997
Jarmain (1945) 436
Jay v. Ladler (1888) 1002
Jefferys v. Boosey (1854) 317, 881, 908, 913, 915, 919
Jenkinson v. Neild (1892) 693
Jenner v. A'Beckett (1871) 859
Jennings v. Stephens (1936) 907
Jenoure v. Delmege (1891) 869
Johnson (1827) 454
Johnson (1840) 647
Johnson v. Freeth (1836) 742
Johnstone v. Orr-Ewing (1882) 993
Jolly (1910) 253
Jones (1809) 87, 89
Jones (1846) 381
Jones (1848) 347
Jones (1870) 443, 444
Jones (1908) 425
Jones (1910) 253
Jones v. Littler (1841) 858
Jones v. Salter (1815) 741
Jordan and Sullivan (1836) 87
Jorden (1872) 245
Joseph v. Joseph and Wenzell (1865) 794

Kay v. Butterworth (1945) 257
Kay v. Marshall (1841) 944
Kearly v. Taylor (1891) 332
Keates v. Merthyr Consolidated Collieries (1911) 682
Keats (1843) 87
Keats v. Keats and Montezuma (1859) 793
Kelly (1847) 284
Kelly (1848) 423
Kelly v. Kelly (1869) 791
Kelly v. Morris (1866) 904
Kendeillon v. Maltby (1842) 874
Kenrick v. Lawrence (1890) 904
Kent Justices (1811) 630
Kerr (1837) 96
Kessal (1824) 431
Kewanee Oil v. Bicron (1974) 986
Kimber v. Press Association (1893) 876
King Features Syndicate v. Kleeman (1941) 983
King v. Arkwright (1785) 947, 950
Kirkham (1837) 424, 425
Kitchen v. Shaw (1837) 647
Knight (1781) 382

Knight (1871) 383
Knight and Thayre (1905) 98
Knight v. Gibbs (1834) 858
Knight's Case (1828) 442
Kopsch (1925) 255

Labouchere (1884) 339
Lady Elibank v. Montolieu (1801) 743
Ladyman (1851) 394
Laitwood (1910) 307
Lancaster v. Greaves (1829) 647
Landow (1913) 307
Lane v. Ironmonger (1844) 738
Larkin [1943] 436
Larkin v. Belfast Harbour Commissioners (1908) 706
Lawrence v. Smith (1822) 898
Lawrence v. Todd (1863) 647
Le Mesurier v. Le Mesurier (1895) 840, 841
Leak v. Driffield (1889) 764
Leather Cloth v. American Leather (1865) 991, 994, 996, 997
Lee v. Dangar (1892) 444
Lee v. Taylor and Gill (1912) 419
Lees v. Whitcomb (1828) 640
Legard v. Johnson (1797) 771
Leggatt (1852) 732
Leng v. Andrews (1909) 685
Lesbini (1914) 425
Leslie v. Shiell (1914) 807
Levy (1819) 317
Levy v. Rutley (1871) 893
Lewis v. Clement (1820) 875
Lewis v. Walter (1821) 874, 875
Lewsi v. Levy (1858) 876
Liardet v. Johnson (1778) 947, 950
Linaker v. Pilcher (1901) 671, 712
Linneker (1906) 305, 307
Linoleum Manufacturing v. Nairn (1878) 1009
Lister (1721) 731
Little (1886) 262, 418
Lock v. Heath (1892) 762
Lolley (1812) 839
Lomas (1913) 287
London Association for the Protection of Trade v. Greenlands (1916) 870
Long (1834) 440, 441
Longbottom (1848) 444
Lord Baltimore (1768) 295
Lord Ferrers (1760) 235
Lord Grey (1612) 317
Lord Mohun (1692) 291, 295
Loveless (1834) 658
Luck (1862) 292
Lumley (1911) 415, 419

Lumley v. Allday (1831) 858
Lumley v. Gye (1853) 694, 699
Lynch (1832) 431
Lynch v. Knight (1861) 858
Lyne v. Nicholls (1906) 859
Lyons v. Blenkin (1821) 810
Lyons v. Wilkins (No. 1) (1896) 694, 695, 698, 703, 705, 706

McAndrew v. Bassett (1864) 996, 997, 998
McCarthy v. Decaix (1831) 839
McCleod (1874) 443, 445
McCord v. McCord (1875) 794
McCulloch v. May (1947) 1009
MacDougall v. Knight (1886) 876
MacFarlane v. Price (1816) 949
McGregor v. McGregor (1888) 765
McGrowther (1746) 267
McGruther v. Pitcher (1904) 975
McIntyre (1847) 455
Mackenzie (1892) 678
Macklin (1838) 290
Macklin v. Richardson (1770) 884, 896
McNaughton (1881) 433
McPherson v. Daniels (1829) 866
Magnolia Metal v. Tandem Smelting (1900) 1009
Makin v. AG for New South Wales (1894) 91, 815
Malcolm v. O'Callaghan (1835) 742
Male and Cooper (1893) 98
Mancini v. DPP (1942) 428
Manley (1933) 298, 317
March v. March and Palumbo (1867) 787
Married Love (1918) 369
Marriott (1838) 460
Marsh (1820) 322, 323
Marsh (1824) 322, 327, 330, 331, 332
Marshall v. Rutton (1800) 770
Marshall's Case (1830) 258
Martin (1827) 432
Martin (1832) 433, 454
Martin (1881) 397
Mary R (1887) 262
Mason (1912) 425
Mason v. Provident Clothing (1913) 685
Massey v. Morris (1894) 331
Massey v. Parker (1843) 742
Mawbey (1796) 652
Mawgridge's Case (1707) 431
Mawman v. Tegg (1826) 903, 905
Maxwell v. Hogg (1867) 994
Mayall v. Higbey (1862) 890
Mayers (1872) 404
Mayor of Bradford v. Pickles (1895) 696

Meade (1909) 265, 418, 420

Meakin (1836) 259

Medland (1851)..381

Meredith (1838) 302

Mersey Docks and Harbour Board Trustees v. Gibbs (1866) 333

Merton (1862) 433

Meters v. Metropolitan Gas (1911) 905

Metropolitan Saloon Omnibus Co v. Hawkins (1859) 855

Mick (1863)..97

Middleton (1873) 383

Millar v. Taylor (1768) 316, 883, 900, 902

Millington v. Fox (1839).. 997

Milner v. Milner (1861)..791

Mitchel (1848) 342

Mitchel v. Reynolds (1711) 940

Mitchell v. Henry (1880) 1002

M'Laren v. Miller (1880) 710

M'Naghten (1843) 239, 240, 241, 243, 244,
                                                          245, 246, 248, 252,
                                                          253, 254, 256, 261

Mogg v. Mogg (1824) 768

Mogul Steamship Co v. McGregor (1892).........................315, 319, 693, 694, 696, 698, 1011

Molton v. Camroux (1849)... 826

Monckton v. Gramophone Co (1912).. 929

Monkhouse (1849) 259, 263

Monks (1870)...457

Monson v. Tussauds (1891) 866

Montgomery v. Thompson (1891)... 1008

Moody v. Tree (1892) 981

Moorhouse v. Lord (1863) 836

Mordaunt v. Moncrieffe (1874) 786, 789

Morfit (1816)...381

Morgan (1895) 98

Morgan v. Seward (1836) 950

Morice v. Bishop (1804) 509

Morison v. Moat (1851)... 984, 985

Morris v. Bramsom (1770)... 946

Morris v. Wright (1870) 904

Mortimer (1908) 136

Mortimer v. Mortimer (1820) 772

Mortimer v. Wright (1840) 808

Morton (1908) 265

Moss v. Moss (1897) 748

Motley v. Downman (1837) 992, 997

Moult v. Halliday (1898).. 684

Mountain (1888) 262

M'Pherson (1857)... 310, 311

Mudd v. GUOC (1910) 709

Mulcahy v. R (1868)..342

Mullins (1848) 319

Mullins v. Collins (1874) 331

Murphy (1833) 437
Murray v. Benbow (1822) 898
Murray v. Bogue (1852) 903
Murray v. Elliston (1822) 896
Murton (1862) 456

Naguib (1917) 838
Napier v. Napier (1915) 749
National Phonographic v. Menck (1911) 975
National Provincial Bank v. Williamson (1876) 764
National Starch v. Munn's Patent Maizena (1894) 1008
Native Guano v. Sewage Manure (1889) 1009
Neilson v. Harford (1841)...945, 946, 948, 950
Newbury v. Jarvis (1817).. 984
Newill (1832) 390
Newill (1836) 417
Newlands v. Paynter (1840)..742
Newman (1913)...73
Newmark v. National Phonograph (1907) 929
Newton v. Reid (1830)...742
Niboyet v. Niboyet (1878)... 840
Nichol (1807) 405
Nichrotherm Electrical v. Percy (1957) 988
Nicols v. Pitman (1884) 899
Nield (1805) 652
Noakes (1866) 443, 445
Nobel's Explosives v Anderson (1895).. 966
Noon (1852) 433
Noor Mohammed v. R (1949) 92
Nordenfelt v. Maxim Nordenfelt (1894) 684
Norris (1840) 391
Norris (1916).. 88
North London Rly v. Great Northern Rly (1883)....................................... 865
Nottage v. Jackson (1883)... 894
Nurse v. Craig (1806) 770

O'Brien v. Marquis of Salisbury (1889) 872
O'Connell (1843) 347
Oddy (1851)...91
O'Donnell (1916) 73
O'Donoghue (1927)...453
Offley v. Clay (1840) 736
Offord (1831)..237
O'Hara, Re (1900) 808, 812
Old v. Robson (1890).. 709
Oliphant (1905) 289
Oneby (1727)..423
O'Neill v. Longman (1863)... 662
Orton (1878)...437
Osborne v. ASRS (No. 2) (1911) 712, 713
Otto v. Linford (1881) 946, 948
Owen (1825) 284

Owens v. Dickenson (1840) 764
Oxford (1840) 238

Page (1847) 62
Palliser v. Gurney (1887) 764
Palmer (1856) 72, 78
Palmer (1913) 425
Pargeter (1848) 459
Parker (1839) 391
Parker v. Alder [1899] 324, 327, 328, 333
Parkes (1794) 377
Parkin v. South Hetton Coal (1907) 684
Parkins (1824) 101
Parmiter v. Coupland (1840) 855
Parnell (1851) 319
Parr v. Lancashire and Cheshire Miners Federation (1913) 700, 704, 714
Parsons (1762) 319
Parsons v. Gillespie (1898) 1008
Patmore (1789) 458
Patterson v. Gas Light & Coke Co (1878) 968
Payton v. Snelling Lampard (1901) 1009
Pearce (1929) 294
Pearce v. Morrison (1904) 765
Pear's Case 376, 377, 379
Pearson (1835) 732
Peirson (1705) 355
Pellecart v. Angell (1835) 290
Pembliton (1874) 227, 390
Perry (1919) 256
Perry v. Truefitt (1842) 994
Pettit (1850) 98
Phetheon (1840) 381
Phillips (1805) 298
Phillips (1842) 350
Phillips (1848) 296
Phillips and Strong (1801) 378, 381
Philpot (1853) 400, 418, 419
Philpott v. St George's Hospital (1859) 515
Pike v. Fitzgibbon (1881) 764
Pike v. Nicholas (1870) 904
Pilkington v. Scott (1846) 640
Pinney (1832) 344
Pitman (1826) 258
Pitts (1842) 457
Plimpton v. Malcomlson (1876) 969
Plimpton v. Spiller (1876) 949
Plummer (1844) 433
Pollard v. Photographic Co (1888) 900
Porter (1873) 412, 433
Porter (1910) 317
Poulton (1835) 446
Powell v. Birmingham Vinegar (1897) 1009

Powell v. Cleaver (1792) 809
Powell v. Kempton Park [1899] 362
Pratt v. Martin (1911) 289
Price (1858) 292, 294
Price (1884) 370
Pridmore (1913) 294
Priestly v. Fowler (1837) 494
Prince (1875) 228, 280, 281, 321, 324, 325, 326,
                                                              327, 333, 405, 407
Prince Albert v. Strange (1849) 899, 985, 986, 988
Pritchard (1836) 235
Procter v. Robinson (1866) 773
Prudential Assurance v. Knott (1875) 864
Pullman v. Hill (1891) 870
Purcell v. Sowler (1877) 876
Purdew v. Jackson (1824) 736
Pym (1846) 455

Quail (1862) 259
Quarmbly (1921) 254
Quinn v. Leathem [1901] 315, 697, 698, 703, 705

R (1992) 732
R v. Barton-upon-Irwell (1814) 648
R v. Stoke-upon-Trent (1843) 643
Race, Re (1857) 809
Ram (1893) 295
Ramsay v. Margrett (1894) 762
Ramsey (1883) 364
Rankin (1803) 431
Ratcliffe v. Evans (1892) 859
Raynard v. Chase (1756) 629
Read v. Friendly Society of Operative Stonemasons (1902) 701
Reade v. Conquest (Nos 1 and 2) (1861) 921
Reade v. Lacy (1861) 921
Reason (1872) 97
Reddaway v. Banham (1896) 994, 1008
Redford v. Bierley (1822) 344, 346
Redgate v. Haynes (1876) 331
Reed (1842) 382
Reeves (1839) 447
Regan (1867) 98
Reniger v. Fogossa (1550) 257
Rennie's Case (1825) 261
Reuters Telegram v. Byron (1874) 987
Rew (1662) 454
Rhodes (1899) 106
Rhodes, Re (1890) 826
Ridgway v. Hungerford Market (1835) 645
Ridley (1811) 458
Rigby v. Connol (1880) 709, 710, 713
Rigmaidon (1833) 443

Riley (1843) 383, 384
Riley v. Warden (1848) 642
Ring (1892) 311, 312
Ringsted v. Lady Lanesborough (1783) 770
Roberton v. Lewis (1960) 928
Roberts (1855) 303, 304, 305, 306
Roberts v. Brown (184) 875
Roberts v. Cooper (1892) 744
Roberts v. Preston (1860) 288
Roberts v. Roberts (1864) 858
Robins (1843) 403
Robinson (1853) 80
Robinson [1915] 307
Robinson King v. Lynes (1894) 764
Robinson v. Robinson (1883) 788
Rodgers v. Nowill (1847) 1003
Rodney (Lord) v. Chambers (1802) 772
Rogers (1894) 311, 312
Rookes v. Barnard (1964) 708
Roper v. Knott [1898] 391
Rose (1884) 282
Rosinski (1824) 405
Rothwell (1871) 425
Routh v. Webster (1847) 864
Routledge v. Lowe (1868) 914, 915
Rowed and Others (1842) 407
Rowlands (1851) 660, 663
Roworth v. Wilkes (1807) 905
Rowton (1865) 89
Royce (1767) 285
Rubel Bronze and Vos, Re (1918) 645
Rubens (1909) 293, 294
Russell v. ASCJ (1912) 709
Russell v. Russell (1924) 789
R.Welsh (1946) 330
Ryder v. Mills (1850) 566
Ryder v. Wombwell (1868) 807
Ryland v. Smith (1835) 736
Rylands v. Fletcher (1866) 333

Sa de Manufacture des Glaces v. Tilghman (1883) 975
St. George (1840) 394
St Helen's Smelting Co v. Tipping (1865) 544
St John Devizes (1829) 637
St John v. St John (1805) 771, 772
Salisbury (Marquis) 475
Salmon (1886) 443
Salmon (1924) 87
Salter (1804) 652
Saltman v. Campbell (1948) 987
Saunders (1838) 404
Saunders and Archer (1576) 296

Saunders v. Mills (1829) 875
Saunders v. Whittle (1876). 645
Sawkins v. Hyperion Records (2005). 928
Saxby v. Easterbrook (1878). 865
Sayer v. ASCJ (1902) 709
Sayre v. Moore (1785) 902, 907
Scofield (1784) 297, 298, 302, 307
Scott v. Morley (1887). 764
Scott v. Scott (1913) 409, 789
Scott v. Sebright (1886). 749
Scott v. Stanford (1867). 904
Scott v. Stansfield (1868) 874
Scottish Co-operative Wholesaler Society v. Glasgow
 Fleshers' Trade Defence Association (1898). 693
Scrimshire v. Scrimshire (1752) 838
Seaman v. Netherclift (1876). 874
Searle (1831) 238
Sedden v. Sedden and Doyle (1862) 788
Seed v. Higgins (1860) 949
Seixo v. Provexende (1866) 1003
Self (1776) 458
Selsby (1847) 659, 661
Selten (1871) 428
Semini (1949) 430
Semple. 377
Senior (1832) 447
Senior (1899) 436, 446
Serne (1887) 414
Serne and Goldfinch (1887). 412
Shakespear, Re (1885) 764
Sharman v. Saunders (1853). 642
Shaw v. DPP [1962] 317
Shaw v. Gould (1868) 836
Shelbourne v. Liver (1866). 663
Shellaker (1914) 92
Shelley v. Westwood (1817) 810
Shephard (1862). 459
Shepherd (1869). 676
Shepherd v. Conquest (1856). 893
Sheppard (1868). 311
Sherras v. De Rutzen (1895). 327, 328, 329, 332
Sherwood (1844) 425
Shillito v. Collett (1860) 811
Shipley (1784). 118
Short (1932). 294
Siddon (1830) 330
Sidney v. Sidney (1865) 787
Sim v. Heinz (1959) 1009
Simonin v. Mallac (1860). 838, 839
Simpson (1845). 262
Simpson (1909) 136
Singer v. Loog (1882). 1002

Singer v. Wilson (1877) 1008
Singh (1933) 257
Singleton v. Bolton (1783) 991
Skeet (1866) 291, 294
Skinner v. Kitch (1867) 663
Slazenger v. Feltham (1889) 998
Sleeman v. Barrett (1863) 636
Sleep (1861) 323, 324
Smith (1826) 458
Smith (1837) 428, 431
Smith (1849) 449
Smith (1865) 425, 459, 460, 461
Smith (1911) 111
Smith (1914) 424
Smith (1915) 106
Smith v. Company of Armourers (1792) 629
Smith v. Dickenson (1804) 985
Smith v. Hayward (1837) 646
Smith v. Marrable (1842) 582
Smith v. Moody (1903) 678
Soares (1802) 284
Sodeman v. R. (1936) 112
Solomons (1909) 380
Somerset v. Hart (1884) 331
Somersett's case (1771) 625
South Wales Miners Federation v. Glamorgan Coal Co (1905) 315, 694, 701
Southern (1821) 322
Southern v. How (1618) 991
Southey v. Sherwood (1817) 898
Southorn v. Reynolds (1865) 997
Spain v. Arnott (1817) 644
Spalding v. Gamage (1915) 1008
Spence, Re (1847) 809
Spencer (1837) 95
Spencer (1867) 444
Spiller (1832) 440
Spilling (1838) 444, 445
Springhead Spinning v. Riley (1868) 673, 864
Stainer (1870) 665
Stanley (1816) 291
Stannard (1833) 89
Stanton v. Hall (1831) 743
Steele v. South Wales Miners' Federation (1907) 712
Stephens (1839) 348
Stephenson (1884) 317
Stockdale v. Hansard (1839) 873
Stocks v. Wilson (1913) 807
Stoddart (1909) 420
Stogdon v. Lee (1891) 764
Stokes (1848) 111, 244
Stokes (1853) 97
Stopford (1870) 263

Stratton (1779) 267
Streeter (1900) 731
Stringer (1933) 446
Stuart v. Bell (1891) 869
Stubbs (1855) 87
Sturgis v. Champneys (1839) 744
Suggate v. Suggate (1859) 791
Sullivan (1836) 433
Summers (1952) 110
Swaine v. Wilson (1890) 709
Swatman v. Swatman (1865) 791
Sweet v. Sweet (1895) 765
Sydley (1664) 298
Sykes (1912) 110
Sykes v. Dixon (1839) 640, 647
Sykes v. Sykes (1824) 993, 996
Symington v. Symington (1875) 788

Tabart v. Tipper (1808) 871
Tacey (1821) 391
Taff Vale v. Amalgamated Society of Railway
    Servants (1901) 698, 700, 701, 702, 706, 711
Taunton v. Morris (1878) 744
Taylor (1839) 95
Taylor (1859) 304, 305, 314
Taylor (1871) 304, 311
Taylor (1875) 290
Taylor (1998) 45
Temperton v. Russell (No. 1) (1893) 700
Temperton v. Russell (No. 2) (1893) 693, 694, 695, 698, 705
Temple v. Prescott (1773) 645, 646
Tetley v. Griffith (1887) 764
Thistlewood (1820) 340, 341
Thomas (1837) 258, 427
Thomas (1841) 379
Thomas (1912) 254
Thomas v. Churton (1862) 874
Thomas v. Hunt (1864) 974
Thompson (1825) 379
Thompson (1862) 379
Thompson (1869) 291
Thompson (1893) 98
Thompson v. Shackell (1827) 871
Thomson DC v. Deakin (1952) 708
Thorley v. Kerry (1812) 854, 857
Thornton (1824) 96, 281, 282
Thristle (1849) 382
Thurbon (1849) 382
Tidd v. Lister (1853) 743, 744
Timmins (1830) 442
Tinsley v. Lacy (1861) 921
Tinsley v. Lacy (1863) 902

Tipping v. Clarke (1843) 900, 984
Tolfree (1829) 731
Tolson (1889) 228, 281, 282, 324, 325, 326, 408
Toogood v. Spyring (1834) 868
Tooke (1794) 340
Towers (1874) 457
Trainer (1864) 443, 444
Trollope v. London Building Trades Federation (1895) 696
True (1922) 254
Truelove (1880) 369
Trusler v. Murray (1789) 907
Trustees of the British Museum v. White (1826) 510
Tuck v. Priester (1887) 894
Tulk v. Moxhay (1848) 580
Tullett v. Armstrong (1840) 742
Turf Fraud case 54
Turlington (1761) 827
Turnbull v. Bird (1861) 871
Turner (1811) 317
Turner v. Mason (1845) 645
Turner v. Performing Right Society (1943) 907
Turner v. Robinson (1833) 645, 890
Turner's (Sir Edward) Case (1680) 744
Tutchin (1704) 336

Udny v. Udny (1869) 836
Underwood v. Barker (1899) 685
University of London Press v. University Tutorial Press (1916) 904
Unwin v. Clarke (1866) 648
USMC v. Brunet (1909) 976

Vacher v. London Society of Compositors (1913) 700, 704, 706
Vantandillo (1815) 268
Vanterstein (1865) 284
Vaux's Case (1591) 295
Vickers v. Siddell (1890) 965, 966
Vincent (1839) 337, 347, 348, 349
Vincent (1842) 349
Vizetelly (1888) 371, 372
Vizetelly v. Mudie's Select Library (1900) 862, 867
Voisin (1918) 99, 100, 106
Vokes v. Heather (1945) 987
Vreones (1891) 304

Wainwright v. Home Office (2004) 900
Waite (1892) 311
Walcot v. Walker (1802) 898
Walker (1784) 235
Walker (1824) 441
Wall (1802) 454
Wall (1907) 706
Wall v. Martin and Taylor (1880) 920

Waller v. Loch (1881). 869, 870
Wallis (1703). 291
Walsby v. Anley (1861) 663, 665
Walsh (1824). 379
Walsh v. Walley (1874) 684
Walter (1799) 321
Walter v. Ashton (1902) 1009
Walter v. Falkirk (1887) 981
Walter v. Howe (1881). 906
Walter v. Lane (1900) 928
Walter v. Steinkopff (1892). 902, 906
Walters (1848) 412
Walters v. Green (1899) 695
Walters v. R (1969) 110
Walton v. Walton (1859). 776
Warburton (1870) 317
Ward (1871). 397
Ward (1872) 227, 390
Ward, Lock v. Operative Printers' Assistants Society (1906) 706
Ward v. Ward (1880). 737
Ward v. Weeks (1830) 861
Ward's Case (1789) 437
Warickshall (1783). 94
Warner, Ex p (1792). 809
Warrender v. Warrander (1835) 770
Wason v. Walter (1868) 874, 876
Watkins v. Major (1875) 389
Watson (1817). 350
Watson (1845). 262
Watson (1872). 249
Watson Laidlow v. Potts Cassels & Williamson (1914) 905
Waught v. R (1950) 106
Weatherby v. International Horse Agency (1910) 905
Weaver v. Floyd (1852) 642
Webb v. Catchlove (1886). 67
Welch (1853) 640
Welch (1875) 227, 390
Weldon v. de Bathe (1884) 760
Weldon v. Weldon (1883) 768, 833
Weldon v. Winslow (1884). 760
Weller v. Deakins (1827). 361
Wellesley v. Beaufort (1827). 809, 810
Wellesley v. Wellesley (1828) 725, 808, 810
Welsh (1869). 425
Werner Motors v. Gamages (1904) 982
West (1848). 447
Western Counties Manure v. Lawes (1874). 859
Westmeath v. Salisbury (1830) 772
Weston (1879). 104
Wheeler (1819) 945
Whicker v. Hume (1858). 836
Whiley (1804) 90, 91

White (1865)...109
White [1910]..307
White v. Mellin (1895)...859
Whiteley v. Adams (1863)... 869
Whitmarsh (1898)..415
Whittle v. Frankland (1863)..639
Whittle v. Henning (1848)... 744
Wildman v. Wildman (1803)...736
Wild's Case (1837)...433
Wilhelm (1858).. 448
Wilkes (1770)...184
Wilkins and Johnson, ex p (1895).. 678
Wilkins v. Aikin (1810).. 905
Willcock v. Sands (1868)..331
Williams (1838)... 404
Williams (1893)... 311
Williams (1923)... 404
Williams v. Bayley (1866)...416, 417
Williams v. North's Navigation Collieries (1906).......................................682
Williams v. Nye (1891)... 970
Williams v. Williams (1819)... 984
Williamson (1807)...439, 440
Williamson (1844)... 442
Williamson (1908)..136
Williamson v. Taylor (1843)...639
Willis (1916).. 88
Wilson (1817).. 93
Wilson v. Wilson (1848)..772, 773
Winans v. A.G. (1904)..837
Wing v. Taylor (1861)..750
Winscom, Re (1865).. 811
Wise Parenthood (1918)... 369
Wise v. Dunnings [1902]...349, 418
Wolfe v. Matthews (1881)...710
Wollaston (1872)...407
Wood (1834)..396
Wood v. Boosey (1867)... 902
Wood v. Bowron (1866)... 665
Wood v. Chart (1870)...906
Wooderson v. Tuck (1887).. 894
Woodrow (1846)..323, 332
Woodward v. Woodward (1863)...765
Woolington v. DPP (1935).. 111
Woolmeston v. Walker (1831)..742
Woolmington v. DPP (1935)... 229, 256, 419, 420
Worthington Pumping v. Moore (1903)...973
Wotherspoon v. Currie (1872).. 997
Wright (1821)..238
Wright v. Vanderplank (1855)..806
Wyatt v. Barnard (1814)... 905
Wyatt v. Wilson (1820)...900
Yorkshire Miners v. Howden (1905)...710

Youle v. Mappin (1861) 648
Young (1838). 286, 296
Young (1866) 437
Young v. Peck (1912) 706
Young v. Timmins (1831) 640
Young and Webber (1838) 429
Yovatt v. Winyard (1820) 984

Zamora (1916) 343

TABLE OF STATUTES

1351
  Treason Act 1351, 25 Edw. III St. 5 c.2 340
1562
  Artificers and Apprentices Act 1562,
    5 Eliz. I c.4. . . . . 626, 630
    s.4 646
    s.5–6 134
    s.6 634
    s.12 634
    s.15. 626
    ss.18–20 626
1565
  Benefit of Clergy Act 1566, 8 Eliz. c.4 141
1597
  Charitable Trusts Act 1597, 39
    Eliz. 1 c.6 507
  Hospitals for the Poor Act 1597, 39
    Eliz. I c.5 473
1601
  Poor Relief Act 1601, 43 Eliz. I c.2 458,
    473, 487, 509
    preamble 507
    s.5 476
    s.7 726
  Charitable Uses Act 1601, 43
    Eliz. 1 c.4 . . . . 473, 507
1603
  Labourers Act 1603, 1 Jas. 1 c.6
    ss 31–33. 626
    s.7 626
1623
  Concealment of Birth of Bastards Act 1623,
    21 Jac. 1 c.27. 448
1624
  Statute of Monopolies 1624,
    21 Jac. 1 c.3 932
    s.2 933
    s.6 . . . . 932, 934, 935
    s.10 933
1662
  Poor Relief Act 1662, 13 & 14 Car. II c.12
    s.21 474
1670
  Coventry (Ambush) Act 1670, 22 & 23
    Car. 2 c.1 . . . . 300, 301, 393, 396

1677
  Statute of Frauds 1677, 29 Car. II c.3
    s.3 634
1695
  Taxation Act 1695, 7 & 8 Will. III c.20
    s.3 935
1696
  Treason Trials Act 1696 788 will III c. 27 . . 74
1702
  Treason Act 1702 I Anne St. 2 c. 17 340
  Witnesses on Trial for Treason, etc. Act 1702,
    2 Anne c.9 284
1709
  Copyright Act 1709, 8 Anne c.21 . . . . .918, 935
    s.1 880
    s.2 881
    s.3 881
    s.5 887
    s.11. 927
  Taxation Act 1709, 8 Anne c.10
    s.1 905
  Trust or Mortgage Estates Act 1708, 8 Anne c.19
    s.7 909
1714
  Riot Act 1714, 1 Geo. I. St. 2 c.5 350
    s.1 350
  Vagrancy Act 1714, 13 Anne c.26 829
1718
  Seduction of Artificies
    Act 5 Geo. I c.27 935
  Poor Relief (Deserted Wives and Children)
    Act 1718, 5 Geo. I c.8 458
1722
  Black Act 1722, 9 Geo.
    1 c.22. . . . . 283, 388, 393, 394, 396
1728
  Merchant Seamen Act 1728, 2 Geo. II c.36
    s.1 634
    s.2 634
1731
  Quarter Sessions Appeal Act 1731, 5 Geo. II
    c.19 475
1734
  Engraving Copyright Act 1734,
    8 Geo. II c.13 881

1736

Charitable Uses Act 1735, 9 Geo.
II c.36 508

Offences against Persons and Property
Act 1736, 10 Geo. II c.16. 388

1739

Importation of Books Act 1739, 12 Geo. II
c.36 909

1745

Stealing from Bleaching Grounds Act 1745,
18 Geo. II c.27 .141

1746

Regulation of Servants and Apprentices Act
1746, 20 Geo. II c.19 646

1747

Regulation of Servants and Apprentices Act
1746, 20 Geo. II c.19 646

1753

Clandestine Marriages Act (Lord
Hardwicke's Act) 1753, 26 Geo. II
c.32 . . . . 751, 752, 753, 754, 776
s.3 753
s.13. . . . . .752, 838

Lord Hardwicke's Act see Clandestine
Marriages Act 1753, 26 Geo. II c.32

1755

Launceston: Poor Relief. Act 1755, 28 Geo. II
c.38 510

1763

Linen and Hempen Manufacturers' Act 1763
3 Geo. III c.34 (Ireland). 141

1766

Regulation of Apprentices Act 1766, 6 Geo.
III c.25 646

1767

Engraving Copyright Act 1766, 7 Geo. III
c.38 881

1769

Malicious Injury Act 1769, 9 Geo. c.29 . . . 388

1774

Exportation Act 1774, 14 Geo. III c.71 935
Fires Prevention (Metropolis) Act 1774, 104
Geo. 3 c.78 390
Madhouses Act 1744, 14 Geo. III c.49 828
Vagrancy Act 1744, 14 Geo. II c.5 829

1776

Criminal Law Act 1776, 16 Geo. III c.43 . . .154

1778

Parish Apprentices Act 1778, 18 Geo.
III c.47 476

1779

Penitentiary Act 1779, 19 Geo.
III c.74 . . . . 154, 155

1782

Poor Relief Act (Gilbert's Act) 1782, 22 Geo.
III c.83 . . . . 475, 486

1786

Returns of Charitable Donations
Act 1786, 26 Geo. III c.58 510

1787

Designing and Printing of Linens Act, 27
Geo. III c.38. . . . . 881, 978

1788

Chimney-Sweepers Act 1788, 28 Geo. III c.48
565

1789

Designing and Printing of Linens Act 1789,
29 Geo. III c.19 978

1792

Libel Act (Fox's Act)1792, 32 Geo.
III c.60 . . . . 335, 337, 853, 855
Middlesex Sessions Act 1792, 32 Geo.
III c.38 . . . . 24, 25

1793

Friendly Societies Act 1793, 33 Geo.
III c.54 653

1794

Designing and Printing of Linens Act 1794,
34 Geo. III c.23 978

1795

Poor Removal Act 1795,
35 Geo. III c.101. 475

1796

Seditious Meetings Act 1996, 36 Geo.
III c.8 . . . . .345, 350
Treason Act 1795 36 Geo. III c.7 340

1797

Illegal Oaths Act 1797, 37 Geo. III, c.79. . . 658

1798

Copyright Act 1798, 38 Geo. III c.56 881

1799

Unlawful Combinations of Workmen Act
1799 39 Geo III c.81 . . . 650, 652, 653, 655
CH and title
Embezzlement Act 1799,
39 Geo. III c.85 . . . . .376, 385

1800

Criminal Lunatics Act (1800),
Geo. III c.93 & 94. . . . . .235, 829
Combination of Workmen Act
1800, 39 & 40 Geo. III
c.106 . . . . 650, 652, 654, 655, 668

1801

Militia (Ireland) Act 1801, 41 Geo. III c.107
s.6 888

1802

Factories Act 1802, 42 Geo.
III c.73 . . . . 519, 558, 559, 562

Parish Apprentices Act 1802, 42
Geo. III c.73. . . . . 462, 519

1803

Malicious Injuries Act (Lord Ellenborough's
Act) 1803, 43 Geo. III
c.58 .139, 300, 302,
386, 396, 397, 441, 447
ss.1–4 448

1806

Cheltenham Improvement Act 1806 46 Geo.
III c.117. .537 CH

1808

Lunatic Paupers and Criminals Act 1808,
48 Geo. III c.96. . . . . .237, 829

1811

Stealing of Linen, etc. Act 1811, 51 Geo. III
c. 41. 122

1812

Charitable Donations Registration Act 1812,
2 Geo. III c.102 511

Charities Procedure Act 1812, 52 Geo. III
c.101 511

Destruction of Stocking Frames, etc. Act
1812, 52 Geo. III c. 16 . . . . .388 CH

Embezzlement by Bankers, etc. Act 1812,
52 Geo. III c.63 . . . . .376, 379

1813

Ecclesiastical Courts Act 1813, 53 Geo. III
c.127 854

Excise Act 1813, 54 Geo. III c.56 881

Wages, etc., of Artificers, etc. Act 1813, 53
Geo. III c.40 630

1814

Apprentices Act 1814, 54 Geo.
III c.96. 630

Copyright Act 1814, 54 Geo.
III c.156 . . . . 887, 890
s.3 888
s.4 888

Sculpture Copyright Act 1814,
54 Geo. III c.56
s.1 891

1816

Custody of Insane Persons Act 1816,
56 Geo. III c.117 237

Malicious Damage (Scotland) Act 1816,
56 Geo. III c.125 388

Millbank Penitentiary Act 1816, 56 Geo.
III c.63

s.13. 122

1817

Night Poaching Act 1817, 57 Geo.
III c.90 386

Seditious Meetings and Assemblies
Act 1817, 57 Geo. III c.19 . . . . .335, 337,
345, 350, 658

1818

Disorderly Houses Act 1818,
58 Geo. III c.70 61

Stuges Bourne Act 1818 473

Vestries Act 1818, (Sturges Bourne's Act) 58
Geo. III c.69 . . . . 473–4, 478

1819

Cotton Mills Act 1819, 59 Geo.
III c.66 . . . . 462, 560

Factories and Cotton Mills Act
1819 559

Pauper Lunatics (England) Act 1819,
59 & 60 Geo. III c.127 828

Poor Relief Act 1819, 59 Geo.
III c.12 . . . . 474, 478

Seditious Meetings Act 1819, 60 Geo.
III & 1 Geo. IV c.86 . . . .345, 346, 347, 350
s.5 345
s.8 345
s.18 345
s.19 345

1821

Cheltenham Improvement Act 1821
1 &2 Geo. IV c.116. 537

Seamen's Arbitration Act6 1821,
1 & 2 Geo. IV c.75. 655

1822

Confirmation of Marriages Act 1822,
3 Geo. IV c.75 753

Hard Labour Act 1822, 3 Geo. IV c.114 . . . 360

Punishment for Manslaughter, etc. Act 1822,
3 Geo. IV c.38 422

Vagrancy Act 1822, 3 Geo.
IV c.40. . . . . .352, 356

1823

Burial of Suicide Act 1823,
4 Geo IV c.52. 421

Clandestine Marriages Act 1823, 4 Geo.
IV c.17 753

Gaols, etc. (England) Act 1823,
4 Geo. IV c.64. . . . . 156, 191

Lotteries Act 1823, 4 Geo. IV c.60 360

Marriage Act 1823,
4 Geo. IV c.76 753

Master and Servant Act 1823,
    4 Geo. IV c.34 . . . . . . 640, 647, 648, 653,
                                654, 655, 656,
                                659, 674, 719
1824
Combination of Workmen Act 1824, 5 Geo.
    IV c.95 . . . . .335, 655, 657, 659, 669
    s.2 655
    s.3 655
Gaols Act 1824, 5 Geo. IV c.85 156
Masters and Workmen Arbitration
    Act 1824, 5 Geo. IV c. 96. 668
Transportation Act 1824, 5 Geo.
    IV c.84 191
Vagrancy Act 1824, 5 Geo.
    IV c.83 . . . . 33, 45, 298, 364
    ss. 3–6. 298, 365, 776
1825
Combination of Workmen Act 1825,
    6 Geo. IV c.129 . . . . 116, 319, 335, 655,
                                656, 657, 660, 661,
                                662, 665, 669
    ss.3–5. 656–7,
                                659, 660–1
Universities Act 1825, 6 Geo. IV c.97. 357
1826
    7 Geo. 4 c.64 61
Criminal Justice Act 1826,
    7 Geo. IV c.64. . . . . 80, 93
    s.9 284
1827
Larceny Act 1827, 7 & 8 Geo.
    IV c.29 . . . . 117, 385
    s.5 385
    s.49 380
Malicious Injuries to Property
    (England) Act 1827,
    7 & 8 Geo. IV c.30 33
    s.24 389
    s.25 390
Spring Guns Act 1827
    (Lord Suffield's Act),
    7 & 8 Geo, IV c.18. 387
1828
County Asylums Act 1828, 9 Geo.
    IV c.40. 831
Lord Landsdowne's Act *see* Offences
    Against the Person Act 1828
Madhouses Act 1828, 7 Geo.
    IV c.34 . . . . .828, 830, 831
Night Poaching Act 1828, 9 Geo.
    IV c.6 387

Offences Against the Person Act (Lord
    Landsdowne's Act) 1828,
    9 Geo. IV c.31 . . . . .117, 302, 395,
                                396, 397, 402, 405,
                                422, 447, 448
    s.2 731
    s.10 430
    s.27 . . . . 395, 644, 797
Passengers in Merchant Vessels Act 1828,
    9 Geo. IV c.21. 607
1829
Larceny (England) Act 1827, 7 & 8 Geo.
    IV c.29 374
Metropolitan Police Act 1829, 10 Geo.
    IV c.44. . . 21, 27, 28, 32, 33, 36, 40, 46, 63
    s.4 33
1830
Forgery Act 1830, 11 Geo. IV & 1 Will.
    IV c.66. 148
1831
Cholera Prevention (England)
    Act 1831, 3 Will. IV c.10
    s.11. 538
Game Act 1831, 1 & 2 Will.
    IV c.32 . . . . 289, 386
Truck Act 1831, 1 & 2 Will.
    IV c.32 . . . . 636, 642, 647, 682
Vestries Act 1831, 1 & 2 Will.
    IV c.60. 478
1832
Reform Act 1832 . . . 148, 336, 385, 531, 756, 979
Representation of the People Act (Reform
    Act) 1832 2 & 3 Will. IV
    c.45 . . . . 148, 331, 385, 478, 531, 756
1833
Criminal Law Act 1833,
    3 & 4 Will IV. c.44 374
Customs Regulation Act 1833,
    3 & 4 Will. IV c.52 935
Dower Act 1833, 3 & 4 Will. IV c.105. 739
    s.2 739
Dramatic Copyright Act 1833, 3 & 4 Will.
    IV c.15 . . . . .884, 896, 920
Factories Act 1833, 3 & 4 Will.
    IV c.103 . . . . 28, 492, 563
Fines and Recoveries Act 1833,
    3 & 4 Will. IV c.74
    s.2 736
Judicial Committee Act 1833, 3 & 4 Will.
    IV c.41 781
Lighting and Watching Act 1833,
    3 & 4 Will. IV c.90. 38

1834
  Chimney Sweepers Act 1834,
    4 & 5 Will. IV c.35 565
  Poor Law Amendment Act 1834,
    4 & 5 Will. IV c.76 . . . . 26, 28, 37, 56,
                          471, 473, 482, 483, 485,
                          492, 493, 497, 499
    ss.1–7. 804
    s.8 804
    s.15. 483
    s.52 . . . . 56, 494
    ss.71–73. 777
    s.109 484
1835
  Lectures Copyright Act 1835,
    5 & 6 Will. IV c.65 . . . . 899, 920
  Letters Patent for Inventions Act (Lord
    Brougham's Act) 1835,
    5 & 6 Will. IV c.83 . . . . 101, 952, 953
    s.4 938
  Marriage Act 1835 (Lord Lyndhurst's Act),
    5 & 6 Will. IV c.54 . . . . 750, 839
  Municipal Corporations Act 1835, 5 & 6 Will.
    IV c.76 .40, 41, 117
    s.76 . . . . 40, 41
    ss.103–107. 4
  Prisons Act 1835, 5 & 6 Will.
    IV c.38 . . . . 28, 37, 156, 157
1836
  Marriage Act 1836, 6 & 7 Will. IV c.85
    s. 7. 755
  Medical Witness Act 1836, 6 & 7 Will. IV
    c.89. 392
  Defendants' Counsel Act 1836, 6 & 7 Will. IV
    c. 114 Geo. V c.117. . . . 7, 61, 77, 78, 79, 101
    s.394
    s.4 94
1837
  Offences Against the Person Act 1837, 7 Will.
    4 & 1 Vict. c.85 . . . . 396, 397, 447
    ss.2–4 396
  Libraries Deposit Act 1837 6 & 7 Will 14
    c.110 888
  Postage Act 1837, 1 Vict. c.35 CH
    s.11. 403
  Wills Act 1837, 7 Will. IV and 1 Vict. c.26
    s.7 . . . . 469, 739
1838
  International Copyright Act 1838, 1 & 2 Vict.
    c.59 909
  Small Tenements Recovery Act 1838, 1 & 2
    Vict. c.71 582

  Vagrancy Act 1838, 1 & 2 Vict. c.38 365
    s.2 365
1839
  Birmingham Police Act 1839,
    2 & 3 Vict. c.10 .41
  Bolton Police Act 1839, 2 & 3 Vict. c.95. 41
  City of London Police Act 1839,
    2 & 3 Vict. c. xciv 49
    s.6 50
  County Police Act 1839, 2 & 3 Vict. c.xciv
    49 CH
  Custody of Infants Act 1839,
    2 & 3 Vict c.54. 811
    ss.1–2. 811
  Designs Registration Act 1839,
    2 Vict. c.17. 979
  Fabric Designs Act 1839,
    2 Vict. c.13 979
  Manchester Police Act 1839,
    2 & 3 Vict. c.87 .41
  Metropolitan Police Act 1839,
    2 & 3 Vict. c.47 . . . . .32, 33, 46, 357
    s.66 45
  Metropolitan Police Courts Act 1839,
    2 & 3 Vict. c.71 .35
  Patents Act 1839, 2 & 3 Vict. c.67 938
  Prisons Act 1839, 2 & 3 Vict. c.56 160
1840
  Chimney Sweepers and Chimneys
    Regulation Act 1840,
    3 & 4 Vict. c.85 565
  County Police Act 1840,
    3 & 4 Vict. c.88 . . . . 39, 40
  Grammar Schools Act 1840,
    3 & 4 Vict. c.77 517
  Infant Felons Act 1840, 3 & 4 Vict.
    c.90. . . . . .235, 819
  Parliamentary Papers Act 1840,
    3 & 4 Vict. c.9
    s.1 873
  Vaccination Act 1840, 3 & 4 Vict.
    c.29. . . . . 490, 491
1841
  Substitution of Punishment for Death
    Act 1841, 4 & 5 Vict. c.56. 150
1842
  Copyright Act 1842, 5 & 6 Vict.
    c.45 . . . . 886, 889, 894, 902, 910,
                          913, 920, 928, 980
    ss. 3–4. 889
    ss.6–10 888
    s.20 897

s.23 897
Liverpool Building Act 1842,
   5 & 6 Vict. c.44. 585
Mines and Colleries Act 1842, 5 & 6 Vict.
   c.122 564
Ornamental Designs Act 1842, 5 & 6 Vict.
   c.100. 980
Parish Constables Act 1842, 5 & 6 Vict.
   c.109 40
Passengers in Merchant Ships Act 1842,
   5 & 6 Vict. 105
   s.6 606
Pentonville Prison Act 1842, 5 & 6
   Vict. c.29 122
Poor Law Continuation and Amendment
   Act 1842, 5 & 6 Vict. c.57. 495
Quarter Sessions Act 1842, 5 & 6 Vict.
   c.38 4
1843
Customs Act 1843, 6 & 7 Vict. c.84
   s.24 935
Evidence Act 1843, 6 & 7 Vict c.85. 101
Libel Act 1843, 6 & 7 Vict.
   c.86. . . . . .337–9, 349,
                   853, 866, 867
   ss. 4–6. 853
Punishment of Death Act 1843, 6 & 7
   Vict. c.10
   s.62 489
Theatres Act 1843, 6 & 7 Vict. c.68. 372
Utility Designs Act, 6 & 7 Vict. c.65 980
1844
Factories Act 1844, 7 & 8 Vict.
   c.15 . . . . 563, 700
Importation Act 1844, 7 & 8 Vict. c.100
   s.1 804
International Copyright Act 1844, 7 & 8 Vict.
   c.12 . . . . 892, 906, 909
Judicial Committee Act 1844, 7 & 8
   Vict. c.69. 938
Poor Rates Act 1844, 7 & 8 Vict. c.40 616
1845
Gaming Act 1845, 8 & 9 Vict. c.109 361
Lunatics Act 1845, 8 & 9 Vict. c.100
   s.90 831
1846
Nuisance Removal Act 1846, 9 & 10 Vict.
   c.96. 539
Sanitary Act 1846, 9 & 10 Vict. c.127 585
1847
Factories Act 1847, 10 & 11 Vict. c.29 566

Foreign Reprints Act 1847, 10 & 11 Vict.
   c.95 911
Juvenile Offenders Act 1847, 10 & 11 Vict.
   c.82. . . . . 117, 172
Town Improvement Clauses Act 1847, 10 & 11
   Vict. c.34 555
Town Police Clauses Act 1847, 10 & 11 Vict.
   89 357
Town Police Clauses Act 1847, 10 & 11 Vict.
   c.89
   s.28 358
1848
Administration of Criminal Justice Act
   (Jervis Act) 1848 11 &12 Vict. c.42
Criminal Procedure Act 1848, 11 & 12 Vict.
   c.46
   s.1 284
Crown Cases Reserve Act 1848, 11 & 12
   Vict. c.78 130,
                     131, 137, 227
District Schools Act 1848, 11 & 12 Vict.
   c. 490
Indictable Offences Act 1848, 11 & 12 Vict.
   c.42. . . . . 45, 80, 98
   s.17. 93
   s.18 93
   s.19 94
Indicatable offences Act 1848 . . . . . .63, 93, 94,
             98, 113, 114, 117, 201
   s.25 113
Nuisance Removal Act 1848, 11 & 12 Vict.
   c.123 539
Passengers to North America Act 1848,
   11 & 12 Vict. c.6. 607
   s.18 607
Public Health Act 1848, 11 & 12 Vict.
   c.63 . . . . 542, 548
Summary Jurisdiction Act 1848, 11 & 12 Vict.
   c.43 . . . . .129, 458
Treason Felony Act 1848, 11 & 12 Vict.
   c.63 . . . . 340, 342
1849
Nuisance Removal Act 1849, 12 & 13 Vict.
   c.11 539
1850
Labour in Factories Amendment Act 1850,
   13 & 14 Vict. c.54. 566
Mercantile Marine Act 1850, 13 & 14 Vict.
   c.93 572
Parish Constables Act 1850, 13 & 14 Vict.
   c.20. 40

1851
    Administration of Criminal Justice Act 1851,
        14 & 15 Vict. c.100
        s.29 . . . . 400, 405, 406
    Birmingham Improvement Act 1851, 14 & 15
        Vict. c.93 555
    Criminal Justice Administration
        Act 1851, 14 & 15 Vict. c.55. 61
    Evidence Act 1851 (Lord Denman's Act),
        14 & 15 Vict. c.99 101
    Lodging Houses Act 1851, 14 & 15 Vict.
        c.34 583
    Poor Law (Apprentices etc.) Act 1851, 14 & 15
        Vict. c.11. 459
    Prevention of Offences Act 1851,
        14 & 15 Vict. c.19
        s.4 400
1852
    Industrial and Provident Societies Act 1852,
        15 & 16 Vict. c.35 716
        ss.2–5 905
    Patent Law Amendment Act 1852, 15 & 16
        Vict. c.83 955
        s.8–9 955
        s.18 955
        s.27 955
1853
    Aggravated Assaults Act 1853. . . . . . . 406, 797
    Betting shops Act 1853. . . . . .361, 362, 366
    Charitable Trusts Act 1853 514
        s.6 514
        s.9 514
        s.15. 514
        s.46 514
        s.60 514
    Evidence Amendment Act 1853 101
    Factories Act 1853 566
    Penal Servitude Act 1853 162
    Smoke Abatment Act 1853. . . . . 395, 405
    Prevention and Punishment of Aggravated
        Assaults on Women and Children Act
        1853 547
1854
    Common Law Procedural Act 1854
        s.79 865
        s.82 865
    Ecclesiastical Courts Act 1854 769
    Merchant Shipping Act 1854. . . . . .571, 572
        Pt.IV. 572
    Merchant Shipping Repeal Act 1854 572
1855
    Charitable Trusts Acts 1855 514

Criminal Justice Act 1855 . . . . 117, 172
Ecclesiastical Courts Act 1855 853
Friendly Societies Act 1855 665
    s.9 711
    s.19 671
    s.24 664
Passenger Act 1855 607
1856
County and Borough Police Act
    1856. . . . . .21, 37, 41, 43, 44, 50
Marriage and Registration Acts Amendment
    Act 1856 756
1857
Divorce and Matrimonial Causes
    Act 1857 . . . . . 759, 780, 784, 787, 788, 796
    s.2 785
    s.8 785
    s.9 785
    s.22 . . . . 784, 789, 795
    ss.24–26 787
    s.27 785
    s.29 795
    s.32 787
    s.33. . . . . 734, 784
    s.35. 785
    s.43 789
    s.50–51 785
    ss.57–59. 783–5
Obscene Publications
    Act 1857 . . . . .365, 367, 368, 369
Penal Servitude Act 1857 162
Punishment of Frauds
    Act 1857 . . . . 376, 379, 380
Summary Jurisdiction Act 1857 . . . . .5, 129
1858
Chancery Amendment Act 1858
    (Lord Cairns' Act) 966, 988
Medical Act 1858. 441
1859
Divorce Court Act 1859 785
Molestation of Workmen
    Act 1859 . . . . 662, 663, 674
Summary Jurisdiction Act 1859 5
1860
Charitable Trusts Act 1860 517
    s.2 514
    s.3 514
    s.5 514
Criminal Lunatics Asylum Act 1860 235
Divorce Court Act 1860. 794
    s.5 795
    s.7 795

Mines Regulation Act 1860
  s.29 638
1861
Accessories and Abettors Act 1861
  s.1 284
  s.2 .... 284, 296
  s.8 296
Consolidation Acts 1861 .... 61, 123,
                124, 212, 221
Forgery Act 1861 374
Larceny Act 1861 374
  s.30 384
  ss.31–37 384
  s.68 379
Malicious Damage Act 1861 .... 388, 389
  s.3390
  s.58 390
Offences Against the Person Act 1861.... 325,
       397, 400, 401, 405, 447, 448
  s.5 422
  s.7 405
  ss.11–14 396
  s.15 .... 396, 422
  s.18 .... 397, 400
  s.20 .... 397, 400
  s.32–3 309
  s.35 446
  s.43 406
  s.47 .... 397, 400
  s.51–2 405
  s.55 405
  s.57 408
  s.58–9 447
  s.61 407
  s.62 406
Statute Revision Act 1861 206
1862
Chancery Regulation Act 1862
  s.1 992
  s.2 992
Companies Act 1862 .... 700, 711
Fine Arts Copyright Act 1862 ...... 886, 891,
          892, 893, 894, 924
  s.1 891
Merchandise Marks Act 1862 997,
       999, 1000, 1007, 1012
  s.11 .... 1000, 1002
Poaching Prevention Act 1862 387
1863
Alkali Act 1863 544
  s.4 544
  ss.7–12 544

s.10 544
Penal Servitude Amendment Act 1863
  s.2 163
1864
Personal Violence (Garotters) Act 1863
          112 CH tit
Chimney Sweepers Regulation
  Act 1864 565
Contagious Diseases Act 1864 .... 354, 357
Factory Acts Extension Act 1864
  s.6(4) 566
  sch.1 566
  sch.2 566
Insane Prisoners (Amendment)
  Act 1864 235
Penal Servitude Act 1864 .... 45, 126,
          162, 163
1865
Criminal Procedure Act 1865
  s.2 76
Prisons Act 1865 .... 163, 164, 166, 175
Union Chargeability Act 1865 497
1866
Contagious Diseases Act 1866 .... 354, 357
Sanitary Act 1866 .... 546, 547, 556
1867
British North America Act 1867
  ss.55–57 911
Councils of Conciliation Act 1867 668
Crown Law Act 1867
  s.11 94
Factory Acts Extension Act 1867 566
Factory and Workshops Act 1867 567
Lunacy Act 1867 175
Master and Servant Act 1867 .... 116, 670,
       672, 675, 676,
       689, 719
Metropolitan Poor Act 1867 .... 495, 497
Reform Act 1867 .... 633, 667, 725,
       760, 766, 874
Workshops Regulation
  Act 1867 .... 566, 567, 568
  s.3(1) 568
  s.8 .... 567, 568
1868
Alkali Act Perpetuation Act 1868 545
Artizans and Labourers Dwelling
  Act 1868 584
Capital Punishment Amendment
  Act 1868 151
Poor Relief Amendment Act 1868 804
  s.4 486

s.37. . . . . 458, 486, 487
s.52 490
Public Schools Act 1868. 523
s.26 523

1869

Contagious Diseases Act 1869 . . . . . . .354, 357
Debtors Act 1869 . . . . 385, 648, 683
Endowed Schools Act 1869 . . . . .524, 525
Evidence (Further Amendment) Act 1869
    s.3 789
Habitual Criminals Act
    1869 . . . . .46, 164, 170, 176
Trade Unions Funds Protection
    Act 1869. 665

1870

Education Act
    1870. . . . . 490, 525, 528, 529, 531, 532
Elementary Education Act 1870. 172
Forfeiture Act 1870. . . . . 4, 340, 421, 430
Forgery Act 1870. 374
Married Women's Property Act 1870 763
    ss.1–5. 760
    s.7 760
    s.9 762
    s.10 761
    s.12 761

1871

Criminal Law Amendment
    Act 1871 . . . . 674, 676, 677, 678, 679
    s.1 674
Merchant Shipping Act 1871. 572
Prevention of Crimes Act 1871. . . 170, 172, 174
    s.7 298
    s.19 . . . . 90, 164
Trade Unions Act 1871. . . . . 116, 670, 671,
                        673, 699, 700, 706,
                        707, 708, 711, 713
    s.2 675
    s.3 671
    s.4 . . . . .671, 672, 704, 708, 709, 710, 711, 713
    s.4(1) 704
    s.4(2) 704
    s.4(4). 680
    s.8 699
    s.9 . . . . 671, 699, 704
    s.13. 700
    s.23 671

1872

Adulteration of Food and Drugs
    Act 1872. .329, 619
    s.2 328
    s.3 328

Arbitration (Masters and Workmen)
    Act 1872. 668
Bastardy Laws Amendment
    Act 1872. 777, 804
Infant Life Preservation
    Act 1872. . . . . .451, 463, 814
Licensing Act 1872. . . . . 174, 328, 331
Merchant Shipping Act 1872. 608
Public Health Act 1872 545

1873

Custody of Infants Act 1873 811
Judicature Act 1873. . . . . 700, 809, 812,
                        849, 864,
                        988, 997
    s.25(8) 864, 865
Merchant Shipping Act 1873. 575
    s.12 575
Vagrancy Amendment Act 1873 . . . . 360, 362

1874

Alkali Act 1874 545
Betting Act 1874 362
Hosiery Manufacture (Wages)
    Act 1874. 643
Infants Relief Act 1874. . . . . .806, 807
    s.1 807
    s.2 807
Licensing Act 1874 .174
Married Women's Property Act
    (1870) Amendment Act 1874
    s.2 761
    s.5 761
Police (Expenses) Act 1874 51
Registration of Births and Deaths
    Act 1874. 815

1875

Artizan and Labourers Dwellings
    Improvement Act 1875 584
Chimney Sweepers Act 1875. 565
Conspiracy and Protection of Property
    Act 1875 . . . . 116, 319, 320,
                        677, 678, 695
    s.3 . . . . 677, 698, 705
    s.7 . . . . 678, 695, 705
    s.7(4). 696
Employers and Workmen
    Act 1875 . . . . 677, 679, 681, 682, 683
Explosives Act 1875 .51
Food and Drugs Act 1875 . . . . 328, 329
    s.6 328
    s.16(1) 329
Friendly Societies Act 1875
    s.28 815

False Accounting Act (Lopes Act)
    1875............................380
Offences Against the Person
    Act 1875.......................406
    s.3 406
    s.4 406
Public Health Act 1875.............548, 549,
                 550, 551, 552, 553,
                 585, 586, 604, 619
    Pt. III 550
    Pt. IX 550
    s.17................................556
    s.51................................ 550
    s.71................................559
    s.72 550
    s.92 550
    s.131.............................. 550
    s.143..............................553
    s.164 550
    s.173............................. 550
    s.293 550
    s.294 550
    s.295 550
    s.296 550
    s.298 550
    s.299 550
Public Stores Act 1875
    s.6 45
Registration of Trade Marks
    Act 1875 .... 1001, 1003, 1004
    s.6 1003
1876
Elementary Education Act 1876..........172
Trade Marks Registration Amendment
    Act 1876
    ss.1–2............................ 1002
Trade Union (Amendment) Act 1876 679
    s.16 673
1877
Prison Act 1877........................ 166
1878
Factory Act 1878...................172, 492
Matrimonial Causes Act 1878 395
    s.4 797
1879
Habitual Drunkards Act 1879
    ....174, 261, 165
Inebriates Act 1879..................261, 265
Penal Servitude Act 1879............... 164
Prevention of Crimes Act 1879.......170, 172
Prosecution of Offences Act
    1879................67, 68, 70, 117 [CH]

s.2 .... 67, 68
s.3 67
s.8 68
[Prosecution of Offences Regulations
    (1880) ....68 CH]
Summary Jurisdiction Act 1879......129, 172
1880
Assault of Young Persons Act 1880...... 406
1881
Alkali etc. Works Regulation Act 1881....545
Ground Game Act 1881................ 387
Newspaper Libel and Registration
    Act 1881 ....339, 877
1882
Bills of Exchange Act 1882 ....215, 614
Interments (felo de se) Act 1882..........421
Married Women's Property
    Act 1882................. 737, 760, 761,
                  763, 764, 776
    s.1 831
    s.1(1) 761
    s.1(2) 763, 764
    s.11...............................761
    s.12 763
    s.13...............................761
    s.17.............................. 762
    s.19 763
1883
Bankruptcy Act 1883 614
City of London Parochial Charities
    Act 1883 515
Patents, Designs and Trade Marks
    Act 1883 .... 956, 964, 981, 1005
    s.2 1004
    s.6 964
    s.11.............................. 964
    s.26(3)........................... 965
    s.27 944
    s.33............................. 965
    s.57 982
    s.59 982
    s.64 1001
    s.72(2) 1003
    s.74(3) 1003
    ss.82–102 964
    sch.2 956
Trail of Lunatics Act 1883 248
1884
Criminal Law Amendment Act 1884
    s.3404
Criminal Lunatics Act 1884 ....175, 236
Married Women's Property Act 1884.... 408

Matrimonial Causes Act 1884 785
    s.5 768
Prosecution of Offences Act 1884 . . . . . 69, 70
Summary Jurisdiction Act 1884
    s.7 94
1885
Criminal Law Amendment Act
    1885. . . . . 87, 90, 104, 107, 354,
                                    55, 358, 405, 406, 407
    s.2 358
    s.3(2) 408
    s.4 406
    ss.4–10 802
    s.5 . . . . 358, 406
    s.11. . . . . 358, 372, 407
    s.13. 358
    s.20 103
Housing of the Working Classes Act
    1885. 588
1886
Guardianship of Infants Act 1886
    s.2 813
    s.3(2) 813
Idiots Act 1886. 833
International Copyright Act 1886
    s.9 894
Shop Hours Act 1886 . . . . 568, 691
    s.3(1) 568
    s.8 568
1887
Coal Mines Regulation Act 1887 116
Merchandise Marks Act 1887. 997,
                                    1007, 1011, 1012
Probation of First Offenders Act 1887. 172
Truck (Amendment) Act 1887
    s.13(2) 642
1888
Law of Distress Amendment Act 1888
    s.7 582
Law of Libel Amendment Act
    1888. . . . . 339, 372, 853,
                                    867, 875
    s.4 877
Local Government Act 1888 . . . . 48, 50
Patents, Designs, and Trade Marks
    Act 1888. 956
1889
Children Act 1889. . . . . .172, 395
Official Secrets Act 1889 343
Poor Law Act 1889 819
    s.1 819

Prevention of Cruelty and Protection
    of Children Act 1889 . . . . 405, 817
    s.1 817
    s.3 817
    ss.4–6 817
    s.37. 817
Technical Instruction Act 1889 532
1890
Housing of the Working Classes
    Acts 1890–1900. . . . . 588, 604
Intestates' Estates Act 1890. 763
Lunacy Act 1890 . . . . .831, 832
    ss. 198–200. 831
Partnership Act 1890 . . . . .215, 614
1891
Custody of Children Act
    1891. . . . . .395, 405, 813, 819
    s.4 819
Slander of Women Act 1891 858
1892
Betting and Loans (Infants)
    Act 1892. 807
Foreign Marriage Act 1892 838
1893
Married Women's Property Act
    1893. 765
Railway Servants (Hours of Labour)
    Act 1893 . . . . 691, 699
Sale of Goods Act 1893. . . . . .215, 614
    s.3 825
1894
Children Act 1894. 172
Finance Act 1894. .471
Merchant Shipping Act 1894 357
Prevention of Cruelty and Protection
    of Children Act 1894 405
1895
Factories and Workshop Acts
    1895. 691
Summary Jurisdiction (Married
    Women) Act 1895. . . . . .395, 797
    s.6 797
    s.7 797
1896
Conciliation Act 1896 690
Public Health Act 1896 553
1897
Infant Life Protection Act 1897 815
1898
Criminal Evidence Act 1898. . . . . 8, 10,
                                    78, 80, 81, 89, 90, 92, 102,
                                    105, 106, 107, 250, 418, 419

Inebriates Act 1898.................174, 265
Marriage Act 1898 756
Prison Act 1898...................168, 169
Vagrancy Act 1898 358
  s.1(1)(b)...........................358
1899
Jurisdiction Act 1899..................172
Poor Law Act 1899
  s.1 819
  s.2 819
  s.3818
Seats for Shop Assistants Act 1899 570
1900
Housing of the Working Classes
  Act 1900....................... 588
  s.4 588
  s.10 588
  s.11.............................. 588
1901
Factory and Workshop
  Act 1901 .... 604 Ch tit
1902
Education Act 1902 533
Licensing Act 1902.....................174
  s.5 797
Musical (Summary Proceedings) Copyright
  Act 1902....................... 897
1903
Motor Car Act 1903 446
Poor Prisoners' Defence Act
  1903.............. 8, 70, 80, 81, 82, 106
1904
Prevention of Cruelty to Children
  Act 1904........................354
1905
Trade Marks Act 1905
  ss.28–31.....................1004, 1006
  s.37............................. 1004
  s.39 1003
  s.54 1003
Unemployed Workmen Act
  1905.............500, 688, 717, 718, 833
1906
Education (Provision of School Meals)
  Act 1906........................534
Street Betting Act 1906 363
  s.1(4)...........................363
Trade Disputes Act 1906 .... 319, 320,
          702, 703, 707, 708, 710
  s.2 706
1907
Criminal Appeal Act 1907 ....128, 135,

              137, 154
  s.1(6) 137
  s.9 136
  s.11.............................. 964
Deceased Wife's Sister's Marriage
  Act 1907........................751
Education (Administrative Provisions)
  Act 1907........................534
Matrimonial Causes Act 1907
  s.1 788
Patents and Designs Act 1907....... 924, 981
  s.19 952
  s.24 977
  s.27 .... 976, 982
  s.38 976
  s.38(4) 976
  s.39 976
  s.53............................. 981
  s.56............................. 981
  s.93 982
Probation of Offenders Act 1907 820
Public Health Acts Amendment
  Act 1907........................553
  Pt.IX............................553
  s.91.............................553
1908
Children Act 1908 .... 87, 172, 354,
           400, 408, 820
  Pt. I.............................815
  Pt. II............................817
  Pt. IV 816
  s.12 446
  s.25 818
Costs in Criminal Cases Act 1908........ 70
Mines Regulation Act 1908............. 691
Prevention of Crime Act
  1908 .... 169, 170, 173
Punishment of Incest Act
  1908 .... 17, 355, 408, 751
1909
Cinematograph Act 1909 372
Housing and Town Planning Act
  1909 .... 590, 596
Probation of Offenders Act 1909 172
Trade Boards Act 1909................. 692
  s.6 692
1911
Copyright Act 1911 ....882, 892,
           897, 924, 983
  s.1(1) 925
  s.1(2) 926
  s.1(2)(d).......................... 929

s.2 892
s.2(1)(i) 927
s.2(2)............................ 926
s.2(3)............................ 926
s.3 925
s.5 927
s.5(2) 927
s.7 926
s.8 982
s.11............................... 982
s.17............................... 926
s.19(2)–(8)........................ 929
s.22 983
s.31............................ 900, 925
s.32 925
National Insurance Act 1911............ 505
Official Secrets Act 1911............ 343, 987
s.1 343
Parliament Act 1911 714
Perjury Act 1911......................216
1912
Criminal Law Amendment
      Act 1912 358
Shops Act 1912...................... 569
s.2 569
1913
Forgery Act 1913 ....216, 374
Mental Defectives Act 1913 ...... 175, 832, 833
Trade Union Act 1913................. 714
s.1(2) 714
ss.3–4 714
1914
Criminal Justice Administration
      Act 1914 .... 87, 117, 172
1916
Larceny Act 1916..................379, 382
s.1(2) 383
s.2 388
s.7 384
s.8 384
s.17.............................. 379
s.17(a) 379
s.20 380
s.33(1) 731
s.43 .... 90, 216, 374
1919
Patents Amendment Act 1919
s.38A(2)........................... 976
Police Act 1919..................... 48, 52
Sex Disqualification (Removal) Act 1919
s.1 822

1920
Administration of Justice Act 1920...... 785
Juvenile Courts (Metropolis)
      Act 1920........................ 822
1921
Deceased Brother's Widow's Marriage
      Act 1921 751
1922
Criminal Law Amendment
      Act 1922........................ 406
Infanticide Act 1922........ 154, 452, 453, 814
1925
Administration of Estates Act 1925...... 763
Criminal Justice Act 1925
s.40(1)............................ 266
Dramatic and Musical Protection
      Act 1925 929
Guardianship of Infants Act 1925
s.1 813
s.4 813
s.5 813
Summary Jurisdiction (Separation
      and Maintenance) Act 1925 797
1926
Adoption Act 1926 818
Judicial Proceedings (Regulation of
      Reports) Act 1926................. 789
Legitimacy Act 1926................... 805
1927
Trade Disputes and Trade Unions
      Act 1927
s.3 706
s.4 715
1929
Age of Marriage Act 1929 749
Infant Life Preservation
      Act 1929........................ 447
1930
Poor Prisoners Defence Act 1930......... 83
Road Traffic Act 1930................. 446
s.15(1)............................ 266
1931
Marriage (Prohibited Degrees of
      Relationship) Act 1931..............751
1932
Children and Young Persons Act 1932
pt.III..............................818
Patents and Designs Act 1932
s.25(2)(i) 967
Town and Country Planning
      Act 1932 597

1933
Administration of Justice (Miscellaneous
Provisions) Act 1933
s.1 113
1934
Torts (Miscellaneous Provisions) Act 1934
s.1 855
1935
Law Reform (Married Women and
Tortfeasors) Act 1935 766
Law Reform (Miscellaneous Provisions)
Act 1935
s.3 764
1937
Matrimonial Causes Act 1837
s.7 749
1938
Infanticide Act 1938 453
1944
Education Act 1944 .534
1947
Town and Country Planning Act
1947 597
1948
Criminal Justice Act 1848
s.31(3) 113
1949
Law Reform (Miscellaneous Provisions)
Act 1949
s.7 789
Registered Designs
Act 1949
s.1 981

1952
Defamation Act 1952
s.4 863
1957
Homicide Act 1957 .154
s.4(1) 422
1960
Payment of Wages Act 1960 643
1961
Suicide Act 1961 420
1964
Criminal Appeal Act 1964 137
1965
Murder (Abolition of the Death
Penalty) Act 1965 154
1967
Criminal Law Act 1967 4
1970
Law Reform (Miscellaneous
Provisions) Act 1970 802
s.4 734
1981
Supreme Court Act 1981
s.72 1000
1987
Minors' Contracts Act 1987 807
1990
Courts and Legal Services
Act 1990
s.8(1) 864
1998
Competition Act 1998
s.70 976

Part One

CRIMINAL LAW

I
General Introduction and Overview

INTRODUCTION

In broad terms, this historical account of the evolving nature of the Victorian and early Edwardian criminal justice system extends across the principal institutions of law enforcement, their procedures and the criminal laws themselves. More specifically, enforcement incorporates the establishment of policing, prosecution responsibilities and practices, the nature of trials, their personnel, and the laws of evidence, sentencing, review possibilities, and punishment. Consideration of the criminal law's sources and form is followed by an analysis of its general conceptual principles, including notions of culpability, moral agency, and the extent to which the law has concerned itself with preparatory activities or assisting in criminal actions. The particular nature and reach of the four primary areas of criminality examined embrace: offences against the state and public order; liability for socially offensive or immoral behaviour; crimes against property interests; and offences against physical integrity, ranging from assault to homicide.

Most basically, the criminal justice system was (and is) the state's institutional response agency to what is deemed to constitute criminal behaviour and therefore open to penal sanction. Except insofar as they relate directly to matters of enforcement, punishment, or formulation of the substantive law, neither the historical interpretation of the social causes nor the demographics of criminality will be considered. However, analysis of the separate elements of criminal justice institutions and laws will frequently involve, at least, brief scrutiny of patently relevant contemporary social, political, and economic circumstances. At the same time, it will be seen that the potential impact of such immediately contextual features was invariably conditioned by the legal profession's extensive level of cultural and institutional autonomy. Consequently, in many respects, it was inevitably from within this legal culture that developments in one criminal justice area could be perceived as having implications for others. Such institutional and substantive interconnectedness, whether or not openly conceded or resisted by contemporary actors and agencies, necessarily occupies a significant place in examining both legal change and stasis within the criminal justice system.

At this preliminary stage it is appropriate to identify one particular feature of the changing quality of nineteenth-century criminal justice: the shifting nature of lay or non-professional engagement in the trial process.[1] Early nineteenth-century Justices of the Peace participated in the criminal justice system in several ways, including summary trial of low level crimes, conducting preliminary hearings prior to trial on indictment, and sitting on Quarter Sessions Benches, although borough Sessions were increasingly led by legally qualified Recorders.[2] For a host of reasons the range of offences triable summarily underwent substantial expansion throughout the nineteenth century (see below).[3] By the early 1900s, over 80 per cent of all prosecutions were tried summarily, with the great majority of these dealt with by lay justices rather than the relatively small number of professional stipendiary magistrates. This conversion of many forms of criminality from indictable[4] to summary while increasing the impact of lay justice, at the same time led to a proportionate diminution in (petty) jury trials.[5] Many crimes previously dealt with by justices and juries at Quarter Sessions were steadily relegated to jury-less summary trial before such self-same justices.

[1] Other than Justices of the Peace, lay participation was also seen in coroners' courts, grand juries, and (petty) juries for trials on indictment. Beyond trial and conviction, was the possibility of Executive review, a rather different species of lay involvement. See generally, below. Although all formal distinctions between felonies and misdemeanours were not finally abolished until the Criminal Law Act 1967, the last of substance, forfeiture on conviction of a felony, was removed by the Forfeiture Act 1870. Except where specifically noted, the felony/misdemeanour distinction was of no consequence after abolition of benefit of clergy in 1827. Stephen, *HCL*, i, 192–4.

[2] For the role of professional judges at Quarter Sessions and the deposing of magistrates, especially in boroughs, see the Municipal Corporations Act 1835, 5 & 6 Will 4, c. 76, ss 103–107 and Quarter Sessions Act 1842 5 & 6 Vict. c. 38. The 1835 Act also enabled boroughs to appoint legally qualified stipendiary magistrates (s 99), a power hardly used. For a contemporary assessment of the position by 1914, G. Alexander, *The Administration of Justice in Criminal Matters* (Cambridge, 1915), 77–82. Also, XI, Pt 3.

[3] See Ch. III.

[4] For the role and impact of juries in criminal trials, see Chs III and XII below.

[5] Decades of the *Justice of the Peace*, published from the late 1830s, offer a generalized running commentary on the topical concerns and practices of the lay bench. For a sustained consideration of the historiographical problems and arguable influence on many aspects of the criminal justice system of magistrates sitting at both Petty and Quarter sessions, see P. King, *Crime and Law in England, 1750–1840: Remaking Justice from the Margins* (Cambridge, 2006), Ch. 1, and *passim*. Also on the functioning of magistrates in the late eighteenth and early nineteenth century Essex, see P. King, *Crime, Justice and Discretion in England 1740–1820* (Oxford, 2000), Ch. 4. For the nineteenth century: C. Conley, *The Unwritten Law: Criminal Justice in Victorian Kent* (New York, 1991); J. Davis, 'A Poor Man's System of Justice: The London Police Courts in the Second Half of the Nineteenth Century' (1984) 27 *Hist. J.* 309; and 'Prosecutions and Their Context' in D. Hay and F. Snyder (eds), *Policing and Prosecution in Britain 1750–1850* (Oxford, 1989), 397. D. Jones, *Crime, Protest, Community and Police in Nineteenth Century Britain* (1992); J. G. Rule and R. Wells, *Crime, Protest and Popular Politics in Southern England* (1997); and T. Shakeshaft, *Rural Conflict, Crime and Poverty 1800–1860* (Woodbridge, 2003). Additionally, P. B. Munsche, *Gentlemen and Poachers: The English Game Laws, 1671–1831* (Cambridge, 1981).

Despite summary trial's overwhelming numerical dominance in the criminal justice system (along with magistrates' initial key filtering role for trials on indictment) the principal authoritative shaping forces of laws and practices were Parliament and the superior courts. Beside supervision of summary jurisdiction, it was in the superior courts where legislation was authoritatively interpreted, where common law doctrines were developed, and general concepts of criminal jurisprudence formulated. Aside from this, is the practical limitation of much of summary justice's administrative history remaining deeply submerged—probably irrecoverable—as a consequence of the absence or obscurity of systematic and detailed court records. Although true to a lesser degree, similar observations may be made of Quarter Sessions proceedings. Moreover, such historiographical difficulties flowing from lack of reasonably comprehensive records are compounded by (or the effect of) the general absence of lawyers[6] from nineteenth-century summary proceedings, and, for most of this period, an accessible appeals system.[7] Thus, while where appropriate, the nature and significance of summary liability and proceedings are reviewed, it is the activities of the superior courts which substantially attract the historiographical focus in analysing most aspects of criminal justice.

An introductory overview of the criminal justice system appropriately begins with locating responsibility for law enforcement. As a central component of any effective system, the necessity of extensive professional policing was far from self-evident in the early nineteenth century. By and large, the enormously variable parish-based or town organized bodies of constables and watchmen were, at least locally, viewed as adequate for most purposes. Enactment of the Metropolitan Police Act 1829 and the installation of professional policing across London took place in a strengthening rationalizing climate affecting the criminal justice system more generally. In turn this was reinforced by specific, rising parliamentary concerns over the demonstrable inefficiency of much of the parish policing system, along with a fair measure of political opportunism.

---

[6] For examples of the relatively early 'intrusion' of lawyers before magistrates, see J. Beattie, *Crime and the Courts in England 1660–1800* (Oxford, 1986), 276–7.

[7] As a further result, much of the extensive discretion witnessed throughout the criminal justice system until early Victorian reforms, persisted as a distinct characteristic of summary proceedings well beyond this period. It was also discretion which some in the superior courts were happy to endorse publicly on the basis that members of the local bench knew 'more about the habits of the people who lived in their districts'. Bramwell, B., 20 March 1865, reported in the *Maidstone and Kentish Journal*; quoted by C. Conley, *The Unwritten Law* (Oxford, 1991) 18. General rights of appeal under the Summary Jurisdiction Act 1857 (on a point of law), and the Summary Jurisdiction Act 1879 (on law or fact) were, in practice, severely circumscribed by the pre-condition that appellants provided security for costs. Much the same was true of Quarter Sessions proceedings. And generally, XI, Pt 3.

Opposition to Metropolitan and provincial reform came from several directions: most basic of all, that the anti-libertarian, intrusive quality of professional policing was too high a price even for a more effective system. Once vanquished by the weighty anxieties of the more exposed propertied middle classes, these libertarian arguments gave way to what was to become a familiar process of centrally enacted facilitative provisions, eventually superseded by mandatory policing requirements. As with the wider processes of nineteenth-century creeping centralization of once local powers, whether through systematized supervision or a complete assumption of responsibility for some function of government, the opposition was often bought off with centrally funded financial inducements.

Aside from such objections of high principle and more lowly concerns of who pays, throughout Victorian times the evolving of professional policing manifested enormous diversity in respect of speed of development, force sizes, and practices. While central government grants provided leverage towards a degree of uniform efficiency, their use over many decades was far from consistent. Indeed, divergence in approaching local policing needs was sometimes depicted as inevitable, if not desirable, by Home Secretaries. Moreover, it was a diversity extending to the very structure of governance and accountability of police forces. Consequently, at the end of the Victorian period, depending on whether it was rural, urban, or Metropolitan, policing could manifest distinctiveness in respect of specific practices, ethos, policy-making procedures, and ultimate accountability. It was a state of affairs which emphatically testified to the haphazard, locally mediated, and only partially centrally driven evolution of English professional policing.

Like policing, the prosecuting of offenders was not, in general, seen to be the central state's business. This conception of the legitimate interests of the state was, if anything, more securely embedded in relation to responsibility for prosecution of offenders than their deterrence or apprehension; whether true or not, the resistance to state responsibility for criminal prosecution certainly survived longer. But the intimate association between policing and prosecutions, noted by parliamentary committees, was undeniable. Nineteenth-century advocates and opposers of reforming policing and prosecutions systems often deployed similar arguments of a libertarian, anti-statist nature, or simply objections as to costs. Indeed, it was often the same individuals who campaigned in both areas: sometimes this was separately in relation to the distinct causes; while in other cases prosecution and police reform were loosely conjoined.

As in policing, local prosecuting practices displayed enormous differences, principally as a consequence of the varying levels of diligence and intervention of magistrates and constabulary. Up to a point, for most of the nineteenth century both sides of the debate on the need and legitimacy of state engagement in prosecutions managed to succeed in defending their ground. An evolving compromise emerged, resting on a mixture of ameliorative measures aimed at encouraging private prosecution: through cheaper or swifter justice by expanding summary liability; funding a state system of rewards for prosecutions; and by awarding victims subsidies to offset the costs of bringing private prosecutions. But, overall, the agency of most radical change in prosecution practices was the professional police. More than uncontrived, the gradual insinuation of professional police into prosecutions followed *ad hoc* local initiatives, and for a lengthy period, in the face of occasional open judicial suspicions, if not outright hostility. To a considerable degree, this default entry of police into the prosecution system, gradually officially recognized and supported by increased funding, deflected much of the force of a succession of parliamentary and other official critiques of the ramshackle, *ad hoc* nature of criminal prosecutions. Consequently, advocates of a structured, nationwide, professional prosecution system were eventually forced to rest content with the establishment of a relatively unengaged Director of Public Prosecutions, whose limited interventionary powers carried very marginal consequences for the system generally.

Looking at the other side of the coin, the protection of defendants' rights, along with striking an appropriate balance of interests between state and individual, also naturally generated extensive differences of opinion across the century. By the 1820s, the entrenched anomalous debarring of felony defendants from the right to counsel had been radically relaxed by the judiciary to permit full examination and cross-examination of witnesses. Participation of lawyers for both defence and prosecution with the consequential rise of adversarialism, transformed the nature of the trial process in two fundamental ways: first, a gradual *de facto* relegation of the interventionary judicial role towards that of neutral umpire; and secondly, the bringing about of a refinement and sharpening of rules of evidence. But though the principle and practice of adversarialism had gained a firm foothold by early Victorian times, because most defendants lacked the means, the majority of trials on indictment continued without the participation of defence counsel.

Furthermore, the desire to embrace adversarialism in criminal trials lacked universal appeal; many lawyers regarded it as more likely to defeat rather than reveal truth; trials would degenerate into a 'war of wit'. But with enactment of the Defendent's Counsel Act 1836, opposition resting on such sentiments was largely extinguished. However, for many subsequent decades, formal recognition of the age of adversarialism remained some distance from the painful realities of most felony trials. On the one side, by mid-century the higher judiciary, through generally insisted that serious offences were prosecuted by counsel. This, together with informal judicial assignment of free defence counsel or encouragement of dock briefs, meant that the majority of Assize cases benefited from a relatively 'balanced' trial.

Yet, at Quarter Sessions, where the overwhelming bulk of felony trials were heard, around half of defendants remained unrepresented at the expiration of the nineteenth century. Consequently, Recorders and Chairmen of Quarter Sessions continued to bear the broad burden of protecting defendants' interests, including testing the credibility of prosecution evidence.[8] Needless to say, it is not difficult to imagine the enormous variability in the level of commitment with which this key informal function was discharged. At summary level, the appearance of defence lawyers remained a relative rarity until well into the twentieth century.

The final major formal procedural shift in the position of Victorian defendants tried on indictment followed the passing of the Criminal Evidence Act 1898. In making all defendants competent to give sworn evidence the 1898 Act threw into strong relief the basic disadvantage encountered by large numbers of unrepresented defendants: should they give professionally untutored evidence or face the inevitable damaging inferences drawn by failing to exercise this new entitlement? Up to a point, this was met by the introduction of basic legal aid provisions. Against powerful opposition from the judiciary and prominent lawyers, long accustomed to and satisfied with informal discretionary procedures, enactment of the Poor Prisoners' Defence Act 1903 constituted a distinctly modest improvement for impecunious defendants seeking professional representation. Judicial resistance to its use in place of comfortable, old procedures, coupled with other restrictions including its unavailability at committal proceedings, ensured that obtaining criminal legal aid remained a haphazard and irregular process. As well as legal right, the opportunities for adequate legal representation continued to rest in good measure on chance and individual judicial temperament.

More broadly, beyond specific defence rights, how was the critical balance struck between protecting defendants from wrong convictions and the powerful social expectation that culpable behaviour should not escape justice? The evolving nature of rules of criminal evidence and attitudes towards appeals offer two further significant markers. Generally, the nineteenth century trend clearly inclined towards narrowing admissibility and asserting the prosecution's duty of proving guilt to a high level of probability. During this period the exclusionary nature of evidence rules underwent more empathetic articulation and refinement. In common with many other features of the criminal justice system, the role of discretion shrank, to be superseded by fixed rules of law. This process was driven by a greater uniformity of judicial practice, principally as a consequence of more extensive law reporting alongside the arrival of treatises seeking to systematize such reported decisions. In good measure, these were responses to the steadily increasing presence and professional demands of prosecution and

---

[8] For the protective or obstructive behaviour of juries, see Chs III and XII.

defence lawyers in criminal trials. The rising numbers of trial lawyers not only modified the trial dynamic and rules of evidence, but also changed the nature of evidence sometimes deployed by the prosecution or the defence—most particularly the use of expert testimony. On the prosecution side, growth of professional policing, and especially detective forces, with the allied emergence of forensic experts, could provide evidence crucial to conviction. More rarely, on those occasions where the defendant was represented, his counsel might seek to defeat prosecutions by drafting in their own expert witnesses.[9]

In sum, the situation of defendants underwent very distinct change over the course of the nineteenth century, moving progressively from a position where unsworn statements constituted an important source of trial evidence to one where several new restrictions worked to exclude defendants' evidence. At pre-trial proceedings, from a formerly interrogatory approach, examining magistrates fell into the practice of cautioning defendants against self-incrimination out of fear for later defence counsel's assertion of a confession's involuntariness. Over the first half of the nineteenth century heightened judicial sensitivity to the twin notions of 'inducements' or 'threats' was probably also in large measure a response to the foundation and expansion of professional policing. Both judges and authors of evidence treatises openly cautioned scepticism when evaluating police testimony. Indeed, mistrust and discomfort over the evidence gained by police interrogation of those in custody eventually openly divided the judiciary: a substantial minority of the Bench sought to exclude any evidence gained after arrest, regarding it as unfair, unseemly, and inherently unreliable; yet for the majority, demonstrable voluntariness of confessions always rendered such evidence admissible. While a degree of consensus arrived with the Bench's collective issuing of the 'Judges Rules' in 1912, their uncertain status and full import continued to generate conflicting interpretations. More generally, in practical terms, the long-celebrated right against self-incrimination was of restricted value: realistically, unrepresented defendants at felony trials had the stark choice of giving unsworn testimony or not mounting a defence. Amelioration of this position and strengthening of the substance of any right against self-incrimination only came through increased levels of legal representation, coupled with judicial clarification of the prosecution's evidential burden and the standard of proof.

[9] The publication of the first edition of A. S. Taylor's *Medical Jurisprudence* (1836) was a hugely significant milestone in making the developing forensic sciences accessible to trial lawyers. *Medical Jurisprudence* rapidly became the standard text in the field for the remainder of the century. 1836 also marked the enactment of legislation enabling coroners in cases of suspicious death to authorize both medical investigations and the provision of expert testimony at inquests. See Ch. VII and XI, Pt 3.

In terms of trial balance, it is difficult to gauge the overall impact of late nineteenth-century changes in the competency of criminal defendants to give sworn testimony. Benthamite arguments that defendants should be regarded as a primary evidential source, and therefore at least competent if not compellable witnesses, were long opposed by claims that defendants would, through fear of adverse inferences, be effectively compelled to give sworn evidence. Thus, it was argued, trials would be transformed into inquisitions, thereby greatly devaluing any presumption of innocence and the right not to self-incriminate. Four decades of steadily rising support for full testimonial competence of criminal defendants became law under the 1898 Criminal Evidence Act, with both the bill's supporters and opponents claiming to be protecting the interests of defendants and seeking to avoid wrongful convictions. However, on the absolutely crucial question of the permissible extent of adverse inferences which a jury might draw from the defendant's failure to give evidence, and the permissible nature of judicial comment, neither the Act nor immediately subsequent appellate decisions offered much clarification. Consequently, individual judicial attitudes and discretion remained major determinants of both the actual substance of any specific defendant's right not to self-incriminate, and whether the burden of proof of guilt truly continued to sit firmly with the prosecution.

Turning to sentencing, appeals, and the nature of punishment, over the course of the nineteenth century and up to 1914, huge changes were effected. In relation to each, judicial discretion—that foundation principle of the pre-reform era—experienced both a decline and expansion. After more than a century of steady resistance to the notion, by 1914, through the establishment of the Court of Criminal Appeal and the growing interventionism of both Home Secretaries and senior Home Office officials, judicial sentencing discretion had become subject to concerted attempts to demonstrate greater apparent consistency and settle commonly employed tariffs. Running against these standardizing ambitions was the legislative expansion of the range of punishments at the disposal of criminal courts: in the final decades of the nineteenth century, broad discretionary opportunities were created for courts to achieve a higher level of sentencing particularity and refinement, whereby a punishment might better match the needs of both offender and society.

Legally challenging or revisiting a trial verdict or sentence, though in theory possible was for most of the nineteenth century a slim chance in reality. Absence of an accessible, effective appeals mechanism by and large represented the majority of the legal establishment's preference for swift and final justice. Any routine employment of an appeals system was long viewed as likely fatally to undermine this supreme objective. Additionally, the question of funding what was anticipated to become the automatic or common practice of appeal by impecunious appellants frequently loomed large in any opposition to a more accessible appeals structure. Moreover, decade after decade, Executive review was often taken to be the trump card against change, rendering any wide-ranging appeals system superfluous. Such was the power of this contention that it required the Beck legal and political fiasco to blast a hole in its credibility and give advocates of reform the boost necessary to haul the 1907 Criminal Appeal Bill through Parliament.[10] Even then, a culture of considerable judicial circumspection for many years characterized the Court of Criminal Appeal's approach to exercising its wide investigative and appellate powers.

Punishment, the final stage in the criminal justice process, underwent radical modification during the Victorian era, in both its nature and, to a lesser degree, its objectives. By the time of Victoria's coronation, for all practical purposes, capital punishment had been erased as the most prominent, if not defining, characteristic of the institution of punishment. The credibility of Paley's intellectual and pragmatic justifications for the broad deployment of the formal threat of death as a general deterrent, had by the mid-1830s been fatally eroded. For the rationalists' camp, rather than a virtue, the huge disparity between a large-scale capital threat and the relatively limited number of executions was viewed as a fundamental weakness: uncertainty of discretionary terror failed to deter, discredited and destabilized the criminal justice system, and brutalized society. In its place, reformers sought certainty, not severity, maintaining that punishments for offences should be calibrated according to moral distinctions, rather than determined almost wholly by judicial-cum-administrative whim. Beside this intellectual and cultural shift, the pragmatic driving force of change lay in the sheer pressure of numbers of capital convictions reached by the 1820s: a stark choice between executing many more capital felons to retain any credible power of general deterrence or abandoning the profligate use of the capital threat.

Except for murder, with the virtual extinction of capital punishment by the 1830s, and steadily shrinking availability of transportation, the ascendancy of imprisonment threw into sharp relief the twin questions of its appropriate nature and function. Two decades of determined, albeit numerically limited, attempts to regenerate morally some longer-term prisoners and transportees by a rich diet of religious instruction coupled with physical isolation, gave way to more openly punitive and retributive nationally organized prison regimes. Begun in the late 1840s, Joshua Jebb's public works prison programme, discredited by an ill-structured remission system, and over-burdened by the drying up of transportation, was eventually superseded by a quarter of a century of prison policy heavily underscored by the ambition of maximum deterrence, efficiently

---

[10] See Ch. IV.

administered by Edmund Du Cane. Like effective policing, under Du Cane's largely undisturbed reign, both prisons and crime became a national concern. Despite a proportionate (to the general population) decline in recorded crime and the prison population during this period, social and political distaste for the monochromatic severity of Du Cane's prisons' policy eventually brought forth in 1895 the Gladstone Report's broad critique, favouring a more personalized, bespoke approach to punishment. Partly on the back of the respectability and credibility gained by advancing medical and social sciences, moral redemption of prisoners returned as a defensible objective.

Yet, while promising penal enlightenment, the ambitious rhetoric of the Gladstone Report was sufficiently hedged by reservations for those minded to act cautiously; this Evelyn Ruggles-Brise, Du Cane's successor, did. In the period running up to 1914, while holding fast to the previous six decades central raison d'être of deterrence and retribution, Ruggles-Brise oversaw a collection of relatively modest innovations, partly inspired by the broad objective of the greater individualism of punishment sought by the Gladstone Report. In focusing on recidivism, inebriety, vagrancy, and juvenile offenders, Ruggles-Brise and the Home Office were addressing the most intractable areas of criminality, problems which became indelibly familiar to successive generations of penal reformers and politicians throughout the nineteenth century. Segregation and differentiation of treatment, long a steady goal of the authorities in dealing with young offenders, were now to be reinvigorated by a broader social welfare ethos taking root in the early 1900s.

Such limited shifts from punishment to welfare or treatment, laced with a widespread dalliance with eugenics, also provided the foundations for the segregation of recidivists, inebriates, vagrants, and the 'feeble-minded'. Whether in the form of domestic, penal, or labour colonies, these groups became the subject of brief, sometimes still-born penal experiments. With the exception of juvenile offenders, by the opening of the First World War, in all essentials, most prisoners remained subject to prison regimes whose core functions were expressed to be punishment and deterrence. After a relatively optimistic interlude of 20 years, following the Gladstone Report, deep scepticism over the moral regeneration of adult criminals once more reasserted itself as the dominant characteristic of penal culture.

Looking at the criminal laws themselves, with the major qualification of strict liability and regulatory offences, the source of the substantive criminal law during the Victorian era remained essentially the common law. Unlike the apparatus and machinery of policing, punishment, and large areas of criminal procedure, both the general and specific rules of criminal law were, and continued to be, judge made. Outside regulatory offences, even those limited occasions of legislative intervention in substantive areas were rarely much more than consolidation exercises, as is well illustrated by the 1861 legislation. By and large, the evolving of the criminal law's general doctrinal and conceptual structures and, to a lesser degree, specific forms of liability, can be viewed as the judicial response to an extensive range of contemporary circumstances, concerns, and other legal developments. These include changes in trial procedure, personnel, and admissible evidence, together with shifts in the nature and objectives of punishment. Additionally, the increasing appearance of trial lawyers was matched by key expansions in law reporting and treatise writing; their combined effect was to place both judicial behaviour and the substantive law itself under new and wider scrutiny.

Beyond these, so to speak, internal influences within the criminal justice system, broader social and economic forces plainly had potential to reshape particular areas of criminal liability. For example, changes in commerce and retailing practices expanded the forms and opportunities for theft and fraud. Growth in working-class political expectations and developing notions of legitimate types of collective protest carried obvious implications for the substance and scope of certain public order offences, even treason. Broader still, after the franchise reforms of the 1860s and 1880s those occupying jury boxes might feel a reinforced willingness to indicate disagreement with either the bringing of particular prosecutions or even the substantive law itself through their 'perverse' verdicts.

What may be loosely dubbed 'general principles of criminal responsibility' embraces three broad areas of law and doctrine: fault, defences, and assisting or preparatory actions. In respect of general conceptual developments in the substance and language of criminal fault, punishment's rationale, while often the mainstay of commentaries and so-called 'speculative' literature, seldom contributed to judicial articulations of the substantive law. This intimate relationship between notions of criminal fault and the function of punishment, while implicitly operating on judicial consciousness, was rarely openly acknowledged and deployed until the late nineteenth century, especially when segregating subjective and objective forms of culpability. While contemporary commentators sought to separate and systematize gradations of moral fault, and identify consistent terminology capturing these distinctions, the judiciary frequently expressed considerable scepticism in the feasibility and desirability of such an exercise. In pragmatic terms, no obvious benefits were seen as likely to follow from jettisoning ancient terminology and soft-edged fault concepts with their intrinsic element of judicial discretion. Moreover, the ubiquitous operation of a fundamental rule of evidence converting foreseeable consequences into results that were presumed to be intended, rather diminished the practical effects and worth of separating objective and subjective fault.

Even the significant growth of strict liability from the 1840s failed to persuade the judiciary of the need to seek anything like a consensus on the necessity of moral culpability for criminal responsibility generally and the weight to be attached to the so-called 'doctrine of *mens rea*'. Indeed, operating in parallel, but never seriously mingling, with what might be called mainstream judicial and other speculation on the language and substance of criminal culpability, were the courts' responses to deployment of the criminal law as a regulatory mechanism in particular social and economic contexts. Here, early nineteenth-century judicial resistance, founded on views running from outrage to disbelief that Parliament could have intended to dispense with fault across wide tracts of penal legislation, gave way to a pragmatic, instrumentalist accommodation by most of the judiciary. But, at the same time, the finding of strict or vicarious liability through application of judicially devised rules of statutory interpretation, left the Bench generous latitude, permitting extensive indulgence of personal attitudes towards fault-free criminal responsibility.

In relation to defences to criminal liability, nineteenth-century judges hardly ventured outside the compass of Blackstone's formulation of the notion of 'will' in approaching any conceptually unified theory. Resort to the formerly significant conceptual language of 'excuse' and 'justification', became inconsistent and seemingly without consequence; so much so, that commentators generally expressed little doubt that the distinction was without legal significance. Rather, their analytical and expositional focus rested on one of two approaches: either, viewing defences as constituting a denial of *mens rea* or voluntariness; or asking whether the actor was able to exercise moral choice and be deterrable by the threat of a criminal sanction. The former approach looked at exculpation through denial of a basic element of criminal responsibility; the latter entailed seeing defences as drawing in extra-responsibility factors. Such lack of anything resembling conceptual agreement amongst commentators doubtless reinforced judicial disinclination to fish in these muddy and deep waters. But while resisting formulation of anything like a conceptual overview of defences, judges could broadly be seen steadily clarifying and objectifying elements of moral agency. This tendency was probably driven by two ambitions: by the 'great principle of deterrence', and the desire for a morally acceptable outcome. Insistence on objective defence standards was frequently viewed as reducing the likelihood of false claims, threatening to undermine specific and general deterrence and fostering inappropriate acquittals. Moreover, objective defence standards were perceived as necessary to stave off the limitless perils of moral indeterminacy in fixing criminal responsibility. This fear proved the principal inhibition to formally relaxing the relatively narrow grounds upon which an insanity defence might be pleaded, and inhabited much judicial and speculative discussion over the boundaries of provocation, necessity, and duress as defences.

A final area of general principles concerns complicity and inchoate liability. Long before the nineteenth century, the criminal law regarded certain forms of preparatory actions or assistance in the carrying out of crimes by others as patently worthy of its attention. Broadly, collusive arrangements with a criminal objective could, without further action, attract conspiracy charges. Preparatory involvement or assistance in the planning or execution of an offence might also attract liability for complicity: criminality as an 'accessory' derived from another party's actions. As a generalization, whereas the judiciary resisted the temptation to extend the reach of complicity liability during the nineteenth century, over the same period, inchoate liability in the form of conspiracy and especially attempt was subject to determined expansion. Complicity's essentially static state was largely the consequence of continued judicial insistence on relatively demanding *mens rea* requirements twinned with the stipulation of an accessory's purposeful engagement with another's criminal actions. However, where a public order or political dimension was involved, the discrete development of unlawful assembly demonstrated judicial readiness to meet particular contemporary social and political challenges of collective criminality.[11]

A similar observation would apply to conspiracy's Victorian career, where common law conspiracy proved a potent weapon against the political and economic ambitions of organized labour. As much or more than its practical effects on the criminal law's scope, clear judicial acceptance of general liability for attempt marked a most significant nineteenth-century conceptual development. Initially in parallel with prosecution of specific legislative forms of attempts, a general common law of attempt steadily established itself as the orthodox approach to criminalizing attempts. It also indicated the common law's retreat, at least in one area, from its strong attachment to consequentialist notions of criminality.

Moving away from general principles and concepts of liability to individual substantive offences, a crude, but historically useful, division can be struck between what might be labelled crimes against the state and social order on the one side, and crimes against person and property on the other. While the latter forms of criminality were by no means untouched by nineteenth-century developments, it was in the area of public order and morality where more novel shifts occurred. Evolving notions of necessary, legitimate social control and public order liability reflected rising contemporary expectations of a peaceful, appropriately regulated, civil society, liberally infused with Christian morality. Furthermore,

---

[11] See Ch. IX.

adequate protection of the person and property could only be seriously maintained in the context of a reasonably well-ordered society, where social morality and expectations broadly corresponded with legal entitlements enforced by the criminal law.

State security and the maintenance of public or civil order are distinct yet obviously linked practical and legal concepts: Parliament, governments, and the monarchy are both vulnerable to, and protected against, treasonable or seditious activities; extreme public disorder can constitute, or lead to, a challenge to these institutions. Nineteenth-century economic and political changes, including franchise reforms, promised greater constitutional stability, wider social consensus, and confidence. In part this was underpinned by a growing professionalism and effectiveness in policing. One consequence was the relegation of treason and sedition prosecutions in favour of public order liability: a shift of emphasis from concerns over state security—conceding the legitimacy of open public political challenge—to a position where purely civil disorder was less tolerated by the authorities as a politico-social phenomenon.

This meshed with rising sensitivity to social immorality, along with ambitions to exercise increasing legal control over its apparent growth. Here, a combination of expanded professional policing and aggressively moralistic religio-economic middle-class forces sought, and often achieved, a more widespread and consistent enforcement of formerly moribund law. Occasionally, such pressures allied to a broader, increased sensitivity to certain manifestations of social immorality, were successful in introducing new forms of criminal liability. Consequently, over the course of the nineteenth century, principally in respect of prostitution, gambling, and obscene publications, the criminal law gained an increasing presence in social regulation, and most especially in the lives of society's lower classes. However, any claim of a consistent, widespread class and economically inspired nineteenth-century push towards a body of criminal laws aimed at achieving a quiescent working class runs up against strong contrary historical evidence. Rather than pursuit of systematic policies, nineteenth-century law-making and enforcement far more often manifested a spasmodic, fragmented legislative and common law creep, usually propelled by transient public scandals or scares.

Evolving social and political attitudes of the early nineteenth century responsible for generating change in the nature and severity of penal measures, were also of patent relevance to the substance and enforcement practices of offences against the person. As intolerance of casual, low level violence grew, so also did expectations for the enforcement of existing measures and creation of new forms of criminal liability. This developing trend over the course of the nineteenth century became particularly marked in respect of the physical abuse of women and children. To a fair degree, the criminal law's increasing intervention, both in terms of rising prosecution rates and introduction of new offences, tracked the distinct changes in the social status and acknowledged moral entitlements of women and children taking place over the century. Beyond society's increased sensitivity to violence and abuse leading to higher levels of prosecutions facilitated by professional policing, new or enhanced forms of liability were introduced to protect certain features of sexual integrity. However, until modern notions of the distinct and broad welfare needs of children gained a secure recognition in the final quarter of the nineteenth century, the highly germane age of legal sexual consent stayed fixed at 12 years. Moreover, the vulnerability of children to predation from within the family remained largely unprotected by criminal sanction until the Punishment of Incest Act 1908.

Though hardly novel forms of criminality, by Victorian times the specific requirements of criminal homicide, including the demarcation point between murder and manslaughter and the scope of felony murder, were far from well settled. Fundamental terminological inexactitudes compounded by conceptual obscurity remained almost as prominent in 1914 as in 1820. To a considerable degree, this followed from a continuous underlying and occasionally explicit lack of judicial and wider consensus on the appropriate culpability distinctions between murder and manslaughter, and most especially the legitimate function of objective fault in murder. Amplifying this absence of consensus on key substantive matters was a combination of long-standing uncertainty and discord inhabiting certain defences of special relevance to homicide charges, particularly provocation and insanity. Here, perverse jury verdicts and Executive intervention further underscored dissatisfaction with the substantive law and the reluctance to always assent to its rigorous enforcement.

Lastly, purely in terms of the number of charges brought, protection of personal and real property was the criminal law's most prominent function, operating principally through a range of dishonesty offences and those dealing with criminal damage. Of dishonesty offences, larceny (stealing) was numerically the most significant generic group. To a fair degree, over the nineteenth century, the common law showed itself reasonably adaptable in meeting changing social expectations and commercial needs in relation to larcenous behaviour. Both the judiciary and legislature demonstrated a steady inclination to increase the criminal law's reach into areas of property right breaches previously regarded as exclusively civil in nature. Again, up to a point, developments in the range of tangible and intangible property requiring protection from criminal violation (along with an expansion of criminal opportunities) were accommodated by judicial willingness to discard or modify redundant doctrine. Most notably, stealing's core concept of breach of possessory rights had become seriously outmoded well before the nineteenth century. But accelerated changes in Victorian economic and commercial needs sometimes exposed the limits of the judicial appetite for vaulting conceptual barriers, highlighting the necessity of direct legislative intervention.

In respect of criminal damage, although occasional attempts to widen the scope of liability were made by dislodging subjective culpability requirements, on the whole, the judiciary showed themselves resistant to this particular expansion of criminality. However, while generally holding the line on fault requirements, a fair crop of decisions showed judges, in some circumstances, virtually extinguish the *de minimis* rule by recognizing as criminal damage the most limited forms of property interference.

OVERVIEW

Taking a wide view of the criminal justice system, during the early decades of the nineteenth century, stark mismatches became increasingly identifiable between evolving social and political expectations and the capacity of the criminal justice system to meet such expectations. Urbanization, often accompanied by social dislocation, generated widespread perceptions of relentlessly rising rates of crime, a belief bolstered by the early deployment of officially produced criminal statistics. Concerns over the ability of a formally severe punishment regime, and most especially the capital threat and transportation, to suppress a vast range of criminality soon broadened into official scrutiny of the whole loose structure of prosecution and punishment. As well as decapitalizing most offences, some (but not all) reforming forces seeking a rational, humanely proportional, and effective system of justice pressed for extensive state intervention in both policing and the process of prosecutions. The scale and duration of resistance to innovations in the nature and responsibilities for these elemental criminal justice features point to several conclusions about contemporary priorities and the true depth of attachment professed by many to a more civil and humane society. In particular, with some justification, much can be made of the role in the early nineteenth century of the expanding professional and middle classes in promoting these profound social changes. Yet over many decades such ambitions were significantly qualified by a marked disinclination on the part of these classes to concede localism in the face of central government moves towards standardization through national structures of superintendence, if not control. Where central intervention was not a threat, local resistance to financing promising criminal justice developments also frequently acted as a powerful brake on achieving what general opinion regarded as beneficial change. Of course, tensions between localism and national responsibilities, control, and funding found in criminal justice matters also characterized practically every other aspect or mechanism of social regulation introduced during the Victorian age.[12]

---

[12] See Vol. XIII, Pt 2.

Increasing general pressure and willingness to resolve social problems through some state agency was manifest in some, but not all, areas of the criminal justice system. Though most pronounced in relation to punishment and policing, in the latter case a fair degree of significant local diversity was tolerated until well into the twentieth century. Yet, while throughout Victorian times the broad direction of social policy was towards centralizing initiatives (with the exception of punishment), in the criminal justice arena pursuit of such ambitions was notably sporadic. This was especially so in respect of the adjudicatory process and substantive law. While occasionally given retrospective statutory recognition, such as the permissible role of defence counsel and the substance of pre-trial rules, procedural developments were almost exclusively of judicial origin. This was principally a consequence of contemporary professional legal culture's implicit and occasionally explicit judgments on the appropriate balance to be struck between the defendant's right to a fair trial and society's reasonable expectations of the trial process. It was particularly true of the migration of many rules of evidence, from a discretionary to a consistent fixed rule basis. Even the core issue of affording defendants legal representation was left largely to judicial resolution until after Victorian times.

As for the criminal law itself, a combination of judicial resistance and parliamentary indifference thwarted sustained attempts at fundamentally reshaping both its form and much of its substance. With certain exceptions, as a consequence, the judiciary and legal profession were left undisturbed to refashion where seen as appropriate both general concepts of criminal responsibility and particular substantive rules. Parliament was even largely content to leave the courts to determine the basis of liability of new socially and economically significant regulation, eventually judged to be 'strict liability' offences. And, except where judicial behaviour chafed particularly sensitive areas of the body politic, as in criminalizing certain activities of organized labour, legislation rarely sought to restrict or modify common law developments. In essence, to an extensive degree, the legal profession's law-making authority and autonomy were left largely undisturbed.

However, especially from the 1870s, in step with the widening acceptance of the legitimacy and necessity of state intervention and responsibility in social welfare matters, it was largely legislative intervention which extended the criminal law's remit in advancing particular interests and protecting vulnerable individuals. This pattern is illustrated, for example, by the common law's distinct reluctance to embrace effective principles of duties of care in relation to child welfare and protection of women from non-fatal spouse abuse. Broadly, throughout the Victorian period, both at a specific and general level, responsibility notions were very gradually refined on a largely pragmatic, *ad hoc*, accretive basis, with a strong disinclination to venturing conceptually beyond immediate case needs.[13] Attempts at wider reconceptualizations, or even authoritative judicial restatements of the nature and justification of responsibility requirements were very much rarities.

In so far as responsibility and punishment concepts were implicitly judicially linked to advancing a socially and civilly progressive society, arguably, this was most apparent in the increased articulated and sometimes covert deployment of objectified responsibility standards. It was an evolving process set against, and probably conditioned by two distinct streams of influence. First, the changing dynamic and makeup of the criminal trial, with the lawyer-led sharpening of each opposing party's rights and responsibilities, alongside the extensive displacement of discretion in substantive matters; and secondly, and more speculatively, the influence of the advancing social and political standing of the individual through franchise reforms. This in turn was reinforced by the recognized economic and political power of organized labour in raising the collective significance of its members in the later decades of the nineteenth century. Put crudely, with the rise in the ordinary citizen's social standing and political power came increased expectations of 'responsibilities', including objectively defined capacities and levels of required social behaviour.

[13] Cf. for example, a similar common law resistance to recognizing wider civil duties of care in industrial accidents, see Vol. XII, Pt 4.

II

Stumbling Towards Professionalism: The Establishment of English Policing in the Nineteenth Century

1. LONDON

The enduring foundations of the 'new police' were laid down in a series of Acts beginning with the Metropolitan Police Act 1829 and concluding with the County and Borough Police Act 1856. Novelty lay in central government's legislative intervention in the establishment of professional police forces: initially prescriptively for the metropolis only, but eventually for the whole of England and Wales. The extent to which actual policing practices changed immediately after the 1829 Act is, as will be seen, contentious. Professionalized policing's impact extended beyond the more effective execution of the previous watch system; without central facilitation or strategic policy, it began assuming the functions of state prosecution authorities and enforcement agents of a new age of public order and respectability.

Gauging the historical nature and significance of these developments, and especially the 1829 Act, demands reflection on a complex amalgam of circumstances, national and local attitudes, and currents of opinion competing for dominance throughout the nineteenth century. Rather than viewing the development of professional policing as primarily a centrally contrived, largely linear process, considerable explanatory emphasis needs to be given to its irregular, haphazard quality and fractured evolution. Moreover, appropriate weight must be attached not only to parochial ambitions and prejudices which long played as significant a role as national political concerns, but also to other major contemporary features of the criminal justice system which exercised a sustained influence on the nineteenth-century shaping of policing.

Unsurprisingly, concerns relating to crime and disorder either initiated or occupied a prominent position in most public or official considerations of policing. From early in the century, some of these anxieties were fuelled by the statistical results of governmental surveys, apparently indicating rising levels of all forms of crime.[1] Whether true or not, the perception of expanding crime rates was both widespread and well established until the late 1840s. Rather less tangible were changes taking place in the populace's social sensibilities and particularly its tolerance of criminality. Public manners and behaviour that may have passed muster in late eighteenth-century England increasingly began to chaff on the sensibilities of the rising middling classes and 'respectable' artisans as the nineteenth century progressed: most especially, the tolerance threshold of petty crime and disorder dropped, which in turn generated expectations of appropriate official counter measures.[2] Allied to such attitudes was a broadening consciousness of shifting social structures and allegiances consequent upon industrial and urban expansion. Unease at these manifest changes and uncertainties was stoked up by periodic eruptions of public disorder, events which vividly brought into action the forces of law and order, and directed sharp, if only short-term, official focus on their nature and adequacy. Consequential parliamentary reviews, especially of the policing arrangements in the metropolis, while having little immediate practical impact, exposed contemporary attitudes found in governing circles. Most particularly, they revealed an entrenched attachment to decentralized, local constabulary or police forces, set against a deep, underlying suspicion of any central government ambitions to establish rationalized, countrywide, uniform policing structures.

Reform Initiatives and Parliamentary Reviews of London's Policing

While provincial policing structures and practices were not entirely static nor beyond central scrutiny, the most significant innovations and highest levels of government attention concerned London's policing. Between 1812 and 1822 six House of Commons' Select Committees affirmed broad, if qualified, satisfaction with the civic jigsaw of parish-based watch systems. The 1812 Report commended the 'zeal and energy' of many parishes as 'exemplary and meritorious'. Indeed, the night watch system was viewed as 'so effectual' as only requiring legislative intervention to give it greater 'uniformity and permanency'.[3] Yet, significantly, such 'uniformity' was seen as best achievable by drawing in each parish watch

---

[1] Statistics related to increased levels of prosecutions and committals. On the problematic nature of such analysis see C. Emsley, *Crime and Society in England* (2004), Ch. 2; King, *Crime, Justice and Discretion*, Ch. 5; but cf. H. Taylor (1998) 51 *Econ. Hist. Rev.* 569. Also, 'Punishment', Ch. V below.

[2] For example, the shift in treatment of low-level offences against the person in the early decades of the nineteenth century offers compelling evidence of this change. Both the level of prosecutions and severity of typical punishments markedly increased during this period. See particularly, King, *Crime and Law in England* and Ch. XII below.

[3] *Report of the Select Committee, PP* 1812, (127), ii, 1.

authority under the 'superintending power' of one of the seven existing district
police offices (below), individually headed by 'pre-existing Boards of Magistracy'.
Furthermore, the Report proposed a unified system of criminal intelligence,
fed by each of the seven Boards and collated by a designated Bow Street official, reporting directly to the Bow Street Magistrates and the Home Secretary.[4]
However, a subsequent, mildly innovatory bill, imbued with much of the rationale of the 1812 Report, was soundly defeated. Parliamentary opponents, including
some with distinctly reformist credentials, such as Romilly and Brougham, characterized the bill's provisions as giving 'new and extraordinary powers to police
magistrates', and obliterating the metropolitan system of local policing.[5]

Further Select Committee Reports followed between 1816 and 1818.[6]
Widespread and powerful distaste for less localized policing, responsible for
defeating the 1812 bill, received strong articulation in the 1818 Report. It was an
underlying constitutional and emotional preference, (expressed earlier by the
likes of Blackstone and Paley)[7] for freedom from excessive executive intrusion,
even at the expense of a more effective policing system. This assumed fundamental choice, between liberty or less crime at the cost of anticipated oppressive
policing, was given high-minded rhetorical expression by the Select Committee:

> It is no doubt true, that to prevent crime is better than to punish it; but the difficulty is
> not in the ends but in the means, and though Your Committee could imagine a system
> of police that might arrive at the object sought for; yet in a free country, or even in one
> where an unrestrained intercourse of society is admitted, such a system would of neces-
> sity be odious and repulsive, and one which no government could be able to carry into
> execution... [A]mong a free people the very proposal would be rejected with abhorrence:
> it would be a plan which would make every servant of every house a spy on the actions
> of his master, and all classes of society spies on each other. The police of a free country
> is to be found in rational and humane laws in an effective and enlightened magistracy,
> and in the judicious and proper selection of those officers of justice, in whose hands,
> as conservators of the peace, executive duties are legally placed. But above all, on the
> moral habits and opinions of the people; and in proportion as these approximate towards

---

[4] *Report*, pp. 4 and 6.

[5] Romilly, *PD* 1812, (s. 1) 23: 950; Brougham, *ibid*. Whilst both Romilly and Brougham were
broadly Bethamite in favouring extensive revision of many aspects of the criminal justice system,
neither (and particularly Brougham) showed much inclination to support reform of policing.

[6] *PP* 1816 (510), v; *PP* 1817 (233), vii; *PP* 1818 (423), viii. The 1816 Report lacks any proposals but contains a substantial body of witness evidence including that of magistrates and commentators such
as P. Colquhoun and J. T. Barber Beaumont. Neither of the two reports from 1817 contains any direct
proposals on the structures of policing, rather they review particular policing questions, including
vagrancy, prostitution, and prisons for juvenile offenders.

[7] Neither Blackstone nor Paley saw organized policing as a key component of the criminal justice system. Blackstone, 4 *Comms*, 350; 3 *Comms*, 325–7; Paley, *Principles of Moral and Political
Philosophy* (17 edn, 1809) 355; vol. ii, 295–7; cf. 306.

a state of perfection, so that people may rest in security; and though their property may occasionally be invaded, or their lives endangered by the hands of wicked and desperate individuals, yet the institutions of the country being sound, its laws well administered, and justice executed against offenders, no greater safeguard can be obtained, without sacrificing all those rights which society was instituted to preserve.[8]

A rather less florid version of such sentiments also concluded the Committee's 1822 Report: it being 'difficult to reconcile an effective system of police, with that perfect freedom of action and exemption from interference, which are the great privileges and blessings of society in this country...'.[9] However, the Committee, chaired by Peel, recently installed as Home Secretary, once again focused its criticism on the 'disunited' structure of London's policing, 'under the control of different and unconnected authorities', and, as before, it favoured the established group of police offices collating criminal intelligence from each parish within their respective districts.[10]

This recurrent pattern of largely fruitless, muted parliamentary and governmental concern over the effectiveness and efficiency of parochial policing in the metropolis must be read against two very different potential reform influences: first, slow, but increasingly significant, Home Office-led institutional developments as one feature of wider executive intervention; and secondly, the public campaign conducted by advocates of police reform. Commencing with the Middlesex Justices Act 1792, a cluster of Home Office initiatives resulted in a steadily growing police force, appointed, funded, and (effectively) directed, by central government, whose functions initially complemented the parish-based watch. Broadly replicating the existing Bow Street model,[11] the 1792 Act established seven police offices, each with a force of six policemen headed by three government paid stipendiary magistrates. Like Bow Street, investigating and 'detecting' crime was their principal function.

---

[8] *Third Report* (1818), pp. 33–44. Allusions to the erosion of civil and political liberties were usually understood to refer to the French (especially that of Paris) policing system. The Ministry of the General Police of the Republic led mainly by the infamous Joseph Fouché in the first two decades of the nineteenth century was essentially a political police force. Its less openly politically successor, the Sûrete (Criminal Investigation Department) functioned from 1812. L. Radzinowicz, *A History of the Criminal Law* (1956), iii, App. 8, 539, 'Certain Political Aspects of the Police of France'. For a broad view of this period of European policing, C. Emsley, *Crime, Police and Penal Policy: European Experiences 1750–1940* (Oxford, 2007). However, successive British governments had no scruple in the domestic use of political spies when considered appropriate. See below.

[9] *Report from the Select Committee on the Police of the Metropolis, PP* 1822 (440), iv. Continuing: 'and Your Committee think that the forfeiture or curtailment of such advantages would be too great a sacrifice for improvements in police, or facilities in detection of crime, however desirable in themselves if abstractly considered' (11).

[10] 1822 *Report*, 8–9.

[11] Sixty constables were based at Bow Street during the late 1770s.

Largely because of the combined operational and supervisory roles of stipendiary magistrates, the police offices were generally not viewed as intrusive central government agencies. Yet, this was undoubtedly a notable development, with some justifiably perceived distinct centralist potential as inherent in such institutions.[12] It was a suspicion that two decades later still enjoyed much currency with the likes of Henry Brougham who treated his Commons' audience to a challenge of the constitutional soundness of police offices. But it was the realities of social demography which led to the 1792 Act: Middlesex's urbanization had meant that the gentry needed to occupy local justices' benches had become embarrassingly scarce on the ground.[13] The notorious 'trading justices', recruited from humbler stock (Burke's 'scum of the earth [barely able] to write their own names'[14]) clearly needed more reputable replacements. Although originally envisaged as having parochial origins, once again, lack of local potential judicial talent ensured that appointments under the 1792 Act steadily became a completely Home Office administrative, if not political, function.[15] Additionally, from the early nineteenth century the Home Office with its clutch of stipendiaries constituted an informed forum[16] for reviewing policing practices, and most especially the benefits of uniformity and co-operation across police office districts.[17]

Turning directly to the public campaign for police reform, a key element for those advocating a less severe system of criminal punishments was the substitution of greater certainty of conviction for that of greatest severity of punishment. And for many (but not Romilly and Brougham) a reorganized police force was regarded as a prerequisite of ensuring that there would indeed be a far greater likelihood of criminals being apprehended, prosecuted, and punished. Prominent amongst those of such persuasion were Patrick Colquhoun and Edwin Chadwick. Both acolytes of Bentham,[18] Colquhoun and Chadwick were indefatigable, self-promoting campaigners and propagandists for a radically

---

[12] Fox characterized the establishment of stipendiaries as a 'new principle, which might be indefinitely extended under various pretexts and effects of which no man could foresee': *Parl. Hist.* 1791–2, vol. 29, 1465.

[13] People characterized by the Duke of Northumberland as 'gentlemen of family and fortune': *Parl. Hist.* 1780–1, vol. 21, 685.

[14] *Ibid.*, 592.

[15] R. Paley, 'The Middlesex Justices Act 1792…' (PhD Diss. 1983, Univ. of Reading), 263–70.

[16] Pelham Papers, BL. Add. MS 33110, vols 215–23; HO 42/118, cited by R. Paley 'An Imperfect, Inadequate and Wretched System' (1989) 10 *Crim. Just. Hist.* 95, 111. On the shift from 'trading justices' to stipendiaries, N. Laudau, 'The trading justices trade', in *Law, Crime and English Society 1660–1830* (ed. Landau, Cambridge, 2002), 46.

[17] In 1798 the Thames River Police was added. Out of strong self-interest, merchants persuaded central government to adopt it two years later. For the steady expansion of mounted and foot patrols based at Bow Street, see the 1828 Select Committee Report, below.

[18] For a detailed exploration of Bentham's theories and proposals on the institution and machinery of policing, see Radzinowicz, *History*, iii, 431–47.

new form of policing which they, like Bentham, espoused as part of a grander (utilitarian) strategy for institutional and social reform. Colquhoun's potential influence was largely confined to the pre-1829 period, Chadwick's primarily to the subsequent two decades.

Colquhoun's *Treatise on the Police of the Metropolis*[19] blended Benthamite social and institutional prescriptions with the realities of his own experiences as a London stipendiary magistrate. His diagnoses of London's ills were frequently dire; his remedies often severely authoritarian. Colquhoun proposed a 'Central Board of Police' whose powers would extend greatly beyond preventing crime and apprehending offenders to embrace inculcating sound moral practices through strictly regulating most aspects of working-class life, including leisure activities. Certainly some of Colquhoun's draconian proposals for extensive police surveillance of what he regarded as the proto-criminal classes could only have powerfully reinforced the phobias of those opposed to police reform. At the same time, linking class and poverty with criminal propensities was, and remained, a common practice. Morally reinvigorating the lower orders was an objective shared by social reformers as apparently disparate as the Evangelicals and dyed-in-the-wool utilitarian and political radicals.[20]

Edwin Chadwick's 'Preventative Police',[21] published immediately after the 1828 Select Committee Report, was very much of this nature. As a principal architect of the severely utilitarian Poor Law Amendment Act 1834, Chadwick regarded poverty as largely the consequence of imprudent and often immoral choices. But, unlike Colquhoun, for Chadwick criminality would be curbed by not only increasing the threat of apprehension but also by making the commission of the offence a more demanding and less pleasurable experience[22]—the stock utilitarian human calculation applied to deterring crime. Benthamite rigour in working through utilitarian logic led to 'Preventative Police' incorporating several innovatory features, including an obligation upon all citizens to avoid carelessly exposing property to the risk of theft, and criminalizing failure to report an offence,[23] measures unlikely to have advanced the cause of police reform. Yet, on key matters, especially the fundamental structural question of police control, Chadwick's proposals were surprisingly fragmentary; possibly a rare occasion on which he felt it strategically advisable to side-step controversy.

---

[19] First published 1795; preface of the 7th and final edition published 1806.

[20] See XI, Pt 1, Ch. V.

[21] (1829) 1 *London Review* 252–308. Originally prepared as a memorandum of evidence for Peel's 1828 Select Committee on the police, but submitted too late to influence the Committee's report.

[22] Chadwick's specific employment of Bentham's felicific calculus: making the effort ('pain') required to commit an offence greater than that needed to achieve the objective ('pleasure') legitimately (271–2).

[23] Chadwick deploys the same argument in his 1839 Royal Commission Report, 67.

Beyond Chadwick and Colquhoun, a modest body of literature supporting some form of centralized police force in London appeared in the decade prior to the 1829 Act, the most thoroughgoing of which was John Wade's *A Treatise on the Police and Crimes of the Metropolis* (1829). In it, Wade presented an unsubtle, loaded choice between the pervasive watch system, a 'poor frittered, disjointed, imbecile thing', and a centralized structure, 'united, energetic…, acting for a common purpose, and under real responsibility for the lives and property of two million persons'.[24] Such a centralized establishment, Wade assured constitutional sceptics, would represent no more than a natural progression from the institutional innovation of the 1792 Act; precisely an embodiment of the thin-end-of-the-wedge argument against which Fox had warned three decades earlier.[25]

Enacting the Metropolitan Police Act 1829

Returning to the Home Office in 1828, Peel determinedly set about bringing change to a 'police establishment [that] the Country has entirely outgrown'.[26] In his Commons speech securing the appointment of a new Select Committee, Peel's familiar central theme was the problem of dealing with rising levels of property crime with a policing system fundamentally defective through 'want of uniformity' and proper co-ordination.[27] Hardly by chance, the Select Committee's composition practically ensured a Report broadly sympathetic to Peel's objectives.[28] Moreover, its terms of reference were a hair's breadth from linking increasing crime with extant policing arrangements: 'to enquire into the cause of the increase in the number of Commitments and Convictions in London and Middlesex, and into the State of the Police of the Metropolis…'.[29] Evidence of the effectiveness of parochial policing was equivocal, as were the reasons for this state of affairs. However, the Committee confirmed Peel's earlier

---

[24] 300–2. See also Sir George Stephen, *Practical Suggestions for the Improvement of the Police* (1829) and cf. G. B. Mainwaring, *Observations on the Present State of the Police of the Metropolis* (1821).

[25] *Treatise*, p. 98.

[26] Peel to Henry Hobhouse, his former Home Office Under-Secretary, 4 February 1828, Peel Papers, BL. Add. Mss 40395, fol. 205. Between 1822 and 1827, as Home Secretary, Peel maintained a steady and active involvement in matters of policing. After his 1822 appointment of 'Chief Constables' to head each of the collection of Police Offices, Peel ensured collection of detailed intelligence of the events in their respective areas of responsibility. In 1826, at Peel's instigation, an internal Home Office inquiry into London's policing produced a London policing model similar to earlier Dublin police prototypes, involving police districts headed by 'divisional' magistrates. N. Gash, *Mr Secretary Peel: The Life of Sir Robert Peel to 1830* (Cambridge, Mass.), 487–92.

[27] *PD* 1828 (s. 2) 18: 799–800.

[28] See Gash, *Peel*, 494, and *House of Commons Journal*, vol. 33, 114.

[29] (1828). The majority of witnesses were associated with various aspects of the watch system yet favoured a centralized policing system.

assessment and characterization of the system as intrinsically defective by virtue of its fragmented, non-uniform, and uncoordinated nature, something which would always defeat the best initiatives and efforts of individual parish forces.[30] Expressed in such form, the prescribed remedy was predictable: a system of centrally directed and regulated police for the metropolis.

Peel's subsequent, felicitously titled bill, the 'Metropolis Police Improvement Bill', was introduced in April 1829 and proceeded, without a division, to receive assent in June. Sweeping away the old watch system, the Act established a new 'Police Office' headed by two government appointed magistrates (soon styled 'Commissioners'), answerable to the Home Secretary, to organize and control an unspecified number of uniformed, paid policemen, funded by a new local authority police rate. While the parochial watch system was to be rapidly replaced, the forces of Bow Street and the district police offices would continue as a parallel and distinct system. For tactical political reasons, the City of London escaped the natural logic of the 1828 Committee's Report on the risible basis of having demonstrated significant recent improvement. This fudge, necessitated by the City of London's powerful political leverage, was finally settled with the 1839 compromise solution of a separate police force modelled on the Metropolitan Police (see below).

Several related questions arise from the shift, if not *volte-face*, in public and parliamentary attitudes represented by the unspectacular, swift process of enactment of the 1829 Act: from a position of resolute, principled opposition to apparent acquiescence in seven years. Was the previous opposition truly converted to the cause of centralization, or did it simply fail to appreciate the import of the 1829 legislation? What were Peel's objectives? Were they limited to reform of the metropolis's policing? Just how great or significant were the changes in the structure and nature of policing introduced by the 1829 Act?

Changes in perceptions and attitudes germane to policing are discernible over the first three decades of the nineteenth century. First, the relationship of central and local government was steadily evolving towards greater centralized responsibility from the many demands generated by urban growth and industrialization. But whilst examples of central government intervention are becoming increasingly common in the early nineteenth century, broad acceptance of the legitimacy of state intervention only begins to establish a firm basis in the years immediately following the First Reform Act.[31] Moreover, the concept of general,

---

[30] July 1828 *Report*, p. 22. Excluding the City of London, then an untouchable citadel of influence.

[31] For example, Education 1833 and 1839, Factory Act 1833, new Poor Law 1834, Prisons 1835. At the same time, it might be suggested that the Home Office under Peel increasingly began to represent part of the vanguard of the coming era of centrally led social reformers. Cf. S. Devereaux,

centralized policing touched a particular political and social nerve not present in the case of regulation of, say, factories or education. Benthamite public service crusaders of the likes of Chadwick, were still some distance from winning the day at this time.[32] Therefore, no politician, especially one endowed with Peel's political acumen, would have expected much assistance from any broad wind of change blowing in the direction of centralization: the notion of locally administered policing still exerted a powerful pull; the particular case for reform needed to be made out emphatically. This was achieved through setting current views on the nature and extent of crime and (dis)order, alongside perceptions of just how the existing system coped, or could cope, with this state of affairs.

Though hardly novel, popular belief in rising crime levels moved from the broadly impressionistic to a firmer (if somewhat uneven) footing in the early decades of the nineteenth century with the commencement of publication of crime statistics. While certainly open to more than one interpretation, reformers like Peel made regular and largely uncontradicted use of them when pressing the case for reform in substantive and procedural laws.[33] References to increasing crime make regular appearances in Select Committee Reports. The long-term popular anxiety this perception generated was intermittently compounded by the specific alarm and unease produced by instances of public disorder. Between 1811 and 1821 outbreaks of substantial public disorder were witnessed in London and the provinces. Most concerning in government and ruling circles was the fact that, in the main, these occurrences were economically or politically inspired.[34] Quelling such disturbances by resort to soldiers, and sometimes also yeomanry and militia, at the very least demonstrated the patent limitations of the policing system. Yet, even by 1822 the unsubtle and inflexible nature of this quasi-military practice did not raise sufficient political apprehension to lead the Select Committee to propose anything beyond a revamping of the watch system. Whatever Peel may have believed at this point, *The Times* appeared to voice the still dominant sentiment that a centralized police force was 'an engine superfluous to the honest

---

'The Criminal Branch of the Home Office 1782–1830', in G. Smith, A. May, S. Devereaux (eds), *Criminal Justice in the Old World and the New* (Toronto, 1998), 270; J. Innes, 'Central Government, "Interference": Changing Conceptions, Practices and Concerns, c.1700–1850', in J. Harris (ed.), *Civil Society in British History: Ideas, Identities, Institutions* (Oxford, 2003), 49.

[32] Peel was a long-term, regular correspondent of Bentham.

[33] See Chs V and VI below.

[34] e.g. (1811–12) Luddite industrial disorders; (1815) Corn Bill riots; (1816) Spa Field riots; (1816) East Anglia Wage riots; (1817) 'Pentridge Rising'; (1819) Peterloo Massacre; (1820) Cato Street Conspiracy; (1820–1) Queen Caroline Riots. Beyond manifestations of social unrest were widely publicised sensational crimes such as the East London serial killings known as the 1811 'Ratcliffe Highway' murders. Crimes of this order naturally raised doubts about the effectiveness of local policing and watch systems. The public concern following these murders was partly responsible for the appointment of the 1812 Select Committee on Policing.

protection of life and property, invented by despotism for purposes inconsistent with full and free enjoyment of those blessings'.[35]

However, the steady undertow of political agitation, including that for franchise reforms, over the subsequent half dozen years eventually succeeded in reversing the logic of such rhetoric. The supremely awkward, long-present dilemma facing the politically dominant classes was quite how to preserve their privileges from the competing dangers of an over-interventionist executive on the one side, and an unruly mob on the other. Protection from the latter at the cost of centrally inspired, if not organized, professional policing had, for many, been regarded as too high a premium. But now, instead of potentially subverting general liberty (and privilege), a centrally organized police force assumed the colours of liberty's staunch defender, with central government acting as guarantor. Reflecting this key change of perception, the Tory *Quarterly Review* was ready to accept that 'a vigorous...well organised...regular police force [was] the base on which men's liberties, properties and social existence repose';[36] a ramshackle, enfeebled watch system meant that serious civil disturbance produced the unedifying deployment of 'red coats and bayonets'.

Yet any radical change in the structure of policing required a firm conviction that the old system was not simply failing to perform adequately but that it was quite beyond redemption. In respect of crime control, the evidence was equivocal, it being likely that in many areas the watch system was rather more effective than reformers chose to concede.[37] And although markedly atypical, the highly refined, multi-tiered hierarchy of the City of London Watch, detailed in the 1822 Select Committee Report,[38] illustrated just what sophisticated levels the watch system might achieve in the hands of a highly motivated and well-funded authority. But the most compelling evidence against the old system was its patent inability to meet the contingent demands of public order disturbances. Not only were its forces such that adequately coordinated action was beyond its natural capacity, more seriously, its raison d'être was local surveillance, deterrence, and occasionally apprehension of criminals. Combining parish forces to meet serious public disorder was demonstrably not a credible solution.

Consequently, whether out of political expediency or genuine scruple over the appropriateness of deploying military forces against public disorder, the only plausible alternative was some form of professional police force; one which was

[35] *The Times*, 31 January 1823.

[36] (1828) 37 *Quart. Rev.* 502.

[37] Particularly Paley, 'An Imperfect Inadequate and Wretched System' and E. Reynolds, *Before the Bobbies: The Night Watch and Police Reform in Metropolitan London 1720–1830* (1998).

[38] 1822 *Report*, 4–7.

sizeable enough to prevent crime and keep public order. Of course, the conclusion of such reasoning was not irresistibly the centralized structure enacted in 1829. Other, more democratically accountable potential schemes might have recommended themselves to Peel had his ambitions been solely effective crime control. Undoubtedly, as Chief Secretary for Ireland between 1812 and 1818, Peel's fundamental and successful reorganization of the Irish police system, which his metropolitan model substantially resembled,[39] had reinforced Peel's centralizing inclinations, both politically and administratively. It is also self-evident that the ruling and propertied classes inevitably used extant policing systems to support and protect sympathetic contemporary political structures. But since early modern times such systems have been both enormously diverse in nature and accountability, and much more than the simple pliant creatures of the ruling classes.[40] Although long feeling the need to change the nature of policing institutions, there is no compelling evidence suggesting that Peel harboured any driving ambition for a uniform, national, centrally directed police force[41] upon which any government and ruling elite might depend to subdue political or economic working-class ambitions. Rather, Peel's broader ambitions lay in a modest, rationalized revision of the inter-linked features of the criminal justice system. As well as policing, these included the relative streamlining and consolidation of criminal law statutes, and significant revision of punishment and prosecution procedures,[42] some of which marked an important shift of jurisdiction from jury to summary trial. In giving great emphasis to police deterrence by beat patrolling, Peel demonstrated that he did not fully accept the Utilitarian credo of more effective deterrence through less severe sanctions, coupled with the virtual 'certainty of detection'. Moreover, in expressly making the deterring rather than the investigating of crime the planned force's operational raison d'être, the inevitable taint of institutional spying might be avoided.[43] This choice of emphasis was reinforced by apparently inexorably rising rates of prosecutions and convictions, which, at least superficially, suggested detection to be of less immediate concern than crime prevention.

Furthermore, in accounting for the politically painless enactment of the 1829 legislation, it is clear that Peel was also much favoured by serendipity. Beyond his considerable political acumen in judging the moment in 1828 when

---

[39] S. Palmer, *Police and Protest in England and Ireland* (Cambridge, 1988), Chs 6 and 7.

[40] e.g. King, *Crime, Justice and Discretion, passim.*

[41] *PD* 1822 (s. 2), 7: 803 and 1829 (s. 2), 21: 741. Also Peel's correspondence with Hobhouse: 9 July, 1826, Peel Papers, 40388, fol. 16; 8 December, 1826, Peel Papers 40390, fols 186–9; 4 February, 1828, Peel Papers, 40395, fol. 205.

[42] See Chs III and V below.

[43] Peel's operational guidance to the Metropolitan Police: *New Police Instructions* (1829), and reprinted in *The Times*, 25 September 1829.

reformist arguments had won over sufficient sceptics, other contemporaneous events likely to benefit Peel were unfolding. One was the tortured issue of Catholic Emancipation which had generated considerable parliamentary heat not long before the Police Bill's Commons' introduction; changes in metropolitan policing arrangements may have assumed a relatively low-key, uncontentious guise. Bearing more directly on potential parliamentary opposition to the Police Bill was the campaign for reform of select parish vestries against which allegations of corruption, incompetence, and extravagance had been accumulating over several years. Such concerns reached a high point a little before Peel's bill. Established early in 1829, a Select Committee on the functioning of vestries heard damning evidence during the period the bill was progressing through Parliament. The sting of the sizeable body of opposition from the vestries to Peel's bill may well have been drawn by a disinclination to fight reform on two fronts simultaneously.[44] Moreover, the evidence given to the 1828 Police Select Committee suggests that many vestry officials and watch committee members were by then persuaded, partly on the powerful ground of cost efficiency, of the benefits of a new centralized policing system. For them, the old structure had become outmoded and its administration tiresome; it was a function of local government that had 'gone as far as an imperfect system will admit'.[45]

Rationalising London's Policing: Implementing the 1829 Act and the Metropolitan Police Act 1839

Between 1829 and 1839 London's policing underwent radical structural change: initially through swift implementation of the 1829 Act, and concluding with enactment of the Metropolitan Police Act 1839, under which the parallel system of policing by Bow Street and the seven district police offices was abolished. In many respects, implementation of the 1829 Act provisions proved to be more contentious than its enactment. Both supporters and opponents of the 1829 Act could hardly have failed to be conscious that the success, or otherwise, of the provisions for London's policing carried implications beyond the metropolis. Moreover, for many individuals and institutions, enactment of the 1829 legislation did not extinguish their opposition to the basic notion of the 'new police', nor force abandonment of hopes of some form of reversion to locally administered policing.

---

[44] For this argument see Reynolds, *Before the Bobbies*, 140–5. On non-Metropolitan eighteenth-century policing, see G. Morgan and P. Rushton, *Rogues, Thieves and the Rule of Law: The Problem of Law Enforcement in North-East England, 1718–1800* (1998).

[45] 1828 *Report*, 260. It is, of course, not unimaginable that Peel had been careful to ensure that the vestry officials who gave evidence were not entirely hostile to the notions of more centralized policing.

In a climate ranging from latent scepticism to active hostility several features of the 1829 Act's implementation merit notice when examining the final stages of rationalizing London's police by the 1839 Act. Most particularly, just what changes of personnel, functions, structures were effected? And what were the consequences in terms of constructing policing roles, and fostering the efficiency and acceptance of the 'new police'?

The broad brush nature of the 1829 legislation[46] gave Peel and his newly appointed Commissioners[47] extensive discretion in practically every dimension of policing, including the force's size, structure, personnel requirements, functions, and deployment policies. Establishment of the general hierarchy, its chain of command, and recruitment of the first force was rapid, exceeding 3000 by May 1830. Predictably, this new policing was far from universally popular. At street level, deterring crime through a policy of greater day-to-day scrutiny, social regulation, and more rigorous enforcement[48] of petty offences, such as vagrancy, loitering, and drunkenness, produced extensive friction between police and the lower social orders. This was partly a result of the higher level of daytime street patrols. Moreover, one approach to crime prevention was, in effect, through 'moralizing' those seen as most susceptible to criminality. Contrastingly, outside regular street contact, working-class radicals soon directly experienced the fairly uninhibited use of truncheons by massed forces of effectively organized police, deployed to quell politically and industrially inspired agitation.[49]

Suspicions that the new Metropolitan Police were little less than a covert military force persisted across a wide political and social spectrum;[50] this was a belief

[46] Section 4 of the Act specified '...a sufficient Number of fit and able Men', approved by the Home Secretary 'to act as Constables for preserving the Peace, and preventing Robberies and other Felonies, and apprehending Offenders against the Peace'.

[47] The first two Commissioners who spent 21 years in post were Colonel Charles Rowan, a Peninsular war veteran, recommended by Wellington, and young barrister Richard Mayne. On Rowan and Mayne, Palmer, *Police and Protest*, 294–6. Originally, as the 1829 Act envisaged, they were appointed as magistrates, but this lingering association with a judicial role and the police office model was soon jettisoned with adoption of the appellation 'commissioner'. 'Scotland Yard', the Metropolitan Police's Headquarters (named after the site of the former pre-Union Scottish Embassy) was chosen for its close proximity to the Home Office. D. Browne, *The Rise of Scotland Yard* (1956).

[48] Facilitated by increasing both the scope of summary offences and powers of arrest of suspicious persons under the Metropolitan Police Act 1829 and earlier legislation, including the Vagrancy Act 1824 and Malicious Trespass Act 1827. See *The Times*, 14 October 1829. Also R. Storch, 'The Policeman as Domestic Missionary' (1976) 9 *J. Soc. Hist.* 482–509; M. Roberts, 'Public and Private in Early Nineteenth Century London' (1988) 21 *J. Soc. Hist.*, 293.

[49] For earlier records of government-inspired police intelligence gathering on such movements between 1795 and 1800, see correspondence N.A. H.O. 65/1. For early twentieth century, see e.g. B. Weinberger, *Keeping the Peace: Policing Strikes in Britain* (Oxford, 1991) and J. Morgan, *Conflict and Order: The Police and Labour Disputes in England and Wales 1900–1939* (Oxford, 1987).

[50] For press characterization of the police as military, see C. Emsley, *The English Police* (1996), 25–6.

in large measure resting on central government control of the force without the mediating administrative involvement of stipendiary magistrates. Beyond such enduring constitutional and political concerns, the more tangible matter of policing costs greatly rankled with parish authorities. Widespread complaints of inferior services delivered for higher charges were eventually met in 1833 by central government conceding the logic of centralization and agreeing to fund one quarter of policing costs.[51]

Continuing broad political sensitivity to the new police's existence and functioning was evidenced by frequent parliamentary scrutiny. Particular examples of apparently disreputable police conduct led to two Select Committee reports in 1833.[52] But the following year a Select Committee produced a strongly favourable stock-taking account of the new police. Comprising many of the 1828 Select Committee, including Peel, the 1834 Committee concluded from a review of the statistical evidence that the principal objectives of better protection of property and a 'methodized system of Police', had been 'practically attained'.[53] More expansively, the Committee lauded the police's 'influence in repressing crime, and the security it has given to person and property as one of the most valuable of modern institutions'.[54] This naturally set the scene for parliamentary attention to policing beyond London.

However, structurally, two outstanding unresolved matters of metropolitan policing—the parallel system and policing of the City of London—continued to attract parliamentary attention and generate considerable political heat. Peel's decision in 1829 to leave Bow Street and the seven police offices untouched can be seen as part of the political price of ensuring enactment of the 1828 Bill. As well as side-stepping confrontation with the vested interest of the particular magistrates concerned, extinguishing their administrative role in deploying police at that charged moment of reform, could easily have been enlisted by the proposed legislation's opponents to reinforce the case against centralist ambitions. Furthermore, the detection and investigative dimension to policing, then undertaken by Bow Street and the police office forces, was still redolent with the odour of despised continental policing practices—something from which Peel was inevitably anxious to maintain a strategic distance and exclude from the new police's declared preventative functions. But, with establishment of the new police firmly accomplished, and such sensitivities and suspicions at least dampened, the 1834 Committee felt able to address directly the matter of the parallel

[51] For local authority resistance to the police rate, Reynolds, *Before the Bobbies*, 153–8.

[52] *PP* 1833 (627), xiii and 1833 (718), xiii.

[53] *PP* 1834 (600) xvi *Report of Select Committee on Police of the Metropolis*, 4.

[54] *Ibid.*, 21. The Report's minutes of evidence reveal substantial continuing dissatisfaction with the absence of the old system of local control and the increased financial burden of the police rate.

system of policing. Its proposals to incorporate the Bow Street horse patrol in the new policing structure were effected in 1836. It took, however, two further Select Committee reports before the system of magistrates directed policing, based at Bow Street and the police offices, was completely dismantled, leaving stipendiary magistrates free to focus on their enhanced judicial functions in their newly designated 'Police Courts'.[55] With this reform, the notion and practice of judicially directed police action, well established in Scotland and other civilian jurisdictions, came to an end in England.

The second sizeable issue of metropolitan policing left unresolved by the 1829 Act concerned the City of London. Successful resistance to Peel's 1829 logic of policing efficiency through a coordinated, unified force, left the square mile at the heart of the metropolis with a highly refined, but nevertheless, ancient watch system completely intact. Although Peel had earlier been 'afraid to meddle',[56] the 1838 Select Committee breezily dismissed the City's great historical lineage as irrelevant to the question of what it took to be the needs of modern effective policing. Moreover, it saw the City's policing 'so much a matter of universal interest' that it ought, 'under the peculiar circumstances of the Metropolis, to devolve upon the government'.[57] Whilst no longer undivided in its opposition to some sort of reform, the notion of absorption into its mammoth neighbour proved highly resistible to the City. Deep, historically entrenched desires to retain control over its policing led the City to impressively outflank original government proposals to extend the Metropolitan Police's reach to include the City. This time, rather than simply relying upon staunch resistance to such developments through political and parliamentary influence, the City authorities successfully introduced private legislation creating a new independent police force, closely resembling the metropolitan structure. However, crucially, the City's new force, headed by a single commissioner, was to be responsible to and under the immediate control of the City corporation, and not the Home Secretary.[58]

[55] PP 1837 (415), xii, *Report of Select Committee on Metropolis Police Offices*; PP 1837-8 (578), xv, *Report of Select Committee Metropolis Police Offices*. The Metropolitan Police Act 1839 2 & 3 Vict. c. 47 greatly enlarged the coverage of the force's jurisdiction from a 10 to 15-mile radius from Charing Cross. The Thames Police were also absorbed into the new force; Metropolitan Police Courts Act 1839 2 & 3 Vict. c. 71. The Select Committee of 1838 maintained that such a change clearly separating judicial and executive functions would 'tend materially to improve the office and elevate the character of the Police Magistracy of the Metropolis were their duties better defined and kept more distinct and apart from those of the Constabulary Force' (334).

[56] Peel to Hobhouse, 8 December, 1826, Peel Papers, 40390, fol. 187. Peel was, of course, well aware that City of London's opposition had been the major factor in forcing Pitt's rapid capitulation over the 1785 Police Bill. Radzinowicz, *History*, iii, 117–21.

[57] PP 1838 (578), xv, p. 329. Debated: PD 1839 (s. 3), 48: 701–2; 49: 340–4.

[58] 1839 Act 2 and 3 Vict. c. 94. But the City Police's autonomy was qualified: under the Act, although the Commissioner was appointed by the City's Common Council, approval of the Home Secretary

2. THE PROVINCES

Provincial Policing until 1856

While subject to periodic criticism and piecemeal local modification, provincial policing in the earlier decades of the nineteenth century never experienced the same level of government scrutiny as that of the metropolis. Though Metropolitan Police reform was not generally held up as a blueprint for the provinces, at the very least, it was an inevitable point of reference for future policing developments elsewhere—if only to assert its inapplicability. Just as within London, provincial policing raised sensitive issues of local social influence and political power. In large towns and cities, along with general municipal government, policing arrangements were increasingly the responsibility of the professional, commercial, and industrial classes. Policing in rural areas, while most directly managed at parish level, also entailed supervision by the established gentry through their role as justices. It was a judicial function, with political overtones, operating both at petty sessions and County Quarter Sessions. But, as a consequence of extensive local authority autonomy, rural and urban policing exhibited an enormous variety of structures and degrees of sophistication, united principally by their common use of part-time constables and watchmen. The limitations and inadequacies of these diverse systems, exposed by occasional episodes of public disorder, were met on an *ad hoc* basis by locally recruited militia or yeomanry, or, exceptionally, by deployment of regular soldiers.

This same combination of outbreaks of economic and politically inspired public disorder, perceived rising crime rates, and ebbing confidence in the old watch systems which had facilitated Peel's Metropolitan Police Act, fed a running debate on the state of provincial policing. With social divisions stoked up particularly by Chartist agitation and implementation of the new Poor Law,[59] rather than entrenched resistance to any change, the core question, both for urban and rural local authorities, soon became *what* type of reformed policing system should be adopted. Distinctions relating to the formal structure of local government, hierarchies of responsibilities and influences, along with particular policing needs, led to provincial urban and rural areas[60] following different

---

was required. Also, either the City or the Home Secretary could call for the Commissioner's dismissal. Home Office approval of regulations governing deployment of the City force was stipulated by the Act. For the political compromise struck on City of London policing, A. Harris, *Policing in the City, Crime and Legal Authority in London 1780–1840* (Columbus, Ohio, 2004), Ch. 5.

[59] See 'Law and Political Economy' XI, Pt 1, Ch. VI and XIII, Pt 2.

[60] The Swing Riots in rural southern England, combined with those in urban areas centring on the Reform Bill crisis at the beginning of the 1830s, led the government to prepare a bill setting

development paths up to the 1856 County and Borough Police Act, and, to a lesser degree, into the twentieth century.

Rural Policing

Until the late 1830s, rural policing attracted practically no direct parliamentary or government attention. Outbreaks of substantial public disorder vividly illustrated at a national level the limitations of the largely amateur watch and parish constable system. But consideration of its effectiveness in countering the standard repertoire of crime was left to local initiatives. A rare, early flicker of central interest in such matters appears in the observations of the 1828 Select Committee on Criminal Committals and Convictions, which noted that 'in the Agricultural counties, the business of detection is often left to a village constable who is perfectly unfit to deal with any but village crimes'.[61] Later official reports became even more unflattering, characterizing the parish constable as 'uneducated... entirely ignorant of duties', and 'ineffective, lazy [and] corrupt'.[62] Experience of the 1830s Swing Riots followed by severe and extensive disturbances induced by the new Poor Laws and Chartism, underscored the limitations of parish policing. These events, along with believed rising rates of local vagrancy, coupled with perceived sinking levels of social deference, encouraged local reform initiatives.

Inhibiting such responses were the developing realities of a broader-based erosion in the local political powers and standing of the county gentry and magistracy. By the 1830s, centrally generated commissions were consistently faulting local government practices, creating new administrative expectations and principles, often at the administrative and political expense of the magistracy.[63] However, whilst exhibiting a considerable breadth of opinion,[64] the governing class of the majority of counties (especially magistrates, Quarter Sessions' chairmen and MPs) accepted the necessity of at least some form of revised policing structures. Beside the exceptional course of procuring specific Local Acts,[65] two

up a national police system. Dampening down of disorder and more pressing government legislative priorities killed off this initiative. D. Philips and R. Storch, 'Whigs and Coppers: The Grey Ministry's National Police Scheme, 1832' (1994) 67 *Historical Research* 75; W. Miles, *Suggestions for the Formation of a General Police* (1836).

[61] *Second Report from Select Committee on Criminal Committals and Convictions*, PP 1828 (545), vi, 423.

[62] *Second Report of the Commissioners on County Rates*, PP 1836 (58), xxvii, 8–9.

[63] Such as in the Poor Law Amendment Act 1834 and the Prisons Act 1835. On this redistributive process, D. Eastwood, *Governing Rural England, Tradition and Transformation in Local Government 1780–1840* (Oxford, 1994), Chs 1–3.

[64] Exacerbated by the example of the new Poor Law administrative machinery, D. Philips and R. Storch, *Policing Provincial England, 1829–1856* (Leicester, 1999), 37–8.

[65] e.g. Emsley, *The English Police*, 35.

approaches to rural policing reform were available: private subscription forces, usually established by the local landed interests; and action under the modest provisions of the Lighting and Watching Act 1833. The 1833 Act granted parish councils power to levy a special rate to employ adequate numbers of day and night watchmen. Aimed at gently encouraging greater levels of rural policing without challenging local autonomy, the extent of adoption of such permissive powers turned substantially on the degree to which local apprehension of crime and disorder exceeded innate parish parsimony.

While these unthreatening local policing initiatives progressed, more ambitious revisions were contemplated centrally. The 1836 observations of the 'Commissioners on County Rates' were indicative of the level of criticism to follow in the coming years. Not only did they regard the typical appointee to parish constable of a type intrinsically unfit for the job, the haphazard structure of rural policing itself was deemed utterly incompatible with efficiency and effectiveness.[66] Such was the government's unhappiness with the general state of rural policing, that the Whig Home Secretary, Lord John Russell announced in May 1836 a Rural Police Bill was 'in preparation' for early introduction, if 'time allowed'.[67] But on reflection, rather than engaging in the inevitable head-on fight entailed with such a bill, Russell accepted Chadwick's proposal for a Royal Commission 'to enquire as to the Best Means of Establishing an effective [rural police]'. Privately, Russell characterized existing arrangements as 'lax, careless, wasteful, injudicious to an extreme, [needing] system, method, science, economy, regularity and discipline';[68] sentiments which had driven the Poor Law reforms of 1834, and with which Chadwick was also closely associated. From the Commission's composition,[69] it was clear that the only outstanding question was precisely what structure for rural professional policing would be proposed.

Distinctly radical and centralist, the Commissioners' 1839 Report proposed the establishment of a force of 8,000 national police, in metropolitan mode, under the control of the Home Office and the Metropolitan Police Commissioners. However, crucially (while probably not Chadwick's own view) the local establishment of such a professional force would be elective and not prescriptive: the choice would remain with each county's Quarter Sessions. To both encourage adoption and underline continuing government interest, the cost would be shared,

---

[66] *Second Report of the Commissioners on County Rates* (1836) 8–9; earlier comments in *Poor Law Commissioners Report*, PP 1834 (44) xxix, 5.

[67] *PD* 1836 (s. 3), 33: 906.

[68] Russell to Chadwick, 9 October 1836, Chadwick Papers 1733/1, quoted to D. Philips, 'A "Weak State", The English State, Magistracy and the Reform of Policing in the 1830s' (2004) 119 *EHR* 873, 876.

[69] Chadwick's fellow commissioners were Charles Rowan of the Metropolitan Police and Whig MP Charles Shaw Leferve, later Viscount Eversley, a County Rates Commissioner.

three-quarters from a county rate and one-quarter from central funds. While reporting their activities to local Quarter Sessions, who would be empowered to produce detailed policing rules, matters regarding the size and general management of the force would be centrally controlled.[70] The widespread hostility which met the Report's 'gigantic tyranny'[71] was both utterly predictable and probably politically useful in emphasizing the relatively mild nature of Russell's subsequent County Police Bill. Attracting little opposition, its parliamentary passage was swift, with the only notable resistance coming from the young Tory Disraeli who, reviving largely exhausted constitutional objections, vividly characterized the expression 'rural constabulary' as 'Gallomanic jargon'.[72]

As with earlier legislation affecting the counties, under Russell's locally more palatable decentralized version of the Commission's proposals, the 1839 County Police Act provisions were facilitative; they enabled county magistrates at Quarter Sessions to adopt powers to create local forces, determine their size, conditions of service and select chief constables, who would be responsible for appointing constables.[73] But, at this stage, such innovation was not baited with central government funding. Both the process and pattern of adoption of the 1839 Act provisions threw up substantial contrasts between counties. Debates on adoption at Quarter Sessions[74] reveal an enormous diversity of local concerns. Financial costs and benefits frequently figured in claims of both advocates and opponents of new policing: would the costs of more prosecutions and necessary increases in prison capacity really be worthwhile? Additionally, constitutional and cultural concerns emerged in some adoption debates, including fears of a shift in influence and power from local Petty Sessions to Quarter Sessions.

By 1856 (before the County and Borough Police Act), two-thirds of counties had embraced the 1839 Act. Adoption practices can be linked to economic, public order, and political factors in some but not all cases. A rough, though far from consistent, correlation appears between public disorder experiences and adoption; but sometimes as important were actual or perceived ratepayers' resistance to anticipated increases in county rates. In general tenor, this long-running debate reveals widespread acceptance of the need for revised policing structures, but not necessarily of the type carrying the Home Office's imprimatur. Yet, even

---

[70] *First Report of the Commissioners*, PP 1839 (169), xix.

[71] *The Times*, 15 November 1836. Russell described the Report's proposals as too extensive for the 'present case', PD 1839 (s. 3), 49: 729.

[72] Quoted by Palmer, *Police and Protest*, 425. Peel did not vote in the bill's debate. Disraeli's Francophobic allusion was commonly echoed in the provincial press. See examples quoted by Philips, 'A "Weak State"', 876–7.

[73] The 1839 Act, 2 & 3 Vict. c. 93 amended by the County Police Act 1840, 3 & 4 Vict. c. 88 dealing with financial and force consolidatory measures.

[74] Philips and Storch, *Policing*, 167–208.

though broadly resigned to the need for improved policing, a significant body of opinion amongst the county elite sought policing improvement through revamping old parish constabularies, facilitated by the Parish Constables Acts of 1842 and 1850.[75] Even to many contemporary minds, those somewhat retrogressive Acts held out the possibility of breathing new life into the parish constabulary. However, only a handful of counties took this option of revising and perpetrating the old system of parish constabulary. Government acceptance of, or at least unwillingness to block, such legislation is open to several interpretations, the most likely of which is a simple lack of any consistent resolve combined with concerns over the strength of residual local attachment to parish policing.[76] Moreover, by the mid-1840s, government statistics were indicating[77] that nationally committal levels had peaked, which opponents of mandatory professional policing argued supported their stance. And, while equivocal, favourable statistical evidence no doubt eased government concerns.

Urban Policing

Rapid establishment of London's professional police system under the Metropolitan Police Act 1829 produced striking contrasts with contemporary policing provisions in large provincial cities and towns, ranging from those with no more than unpaid constables to others with substantial cohorts of full-time professional police. Extensive growth in urban manufacturing centres had rendered local government structures generally inadequate. Tory and Whig leaders alike understood that anomalies in local government arrangements abounded, including those for policing. Following the Report of the Commissioners on Municipal Corporations[78] into the general functioning of corporations, the Municipal Corporations Act 1835 enacted a cluster of measures increasing the local accountability of borough government; essentially, awarding greater powers to the enlarged professional, business, and trades classes. Just one provision of the Act (s 76) dealt with policing, requiring each borough council to establish a Watch Committee responsible for appointing sufficient paid constables to keep the peace, prevent serious crime, and apprehend offenders. Although expressed as mandatory, the complete lack of regulations governing any aspect of policing under the Act indicated either the Whig administration's strong confidence in

---

[75] For parliamentary attempts to revive parish constabulary, see C. Steedman, *Policing and the Victorian Community: The Formation of English Provincial Police Forces 1856–80* (1983), 18–19.

[76] For the range of models under the 1839 and 1840 Acts, Emsley, *The English Police*, 43–9.

[77] Above, n. 1.

[78] *PP* 1835 (116), xxiii, 43.

the efficiency of municipal government,[79] or, more likely, absence of sufficient political support for such an erosion of corporate autonomy.

Certainly, as with counties, the rate and extent of compliance with the 1835 Act was slow and extremely varied. Save for some significant exceptions,[80] most corporations saw no pressing need to abandon familiar institutions and fully introduce new, expensive, potentially intrusive, forms of policing. After all, even the unnerving spectre of occasional large-scale public disorder could still be met by the temporary drafting in of sizeable detachments of either Metropolitan Police or soldiers. However, unusual circumstances combined to defeat such expedients in the summer of 1839 for Birmingham, Bolton, and Manchester. Here, against a backdrop of widespread Chartist agitation and disorder, central government was provoked to take on a fermenting brew of local indecision, internal wrangling, historical anomaly and a clutch of radical local politicians. An anxious Whig administration, with overwhelming parliamentary support, drove through short-term legislation imposing on these cities centrally appointed commissioners and police forces broadly on the metropolitan pattern.[81] Such measures were taken within days of Russell's introduction of the purely facilitative County Police Bill, underscoring the Whig government's relative political impotence and probable lack of ambition to force the pace of rural policing reform beyond that acceptable to the county ruling classes.

Provincial Policing: Establishing Uniformity through the County and Borough Police Act 1856

The responses to the explicitly permissive County Police Acts, and the *de facto* permissive nature of s 76 of the Municipal Corporations Act, had ranged from enthusiasm to entrenched hostility. Consequently, by the early 1850s the form and effectiveness of policing in both urban and rural provincial England and Wales remained subject to wide variations. By then, the practice of government to set national uniform standards in many areas of social and economic activity, including industrial production and public health, had become almost commonplace, although not without frequent initial resistance, and in respect of the Poor Laws, sustained opposition. More germanely, for many, central government's role in the criminal justice system needed extending. By the 1850s

---

[79] J. Prest, *Liberty and Locality* (Oxford, 1990), *passim*.

[80] For the pattern of compliance, D. Taylor, *The New Police in Nineteenth Century England* (Manchester, 1997), 32–5; J. Hart, 'Reform of the Borough Police 1835–1856' (1955) 70 *EHR* 411. But cf. D. Wall, *Chief Constables* (1998), 32–3.

[81] Manchester Police Act 1839; Birmingham Police Act 1839; Bolton Police Act 1839. For the political background, Palmer, *Police and Protest*, 411–20.

policies on prisons were being nationally set by Jebb;[82] by which time it had also become unremarkable to assert that 'it was quite as much the duty of the government to prevent crime as to punish it'.[83] Correspondingly, the effectiveness of local policing had moved from being a parochial matter to one of national concern. Moreover, almost annual instances of public disorder, exposing the shortcomings of many local police forces, constituted frequent sharp reminders of this state of affairs. In such a climate, Palmerston took the familiar route in 1853 of appointing a Commons Select Committee on Police. Adopting well-established practice, the Committee's composition and witnesses[84] were selected to ensure support for a uniform policing system. The Committee duly obliged: recommending a new obligatory uniform system for all counties; that policing of small boroughs be incorporated in county forces; that larger boroughs should work closely with county forces; and that central government should contribute towards the costs.[85]

Following two abortive attempts,[86] Palmerston's successor as Home Secretary, Sir George Grey, introduced the County and Borough Police Bill early in 1856. But while the rhetoric of staunch resistance from boroughs and counties had centred on the principle of local autonomy, for many, its true substance proved to be one of money—something of which Grey was well seized. Under his bill, acceptance of compulsory, fully manned, centrally inspected, 'efficient police forces' would be rewarded by a government funding subvention of one-quarter, matching that supporting the Metropolitan Police. Opposition manifested during the bill's second reading, largely from boroughs, continued to insist on the undemocratic, anti-local government nature of the shire proposals: in contrast with the administration of county police by Quarter Sessions, borough policing was in the hands of elected representatives. But by this stage in the history of policing the basic case for professional policing was conceded by most, ensuring that the outcome of this crucial debate was overwhelmingly[87] in support of the bill; with the prevailing parliamentary mood accepting at least the legitimacy of central insistence on basic national policing. This also found voice in the

[82] See Ch. V below.

[83] R. Palmer, *PD* 1856 (s. 3), 140: 243. See also (1852) 96 *Edin. Rev.* 1 at 27 and *The Times*, 7 December 1853, p. 8.

[84] On the Committee's composition and evidence, Emsley, *The English Police*, 50–1.

[85] *Second Report of the Select Committee on Police*, PP 1852–3 (715) xxxvi.

[86] Introduced in June 1854, Palmerston's first bill sought an even greater level of centralized involvement and consolidation of county and borough forces than proposed by the Select Committee. A regime of government inspection and uniform standards, regular reports from county and borough Chief Constables, loss of much municipal independence, along with the absence of any central funding, combined to generate sufficient opposition to sink the bill. A proposed second bill applying to counties only was immediately lost a few days later.

[87] 259 votes for, 106 against. Of the borough MPs, 83 voted for, 69 against.

provincial press debates, with one local newspaper capturing the sentiment by asserting that effective policing was 'as necessary to the proper management of a town as gas lighting', and entailed no greater 'danger to general freedom'.[88]

The 1856 Act's compromised blend of centrally supervised and locally administered policing was achieved in a period when no particularly prominent political or social features pressed the government or its supporters for legislative action, and when committal statistics continued to show a downward trend.[89] Rather, the 1856 legislation was enacted against a background of several lower-level conditioning events, assumptions, and concerns. Most particularly, central and local governments' spheres of interest and responsibility had been gradually and pragmatically redefined in the previous two to three decades; and for most, the spectre of intrusive and oppressive state police had been largely vanquished. In little more than two decades, from the initial examples and experiences of London, the reformed borough and county forces, professional policing had become an established, increasingly familiar and unremarkable fact of life. Moreover, although not an argument deployed in the 1856 debates, the broad belief had firmly taken root that professional policing both improved crime prevention and caught more criminals. Certainly, the apparent decline in recorded crime was, at least, capable of an interpretation favourable to professional policing. Less tangibly, but especially appealing to the middle and 'respectable' classes, the new police showed distinct promise as an agency well capable of promoting the cause of a more orderly, better regulated society. The new police had become a daily reminder and embodiment of the criminal law and a powerful expectation of social stability. As *The Times* eulogized, for many the 'sworn professional policeman...exerts the strength of a dozen rioters and paralyses the opposition by the power which is felt to be at his back'.[90]

With the County and Borough Police Act, central government had gained the authority and some of the machinery necessary to insist on adequate provincial policing. However, the management and operation of such forces remained an

---

[88] *Brighton Examiner* 18 March 1856, quoted by Taylor, *The New Police*, 38. For contemporary press comments, Palmer, *Police and Protest*, 510 and 513.

[89] Three background factors have been commonly identified as having potentially encouraged government action and softened opposition: (i) Between 1854 and 1856 the Crimean War both absorbed army resources available for domestic disorders in garrison towns, and later caused the government to resolve to refocus army organization on purely military deployment. (ii) The virtual ending of transportation of convicts to Australia in 1853 led to the scheme of domestic 'penal servitude' and the 'ticket of leave' system, which generated civic concerns: P. Bartrip, 'Public Opinion and Law Enforcement: The Ticket of Leave Scares in Mid-Victorian Britain', in V. Bailey (ed.), *Policing and Punishment in Nineteenth Century Britain* (1981), Ch. 7. (iii) Expansion of the railways increased the mobility of both criminals and troops; crime began to take on a national as well as a local character.

[90] *The Times*, 7 December 1853, p. 8.

organic element of standard local government bodies for counties and boroughs. Consequently, over the subsequent decades development of police forces and the nature of policing would remain subject to, and the product of, markedly differing conceptions of policing, both at a local and national level.

3. ACCOUNTABILITY AND EXPANDING CAPABILITIES

Acceptance of a Policed State

Despite core, structural requirements of the 1856 legislation, and essentially common objectives, the development of provincial and metropolitan policing over the subsequent half-century continued to exhibit substantial diversity. One new force for standardized policing organization and practices was the system of annual inspections and reports by Home Office appointed Constabulary Inspectorate, established under the 1856 Act. Until the 1870s, policies and practices conducing to 'efficient policing' were almost exclusively initiated by the three member Inspectorate; but the potential for more extensive Home Office involvement was clearly always present. Early reports reveal police forces to be 'infinitely varied in their outlook, efficiency, status and popularity..., in their standards of discipline, and rates of pay... [But] the Metropolitan Police remained an entity within itself...'.[91] For some time, smaller boroughs were prime targets of critical reports because of their perceived 'slackness and apathy' and apparent 'desire to evade for as long as possible the performance of their [statutory] duties'.[92]

An obviously important element in developing the reputation of professional policing and sustaining expansion was the ability to demonstrate success. At the very least, supporters whether in central or local government needed to adduce evidence that the new police were superior to the old system. Extensive early recruitment and retention problems, as well as handicapping the refinement of policing skills, worked against fostering a favourable public image. Yet, by the 1860s, through the combined effect of increased arrests[93] and assumed stronger

[91] 'Efficiency' under the 1856 Act covered 'numbers and discipline'. For inspectors' early reports, see T. Critchley, *A History of Police in England and Wales* (1978), 124, 118–123, and Steedman, *Policing the Victorian Community*, 38–41, 56–9.

[92] J. Hart, 'The County and Borough Police Act 1856' (1956) *Public Administration* 413. On the expansion of police forces, see J. Martin and G. Wilson, *The Police: A Study in Manpower, The Evolution of the Service in England and Wales 1829–1965* (1969), 32. For recruitment, training, working conditions, and professionalization of the police, see Taylor, *The New Police*, 47–77, and H. Shpayer-Makov, *The Making of a Policeman* (2002).

[93] In general, common law powers of arrest changed relatively little during the nineteenth century. Broadly, any person could lawfully arrest someone who was committing a felony or breach

general deterrence, the police were being credited with a steady, continuing countrywide decline in serious crime levels.[94] Whether or not this decline was properly attributable to policing, the general perception was that it was. However, such recognition or belief did not necessarily carry with it unqualified endorsement of the full range of roles which the police had by then assumed.

Most particularly, just how broad the concept of policing should be, and quite how it should be executed, were matters which generated long-term friction between the police and predominantly working-class sections of the population. Beyond seeking to prevent serious offences against person and property, policing soon took on other, contentious functions. The gradual informal assumption by police forces across the country of the role of local prosecuting authorities encountered mixed reactions at all social levels, with open judicial unease or even hostility occasionally expressed.[95] Similar levels of disquiet in many quarters greeted police involvement in the supervision of early released prisoners on licence, authorized under the Penal Servitude Act 1864.[96] Added to this was a more systematic enforcement of laws[97] against gambling, prostitution, itinerant trading, drunkenness, and vagrancy. At the same time, increasingly high levels of less visible, but serious, white collar crime went undetected or not subject to prosecution.[98] In part, this is ascribable to the relative covert nature and obscurity of the criminality and highly restricted investigative capacity of the police until the 1870s (see below). And while it has frequently been asserted that social

---

of the peace, or one suspected of carrying out a felony. However, if it transpired that no felony had been committed only a constable would be immune from an action for false imprisonment. Beyond this basic position, powers and procedures for arrest under warrant (usually issued by a magistrate) were revamped and consolidated in 1848 under 11 & 12 Vict. c. 42. However, by far the most significant nineteenth-century developments were enacted by legislation which expanded both arrest and search powers. Through a combination of specific and general Acts, police entitlement to arrest or search was extended to lesser offences, especially relating to property. Stop and search powers under s. 66 of the Metropolitan Police Act 1839 and s 6 of the Public Stores Act 1875 were prominent examples. On the judicial interpretation of these powers, see L. Leigh, *Police Powers in England and Wales* (1975), 129–40. Important earlier wide statutory authorization of arrest for low-level criminality was provided by the Vagrancy Act 1824. See Ch. X below.

[94] V. Gatrell, 'The Decline of Theft and Violence in Victorian and Edwardian England', in V. Gatrell et al., (eds), *Crime and the Law* (1980). Cf. Taylor (1998) 51 *Econ. Hist. Rev.* 569 for the suggestion of a broad-based official understanding, driven by government thrift, to understate the levels of crime in order to inflate the appeal and effectiveness of the police and criminal justice system. Supporting evidence adduced for the theory is severely limited.

[95] See Ch. III below.

[96] See Ch. V below.

[97] S. Petrow, *Policing Morals, 1870–1914* (Oxford, 1994), *passim*; D. Miers, *Regulating Commercial Gambling* (Oxford, 2004), *passim*, esp. Chs 2, 9, and 10.

[98] G. Robb, *White-Collar Crime in Modern England: Financial Fraud and Business Morality 1845–1929* (1992).

class materially affected the criminal law's enforcement, the extent to which the offender's social background was a factor in determining police involvement and prosecution defies confident assessment.

On the other hand, imposing middle-class mores and codes of behaviour on the working classes by establishing a firm grip on the society and economy of the streets was a predictable recipe for resentment and resistance. Quite how far it materialized frequently turned on the zeal which drove local policing policy, along with the extent of good sense and discretion exercised by beat contables. Undoubtedly, the combination of a rapidly expanded police force armed with facilitative legislation produced a markedly more 'policed' society, with working-class street culture attracting particular scrutiny and intervention. Complementing the coercive, intrusive, and often irksome nature of this kind of policing was a host of ancillary functions developed by, or imposed upon, the police. Some, such as rendering first aid, locating missing persons, and charitable works, sprang from a mixture of common humanity and political calculation. As many, including Chadwick,[99] well understood, extending police activities to socially benign 'collateral services' not only directly benefited the community, but also eased the process of acceptance of the institution of professional policing. While not exactly making the policeman part of the community, activities of this nature might foster the view that the police served, as well as coerced, the community.[100] One illustration of an attempt at a balanced approach to policing of a different kind was the establishing of a relatively tight body of rules of interrogation aimed at ensuring that the extensive arsenal of stop-and-search powers was deployed in a responsible and least provocative fashion.[101]

At the start of the First World War, the range of responsibilities assumed by the police had grown from the maintenance of 'law and order' to include emergency and miscellaneous civil duties.[102] Although hardly immune from criticism,[103] amongst the middle and upper classes the second half of the nineteenth century saw a consolidation of the broadly favourable reputation gained first by the metropolitan force and later by provincial police. At least for these sections of society, 'the blue coats—the defenders of order—[were] becoming

[99] Chadwick, 'On the Consolidation of Police Force and the Prevention of Crime' (1868) 77 *Fraser's Magazine* 1.

[100] Amongst the additional functions given to the police was supervision of released prisoners. The Convict Supervision Office, Scotland Yard, was established in 1880. See Ch. V below.

[101] Especially under the 1829 and 1839 Metropolitan Police Acts, and the Habitual Criminals Act 1869. W. Miller, *Cops and Bobbies* (1999), 56–66, and see Ch. III below.

[102] Such as highways, gas supplies, and inspection of weights and measures.

[103] Two Royal Commissions on the Police in 1855 and 1906 dealt with a wide range of complaints against the Metropolitan Police. See below.

the national favourites'.[104] So much so, that by the end of the century it was almost routine to assert that the English police were the world's finest—subject to ever present reservations as to their cost.[105] However, whilst society's better off had generally embraced the growth of professional policing, the benefits for the working classes were rather less apparent. Arrival of professional policing brought heightened levels of official superintendence, along with the selective curtailment and attempts at what was viewed as improving cultural and social mores.[106] Consequently, replacing working-class suspicion and hostility with a broad but often guarded acceptance of professional policing was a more extended and gradual process, with relatively common individual acts of violence towards the police periodically erupting into large-scale conflict.[107]

In London, particularly during the 1880s, the fine demands of achieving a measured balance between firmness and flexibility needed for unruly crowd control saw the undoing of two successive Metropolitan Police Commissioners.[108] To a large degree, acceptance of the new police accompanied the rising standard of living of the skilled and semi-skilled working classes—when a mean subsistence could be escaped by joining the swelling the ranks of the 'respectable'[109] working classes. Indeed, the prominent moral crusades pursued through the police from time to time to suppress, if not eradicate, the vices of drink, gambling and prostitution, may have enjoyed 'respectable' working-class approval. However, it is more than a little doubtful whether, even by the early 1900s, *The Times* truly captured common working-class sentiment when observing that the metropolitan policeman was 'not merely guardian of the peace... [but] the friend of a mass of people who have no other counsellor or protector'.[110]

Beyond the metropolis, a broadly similar picture of steadily evolving attitudes and perceptions emerges: for society's materially advantaged and least likely to be subject to police scrutiny and coercion, came the relatively early belief in the

[104] *Punch*, 1851, July–December, 173; quoted by Emsley, *The English Police*, 62.

[105] e.g. 1900 PD (s. 4), 85: 1559.

[106] Petrow, *Policing Morals, passim*. For evidence of the inertia of tradition and slow pace of change in local policing and prosecution practices, see Conley, *The Unwritten Law, passim*.

[107] Although the accuracy of recorded figures is open to dispute, the statistics for the annual rates of general assaults and for those on the police between 1860s–1914 show a very distinct reduction. V. Gatrell, 'The Decline of Theft and Violence in Victorian and Edwardian England'. There is no comparable information for pre-professional periods.

[108] V. Bailey, 'The Metropolitan Police, the Home Office and the Threat of Outcast London', in V. Bailey (ed.), *Policing and Punishment in Nineteenth Century Britain* (1981); and R. Vogler, *Reading the Riot Act* (1991).

[109] F. Thompson, *The Rise of the Respectable Society* (1988), 198.

[110] *The Times*, 24 December 1908, quoted by Critchley, *History of Police*, 326.

overall benefits of professional policing; and for the working classes, there followed a gradual erosion of suspicion and resistance to the police, who were, in many respects, the front line proselytes and enforcers of middle-class values and mores.[111] As in London, the popularity and acceptance of policing would turn largely on the sensitivity and flexibility with which local constables exercised their discretionary powers. Relief from the commonplace aggravations of petty theft and casual violence (not uncommon under the watch system) might be regarded as a worthwhile exchange for the officious intrusiveness of the professional constable. On a larger scale, from the 1860s to the early twentieth century, in a variety of locations, periodic eruptions of violence between police and political or industrial demonstrators undoubtedly soured police–working class relations. Many of these encounters drew charges of police misconduct, some of which were found on official inquiry to be well justified, while other allegations were rejected.[112]

More widely, deployment of police raised the fundamental issue of impartiality. Like both government and institutions of the criminal justice system, the police were naturally anxious to be perceived as objective and impartial. For, as was patently obvious from the inception of professional policing, the consent and cooperation of the policed was going to be a key element in its efficiency. However, as the enforcers of many laws, either aimed at or inevitably most likely to affect the lower classes, the social and political neutrality of the police was immediately suspect. Aside from occasional, essentially local instances, allegations of partiality were most insistent in relation to the policing of industrial conflicts. Here, the suspicion of bias sometimes not unsurprisingly rested on the clear association between the membership of a police committee and business interests subject to an industrial dispute. At the same time, long-running agitation within police ranks, largely concentrating on the steady push for reasonable pay and pension rights through unionization, attracted either police authority or Home Office concessions or countermeasures. A broad swathe of radical organized labour, including membership within police forces, was not a situation to be lightly contemplated by central or local government. Most fundamentally, police political neutrality was to be equated with unqualified and unquestioning dependability when called upon to render physical support to the government of the day. Consequently, following the immediate post-War police strikes, the Police Act 1919 sought to provide a formal statutory solution, through creation

---

[111] R. Storch, 'The Policeman as Domestic Missionary' (1976) 9 *J. Soc. Hist.* 481 and D. Taylor, *Policing the Victorian Town* (2002), Ch. 5.

[112] Emsley, *The English Police*, Ch. 5 and provincial anti-police sentiments examined by Taylor, *The New Police*, 108–24.

of a Police Federation as a representative body, coupled with the prohibition of strikes and association with any union or other labour organization.[113]

Control and Accountability: Chief Constables, Police Authorities and the Home Office

After 1856, acceptance of professional policing and its particular local structures rested as much on the machinery of control and accountability as on actual policing practices.[114] Clearly, friction and conflict over this machinery principally engaged the politically active middle and governing classes, rather than society's lower orders. Three forms of police authority existed after 1856: for London, Metropolitan Police Commissioners were answerable to the Home Secretary;[115] for the provinces, Quarter Sessions governed county forces, with borough police the responsibility of Watch Committees made up of elected councillors. In the succeeding decades, each institution became the subject of largely political dispute. For the metropolitan and county police the contentious issue was lack of direct democratic control; for boroughs the dominant dispute centred on the professional relationship between watch committees and their chief constables.

Challenges to the Home Secretary's policing role in London were at their most cogent and insistent during the periods leading up to, and immediately after, the establishment of the London County Council under the 1888 Local Government Act. In the absence of any unified local government body for London in 1829 political accountability for a police force had gone to the Home Secretary almost by default; although, no doubt, because of London's strategic position, Peel would have insisted on central government control. Now, with two recent resignations of Metropolitan Police Commissioners, parliamentary and extra-parliamentary claims that London police control should logically be a democratic function of local government, as in the boroughs, defenders of the status quo were pressed to make out their counter-case. Initially, this focused on the unique national and imperial nature of London[116] and its special policing needs. These suggestions, supported by instances of past public disorder in the capital, were sharpened by contemporary unease over Irish

---

[113] G. Reynolds and A. Judge, *The Night the Police Went on Strike* (1968), *passim*.

[114] On the constitutional independence and accountability of individual constables, G. Marshall, *Police and Government* (1965), Chs 2 and 3.

[115] Under the City of London Police Act 1839, the Commissioner of the City of London police enjoyed even greater autonomy than a county chief constable, dismissal being by either the Crown (effectively the Home Secretary) or by the City's Court of Aldermen. J. W. Nott-Bower, *Fifty Years of Policemen* (1926), 173.

[116] On the nationally strategic importance of the Metropolitan Police, see H. Evans, 'The London County Council and the Police' (1889) 55 *Contemporary Review* 448.

Nationalist mainland threats.[117] A second, more openly partisan line, concerned the possible leftist political complexion of future London County Councils; a fear to be overwhelmingly borne out by the 1889 elections. This extinguished any remote possibility entertained by Salisbury's government of surrendering central responsibility for London's police to a body whose political fitness and administrative capacity to control the metropolitan force the Tories fiercely disputed.[118]

Out in the shires, instead of the Home Secretary, the target of criticism was the undemocratic and ineffectual nature of Quarter Sessions police committees. For some, it was a failing in accountability aggravated by the generally relaxed control exercised by county committees over their chief constables, most of whom had come to enjoy extensive professional autonomy in the development of their police forces.[119] Under the County Police Act 1839, s 6, county chief constables were responsible for the appointment, discipline, and dismissal of constables. Quarter Sessions committees were invested with the rarely exercised residual power of giving their chief constables 'lawful orders'. A shared social background (usually gentry–military) between chief constables and county magistrates, coupled with broadly common notions of appropriate policing practices and policies, generally conduced to natural and unforced professional harmony. While under the Local Government Act 1888 changes in the constitution of county police committees introduced a political component of 50 per cent of elected county councillors, the position of chief constables and level of positive control exercised by the new standing committees underwent no discernible change (as was true of their social composition and attitudes) for several decades.[120]

Both the structure of borough Watch Committees and the operational relationship with their chief constables presented a striking contrast with the contemporary situation in the counties. Although the 1856 Act recognized the role of borough chief police officers, it gave them no powers. Like county chief constables, Watch Committees had responsibility for all police appointments, prescribing police regulations, including rates of pay, matters of discipline, and dismissal. Rather than a quarterly event, meetings between Watch Committees and their chief constables generally occurred far more frequently, an indication

[117] e.g. Harcourt, as Home Secretary, to Spencer 4 March 1883, Harcourt Mss (Bodleian Library, Oxford) Box 41, 138.

[118] J. Davis, *Reforming London: The London Government Problem 1855–1900* (1988), 115–22 and Emsley, *English Police*, 85–6. Lord Salisbury's sympathetic comments on greater police centralization in the 1888 Lords' debate, *PD* 1888 (s. 3), 329: 1653.

[119] Wall, *Chief Constables*, 91. The Home Office view in 1876 was that 'the head constable of a borough police force holds an inferior position as compared with the chief constable of a county force': *Home Office Printed Memoranda and Reports*, 1 May 1876, N.A. H.O. 347/3.

[120] C. Zangerl, 'The Social Composition of the County Magistracy' (1971) XI *Journal of British Studies* 113.

of the greater level of potential and actual involvement in operational control by such police authorities. Moreover, the great majority of borough chief constables could claim only modest social origins, generally owing their position to rising through the ranks.[121] Consequently, for most of the nineteenth century, Watch Committees commonly viewed their chief constables, like any other executive servant of the borough, as very much subject to committee-led policy-making. While few in number, recorded examples of conflict between police authorities and chief constables were almost exclusively confined to boroughs.[122] However, by the end of the nineteenth century, the controlling ability of Watch Committees was distinctly waning. Going beyond issuing wide policy directives by seeking to exercise close control over detailed and general operational practices, was often inhibited by the realities of councillors' short-term tenure and restricted knowledge. Set against this was the accumulated experience and increasing professionalism of borough chief constables.[123]

By the early 1900s, a further significant factor conditioning the ability of boroughs and counties alike to control their police forces was the Home Office's rapidly rising involvement in policing matters outside the metropolis. The broad consequence of its inspection system was a modest measure of standardization of policing practices, including manning levels and just what non-criminal justice roles the police might properly perform.[124] Expansion of Home Office direct communication with chief constables also occurred, especially in relation to the handling of public disorder which might threaten or generate large-scale industrial paralysis;[125] it was a practice probably enhanced by the criminal branch of the Home Office achieving department status in 1870.[126] Additionally, the Home Office began to initiate legislation empowering police forces directly to carry out specific functions.[127] As with other[128] aspects of the criminal justice system, the pace and extent of Home Office involvement in policing affairs outside London

---

[121] Wall, *Chief Constables*, 108–20.

[122] Critchley, *History of Police*, 143; Emsley, *The English Police*, 89–91, and generally M. Brogden, *The Police: Autonomy and Consent* (1982).

[123] Cf. most especially R. Reiner, *Chief Constables* (1992), 12–14; and see also Wall, *Chief Constables*, 95–6.

[124] The importance of being certified 'efficient' increased when the central subvention rose from ¼ to ½ of the costs of police pay and clothing under the Police (Expenses) Act 1874.

[125] Particularly, Churchill's interventions as Home Secretary in the industrial disputes between 1910 and 1912. Morgan, *Conflict and Order*, 44–9 and D. Englander, 'Police and Public Order in Britain 1914–1918', in C. Emsley and B. Weinberger (eds), *Policing Western Europe...1850–1940* (Westport, 1992), 90.

[126] J. Pellew, *The Home Office 1848–1914* (1982), 57.

[127] Such as the Explosives Act 1875.

[128] e.g. prisons, where the centralizing momentum issued from Du Cane and the prisons administration, with the Home Office acquiescence.

was cautious and relatively limited. Until the early twentieth century, neither Home Secretaries nor their permanent officials[129] exhibited any systematic ambitions to establish a powerful presence in police affairs.[130] Yet, certainly, during the 1870s and 1880s, Home Office concerns relating to its extremely limited powers over provincial policing occasionally surfaced.[131] One prominent manifestation of this intermittent interest was an abortive attempt in the 1888 Local Government Bill to empower the Home Secretary to stipulate the size of each police force.[132]

However, although expressed somewhat robustly, far more indicative of the Home Office mindset was Harcourt's jibe that central government insistence on police authorities appointing 'more police than [local authorities] want is like the old story of compelling the Brahmins to develop butchers' shops because beef is thought to be good for them'.[133] Home Office moves towards embracing greater centralization of policing policy were eventually driven by the experiences of early 1900s political and industrial agitation, and the police strikes of 1918–19, coupled with the ever compelling centralist appeal of administrative convenience.[134] Home Office mobilization and direction of police forces in response to large-scale pre-War strikes[135] was also illustrative of changing government perceptions of its competence and responsibilities across a far wider political and social spectrum. Such changes ran in tandem with substantial moves towards national uniformity of police service training and conditions proposed by the Desborough Committee,[136] embodied in the 1919 Police Act, and largely implemented and enforced by the Home Office.

From Prevention to Detection

A final and particularly significant feature of the nineteenth-century evolution of police forces requiring review is the hesitant adoption of covert policing. Entrenched suspicions of the inherently anti-libertarian nature of professional

---

[129] Pellew, *Home Office*, 5–33; H. Parris 'The Home Office and the Provincial Police, 1856–1870' (1961) *Public Law* 235; E. Troup (Permanent Under Secretary from 1908–22) became a highly formative influence in Home Office policy, including a more uniform and interventionist approach to policing. See Troup 'Police Administration, Local and National' (1928) 1 *Police Journal* 5.

[130] Cf. Steedman, *Policing the Victorian Community*, 27–32.

[131] In 1874 an increase in central government support for police costs from ¼ to ½ was partly motivated by the desire for greater leverage.

[132] *PD* 1888 (s. 3), 327: 1053; and 328: 797–861.

[133] 1883, quoted by Critchley, *History of Police*, 130. Harcourt was Home Secretary 1880–5. In the 1888 Local Government Bill debates, Harcourt lambasted the Inspectors of Constabulary as being 'absolutely useless', *PD* 1888 (s. 3), 327: 1053.

[134] Emsley, *The English Police*, Ch. 6.

[135] Weinberger, *Keeping the Peace*, Ch. 3.

[136] Critchley, *History of Police*, 182–98.

policing were not just a major political inhibition in the general establishment of police forces, they were especially antithetical to the notion of the plain-clothes detective; a figure who embodied the essence of un-English official intrusiveness and subterfuge. Consequently, it is likely that partly to assuage such fears and partly out of a firm belief in its efficacy, the principal function of the metropolitan and provincial constable was initially identified as one of deterring crime through open, uniformed patrol. However, predictably from early days, the need for catching criminals by more subtle policing methods was well understood by the Metropolitan Police establishment, who soon deployed plain-clothes officers; a practice earlier pioneered at Bow Street and other stipendiary magistrate-led district police offices and one which continued until 1839.[137] By 1842, emerging public acceptance of the new institution of policing, reinforced by recent high profile events, caused the Home Office to authorize the Metropolitan Police Commissioners' appointment of a small detective branch of two inspectors and six sergeants.[138] Though compared with the pre-1839 position, a decidedly limited establishment, it constituted at least a degree of open official recognition that crime prevention needed to be complemented by detection.

Virtual stagnation in the size of the metropolitan detective branch ended in 1869 with its dramatic expansion in response to public criticism of apparently rising levels of certain types of criminality, allied to publicly expressed doubts over uniformed policing efficiency. An 1868 Home Office Departmental Committee recommendation for a substantial increase in detective numbers (combined with direct London vestry and district board pressure early in the following year) led to a substantial boosting of the central detective force. Rather than coping with 'ordinary crime', the Committee's dominant anxiety over 'wholly inadequate'

---

[137] e.g. *Report from the Select Committee on the Petition of Frederick Young*, PP 1833 (627), xiii, and *Metropolitan Police Offices*, PP 1837 (451), xii. Distaste for police surveillance in the 1830s is evidenced by the response and language of the 1833 Select Committee Report on the covert and instigatory activities of Sgt Popay. It characterized the general use of non-uniformed police officers ('Spies') as 'most alien to the spirit of the Constitution'. Their exceptional use could only legitimately be sanctioned as a last resort to detect crimes or prevent a breach of the peace (3). See also the extensive number of detailed Metropolitan Police reports to the Home Office on public meetings of Chartists and sympathisers, and trade unionists for 1839. N.A. H.O. 44/52, 1–245. And the enquiry into PC Culley and the Coldbath Fields Meeting, PP 1833 (718) xiii. On the functioning of the Bow Street Runners, see J. Beattie, 'Early Detection: The Bow Street Runners in Late Eighteenth Century London', in C. Emsley and H. Shpayer-Makov (eds), *Police Detectives in History, 1750–1950* (Aldershot, 2006), 15. For their provincial deployment, see D. Cox, 'A Certain Share of Low Cunning': *An analysis of the work of Bow Street Principal Officers, 1792–1839, with particular emphasis on their provincial duties* (PhD Thesis Cornell University, 1991).

[138] The extent of Metropolitan plain clothes police actually deployed before 1842 is unclear. R. Morris, '"Crime Does Not Pay": Thinking Again About Detectives in the First Century of the Metropolitan Police' in Emsley and Shpayer-Makov (eds), *Police Detectives in History 1750–1950*, 79. Petrow 'The Rise of the Detective in London, 1869–1914' (1993) 14 *Crim. Just. Hist.*, 91, 92n.

numbers of policemen was their ability to counter 'conspiracies' and 'secret [trade] combinations',[139] increasingly of considerable economic and political significance for governments. But despite this, underlying concerns over the supervision and obvious potential corruptibility of detectives habitually in close contact with criminals, continued to dampen official enthusiasm for increasing detective force strength. Such suspicions were publicly borne out by the 1877 'Turf Fraud' case, involving corruption charges against three senior central detectives.[140] Following a Home Office Departmental Commission of Enquiry, the Metropolitan Police detective branch was re-created as the Criminal Investigation Department in 1878. Headed by Howard Vincent,[141] the newly appointed Director of Criminal Investigation, the force steadily increased in size to around 290 men by 1884 when Vincent resigned.

It was a modest expansion momentum very publicly checked by an early judicial reprimand coupled with explicit Home Office circumscription arising from detectives' use of an agent provocateur to assist in convicting a chemist of supplying abortifacients. Responding to parliamentary questioning, the Home Secretary, Sir William Harcourt, regarded the occasions on which such 'artifice' would be justified as 'rare indeed'; and then only to be resorted to under Home Office authority.[142] Limited, largely anecdotal, evidence suggests that judicial tolerance of dubious investigatory practices varied substantially. Most particularly, failure to issue a caution to suspects prior to confessions (or other incriminatory statements) led to some judges excluding such evidence, while others would not bar its admission. The position was eventually partially regularized by the Home Office's 1912 request for judicial formulation of what became known as the 'Judges Rules'.[143]

---

[139] Confidential Home Office Departmental Committee to enquire into the System of Police Report, p. 21, *Home Office Printed Memoranda and Reports* N.A. H.O. 347/1,475. In his evidence to the Committee Sir Richard Mayne, Metropolitan Police Commissioner, identified 'good detectives' throughout large city provincial forces, including Liverpool, Birmingham, Manchester, and Bristol, Evid. mins (87). The provocative almost hostile tone of questioning by parliamentary counsel and Home Office legal adviser, Henry Thring, included references to detectives as 'spies' and a 'spy system' (88–9). Parallel development of detective branches in provincial forces was subject to substantial variation in the rate of development and size of force. But the Metropolitan use of detectives was undoubtedly influential, as witnessed by their requested use outside London. Public order concerns relating to labour disputes was an important factor in revamping the organization and clarifying the powers of special constables. Confidential memo 20 December 1867, N.A. H.O. 347/3 573; January 1868, 577.

[140] See D. Ascoli, *The Queen's Peace: The Origins and Development of the Metropolitan Police 1829–1979* (1979), 143–7.

[141] 29-year-old Vincent, a barrister and former army officer without policing experience.

[142] Comments in *Titley*, by Stephen J., *The Times*, 14 and 17 December 1880. Home Secretary, Harcourt, *PD* 1881 (s. 3), 257: 443–4, 941–2.

[143] E. Williams, 'The Modern View of Confessions' (1914) 30 *LQR* 294. And Ch. III.

More generally, essential enhancement of the operational organization of the Criminal Investigation Branch only got seriously underway in the first decade of the twentieth century; with the coincidence of a sympathetic Commissioner of Police, a favourable Home Office attitude, and a moderately sanguine public climate.[144] However, sustained unease at the suspect metropolitan detective culture of clandestine irregular and illicit practices persisted well into the twentieth century, a concern which surfaced in the generally laudatory 1929 Report of the Royal Commission on Police Powers and Procedure:

> Some of the CID (Scotland Yard) evidence...leaves a somewhat disquieting impression upon our minds. There is, we fear, a tendency amongst this branch of the service to regard itself as a thing above and apart, to which the restraints and limitations placed upon the ordinary Police do not, or should not, apply.[145]

By way of a final, distinct development, the spectre of secret political police became a (limited) corporeal reality with the formation in 1884 of a 'Special Irish Branch' of the CID, as a response to the resurgence of Fenian terrorism.[146] In its rapidly acquired wider remit (and title), artifice, and subterfuge were virtually the raison d'être of Special Branch, as with any secret service. The relatively relaxed stance of British governments during the earlier parts of the nineteenth century[147] towards a kaleidoscope of exotic political exiles and other foreign groups, experienced marked changes between the century's closing decades and 1914. With full Home Office encouragement and authority, the police Special Branch developed an increasingly active and expanded interest in an ever disparate collection of suspect groups, ranging from foreign anarchists, nihilists, and spies, to homegrown Socialists and Suffragettes.[148] Yet, against this fermenting background, in

---

[144] Petrow, *Policing Morals*, 62–6 and the *Royal Commission upon the Duties of the Metropolitan Police, Report*, PP 1908 [Cd. 4156]l.

[145] [Cmnd. 3297] p. 102, para. 269, on interrogation practices.

[146] State use of spies and surveillance techniques had a pedigree stretching back more than two centuries. Report of the Select Committee on the Post Office, *PP* 1844 xiv. F. Smith, 'British Post Office Espionage 1844' (1970) *Historical Studies* 4; D. Mack Smith, *Mazzini* (New Haven, 1994). The availability and use of 'secret service money' by Home Secretaries to 'preserve the public peace' was a somewhat ill-defined, open secret. Well-known examples of the use of spies and agents provocateur from the early nineteenth century include the activities of W. Richards ('Oliver') in the Pentridge Rising (1817) and G. Edwards in the Cato Street Conspiracy (1820). For example, Lord John Russell, *PD* 1845 (s. 3), 77: 987. Generally, D. Vincent, *The Culture of Secrecy: Britain 1832–1998* (Oxford, 1998); B. Porter, *The Origins of the Vigilant State: The London Metropolitan Police Special Branch before the First World War* (1987), *passim*.

[147] See P. Thurmond Smith, *Policing Victorian London* (1985), Ch. 4.

[148] See Porter, *The Origins of the Vigilant State* and C. Andrew, *Secret Service: The Making of the British Intelligence Community* (1985).

1914 the Home Secretary felt perfectly able and most emphatically to assure his Commons audience that no 'political police' operated in Britain.[149]

4. CONCLUSIONS

The nineteenth-century establishment, development, and growth of professional policing in England and Wales was one of the most significant institutional changes in the whole apparatus of criminal justice: over less than half a century, the new police radically altered the processes and practices of deterring, detecting, and prosecuting crime. Change did not take place in any predicable uniform or linear fashion. Instead, following the innovation of the Metropolitan Police Act 1829, the evolution of policing was irregular and frequently hesitant, representing the outcome of many decades of political compromise and accommodation between local and central interests set against shifting transient concerns.

With varying degrees of intensity, the introduction of new professional policing faced opposition from several quarters on a variety of grounds. Suspicions at all social levels (including the judiciary) as to the inherently intrusive, alien nature of policing were far from fully dispelled by the actual practices adopted by some new forces. More tangibly, the steady ceding of local political, civic, and legal autonomy from councils and magistrates to central government supervision or regulation across a broad range of functions[150] (including policing) was almost inevitably staunchly resisted locally. Yet, here, as in other areas of responsibility, the promised flow of central funding was the eventual balm most often employed for dissolving or appeasing opposition. However, not only did the prospect of large-scale professional policing for many decades prove unappetizing locally, after 1829 central government interest and resolve on matters of policing displayed enormous fluctuations. Legislation, facilitative or prescriptive, issued in fits and starts, in much the same fashion and pace as other nineteenth-century centralist engagements. The haphazard, not to say, accidental quality of some policing developments was particularly marked in relation to the expansion of detective and prosecution functions. Unease at the employment of detectives lingered throughout Victorian times; with reservations being partly overcome by even greater distaste for the covert activities of organized labour. In respect of prosecuting offenders, while from mid-century police forces assumed a prosecutorial role, this was largely through default and based on local accommodations.[151]

---

[149] PD 1914 (s. 5 HL), 61: 1874, and 62: 121.
[150] e.g. prison construction and administration at Ch. V below. Poor Law reforms 1834, and subsequent health and housing interventions. See Vol. XI, 1 and Pt 2, Ch. VI below.
[151] See 'The Trial'—Prosecution, Ch. III below.

It plainly followed successive decades of central government's unwillingness (or indifference) to resolve long-standing inadequacies in the system, where rising levels of defendant representation[152] coupled with a steady sharpening of evidence requirements[153] increasingly placed a premium on skilled, methodical prosecution preparation. And, paradoxically, it was a relative neglect of the machinery of prosecution which continued against a background of innovatory penal measures enacted after the 1850s to protect vulnerable sections of society, especially women and children from sexual predation and violence.[154]

Overall, while it might be reasonably contended that police forces were, from time to time, deployed in the cause of topical strategic political, economic, or social objectives, especially in the second half of the nineteenth century, these were largely secondary or incidental to the police's originally conceived functions. The historical evidence of professional policing's fitful, organic rather than calculated, systematic development weighs heavily against claims of sustained political ambitions for their large-scale instrumentalist or centralist function and local use considerably beyond immediate criminal justice objectives.

---

[152] See 'The Trial'—Defence, Ch. III below.

[153] See 'The Trial'—Criminal Evidence, Ch. III below.

[154] See 'Offences Against the Person'—Sexual Offences, Ch. XII below. Yet, at the same time, the strength of police forces considerably increased. In the case of the Metropolitan Police from around 3000 in 1830, force strength had risen to approximately 9000 in 1870, and reached in excess of 19,000 by 1910. Emsley, *The English Police*, App. 1. Even allowing for population expansion, the police/civilian ratio dramatically decreased by the end of the century. Martin and Wilson, *Study in Manpower*, 32.

III

The Trial: Adversarial Characteristics and Responsibilities; Pre-trial and Trial Procedures

1. PROSECUTION

'Everybody's Right to Prosecute, ... Nobody's Business to do so'

The nineteenth-century institution of criminal justice inherited the long-established convention that while the trial and punishment of offenders was the state's business, the detection and prosecution of criminals was generally the aggrieved citizen's responsibility. Extensive reserve 'powers vested in the Attorney-General...to undertake, control, and terminate any criminal prosecution', were rarely exercised, as though 'the detection of guilt and the security of innocence were no part of those great social interests which the prerogatives of the Crown were especially intended to protect'.[1] This apparent, startling paradox, as much the consequence of omission[2] as calculated political preference, was sustained by similar fears and beliefs to those long antagonistic to the establishment of professional policing.[3] At the same time, in large measure, forces that campaigned for professional police saw the inadequacy of parochial policing as bound up with an insufficiently active magistracy. Although a system of state or public prosecutors might conceivably operate without the assistance of a

---

[1] Draft Report written by John Phillimore, MP, QC, chairman of the *Commons Select Committee on Public Prosecutors; Report*, 1 May, *PP* 1856 (206), vii. The final report, drafted by another member of the Committee, opens with a much less rhetorically critical characterization of the system. Of contemporary practitioners' texts, by far the most extensive discussion of 'the Prosecutor' is found in J. Chitty, *A Practical Treatise on the Criminal Law*. The work's first chapter is devoted to analysing the nature of obligations and inducements to prosecutors, concluding that prosecution is a 'moral obligation' involving 'security and happiness of the people in general...interweaving [the prosecutor's] own advantage with public benefit' (2nd edn, 1826), i: 1–5. On the Attorney-General's initiation and termination of prosecutions, see XI, Pt 3.

[2] Stephen, *HCL*, i, 496 (below).

[3] See 'Policing', Ch. II.

professional agency of criminal investigation, operational practicability strongly argued for such a complementary development.

Throughout the nineteenth century, significant changes occurred in the roles and personnel of law enforcement, along with a drip feed of ameliorative state measures. Such developments took place against a background of several decades of the steady push of reformers successfully resisted by defenders of the status quo. Aside from a victim's personal inclination[4] and means, the likelihood of prosecution turned substantially on the attitudes and practices of local magistrates and constabulary. Enormous variation in the levels of ability and involvement[5] of the magistracy was manifest in the extent of their willingness to activate the local constabulary[6] into investigating crime and bringing offenders before the justices. Moreover, the late eighteenth and early nineteenth centuries saw the role of magistrates evolve in a judicial direction. The range of summary jurisdiction increased as did their pre-trial role for serious offences, from one of assisting the prosecution in marshalling its evidence to one of determining whether a *prima facie* case was established.[7]

Whilst the theory of private or citizen's criminal prosecution satisfied the nonstatist libertarian inclinations of many, its predictable operational consequences were less palatable, attracting a steady barrage of criticism from individuals and official bodies alike. The 1818 Commons Select Committee on the State of the Police of the Metropolis entertained

no doubt, that the early detection and speedy punishment of offenders are much frustrated by the present system, which forces the individual, in a great degree, to prosecute

---

[4] On the practice of magistrates' use of recognisance in an attempt to ensure the victim or any other potential prosecutor continuing a prosecution, see King, *Crime, Justice and Discretion*, 43–6.

[5] D. Eastwood, *Governing Rural England*, Ch. 4.

[6] No general expectation existed that parish constables would investigate a crime on their own initiative. See C. Herrup, *The Common Peace* (Cambridge, 1987), 68–70 and King, *Crime, Justice and Discretion*, 73–5. The directability of constables by magistrates was also certainly subject to local variation. According to Henry Dover, Chairman of Norfolk Quarter Sessions, before professional policing 'the parish constable was his own master; you could hardly say that he was responsible to the Magistrates; he would not move in a doubtful case unless he was paid for it': *First Report of the Select Committee on Police*, Mins of Evidence, PP 1852–3 (603), xxxvi, p. 107.

[7] On the termination of the police-directing powers of Metropolitan Police offices, see Ch. II above. For analysis of magistrates pre-trial role, see 'Evidence' below. For a discussion of the failure of magistrates to develop a system of direct control of newly emerging police prosecution practices, see W. Cornish, 'Defects in Prosecuting—Professional Views in 1845', 305 in *Reshaping Criminal Law* (1978). More generally, some opinion maintained that public prosecutors (along with professional policing) were one manifestation of an inquisitorial system of justice. While true, an inquisitorial system was not an inevitable corollary of public prosecutors. For an analysis of this link, Stephen, 'The Characteristics of English Criminal Law' *Cambridge Essays* (1857), 1, 50–9.

at his own expense for the injuries which he may have sustained in person or property; justice is often thereby prevented taking its course; prosecutors no less than witnesses are tampered with, and some are induced to submit to the loss they have suffered, by motives of ill-judged compassion, others from feelings of apprehension of further injuries: all these causes conspire to give a degree of impunity to offenders, which is greatly injurious to the public peace.[8]

Highly placed legal practitioners also frequently registered fundamental rejection of the principle of private prosecution. Eight years before his appointment as Chief Justice of the King's Bench, Lord Denman observed that the notion 'that the administration of justice should in almost every instance be set in motion by individual feelings of resentment and placed under the guidance of ordinary magistrates, or perhaps even of inferior persons, is a strange abandonment of the public interests to chance'.[9] Similarly, two decades later, in evidence to the Criminal Law Commissioners, Lord Denman argues, 'The injured party may be helpless, ignorant, interested, corrupt. He is altogether irresponsible; his dealing with the criminal may effectually defeat justice.'[10] And adopting much the same standpoint, the Commissioners favoured appointment of public prosecutors.[11]

Such realities had long been widely understood and tolerated by both courts and governments; it was a toleration tempered by a creeping strategy of *ad hoc*, ameliorative measures, spanning 200 years, beginning in the early eighteenth century. Central funding of prosecutions of some felony cases at the Old Bailey from the 1720s[12] had been swelled by increasingly numerous examples of

---

[8] *PP* 1818 (423), viii, p. 32. And earlier Report, *PP* 1812 (127), ii, p. 7.

[9] (1824) *Edin. Rev.* 40, 191, and also Romilly, *Memoirs* (1840), 1, XVI. Denman enjoyed wide experience of politics and legal practice: MP from 1818 and Attorney-General in the Whig Government 1830–2; Old Bailey judge 1822–30, Lord Chief Justice 1832–50.

[10] *Criminal Law Commissioners Eighth Report, PP* 1845 (656), xiv, App., 211.

[11] *Ibid.*, 24–5. But they were reluctant to offer specific proposals. Supported in *The Times*, 29 August 1845, p. 4 and 25 January 1848, p. 4.

[12] Beattie argues that such funding was prompted by the Whig Government anxiety to defend the Revolution and Hanovarian succession, *Policing and Punishment in London 1660–1750* (New York, 2001), 394. A close legal associate of Brougham, Denman was an advocate of reform of several areas of criminal law, including the provision of full defence counsel, see 'Defence' below. For Brougham's early proposals on Old Bailey public prosecutors, *Select Committee on Public Prosecutors*, Evd, 3–4. Charles Phillips, a leading criminal law barrister and acolyte of Brougham, made similar proposals in correspondence with Brougham, hoping for personal preferment. Brougham Papers, University College, London, 3 July 1834 (28, 437) and 26 August 1834 (36, 815). As the *Law Magazine* (1835, 13, 281) sarcastically observed, any possibility of this fizzled out with the Whig Government's exit in late 1834. By the 1830s the use of prosecution counsel was probably still only around 5% of cases, lower than the participation level of defence counsel. At the Old Bailey representation rates were higher: nearly 9% prosecuting and about 25% defence. J. Langbein, *The Origins of Adversary Criminal Trial* (Oxford, 2003), 170n and D. Cairns, *Advocacy and the Making of the Adversarial Criminal Trial* (Oxford, 1998), 118. On the development of the Old Bailey Bar during this period, see A. May, *The Bar and the Old Bailey 1750–1850* (Chapel Hill, 2003), Ch. 2.

prosecutions of coining and forgery offences, carried out by lawyers acting for the Mint and Bank of England.[13] Prosecutions for treason and sedition led by the Attorney-General were well established exceptions where the Crown's interests were recognizably most directly challenged. Driven by the ambition for cheap and swift justice, a series of legislative interventions increasing the scope of summary trial, incidentally eased the burden of private prosecution of certain offences, including some thefts and assaults. In the case of London and a few large cities, gradual expansion of the ranks of stipendiary magistrates added to this effect.[14] A second line of approach to encourage prosecutions was the paying of substantial rewards to those responsible for the conviction of certain types of offenders.[15] However, incentives of this nature not only generated prosecutions, but also spawned extensive, and notoriously corrupt practices.[16]

Fewer such risks attended the judicially administered award of costs and compensation. Running from the mid-1700s into the twentieth century, a trickle of increasingly wide powers were given to courts authorizing the payment of prosecution expenses and allowances to compensate for the sheer unpleasantness of bringing criminal proceedings.[17] The importance of such measures rose with the gradual expansion in the use of lawyers to prosecute in criminal trials. Supplementing this calculated employment of prosecution counsel was the informal judicial practice, at the opening of trials, of spontaneously drafting available counsel into representing unrepresented prosecutors. In large measure this was born of a judicial disinclination to act as prosecutor in serious cases. No doubt, the rising number of fully briefed defence counsel empowered to address the jury by the Defendants' Counsel Act 1836, added greatly to the discomfort of unprepared judges who found themselves obliged to present extempore prosecution cases. This judicial frame of mind was emphatically aired by Maule J.:

The fiction of law in criminal cases is, that the judge is counsel for the prisoner; but here it is sought, not only to upset and to reverse that doctrine, and make me counsel for the

[13] D. Hay and F. Snyder, 'Using the Criminal Law, 1750–1850', 3, 21–2; *Policing and Prosecution in Britain 1750–1850* (Oxford, 1989). On the Solicitor to the Treasury, see J. Ll. Edwards, *The Law Officers of the Crown* (1964), 371–3.

[14] Radzinowicz, *History*, ii: 123–37 and J. Davis, 'A Poor Man's System of Justice: The London Police Courts in the Second Half of the Nineteenth Century' (1984), *History Journal*, 319.

[15] For the public and private reward system see Radzinowicz, *History*, ii: Chs 3 and 4.

[16] King, *Crime, Justice and Discretion*, 47–52, 180–1 and Langbein, *Origins*, 147–77, on the practices and judicial reactions to 'thief-takers' manufacturing evidence.

[17] For the nineteenth century, see 1818, 58 Geo. III, c. 70; Peel's 1826, 7 Geo. IV, c. 64 covering costs of committal proceedings and some frequent misdemeanours such as certain forms of assault, attempt, and receiving. Peel saw the changes as opening up the 'avenues of justice in instances in which the poorest classes are the sufferers…' *PD* 1826 (s. 2), 14: 1230; 1851 14 and 15 Vict. c. 55; and the five Consolidation Acts, 1861. As Stephen remarked, the legislation was 'in some points, capricious, as the misdemeanours in respect of which costs may be given are chosen without much reference to principle', *HCL*, i, 499.

prosecution, but to throw the whole burden of the prosecution on me, and leave me to make out the best case I can against the prisoner by a careful and diligent perusal of the depositions. But I will not do it. It is indecent. I will be counsel for the prisoner, and let the depositions be handed to some counsel to conduct the prosecution.[18]

Manifest from the mid-1830s, this strengthening disgruntlement of Assize judges ensured that by the 1850s practically all prosecutions before them were carried out by counsel.[19]

Operating alongside largely centrally initiated funding measures were prosecution associations, a phenomenon directly attributable to the problems engendered by the system of private prosecution. Appearing first in significant numbers during the 1770s,[20] this formation of prosecution associations was a practical response to widespread unease at the inadequacy of the system of law enforcement, coupled with the frequently formidable challenges facing individuals bringing prosecutions.[21] Subscribing to a local association offered a form of indemnity against a victim having to face alone the full costs and vicissitudes threatened by a personally instituted prosecution. Growing awareness in the eighteenth century that prosecutions of indictable offences might be contested by solicitor and counsel is likely to have increased the appeal of forming associations with the obvious attraction being able to entrust cases to professional hands. While indicative of a broad dissatisfaction, largely amongst middling property owners, with the limited machinery of public law enforcement, it is rather doubtful whether any significant overall effect was achieved by associations, with

---

[18] *Page* (1847) 2 Cox 221. Similarly, Coleridge, J. in *Anon* (1843) 1 Cox 48 and Cresswell J. in *Hezell* (1844) 1 Cox 348. See the supporting comments in *The Times*, 18 June 1847 and (1847) 9 *LT* 256 and 283.

[19] Also the critical comments of Tindal CJ and Park J. in evidence given to the *House of Lords Select Committee on County Rates*, PP 1835 (206), xiv, p. 72; and Lord Lyndhurst in evidence to the *House of Lords Select Committee on the Criminal Law Administration Bill*, PP 1847–8 (523), xvi, 425; QS 307–8. Though subject to a gradual decline, Quarter Sessions recorders and chairmen continued to prosecute throughout the remainder of the century. See the *Fifth Report of the Judicature Commission*, PP 1874 [C. 1090], xxiv, 307, App. 1, pp. 14 and 25. For the rapidly rising proportion of prosecutions employing counsel at the Central Criminal Court (a combination of higher and lower judiciary), see M. Feeley, 'Legal Complexity and the Transformation of the Criminal Process…' (1997) 31 *Israel LR* 183, 195 fig. 1. Yet by 1912, around 40% of all prosecutions were unrepresented by counsel. As most serious charges were heard by the senior presiding judge, and these prosecutions would be conducted by counsel, the level of professional unrepresented prosecutions of far less serious offences would have been even higher than 40%.

[20] Estimates of the number of associations established between the 1770s and 1840s substantially vary, from between 600 to 4,000. See D. Philips, 'Good Men to Associate and Bad Men to Conspire, Associations for the Prosecution of Felons in England 1760–1860', in Hay and Snyder (eds), *Policing and Prosecution*, 113, 120.

[21] A few societies had special axes to grind, such as the Society for the Suppression of Vice, by Stephen Lushington, *PD* 1821 (s. 2), 5: 1491.

their low activity levels, averaging two prosecutions a year.[22] Moreover, their success rate may have been no greater than unassisted prosecutions.[23] The eventual arrival of professional policing throughout the country, followed by their accelerating involvement in prosecutions, brought about a rapid decline in the number of associations by the mid-nineteenth century.[24]

Police: Public Prosecutors by Default

Indeed, the introduction of professional policing between 1829[25] and 1856 was soon by far the most significant factor in ameliorating the fundamental problems inherent in private prosecutions. Whilst probably not even a subordinate motive[26] driving the initial establishment of professional policing, their assumption of a prosecutorial role must, to many, have been at least a foreseeable outcome. Even with the early explicit emphasis on patrolling, surveillance, and deterrence, a beat constable would in many, if not the majority of cases, be the individual most familiar with the evidence, and would often after arrest be expected to bring the defendant before a magistrate.[27] Recognition of the supplemental need for police detection would, inevitably, have strengthened such police inclinations to assume a prosecutorial role; it may even have been a factor motivating expansion of the detective role. Police prosecutors relieved considerable numbers from the burden of private prosecution and, at the same time, arguably boosted the criminal justice system's credibility and power to deter. But, as a substantial palliative, they incidentally probably delayed the stage at which radical government intervention became unavoidable.

Government inaction on criminal prosecutions, if not an unbroken policy, was the defining response throughout most of the nineteenth century. This remained true in the face of a succession of official reports and commentaries

---

[22] Philips, 'Good Men to Associate', 143.

[23] King, *Crime, Justice and Discretion*, 55–6 and Beattie, *Crime and the Courts*, 50.

[24] No inevitable correlation existed between membership of an association and support for the introduction of professional policing. Compare Philips, *op cit.*, 147–50 with A. Shubert, 'Private Initiative in Law Enforcement', in V. Bailey (ed.), *Policing and Punishment in Nineteenth Century Britain* (1981), 25, 34–9. For a while, some associations formed loose links with the new local police expecting preferential services in exchange for financial rewards: Philips, 'Good Men to Associate', 150–1.

[25] Prior to the Metropolitan Police Act 1829, the police serving Bow Street and the other seven London Police offices frequently prosecuted before stipendiary magistrates.

[26] In an 1826 Commons' speech, Peel indicated his support for at least the 'theory of public prosecutors': *PD* 1826 (s. 2), 7: 1231.

[27] For an early declaration of this expectation by a Metropolitan Stipendiary, see *The Times*, 3 October 1829. Peel's 1829 *General Instructions* put the 'prevention of crime' before 'detection and punishment': 'Policing', Ch. II.

which ensured that critics of private prosecution never lacked ample campaign-ing ammunition. Between 1812 and 1853, practically every official examination of metropolitan or provincial policing expressed disquiet over the fundamental operational inadequacies of the prosecution process. More specific and extended analyses of the prosecution system (especially the Criminal Law Commissioners Eighth Report (1845) and the Select Committee on Public Prosecutors (1854/6)) were equally unsparing. Evidence of legal luminaries given to the Select Committee on Public Prosecutors consistently dismissed the existing system: for Lord Brougham, 'nothing can be more ineffectual'; and for C. S. Greaves, it was an 'immense public evil';[28] with the Committee concluding the system to be 'greatly defective and urgently requires amendment'.[29] Twenty years on, these sentiments were echoed by a Committee of the Judicature Commission, whose members included Blackburn J. and Lord Cockburn CJ.[30] Such official discon-tent was paralleled by a steady reform campaign in the press and periodicals.[31] However, whilst the system's powerful opponents were broadly united in the substance of their criticism, rather less unanimity was apparent in respect of a remedy. But although the range of reform proposals was wide, a fundamental division lay between proponents of some form of public prosecution system and those like Greaves and Stephen, favouring a less radical approach of using exist-ing legal personnel boosted by more generous levels of public funding.

The Select Committee on Public Prosecutors proposed the establishment of full-time 'district agents' to prepare and conduct the preliminary stages of pros-ecutions as far as the grand jury hearing, after which they would select and brief counsel. Prosecuting district agents would be subject to the advice and super-vision of part-time 'circuit counsel', covering all districts within each Assize circuit.[32] To thwart the corrupting effect of unlawful compromises between vic-tims and defendants, solicitors would be required to notify district agents of the initial intention to pursue prosecutions.[33] Even more thorough-going proposals

---

[28] Brougham, *Minutes of Evidence of the Select Committee on Public Prosecutors*, PP 1854/5 (481), xii, 1; Greaves, *Evd.* p. 29.

[29] *Report* (1856), viii.

[30] PP 1874 [c. 1090], xxiv, 307. On the report see P. B. Kurland and D. M. Waters, 'Public Prosecutions in England, 1854–1879' (1959) 9 *Duke LJ* 493, 546–9.

[31] For example, *The Times*, 17 December 1850, p. 4; 19 December 1850, p. 5; 12 March 1868, p. 12; 4 September 1874, p. 7; 24 December 1879, p. 9; (1843) 2 *LT* 259 and (1852) 18 LT 228; (1858) 100 *Edin. Rev.* 343; (1873) 13 *Fortnightly Rev.* 316; (1868) 127 *Quart. Rev.* 44.

[32] On the perpetually worrying question of patronage and control, district agents were to be appointed by the Home Secretary, while advisory counsel would be appointees of the Attorney-General.

[33] *Report*, viii–ix. See *Criminal Law Commissioners Eighth Report* PP 1845 (656), xiv, Evidence on such compromises and the bribery of prosecutors: 238. An important Select Committee wit-ness, vastly experienced and knowledgeable practitioner and author, Greaves soon after produced

emerged from the Judicature Commission's Committee: a Metropolitan Chief Public Prosecutor supervising national district prosecutors responsible for prosecuting practically all felonies and misdemeanours across the country.[34] Most radically, in a minority report, Lord Cockburn, long politically unencumbered, proposed that all offences be publicly prosecuted because 'Every act which the law constitutes a crime is…an offence, not against the individual…but against the Community or State'. As for the cost of such a policy, Cockburn loftily declared 'the question should not be considered as one of pounds, shillings and pence' for '[n]o economy can be more ill-judged than that which would make the prosecution of offenders with a view to the suppression of crime a matter of pecuniary consideration'.[35]

Decades of drift were littered with abortive private parliamentary initiatives,[36] fuelled by an extensive clutch of severely unflattering official analyses of the prosecution system. An interruption of sorts came in 1879 with a government Bill providing for the establishment of a 'Solicitor for Public Prosecutions'. Neither resembling the 1855 Select Committee scheme, nor that of the Judicature Commission, the resulting Prosecution of Offences Act established the office of Director of Public Prosecutions, charged with the vague duty of ensuring the prosecution of important or difficult, but undefined cases.[37] Disappointed advocates of a public prosecution system, such as *The Times*, were left to reflect on the essentially unchanged post-1879 position where 'the State [still] regards the

---

A Report on Criminal Procedure to the Lord Chancellor PP 1856 vii. Here, while agreeing with the Select Committee on the need for official prosecutors, he saw them as best deployed supervising the police in investigation and arrest, and conducting proceedings before magistrates. For Greaves, their role would usually terminate with instructing of the victim's publicly funded solicitors, or solicitors appointed by magistrates where no active prosecutor existed. Cf. Stephen whose practical solution was primarily to attract able solicitors and barristers by paying them civil level costs, describing 'criminal law fees as wretchedly small', *General View*, 172.

[34] *Report, PP* 1874 [c. 1090], xxiv, 301, 319. Public prosecutors would have responsibility for selecting and briefing counsel.

[35] *Ibid.*, 327–8. The Cockburn proposals received support from *The Times*, 4 September 1874, p. 7. Twenty years before, Cockburn, as Palmerston's Attorney-General, had sunk Phillimore's no more revolutionary second bill on the grounds of expense and it being 'entirely new and foreign to the present system'. Cockburn later found similar measures unobjectionable when they appeared in the Select Committee proposals: *Evidence*, 185.

[36] Especially the early 1870s' bills of Russell Gurney (1871) and William Harcourt (1870). See generally Kurland and Waters 'Public Prosecutions'. A government bill introduced in 1873 containing some measures similar to the 1879 bill was withdrawn through lack of time.

[37] According to government spokesmen, the provisions were aimed at large-scale fraud and collusive arrangements to terminate prosecutions. This was the view of Cross, the Home Secretary in a confidential Cabinet briefing paper 'Public Prosecutors', *Home Office Printed Memoranda and Reports*, N.A. H.O. 347/14, 431–3. From this paper it is clear that Cockburn's elaborate, comprehensive prosecution scheme had little support. Cross broadly took Bramwell B.'s line that the police undertook prosecution 'duties very well'.

prosecution of crime with something like unconcern, and [where] private individuals are free to gratify their passions in a field from which passion should be excluded... The great fault of our existing system is that while it is everybody's right to prosecute, it is nobody's business to do so'.[38]

In a strict sense *The Times* was correct, but by then the *de facto* position was very much otherwise, with the police having substantially assumed the role of public prosecutor. This accretive process, following the professionalization of policing,[39] was viewed by some,[40] particularly in the early days, with suspicion and ill-concealed distaste. Several of the 1855 Select Committee's witnesses were severely critical. Supporting a new system of public prosecution, Cockburn regarded it a 'great scandal' that the police 'as inferior ministers of the law', conducted prosecutions. For him, the linkage between promotion and successful prosecutions led to 'over-zealous' conduct, coupled with temptations to invent or distort evidence.[41] Similarly, Greaves saw the appropriate police role as limited to arrest and detention.[42] John Phillimore, Chairman of the Select Committee, and author of two (1854 and 1855) failed public prosecutors bills, unsparingly characterized the police as 'a class amongst whom were to be found some of the most hardened and profligate of mankind, and over whom the most incessant vigilance was requisite to prevent flagrant and cruel abuses of authority'.[43]

Yet, such extreme misgivings came to nothing in the face of the sustained failure of national alternatives. Needs were met by the steady development of a wide range of *ad hoc* local arrangements of highly variable effectiveness involving police, magistrates' clerks, and nominated solicitors.[44] What amounted to local prosecuting cartels sometimes came under fierce criticism for indifferent

---

[38] 24 December 1879, p. 9. And Stephen, *HCL*, i, 497.

[39] An early recorded acknowledgement of this appears in Metropolitan Police Commissioner Mayne's evidence to the Criminal Law Commissioners: *Third Report of the Royal Commission on Criminal Law*, PP 1837 (79), xxxi, App. 1, *Mins of Evidence*, 21 February 1837, p. 23, endorsed by Joint Commissioner Rowan. Also, *Report of the Select Committee on the Police of the Metropolis*, PP 1834 (600), xvi, p. 59. During the 1879 bill Debates, the Home Secretary revealed that it was Home Office practice to liaise with chiefs of police in complex cases or those which had aroused public interest, *PD* 1879 (s. 3), 244: 973.

[40] e.g. (1844) 2 *LT* 356. Support for the police as prosecutors appears in the *Evidence* to the *Criminal Law Commissioners Eighth Report*, PP 1845 (656), xiv, 290, 302, and 309.

[41] 1856 *Select Committee Report, Evidence*, p. 186. Yet, in 1862, as LCJ, Cockburn suggested the acceptability of the practice in summary proceedings was entirely up to magistrates to determine. *Ex p Leamington Local Board* (1862) 5 LT 637. Additionally, the Attorney-General felt obliged to comment, 'one knows perfectly well the class of men from whom policemen are selected'.

[42] *Evidence*, 31.

[43] *PD* 1855 (s. 3), 137: 1651. On the widespread scepticism relating to police testimony on confessions, see 'Evidence', 'Confessions' below.

[44] For national variations in practice in the mid-1840s, and 1850s, see *Report of Select Committee on Public Prosecutors* (1854/6) questions 76, 106, 975 and 2767, and on the *Criminal Law Commissioners Eighth Report* (1845), Cornish, 'Defects in Prosecuting', 305, 307–9. The practice of using police

standards of practice unchallenged by open competition for briefs.[45] And within two decades, a marked softening of hostility towards police prosecutors is apparent, as, for example, in the observations of the Judicature Commission Committee. Here, magistrates' committal proceedings were viewed as 'satisfactorily conducted by the police'.[46] Soon after, the imprimatur of official recognition of the police role in prosecutions was implicitly given in the Prosecution of Offences Act 1879, which permitted the DPP to advise and assist 'chief officers of police... concerned in any criminal proceedings'.[47] Moreover, through their key responsibilities in the connected processes of detention, arrest, and prosecution, the police inevitably played a central role in shaping the social understanding of crime. Most especially, in relation to prosecution of a host of 'social' offences, including vagrancy, public disorder, and drunkenness, the police greatly facilitated attempts to impose governing and middle-class notions of an orderly and civilized society.[48] At the same time, by increasing the accessibility of the prosecution process for victims of crime, police participation boosted both their own standing and the ability of individuals of all classes to exercise some control over their lives and environments.[49]

Director of a Few Public Prosecutions

Such practical developments and benefits eased the pressure for structured change of the prosecution system and fed professional inertia resistant to change, most especially amongst solicitors and magistrates' clerks, the principal beneficiaries of the status quo. Predictably, any parliamentary intrusion jeopardizing local accommodations and often lucrative professional practices forged and refined over the preceding decades, was staunchly resisted.[50] Harcourt, for

advocates in summary proceedings was judicially criticized by Lord Coleridge CJ in *Duncan* v. *Toms* (1887) 56 LJMC 81 and Hawkins J. in *Webb* v. *Catchlove* (1886) 3 TLR 159.

[45] For example, 'Public Prosecutors' (1861) 5 *Sol. J.* 155.

[46] *Report*, 321. As the basis of perceived bias, committee disapproval was levelled at the practice of the police prosecuting cases where they also acted as witnesses. Any investigatory inclinations by magistrates were by then largely extinct, thereby adding to the importance of preliminary police activities. See Stephen, *HCL*, i, 494 and 497.

[47] Section 2. Under s 3 of the Prosecution of Offences Act 1884, the 'chief officer of every police district' was required to inform the director how all indictable offences in that district had been dealt with over the previous year.

[48] Generally, J. Davis, 'Prosecutions and Their Context' in Hay and Snyder, *Policing and Prosecution*, 397.

[49] On the wide social class base of prosecutors from the late eighteenth century and throughout the nineteenth century, King, *Crime, Justice and Discretion*, 35–42; J. Brewer and J. Styles, *An Ungovernable People* (1980), 48; Davis, 'Prosecutions and Their Context', 413–19.

[50] *Criminal Law Commissioners Eighth Report* (1845); *Evidence*, e.g. 246–7, 256–7, 303, 306, 333–4; *Select Committee on Public Prosecutors PP* 1854–6 (206) vii, 100, 120; and consultation by Home

one, experienced little difficulty in identifying the major obstacle to change: 'the most formidable body except the licensed Victuallers in the country...I mean Solicitors'.[51] Vested interests aside, no galvanizing dissatisfaction was to be found amongst the Bar or judiciary, sufficient to motivate any governmental legislative intervention. As Lord Chancellor Cairns indicated when supporting the limited measures of the Prosecution of Offences Act 1879, the system generally functioned well enough and most practitioners saw no case, nor had the appetite, for substantial change.[52] Reinforcement of this position came from recurrent concerns over patronage and political misuse. Settling just who should appoint public prosecutors, whether centrally (Home Secretary or Attorney-General) or locally,[53] would always be highly contentious. Added to this, lingering unease provoked in many by the prospect of centrally and politically controlled prosecutions, gained potency with the franchise reforms of 1867 and 1885. For some, this '[t]yranny of numbers over intelligence and property', conducing to 'democrative despotism', would only be reinforced by the 'terrible engine' of a public prosecutor.[54]

But any such fears which might have survived the restrictive 1879 legislation would have been rapidly extinguished by the ultra-cautious performance of Sir John Maude, the first Director of Public Prosecutions. Maude's strict and constricting reading[55] of his brief comfortably undershot not just the low expectations of many advocates of a full blown system of state prosecutors but also wider, more sanguine, public expectations of the office. Sustained criticism[56] of Maude was met in 1884 by the setting up of a Commons Select Committee,

Office 1872 and 1873 (e.g. proposals set out in (1872) 53 *LT* 276) with judges, magistrates, and quarter sessions revealing limited desire for fundamental change. See e.g. (1871) 50 *LT* 453; (1875) 10 *LJ* 568. The 1848 Administration of Criminal Justice Act (Jervis Act) sought to ensure regular and uniform judicial practice by magistrates at committal proceedings, see 'Evidence' below.

[51]   *PD* 1879, (s. 3), 243: 977.

[52]   *PD* 1879, (s. 3), 246: 1336. See also similar sentiments expressed in the bill's Commons Debate by the Attorney-General, Home Secretary, and the future Lord Chancellor Herschell, *PD* 1879 (s. 3), 244: 970–82.

[53]   See the *Judicature Commission Report*, App. 1, p. 25 for a list of counties and cities with locally appointed public prosecutors; and *Report on Public Prosecutors*, p. iv.

[54]   (1869) 47 *LT* 350.

[55]   The Prosecution of Offences Regulations 1880 (HC Paper 177) under s 2 of the 1879 Act, provided for prosecution where formally carried out by the Treasury Solicitor and 'other cases' for the proper conducting of which, in his opinion, the ordinary mode of prosecution is insufficient. And see the Director's limited, purely supplemental role, envisaged by the Home Secretary and Lord Chancellor in cases of 'remarkable fraud' or cases of collusion. *PD* 1879 (s. 3), 243, 976; 246, 1336. Under s 8 of the 1879 Act, regulations were made by the Attorney-General with the approval of the Lord Chancellor. Maude's brief report on the initial three years' operation of his department was a largely statistical analysis of approximately 2300 applications and approval of approximately 800 interventions (HC Paper 241, 1883).

[56]   See T. Mathew, *The Office and Duties of the Director of Public Prosecutions* (1950), 9–11.

chaired by Harcourt, then Home Secretary, to enquire into the 'action and position of the Director of Public Prosecutions'. Damningly, it concluded that the office of the Director of Public Prosecutions carried out very few functions not already within the remit of the Treasury Solicitor and Treasury Counsel. Enacted by the Prosecution of Offences Act 1884, the Committee's solution was to combine the two offices and posts into the Director of Public Prosecutions and Solicitor to the Treasury.[57]

The core question of exactly when the Director of Public Prosecutions should intervene continued to generate considerable division, something well demonstrated by the contrast between the Harcourt Committee recommendations and the approach finally embodied in the 1886 revised regulations governing the activities of the Director of Public Prosecutions. Harcourt's interventionist credentials, favouring public prosecutors, were evident in the Select Committee's suggested measures requiring the Director to prosecute in every capital case and, most significantly, in 'all other cases in which he has reason to think that the prosecution will not be efficiently conducted by the ordinary machinery of the locality...'. Of course, as the Committee owned, this provision had the clear potential to lead to a 'considerable increase in the number of prosecutions'[58] conducted by the Director. But, doubtless to ensure closer adherence to the original conception of a very limited Director's role, the actual 1886 Regulations resorted to 'public interest' as the base criterion of intervention;[59] a formulation implying a narrow range of cases, whilst still endowing the Director with substantial discretion. As an attempt to clarify the grounds for intervention, the 1886 Regulations were a signal failure,[60] with criticism unstaunched on two distinct fronts: first, the

---

[57] *Report*, 1884 [c. 4106]. Membership of the Committee included the Attorney-General and Solicitor-General, Farrar Herschell. The offices were separated by the Prosecution of Offences Act 1908 to cope with the vastly increased administrative burden as a result of expanded civil law responsibilities of the Treasury Solicitor. The root problem was that under the initial arrangement the Director or Public Prosecutions' office was purely advisory with the business of prosecution the responsibility of the Treasury Solicitor's staff.

[58] *Select Committee Report*, vii. As well as author of a failed public prosecution bill, in the early 1870s, the Liberal Harcourt had been a severe critic of the narrowly conceived Tory Government's 1879 bill: *PD* 1879 (s. 3), 244: 978.

[59] Besides capital cases, and offences formerly prosecuted by the Treasury Solicitor, or at the request of the Attorney-General or Home Secretary, the Director was required to prosecute where it appeared that the offence or its circumstances was of 'such a character that a prosecution in respect thereof is required in the public interest and that owing to the importance or difficulty of the case or other circumstances the action of the Director of Public Prosecutions is necessary to secure...prosecution...' (1886) Regulations 1(d). Harcourt's Committee had been critical of just such vague criteria which gave extensive discretion to the Director.

[60] Annual Reports between 1887 and 1915 are printed as House of Commons papers. See citations of Edwards, *op cit.*, n. 43.

familiar one of excessively circumscribed and opaque conditions of intervention; and a new one relating to the professional standards of the Director's office. The latter developed into a running, open feud between Lord Coleridge CJ and the Director, Sir Augustus Stephenson, with the Lord Chief Justice publicly censuring both the Director's choice of cases and standard of preparation.[61] Not until well into the 1890s did the narrowly conceived remit of the office itself, rather than the office holder, become the principal source for dissatisfaction.[62]

Consistent with the Home Secretary's assurances offered during the 1879 debates, the focus of successive Directors became substantial and complex frauds, along with illegal collusive arrangements. And while establishment of the office of Director of Public Prosecutions effectively marked defeat for advocates of a fully functioning public prosecution system, at the same time it constituted a distinct and further erosion of the taboo against a public prosecutions system. But for practical assistance in a wider range of cases, private prosecutors were obliged to wait for the financial support provided by the Costs in Criminal Cases Act 1908.[63] By the early 1900s, through the combined effects of increasingly generous levels of public funding and the nationwide assumption by the police of a prosecutorial role, the burden of private prosecution had, largely, become a public one. And while lacking clear structure, a measure of superintendence and regulation of the machinery of this organically developed institution of public prosecution existed in practice, in both direct and indirect forms. Beyond the Attorney-General's overall constitutional responsibility, the Prosecution of Offences Acts 1879 and 1884 had established advisory and reporting mechanisms between the DPP and chiefs of police, obliging the latter to account annually for their prosecutorial actions. Potential regulation of prosecution practices by the courts existed through their treatment of costs, employment of rules of evidence, and, occasionally, explicit public censure. Additionally, many magistrates exercised a form of supervision of police prosecution practices through membership of city watch committees or county police committees. More remotely, a dimension of accountability lay with the Home Secretary though his administrative control of police practices, and responsibility for appointment of stipendiary magistrates, Chairmen of Quarter Sessions, and Recorders.

---

[61] Edwards, *op cit.*, 378, 381–4.

[62] *The Times*, 19 May 1894.

[63] Prior to the Act, see DC *Report on Allowances to Prosecutors and Witnesses in Public Prosecutions*, PP 1903 [Cd. 1650]. The Act provided for payment at the court's direction of prosecution or defence costs out of local funds. Both summary and indictable defences were covered by the Act. Assistance for impecunious defendants could be granted under the Poor Prisoners' Defence Act 1903.

2. DEFENCE

The Participation of Lawyers

At the beginning of the eighteenth century, a party charged with an indictable offence had faced grave difficulties in mounting a defence. Not only did defendants frequently have no detailed advance knowledge of the precise charge for indictable offences, they would also lack the earlier depositions of prosecution witnesses. In the case of a felony, the defendant would usually have to organize his defence from the confines of a jail. Moreover, unlike defendants charged with treason or misdemeanours, at a felony trial a defendant was denied access to legal representation and expected to conduct his own 'plain and honest Defence'. From this position, in the following century running up to 1820, criminal trials on indictment underwent fundamental change, both in respect of the roles of the *dramatis personae* and the rules which regulated them. This was true of the judge, prosecution, and most especially the defendant. It was a process of change in large measure wrought by the relatively small, but slowly swelling ranks of lawyers participating in trials from the early eighteenth century, initially almost exclusively acting for the prosecution. However, by the 1730s, counsel were also being permitted to appear in felony trials for the defence in London and at provincial Assizes. By the 1800s, between a third and a quarter of all trials at the Old Bailey witnessed defence counsel in action, a figure approximately double that of cases led by prosecution counsel.[64] Accounting for this modest relaxation of the prohibition of defence counsel at felony trials and the steadily strengthening infiltration of lawyers is a largely speculative exercise. Most plausibly, early eighteenth-century appearances of prosecution counsel in trials of murder and other serious offences encouraged judicial admission of defence counsel, both to achieve a better sense of fairness and balance, and to expose certain forms of highly dubious prosecution evidence to greater forensic scrutiny. Certainly, with a more thorough, professional presentation of the prosecution case in trials of complex offences, such as forgery, the risks of inadequately staged defences and incorrect verdicts became apparent.[65] From their admission of defence counsel

---

[64] See J. Langbein, 'The Criminal Trial before the Lawyers' (1978) 45 U Ch LR 263, and *Origins* 169–70; J. Beattie, 'Scales of Justice: Defence Counsel and English Criminal Trials in the Eighteenth and Nineteenth Centuries' (1991) 9 *Law and Hist. Rev.* 221, 228–9. On the problematic nature of Old Bailey Sessions Papers for assessing the use of counsel, Beattie, *ibid.*, 228; Langbein, *Origins*, 169–70n; cf. S. Landsman, 'The Rise of the Contentious Spirit: Adversary Procedure in Eighteenth Century England' (1990) 75 *Cornell LR* 498, 607, table II, suggesting a lower proportion.

[65] On the risky nature of evidence from accomplices and professional thief-takers, see Beattie, 'Scales' (1991), 226; Langbein, 'Trial before the Lawyers', 313; *Origins*, 148–77; on forgery,

it is reasonable to infer that the judiciary collectively felt that trial judges alone could not fulfil this protective function.

By 1820, the early eighteenth-century judicial discretion permitting counsel to sit with and advise felony defendants on how best to conduct their defence, had mutated into a wide defence role; this all but obliterated the former rule against full defence counsel. Not only was defence counsel now permitted to assume the former judicial function of examining and cross-examining, and speak on legal issues, he was recognized as appropriately completely partisan: as Chitty noted, it was his 'business to see that the [defendant] lose no advantage'.[66] The one surviving substantial restriction on full defence rights denied counsel the valuable opportunity of addressing the jury. In those felony trials where counsel participated, the nature of trial on indictment had been transformed from a judge-led examination of the prosecutor's and defendant's cases to a contest between opposing parties—an adversarial contest. Under such a system, counsel's examination of witnesses would probably be better focused and more conducive to advancing their client's claims; and cross-examination was likely to be better informed and more destructive of the opposition's case. However, throughout the nineteenth and well into the twentieth century, the judicial role remained hybrid in nature; because the majority of trials on indictment still involved unrepresented defendants, a substantial remnant of the judge's former paternalistic function continued: requiring him to speak on the law; 'examine witnesses for the defend-

---

see R. McGowan 'Knowing the Hand: Forgery and the Proof of Writing in Eighteenth Century England' (1998), 24, *Historical Reflections* 385. Furthermore, a dramatic increase in the number of barristers occurred , with many seeking fresh outlets for their talents. Between the 1770s and 1840s the size of the Bar more than quadrupled, with the number of additional practitioners estimated as increasing by two and a half times. Expansion slowed considerably during the second half of the nineteenth century. D. Duman, *The English and Colonial Bars in the Nineteenth Century* (1983), 6–9, and tables 1.2 and 1.3.

[66] *Chitty* (1826), ii: 407. Similarly, the *Criminal Law Commissioners, Second Report* (1836), 8. For criticism of unrestrained cross-examining counsel, 'going all lengths,...frequently without any instructions to warrant an attack upon the character and demeanour of the witness...', see J. P. Collier, *Criticisms on the Bar; Including Strictures on the Principal Counsel Practising in the Courts* (1819), 112. A number of celebrated trials, particularly from the 1840s, exposed in very public fashion the problems of the professional limits and responsibilities of advocates. *Courvoisier* (1840) raised the fundamental question of defence of an accused believed by his advocate to be guilty. Charles Phillips' robust defence of Courvoisier despite such a belief attracted widespread and sustained criticism. The notorious case of *Palmer* (1856) wrestled with the legitimacy of counsel asserting his personal belief in the defendant's innocence. Again, wholesale condemnation of the practice from the Lord Chief Justice downwards left little doubt of the appropriate professional ethics. See Cairns, *Advocacy*, Ch. 6. Also Stephen's written account of the Bar's often unwritten professional ethos which distinguishes 'between honourable and dishonourable attack and defence...between honourable and dishonourable warfare': *General View*, 167–8 and 'The Morality of Advocacy' (1861) 3 *Cornhill Mag.* 447–57. And generally on the Bar's professional reputation and ethos XI, Pt 4.

ant; [and] to advise him for his benefit'.[67] Moreover, the presence or absence of a defence advocate might be expected to influence the substance of a judge's summing up. Although a 'moderator' his summing up 'may, and generally does indicate his opinion',[68] it might be hazarded that judges were probably more circumspect in their willingness to express outright an unfavourable assessment of unrepresented defendants. But whether with or without defence counsel, many key trial features changed, or were in the process of changing as a consequence of the general incursion of lawyers, most particularly the treatment of evidence.

Establishing new rules, or sharpening old rules of criminal evidence was an almost inevitable consequence of the involvement of trial lawyers deploying their forensic skills to undermine or dismember the opposition's evidence. Testing the opposition's case and putting the best gloss on one's own evidence was soon counsel's raison d'être. In broad terms, before the arrival of counsel, practically all evidence was regarded as admissible. Greater scepticism and scrutiny narrowed the nature and forms of admissible evidence, and in many instances the discretionary nature of admissibility moved to a fixed rule basis. Likewise, central issues relating to the presumption of innocence, and the onus and standard of proof, were thrown into stronger relief by the presence of opposing counsel. Unlike judges, lawyers could investigate and organize the adduction of evidence. With counsel's presence came greater attempts to discriminate more clearly between mere assertion, argument, and verifiable evidence. In sum, new procedures seeking to ensure a proper, balanced admission, employment, and treatment of evidence were installed.[69]

However, whilst by the 1820s, felony trials had sustained radical modification, transformation to an uninhibited adversarial system was still highly contentious. The dispute between reformers and defenders of the status quo would be given full vent in a series of campaigns fought across 15 years over legislative initiatives aimed at giving accused felons the entitlement to full trial counsel. Successive reform bills[70] introduced during the 1820s perished largely at the hands of a hostile Tory administration and Commons, along with opposition

---

[67] *Chitty, ibid.*, and Blackstone, *Comms*, iv, 349–50. Brougham, amongst others, maintained that after the 1836 Act public prosecutors would relieve judges of having to deal with defence counsel speeches: Brougham to Lyndhurst, 20 December 1836, *Lyndhurst Papers*.

[68] Stephen, *General View*, 161. Supporting Stephen's observations, *O'Donnell* (1916) 12 Cr App R 219. Throughout Victorian times, and beyond, the judiciary permitted themselves enormous latitude in the substance and style of summing up. Some judges routinely either omitted any summing up or provided no more than the most perfunctory comment. For example F. W. Ashley, *My Sixty Years in the Law* (1936), 97. Certainly, where the facts were clear and the law simple, the Court of Criminal Appeal found the practice unobjectionable: *Newman* (1913) 9 Cr App R 134.

[69] See generally 'Evidence', below.

[70] Between 1821 and 1828, six bills were introduced. Parliamentary support came from familiar Whig reformers including Mackintosh, Lushington, and Denman.

from most of the Bar and Bench.[71] Underpinning the case for full defence counsel was the belief that an adversarial procedure was the most effective method
of achieving the core aim of a criminal trial—the correct verdict through the
exposure of truth. It was an assertion powerfully supported by the long-established right to full counsel in civil proceedings, and in trials for treason and
misdemeanours.[72]

But the case against reform lacked neither force nor able advocates. First as
Solicitor-General, and then Attorney-General, Sir John Copley bore principal
responsibility for marshalling the anti-reformist arguments, directly challenging
claims that adversarial combat was the most effective method to 'investigate the
truth'. In what closely resembled a case for rolling back decades of change and
returning to an inquisitorial style of trial, Copley characterized criminal trials as
occasions where there should be 'no extraordinary excitement [but] temperate,
candid inquiry…', where the judge jealously watched over the defendant's interests. Admission of full counsel would transform the trial into 'a war of wit',[73] convert the court into an 'arena for two ingenious combatants', and permit 'passions
instead of reason' to dominate; rather than revealed, truth would be disregarded
or even defeated.[74]

But rhetoric of this nature proved insufficient to hold back the general reformist inclinations of the Whig administration of the early 1830s, especially with
Brougham, as Lord Chancellor, and Denman established as Chief Justice of the
King's Bench from 1832.[75] Eventual success of William Ewart's fourth Defendants'
Counsel Bill in 1836 followed two earlier defeats in the Lords. Here, resort to
the common law's long distilled certitudes on the comprehensive protective role
of judges relented to the measured scrutiny of those wishing to embrace a fully
adversarial trial. Whilst many elements appear in the Commons' and Lords'

---

[71] Discussed by May, *The Bar*, 183–94.

[72] e.g. *PD* 1821 (s. 2), 4: 1513, and 1824 (s. 2), 11: 182.

[73] *PD* 1824 (s. 2), 11: 208. As the *Legal Observer* noted, some 'Chairmen of Quarter Sessions, probably fatigued by the brawling of some hard-fighting junior, cannot endure the thought of giving him
unlimited time and scope for his tounge' (*PD* 1835 (s. 3), 10: 225).

[74] *PD* 1824 (s. 2), 11: 206–8 and 193; *PD* 1821 (s. 2), 4: 1513. In general a view informing Langbein's
Origins, passim. Cf. Cairns, *Advocacy*, 68–9; Beattie, 'Scales', 253. Copley did not account for the
right to full counsel in misdemeanour and treason trial, and particularly why defendants facing
less serious misdemeanour charges enjoyed the right to full counsel. For treason, see A. Shapiro,
'Political Theory and the Growth of Defensive Safeguards in Criminal Procedure: The Origins of the
Treason Trials Act of 1696' (1993) 11 *Law and Hist. Rev.* 215. Chitty notes, 'In prosecution for treason,
it was feared that the very weight of the charge would tend to depress the prisoner…', *Criminal Law*
(1826), i: 408.

[75] The broadly reformist legal press largely supported the campaign, while, in the main, the legal
profession, including the judiciary, opposed change. For a survey of contemporary legal periodical
comment, see May, *The Bar*, 181–3.

debates, the Whig reformers' creed was most cogently and relentlessly rehearsed in the Criminal Law Commissioners' Second Report, calculatedly published on the eve of the Lords' debate on Ewart's fourth bill.[76]

From the Report's opening paragraphs, the Commissioners sought to demonstrate the common law's illogicality, inconsistency, and a-typicality in the civilized world. In pursuing a trial's central objective of 'discovery of truth', permitting full counsel 'has obtained in every civilized age and country [including] by our own law in all judicial proceedings except trials for Felonies'. The right to counsel was 'essential to the attainment of truth', with the common law exception of felony trials an anomalous survivor from a 'remote and illiterate age'.[77] It was a visible distortion of reality to characterize the nature of the defendant's case as an 'honest, artless' narration of facts, requiring no skill. Moreover, how many defendants had the necessary 'coolness and talent' required to expose the 'improbabilities and discrepancies' in evidence, especially where 'facts' were circumstantial and did not 'speak for themselves'?[78] The frequently repeated claim that the judge was the defendant's counsel was a 'vulgar notion' almost 'too extravagant to require comment'; it was 'impossible that any Judge, however transcendant his talents' could properly present the defendant's case.[79] Furthermore, as a matter of principle, if the judge is 'an efficient Counsel, he transgresses his proper power as a Judge; if he is an inefficient Counsel, the Prisoner is not properly defended... [A] Judge is only so far Counsel for the Prisoner as to see that he is fairly treated. If that is the amount of the Judge's defence, he is not an adequate counsel'.[80]

Voicing the contemporary reform ethos, the Commissioners sought effectiveness in deterring and punishing crime by removing vague, discretionary powers, and substituting clear and objective procedures, conducing to 'the more certain punishment of guilt, as well as the more complete defence of innocence'.[81] The subtle checks and balances operating between protective, paternalistic judges and self-restrained[82] prosecution counsel, allegedly then underpinning felony trials, were regarded as unlikely to achieve such aims. Judges who were less than

---

[76] Following frequent political practice, witnesses were mainly selected to give supporting evidence. Known to be largely hostile to the bill, the judiciary were not consulted. However, some leading members of the Bar hostile to reform (on grounds similar to those voiced by Copley) did give evidence, including Sjts D'Oyley and Spankie, *Report*, PP 1836 (343), xxxvi, Apps.

[77] *Report*, 2 and 14, and 6n.

[78] Similarly, Lushington, *PD* 1824 (s. 2), 11: 210.

[79] *Ibid.*, pp. 6, 3, 9, 7, 8.

[80] *Ibid.*, p. 9, quoting Ewart's evidence. See similarly, S. Smith (1827) 45 *Edin. Rev.* 82; attribution *Wellesley Index* vol. 1, 468; Lushington, *PD* 1824 (s. 2) 11: 240; and Mackintosh's comments on the discretionary or 'casual feelings of a judge', *ibid.*, 185.

[81] *Ibid.*, p. 16, Ewart's evidence.

[82] Regarded by the Commissioners as 'injurious to the interests of justice; in as much as they frequently occasion the acquittal of guilty persons', *ibid.*, p. 16. In the 1824 Commons debates, John

fully briefed and uncommitted prosecutors did not conduce to, but inhibited, the 'attainment of truth', making less likely the conviction of the guilty and protection of the innocent. Like unpopular excessive punishment,[83] the dangers of jury nullification of charges, or the complete failure to prosecute, concerned the Commissioners. In respect of representation, they saw the vital matter of the public image of criminal justice as damagingly compromised by a law which 'closes the Lips of the Prisoner's advocate'. Rather than 'moderate and just' this restriction appears to jurors and the 'generality of people…harsh and unreasonable' and was likely to lead jurors to 'show undue favour' to defendants.[84]

Assuming the rights to full counsel were granted, just what general balance should be struck in felony trials between prosecution and defence? Most especially, which side should have the 'last word'? The Commissioners regarded as unfair to defendants the existing position for misdemeanours and civil trials, whereby counsel for the prosecution or plaintiff enjoyed the substantial tactical benefit of the right to address the jury in response to defence evidence; it was a 'last word' advantage denied the plaintiff or prosecution only where the defence failed to call evidence and relied exclusively on counsel's cross-examining skills and his address to the jury. In the Commissioners' view, avoidance of this tactical penalty for defendants in felony trials (which inhibited the 'attainment of truth') required specific provisions ensuring defendant's counsel could freely call witnesses without forfeiting the right to reply to the prosecution's response.[85] However, on the claimed grounds of consistency between civil and criminal law, the Lords, led by Lord Lyndhurst[86] (the ennobled Sir John Copley) and Lord Abinger[87] excised the 'last word' provision from the 1836 bill.[88]

North characterized prosecution restraint as an 'obligation of honour and mercy…to offer a plain, colourless statement of the case without a single attempt to aggravate', PD 1824 (s. 2), 11: 190.

[83] See the Commissioners' views on 'Punishments', *Report*, 19–38, which they regarded as linked to felony defence counsel.

[84] *Report*, 17. For concern over the need for the system of criminal justice to enjoy broad public approval, for example, Lushington, PD 1824 (s. 2), 11: 211 and 1825 (s. 2), 12: 971; Denman, PD 1826, (s. 2), 15: 632.

[85] *Report*, 16–17. Five years earlier the Common Law Commissioners had proposed giving defendants in civil trials the right to a closing speech: *Third Report into the Practice and Proceedings of the Superior Courts of Common Law*, PP 1831 (92), x, 375, 442. Eventually enacted under the Common Law Procedure Act 1854, s 18.

[86] Cairns, *Advocacy*, 110n. Lord Lyndhurst credited his conversion to the faith of full counsel to time spent between 1831 and 1834 trying criminal cases whilst Chief Baron of the Exchequer, PD 1836 (s. 3), 34: 764.

[87] Chief Baron of the Exchequer, formerly James Scarlett.

[88] Entitlement to a closing speech in criminal trials was given to defendants by the Criminal Procedure Act 1865, s 2, thereby enabling defendants' counsel to comment on the evidence of defence witnesses and the prosecution's cross-examination.

The Defendants' Counsel Act 1836: Rights and Realities

Whilst formally opening a new chapter in criminal trial procedure and the rights of defendants, in practice the Defendants' Counsel Act 1836 introduced no dramatic change in the nature of felony trials. True, the Act demarcated an expanded age of adversarialism,[89] but for several reasons the immediate effects were limited and gradual in maturing. First, to a powerful degree, excision of the defendant's 'last word' provision from the 1836 Act almost obliged defence counsel to continue excluding defence evidence in order to retain the considerable benefit of addressing the jury at the end of the prosecution case.[90] But such a tactic denied juries hearing not only defendants' unsworn statements of events but also any witness evidence. This was an outcome some distance removed from the assertions of the Criminal Law Commissioners, and others, that unrestricted adversarialism was the enlightened route to the 'attainment of truth'. In such circumstances, the essence of defences became the undermining of prosecution evidence:[91] exposing its inconsistencies, lacunae, impugning motives of witnesses, and by innocently accounting for what remained consistent with the defendant's guilt.[92]

Secondly, considerable ambiguity followed the Act concerning the appropriate judicial role where, as in the overwhelming majority of cases, the prosecution was unrepresented. If the defendant was represented by counsel, should the trial judge seek to take on a more forensic prosecutorial role, drawing a jury's

[89] It has been forcefully contended that the adversarial system was a response to failure to develop an effective pre-trial investigation: Langbein, *Origins*, at e.g. 333. Developments in felony trials appear to have been almost inevitable: first, the principle of adversarialism was well entrenched in civil proceedings and misdemeanour trials by the time lawyers made their presence felt in felony trials; secondly, as shown by the patchy performance of local magistrates and widespread resistance to professional policing, the general political and criminal justice culture in England was broadly hostile to the professionally organized investigation and prosecution of offences; and thirdly, later changes improving investigation and pre-trial procedures produced no obvious curbs on the development of adversarial practices.

[90] Confirmed by the extensive restrictions on introducing defence evidence set out in a judicial practice direction reproduced in (1837) 17 *LM* 470, 'Prisoners' Counsel: Practice Memorandum'. Moreover, as in civil proceedings, defence counsel's speech could not incorporate any claim unsupported by evidence adduced.

[91] A judicial Practice Memorandum effectively restricted the defence's use of pre-trial depositions to undermine the credibility of prosecution witnesses by identifying inconsistencies between deposition evidence and that given at trial. For the background to this restriction and on the post-1836 Act development in criminal advocacy, Cairns, *Advocacy*, 117–24 and Ch. 6.

[92] It was soon ruled that the defence had only one opportunity to address the jury: either by counsel or the defendant, not both. Coleridge J. in *Boucher* (1837) 8 Car. & P. 141. On the central claim of the proper professional role of counsel in 'truth' finding, see May, *The Bar*, Ch. 8; for the claim that the Criminal Bar adopted the objective of procedural justice for defendants rather than identifying 'truth', cf. Cairns, *Advocacy*, Ch. 4, and *passim*.

attention to what he regarded as deficiencies in defence counsel's speech? Indeed, as seen, judicial recognition of the potential invidiousness of their position, along with possible concerns at being unable to match defence counsel's fully briefed performance, almost certainly motivated successful judicial demands in 1830s and 1840s for counsel to appear in all Assize prosecutions.[93]

The third and harshest reality limiting the impact of the 1836 Act was that while it granted the procedural right to full counsel in felony trials, the inability to pay counsel's fees meant that the practical position for the majority of defendants remained unchanged. For some time to come, except for murder and fraud charges, trials would generally be swift, almost perfunctory.[94] By initially incorporating in his bill provisions for the judicial assignment of counsel to all impecunious defendants,[95] Ewart, at least, was consistent in his assertion that defence counsel was vital for the 'attainment of truth'. Occasionally other ineffectual voices were raised in the name of 'justice' supporting legal assistance to ensure a 'fair trial' for every defendant, 'though he be the poorest and meanest wretch that crawls upon the face of this earth...',[96] including Stephen who observed that 'To call upon the common run of criminals to defend themselves is a sort of mockery'.[97] Moreover, rather than beneficial, judicial reluctance to question defendants directly on the substance of their defences, could leave the undefended in a tongue-tied and 'absolutely pitiable' state.[98] While during the course of the nineteenth century a succession of measures was enacted increasing the financial support of prosecutions, none was forthcoming for the provision of defence lawyers. Instead, impecunious defendants mainly went undefended, whilst a minority enjoyed the benefit of counsel through two largely discretionary judicial practices.

[93] See 'Prosecution', above.

[94] Into the 1840s, and beyond, the rapid speed of trials generated disquiet and criticism in many quarters. The leading criminal law solicitor, Thomas Wontner, famously estimated the average duration of an 1830s Old Bailey trial to be under nine minutes: T. Wontner, *Old Bailey Experience* (1833), 59 and May, *The Bar*, Ch. 6, *passim*. Similarly, (1833) 10 *LM* 275. As well as through increased rates of professional representation, the length of criminal trials was also expanded by the gradual rise in the use of expert witnesses. Prosecutions for poisoning were usually particularly dependent on expert forensic evidence. For a detailed account of one of Victorian England's most celebrated examples, *Palmer* (1856), see Stephen, *HCL*, *iii*, 389–425. For experts and the insanity defence, see below. At the end of the century the effects of enactment of the Criminal Evidence Act 1898 added to this trend. Cf. The Gorell Committee *Report* 1909, [Cd 4976] 13.

[95] At the House of Lords Select Committee stage the 1835 Bill was opposed by members of the bar on the grounds of professional self-interest and procedural inconvenience, *PD* 1835 (s. 2), 46: 317. Such a provision was excluded from the 1836 Act.

[96] (1843) 1, *LT* 635; also (1846) 7, 421; (1857) 30, 195; and (1866) 41, 594.

[97] 'Characteristics of English Criminal Law', 56. Similarly, 'The Practice of Interrogating Persons Accused of Crime' *Juridical Society, 1855–58* (1858), 456, 474.

[98] Stephen, *General View*, 196.

For serious offences, usually murder, counsel might be provided by a judge, requesting 'some member of the Bar present to give his honorary services'.[99] However, not only was the judicial practice relatively rare, it was variable; even in some cases of murder, trial judges occasionally failed to assign counsel.[100] But when provided, the quality of representation was frequently of doubtful value to the defendant, usually because of the short time available to prepare the defence, lack of an instructing solicitor, or, most likely, assignment of an inexperienced or newly fledged barrister. As Grantham J. later observed, 'my difficulty is to get a man that I think can do it properly. [An] inexperienced barrister…almost invariably runs his man in'.[101] The alternative 'dock brief', whereby a defendant might choose from the dock any available counsel in court for a fee of one guinea, was a hardly more impressive means of securing representation for the poor. Unlike assignment of counsel, a dock brief could apply to any offence, but the procedure was not widely favoured or even known of[102] during the nineteenth century. Besides the initial problem of raising the not insubstantial fixed fee of one guinea,[103] there remained many of the same deficiencies affecting assignment of counsel. Moreover, dock briefs also gained some notoriety, at the Old Bailey, where 'counsel are to be found who sign briefs marked with guineas when they receive only shillings, and who take a number of briefs positively at so much a dozen'.[104]

By mid-century, representation levels at trials presided over by High Court judges had steadily risen to a position where the overwhelming majority of defendants were represented. This was a consequence of at least two factors. First, most serious offences were heard by superior court judges, whether at provincial Assizes or at the Old Bailey, making resort to a dock brief, assignment of counsel, or engagement of counsel at full cost, more likely. Secondly, since their campaign to ensure all prosecutions before them were presented by counsel, along with expectations of unrestrained adversarialism after the 1836 Act,

[99] *Archbold's Pleading and Evidence* (12th edn, ed. W. N. Welsby, 1853), 129.

[100] For a review of judicial practices, D. Bentley, *English Criminal Justice in the Nineteenth Century* (1998), 110–13.

[101] Giving evidence to the *SC Report on the Poor Prisoners' Defence Bill*, PP 1903 (264), vii, 580–90. And experiences of G. Coleridge, *Some and Sundry* (1931), 187–8.

[102] It was unclear whether dock briefs were ever available in summary proceedings, nor does any reference to the procedure occur in contemporary practitioners' manuals. See e.g. *Chitty* (2nd edn, 1826) and *Archbold* (12th edn, 1853). A third procedure of some antiquity available to a defendant with assets worth less than £5, 'defence in *forma pauperis*' appears to have been practically defunct by the nineteenth century *Chitty*, (1826), i: 412, and *Archbold* (1853), 128).

[103] The financial concessions made by the Bar during the nineteenth century in accepting the practice were far from professionally ruinous. By mid-century, one guinea was the usual basic prosecution fee paid to counsel at the Old Bailey, Assizes and Quarter Sessions: *Report of Departmental Committee on Allowances to Prosecutors and Witnesses*, PP 1903 [Cd. 1650], lvi, 357, 583.

[104] (1871) 51 *LT* 327, calling for 'sweeping investigations [into] the Criminal Bar'. Earlier examples include (1843) 2 *LT* 46; (1844) 4 *LT* 186. And see XI, Pts 3 and 4.

judges would have felt much more inclined to try and ensure the appearance of defence counsel.[105] Trials at Quarter Sessions and the Old Bailey without a presiding High Court judge, were different with half of defendants still unrepresented by the end of the nineteenth century.[106] Besides trying offences less serious than those heard by Assizes, at Quarter Sessions no universal practice had developed of prosecutions being carried out by counsel.

The consequences of the absence of legal representation could be aggravated by one further factor: whether the defendant was at liberty on pre-trial bail. Clearly, without legal representation, organizing a defence (including witnesses) whilst in custody could be problematic. Prior to the Administration of Criminal Justice Act 1826, for felonies a heavy presumption operated against pre-trial bail. Unless a capital felony, in a minority of cases this presumption might be dislodged where a prisoner of sound reputation could provide sureties, and particularly if the prosecutor's evidence was less than compelling.[107] For lesser offences, provided sureties could be offered, granting bail was usual. After 1826, the presumption against bail remained for felonies where a charge was 'supported by positive and credible evidence'. But two magistrates retained the general right to order bail, especially where the prosecution case was undermined by defence evidence.

Fear of the defendant absconding as the principal ground for failing to grant bail did not become openly articulated until mid-century.[108] Yet, until 1898, poor prisoners were almost inevitably disadvantaged by their inability to provide sureties, even though there was no serious risk of them failing to answer their bail. Under 1898 legislation, sureties could be dispensed with so long as this would not 'tend to defeat the ends of justice'.[109] However, despite frequent prodding by the Home Office and higher judiciary, the impact of the legislation on magistrates' practices was limited.[110]

---

[105] This impression is gained from Old Bailey Sessions Papers between 1860 and 1902, showing defence counsel appearing in practically all cases heard by a High Court judge. This is equally true of reports of provincial Assize trials.

[106] In 1856 the Law Times reported that at Bath Quarter Sessions no prisoners were represented by counsel (1856) 28 LT 74. Representation rose from approximately one-third in mid-century to over a half by 1900. For the Central Criminal Court the representation rate of defendants, even after enactment of the Poor Prisoners' Defence Act 1903 (below) was under 40% in 1912. Feeley, 'Legal Complexity' (1997), 195. And XI, Pt 3. Also the confirmatory comments of C. Kenny, Outlines of the Criminal Law (Cambridge, 1904), 478.

[107] 1826 7 Geo. IV c. 64. For practices between 1800 and 1834, see O.B.S.P. On securing release through a writ of habeas corpus, XI, Pt 2.

[108] For example Robinson (1853) 23 L.J. Q.B. 286. The Indictable Offences Act 1848 11 & 12 Vict. c. 4 empowered a single magistrate to grant bail in felony cases, and required bail be given for all except specified misdemeanours.

[109] 1898 61 & 62 Vict. c. 7.

[110] e.g. Home Office circulars cited in Stone's Justices' Manual (46th edn, 1914), 18–19; and comments in (1910) 128 LT 511.

The Criminal Evidence Act 1898 and the Poor Prisoners' Defence Act 1903

By making all defendants competent to give sworn evidence, the Criminal Evidence Act 1898 irresistibly revived the issue of defence representation. Following the Act, the unrepresented defendant faced the dilemma of whether, and how, he would give evidence and respond to cross-examination.[111] No group of individuals collectively understood this better than the Bar. Yet though endorsing the idea of legal representation for poor defendants, their specially appointed committee of 1899 pursued the matter no further. However, in 1903, despite lacking campaigning support from the Bar Council,[112] seven KCs and MPs introduced the Poor Prisoners' Defence Bill,[113] which provided for the gratuitous representation of all defendants by counsel and solicitor. Comprising a mixed group of judges, practitioners, and administrators, the Select Committee witnesses were divided on the bill's merits. Along with the DPP and Grantham J., the vastly experienced Treasury counsel, Sir Harry Poland, KC, was the Committee's principal witness. Each witness, and most emphatically Poland, saw the bill as superfluous, firm in the belief that the existing system of assignment of counsel or defence by trial judge ensured that 'a man gets real justice . . . in the large majority of cases'.[114] Against this perception, support for the bill came both from Quarter Sessions benches,[115] with their relatively high levels of unrepresented defendants, and from Channell J., on the grounds that representation of defendants 'would tend to increase confidence in fairness with which justice is administered'.[116] Whilst broadly in favour of improving the representation of defendants, the Select Committee modified the bill in two significant respects. First, believing

[111] 61 & 62 Vict. c. 36. Before 1898 many specific statutory exceptions to the rule existed, see 'Evidence' below. Attempts failed at the Committee stage of the 1898 bill to include provisions to provide poor prisoners with counsel, PD 1898 (s. 4), 60: 720–1, 748.

[112] Special Committee Report (1899) 63 JP 115. The 1899 Bar annual general meeting approved the Special Committee Report, but took no further measures to ensure legislative action, ibid., 127. According to the bill's Select Committee, the Law Society had shown no interest in the bill's proposals. Report, v.

[113] The scheme was seen as unnecessary and opposed by several London Bar Messes NA, LC 02/148. Bentley, Criminal Justice, 128. Favourable press comments include The Times, 2 April 1903, and (1903) 38 LJ 139, which expressed disappointment that proposals would not cover summary proceedings (p. 140). And similarly nine years earlier (1894) 29 LJ 275.

[114] Report and Special Report from the Select Committee on Poor Prisoners' Defence Bill, PP 1903 (264), vii, 6–8. The DPP regarded the bill as unnecessary with the existing 'extremely good system to secure the safety of innocent persons' (p. 53).

[115] H. Buszard, KC, Recorder of Leicester, (p. 36) and Viscount Cranbourne, Chairman of East Herts Quarter Sessions (p. 15). The Committee regarded the lack of a legally qualified Chairman of County Quarter Sessions as a strong reason for ensuring defendants were represented.

[116] In a letter to the Select Committee, Report, 36.

them to be unworkable,[117] the Select Committee jettisoned the provisions for gratuitous lawyers' services in favour of public funding. Secondly, for unspecified reasons,[118] the Committee restricted availability of aid to those certified by committing magistrates as appropriate because of the nature of defence evidence.[119]

The Poor Prisoners' Defence Act 1903 enjoyed neither judicial popularity nor clarity. Some judges continued to view the dock brief system as adequate, treating the new provisions as completely unnecessary.[120] Others, such as Wills J., regarded the Act as 'without doubt, one of the worst-conceived and worst-drawn pieces of legislation I ever saw'.[121] Certainly, on more than one occasion in its first year, interpretation of the Act required the public intervention of Lord Alverstone CJ. Making explicit the Act's implicit philosophy, Lord Alverstone confirmed that it 'was not intended to give a prisoner legal assistance to find out if he has got a defence [but] in order to make clear that defence...The Act was passed in the interest of innocent persons and such should be advised in future not to reserve "their defence" but to disclose it at once, so that it can be investigated'.[122] Effectively, the price of taking publicly funded legal representation was potentially to place defendants in a position inferior to those able to pay for counsel.

Moreover, an unrepresented defendant at committal proceedings, through confusion, miscalculation, or agitation, might prejudice his entitlement to professional assistance by failing to disclose material evidence. Such risks were compounded by the quickly established frequent practice of magistrates of leaving the question of legal aid to trial courts, by which stage thorough defence preparation and recovery of all relevant evidence was frequently impossible.[123] Besides the defence disclosure requirement, widespread dissatisfaction existed with failure of the 1903 Act to cover committal proceedings and summary trials. However, it was a dissatisfaction which was not felt greatly either by successive

---

[117] Sir Harry Poland doubted the value of inexperienced solicitors and barristers who he regarded as 'very dangerous at times', *Report*, 25. And see the DPP's comments, *Report*, 56.

[118] Probably a combination of the desire to limit public costs and acceptance of the judicial view that only defendants who openly revealed their defence at an early stage deserved public support. See this view expressed by Wills, Grantham, and Channell JJ reported in (1903) 67 *JP* 583–4.

[119] Under the 1903 Act certificates of aid would be granted, if 'desirable in the interests of justice', for solicitor and counsel by committing magistrates, or later at Quarter Sessions or Assizes. The qualifying requirement of poverty was undefined by the Act.

[120] Bigham J. (1904) 68 *JP* 76.

[121] *The Times*, 28 October 1904. And observations of McCardie J. In G. Pollock, *Mr Justice McCardie* (1934), 62.

[122] 23 July 1904, quoted in *PD* 1929, (s. 5 HL), 231: 146; and 9 November 1904, reported (1904) 68 *JP* 557.

[123] Especially where no aid was granted for a solicitor. See *First Report of the Committee on Legal Aid for the Poor*, 1926 [Cmnd. 2638] para. 13; and B. Abel-Smith and R. Stevens, *Lawyers and the Courts*, (1967), 153. In his evidence to the 1903 Select Committee, Recorder Buszard, expressed little enthusiasm for the use of magistrates, noting that he 'would not care to trust...discretion to magistrates in county towns', *Report*, 38.

governments or significant sections of the legal profession. Parliamentary[124] and extra-parliamentary[125] efforts to widen the availability of criminal legal aid produced only the most meagre results until enactment of the Poor Prisoners' Defence Act 1930.[126]

3. REGULATING THE TRIAL: CRIMINAL EVIDENCE: REFINING AND FORMALISING ITS EXCLUSIONARY AND PROTECTIVE EMPHASIS

The philosophical and pragmatic scrutiny visiting most areas of the criminal law during the nineteenth century, carried significant consequences for much of the law of criminal evidence. As elsewhere, the blend of utilitarian rationalism[127] and growth of adversarial assumptions were powerful forces in unseating or disturbing established law and practices. While the efficient ascertaining of the relevant facts at a trial was common cause amongst lawyers, just how this was to be achieved attracted rather less of a consensus. Beyond policy questions relating to the best techniques and rules for identifying judicial facts and exposing untruths, lay the considerable issue of the balance to be struck between protecting defendants from the risks of wrong convictions and social demands of ensuring that criminals did not escape conviction and punishment. Subject to the major exception of the defendant's own competency to give evidence, the broad emphasis of nineteenth-century developments in criminal evidence was towards narrowing the range of admissibility and increasing clarification of the prosecution's burden of proving its case to the required high standard. On the whole, although not an inevitability, such developments favoured the defendant by restricting the types and sources of evidence from which the prosecution might establish its case.

---

[124] Most substantially, the 1919 Bill to establish a Public Defender's Department, staffed by barristers and solicitors for the defence of any defendant charged with an indictable offence, PD 1919 (s. 5 HC), 117: 1351; and 1925 (s. 5 HC), 189: 723. *The Findlay Committee on Legal Aid for the Poor* (First Report 1926) did not regard the 1903 provisions as 'in any serious respect unsatisfactory, but recommended an extension of the power to grant aid to summary trials (paras 9 and 14).

[125] An early campaign group was the Central Legal Aid Society, whose well-publicized inaugural meeting took place at the Mansion House in May 1907, presided over by the Lord Mayor of the City of London and included a mixture lawyers, MPs, and clerics. The society's broad aim was free legal advice and representation at all trials (1907) 42 *LJ* 315, and Abel-Smith and Stevens, *Lawyers and the Courts*, 153–4.

[126] By judicial fiat, in 1907 the newly established Court of Criminal Appeal ensured that all appellants should be represented. The 1930 Act's provisions eliminated the defence disclosure requirement, granted assistance if 'desirable in the interests of justice' (mandatory for murder charges) and extended the power to grant representation for summary trials and committal proceedings for serious charges or if desirable in the interests of justice.

[127] On the 'rationalist model of adjudication', particularly, W. L. Twining, *Rethinking Evidence* (Oxford, 1990), 71 *et seq.*

The broadly exclusionary character of the law of evidence was relatively firmly established by the beginning of the nineteenth century,[128] after which followed a period of consolidation and refinement of these general exclusionary principles. It was a period when underlying rationales were articulated and exclusionary rules shed any discretionary elements to become fixed rules of law. The practising lawyer's need for a comprehensive and principled treatment of the rapidly expanding body of reported evidence case law from the late eighteenth and early nineteenth century was met by publication of a cluster of specialist evidence treatises. These works both assisted and accentuated the 'self-multiplying effect of the detailed development of the rules' by case law;[129] specific rules could be justified or criticized on the basis of more general principles elaborated by writers. And while evidence texts were rarely alluded to in reported judgments, it is extremely likely that both counsel and judges made frequent resort to them: by counsel as a source of argument to undermine or defend existing authorities; by judges to assist or reinforce their responses to assertive counsel. Starkie's 1824 *Treatise* offered what soon became the leading expression and defence of an exclusionary system of evidence law forged on 'general grounds of utility and convenience': a system which admitted 'every light which reason and experience can supply for the discovery of truth, and reject[s] only that which serve[s] not to guide, but to bewilder and mislead [juries]'.[130] Furthermore, discarding a discretionary approach to exclusion in favour of fixed rules 'brought stability...and the feeling of security [engendered by rights removable] only by the authority of the law, and not at the pleasure of a tribunal'.[131]

This shift, during the late eighteenth and early nineteenth century, from a substantially discretionary approach to exclusion to one governed by fixed rules and uniformity of judicial practice, probably owed its impetus to a combination of three principal factors: greater uniformity of judicial practice following increased levels of law reporting; the arrival of treatises offering systematic treatments of evidence law underwritten by the assumption that adversarialism

---

[128] Wigmore describes the period 1790–1830 as when the 'full spring-tide of the system has now arrived', *A Treatise on Evidence* (3rd edn, Boston, 1940), i: 238.

[129] *Ibid.*

[130] *A Practical Treatise of the Law of Evidence*, vol. 1, iii–iv. Also, Thayer, *Preliminary Treatise on Evidence* (Boston, 1898), 517–18. Bentham's advocacy of the 'Natural System' of wide admissibility and powerful aversion to exclusionary rules of evidence appear in Dumont's edition of *Traité* (1823, Paris; English edn, 1825), and *Rationale of Judicial Evidence* (ed. J. S. Mill, 1827). Denman's important review article of *Traité* was published in (1824) 40 *Edin. Rev.* 169. Although Starkie makes no mention of Bentham, in all likelihood, he had knowledge of the *Traité*. On Bentham, see W. L. Twining, *Theories of Evidence: Bentham and Wigmore* (1985), Ch. 2.

[131] W. Best, *Treatise on the Principles of Evidence* (1849), 31. And, rules of evidence are primarily 'rules of law...not to be enforced or relaxed at the discretion of judges' (129); and C. Allen, *The Law of Evidence in Victorian England* (Cambridge, 1997), 24–5.

was the essential central mechanism for testing evidence and truth finding; and thirdly the increased participation of lawyers, involving the possibility of legal challenge and more vigorous levels of cross-examination by defence counsel. Surveying recent history from the mid-century point, Best notes: 'objections to the admissibility of evidence were much more frequently taken, the attention of judges…more directed to the subject of evidence, their judgments better considered, and their decisions better remembered'.[132] Adversarialism's change of trial dynamic entailed the relative relegation of the judicial role, along with its effect of interposing counsel between judge and jury. Added to this was defence counsel's regular insistence on the enforcement of exclusionary rules originally judicially introduced to protect defendants where judged necessary.

More generally, the exclusionary nature of the law of evidence was in large measure driven by judges' and lawyers' scepticism over a jury's ability to make a balanced judgment of the worth of some forms of evidence. Judicial discretion in controlling its admission was probably seen as adequate when judge and jury enjoyed a closer working relationship. Modification of this relationship by the onset of adversarialism is likely to have encouraged judicial acquiescence in a more rigid application of rules of exclusion. Three areas of development of criminal law evidence merit review. First, the most direct manifestations of the exclusionary emphasis in criminal evidence, maturing during the course of the nineteenth century, were rules relating to hearsay, corroboration, character, and similar fact evidence. Secondly, during the nineteenth century treatment of a defendant's evidence produced before and during trial underwent changes of both an inclusionary[133] as well as exclusionary character. Lastly, significant developments concerning the burden and standard of proof at different stages of the prosecution process illustrate the alternative strategy to ensuring accuracy in adjudication: rather than exclusion because of the type or circumstances of particular evidence, the chances of correct verdicts were to be increased by clarification of the onus of proof and the affirmation of individual rights by resort to a high standard of proof.

---

[132] *Treatise*, 133. And Langbein, 'Historical Foundations of the Law of Evidence: A View from the Ryder Sources' (1996) 96 Col LR 1168, 1194–202; Beattie, 'Scales of Justice', 236–50; T. P. Gallanis, 'The Rise of Modern Evidence Law' (1999) 84 Iowa LR 499; Feeley, 'Legal Complexity' (1997), rates of challenge on matters of law, 211, fig. 8; rates of defence cross-examinations, 213, fig. 9. Cf. J. Oldham, *The Mansfield Manuscripts* (Chapel Hill, 1992), i: 144.

[133] One area was testimony of scientific or medical experts. Admissibility of such opinion evidence, recognized, *inter alia*, by Lord Mansfield in the late 1700s (*Folkes v. Child*) (1782) 3 Doug. 157) played an especially significant role mainly in prosecutions from the 1850s. For the Central Criminal Court, see Feeley, 'Legal Complexity' (1997), 209, fig. 7. See also 'Insanity' Ch. VII below, and 'Coroners Courts', XI, Pt 3.

Hearsay, corroboration, character
and similar fact evidence

(1) HEARSAY

At the outset of the nineteenth century, the categories of exceptions to the hearsay rule were, by and large, established, remaining essentially unchanged into
the twentieth century. However, the justification for the hearsay rule was then in
the process of shifting away from one based on the absence of the truth-affirming
properties of an oath, to one emphasizing the untestability of hearsay evidence
by the rigours of cross-examination.[134] Exclusionary rules of evidence inhabited both eighteenth-century civil and criminal evidence law. Especially in the
case of hearsay, the progression from discretionary exclusionary status to fixed
rules of evidence may have commenced in criminal courts as a consequence of
defence counsels' increasingly insistent trial adversarialism, determined to prove
cross-examination to be the 'greatest legal engine ever invented for the discovery
of truth'.[135]

(2) CORROBORATION

For most of the nineteenth century the reception of accomplice evidence was by far
the most important situation where the issue of corroboration arose.[136] The paradox
of a significant element of law enforcement depending on the evidence of criminal
accomplices had been firmly accommodated by the eighteenth century.[137] So also
had the contrast between the exclusion of defendants from giving sworn evidence
(in large part because of likely self-interest) and the admissibility of patently suspect and highly partial sworn accomplice evidence. Beyond the extensive system
of public and private rewards open to all-comers, aimed at boosting levels of prosecutions, lay the particular matter of accomplice evidence bought at the cost of
immunity from prosecution. Two related questions arose: what practices or rules
governed the acceptance of evidence from accomplices or 'Crown witnesses'?; and
how was such presumptively unreliable evidence to be treated by the courts?

   If not initiated by the accomplice himself, official encouragement to give
evidence as a Crown witness might come from examining magistrates. Clearly,

---

[134] T. Peake, *Compendium of the Law of Evidence* (1801), 7; W. Evans (trans.), Pothier's, *A Treatise
on the Law of Obligations* (1806), vol. II, 141; Starkie, *Treatise* (1824), 43.

[135] Wigmore, *Treatise*, v: 29, para. 1367. Gallanis 'Modern Evidence' and Langbein, *Origins*, 243–5.
Also Bentley, *Criminal Justice*, 213–20 for nineteenth-century technical developments in the principal exceptions to the hearsay rule.

[136] For most of the nineteenth century the other cases were treason and perjury.

[137] Radzinowicz, *History*, ii: 33–137; Langbein 'Shaping', 1983, 84–96. The elaborate system of
rewards and pardons was steadily dismantled with the establishment of professional policing over
the first half of the nineteenth century.

such encouragement carried the danger of rendering the self-implicating evidence inadmissible under the confession rules should a magistrate eventually decide against recommending accepting an accomplice as a Crown witness (see below). Moreover, no final, binding decision on such acceptance and on immunity from prosecution rested with an examining magistrate; that was for the trial judge's[138] determination. However, the risk of discrediting the whole procedure of Crown witnesses was a powerful incentive for judges not to be too ready to resist an examining magistrate's recommendation.

Obvious tensions between notions of fairness to defendants and the practical needs of the criminal justice system caused the judicial view and treatment of the evidence of accomplices to undergo change in the late eighteenth and nineteenth century. English law's general shunning of corroboration requirements at one time encouraged judges to require the suspected partial evidence of accomplices to be inadmissible without corroboration.[139] But, possibly because of a later perception of its excessive generosity towards defendants, the rule was revised, permitting uncorroborated evidence from accomplices to be heard by juries, subject to any judicial comment as to credit thought warranted by the particular circumstances.[140] Quite how juries should regard such evidence now turned substantially on judicial discretion: how individual judges regarded accomplice evidence, and what they felt to be an appropriate level of judicial influence over its reception by juries. Moreover, for much of the nineteenth century the willingness of judges to exclude uncorroborated accomplice evidence from consideration of juries remained subject to uncertainty and judicial conflict.[141] By mid-century it was almost universal practice to warn juries to require corroborative evidence.[142] Nevertheless, until the early 1900s individual judges enjoyed an

---

[138] Magistrates gave accomplices 'merely an equitable claim to the mercy of the crown…upon certain conditions of a most candid disclosure' by the accomplice. *Chitty* (1816), i: 83. Judges granted leave 'almost [as] a matter of course', *Barnard* (1823) 1 Car. & P. 87.

[139] Both new and established sexual offences were subject to particular concerns relating to malicious and fabricated claims. Charges of rape had long been regarded as more likely to succeed with the corroborative support of an early complaint by the victim. For example, *Russell* (4th edn, 1865), i: 922–4. Authority confirming the appropriateness of a judicial warning to juries on the dangers of conviction appear in early twentieth-century judgments. For example, *Graham* (1910) 4 Cr App R 218, and *Salmon* (1924) 18 Cr App R 50. The creation of several new sexual offences against women and children by the Criminal Law Amendment Act 1885 was accompanied by particular corroborative requirements. Similarly, under the Children Act 1908 and the Criminal Justice Administration Act 1914.

[140] *Atwood and Robbins* (1788) 1 Leach 464. Langbein's analysis suggests a collective judicial error that assumed competency was the only ground for excluding evidence, thereby ignoring the trial judge's power to exclude specific evidence of a generally competent witness (*Origins*, 212–17).

[141] Cf. e.g. *Jones* (1809) 2 Camp. 131; *Stubbs* (1855) 7 Cox 48; *Boyes* (1861) 1 B. & S. 311 with *Jordan and Sullivan* (1836) 7 Car. & P. 432; *Keats* (1843) 7 JP 484; *Cunnings* (1861) 56 CCC Sess. 378.

[142] Best *Treatise* (1849), 196–7; *Archbold* (11th edn, 1849), 163.

unfettered discretion in the treatment of accomplice evidence, ranging from its complete exclusion, to its admission without comment.

Settling just what powers a trial judge should possess in this respect generated a series of Court of Criminal Appeal judgments, displaying both judicial confusion as to what the law had been, and disagreement as to what it ought to be. By 1916 the Court of Criminal Appeal, while denying a trial judge the right to withdraw uncorroborated accomplice evidence from a jury's consideration, asserted the Appeal Court's power to quash any conviction regarded as unreasonable or unsupportable on the evidence.[143] Defendants had by then become distinctly less vulnerable to conviction on the basis of accomplice evidence: not only were the requirements of corroborative evidence more stringent, and verdicts open to complete appellate review, but defendants had also become competent witnesses capable of giving sworn evidence contradicting an accomplice's. Furthermore, the availability of legal aid to some defendants increased the likelihood of defence counsel being able to cross-examine an accomplice and discredit his evidence.

(3) EVIDENCE OF CHARACTER

Both defence and prosecution may have good, though opposed, reasons for adducing evidence of the defendant's character. The presumed likelihood of juries being unduly impressed by either type of evidence and diverting their attention away from other more direct and cogent evidence, caused a judicial fashioning of rules of admissibility. In broad terms, rules protecting the defendant against evidence of bad character were strongest during the second half of the eighteenth century. As an accused's ability to conduct his defence was, in some respects, strengthened during the nineteenth century, the position became less favourable in relation to bad character evidence.

---

[143] Just what constituted corroboration remained unsettled until the mid-nineteenth century when the standard practice became a requirement of evidence which tended directly to implicate the defendant, not just confirm that the accomplice was likely to be telling the truth. Best, *Treatise* (1849), 197 and *Archbold* (1849), 163 records this of recent origin. The practice finally became law in *Baskerville* [1916] 2 KB 658. But even if the trial judge had given the necessary jury warning of the dangers of uncorroborated accomplice evidence, *Everest* (1909) 2 Cr App R 130 required a directed acquittal if accomplice evidence was uncorroborated by evidence implicating the defendant. This was seemingly confirmed by the less than clear judgment in *Cohen* (1914) 10 Cr App R 91. *Contra Tate* (1908) 2 KB 680; *Willis* (1916) 1 KB 933; *Blatherwick* (1911) 6 Cr App R 281, where Lord Alverstone noted that if a 'strong caution [is given] we cannot interfere' (282). Without a proper trial warning or corroboration, the appeal court would automatically quash a conviction: *Norris* (1916) 12 Cr App R 156. Some of these rulings were made against the background of the House of Lords' recent reaffirmation of a judge's overall discretion to exclude strictly admissible evidence on the grounds of its likely prejudicial effect exceeding its probative value: *Christie* (1914) AC 545. Lord Reading described it as the 'constant practice' of judges indicating to the prosecution counsel where such evidence should not be brought forward (564–5).

By the nineteenth century the practice of defendants claiming good character, sometimes through a host of favourable witnesses, was well established. However, quite what function good character evidence might serve was disputed amongst some treatise writers. Phillips regarded character evidence as 'entitled to great weight…in every case of doubt'. Roscoe conceived of it as serving a broader function, with germane evidence of good character always an ingredient of the defence which should go to the jury.[144] However, the general run of nineteenth-century cases appeared to correspond with Phillips' view.[145] A second contentious issue was the precise scope of admissible character evidence. As an increasingly exasperated Lord Ellenborough is recorded as reminding an unfortunate defence counsel and defence witness, 'What was [the defendant's] general character for integrity is the question…It is reputation; it is not what a [witness] knows. There is hardly one question in ten applicable to the point'.[146] Consequently, character witnesses were not to testify as to their personal impressions or knowledge of the defendant or his good character; they might only speak of other people's knowledge and views of the defendant. Underpinning this restriction was the assumption that general opinion 'arising from a man's disposition in society' was a more reliable guide to character. Yet, as Best observed, this rule 'appears to rest rather on authority than reason'. And, as Stephen argued, it was too diffuse to be easily contradicted, thus 'if a man gains a reputation for honesty or morality by the grossest hypocrisy he is entitled to give evidence of it…'.[147] Moreover, the rule assumed indivisibility of character, lacking the cogency and force of specifically based character evidence to address particular types of alleged criminality. In consequence, despite a strong attempt in *Rowton* to take Ellenborough's line and insist on its observance, the rule was 'in practice seldom strictly enforced'.[148]

The routes via which evidence suggesting bad character, the counterweight to evidence of good character or reputation, might come before a jury increased during the nineteenth century. Endeavours to establish good character, whether by defence witnesses or cross-examination of prosecution witnesses, might be

---

[144] S. M. Phillips, *A Treatise on the Law of Evidence* (1822), 176–7; H. Roscoe, *Digest of the Law of Evidence in Criminal Cases* (1835), 73.

[145] e.g. Lord Ellenborough in *Davison* (1808) 31 St. Tr. 99 at 216: 'highly important if the case…hangs in even scales'; *Haigh and others* (1813) 31 St. Tr. 1092, Le Blanc J., at 1122. Criticized for example in *Best* (5th edn, 1870), 360 and *Russell* (8th edn, 1923), ii: 1957 citing the support of *Stannard* (1833) 7 Car. & P. 673.

[146] *Jones* (1809) 31 St. Tr. 251 at 309–10.

[147] J. Pitt Taylor, *Treatise on the Law of Evidence* (7th edn, 1878), i: 320; Stephen, 1 *HCL* i 450 and *Digest of Evidence* (1876), 167.

[148] *Rowton* (1865) 10 Cox 25, a majority of 11 to 2 judges. On the practice of ignoring the rule see Taylor and Stephen, *ibid.*, and the comments in *Rowton* of Lord Cockburn CJ (at 30) and Earle CJ (at 32–3) the latter expressly agreeing with Taylor's observations. Cockburn claimed to be a captive of strong precedent, despite his acknowledgement of contrary practice. After the Evidence Act 1898, the defendant could claim good character in sworn evidence.

rebutted by general evidence of bad character, including previous convictions. Moreover, with the gaining of competency under the Criminal Evidence Act 1898, a defendant choosing to give evidence laid himself open to cross-examination as to his character if the defence sought to establish good character by its own cross-examination of prosecution witnesses. But more significant nineteenth-century developments relate to the admission of similar fact evidence. Here, unlike the rules governing the giving and rebutting of character evidence, the defence's actions at trial are not the initiating or triggering mechanism; the admissibility of similar fact evidence is totally independent of the defence's trial conduct and outside its control.[149]

(4) SIMILAR FACT EVIDENCE

Beyond the broad question of evidence of the defendant's dubious character or reputation and general propensity to commit crime, arose the more tightly focused issue of the legitimacy of admitting evidence of previous convictions or conduct to assist in proving the present charges. Except where the prosecution could rebut a defendant's undeserved claim of good character by introducing evidence of previous convictions, on what other occasions could this be done? A cluster of early nineteenth-century cases and treatises affirmed the judicial attitude that evidence of the defendant's previous convictions might be introduced by the prosecution. This could occur when such evidence went beyond showing mere propensity to commit crimes of the nature charged and was directly relevant in establishing an element of the prosecution's case.[150]

The steady nineteenth-century expansion of categories of cases allowing evidence of previous convictions raised a fundamental doctrinal question: whether admissibility was indeed purely a matter of materiality or relevance to be determined in each case, or whether particular instances were to be judicially recognized on the grounds of expediency and a tendency to prove an element of the prosecution's case. Lord Campbell CJ probably favoured the latter view when

---

[149] Defendants with previous convictions or previous discreditable behaviour became vulnerable under two broad types of statutory provisions: (i) various statutory provisions (e.g. the Criminal Law Amendment Act 1885) making defendants competent witnesses for certain offences without protection from cross-examination as to credit; (ii) specific enactments which allowed in evidence of previous conduct to prove an element of the offence charge; e.g. in relation to receiving. The Prevention of Crimes Act 1871, s 19, re-enacted in the Larceny Act 1916, s 43. For the decline in the use of defence character witnesses over the nineteenth century, see Feeley, 'Legal Complexity', 214, fig. 10. Much of the steep decline after 1855 can probably be attributed to the effective hiving off of most lower-level larcenies to summary jurisdiction. For the majority of these largely unrepresented defendants, evidence of previous good character was the only line of 'defence' they were capable of offering.

[150] Cole (1810) reported in Phillips Evidence (1814), 69–70; Tattersal's Case (1801) noted by Lord Ellenborough CJ in Whiley (1804) 2 Leach 983 and in D. Bentley, Select Cases from the Twelve Judges' Notebooks (1997), 89; and Starkie, Treatise (1824), ii: 381.

expressing mid-century unease at extrapolating the trend of earlier cases 'generally to the criminal law'.[151] However, late-nineteenth century confirmation of
the former analysis authoritatively appeared in *Makin*, showing that rather than
a rule of exclusion, subject to exceptions, the doctrinal basis for admitting evidence of previous convictions or conduct arose from its relevance to a fact in
issue, unless relevance came solely from disposition.[152]

The declared basis of the general rule against bad character evidence (including evidence of previous offences or conduct) was unpreparedness and lack
of materiality. Thus, during the early nineteenth century exchange in *Whiley*,
defence counsel's claim that evidence of the defendant's previous misconduct
was not material and given without notice adequate for preparation of a rebuttal, was dismissed by Lord Ellenborough as 'not correct' because such evidence was
material and predictable.[153] Both doctrinally and technically this view was probably faithful to the mechanism for the protection of defendants fixed by judges
in the eighteenth century. However, refinements in the notion of materiality or
relevance, consciously engineered by the Twelve Judges early in the nineteenth
century, effectively cut back the protection offered by the original character rule;
the genie of wide-ranging inclusivity was out of the bottle. As Phillips noted, the
weight of such relevant evidence might vary enormously, but that is a 'question
entirely for the jury'.[154] Initially, any judicial concerns for the prejudicial effect of
such adverse evidence outweighing its probative value could only be addressed
by encouraging the prosecution not to present such evidence.[155] Additionally, a
judge might rule some character evidence inadmissible as being too remote in
time or circumstance to have direct probative value. Individual judicial attitudes
and willingness to intervene could be of pivotal importance.[156] However, clear
recognition of the rationale of exclusion and judicial power to exclude evidence

---

[151] (1851) 2 Den. 264, 502. In *Makin* counsel for the Crown adopted the former argument; counsel
for the defendant the latter. A policy-driven approach could be construed from Lord Ellenborough's
comments in *Whiley* relating to the inherent problems of proving guilty knowledge of forged notes
in uttering cases.

[152] [1894] AC 57, 68. Also J. Stone, 'The Rule of Exclusion of Similar Fact Evidence: England' (1932)
46 *HLR* 954; Wigmore, *Treatise* (3rd edn), ii: Ch. XIII, for an extensive list of authorities categorized
according to the nature of the relevance to the crime charge.

[153] (1804) 2 Leach 983. Forgery and uttering offences were widespread and treated with considerable seriousness. In *Whiley* the prosecutors, the Bank of England, deployed four counsel, including
Garrow. See also the opinion of the Twelve Judges in *Ball* (1808) 1 Camp. 325.

[154] *Evidence* (5th edn, 1822), 181.

[155] See comments in *Christie* (1914) AC 545: Lord Reading's reference to the 'constant practice
for judge[s] to indicate his opinion to counsel for the prosecution that evidence which, although
admissible...has little value in its direct bearing upon the case, and might...operate seriously to the
prejudice of the accused, should not be given against him, and, speaking generally, counsel accepts
the suggestion' (564), and Lord Moulton (559).

[156] Roscoe, *Criminal Evidence* (6th edn, 1862), 90 and cases cited.

on the grounds of prejudicial effect exceeding probative value did not arrive until well into the twentieth century.[157]

Evidence of the defendant

Of the several substantial changes occurring in the rules of criminal evidence during the nineteenth century some of the most striking related to the defendant: essentially, the previously powerful expectation that the defendant, through his or her unsworn statement, would be a major source of evidence was considerably eroded. This process of change occurred in three related areas: (i) the pre-trial examination conducted by magistrates; (ii) extra-judicial questioning at arrest or in custody; and (iii) at trial. The only significant reversal of this exclusionary trend of diminishing the defendant's evidential role occurred with the enactment of the Criminal Evidence Act 1898, making the defendant generally competent (and practically obliged) to give sworn evidence.

(1) MAGISTRATES' PRE-TRIAL EXAMINATION

Although examination of felony suspects under the Marian statutes of 1554 and 1555 was originally conceived to be most decidedly inquisitorial, by the beginning of the nineteenth century the nature of the occasion had become somewhat more benign towards the defendant, with examining magistrates assuming a clearer judicial role. Rather than principally aimed at marshalling prosecution evidence, the examination had broadened into a better balanced assessment of whether the available evidence constituted a *prima facie* case against the defendant.[158] In large measure, such developments were probably attributable to the steady in-filtration of lawyers and the increasingly public nature of committal proceed-ings.[159] As Chitty records, the guilt of an offender was not to be 'wrung out of himself,... And, indeed, the examination has been considered rather as a privilege

---

[157] For an early discussion of the modern rationale of exclusion, see S. Phipson, *Law of Evidence* (6th edn, 1921), 159. Cf. *Taylor* (10th edn, 1906), i: 256 which bases exclusion on the old grounds of the unfairness of 'taking the prisoner by surprise' and similar to Phillips, *Evidence* (1822), 179. On the judicial power to exclude unduly prejudicial evidence, see *Noor Mohammed* v. *R* [1949] AC 182, 192. In relation to similar fact evidence see the Court of Criminal Appeal's early recognition of cases where 'though in strictness the evidence is admissible, the judge may be of opinion that it is of so little real value and yet indirectly so prejudicial...or is so remote, that it ought not to be given', *Shellaker* [1914] 1 KB 414, 418; similarly *Hewitt* (1925) 19 Cr App R 64, 66.

[158] *Chitty* (1826), i: p, 89 and the *Criminal Law Commissioners, Eighth Report, Digest*, Ch. 1, sec-tion 7, article 1. As Bentham maintained, the Marian procedure was clearly at odds with any general common law notion of the right not to self-incriminate: *Rationale* (1827), Bowring, *Works*, vii, 459. On 'prima facie', below.

[159] The presence of lawyers (by concession rather than right) and signs of a change of attitude amongst examining magistrates are evident at least from the mid-eighteenth century: Beattie, *Crime and the Courts*, 273–80.

in favour [sic] of the...accused afforded by law for the benefit of an innocent man [to] clear himself'.[160] Whilst approaching the (unintentionally) ironic, the claim reflects wider contemporary judicial sensitivity to securing voluntary and truthful incriminating evidence (see 'Confessions' below).[161] Therefore, to lessen the risk of exclusion of evidence on the basis of involuntariness at trial, 'In practice [the defendant was] generally cautioned that he is not bound to accuse himself, and that any admission may be produced against him at his trial'.[162] However, such was the level of anxiety of many examining magistrates over the exclusion risk, that defendants would be directly advised against offering incriminating evidence.[163] It was a 'prevalent error' eventually censured by Lord Denman CJ:

A prisoner is not to be entrapped into making any statement; but when [he] is willing to make a statement, it is the duty of magistrates to receive it; but magistrates before they do so ought entirely to get rid of any impression...that the statement may be made for his own benefit; and the prisoner ought to be told that what he thinks fit to say will be taken and may be used against him on his trial.[164]

The common law transformation of the pre-trial examination from interrogatory to judicial enquiry received statutory recognition and uniform force in the Jervis Acts of 1848, under which defendants were offered the opportunity to respond to the prosecution evidence followed by a caution along the lines indicated by Lord Denman.[165] Stephen regarded this protection of defendants as both 'highly

---

[160] (1816), 84–5; (2nd edn, 1826), 83–4.

[161] Reaching its zenith in *Wilson* (1817) 1 Holt 597, with Richards LCB regarding magisterial examination a 'form of compulsion' because it imposed an obligation on the defendant to tell the truth. Consequently, evidence so gained was inadmissible at trial. However, a slightly modified re-enactment of the Marian legislation in 1826 (Criminal Law Act 1826, 7 Geo. IV, c. 64, extending powers to misdemeanours as well as felonies) along with subsequent contrary decisions (including *Ellis* (1826) Ry. and Mood. 432 and *Green* (1832) 5 Car. & P. 312) marked a retreat to a less extreme position permitting examination.

[162] *Chitty* (1826), 84.

[163] Cottu observed: 'Scarcely a single question is put to the defendant; if asked to give an account of himself, he answers, if he thinks proper; and the magistrate feels himself under no obligation to point out his contradictions either with himself or his witness. Nor is he asked for any explanation of the charges...against him' (*Administration* (1822), 37).

[164] *Arnold* (1838) 8 Car. & P. 645–6. Pitt Taylor described the magistrates' practice as 'rather to be admired for romantic generosity than for wisdom, or any beneficial consequences resulting therefrom to the public': *Treatise* (1848), 595. Also the *Criminal Law Commission's Eighth Report*, (1845), App. A, 242 and 256. Lord Denman's evidence reflects a similar distinction between admissible, voluntary, or spontaneous admissions and those gained by undue pressure. He criticized the police 'who fancy themselves bound to stop the prisoner's mouth' (p. 211) See also Denman's early criticism of over-scrupulous confession rules in (1824) 40 *Edin. Rev.* 169.

[165] Indictable Offences Act 1848, s 18, 11 & 12 Vict. c. 42. (The other two Jervis Acts were c. 43 and c. 44.) Section 17 of the Act confirmed the generally established practice of ensuring that all evidence was taken in the presence of, or made known to the defendant, and that he had the opportunity

advantageous to the guilty', but at the same time, 'It contributes greatly to the dignity and apparent humanity of a criminal trial. It effectually avoids the appearance of harshness.'[166] Whilst the Jervis Acts were enacted with the general objective of bringing a standard code of procedure to magistrates acting 'out of sessions', significant latitude was left untouched in respect of permitting legal representation, which remained at the magistrates' discretion.[167] Evidence published in the Criminal Law Commissioners' Eighth Report (1845) revealed a diversity of views and practices in respect of the permitted presence of lawyers and the exercise of magistrates' discretion.[168] Subsequent indirect legislation left the discretionary status uncertain beyond 1914.[169]

(2) CONFESSIONS

Well before the beginning of the nineteenth century 'a peculiar delicacy [was] observed in the reception' of defendants' confessions in other circumstances, whereby they would be inadmissible as evidence of guilt unless voluntary: made free of promises or threats.[170] However, according to *Warickshall* the rule was founded exclusively on the grounds of reliability, or accuracy of evidence rather

---

of cross-examining witnesses: Lord Denman in *Arnold*. Section 27 restricted the defendant's right (enacted in the Prisoners' Counsel Act 1836, c. 114, ss 3 and 4) to copies of all depositions. Examining magistrates were eventually required to take and furnish copies of depositions of defendants' witnesses by the Crown Law Act 1867, s 11 (30 and 31 Vict. c. 35). On the background of the legislation, J. Freestone (1980) *Crim. LR* 5 and W. Pue 'The criminal Twilight Zone: Pre-Trial Procedures in the 1840s' (1983) 21 *Alberta LR* 335. As both Sir John Jervis (*PD* 1848 (s. 3), 96: 4) and the annotated copy of the bill confirm, s 18 was based on pre-existing practice and the decisions of *Howes* (1834) 6 Car. & P. 404 and *Hearn* (1841) 1 Car. & M. 109.

[166] *HCL*, i, 441. From early in his career as a commentator, Stephen frequently contrasted the benefits and costs of the English accusatorial system with the more 'oppressive' French inquisitorial procedure, e.g. 'The Criminal Law and the Detection of Crime' (1860) 2 *Cornhill Mag.* 697, developed in the *General View, passim*.

[167] See s 19 of the Indictable Offences Act and *Cox and Coleridge* (1822) 1 B. & C. 37. Abbott CJ, Bayley and Holroyd JJ characterized committal proceedings as non-conclusive and magistrates did not 'act as a court of justice'.

[168] The presence of lawyers and the nature of the committal examination were intimately linked. Many witnesses, including lawyers and magistrates' clerks, viewed the judicial rules governing the defendant's examination as 'unnecessarily fastidious' (p. 268), 'absurd and impolitic' (p. 324), involving 'excessive precautions' (p. 312). Magistrates were intimidated by counsel's habit of asking 'Was the prisoner regularly cautioned?' (p. 256). Prosecution witnesses could expect to suffer the 'vituperation of counsel' (p. 252). Consequently, practice was 'variable' (pp. 333, 273) with some Benches 'more frequently' choosing to exclude lawyers (p. 278) whilst others were sufficiently robust to 'very rarely' refuse admission, even though lawyers were 'very interventionary' (p. 309).

[169] See the discussion of the effects of judicial construction of s 7 of the Summary Jurisdiction Act 1884 in *Stone's Justices' Manual* (25th edn, 1889), 842 and contrary Home Office advice, cited in (46th edn, 1914), 1264.

[170] *Chitty* (1826), i: 571, and *Warickshall* (1783) 1 Leach 263. Foster characterized confessions as the 'Weakest and most Suspicious of all Evidence': *Crown Law* (1762), 243. For arrest powers, see Ch II above.

than out of 'regard to public faith' in the criminal justice system. Therefore the rule related only to the inadmissibility of the confession itself and did not taint forms of derivative evidence, because 'they rest on their own foundations'. Initially, confessions might be regarded as involuntary regardless of the status of the party offering an inducement. But despite early conflicting judicial opinion, by the late 1830s it was accepted that only inducements offered by parties with the power to influence the prosecution might render confessions inadmissible.[171] For the remainder of the century certain aspects of the rules governing the inadmissibility of defendants' confessions and incriminating statements were subject to substantial judicial uncertainty and division: most particularly, just what constituted a threat or inducement, and the legitimacy of police interrogation.

During the first half of the century, because of the claimed inherent difficulty in gauging the impact of a specific threat or inducement on any particular defendant, a high level of judicial sensitivity to perceived involuntariness was manifest; practically any comment directed at the defendant had the potential to exclude incriminating statements. A sharp contemporary critique of the position appeared in Phillip's leading evidence text:

There is a general feeling, which seems to be well founded that the rule has been extended much too far, and been applied in some cases where there could be no reasonable ground for supposing that the inducement offered to the prisoner was sufficient to overcome the strong and universal motive of self preservation. The doctrine has also been attended with much inconvenience, in consequence of the nice distinctions and numerous, and sometimes contradictory decisions, to which it has given rise.[172]

Indeed, sympathy for such a view surfaced in *Baldry*[173] where the Court for Crown Cases Reserved emphatically sought to terminate both the uncertainty and indulgence of confessions law: Pollock CB was anxious that courts should no longer 'torture expressions' to detect threats or inducements; Parke B. looked 'with some shame to the state of the law' (along with Erle J.) and endorsed Pitt Taylor's comment that 'justice and common sense seem to have been sacrificed on the shrine of mercy'.[174]

---

[171] *Spencer* (1837) 7 Car. & P. 776; (1837) 7 Car. & P. 776; *Taylor* (1839) 8 Car. & P. 733. See Ch. VI below.

[172] S. M. Phillips and A. Amos, *A Treatise on the Law of Evidence* (8th edn, 1838), 424. The section cited was not present in the previous edition. A note to the text refers the reader to Bentham's *Rationale of Judicial Evidence*. Phillips acknowledges that Amos 'took a greater part of the work' for this revised section of the text. Amos left the Criminal Law Commission in 1837 to serve on the Indian Council. He returned to act as a Criminal Law Commissioner between 1845 and 1849. See 'Codification', Ch. VI below.

[173] (1852) 5 Cox 523, Lord Campbell CJ at 532 and Parke B. at 530.

[174] *Ibid.*, 530 and 531. See Pitt Taylor, *Treatise* (1848), i: 597. Pitt Taylor had previously advocated Bentham's approach to confessions. See (1842) 28 *LM* 1, 16–18. On Pitt Taylor's position in the 'Rationalist Tradition' of evidence scholarship, see Twining, *Rethinking Evidence*, 50–1. Lord

Although rarely judicially expressed at the time, it is likely that the 'peculiar delicacy' in the reception of confessions was partly a reaction to the rapidly swelling ranks of professional police witnesses from the 1830s and 1840s, with those suspicious of their methods including many members of the judiciary. From the vantage point of the early 1860s, Stephen perceptively suggests that while Bentham's proposal to expose all confession evidence to jury scrutiny would 'for the interests of truth, be the best rule', there was the crucial issue of the law's popularity:

It must never be forgotten that the poor and ignorant are the persons most affected by the administration of criminal justice; and the ministers of justice, with whom they have most to do, the police, have just that amount of intellectual and social superiority to day-labourers and the lower class mechanics, which makes them the object of peculiar jealousy, and renders it desirable to take special precautions against abuses of their power. Their rough and ignorant zeal would frequently lead them into acts of real oppression, if the law of evidence were altered so as to make such oppression useful. It must be also remembered that to require the legal punishment, even of the criminal, is no light thing. It is not less important that the sympathies of the community should go with the punishment and all concerned in its infliction, than the crime should be punished; and this would not be the case if evidence obtained by threats or promises were admitted unless at the same time, those who have made use of the threats or promises were punished, which it would be practically very difficult to do. For these reasons it would, perhaps, be wise not only to maintain the rule, but to extend it to cases of confessions extorted by spiritual terrors or obtained by fraud.[175]

Baldry had produced only a limited degree of judicial uniformity and 'common sense' on the question of what constituted a voluntary confession. For while the focus of most pre-*Baldry* decisions related to the potential of a 'caution' to threaten or induce confessions, the actual practice of police interrogation was not in itself usually a source of contention. Indeed, for many judges questioning without a caution, whether or not in custody, was not necessarily fatal to a confession's admission.[176] However, some judicial opinion clearly began to favour a

---

Denman, who while broadly favouring reform of evidence law saw certain protective rules, including those on confessions, as essential. For Denman, Bentham's 'mode of treating...accused persons, does not appear to us quite philosophical. In his balance, their interests and safety seemed to weigh very little against his eagerness for the detection of crime, and the infliction of punishment' (1824) 40 *Edin. Rev.* 169, 179.

[175] *General View*, 323–4 and also Stephen's paper on confessions delivered to the Juridical Society in 1857 (1858), i: 456. Essentially, Bentham argued that the most accurate decision making by courts would follow from admission of the widest range of evidence, its weight being assessed by juries: *Rationale*; Bowring, *Works*, VI, Section 3 'confessorial evidence'. Also, A. Lewis, 'Bentham's 'View of the Right to Silence' (1990) 43 *Current Legal Problems* (ed. R. Rideout and B. Hepple), 135.

[176] *Thornton* (1824) 1 Moody C.C.R. 27. In *Kerr* (1837) 8 Car. & P. 176 and *Dickenson* (1843) 1 Cox 27. Both judges suggested, though not essential, cautioning was desirable.

caution prior to questioning;[177] others, including Lord Denman CJ, were 'strictly opposed to the practice of questioning the prisoner by any person in authority', as was his successor Lord Campbell CJ who declared in *Baldry* that 'Prisoners are not to be interrogated'.[178]

More generally, some authoritative voices, like Pitt Taylor's, with direct access to the judicial ear, pungently expressed the scepticism with which police evidence should be approached:

With respect to *policemen, constables,* and others employed in the suppression and detection of crime, their testimony against a prisoner should usually be watched with care; not because they intentionally pervert the truth, but because their professional zeal, fed as it is by an habitual intercourse with the vicious, and by the frequent contemplation of human nature in its most revolting form, almost necessarily leads them to ascribe actions to the worst motives, and to give a colouring of guilt to facts and conversations, which are, perhaps, in themselves consistent with perfect rectitude. 'That all men are guilty, till they are proved to be innocent', is naturally the creed of the police; but they are apt to consider his acquittal as a tacit reflection on their discrimination or skill and, with something like the feeling of a keen sportsman, they determine, if possible, to bag their game.[179]

Continuing suspicions and disapproval of police interrogation, with or without a caution, of those in custody emerge in a succession of judgments[180] during the 1860s and 1870s, based on articulated judicial fears of the types of distortion, falsification, or unfairness identified by Stephen and Pitt Taylor. But it was censure without any sanction, for confession evidence was not at this time ruled inadmissible as a consequence of the practice of interrogation or police failure to caution. No doubt the Jervis legislation created a dilemma for judges: in one sense by confirming the prohibition of magisterial interrogation, it could be (and was later) regarded as, *a fortiori*, an implicit condemnation of such police practice; at the same time, the predictable practical effects of eliminating both police and magistrates' interrogation and likely sources of incriminating evidence was almost certainly a powerful restraint on some judges against rejecting police interrogation. From the 1880s, the judiciary were openly divided, with one section of judicial opinion moving to exclude evidence gained as a consequence of

---

[177] Including Pollock CB in *Baldry* at 530, on charging.

[178] *Criminal Law Commissioners Eighth Report*, Evidence, 211. Denman's *Edinburgh Review* article characterizes judicial interrogation as being unfair on prisoners and compromising the dignity and standing of the court: '[E]very generous and feeling mind listens with silent indignation, and retires from the debate with diminished respect for the law, and a diminished sense of his own security'. Campbell in *Baldry* (1852) 2 Den. 430 at 436. Unlike Denison's version, Cox's report does not contain this remark.

[179] *Treatise* (3rd edn, 1858), i: 68 and 78.

[180] e.g. *Stokes* (1853) 17 *The Jurist* 192; *Mick* (1863) 3 F. & F. 823; *Reason* (1872) 12 Cox 228. Lord Cockburn CJ in 'The Yeovil Murder' (1877) 41 *JP* 187.

police interrogation[181] on the grounds that no-one, including 'judge or jury' or the police had the right to examine a party after arrest. Set against this view, and running in parallel over the succeeding two decades, was a more authoritative line of appeal decisions affirming police entitlement to question suspects after arrest without prejudicing the admissibility of confessions shown by the prosecution to have been voluntary.[182] The legal basis for possible rejection of confessions gained by interrogation was eventually identified by Channell J. as being a judge's general discretionary power to exclude evidence.[183]

An important source, if not the genesis of this late nineteenth-century judicial dispute over the propriety and legality of police interrogation, was probably Hawkins J.'s foreword to Sir Howard Vincent's 'police code', a widely employed policeman's manual of professional conduct, originally published in 1882. Here, Hawkins recorded the familiar comparison with the inability of 'judge, magistrates, [or] jurymen [to] interrogate an accused...unless he tenders himself as a witness. Much less, then, ought a constable...'. From the moment a policeman determines to make an arrest, it was 'very wrong' to question the accused. Rather, 'Keep your eyes and your ears open, and your mouth shut...Never act unfairly to a prisoner by coaxing him...to divulge anything. If you do, you will assuredly be severely handled at trial, and it is not unlikely your evidence will be disbelieved.'[184] Here, and elsewhere, *unfairness*[185] rather than unreliability appears to be the basis

---

[181] Smith J. in *Gavin* (1885) 15 Cox 656 and Cave J. in *Male and Cooper* (1893) 17 Cox 689 and *Morgan* (1895) 59 JP 827; Hawkins J. in *Histed* (1898) 19 Cox 16. In the earlier case of *Hassett* (1861) 8 Cox 511, at the invitation of Christian J., the prosecution withdrew confession evidence gained from interrogation.

[182] Beginning with *Thompson* [1893] 2 QB 12; also earlier in *Hassett* (1861) 8 Cox 511 and *Regan* (1867) 17 LT 325. Revealingly, after delivering the judgment of the Court for Crown Cases Reserved, Cave J. expressed strong personal scepticism about the general value of confessions (p. 18). See the extensive review of authorities in *Ibrahim* v. *R* (1914) AC 599.

[183] *Knight and Thayre* (1905) 20 Cox 711 and *Booth and Jones* (1910) 5 Cr App R 177: 'inasmuch as a judge even cannot ask a question, or a magistrate, it is ridiculous to suppose that a policeman can. But there is no actual authority yet that if a policeman does ask a question it is inadmissible' (179). The general power to exclude was adverted to in the Court of Criminal Appeal case of *Gardner and Hancox* (1915) 11 Cr App R 265 at 270. The consequences of breach of the provisions of the Jervis Acts also remained unclear. *Pettit* (1850) 4 Cox 164, a case of failure to caution, ruled the confession necessarily involuntary and, therefore, inadmissible. *Berriman* (1852–5) 6 Cox 388 where questioning took place after cautioning, held the responses were potentially excludable if gained by unfairness. Taylor, *Treatise* (1906) suggests breaches of the 1848 Acts rendered the evidence subject to common law rules of exclusion or admission (629–30).

[184] Throughout the nineteenth century the operative notion of fairness was narrowly confined when determining the exclusion of confessions. A wide range of harsh or unfair practices employed to gain confessions was consistently ruled as constituting neither an inducement nor threat and therefore insufficient to exclude confession evidence. Bentley, *Criminal Justice*, 226–7; and Roscoe's *Digest* (12th edn, 1898), 'Confessions obtained by artifice or deception', 43–4.

[185] Reproduced in the *Report of the Royal Commission on Police Powers and Procedures* 1929 [Cmnd. 3297] App. 8. Also, *Report*, 60–1. The phrase 'ears open...mouth shut' appears in Cave J.'s judgment in *Male and Cooper* (above, n 181).

of Hawkins' objection to questioning; but his reference to likely lack of credibility implies that such evidence would still be admissible.

Extra-judicial attempts to resolve this confused state of affairs commenced in 1906 with a letter from Sir Charles Rafter, Chief Constable of Birmingham, to Lord Alverstone CJ, seeking advice on how to proceed in the face of conflicting local judicial attitudes to police questioning. Following a specially convened meeting of the judiciary, Lord Alverstone assured Sir Charles that 'no difference of opinion whatsoever' existed; but while indicating that cautions were properly to be given before any charges were made, no guidance was offered on the propriety of subsequent questioning. Similar requests from other police forces ultimately resulted in the judges of the King's Bench Division formulating and issuing in 1912 the first four of the 'Judges' Rules'.[186] As the immediately subsequent continuation of case law demonstrated, the Rules failed to achieve their object, partly in consequence of an ambiguity in their drafting, and partly because of uncertainty over their status. The first problem stemmed from an apparent conflict between Hawkins' police code proscription of questioning defendants and the Judges' Rules[187] which appeared to permit the practice. The latter question of status was identified by the Court of Criminal Appeal in *Voisin* (1918): 'These rules have not the force of law, they are administrative directions, the observance of which the Police authorities should enforce on their subordinates as tending to the fair administration of justice.' Failure to do so could result in rejection of 'statements obtained . . . contrary to the spirit of these rules'.[188]

As had been true throughout the nineteenth century, judicial opinion was divided first on the legality, then on the propriety, of interrogation. For some commentators, concerns over the intrinsic unreliability of confession evidence rendered it objectionable. For others, the unwholesome image of a criminal justice system that implicitly condoned the practice of coercing self-incrimination argued for the exclusion of any confession gained in the course of interrogation; yet others, 'less tender to the prisoner', and anxious not to acquit the guilty, would not condemn questioning.[189] The 1929 Royal Commission on Police Powers appeared to conclude that by virtue of the psychological dynamic of police questioning, suspects were inherently subject to a form of coercion which rendered all incriminating

---

[186] *Report of the Royal Commission* (1929), 69 and App. 10. A further five rules were added in 1918.

[187] Rule 3 provided 'Persons in custody should not be questioned without the usual caution being first administered', which carried the 'corollary that prisoners may be questioned': *Report*, 1929, 60.

[188] (1918) 13 Cr App R 89 at 96. Cf. the Court of Criminal Appeal in *Gardner and Hancox* (1915) 11 Cr App R 265 at 269: 'the police have been told over and over again from the bench that they have no right to cross-examine a prisoner after he has been arrested and charged'. The court went on to suggest that judges 'ought to refuse to admit' such evidence (at 270).

[189] See Lord Sumner in *Ibrahim*, 618; and *Report* (1929), 61.

statements, in one sense, involuntary. Consequently, whilst judicial discretion was not to be denied, for the Royal Commission, the solution was to proscribe questioning in custody (not because of unreliability) as in breach of the rule against self-incrimination, the 'maxim fundamental to our criminal law', enforced by 'a rigid instruction' to the police, issued by the Home Office.[190]

(3) AT TRIAL: SELF-INCRIMINATION, COMPETENCY, AND 'MORAL TORTURE'

Whilst claiming a long pedigree,[191] until the early nineteenth century, an accused's right against self-incrimination was, in many respects, more theoretical than real. Beside the substantial inroads made by the Marian legislation governing magistrates' pre-trial examinations, unrepresented defendants at felony trials were faced with the practical choice of defending themselves by giving unsworn testimony or, effectively, denying themselves a defence. For most defendants, rebutting charges by reliance on cogent cross-examination of prosecution witnesses was quite unrealistic. This was also often true of the defendant's ability to organize and produce defence witnesses. Not only was the function of the Marian procedures largely one of assembling prosecution evidence, but little official assistance in gathering defence evidence existed at the pre-trial stage. Consequently, without counsel the defendant's 'testimonial and defensive function were inextricably merged'.[192] At felony trials the 'assumption was clear that if the case against him was false the prisoner ought to say so and suggest why, and if he did not speak that could only be because he was unable to deny the truth of the evidence'.[193] Only in the early nineteenth century could a privilege against self-incrimination be realistically asserted.[194] This was the consequence of the extensive role by then conceded to defence counsel, combined with the common law modification of pre-trial examinations whereby the defendant's silence was almost encouraged. Even in the majority of felony trials where the defendant remained unrepresented until the end of the nineteenth century, the changes established by the 1800s relating to fixing the prosecution's burden and standard of proof (see below) generally reinforced a defendant's ability to elect not to make an unsworn

---

[190] *Report*, citing the authority of Wigmore, 61; also 65 and 119. For an analysis of developments following *Voisin* and the 1929 Royal Commission Report, see I. Brownlie, 'Police Questioning, Custody and Caution' (1960) *Crim LR* 298, and P. Devlin, *The Criminal Prosecution in England* (1960), Ch. 2.

[191] Blackstone, *Comms*, iv, 296 and R. H. Helmholtz, *Privilege Against Self-Incrimination* (Chicago, 1997), *passim*.

[192] J. Langbein 'Privilege Against Self-Incrimination' (1994) 92 *Michigan LR* 1047, 1048 and generally.

[193] Beattie, *Crime and the Courts*, 349.

[194] To these should be added the piecemeal nineteenth-century legislation gradually increasing financial support for the expenses of defence witnesses.

statement at trial. As has been seen, the nineteenth-century development of pre-trial cautioning and rules of confession evidence, after early apprehension over reliability, became increasingly driven by notions of fairness to the defendant and the public image of such. The privilege against self-incrimination was recognized by the 1929 Royal Commission as one manifestation of these concerns.

As a general rule, until the mid-nineteenth century, defendants in criminal (and both parties in civil) proceedings were de-barred from giving sworn evidence. It was reasoned that personal interest would probably undermine the credibility of their evidence or tempt them to commit perjury. Pitt Taylor caustically observed that the law presumed 'not only that [defendants] sooner than make a statement which might prejudice themselves, would commit deliberate perjury but that...juries would be incapable of detecting the falsehood. A more unfounded calumny upon the veracity of witnesses, and the intelligence of juries cannot well be imagined'.[195] However, defendants in treason or felony trials might resort to several other methods of giving evidence, the principal[196] of which was through an unsworn oral or written statement. Whilst enjoying considerable latitude in terms of what might be incorporated in the statement, and not subject to cross-examination, the credibility of unsworn statements was still open to challenge, either by the recall of prosecution witnesses or by pointedly sceptical judicial comment. After some judicial equivocation, the entitlement of represented defendants to make an unsworn statement was eventually largely lost after the enactment of the Defendants' Counsel Act 1836.[197]

The Act might be seen as likely to have reduced the force of any call (such as by Bentham) for making defendants in criminal trials fully competent to give evidence. But in practical terms, that would be to ignore the plight of the majority of defendants who remained unrepresented after 1836. The impetus for reform in criminal cases in large measure followed in the wake of a succession of civil reforms during the 1840s and 1850s,[198] making parties to, or with an interest in, a

---

[195] *Treatise* (2nd edn, 1855), 1040.

[196] Besides problems of organization, for a defendant in custody pending trial, the costs of calling defence witnesses could rule out potential defences.

[197] This put felony trials in the same position as misdemeanours: *Parkins* (1824) 1 Car. & P. 548. When represented, either the defendant or his counsel could address the jury, not both. *Boucher* (1837) 8 Car. & P. 141. The right to make unsworn statements was neither expressly nor implicitly terminated by the Act. On the various judicial views, see Bentley, *Criminal Justice*, 156–9.

[198] Particularly the Law of Evidence Act 1843 (known by its principal sponsor's title: Lord Denman's Act) and the Evidence Act 1851 (Lord Brougham's Act) and the Evidence Amendment Act 1853. The combined effect of this legislation removed the bar of incompetency of parties in civil suits, or those with a personal interest or conviction of a crime. Pitt Taylor, as a proselyte of much of Bentham's inclusionary approach to evidence, prepared the 1851 bill. He ascribed the Denman and Brougham Acts to Bentham's critique: 'When Bentham's work of Evidence first made its appearance, the world in general regarded the author as a gentleman who delighted in paradox and wrote bad

civil action competent witnesses. In criminal cases, from the late eighteenth century the defendant had become potentially more secure and insulated from the role of evidence-provider through the increasing concession of representation coupled with the heightened judicial sensitivity to confessions and the questioning of defendants. Following civil law, changes making defendants competent as witnesses could be construed as a development which promised not only the liberation, but also the endangerment of defendants.

Emboldened by the apparent success of civil reforms (or at least the absence of the frequently predicted perjury epidemic), between 1858 and 1878 several abortive attempts were made to bring revisions effected in civil actions to criminal law proceedings. Both the proposed extent of change and the nature of supporting or oppositional arguments varied considerably. The general claim of enhanced effectiveness in truth-finding underpinned much reformist rhetoric. Leading supporters of competency, including Brougham, Pitt Taylor, Lowe, and Stephen (in differing degrees) inclined towards either Bentham's proposal of making defendants compellable witnesses or, at least, permitting a potentially fatal adverse judicial comment on a defendant's failure to give evidence. At the same time, advocates of reform maintained that innocent defendants stood to gain from these changes, as greater weight would be attached to sworn testimony, which might be judicially related to specific elements of the prosecution's case. Ranged against such arguments were broad parliamentary and press claims of the inherently oppressive inquisitorial consequences of competency. Even without comment, it was urged juries would spontaneously draw their own adverse inferences from a defendant's failure to give sworn, cross-examinable, evidence; and where the whole complexion of the trial process would be transmogrified by judges assuming a prosecutorial/inquisitorial role.[199]

Over the succeeding two decades, culminating in the Criminal Evidence Act 1898, both government and the bulk of informed opinion moved from opposition (or indifference) to support for competency. Initially, reforms of competency were just one component in broader codifying ambitions; latterly, they became the focused objective of government-initiated legislation.

English. But truth...at length prevail[ed]...Mr Bentham's opinions were [eventually] recognised as correct and finally in a great measure adopted by the Legislature': *Treatise* (3rd edn,1858), ii: 1081. In his *A Report on Criminal Procedure* (1856), Greaves appeared to accept the foundational premise that the civil and criminal law's common aim of discovery of the truth suggested a *prima facie* assumption of common rules (p. 110). Similarly, Pitt Taylor, in a paper to the 'Society for Promoting the Amendment of the Law', maintained that 'so far as practicable' the law of evidence for civil and criminal law should be the same (1860–1) 5 *Solicitors' Journal and Reporter* 363.

[199] Generally, Allen, *Law of Evidence*, Chs 4 and 5.

In accordance with government strategy, Stephen's specially commissioned 1878 draft Criminal Code was turned over for review by a Code Commission comprising Lord Blackburn, Lush LJ, Barry J., and Stephen.[200] Unlike Stephen's proposal permitting cross-examination of defendants only as to credit,[201] the Commission's treatment of the defendant's competency more closely resembled that of ordinary witnesses. Although attracting a fair spread of support as well as individual criticism, the provision was lost when the complete bill was withdrawn. Attempts to resurrect modified code bills incorporating broadly similar competency provisions were equally unsuccessful, as were two 1884 bills dealing solely with competency.[202] Despite clear government reforming resolve, sustained over the decade between 1885 and 1895, a whole series of bills failed, substantially because of the machinations of Anglo-Irish politics and the tactical opposition of Irish Nationalist Members of Parliament.[203]

While by 1896 the hurdle of Irish Nationalist obstruction had been cleared by excluding Ireland from proposed reform measures, on the home front oppositional forces were being marshalled by Sir Herbert Stephen, son of Fitzjames Stephen. Sir Herbert's campaign in the two years running up to the 1898 bill usefully captures and summarizes the core anxieties which for many still made the competency of criminal defendants a fundamentally resistible development. In his provocatively entitled 'A Bill to Promote the Conviction of Innocent Prisoners',[204] Stephen offered an empirical challenge to a leading feature of the reformist case. From the vantage point of a practising barrister and, latterly, Clerk of Assize of the Northern Circuit, he cited his critical experience of the operation of the Criminal Law Amendment Act 1885, one of the[205] principal statutory competency exceptions permitting defendants to give sworn evidence. His observations

---

[200] Generally, K. Smith, *James Fitzjames Stephen* (Cambridge, 1988), Ch. 4.

[201] Subject to judicial discretion as thought 'proper': s 523. On this, the Report records that the Commission was 'divided in opinion', p. 37. Similarly, Sir John Holker, the Attorney-General, saw the matter as 'evenly balanced', *PD* 1879 (s. 3), 245: 321.

[202] The government-sponsored Law of Evidence in Criminal Cases Bill, *PP* 1884 (4) iii, 525, and Lord Bramwell's Law of Evidence Amendment Bill, *PP* 1884 (130), iii, 521. Both bills were unsuccessfully resurrected in the following session.

[203] See C. Jackson, 'Irish Political Opposition to the Passage of Criminal Evidence Reform at Westminster, 1883–98', in J. F. McEldowney and P. O'Higgins (eds), *The Common Law Tradition: Essays in Irish Legal History* (Blackrock, 1990), 185.

[204] (1896) 39 *Nineteenth Century* 566.

[205] 48 and 49 Vict. c. 69, s 20, including offences of rape, indecent assault, or abduction. The 1885 Act and a series of other statutory exceptions to the incompetency rule dating from the 1870s were largely justified on the basis of the offences involved placing the onus of [dis]proof on the defendant. See Taylor, *Treatise* (9th edn, 1895), ii: 885 n. 6. A decade earlier Fitzjames Stephen had suggested that the 1885 Act competency provision worked satisfactorily: (1886) 20 *Nineteenth Century* 453, 'Prisoners as Witnesses'. Cf. (1886), 20 *LJ* 323.

on the workings of the 1885 and similar Acts led him to conclude that, especially under cross-examination, testifying defendants tended to create prejudicial impressions. At the same time, those who failed to avail themselves of the right were exposed to critical judicial and prosecution comment. Either course greatly increased the likelihood of wrong convictions. As a member of the generally pro-reform Bar Council committee, in the following year Stephen issued a minority report, again lamenting official neglect of critical evidence from practising lawyers.[206] Finally, in 1898, anticipating a new government bill, he published *Prisoners on Oath: Past, Present and Future*, a detailed recapitulation and rebuttal of each reformist claim pressed into service over the previous year.

As in earlier parliamentary debates, both sides fought under the banner of defendants' protection: reformers asserted the bill's ability to permit defendants to gain maximum credit for their evidence,[207] which only cross-examined, sworn testimony could offer, and from which no 'innocent man will shrink';[208] opposers wished to save inarticulate and unprepossessing defendants from the unedifying spectacle of, effectively, forced self-incrimination or panic-induced perjury. Both sides regarded the experience of the previous 26 Acts permitting defendants and spouses to give sworn evidence as supporting their cause. For the government, the Attorney-General promoted the bill as a rationalizing measure eliminating the anomalies of 'two systems'; for the opposition, the empirical evidence presented by practitioners suggested what amounted to a disadvantageous reversal of the onus of proof, exposing defendants to what, 40 years before, Lord Campbell had characterized as 'moral torture'.[209] Such was the government concern over the potential effects of Herbert Stephen's campaign that during the passage of the successful 1898 bill, both the Lord Chancellor and Attorney-General felt obliged directly to contest the validity of his claims of wrongful convictions.[210] Certainly

---

[206] See *The Times*, 16, 19 and 24 April 1897, for letters endorsing Stephen's claims.

[207] For example, Pitt Taylor (1860–1) 5 *Sol. J.* 363, 364.

[208] Attorney-General, *PD* 1898 (s. 4), 56: 979.

[209] *PD* 1859 (s. 3), 152: 763. Similarly, for example, F. Worsley, *An Examination of Mr Pitt Taylor's Thesis...* (1861) and A. Elliot (attrib., *Wellesley Index*) 'The Code of Criminal Law' (1879) 150 *Edin. Rev.* 524, 550.

[210] *PD* 1898 (s. 4), 56: 981. Home Office memoranda reveal evidence that the 1885 Act provisions probably did 'increase the number of shaky convictions'. Claims were made of growing opposition from the Bar and Judiciary: (1896) 31 *LJ* 250: 'beyond doubt amongst lawyers there is a growing disposition to oppose the Bill in toto...'. The attitude of most of the judiciary remained unclear. In 1897 the Attorney-General claimed support of practically all judges: *PD* 1897 (s. 4), 48: 783–4. During the bill's second reading in response to the Attorney-General's denial of judicial opposition, Lloyd Morgan MP specifically identified six of the QBD judges as against the bill with two more 'doubtful', and two or three Court of Appeal Judges as opposing the bill: *PD* 1898 (s. 4), 56: 997.

In the early 1880s, considerable judicial uncertainty existed in relation to the defendant's right to make an unsworn statement. Lord Cockburn ruled in *Weston* (1879) 14 Cox 346 that counsel

many speakers opposed to the bill claimed that a majority of lawyers through-out the profession were hostile to the bill.[211]

However, parliamentary opposition to the bill was confined to 80 MPs at the second reading. The still live issues involved the government's shifting attitude on the extent to which defendants might be cross-examined, and who, if anyone, might comment on a defendant's failure to give evidence. Francophobic refer-ences were, as always, an entertaining, stock response of the majority of com-mentators, even when broadly favouring reform, like *The Law Journal*:

> All continental systems of law permit—nay, they pivot on—the admissibility of evidence of the accused. And it is perhaps owing to what to English minds is the indecency of the French prosecuting system that people are indisposed to sanction readily a change which may lead us by two swift steps into what we regard as a pernicious course of legal procedure.[212]

For *The Law Journal*, and others, avoidance of this peril demanded restraint on both power to cross-examine and to make adverse comment on defendants declining to testify. Meeting the former concern, the government bill incorpo-rated provisions protecting defendants from cross-examination as to credit, unless attacks were made on the character of any prosecution witness. As for the latter issue, both the Attorney-General and Solicitor-General eventually con-ceded a bar on prosecution comment on a defendant's failure to give evidence, but leaving a trial judge unfettered discretion to make observations.[213]

The 1898 Act constituted a compromise between the occasionally advo-cated Benthamite stance of competency plus compellability of defendants, and those who favoured protecting defendants from what they regarded as the

---

could relay anything that the defendant might choose to, thereby eroding some of the disability of incompetency. This was compounded by some judicial support for permitting represented defend-ants to make unsworn statements. Meetings of the Council of Judges failed to achieve judicial con-sistency in respect of either innovation throughout the remainder of the century. Roscoe's *Digest* (12th edn, 1898), 191–2. The 1898 Act preserved the right to make unsworn statements.

[211] e.g. *PD* 1898 (s. 4), 56: 985, 995, 1032; (s. 4), 60: 306. On the legal climate of opinion before and during the 1898 legislation debates, *The Times*, correspondence columns, especially the period from April to December 1897 (e.g. 21, 22 April, p. 9; 24 April, p. 13; 29 June, p. 4; 25 October, pp. 11, 29; 28 December, p. 9. Also Lord Alverstone (as Attorney-General, an earlier promoter of bills) *Recollections of Bar and Bench* (1914), 176–9. The position of the great criminal advocate, Sir Harry Poland is subject to conflicting views: cf. C. Biron, *Without Prejudice* (1936), 218–19, with E. Bowen-Rowlands, *Seventy-Two Years at the Bar* (1924), 27–8. Bowen-Rowlands' book is essentially a biog-raphy based on several interviews with Poland.

[212] (1896) 31 *LJ* 250 (and 631) reviewing Stephen's 'A Bill to Promote'. See also *PD* 1898 (s. 4), 56: 994.

[213] *PD* 1898 (s. 4), 60: 671–3. In the 1880s and 1890s many colonial legislatures enacted legislation making the defendant a competent witness in criminal cases, but proscribed any judicial comment on the failure to give evidence: A. R. Butterworth, *The Criminal Law Evidence Act 1898* (1898), 18 and Apps 93 *et seq*. On this, see *PD* 1898 (s. 4), 56: 1017.

self-incriminatory perils of entering the witness box, either because of the risk of unreliable testimony or because it (effectively) amounted to a dilution of the basic protection against self-incrimination. While the Act sought to confine the hazards of the defendant's cross-examination to undermining his account of germane events, considerable trust was vested in the judiciary by leaving unregulated their ability to comment on a defendant's failure to submit himself to the rigours of cross-examination.

On this key dimension to competency, appellate courts subsequently exhibited extreme reluctance to fetter a judge's discretion. Setting the judicial tone for half a century, Lord Russell CJ indicated: 'The nature and degree of such comment must rest entirely in the discretion of the judge who tries the case...', a view later endorsed by the Court of Criminal Appeal, confirming that such exercise of discretion was not open to review.[214] Whilst enjoying substantial freedom, a jury's inference from a defendant's failure to give evidence, in all likelihood would be crucially influenced by the judicial response: a judge might choose to make no mention of it; explain that it was the defendant's right to remain silent; or adopt the Benthamite assertion that innocence always claimed the right to speak. For the defendant it would be largely a matter of luck which approach his trial judge favoured. Furthermore, after 1898 whether or not to give sworn testimony would remain for some considerable time a dilemma faced by defendants without counsel in over half of jury trials. Even the ameliorative measures found in the Poor Prisoners' Defence Act 1903 were substantially contingent upon a defendant's early disclosure of his defence; a condition demanding that defendants both understood and gave evidence on the central elements of their defence.

Undoubtedly, making defendants competent could be presented as constituting a natural progression in an avowedly truth-seeking adversarial system, at least when the defendant enjoyed representation. This was a critical supporting argument for the 1903 legislation. At the same time, it is readily apparent from parliamentary, press, and journal debates that by the 1880s a considerable body of influential opinion had come to regard the criminal defendant's inability to give sworn evidence as inhibiting full adversarial exposure of all relevant evidence. Most particularly, incompetency was increasingly viewed as protecting the guilty from conviction, an assumption borne of common experience pithily captured in Bentham's well worn adage: that innocence claims the right to speak, while guilt invokes the privilege of silence. Echoing this sentiment when advocating

---

[214] Lord Russell in *Rhodes* (1899) 1 QB 77 at 83, confirmed in *Voisin* (1918) 1KB 531. Also *Smith* (1915) 84 LJ KB 2153, where counsel for the appellant claimed that the judge 'practically...direct[ed]' a conviction (2155), Lord Reading CJ observed that it was not for the CCA to 'say how far he should have proceeded in such comments' (2157). The Privy Council in *Waugh* v. *R* (1950) AC 203 recognized that the discretion was open to review.

competency legislation in 1886, Lord Bramwell did not mince words: it was 'not a Bill for the benefit of prisoners. [M]ore convictions would take place under it than they had before. [It was a] bad Bill for the guilty and a beneficial Bill only for the innocent.'[215] Similarly, the competency provision inserted at committee stage in the Criminal Law Amendment Act 1885 recommended itself to the Attorney-General because it would 'enable the innocent to get off and aid the conviction of the guilty'.[216] It was an attitude implicit in much support for the 1898 bill, typi-fied by the Attorney-General's declaration that 'No innocent man will shrink from giving evidence'.[217] Coupled with the long-running, post-Victorian judi-cial uncertainty on how to respond to police interrogation,[218] the role of judicial discretion in the aftermath of the 1898 Act was still exceedingly prominent in determining just how significant the privilege of self-incrimination remained.

The burden and standard of proof

In criminal trials the presumption of innocence was well entrenched long before the nineteenth century.[219] However, rather less clear was the weight of evidence required from the prosecution to overturn the presumption of innocence and convict the defendant: just what was the standard of proof of guilt, and what terms could be used to encapsulate this consistently? Compounding this uncertainty was a marked vagueness surrounding the evidential standards to be applied by exam-ining magistrates and Grand Juries (see below) during pre-trial procedures. Most particularly, was the standard of proof required to pass through either (or both) of these pre-jury trial qualifying stages the same or different from that necessary to convict at trial? Each of these stages raised distinct questions of theory and policy, but the most significant and contentious related to the trial itself.

(1) THE BURDEN AND STANDARD OF PROOF AT TRIAL

Together, the burden and standard of proof function as the fulcrum of a criminal trial. Fundamentally, setting the standard of proof for conviction entails striking the desired balance between the relative evils of wrong convictions and wrong acquittals—a balance between the practical functioning of the criminal justice system and the reasonable expectations and safeguards of individuals. Romilly provided a neat nineteenth-century articulation of the core objective which a

[215] Law of Evidence Amendment Bill, *PD* 1886 (s. 3), 303: 1471.

[216] *PD* 1885 (s. 3), 300: 906. Harcourt saw the provision in the same light, *ibid.*, 908. The provision's broader ramifications did not escape some committee members: 'a most startling change' in the law of evidence (1910); a 'very serious alteration in the jurisprudence of this country' (1906).

[217] *PD* 1898 (s. 4), 56: 979.

[218] Above, 'Confessions'.

[219] e.g. Thayer, *Evidence*, 551–4.

high standard of proof sought to achieve: 'When guilty men escape, the law has merely failed; when an innocent man is convicted it does a great harm; it creates the very evil it was to cure and destroys the security it was made to preserve.'[220] In essence, a wrong conviction was to be regarded, socially and morally, as substantially worse than wrongful acquittal.

The impetus towards adopting a common standard and expression indicating the appropriate degree of proof of guilt was probably a judicial desire for the security of consistency in the face of the increasing presence of defence lawyers.[221] It was a trend that would be enhanced by the rising level of case reporting along with the consequent growth in publication of practitioners' evidence manuals. But at all events, rather than signify a raising of the standard of proof, the process of adoption of the beyond reasonable doubt standard was one of seeking a greater degree of uniformity and compliance with what had hitherto been the widely understood expectation.

Although making occasional appearances in trial reports, particularly in the late eighteenth century,[222] the 'beyond reasonable doubt' formulation received its earliest accessible legal analysis in the first edition of Starkie's *Practical Treatise on the Law of Evidence* (1824).[223] Indicative of his claim's speculative nature, Starkie

---

[220] *Observations on the Criminal Law of England* (1810), note D, in response to Paley's comment that the wrongly convicted 'may be considered as falling for his country...'. *The Principles of Moral and Political Philosophy* (1809 edn), 310. For Bentham's equivocal position, see Twining, *Theories of Evidence*, 96–100.

[221] Indeed in 1856 Stephen maintained that there could be 'no doubt that the standard of certainty required has risen of late years'. In his opinion the increasing presence of defence counsel was the principal cause of this: *Cambridge Essays* (1857) 'The Characteristics of English Criminal Law', 1, 34.

[222] Langbein, *Origins*, 264n. Assessing the extent to which standards of proof at summary trials followed those of higher courts is highly problematic. Standard practitioner manuals of the nineteenth century indicate that the rules of evidence, including standard of proof, were (at least in theory) the same as in superior courts. For example, *Burn's Justice of the Peace* (1836), i: 1099; *Stone's Justices Manual* (6th edn, 1855), 120–5. By way of exception to the general burden of proof, a significant cluster of summary offences existed from the eighteenth century relating to the possession of certain goods. Defendants could be convicted of such offences on failure to provide a satisfactory account of their possession. For the claim that creation of these offences was a parliamentary response to the increased difficulty of convicting for theft at trials on indictment where prosecution evidence became increasingly subject to defence counsel challenges, see B. Smith, 'The Presumption of Guilt and the English Law of Theft, 1750–1850' (2005) 23 *Law and Hist. Rev.* 133; and 'Did the Presumption of Innocence Exist in Summary Proceedings?', *ibid.*, at 191. For a detailed challenge to this interpretation of the origins and use of the possession offences, see N. Landau, 'Summary Conviction and the Development of the Penal Law', *ibid.*, at 173.

[223] e.g. 'Even the most direct evidence can produce nothing more than such a high degree of probability as amounts to moral certainty' (450). In criminal trials 'It is sufficient if they produce moral certainty to the exclusion of every reasonable doubt' (514). Starkie had been elected Downing Professor at Cambridge the year before. Cf. *Chitty* (1826), i: 559, 'What degree of proof?'. For the strong link between the earlier contemporary moral philosophy and epistemological theory, and

offered no supporting citations. Indeed, until well into the second half of the nineteenth century, many judges employed simple terms common throughout the previous two centuries,[224] revolving around notions of 'belief' in, or 'satisfaction' of, guilt.[225] From the varying treatments of the topic by different leading evidence texts, such as by Taylor and Best, the absence of the universal acceptance of the 'beyond reasonable doubt' formula is still apparent in the mid-nineteenth century.[226] By the early 1860s Stephen's first major published work, *A General View of the Criminal Law*,[227] refers to 'no doubt which [the jury] will call reasonable'. Although citing no supporting authority, among the seven illustrative case studies incorporated in the *General View* is the notorious 1855 poisoning trial of Dr William Palmer; here Lord Campbell CJ instructed the jury that they were 'not to convict [Palmer] on suspicion, even on strong suspicion. There must be a strong conviction in your minds that he is guilty of this offence, and, if you have any reasonable doubt you will give him the benefit of that doubt.'[228]

Whilst formulaic deviations from the 'reasonable doubt' standard continued into the twentieth century, they were tolerated provided the judicial direction was believed to accord with the substance of the standard of reasonable doubt. One example which caused considerable discomfort to some contemporaries was Pollock LCB's 1864 reference to 'that degree of certainty with which you decide upon and conclude your most important transactions in life'. The Chief Baron's observation induced reporters Foster and Finlason to record the subsequent orthodox 'beyond reasonable doubt' direction in *White* 'entirely for the sake of this clear and decided declaration of the real rule of law, as to sufficiency of proof in criminal cases'.[229] This episode typifies the elusive, normative quality of a reasonable doubt standard and the dangers attached to attempts to communicate

the conceptual development of the law of evidence, see B. J. Shapiro, *Beyond Reasonable Doubt and Probable Cause: Historical Perspectives on the Anglo-American Law of Evidence* (Berkeley, 1991).

[224] Shapiro, *op cit.*, 18–24.

[225] e.g. Parke J. in *Higgins* (1829) 3 Car. & P. 603 and Alderson B. in *Howlett* (1836) 7 Car. & P. 273.

[226] Taylor *Treatise* (1848), 266. In his *Treatise* (1849) Best adopts Starkie's analysis, but is unable to offer any more authoritative case law support for this formulation beyond the unreported direction of Parke B. (the book's dedicatee) in *Sterne* (1843), 100.

[227] *General View*, 325. By this time Stephen was Recorder for Newark-on-Trent. For his earlier use of 'beyond all reasonable doubt', see *Cambridge Essays* (1857), 26.

[228] *Ibid.*, Palmer's Trial, 357–90. While his 33-page extract from published proceedings does not include Campbell's direction, it is impossible to believe that Stephen was unaware of it.

[229] *Muller*, October 1864, reported in CCC Sessions Paper, vol. LIX, part 360, 461, without Pollock's offending direction, which is cited in *White* (1865) 4 F & F 383n. In *White* Martin B. directed the jury on the need to be 'satisfied beyond reasonable doubt'. Pollock had used a similar direction to that in *Muller* in later cases, including *Exall* (1866) 4 F & F 922. Foster and Finlason's commenting on *Muller*, note that 'of later years there has been observed a dissatisfaction with [beyond reasonable doubt] practical results in some cases, and its tendency to secure acquittals in…capital cases, and a disposition to get rid of it…by the substitution…of a much looser rule'.

its meaning to juries in more transparent and comprehendible terms. Though conceding the indefinite nature of 'reasonable', Stephen, speaking with the experience of a trial judge, maintained that its practical value lay in it being 'an emphatic caution against haste in coming to a conclusion adverse to a prisoner. It may be stated otherwise, but not, I think, more definitely, by saying that before a man is convicted...every supposition not in itself impossible which is consistent with his innocence ought to be negatived.'[230] Judicial vacillation on the wisdom of attempting to elucidate the meaning of 'beyond reasonable doubt' remained a frequent feature of the subsequent history of the expression.[231]

(2) ONUS AND STANDARD OF PROOF FOR DEFENCES

The evidential requirements for rebutting (the equivalent of) a *prima facie* case against the defendant remained generally murky until well beyond the nineteenth century. In part this was a consequence of the absence of clarity surrounding the central question of the standard of proof required to convict. However, two further factors combined to obscure the rebuttal issue and inhibit its resolution: first, until the presence of defence counsel became a fairly frequent occurrence, refinements of this nature were unlikely to be raised by a defendant and only in an unstructured fashion by trial judges; secondly, and most significantly, was the wide-ranging doctrinal force of the presumption of intended consequences. Besides its crucial effect on the development of the substantive law (see below), the presumption constituted both a pragmatic recognition of the practicalities of proof at criminal trials and the balance which the law chose to strike between social and individual needs and expectations. Best's *Treatise* well expressed this choice in the late 1840s:

[T]he safety of society, joined to the difficulty of proving psychological facts renders imperatively necessary a presumption which may seem severe; viz., that which casts on the accused the onus of justifying or explaining acts prima facie illegal. It is on this principle that sanity is presumed [and an accused is] bound to prove [a defence of insanity]. So a party who is proved to have killed another is presumed in the first instance, to have done it maliciously...until the contrary is shown.[232]

---

[230] *HCL*, i, 438 and *General View* (2nd edn, 1890), 138. Stephen appears to imply that the standard whilst appropriate when the law was extremely severe and capricious, might no longer be true, *HCL*, i, 438–9.

[231] Compare *Sykes* (1912) 8 Cr App R 234 with *Abramovitch* (1914) 11 Cr App R 45. A direction almost identical to Pollock's in *Muller* was ruled as 'unexceptionable' in *Walters v. R* [1969] 2 AC 26. Indeed, simple directions resembling those employed before the nineteenth century regained acceptability during the twentieth century. For example, 'completely satisfied' and 'sure' in *Summers* [1952] 1 All ER 1059, *Hepworth* [1955] 2 QB 600, and *Ferguson v. R* [1979] 1 WLR 94.

[232] (1849), i, 344–5. Similarly, (11th edn, 1911), 411. The conveniences and practicalities of criminal presumptions were also increasingly recognized throughout the nineteenth century in two further

It appears reasonably clear that Best (and *Archbold*)[233] was seeking to provide a *general* account of the position of the defendant in relation to exculpatory grounds or defences; and while they were, and remained, the most established instances, the insanity defence and presumed malice were illustrative and not exhaustive examples.[234]

But even in these well-recognized cases, practically no indication appears in nineteenth-century authorities of what *standard* of rebutting evidence must be offered by the defendants; no distinction is made between the legal burden of proof and that of adducing evidence judicially regarded as worthy of a jury's consideration—in effect, sufficient to raise a reasonable doubt as to guilt.[235] The evidential difference in the standard of evidence required to establish insanity, as compared with other defences, seems to underlie insanity's frequent distinct identification and treatment by some nineteenth-century commentators, such as Stephen. His closest approach to suggesting that defendants do not generally need to prove defences appears in the *History* (1883): when discussing the implications of the prosecution's burden of proof, Stephen maintains it includes negating 'every supposition not...itself improbable which is consistent with...innocence'.[236] Elsewhere, in texts and draft legislation, Stephen consistently declared the need for defendants to 'prove' insanity, whilst never suggesting any particular evidential requirement for other defences, except in murder where 'the burden of proving circumstances of excuse, justification, or extenuation' was on the defendant.[237] Clarification of the law (and probably change as well) would come with *Woolmington v. DPP*, when the House of Lords both asserted

---

ways: by statutory exceptions relieving the prosecution of proving a negative fact by placing the burden of proof on defendants, such as 'proving authority, consent, lawful excuse and the like'; and by common law exceptions of similarly reversing the onus 'where the subject-matter of the allegation lies peculiarly within the knowledge' of the defendant. See Taylor, *Treatise* (1848), i: 267–70, and subsequent editions.

[233] *Archbold*, like Best, appears to deploy insanity as illustrative of the general rule of the onus in defences. See e.g. (25th edn, 1918), 18–19.

[234] In *M'Naghten*, when speaking of proving the defence of insanity, Tindal CJ used language similar to that employed when directing on the general question of burden and standard of proof: 'clearly proved'; 'proved to [the jury's] satisfaction' (1843) 10 Cl. & Fin. 200, 210. And see the emphatic directions of Rolfe B., in *Stokes* (1848) 3 Car. & K. 185, and Bramwell B. in *Dove, The Times*, 17 July 1856; *Oliver Smith* (1911) 6 Cr App R 19. For the presumptions of *mens rea*, see e.g. *Foster*, 255; Tindal CJ in *Greenacre* (1837) 8 Car. & P. 35, 42; Starkie, *Evidence* (2nd edn, 1833), ii: 522. An attempt to extend the presumption beyond murder seems to have been resisted in *Davies* (1912) 8 Cr App R 211.

[235] Rolfe B. in *Stokes* (above) directed the jury 'must be satisfied' that the defendant was insane: 'If the matter be left in doubt it will be their duty to convict.'

[236] *HCL*, i, 438.

[237] *General View*, 91; *A Digest of the Criminal Law* (1877) 152, Art. 230, 16, Art 28; similarly Homicide Amendment Bill, 1874, s 24; and Draft Code Bill, 1879, Part III, s 22.

the general prosecution burden of proving the fault element in offences, and the special position of the defence of insanity in respect of burden of proof.[238]

(3) MAGISTRATES' PRE-TRIAL EXAMINATION

By the 1820s, the role of the pre-trial examination by magistrates had evolved from the strict Marian concept of gathering prosecution evidence to one where the defence might seek to undermine the prosecution case or even boost the defence case.[239] Uncertainty surrounds the extent to which magistrates were prepared to discharge examined defendants on the grounds of insufficient evidence to commit, or, indeed, whether any particular level of incriminating evidence needed to be established. Clearly, existence of such a standard was a prerequisite of any discharging power for failure to achieve it. Although the Marian legislation set no committal standard, at least by the eighteenth century magistrates are recorded as discharging suspects on the grounds of insufficient evidence.[240] Whilst some early nineteenth-century authority suggest that a *prima facie* case must be shown for committal, somewhat inconsistently, discharge would apparently have not necessarily followed failure to adduce such evidence.[241] However, certainly by the 1840s, the actual practice of committal proceedings had evolved into a thorough and wide-ranging enquiry, where examining magistrates acted as a 'preliminary judge'.[242] And as Pitt Taylor noted, after the prosecution evidence was heard in

---

[238] [1935] AC 462, 481. In identifying the unique position of the insanity defence, by implication, the House of Lords established the ground for later rulings placing the evidential burden on defendants of raising other exculpatory circumstances. The standard of proof placed on the defendant pleading insanity was not settled until *Sodeman* v. *R* [1936] 2 All ER 1138, requiring the 'balance of probabilities', that employed in civil actions.

[239] *Chitty*, notes that the 'justice ought to take and certify...the information, proof, and evidence which tend in favour of the prisoner, as those which are brought forward against him. And though formally his witnesses could not be examined upon oath, they are now placed on a footing with those whom the prosecutor adduces', (1816), i, 79. Also Cottu, *Administration* (1822), 34.

[240] See Beattie, *Policing and Punishment*, 107 and Langbein, *Origins*, 47 and 273.

[241] See *Chitty* (1816), i: 89. *Chitty* does not define 'prima facie'. However, a modern definition is proposed by Starkie, *Treatise* (1824), vol. 1, 451 and 453: '"prima facie" evidence is that which not being inconsistent with the falsity of the hypothesis nevertheless raises such a degree of probability in its favour, that it must prevail if it be accredited by the Jury, unless rebutted, or the contrary is proved'. Chitty remarks that it is 'not usual for the magistrate to discharge him, even when he believes him to be altogether innocent'. On the eighteenth and early nineteenth-century practice of a *second* pre-trial hearing and the appearance of lawyers, see King, *Crime, Justice and Discretion*, 94–9; Langbein, 'The Prosecutorial Origins of Defence Counsel in the Eighteenth Century. The appearance of solicitors' (1999) 58 *CLJ* 314. In *Cox and Coleridge* (1822) 1 B. & C. 37, Bayley J. observed that 'a magistrate is clearly bound...not to commit anyone unless a prima facie case is made out...' (50 and 20). In their Eighth Report (1845) the Criminal Law Commissioners' draft 'Act of Procedure', which purported to be largely a digest of existing law, employs the 'prima facie' standard for examining magistrates (citing *Cox* v. *Coleridge*). A subsequent section on powers of discharge refers to the need for 'a strong presumption of guilt'. An examination of all the evidence is contemplated by the provisions of the draft Act. See Ch. 1, s 7, Arts 1, 2 and 5.

[242] Stephen, *HCL*, i, 221.

open court, the defendant or 'his legal adviser, has then an opportunity of cross-examining the witnesses, of calling others to contradict them and of making any statement, with the view of explaining, justifying, or disproving the charge'.[243] Acceptance of the 'judicial' complexion of committal proceedings in turn facilitated fuller recognition of not just the power, but the duty to dismiss charges unless supported by evidence upon which a reasonable jury might convict the defendant.

Formal confirmation of this evolution came with the first Jervis Act 1848 (s. 42, s. 25) which expressly authorized discharge if the evidence was 'not sufficient'—if it failed to raise 'a strong or probable presumption of guilt'. While obviously construable as a *prima facie* standard, the term was not used, nor was any direct interpretation of this provision offered by *Stone's Justices' Manual*, the semi-official guide for proceedings in magistrates' courts.[244] However, from 1900, in relation to the role of Grand Juries, the text refers to the 'prima facie case' determined by committing magistrates.[245] As will be suggested (see 'Grand Jury' below), the Jervis Act requirements on levels of committal evidence appear to have been an attempt to ensure that the Grand Jury 'true bill' standard operated as a filter at an earlier stage, thereby eliminating the personal hardship and institutional costs of insubstantial accusations proceeding further.

(4) THE GRAND JURY

The final vestiges of Grand Jury hearings to determine whether an accused should face jury trial were eventually abolished in 1948.[246] However, this ancient procedure was widely regarded as, at least, superfluous from more than a century before. Its virtual indestructibility was a consequence of the familiar brew of low political visibility, shortage of parliamentary time frustrating reform initiatives, and misplaced sentiment. Following magistrates' committal proceedings, Grand Juries constituted a second stage filter on the way to jury trial.[247] It was

---

[243] 'Defects of Criminal Procedure' (1844) 31 *LM.* 241 reproduced in *Criminal Law Commissioners' Eighth Report*, App. C.

[244] But the term did have contemporary currency, e.g. Stephen, *General View*, 175.

[245] (22nd edn) 89. Atkinson's *Magistrates Practice* (12th edn, 1915), simply quotes the Jervis Act provisions (172). The 1869 edition (v: 405) of the voluminous *Burn's Justice of the Peace* unhelpfully cites *Chitty*, followed by the requirements of the 1848 Act.

[246] Criminal Justice Act 1948, s 31(3) and the Administration of Justice (Miscellaneous Provisions) Act 1933, 23 and 24 Geo. V. c. 36, s 1.

[247] Alternatively, but unusually, the prosecutor might directly prefer a 'voluntary bill' of indictment from the Grand Jury. A Coroner's Court inquest accusing a party of murder or manslaughter could serve as an equivalent to a Grand Jury indictment. On rare occasions, in cases of 'high misdemeanours', such as libel and sedition, the Grand Jury could be bypassed by an 'information' filed in the Queen's/King's Bench Division by the Attorney-General or the Master of the Crown Office. See Kenny, *Outlines* (8th edn, Cambridge, 1917), 453–4.

Grand Juries consisted of at least 12 but not more than 23 jurors. Although no formal qualifications were required of jurors, those serving Quarter Sessions and the Central Criminal Court were

rendered increasingly obsolete as the nineteenth century progressed and magistrates' committal proceedings ceased to be a crude preliminary hurdle for prosecutors and evolved into a more carefully structured procedure under which the full range of evidence was scrutinized to ensure the existence of what amounted to a *prima facie* case against the defendant. The Grand Jury's role entailed a reexamination of solely prosecution evidence, in private, without the defendant's presence, to determine whether a *prima facie* case existed.[248]

Slashing attacks on the perceived disutility of Grand Juries were almost as common as attempts to legislate them out of existence.[249] In his damning evidence to the Criminal Law Commissioners, Pitt Taylor concluded:

We would abolish grand juries; not only because we consider them to be utterly useless, but because we can see that in many cases they defeat the ends of justice; in many they are instruments of oppression and in all they create a large expense and are productive of much inconvenience.[250]

The overwhelming weight of evidence from a wide spread of professional respondents whose evidence appeared in the Criminal Law Commissioners' Eighth Report favoured the Grand Jury's complete abolition, or at least extensive curtailment of its use.[251] At the beginning of the twentieth century Kenny pithily expressed the essential anomaly of the system:

[T]he sole function of a modern grand jury is to repeat badly what has already been done well: to hear in secret, imperfectly, and in the absence of the accused, one side of the

chosen on the basis of liability for 'reasonable' property rates: *DC Report Committee on Jury Laws*, *PP* 1913 [Cmnd. 6817], xxx 403. For Assizes, those selected were usually 'gentlemen of the highest position in the county', who were almost inevitably JPs: S. Harris and F. Tomlinson, *Principles of the Criminal Law* (2nd edn, 1881), 346.

[248] The position remained obscure beyond the nineteenth century. In 1816 Chitty noted that the Grand Jury should be 'convinced of the guilt of the defendant' (137). From 1835–62 successive editions of Roscoe's *Digest* observe that the standard is the 'same evidence…necessary to support the indictment at trial' (3rd edn), 323. From 1862 (6th edn) onwards this work refers to a 'prima facie' case (177). No supporting authority is offered to account for this change. All editions of *Archbold* to the end of the century used the term 'sufficiently proved'—the Jervis Act standard for committing magistrates. A change to 'prima facie' occurs in the 1900 (22nd edn), 589. A further change, again without apparent reason, appears in the following edition (23rd edn, 1905), when references to both 'prima facie' and 'probable evidence' (99) occur. Whilst the concept seems to have been accepted fairly early, the expression 'prima facie' was not the universal currency in criminal proceedings during the nineteenth century.

[249] See Bentley, *Criminal Justice*, 133–4 for an outline of failed bills.

[250] *Eighth Report*, 1845, App. C, 357, reproducing Pitt Taylor's article published in (1844) 31 *LM* 241, 242; also (1844) 3 *LT* 172, and (1848) 10 *LT* 447. Similarly, W.C. Humphreys, *Observations on the Inutility of Grand Juries, and Suggestions for their Abolition* (1842), and (Lord) Denman (1828) 48 *Edin. R.* 411 and *The Times*, e.g. 19 April (1845), p. 4 and 24 April 1860, p. 6.

[251] *Eighth Report*, (1845), App. A.

case, after both sides of it have already been heard fully in open court...A bad tribunal is laboriously brought together in order to revise the work of a better one.[252]

Survival of the Grand Jury probably owed much to a long enduring and influential sentiment sometimes expressed by lawyers of considerable gravitas, including Denman and Stephen, that involvement of the 'higher and middle classes in the administration of justice' was socially most beneficial.[253] Added to this, in the early twentieth century Lord Alverstone was one who offered the 'strongest' reaffirmation of the extra-legal, libertarian argument that the 'Grand Jury is, in fact, a great protection in certain classes of cases where persons are charged with criminal offences to which there attaches no real criminality'.[254] Small wonder then, that with such powerful advocates the institution survived until the 1940s.

4. FORMS OF TRIAL: THE RISE OF SUMMARY TRIAL AND DECLINE IN JURY TRIAL

The steady, insistent expansion of summary trial at the expense of trial on indictment has already been remarked upon. The driving forces behind the change were diverse. One early important motivating factor was the desire to segregate young persons from exposure to the 'evils of idleness and contamination of bad association'[255] when held in local prisons for weeks or months pending jury trial. Swift justice by local magistrates was regarded as an important device in avoiding such contamination. Added to this was the more general pragmatic ambition of achieving a higher prosecution rate of petty offences at the lowest cost. In turn, raising prosecution rates and increasing the likelihood of punishment was seen as enhancing the law's powers of deterrence. Beyond expanding summary jurisdiction by making formerly indictable offences triable summarily, strict and vicarious criminal responsibility, largely a nineteenth-century legislative innovation, also became principally the province of summary trial. And from the end of the nineteenth century, to this broad regulatory function was added a steadily expanding catalogue of summary road traffic offences. As a final factor, during Victorian times the scale of prosecution of established summary offences of a social-moralistic

---

[252] *Outlines* (1902), 456. Also, similarly critical, for example, T. Crispe, *Reminiscences of a KC* (1909), 249–50 and Sir H. Dickens, *Recollections of Sir Henry Dickens* (1934), 206–8. At the beginning of the nineteenth century a substantial number of bills were being dismissed by Grand Juries (e.g. Beattie, *Crime and the Courts*, 401–6 and table 8.1) but by the end well below 1% of bills were being rejected: *Judicial Statistics, PP* 1900 [Cd. 123], ciii, 1.

[253] Denman, *Criminal Law Commissioners', Eighth Report*, 1845, App. A, p. 212 and Stephen, *General View*, 158. But according to Maitland, they were 'usually county justices' and thus very much involved in criminal justice: *Justice and Police* (1885), 165.

[254] *Recollections of Bar and Bench* (1914), 291–2.

[255] Criminal Law Commissioners, *Third Report*, (1837), p. 6; also *Eighth Report*, (1845), p. 161.

nature (including vagrancy, prostitution, and intoxication) grew as new professional police forces established themselves, going beyond the apprehension of offenders by gradually assuming a wide-ranging prosecutorial role.

In the main, this process of almost relentless expansion[256] in the volume and range of summary offences was achieved in the face of sustained yet relatively ineffectual opposition. For example, throughout the nineteenth century, some regularly and cogently argued that such developments would erode moral values previously reinforced by the formality and ritual of jury trial.[257] On a different tack, it was frequently maintained that local justice might be less impartial where the material interests of magistrates were even indirectly at stake. Moreover, it was suggested that even perceived partiality without substance threatened that vital public confidence necessarily underpinning the criminal justice system.[258] Voiced since Blackstone's time, others raised constitutional objections to the increased use of summary procedures, claiming defendants were denied their basic rights to protection by jury trial. But, in the main, these oppositional voices were quelled by what were regarded as the more compelling claims of swifter and cheaper justice.[259] Furthermore, the post-decapitalizing period saw a refinement in the calibration of punishments for sub-categories of crimes, such as larceny. This almost inevitably meant a drastic diminution in the prescribed maxima for less serious forms of such offences was accompanied by their relegation to summary trial. At the same time, long-running concerns over the professional competency and common eccentricities of the lay magistracy assumed even greater significance as their judicial burden and importance grew. While no concerted attempt was made to provide legal education for the lay magistracy,[260] such concerns were

[256] According to *The Times*, 'with the most precipitate recklessness' 6 April 1844, p. 4.

[257] See such apprehensions cited by L. Radzinowicz and R. Hood, *A History of the Criminal Law, v: The Emergence of Penal Policy* (1986), 620n.

[258] Beyond the Game Laws were the increasingly prominent summary offences relating to labour relations, especially under the Combination Act 1825, Master and Servant Act 1867, and Conspiracy and Protection of Property Act 1875. Instances of legislation enacted to combat potential local partiality were provisions in the Trade Union Act 1871 and Coal Mines Regulation Act 1887. More broadly, on magistrates and penalties for breach of employment contracts, see R. Steinfeld, *Coercion, Contract and Free Labor in the Nineteenth Century* (Cambridge, 2002).

[259] Blackstone saw the steady growth of summary jurisdiction as threatening the 'disuse of our admirable and truly English trial by jury'. Especially, in the case of excise and revenue offences, he regarded summary power over individual's property as 'increased to a very formidable height', *Comms*, iv, 278. Opposition to widening the scope of summary trial was at its strongest between the 1820s and 1840s. For the several Committee Inquiries of this period favouring an expansion of summary jurisdiction and the initially unsuccessful attempts at legislation, see Radzinowicz and Hood, *Penal Policy*, 620–1 n and T. Sweeney, 'The Extension and Practice of Summary Jurisdiction in England, 1790–1860' (Phd, Thesis, Cambridge University, 1985).

[260] Nineteenth-century magistrates took their law from two main sources: practice works, especially Burn's long lived, multi-volumed, *Justice of the Peace*, later overtaken by *Stone's Justices Manual*; and from justices' clerks, who would similarly rely on such works.

addressed principally by two strategies: through facilitating the appointment of stipendiary magistrates outside the Metropolis under the (largely ignored) Municipal Corporations Act 1835;[261] and by detailed legislative regulation under the Jervis Acts 1848 (and subsequent legislation) of all summary proceedings.

As numerically the most significant offence, larceny's procedural career offers the clearest and most emphatic illustration of the growth in summary justice. After modest innovations in 1827, further legislation in 1847 and 1855 greatly expanded summary jurisdiction.[262] By this stage, with defendants' consent, magistrates were empowered to deal with certain forms of larceny regardless of the property's value, and impose sentences of up to six months' imprisonment. In consequence, a dramatic relocation of business occurred from Quarter Sessions to magistrates' courts; with trials on indictment dropping by more than half in the mid-1850s, from 21,000 to less than 10,000, and summary trials rising from 3,000 to 35,000. Further increases in summary jurisdiction generated smaller, but still notable, shifts in trial numbers from Quarter Sessions to Petty Sessions.[263] By 1900, 88 per cent of all non-violent larcenies were tried summarily;[264] and 81 per cent of all prosecuted offences were dealt with summarily.[265]

Beyond the formalistic business of summary trial, the role of both lay and (later) stipendiary magistrates also incorporated the significant, but often hidden function of local social-legal arbitrator or mediator. Though suffering a relative decline in local standing and power,[266] nineteenth-century magistrates perpetuated this quasi-judicial activity. And while by no means inconsequential in urban areas, it was a role which constituted a singularly important feature on the rural social landscape, and properly attracts the attention of modern socio-legal historians.

A second broad issue relating to mode of trial and law-making is that of the potential impact of juries on the application of the law and the possibility of their

---

[261] For stipendiary magistrates, see XI, Pt 3.

[262] 1827 7 & 8, Geo. IV c. 29. Of particular significance were the Juvenile Offenders Act 1847, 10 & 11 Vict. c. 82 and the Criminal Justice Act 1855, 18 & 19 Vict. c. 126. Initially, for offenders up to 14 years old, and eventually of any age, the Acts opened up to summary trial simple larcenies, offences which made up more than 50% of all larcenies previously heard at Quarter Sessions: *Judicial Statistics 1857, Part I, PP* 1857–8 [2407], lvii, 383.

[263] This jurisdiction was widened further to cover all offences (except homicide) for children under 12 and adults for property offences, eventually, up to £20: 1879 42 & 43 Vict. c. 22; 1914 4 & 5 Geo. V, c. 58. For common assault, 1828 9 Geo. IV, c. 31.

[264] V. Gatrell, 'The Decline of Theft and Violence in Victorian and Edwardian England', in V. Gatrell, B. Lenman, and G. Parker (eds), *Crime and the Law: The Social History of Crime in Western Europe since 1500* (1980), 274.

[265] *Judicial Statistics for 1902, PP* 1904 [Cd. 2010] *Part 1, Criminal Statistics*, p. 37. Similarly, *Introduction to the Criminal Statistics for the year 1912*.

[266] Eastwood, *Governing Rural England, passim.*

influence on the law's substance. Judicial control over the application of substantive law while notionally considerable, was (is) in practice ultimately limited in the face of any jury which chose to act against judicial advice, however emphatic. The highly misleading common designation of trial roles, whereby judges settle law while juries determine facts, not only conceals the legitimate law/fact-finding function of juries in some offences, but also the ability of the jury's general verdict to submerge totally any wilfully illicit construction of law.[267] Acknowledging this, Mansfield observed: '…by means of a general verdict [juries] are intrusted with a power of blending law and fact and following the prejudices of their affections or passions'.[268] Indeed, rather than the subject of condemnation, widespread and routine jury mitigation or nullification of the harshness of eighteenth-century penal legislation became lauded as proof of the jury's great institutional value in the administration of criminal justice.[269] 'Partial' verdicts to push criminality under low capital thresholds, or merciful acquittals in the face of overwhelming evidence, were extensively deployed by juries well into the nineteenth century. It was a practice which also provided valuable ammunition for those, such as Romilly and Mackintosh, seeking to replace alleged ineffective penal severity with a more rational and morally discriminatory structure, in line with public sympathy—that vital ingredient of any successful criminal justice system.[270]

Even after the reforms and revisions effected from the 1820s to early 1840s, greatly diminishing the law's harshness, jury mitigation remained a characteristic of a significant number of criminal trials, albeit on a less prominent scale. Evidence of its extent is to be gleaned from case reports and the steady flow of critical comment issuing from some quarters. First published in 1845, Sir George Stephen's moderately successful *The Juryman's Guide* unsparingly flayed jurymen who through 'weakness and cowardice…betray themselves'; a '"merciful jury" [was] a self-degraded and…perjured jury; mercy is not their prerogative…'. Rather than diminishing, Stephen feared it was a 'weakness…daily increasing…to that degree that it [is] often the subject of discussion'.[271] On the basis of

---

[267] *Shipley* (1784) 4 Doug. 73, 163. More generally, Thayer, *Treatise*, Ch. 5 and W. R. Cornish, *The Jury* (1968), *passim*. Sir William Harcourt's affirmation of this position in 1890 attracted challenges from several including Sir Harry Poland and (the eventual) Darling J. For example, *The Times*, 28 May 1890, p. 7 and 7 June 1890, p. 17.

[268] e.g. the presence of 'gross negligence' in manslaughter trials.

[269] Comments of the *Select Committee on the Criminal Laws*, PP 1819 (585), viii, 24–7, 93–9. Generally, T. Green, *Verdict According to Conscience* (Chicago, 1985).

[270] Romilly, *PD* 1811 (s. 1), 19: Apps 7–8, 61. Mackintosh, *PD* 1819 (s. 1), 39: 784, 788–9, 794–5; *PD* 1825 (s. 2), 9: 403. Also, 'Petition of Jurymen', *PD* 1824 (s. 2), 11: 180–1, 210–11. And the Criminal Law Commissioners, *Second Report* (1836), 17, 27–8. And more generally on the use of juries in civil and criminal cases XI, Pt 3.

[271] At pp. 2, 3, 134–9. A revised edition, published in 1867, carried a prefatory disclaimer that there were 'some observations…to which the Editor does not give his entire concurrence…'. Similarly,

the relative frequency with which the subject was visited by the press, and most particularly *The Times*, this last remark appears to have some substance. Available evidence suggests that, rather than an actual increasing incidence of jury way-wardness, much more likely was a slower than anticipated falling away of the practice. Especially during the 1840s and 1850s, *The Times* leader writers left the nation in no doubt about the illicit behaviour of some criminal juries. The cata-lyst for one of its most sustained and forceful denunciations was Lord Denman's incautious and ambiguous observations in a parliamentary exchange in June 1841, relating to decapitalizing rape. Hansard reported the Lord Chief Justice as reflecting 'Was it fit still to ask juries as an alternative, whether they would com-mit perjury [by acquitting] or that which they considered to be murder?' by con-victing.[272] With affected mock disbelief, *The Times* splenetically lamented:

That sentiments so atrocious, sophistry so pernicious, and immorality so shameless, should have been spoken of by the Lord Chief Justice as commonly influencing English Juries, without so much as a protest against their wickedness, and that the prevalence of such sentiments should have been recognised in such a quarter as a sufficient legislative ground for lowering the standard of punishments, is more than we are capable of believing.[273]

Jurors who adopted their 'private sympathies or *theories* rather than their oaths for a sufficient standard of duty [manifested] depravity [that made] them far fitter companions for the prisoner . . . than judges of his offence'.[274]

Over succeeding decades occasions markedly decreased on which *The Times* felt it necessary to vent its general anxieties over jury behaviour in crim-inal trials;[275] whether this was due to a growing acceptance (or resignation) of

J. Brown, *The Dark Side of Trial by Jury* (1859). Cf. the milder comments on such jury practices in T. H. Cornish's rival *The Juryman's Legal Hand-Book* (1843), 105–6.

[272] *PD* 1841 (s. 3), 58: 1555–6. The Report continued 'His own opinion was, that juries manfully did their duty, and that it was as often the fault of the judge who contemplated with horror the depriv-ing a fellow creature of life as of juries, that persons accused of [rape] were frequently acquitted.' Rape was decapitalized soon after, probably partly in response to such jury resistance: *ibid.*, 1486, 1552 and 1568; and 57: 50–7, 1408. Decapitalizing rape by no means removed the reluctance of juries to convict, or, indeed, for prosecutions to be brought. On the nineteenth century, see Conley, *The Unwritten Law*, 81–95.

[273] *The Times*, 19 June 1841, p. 4. Jury trial in preference to the move to summary justice never lacked advocates in the press, e.g. (1849) 13 *LT* 355 and (1850) 14 *LT* 479.

[274] *Ibid.* This newspaper's systematic coverage of Assize proceedings from the 1830s by legally qualified reporters gave its 'Leaders' on the law an added authority beyond that already enjoyed by the paper. The bulk of middle range offences were tried at Quarter Sessions and consequently almost completely unreported.

[275] e.g. the applauded firmness and forceful analysis of evidence in the jury direction of Wightman J. were contrasted with the unflattering account of Willes J.'s studied neutrality: *The Times*, 20 March 1863 p. 9. *The Times* accepted that there was a 'certain rough truth' in the 'very

perceived quirky jury practices, or a change in jury behaviour, is very difficult to hazard. However, *The Times* continued to provide a running commentary on specific instances where juries and even judges were apparently failing to apply the full rigour of the law.[276] Most notable in these commentaries was the treatment of homicide, and a perceived over-willingness of some juries to convict many on murder charges of the lesser, non-capital offence of manslaughter:

According to the frequent interpretation of modern juries, the distinction between murder and manslaughter has become so exceedingly subtle, that in some instances we own our utter inability to discover it. Nearly every Assize furnishes a few cases in which the verdict, rather than the evidence, appears to afford the only reason for classing as the minor offence what we should have otherwise considered the greater.[277]

Beyond a claimed general amiable weakness, to call it by no harsher name, the 'magic twelve'[278] in benevolently interpreting the circumstances of killings, *The Times* became particularly exercised by some juries' treatment of insanity and provocation defence pleas.[279] More generally, in 1908 *The Times*, after mulling over the quixotic behaviour of juries, concluded:

We are rapidly becoming the most emotional of people, and one of the most mischievous forms of uncontrollable feeling is an outburst of enthusiasm, or it may be the opposite, as to someone on his trial. To-day it may be for the innocent and to-morrow for the guilty.[280]

All in all, recorded jury practices clearly argue that analysis of the contemporary substantive law and conceptual controversies should be tempered by awareness of the particular contextual variations and realities in the law's enforcement.

---

prevalent opinion that Quarter Sessions are a more satisfactory tribunal for the repression of crime than the Assizes [because] Her Majesty's Judges have too much subtlety and refinement, [and] share too little sympathy with the interests of honest men against thieves and ruffians, and leave the juries too much to themselves...': 7 March 1864, p. 8.

[276] Typical of its criticism of juries' 'under' convictions (for lesser offences) and for judges 'under' sentencing, see e.g. 26 March 1853, p. 4. For undoubtedly 'disgusting' incompetence in conducting an Exeter Assizes murder trial, leading to acquittal of two defendants in the face of overwhelming evidence of guilt, Talfourd J. was subjected to several slashing attacks in *The Times* leaders, which 'look[ed] forward with indescribable apprehension to his further administration of justice', 27 March 1850, p. 5. Also, 26 March, p. 4 and 29 March, p. 4. References to the 'perjury and cowardice' of juries and sometimes 'inexcusable laxity' of judges were no strangers to the young Fitzjames Stephen's regular *Saturday Review* commentaries, e.g. 10 April 1858, p. 370; 18 April 1857, p. 357; 29 August 1857, p. 199.

[277] *The Times*, 22 July 1847, p. 4. Similarly, 31 August 1846, p. 5; 22 June 1847, p. 4; 12 August 1847, p. 5.

[278] *The Times*, 19 June 1846, p. 5.

[279] e.g. 1 July 1850, p. 4; 11 August 1855, p. 6.

[280] *The Times*, 31 July 1908, p. 13.

Yet, while recognizing the continuing inclination of juries to assert a degree of moral independence in applying the law, identifying the possible impact of such behaviour on the judicial development of substantive rules is necessarily far more speculative and problematic, carrying a distinct risk of characterizing the tail as the dog.[281]

---

[281] Considered in 'Homicide', Ch. XII and 'Defences', Ch. VII below; and the jury's explicit normative role in constructing objective standards, including 'reasonableness' and the concept of 'gross negligence'. The general effect of jury recommendations to mercy on judicial and Executive action is difficult to gauge. As an illustration, between 1861 and 1881, of 564 convicted of capital offences (overwhelmingly murder) 243 were recommended for mercy by juries. Of these 68 were executed; of those not recommended by juries 235 were executed. Table, *Home Office Printed Memoranda and Reports* N.A. H.O. 347/8, 243. Of course, most mitigating factors influencing juries would also have been relevant to judicial recommendations and ultimate Executive response.

IV

Sentencing and Review

1. SENTENCING: CURBING JUDICIAL DISCRETION

The Legislative Framework

Prior to the large-scale decapitalizing of offences, judicial sentencing discretion figured most prominently in the process of reprieve and substitution of an alternative punishment to death. The capital threat and the extensive power of reprieve were typically replaced by a wide judicial discretion of sentencing to transportation for a period of between seven years and life, or imprisonment for up to seven years.[1] Legislative replacement of the capital penalty with transportation and imprisonment was undertaken largely on a fragmented, frequently *ad hoc* basis, with no attempt to devise a generally coherent or systematic punishment structure across a wide spread of offences of varying seriousness.[2] At this stage, reformist energies were deployed principally in addressing the capital question[3] and, to a lesser degree, the nature or substance of the alternatives of imprisonment and transportation. Yet, while the practicalities of legislative change in individual penalties were being addressed in this isolated fashion, broader strategic punishment issues came under the severe periodic scrutiny of the Criminal Law Commissioners between 1833 and 1849.

Predictably, from the outset the Commissioners were unsparingly critical of both the wide discretionary basis of sentencing practice and punishment scales. Applying their stock Benthamite yardstick of maximum deterrence achieved

---

[1] An early example of this formula relating to stealing is found in one of Romilly's few successes in decapitalizing punishment: 1812 51 Geo. III c. 41. Specific legislation authorized the very frequent executive practice of commuting a sentence of transportation to a lengthy term aboard one of the prison hulks, or in Millbank or Pentonville: 1816 56 Geo. III c. 63, s 13 and 1842 5 & 6 Vict. c. 29.

[2] See a detailed review of the legislative conversion of most formerly capital offences to a non-capital basis, *First Report, Criminal Law Commissioners, PP* 1834 (537), xxvi and D. A. Thomas, *The Penal Equation: Derivations of the Penalty Structure of English Criminal Law* (Cambridge, 1978), 9–18.

[3] For example, Mackintosh's 1819 Committee accepted a very wide judicial discretion to substitute imprisonment with hard labour where it appeared 'expedient' (*Report*, pp. 15–16).

through certain and properly proportioned punishment, the existing institution was found wanting in most respects: broad offence definitions covering vastly different degrees of criminality and moral culpability were subject to wide latitude in sentencing; piecemeal, unreflective, and unstructured reforms had produced a state of affairs where 'the degrees of guilt have been confounded, and the relative proportions of punishment destroyed'.[4] It was a virtual moral homogeneity later reflected upon by C. S. Greaves and ascribed to the heavily blinkered legislative practice of fixing the punishment of an individual offence without 'reference to other offences [or] a view to establishing any congruity in the punishment of them...'.[5] As a response to this penal incoherence, the Commissioners offered a graduated scale of punishments assigned to designated classes of offences sharing similar 'degrees of guilt', with the operation of judicial discretion recognized as legitimate for 'various innumerable intermediate cases' defying classification.[6] Beyond marginal influence on the 1861 Consolidation Acts, the Commissioners' work of rationalizing sentencing largely perished with their general codification proposals. Greaves, the vastly experienced criminal lawyer and draughtsman of the 1861 legislation, occupied a critical position somewhere between the Commissioners and the existing system. Unlike the Commissioners, he was not doctrinally opposed to wide judicial discretion; but, in common with them, he was powerfully inclined to construct a rationally organized and comprehensive penalty structure. This objective was denied him by sustained opposition in both Houses of Parliament.[7] Consequently, the penalty structures of the 1861 Acts did little more than reflect the reformed legislation of the 1820s and 1830s. As Greaves noted: the Consolidation Acts were 'chiefly re-enactments of the former law, with amendments and additions'.[8]

---

[4] *Fourth Report*, PP 1839 (168), xix, xvi; *First Report*, 32; *Second Report PP* 1836 (343), xxxvi, 19 and 37. Similarly others, including Blackstone, a century before: *Comms*, iv, 3–4.

[5] C. S. Greaves, *The Criminal Law Consolidation and Amendment Acts—Notes and Observations* (1861), xlvi. Similarly, *Seventh Report PP* 1843 (448), xix, 97.

[6] For example, *Second Report* (1836), 37, *Fourth Report* (1839), viii, *Seventh Report*, 92–4. Shifting views on the classification of offences, punishment levels and tolerable range of judicial discretion, are apparent from the substantial variations appearing in the Commissioners' Reports: *Fourth Report* (1839) 15 classes; *Seventh Report*, 45 classes; *Second Report pp* 1846 (709), xxiv, 13 classes; *Third Report PP* 1847 (830) xv, 31 classes; Fourth Report (1848), 18 classes. Relative to earlier formulations, the Fourth and final Report proposals covering classes of punishment, increased judicial discretion by removing many previous limitations requiring minimum sentences. The Second Royal Commission dates from 1845.

[7] *Notes and Observations*, xlv and *passim. Ibid*, ix–xxxv, provides a valuable and authoritative account of the failure of the Commissioners' codifying bills, the legislative process, and antecedents of the 1861 Acts. Greaves observed that the 'manner in which Acts...are framed is a disgrace' (liv).

[8] *Notes and Observations*, xi.

Sentencing Practices

With a penalty structure substantially unreformed since the decapitalizing initiatives of the 1830s, and one which left largely intact judges' very wide discretionary sentencing powers, after the 1861 Consolidation Acts credibility of the system rested on just how such a discretion was exercised. Establishing imprisonment as the principal form of punishment increased the visibility of apparent sentencing anomalies and disparities between different judges and courts. Almost inevitable differences existed between the perceptions of different High Court judges, Recorders, and Chairmen of Quarter Sessions, as to the relative gravity of different offences carrying similar punishment maxima. Differences could also be expected in relation to the perceived function of punishment: just what the appropriate emphases or weighting should be between deterrence, retribution, and reform.[9]

Although public concern over idiosyncratic sentencing practices only became troublingly insistent from the 1870s, earlier recorded examples surfaced from time to time. For instance, in 1843, reviewing the Criminal Law Commissioners' Seventh Report for the *Law Magazine*, John Pitt Taylor acidly characterized the sentencing practices of Gurney B. and Maule J. as manifestly 'form[ing] distinct codes of criminal jurisprudence'.[10] In much the same vein, *The Times* regularly felt compelled to comment on blatant sentencing disparities.[11] Furthermore, what was regarded as mischievous leniency attracted at least as much condemnation as disproportionate severity, especially the alleged inclination of judges to value property more highly than the person.[12] In respect of theft, numerically the most significant group of offences, following the 1833 legislation removing residual capital provisions, the available punishments ranged from whipping or a fine to 14 years' transportation. Even allowing for variations in defendants' antecedents, manifest sentencing disparities remained commonplace, especially up to the mid-1850s when transportation effectively ended. After this there long

---

[9] At the Old Bailey where several judges operated in close proximity, sentencing contrasts could be particularly vivid, see XI, Pt 3.

[10] ('JPT') Probably John Pitt Taylor, 'The Seventh Criminal Law Report' (1843) 30 *LM* 1, 46. The *Law Times* was also a steady critic of patent variations in sentencing, e.g. (1844) 2 *LT* 485 and 3 *LT* 24.

[11] e.g. 24 August 1846, p. 4; 2 December 1862, p. 8.

[12] William Reade 'Punishment of Crimes of Violence' (1867) 23 *LM* 95. The Criminal Law Commissioners expressed marked concern over the position at Quarter Sessions where most felonies were tried. They regarded Quarter Sessions ('fluctuating bodies') as especially in need of 'particular and distinct rules': *Seventh Report*, 99–100. Somewhat more pungently, magistrates were described as a 'fluctuating and irresponsible body of men, who grow turnips, preserve pheasants and have stacks of corn and flocks of sheep of their own', Anon, 'Crimes and Criminals' (1849) 42 *LM* 13.

continued to be an abundance of Assize and Quarter Sessions judges who felt obliged to impose substantial custodial sentences for relatively trivial instances of theft. However, the steady relegation of different forms and values of larceny offences to summary status drove down punishment levels of the overwhelming majority of thefts to a fine or short-term custody.[13]

Political concern carrying sufficient potential to effect changes in sentencing practice, whilst occasionally registered in the 1860s and 1870s, found its most forceful expression in 1883 with Harcourt's Commons description of sentencing disparities as 'one of the great scandals of our criminal jurisprudence'. The year before as Home Secretary, Harcourt had suggested that 'too often…a man's sentence…depend[ed] very much on the accident of the Judge before whom he was tried'. As a remedy for this 'scandal' he proposed more extensive judicial consultation.[14] Additionally, Sir Edmund Du Cane had in 1883, published a critique of sentencing practices in the *Fortnightly Review*, censuring what he regarded as wild sentencing variations amongst different courts.

Du Cane followed up this public expression of dissatisfaction by lobbying Harcourt for an 'authoritative investigation of the subject'.[15] Consultation with Lord Chancellor Selborne led Harcourt to draft a memorandum circulated amongst the judges noting extreme variations in sentencing practices, and indicating an objective of greater 'harmony and unity' in sentencing. This was to be achieved through the Home Office, in consultation with the judiciary, establishing 'general rules' of sentencing. Further prodding from Harcourt resulted in Lord Coleridge CJ convening a meeting of judges in 1885. While unanimously assenting to the proposition that judicial consultation might assist in preventing sentencing disparities, the judges expressly rejected any notion of fettering their discretion. It was a response most publicly and emphatically reiterated by (the then) Stephen J. in the columns of *Nineteenth Century*.[16]

---

[13] Gatrell, 'Decline in Theft and Violence', table B3, 370. But for detailed illustrations of the effects of recidivism on sentence for low level criminality, see Emsley, *Crime and Society in England* table 10.6, 282–3. In respect of sentencing for woundings, Gatrell, table B1, 368 suggests a judicial culture of relative leniency for non-fatal offences against the person. See also the contrasting practices of contemporary Old Bailey judges recorded in the *OBSP* 1835–1914.

[14] *PD* 1883 (s. 3), 277: 1227, and 1882 (s. 3), 267: 431–2. A view also expressed in private correspondence, where Harcourt refers to the 'experience which convinces me every day of the fallability of the sentences of Judges and…of Juries…': A. G. Gardiner, *The Life of Sir William Harcourt* (1923), 400.

[15] Sir E. Du Cane, 'The Duration of Penal Sentences' (1883) 39 *Fortnightly Review* 856. Du Cane also wrote directly to Lord Chief Justice Coleridge on sentencing matters in 1885. For Home Office engagement, see Radzinowicz and Hood, *Penal Policy*, 747–51.

[16] 'Variations in the Punishment of Crime' (1885) 17 *Nineteenth Century* 755. One of Stephen's targets was Harcourt's and Du Cane's proposal for shorter sentences on the grounds of the apparently declining crime rate and prison population. Stephen's argument was essentially, why change a successful formula? On discretion, consistent with earlier published views, Stephen claimed there

One important element fuelling discontent over sentencing was the judicial attitude towards recidivists, a problem which steadily gained prominence following the ending of transportation. In many respects, the question provided a focus for more general unease over sentencing disparities. The 1863 Royal Commission on the Penal Servitude Acts favoured punishing recidivists with increasingly heavy sentences, an approach partly reflected in the Penal Servitude Act 1864. Wider application of the principle of 'cumulative' sentencing was persistently pressed for by several individual campaigners during the 1860s and 1870s.[17] Its enthusiastic adoption by a number of Quarter Session benches eventually became the subject of parliamentary exchanges,[18] in good measure as a consequence of the public opposition to the principle by former MP, Charles Hopwood, 'The Lenient'[19] Recorder of Liverpool. Hopwood maintained that long sentences of penal servitude imposed as a consequence of cumulative calculation were not merely unjust for punishing past criminality, but also that they were less effective than shorter sentences in preventing recidivism. His claims attracted both support and criticism in the Commons[20] and, most significantly, in 1890 in the Lords, with Lord Coleridge expressing scepticism over the practice of cumulative sentencing.[21] Though Lord Halsbury, LC accepted the evident need for

was an exaggerated level of disparity, frequent informal judicial discussions on sentencing, and the existence of relatively clear tacit norms of sentencing. He argued that the infinite range of circumstances of each offence and offender rendered impossible anything more than the widest guidelines; and that the rigidity of detailed rules would lead to greater sentencing injustice: *HCL*, ii, 90. Cf. the younger Stephen's keenness on a more structured sentencing regime: 'The Punishment of Convicts' (1863) 8 *Cornhill Mag.* 189.

[17] Particularly Barwick Baker, reformer and magistrate, *War with Crime* (H. Philips and G. Verney (eds), 1889); Sergeant Cox (1869) 46 *LT* 404 and 493; *The Principles of Punishment* (1877) in which judicial sentencing conferences were proposed (xix); also D. A. Thomas, *Constraints on Judgment*, 13–16; and below, 'Punishment' Ch. V.

[18] e.g. '[I]t is rather at Quarter Sessions than at Assizes that the habit of passing very considerable terms of penal servitude after previous convictions is followed': Lord Herschell, *PD* 1890 (s. 3), 343: 928.

[19] For this contemporary sobriquet, see H. Jager *Brief Life* (Liverpool, 1934), 156.

[20] *PD* 1889 (s. 3), 336: 1003–56. The debate was on a motion for the appointment of a Royal Commission on achieving 'greater equality of sentences' and a 'more systematic punishment of repeated offences'. Opposing the motion, Home Secretary Matthews defended the existing system, principally on the basis of a believed substantial decline in serious offences (1026–9).

[21] *PD* 1890 (s. 3), 343: 942–5. When sentencing 'I am compelled to inflict [punishment] for the particular offence for which the prisoner is being tried...I am perhaps an offender in disregarding repeated convictions [for] what I should call peccadilloes rather than serious crimes' (943). Lord Halsbury LC indicated the matter warranted 'finding some mode of fixing a standard or principle...' (942). Lord Herschell, later Lord Chancellor, was the mover of the Lords' motion for the appointment of a Royal Commission on sentencing. Lord Coleridge is reported as observing when on Assize, that his view on cumulative sentencing was gradually being accepted (1890) 90 *LT* 123. Government criminal statistics for the period 1894–1900, (tables II and IV) suggest that cumulative sentencing for recidivist petty offenders declined during this period. For the mixed

clarification, it was eventually his successor as Lord Chancellor, Lord Herschell, who in 1892 invited the Lord Chief Justice and the Council of Judges to review perceived sentencing inequalities. On this occasion the judges' response was both rapid and radically different from previously recorded views. Doubtless conscious of persistent and steadily building political concerns, not only did the Council accept the existence of a 'great diversity' in sentencing practices, it proposed the establishment of a court empowered to examine and change sentences.[22]

Machinery for Review

While such a court had the clear potential to influence and produce less variable sentencing practices, no legislative action followed. In part, at least, this was probably a consequence of the aim of many to ensure that sentencing disparities were dealt with directly by the judiciary through establishing agreed sentencing principles or even a tariff. Considerable influence might also have been anticipated from the long-standing, broader, campaign to set up a Court of Criminal Appeal (see below), whose powers would include review of not just sentences but convictions.[23] However, in 1901, before the Court of Criminal Appeal became a reality, the Lord Chief Justice, a staunch opponent of its creation, took the tactical initiative. Lord Alverstone with a Committee of Queen's Bench judges, whilst denying widespread sentencing disparities, constructed a set of 'normal punishments' for a core group of offences against person and property which also attempted to distinguish between types of offenders, including recidivists who were to expect heavier sentences. Though marking a distinct shift of judicial principle, in practical terms the guidelines had a negligible impact because they were not circulated to Quarter Sessions, where the overwhelming majority of indictable offences were tried and where sentencing disparities were most notorious. In all likelihood, this curious lack of wider dissemination probably stemmed from Home Office dissatisfaction with what it regarded as a lack of severity manifested in the guidelines covering offences against the person and categories of recidivists.[24]

press response to Hopwood's campaign, see Radzinowicz and Hood, *Penal Policy*, 747 n; also M. Crackenthorpe, 'New Ways with Old Offenders' (1893) 34 *Nineteenth Century* 614.

[22] *Return of Report of the Judges in 1892 to the Lord Chancellor recommending the constitution of a Court of Appeal and Revision of Sentences in Criminal Cases, PP* 1894 (127), lxxi. See particularly the critique of Crackenthorpe, 'New Ways' and also the extensive range of contemporary and subsequent comment cited by Radzinowicz and Hood, *Penal Policy*, 754–5.

[23] An informed and persistent public advocate of judicially agreed sentencing standards was Montague Crackenthorpe, e.g. 'Can Sentences be Standardised?' (1890) 47 *Nineteenth Century* 103.

[24] Moreover, senior Home Office officials were then inclined towards indeterminate sentencing for professional recidivists, seen as a solution to criticisms of variations in sentencing practices

Established principally for reasons other than the harmonization of sentencing, the Criminal Appeal Act 1907 nevertheless incorporated provisions for the review of sentences, leading to their possible increase or reduction. Despite giving early indications of its intention to 'standardize sentences', in its initial years, the Court of Criminal Appeal exhibited decided reluctance to interfere with their type or length, or to offer sentencing principles. The new Court was led by Lord Alverstone CJ, who had energetically resisted its creation, including its proposed powers of sentence review (see below). Formulation of review principles and emergent features of a tariff began appearing by 1912. In good measure these eventual moves were necessitated by earlier preventive detention legislation,[25] and probably also, in part, by Churchill's constant agitation and intervention as Home Secretary (between 1910 and 1912) in the cause of what he regarded as sentencing justice. Appearing to have enthusiastically accepted advice to 'keep an eye on the sentences passed by fat headed people and reduce them fearlessly whether they emanate from the Ermine or only the great unpaid', Churchill liberally deployed the royal prerogative in an attempt to educate the judiciary in standards of sentencing.[26]

By 1914, two fundamental features of sentencing and punishment had undergone overwhelming change over the preceding century: the overall severity of punishment had radically diminished, and the vast range of sentencing discretion enjoyed by the courts had been both substantially eroded and enlarged on several different fronts. Discretion shrank through the intervention practised by increasingly experienced senior Home Office officials;[27] a feature which would become more pronounced with the progression of the twentieth century, as would the role of the Court of Criminal Appeal in setting sentencing standards. In the other direction, the range of types of sentences underwent expansion, offering courts a greater level of sentencing refinement in matching punishments and offenders.

2. APPEALS AND EXECUTIVE REVIEW

The Desire for Swift, Certain and Final Justice

In the early nineteenth century, the opportunities for judicial review of a conviction were, both in legal and practical terms, decidedly limited. This position

---

for recidivists. For an analysis of internal Home Office memoranda and judges guidelines, see Radzinowicz and Hood, *Penal Policy*, 757–8 and R. S. de Vere, 'Discretion in Penalties' (1911) 27 *LQR* 317.

[25] H. Cohen (1918) *Quart. Rev.* 342; Thomas, *Constraints on Judgment*, 91–4.

[26] Quoted by Radzinowicz and Hood, 770–5.

[27] See 'Punishment', Ch. V below.

changed only marginally prior to establishment of the Court of Criminal Appeal in 1907.[28] Before this three routes by which a convicted person might challenge a verdict were notionally open. First, through the writ of error a defendant might challenge a conviction by jury trial on the narrow technical ground of an error apparent on the face of the record.[29] Its value was particularly limited by the procedure's inability to scrutinize key areas of likely judicial error, including treatment of evidence, direction, and summing up. Moreover, without access to a lawyer, the procedure was a wholly unrealistic prospect for any defendant. Motions for a new trial were a second, even more limited, remedy in that they applied only to convictions for misdemeanours tried in the King's Bench.[30] Reserving a point of law was a third possibility. Depending entirely on the trial judge's inclination, the procedure for reserving a point of law for the collective consideration of the criminal law judges was (despite modifications) a creaking relic of a bygone age of almost total professional autonomy and practical lack of accountability.

As much as occasionally determining a convicted individual's fate, or a change of doctrinal direction, the old practice of reserving cases also served as a training ground and 'post-prandial' entertainment for members of the Bar and Bench. Besides resting purely on a trial judge's discretion, the process of reserving a point of law suffered from other deficiencies, including the secrecy of its proceedings, the frequent absence of reasons for judgments, the exclusion of Quarter Sessions, and the practical need for legal representation. Furthermore, the absence of any power to order a new trial would necessarily result in a successful applicant being given a complete pardon, however strong the prosecution evidence might have been.[31] Indeed, the procedural defects involved in reserving cases was the one

[28] For a detailed table of attempts to enact criminal appeals legislation since 1844, see H. Cohen, *The Criminal Appeal Act 1907* (1908), App. A.

[29] Stephen, *HCL* i, 214 and 312; Chitty, *Criminal Law* (2nd edn, 1826), i, 743. For summary trials substantial modifications were enacted during the nineteenth century, widening the avenues of appeal open to defendants. By 1879, appeals to Quarter Sessions for re-hearing of cases were permitted. See particularly the Summary Jurisdiction Acts 1848, 1857, and 1879; and R. Pattenden, *English Criminal Appeals 1844–1994* (Oxford, 1996), 211–15. However, especially because appellants were obliged to provide security for costs, few appealed.

[30] On any aspect of the merits of the case to 'further the ends of justice'. However, if an aspect of the trial was so irregular as to amount to a 'mis-trial', a 'new' trial could be granted by any Assize or Quarter Sessions. Chitty, *ibid.*, 652. The limitation to misdemeanours may have derived from the more general aversion to second trials and principles of double jeopardy: P. Devlin, *Trial by Jury* (1966), 75–8.

[31] See the critical evidence of Lord Denman CJ and Parke B. in the House of Lords SC Report, *PP* 1847–8 (523) xvi, 423; and C. S. Greaves, 'The Bill to Provide an Appeal in Criminal Cases' (1845) *LM* 129. Denman favoured removing from the trial judge control over the reserving of cases. The Select Committee evidence suggested that it was the practice for Chairmen of County Quarter Sessions to occasionally informally consult local Assize judges on points of law. More generally

area where defenders of the status quo and its more severe critics occupied some limited common ground. As a consequence, restricted, though *potentially* useful, revisions of the process were, on Lord Campbell's initiative, enacted in 1848. Henceforth, under the Crown Cases Reserved Act, the newly constituted Court for Crown Cases Reserved (composed of at least five judges) would sit in public, hear reserved points of law, including those from Quarter Sessions, and provide reasons for its judgments.[32]

However, the bulk of the legal establishment was implacably resistant to the central reformist objective of providing a considerably more effective system for challenging convictions on questions of fact and allowing new trials. The case for wider reform to remedy 'great injustice' had been advanced three years before the 1848 Crown Cases Reserved Act by the Criminal Law Commissioners. They were in no doubt that 'cases not unfrequently [sic] occur when the convict is either altogether innocent, or not guilty of the aggravated offence charged'.[33] On more than one occasion *The Times* leader writers advocated broader rights of appeal.[34] In 1848, three leading advocates of change, Fitzroy Kelly, Greaves, and Pitt Taylor, made full use of the opportunity to present their case to a House of Lords' Select Committee. Greaves and Kelly favoured an 'absolute and unconditional Right to every Prisoner...to appeal...Upon Facts and Law'. Appeal on mistakes of fact was especially crucial because they 'more frequently took place [and] generally go to the entire Guilt or Innocence of the Prisoner'. The proposed solution would be to put criminal defendants on the same footing as those in civil courts by providing the right of appeal for a new trial.[35]

on reserve cases procedure 1757–1828, see Bentley (ed.), *Select Cases from the Twelve Judges' Notebooks*.

[32] Crown Cases Reserved Act 1848, 11 & 12 Vict. c. 78. The Act required that at least one of the five judges was a Chief of one of the three common law courts. Over the 60 years of its existence the Court for Crown Cases Reserved annual number of hearings varied between the mid-30s and under 10. Quarter Sessions cases made up a substantial proportion of these, and largely accounted for the rise in hearings after 1848. Bentley, *Select Cases*, App. 3(b). See the critical comments in (1895) 100 *LT* 29. Stephen's early 1880s' estimate was fewer than 20 cases a year: *HCL*, i, 312.

[33] *Eighth Report* (1845), 20. The 'zealous exertions' of the Home Secretary was 'the subject of popular jealousy or suspicion'. Moreover, it was inaccessible to many without means (p. 22).

[34] e.g. 16 September and 13 November 1847, p. 4.

[35] Greaves, *Report*, 13–17; Kelly, 26–8; Pitt Taylor, 37–8. Unlike the former, Pitt Taylor did not support an absolute right of appeal on facts. Greaves in particular was subject to an extremely lengthy, detailed, and generally searching examination of his position by the Committee's Chairman, Lord Campbell. An appeals sceptic, Campbell scored some telling points on the impractical aspects of Greaves' proposals. On Kelly's bill (prepared by Greaves) see *PD* 1844 (s. 3), 75: 11. The *Law Times* frequently urged a full right of appeal on questions of fact, e.g. (1844) 2, 276; (1847) 10, 40 and 173; (1848) 11, 339. Stephen argued strongly against the analogous case of new trials for criminal as well as civil cases: *General View* (1863) 226–9. He concluded that it would 'extend too far the litigious theory of criminal justice, which already exercises quite influence enough on our law' (229).

Opposition to this and other changes beyond those of the 1848 Act was buttressed by a phalanx of legal luminaries more often associated with reform, including Brougham, Campbell, and Denman. They, and more predictably, the judiciary, even doubted whether wrong convictions were more than a 'very rare' occurrence. In any event, several weighty practical and conceptual objections were anticipated. Giving an unrestricted right of appeal would swamp the existing judiciary and require a swelling of their ranks at considerable public expense. Moreover, as the majority of likely appellants were impecunious, how other than at public expense would the professional costs of an appeal be funded? Additionally, individual prosecutors already facing the aggravation and cost of the initial prosecution would have the further disincentive of potential appeals and their consequent expense and disruption. For proposed new trials these problems were compounded by the inherent difficulties of locating prosecution and defence witnesses once more, along with the inevitable problem of stale or imperfectly recalled evidence. Finally, it was argued that the widely accepted belief in the deterrent power of swift and sure justice would be undermined by protracted appeals procedures and re-trials.[36] With varying emphases, these contentions formed the basis of the successful anti-reformist stance until the early twentieth century and the setting up of the Court of Criminal Appeal.

The Prop of Executive Review

Beside such objections, the key supposition responsible for the longevity of the largely unreformed appeals system was the adequate functioning of executive review. Acting as an appellate longstop for those 'few' cases of wrongful conviction, the Home Secretary might recommend a pardon or commutation of sentence. Depending largely on the initiative of the defendant or his friends, or occasionally that of the trial judge (who was routinely consulted), the system governing the Home Secretary's exercise of the royal prerogative became less haphazard and variable as the nineteenth century advanced; investigative procedures followed by Home Office officials and conventions governing the exercise of discretion steadily became formalized.[37] This was apparent from the very close and searching questioning of the Home Secretary, Spencer Walpole, by

[36] *House of Lords Report, SC Report,* PP 1847–8 (523) xvi, 423. Brougham (p. 49), Wightman J. (p. 53), Parke B. (pp. 3–9), Alderson B. (p. 9), Denman (pp. 44–6).

[37] Sir William Harcourt, *PD* 1883 (s. 3), 277: 1223; Chadwick, *Bureaucratic Mercy, passim*; S. Devereaux, 'The Criminal Branch of the Home Office 1782–1830', in G. Smith, May, and Devereaux (eds) *Criminal Justice in the Old World and the New* 270.

the 1866 Royal Commissioners on Capital Punishment.[38] Moreover, at this time the absence of a full criminal appellate system was exercising *The Times* leader writers, who regarded resort to the Home Secretary as no more than a 'clumsy expedient' for cases manifesting the 'grossest misinterpretation of evidence, or the most palpable prejudice on the part of either judge or jury...'.[39] Yet, overall, the system enjoyed broad and, sometimes, enthusiastic support. As Walpole glowingly related, although the Home Secretary did 'not in the least degree rehear cases...justice is most perfectly administered there'. A hardly less generous commendation came from Sir John Walton. In his 1898 (pre-Beck Inquiry, below) comparison with an appeal court, he regarded the Home Office procedure as 'infinitely more elastic, more subtle and efficient in its administration and infinitely more in the interests of the accused person'.[40] But a few years after, it was he, who as Liberal Attorney-General, was charged with piloting the 1907 Court of Criminal Appeal bill through the Commons.

Indeed, identification of the allegedly manifest shortcomings of executive intervention was almost a prerequisite of support for an improved judicial system of correcting miscarriages of justice. Greaves, for one, offered a powerful public critique of the Home Secretary's role on several occasions, including his Select Committee evidence in 1848, and his 1856 Report on Criminal Procedure to the Lord Chancellor. In the latter, he described Executive review as a 'system...such as cannot fail to lead to mischievous results': new evidence was not tested; the often inadequate investigation was private; no notice of review was given to the prosecution; and no reasons were given for any consequent action. At the very least, Greaves maintained, the Home Secretary needed greater investigative powers, coupled with the ability to order a new trial when the original verdict was, or became, subject to doubt.[41] Though against new trials and not consistently favouring full-blown judicial review, Stephen was also another severe critic of the existing system of executive appeal: the procedure was 'strange and unsatisfactory in the extreme...The mode of administration is wrong, because under it a function which is really judicial is discharged by an irregular, irresponsible and secret tribunal, consisting of a single statesman who has no special acquaintance with law and no judicial experience, who can neither examine witnesses nor

---

[38] *RC on Capital Punishment*, Report *PP* 1866, (3590), xxi, pp. 66–73. And Stephen's critical description of the procedure in 1863, *General View*, 224–31. Of all the witnesses who gave an opinion on appeals, only Fitzroy Kelly supported a new Court of Criminal Appeal.

[39] *The Times*, 5 September 1866, p. 7; and on 'executive mercy' 31 October 1862, p. 6.

[40] *PD* 1898 (s. 4), 55: 47. At the time, the Home Office was considering the benefits of giving Home Secretaries the power to order a new trial as an alternative to pardoning: *Home Office Printed Memoranda and Reports*, N.A. H.O. 347/16, 129–31.

[41] *PP* 1856 (456) i, pp. 51–2; 1848 SC (Lords), *ibid.*, p. 15.

administer oaths...'.[42] Stephen's 'true remedy' in 1863 was a hybrid 'court of law, charged with the duty of doing openly and judicially what the Home Secretary does in secret'. It would comprise the Home Secretary, the trial judge, and one other judge, with power to hear any witness, including the defendant. However, for some, the core objection to this was most cogently and memorably later articulated by Lord Penzance:

[B]ad as this system is in practice, it is equally vicious in theory. [Justice] should be done in the name of justice, not in the name of mercy. Mercy begins where justice ends; and this is a system of eking out imperfect justice by irregular mercy.[43]

Indirect and candid confirmation of this claim came a few years later from Harcourt during his term as Home Secretary: 'The fact is that the exercise of the prerogative does not depend on principles of strict law and justice. Still less does it depend on sentiment in any way. It is really a question of policy and judgment.'[44]

Yet throughout the century whatever defects and inadequacies in Executive review might be identified, they were politically and professionally easier to stomach than the proposed alternative of a fully empowered Court of Criminal Appeal. Over the course of the second half of the nineteenth century, successive, largely private members' bills, incorporating various procedural permutations for the establishment of a judicial appeal on questions of fact, met the same fate on essentially the same grounds as raised in the 1840s.[45] Legislative endeavour came closest to success with the 1879 Criminal Code bill. The signs were propitious: this was a government bill the provisions of which had been fashioned by a panel (latterly) made up of judges. The powers of the proposed Court of Criminal Appeal met most reformers' requirements: to order a new trial; to hear appeals from a trial judge's refusal to reserve a point of law; and a right for trial judges to order a new trial where the jury's verdict was against the weight of evidence. Additionally, the Home Secretary would be empowered to require a new trial where, on the basis of fresh evidence, doubt existed as to a conviction's soundness.[46] Though lost, along with the Code generally, the episode revealed

---

[42] *General View*, 225 and 230. Cf. (1877) 2 *Nineteenth Century* 736, 758, and *HCL* i, 313. For Stephen's shifting views on the advisability on a Court of Criminal Appeal, see Smith, *James Fitzjames Stephen*, 96, and below. Similarly, Bramwell B., an opponent of appeals on facts, *Report of Royal Commission on Capital Punishment*, Evidence, 34.

[43] *PD* 1870 (s. 3) 200: 1150. On the entirely secret nature of the proceedings: *Home Office Printed Memoranda and Reports*, N.A. H.O. 347/22, 765, 1 October 1905.

[44] *PD* 1885 (s. 3), 294: 1156.

[45] For an account of the attempted legislation, see Pattenden, *op cit.*, 6–16.

[46] The conduct of the Home Office in dealing with petitions in the previous year had generated public criticism: B. Moseley, 'The New Criminal Code' (1878) 4 *LM* 55.

that a number of senior judges had been persuaded of the merits of revamping appeal powers and procedures.[47] But changes in the Commons and on the Bench long ensured that further efforts to revive appellate reforms met with a fatal combination of indifference and positive hostility.

Political Expediency and Establishing the Court of Criminal Appeal

Eventual establishment of the Court of Criminal Appeal was substantially the product of political default. Defenders of the status quo were spectacularly denied their fall-back claim of a tolerably effective system of Executive review by the Beck affair. Whilst generously spared the Committee of Inquiry's outright censure, Home Office procedures for review of petitions were exposed as unreliable, in large part due to ill-trained lower level officials.[48] In a climate of public outrage and political recriminations generated by Beck and other cases,[49] the Committee's recommendations for improvement of staff training and procedures had practically no chance of shoring up the Home Office's sagging credibility.[50] Reflecting on the strength of this widespread scepticism, *The Times* found 'truly alarming'

---

[47] While objecting to many aspects of the 1879 Code, Lord Cockburn CJ was uncritical of the appeals provisions. Both his successor, Lord Coleridge, and Lord Esher MR, fully endorsed similar proposals in 1883: (1883) 75 *LT* 107. Predictably, Lord Bramwell opposed such a reform on the grounds of appeals or 'second trials' undermining the responsibility of juries and diminishing the deterrence power of speedy, unchallengeable (on fact) convictions: 'Criminal Appeals' (1883) *The Economist* 395 (attrib. C. Fairfield, *A Memoir of Lord Bramwell* (1898)). After elevation to the Bench, Stephen's principal objection was that a Court of Criminal Appeal would add a further tier to the judicial proceedings, making an appeal almost an expectation: *General View* (2nd edn, 1890), 174–5. By 1892, the Council of Judges favoured limiting appeals on facts to referrals by the Home Secretary. The Council also supported establishment of an appeal court with powers to quash convictions where further exculpatory evidence came to light: *Return of Report of the Judges in 1892 to the Lord Chancellor*, *PP* 1894 (127), 71 179; and similarly (1895) 30 *LJ* 333.

[48] 'Report of the Committee of Inquiry into the Case of Mr Adolf Beck', *PP* 1905 [Cd. 2315]. With one of history's incidental ironies, Sir Spencer Walpole, a member of the Beck Committee, participated in the exposure of the inadequacies of procedures once eulogized by his father (above). The Beck saga began in 1896 at Beck's Old Bailey trial for several frauds, where the Common Serjeant erroneously ruled certain evidence inadmissible; evidence which would have proved the case to be one of mistaken identity. The trial judge refused to reserve the point of law. Three years after Beck's release, in 1904 he was again convicted, once more based on mistaken identity evidence. The arrest of the actual fraudster, who had committed the earlier and later offences, along with the exemplary tenacity of Detective Inspector Kane, unearthed a catalogue of Home Office errors. For his trouble, Beck was rewarded with two pardons and £5000.

[49] Particularly the case of Birmingham solicitor George Edalji, a cause taken up by Sir Arthur Conan Doyle, which resulted in an inquiry in 1907 and eventual pardon of Edalji, *PP* 1907 [Cd. 3503]. Also the Staunton case, H. L. Adam, *The Penge Mystery, the Story of the Stauntons* (1913).

[50] By 1905 the Home Office was receiving around 5000 petitions annually [Cd. 2315], App. 60. Beyond criticism by the general press, see (1904) 118 *LT* 100, 182, 1207, 316 and 346; and (1904) 30 *LM*. 399, demolishing Sir Godfrey Lushington's post-Beck Inquiry defence of the Home Office.

the ease with which a 'large number of well-meaning persons...take for granted [the] innocence of everyone convicted'. Characterizing the Home Secretary's situation as now 'almost unbearable', with public opinion regarding miscarriages of justice as practically an 'everyday occurrence', Herbert Gladstone capitulated to public and political clamour for the setting up of a Court of Criminal Appeal empowered to take appeals on fact, law, and sentence.[51]

Yet the political demands of the moment by no means cooled the oppositional ardour of many, including most importantly Lord Alverstone CJ, who (in tandem with Lord Halsbury), tenaciously fought the proposed government legislation through the House of Lords.[52] The Lord Chief Justice's opposition focused on appeals on questions of fact. In a politically astute manoeuvre, he and Halsbury swiftly acted on the 1905 Beck Committee recommendation to remove a trial judge's discretion to prevent the reserving of a point of law. Successfully passing through the House of Lords, the Alverstone bill also gave the Court for Crown Cases Reserved power to order a re-trial or allow a conviction to stand if the court believed 'no miscarriage of justice' had occurred. And seeking to bolster his position, the Lord Chief Justice had assured their Lordships that the provision had been 'most carefully considered by the Judges of the King's Bench'.[53] But

---

[51] *The Times*, 30 July 1907; *PD* 1907 (s. 4), 175: 193. Gladstone refers to trial by 'less responsible papers where the "case for the accused" is set forth with every kind of literary and editorial garnishing' (194). The Attorney-General did not mince his words, conceding that no 'jurist' could any longer regard the Home Office as 'correspond[ing] in any satisfactory degree to a tribunal of criminal appeal' (227). For the Commons Debate on the Beck Inquiry, see *PD* 1905 (s. 4) 143: 679–704, 1039–52.

[52] The government's first bill was introduced by Lord Chancellor Loreburn, *PD* 1906 (s. 4), 154: 992. One of Lord Loreburn's supporting arguments was the lack of criticism by 'Bar or Bench' of the 'revision of trials' for misdemeanours via the Certiorari procedure (996). Though passing the Lords, it was withdrawn before its second Commons reading for further amendment. In Lord Alverstone's speech and arguments, *PD* 1906 (s. 4), 157: 1078, he disputed the civil law analogy, citing the unique pre-trial filters of magistrates and grand juries; knowing they could be overturned, it would lessen a jury's sense of responsibility (1079–80); evidence by deposition and transcript was less easy to judge than fresh oral testimony (1081); costs would limit appeals to the well off (1082); the certainty and finality of jury verdicts regularly arrived at would be fundamentally undermined (1086). On this see Bingham J.'s public protest at the proposed criminal appeal legislation, *The Times*, 20 April 1906; and, subsequently, Sir Harry Poland's introduction to H. Cohen, *The Criminal Appeal Act 1907* (1908). For a reply to similar arguments in an earlier pamphlet of Poland and Cohen, see N. Sibley, 'Appeal on Matter of Fact in Criminal Cases' (1907) 32, *LM* 314. And also Lord Alverstone, *PD* 1906 (s. 4), 160: 1002–5, and 180: 246–9 and Lord Halsbury, *PD* 1907 (s. 4), 179: 1473–6; 180: 235–40, 252–3. The revised bill was pushed through the Commons in 1907. The Lords' Tory majority acquiesced in the face of the Liberal Government's clear resolve.

[53] *PD* 1905 (s. 4), 148: 640. Broadly supported by *The Times*, e.g. 24 May 1906, p. 9. In proposing the power to order new trials rather than a re-hearing, Lord Alverstone expressly aligned himself with the route adopted by the 1879 *Code Commission* (157, 1082). The Criminal Appeal Act 1907, 7 Edw. 7, c. 23, provided for the Court of Criminal Appeal to affirm, amend, or quash verdicts, and to confirm, reduce, or increase sentences. In cases of appeal on fact, the leave of the Court of Criminal Appeal

Lord Alverstone's hopes of pre-empting wider appellate reforms proved unrealistic. In the face of a new government persuaded of the merits of more radical change, and, crucially, of the political unavoidability of such, Alverstone's tactic was thwarted.

Section 9 of the 1907 Act met most reform demands by equipping the Court of Criminal Appeal with extensive investigative powers, including hearing trial witnesses, new witnesses, and specialist evidence. However, the envisaged (or at least hoped for) active engagement of the new Court in 'get[ting] at the truth'[54] was not to materialize. Broad judicial antagonism towards the 1907 legislation, coupled with instinctive adherence to the primacy and finality of jury verdicts, almost inevitably set the Court of Criminal Appeal against an investigative role that even remotely resembled a re-hearing of cases. Instead, a long-lived narrow form of appellate review of convictions rapidly became established. Appeals attacking a conviction as unreasonable were typically met with the sentiment that juries are the 'judges of fact. The Act was never meant to substitute another form of trial...'. Convictions would stand so long as there was evidence on which a jury might convict.[55] Though appeals on the grounds of new evidence were underwritten by extensive investigative powers, the court was only obliged to deploy such powers where it was 'necessary or expedient in the interests of justice'. In construing this requirement, the court, and especially Lord Alverstone, was again powerfully influenced by the desire not to re-hear cases, thereby 'substituting a trial by judges for a trial by jury'.[56] Doubtless the judiciary also regarded frequent revision of jury verdicts as likely to undermine that lauded institution's standing.

or the trial judge's certificate was required; and for appeal against sentence, leave by the Court of Criminal Appeal (s 3). The Act gave no power to order a re-trial nor for the prosecution to appeal against verdict or sentence. On calls for the power to order a retrial, see e.g. *The Times*, 30 September 1911, p. 9 and 30 August 1913, p. 3. The Act abolished the virtually moribund writ of error procedure and power of the High Court to grant a new trial for misdemeanours tried there. The powers of the Court for Crown Cases Reserved on questions of law was assigned to the new court (s 20).

[54] *PD* 1907, (s. 4), 174: 1010.

[55] *Simpson* (1909) 2 Cr App R 128, 130. Darling J. conceded that the 'case was not a strong one', also e.g. *Williamson* (1908) 1 Cr App R 3. For contemporary criticism, see H. Cohen, 'The Court of Criminal Appeal' (1918) 456 *Quart. Rev.* 342.

[56] *Colclough* (1909) 2 Cr App R 84, 85; *Mortimer* (1908) 1 Cr App R 20, 22; *Dutt* (1912) 8 Cr App R 51, 57. This sentiment is implicit in Lord Alverstone's 1914 autobiography *Recollections of Bar and Bench*: while supporting the 'further consideration of points of law which might have been raised at the trial or erroneous direction or for the reconsideration of... sentence', he was 'strongly opposed to the idea that there should be an appeal on the facts...' (270). This hostility is exposed in an unqualified fashion, with no reference to the court's powers (with leave) to hear appeals on 'a question of fact alone', or to investigate fresh evidence or review the cogency of trial evidence. Indeed, Lord Alverstone's remarks that 'Fortunately, this proposal [to appeal on facts] was dropped', come very close to a distorted account of the 1907 provisions. Alverstone's praise for the Act is reserved for

General impatience and dissatisfaction with the Court of Criminal Appeal's very cautious early years led Churchill, as Home Secretary, to make vigorous use of prerogative intervention. Indeed, his readiness to write off the customary practice of consultation with the judiciary earned him substantial parliamentary censure.[57] But at the Home Office Churchill's robustness was little more than a passing, uncomfortable, phenomenon. In the immediately subsequent decades, the Court of Criminal Appeal was left relatively undisturbed. The backbone of nineteenth-century opposition to reform had been judicial distaste for gainsaying jury verdicts on the basis of an appellate re-evaluation of evidence. Despite the transparently clear legislative objectives of the 1907 Act, in many respects this ethos endured little change into the second half of the twentieth century, eventually attracting legislative intervention aimed at ensuring judicial acceptance of a wider appellate role.[58]

sentencing: 'It has tended to render sentences much more uniform, and has caused Judges of the High Court and Chairmen of Quarter Sessions to be more careful in their summing up of the facts to the jury' (271). And similarly, later members of the Court of Criminal Appeal, e.g. Humphreys J., *Criminal Days* (1946), 53–5.

[57] Particularly *PD* 1911 (s. 5 HC), 27: 238–60.

[58] See s 1 of the Criminal Appeal Act 1964, and Pattenden, *English Criminal Appeals,* 130–51. The enormity of the change in respect of finality of jury verdicts figures prominently in Sir Harry Poland's critique of the 1907 Act. Cohen, *The Criminal Appeal Act 1907*; Poland's Introduction, 10–12. The 1907 Act, s 1(6) provided for an appeal to the House of Lords if a certificate from the Attorney-General certified that the decision of the Court of Criminal Appeal involved points of exceptional public importance and that it was desirable in the public interest that a further appeal would be brought. The new procedure was first deployed by the Crown in *Ball* (1911) AC 47 on a question of similar fact evidence law. No such power had been given under the Court for Crown Cases Reserved Act 1848. Before the 1907 Act, criminal appeals could only be taken to the House of Lords through the writ of error procedure. Used extremely rarely, it was last witnessed in the Titchborne claimant's case, *Castro v. R* (1883) 6 App Cass 229.

V

Punishment: Death and Transfiguration

1. THE CAPITAL QUESTION

Paley's 'Glorious Uncertainty'

At the opening of the nineteenth century the dominant characteristic of the institution of punishment was the considerable distance between the law's formal severity and the realities of its enforcement. The immediate consequences of the huge range of capital statutes, largely of eighteenth-century origin, were their extensive modification by the intervention of broad discretionary mitigatory practices aimed at achieving individual justice whilst retaining general deterrence. Most especially, from the early 1700s, the discretionary commutation of death sentences and substitution of lengthy periods (sometimes life) of transportation provided an important secondary punishment.[1] Thus, in 1805 instead of a grim harvest of 350 hanged felons from a strict application of the capital laws, only 68 actually suffered such a fate. Twenty years on, with rapidly climbing numbers of capital convictions, the effects of mitigatory practices reduced around 5000 sentenced to death to 360 executions.[2] This ever-widening disparity between law and practice increasingly tested the credibility of Paley's utilitarian underpinnings of the edifice of discretionary capital justice: his 'glorious uncertainty' thesis whereby great general deterrence might be achieved with the exemplary execution of relatively few, 'whilst the dread and danger hang over the crimes of many'. Moreover, under Paley's doctrine of mock heroism 'he who falls by a mistaken sentence may be considered as falling for his country'.[3] It was a growing

---

[1] On the crucial role of transportation in the development of penal practices, see Beattie, *Crime and the Courts*, Ch. 9 and below at section 2. The value of the mitigatory device of benefit of clergy was greatly reduced in the eighteenth century. Many capital statutes of the period expressly excluded its availability or confined its use. Benefit of clergy was completely abolished in 1827: Stephen, *HCL*, i, 470.

[2] Calculations by V. Gatrell, *The Hanging Tree* (Oxford, 1994), App. 2, table 2. Between 1805 and 1825 the pardoning rate had risen from just over 80% to 93%. For fluctuations in the percentage of those condemned and hanged in the late eighteenth century, see, *ibid.*, table 1.

[3] *The Principles of Moral and Political Philosophy* (1785), book vi. A cruder version of Paley's theory appears in Blackstone's successor to the Vinerian chair, Robert Chambers', *A Course of Lectures on English Law* (1767–73), ed. T.M. Curley (Oxford, 1986).

disparity that also put Paley's staunchest defenders on their mettle over the suc-ceeding two decades, during which the threat of capital punishment balanced by merciful discretion were ousted by a system contrived to produce both certain and proportional punishment, uniformly applied. As will be suggested, in broad terms these were changes driven by an increasing distaste amongst the governing and growing middle classes for corporal punishment,[4] combined with the ever imminent threat of the credibility of the Paleyite system self-destructing.

Though subject to considerable criticism in the second half of the eighteenth century,[5] the extensive body of capital crimes first came under serious parliamen-tary review between 1808 and 1818 during Romilly's campaign[6] to eliminate what were regarded by reformers as the more extravagant excesses or anachronisms amongst capital statutes. Enjoying only the most limited success, Romilly's activ-ities did, however, generate parliamentary and extra-parliamentary examination of the rationales held to by both the advocates of change and adherents of the existing system; these were arguments and counter-claims that would be regu-larly deployed over the succeeding 20 years or so.

Reformers challenged both the pragmatic and moral claims of the system: discretionary 'terror' did not deter capital crime; statistical and empirical data demonstrated a decline in executions and rise in the level of capital crime;[7] wild

---

[4] For the lead up to the extinction of the use of the pillory in 1837 (7 Wil. 4 and 1 Vict. c. 23) and decline in the use of public whippings, see R. Shoemaker, 'Streets of Shame? The Crowd and Public Punishments in London 1700–1820', in S. Devereaux and P. Griffiths (eds), *Penal Practice and Culture 1500–1900 Punishing the English* (2004), 232. On the practice and reform of corporal punishment (including flogging) in the nineteenth century, see Radzinowicz and Hood, *Penal Policy*, Ch. 21. For an early twentieth-century account of the nature and practice of flogging, see C. Whiteley (Common Serjeant at the Central Criminal Court) *Brief Life* (1942), 145–87. While the pillory was abolished in 1837, use of local stocks for punishing low level offenders and vagrants continued beyond mid-century: B. Davey, *Lawless and Immoral: Policing a Country Town 1837–57* (Leicester, 1983). More generally on early nineteenth-century society's rising intolerance of violence, see 'Offences against the Person', Ch. XII, below.

[5] Most prominently W. Eden, *Principles of Penal Law* (1771), Blackstone, *Comms*, iv (1765–9), 17–19; Romilly, *Observations on a Late Publication Entitled Thoughts on Executive Justice* (1786); Bentham, *Introduction to the Principles of Morals and Legislation* (1789). For parliamentary disputes over the enactment of capital statutes, see J. Innes and J. Styles, 'The Crime Wave: Recent Writing on Crime and Criminal Justice in Eighteenth Century England' (1986) 25 *J. of British Studies* 380; and more generally in the eighteenth century, Beattie, *Crime and the Courts*, 513–39, 582–92. New capital offences were still being enacted in the early nineteenth century, e.g. Lord Ellenborough's Act 1803 43 Geo. III, c. 58 for certain aggravated woundings.

[6] For a detailed account of Romilly's parliamentary performances and generally favourable press reception, see Radzinowicz, *History* i: 322–35 and Ch. 16.

[7] From their initial publication in 1810, official statistics on the incidence of criminal committals dating back to 1805 were enlisted in controversies over most aspects of criminal justice, including the efficacy of the threat of capital punishment, and the necessity of professional policing; they were used by both advocates of reform and defenders of the status quo. The inherent shortcomings of statistical evidence on the levels and nature of criminal activity were of secondary importance when

variations in judicial practice[8] suggested chance to be a principal determinant of ultimate punishment; the law's severity often made prosecutors reluctant to pursue capital charges and frequently inhibited jurors from strictly carrying out their duties, such as to constitute a 'universal confederacy amongst the middling classes not to punish [many] offences by death'.[9] Furthermore, harsh and inhumane penal law brutalized a nation and demoralized society, imbuing it with a greater tolerance of violence and disorder.[10] In essence, the law's severity allegedly inhibited and corrupted the process of prosecution, required a high level of discretionary mitigation, which both lowered deterrence and generated a destabilizing and corrosive perception of injustice suffered by those individuals ultimately selected for execution. Remedying this state of ineffective deterrence, coupled with endemic injustice, demanded a penal regime where certainty of punishment prevailed over severity; a system enforced by a 'vigilant and enlightened police, rational rules of evidence, and clear and unambiguous laws'.[11]

To the extent that it aimed at removing the worst excesses of capital legislation, the reformist critique was accepted by a majority of the House of Commons between 1808 and 1818, though, as Thomas Denman later noted, Romilly's 'projects were still assaulted by the whole tribe of ministerial lawyers..., from the Lord High Chancellor down to the meanest candidate for a Welsh judgeship'.[12] Effective defence of the existing system fell to the Lords, frequently under the formidable dual leadership of Lord Ellenborough CJ[13] and Lord Chancellor Eldon,

considering their role in fashioning social and political perceptions of the efficiency of the criminal justice system: rather than accuracy, what statistics were believed to establish by contemporary observers was the formative force in influencing penal policies. Up to the early 1840s, Government statistics were seen as demonstrating an apparently inexorable rise in committals, reinforcing the common belief that the 'progress of wickedness is so much more rapid than the increase of the numbers of the people', A. Alison (1844) 56 *Blackwood's Edin. Mag.* 1. R. Jackson, *Considerations on the Increase of Crime* (1828) and 'The Growth of Crime' (1844) 1 *LM* 117. But cf. e.g. the more sanguine 'Moral Economy of Large Towns' (1839) 6 *Bentley's Misc.* 476. Generally, V. Gatrell 'The Decline of Theft and Violence in Victorian and Edwardian England', in V. Gatrell et al. (eds), *Crime and the Law* (1980), 238. On the problematic use of criminal statistics, see citations in 'Policing', Ch. II above and Radzinowicz and Hood, *Penal Policy*, Ch. 4.

[8] King, *Crime, Justice and Discretion*, Ch. 9; Beattie, *Crime and the Courts*, Ch. 8.

[9] Sir William Grant, MR, *PD* 1811 (s. 1) 19: App. lxvii. See Holdsworth, *HEL* vol. 13, 656 for Grant's interesting career profile.

[10] e.g. Romilly: the effect of the spectacle of capital punishments is to 'torture the compassionate and to harden the obdurate', *PD* 1814 (s. 1), 28: 138 and W. Wilberforce, *PD* 1819 (s. 1), 39: 808.

[11] Romilly, *PD* 1812 (s. 1), 21: 198–202. For the ambivalent attitude of Romilly and other penal reformers to establishing a professional police force see 'Policing' above.

[12] (1824) 40 *Edin. Rev.* 169, 182.

[13] Denman implies that Ellenborough's actions were unconstitutional: 'Lord Ellenborough... favoured the House of Lords, for the first time, with an unasked opinion respecting a matter, not of law, but of legislation, declaring against any abridgement of the [judges'] own powers of life and death'. *Ibid.*

both conservative lawyer–politicians of the deepest dye. Romilly's extremely limited legislative success was achieved only with their Lordships' concurrence.[14] On most occasions Ellenborough gave the shortest of shrift to 'that speculative and modern philosophy which would overturn the laws that a century had proved to be necessary—on the illusory opinions of speculatists', such as Romilly.[15] The Lord Chief Justice's fervent attachment to Paley's doctrine of prevention of crime through selective terror was personal as well as intellectual, for the widely venerated cleric and moral philosopher had been both Ellenborough's friend and his father's chaplain. Reported to have declared that 'Paley formed my character', Ellenborough had at one time 'corrected for Paley the proof-sheets of some of his works as they were passing through the press'.[16] At the core of Lord Ellenborough's opposition to change was his unbending belief in the superior virtues of the exercise of broad judicial discretion in sentencing: only through the operation of flexible and virtually unfettered sentencing powers could justice be effected; only judicial discretion enabled the appropriate sentence to be meted out in the infinitely variable circumstances of offender and offence;[17] only a judge could subtly

[14] Repealing 1565, 8 Eliz. c. 4, a little used statute on pick-pocketing; 1745, 18 Geo. II c. 27 and 1763, 3 Geo. III c. 34, stealing from bleaching-grounds. Repeal of the latter two Acts was supported by Lord Ellenborough following parliamentary petitions from 150 proprietors of bleaching-grounds claiming the law's severity prevented effective enforcement: (1810–11) 66 *Journals of the House of Commons* 123.

[15] Quoted by Campbell, *Lives of Chief Justices* (1874), 4, 294; and see *PD* 1811, (s. 1), 19: App. XC. Romilly's stance was representative of the majority of the most prominent penal theorists and commentators of the late eighteenth and early nineteenth century, who saw the absence of clearly structured and proportional punishment as much in need of statutory revision. Almost all regarded punishment as a means of preventing crime rather than as serving a retributory function. Common to all is the acknowledged influence of C. Beccaria, *On Crimes and Punishment* (trans. 1764), a manifesto for a penal system resting on consistently applied humane, rationally constructed laws. Effectiveness in crime prevention required swift enforcement of clear and certain laws, allied to appropriate proportionality between crime and punishments. Extensiveness of harm to the individual or society would regulate levels of punishment. See Blackstone, *Comms*, iv, 3–17; Eden, *Principles of Penal Law*, 3–14, 267; H. Dagge, *Considerations on Criminal law* (1772), i: 77 *et seq*. Bentham's *An Introduction to the Principles of Morals and Legislation* (1789), rather than a penal code, was an exhaustive comprehensive manual for assiduous codifiers. In relation to punishment, Bentham provided an elaborate moral arithmetic by which the appropriate type and amount of punishment might be 'scientifically' arrived at. Not wholly untypical of even the reformist Whig intellectual response, was Francis Jeffrey's 1804 *Edinburgh Review* measured dismissal, as sheer 'foppery', of Bentham's system of classified groups and sub-groups of features germane to crime and punishment: (1804) 4 *Edin. Rev.* 1, 18. A more modest classificatory approach in relation to scales of punishment appeared in successive proposals of the Criminal Law Commissioners (see 'Sentencing', Ch. IV above).

[16] *Ibid.*, 201. Campbell does not indicate the works in question, but the dedicatee of *Moral and Political Philosophy* was the Bishop of Carlisle, Ellenborough's father.

[17] Of Bentham's sentencing proposals, Ellenborough observed that 'a system of innovation...by persons speculating in modern legislation, that a certainty of punishment is preferable to severity, that it should invariably be proportioned to the magnitude of the crime; thereby forming a known

discern who 'morally speaking, are fit objects' for capital punishment—a claim not wholly consonant with the interventionary role of executive justice.[18]

Probably, as a principal consequence of the combined effects of an economic recession and the demobilization of several hundred thousand soldiers and sailors after Waterloo,[19] the already rising level of capital crime increased momentum immediately after 1815. For true believers in the effectiveness and wider virtues of the existing system, holding a firm penal line was never more vital; if anything, rather than continue to tolerate a decade-by-decade reduction of the execution proportion, an increased severity in capital enforcement might now be demanded.[20] For reformers, the situation was irrefutable evidence of a discredited system in terminal decline, faced with the spectre of attempting to regain credibility through a dramatic increase in the ratio of executions of those capitally convicted. Parliament was galvanized by an avalanche of petitions, notably from the Corporation of London, commercial organizations, and campaigning Quakers,[21] expressing alarm at the law's apparent inability to protect property and person because of its severity and unenforceability. Additionally,

---

scale of punishment commensurate with the degree of offence. Whatever may be my opinion of this doctrine, I am convinced of its absurdity in practice', *PD* 1811 (s. 1), 19: App. XC. The need for judicial discretion in sentencing and the believed inability to set fixed tariffs, was an element of Francis Jeffrey's extensive criticism of Bentham's proposals on punishment in the *Edinburgh Review* (1804). K. Smith, *Lawyers, Legislators and Theorists* (Oxford, 1998), 38–40. The real issue between reformers and judges was not the need for judicial discretion but its extent. See Sir William Grant's comment on this point, *PD* 1811 (s. 1), 19: App. LXVIII.

[18] Colonel Frankland, *PD* 1811 (s. 1), 19: 628. Frankland was amongst the most persistent, articulate, and effective Commons defenders of the status quo. By a questionnaire addressed to the Recorder and Common Serjeant of the City of London, he sought to demonstrate a consequential increase in pick-pocketing following its repeal as a capital offence in 1808. See *PD* 1811 (s. 1), 19: 642. Both reformers and retentionists not only invoked the support of legal luminaries but also felt uninhibited in their ability to criticize them. Thus, in the Commons for example, Blackstone's unflattering observations on elements of the penal system were written off by Tories as a 'few sentences brought in as ornamental flourishes at the end of a lecture, to enliven the students of a college': Frankland, *PD* 1813 (s. 1), 25: 584.

[19] And, as barrister John Miller reflected in the *Quarterly Review* (1821), the increasing 'relaxation of the bonds of social and domestic union, which dense population and commercial habit everywhere produced' (24, 241).

[20] For example, Miller's rejection of the 1819 Committee Report and call for an increased level of enforcement of capital provisions: *An Inquiry into the Present State of the Statute and Criminal Law of England* (1822). Similarly, M. Madan, *Thoughts on Executive Justice* (1784).

[21] See *PD* 1819 (s. 1), 39 and 40. And (1818–19) 74 *Journals of the House of Commons*. Driven by concerns regarding the law's unenforceability as a consequence of the lack of public sympathy and support, the Corporation of London's petition characterized the law as one which 'produces evasions, dangerous to the community', with the levels of crime continuing to rise so long as the law failed to represent the 'morals and religious sentiments of the nation'. Radzinowicz, *History*, i: App. 4. Petitioning Quakers sought a complete termination to capital punishment on the grounds of 'justice' and the tenets of Christianity, *PD* 1819 (s. 1), 39: 396.

the relatively regular executions of forgers had increasingly generated public disquiet, such as to cause Sir James Mackintosh to reflect in 1819 that 'executions for forgery have chiefly contributed to produce a general call for reformation in the penal system'.[22]

Boosted by this manifestation of public concern, a radical Whig group, led by Mackintosh and Sir Thomas Fowell Buxton, successfully sought the appointment of a Commons' Select 'Committee of Inquiry into the Criminal Law', charged with considering 'so much of the criminal law as relates to capital punishment in felonies'. Faced with a legislative cul-de-sac in the Lords, this parliamentary manoeuvre gained reformers prominent public exposure of their cause. It was also an opportunity which Mackintosh and his acolytes exploited without scruple, ensuring the greatest representation of both like-minded members on the Committee, and of witnesses likely to offer evidence supporting reform.[23] The rapidly produced report constituted the first extended, highly detailed parliamentary analysis of the state of crime and punishment, coupled with an attempt to gauge public opinion[24] on the law and its enforcement.

Mackintosh had given great emphasis to the importance of the latter in his Commons' proposal for the Select Committee's establishment. Penal laws would fail so long as they were 'inconsistent with the deliberate and permanent opinion

[22] Mackintosh to Lord Grenville, 15 April 1819, Dropmore Papers, BL Add Mss 58964, F. 155. Quoted by P. Handler, 'Forgery and Penal Reform in England, 1818–1830' (PhD dissertation, Univ. of Cambridge, 2002).

[23] PP 1819 (585), viii. Beside Mackintosh and Buxton, amongst the Committee's prominent advocates for reform were Brougham, Bathurst, Scarlett, Russell, and Wilberforce. The Committee's 61 witnesses were selected on the basis of their knowledge of, and acquaintance with, the administration of the criminal law, coming from a variety of professional bodies and social classes, including traders, merchants, bankers and insurance brokers, magistrates and their clerks, and prison warders. Not only were judges excluded from Committee membership, no judges (except the retired and sympathetic Chief Baron, Sir Archibald MacDonald) were called to provide evidence. Unconvincingly, such exclusion was justified by the Committee on the basis that it would be 'unbecoming' for judges to censure law which they were obliged to enforce. More tellingly, judges were described as too remote from the motives and causes which affected the bringing of prosecutions (Report, 9). Neither, implied Mackintosh, could judges give useful evidence of the effects of capital punishment upon the 'morality of the country', PD 1819 (s. 1) 40: 1519. Romilly had also ignored what he had regarded as the 'most unconstitutional doctrine' of consulting the judiciary on proposed penal legislation. Privately, he noted, 'I know the severity of Lord Ellenborough's disposition and had therefore avoided consulting him before I brought either bill in', Memoirs, 2, 177 and 246. Romilly's actions did not go unremarked upon, PD 1811 (s. 1), 19: App. LXX1. Predictably, criticism of the 1819 Committee arose both in Parliament (e.g. PD 1821 (s. 1), 5: 953), and elsewhere, including John Miller's Quarterly Review (1821)) critique of the Committee's Report. Miller observed 'neither have the Committee informed us…by what accident they assembled a cloud of witnesses whose opinions so exactly tally' (24, 219). In reality, the evidence of many witnesses was equivocal; something often ignored in the Committee's Report.

[24] For a contemporary general view of the phenomena, see W. Mackinnon, On the Rise, Progress and Present State of Public Opinion (1828).

of the public'. For Mackintosh and most of his kind, that was the 'well-grounded persuasion of that numerous and respectable class of society', or 'the virtuous feeling of the community'.[25] In seeking to achieve this, the Report[26] included proposals for two bills: one to abolish a combination of obsolete statutes and certain capital statutes relating to forms of stealing (previously the subject of Romilly's abortive reform bills) and a second bill generally consolidating and decapitalizing some forms of forgery. Although failing to make parliamentary headway under Mackintosh's patronage, (again because of Lords' opposition),[27] the proposals subsequently formed the basis of some of Peel's limited, but worthwhile, amending and consolidating reforms of the 1820s.

Quite how accurate the general campaigning claims of reformers were, that the criminal law's enforcement was being undermined by its nominal ferocity, is questionable. Whilst a majority in the Commons since Romilly's time had manifestly been persuaded of the need for at least some amelioration of the capital laws, the perceptions and opinions of their constituents, that 'numerous and respectable class of society', are more obscure. Certainly, the large body of parliamentary petitions offered relatively narrow views of discontent, largely resting on humanitarian or religious objections, or on the need to protect property and commercial interests. Furthermore, evidence from the 1819 Committee witnesses gave support to claims of manipulation of evidence by juries and judges to produce non-capital verdicts and of the reluctance of victims to pursue capital prosecutions. Yet, whatever prosecutorial timidity may have existed in some quarters, this could not gainsay the overall climbing rate of capital prosecutions and convictions. Undoubtedly, some reformist agitation was powered by an effective brew of both commercial and ethical concerns, as illustrated by the 1819 Corporation of London petition.[28] But claims of reformers and essayists to be echoing a growing public sensitivity to harsh penal laws defy easy verification.[29] Evidence of rising levels of capital prosecutions was of equivocal significance: it undermined neither humanitarian nor ethical objections, nor even those claims relating to failed deterrence and lack of public credibility of the criminal justice

[25] *PD* 1819 (s. 1) 39: 784 and 40: 1536. Similarly 1823 (s. 1) 9: 397.

[26] *'Report from the Select Committee on Criminal Laws' PP* 1819 (585) viii. For a detailed review of the Report, see Radzinowicz, *History*, i, 547–51.

[27] It has been claimed that while the majority of Lord Liverpool's Cabinet favoured supporting the 1819 Report, a minority led by Lord Eldon opposed it. A. Alison, *Lives of Lord Castlereagh and Sir Charles Stewart* (1861) vol. 3, 84.

[28] To a substantial degree, Quaker organized. On the extensive involvement and political skill demonstrated by Quakers in the movement for reform of the capital laws, see Gatrell, *The Hanging Tree*, 396–416, and generally Chs 12–16 for the view that, at least, in the early decades of the nineteenth century, reformist public opinion was more a campaigning construct than a matter of substance.

[29] On public sensibilities and the decline of many forms of corporal punishment by the beginning of the nineteenth century, see Beattie, *Crime and the Courts*, 613–16.

system.[30] Execution of a sinking proportion of capital offenders not only lowered the capital odds for those convicted but also transmitted a weaker, even less convincing deterrence signal, especially if, as was increasingly argued, the secondary punishment of transportation held no great terrors for felons (see below). Moreover, the very process of discretionary judicial and executive selection of those who should hang was, over the years, frequently characterized by reformers as the antithesis of 'justice'. Rather than discretion, they asserted that law alone should determine who would suffer capital punishment.[31]

Cutting Back Capital Offences: Peel and Russell

Peel's central role in the penal reforms effected in the 1820s is readily apparent. Decidedly less clear is the extent of his ambitions relating to the pace and substance of such changes. Between 1819 and Peel's arrival at the Home Office in 1822, attempts at implementing any of the Select Committee's report were almost totally fruitless. As an alternative strategy, efforts led by Mackintosh to shackle the government to a programme of penal reform by Commons' resolutions enjoyed limited success. An effective Commons' resolution in 1822 to balance moderation of the criminal law's severity against a strengthening of the police and improvement of the range of secondary punishments, was followed in 1823 by an unsuccessful motion overtly targeted at reducing the range of capital offences.[32] Peel opposed both resolutions, indicating the government's intention to carry out its own extensive review of penal laws; it was an undertaking which some were not wholly assured by, including Mackintosh, who dubbed Peel a 'great friend to general principles, but one [who] had an exception for every particular case'.[33] In respect of the capital question it was a scepticism partly borne out in subsequent years of Peel's Home Office tenure. Between 1823 and 1830, by a process of repeal and valuable consolidation,[34] the number and range of capital statutes and

---

[30] For they could be, and were, ascribed to improved funding of prosecutions.

[31] e.g. Romilly, PD 1811 (s. 1), 19: 12, and 22; Mackintosh 1823 (s. 2), 9: 411.

[32] PD 1822 (s. 2), 7: 790 and 1823 (s. 2), 9: 397.

[33] PD 1823 (s. 2), 9: 431. Cf. Scarlett at 430 and Denman who observed the following year that Peel's 'five Acts...for effecting Sir Samuel Romilly's proposals, have not been so much celebrated as they deserve because they still leave one great reformation unaccomplished, we allude to the abolition of capital punishment in the case of forgery; for in parliamentary tactics, it is well understood that those who fight for principles, must complain as if nothing was done, while anything still remains to be done' (1824) 40 Edin. Rev. 169, 183.

[34] On the feasibility and process of consolidation, see the Report and Further Report of the Select Committee on the Criminal Law of England, PP 1824 (205) iv, p. 39; (444) iv, p. 347. The 1824 Committee was appointed, with Peel's agreement, on a motion of Stephen Lushington. Forgery was selected as the focus of the feasibility study because of its complexity and contentiousness as a capital crime. On the process of consolidation, see K. Smith, 'Anthony Hammond: "Mr Surface Peel's" Persistent Codifier' (1999) 20 JLH 24.

offences was radically cut back, while leaving untouched a very substantial group of the most commonly used capital offences.[35]

Peel viewed his selective culling of capital statutes as striking an appropriate balance between proportionality of punishment and the needs of general deterrence. Defending an 1830 consolidating bill which broadly retained capital punishment for forgery, Peel demonstrated a largely undiminished faith in the efficacy of Paleyite deterrence: 'to continue the severity of the law in its letter, but gradually to ameliorate its practical application'.[36] It was a view to which Peel and his supporters (particularly in the Lords) adhered in the face of principled assaults on two fronts: first, a regular and heavy flow of parliamentary petitions, including one from over 200 provincial bankers;[37] and secondly, the strident advocacy of partisan press and periodicals, founded on an amalgam of pragmatic and humanitarian concerns. Peel's declared objective was to review and reform steadily on all interdependent criminal justice fronts, including improved prevention and deterrence of crime, better financial support and simpler prosecution procedures, and more effective secondary punishments. For Peel, capital punishment could not be considered in isolation from such measures, and especially what might replace it as the mainstay of deterrence. Here he saw little immediate prospect of transportation or prison effectively performing this role.[38]

---

[35] Listed in Radzinowicz, *History*, i: 574–85. Many of Peel's early statutory reforms that passed without a 'whisper of dissatisfaction', had been proposed by Romilly and later Mackintosh. Denman, the lawyer-politician reflected on the swift changes of political attitudes caused by public opinion: 'Common sense requires an obvious improvement: an opposition member brings it forward, and is overpowered by sarcasms, invectives, and majorities. But public opinion decides at once in its favour, and gradually diminishes the majority in each succeeding year, till the scale is turned, and independent men of all parties become anxious to see the alteration effected. Suddenly the minister proposes the reprobated project as a government measure, and converts, while he laughs at, his former adherents' (1824) 40 *Edin. Rev.* 169, 182–3.

[36] *PD* 1830, (s. 2), 24: 1044, and 1179. Continuing a long-term trend, the percentage rate of executions of capital offenders steadily declined in the early decades of the nineteenth century. On Peel's record as Home Secretary in commuting death sentences, and his political concerns not to increase the level of executions, see Gatrell, *The Hanging Tree*, Ch. 21 and App. 2, tables 1 and 2. Peel's commutation record is open to dispute. While some maintain Peel displayed severe tendencies (Gatrell), others provide strong rebutting evidence: S. Devereaux, 'Peel, Pardon and Punishment: The Recorder's Report Revisited', in Devereaux and Griffiths (eds), *Penal Practice and Culture*, 258.

[37] Petitions listed in (1830) 85 *Journals of the House of Commons* and (1830) 62 *Journals of the House of Lords*. Executive recognition of the widespread unpopularity of the capital forgery laws ensured that no convicted forgers were executed after 1830. The attitude of bankers to the use of capital forgery laws was clearly regarded by retentionists and reformers as of considerable significance and a source of serious parliamentary dispute. Peel skilfully produced a case suggesting that those materially 'most interested' in the question—London bankers and the Bank of England—were against the decapitalizing of the forgery laws, *PD* 1830 (s. 2), 24: 1044–55; (s. 2), 25: 48, 587 and 840–54.

[38] For example, Peel to Sydney Smith, March 1826, *Sir Robert Peel from his private correspondence*, ed. C.J. Parker (1891) vol. 1, 402, and *PD* 1823 (s. 2), 8: 1440. For the dismal results of the Millbank penitentiary venture at this time see 'Prisons, transportation and institutional detention' below.

Even in the mid-1830s, when in opposition, with the Metropolitan Police established and beginning to make its mark, Peel showed no great inclination to relinquish his attachment to Paleyite penal philosophy;[39] something not wholly consistent with the retentionist claim that organized, invasive policing was *the* alternative to the broad use of the capital threat. Taken collectively,[40] Peel's wide range of criminal and penal law reform measures constituted a significant change in the culture and administration of law enforcement, one quite beyond shoring up the old non-centralist approach. However, in respect of capital punishment Peel exhibited a level of reforming caution distinctly beyond that justified by the objective evidence accumulating before and during his tenure as Home Secretary. Here his political judgment on the continuing practical and symbolic function of capital punishment proved deficient, leaving him in the wake, rather than the vanguard, of widespread parliamentary and public attitudes.

More generally, the campaign against the 'bloody code' was directed against the cumulative outcome of eighteenth-century penal legislation. Rather than seeking to mis-characterize the era as one of a concerted, focused move-ment towards a comprehensive body of criminal laws capitally enforced, early nineteenth-century reformers looked to the accretions of this sustained, ill-or-dered legislative activity. On the whole, it was rightly recognized that this corpus of penal legislation was enacted from a variety of motives, by a diverse group of instigators.[41] They ranged from individuals with narrow local grievances to government-led legislative initiatives. A prominent example of the latter was reform of the forgery laws aimed at meeting the perceived threat to the security and standing of financial institutions basic to national commercial integrity.[42] Independent of Peel's steady, incremental legislative ambitions and actions, the

---

[39] On Peel's multi-faceted attitude towards judicial discretion, including that relating to recom-mended commutation of capital sentences, see B. Hilton, 'The Gallows and Mr Peel', in T. Blanning and D. Cannadine (eds), *History and Biography Essays in Honour of Derek Beales* (Cambridge, 1996), 88.

[40] See elsewhere, 'Policing', Ch. II, 'Consolidation', Ch. VI, 'Prosecution', Ch. III, and 'Imprisonment' below.

[41] Some accounts of the origins and functions of eighteenth-century penal legislation depict the criminal justice system as a key instrument of political and social hegemony by a landed and gov-erning elite: most powerfully argued by E. P. Thompson, *Whigs and Hunters: The Origins of the Black Act* (1975) and D. Hay, 'Property, Authority and the Criminal Law' in Hay et al. (eds), *Albion's Fatal Tree* (1975), 17. Subsequent studies and interpretations have considerably eroded the force of such hegemonic claims, emphasizing extensive working and middling-class engagement in prosecution and jury discretion. King, *Crime, Justice and Discretion, passim,* who characterizes the eighteenth-century justice system as one of not simply terror and exploitation, but of 'struggle, of negotiation, of accommodation', with practically every social group shaping the system and being shaped by it (373). And J. Langbein, 'Albion's Fatal Flaws' (1983) 98 *P & P* 96.

[42] Analysed by R. McGowen, 'Making the "bloody code"? Forgery legislation in eighteenth cen-tury England', in *Law, Crime and English Society 1660–1830,* ed. N. Landau (Cambridge, 2002).

operating dynamic of the system ensured that the years between 1824 and 1831 witnessed not just a decline in the proportion executed of those sentenced to death, but also in the absolute numbers hanged.[43]

Arguably, the punishment of forgery was the retentionist's final defensive redoubt. Peel's 1830 Forgery Act consolidated the law whilst retaining capital punishment for most forms of the offence, the value of which ambitious reformers, such as Brougham, 'rated at [zero]'.[44] Retention of the law's strong capital complexion once again owed much to the incumbent Lord Chancellor and Lord Chief Justice who galvanized the House of Lords into excising Mackintosh's Commons' amendment seeking to eliminate hanging for all forgeries except that of wills. In the event, it was the last parliamentary success at staunching the ever-strengthening flow of support for removing capital punishment from the calendar of mainstream punishment; when the threat of death and discretionary intervention would rapidly cease to be a defining characteristic of the criminal justice system. The entry of Earl Grey's Whig administration in November 1830, inaugurated an anticipated (though, at first, hesitant) change in government attitude towards the capital question. While not introducing reforming measures, the government (initially with Denman as Attorney-General and Brougham as Lord Chancellor) broadly supported the initiatives of private members' bills. Acquiescing in (and possibly capitalizing on) the large body of press, periodical, commercial and public opinion favouring reform, during the 1830s, the Whigs oversaw enactment of a series of bills replacing Peel's gradualist legacy with a more radical pace of change.[45] No doubt, these reforms were driven by a substantial measure of political opportunism in seeking to match leading features of the criminal justice system with perceived public opinion. However, the Whig government reforms also owed much to a combination of the humanitarian, religious, and utilitarian principles long espoused, and consistently campaigned for, by many of the administration's leading members and supporters. In many respects, the critical political facilitator of this period was Lord John Russell.

While early legislation that cut back the range of capital offences was often the outcome of private initiative, especially from the likes of William Ewart,[46] with the installation of Russell at the Home Office in 1835 there came a markedly greater government interest and involvement in penal affairs. Boasting a reformist

---

[43] *PP* 1831–2 (282), xxiii, p. 133.

[44] *PD* 1830 (s. 2), 24: 1058. Originally suspended pending parliamentary legislative reform, as a matter of practice execution for forgery permanently ceased by 1830.

[45] For a detailed account of contemporary public press and parliamentary opinion, see Radzinowicz, *History*, i: 590–607.

[46] *Ibid.*, 600–7. More generally, the Representation of the People Act (Reform Act) 1832 was responsible for the influx of a considerable body of independent, largely reformist, MPs.

pedigree that included previous active support of Romilly and membership of the 1819 Committee, Russell soon redirected the attention of the Criminal Law Commissioners to evaluating the use of capital punishment. Reporting in 1836, the Commissioners predictably deployed the largely stock reformist arguments rehearsed over (arguably with changing emphases) the previous two decades. Still regarded as enjoying credibility amongst many, Paley's thesis was deconstructed and rejected on the grounds of patent ineffectiveness and injustice for those selected for sacrifice: deterrence could only operate effectively if penalties were definite and known and not the unpredictable outcome of judicial and executive discretion; statistical evidence for 1834 and 1835 suggested that repeal of capital punishment for certain offences had met with a diminution in commission rates. Beyond empirical evidence, the Commissioners (like reformers) freely invoked the force of what they claimed to be public opinion. It was 'peculiarly expedient' that courts and punishment should in great measure accord with popular feelings'; failure to calibrate law with 'popular sentiments' was a precarious strategy, eroding its necessary general support and particularly that of those involved in its administration. Moreover, capital punishment could expediently be retained for high treason or offences involving expressly defined aggravated acts of violence or those endangering life, because in such cases death could be inflicted 'without shocking the feelings of society'.[47]

With little Commons' opposition and the parliamentary assistance in the Lords of Lord Chancellor Cottenham and Lord Denman CJ, Russell rapidly brought about the enactment of seven bills closely following the Commissioners' proposals for reducing the range of capital offences.[48] As with the Commissioners, the core of Russell's justifications was one of gaining maximum deterrence along with aligning the penal law with alleged public sentiment, an aim requiring greater proportionality between crime and punishment. On the ever-contentious issue of the capital threat and forgery, to bolster the reformist case Russell employed statistical evidence apparently demonstrating the increased conviction rates of non-capital forgery, and gained the personal endorsement for reform from the Governor of the Bank of England.[49] By 1841, with one limited exception,

---

[47] *Second Report of His Majesty's Commissioners on Criminal Law, PP* 1836 (343), xxxvi, p. 183. On the Criminal Law Commissioners, see Ch. VI below.

[48] For details of the bills, see Radzinowicz, *History*, iv: 317–19 n. The Commissioners had counselled a delay in legislation, pending a more general revision of the criminal law. See *Correspondence between His Majesty's Principal Secretary of State for the Home Department and the Commissioners, PP* 1837 (76), xxxi, 37, p. 31 at p. 35, and generally.

[49] *PD* 1837 (s. 3), 37: 717–33. In 1830 the Bank of England had been solidly behind Peel's resistance to the decapitalizing of forgery. On forgery and the prosecution practices of the Bank of England, see R. McGowen, 'Managing the Gallows' (2007) 25 *Law and History Review* 241 and P. Handler 'The Limits of Discretion: Forgery and the Jury at the Old Bailey, 1818–21', in J. Cairns and G. McLeod

no property offences attracted the death penalty unless accompanied by violence. For all practical purposes, capital sentences were reserved for major crimes of violence and sodomy, with an annual execution rate of murderers averaging around 10 cases.[50]

Narrowing the Capital Scope of Murder and Ending the Public Spectacle of Hangings

Campaigns to hone down or totally abolish capital punishment must be viewed against the reality that after 1841 (except for treason or cognate offences) only murderers were hanged; and even here it was a proportion of those convicted. At this stage the abolitionist cause had begun to resemble more of an emotional or ethical exercise than one concerning the practicalities of actual punishment. Yet a 1837 Commons' motion for the abolition of capital punishment in all cases except murder (proposed by Ewart, seconded by fellow radical Hume) came within one vote of success. Supported by a blend of religious, ethical, and utilitarian arguments, Ewart's proposal was resisted by Russell who invoked the likelihood of the hostile 'feelings of the public at large...and of the judges'.[51] As before, only the most limited assessment can be offered of the extent to which public opinion corresponded with its parliamentary depictions. Almost inevitably, such assessments are restricted to the views of the articulate professional and upper classes. However, any genuine political concerns relating to the effective functioning of the criminal justice system would necessarily also have embraced the swelling, post-Reform Act middling classes, from whose ranks came a large proportion of prosecutors and jurymen.

More generally, the 1840s were the high season of the abolitionist movement, witnessing the appearance of a substantial body of tracts, pamphlets and journal

(eds), *The Dearest Birth Right of the People of England* (Oxford, 2002), 155. Piloting the bills through the Lords, with Benthamite directness, Denman identified the underlying 'great principle of the bills [as] that crime should be visited with certain punishment' *PD* 1837 (s. 3), 38: 1775.

[50] Excepting treason, piracy, and certain forms of arson of military installations. See *Fourth Report of Her Majesty's Commissioners on Criminal Law*, App. 4, *PP* 1839 (168), xix p. 235, as modified by the Substitution of Punishment for Death Act 1841, 4 and 5 Vict. c. 56; and on levels of executions, *PP* 1838, xxxviii, p. 246. By the 1860s fewer than half of convicted murderers were executed: *Judicial Statistics*, *PP* 1862 (3025) lvi, p. 491.

[51] *PD* 1837 (s. 3), 38: 912–14. Besides support from dyed-in-the-wool total abolitionists, such as Buxton and Lushington, Brougham was also 'strongly inclined to question the propriety' of any use of capital punishment, deploring its 'tendency to brutalise those who witnessed it', *ibid.*, 1788. Three years later, Ewart's motion seeking the complete abolition of capital punishment (on the grounds of both public support and the projected further diminution of decapitalized offences) suffered defeat by a substantial margin. Again, Russell and others claimed public sentiments were against abolition of hanging for murder, *PD* 1840 (s. 3), 52: 927–9. A similar response and fate met Fitzroy Kelly's 1841 attempt to remove the capital penalty for every offence other than treason and murder, *PD* 1840 (s. 3), 55: 741 and 1079–82. And in the following year, *PD* 1841 (s. 3), 56: 462 and 57: 1408.

articles. These included contributions from the pens of the most prominent of the contemporary literati, advocating the total abolitionist cause from a variety of standpoints, not least religious, ethical, and utilitarian. But over subsequent decades, with an annual execution rate for murder frequently under 10, the abolitionist campaign lost momentum and literary vigour, with some writers and journals switching allegiance and aligning themselves with the status quo. Several prominent murder trials of the period which provoked published affirmations of the necessity of capital punishment, are also likely to have taken their toll on the abolitionist cause. Additionally, in the mid-1850s the retentionist camp enlisted the formidable polemical skills of Fitzjames Stephen. Writing most frequently in the columns of the *Saturday Review*, though favouring a more tightly focused definition of murder, the rising young barrister unsparingly lacerated abolitionist arguments, whether religious, ethical, or utilitarian.[52] But probably most significantly, the spectacle of public hangings became identified by many as the most objectionable feature of capital punishment. As opposition focused on this specific aspect of capital punishment, the broader abolitionist cause was inevitably weakened.

While total abolitionists failed to end capital punishment for murder (and other exceptional offences), those advocating its removal from public view eventually enjoyed success with enactment of the Capital Punishment Amendment Act 1868.[53] The Act, however, by no means marked a natural or inevitable compromise between abolitionists and retentionists. Tactically, some abolitionists feared elimination of what they regarded as the deeply repellent spectacle of the execution, followed by degrading public behaviour, would undermine a central plank of their cause, thereby prolonging the use of capital punishment. Consequently, all four abolitionist members of the 1865 Royal Commission on Capital Punishment voted against private executions. At the same time, for staunch retentionsts, private executions threatened loss of a claimed vivid and powerful dimension to general deterrence: in Bentham's terms, a 'speaking image of the law [producing a] better and more awful effect'.[54] Yet, the rising sensibilities of an expanding middle class took their toll. Furthermore, a growing governing

[52] For a general review of contemporary literature on capital punishment, see Radzinowicz, *History*, i, 329–30 n, and 337–40. On Stephen and the *Saturday Review* articles on capital punishment, see Radzinowicz, *Sir James Fitzjames Stephen*, (1957) and Smith, *James Fitzjames Stephen* 58–9. Stephen argued for substantial modification of the royal prerogative of mercy (see 'Appeals' Ch. IV above). On the gradual, post-1860 growth of bureaucratic expertise and formalization of Home Office practices, see Chadwick, *Bureaucratic Mercy, passim*.

[53] 31 Vict., c. 24. On contemporary public and parliamentary opinions and committees, see Radzinowicz, *History*, iv: 343–52.

[54] 'Principles of Penal Law', Bowring *Works*, i: 549–50, and cf. Stephen 'Public Executions' (1856), 2 *Saturday Review* 336, and Henry Mayhew, 'On Capital Punishments' (1856) *Society for Promoting the Amendment of the Law* 47.

class belief in the corrupting or de-sensitizing power of public corporal and capital punishment, was reinforced by a succession of executions constituting 'most disgusting exhibition[s]'.[55] Eventually this climate of opinion generated a House of Lords' Select Committee to examine the 'present mode' of executions. In its 1856 Report the Committee favoured relocating capital punishment inside prisons, or similar establishments, to be witnessed by a specified collection of officials and a restricted number of invited spectators.[56] A further decade of inaction ended with the establishment of the 1865 Royal Commission, charged with reviewing both the mode and the extent of capital punishment. Reporting in 1866, a majority of the Commission regarded evidence from a wide range of foreign jurisdictions as conclusive of the advisability and feasibility of an end to public executions;[57] a view which aroused little dissent and one given legislative force within two years.

The disappearance of capital punishment behind high prison walls constituted a removal from public view of the last, most vivid and direct form of corporal punishment. It was a final relinquishment of what had for some time been an outmoded and discredited ritual—arguably since the 1830s when, in practice, murder became the only capital crime. Whatever power public capital punishments might have once possessed, of providing an awful assertion of the ultimate coercive and confirming state sanction, it had become increasingly discordant with contemporary sensibilities and superfluous to political needs; it had come to be regarded as both uncivilized and impolitic.[58] Broad use of capital punishment had become discredited in that its unique ability to deter crime had long been

---

[55] Russell, PD 1837 (s. 3), 38: 911; and e.g. Rich, PD 1841 (s. 3), 56: 648; Milnes, PD 1845 (s. 3), 81: 1412; Bright, PD 1849 (s. 3), 104: 1076; the Bishop of Oxford, PD 1854 (s. 3), 133: 311 and 1856 (s. 3), 142: 247, responsible for establishing the 1856 Select Committee of Enquiry.

[56] Report from the Select Committee [on] carrying into effect Capital Punishments, PP 1856 (366) vii, p. 9. The Committee regarded evidence of continental and North American practices as strongly indicating an end to public executions.

[57] Report of the Capital Punishment Commission, PP 1866 (3590), xxi, p. 1. Establishment of the Commission was proposed by Charles Neate, MP, a long-standing abolitionist and eventual member of the 12-man Commission, along with fellow abolitionists Ewart, Bright, and Lushington.

[58] For a broadly supporting analysis of the evidence of causal changes in culture and public sensibility towards punishment, and especially corporal and capital punishment, see D. Garland, Punishment and Modern Society (Oxford, 1990), 225–34 and D. Cooper, The Lesson of the Scaffold: The Public Execution Controversy in Victorian England (1974). For an instrumentalist view that change in forms of punishment was driven overwhelmingly by strategic political and professional ambitions, adapting institutions of control to intellectual and professional innovation, see notably, M. Foucault, Discipline and Punish (1978) (see 'Prisons' below). Evolving ideologies, along with developing socio-economic structures, inevitably help shape criminal justice perceptions and practices. However, it is highly improbable that (as Foucault appears to maintain) wider shifting cultural forces and ethical traditions did not significantly interact with ideologies and structures in the process of transforming penal law. In essence, 'punishment has an instrumental purpose, but also a cultural style and an historical tradition, and a dependence upon "institutional, technical and discursive conditions"', Garland, ibid., p 19.

exploded by various forms of empirical counter-claims. Moreover, increasingly centralized prison administration had encouraged the belief that beyond punishment's functions of deterrence and retribution lay a realm of possibilities for the moral reorientation of the criminal classes. Capital punishment for murder survived because it chimed with broad public sentiment, and consequently was politically unthreatening; or as the Criminal Law Commissioners observed in 1836, it did not 'shock...the feelings of society'. Unlike all other formerly capital crimes, capital punishment for murder was sustained by its long retributivistic appeal, as being a 'just', proportionate response. As Russell remarked in 1840, for murder there was 'an important retributive function satisfied by capital punishment which the public would not be safely denied'.[59] And, while losing its graphic public image by removal to an acceptable 'emotional and physical distance', out of public sight was never intended to be completely out of the public's mind.

Though indefatigable abolitionists, such as Ewart and Bright, soldiered on with periodic abortive parliamentary initiatives,[60] the appeal of their cause not only wilted through public indifference, but by an inability to recruit much new blood, particularly amongst prominent contemporaries. Indeed, some eminent public figures, (especially John Stuart Mill) alignment with retentionism in the 1860s boosted the intellectual and philosophical credentials of capital punishment.[61] A more broadly supported quasi-abolitionist strategy was to refine and narrow the concept of murder, thereby diminishing the number of cases subject to capital punishment. Adopting this approach, the 1865 Royal Commission chose to divide murder into 'first or higher degree' capital murder, and non-capital murder. This avoided directly tackling the conceptual and doctrinal problems wrapped up in the common law definition of murder. However, the proposals' demise was ensured by their opaque or self-contradictory drafting, combined with parliamentary and judicial disagreement over quite where the line should be drawn between the two categories. For much the same reasons, a similar fate overtook a host of private and government bills brought forward in the 1870s and early 1880s.[62] Separating convicted murderers who morally merited

[59] *PD* 1840 (s. 3) 52: 929.

[60] Radzinowicz and Hood, *Penal Policy*, 672–6, 685–8.

[61] *Ibid*. At the time a Liberal MP, Mill supported removal of murderers from the 'catalogue of the living' for its unique power of deterrence. Abolition would bring 'an effeminacy to the general mind of the country'; capital punishment of murderers 'show[s] most emphatically our regard for [life]', *PD* 1868, (s. 3) 191: 1050–5. Mill's reference to 'effeminacy' has resonances of Colonel Frankland's parliamentary comments half a century earlier, *PD* 1811, (s.1) 19: 647. On public apathy, see the 1894 *Report* of the Howard Association; since 1866, the reinvented Society for the Abolition of Capital Punishment.

[62] See 'Homicide' Ch. XII below. For an early twentieth-century private members' attempt to modify the law of murder, see the Law of Murder Amendment Bills of 1909 and 1910, *PP* 1909 (58), iii, p. 423 and 1910 (53), ii, p. 431.

non-capital punishment from those destined for the gallows continued to be a matter of executive discretion informed by judicial advice until well into the twentieth century.[63]

2. PRISONS, TRANSPORTATION, AND INSTITUTIONAL DETENTION

Early nineteenth-century England faced an increasingly uncomfortable, not to say alarming, conjunction of three social and political realities: first, an apparently inexorable rise in recorded crime, prosecution rates, and convicted criminals; a phenomenon that 'excited the alarm and baffled the efforts of Philanthropist and Statesman';[64] secondly, the diminishing reputation of the capital threat, the centrepiece of the institution of punishment; and, thirdly, the flagging confidence in the general deterrence power of transportation. One significant government response was its reinvention of the prison. Rather than punishment, eighteenth-century local prisons were essentially institutions for pre-trial detention. However, hostilities with America in the 1770s caused an interruption to the transportation of convicts forcing on the British government the 'temporary' expedient of prison 'hulks' along with a programme of revamping local prison or houses of correction.[65] Development of existing houses of correction for confinement of convicted felons was directed by the Penitentiary Act 1779.[66]

---

[63] Aside from the indirect effects of the Criminal Appeal Act 1907, see below for the provisions of the Infanticide Act 1922 and Homicide Act 1957. Capital punishment for all forms of murder was finally abolished (after initial suspension) under the Murder (Abolition of Death Penalty) Act, 13 and 14 Eliz. 2, c. 71. Though ultimately not subject to formal regulation, the determining criteria employed by Home Secretaries when reviewing convictions were, to a fair degree, both known and consistently applied. From an extensive range of potentially germane factors, four dominate: (i) mental infirmity outside the narrow cognitive deficiencies recognized by the M'Naghten rules; (ii) cases of infanticide; (iii) absence of an intention to kill or cause serious harm; (iv) provocation not recognized by the legal defence of provocation. For the relevant parliamentary statements by successive Home Secretaries and Home Office memoranda, see particularly, Troup, *The Home Office*, 55–71; *Home Office Printed Memoranda*, N.A. H.O. 347/8 (1882) 208–29, and Radzinowicz and Hood, *Penal Policy*, 676–85. On broader questions of policy and practice, see Chadwick, *Bureaucratic Mercy*, Chs 6–8. See further, 'Homicide' Ch. XII below for the substantive law developments relating to murder and defences.

[64] *Report of Select Committee on the best mode of giving Efficiency to Secondary Punishments*, PP 1831–2 (547), vii, p. 3. Aside from various forms of detention and corporal punishment (above) fines could be, and were, commonly imposed for a vast range of summary offences. Their use also extended to many more serious, indictable offences. For an assessment of the benefits and disadvantages of fines, see the *Criminal Law Commissioners Seventh Report*, PP 1843 (448), xix, p. 109. And on the enforcement of fines, see Radzinowicz and Hood, *Penal Policy*, 648–51.

[65] (1776) 16 Geo. III c. 43.

[66] The Penitentiary Act 1779, 19 Geo. III c. 74 promoted by the distinguished trio of Blackstone, Eden, and Howard. See Beattie, *Crime and the Courts*, Ch. 10, *passim*.

Local response to the legislation varied substantially; furthermore the scheme sanctioned by the Act for building two national penitentiaries (one for men and one for women) for the rehabilitation of offenders foundered through a combination of conflict over costs, design, and waning enthusiasm. This latter cause sprang largely from the recommencement of transportation, thereby relieving the immediate pressure for disposal of those convicted of more serious offences. But despite the collapse of this national initiative, the principle and practice of imprisonment as punishment had gained broad acceptance.

More than 35 years after the failure of the 1779 scheme, a national prison finally materialized. Located in central London, and opened in 1816, Millbank national penitentiary or prison distinctively marked the entry of central government into the arena of prison administration. Yet nothing remotely resembling a national strategy for prisons followed this physically and politically monumental event for several decades. A number of reasons account for this. One was that whilst doubts were widespread as to the power of transportation to deter, its great virtue of removing increasing numbers of convicts from England remained unchallengeable. Further, the funding, control, and regulation of prisons and houses of correction had been, and remained, largely in the hands of the local magistracy in Quarter Sessions. Only when crime was centrally perceived as a matter of national interest did government action follow. And finally, beyond the detention of debtors, petty criminals, and those awaiting trial, no consensus existed as to the functions of prison for those serious criminals suffering substantial periods of confinement.

Such uncertainty and conflicting opinion appears in the 1820s, when leading Quakers inspired faith in a redemptive and reformatory role for prisons;[67] but frequently this was displaced, or relegated, in official reports by the language of deterrence and retribution. This was true of the 1822 House of Commons Select Committee on Prisons with its emphatic declaration that prisons should be an 'object of terror, and may operate as real punishment...'.[68] Yet, at the same time,

---

[67] Reform as the leading objective appeared in the Holford Commitee, *First Report*, PP 1810 (199) iii, 567 p. 606. The proposals of the Holford Committee (which included Romilly and Wilberforce) were responsible for the building of Millbank. See also, e.g., the reformist emphasis in *Report on Cold Bath Field Prison*, PP 1809 (216) iv, p. 19, and *Report on Lancaster Prison*, PP 1812–13 (3), v, 28. At the beginning of the nineteenth century, before the coming of centrally financed national prisons, two types of criminal prisons existed: houses of correction, (initially for vagrants and the like) and gaols for those being held awaiting trial. These local prisons were funded by rates and subject to local inspection.

[68] *Report PP* 1822 (300), iv, 3. Reform is recognized as an important objective in the *Select Committee Report on Millbank*, PP 1823 (533) v, p. 12: 'punishment which may strike terror in evil doers, and operate by example in the prevention of crime [and] confinement...sufficiently long to ensure a change being effected in the evil habits and opinions of the prisoners'. The Committee saw the power to reform as relevant largely to the young and first offenders 'whose hearts are not hardened by guilt' (p. 13).

the preamble to the Gaols Act 1823 spoke of the aim to 'improve the Morals' of prisoners, as well as ensuring the 'proper measure of punishment'. However, relatively less charged or uncontentious areas of prison administration did engage the government's attention. Though lacking any enforcement mechanism, the 1823 Act was, nevertheless, innovative in its attempt to establish uniform practices in all local prisons, involving proper classification of prisons, inspection by visiting justices, and a regime of 'regular labour [and] religious and moral instruction'.[69] With the Prisons Act 1835, central government's involvement edged forward from the tentative, permissive approach of the 1823 Act, to a regulatory stance through the setting up of a Home Office appointed prison inspectorate. But wide local variations long persisted in the penal aims and practices of local prisons.[70]

Experiments in Reform

Although fuelled by a combination of humanitarian, evangelical, and Quaker reformative beliefs, the Millbank experiment turned sour by the early 1820s. Seeking redemptive 'improvement of the mind' through 'seclusion, employment, and religious instruction' had exhibited little evidence of moral reclamation. Problems of recruitment and retention of competent staff were further aggravated by Millbank's structurally uneasy management relationship between the Governor and Chaplain, one which predictably generated friction on matters of jurisdiction over prison discipline and the role of religious teaching. Rising levels of mental degeneration among inmates, coupled with deaths from scurvy as a consequence of poor diet, provoked Select Committee recommendations for measures to improve prisoners' physical and mental well-being. Whilst not rejecting the function of religious indoctrination, the Committee proposed the teaching of literacy skills based on non-religious sources, along with 'games and sports'. Moreover, utilitarian notions of a 'stock of rewards and punishments' were freely and liberally commended.[71] Regime modifications at Millbank attempted to

[69] Peel's 1823 and 1824 Gaol Acts also abolished gambling and the sale of liquor in prisons, provided for the appointment of salaried governors, noted the benefits of teaching literacy skills, and required separate beds for each inmate. The 1823 Act insisted upon the strict separation of men and women prisoners and that the latter be supervised by women prison staff. Although uniformally observed in state prisons, at the local level this provision was unevenly applied. Driven partly by the perception of female criminality differing fundamentally from that of men, and partly by the belief of the increased tractability of segregated prisons, a number of women's state prisons were established during the nineteenth century, beginning with Brixton in 1853. S. McConville *A History of English Prison Administration* (1981), 425–7.

[70] The 1835 Act required that all prison rules, regulations, and diet details be submitted for approval to the Home Secretary.

[71] *Select Committee Report on Millbank*, PP 1823 (533) v, p. 4; *Report*, PP 1824 (408), iv, 6. The Gaols Act 1823 limited solitary confinement to the night and for disciplinary purposes.

straddle the twin objectives of individual reform and general deterrence. While failing to achieve the former, official comment in the early 1830s noted that at least the prison was 'generally dreaded for the strictness of the discipline...and the irksome confinement'.[72]

In good measure, the failing fortunes of crusaders for moral reclamation of prisoners enjoyed a temporary reprieve through the incidental effects of the Prisons Act 1835, whose declared function was one of achieving greater uniformity of prison management and practice. As a further modest step in central government involvement, the Act set up a system of five 'Inspectors of Prisons' charged with ensuring a uniformly sound prison management. It was a role performed through inspection, encouragement, public censure and report. Appointed to the two senior inspectorates were William Crawford, and the Reverend Whitworth Russell. Both offered experience and considerable knowledge of the prison system; both were strong believers in the redemptive powers of high levels of religious instruction; and both were staunch devotees of the 'separate system' of prisoner isolation.[73] Reinforced by the 1835 House of Lords' Select Committee's explicit endorsement of extreme prisoner isolation,[74] over the succeeding dozen years Crawford and Russell exercised a powerful influence in directing penal policy towards incorporating the separate system. In Millbank's case, on Crawford's and Russell's recommendation, the level of separation and dosage of religious instruction were increased, with the centrality of the latter underscored by appointment in 1837 of a chaplain-governor. Though failing to improve rates of non-recidivism, the regime's increased severity excelled in producing a high incidence of mental breakdown amongst inmates. In 1843, within a year of an unflattering parliamentary report, the Millbank experiment was terminated, with the prison thenceforth serving as a centre for assessment and dispersal of prisoners.

While demonstrably unfulfilled at Millbank, reformist optimism for fresh central government initiatives remained undimmed. Established in 1838, following

---

[72] *Report of the Select Committee on the Best Mode of Giving Efficiency to Secondary Punishments*, *PP* 1831–2 (547), vii, 10.

[73] Crawford was a founding member of the Society for Improved Prison Discipline, and an author of an extensive and influential *Parliamentary Commission's Report on US Penitentiaries*, *PP* 1834, xlvi, p. 349. And see U. R. Henriques, 'The Rise and Decline of the Separate System of Prison Discipline' (1972) 54 *P & P* 61. Russell was the cousin of the Home Secretary, Lord John Russell, and formerly chaplain at Millbank.

[74] *Second Report of Select Committee of the House of Lords on Gaols and Houses of Correction*, *PP* 1835 (495) xi, p. iv. As well as 'entire separation, except during the hours of labour and of religious worship', silence was also to be 'enforced'. However, unlike zealous separationists such as Russell and Crawford, the House of Lords' Committee aim was to avoid 'frightful contamination' of the 'comparative innocent' by 'depraved and systematic criminals'. Similarly, *Report of Select Committee on Secondary Punishments*, *PP* 1831–2 (547), vii, 10. Russell and Crawford regarded isolation as essential to increasing the receptivity of prisoners to religious and moral salvation.

a 1835 Select Committee proposal, Parkhurst reformatory aimed, through a 'course of moral, religious and industrial training', to equip redeemable juvenile offenders for transportation and a new life in the antipodes. By the mid-1840s, despite careful sifting of entrants, the familiar combination of an extremely harsh disciplinary regime, poor diet, and a hopelessly inadequate trade education, defeated any real chances of success.[75] Built before the Parkhurst ideal had met with failure, Pentonville prison constituted the apotheosis of Russell and Crawford's tenaciously advocated separate system.

Opened in 1842, Pentonville was intended to perform a similar role for adult criminals to that of Parkhurst for juveniles. However, in seeking to reclaim the souls and sound characters of its inmates in preparation for eventual transportation, the Pentonville regime elevated the separate system to unmatched levels of thoroughness: silence and isolation were engineered into the building's design and fabric; over 500 prisoners left their individual cells for physical exercise in individual yards and gained spiritual enlightenment from frequent occupation of their own partitioned chapel stall; regularly patrolling prison warders did not speak to prisoners, but maintained unbroken silence by donning felt overshoes. More than generous helpings of evangelical fervour, mixed with sustained isolation, rapidly proved a too powerful brew for some prisoners.[76] Just as at Millbank, a rising incidence of mental instability amongst prisoners soon followed, eventually bringing about a reduction of solitary confinement from 18 months to nine months. Swelling public criticism[77] of the regime's severity,[78] without any demonstrable compensating reduction in recidivism, terminated the experiment in 1849. Pentonville followed Millbank's fate of becoming a sorting house for prisoners destined for other venues. Acting partly as an epitaph for those experiments, Carlyle's 'Model Prisons' characteristically flayed advocacy of deterrence and, most especially, prisoners' moral regeneration as that 'mournfullest twaddle' of those 'preaching and perorating from the teeth outward!'[79]

Ending Transportation: Deterrence by Imprisonment

With Russell's suicide at Millbank, and Crawford's natural death at a Pentonville board meeting, both in 1847, whatever credibility remained in the separate

[75] Radzinowicz and Hood, *Penal Policy*, 148–55.

[76] For a vivid evocation of the Pentonville regime, see M. Ignatieff, *A Just Measure of Pain* (1978), 3–9.

[77] Particularly Sir Peter Laurie *Killing no Murder or the Effects of Separate Confinement on the Bodily and Mental Conditions of Prisoners* (1846).

[78] e.g. *The Times*, 25 and 29 November 1843.

[79] *Latter-Day Pamphlets* (1850), 84. Neither would Jebb's greater emphasis on deterrence be in line with Carlyle's neo-Kantian retributive beliefs in criminals receiving their just deserts.

system was further eroded with Pentonville's redesignation. By virtue of Home Office powers to regulate and approve local prison design since 1839, Pentonville had functioned as a model for over 50 new or rebuilt local prisons. However, whilst pursuit of moral and spiritual regeneration through a rich diet of religious instruction and an extreme separation system lost momentum, belief in its retributivistic and deterrent power remained undiminished. By the 1840s, developments in penal strategy had become increasingly conditioned by problems relating to the system of transportation, allied to growing doubts over its future: if the disposal of 4000 convicts a year (the peak reached during the 1830s) were to be terminated, just how could such substantial numbers be accommodated for long periods in England?

While in contemporary estimation enjoying the inestimable benefit of ridding the country of great numbers of convicts, transportation suffered from certain drawbacks as part of a broader penal strategy, especially the difficulty of uniform regulation and doubts over its power, 'to terrorize' would-be offenders. Lord Ellenborough was not alone in subscribing to the belief that 'transportation to Botany Bay, is nine times in ten, looked upon as no more than a summer's excursion, or an easy migration, to a happier and better climate'.[80] It was a view resonating in some of the evidence taken by, and reflected in the 1831 Select Committee on Secondary Punishments' report, causing it to propose a severely punitive period of productive hard labour before transportation.[81] Six years on, the powerful Molesworth Select Committee (whose membership boasted the Home Secretary Lord John Russell, Fowell Buxton, and Peel) produced a thoroughgoing condemnation of most aspects of the system: highlighting its enormous administrative variations, inequalities, corruption of convicts, and, most concerning, its high costs and low powers of deterrence. Unanimously recommending an immediate end to transportation, the Committee proposed to substitute a punitive regime of imprisonment with hard labour, either in England or in penal colony prisons.

For an amalgam of reasons (principally the change of party in government and other legislative priorities) this course was not immediately followed. But the rate of transportation declined to around 500 a year by 1852, and completely ceased in 1867. On the home front, besides the grounds offered by the Molesworth Committee, some maintained that transportation was inhuman and (frequently)

---

[80] *PD* 1811 (s. 1) 19: App. CXX. Similarly, Sydney Smith's satirical characterization in an 1826 letter to Peel: *Sir Robert Peel: From his Private Papers* (ed. C. S. Parker (1891), i: 400.

[81] *PP* 1831–2 (547), vii, 12. The Committee accepted that those with families 'dread it extremely'. But 'single men [regarded transportation] rather an advantage than a punishment' (p. 17). In reality, more than 50% of those transported were under 24, and around 75% were single. L. L. Robson *The Convict Settlers of Australia* (Melbourne, 1965), 179. Also Anon. 'Secondary Punishment' (1832) 3 *LM* 13–14, and an earlier critical report by a special Commissioner, J. T. Bigge, *PP* 1822 (448) xx.

disproportionately severe for the offences committed; others argued that the great enterprise of colonizing distant realms of the Empire should no longer be burdened with the most dangerous or incorrigible offenders. This claim was further strengthened when the penal settlement on Norfolk Island, used from 1825 for the worst convicts and those re-offending in Australia, closed in 1850. Nevertheless, advocates of transportation could still be located amongst those believing in either its enduring power to reform or ability to deter. Yet, ultimately, the increasingly politically powerful, self-interested opposition of established colonists became a decisive factor in overcoming the residual support which transportation enjoyed in the mother country up to the 1860s.[82]

Following the Molesworth Committee's round condemnation of transportation, Russell had caused plans to be drawn up for establishing national long-term prisons, and secured enactment of the enabling Prisons Act 1839. Creation of a sufficient number of new prisons to replace transportation and the prison hulks[83] was entrusted to Captain Joshua Jebb in 1838. Late of the Royal Engineers, Jebb was originally recruited as a Home Office adviser on the establishing of the separate system in prisons. Despite friction between himself and the more ideologically driven Crawford and Whitworth Russell, the pragmatic Jebb made his mark, and was rewarded by appointment to the key position of Surveyor-General of Prisons in 1844. Peel's second administration, between 1841 and 1846, signalled rather less commitment to new prisons and a more benign view of transportation's future, carrying out ameliorative reforms to meet some of the shortcomings castigated by Molesworth.

---

[82] Molesworth, *Report PP* 1837 (518), xix: A. G. Shaw, *Convicts and the Colonies* (1966); Robson, *The Convict Settlers of Australia* R. Hughes, *The Fatal Shore: A History of Transportation of Convicts to Australia 1787–1868* (1987); J. Cobley, *The Crimes of the First Fleet Convicts* (1984). For a comprehensive review of relevant parliamentary papers, see Radzinowicz and Hood, *Penal Policy*, 468–5.

[83] Originally a temporary expedient to cope with appalling prison overcrowding caused by the interruption of convict transportation in 1775, prison hulks survived until 1857 in England, 1863 in Bermuda, and 1875 in Gibraltar. Moored in the Thames estuary, at Portsmouth and Plymouth, the hulks were administered in a semi-autonomous fashion under the generally lax control of a superintendent of hulks, who was obliged to produce bi-annual reports and make recommendations for the ultimate pardoning or transportation of prisoners. Convicts were required to work on heavy labour projects for the Admiralty or Royal Arsenal. Except for juvenile offenders, no attempt was made to separate or segregate prisoners or to effect their reform. Until the mid-1840s, hulks remained the principal (70%) accommodation for convicts. Their use decreased with the opening of Pentonville and the slow growth of purpose-built public works prisons. By the time of the publication of the highly condemnatory *Report of an Inquiry into the General Treatment and Conditions of the Convicts in the Hulks at Woolwich*, PP 1847 (149), xlviii, 63, the hulks accommodated marginally more than 30% of convicts. Despite being subject to substantial and persistent criticism by the Directorate of Convict Prisons, their usefulness as a source of cheap labour for Admiralty projects prolonged their use until a combination of decay and fire damage terminated their use in England. McConville, *History*, 197–203, 393–6.

The arrival of Russell's first government in 1846, led to renewed instructions aimed at substantially reducing levels of transportation with a compensatory expansion of public works prisons at home. Sir George Grey, Russell's reformist Home Secretary, prompted Jebb to establish a hard labour public works project for convicts at Portland, which began operation in 1848.[84] Much as proposed by the 1831 Select Committee on Secondary Punishments, under this hybrid scheme, after completion of a period at Portland, prisoners would be transported. However, reception of the output of public works prisons was limited to Western Australia where the colony was at a relatively early stage of development. Taking around 500 a year, the last group of transportees to Western Australia departed in 1867. The public works prison regime offered a staged approach to processing prisoners, blending an initial period of separation with later hard manual work on labour-intensive projects, such as the construction of fortifications and sea walls. Finally, the prisoner would be transported, or, for the majority, conditionally released with a 'ticket of leave'. The scheme's claimed benefits were manifold: general deterrence and the potential reform of social attitudes, if not morals, coupled with potentially self-financing prisons.[85]

With Jebb's elevation in 1850 to chairman of the newly created Directorate of Convicts Prisons, policy shifted onto a new footing. Anticipating the end of transportation, a centrally coordinated, national strategy for prisons was developed, with further public works prisons opened up at Portsmouth, Chatham, and

[84] The proposal was strongly opposed by Russell and Crawford, most especially on the grounds of the necessary association and consequential contamination of prisoners involved in public work projects. *Select Committee on Execution of the Criminal Laws*, PP 1847 (447), vii, Minutes of Evidence.

[85] Cf. *Fifth Report of the Surveyor-General of Prisons*, PP 1852–3, li, 1, 64; and McConville, *History*, 381–92. From the outset, women prisoners were never subjected to the physical rigours of hard labour nor the tread wheel. In general, the treatment of women, both in state and local prisons, differed from that handed out to male inmates. This reflected the evolving nineteenth-century image of 'normal' womanhood as incorporating large elements of domesticity, passivity, conformity and, possibly above all, virtue. Belief in the inherent physical vulnerability of most women, their impressionability and susceptibility to personalized measures, translated into less severe manifestations of daily prison life. This included less rigidity in the enforcement of discipline, the absence of disciplinary corporal punishment, and a greater unwillingness to subject recalcitrant women prisoners to the full range of available physical restraints. L. Zedner *Women, Crime and Custody in Victorian England* (Oxford, 1990), *passim* and S. McConville, *English Local Prisons 1860–1900* (1995), 340–50. On earlier trial and punishment practices of women offenders, see King, *Crime and Law in England 1750–1840*, Chs 5 and 6 and D. Palk, *Gender: Crime and Judicial Discretion 1780–1830* (Suffolk, 2006). During (and before) the nineteenth century, the proportion of women tried for both indictable and summary offences fell, as did the proportion of women in local and state prisons. In the case of serious offenders in state prisons, between the late 1870s and 1914 the proportion dropped from approximately 15% to 3%. The basis for the apparent long-term decline in female criminality is problematic; whether it is a true manifestation of decline or one of redesignation of antisocial or delinquent behaviour is contentious. M. Feeley and D. Little 'The Vanishing Female: The Decline of Women in the Criminal Process 1687–1912' (1991) 25 *Law and Society Review* 719.

Dartmoor. While broad acceptance greeted the scheme's expansion, the qualifying basis of a prisoner's release became highly contentious. The practice of remitting part of a sentence and granting a conditional release ('ticket of leave') was a long-established tool of prison discipline. Rationalizing sentencing and devising equivalence tables for the conversion of sentences of transportation into terms of imprisonment generally raised the visibility of remission, most especially just how it was, and ought, to be earned. Against persistent and widespread demands that early release should only follow clear moral regeneration, or at least an exemplary prison record, the more pragmatic approach of Jebb and the Home Office won the day, permitting less virtuous levels of behaviour to qualify for remission.[86]

From 1853 until Jebb's death ten years on, the ticket of leave system attracted a steady and sometimes fierce degree of criticism. Public apprehension grew at the practice of prisons disgorging large numbers of those who formerly would have been transported. The absence of anything resembling systematic post-release supervision by either prison authorities or the police furthered public suspicion. Against a national background of (relative to population growth) falling levels of crime, attribution of perceived localized crime waves to ticket of leave men (particularly the London 'garrotting panic' in the early 1860s) led to specific legislation to allay public fears.[87] Earlier incidents of rioting prisoners had already cast a shadow over prison administration. Most particularly, successive days of severe disturbances in February 1861 at Chatham, had culminated in several hundred inmates being quelled by a combined police and military force of over 500. Followed by the 'garrotting panic', such events were taken as manifest confirmation by many of Jebb's failure effectively to transform a penal system that until then had been heavily reliant on transportation. To these perceived

---

[86] *Ibid.*, and the Penal Servitude Acts 1853 and 1857. Even under the less generous 1857 Act, a sentence, e.g., of 15 years or more could attract one-third remission. 'Penal servitude' had no defined meaning. Sentencing and remission anomalies, together with the perceived largely lost opportunity of a new start in Australia, caused a spate of prison protests between 1853 and 1858, *PP* 1854 (1825), xxxiii, 1856 (2126) xxxv, 79.

[87] The Garotters Act 1863 authorized and revived the practically defunct practice of flogging with up to 150 strokes in total. For the apparent public popularity of flogging in the late nineteenth century, see L. Pike, *A History of Crime in England* (1876), vol. 2, 574–8. The Penal Servitude Act 1864 provided for a structured system of police supervision of 'ticket-of-leave' men. Not only were women entitled to earn remission more swiftly, under the scheme's rules, they were also not subject to regular police supervision. P. W. Bartrip, 'Public Opinion and Law Enforcement: The Ticket-of-Leave Scares in Mid-Victorian Britain', in V. Bailey (ed.), *Policing and Punishment in Nineteenth Century Britain* (1981); J. Davis, 'The London Garrotting Panic of 1862: A Moral Panic and the Creation of a Criminal Class in Mid-Victorian England', in V. Gatrell, V. Lenman, and G. Parker (eds), *Crime and the Law* (1980); and R. Sindall, *Street Violence in the Nineteenth Century: Media Panic or Real Danger?* (Leicester, 1990). On the fall in offence levels relative to population growth, see Gatrell, 'Decline of Theft and Violence'.

shortcomings were added empirically based claims by influential parties, such as Henry Mayhew, that Jebb's prisons were having no great impact on recidivism rates. More impressionistically, Henry Maine reflected that 'All theories on the subject of Punishment have more or less broken down; and we are at sea as to first principles'.[88]

Sliding confidence in Jebb was eventually met in 1863 with the appointment of the House of Lords' Select Committee Inquiry into prison discipline, chaired by Lord Caernarvon, and a Royal Commission to examine the 'operation of the Acts relating to Transportation and Penal Servitude'. The combined effect of two subsequent reports was the rapid enactment of the Penal Servitude Act 1864, which ushered in a nationwide, self-consciously more directly punitive era of prison regimes.[89] The 1864 Act provided for structured police supervision of ticket of leave men, procedures which would prove a foot in the door for later legislation aimed at recidivists in general. In response to the Commission's view that generally punishment failed to deter because it was not 'sufficiently dreaded', the Act also stipulated minimum penal servitude sentences of five years for many first offenders and seven years for anyone with a previous felony conviction.[90] On top of this, provisions of the Prisons Act 1865, incorporating many of the Royal Commission's and Caernarvon Committee's proposals, sought to ensure that extended periods of imprisonment would be ever more punitive.[91] Moral regeneration of prisoners had already been explicitly subordinated to deterrence

---

[88]   Mayhew, *The Criminal Prisons of London* (1862); Maine, *Speeches* (1864), 123.

[89]   *Report of the Select Committee of the House of Lords on the Present State of Discipline in Gaols and Houses of Correction PP* 1863 (499), ix, 1; and *Report of the Commissioners Appointed to Enquire into the Operation of the Acts Relating to Transportation and Penal Servitude, PP* 1863 (3190), xxi, 1.

[90]   The Penal Servitude Amendment Act 1863, 27 Vict. c. 47, s 2. Jebb, the Home Office and the Royal Commission had favoured supervision being carried out by the prison authorities. Radzinowicz and Hood, *Penal Policy*, 246 *et seq.*

[91]   Common to every official and parliamentary report of this whole era, is a singular lack of any sustained attempt to distinguish between punishment imposed for retributive and deterrence purposes. The broad drift of justifications for penal proposals, whilst explicitly based on deterrence, are often overlaid with retributory rhetoric. The relatively clear utilitarian-deterrence rationale underpinning the range of Criminal Law Commissioners' recommendations relating to punishment is not found in all (nominally) utilitarian theorists of the second half of the nineteenth century. Appearing in the *General View* (1863), Fitzjames Stephen's denunciatory theory of punishment (the need to gratify and reinforce common moral outrage) was probably ultimately utilitarian in so far as seeking to maintain an efficient crime controlling system. However, for Stephen, besides general deterrence, punishment's key function was one of fostering moral approval and social solidarity. Similarly, S. Amos, *The Science of Law* (1874), 28 and F. Pollock, *A First Book of Jurisprudence* (1896). Smith, *James Fitzjames Stephen*, 54–60. For direct assaults on utilitarian/deterrence theories of punishment of the second half of the nineteenth century (principally J. S. Mill, *Utilitarianism* (1863), Ch. 5) see particularly the 'British Idealists' retributive claims of F. H. Bradley, *Ethical Studies* (1876), Essay 1 and T. H. Green, *Lectures on the Principles of Political Obligations* (1881).

by Jebb, and now it would be further relegated: strict compliance of all prisons and a broader deterrence was to be achieved by harder and more tedious labour (including tread-wheels and hand cranks) along with a physically more uncomfortable environment.[92] Enforcement of provisions of the 1865 Act represented one further step in ensuring nationally uniform prison regimes and standards: failure to comply with either statutory requirements or Home Office regulations threatened withdrawal of central funding or even closure of a local prison.

Du Cane, Uniformity of Punishment and the Nationalization of Prisons

Jebb's successors, in 1863, were Edmund Henderson and Edmund Du Cane, a friend and one of Henderson's deputies. Both shared Jebb's Royal Engineers background and both had similar experience in managing criminals in Western Australia. Du Cane succeeded Henderson in 1869, with the latter's appointment as Commissioner of the Metropolitan Police. Du Cane became the dominant figure in prisons' administration for over two decades until retirement in 1895. As he frequently reiterated, punishment was 'more to deter others than the individual'; and such general deterrence came most effectively from uniformity of penal servitude applied with no discretion.[93] Discipline and general order were achieved through specific mechanisms devised to reward a prisoner or to add to a prisoner's punishment. Beside the routine disciplinary effects of a largely silent work and exercise regimen, and the sheer exhaustion induced by hard labour, resort could be made to flogging, birching, or extended periods in solitary confinement.

However, of considerably greater disciplinary importance was the granting or withholding of remission.[94] Deep and widespread concerns over 'habitual' offenders and 'ticket of leave' practices had led to systematized registration and post-release supervision under the Habitual Criminals Act 1869 and Prevention of Crimes Act 1871.[95] Eligibility for remission under Du Cane became a methodical

---

[92] For a detailed analysis of the Caernarvon Committee's proposals, the extent of their implementation in the Prison Act 1865, and subsequent national policies, see McConville, *English Local Prisons, passim.*

[93] Especially the Kimberley *Commission on the Penal Servitude Acts,* 1879 [C. 2368], *PP* 1878–9, xxxvii, 1. On the dynamics of the relationship between Du Cane, senior Home Office officials and local prisons Visiting Committees of magistrates, see McConville, *English Local Prisons,* Chs 10–12.

[94] The overwhelming majority of prisoners in local prisons served terms of less than six months. Consequently, remission was not relevant to most local prisoners.

[95] For the influential role played by the Social Science Association in the enactment of this legislation aimed at the believed class of hardened, professional criminals and recidivists, see

book-keeping exercise, the subject of a ledger account of marks earned for work carried out. Reward marks also progressively eased the sheer mental and physical grimness of daily survival, with the more industrious and compliant prisoners moving after three years into a class which enjoyed limited additional periods of exercise, visits and letters, and slight improvement of diet. Indeed, the question of appropriate diet and the awkward, ever-present, issue of 'less eligibility' had long troubled prison authorities. Public opinion and some penal philosophers demanded that prison diets, at best, should be no more generous than those experienced in workhouses or by common labourers. Considered by some as too generous under Jebb, the question of appropriate diet was settled by a special committee on 'Convict Prison Dietaries' at barely more than starvation levels: 'sufficient to preserve health'; but at the same time, diet should 'minister to their correction by being unattractive and monotonous'. Such dietary privations remained an element of punishment and a fundamental feature of prison life until the end of the century.[96]

Although subject to periodic parliamentary investigation, Du Cane (eventually) ran a national system of prisons with neither a structured procedure of external scrutiny nor any apparent willingness to modify policies that periodically attracted adverse comment. Moreover, as well as successfully resisting proposals of even officially appointed bodies,[97] the former sources of information on the system's functioning published under Jebb were rapidly pruned, thereby greatly constricting external review of the internal processes of prison governance. In large part, Du Cane's policies emerged and operated as a consequence of government default as much as any positive, centrally driven ambitions. It was a state of affairs which successive governments and Home Secretaries found expedient to leave largely undisturbed. Rather than an agent of Liberal or Tory ideology, Du Cane was long tolerated as a safe and experienced administrator who could be trusted to act within fairly broad common policy limits and to achieve an acceptable measure of 'success' or containment. Nationalization of prisons was one important manifestation of this relationship. Justifiably, local prison autonomy had been under steady scrutiny and gradual erosion since Peel's time.

L. Goldman, *Science, Reform and Politics in Victorian Britain* (Cambridge, 2002), Ch. 5. Use of the police supervision system of 'habitual' criminals declined rapidly in the following years through a combination of inadequate police resources and judicial reservations on its effectiveness or justification. Radzinowicz and Hood, *Penal Policy*, 254–61.

[96] Du Cane, *The Punishment and Prevention of Crime* (1885), 1 and 155.

[97] *Report of the Departmental Committee on Prison Dietaries* [C. 9166], *PP* 1899, xliii, 1. The Committee found deficiencies in the quantity, nutritional value, and variety of prison food. On the less than creditable performance of many in the prison medical service, see McConville, *English Local Prisons*, Ch. 7.

National prisons took the most serious offenders sentenced to penal servitude, but the overwhelming bulk of offenders served out their sentences (of mainly weeks or months) in local prisons. While the Prisons Act 1865 prescribed conditions and regulations for all prisons, it only gave Henderson, Du Cane and the Home Office, coercive financial power; no ability existed to exert direct and positive control over local prison administration.[98] The Prison Act 1877 equipped Du Cane, as chairman of the newly created Prison Commission, with just such centralized administrative responsibility and power.

Momentum for central control of prisons had been steadily building before Du Cane's ascendancy; but his administrative acumen and strategic ambitions for prisons in general, coupled with broader political factors, were the essential galvanizing conditions for legislative intervention. As with many other areas of administrative centralization in the nineteenth century, the elevation of local problems to matters of national concern often went hand in hand with the assumption of financial responsibility. Local inability or unwillingness to levy sufficient rates to fund prison construction or improvements had necessitated central financial support. Increasing government regulation of prison conditions was accompanied by substantial emasculation of local magistrates' supervisory powers. This argued for the assumption of full central administrative responsibility, as did the widespread perception of crime and crime control as a national phenomenon.

Characterization of crime as a matter of national concern, met by incremental increases in centralized powers, was also the pattern for the imposition of professional policing in all areas of the country. But government indifference aside, the prospect of a national police force would have been perceived as an infinitely more centrally intrusive move than such a development for prisons. The final step to nationalization of prisons owed much to Du Cane's faith in the overwhelming virtues of centralized, uniform prison policies and administration, particularly his own. Du Cane's nationalization plans had offered a Tory government an inestimable benefit: the chance to redeem a clear election pledge to cut back both local rates and government taxes. As promoted by Du Cane, nationalization could eliminate expensive, under-used prisons, produce rapid cost-effective amalgamations, and increase revenue from an expanded, professionally run prison labour scheme. While challenged on constitutional grounds, expressed

---

[98] While highly critical of the inefficiency and lax administrative practices of many local prisons (xiv–xvi), the Caernarvon Report stopped short of proposing nationalization. Jebb, for one, in his evidence to the Committee advocated giving the Home Secretary greater powers to control the administration of local prisons. Du Cane's control of local prisons ended residual local avoidance of the strict separation regime required by early legislation for all prisoners, including those serving short sentences.

scepticism over projected financial savings, and by resistance from demoralized local magistrates, the nationalization bill never faced seriously endangering
opposition. Although failing to achieve the administrative miracle of a cost-
free, streamlined revamping of the prison system, Du Cane's undeniable legacy
was the significant raising of management efficiency and modernization of the
very fabric of the prison system. Moreover, with a steady downturn in recorded
crime and committal levels since the mid-1840s,[99] and dramatic falls in prison
populations,[100] general opinion now 'asserted that there never was...a time in
which life and property were so secure as...at present'.[101] Indeed, such was the
optimism that infected some areas of officialdom, by the end of the century it
could be recorded that society had experienced a 'great change in manners; the
substitution of words without blows for blows with or without words;...a decline
in the spirit of lawlessness'.[102]

Consequently, it was hardly surprising that through a powerful combination
of personality, a detailed command of his responsibilities, acquiescing Home
Secretaries, frequently quiescent Home Office officials and, not least, an apparent
measure of success, Sir Edmund Du Cane came tantalizingly close to serving out
his days, unchallenged as an administrative potentate, until natural retirement.
However, two years out from the event, a process of de-thronement got underway with a press campaign, nominally addressed to Asquith, then Liberal Home
Secretary, calling for extensive reform of the prison system to reflect a less punitive and pernicious, more positive view of the role that prisons might perform.
Though Du Cane did not lack public defenders, with parliamentary support
the periodical and newspaper debate gained sufficient momentum to persuade
Asquith of the necessity for some form of public review.

The extent of this pressure was expressly confirmed by the departmental committee appointed by Asquith and chaired by Herbert Gladstone; at the beginning
of its Report the Committee noted the 'sweeping indictment' against the whole
prison system advanced in the press.[103] Du Cane's identified 'achievements' were

[99] Broadly continuing until 1914. S. Redgrave, Criminal Registrar, 'Criminal Tables for the Year 1845' (1846) 9 *J. of Stat. Soc.* 177; Radzinowicz and Hood, *Penal Policy*, 113.

[100] During Du Cane's long reign from the early 1870s to the mid-1890s the number of convict prisoners dropped from c. 12,000 to c. 5000.

[101] Pike, *A History of Crime in England* vol 2; 480. Similarly, *The Times*, 3 November 1881, p. 7.

[102] Proportionate to population growth. Criminal Registrar (1901) Report for 1899, 36; Gatrell, 'Decline', 241. Similarly, *The Times*, 6 February 1899, p. 9 and Radzinowicz and Hood, *ibid.*, 115.

[103] *Report from the Departmental Committee on Prisons PP* 1895 [C. 7702–1], lvi, 1. Son of the Liberal Prime Minister, Herbert Gladstone, was parliamentary Under Secretary at the Home Office from 1892–4 and later Home Secretary. Committee membership included a magistrate, Chairman of Quarter Sessions, an Irish Nationalist, a doctor, and the future Lord Haldane. As well as visiting a substantial range of convict and local prisons, the Committee took evidence from a broad span of witnesses including Du Cane himself, Home Office officials, the two prison commissioners, prison

marshalled so as to underline their deficiencies: the 'masterful' creation of an 'absolute system of uniformity...discipline and economy' which was 'admirable for coercion and repression'. However, in the Gladstone Committee's view there had been an 'excessively defiant' regard for the 'reformatory side', which, with deterrence, should be 'primary and concurrent objects'. Instead of uniform treatment as a 'hopeless or worthless element in the community'—as 'irreclaimable', prisoners should be subject to an 'elastic', more individualized system, designed to 'awaken...higher susceptibilities..., develop moral instincts [and] to train them in orderly and industrial habits...'.[104] Such redeeming of the redeemable would require several radical shifts of policy: most especially, a greater discrimination was required to produce the appropriate categories of prisoners and appropriate prison response. Addressing the 'headsprings of recidivism', the Committee identified 17–19 years as the 'most fatal years', when the 'most determined effort should be made to lay hold of those incipient criminals and to prevent them by strong restraint and rational treatment'. And even for 'irreclaimable' recidivists and those serving long sentences, the severity of punishment was to be eased, with reconsideration of the initial nine-month solitary confinement period, and a staged and supervised relaxation of the prohibition on socializing.

A Discriminatory Approach: Punishment or Treatment?

The outcome of the Gladstone Report first appeared in the Prison Act 1898, whose provisions were largely the combined consequences of the detailed responses of the Prison Commissioners and spirited, highly disputatious parliamentary debates.[105] Critical opinion polarized between those who regarded reform proposals as either subversively lenient in the treatment of prisoners or utterly inadequate to remedy the indiscriminate harshness of the Du Cane era. Beyond amalgamation of the two boards of national and local prisons, the 1898 Act was a cautious, facilitative measure leaving undisturbed much of Du Cane's uniformity and emphasis on deterrence, but expressly requiring that the treatment of prisoners reflect their 'sex, age, health, industry and conduct'. Such consequential changes could be accompanied by discretionary Home Office administrative procedures without recourse to the open, public process of further legislation.

---

medical officers, governors, and ex-prisoners. For details of the press campaign, see Radzinowicz and Hood, *Penal Policy*, 573–6 and McConville, *English Local Prisons*, 554–84, and 649–60 on the press response to the Committee's Report.

[104] *Report*, 7, 8, 12, 13, 18 and 22. For habitual criminals, drunkards, and the mentally impaired, provision of specialized institutions was proposed.

[105] For a detailed account of the enactment of the 1898 Act, see McConville, *English Local Prisons*, 697–757.

Evelyn Ruggles-Brise's appointment as Du Cane's successor in 1895[106] was of central importance in determining just how far the Gladstone Report objectives would be realised through the empowering 1898 Act. While exhibiting a distinctly different administrative style—more open and collective—Ruggles-Brise led no innovative leap in prison penal policy. As presaged by the Commissioners' cautious 1896 response to the Gladstone Report, for the general run of prisoners, daily existence improved slowly and only to a limited degree. At odds with the broader Gladstone philosophy, Ruggles-Brise held to the dominant roles of retribution and general deterrence. Informed by a combination of humanitarian beliefs and concerns over prisoners' psychological welfare, a trickle of concessions were introduced over several years. By earning these, prisoners could gain certain benefits relating to diet, communication, socialisation, visits, and the range of available prisoners' reading materials. Following the introduction of Boards of Visitors in 1898, the frequency and severity of disciplinary flogging dropped dramatically. Additionally, though initially resisted by the Commission, the periods of separate confinement for different categories of prisoners were reduced from nine months in 1895 to between one and three months by 1910.[107]

The discriminatory penal philosophy embedded in the Gladstone Report and given an inchoate form in the 1898 Act, eventually fed into several distinct initiatives including preventive detention, borstals, probation and aftercare, treatment of inebriates, and arrangements for the mentally deficient.

(1) RECIDIVISM

Although imbued with a restrained optimism in the reformability of some offenders, the Gladstone Committee Report also recognized the disposal problem associated with a large body of persistent offenders for whom there was no reasonable hope of redemption. Indeed, the Committee identified recidivism as the 'most important of all prison questions and the most complicated'.[108] Beyond the vaguest of proposals for lengthy periods of detention under a regime less severe than penal servitude, the Committee dropped the matter into the collective lap of the Prison Commissioners and Home Office. An eventual response was the Prevention of Crime Act 1908. This established a two-stage system of sentencing

---

[106] Before appointment as Chairman of the Prison Commission and Convict Prison Directorate, Ruggles-Brise had been Private Secretary to four Home Secretaries and a Prison Commissioner since 1891. He retired from the prison service in 1921. Like many of his colleagues, his professional relationship with Du Cane had been remote. For an assessment of Ruggles-Brise's role, the Prison Commission, and his relationship with the Home Office, see W. J. Forsythe, *Penal Discipline, Reformatory Projects and the English Prison Commission 1895–1939* (Exeter, 1991), Ch. 3.

[107] Routine separate confinement was abolished in 1922 after Ruggles-Brise's retirement. For Churchill's performance and the campaigning role of the novelist and lawyer John Galsworthy to reduce the periods of solitary confinement, see Radzinowicz and Hood, *Penal Policy*, 591–5.

[108] *Report*, 5.

under which a person convicted of being an 'habitual offender' was subject to a further sentence of at least five years' preventive detention, to be served after the expiration of the initial sentence.

Much of the intervening 13-year period between the Gladstone Committee and the Act of 1908 had been characterized by extensive, principled, and frequently heated exchanges between the advocates and opponents of such a system. There was an initial definitional hurdle of 'habitual criminal': should it include persistent petty offenders as well as those repeating serious offences, or both? Beyond this was a cluster of further questions which divided supporters as well as opponents: What attempt, if any, would be made to determine individual causes of recidivism? Should protective eugenic measures be enlisted? Should preventive detention be fixed or indeterminate? If the latter, who should settle the appropriate point of release?[109] More broadly, as a matter of penal philosophy a dyed-in-the-wool utilitarian might demand that habitual criminals should never be released to threaten further criminal activity. However, most parties involved in the system's operation and direction appeared to be guided by an innate sense that punishment had to meet retributive values.

The unresolved, or unresolvable, nature of such issues fatally undermined the compromised provisions finally constituting the 1908 Act. Within two years a sceptical, not to say hostile, Winston Churchill had characterized preventive detention as little more than an extended form of penal servitude. Even when assured of the intended distinctions, Churchill, as Home Secretary, drastically reduced the range of candidates for preventive detention to the 'worst class of professional criminals'. The Act's operation was further marginalized by its unpopularity with the judiciary and the common aversion amongst juries to identifying defendants as 'habitual criminals', thereby facilitating what they regarded as disproportionately lengthy sentences. Moreover, quite contrary to its original conception, reform objectives gradually insinuated themselves amongst the social protection objectives of preventive detention, thereby opening up an additional avenue for discrediting the system. Although not without loyal enthusiasts, and surviving until the 1960s, the procedure never made a significant penal impact.

(2) JUVENILES

The Gladstone Committee displayed considerable empathy for young offenders, urging a distinct discriminatory approach to their 'punishment'. It was an

---

[109] For a detailed account of the pre- and post-1908 Act position, see Radzinowicz and Hood, 265–87. Previous legislation on habitual criminals focused largely on a system of post-release police supervision, with specific penalties for re-offending within a specified period. The system's dependence on long-term supervision proved impracticable. See above for the Habitual Criminals Act 1869 and Prevention of Crimes Acts 1871 and 1879.

attitude with long roots.[110] Throughout the century, appalling social conditions, aggravated by feckless parents and early association with criminality were frequently identified by commentators and committees as major sources of criminality. The vague Gladstone prescription of 'strong restraint and rational treatment' had in earlier decades inspired a mixed bag of initiatives with varying levels of success. As has been seen, the innovatory Parkhurst experiment from the 1830s was defeated by a combination of unsure targeting, confused aims, and poor instruction. During the second half of the nineteenth century, moralizing and training errant juveniles fell largely to privately run reformatories and industrial schools, partly state funded and government inspected. Offenders under 16 could be sentenced to a term of imprisonment followed by two to five years in a reformatory. Vagrant children up to 14 or those beyond parental control were eligible for industrial schools, successors to Lord Shaftsbury's ragged schools. While the basis for calculating claims of high success rates for such regimes is open to extensive doubt,[111] there was nonetheless a trend, discernible from the mid-nineteenth century onwards, towards removing children from the operation of adult penal sanctions and institutions.[112] However, partly because of its more direct challenge to the criminal justice system and the fundamentals of adult liability, no corresponding development occurred relating to the basis of juvenile criminal responsibility.[113]

Government supported growth of separate reformatories and industrial schools affirmed the distinction between reformist and preventative endeavours. Removal of the requirement of a short spell of initial imprisonment before entry into a reformatory school and similar regimes threatened their distinctiveness by 1900. Yet the final step of amalgamation would wait until 1933. The use of

[110] For a survey of the early law, policies, and practice of punishing young offenders, see King, *Crime and Law in England*, Chs 2–4, and also XIII, Pt 4.

[111] Until 1899, the period spent at reformatory school had to be preceded by the 'shock' of a minimum of 14 days' imprisonment. Absconding or poor discipline could attract a sentence of up to three months' hard labour. Courts were empowered to order a child's parents to contribute towards maintenance at reformatory schools and industrial schools. See generally, J. A. Stack, *Social Policy and Juvenile Delinquency, 1815–1875* (1974). The alternative or additional punishment of whipping was available to all courts for juveniles under 16 until 1948. For the campaigning role of Mary Carpenter (author of *Reformatory Schools for the Perishing and Dangerous Classes* (1851)), see R. Watts, 'Mary Carpenter: Educator of the Children of the "Perishing and Dangerous Classes"', in M. Hilton and P. Hirsch (eds), *Practical Visionaries. Women, Education and Social Progress 1790–1930* (Harlow, 2000), 39. For religious inspiration generally, see XI, Pt 1.

[112] Radzinowicz and Hood, *Penal Policy*, Chs 6 and 7. For the internal official debate on the welfarist-responsibility distinction, see M. Wiener, *Reconstructing the Criminal* (Cambridge, 1990), *passim*.

[113] The Gladstone Committee proposed raising the age of eligibility for reformatories to 18 (p. 30).

such discrete institutions also facilitated a more general, widely held, objective of reducing the number of children in prison. Driven by a range of pragmatic, moral, and humanitarian motives, from a peak of over 12,000 in the mid-1850s, the number had sunk to just over 1000 by 1903. In considerable measure this was a consequence of legislation beginning in the 1840s aimed at enlarging summary jurisdiction to include offences of juveniles formerly only triable on indictment. Within two years, the Children Act 1908 (see below) pushed this drastically reduced number down to around 150 imprisoned children.[114]

More generally, during the decades leading up to the outbreak of the First World War, the penal system and particularly those elements concerned with juvenile criminality, underwent substantial official scrutiny. Partly in response, a welfarist Liberal government included in its legislative programme a cluster of measures aimed generally at child welfare, including that of juvenile offenders. Its principal political mentor was Herbert Gladstone, Home Secretary from 1905. The cornerstone of these measures was the Children Act 1908, powerfully affirming the principle that young offenders were to be the subject of special treatment throughout the criminal justice system, including the establishment of juvenile courts. The Act also required that no one under 14 would be imprisoned, or if aged 14–15, then only in the most exceptional circumstances. Enactment of the Probation of Offenders Act the year before was aimed at reforming offenders (both adult and juvenile) and preventing recidivism by a regulated mechanism of advice, supervision, assistance, and basic 'civilizing' from social workers.[115] Broadly, these institutional reforms and innovations for the treatment of young offenders followed two distinct initiatives. For those under 16 the management and methods of industrial and reformatory schools were subject to a searching Home Office Departmental Committee review, the outcome of which was a determined attempt at revising institutional ethos and practices. Accumulated, stultifying rigidities were to be jettisoned; welfarist individualism was embraced

[114] See also especially the Juvenile Offences Act 1847, the Criminal Justice Act 1855, the Summary Jurisdiction Acts 1879 and 1899, and the Criminal Justice Administration Act 1914. Additionally, with varying degrees of emphasis, a succession of Home Secretaries from the 1870s actively encouraged a diminished use of imprisonment by courts for juveniles. From the 1870s, state intervention in the welfare of children moved forward on a broad front: the compulsory elementary education of children (Elementary Education Acts 1870 and 1876); the broader regulation of children's working conditions (Factory Act 1878); protection from cruelty and neglect (Prevention of Cruelty to Children Acts 1889 and 1894).

[115] Described in the *Report of the Departmental Committee on the Probation of Offenders Act 1909.* For the antecedents of the 1907 Act, see the Prevention of Crime Acts 1871 and 1879, and the Probation of First Offenders Act 1887. See generally, D. Bochel, *Probation and Aftercare: Its Development in England and Wales* (Edinburgh, 1976) and Radzinowicz and Hood, *Penal Policy*, 633–47. By 1914, well in excess of 10,000 probation orders a year were being made by the courts.

with the hope of enhancing the healthier mental and moral development of these institutionalized children.[116]

For young adults, aged 16–21, Herbert Gladstone translated the 1895 Report proposals into provisions of the Prevention of Crime Act 1908. The Act enabled higher courts to impose indeterminate sentences of between one and three years detention on young adults when convicted of offences for which they could be imprisoned or suffer penal servitude. Candidates for this innovatory 'borstal' training were to be those who 'by reason of... criminal habits and tendencies or associations with persons of bad character, [it] was expedient... should be subject to detention and [such] instruction and discipline most conducive to... reformation and the repression of crime'. Enactment of these flexible criteria followed what were regarded as encouraging experimental detention training schemes first begun in 1900, under Ruggles-Brise's supervision, at Bedford, Borstal (Kent), Lincoln, and Dartmoor.

At these borstals, through a blend of prison-type discipline and appropriate instruction, both young men and women were to benefit from improved physical and moral wellbeing, and acquire trade skills and industrious habits. Additionally, young women would be trained in a range of domestically useful skills. Considerable emphasis was to be given to individual assessment and progression of 'trainees', and to beneficial personal staff influence. Release could take place at any time after three months for women and six months for men. Post-release assistance and supervision, strongly favoured in the Gladstone Report, was carried out by the specially established Borstal Association. Early difficulties in recruiting knowledgeable and sympathetic staff, and in ensuring that courts made full and proper use of the system, were substantially overcome by the 1920s.[117] By this time the therapeutic element had achieved ascendancy over the penal, and the institutions had gained an ethos a little closer to Ruggles-Brise's 'long curative detention', likened by him to the needs of 'habitual inebriates'.[118]

(3) INEBRIETY AND VAGRANCY

Recidivism amongst three particular categories of offenders had been especially intractable throughout the nineteenth century, and before; these were inebriates,

[116] *Report of the Departmental Committee on Reformatories and Industrial Schools* [C. 6838], *PP* 1913, ixl, 1; J. Carlebach *Caring for Children in Trouble* (1970), 81–94, 113–32. The Committee was set up by Churchill, as Home Secretary, in 1911. On attempts to identify criteria for the appropriateness of reformatory, industrial school, or probation, see V. Bailey, *Delinquency and Citizenship: Reclaiming the Young Offender 1914–1948* (Oxford, 1987), Ch. 2.

[117] As well as judicial over-use of the scheme for short periods and reluctance to resort to high maximum indeterminate sentences, Churchill expressed considerable distaste for what he regarded as a repressive, class-based scheme. R. Hood, *Borstal Re-Assessed* (1965) and Forsythe, *Penal Discipline, Reformatory Projects and the English Prison Commission*, Ch. 4.

[118] *Report on the Fifth and Sixth International Penal Congress* 1900, p. 104.

vagrants, and the 'feeble minded'. Treatment of the persistent low level criminality or anti-social behaviour by members of these groups with standard forms of punishment had lacked conviction. In each case the ethical or practical appeal of deterrence, retribution or reform was, at best, subject to considerable scepticism. By the early twentieth century, against a background of scientifically informed prison and government bureaucracies, the response to each (often overlapping) category of 'inadequate' offender had evolved from a largely undiscriminating penal approach to one of specialized therapy or at least segregation.

Over the whole of the nineteenth century, intoxication was a frequently designated major cause of pauperism and criminality.[119] However, by the 1870s, despite the increasing strength of the temperance movement, the moral reprehensibility attached to habitual intoxication had given substantial ground in official quarters to regarding the condition as a pathological disorder. Allied to this, the often appalling social consequences of excessive drinking now caused officialdom to focus increasingly on regulating the sale of intoxicants. Consequently, rather than punishment, inebriety was seen as more appropriately treated therapeutically. The modest provisions of the Habitual Drunkards Act 1879 provided for the voluntary commitment by magistrates of those declared habitual drunkards for up to 12 months to a licensed private institution. Not only did the Act fail to deal with criminal offenders, because of the costs involved, it was, effectively, only relevant to those able to fund their own treatment. Distinctly more radical proposals were produced by a Home Office departmental committee set up in 1892, which, in a modified form, led to the Inebriates Act 1898. Under this Act, courts could commit an offender to an inebriates' reformatory for up to three years where an offence had either been committed under the influence of alcohol or the offender was found to be an habitual drunkard.[120] The legislation's prime

---

[119] e.g. *Report of the Select Committee of Inquiry into Drunkenness, PP* 1834 (559), viii, 315, 320; *Report from the Select Committee on Public Houses, PP* 1854 (367), xiv, 231, at p. 245; *Second Report from the Select Committee of the House of Lords on Intemperance, PP* 1877 (271), xi, p. 357 at p. 395; and the *Final Report of the Royal Commission on Liquor Licensing Laws* 1896–99, *PP* 1899 [C. 9379], xxxv, p. 1 at p. 92. More generally, and on the oppositional roles of temperance societies and the highly influential liquor trade, see B. Harrison, *Drink and the Victorians* (1971) and L. Shiman, *Crusade Against Drink in Victorian England* (1988). The major restrictions on the sale and consumption of alcohol were contained in the Licensing Acts of 1872 and 1874, which facilitated police and Home Office supervision of public houses and further regulations under the Licensing Act 1902. For the interactive relationship between the Home Office and the Metropolitan Police in the fashioning and enforcement of the regulations, see Petrow, *Policing Morals*, Chs 7 and 8.

[120] *Report from the Departmental Committee on the Treatment of Inebriates PP* 1893–4 [C. 7008], xvii, 17, 597. The Committee's proposal for the compulsory committal of non-criminal inebriates to distinct institutions was abandoned. The Gladstone Committee regarded habitual drunkards as 'not criminals in the ordinary sense and should stand by themselves in the special category. [They] should be dealt with as patients rather than criminals' (pp. 31–2). Also the *Report from the Departmental Committee on Habitual Offenders, Vagrants, Beggars, Inebriates and Juvenile Delinquents (Scotland), PP* 1895 [C. 7753], xxxvii, 1. As a further move against habitual drunkards, the Licensing

target was highly recidivistic women inebriates who rapidly became the overwhelming majority of occupants of both local and state reformatories. But the scheme foundered through a combination of problems including defining 'habitual drunkard', under-use or misuse by the courts of their committal powers, together with poor results. As a result, within two decades the experiment was terminated with closure of the system's 15 reformatories.[121]

Broadly, mental impairment short of that required for a defence of insanity had no formal effect on an offender's criminal liability and eligibility for punishment, including imprisonment. Removing or segregating 'feeble minded' prisoners from the standard prison regime was viewed as undermining Du Cane's insistence on uniformity of treatment and discipline. However, the disruptive tendencies of such prisoners, coupled with the growing ascendancy of prison medical officers, first led to local innovations followed by a general power to remove some 'feeble minded' to special institutions.[122] Despite extensive disagreement over the extent of the problem, the general desire amongst Home Office and prison officials for greater discrimination of treatment amongst prisoners in the post-Gladstone Report period culminated in the Royal Commission on the Care and Control of the Feeble Minded, 1904–8. Most significantly, the Commission accepted the fundamental distinction between detention for punishment and detention for mental incapacity; and that they were 'two procedures…in large degree incompatible'.[123] Basing its proposal principally on an hereditary view of feeble mindedness, the Commission urged the establishment of a 'Board of Control' to oversee the creation and administration of specialized labour colonies. This widely supported eugenists' approach gained legislative force in the mainly unopposed Mental Deficiency Act 1913, which provided for care and control of defined offenders and non-offenders in specialist institutions.[124]

Act 1902 provided for the fining and possible detention of black-listed inebriates who attempted to purchase alcohol.

[121] C. Harding and L. Wilkins ' "The Dream of a Benevolent Mind": the Late Victorian Response to the Problem of Inebriacy' (1988) 9 *Criminal Justice History* 189; Petrow, *Policing Morals*, Chs 7 and 8; Zedner, *Women, Crime and Custody*, Ch. 6.

[122] The Prisons Act 1865 required all prisoners to be regularly medically inspected, but under the Lunacy Act 1867 only those certified insane could be removed to an institution such as Broadmoor. The Criminal Lunatics Act 1884 removed the inflexibility of the 1867 Act, giving the Home Secretary powers to regulate the treatment of mentally impaired prisoners. Partly through prison authority concerns over undermining discipline and also because of the reluctance of asylums to receive such individuals, the powers were infrequently exercised.

[123] *Report of the Royal Commission on the Care and Control of the Feeble Minded*, PP 1908 [C. 4202], xxxix, 159, 314.

[124] Those subject to 'mental defectiveness, not amounting to imbecility'. For the political and legislative background, and broader public debate on the 1913 Act and eugenics, see Radzinowicz and Hood, *Penal Policy*, 326–38. On the subsequent history of the Act, see K. Jones, *Asylums and After: A Revised History of the Mental Health Services* (1993).

In general terms, vagrancy, feeble mindedness, and inebriety shared much common ground. Beyond the desire for an itinerant life or one of pure idleness, vagrancy was frequently a manifestation of inebriety and sometimes feeble mindedness. Whatever its root cause, vagrancy had long been regarded by the authorities as a social and economic pestilence. Its particular intractability lay in vagrancy's intimate relationship to poor relief: devising an effective legal and practical strategy for effectively separating the deserving from the undeserving. Formulating a process of providing relief for the genuinely destitute but penalizing the wilfully idle, eluded the courts, Parliament, and poor law authorities throughout the century.[125] As well as offending work ethic sensibilities, the local presence of vagrants was typically viewed as a preliminary to casual, opportunistic petty crime. Such apprehensions generated a series of increasingly restrictive measures providing for the arrest, summary conviction, and imprisonment of 'suspicious' or 'suspected persons'. Moreover, begging was often regarded as an initial step of a predictable and progressive descent into serious forms of criminality; vagrancy was proto-criminality, and vagrants proto-criminals. Furthermore, not only did their presence in the casual wards of workhouses disrupt and undermine the grinding, grim, disciplined administration of poor law relief, their frequent and brief spells in local prisons were regarded as a thorough-going nuisance and a very substantial distraction by prison authorities.[126]

As much as under the earlier severe Poor Law regime, in the final decades of the nineteenth century increasingly broad state welfare provisions were most distinctly not intended to underpin the perceived pleasures of the voluntary idle. For the 1906 Departmental Committee on Vagrancy, the solution to the vagrancy problem lay in establishing penal colonies in England, where the now designated

---

[125] The 'less eligibility' calculation was a central source of difficulty. Essentially, to reflect the nature of their institutions and to deter opportunistic migration from workhouses to prison, the living and working conditions (and especially diet) for inmates of prisons were to be kept more severe than those of workhouses. In turn, workhouse conditions were supposed to be no better than those of a common working labourer. To deter abuse of the workhouse casual ward system by itinerant vagrants, successive attempts were made to make them distinctly more unattractive than that for longer-term residents. Maintaining these relativities between workhouse and prison greatly taxed the ingenuity of central government, the Poor Law Commissioners, and local boards of guardians throughout the nineteenth century. M. Crowther, *The Workhouse System 1834–1929* (Athens, Georgia, 1981), *passim*.

[126] For powers of arrest and conviction on 'suspicion', see the Habitual Criminals Act 1869 and the Prevention of Crimes Act 1871. Official and other estimates of the vagrant prison population during the course of the nineteenth century vary enormously. In the early 1830s around 20% of prisoners were classed as vagrants. *PP* 1895 (441), xii, 398–9. At the beginning of the twentieth century, evidence taken by the Departmental Committee on Vagrancy suggested the figure to be in excess of 25%. *Report, PP* 1906 [C. 2852], ciii, p. 25. The majority served less than 14 days.

'incorrigible rogues' would be separated for detention between six months and three years. While attracting extremely wide political and public support, the hybrid nature of the initiative provoked sufficient parliamentary caution to stall the full passage of proposed legislation.[127] Immediate post-War social and economic developments radically diminished the scale of the vagrancy problem and with it the strong political appeal of penal labour colonies.[128]

Strategic Overview of Punishment

The institution of punishment underwent the most radical of changes over the century or so leading up to the First World War. Capital punishment's dominant symbolic role was terminated by the 1830s; disposal of substantial numbers of convicts by transportation came finally to an end in the 1860s. With the opening of Pentonville, prisons were perceived as the principal future mechanism for punishing, deterring, and morally reclaiming criminals. Elevation of prisons to this central function involved the broadest of reforms: a steady drive for centralized administration and scrutiny; uniformity of rules and treatment of prisoners; increased professionalism of all levels of prison staff; and, until the late 1890s, the largely undiscriminatory pursuit of the depersonalization of prisoners.

In varying degrees, all these features were in place by the 1840s. But while the presence of these characteristics is largely undisputed, just how and why such developments took place, and what they represented on a broader social and political plane, is highly contentious. Instrumentalist and structuralist historiographies of punishment, and especially prisons, have offered revisionist interpretations, the most potent and imaginative of which is in Foucault's *Discipline and Punishment*.[129] In essence, such accounts argue that criminal law policies sought to perpetuate existing social power structures; penal strategies, and most particularly the new prisons, were developed through an unstated consensus of ruling class interests between the 1770s and 1840s, constituting a 'carceral archipelago', aimed at more effective social control of the working classes. Enlisting professionals armed with knowledge of the emerging behavioural sciences, prison authorities (along with other 'total' institutions including workhouses,

---

[127] *A Bill to Amend the Vagrancy Act 1824 and to facilitate the Establishment of Labour Colonies*, PP 1909 (213), v, 571.

[128] E. Ruggles-Brise, *The English Prison System* (1921), 149–51; Radzinowicz and Hood, *Penal Policy*, 362–75; Petrow, *Policing Morals*, 83–116.

[129] M. Foucault, *Discipline and Punish: The Birth of a Prison* (1977). Also D. Rothman, *The Discovery of the Asylum* (1971); M. Ignatieff, *A Just Measure of Pain* revised in 'State, Civil Society and Total Institutions: A Critique of Recent Social Histories of Punishment', in D. Sugarman (ed.), *Legality, Ideology and the State* (1983)); D. Garland, *Punishment and Welfare: A History of Penal Strategies* (Aldershot, 1985).

reformatories, and lunatic asylums) sought to produce social compliance and unqualified acceptance of the work (capitalist) ethic. Apparently disinterested philanthropic, humanitarian, and religious driving forces of change are regarded as little beyond subterfuges, disguising a deeper, hegemonically inclined, tacit governing class consensus.[130] Thus, former misleading historical accounts should be regarded as either tendentious or the product of fundamental misinterpretation.

Foucaultian interpretations clearly merit careful examination. Such scrutiny suggests that revisionist historiography of this genre is open to several different forms of objection. First, and most elusive, is the question of ruling class consensus. From their very nature, such claimed deep power structures defy easy excavation and exposure. However, beyond the broadest common concern of the ever-widening well-to-do classes to retain and increase their wealth and influence, little consensus as to quite how this should be achieved was ever manifest. Indeed, as has been seen, conflict and diversity characterize relations and opinions across the disparate elements of the governing classes throughout most of the nineteenth century on questions of punishment. Consequently, formulation of most penal policy, including that governing prisons, was subject to national divisions of opinion and frequent local resistance to central regulation, either on the grounds of concerns over local autonomy or strong disinclination to increase the burden of local rates.[131] A second broad objection is Foucault's mono-causal prominence of social political power, with its virtual dismissal of the existence of other motivating interests found in developed civil societies. The ability of embedded cultural traditions and value systems in regulating and shaping the political process is largely ignored, as is the range of non-state punitive or institutional methods of social control.[132]

More generally, substantial empirical doubts arise: the claimed Foucaultian process of transformation corresponds neither with the discernible motives underpinning changes nor their outcomes. Looking at the last two decades of Foucault's period, while the Millbank and Pentonville episodes do indeed resemble his 'total institutions', not only was their appeal both practically limited and

---

[130] Foucault's focus is institutions, Hay's (1975) is both prosecution and punishment. However, in some basic respects, Foucault's account of nineteenth-century penal development is the very antithesis of Hay's interpretation of the techniques of eighteenth-century elite hegemony through the criminal justice system. For Hay's ruling elite, social control came through the reinforcing symbolism and daily practice of merciful discretion; Foucault's professional punishment machine is actively, uniformly, ever socially intrusive; Hay's punishment process and social control thrives on enormous institutional variation and latitude, mediated by discretionary intervention.

[131] On local prisons, see McConville, *History, passim* and M. DeLacey, *Prison Reform in Lancashire 1700–1850* (Manchester, 1986), and in relation to women's prison conditions, see Zedner, *Women, passim*.

[132] Ignatieff, 'State, Civil Society'; and Davis, 'The London Garrotting Panic'.

short lived, their most persistent advocates were patently propelled by divine inspiration rather than hegemonic class ambitions. Beyond Foucault's immediate period of transformation it has been seen that the Jebb and Du Cane regimes were explicitly premised on retribution and deterrence, with notions of moral discipline and regeneration well subordinated. Moreover, while at first blush the post-Gladstone Report era appears to offer a later, greater correspondence with some of Foucault's claims related to the earlier part of the century, the empirical evidence suggests otherwise. Replacement in the 1880s of crude neo-Darwinian determinism, with positivist theory recognizing the function of environment in generating criminality amongst the criminally predisposed, offered a potentially more optimistic prognosis for the institutional intervention and moral capture of offenders.

Such hopes certainly resonate in many of the Gladstone Report's proposals just as they inform the Liberal social welfare policies and legislation of the early twentieth century. Yet, while viewed by some[133] as constituting a radical, far-reaching reconceptualization of criminality, powered by the credibility then enjoyed by positivistic biological and sociological sciences, the weight of historical evidence does not easily bear such an interpretation. Rather than abandoning 'classical' notions of moral culpability, individual fault and proportional punishment, the Gladstone Committee saw positivist sciences as a potential ally in refining this basis of responsibility and punishment. For those particular groups identified in the 1895 Report and in subsequent enabling legislation as appropriate subjects for the application of positivist-welfarist intervention, the measures were applied in diluted forms and often short-lived: borstals were initially distinctively penal rather than individualistic in approach; regimes for inebriates suffered rapid extinction; labour colonies for vagrants hardly left the drawing board; preventive detention, though supported by eugenic claims of innate criminality, with its emphasis on preventative not therapeutic incarceration, proved to be of very limited application.[134] For the bulk of the population of prisons and allied institutions punishment or incarceration remained essentially punitive, with therapeutic measures playing a largely peripheral, ameliorative role.[135]

[133] e.g. Garland, *Punishment and Welfare, passim.*

[134] Radzinowicz and Hood, *Penal Policy,* Ch. 1 and 597–9; Forsythe, *Penal Discipline;* A. Rutherford, 'Boundaries of English Penal Policy' (1988) 8 *OJLS* 132.

[135] e.g. from 1919 for male prisoners and from 1923 for women prisoners, some prison clinics offered psychoanalysis for selected inmates. M. Hamblin Smith, *Prisons and a Changing Civilisation* (1934) and G. Pailthorpe, *What we Put in Prison* (1932).

VI

The Sources and Form of the Criminal Law: The Medium of Change and Development: Consolidation or Codification?

1. SOURCES OF THE CRIMINAL LAW

Where would judges and lawyers find the criminal law during the early decades of the nineteenth century? How accessible and well articulated was it? The bearing of such basic questions on the law's development hardly needs labouring. Whether settling novel or well-worn issues, judges and lawyers would have resort to available law reports, relevant statutes, and, most importantly, criminal law treatises.[1] Alongside matters concerning the sources of law was the related issue of precedent. Certainly, by the beginning of the nineteenth century a fairly well developed system of law reporting had been established, albeit with variations in style, status, and presentation. In the case of criminal law, the reports of the informal procedure of reserved Crown cases were generally brief, lacking counsels' arguments and much judicial deliberation. These features of the criminal law's most authoritative rulings could only handicap conceptual development.[2] Moreover, although by the end of the eighteenth century a system of binding precedent was beginning to take on a recognizable shape, it was still some distance from the level of developed formality achieved by the mid-nineteenth century.[3] Until then, a fair degree of latitude persisted, notionally facilitating judicial creativity where circumstances permitted and a court was minded not to be trammelled by

---

[1] The significance of 'higher journalism' to legal development also grew. General journals of high standing, most particularly the *Edinburgh Review*, and *Quarterly Review*, published a sizeable number of exceedingly well-informed articles on a range of legal topics. Law journals began to appear on a sustained basis from the early 1800s and most importantly from the late 1820s with the publication of the *Law Magazine* in 1828. See below, generally.

[2] See below and Holdsworth, *HEL*, vol. 12, 110–17; vol. 13, 423; and W. T. S. Daniel, *The History and Origin of the Law Reports* (1884). Also, XI, Pt 4. Reports of State Trials was the major exception.

[3] J. Evans, 'Change in the Doctrine of Precedent During the Nineteenth Century', in L. Goldstein (ed.), *Precedent in Law* (Oxford, 1987), 35.

expectations of *stare decisis*. But more than earlier case-law, what bound courts were entrenched principles and doctrines recorded by institutional works.

As the century progressed, and the notion of binding precedent solidified, there followed not only gradual changes in the styles and substance of judgments, but also an emphasized significance of institutional works and new legal treatises. Treatises became not simply a source of statements of law and occasionally half-apologetic, speculative conceptual propositions, but additionally a convenient reliable compendium of an expanding body of relevant case-law. Beyond this, the role of the treatise, written principally for practitioners, was particularly important in the development of the form and substance of the criminal law: the process of distillation of case-law and other authority occasionally led an author to conceptualizing—or reconceptualizing—areas of law hitherto not subject to this form of judicial treatment. Resting at the right hand of judges and practising lawyers, treatises probably exercised steady and extensive, if often unspoken, influence. Both the range and style of criminal law treatises underwent significant change during the nineteenth century.

Growth of Criminal Law Treatises

Prior to the appearance of Stephen's *General View* in 1863, Blackstone's treatment of the criminal law in *Public Wrongs* constituted the law's single most influential principled exposition. Rather than a comprehensive treatise, *Public Wrongs* offered an analysis, based on English and Continental institutional texts, of criminal justice principles and doctrines in an accessible style, of interest to, and digestible by the educated non-lawyer, as well as lawyers. After providing a substantial introductory discourse on the criminal justice system's general philosophy, Blackstone constructed a unified theory of culpability factors that exercised a powerful influence on the conceptual structure of judicial analysis and successive generations of practitioner texts throughout the nineteenth century.

Looking back from the 1880s, Stephen observed that 'since...Blackstone hardly any work has been published in England upon criminal law which aims at being more than a book of practice..., arranged with greater or less skill—usually with almost none'.[4] However, in terms of organization and structure, William Oldnall Russell's *Treatise on Crimes and Misdemeanours*, first published in 1819, marked a useful advance on previous practitioner works. Unlike his predecessors,[5] Russell

---

[4] *HCL*, ii, 218–19. Stephen's view on Blackstone is rather better informed than Austin's dismissal of *Public Wrongs* as no more than a 'slavish blundering copy' of Hale. See more generally, S. Milsom, 'The Nature of Blackstone's Achievement', *Studies in the History of the Common Law* (1985) 197–208.

[5] Particularly Edward Hyde East's *Pleas of the Crown* (1803). Later described by Amos as giving the 'world the contents of eleven sets of MSS of deceased judges'. With no rival, East's treatise was

appears to have been more aware of the value and possibilities for conceptual development by adopting Blackstone's analysis of general principles of liability. In tandem with *Russell*, throughout the nineteenth century and beyond, was J. F. Archbold's *Law and Practice Relating to Pleading and Evidence in Criminal Cases*, originally published in 1822. With John Jervis taking on the editorship in 1831, *Archbold*, the advocate's 'bible', also followed *Russell* in incorporating an abbreviated version of Blackstone's introductory general principles. *Russell* was the more compendious work, giving greater attention to reproducing the facts and rulings of authoritative case law; *Archbold* provided a concise synthesis of substantive law, principles, and procedure. As the two major practitioners' works, *Russell* and *Archbold* were largely passive rather than speculative in style, recording rather than seeking to shape or lead judicial opinion[6] and the law's development.

Stephen's treatise contribution to criminal law literature came in two forms: broadly theoretical and practitioner orientated; in the former category lay the *General View of the Criminal Law of England* (1863) and the *History of the Criminal Law of England* (1883); the *Digest of the Criminal Law* (1877) was of the latter variety. The *General View* constituted a measured attempt of no mean achievement to place the study of criminal law amongst the emerging, empirically based social sciences; and (like Blackstone) it aimed to reveal the criminal law's general relevance to any interested observer of society's workings: to make the study of criminal law into an 'art founded on science, the art of making wise laws, the science of understanding and correctly classifying large departments of human conduct'. Stephen's prefatory remarks to the *General View* ensured that no reader would be left in any doubt as to the author's belief in the importance of the book's subject-matter and range:

Its object is to give an account of the general scope, tendency and design of an important part of our institutions, of which surely none can have a greater moral significance, or be more closely connected with broad principles of morality and politics, than those by which men rightfully, deliberately, and in cold blood, kill, enslave, and otherwise torment their fellow-creatures.[7]

Stephen's more mature, occasionally modified, views on criminal responsibility appear in his *History of the Criminal Law of England*, completed in 1882 and

---

an instant success and 'bore an exorbitant price until it was superseded by Russell's'. *Ruins of Time*, 5 and xxiv.

   [6] On the relationship of literary form and legal theory and principles, see A. W. B. Simpson, 'The Rise and Fall of the Legal Treatise: Legal Principles and the Forms of Legal Literature' (1981) 48 *Univ. of Chicago LR* 632; and M. Lobban, 'The English Legal Treatise and English Law in the Eighteenth Century' (1997) 13 *Scripta Historica* 69.

   [7] *General View*, 337 and vi.

published the following year. Here, Stephen's accumulated experience as an Indian legislator, a frustrated author of several codifying measures, and two years on the High Court Bench, combined to produce shifts of emphases and in some cases a fuller, clearer conceptual analysis. The essence or conclusions of some of the discussions found in the *History* are pre-empted by Stephen's 1877 *Digest of the Criminal Law* in which, although a practitioners' manual, Stephen is unable to resist a discursive general introduction, including codification propaganda.

1863 not only witnessed the publication of Stephen's *General View*, but also of Austin's *Lectures on Jurisprudence*. However, whilst benefiting from the earlier published *Province of Jurisprudence Determined* (1832), Stephen was denied prior access to *Lectures* which contained Austin's most pertinent thoughts on criminal responsibility.[8] Encounters of more general, late nineteenth-century jurists with criminal law concepts frequently reveal indebtedness to Austinian thinking, sifted through the mesh of Stephen's analysis. As will be seen, such writers, including Clark, Markby, Salmond, and Holland, who, though not offering full-scale criminal law treatises, contributed to the body of available literature and analysis on some of the period's central criminal law concerns. Marking the arrival of the new century, C. S. Kenny's *Outlines of Criminal Law* was the first work of its kind. Derived from undergraduate lectures and primarily, though not exclusively, intended as an academic student text, it constituted a systematic treatment of theory and substance, becoming the prototype of several generations of treatises. Especially in relation to culpability requirements, the Stephen and Austinian legacies are plain, both through direct and indirect references. *Outlines* provided readers with a lucid, often original account of general principles, quickly gaining a wide audience beyond undergraduates.

Legislative and Proto-legislative Potential Influential Sources

Beyond the source and influence of standard treatises and practitioner works, lay two further distinct, though related areas of nineteenth-century criminal law activity of clear relevance to the broader conceptual and doctrinal milieu of the

---

[8] J. S. Mill's *Utilitarianism* was also published in the same year. The preface to Stephen's work is dated June 1863. Sarah Austin's preface to *Lectures on Jurisprudence*, the first publication of the lectures and notes particularly relevant to criminal responsibility, is dated April 1863.

Stephen's broad adherence to Austinian positivism reveals itself both expressly and implicitly not only throughout the *General View*, but in his comparative review of the 1861 edition of the *Province* with Maine's *Ancient Law* (1861) 114 *Edin. Rev.* 456. For Stephen, the core value of Austin's positivism was his objective of clearing up the analytical muddle 'which is continually arising between an actual and ideal state of things; between the rights or powers protected by laws which do exist, and those which upon some principle or other ought to exist, and this confusion has given the tone to almost all the controversies upon such subjects which have agitated and still continued to agitate mankind' (470).

period. Of immediate and direct significance, the long-running digest and codification analyses of the Criminal Law Commissioners provided a rich, unrivalled
critique of most principal areas of the criminal law. To a rather lesser degree,
such comments may also be made of the 1879 Code Bill Report. Of more tangential relevance, are Macaulay's Indian Penal Code, originally drafted in 1836, and
Wright's 1877 Draft Jamaican Penal Code. Both colonial codes, unlike the work
of the Criminal Law Commissioners, offered (relatively) historically and politically unburdened, *de novo*, constructions of a penal code, drawing on a range
of foreign jurisprudential sources and experiences. Later Reports of the English
Criminal Law Commissioners contain express acknowledgements of their intellectual debt to the Macaulay Code. Identifying the extent to which law-making
and practice may have been influenced by this wealth of background contextual materials is reviewed in the context of the substantive law's examination (see
below).

Style and Substance of Criminal Law Judgments

(1) STYLE

Judges of the stature of Mansfield were conscious of the need for clear public
articulation of the principles of criminal responsibility: 'it is of great consequence to explain [the legal principles of judgments] with accuracy and precision in open court, especially if the questions be of great tendency, and upon
topics never before fully settled [so] that the criminal law may be fully settled
and known'.[9] However, as the vastly experienced criminal lawyer and jurist C. S.
Greaves acidly observed many decades later, the reality of criminal judicial practice was far removed from Mansfield's objectives, comparing badly with usually
more fully argued civil suits:

In the majority of [criminal] instances, no argument by counsel takes place, but the question reserved is discussed among the judges themselves...We must be pardoned in suggesting that occasions may peradventure arise where it would be advantageous that the
case should be argued by counsel, who may have had an opportunity of searching into the
authorities, and who cannot fail to have an interest in putting the question in favour of
the prisoner in the strongest point of view. [Yet] generally speaking, no judgment with the
reasons for it is pronounced...When we remember what admirable judgments [judges]
have delivered in civil cases: we cannot but deeply lament the inestimable store of criminal law that has been lost for ever by these decisions and the grounds of them not being
publicly promulgated.[10]

---

[9] *Wilkes* (1770) 4 Burr. 2527, 2549.
[10] (1845) 2 *LM* 129, 139. Greaves was referring to the reserved cases procedure. The *Law Times*
identified (propertied) class interest and influence as responsible for greater judicial attention being
given to civil law (1855) 25 *LT* 18.

Lack of relatively accessible, frequently used formalized appeals procedures clearly worked against the production of more generalized judicial speculation; it was a characteristic of the criminal justice system expressly registered by the Criminal Law Commissioners in their early Reports. Even after the changes introduced by the establishment of the Court for Crown Cases Reserved in 1848, the regular absence of legal representation for either defence, prosecution or both, inevitably impoverished the range and depth of legal argument, thereby diminishing the chances of judicial innovation. Without counsel of reasonable quality the need to justify opinions by resort to larger-scale reasoning was decidedly less pressing. Moreover, there was no right of appeal to the Court for Crown Cases Reserved; cases were reserved entirely at the trial judge's discretion. This feature of the system, alone, meant that the pace and areas of theoretical development were largely governed by judicial interest and inclination. Moreover, the creation of the Court for Crown Cases Reserved produced no apparent effect on the style and substance of reported first instance judgments; overwhelmingly they remained brief to the point of perfunctoriness.

Even following the demise of the Court for Crown Cases Reserved in 1907, from the Court of Criminal Appeal's earliest days, any expectations of an enriched, more forthcoming era of judicial criminal jurisprudence proved groundless. As before, judgments displayed a persistent disinclination, if not resistance, to engage in conceptual speculation and policy review. As one commentator with unconcealed irony much later noted, the 'judgments of the Court present a trifle too frequently an air of thinness in their articulation':[11] it was an appellate culture where function was exceedingly narrowly conceived; where, according to a former distinguished member of that court in its latter days: 'Discussion of general principles is not encouraged. Cases relating to mens rea as an element of crime live in a shambles from which academic writers try to rescue them.' Culturally, the 'Court of Criminal Appeal had the air of a place where regimental officers foregathered and staff wallahs were not highly thought of'.[12]

(2) SUBSTANCE

More specifically, during the nineteenth century to what extent were criminal law judgments and counsels' arguments based on precedent and other authority? Law reports reveal that a substantial proportion of first instance decisions were settled without express resort to any authority but simply on a bare judicial assertion of the law. Institutional works make only sporadic express appearances in judgments, and were deployed hardly more frequently by counsel. Direct references to established practitioner texts such as *Russell* and *Archbold* figured no

---

[11] D. S. Davies (1951) 1 *JSPTL* 425, 434, 436; and also (1937) 121 *Nineteenth Century* 531.

[12] Lord Devlin, *The Judge* (Oxford, 1979), 186–7.

more often than institutional works. Of course, the impact of the vague convention against citation of texts of living authors might partly account for the virtual absence of citations of early editions of *Russell* and *Archbold*, but their later consistent rarity of appearance points to a far deeper judicial disinclination expressly to acknowledge their existence.

Undoubtedly, influence is very likely to have been unacknowledged in many cases, or even through unconscious absorption of textbook opinions. Certainly, doctrinally, the common law's developmental process tended to deny or obscure such innovation from view: an open adoption of extra-judicial opinion would have been regarded as a visible compromise of doctrine. However, examination of textbook formulations of principles (see below) suggests that judges and counsel rarely extracted more than the previous judicial formulation of a principle cited by any particular text. One of the few substantial exceptions to this state of affairs was Stephen's *Digest of the Criminal Law*, which, from the late 1880s (during the author's lifetime), began to make the odd appearance in judgments and counsel's arguments. And, indeed, Lord Coleridge felt obliged in *Dudley and Stephens* to allude to Stephen's views on a necessity defence put forward in both his *History* and *Digest*.[13] Doubtless, Stephen's judicial status greatly assisted in raising him above the heads of other mere commentators.

Arrival of the Court of Criminal Appeal brought a provision in the Criminal Appeal Act virtually ensuring that all cases before the court were argued by counsel for both sides. Yet over the subsequent half century this and other procedural changes accompanying the Court of Criminal Appeal's establishment produced little discernible change in the style and substance of criminal appeal judgments. Not only was this true of judicial behaviour, but despite the growth in volume and quality of published legal analyses, counsels' arguments displayed very limited incorporation, or acknowledgement, of relevant contemporary texts and other legal literature in cases where principle was in contention. To what degree this was a manifestation of counsel responding to the actual or perceived appellate ethos of the Court of Criminal Appeal or Divisional Court is exceedingly difficult to assess. However, the continuing scarcity of citation even of leading practitioner works, including *Russell* and *Archbold*, points to the understood or unspoken futility of attempts to argue appeals on broader conceptual grounds by resorting to more speculative, non-practitioner treatises or journals.

Such an apparent, narrow judicial self-sufficiency in settling matters of doctrine or principle, by usually confining analysis to precedent or analogical deduction, was not limited to criminal appeals, but to a large degree was replicated in

---

[13] Another early judicial reference to the *History* three years after publication occurs in *Burns* (1886) 16 Cox 355.

civil cases.[14] This suggests the judicial mind-set and culture were of a more universal character and not peculiar to criminal matters. The judicial 'strong aversion for and distrust of theory and principle'[15] between 1800 and the end of the first half of the twentieth century has not been simply implicit, but, from time to time, openly confessed. For Lord Devlin this judicial attitude was no more than an expression of a far broader cultural preference:

[The English] like what they call practical and commonsense solutions...and they pick their judges with that object in view. But the consequences of that is, I think, that in England you cannot have the judges—certainly not the judges of first instance—to build up unaided a coherent system of law...The practice and tradition of extempore judgments means that they throw off things that are better left unsaid.[16]

And doubtless, the occasional openly expressed view that academics were failed barristers[17] was widespread and slow to dissipate amongst judges and practitioners.

2. THE CRIMINAL LAW'S FORM: CODIFICATION: SHIMMERING VISTA OR THREATENING SPECTRE?

As has been seen, broad-fronted agitation for amelioration of the criminal law's severity in the opening decades of the nineteenth century raised a host of incidental and related issues, not least the constitutionally and doctrinally sensitive question of the law's sources and form. Campaigners for greater proportionality of punishment had in their immediate sights extinction of the endless tracts of capital statutes, as heavily mediated by daily doses of common law discretion and pragmatism. As a substitute for ineffective, severe, unsystematic obscure laws, reformers sought salvation through a humane, rationally constructed, and

---

[14] S. Hedley, 'Words, Words, Words; Making Sense of Legal Judgments 1874–1940', in C. Stebbings (ed.), *Law Reporting in Britain* (1995). Whilst civil judgments became longer, references to textbooks and similar sources became less and less common between 1875 and 1940. At the same time, arguments became more technical and prolix with less resort to general moral assertions, a change which in part at least could be attributed to the availability of a greater range of contemporary textbook analysis. See generally, P. S. Atiyah, *Pragmatism and Theory in English Law* (1987), Ch. 4 and *From Principles to Pragmatism* (Oxford, 1978).

[15] Lord Macmillan, *Law and Other Things* (1937), 80 and Atiyah, *op cit.* (1987) 4.

[16] (1958) 4 *JSPTL* 206.

[17] Lord Alverstone. Quoted in *Holmes–Laski, Letters*, ed. M. De Wolfe Howe (Camb. Mass., 1953), 1439, May 1933 and Hedley, *loc cit.* 177. The DNB biographer of Lord Alverstone characterized his subject as: 'Not a very clever man, nor a learned lawyer...The Reports will be searched in vain for judgments that are valuable as expositions of the law', *Dictionary of National Biography*, 1912–21, 562. Cf. Lord Goff who appears to give greater and earlier credit to the influence of legal commentators. 'The Search for Principle' (1983) LXIX *Proc. Br. Acad.* 169 and 'Judge, Jurist and Legislature', Child and Co, Oxford Lecture, 1986.

clearly articulated system of offences and punishments. However, the slipshod haphazard nature of much penal law had put statutory legislation in particularly bad odour; Blackstone echoed common sentiments in describing such legislative practices as 'quackery in government'.[18] But because the law's obscurity, severity, and absence of proportionality was principally the consequence of a large, accreted mass of penal statutes, the undoing of this state of affairs necessarily required further legislative intervention.

With the massive exception of Bentham, most late eighteenth and early nineteenth-century solutions offered variations of the hallowed Baconian legislative prescription of consolidation and revision: maintaining the law's accessibility and certainty through the periodic excision of obsolete provisions along with the compilation of statutory digests.[19] True to this formula, late eighteenth-century critiques such as Eden's *Principles of Penal Law* and Dagge's *Considerations on Criminal Law* advocated a programme of statutory amendment and consolidation to be executed by special commissioners.[20] Similarly, in urging more effective and humane criminal laws—a 'total revision and reformation of our penal laws'— Romilly has recourse to Bacon's recommendations for statutory consolidation and revision rather than seeking to formulate a 'perfect code'.[21] However, particularly in respect of punishment, the revisions contemplated by those such as Eden, Dagge, and Romilly went beyond matters of form; quite how far was to become the core contention in the early nineteenth-century reform debates leading up to, and including, Peel's legislative initiatives. Here, the obsolescence of the majority of capital statutes was one of claimed ineffectiveness in the social and political context of the early nineteenth century.[22] But even progressives such as Romilly drew the line at wholesale reconstruction, or even restructuring. Consequently, even though late in his life Romilly was happy to endorse Bentham's hostility to unprincipled 'judicial legislation', he remained unconverted by Bentham's codification schemes. For Romilly, they lacked the potential to translate into practical working provisions: 'we are not able to discover the traces of these works in the improved conditions of any portion of the human race'.[23]

Except for Bentham, the common law was not the principal target of reformers; for Bentham the common law was the central problem. In its stead, Bentham

---

[18] *Comms*, iv, 17 and *Comms*, i, 10.

[19] Analysed by D. Lieberman, *The Province of Legislation Determined* (Cambridge, 1989), Ch. 9. *passim*.

[20] *Principles of Penal Law* (2nd edn, 1772), 312–13, 306, 19, 67; *Considerations on Criminal Law* (2nd edn, 1774), 78. See Smith, *Lawyers, Legislators and Theorists* 25–8, 73.

[21] *Observations on a Late Publication* (1786), 41–2, 105–7. Legislative revision more than consolidation was Romilly's principal focus.

[22] See 'Punishment I', Ch. V, above.

[23] 'Bentham on the Codification' (1817) 29 *Edin. Rev.* 217, 219, attrib. *Wellesley Index*, vol. 1, 457.

offered a complete, reconceptualized body of penal laws driven by the foundational principle of utility. Though initially flirting with digesting common law into statute, followed by statutory consolidation, Bentham rapidly jettisoned such ameliorative schemes for a complete, *de novo* legislative programme posited on utilitarian principles. Efficacy of law resting on utilitarian principles demanded an integrated relationship between form and substance. To guide the calculating actor, law needed to be readily accessible, to be knowable: 'The notoriety of every law ought to be…as extensive as its binding force'. Law was to be rational and comprehensive, structured for the interpreter to move deductively from general principles to the particular instance in issue. A complete code would contain 'no terrae incognitae, no blank spaces: nothing is at least omitted, nothing unprovided for'. Conceptual and terminological clarity required 'perpetual and regular definition';[24] grammar and legislation must work in concert;[25] form and content were an indivisible whole.

By the time Peel's most significant consolidating phase had got underway, the literature on the medium of law-making and reform had grown substantially, both in terms of general works and those devoted to criminal law. Though none remotely approached the top-to-bottom radicalism of Bentham's codification schemes, some crossed the jurisprudential rubicon in advocating not just revisions of both form and substance of statute law, but also the common law.[26] One such work was Horace Twiss's *An Enquiry into the Means of Consolidating and Digesting the Laws of England* (1826), the most extended, thorough-going of the period's analyses of the machinery of law revision. Twiss saw the process of reviewing statute law as 'no irreverent innovation, of modern hardihood', and while agreeing that 'eminent officers of the law' were prudent in resisting 'patrons of hazardous inventions', the need for careful reassessment of possible reforming procedures was patent. For Twiss, a succession of graduated measures might begin with statutory classification and indexation, proceed onwards to consolidation enactments, followed by government resourced abridgments of common law treatises, after which both consolidated statutes and abridgements could be jointly digested. As a final stage, such digests could be 'authenticated' by 'enactment, or by judicial authority'. Rather than adopting usual legislative procedures, Twiss advocated 'a simple declaration of Parliament, that the digest, as finally settled…, should be deemed to be the law of the land…with respect to the common as the statutory law therein contained'. Like Eden, Twiss would have assigned the

---

[24] *Comment*, 346–7.
[25] *Laws in General*, 245; quoted by Lieberman, *op cit.*, 262.
[26] On criminal law revision schemes, see Smith, *Lawyers, Legislators and Theorists*, 78–84.

task to a specially appointed 'continuing and constantly working' Commission of lawyers.[27]

Still more provocative and disturbing for traditionalists was the successful property lawyer, James Humphrey's *Observations on the Actual State of the English Laws of Real Property within the Outlines of a Code* (1826). While talk of revising the forms and functions of statutes and cases for the criminal law was the thin end of legal radicalism's wedge, this work was decidedly the thick end. Though *Observations* by no means proposed a Benthamite, *de novo* system, the predictable professional response was vociferously antagonistic and widespread, revealing the broad extent of professional hostility to anything remotely smacking of codificatory revisions.[28] The considered Establishment case against such heterodoxy was eventually voiced by John Park in his Savigny-based[29] *Contre-Projet* (1828), which asserted that rather than deducing law through the application of basic, *a priori*, principles, common law was properly the accretive product of reasoning through analogy. According to Park, law had, and should have, a malleable, 'plastic' quality that ought to remain with, and be at the service of, those who are 'daily conversant in the business of jurisprudence, and daily experiencing its practical workings and defects'. Far from reducing the sheer bulk of law, Park maintained codification was a potent means of increasing it. Pithily concluding an otherwise rather turgid defence of the common law, he characterized codifiers as slavishly obsessed by form and symmetry: 'the lover must become the husband to find out, perhaps too late, how small a portion of perfection form alone constitutes'. And allying himself with Savignyean sentiments via a teasing allusion to Bentham, Park asserted that the '*benefit* of codification is a question of time, place, and circumstance . . . it cannot be argued in the abstract'.[30]

---

[27] 'Introduction', 1–6, 65, 76. Twiss is best remembered as Lord Eldon's biographer.

[28] M. Lobban, *The Common Law and English Jurisprudence 1760–1850* (Oxford, 1991), 195–201 and B. Rudden, 'A Code Too Soon: The 1826 Property Code of James Humphreys...', in P. Wallington and R. Merkin (eds), *Essays in Memory of F.H. Lawson* (1986) 101.

[29] On the deployment of the German Historical School philosophical underpinnings in defence of common law reasoning and law-making during this period, see R. Lettow, 'Codification and Consolidation of English Law in the Age of Peel and Brougham' (1992 M. Litt., Oxford), Ch. 5; and R. Reimann, 'The Historical School Against Codification' (1987) 37 *Am. J. of Comp. Law* 95. The broadly liberal-conservative stance of the *Law Magazine* during the 1830s and 1840s owed much to the intellectual affiliations of Abraham Hayward. The journal's co-founder, and soon sole editor, Hayward, had strong personal links with the German Historical School, including the writing in 1831 of an English translation of Savigny's *Vom Beruf unserer Zeit für Gesetzgebung und Rechtswissenschaft*, the foundational text opposing the advocates of German codification. Lettow, 105–11. For Austin's sympathy for, and possible influence by, the German codifiers (including Thibaut), see. W. Rumble, *The Thought of John Austin* (1985), 31–4 and Lobban, *The Common Law* (1991), 227–34.

[30] *A Contre-Projet to the Humphresian Code and to Projects of Redaction of Messrs Hammond, Uniacke and Twiss* (1828) addressed to J. Hodgson, one of the Commissioners for 'revisal of the English property law', xiv, 156, 87, 89. From 1831, Park was professor of law at King's College,

It was in such a professional and intellectual milieu that Peel's criminal law consolidation legislation progressed through the 1820s, and beyond. Though earlier measures appeared,[31] Peel's most significant period of consolidatory activity followed his Commons' reforming manifesto delivered in 1826. Despite a residual adherence to Paley's 'glorious uncertainty' philosophy when it came to the enforcement of punishment, Peel claimed as axiomatic that penal law itself should be 'precise and intelligible'; only this would ensure 'the security of property—the prevention of crime—[and improvement of] the moral habits of the people'. As Peel graphically demonstrated to his audience, this was patently not the state of penal statutes. Such deficiencies were seen as substantially contributing to the law's apparent failure in preventing a doubling in the rates of recorded crimes and convictions over the previous seven years. Part of the remedy lay in 'reparation...for past neglect', through a programme of statutory consolidation and simplification, plus the correction of 'glaring defects' or omissions.

Potential disquiet or suspicion at the apparent radical nature of these ambitions were calmed by liberal applications of the balm of 'Lord Chancellor Bacon['s]' unchallengeable wisdom: like Bacon, Peel aimed to give law 'rather new light than any new nature'; to 'substitute more reasonable law...agreeable to the time', including less severe penalties; and, adopting Bacon's apt horticultural analogy, to reform that 'tendeth to pruning and grafting the law, and not to ploughing up and planting it again'. Underscoring his awareness of the subject's sensitivity, Peel adopted two linked strategies. First, he assured the Commons (and his wider audience) that he would not 'rush' the pace of such consolidation, but would proceed subject by subject, commencing with a bill on theft (and allied offences), the largest area of criminality; moreover, each change needed time 'to digest' by the 'various authorities'. Secondly, well aware of the thwarted ambitions of Romilly's

London. Though regarding it as a 'very valuable work', the (1828–9) 1 *LM* 613, commented 'What could induce him to invent such a name' (615). And cf. the sniping nature that the pro- and anti-codification campaign took between the Benthamite leaning *Jurist* and the *LM* (1829) 2 *LM* 227. A good portion of Park's fire had been drawn by the work of the appallingly industrious Anthony Hammond whose mammoth consolidating and codifying efforts had been first thrust into public view with the publication of the 1824 Report of the Select Committee considering the expediency of consolidating and amending the Criminal Law. Hammond's very substantial analysis of the law of forgery, with legislative proposals, formed the Report's Appendix. On Hammond's, would-be involvement in Peel's consolidatory efforts, see below and K. Smith, 'Anthony Hammond: Mr Peel's Persistent Codifier' (1999) 20 *JLH* 24.

   [31] Especially the Acts consolidating and revising secondary punishment, 1823 4 Geo. IV 4, c. 64 and 1824 5 Geo. IV, c. 84. In relation to form, Mackintosh's 1819 Select Committee's Report in no way suggested anything beyond statutory revision and some consolidation. He expressly disclaimed further ambition: the common law was a system 'admirable in principle, interwoven with the habits of the English people...', *PD* 1819 (s. 1) 39: 783. Lushington's 1824 Select Committee on statutory consolidation and amendment had been established with Peel's support.

legislative career, Peel made much play of, and gave lavish credit to, the consultative involvement in drafting the theft bill of several members of the bench, including the Lord Chief Justice.[32] At no point in Peel's extensive speech was any allusion made to the state or role of the common law. Such assiduous preparation rewarded Peel with the continued assent of Commons, Lords, and press,[33] along with sustained judicial collaboration.[34] By 1830, a clutch of consolidating and revising statutes had been enacted, spanning the core offences of theft, criminal damage, offences against the person, and forgery, replacing in excess of 320[35] individual statutes. It was an achievement prompting the *Law Magazine*'s former editor, Abraham Hayward, to suggest that anyone doubting the Acts' value ought to 'compare one of the best Treatise on criminal law composed prior to [the consolidation Acts] with one composed subsequently'.[36]

Though Peel's final major consolidation measure on forgery attracted widespread hostility for its inadequate response to the public appetite for the relegation of capital punishment,[37] as far as the law's form was concerned, the *Law Magazine* felt able to certify in 1830 that 'Codification...has become a dead letter in England...'.[38] But even where, as in the *Foreign Quarterly Review*, a chilly reception was given to the codificatory proposals from the 'firm of Bentham and Dumont', conceding the benefits of a more 'comprehensive consolidation and digest of criminal law' was becoming unexceptional.[39] The mood for more innovative and extensive law reform soon took legislative form in 1832 with Grey's Whig administration, as initially galvanized by its more radical supporters. Peel's moderate consolidation revisions were themselves quickly revised, greatly

---

[32] *PD* 1826 (s. 2) 14: 1214–39.

[33] Newspaper and periodicals naturally lacked a single voice. For example, in 1828 the *Quarterly Review* reflected on Peel's 'judicious caution which has restrained him from pushing his reforms beyond the point' approved of by the 'practical executors and ministers of the law' (1828) 37 *Quart. Rev.* 147; 38 *Quart. Rev.* 244, also (1832) 43 *Quart. Rev.*170. Initial support came from the *Morning Chronicle*, 3 October 1826 but cf. 31 January 1828. A surprising endorsement was issued by the *Westminster Review* (1827) 7 *West. Rev.* 91.

[34] e.g. *PD* 1827 (s. 2) 17: 592 and 1261.

[35] Greaves, *Introduction*, v–vii and Radzinowicz, *History*, i: 575. For a detailed account of Peel's consolidations and repeals, see *ibid.*, 574–87.

[36] *Juridical Tracts*, Part 1 (1856), 58.

[37] e.g. (1830) 52 *Edin. Rev.* 398 and 545; and (1831) 54 *Edin. Rev.* 183 by Empson; the *Morning Chronicle*, 7 September 1831; (1832) 17 *West. Rev.* 52. See also the 'The Capital Question' above Ch. V.

[38] (1830) 4 *LM* 244.

[39] (1830) vi *Foreign Quarterly Rev.* 321; and see also (1830) 52 *Edin. Rev.* 479 and n. 23 above. Even Bentham, though predictably deeply scornful of Peel's reforming pace, felt able to confess that it was no longer 'considered as a mark of disaffection towards the state, and hostility to the social order and to the law in general, to express an opinion that the existing law is defective, and requires a radical reform...[A] new spirit is rising in the profession itself', Bowring *Works*, vi: 203.

narrowing the range of capital offences.[40] The less focused, less pressing issue of the criminal law's form attracted a different response from a coterie of leading Whig lawyers.

Installed as Lord Chancellor in 1830, Brougham's position on the subject was clearly of great moment. Despite long-standing admiration of, and friendship with, Bentham, he was some distance from embracing the great philosopher's Pannomionic schemes for dismantling common law institutions to make way for thorough-going utilitarian-based structures and institutions. Typical of most 'Edinburgh' Whig-lawyers, Brougham's Benthamite credentials were pragmatic-ally severely trimmed to following a utility-rationalist driven approach to assessing the function and state of the law and legal institutions. The limits of Brougham's ambitions had emerged in his 1828 Commons' monumental flight of reforming rhetoric. While the 80-year-old Bentham's censorial jurisprudence received a glowing commendation for its premier role in exposing a very broad canvas of legal imperfections, inadequacies, and abuses, it was not going to fuel the law's total reconstruction. Instead, ineffective, anachronistic, and anomalous outgrowths of the law were to be pruned, leaving the common law substantially untouched and unreconstructed; most assuredly this was reform, not root and branch revolu-tion. For a disappointed Bentham, Brougham's great 'mountain is delivered and behold—the mouse'.[41] Such momentum as was generated by Brougham's perform-ance eventually manifested itself in the establishment of two Royal Commissions, the second of which was to address the state of the Criminal Law.

The Criminal Law Commissioners 1833–49

In June 1833, during the course of opposing a non-government bill amending the law of robbery, George Lamb, Under-Secretary of State at the Home Office, observed that

On the whole…it would be much better at once to appoint a general committee for the revision of our criminal code than to go on thus, step by step, adopting measures at the suggestion of individual Members without knowing where this mitigation of punish-ment was to stop or upon what general principle it was to be regulated with regard to particular crimes.[42]

Whether this was no more than a completely personal, extempore comment, or whether it was a conscious trailing of an issue then under government review, is impossible to say. Certainly, as the brother of the Home Secretary,

---

[40] See 'Punishment', Ch. V above.
[41] Brougham's speech, *PD* 1828 (s. 2) 18: 241. Bentham, Bowring *Works*, 10, 588 and *West. Rev.* xi, 448.
[42] *PD* 1833 (s. 2) 18: 616. Several members endorsed the suggestions, *ibid.*, 618–20.

Lord Melbourne, it is highly likely that Lamb would have been privy to any active consideration of the appointment of such a Committee or other review body by the Home Office or Lord Chancellor's officials. Whatever the immediate background, Brougham soon after engineered the appointment of a Royal Commission on the criminal law.

Behind Brougham's initiative were the insistent promptings of Henry Bellenden Ker, a well-regarded conveyancer and skilled freelance draftsman of several private bills. A confidante and adviser to Brougham, Ker had pressed Brougham on several occasions in late 1832 and early 1833 to support some form of codification venture. More specifically, Ker revealed that he had discussed with the Jurist, John Austin, a 'complete digest of the existing law' and also a 'revision and digest of statute law', which might be followed by a 'code', by which stage the need for alterations to the law might be assessed; such a project might extend to both the criminal and civil law. Expressing his own 'zeal and eagerness' for the project, Ker furnished Brougham with copies of a clutch of codification schemes from the 1820s, including Twiss's, while at the same time commending Brougham's attention to recent New York codification initiatives.[43]

Besides Austin and Ker (cuttingly dubbed the Commission's 'conveyancing member' by the *Law Magazine*),[44] appointed as Criminal Law Commissioners were Thomas Starkie, William Wightman, and Andrew Amos. Starkie, a King's Counsel, author of the period's leading treatise on evidence, former Cambridge Senior Wrangler and later occupant of the Downing Chair at Cambridge from 1824 until 1847, was clearly no intellectual slouch. Wightman, a Junior Treasury Counsel and member of the Common Law Courts Commission, was elevated to the Queen's Bench eight years later. Amos was appointed foundation Professor of English Law at University College, London, with Austin as Professor of Jurisprudence. Along with Starkie, Amos lectured extensively on the common law, and also sat as Recorder at Oxford and Banbury.[45]

Whether Brougham sought any particular proposals from his Commissioners is unclear. However, both tactically and technically the Commissioners' original membership was exceedingly well constructed, with reasonable claims to considerable experience of practice represented by all members except Austin, coupled

[43] Brougham Mss, University College, London, (24 December 1832), 11, 562; (31 December 1832), 13, 749; (undated) 13753.

[44] (1838) 19 *LM* 421. The journal regarded him as unfit, asking why this 'gentleman has twice been selected for enquiries lying beyond the pale of his particular pursuit'.

[45] The original Commission issued eight Reports on the criminal law between 1834 and 1845, and a Report on general consolidation of statute law in 1835. A second Commission appointed in 1845 to review and revise earlier Reports and provide a draft codification bill produced five Reports between 1845 and 1849 covering substantive law and eventually procedure. Ker and Starkie were the key members of the first and second Commission, providing unbroken service for the whole period.

with the powerful analytical and conceptual ability of Starkie, Amos and Austin. Moreover, Starkie enjoyed the esteem of Peel's public thanks for his assistance in preparation of the consolidation bills.[46] Originally, the Commissioners were required to 'digest' into a single statute all criminal statutes, to 'digest' into statute 'the common or unwritten law', and to report on the expediency of combining both statutes into a single code. However, as a result of pointed comments in their First Report, Melbourne widened the Commissioners' remit in July 1834 to permit consideration of 'necessary' or 'expedient partial alterations' of the law.[47]

The Commissioners' First Report amply displayed their reformist mettle, characterizing the basis of liability to be devoid of general organizing principles and fundamentally failing to reflect the distinct degrees of criminality in proportional levels of punishment; this the Commissioners ascribed to the law's form. With uncompromising utilitarian rigour, the Commissioners argued that 'so long as a large proportion of the penal law is merely oral and dependent on the examination and consultation of precedents, it must be, to the mass of society inaccessible, and unintelligible. [Consequently] it cannot possess the efficiency of written and certain rules and specific penalties in deterring men from the commission of crimes...'. As a first stage solution to this state of affairs the common law and statutes should be digested into 'one body of law', a measure which the Commission felt would 'tend greatly to the improvement of the jurisprudence of the country'.[48]

Over the subsequent 15 years from the first to the last report, in tone and substance, the reports offered a blend of consistency and inconsistency of approach. With varying degrees of directness and emphasis, they adhered to the view of superiority of statute law over common law as a medium of law-making, a claim given its most emphatic expression in their 1835 Report on general statutory consolidation.[49] Permitting themselves a very rare express note of dissent

---

[46] 'He could name, among many others, Mr Starkie, Mr Russell and others, and all the judges', *PD* 1827 (s. 2) 17: 939.

[47] *Second Report, PP* 1836 (343) xxxvi, p. 2.

[48] *First Report PP* 1834 (537), xxvi. 25 and 35. A sentiment echoed by Brougham on the Report's publication, *PD* 1834 (53) 24: 835. The Commission's 1835 Report on the consolidation of statute law generally, requested by Melbourne in 1834, was equally emphatic in its support for statutory consolidation of civil as well as criminal law. Bacon's authority is judiciously inserted at several points in the Report, *PP* 1835 (406), xxxv, at e.g. 6, 7, and 22.

[49] Before Austin's resignation in 1836, Brougham suggested that Austin quickly found himself out of step with his fellow Commissioners, who regarded his views as 'too abstract and scientific', 'John Austin' (1860) *LM* 165. Austin found the Commission's remit incapable of sanctioning the 'fundamental reforms from which alone any good could come'; these would be a 'complete map of the whole field of crime, and a draft of a Criminal Code', Sarah Austin, *Lectures on Jurisprudence* (4th edn), preface, 11. And see Austin's discussion of the criminal law codification in *Lectures*, xxxvii–xxxix and 'Notes of a Criminal Code', 1056–73, 1129–37, below, *passim*. Sarah Austin indicates (11)

from Bacon's venerated wisdom, the Commissioners observed that statutes 'possess such manifest advantages in point of clearness and certainty over unwritten law, as almost to exclude a comparison of their excellence and utility'.[50] A particular Benthamite *bete noir*, the *ex post facto* nature of common law was subject to frequent assaults throughout several reports, both for its inefficiency in deterring crime and its inherent 'injustice' and 'odium'.[51] Such judicial 'constructive enlargement' through the technique of 'analogical reasoning' produced a mass of frequently conflicting case law, largely unstructured by general principles, and inadequate to the 'requirements of a civilised nation'.[52]

Yet by 1843, a collective shift in attitude was manifest; common law principles and the mechanism of law-making were now regarded rather less harshly: common law rules were 'susceptible of precise distinction and arrangement'; whereas 'with respect to statutory enactments, the difficulty is much greater [because] the meaning of a statute so frequently depends on the context' which is often very 'specific', defying generalized relevance. Moreover, common law 'terms of art' were to be preserved because the substance of 'new ones, can rarely, if ever, be attended with any preponderating advantages'. Additionally, such a general 'written exposition' of slightly revised existing law would enjoy 'great advantages' while the 'disadvantages necessarily incident to any experimental change in legislation are avoided'.[53]

Occasionally, the Commissioners allowed themselves the indulgence of expressing just what system of change they might effect, freed from the shackles of their official remit. In January 1837 writing to Lord John Russell, then Home Secretary, airing concerns over the advisability of partial reform and the risks of creating 'new anomalies and inconsistencies', the Commissioners pronounced the criminal law so defective as to warrant 'an entire revision and reconstruction of the whole fabric...'.[54] Two years on, they compare their restricted objectives with

that 'Notes' were written during her husband's period as a Commissioner. Cf. L. and J. Hamburger, *Troubled Lives: John and Sarah Austin* (Toronto, 1985), 51 and 215.

[50] *1835 Report*, 22. The Commissioners were provoked by Bacon's claim of the higher frequency of 'doubts' in statute law than from the common law. However, indicating the perceived sensitivity of the broad issue of such reforms, the Commissioners felt obliged to align themselves with Baconian doctrine by suggesting their proposals to be 'in accord, for the most part' with Bacon's (p. 24).

[51] *Fourth Report PP* 1848 (940), xxvii, 6; *First Report* (1834), 25; *Fourth Report PP* 1839 (168), xix, xiv.

[52] *First Report*, 25; *Fourth Report* (1848), 6; *Fourth Report* (1839), viii.

[53] *Seventh Report PP* 1843 (448), xix, 2, Starkie and Ker.

[54] *Correspondence, PP* 1837 xxxi, p. 39. In the previous October Russell had told the Commissioners that it was not 'expedient' to wait for a general digest before going ahead with his programme of decapitalization; the digest would 'take an age' to complete (p. 35). The Home Office view of the Commissioners' legitimate area of activity was firmly indicated two years before by Phillips, Russell's Under Secretary, and successor of Hobhouse, a key figure in Peel's consolidation programme. Phillips suggested that the Commission should confine their digest to statute law, with Amos being

'formation of a new system', where 'rules and definitions' would be expressed in
'uniform language' and different 'classes of crime' would 'always bear a just proportion to each other' to 'ensure the complete harmony of the whole'.[55] A further
four years into their labours, there is talk of the benefits of 'total remodelling'
and 'deduc[ing] a system of rules more general, consequently more compendious
and more uniform and apparently more scientific and practical'. Additionally, on
occasion, the Commissioners indicated a Benthamite awareness of, and concern
for, the points of intersection between civil and criminal law, where uniformity
of language and principle was essential.[56]

Running against such relatively radical leanings, sometimes translated into
proposals, are several telling counter-indications and recommendations appearing in the Reports. While often unsparing in their criticism of the common
law's state and basic law-making processes, the Commissioners adopted a more
measured, if somewhat equivocal, line in respect of what they regarded as the
legitimate law-making role of judges. A 'digest or code' could 'never supersede
the necessity for judicial construction which, rightly understood and applied
within certain limits, is not only necessary but beneficial'.[57] Crucially, 'certain
limits' are never directly confronted when the Commissioners are considering
the appropriate mechanism for post 'digest or code' additions or alterations to the
law. Though not free from ambiguity, the proposals appear exclusively directed
at incorporation of statute-based changes into the law. Procedures for absorbing
subsequent judicial interpretation of statutory enactments (let alone elaboration
of digested common law) are fudged or at least never clearly addressed.[58] The

told to 'steer clear of codification' because several judges were opposed to it, 25 November 1835,
Brougham Mss, 10, 190.

[55] *Fourth Report* (1839), vi, by Starkie, Ker, Wightman, and Jardine, a barrister and replacement
for Amos.

[56] *Seventh Report* (1843), 10, 11–12, by Starkie and Ker. On the relationship of criminal and civil
law, see also the *Fourth Report* (1839), vii.

[57] *Fourth Report* (1839), xvi. Again, Bacon's authority is cited in support of the Commissioners'
views. Also, *Second Report PP* 1846 (709), xxiv, 6, Ryan, Starkie, Richards, Ker, and Amos. Austin's
position on judicial 'legislation' was ambivalent, lacking Bentham's inflexible opposition. Discussed
by Rumble, *Austin*, Ch. 4. On this fundamental question see the Whig-Liberal (probably corresponding to Brougham's) analysis of William Empson, Professor of Law at the East India College,
and sometime editor of the *Edinburgh Review*, (1831) 54, *Edin. Rev.* 183, 230–1, attrib. Wellesley *Index*,
vol. 1, 475.

[58] *Seventh Report* (1843), 13–14; *Second Report* (1846), 6. The proposals for periodic public notification of changes of law by some 'official document' and their embodiment in the 'Digest' by
Parliamentary authority do not comfortably extend to judicial legislation. Neither is it apparent
what body would amend the Digest. Pitt Taylor in the *Law Magazine* endorsed the appointment
of a Commissioner to provide Parliament with an annual update of judicial decisions interpreting the code which would be embodied in the Digest every three years. Pitt Taylor believed
both 'bench and bar would cheerfully transmit the best information' (1843) 30 *LM* 17. Austin had

broadly less radical tone of the Commissioners' later reports suggests either a cooling of initial radical ardour or, more likely, a pragmatic recognition of the generally conventional limits to revision of the law's form imposed by professional and political attitudes. This had occurred before the long-serving core Commissioners, Starkie and Kerr,[59] were rejoined by Amos in 1845 after his Indian interlude when succeeding Macaulay as Legal Member of the Governor-General's Council.[60]

More generally, like Peel, the Commissioners sought a reformulation of criminal law to increase accessibility ('knowability') and, thereby, its effectiveness in deterring crime. Drawing the common law into a more comprehensive and ambitious digest programme immediately raised the fundamental question of the status and standing of both existing and future common law. The solution of a 'wider exposition' of common law, digested alongside statute law, offered an accessible authoritative restatement and perpetuation of extant common law wisdom. Common law reasoning and the judicial role would necessarily be altered to the extent that the Digest exposition became the exclusive source from which future reasoning and development would proceed. However, as the Commission Digest's articulated general principles and substantive provisions demonstrate, considerable potential scope for judicial development would remain.[61] It was a rationalistic response of experienced practical lawyers seeking to secure a better functioning, publicly more accessible, criminal law capable of both preventing and punishing crime more effectively. In line with other areas of contemporary criminal law reform initiatives, the Commission's objectives were the revamping not elimination of the common law system of law-making.[62]

earlier proposed a provision for judicial involvement in reviewing the code or digest, *Lectures on Jurisprudence*, vol. 2, 675. He later suggested a 'Permanent Commission of Legislation' (1847) 85 *Edin. Rev.* 257. On such revisionary bodies see below.

[59] In correspondence with Brougham, Ker later expressed his general aversion to Benthamite codification schemes. On this and the more general issue of the relatively limited influence of Bentham on the Commissioners and their work, see M. Lobban, 'How Benthamic Was the Criminal Law Commission' (2000) 18 *Law and History Rev.* 427, 428–30 and *passim*.

[60] Further Indian codification experience was introduced with the appointment in 1845 of Sir Edward Ryan, former Lord Chief Justice of Calcutta, as Chairman of the Second Criminal Law Commission. Ryan became a member of the second and third Indian Law Commission in 1853 and 1861. On the drafting and final enactment of the Indian Penal Code, see K. Smith, 'Macaulay's Utilitarian Penal Code: An Illustration of the Accidental Function of Time, Place and Personalities in Law Making', in W. M. Gordon and T. D. Fergus (eds), *Legal History and the Making* (1991), 145; and more generally, S. Kadish, 'Codifiers of the Criminal Law' (1978) 78 *Col. LR* 1098.

[61] For analysis of the Commission's substantive provisions and a consideration of their radical amendments, see 'Criminal Fault', 'Defences' etc. Ch. VII below.

[62] In many respects this solution strongly resembled the liberal Tory John Miller's 1822 *Inquiry* approach, favouring the digesting of statutes and common law, *An Inquiry into the Present State of the Statute and Criminal Law of England*. Examined by Smith, *Lawyers, Legislators and Theorists*, 79–80.

Reception of the Criminal Law Commissioners and Responses to their Reports

Predictably, the creation of the Criminal Law Commissioners aroused suspicions and concerns of the nature which greeted the private revision or codification schemes of the 1820s. Terminological confusion on quite what constituted a 'digest' or 'code', and whether the latter necessarily meant 'new' law, served only to aggravate unease as to just what the Commissioners (for many, the creature of an unsettling, quixotic, Lord Chancellor) might be about.[63] The reception of the Commissioners' First Report was indicative of future attitudes. In presenting the Commissioners' First offering to the Lords, Brougham was typically unsparing in his support: the 'digest' was 'above all praise'; this 'most masterly digest…would teach all men, lawyers and [non] lawyers, what the Criminal Law of the country really was'.[64] Significantly, Brougham's ambiguous, interchangeable references to 'code' and 'digest' fed confusion and suspicions about the nature and extent of the Commissioners' activities for years ahead. An exchange between the Chancellor of the Exchequer and several members of the Commons in the following year typifies this terminological problem.[65]

True to its colours, the *Law Magazine* found the First Report to be 'deficient in all main requisites—in sound reasoning, accurate knowledge, logical connection of parts, and comprehensiveness'. Indeed, the whole project was questionable: why employ five Commissioners when a 'Book on Criminal Law might be composed by one—Mr Starkie'? Not only did the reviewer (almost certainly Abraham Hayward) challenge the Commissioners' accuracy in their dismissal of the value of modern treatises, more fundamentally, he questioned the importance of the core axiom requiring that criminal law be readily accessible and 'knowable': 'it was idle to suppose that people, particularly the lower orders, take their notions as to the criminality of criminal actions from books'. Furthermore, deep scepticism was expressed over the value of seeking to comprehensively provide legal definitions, a quest which would gain the approval of only 'speculating jurists' but not 'practical jurists' who know 'all operative law' may not be turned into 'written law'.[66] Returning to the theme a year or two later, the *Law Magazine* lambasted the Commissioners' efforts as 'little more than…long, loose, clumsy,

---

[63] e.g. (1833) 10 *LM* 492 and (1830) 6 *Foreign Quart. Rev.* 321, 331.

[64] Responding, Lord Wynford perceived the dangers of a code to be, as in France, where 'shortness…almost put absolute power into the hands of Judges', *PD* 1834 (s. 3), 24: 835–6.

[65] *PD* 1835 (s. 3) 29: 425. Several MPs thought that a full-time Commissioner could carry out the work more swiftly.

[66] (1835) 13 *LM* i–5, 44, 51. Cf. (1835) 15 *LM* 15, 236. It was later that year after publication of this article, that Phillips issued the recorded Home Office restraint on the Commissioners' endeavours.

common-place statements of exhausted controversies, with which the public has been bored to satiety'.[67]

However, with the moderated proposals manifest in the Fourth Report's publication in 1839 such broad hostility subsided. Indeed, the *Law Magazine* positively beamed approval at what it regarded as the greatly reduced ambitions of the Commissioners. Instead of threatening a 'Code Napoleon', the Commissioners had adopted a 'far more temperate and self-denying tone' than emerged in their First Report. Endorsing the Commission's view that a 'statutory declaration of crimes and punishments [was] essential for the good administration of [existing] penal laws', the *Law Magazine* expressed relief that there would be no resort to the 'fabrications of Bentham'. Overall, the Commissioners' Fourth Report would be 'introductory to many valuable improvements in the legislation of this country'.[68] While the Commissioners had certainly adopted a more restrained tone by the Fourth Report, rather than a reduction of scale, the Commissioners' ambitions were benefiting from clarification. For, in common with others, the *Law Magazine* had, at least in part, misconstrued the Commissioners' original objectives.

By the early 1840s the Commissioners' Reports were enjoying a consistently strong measure of support from both the *Law Magazine* and *Law Review*. The former even permitted Pitt Taylor, a confirmed reformer, to offer the 'highest praise' for the Seventh Report. More lavish still was the 1845 *Law Magazine*'s judgment of the Digest as a 'truly great work', which, if enacted would 'yield a moral benefit…vitally need[ed]'. By now the Commissioners' practical credentials were never doubted; they well understood that the criminal law was based on a 'broad philosophy', and built on the roughest facts; it could not be a product of the 'closet or guided alone by the light of parliamentary inspiration'.[69] Similarly, from its establishment in 1844, the *Law Review* generally applauded the enterprise. In part this was initiated by using Starkie to review anonymously the Seventh Report.[70] And like the *Law Magazine*, by 1845 the *Law Review* was

---

[67] (1837) 17 *LM* 224. As seen, at this time Russell, as Home Secretary, had told the Commissioners that his priority was a range of decapitalizing measures, not general digesting or codification schemes.

[68] (1839) 22 *LM* 1, 3, 6, and 60. Similarly (1840) 24 *LM* 1–4. The article was signed 'H', presumably Hayward.

[69] (1843) 30 *LM* 1, 12, 18, 48. Pitt Taylor expressed disapproval of the wide judicial discretion in respect of punishment (23–6), and (1845) II, 88–92. 224. By 1845 the *Law Magazine* was critical of the Commissioners' insufficiently radical treatment of the legal terminology (89). The article was signed 'S'.

[70] (1844–5) 1, 438. Starkie felt obliged to deploy Bacon in describing the great benefit of such law reform. The article is attributed to Starkie in the *Law Review*'s obituary of him (1849) 10 *Law Rev.* 202.

even critical of the Commissioners' timidity in not tackling 'undigested' common law terminology.[71]

Brougham's relative neglect of the Commissioners following his fall from government was very publicly terminated in 1843 when Peel's second administration appeared to be cooling in respect of the Commissioners' continued existence. Brougham's published *Letters on Law Reform to the Right Honourable Sir J.R. Graham*, then Home Secretary, emphatically reaffirmed his attachment to the project of a combined digest of statute and common law. Both here, and the following year in the Lords, Brougham, unhelpfully, also chose to air his determination to 'leave as little as possible to the Judge's discretion...'.[72] Whilst supporting the digesting of statutes, as Chancellor, Lord Lyndhurst, expressed keen awareness of judicial opposition to a similar treatment of the common law; for him, it was a situation demanding 'time for reflection and the careful gauging of [judicial] opinion'.[73] This process of reflection began in the following year with the establishment of a Second Criminal Law Commission, chaired not as before by Starkie, but by Sir Edward Ryan, charged with revising the previous Reports and completing a draft code on criminal procedure.[74] In June 1848, within three months of the publication of the Fifth and final Report of the Second Commission, Brougham introduced the Report's draft Digest bill, combining statute and common law, into the Lords by way of a provisional run for the next parliamentary session.[75] Despite the growth of support in the periodical press

[71] (1845–6) 2 *Law Rev.* 249–51. The *Law Review* expressly disclaimed sympathy for an anti-'speculative' digest article it chose to publish (1846) 4 *Law Rev.* 78.

[72] *PD* 1844 (s. 3) 74: 993, continuing: 'I would have the law speak through the judge...and not the judge make the law he delivers'. Brougham also indicated that he 'favoured...a general digest of the whole Common Law', both civil and criminal. And also *PD* 1843 (s. 3), 71: 753. In his *Letters* (1843) Brougham argued 'Nothing can be worse than leaving the definition of the law to the judges, [although] its application and interpretation must of necessity be left to them' (34–5). The recently established *Law Times* expressed full support for this stance (1843–4), 2, 31. Lord Chancellor Lyndhurst spoke of 'expressions of doubt and suggestions of difficulty' from 'persons connected with the administration of justice' in respect of digesting the common law (1009). Lord Denman CJ, Brougham's long-standing reformer comrade-in-arms, was notably reticent in throwing his weight behind Brougham's sentiments. He was anxious to remove 'existing evils' from the law's substance (1012). Less circumspect, Lord Campbell 'hoped, before long to see...a written criminal code' including the common law (1013). But the current digest required further 'revision' (1015).

[73] *Ibid.*, 1008.

[74] As Amos later reflected with some justice, the 1848 Administration of Criminal Jervis Act (Jervis ed) exhibited such an 'unmistakable family likeness' to the Commissioners' procedure code as to warrant the Acts bearing the appellation 'Starkie', *Ruins of Time* (1854), xvi. Ryan had co-authored with W.D. Russell a volume of Court for Crown Cases Reserved judgments, 1799–1825. In 1846 he was also appointed a railway commissioner, DNB, vol. xvii, (1888–9).

[75] Second reading, *PD* 1848 (s. 3), 99: 990. The bill ended its career in a Select Committee.

for the Commissioners' work, the parliamentary campaign was largely left to Brougham's own dogged efforts.[76]

Prospects revived in the autumn of 1852: urged on by *The Times* to carry out what the 'Whig Ministry could not prevail on themselves to finish',[77] Greaves and Lonsdale (the long serving Secretary of the Criminal Law Commissioners) were directed by Tory Chancellor, Lord St Leonards, to prepare several 'codification' bills based on the Commissioners' Reports,[78] beginning with an Offences Against the Person Bill. Chaired by the Lord Chancellor, the bill's Select Committee boasted Lords Lyndhurst, Brougham, Campbell, and Cranworth, amongst others. The exit of Derby's short-lived administration and entry of Aberdeen's did nothing to halt this modest momentum. As St Leonard's successor, Cranworth renewed the former Chancellor's instructions to Greaves and Lonsdale, with Lord Campbell CJ, endorsing preparation of the 'whole code' as soon as possible.[79] Small wonder that in this bi-partisan 'codification' climate, Brougham thought that there was 'every reason to expect that the country was on the eve of receiving a sound and well-digested code of criminal law'.[80] Following frequent, though not inevitable practice, in the autumn of 1853 the opinions of the judges were solicited on the Offences Against the Person and Larceny Bills. Both in relation to the practicality and general desirability of the combined digest of the criminal law, the judges were uniformly hostile. Recurring throughout the judges' responses was the assertion that little or no practical benefit could be gained by what was regarded as surrendering the common law's flexibility and adaptability; indeed, many of them saw considerable disbenefits as almost certain to follow. In essence, a Code would hinder the law's natural accretive growth and development; statutory consolidation was urged as the appropriate reform strategy.[81]

In the immediate aftermath both the Lord Chancellor and Judiciary were subject to some especially stinging comments from legal and general journals. For one thing, rather than simply request 'detailed' observations on the bills, Cranworth had also sought opinions on the fundamental question of a combined

---

[76] e.g. Brougham, *PD* 1851 (s. 3), 113: 954; 1851 (s. 3), 116: 121; and 1852 (s. 3), 120: 343. See also the *Law Review's* criticism of government inactivity, (1851) 14, 187–90. And see also (1852) 16 *Jurist* 197. *The Times* spoke with 'admiration and envy' of the New York Code, and looked forward to similar 'enlightenment' in England, 30 November 1850.

[77] '…although it had cost the country £40,000', 19 November 1852, p. 4.

[78] Greaves, *Introduction*, x. See *PD* 1853 (s. 3), 124: 8. Lord Campbell 'rejoiced' at this step towards 'codify[ing]' the law (9).

[79] *Ibid.*, xi.

[80] *PD* 1853 (s. 3) 129: 159.

[81] *Copies of the Lord Chancellor's Letters to the Judges and of their Answers…*, 1854 *PP* (303), liii, 391. On the loss of flexibility and the consequential dangers etc., for example, see Pollock LCB 6; Parke B. 7; Alderson B. 9; Maule J. 18; Cresswell J. 21; Talfourd J. 37. Specific drafting criticisms were responded to by Greaves and Lonsdale in 'A Letter to the Lord Chancellor, containing Observations on the Answers of the Judges to the Lord Chancellor's letter' (1854).

digest of statute and common law: whether such a 'measure [was] likely to prod-uce benefit in the administration of criminal justice, or the reverse'. This, the *Law Review* regarded as 'too loose in its shape' and 'seemed to say, come and help me to defeat this measure'.[82] As for the judges, 'Never...was there exhibited in such striking colours the contrast between men's competency within the limits of their own province, and their incapacity beyond those bounds—between judges exercising judicial functions and judges turned law givers...'.[83] Unsurprisingly, Brougham's personal frustrations were given full vent after an initial restrained, historically informed lament in the Lords. In an unattributed scathing critique appearing in the *Edinburgh Review*, Brougham accused the judiciary of putting their own convenience and self-interest, in not having to master new laws, before the public benefit of law reform; 'Satire, sarcasm, irony and something akin to petulance, each play their several parts [and] only...accentuate [that] facts and logical reasoning...are sparingly used...'.[84]

When pressed by St Leonards, Cranworth not only dithered as to the course to be adopted, but suggested that as the originator of the bill, it was for St Leonards to make the running. The whole matter of a digest or code was effectively con-signed to oblivion through a Lords' Select Committee which later reported it inexpedient to proceed further.[85] For Cranworth the future lay in production of a 'Code Victoria', a grandly styled project of relatively modest scope, involving gen-eral statutory revision and consolidation, to be assigned to a specially appointed body. It was a measure that many of the judges had indicated to be an acceptable reform route, and which had got underway in 1853, prior to the judicial rebuff of the Digest bills.[86]

---

[82] Copies of the 'Lord Chancellor's Letters' (1854) 20, *Law Rev.* 110, 112. Brougham made pre-cisely this point in the following Lords' debate, *PD* 1854 (s. 3), 131: 349. The *Law Review* acquitted Cranworth of any sinister purpose, ascribing his error of judgment to 'too little confidenc[e] in his own powers, and too little reliant upon the authority of his own position...'. It was Lord St Leonards who proposed consulting the judiciary, *PD* 1853 (s. 3), 129: 158. Cranworth admitted to being 'stag-gered at the difficulty of the task' of digesting before writing to the judges, *PD* 1854 (s. 3), 131: 342.

[83] (1854) 20 *Law Rev.* 142–5.

[84] (1854) 99 *Edin. Rev.* 573 at 576–81, attrib. *Wellesley Index* 1, 503. There is evidence that another attack on the judges' behaviour in the (by then) more liberal Tory *Quarterly Review* was also by Brougham (1854) 'Criminal Law Digest' 461, attrib. *Wellesley Index* 1, 737. For Brougham's Lords' response, see *PD* 1854 (s. 3), 131: 346. For similar comments on the judiciary, see also (1854) *Law Rev.* 120 and 426. Three years before, on the issue of judicial opposition to law reform, the *Law Review* had advised the judges 'not to push the advantages of their position too far' (1851) 15 *Law Rev.* 372. Cf. *The Times'* equivocal stance, 8 March 1854, p. 8.

[85] *PD* 1854 (s. 3), 1, 131: 332–55; 134, 1441–2. At this stage, Lord Campbell 'despaired' that a 'crim-inal code' could ever be enacted by standard legislative procedures (1442) *Report from the Select Committee* (p. 339); 1854 *House of Lords Session Papers*, vol. 21, 1.

[86] Cranworth spoke of his plan for a 'Code Victoria' and Ker's participation, February 1853, *PD* (s. 3), 124: 64–6. It was less than obvious how the St Leonards' Digest bills, by then adopted by Cranworth, would mesh with the criminal elements of the 'Code Victoria'. From the beginning, Ker's suitability

Under-resourced and feebly led by Ker, the Statute Law Board was reincarnated as the Statute Law Commission in 1854, whose membership was now boosted by the likes of former Chancellors and Law Officers, though still headed by Ker. Many members had previously made up a significant part of the Lords' Select Committee on the Digest Bills; Amos mockingly likened this change to 'from being grubs of criminal law, they were transmuted into butterflies, licensed to range over the wide expanse of legislative creation'. He also rightly observed that their brief (albeit including civil law) was strikingly close to that empowering the first Criminal Law Commissioners.[87] However, vacillation on the part of Cranworth and Ker, combined with a palpable absence of sustained commitment from the bulk of the distinguished group of Statute Law Commissioners, conduced to an almost inevitable result. Four Reports, issued between 1855 and 1859, reveal a fundamental inability to resolve both the proper scope of the Commission's work and *modus operandi*; recurrent disagreements relating to such matters crippled the operation and output of the whole venture and its ultimate value.[88]

Running from 1833, the final modest outcome of this era of the most earnest and sustained efforts to recast the criminal law's form were the 1861 Consolidation Acts. As Greaves, their principal architect and member of the Statute Law Commission, acknowledged, their successful passage through the parliamentary mill in no small measure rested on the assurance that little in language or substance of the consolidated statutes had been altered.[89] Effectively, almost nothing had changed from the climate which fostered and restricted Peel's familiar consolidating formula. Greaves's ascription of the general failure of the Criminal Law Commissioners' project to inherently hostile parliamentary procedures, political and broad professional hostility or indifference, was amply justified. The political and legislative focus had long been amelioration of the scale of punishments coupled with the steady modification of generally acknowledged procedural deficiencies. By comparison, obscurities in the substantive law were almost celebrated in the growing range of practitioners' manuals, as well as fuelling and funding the expansion of the numbers of criminal lawyers. Judicial obstruction

and competence were subject to slashing attacks in the (1854) 19 *Law Rev.* 111; and also the *Morning Chronicle*, 16 February 1854. The *Law Magazine* was equally unsparing (1856–7) 1 *LM* 122 and 455; 3 *LM* 317; 4 *LM* 328. In 1859 the Commission's final Report was characterized as 'utterly valueless'; the whole enterprise was 'futile' when undertaken by 'political pretenders' and 'incapable minds busy begetting cripples [or] delivering abortions…' (1859) 7 *LM* 452.

[87] *Ruins of Time*, xx–xxi.

[88] For an analysis of the Statute Law Commission's composition and Reports, see A. H. Manchester 'Simplifying the Sources of Law: An Essay in Law Reform' [1973] *Anglo Am. LR* 395.

[89] *PD* 1860 (s. 3), 158: 998, 1200; (s. 3), 159: 270; (s. 3), 160: 893; (1861) (s. 3), 161: 439; (s. 3), 163: 930, 1376; (s. 3), 164: 370.

of digesting or codifying the common law was both predictable and natural; the Bench's deep reluctance to accept an apparent diminution in its creative powers and standing could only have been reinforced by Brougham (and others) openly seeking to redefine their role by cutting back the judicial common law legislative function. Little wonder that Amos declared 'codiphobia' was endemic throughout a common law nurtured profession, and why government law reform policy was half-hearted and easily compromised, often appearing 'crab-like and retrograde'.[90]

The fate of the Criminal Law Commission's Reports and Digest Bills, along with that of the Statute Law Commission, confirmed entrenched attitudes of the legal profession and Parliament in relation to the respective criminal law-making roles of each institution. As had been the case long before even Peel's time, regulation of the nature and measure of punishment was Parliament's function. Formal changes of punishment throughout the nineteenth century were necessarily effected by legislation. This was equally true of the establishment and modification of the machinery of criminal law enforcement. The common law heartland of the criminal justice system was substantive criminal law and principles, as mediated through its evidence rules and doctrines. These perceptions of respective institutional functions remained essentially unchanged until the end of the nineteenth century. As Cranworth observed in 1863, statutes were 'simply a supplement to rectify the omissions of the unwritten law';[91] a philosophy which *The Times*, amongst others, had regularly pulverized in editorials from the late 1850s to early 1860s.[92]

Codification by Private Enterprise: Stephen

Dissatisfaction with the modest advances gained in the criminal law's form and accessibility by the 1861 legislation was implicit in Lord Chancellor Westbury's 1863 speech on law revision. From the mid-1850s, first as Solicitor-General, and then Attorney-General, as well as a Statute Law Commissioner, Richard Bethell had shown interest in law revision, including case law digestion.[93] Once installed on the woolsack, he proposed enacting a general (both criminal and civil) programme of purging, revising, and digesting not only statute, but also common law reports. In the latter case, there would be a weeding out of contradictory decisions and settling 'those which ought to remain', as consistent with the 'existing

---

[90] *Ruins of Time*, xvii and xi.

[91] PD 1863 (s. 3), 171: 794 and Westbury, 776.

[92] e.g. 17 July 1858, p. 9; 5 February 1859, p. 8; 29 August 1860, p. 8; 13 June 1863, p. 11.

[93] T. A. Nash, *Life of Richard Lord Westbury* (1888), ii: 62–4.

condition of society'. Thus, 'purified and refined', case law would be 'brought into a moderate compass' and digested alongside statute law. At the same time, somewhat disingenuously, Westbury assured their Lordships that he was not advocating 'codification', for that would 'imply a re-writing of the law'.[94] Of course, while strictly true, indirectly the process of choosing between conflicting authorities and gauging what was consistent with the 'existing condition of society', licensed just such a 're-writing' exercise. With Westbury's early resignation, his ambitious project lost momentum and never proceeded beyond a First Report, the equivocality of which prompted an exasperated *Law Magazine* to declare the 'nation is wearied out and demands a reform, which will render our system clear, concise, simple, intelligible to all'.[95]

As an admirer, Stephen was doubly saddened by Westbury's fall from high office. Beside the loss of his reforming zeal, Westbury's grand programme had held out the promise of possible preferment for Stephen as one of the Chancellor's 'body of redacteurs'.[96] Furthermore, publication of *A General View of the Criminal Law of England*, Stephen's most public entry into criminal law jurisprudence and reform, broadly coincided with Westbury's Lords' announcement. Quite how much notice Stephen had of Westbury's intentions is difficult to gauge. It is not unlikely that he was aware of at least the general nature of Westbury's ambitions. Certainly the *General View* contains much in sympathy with them, including the proposals for a 'Ministry of Justice', headed by the Lord Chancellor, charged with superintendence of all criminal legislation. More radically, such a ministry was to have responsibility for law reporting, from which digests of general principles and rules would be extracted. But, though critical of the law's disorganized form, Stephen regarded 'English judges [as] one of the best subordinate legislators in the world', arguing for their active participation in authenticating such digests.[97]

---

[94] *PD* 1863 (s. 3), 171: 795, 785–8. In common with practically all previous consolidators and digesters, Westbury felt obliged to 'take Lord Bacon as my guide' (786, 777, 789). As an agency for the annual revision and authentication of case law, Westbury referred briefly to a 'Department of Justice'.

[95] *Report*, PP 1867 [C. 3849], xix, 65. (1868) 25 *LM* 237, 256 and (1867) 126 *Edin. Rev.* 347. A Royal Commission (which included Cranworth, Cairns, Westbury, Roundell Palmer, and Robert Lowe) to consider the 'expediency of a digest' was appointed in 1866 and produced one report the following year. No further action followed. In 1860, Bethell, as Attorney-General, had appointed a team of two to 'expurgate' all obsolete statutes, an exercise carried out for several years under the Statute Revision Act 1861. Initiatives by the Statute Law Committee from 1868 for statutory tidying continued throughout the remainder of the century. For a concise outline see 'Memo relating to Statute Law Revision', PP 1891 [C. 6420], lxiii, 873.

[96] Smith, *James Fitzjames Stephen*, 76 n. 27.

[97] *General View*, 326–36. And to underline the absence of any attempt to restrict judicial creativity, Stephen observed that the power to overrule case law would remain untouched in relation to its digested form. Early published criticism by Stephen of the 'unfathomable mysteries of the common

In broad terms, like Westbury's, the substance of Stephen's solution differed little from the final approach of the Criminal Law Commissioners.[98]

In 1872, on his return from three years in India as Law Member of the Governor-General's Council, Stephen embarked on a course of privately inspired codification initiatives, having scorned the idea a decade earlier in the *General View*. His Indian experience had clearly reinforced existing inclinations towards recasting the law's form. In India, Stephen had both broken a log-jam of stalled legislation accumulated under Maine, his predecessor, and also generated his own legislative programme. According to Sir Courtney Ilbert, Stephen's later successor, 'His tenure of office lasted only half the ordinary span but he compressed into it enough work for five law members—He left the Legislative Council breathless and staggering, conscious that they had accomplished unprecedented labours'.[99] Stephen's post-Indian frame of mind relating to remodelling the criminal law's form was pithily summed up in his address to the Social Science Association in November 1872; here he suggested that 'to compare the Indian Penal Code with English criminal law is like comparing cosmos with chaos'.[100]

Active engagement with anything resembling codification of English law occurred within a few weeks of his return from the subcontinent. Exceedingly well connected through family and friends, and enjoying a rising reputation as a criminal jurist, Stephen was an obvious choice to assist his cousin, Russell Gurney, in drafting a Homicide bill. Encouraged by the radical MP John Bright, Gurney, fellow MP and Recorder of London, sought a narrower, codified reformulation of homicide. First introduced in 1872, on its reintroduction in 1874 the bill was sent to a Select Committee which declared the project unsatisfactory on two principal grounds: that enactment of a penal code should commence with principles and rules of more general relevance to larger classes of crime; and the familiar argument that changes in the law of this nature were most appropriately the business of the whole House.[101] Also familiar and carrying similar significant weight in the Committee's deliberations was the judicial reaction.

---

law' appeared in his 1856 *Saturday Review* articles (vol. i, 252, vol. ii, 545). Also 'The Characteristics of English Criminal Law', *Cambridge Essays* (1857).

[98] However, Stephen's reform credentials were challenged by *The Times*, 8 February 1865, p. 9 in directly rejecting his *General View* observation on the 1861 Consolidation Acts as 'tolerably well fulfil[ling] the main purpose of codification'.

[99] 'Sir James Stephen as a Legislator' (1894) 10 *LQR* 222, 224. More generally on Stephen's Indian codification, see Smith, *James Fitzjames Stephen*, Ch. 6, 'India and the Imperial Ethic'.

[100] His speech is reported in (1872) xii *Fortnightly Rev.* 644, 654. Cf. Austin's comments on the 'empires of chaos and darkness' in *Lectures on Jurisprudence* (1863), Lecture 39.

[101] *Special Report from the Select Committee on Homicide Law Amendment Bill PP* 1874 (315), ix, 471. Robert Lowe, the Committee's chairman, ten years before had used a flattering review of the *General View* to discuss the great need for criminal law reform (1865) 121 *Edin. Rev.* 109, attrib. Lowe, *Wellesley Index*, i: 514. The *Law Times* declared the Committee's conclusions to be 'ingenious but

As in 1853, judicial opinion had been canvassed, and again the response had been mainly hostile to change. Occupying the vanguard of judicial opposition was Lord Chief Justice Cockburn, whose main objection was that partial codification required the unsatisfactory practice of incorporation of references to non-code sources of law; it was an argument previously fielded by Cockburn as Attorney-General to undermine the chances of the proposed wider digest reforms of the 1850s.[102] But as Stephen later pointed out, the suggested dilemma of codification *en bloc* or no codification was fallacious; a staged transition during which common law concepts could be phased out was quite feasible. Yet, as before, the core of explicit judicial antagonism was the expectation that codification would remove the essential flexibility of the common law to meet both the exigencies of social change and novel situations. Additionally, as Stephen openly suggested, fears for the judiciary's general standing were probably just as potent in motivating their opposition. Giving evidence before the Select Committee over two days, Stephen pulled no punches, insisting (much in the vein, but without the invective, of Brougham) that it was quite natural that judges should feel an 'irresistible temptation' to work with a familiar system of unwritten rules rather than accept the upset and restrictions of change. However, for Stephen, 'this quasi-legislative authority should not be left in the hands of the judges' in its present form; it was a stance which represented a distinct shift from that taken less than a decade before in the *General View*.[103]

Stephen's further session before the Committee, responding to evidence given on culpability and other issues by senior common law judges, Blackburn J. and Bramwell B., two of the day's most acute and forceful judicial minds, was marked by startling and characteristic candour. Although much of Stephen's testimony defending the Bill related to the proposed drastic modification of the felony-murder rule, parts of it sought to refute key judicial assertions on the need for definitional 'elasticity'. In this respect, Stephen scored a direct hit by demonstrating the starkly conflicting nature of the testimony of Bramwell and Blackburn on certain aspects of culpability.

'Amazing' is the only proper epithet to apply to the vigour and tone of Stephen's reply to the criticisms of the Bill made by [Bramwell and Blackburn]. Seldom in the history of English law can a member of the Bar have dared to shake occupants of the Bench so

cowardly' (1874) 57 *LT* 243. Aimed at eliminating felony murder and incorporating specific measures on insanity, duress and the like, the Bill was, effectively, a self-contained homicide code capable of operating with little reference to common law principles outside the code.

[102] Here, and later, Cockburn claimed *principled* support for such reforms always ended in *detailed* opposition. For his similar tactic in relation to fusion of civil courts, see XI, Pt 3.

[103] As well as Cockburn, the Committee took evidence from Blackburn J. and Bramwell B. The latter's criticism related to detail rather than conception.

thoroughly as he did on this occasion. He was not satisfied with trouncing them separately; with a devastating show of logic, he truculently and sarcastically used the one to knock the other down.[104]

Of course with the experience of India deeply imbibed, Stephen was less inclined to observe the niceties of Bar and Bench etiquette when expressing opinions on English law's irregular and unsystematic form. But while, doubtless, feeling intellectually vindicated, publicly out-witting members of the judiciary was never going to save the Bill from extinction.[105]

Rather than deterred by the experience of the Homicide Bill, Stephen eventually embarked on a full-scale criminal law codification initiative. Partly as a preliminary to an intended second edition of the more discursive *General View*, Stephen produced *Digests* of the *Criminal Law* (1877) and *Evidence* (1876). Not only would these practitioners' works generate income, they also carried the twin promise of enhancing Stephen's reputation as a skilled expositor of criminal law and of serving as the basis for a criminal code. Work on the *Digest of Criminal Law* painfully confirmed his impression of the problematic nature of producing a clear, accessible account of the substantive law. His contemporary reflections on the two leading practitioners' works, *Russell* and *Archbold*, vividly convey Stephen's mood. The former's unsystematic layout and arrangement were 'enough to make one go crazy', with the case law 'like the stores at Balaclava in the winter of 1854–1855. Everything is there nothing is in its place, and the few feeble attempts at arrangement... serve only to bring the mass of confusion to light'. *Archbold*, the advocate's bible, faired no better: 'to try to read it is like trying to read a Directory arranged partly on geographical and partly on biographical principles'.[106]

By late 1876 Stephen was using public lectures and press coverage to campaign for criminal law codification. One such meeting addressed by Stephen, well capturing the width of support for some form of codification, was organized in February 1877 by the Trades Union Congress Parliamentary Committee. Most successfully assuming the unfamiliar guise of populist orator and trades union 'bed fellow'[107] before a 'densely crowded' hall of 'working men', Stephen asserted

---

[104] D. S. Davies, 'Child-Killing in English Law', in L. Radzinowicz and J. W. C. Turner (eds), *The Modern Approach to Criminal Law* (1945), 301, 326–7.

[105] Stephen's 1872 Evidence Code Bill enjoyed an even briefer career. As the Attorney-General, Sir John Coleridge explained, the bill (strongly resembling Stephen's recently enacted Indian Evidence Act) was the work of '[my] friend Mr Fitzjames Stephen,...employe[d] in consequence of the kind liberality of the Chancellor of the Exchequer', *PD* 1873 (s. 3), 217: 1559. The bill's introduction was no more than a parliamentary marker. Absence of practical and political need ensured the bill was not revived in the subsequent parliamentary session. In 1872, the *Law Times* had expressly called for the Indian Evidence Act to form the basis of an English code of evidence (1872) 53 *LT* 312.

[106] *Digest* (1877), 366 and x.

[107] Stephen to Lytton, 3 May 1878, Stephen Papers, Cambridge University Library.

the criminal law's need for 'wide and extensive amendment...in its form but also in its substance'; change that was sympathetic to the 'present state of knowledge and feeling'. Significant endorsements came from R. S. Wright, Frederic Harrison, and Sir George Bramwell, with the latter now expressing 'no misgivings' that codification 'was the right thing to do'. As the meeting's chairman, Lord Coleridge (then Chief Justice of Common Pleas) saw a 'code worthy of the country' as unlikely to survive ordinary parliamentary procedures; instead, the public was enjoined to encourage Parliament to surrender its 'authority into the hands of a commission of distinguished men who alone could form a true sense of what was required'.[108]

Capitalizing on such powerful publicity, early in the following year Stephen wrote to both Holker, the Attorney-General, and Lord Chancellor Cairns, proposing the preparation of a draft code of the greater part of the substantive and procedural common law, based on his *Digest*. Taken with the proposal, Holker was instrumental in Cairns instructing Stephen in August to draft bills for a penal code and (later) for one on procedure.[109] The following May, the Criminal Code (Indictable Offences) Bill was introduced into the Commons by the Attorney-General, soon attracting fulsome endorsement from *The Times*.[110] After its second reading, the bill became the subject of a Royal Commission composed of Lord Blackburn, Mr Justice Barrie, Lord Justice Lush, and Stephen. The Commission sat from November 1878 to May 1879, 'daily during nearly the whole of that time, and discussed every line and nearly every word of every section'.[111] While the bill underwent a wide range of detailed amendments, this, essentially,

---

[108] Reported in (1877) 62 *LT* 265–6. Also, Stephen to Lord Broadhurst 4, 9, and 11 December 1876; 15 and 23 January 1877. Broadhurst Papers, London School of Economics and Political Science. The Committee, whose membership included Maine, noted that Wright had executed the work in a 'highly skilful manner' (p. 3). On Wright's work for the Statute Law Committee, see below, n. 119. Wright, barrister and fellow of Oriel College, Oxford, was an established adviser to the Trades Union Congress on labour legislation, and author of *Law of Criminal Conspiracies and Agreements* (1873). For the Trades Union Congress's apprehension over the organized labour provisions of the 1879 Draft Code, see M. L. Friedland, 'R. S. Wright's Model Criminal Code' (1981) 1 *OJLS* 322–4.

[109] Lord Chancellor's Office files, NA. LCO. 1/42. Letter 20 January 1877. Holker's communications with Cairns revealed Holker's very strong advocacy of the Code and Stephen's participation, 5 March and 1 June 1877. On 10 and 26 May, Stephen also wrote directly to Cairns. Stephen told his friend Lord Lytton, that he had been 'pressing the Lord Chancellor to let me draw an English Penal Code for him', 19 July 1877, Stephen Papers.

[110] *PD* 1878 (s. 3), 239: 1936. The Bill contained many reforms in the law of homicide, larceny, and evidence, together with the establishment of a Court of Criminal Appeal. It was confined to indictable offences. Because the 'labour of passing an [even larger] measure through Parliament would be too vast and overwhelming', summary jurisdiction had not been included, *ibid.*, 1940. Also, *The Times*, 13 June 1878, p. 9, declaring it would be a 'scandal if any time be wasted in the process of substituting [the Code] for the [present] superannuated machinery'. Similarly, 10 June 1878, p. 9.

[111] *HCL*, i, vi.

judicial Commission expressed absolutely no reservations on the advisability and benefits of a criminal code. Codification would bring about the 'reduction of the existing law to an orderly written system freed from the needless technicalities, obscurities, and other defects which the experience of its administration has disclosed'.[112] However, the more pressing 'condition of public business' consumed available parliamentary time and denied the bill a third reading. Though reintroduced in February 1880, the bill's remaining momentum was effectively dissipated with a Spring change of government.

The fate of Stephen's great codification initiative was settled by a combination of several factors, some familiar and some unique. In this latter category the Irish question's absorption of much parliamentary time and moral energy was at the expense of measures of lesser moment. Criminal law reform being a frail craft even in favourable conditions, the Code Bill was predictably 'wrecked in an Irish storm in the Grand committee of the Commons'.[113] And although in the following year Gladstone himself indicated his willingness to take up the code, it was not salvaged.[114] More familiar in its role of defeating this most promising of all English criminal codification attempts was the hostile nature of standard parliamentary procedure to the passage of such measures, especially when many changes of the law were to be effected. Years later, Sir Harry Poland was no more than graphically expressing common-place scepticism (like Greaves, Brougham, Campbell, and Stephen before him) when likening the naivety necessary to believe a criminal code could be got through the Commons with that of 'expecting to find milk in a male tiger'.[115] Overcoming this fundamental difficulty required a level of sustained government commitment which even the 1879 Code Bill never enjoyed. It is very doubtful whether professional and some judicial resistance to the Code Bill was of more than marginal significance. On this occasion, open judicial opposition was confined to Lord Cockburn CJ.

On the same day as the Commission's Report was published, Cockburn furnished Holker with 'Comments and Suggestions in relation to the Criminal Code (Indictable Offences) Bill'. As in the 1850s and 1874, Cockburn oozed sympathy for the general notion of codification, whilst feeling compelled to express opposition to the undesirable practice of partial codification. Both Holker and Stephen

---

[112] *Report*, 47.

[113] M. D. Chalmers (1886) 2 *LQR* 125, 126.

[114] *PD* 1881 (s. 3), 262: 1937. Writing privately to Stephen on 17 July 1882 (Stephen Papers) Holker reports that Harcourt, the Home Secretary, would try to push through the Code's procedural element. Though announced in 1882 as part of the government's programme, nothing came of it. From early days, *The Times* predicted that rather than criticism, government neglect would defeat the Code, 7 May 1879, p. 11.

[115] Attributed to Poland in the Preface of *Archbold* (22nd edn, 1900).

intended to brook no such opposition: Holker brusquely rejected Cockburn's objections in the Commons; Stephen published a detailed and measured rebuttal a few months later in the *Nineteenth Century*.[116] His appointment as a High Court judge the year before provided a rare public spectacle of an open clash of judicial opinion on principles of legislation and the role of the judiciary. Unlike earlier generations of judicial discontent, loss of the common law's intrinsic virtue of flexibility did not form the mainstay of Cockburn's assault on the Code;[117] rather, the core of his dissent was the Code's incomplete substantive coverage along with lack of autonomy and independence from common law principles; consequently, he regarded it as untenable as a comprehensive code.

Claims of the inherently defective nature of partial codification had, as has been seen, figured previously in Cockburn's rejection of the 1874 Homicide Bill. With some justification, Stephen argued that earlier legislation, including the 1861 Consolidation Acts, despite incomplete coverage of all the relevant law, had proved its value. Moreover, it was quite coherent to extract from the common law ill-defined specific offence definitions, whilst retaining broad common law defences or exculpatory principles of justification and excuse. Essentially, Stephen supported the retention of the flexibility to deal with occasional unpredictable

---

[116] Holker to Stephen, 8 July 1879 'I think nothing of Cockburn's criticisms and I do sincerely hope you may be able to hold him up to ridicule'. Also, *PD* 1879 (s. 3), 247: 953. Writing to a long-standing confidante later in the year, Stephen discusses his forthcoming publication in the *Nineteenth Century*, 'I have tried to make it profoundly respectful, and even flattering to his vanity, but I have had to struggle with what in sermons is called the Old Man—...this monster of vanity, and of pure pique at not being a member of the Criminal Code Commission, has written what he probably regards as an effective attack on the Code. He has succeeded in proving nothing, except that wounded vanity will induce him to take a great deal of trouble and that he has really never given any serious thought to this subject or attempted in any way to understand its difficulties. I hope, however, I have been able to keep this old man in the sense of corrupt human nature, pretty quiet— and to heap the Old Man Cockburn (he is in his 78th year I believe) with all the respect which certainly is due to him, both as the High Priest for the time being and as one of the very cleverest fellows (with all his faults) in all England', Stephen to Lady Grant Duff, 11 December 1879 (Stephen Papers). Evidence of Cockburn's annoyance at being left out of the Commission appears in a letter from Lord Chancellor Cairns to Cockburn, clearly attempting to smooth ruffled feathers, 15 July 1878, NA, LCO 30/51. Cockburn's objections were largely endorsed by the 1879 67 *LT* 188. The *Edinburgh Review* regarded the Code as a 'magnificent piece of legislation' (1879) 150 *Edin. Rev.* 524 at 556. See also the *Law Magazine*'s general approval of the project: (1879) 4 *LM* 31. For earlier positivist accounts of the benefits of codification, see S. Amos, *An English Code* (1873) and, less radically, T. E. Holland, *Essays Upon the Form of the Law* (1870).

[117] The Code Commissioners, including Blackburn, explicitly adopted Stephen's analysis: the value of the common law's 'elasticity' had 'to say the least been largely exaggerated', and did not constitute a significant 'objection to codification'; 'the elasticity so often spoken of as a valuable quality would if it existed, be only another name for uncertainty'; in reality, the criminal law was largely 'extremely detailed and explicit and leaves hardly any discretion to the judges', *Report of the Royal Commission PP* 1878–9 [C. 2345] xx, 168.

instances of injustice, while diminishing the common law's potential for arbitrary and oppressive expansion.[118]

Doubtless, Cockburn's opposition did not only undermine the bill's prospects,
it would also have furnished sceptics and those opposing the bill with some useful ammunition. However, Cockburn's death in the autumn of 1880 inevitably
weakened this effect, especially as his successor, Coleridge, was more sympathetic and professionally closer. Allied to this was the not inconsiderable symbolic significance of the Code having been reformulated and endorsed by a largely
judicial commission. Consequently, in all likelihood, the Cockburn 'effect' was
ultimately slight. Aside from the key negative influence of standard parliamentary procedures, other contemporary forces and circumstances may well have
worked against the Code's enactment. Not the least of these was the view taken
of Stephen by many influential officials from the Lord Chancellor's Department
and Home Office, who may have regarded Stephen as something of a self-seeking interloper, attempting to interfere with the existing gradual and staged pace
of change. Such feelings were a possible legacy of Stephen's own private initiatives having upstaged high officialdom's collaboration in the work of the Statute
Law Committee, which, since its establishment in 1868, had been steadily inching towards the possibility of codifying reforms. Moreover, the Committee had,
prior to Stephen being asked to draft his Code, commissioned its own report, and
for this job, rather than Stephen, had chosen the lesser-known barrister Robert
Samuel Wright.[119] Although owing much to previous connections, the choice was
also prompted by reservations over the quality of Stephen's draughtsmanship

[118] 'The only result which can follow from preserving the common law as to justification and
excuse is, that a man morally innocent, not otherwise protected, may avoid punishment. The worst
result that could arise from the abolition of the common law offences would be the occasional escape
of a person morally guilty.'
   In contrast, 'The continued existence of the undefined common law offences is not only dangerous to individuals, but may be dangerous to the administration of justice itself. By allowing them to
remain, we run the risk of tempting the judges to express their disapproval of conduct which upon
political, moral, or social grounds, they consider deserving of punishment by deciding upon slender
authority that it constitutes an offence at common law; nothing, I think could place the bench in a
more invidious position, or go further to shake its authority' (1880) 7 *Nineteenth Century* 136, 154.
[119] Later to become Mr Justice Wright. Friedland, 'R. S. Wright's Model Criminal Code'. Wright's
Jamaican Code—vetted by Stephen at the Colonial Office's request—contained a more innovatory
and comprehensive approach to codification than Stephen's own work, having much in common
with Macaulay's Indian Code. In part, this was attributable to the fact that the Jamaican Code was
not for home consumption—experimentation in foreign parts was clearly more readily acceptable to the British Parliament. In 1877 Wright produced a Report on Criminal Law Statutes for the
Statute Law Committee, *Papers relative to the Proceedings of the Statute Law Committee respecting Consolidation*, July PP 1878 (320), lxiii, 265. Stephen's other competition was the private bill
of solicitor, E. D. Lewis. See K. Smith and S. White 'An Episode in Criminal Law Reform through
Private Initiative', in P. Birks (ed.), *The Life of the Law* (1993), 235. The Statute Law Committee looked

and especially his general tractability. Failure to turn the Lord Chancellor against Stephen's enterprise probably ensured a degree of official coolness that is unlikely to have enhanced the Code's chances.

Beyond such possible animus were mundane practical matters; more specifically, the whole legal profession was just beginning to acclimatize to the radical procedural changes recently introduced by the Judicature Acts; the prospect of further innovation on the scale of a new penal code must have proved singularly resistible to many practitioners. Furthermore, despite the Code Commission's overwhelming judicial make-up, unease remained within the legal profession, with this particular current of change perceived as likely to threaten the judiciary's established role as common law legislators. More abstractly, some perceived the proposed code as the vanguard of a transition from an organically developed common law system to one exhibiting a widespread codified complexion; a change which 'impli[ed] a mental and almost moral metamorphosis of the whole legal intellect of the country';[120] an identification of national culture with law's form, where, in England, a code would constitute the substitution of 'mechanism for organism'.[121]

Stephen's response to grand national metaphysics of this order was that codification did not arrest the law's development and that, in general, reform more properly lay with parliament; furthermore, the 'elasticity' of the common law was 'a form of expression which conceals a power vested in human beings by describing it as a quality inherent in a collection of words';[122] and finally, that in any case much of the so-called 'elasticity' was far from elastic in nature, binding the judiciary quite as tightly as any statute. Even Pollock, whose deep common law instincts were not the most natural allies of codification, found Stephen's position the more convincing. While seeing in the common law great benefits of ethical refinement and adaptability, Pollock admitted in a letter to Oliver Wendell Holmes, that Stephen 'met the supposed scientific objection with (as I think) the right answer: that laws exist not for the scientific satisfaction of the legal mind, but for the convenience of the lay people who sue and are sued'.[123]

---

to a gradual phased move to codification, first by amending and consolidating the law, Committee memo, 2 January 1878, LCO 1/42; Friedland, 321.

[120] S. Amos, *The Science of Law* (1874). Amos was Professor of Jurisprudence at University College London and son of the Criminal Law Commissioner Andrew Amos.

[121] Maitland's 'Introduction', to O. Gierke, *Political Theories of the Middle Age*, xv (1900), on Savigny's theory of the association between national culture and the law's form.

[122] (1880) 7 *Nineteenth Century* 136, at 152.

[123] *Essays in Jurisprudence and Ethics* (1882), 287; and Pollock's discussion of codification in the introduction to his *Digest of the Law of Partnership* (1877). Pollock to Holmes, 26 July 1877, *Pollock-Holmes Letters* (ed. M. De Wolfe Howe, Camb., Mass., 1942).

On a broader plane, what might be called 'national forces' of the kind which propelled countries, such as France and Germany, towards codification in the nineteenth century, were absent from English political consciousness. In these countries codification carried clear political symbolic significance, acting as an important means of achieving a national unity and identity. It was a dimension of codification that had not escaped Stephen, but for him it was moral as much as political. In an age of rising scientific knowledge and correspondingly increasing religious scepticism, he regarded a criminal code as constituting a powerful collective moral statement, able to reinforce common feelings against criminality; something that

would represent nothing less than the deliberate measured judgment of the English nation on the definition of crimes and on [their] punishments...that judgement representing the accumulated experience of between six and seven centuries...The criminal law may then be regarded as a detailed exposition of the different ways in which men may so violate their duty to their neighbour as to incur the indignation of society...I think that there never was more urgent necessity than there is now for the preaching of such a sermon in the most emphatic tones. At many times and in many places crime has been far more active and mischievous than it is at present, but there has never been an age...in which so much genuine doubt was felt as to the other sanctions on which morality rests.[124]

However, instead of national moral retrenchment, the promise of commercial convenience[125] was the compelling benefit motivating the only successful nineteenth-century codification initiatives in the form of the Bills of Exchange Act 1882, the Partnership Act 1890, and the Sale of Goods Act 1893. Beside the instantly comprehensible and powerful imperative of commercial convenience to the 'mercantile community', the 1882 bill's aim was to 'reproduce...the existing law, whether...good, bad or indifferent in its effects'; any amending reforms were strictly the business of Parliament.[126] After the experience of the 1882

[124] HCL, iii, 366–7. On the political dimension to codification, see Ilbert, *Legislative Methods and Forms*, 18–19, 148 n. Ilbert, a leading parliamentary draftsman, was a later legal member of the Indian Governor-General's Council. Stephen was not 'specially flattered' by this. Stephen to Lady Grant Duff, 20 February 1882; Stephen Papers.

[125] In the case of the Bills of Exchange Act 1882: 'Mercantile men were anxious that the law upon these subjects should be brought into a more convenient and accessible form', Sir John Lubbock MP (President of the Institute of Bankers), PD 1882 (s. 3), 266: 1202. Lubbock emphasized the bill 'contained no new provisions'. The bill's Select Committee composed merchants, bankers, and lawyers.

[126] M. D. Chalmers, 'An Experiment in Codification' (1886) 2 LQR 125, 126. Chalmers was draftsman of the 1882 and 1893 bills; Pollock drafted the 1890 bill. As Chalmers notes, 'codification' meant the systematic and authoritative restatement of the law from all sources in a given branch of law; the 'propositions of a code are law'. Chalmers later became Law Member of the Indian Governor-General's Council.

legislation, Chalmers, its author, rightly estimated that any such 'extension of codification...would merely produce a slight flutter in the legal dove-cote'.[127] But although true of elements of the civil law, no further criminal law initiatives followed; unlike areas of civil law, no political or professional constituency existed to press criminal justice's particular cause. Ironically, Stephen's own highly accessible *Digest of the Criminal Law*, along with other texts, lessened the practical need for a criminal code.

At the beginning of the twentieth century, Sir Courtney Ilbert, Parliamentary Counsel to the Treasury, reflected on the impossibility of viewing 'without a certain degree of humiliation, the entire cessation during recent years of any effort to improve the form of English [criminal] law, and the apathy with which that cessation has been regarded'.[128] It was, however, an apathy which, if not totally vanquished, was greatly modified in the sense that defined areas of criminal law were made the subject of 'code digests' a few years after Ilbert's observations. More specifically, the Perjury Act 1911, Forgery Act 1913, and the Larceny Act 1916 were produced in a fashion much resembling that adopted in the late nineteenth century for areas of the civil law, and much commended by Chalmers. Now a standing joint 'Codification Committee' of Lords and Commons 'endeavoured to ensure' that bills always reproduced the law. Absence of innovative, new law was the fundamental feature of such bills digesting statute and common law into authoritative codes. Express affirmation of this unadulterated quality became a prominent feature of the legislative process. Thus, on the Larceny Bill's second reading, Lord Chancellor Buckmaster most emphatically repeated his assurance that the bill had 'faithfully consolidated the existing law and not imposed anything new...'.[129] It was a procedure whereby changes to the law's substance not only lay exclusively in parliamentary hands, but the initiatives for such were necessarily parliamentary in origin. Judicial creativity, as the example of the Larceny Act well demonstrates, rather than diminished, simply took a different course whereby the law restated in the Act was judicially construed with the assistance of earlier authorities considered to be relevant though no longer binding.[130]

---

[127] *Ibid.*, 129. The 1879 English Draft Code eventually formed the basis of criminal codes of several self-governing colonies, including Canada and some Australian states. Listed by Ilbert, 200.

[128] *Legislative Methods and Forms* (Oxford, 1901), 162.

[129] Sir George Cave, Solicitor-General, on the Larceny Bill's second reading, *PD* 1916 (s. 5 HC) 86: 65.

[130] See e.g. Lord Reading CJ in *Dymond* (1920–1) 15 Cr App R 1, 4–5.

VII
General Principles of Criminal Law

Two distinct areas of analysis are included within what is frequently termed 'general principles of criminal law': one relates to the notion that at least most major examples for criminal responsibility are constructed from, and governed by, an identifiable body of common principles. For present purposes, consideration of general principles of criminal law, sometimes termed the 'General Part', will include common fault concepts together with the substance and structure of general defences. Criminal fault represents the most distinctive and varied incriminatory component of liability and, broadly, the exculpatory mechanisms of defences represent the other side of the conceptual coin.[1] A second dimension of general principles embraces auxiliary or complementary forms of criminal liability, spanning and operating alongside specific offences; the most significant of these are inchoate liability (incitement, conspiracy, and attempt) and complicity or secondary liability. To a greater or lesser degree, all of these areas of 'general principles' underwent significant development in the nineteenth century.

1. GENERAL PRINCIPLES OF CRIMINAL FAULT AND DEFENCES

Milsom maintains that nineteenth-century law treatises were 'expansions from [Blackstone's] reduction and simplification of the mechanical learning of practitioners. [T]here was a sense of discovery, of intellectual compulsion. The writers saw themselves as finding the pattern which fitted the rules, the judges as finding rules which fitted the pattern. Something absolute was emerging'.[2] In respect of the criminal law, Milsom's elegant characterization is, to a fair degree, borne out by the evidence, insofar as it concerns 'writers'; however, as will be suggested, judicial efforts to operate within an expressed 'pattern' or general

---

[1] Other general elements of what is commonly termed '*actus reus*', principles of causation and special issues relating to liability based on omission, are considered in 'Homicide', Ch. XII below. The elusive notion of voluntariness of action is reviewed in the context of individual defences.

[2] S. Milsom, 'The Nature of Blackstone's Achievement', *Studies in the History of the Common Law* (1985), 197, 206–8.

conceptual framework were far more noticeable by their overwhelming absence than by any routine observance. Attempts at constructing a 'general part' for nineteenth-century criminal law doctrines and principles appropriately begins with Blackstone's greatly influential claim of an ordered, coherent, unified body of principles:

[First], the general nature of crimes and punishment; secondly, the persons capable of committing crimes; thirdly, their several degrees of guilt, as principals or accessories; fourthly, the several species of crimes, with the punishment annexed to each by the laws of England; fifthly, the means of preventing their perpetrations; and sixthly, the method of inflicting those punishments which the law has annexed to each several crime and misdemeanour.[3]

Even Bentham conceded that Blackstone's 'technical arrangement and structure' produced valuable gains in systematizing principles of law.[4] Moreover, Stephen, who regarded Blackstone as 'neither a profound nor accurate thinker', compulsively prone to 'over strained praise', granted that Blackstone 'first rescued the law...from chaos. He did...exceedingly well...what Coke tried to do, and did exceedingly ill, about 150 years before'.[5] Blackstone frequently acknowledged the influence of continental authors; in respect of criminal law the dominant inspiration was Beccarian utilitarian penal philosophy: the desirability of a discriminating proportionately between deterring punishment and different levels of criminal immorality; applying similar punishments to crimes of 'different malignity' was 'absurd and impolitic...a kind of quackery in government; the objective should be swift enforcement of clear and certain laws'.[6]

By contrast, Bentham's own *de novo* structure of criminal responsibility offered an exhaustive, logically informed system of general principles that could be worked through in infinite detail to specific forms of liability; where Bentham provided 'definition', Blackstone was content with 'declaration'.[7] Bentham's analysis emphatically boosted criminal law theory's ability to distinguish between general and specific conceptions of liability. But while Bentham's schemes held out the promise of a rational and comprehensive structure, it was Blackstone's analysis which was taken up by most nineteenth-century treatise writers, and, implicitly, the judiciary. However, though Bentham's general

---

[3] *Comms*, iv, 42.

[4] *Comment on the Commentaries*, 180.

[5] *HCL*, i, 214. Cf. e.g. a contemporary critic of Blackstone's approach: John Reeves (*History of English Law* (1787)) who denied the existence and operation of overarching common law theories and principles.

[6] *Comms*, iv, 12–18. C. Beccaria, *Of Crimes and Punishment* (trans. 1768/8).

[7] For a contrasting analysis of Blackstone and Bentham's proposals on criminal responsibility, see Smith, *Lawyers, Legislators and Theorists*, Chs 1 and 2, *passim*.

institutional proposals were largely sunk by direct hostility or plain indifference, his frequently revealing critique of the common law system regularly informed criminal law reform initiatives throughout the nineteenth century.

Concepts of Criminal Fault—Mens Rea

SPECULATION ON THE NEED FOR AND NATURE OF FAULT

In respect of criminal fault, both early nineteenth-century judicial observations and limited commentaries demonstrated practically no inclination to broaden legal analysis beyond the specific circumstances in question. Certainly, other than asserting the need for criminal fault, neither judges nor contemporary commentators revealed interest in issues such as conceptually separating advertent from inadvertent fault, or distinguishing intention from subjective recklessness. During this period both legal texts and reported judicial observations suggest a severely limited, irregular awareness of the potential desirability of openly employing clearer, more refined general fault gradations in the substantive criminal law: clearer both in a conceptual and terminological sense.

The potential for, and value of, such developments to a considerable degree went hand in hand with the widening choice of punishments available to the courts; this offered the means and motive for drawing distinctions in degrees of culpability. Lack of ability to discriminate in terms of punishment between levels of fault in the hierarchy of offences had been a common source of complaint by many eighteenth-century commentators, including Blackstone, Eden, and Dagge; in part, it was also a sentiment reflected in techniques of jury nullification, along with judicial and executive clemency.[8] Distinguishing cause from effect is problematic, but it is most likely that the desire for a greater range of punishment was premised on the assumption that a greater level of formally drawn distinctions was possible between various degrees of immoral, culpable actions and consequences. However, the continuing presence for much of the early nineteenth century of a substantial, though diminishing, corpus of capital laws, exercised a strong influence on styles of judicial construction of fault requirements for statutory and common law offences. Most importantly, these background factors also powerfully militated against the willingness of courts and commentators to claim (or seek) *general* conceptual currency for culpability terms honed and employed in fact-specific contexts. Invocation of the need for *mens rea*—some form of criminal fault—was commonplace. Yet, certainly no sustained considerations (or reflections on the role of moral fault in the ascription of criminal responsibility or, for example, on the nature and function of

---

[8] See 'Punishment', Ch. V above.

distinguishing advertent and inadvertent fault) are to be found in contemporary judgments or commentaries, such as *East* and *Russell*.

Bentham's and Austin's detailed systematic identification of the centrality of both the rationale(s) of criminal fault, together with its operation through clear and consistent terms, unsurprisingly, had little direct impact on judicial consciousness or even contemporary practitioner treatises.[9] Greater prominence and potential influence of the fault analyses of Bentham and Austin came indirectly through the several extensive reviews undertaken by the Criminal Law Commissioners when seeking to digest and codify the law. Their encounters with conceptual and practical questions of criminal fault and attempts at a systematic reconstruction of fault requirements owe much to Benthamite rigour and Austinian[10] fault concepts. The Commissioners' First Report had been deeply disparaging of the 'remarkable' absence of general principles in judgments and the paucity of principles in works of authority; and even where general principles were expressed, they were often outdated or 'contradictory'.[11] Directly addressing the vague doctrine of *mens rea* and general concepts of fault six years later, the Commissioners identified what they regarded as the fundamental need for a systematic and rational linkage between punishment's underlying deterrence objective and the fault elements of criminal liability; part of this endeavour would be settling consistent fault terminology.

Austin's likely influence appears in the Commissioners' analytical distinction (significantly not clearly identified by Blackstone) between an actor's mental state in relation to an 'act' and any 'consequence': 'intention to do acts exists for all criminal purposes, where it is wilfully done, though the act itself was merely intended as a means of obtaining some ulterior object'.[12] Like Austin, the Commissioners sought to demarcate clearly subjective and objective forms of fault as representing different degrees of immorality. In common with Austin, on the grounds of a sufficient moral parity, the Commissioners expressed no inclination when settling degrees of fault to separate (purposeful) intention from 'conscious' risk taking.[13] Some later attempts by the Commissioners to formulate general fault principles and consistently employed fault terms, although following similar objectives and resting on essentially the same conceptual framework,

---

[9] See Smith, *Lawyers, Legislators and Theorists*, Chs 1–3, *passim*; Ch. 4, 122–7.

[10] Austin was one of the original Criminal Law Commissioners.

[11] *First Report* (1833), 3.

[12] *Fourth Report* (1839), xv.

[13] In arriving at this view the Commission spent much time picking over Foster's exploration of 'malice aforethought' (see 'Homicide', Ch. XII below), *ibid.*, xxiii–xxiv. Austin's term, 'advertent' fault, was not adopted by the Commissioners who favoured 'conscious risk taking'; the term 'subjective recklessness' appeared more commonly later in the century.

were distinguished by their opacity rather than illumination; this was especially true of parts of the Seventh Report where complex efforts to modify and retain ancient fault terms, including 'malice', provoked former Commissioner Amos's apt description, 'bilingual ambiguity'.[14]

In the 1860s, Stephen exhibited a cautious approach to endorsing any general principles of *mens rea*. This was the likely product of his belief that fault's exact content or form could only be determined on the basis of individual offences, and settling definitional requirements of particular crimes could not usefully be aided by the judicial invocation of any general mantra of *mens rea*. His long-standing hostility to the notoriously wide felony-murder rule[15] is an outstanding illustration of his opposition to the use of imprecise generalized notions of fault. But even on the basic question of fault terminology, his *General View* failed to offer a distinct, conceptual contrast between subjective and objective fault in the fashion of Austin and the Criminal Law Commissioners. Distinctions, although recognized, appear in Stephen's examination of murder rather than alongside his discussion of the term 'malice', which at some point he appears to use as a general term for all species of criminal fault, both objective and subjective.[16] Of 'malice', Stephen concluded that despite its undoubted imprecision and confusing use it had continuing value insofar as it was sufficiently flexible to meet any 'new cases that may arise'. This was a surprising conclusion bearing in mind the critical observations in some of the Criminal Law Commissioners' Reports, with which it would be reasonable to assume Stephen was familiar. But at this stage whilst calling for the clarification and general sorting out of legislation, such as the 1861 consolidation Acts ('full of needless intricacy and hardly intelligible technically'), Stephen did not favour wholesale, systematic reformulation of fault terms and codification.[17]

Twenty years on, Stephen's *History* provides a more thoroughgoing treatment of the subject. On the broad issue of the relationship of criminal law and morals, rather than claim, as was frequently done at the time, that the imposition of liability was subject to a general *mens rea* principle requiring personal moral blameworthiness of some sort, Stephen recognized its desirability but made no attempt to give such an expectation the status of a presumptive principle.[18] He dismissed

---

[14] *Ruins of Time*, 115. For an analysis of the conceptual shifts and terminological changes over the lifetime of the Criminal Law Commissioners, see Smith, *Lawyers, Legislators and Theorists*, Chs 4 and 5, *passim*.

[15] Essentially, death caused in the course of committing a felony constituted murder. See 'Homicide' below, Ch. XII.

[16] e.g. 81n and 85.

[17] At 150 and 152.

[18] But cf. Stephen in *Tolson*, below.

the maxim *actus non facit reum nisi mens sit rea* as highly misleading in that it implied 'laudable motives' prevented an act from being criminal; or that immorality was essential to liability. With a touch of irreverence doubtless calculated to catch the eye, he suggested that:

Legal maxims in general are little more than pert headings of chapters. They are rather minims rather than maxims, for they give not a particularly great but a particularly small amount of information…[In truth, the maxim meant] no more than the definition of all or nearly all crimes contains not only an outward visible element but a mental element, varying according to the different nature of different crimes…[and] the only means of arriving at a full comprehension of the expression 'mens rea' is by a detailed examination of the definitions of particular crimes, and therefore the expression itself is unmeaning.[19]

It is clear from this and other comments that Stephen's broadly positivist account, denying the core need for *any* immoral behaviour as the basis of criminal responsibility, also carried clear implications for the developing sizeable body of strict liability offences and, arguably, for defences. However, as will be seen, Stephen J.'s judicial view of the maxim was rather less dismissive a half dozen years later in *Tolson*.[20]

Turning to the terminology of fault, whilst recognizing the basic distinction between subjective and objective culpability, Stephen never offered a direct, relatively clean-cut, analysis of intentionality and subjective recklessness to rival that of the Commissioners and Austin. 'Intention' was narrowly conceived of as being the 'result of deliberation upon motives, and is the object aimed at by the action caused or accompanied by the act of volition'.[21] The adjacent territory of 'oblique intention' or subjective recklessness, was indirectly tackled through a consideration of 'malice' and given a meaning (depending on the context) extending from 'intention' to 'indifference' as to consequence.[22] Bearing in mind his detailed treatment of other areas of criminal responsibility, Stephen's comparative lack of analytical rigour on the question of fault terminology might appear surprising, all the more so considering his draughtsman's experience on the Homicide Bill[23]

---

[19] *HCL*, i, 94–5. The dispute over the existence or otherwise of a general principle of *mens rea* was of practical significance in the nineteenth century when approaching the expanding problem of statutory interpretation of regulatory offences. A core principle of fault or immorality as embodied in the doctrine of *mens rea* was of distinct importance and frequently enlisted by the judiciary when construing individual offences. See 'Strict Liability', Ch. VIII, below.

[20] See 'Strict Liability'.

[21] *HCL*, i, 110.

[22] *Ibid.*, 118–21.

[23] And his Indian legislation. His 1872 Homicide Bill was intended to be a consolidatory and amending provision, incorporating specific measures on insanity, duress and the like. In effect,

and 1879 Draft Code,[24] together with the availability of the Commission Reports and Austin's work. Yet, holding in mind Stephen's strong pragmatic streak, the *General View* and *History*, as well as the *Digest of Criminal Law*, had their part to play in enlightening the influential, and especially the legal profession, with the hope of eventual modification of the law itself. Matching Austin's higher level of analytical abstraction, Stephen might have calculated, could easily have risked limiting the appeal, comprehensibility, and chances of effective influence and legal change.

First published at the opening of the twentieth century, C. S. Kenny's *Outlines of Criminal Law* was an accessible, case law orientated work based on his lectures to Cambridge undergraduates. Kenny offered readers a valuable, often original account of the general principles of criminal law; one that was quickly to achieve a wide readership beyond undergraduates. In respect of basic culpability requirements, though not slavishly followed, the Austinian legacy is plain. Kenny contrasts what he suggests 'intention' signifies in law and its more appropriate meaning in 'popular parlance': in law 'intention', like 'malice', extended to 'all consequences... which the doer of the act foresees as likely to result from it', whereas in the non-legal sense, 'intention' connoted 'purpose' or 'desire'.[25] It

---

it was to be a self-contained homicide code, that could be operated with little or no reference to common law principles existing outside the code. In defining the fault requirements of murder and manslaughter, Stephen's bill employed both a subjective/objective fault distinction and stipulated a particular degree of subjective recklessness. As an alternative to intention to cause death or GBH, sufficient culpability for murder existed if there was 'knowledge' that an act 'will or probably may cause death or GBH' (s 25, 'malice aforethought' was not used). Striving for clarity, the term 'malice' was jettisoned; the Committee agreed with Stephen that 'malice', and especially 'malice aforethought', were 'unlucky words' that had suffered 'various torturings... and twisting... to mean what [they] never did mean' (Minutes, 113).

[24] 'Malice' was similarly avoided in the 1879 Draft Code. *Report of the Royal Commission*, 1879 [C. 2345], 383. Great play was made of this by the Attorney-General during the bill's Commons' introduction: 'The next amendment in the code to which I will call attention—and I think I shall be considered justified in calling it an amendment—is the omission from the definitions of offences comprised in it of all mention of malice, of all use of that word, or any of its derivatives. This omission has been decided on, because of the legal and popular sense of malice are irreconcilably indifferent, and all the efforts of Judges are frequently unavailing to make juries understand and appreciate this indifference... The word "malice" is largely used in our existing criminal law; but it is a word which is full of danger, and the source of infinite confusion and difficulty', PD 1878 (s. 3), 239: 1945.

[25] Cf. R. S. Wright's 1877 Draft Jamaican Penal Code [C. 1893] use of generally defined fault terms; something with which Stephen originally expressed disagreement, but later relented on. Wright separated subjective and objective fault requirements under the headings of 'intent' and 'negligence': with 'intent embracing acting with a particular "purpose", and with the belief that certain consequences will "probably" occur' (s 10(i), (ii)). Wright, a young barrister and a fellow of Oriel College, Oxford was author of the still valuable *Law of Criminal Conspiracies and Agreements* (1873) and was later appointed a High Court judge. His draft criminal code was commissioned

is noteworthy that Kenny unlike previous writers frequently employs the term 'recklessness' when alluding to action taken by one who foresees the risk of criminal consequences.[26] However, somewhat unconvincingly he asserts the existence of the general doctrine of *mens rea* by characterizing strict liability as a 'slighter degree of mens rea'.

ESTABLISHING SPECIFIC FAULT TERMS AND JUDICIAL PRACTICE

Looking back from the early 1900s at the theoretical, proto-legislative and judicial analyses of fault concepts, several features stand out. First, throughout the nineteenth century there was a broad consensus amongst theorists and proto-legislators on the need to clarify and systematize fault concepts; but it was not until the 1870s that this consensus extended to accepting that discarding old terminology was a necessary part of the process. Though offering diverse reasons, even Austin, most of the Criminal Law Commission Reports, and the young Stephen showed a considerable reluctance to abandon fault's linguistic heritage. In Stephen's case, his initial (1863) notion of retaining 'malice' (the most notorious transgressor of linguistic certainty) as an aid to future judicial development of fault concepts showed that even amongst the most informed of contemporary criminal lawyers, a high tolerance of conceptual laxity existed. However, within a decade this attitude had necessarily changed, as evidenced by his draft Homicide Bill, and subsequent abortive legislative measures. The arrival of university-based commentators largely removed any lingering sympathy for the linguistic *ancien regime*, who instead insisted on the installation of fault concepts expressed in language corresponding with 'popular' meanings.

Judicial recognition of the conceptual distinctiveness of subjective and objective forms of fault advanced, albeit erratically. The fundamental rationale for doing so appeared in most cases to be taken as too self-evident to need articulation. Largely by implication, with occasionally express confirmation, it would seem that the determining factors included the following: (i) the perceived higher level of immorality entailed in the advertent, as compared with the inadvertent, infliction of criminal harm; (ii) a greater potential for deterring an actor who consciously seeks or is aware of likely criminal consequences; and (iii) that the very existence of criminal 'harm' may be contingent upon an actor's subjective fault—as generally true in non-fatal offences against the person and offences of dishonesty.

---

by the Colonial Office in 1870 initially for Jamaica, but also as a possible basis for wider colonial use. Friedland, 'R. S. Wright's Model Criminal Code (1981) and Ch VI above.

First published 1902 (1904 edn), 148. Cf. different treatments of fault terms by Clark, Markby, and Salmond. Smith, *Lawyers, Legislators and Theorists*, 152–6, 188–90.

[26] *Ibid.*, 147–8, 165.

Settling on a generally acceptable concept of criminal 'intention', and particularly whether it embraced subjective recklessness, was especially problematic. Confusion and disagreement were fuelled by commentators not always separating the expositional from the censorial—the existing state of affairs from that thought desirable. Although well aware of their difference, Austin (broadly in line with Bentham) endorsed a wide notion of intention, implicitly rejecting the value of registering an analytical or practical distinction between purpose and foresight. To a considerable degree, this mimicked the breadth of subjective fault most frequently covered by judicial use of the terms 'wilful' and 'malicious'. In taking this line, Austin stood alone amongst leading nineteenth-century commentators. From Macaulay, through the Criminal Law Commission Reports to Kenny, all distinguished analytically between acting with a criminal design or purpose and acting with foresight of a criminal outcome. The common rationale for this was its correspondence with the generally understood or 'popular' meaning of 'intention'. It also corresponded to the most frequent judicial construction of the statutory use of 'intention' (below). Beside the linguistic objection of foreseen but undesired consequences being awkwardly labelled as 'intended', the most powerful reason for not taking Austin's wide view of 'intention' was the challenging question of the point at which the foreseen likelihood of criminal harm eventuating became too slight to qualify as 'intention'. The most favoured terms employed to indicate the appropriate level of likelihood were 'probable' and 'likely' which (as with any other quantitative terms) entailed the difficulty of communication of meaning to juries and application of that meaning to the calculating actor in question.

Conceptually, however, the most significant feature was the shifting of subjective recklessness onto a more open, conscious risk-taking basis from what previously resembled a broad moralistic test. Yet the question of the qualifying degree of foresight of risk-taking still remained an analytical (if not practical) problem addressed seriously only by some commentators, particularly Austin and the Commissioners. However, the combined effects of the presumption of intended consequences[27] and the defendant's lack of full testimonial status until the end of the century, meant that the issue lacked obvious practical consequences, thereby ensuring continued judicial neglect.

Analysis of objective and constructive fault was characterized by the absence of rigour common to treatments of subjective fault. Again, it was the endeavours of the Criminal Law Commissioners which showed the widest awareness of underlying issues posed by the distinctions and values embodied in objective and constructive fault liability. But even the Commissioners, for whom deterrence

---

[27] See 'Criminal Evidence' and 'Homicide' Chs III and XII.

was the primary function of punishment, never felt the need to go beyond asserting, almost as self-evident, the deterrability of negligent actors. As for its nature,
most commentators depicted negligence as a culpable state of mind which not
only gave implicit credence to claims of its deterrability, but also carried the
potential to head off doctrinal objections over the legitimacy of criminal liability which did not appear to comply with the spirit of the venerable maximum of
actus non facit reum nisi mens sit rea. Yet no hint of such doctrinal inhibitions
is to be found amongst any of the criminal law's principal nineteenth-century
doctrinal commentators. Indeed, the several proposed extensions of non-fatal
offences against the person to include negligently inflicted harm suggest that a
more systematic and symmetrical approach to criminal liability could be pursued without great concerns, either over falling foul of the maxim or because it
was already regarded as a largely spent doctrinal force.

In respect of the standard of objective non-compliance, not only was there an
understandable lack of terminological consensus, but the relevance of the actor's
personal capacities and ability to achieve a 'reasonable' standard of foresight and
conduct was never broached. Whether resting punishment on a deterrence or
retributive basis, the inherent inability of the dull-witted to perceive that which
most others could perceive would arguably have suggested punishment was
inappropriate. Clearly, the performance of everyday activities would need separating from specially undertaken roles where the possession of specific skills
were implicitly claimed. No reflections of this nature appeared amongst commentators; rather, the standard, expressed in a variety of forms, was uniformly a
completely objective one.

Constructive fault's two principal creations (felony-murder and unlawful act
manslaughter) were, with varying degrees of vigour, given fairly short shrift—
particularly felony-murder—by practically all commentators. Once more, the
most cogent and searching analyses of the underlying consequentialist punishment philosophy embodied in felony-murder and unlawful act manslaughter are
found in the Reports of the Criminal Law Commissioners. Yet the retributive
satisfactions to be had from punishing actors for the eventual harm caused by
their culpable initial behaviour were, even to those professedly driven by rationalistic ambitions, not easily resisted; consequently, pruning of the felony-murder
rule's worst (potential) excesses was often the compromise response between
the conflicting inclinations of head and heart.

Away from speculative commentaries, in the criminal courts one of the intellectual and emotional legacies of the eighteenth-century's savage penal code was
a judicial mind-set generally anxious to construe criminal provisions in a strict,
legalistic, and pernickety fashion. While this interpretive policy mitigated the
law's capital rigour, its immediate and long-term effects were undoubtedly hostile

to the growth of a wider, conceptual treatment of criminal fault. Fact-specific statutory provisions and narrowly confined interpretive judgments were effort-lessly delivered by a judiciary against a background of the vaguest and unprin-cipled 'principles' of criminal fault. But, unsurprisingly, removal of the criminal law's most extravagant punishment in the early decades of the nineteenth century produced no rapid change in a judicial and wider legal culture largely indifferent, if not positively resistant, to speculative conceptualization. This remained little changed after revamping the criminal appeals' system with the establishment of the Court for Crown Cases Reserved. Despite the 1848 Act's express requirement that the Court formulate and articulate principled grounds, few developments were discernible in the subsequent limited flow of appeal judgments over the second half of the nineteenth century. Similar comments might also be levelled at the performance of the Court of Criminal Appeal for several decades into the twentieth century.[28]

On many fundamental questions, the judicial articulation of fault concepts and policy proceeded at an exceedingly modest pace, and one substantially behind contemporary theorists. This was particularly apparent until the 1870s when the courts began to offer *relatively* clear accounts of the notion of subject-ive recklessness,[29] and when the likes of Blackburn J. and (later) Stephen J. were active in both judicial and (proto-) legislative matters concerning criminal fault. Yet, on several grounds, the sluggish judicial response was more apparent than real; that although culturally, steadily resistant to conceptual innovation (as more than once shown by the judges' collective formal negative reactions to legislative proposals), there were neither compelling practical grounds for change, nor an easy or obvious route through which change might be effected. While uttered in the mid-twentieth century, it is apt to note Lord Devlin's reflections that the English 'like what they call practical and commonsense solutions...and...pick their judges with that object in view'.[30] But it might be added that, as has been seen, neither was there anything resembling an obvious consensus in many areas amongst contemporary commentators to which a willing and innovative judi-ciary might have turned for enlightenment.

From a stance of practical need, 'malice' and similarly plastic terms offered the judiciary a not wholly unwelcome normative flexibility in ascribing fault and criminal responsibility. Moreover, judicial need and desire to distinguish intention from subjective recklessness was severely limited, partly because of

[28] Very few criminal cases ever reached the House of Lords, even by the mid-twentieth century.

[29] See *Ward* (1872) 1 *LR* 356; *Pembliton* (1874) 2 *LR* 119, and *Welch* (1875) 1 QB 23. On the general judicial development of subjective notions of fault, see Smith, *Lawyers, Legislators and Theorists*, 159–71; and cf. J. Horder, 'Two Histories and Four Hidden Principles of Mens Rea' (1997) 113 *LQR* 95.

[30] (1958) 4 *JSPTL* 206. And also 'Sentencing', Ch. IV above.

an implicit broad moral equivalence given to the two mental states and partly on evidential grounds: that foreseen possible consequences would for all practical purposes be irrebuttably presumed to have been intended. Even resort to the period's most prominent speculative literature would not always have provided unequivocal guidance; for, as noted in Austin, most of the Criminal Law Commissioners' Reports, and the younger Stephen, whilst seeking conceptual and terminological clarity also conceded benefits in not jettisoning the terms of art relating to fault. Only with codificatory initiatives from Stephen in the 1870s did disenchantment with fault's *ancien regime* prompt any concerted attempt by the judiciary at conceptual and linguistic re-evaluation.

Most marked of the contrasts between contemporary judicial and non-judicial treatments of criminal fault was the almost complete absence of judicial analyses of the policy rationales for even the fundamental division of advertent from inadvertent fault, or the basis for several forms of constructive fault.[31] Certainly, no consistent adherence to the view emerged that the doctrine of *mens rea* demanded that all criminal responsibility rested on subjective fault. Indeed, fundamental questions right down to the function of fault in a criminal justice system remained almost entirely judicially unaddressed. Most basically, this included whether the doctrine's function was to underpin individual justice, fairness, and personal desert, or to demarcate actors whose conduct was deemed subject to choice and calculation and, thereby, open to deterrence. Even amongst the extended judicial reflections found in *Tolson* and *Prince*,[32] practically nothing emerges in respect of the function as well as the substance of the doctrine of *mens rea*. Judicial constructors of strict and vicarious liability displayed a similar unwillingness to offer any principled account of the perceived basis and function of these particular species of inculpatory devices.

Such comments are equally merited by the judicial treatment of fault concepts well into the twentieth century.[33] In some respects, both conceptually and terminologically, this period witnessed greater instability and inconsistency. As in the early nineteenth century, 'intention' was still occasionally and unpredictably narrowly construed to cover only purposive intention; more than ever 'recklessness' was judicially credited as a form of objective *or* subjective fault. In part, this was a resonance of a long-rooted judicial ambivalence over the relative immoral qualities of subjective and objective 'recklessness': whether the culpability manifested by each merited distinction for the purpose of ascribing criminal responsibility.

---

[31] For the judicial treatment of objective and constructive fault, see Smith, ibid., 85–92, 191–200, and 'Homicide' Ch. XII, below.

[32] *Tolson* (1889) 23 QBD 168; *Prince* (1875) 2 *LR* 154, and 'Strict and Vicarious Liability', Ch. VIII, below.

[33] Smith (See ns 29 and 31), Ch. 9.

Judicial responses towards murder's fault element, through a form of conceptual pincer movement, manifested a tendency to shift towards a common negligence basis. From one side came a diminution in the harshness of felony-murder by requiring what constituted a form of negligence in respect of serious harm; from the other, there was a relaxation in the demands of the offence's more general *mens rea* requirement by suppressing the subjective dimension of malice aforethought. It was a process facilitated (both before and after *Woolmington*) by the equivocal nature and status of the presumption of intended consequences, an equivocality that ran through judicial thinking leading up to and culminating in the conceptual debacle of *DPP v. Smith*.[34]

Moral Agency—Defences to Criminal Liability

GENERAL PRINCIPLES: A UNIFIED THEORY?

Most significantly, in 'Persons Capable of Committing Crimes' Blackstone offered a unified conceptual account of general defences by resort to the notion of 'will':

All the several pleas and excuses, which protect the committer of a forbidden act from … punishment … may be reduced to this single consideration, the want or defect of *will*. An involuntary act, as it has no claim to merit, so neither can it induce any guilt: the concurrence of the will, when it has its choice either to do or to avoid the fact in question, being the only thing that renders human actions either praiseworthy or culpable … there must be both a will and an act.

Following this general statement, Blackstone elaborated the cases where there would not be an appropriate level of 'will':

Now there are three cases, in which the will does not join with the act: 1. Where there is a defect of understanding. For where there is no discernment, there is no choice; and where there is no choice, there can be no act of the will, which is nothing else but a determination of one's choice, to do or to abstain from a particular action: he therefore, that has no understanding, can have no will to guide his conduct. 2. Where there is understanding and will sufficient, residing in the party; but not called forth and exerted at the time of the action done: which is the case of all offences committed by chance or ignorance. Here the will fits neuter; and neither concurs with the act, nor disagrees to it. 3. Where the action is constrained by some outward force and violence. Here the will counteracts the deed; and is so far from concurring with, that it loaths and disagrees to, what the man is obliged to perform.[35]

---

[34] [1961] AC 290; and *Woolmington* v. *DPP* 1935 AC 256. See Trial, Ch. III.

[35] *Comms*, iv, 21. While owing much to Hale's *Pleas of the Crown* (1736 edn, 1 PC 14–15), Austin was wide of the mark in describing Blackstone's efforts as no more than a 'slavish and blundering copy' of Hale. As seen ('Homicide', Ch. XII, below) Foster's *Crown Cases* brought to murder the conceptual account of 'malice aforethought': 'a heart regardless of social duty and fatally bent on mischief'.

This broad amorphous, normative notion of 'will', as the essential prerequisite of liability embraced a range of diverse situations where the actor was regarded as not properly criminally blameable or culpable.

As will be seen, Blackstone's theory of will or voluntariness apparently combining (but never clearly separating) elements of the concept of *mens rea*, exercised extensive influence over both later commentators and judges. In the case of treatises, Blackstone's view of 'will' was adopted almost wholesale by *Russell*, and, to a lesser degree, in the early twentieth century by Kenny's *Outlines*. Overall, while the particular qualifying bases of individual defences were refined during the course of the nineteenth century, practically no judicial analysis was devoted to constructing any *general* conceptual basis of moral agency. Even in respect of the relatively frequently reviewed defence of insanity, case law reveals little outside persistent judicial concern that the law's power of deterrence should not be eroded by too wide a drawing of an insanity defence. Fundamental structural questions on the relationship of defences to *mens rea* or voluntariness and possible unifying theories of excuse and justification remained quite beyond express judicial interest. But in several respects neither was analysis of such matters greatly advanced by contemporary commentators from the state of affairs bequeathed by Blackstone and, to a lesser degree, Bentham.

Especially in respect of murder and manslaughter, at one time a conceptual and practical distinction was made between defences classified as 'excuses' and those as 'justification'. However, with the practical consequence (see 'Homicide' at Ch. XII below) largely disappearing by the late eighteenth century, calculated references to the distinction by judges and commentators became infrequent. Throughout the nineteenth century, any resort to the earlier conceptual language of justification and excuse was casual and sporadic, often inconsistent, and largely undefined. For Blackstone the presence or absence of 'fault' was the basis of both justification and excuse. In the context of homicide, Blackstone characterized behaviour as justifiable where there 'is no kind of fault whatsoever, not even in the minutest degree', with acquittal accompanied by 'commendation rather than blame'. For East, 'justification is founded upon some positive duty'. Excuse, notes Blackstone, 'imports some fault, some error..., so trivial however, that the law excuses it from the guilt of felony, though in strictness it judges it deserving of some little degree of punishment'. A defendant was excused because 'it is highly just and equitable'; or, according to East, because behaviour was 'due to human infirmity'.

East's *Pleas of the Crown* (1803) contains some general theoretical speculation, but its chief value (a 'very arduous undertaking [becoming a] burthen which has already broken in too much upon my private life', according to its author, preface vii–viii) lay in its use of 'eleven sets of MSS of deceased judges' (Amos, *Ruins of Time*, 5). East did not adopt Blackstone's analysis of defences.

But, by the beginning of the nineteenth century, judges had informally discarded the notion that any penalty significance should be attached to the distinction between justification and excuse. Moreover, when considering a necessity defence and homicide, East dismisses concerns over necessity's status, whether 'excusable' or 'justifiable', as 'not worth examination'.[36] It was a comment later expressly endorsed by the Criminal Law Commissioners,[37] who eventually consciously 'avoided laying down distinctions between justifiable and excusable homicide'.[38] Stephen, too, wrote off such matters as having 'some historical interest, though at present it involves no legal consequences'.[39]

Instead of justification and excuse, commentators articulated defences on a diversity of bases separable into two broadly distinguishable categories: those entailing a denial of an elemental feature of criminal responsibility, whether *mens rea* or voluntariness; and those defences resting on the presence of absence of some other 'superadded' quality, most especially moral choice or deterrability. And even then there were crossover features, particularly in Blackstone's case. His overarching liability requirement of a 'vicious will', incorporated *mens rea* in the form of cognition or knowledge and also morally free choice. There could be an absence of 'vicious will' because of lunacy, mistake of fact, 'compulsion or necessity'. For lunacy and mistake the substance of Blackstone's explanation was a denial of *mens rea*; but 'compulsion and necessity' involved the non-concurrence of 'will' and 'deed', a claim of moral involuntariness. His unifying normative concept for 'pleas and excuse' was absence of 'choice', it 'being the only thing that renders human actions either praiseworthy or culpable'.[40]

---

[36] *East*, 1 PC, 219–21, and 294; Blackstone, *Comms*, iv, 182 and 27. The forfeiture distinction between excusable and justifiable homicide was effectively removed in 1828. See 'Homicide', Ch. XII below.

[37] *Fourth Report* (1939). In respect of 'self-protection' the Report notes: 'this is one of the instances of homicide which have been termed excusable, in contradistinction to justifiable, though the difference, as Mr East observes, is not worth examination', xxxvii, Art. 39.

[38] This they saw as pointless after the abolition of the forfeiture rules, *Second Report* (1846), 33n and *Fourth Report* (1848).

[39] *HCL*, iii, 11. Yet the issue was not entirely extinct in the judicial mind, for omission of reference to 'justification' and 'excuse' in Stephen's draft of the 1872–4 Homicide Bill drew Blackburn J.'s specific criticism at the Select Committee inquiry. Stephen's response to the Committee was that use of the terminology would be completely otiose: 'you have only to do with whether it is criminal or not, and the words "justification or excuse" would introduce quite a needless distinction'. But cf. the 1879 Code Bill Report, 7.

[40] *Comms*, iv, 20–1. Both before and throughout the Victorian age, the potential criminal responsibility of infants was determined by age: those under seven years were conclusively presumed to lack any necessary criminal fault; between seven and 14 this presumption was rebuttable by contrary evidence of 'mischievous discretion'—the ability to 'discern between good and evil', *Comms*, iv, 23. No consistent rationale for these rules was offered by courts or commentators. See 'Punishment', Ch. V.

In contrast, rather than a substantially moralistic or elemental account, Bentham's and Austin's general exculpation rationale was the instrumentalist one of deterrence: could the threat of a criminal sanction have prevented the actor's behaviour? For Bentham, where there was insanity, 'though [the threat] were conveyed to a man's notice, [it] could produce no effect on him'.[41] Austin offered a slightly different route to the same conclusion: lack of *mens rea* was inferred in cases of insanity and, consequently, the threat of punishment was 'necessarily ineffectual'.[42] Moreover, for Austin, in these cases not even *prima facie* liability was incurred from which a defendant needed 'exemption'.[43] Duress and necessity were similarly regarded by both Bentham and Austin as cases where (the threat of) punishment would be gratuitous: where the defendant was motivated by another threat 'more proximate and more imperious than any sanction'.[44] Though successive Reports from the Criminal Law Commissioners produced variations in emphasis and analysis, they leaned clearly in the same direction as Bentham and Austin, expressly accounting for insanity, duress and necessity, and mistake on the basis of the 'great principle' of deterrability. Consequently, criminal agency required freedom of action and informed choice: 'the power of electing to abstain from what is forbidden rather than suffer the consequences of offending'. However, blameworthy self-induced incapacity, 'attributable to the want of exercising due and reasonable caution', suspended operation of the 'great principle'.[45]

Stephen's understanding and accounts of defences, though lacking any clear attempt at an overarching analysis, were modified in the 20 years between the appearance of the *General View* and the *History*, with his *General View* treatment owing as much or more to Blackstone as to Austin or Bentham. According to the *General View*, self-defence and actions under duress were lawful because the defendant's mental state was not 'malicious or wicked'; this was also true for insanity where the presumption of 'will, intention; or malice' was rebutted.[46] These explanations centred around negation of either *mens rea* or voluntariness. By the early 1880s, in the *History*, insanity was again accounted for as involving either the defendant's lack of voluntariness or absence of *mens rea*. But

---

[41] *Introduction to the Principles of Morals and Legislation* ('IPML'), Ch. XIII, section 9. Also in respect of infancy and intoxication. Bentham adds that references by others to the absence of the 'free use of their will' was neither here nor there as utility of threat and punishment was the fundamental issue.

[42] *Lectures*, 492–5, 504–7. Also covering mistake of fact and infancy.

[43] *Ibid.*, 515.

[44] *Ibid.*, 515. Bentham *IPML*, Ch. XIII, section 11.

[45] *Seventh Report* (1843), 17. Similarly in later Reports.

[46] *General View*, 85–6, 91, 117. For insanity the onus of proof was on the defendant to establish that he did not know the nature of the act or that it was 'wrong'.

while duress entailed the presence of 'compulsion', this did not negate voluntariness. Moreover, though denying conceptual consequences, Stephen sometimes employed the terminology of justification and excuse: both insanity and duress were characterized as 'matters of excuse';[47] the 'rights' of reasonable self-defence and the prevention of offences were instances of 'justified' behaviour. Though not always explicit, Stephen's underlying general defence rationale was in essence utilitarian deterrence based.[48]

Finally, Kenny's theoretical eclecticism involved a long-standing attachment to Blackstone's framework of 'exceptions from responsibility', blended with instrumentalist elements. Taking Blackstone's 'will' to correspond 'roughly with Austin's Intention', insanity and mistake were regarded as 'defences' where there was 'no sufficient mens rea'.[49] 'Duress' might 'excuse' because the will is 'overborne by compulsion'. 'Necessity' according to Kenny, was recognized sometimes because 'actual guilt' is 'almost or altogether absent' and sometimes because the threat of punishment could not deter,[50] adding for good measure that in both cases there was 'unquestionably [a] lack of the necessary *mens rea*'.[51]

Overall, during the course of the nineteenth century it is clear that individual commentators conceded only limited significance to general defence concepts. However, it is equally clear from their disparate accounts of defences that any judicial attempt at conceptual speculation or development, whether in respect of an individual defence or of a more general character, would not have lacked choice for inspiration or support. Indeed, the very diversity of commentators'

---

[47] *HCL*, ii, 97, 99. 'Matters of excuse are exceptions to the general rule that people are responsible for actions falling within the definition of crime'.

[48] On duress, see below. The three roughly contemporary post-Stephen accounts of Clark, Markby, and Salmond offered contrasting analyses, though, in common, none made general resort to a deterrence rationale. Clark's treatment of defences identified two facets of impaired voluntariness: 'unconsciousness' and 'constraint'. Insanity was cited as a prime instance of 'unconsciousness', 'certainly as to the most immediate consequences' of behaviour, with cases of constraint include[ing] self-defence, necessity, duress and irresistible impulse' (*An Analysis of Criminal Liability (1880)*, 27–8). Markby's analysis of insanity rested exemption on a 'humane and just' basis (*Elements of Law* (1905), 349) whilst more generally asserting that the rationale of defences was distinct from issues of *mens rea* (*ibid.*, 350–4). Contradicting this, Salmond's quasi-Blackstonian account maintained that the theory of *mens rea* incorporated 'an essential element…namely freedom of choice' without which 'an act…is not wrongful (*Jurisprudence* (1907), 391) and, like Markby, made no attempt to link this requirement to the potential ineffectiveness of deterrence.

[49] *Outlines* (1904), 49, 51, and 65 (mistake).

[50] *Ibid.*, 74.

[51] *Ibid.*, 77. Similarly for mistake (65). From Blackstone to Kenny, substantial changes in the collective terms used to describe defences occurred: Blackstone, 'Of the Persons Capable of Committing Crimes; Bentham, examples of where 'punishment must be inefficacious'; Austin, 'Grounds for Non-Imputability'; Stephen's *Digest*, 'general exemptions to liability'; Kenny, 'exemptions from responsibility' on the grounds of no 'guilty mind'.

views might well have encouraged or reinforced the judicial attitude that such conceptual speculation was a futile exercise, guaranteed to satisfy few and create potential practical hazards in future cases.

On the judicial front, as the century progressed, moral agency, as delineated in 'defences', steadily assumed a more objectively defined quality. Driven to a substantial degree by the 'great principle of deterrence', objective qualifying standards for defences had considerable intrinsic appeal. They offered relative clarity, ease, and uniformity of application, and lessened the chances of fakery. Moreover, objective standards were consonant with the limitations of contemporary trial rules relating to procedure and evidence. This objectivist tendency had long been powerfully represented in the presumption of intended consequences. Objectifying elements of moral agency also promised to head off the perceived unlimited perils of indeterminacy in the criminal law, something threatened in relation to duress, provocation, and insanity defences. Additionally, neither self-induced nor blameworthy impaired volitional control was permitted to deny moral agency. This regulator on the availability of defences was, in various guises, judicially established in cases of intoxication, mistake, automatism, and, less clearly, in relation to duress. In this sense, where the defendant was by a specific defence's qualifying conditions free of fault, exculpation was also a 'just' outcome.

In these approaches, the deemed absence of disqualifying fault, or the reasonableness of behaviour, became the common device whereby the collective and social aims of wider deterrence might be tempered by *objective* notions of individual fairness. No great compromise was entailed in this twin pursuit because the broad nature of reasonableness of behaviour also went to the credibility of defence claims, thereby holding in check the risks of encouraging fakery and abuse.

SPECIFIC DEFENCES

(1) *Insanity*

Uncertainty over the nature and extent of moral agency necessary to incur criminal liability was well demonstrated by the highly prominent treason trial[52] of James Hadfield in June 1800. If anything, the deliberations in *Hadfield* compounded rather than eased this uncertainty. Hadfield faced charges of high treason through his shooting at George III at 'Drury-Lane' theatre. Caused by head wounds sustained during military action some years before, Hadfield's malady manifested itself in a combination of delusions and depression, coupled with a

---

[52] Before a 'special commission' of Lord Kenyon CJ, Grose, Lawrence, and LeBlanc JJ. (1800) 27 St. Tr. 1281.

calculated objective of ending his own life through the circuitous route of being executed for treason. Previous reported insanity defence authorities veered between requiring such a lack of cognitive powers as to prevent the defendant appreciating the nature of his actions or an inability to distinguish right from wrong;[53] or, in some cases, an extreme volitional defect preventing the defendant from exercising self-control.[54] Though well aware of the nature of his actions and (probably) that they were wrong, Hadfield was acquitted on the apparent basis of an insane, delusion-induced depression, with Lord Kenyon's loosely formed jury direction referring to an 'act…not so under the guidance of reason, as he be answerable for this act'.[55]

The contemporary significance of *Hadfield* was more procedural than substantive, in that while satisfied that he should not be criminally responsible, the trial court was naturally extremely concerned[56] about Hadfield's disposal. As a consequence of no clearly established legal procedure[57] existing for the safe confinement of a party acquitted of a crime on the grounds of mental incapacity, legislation[58] was rapidly enacted 'for the safe custody of insane persons, charged

[53] See particularly *Arnold's Case* (1731) 16 St. Tr. 764 and *Lord Ferrers* (1760) 19 St. Tr. 947, discussed by N. Walker, *Crime and Insanity in England*, vol. 1 (Edinburgh, 1968), Ch. 3.

[54] Cf. *Walker* (1784) OBSP 388 and *Broadric, The Times*, 18 July 1795, cited by Walker, *op. cit.*, App. F., 275.

[55] (1800) 27 St. Tr. 1281, 1355. The formal verdict was the opaque 'Not Guilty, [Hadfield] being under the influence of insanity at the time the act was committed'.

[56] Lord Kenyon CJ: 'Something must be done that he may be prevented from committing farther mischief. Mr Justice Grose—at present he must not be discharged. Mr Attorney-General—it is laid down in some of the books, that by the common law the judges of every court are competent to direct the confinement of a person under such circumstances. Lord Kenyon—that may be, Mr Attorney-General; but at present we can only remand him to the confinement he came from; but means will be used to confine him otherwise, in a manner much better adapted to his situation' (1800) 27 St. Tr. 1281, 1355–6).

[57] Cf. Blackstone, *Comms*, iv, 25.

[58] Criminal Lunatics Act (1800), Geo. III, c. 93 and 94. The legislation was made retrospective in effect so as to apply to Hadfield and others confined under the previous uncertain powers. Under the Act, 'Fitness to plead' was settled to mean 'whether the prisoner has sufficient understanding to comprehend the nature of [the] trial, so as to make a proper defence…', *Pritchard* (1836) 7 Car. & P. 303.

Broadmoor, the principal asylum for criminal lunatics was opened in 1863 (Criminal Lunatics Asylum Act 1860). The Insane Prisoners (Amendment) Act 1864, 27 & 28 Vict. c. 29 made it the Home Office's responsibility to assess the sanity of convicted prisoners, and those held pending trial; this responsibility was assumed by the Prison Commission in the 1870s, which acted on the advice of medical specialists appointed by the Home Office from the early 1860s. These procedures produced a substantial impact on the numbers of prisoners found unfit to plead. The Insane Prisoners Act 1840 enabled the Home Secretary (on the certification of two doctors and two magistrates) to commit a prisoner unfit to plead to an asylum. Judicial disquiet at denying such prisoners a public trial eventually caused the Home Office in 1885 to revise its practices so as to generally avoid use of these Executive committal powers. The 1840 Act permitted the Home Secretary to adopt the procedure

with offences', whereby those acquitted on a special verdict were to be held in 'strict custody, in such place and in such manner as to the court shall seem fit'. Thus, the law was able to acquit the accused of both moral and criminal responsibility for his actions, but at the same time provide the court with the power to ensure the accused remained in suitable custody.

Substantively, the immediate impact of *Hadfield* appears to have been slight. In view of the established nature of some form of insanity defence,[59] it is surprising that *East* hardly touched on the subject in the whole of his treatise, with the recent decision of *Hadfield* attracting only a brief procedural reference.[60] Sixteen years on, *Russell* was (unsurprisingly) clearly in some difficulty in construing Hadfield's acquittal, eventually interpreting the decision as based on Hadfield not constituting a 'rational and accountable being'.[61] Indeed, as *Russell* conceded:[62]

the great difficulty…is to determine where a person shall be said to be so far deprived of his sense and memory as not to have any of his actions imputed to him; or where, notwithstanding some defects of this kind, he still appears to have so much reason and understanding as will make him accountable for his actions.

These comments well demonstrate the normative dilemma of what constituted the 'normal' accountable actor and the absence of any judicial or intellectual consensus on the underlying basis of the defence, most particularly, whether it was founded on cognitive or volitional defects. The former roughly approximated to the absence of *mens rea*, the latter to notions of voluntariness of action; the ability to distinguish right from wrong could accordingly be construed as either a purely moral standard or as a calculation based on utility, in the sense that lack of awareness of wrongfulness would make the threat of a sanction 'inefficacious'.

In general conceptualization, *Russell* followed Blackstone in identifying 'a deficiency in will' arising from a 'defective or vitiated understanding' as the basis of the defence.[63] Certainly the so-called, undiscriminating, 'wild beast' characterization of criminal insanity was no longer extant even in Hale's time,

---

after conviction, even where a plea of insanity had been rejected at trial. After the Criminal Lunatics Act 1884, the Home Secretary's powers became obligations, exercised on the advice of Home Office appointed medical specialists. Walker, *Crime and Insanity*, 226–8, 207–10.

[59] Walker, 72 for the estimate of an annual rate of four successful and eight unsuccessful insanity pleas between 1750 and 1800. For an analysis of the final decades of the nineteenth century, see Chadwick, *Bureaucratic Mercy*, 402.

[60] *East*, 2PC 1023.

[61] (1819 edn), 19.

[62] In both the 1819 (at p. 12) and 1826 (at p. 8) editions. Cf. the 1825 edition of *Hawkins*, which in its brief general treatment of the defence, whilst including a note on the 1800 legislation, omits any reference to the reported case law of the previous 150 years.

[63] *Comms*, iv, 24. Blackstone later refers to 'total idiocy; or absolute insanity' (25).

it being acknowledged that if a 'lunatic hath lucid internals of understanding, he shall answer for what he does in those intervals, as if he had no deficiency'.[64] More generally, Blackstone followed Coke in seeing the prosecution and punishment of the mentally incapacitated as being not only individually inappropriate, but of political, social, and practical unsoundness: a 'miserable spectacle both against law, and of extreme inhumanity and cruelty, and can be no example to others'—a mixture of humanitarian and utility concerns.

In the four decades following *Hadfield*, while few reported decisions appear, speculative activity relating to the concept of excusing criminal responsibility on the grounds of mental disability can be seen in both parliamentary[65] and academic contexts.[66] On those occasions where judicial opinion surfaced, a lack of consensus is apparent, no doubt in part the consequence of differing attitudes towards the proper basis of the defence.[67] Disagreement in the Commons was apparent during the passage of the *Hadfield* generated legislation; there was no consensus on whether the defence rested on an individualistic basis of requiring moral capacity and fault, or the rather more utility inspired notion relating to the (in)effectiveness of threatening to punish those whose malady would render threats of sanctions pointless.[68] By the 1830s it was this combination of judicial vacillation as to the appropriate legal test and fundamental dilemma of how the law should regard volitional or 'moral madness', which drew from some commentators accusations of judicial unintelligibility 'surpassing in absurdity'.[69]

[64] *Ibid.*, citing *Hale*, 1 PC 31.

[65] Most parliamentary and legislative activity concerned the provision of proper and secure accommodation for 'criminal lunatics'—whether tried, suspected of offences, or even believed to have such propensities. For example, the 1807 *House of Commons Select Committee Report on the State of Criminal and Pauper Lunatics*, noted that by the time of the *Report* 27 criminal lunatics had been detained under the Hadfield-inspired 1800 legislation, and that the building of regional centres of detention was required, PP 1807 (39), ii, 69. Also *Report*, PP 1816 (398), vi, 349; PP 1828 (407), i, 407; Legislation 48 Geo. III c. 96 and 56 Geo. III c. 117. See also XIII, Pt 4.

[66] Walker, *Crime and Insanity*, 89.

[67] e.g. in *Bowler* (1812) *OBSP* 527 where Le Blanc J.'s insanity defence direction was based on the inability to distinguish right from wrong, or delusions preventing an actor understanding the nature of his actions. But in *Bellingham* (1812) *OBSP* 272 the defence was given a narrower scope based entirely on knowing right from wrong. For the context of this case, see K. Goddard, *A Case of Injustice? 'The Trial of John Bellingham'* (2004) 46 *American JLH* 1. Similarly, *Offord* (1831) 5 Car. & P. 168.

[68] *Parliamentary History* (1819 edn), xxxv, 392–3.

[69] 'Medical Jurisprudence—Insanity' (1830) 3 *LM* 158. On the issue of 'moral insanity' the writer noted: 'In modern murders, for example, there is found an abasement and hebetude of intellect scarcely consistent with moral responsibility; in others, a miscalculation of the chances of impunity hardly explicable in a creature capable of reflection; with others, the motive is so trifling and inadequate, that few persons under its influence would be at pains to cross the street; with others, absolutely no motive whatever. All these persons, though in various degrees…partially insane…yet every one of them would be executed' (161–2).

The subsequent decade, or so, leading up to the judicial enunciation of what became known as the M'Naghten Rules saw very limited reported case law on the insanity defence. One of the few authorities of this period, *Oxford*,[70] confirmed the continuing fluidity of judicial opinion with Lord Denman CJ ruling that:

> If some controlling disease was in truth the acting power with him, which he could not resist then he will not be responsible...The question is, whether the prisoner was labouring under that species of insanity which satisfies you that he was quite unaware of the nature, character and consequences of the act he was committing, or in other words whether he was under the influence of a diseased mind and was really unconscious at the time he was committing the act, that it was a crime.

Such a confusing amalgam of volitional and cognitive defects made plain the need for some carefully measured and authoritative judicial articulation of the insanity defence. Aggravating the judiciary's manifest inability to agree upon the defence's conceptual basis—particularly whether it was either cognitive or volitional, or both—was the growth in scientific interest in and knowledge of mental disorders.

Expanding medical interest in the subject generated an expectation that judges would clarify the extent to which the defence of insanity was to be settled by lawyers rather than by representatives of the medical fraternity.[71] Automatic exculpation from criminal liability on the basis of medical opinion was a growing[72] challenge to the trial process and judicial control, a threat which it was felt clearly needed to be met. But if courts were to claim competency to continue to determine criminal (non-)responsibility in all cases, then on what basis

---

[70] (1840) 9 Car. & P. 525, cited in *Russell* (3rd edn, 1843), 11. On the medical profession's increasing tendency to incorporate notions of 'will' into the insanity defence, see J. Eigen, *Witnessing Insanity: Madness and the Mad—Doctors in the English Court* (New Haven, 1995), Chs 3 and 6. On the conduct of the trial see Campbell, who was prosecuting counsel, in *Life of Lord Campbell*, ed. Hardcastle (1881), vol. 2, 133. See also XIII, Pt 4.

[71] Cf. the M'Naghten Rules (below) question and answer 'V' on the permitted role of medical witnesses. According to Tindal 'when the facts are...not digested, and the question becomes substantially one of science only, it may be convenient to allow the question to be put in general form...'. In *Wright* (1823) R. & R. CCR, 456, the judges collectively observed that 'A witness of medical skill might be asked whether, in his judgment [certain] appearances [and behaviour] were symptoms of insanity...Several of the judges doubted whether the witness could be asked his opinion on the very point which the jury were to decide...'. Similarly, in *Searle* (1831) 1 M. & Rob. 75.

[72] For Home Office powers especially from 1840, see above. For the proposals for alleged criminal lunatics to be excluded from the criminal process, see R. Smith, *Trial by Medicine: Insanity and Responsibility in Victorian Trials* (Edinburgh, 1981), 79. Cf. Stephen's early *General View*, encapsulation of the importance of an open, legal determination of the issue: 'no one shall be punished [or acquitted] unless his guilt [or innocence] can be proved on grounds which the bulk of the nation at large can understand' (213).

was this to be done? Most centrally, what mental attributes or capacities were essential for the identification of moral agency and ascription of liability? Could such capacities be reliably and convincingly isolated by the trial process? The fundamental nature of such questions was obvious, generating by far the most extensive body of nineteenth-century literature on any single issue of criminal responsibility.[73]

A collective judicial formulation of the insanity defence: the M'Naghten Rules Like *Hadfield*, the M'Naghten Rules sprang from a high-profile shooting, on this occasion resulting in the death of Edward Drummond, Peel's private secretary.[74] As befitted the occasion, the bench was occupied by Tindal CJ, flanked by Williams and Coleridge JJ. Leading for the defence (a future Lord Chief Justice) Alexander Cockburn, then a Queen's Counsel, not only took the court on an extensive tour of all possible relevant judicial authorities, but also discoursed impressively on contemporary scientific knowledge of human psychology and mental maladies, setting the 'doctrines of mature science' against ancient 'maxims'.[75] With consummate subtlety and full-blown rhetorical skill, supplemented by choice use of expert medical evidence, Cockburn was able to present the deluded defendant as having lost both the power of self-control and ability to discern right from wrong.[76] Effectively, as in *Hadfield*, what was in substance a plea of insanity based on defective volitional powers was successfully passed off as legal insanity by interweaving such claims with notions of cognitive impairment. Tindal's perfunctory summary and direction, whether through reasons of his own bewilderment or policy preference, made no attempt to dismantle or challenge Cockburn's

---

[73] e.g. Stephen's *History* treatment of the topic runs to over 60 pages, as against his combined *mens rea* and other defences section of less than half the size (*HCL*, ii, Ch. XIX).

[74] The insanity defence increasingly became closely linked with murder and the debate over capital punishment. See frequent comments to this effect by witnesses giving evidence to the 1866 Royal Commission on Capital Punishment.

[75] (1843) 4 St. Tr. (NS) 847, 878. See particularly references to I. Ray, *A Treatise on the Medical Jurisprudence of Insanity* (1839); J. Prichard, *On the Different Forms of Insanity in relation to Jurisprudence* (1842); L. F. Winslow, *On Insanity in Criminal Cases* (1843). M'Naghten was a paranoiac who experienced delusions of persecution by a range of parties including the police and the Tories. See the comment on the case's range of medical speculation in (1843) 74 *Quart. Rev.* 416. Cockburn's extensive use of expert medical testimony well illustrates the degree of acceptance that such testimony had by then achieved and its deployment by defence counsel. See Eigen, *op. cit.*, for an examination of this process from 1760–1843 and T. Ward, 'The Law, Common Sense and the Authority of Science: Expert Witnesses and Criminal Insanity in England, 1840–1940' (1997) 6 *Social and Legal Studies* 343. And more generally, T. Forbes, *Surgeons at the Old Bailey* (New Haven, 1985).

[76] (1843) 4 St. Tr. (NS) 847, 887, 892, 900, and 904. Also: '...the intellect had become diseased, the moral sense broken down and self control destroyed...the victim of ungovernable impulses' (875).

assertions: rather, he emphasized the need for the defendant to understand that he was in 'violation of the law of God or of man'.[77]

M'Naghten's acquittal generated disquiet in Parliament and beyond, e.g. *The Times*: 'in a spirit of humble and honest earnestness, of hesitating and admiring uncertainty, and of almost painful dubitation ask[ed] those learned and philosophic gentlemen to define, for the edification of common-place people like ourselves, where sanity ends and madness begins…'.[78] In the Upper Chamber, Lord Lyndhurst LC indicated surprise (whether feigned or genuine) that anyone should doubt that the law was anything other than clearly[79] laid down; his Lordship saw the jury's verdict as consistent with the knowledge of 'wrong' test endorsed in *Hadfield*. However, in a gesture intended to assuage concern expressed by many of their Lordships,[80] Lyndhurst offered to summon Her Majesty's judges to appear before the House and deliver authoritative clarification of the insanity defence. The offer was taken up and, after some prompting, the judges attended on their Lordships with responses to written questions put to them on the nature of the defence. Despite a sizeable degree of ambiguity,[81] in essence the rules formulated[82] a synthesized 'restatement' of some earlier case law. This entailed asserting more strongly a narrow knowledge or cognitive basis, of the defence, and, by implication, denying the relevance of ineffective volitional control. The rules also constituted a judicial affirmation that the determination of criminal responsibility was to remain one of legal rather than medical adjudication. Against a background of an immature science of psychiatric medicine replete with internecine disputes among its practitioners, any other conclusion would have been truly remarkable.

---

[77] (1843) 4 St. Tr. (NS) 847, 925. Cf. in Clark and Finnelly's Reports, 200, 202, which reads 'both of God and man'. For the trial's background, see R. Moran, *Knowing Right from Wrong* (New York, 1981).

[78] 6 March 1843, quoted by Walker, *Crime and Insanity.*, 93. According to the *Law Times*, the verdict generated a 'tempest of public indignation' (1892), 59, 93.

[79] *PD* 1843 (s. 3), 67: 716: 'clear distinct [and] it will be quite impossible beneficially to alter the law…'. Punishment was appropriate both to punish immoral behaviour and to deter others (722–3). Also, Lords Brougham and Cottenham, 729–38.

[80] *PD* 1843 (s. 3), 67: 716.

[81] With the exception of Maule J., Tindal CJ gave the collective opinion of all the judges. For a full account of the questions and answers, see Walker, *Crime and Insanity*, 97–102 and T. Barnes, 'A Century of the M'Naghten Rules' (1944) 8 *CLJ* 300, 300–6.

[82] A defence of insanity was available if the defendant did not know the 'nature and quality of his act', or, if he did know this, he did not know that it was 'wrong'. The rules' neglected third limb covers what was termed 'partial delusion', where even though the defendant knew the nature of the act and that it was wrong, he was suffering from other forms of delusion, such as the circumstances which motivated his actions. In such cases the defendant was liable to the extent that he would be in the imagined circumstances. It is not clear quite what this element adds to the rule concerning the 'nature and quality' of an act or consequences. Moreover, it is obvious that a defendant could not always be treated on the basis of the facts as imagined by him, as, for example, where he cuts off a broom head whilst believing himself to be decapitating his brother.

As thoroughly demonstrated by Cockburn at M'Naghten's trial, contemporary medical opinion took a flexible, more comprehensive approach than the criminal law to what mental abnormalities might properly be regarded as excluding responsibility. By and large, it rejected compartmentalization of the reasoning faculty whereby 'partial delusion' or defective volitional control might be legally isolated from functioning cognitive discernment. Non-judicial commentators of the period were by no means inclined to adopt this view. In particular, Austin, along with the Draft Indian Penal Code and the 1843 Criminal Law Commission's Seventh Report, gave no support to an insanity defence extending beyond that set out in the M'Naghten Rules. When directly considering insanity, Austin holds firmly to a knowledge-based, instrumentalist account. An afflicted actor is exempt from liability because 'he was not capable of unlawful intention or inadvertence [or] he was ignorant of the law' and therefore was not open to deterrence by the threat of punishment: 'For in order that I may adjust my conduct to the command or prohibition of the law, I must know... what the law *is*; I must distinctly apprehend the *nature* of the conduct which I contemplate...'.[83] Recognition of an impaired volitional dimension to insanity is implicitly dismissed in his comment on Blackstone's analysis of the defence, regarded by Austin as 'hardly worth powder and shot'. The source of his irritation was Blackstone's use of 'will', by which he seemed to have meant 'intention or inadvertence', as well as 'will' in the sense of volitional power attributed to the word by Austin.[84]

Of course, with publication not until the early 1860s, Austin's *Lectures* had no potential (beyond his small 1830s audiences at University College and the Temple) influence on the formulation of the M'Naghten Rules. But both Macaulay's Draft Indian Code and the Criminal Law Commissioners' Seventh Report were available before the judges addressed their Lordships. Without the benefit of commentary, Macaulay's Draft Code sets out a knowledge-based test similar to that later adopted in the M'Naghten Rules, but 'wrong' is expressly made to cover moral or legal wrongfulness.[85] Published a week or so after the verdict but before[86] the collective formulation of the M'Naghten Rules, the Criminal Law

---

[83] *Lectures*, 506. The deterrence basis was maintained by Brougham in the M'Naghten inspired debate, *PD* 1843 (s. 3), 67: 729.

[84] *Lectures*, 511: '...it is clear that there must be a will going with the act, although the party may not be conscious of a wrong...By a wicked will [Blackstone] means unlawful intention or inadvertence'. Also 'Notes' in *Lectures*, vol. 2, 1095 and Austin's puzzling comments (510) on Bentham's non-deterrability claim (*IPML*, Ch. XIII, section 9), which would not exclude volitional defects. Bentham characterized insanity affecting liability as clear cut: 'as conspicuous and unquestionable as lameness or blindness' (*IPML*, Ch. VI, para. 18).

[85] Section 84.

[86] 11 March 1843, two days before the House of Lords' debate on the trial verdict. The Report would certainly have been in the hands of the Lord Chancellor and available to Tindal CJ and his judicial brethren.

Commissioners' Seventh Report provided a broadly Austinian, yet fuller, analysis of the nature and scope of the defence. As with some other defences, absence of criminal responsibility is predicated on 'prevention of injury through fear of suffering', thereby requiring an informed, free-acting agent possessing the 'power of electing to abstain from what is forbidden'; such power being absent where through disease of the mind an actor is 'unconscious either of what he does, or that what he does is wrong', in a 'legal or moral sense'.[87] Whilst the deterrence theory directly links up with the actor's awareness that the behaviour is *legally* wrong, the connection of awareness of the *moral* wrongfulness of an act with the threat of a legal sanction is not expressly argued by the Commissioners. Presumably it would have been claimed that knowledge of the immoral nature of an act would indicate an expectation by the actor of likely legal wrongfulness too.

In respect of 'partial insanity', a term much associated by judges and commentators with delusions and diminished volitional control, the Commissioners entertained great reservations: such a plea was 'not only inconsistent with the general principle of incapacity, but attended with great danger to society [because] it would be impossible to prescribe any certain test...for distinguishing degrees of insanity.[88] This concern over indeterminacy and diluting the criminal law's power to deter would-be offenders, of course, applied to the insanity defence more generally:

It is, no doubt far from impossible that one not entitled to exemption may do wrong under the hope of sheltering himself under this plea, and even that he may succeed in his object, in consequence of the difficulty of distinguishing between partial and total insanity, and the degree of favour which the plea frequently meets from juries.

This was a hint that juries were regarded as either overzealous in acquitting on the basis of such mental incapacity or too open to manipulation by defence counsel, when present. However, even on utilitarian grounds, a narrowing of the defence which might involve 'condemning the innocent' was seen to be mistaken: 'increased security would be too dearly purchased at such a price, even if it could be so purchased. But, in truth, it could not: so barbarous a law could not be executed.'[89] It was an instance where exempting a party on the grounds of personal justice or fairness could also be accounted for on instrumentalist grounds.

---

[87] *Report*, 17–18, Art. 1 (at 31): 'No person shall be criminally liable for any act who, at the time of such act, by reason of any disease, disorder, or delusion of mind, or of weakness or unripeness of understanding, is either unconscious of what he does, or unable to discern that what he does is wrong, and, therefore, knows not that he offends against the laws of God or man'.

[88] *Ibid.*, 18–19.

[89] *Ibid.*, 19. Cf. Bentham's argument that defences, such as insanity, rest on the non-deterrable state of actors. *IPML*, Ch. XIII, section 9.

Following M'Naghten: the response to volitional impairment Over the remainder of the century, and beyond, one[90] particular dimension of the M'Naghten Rules was subjected to extensive and substantial discussion, by both the judiciary and commentators: the degree to which impaired volitional control should be, and was, recognized by the insanity defence. Yet, insanity was not the only context in which the criminal law encountered the effects of defective volitional control; the question of the legal consequences of such impairment also arose in relation to the long-established partial defence of provocation[91] and also infanticide, or child murder. Provocation never generated the same level of judicial anxiety as impulsive insanity for several reasons: it could, and was, increasingly limited by objectively determined boundaries; it did not require human and judicial under-standing beyond (relatively) common experience; and never entailed the threat-ening and intrusive involvement of medical expertise. Child killing by mentally disturbed mothers, while raising similar legal and conceptual questions to an insanity defence, was frequently side-stepped through the nineteenth century by a combination of natural social and judicial sympathy and the deployment of alternative non-capital charges.[92] Moreover, its highly specific circumstances meant that *de facto* recognition of the mitigatory effects of mental disturbance caused by childbirth carried no wider implications (or threats) for the criminal justice system.

Returning to the insanity defence, the evidence adduced at M'Naghten's trial had displayed distinct elements of defective self-control, subtly woven by Cockburn into the fabric of the defendant's powers of perception. However, while the rules themselves made no express allowance for volitional impairment, this failed to quell periodic attempts, both within and outside the courts, to extend coverage of the insanity defence to such cases. It was this particular issue which generated the greatest volume of criticism of the M'Naghten Rules from the over-whelming mass of vocal medical opinion. The extent of hostility and acrimony between some members of the two professions was later well evidenced by (the then) Mr Justice Stephen's candid admission of concern over the possible effect on his own objectivity of the 'harsh and rude' attacks 'upon a small body of which he himself is a member'. For Stephen, it was a territorial dispute involving con-fusion over what were legal and what were medical issues, with many doctors

---

[90] A second lesser issue was the meaning of 'wrong'. Subject to a few reported exceptions, the judicial view throughout the remainder of the century was that criminal capacity required under-standing of what was morally wrong. However, for some commentators, including the Criminal Law Commissioners, the question was a source of dispute. See Smith, *Lawyers, Legislators and Theorists*, 223–5.

[91] See 'Homicide' and 'Provocation', Ch. XII below.

[92] See 'Homicide, Abortion and Infanticide', Ch. XII below.

claiming that legal responsibility in the case of insanity was a scientific question which judges and lawyers perversely determined by employing narrow and anti-quated notions of cognition. Against this, the legal profession counter-claimed that doctors were attempting to dictate what mental maladies ought to excuse, something properly regarded as a question of law not medicine. At the same time, Stephen strenuously objected to the treatment sometimes handed out to 'medical writers' appearing as witnesses:

...in courts of justice, even by judges, in a manner which, I think, they are entitled to resent. Sarcasm and ridicule are out of place on the bench...particularly when they are directed against...a man of science who, under circumstances which in themselves are found trying on the coolest nerves, is attempting to state unfamiliar and in many cases unwelcome doctrines, to which he attaches high importance.[93]

Small wonder then, with an accumulating body of medical and, later, legal litera-ture supporting the view that the insanity defence was too narrowly conceived, that defence counsel occasionally sought to draw in evidence of the defendant's defective powers of self-control. But until the century's closing decades, the judi-cial response was one of almost uniform hostility. Rolfe B. set the tone five years after M'Naghten:

It is true that learned speculators, in their writings, have laid it down that men, with a consciousness that they were doing wrong, were irresistibly compelled to do some unlaw-ful act. But who enabled them to dive into the human heart, and see the real motive that prompted the commission of such deeds?...[It] would be a most dangerous doctrine to lay down that, because a man commits a desperate offence, with a chance of instant death, and the certainty of future punishment before him, he was therefore insane: as if the per-petration of crimes was to be excused by their very atrocity.[94]

The most sustained and characteristically trenchant judicial opposition to a wider defence came from Bramwell B., in 1859:

A morbid and restless (but resistible) thirst for blood would itself be a motive urging to such a deed for its own relief. But if an influence be so powerful as to be termed irresist-ible, so much the more reason is there why we should not withdraw any of the safeguards tending to counteract it. There are three powerful restraints existing all tending to the assistance of the person who is suffering under such an influence: the restraint of reli-gion, the restraint of conscience, and the restraint of the law. But if the influence itself

---

[93] HCL, ii, 125.

[94] Stokes (1848) 3 Car. & K. 185. Also in Allnutt, The Times, 16 December 1847. Followed in Barton (1848) 3 Cox 275. While Parke B. acknowledged the M'Naghten Rules did not have the 'concurrence of medical men', he expressly indicated his complete agreement with Rolfe B.'s views on 'irresistible impulse' (276); and similarly Brough (1856) 1 F. & F. 667n.

is to be held a legal excuse rendering the crime dispunishable, you at once withdraw a most powerful restraint—that forbidding and punishing its perpetration.[95]

Countervailing judicial views, recognizing anything resembling a defective control or volition element in the defence of insanity, were both exceedingly sparse and lacking such pungency, but not entirely absent. For example, in the early 1870s'[96] decision of *Jorden*,[97] Martin B. directed that in the case of emotional impulses which 'according to the medical evidence [the defendant was] unable to resist, [it] would be safe in such a case to acquit the accused on the ground of insanity'. And later in *Duncan*, Lawrance J.'s direction posed the question: 'Was the prisoner unable to control his actions in consequence of a disordered mind?'[98] But such directions were atypical and at odds with the general run of reported decisions. Even members of the Bench, probably sympathetic to widening the M'Naghten rules, such as Byles J., indicated change could only be effected through legislation.[99] Unsurprisingly, resistance from the Bench by no means prevented a determined jury set on finding insanity, especially where defence counsel had adduced plausible expert medical evidence to support the plea.[100]

---

[95] *Haynes* (1859) 1 F. & F. 666. See also Bramwell in *Dove* (1856) *The Times*, 17–20 July 1856 and C. Williams, *Observations on the Criminal Responsibility of the Insane. Founded upon the Trials of James Hill and William Dove* (1856). Also, *Burton* (1863) 3 F. & F. 772, where former Criminal Law Commissioner, Wightman J. observed, 'It is hardly necessary to have recourse to science to learn that the moral faculties may be diseased while the intellectual faculties are sound', and further *in arguendo*. Consistently with the Criminal Law Commission's view, Wightman regarded the defence of 'uncontrollable impulse' as a 'most dangerous doctrine, and fatal to the interests of society and security of life'.

[96] A scattering of earlier judicial references supporting the inclusion of volitional defects includes *Frost* (1844), *Dickinson* (1844), and *Brixey* (1845), cited by A. S. Taylor, *General Principles of Medical Jurisprudence* (1861), 893–6. Also, Erle J. in *Adams*, *The Times*, 26 July 1856, p. 11.

[97] (1872), cited by Taylor, *Medical Jurisprudence* (1873), 881.

[98] 1890. Cited by A. Wood Renton, *Law and Practice of Lunacy* (1894) who commented, 'On the whole, the latitudinarian school of judicial thought in regard to the interpretation of the answers in McNaughten's [*sic*] case is now on the ascendant' (902). Similarly R. Wilson (1902) 18 *LQR* 21.

[99] *Watson*, *The Times*, 13 January 1872, p. 13; and below. Three weeks after *Watson*, Bramwell B. published in *The Spectator* (3 February) an article implicitly critical of Byles' more liberal stance, 'The Object of the English Criminal Law'.

[100] In *Blampied*, *The Times*, 24 July 1875, p. 13. Brett J. emphatically denied the views of the standard medico-legal text, Taylor's *Medical Jurisprudence* cited by defence counsel supporting volitional defects as constituting the defence of insanity. Despite this, the jury found the defendant to be insane. Cf. *The Times* editorials, e.g. 1 July 1850, p. 4 and 11 August 1855, p. 6. Alfred Swaine Taylor's *Medical Jurisprudence* first appeared in 1836, five years after his appointment as lecturer in 'medical jurisprudence and chemistry' at Guy's hospital. The promised sections covering insanity were eventually published in 1844. Here Taylor's critique on the narrowness of the M'Naghten Rules argued that their 'relaxation was imperatively necessary' (647) to include 'sudden destructive impulse'. Until well into the twentieth century, *Medical Jurisprudence* was the standard reference text for lawyers engaged in medico-legal areas—including those advancing the insanity defence. By

Paralleling (and occasionally even provoking) the mainstream judicial rejection of what was frequently dubbed a plea of 'irresistible impulse' were parliamentary initiatives underpinned by the observations of commentators.[101] Combining the former and the latter, Stephen emerges as the most persistent adherent and propagandist of the cause of 'irresistible impulse'. From the mid-1850s[102] for over 30 years he can be seen maintaining broadly the same stance: first, that 'insane impulsiveness' is indirectly addressed by the M'Naghten Rules because such a malady raised the presumption that the defendant did not know his act was wrong; and secondly, if this were not true, then the law should recognize it to be so.[103] The basis of Stephen's attitude was his relatively deep immersion in contemporary medical literature which argued for a theory of integrated personality: in essence, a mutuality and dependency of the several facets of human personality and intelligence, of a nature that serious mental incapacity almost necessarily impaired all principal aspects of personality; and that fundamentally defective ability to understand and reason almost invariably affected the power of self-control, and vice versa.[104] In the succeeding two decades, through

1860, Taylor claimed that the actual treatment by the courts of insanity pleas was much more flexible than required by the M'Naghten Rules, e.g. (7th edn, 1861), 901. See also XI, Pt 3.

[101] Indicative of the general resistance to an impaired volition insanity defence is that neither before nor after articulation of the M'Naghten Rules was any support given to the concept by the often innovative Criminal Law Commissioners. In 1856, Andrew Amos, one of the longest-serving members, expressed considerable scepticism in respect of the 'notion [which] has recently been propagated of a moral, or instinctive insanity, [where there is] simply a perversion of the moral sentiment, the individual labouring under an impulse to commit certain outrageous and extravagant acts, such impulse being irresistible. [B]ut it may be doubted whether, in the absence of any lesion of intellect, the power of self-control is ever really lost, and punishment can be attended with no salutary dread…'. Amos notes in passing the support of Brodie's *Physiological Inquiries* and Mayo's *Croonian Lectures* (1853) where *mitigated* punishment in such cases is supported, *Ruins of Time*, 36–7.

[102] See his Juridical Society paper, 4 June, 1855. 'On the Policy of maintaining the limits at present imposed by law on the Criminal Responsibility of Madmen', *Papers read before the Juridical Society*, vol. 1 (1855 and 1856). Here Stephen reviews the arguments of Winslow, Prichard, Ray, and Taylor, authors of the leading contemporary medico-legal treatises. Stephen's other articles of this period include 'Are Madmen Responsible?', *Saturday Review* (1856) ii: 100 and 'Responsibility and Mental Competence', originally delivered at the National Association for the Promotion of Social Science, Annual Meeting, York, September 1864, reproduced in (1865) 18 *LM* 26.

[103] Stephen was, of course, not alone in this belief. For example, support for this view is found in (1855) 26 *LT* 145, (1856) 28 *LT* 47, and (1863) 38 *LT* 294.

[104] 'I understand by the power of self control the power of attending to general principles of conduct and distant motives and of comparing them calmly and steadily with immediate motives and with the special pleasure of other advantage of particular proposed actions…[T]he absence of the power of self-control would involve an incapacity of knowing right from wrong [because] knowledge and power are the constituent elements of all voluntary action and if either is seriously impaired the other is disabled. It is as true that a man who cannot control himself does not know the nature of his acts as that a man who does not know the nature of his acts is incapable of self control', *HCL*, ii, 171. Stephen was particularly influenced (though not uncritically) by the works of Henry Maudsley, Professor of Medical Jurisprudence at University College, London and the period's most

his roles as legislative draughtsman, judge, and author, Stephen was uniquely placed in endeavouring to influence the run of events and seek to have his own way on the scope of the insanity defence.

The most significant instances of official public and legislative interest in the insanity defence are to be found in the deliberations of the Capital Punishment Commission (1866),[105] the 1874 Homicide Bill Committee Report, and the 1879 Criminal Code Commission Bill and Report. In the Capital Punishment Commission proceedings the only clear support for embracing defective volitional control as part of the insanity defence came from medical professionals.[106] Much in the fashion of his remarks in *Haynes*, Bramwell B. voiced the most robust rejection of any such enlargement of the defence: little credence could be given to the views of 'mad doctors' who spoke of 'uncontrollable impulse'. On the suggestion from one Commissioner, Home Office Under Secretary, Horatio Waddington, that certain defendants undoubtedly did suffer from an 'uncontrollable impulse' to kill, Bramwell insisted that whilst 'there may be such a thing [...] I vastly disbelieve in it'.[107] Pushing the deterrence theory to its limits, and beyond, Bramwell saw the 'unhappy madman' as the person 'who requires the threat [of punishment] more than anybody else, because, from the condition of his mind, he is more likely to have some temptation to commit the offence, [without] intelligence to deter him'. And when questioned as to the public perception and 'sense of justice' in respect of 'punishing men of weak intellect', Bramwell indicated that: 'I am not aware of any justice in this matter, *ultra* expediency'.[108]

---

distinguished English author on psychiatric medicine. Stephen also solicited T. H. Huxley's views on the subject, Stephen to Huxley, 13 May 1881, Huxley Papers, Imperial College. Stephen's earlier *General View* treatment of the insanity defence at times appears to combine uncontroversial statements of law with examples of what he must have understood to have been kite-flying. His general description of the defence more than once suggests the law covered both cognitive and volitional impairment, such that the defendant 'could not know it was wrong, or could not help doing it' (91). Particularly noticeable is that unlike previous and most subsequent accounts of the defence, Stephen treats the 'defence' as negating either *mens rea* or voluntariness (86 and 89). And in a specific section on 'impulsive insanity' he notes that where actions are truly 'irresistible' an acquittal should follow 'because the act was not voluntary'. Without supporting authority, Stephen resorts to infanticide as the 'commonest and probably the strongest example' (94–5).

[105] Though called as a witness before the Capital Punishment Commission, Stephen's evidence in relation to insanity was almost exclusively directed at a possible defence of infanticide, *Minutes*, 254–61, 277–98.

[106] *Report and Minutes before the Royal Commission on Capital Punishment 1864–6*, PP 1866 [3590], xxi, *Minutes of Evidence* of Tuke, 323–4; Hood, 369–81; and Tallack, 152–78.

[107] *Minutes*, 25 and 22. Waddington also referred to the existence of kleptomania. His detailed questioning of Drs Tuke and Hood on the nature of 'irresistible impulse' sometimes gave the impression of an advocate seeking to demonstrate the credibility of such a defence.

[108] Unabashed, when pressed by a member of the Committee, he conceded that it was 'almost a logical conclusion from my argument...that the greater the temptation under which a person

Bramwell's opinion was vented once again at the Committee stage of the 1874 Homicide Bill, where his most immediate target was Stephen's attempt to incorporate an explicit 'uncontrollable impulse' provision allowing a defence to 'homicide' if the defendant when committing the act was 'prevented by any disease affecting his mind...from controlling his own conduct'.[109] Furthermore, Stephen's bill had boldly contrived to link insane delusions with volition: 'If a person is proved to have been labouring under any insane delusion at the time when he committed homicide it shall be presumed, unless the contrary appears or is proved, that he did not possess a degree of knowledge or self-control here and before specified.' Giving evidence to the Committee, Stephen depicted these provisions as no more than consonant with the actual practice of courts, if not the expressed theory. True to form, Bramwell 'vehemently protest[ed] against' such an innovation and 'would control [impulses] by the fear of hanging, mad or not mad'. At his second lengthy session before the Committee, Stephen, no doubt with some satisfaction, pointed out (having by then carefully scrutinized earlier evidence of Bramwell and Blackburn) that whilst the former distinguished member of the bench had fulminated over the claimed broadness of the bill's insanity provisions, the latter had regarded them as possibly erring on the narrow side.[110]

Providing an instance of one of legal history's satisfying ironies, the final brick of opposition to the bill was laid in place by M'Naghten's counsel, Alexander Cockburn, now Lord Chief Justice. In a memorandum sent to the Committee at the end of its hearings, Lord Cockburn sought, as on previous occasions, to assure all parties that though a 'strong supporter of codification' and reform, he was hostile to 'particular incomplete' efforts, such as this bill. But in respect of the proposals dealing with 'the absence of the power of self-control', he:

concur[red] most cordially..., having been always strongly of opinion that, as the pathology of insanity abundantly establishes, there are forms of mental disease in which, though the patient is quite aware he is about to do wrong, the will becomes overpowered by the force of irresistible impulse, the power of self-control when destroyed or suspended by mental disease becomes, I think an essential element of responsibility.

---

is to commit an offence, the greater ought to be the restraining considerations upon him' (25). Yet Bramwell's views on the deterrability of the insane were given some credibility by Dr Tuke who agreed that 'some insane people most decidedly are restrained by the fear of punishment' (2402). Dr Hood also accepted that he had encountered 'many convicts feigning insanity' (2944). On Bentham's allegiance to Bramwell's attitude, *IPML*, Ch. XIV, sections 8 and 9.

[109] Special Report of the Select Committee, PP 1874 (315), ix, section 24(d). Belief in potential deterrence was the principal rationale behind the Trial of Lunatics Act 1883, 46 and 47 Vict., c. 38 which changed the verdict after a successful insanity plea to 'guilty, but insane'. For Queen Victoria's role in instigating this change, see Walker, *op. cit.*, p. 189. *The Times* later described notion of deterring lunatics as 'fantastic', 17 October 1895, p. 9.

[110] *Minutes*, 2, paras 10, 26–7, and 45.

However, as in the case of insanity, he saw this 'new principle' as properly applicable to all offences, not just homicide.[111] Whatever the extent of the Lord Chief Justice's genuine allegiance to recognizing impaired volitional powers, at no stage during his occupation of this high office was it ever manifested through support for a *judicial* interpretation of the M'Naghten Rules along the lines pursued by Stephen. This was certainly a course legitimately open to any Lord Chief Justice bearing in mind the judicial origins of the rules, and a course that a Lord Chief Justice might have adopted were he so minded.

Legislative initiatives and Executive review The concluding scene of nineteenth-century proto-legislative activity concerning the insanity defence was played out, again with Stephen as principal participant, against the backdrop of the 1879 Draft Code. In place of a direct and open provision recognizing volitional impairment, Stephen's own initial Draft Code of 1878 contained a painfully awkward section expressly based on the criterion of potentially effective deterrence.[112] Clearly this was Stephen's attempt to meet the opposition (such as Bramwell) on their own ground. But the manoeuvre failed, with the 1879 Code Commission (which included Lord Blackburn) excising the provision and any reference to 'impulsive insanity'. The extent of the likely dispute amongst the Commission's members is plain from the Report's frank admission that the 'framing of the definition has caused us much labour and anxiety; and though we cannot deem the definition to be altogether satisfactory, we consider it as satisfactory as the nature of the subject admits of'. The Commission's reflections well identify the sources of its reluctance to widen the scope of the insanity defence. When accounting for the removal of Stephen's 'impulsive insanity section', the Commission proposed what amounted to an early diminished responsibility rationale through a regime of reduced punishment levels:[113]

The test proposed for distinguishing between such a state of mind and a criminal motive, the offspring of revenge, hatred, or ungoverned passion, appears to us on the whole not to be practicable or safe, and we are unable to suggest one which would satisfy the requisites

---

[111] *Ibid.*, 63. App. No. 1, Memorandum of the Lord Chief Justice. Lord Cockburn expressed disapproval of the proposed ancillary presumptive provision to s. 24(d) (p. 66). As for Cockburn's judicial approach to mental impairment beyond trials: in the prominent case of *Watson* (1872) an insanity defence failed; Home Office documentation shows that eventual commutation of the death sentence rested on evidence of 'uncontrollable maniacal frenzy' and the support of the trial judge (Byles J.) together with that of Lord Cockburn. See Chadwick, *Bureaucratic Mercy*, 252–5.

[112] '(C) if [the defendant] is in such a state that he would not have been prevented from doing that act by knowing that if he did do it the greatest punishment permitted by law for such an offence would be instantly inflicted upon him…'.

[113] *Report*, 18. The distinguished American codifier David Dudley Field published broadly similar proposals in (1873) 2 *LM* 779.

and obviate the risk of a jury being misled by considerations of so metaphysical a character. It must be borne in mind that, although insanity is a defence which is applicable to any criminal charge, it is most frequently put forward in trials for murder, and for this offence the law—and we think wisely—awards upon conviction a fixed punishment which the judge has no power to mitigate. In the case of any other offence, if it should appear that the offender was afflicted with some unsoundness of mind, but not to such a degree as to render him irresponsible—in other words where the criminal element predominates, though mixed in a greater or less degree with the insane element—the judge can apportion the punishment to the degree of criminality, making allowance for the weakened or disordered intellect. But in the case of murder this can only be done by appeal to the executive, and we are of opinion that this difficulty cannot be successfully avoided by a definition of insanity which would be both safe and practicable, and that many cases must occur which cannot be satisfactorily dealt with otherwise than by such an appeal.

Here the Commission was consciously venturing into conceptually deep waters: in 'irresistible impulse' cases the actor may have had the necessary *mens rea* but arguably lacked the equally essential attribute of voluntariness. This raised the potentially open-ended question of when were actions 'voluntary'? or just *how* voluntary they needed to be for the proper attribution of responsibility. If such 'impulsive' behaviour were viewed as involuntary in a narrow Austinian sense, then there was no 'act' and therefore could be no liability. But excluding responsibility on the basis of a looser indeterminate moral involuntariness presented a conceptually dangerous spectre which the Commission firmly reinterred.

The general suspicion, not to say judicial alarm, greeting attempts to regularize and formulate a broader version of the insanity defence was predictable. As has been seen, determining a person's mental state for normal *mens rea* purposes was subject to the handicaps of nineteenth-century trial practices and evidential rules which excluded defendants from full participation until the Criminal Evidence Act 1898. But gauging a defendant's strength of volitional control or capacity at the time of the offence appeared a formidably daunting and dangerous proposition. It could reasonably be regarded as the thick end of a deterministic wedge capable of making the deepest of subversive inroads into the fundamentals of the whole structure and philosophy of penal law based on the assumption of a free-acting agent. As such it would be capable of undermining penal law, whether of a deterrence or retributive complexion.

At the same time, the prospect of admitting an ever-widening range of scientific and medical evidence by which defendants might be extricated from both blame and judicial disposal was undoubtedly seen by the bulk of the judiciary as carrying the potential to undermine the system's power to deter. Moreover, where might this degree of crypto-deterministic, particularization of the defendant's qualifying 'excuse' lead in other areas, such as provocation, duress, and necessity? For the criminal justice system was, in large measure, founded on the formulaic identification and punishment of (objectively) free-acting and informed agents who had 'voluntarily' transgressed. Any exculpatory recognition of weak resistance to criminal temptation would seemingly question the legitimacy of the whole institution. At its most basic, how might the lazy, avaricious, and unscrupulous actor be confidently and clearly segregated from one with clinically recognized levels of irresistible criminal proclivities? And just what credence could properly be given to the diagnoses of clinicians? Far better then, it might have been reasoned, to opt for an informal, flexible, case-by-case Executive review approach to accommodating extreme behaviour indisputably driven by what could be regarded as 'insane impulses'. In essence this was the 1879 Commission's stance, and one which can be found represented elsewhere during this period. In many respects, it constituted a pragmatic compromise between deep concerns over eroding the criminal law's relative certainty and, crucially, believed power to deter, along with recognition that individual justice should not be completely sacrificed to the greater good of preserving the system's overall utility.

In broad terms, this attitude represented the established late nineteenth-century Home Office practice in murder cases, where evidence had been unsuccessfully adduced at trial supporting claims of the defendant's mental incapacity or derangement. Depending on the particular circumstances and evidence, the Home Secretary might commute the capital sentence to one of incarceration, usually, but not always,[114] in an institution for the criminally insane. The core of this policy, openly articulated in 1886 by former Home Secretary, William Harcourt, was that 'Neither he nor his immediate Predecessors in Office had thought that they were bound by the strict legal interpretation of insanity as laid down by the Judges in the House of Lords, which he had always thought was much too narrow;...a much more liberal interpretation had been adopted in all cases where the prerogative of mercy was to be exercised'.[115]

---

[114] General deterrence remained a factor, rendering it justifiable to hang killers lacking 'fully morally responsible volitional control' because it 'has a refraining influence on others of similar abnormal proclivities...', Sir Kenelm Digby, Home Office, Permanent Under Secretary, 17 December 1895, *Home Office Printed Memoranda and Reports*, N.A. H.O. 347/18, 119.

[115] At the time of the Commons' statement, Harcourt was Gladstone's Chancellor of the Exchequer. See above for the gradual nineteenth-century legislative increase in Home Office powers and responsibilities in relation to 'insane criminals', ensuring that they were not tried, or if tried and convicted, then not punished. For a detailed analysis of Home Office attitudes and practices in relation to the insanity defence revealed by internal documentation, see Chadwick, *Bureaucratic Mercy*, Ch. 6. In this process of 'medical development and bureaucratic accommodation', from the 1860s the Home Office made increasing and extensive use of its own expert advisers both on questions of defendants' fitness to plead as well as the defence of insanity. On the practice of Home Office intervention, see e.g. *The Times*, 4 January 1864; p. 7; 15 January 1864, p. 8; 16 February 1864, p. 10.

Indeed, even Bramwell in his evidence to the 1866 Capital Punishment Commission volunteered both recognition and endorsement of a flexible approach to the application of the M'Naghten Rules, where the 'practice of juries which has met with the sanction of Judges' had been to acquit those where 'public feeling' required it.[116] Also in *Dove*, Bramwell dealt with a claim of loss of self-control by reducing the question of liability in his jury direction to 'could he help it?'[117] Less surprisingly, Stephen himself in the early 1880s' case of *Davis* went as far as any puisne judge of the time might prudently have gone in subtly insinuating impaired volition (absence of 'calmness and reason') into a jury direction by giving it a knowledge-of-wrong-veneer:

As I understand the law, any disease which so disturbs the mind that you cannot think calmly and rationally of all the different reasons to which we refer in considering the rightness or wrongness of an action, any disease which so disturbs the mind that you cannot perform that duty with some moderate degree of calmness and reason may be fairly said to prevent a man from knowing that what he did was wrong.[118]

As a consequence, before the end of the nineteenth century, commentators like Markby were prepared to maintain that such judicial practice transmuted the M'Naghten Rules into a general, soft-edged normative question for the jury, 'namely, whether, under all the circumstances, the prisoner ought to be punished'.[119] In fact, one nineteenth-century draft code provision came very close to proposing this. Unshackled by concerns over the usual level of scrutiny

---

[116] *Minutes*, 24. But at the same time Bramwell would not agree to any formal change in the law to make it harmonious with such 'public feeling'. See also similar arguments by Bramwell in (1885) 18 *Nineteenth Century* 893, where he made reference to kleptomania afflicting 'a well-to-do-person' (898). And below.

[117] *Dove, The Times*, 17–20 July 1856. See also the account of the case based on Bramwell's trial notes lent to Stephen in the *General View*, 391 and *HCL*, iii, 426. The commentaries differ in presentation but not greatly in substance. For the common currency of Bramwell's 'could he help it?' test, see T. E. Crispe, *Reminiscences of a KC* (1909), 150.

[118] (1881) 14 Cox 563, 564. On Stephen's judicial practice in relation to the insanity defence, see the remarks of a medical expert published in *The Times*, suggesting Stephen would not allow a defendant's apparently sound *cognitive* ability to necessarily defeat a plea of insanity: *The Times*, 31 August 1894, p. 5.

[119] *Elements of Law* (1st edn, Oxford, 1871), 129–30 and (6th edn, 1905), 350–1. Similarly, the conclusions of the jurist A. Wood Renton, in 'The Legal Test of Lunacy' (1890) 6 *LQR* 318–19 and *An Examination of the Irresistible Impulse Theory* (Edinburgh, 1886). Also Stephen's observations on trial practices, *HCL*, i, 186. Kenny, *Outlines* (1904), 56–7 raised the example of kleptomania, apparently then sometimes put forward in the lower courts by 'well-to-do-persons accused of trivial acts of theft'. (1892) 93 *LT* 60 observed when considering the exclusion of 'irresistible impulse' that: 'Many of the judges readily admit that the rules in Macnaghten's case [*sic*] require 'manipulation', and manipulate them at Nisi Prius with the full sympathy of juries of assize'. Also, *The Times*, 1 September 1894, p. 9. Indeed, such was the belief that the general judicial practice achieved the appropriate results, that the Medico-Legal Association appeared willing to allow the formal insanity

and self-interest which attended draft legislative provisions destined for home consumption, Wright's Jamaican Code (with Stephen's express concurrence)[120] provided a defence where the accused was 'under the influence of a delusion of such a nature as to render him, in the opinion of the jury, an unfit subject for punishment of any kind in respect of such an act'.[121] Consequently, towards the end of the nineteenth century *The Times* was well justified in declaring that there was 'no longer [a] common legal view' on the scope of the insanity defence.[122]

If anything, judicial division on the legitimacy of widening the insanity defence became more overt in the early twentieth century.[123] Initially, neither Lord Alverstone CJ nor his successor, Lord Reading, was anxious to remedy this uncertainty by any express articulation of principle, whether including or excluding volitional impairment as part of the M'Naghten Rules. Occasionally, lesser members of the Bench might venture a contentious opinion. Alongside Lord Alverstone in the Court of Criminal Appeal, Channell J. openly confessed to following Stephen's judicial course in *Davis* (1881), taking the view that lack of ability to form a 'reasonable judgment as to what is right or wrong relieves from responsibility'.[124] However, whilst accepting the relevance of evidence of incapacity which prevented the defendant 'from exercising self-control', Lord Alverstone put off any authoritative ruling until an appropriate occasion when the 'court will not shrink from the duty of deciding those matters of controversy and deciding the law'.[125] A decade later, Lord Reading showed a similar inclination to put off providing a clarificatory ruling.[126]

In addition to conflict of judicial opinion, individual judges, such as Darling J., displayed inconsistency, with evidence of 'impulsive homicidal mania' accepted

rules to die a 'natural death' (1896) 42 *Journal of Mental Science* 217, cited in Wiener, *Reconstructing the Criminal*, 276.

[120] Letter, January 1875, CO 137/480/613. Also, Friedland, *loc cit.*, 331.

[121] Section 38(ii). Subsection (i) also sets out a 'knowing the nature of consequences of the act' test. Wright reveals the strong influence of the North German Code provisions dealing with the need for 'free volition' as a requirement of criminal responsibility. He also appeared to endorse the view that fewer problems would be encountered if the defence were not set out in a detailed form, 'Notes on Part I of the Draft', Report, 103–4.

[122] 17 October 1895, p. 9. In 1894 *The Times* had published a series of letters debating the need for widening the insanity defence and the appropriate weight to be ascribed to medical evidence: e.g. 25 August, p. 3; 31 August, p. 5; 8 September, p. 12; 22 September, p. 12; 10 October, p. 14; and 17 October, p. 14.

[123] Home Office commutation policy and practice for convicted murderers where there had been strong evidence of derangement, short of that satisfying the M'Naghten Rules, was also by no means predictable or uniform. See Chadwick, *op. cit.*, Ch. 6, *passim*.

[124] *Jones* (1910) 4 Cr App R 207.

[125] *Ibid.*, 214 and 218. Also Bray J. in *Fryer* (1915) 24 Cox 403, who, like Channell J., expressly followed Stephen; and also *Jolly* (1919) 83 JP 296.

[126] *Holt* (1920) 15 Cr App R 10.

in some cases[127] yet characterized as the 'last refuge of a hopeless defence' in others.[128] Such equivocation was at least formally terminated shortly after Lord Hewart's installation as Chief Justice, when in *True* (1922) he indicated that in the 'view of this Court there is no foundation for the suggestion that the rules derived from the M'Naghten case have been in any sense relaxed'.[129] But, to meet the parliamentary agitation generated by the Home Secretary's subsequent reprieve of True, the Atkin Committee was set up to review, inter alia, the insanity defence.[130]

The Committee's Report proposed augmenting the M'Naghten Rules with a provision whereby a 'person charged criminally...is not responsible for his act [if] committed under an impulse which the prisoner was by mental disease in substance deprived of any power to resist'.[131] Government inaction prompted the Criminal Responsibility (Trials) Bill (1924) tabled by the ennobled Darling J.,[132] which aimed to enlarge the M'Naghten Rules to include defendants 'wholly incapable of resisting the impulse to do the act'. The bill's highly placed, effective, opposition included Haldane LC and Lord Hewart, with the latter boasting the support of 12 of the 14 King's Bench judges. Consistent with his post-trial action in *True*, Lord Hewart maintained change to be unnecessary, with Executive clemency providing adequate safeguards. Furthermore, he preferred to regard alleged previous judicial endorsements of Stephen's support for 'irresistible impulse', in reality as 'not...adopted, but coquetted with'.[133]

In fact, the Lord Chief Justice's opposition to any formal change of the M'Naghten Rules enabling them to embrace volitional impairment became both frequent and fervent. With powerful nineteenth-century resonances, from the Bench he characterized the potential development as involving: 'the fantastic

---

[127] *Hay* (1911) 22 Cox 268.

[128] *Thomas* (1912) 7 Cr App R 36. See also Darling J. years later in *Quarmby* (1921) Cr App R 163, 164.

[129] *True* (1922) 16 Cr App R 164. Lord Hewart implicitly criticized Macardie J.'s trial direction which accepted impaired self-control as within the Rules. *In arguendo*, Greer J. indicated that 'uncontrollable impulse' could come within the Rules.

[130] *PD* 1922 (s. 5 HC) 155: 201 where the Home Secretary revealed that as well as the trial judge, Lord Hewart had emphasized the existence of strong medical evidence of True's broader-based insanity. Appointed by Birkenhead LC, the Committee contained no medical members and was almost exclusively composed of lawyers.

[131] *Report* (1924), [Cmnd. 2005]. This was the BMA's proposal. More far-reaching changes were supported by the Medico-Psychological Association which advocated complete abrogation of the M'Naghten Rules and the jury settling criminal responsibility where the defendant was insane at the time. No criteria for the determination of sanity were suggested. In many respects the proposal regularized what had been and was to continue to be the reality of jury verdicts.

[132] *PD* 1924 (s. 5 HC) 57: 222.

[133] Lord Hewart's speech, reproduced in *Essays and Observations* (1930), 225, 228.

theory of uncontrollable impulse which, if it were to become part of our criminal law, would be merely subversive. It is not yet part of the criminal law, and it is to be hoped that the time is far distant when it will be made so'.[134] Extra-judicially, he warned that: 'Lawyers, and statesmen will hesitate long before they open the door to a quite incalculable flood of mischief for the purely academic purposes of giving logical sufficiency to a formula, or a superior degree of correctness to verdicts which in practice are already rational.'[135]

Such implacable resistance to a *formal* broadening of the insanity defence rested on a combination of several factors, some novel and some carried forward from the previous century. First, as has been seen, in the nineteenth century whilst a considerable body of medical opinion was in varying degrees critical of the defence's essentially cognitive basis, there was no consensus on the defence's appropriate scope.[136] Moreover, as Lord Hewart noted, many advocates of reform (including the Atkin Committee) were forced to concede that in practice mentally irresponsible defendants were, as a result of Executive review, subject to mitigated punishments or non-prison institutionalization. Secondly, not all medico-legal opinion unreservedly pressed for change. Even Taylor's *Principles and Practice of Medical Jurisprudence*, the standard medico-legal text, urged a cautionary approach:

The doctrine of irresistible impulse and the theory of impulsive insanity have been strained to such a degree as to create in the public mind a distrust of medical evidence on these occasions. It is easy to convert this into a plea for the extenuation of all kinds of crimes for which motives are not apparent, and thus medical witnesses expose themselves to rebuke. They are certainly not justified in setting up such a defence unless they are prepared to draw a distinction between impulses which are 'unresisted' and those were are irresistible.[137]

---

[134] *Kopsch* (1925) 19 Cr App R 50, 51–2.

[135] Lecture delivered before the Medical Society of London, 16 November 1927, reproduced in Hewart's *Essays and Observations*, 222. See a similar espousal of the pragmatic approach by Travers Humphreys in (1921) 1 *CLJ* 302. Also in (1928) 44 *LQR* 20. Practitioners, such as W. C. Sullivan, Medical Superintendent at Broadmoor, admitted the insanity defence, as actually administered, 'worked no great injustice', *Crime and Insanity* (1924), 230.

[136] Cf. e.g. the evidence of BMA and Medico-Psychological Association to the Atkin Committee. Leading contemporary medical commentators such as Charles Mercier, though favouring mitigation of punishment, were cautious in their approach to recognition of impulsive disorders. See e.g. his evidence to the *Royal Commission on the Care and Control of the Feeble-minded* (1908) [Cmnd. 4202] and *Crime and Insanity*, 251–3. H. Oppenheimer's influential text *The Criminal Responsibility of Lunatics* (1909) expressed doubts as to whether 'irresistible impulses' could occur in a state of consciousness and whether such could reliably be ascertained as part of the trial process (182–94).

[137] 7th edn, 1920 by F. J. Smith, physician and lecturer in medical jurisprudence at the London Hospital, i: 884–5. Similarly, 'to distinguish between an uncontrollable impulse and an uncontrolled one' was the fundamental reason why judges had 'refused to accept uncontrollable impulse as an

Most disturbing of all for Lord Hewart and other sceptics was the perpetually perceived threat of transforming the *legal* question of whether a defendant was properly responsible for his actions into a *medically* determined one. The crudeness of the M'Naghten Rules kept the question within a range of understanding and determinacy acceptable to most lawyers and jurists. But identifying irresponsibility on the grounds of impaired volitional powers threatened a more scientific, sophisticated examination of human mentality, and, consequently, a greater or complete reliance on medical opinion. The pragmatic approach of arriving at the 'right' result through a 'practical' and relatively sharp-edged intellectual test of knowledge as the basis of responsibility carried no such threats to the *legal* ascription of liability. Moreover, questions relating to the ultimate disposal and punishment of defendants could be determined after a further, more subtle Executive examination of the evidence of an actor's mental capacity and maladies.

Finally, almost acting as a coda to the long-running dispute over the insanity defence, was the question of automatism. From the early nineteenth century, specialist medical discourse had recognized impaired mental capacity outside the orthodox analytical distinction made between cognitive and volitional defects. Such unconscious, dissociated, or automatous states most commonly included somnambulism and epileptic interludes. Like impaired volitional control, claims of automatous behaviour were framed in terms of an insanity defence; and, as with impaired volition, they were generally met with intense scepticism from both judges and, usually, juries.[138] One of the earliest reported judicial encounters with a defence plea of 'automatism' arose in the 1912 theft case of *Chetwynd*.[139] Here, Scrutton J.'s response to evidence of 'mental automatism which is midway between somnambulism and a minor form of epilepsy', was to treat the plea as one of insanity, a course confirmed a few years after by the Court of Criminal Appeal.[140] Associating automatism with epilepsy became an almost inevitable

excuse'. A. L. Goodhart, 'Recent Tendencies in English Jurisprudence' (1929) 7 *Can. Bar Rev.* 289, reprinted in *Essays* (Cambridge, 1931), 47.

[138] On Home Office anxiety to ensure that the law 'commend[ed] itself to popular sentiment': *Home Office Printed Memoranda and Reports*, N.A. H.O. 347/18, 119; 17 December 1895. J. Eigen's post-*M'Naghten* collection of Old Bailey case studies reveals the wide-ranging nature and relative frequency of medical testimony on insanity and a distinct proto-automatism defence, *Unconscious Crime, Mental Absence and Criminal Responsibility in Victorian London* (Baltimore, 2003), esp. Ch. 6. Just one case, based on evidence of epilepsy, is identified where the terms of the jury verdict recognized automatism: 'not guilty on grounds of unconsciousness', *Carr* (1875–6) *OBSP* 495. This was taken by the trial judge to amount to an acquittal on the grounds of insanity, Eigen, 140–6 and App., table A.2.

[139] (1912) 76 *JP* 544.

[140] *Perry* (1919) 14 Cr App R 48.

analysis, following the practice of leading medico-legal authors.[141] The conceptual leap of ascribing an automatous state to a 'non-insane' category, with the consequence of a complete acquittal and the defendant's unconfined discharge, was several decades away.[142]

(2) Intoxication

States of intoxication range from 'mere exhilaration down to unconsciousness'.[143] For early commentators, the severe effects of intoxication were often allied to those of insanity: according to Blackstone, the 'artificial, voluntary contracted madness... depriving men of their reason [putting] them in a temporary phrenzy'.[144] Such a classificatory perception was carried through in *Russell's* treatment where intoxication is identified as one of four examples of actors who are *non compos mentis*—'a species of madness'. Yet, at the same time, both Blackstone and *Russell* asserted voluntary intoxication, unlike insanity, could not excuse an actor from liability.[145] Moreover, both maintained that intoxication could be an 'aggravation of whatever [the offender] does amiss',[146] 'aggravation' being reflected in severity of sentence, where possible.

Responding to the effects of intoxication raised a conflict between a reluctance to derogate from the fundamental requirement of a 'voluntary', free-acting agent, and the powerful intuitive demand to punish harm caused by a party who was in some less specific way blameworthy. As Stephen observed, 'the reason why drunkenness is no excuse for crime is that the offender did wrong in getting drunk'.[147] An additional worry was defendants using a superficial state of intoxication to feign absence of *mens rea*; for 'how easy it is to counterfeit this excuse'.[148] However, with the gradual, increasing sophistication of trial

---

[141] e.g. in that period, Mercier, *Crime and Insanity* (1911), 62–6.

[142] *Kay* v. *Butterworth* (1945) 110 *JP* 75; *Harrison-Owen* [1951] 2 All ER 726.

[143] Kenny, *Outlines* (1929), 63. Warming to this characterization, he added: 'Hence the familiar division into four successive steps—jocose, bellicose, lachrymose, comatose' (n. 63).

[144] *Comms*, iv, 25.

[145] Blackstone, *ibid.*; *Russell* (1819), 11; (1826), 7; *Hale* 1 PC 32, noted that there was 'no privilege by voluntary contracted madness'.

[146] *Ibid.*, and see *Coke*, Inst., 247. The validity of the aggravation claim at the time is open to some doubt. See Singh (1933) 49 *LQR* 528.

[147] *HCL*, ii, 165. Or in Bacon's terms: 'imperfections came by his own default', *Maxims*, reg. 5. See *Reniger* v. *Fogossa* (1550) 1 Plowd. 1, 19. Cf. Paley's suggestion that the level of criminality and moral guilt coincide and are to be fixed by the actor's degree of awareness when he was getting drunk that, when drunk, he would commit the criminal act: *Principles of Moral and Political Philosophy* (1785) Book IV, Ch. 2.

[148] Blackstone, *Comms*, iv, 26. Blackstone prefaced his conclusion with a summary of national climates and their relationship to the physiological and jurisprudential effects of alcohol: 'The same indulgence, which may be necessary to make the blood move in Norway, would make an Italian mad. A German therefore, says... Montesquieu, drinks through custom, founded on constitutional

procedures and techniques of eliciting evidence of states of mind, the force of
this concern would diminish.

Throughout the nineteenth century, intoxication was recognized both as a
distinct widespread social problem and a significant factor in inducing many
forms of criminal behaviour.[149] But, in suggesting that drunkenness could be an
aggravating factor, *Russell* was recording the tail end of this belief. Already,[150] at
least some judicial opinion recognized two concessions to drunken agents: on a
charge of murder, in determining the presence of calculated intent, intoxication
could be taken as negating evidence;[151] and secondly, in cases of provocation a
defendant would not be debarred from benefiting from the defence because of
his 'more easily excitable' state, despite the prior fault of getting intoxicated.[152]
Moreover, by 1830, it was not only accepted that intoxication might be germane
in deciding the genuineness of a claimed belief of acting in self-defence,[153] but
also that a drunken mistake as to the ownership of property would not lead to
liability for stealing.[154]

Of course, the general resistance of English law to excusing criminal conduct on the basis of intoxication concerned *voluntary* intoxication. Less or no
moral opprobrium attached to a party who had got into such a state *involuntarily*.
Following the authority of *Hale*, *Russell* suggested intoxication would be 'involuntary' where, for example, it was the result of the 'unskilfulness of [a] physician or by the contrivance of...enemies'.[155] More conceptually interesting was
the further category of someone suffering from alcoholism. Here, even though
the 'habitual or fixed frenzy...was contracted by the vice and will of the party' an
alcoholic would be regarded as being involuntarily intoxicated, a merciful conclusion bearing in mind the defendant's admitted prior fault. One interpretation

necessity; a Spaniard drinks through choice, or out of mere wantonness of luxury: and drunkenness, [Montesquieu] adds ought to be more severely punished, where it makes men mischievous and
mad, as in Italy and Spain, than where it only renders them stupid and heavy, as in Germany and
more Northern countries'. On such reasoning, English law was clearly severe in its attitude towards
intoxication.

[149] See 'Punishment', 'Inebriates', Ch. V, above.

[150] See *Grindley* (1819), cited by *Russell* (1826 edn), 8n. However, cf. *Carroll* (1835) 7 Car. & P. 145.
Cf. *Hill* (1790) *OBSP* 276, which appears to suggest that the defendant's drunkenness was relevant to
a charge of theft. See also *Thomas* (1837) 7 Car & P. 817.

[151] *Grindley* (1819).

[152] *Thomas* (1837) 7 Car. & P. 817. This is one possible construction of a judgment not without
ambiguity.

[153] *Marshall's Case* (1830) 1 Lew. 76. See also *Crossfield* (1796) 26 St. Tr. 122, noting that whilst
intoxication was no defence it 'undoubtedly...will weaken or destroy any inference to be raised
from the [defendant's] actions'.

[154] *Pitman* (1826) 2 Car. & P. 423.

[155] 1819 edn, 11–12. *Hale*, IPC 32.

might be that such a condition, though initially voluntarily induced, was viewed as akin to pathological insanity.

Association of the effects of intoxication and insanity continued throughout the nineteenth century, in that courts and commentators frequently employed the similarities and dissimilarities between the two to define intoxication's exculpatory scope. The similarities were obvious: both conditions could produce cognitive or volitional impairment erupting into violence, and both claims carried the worrying potential for fakery, along with concerns over erosion of the law's power of deterrence. Distinguishing the two conditions were notions of voluntariness and fault: the actor's intoxicated state was self-induced; his capacities were self-disabled. Furthermore, in most cases, the condition was transient.

Limited concessions to the effects of intoxication marked out an oblique route to resolving the more alarming central issue of whether evidence of intoxication might be admitted to establish the absence of the necessary mental element. Unwittingly or not, admitting evidence of the effects of intoxication on the defendant's mental state for particular defence purposes, as in provocation, logically pointed to similar treatment of such evidence in relation to culpability requirements. This was recognised in *Cruse*[156] where, on a charge of injuring with intent to murder, Patteson J.'s jury direction emphasized that: 'although drunkenness is no excuse for any crime whatever, yet it is often of very great importance in cases where it is a question of intention. A person may be so drunk as to be utterly unable to form any intention at all, and yet he may be guilty of very great violence'.

Quite what Patteson J. meant by 'cases where it is a question of intention' was of key importance in determining the nature and extent of the shift away from an unqualified 'no defence' approach. Coleridge J. probed a little further a decade later in *Monkhouse:*[157]

Drunkenness is ordinarily neither a defence nor excuse for crime, and where it is available as a partial answer to a charge, it rests with the prisoner to prove it; and it is not enough that he was excited, or rendered more irritable, unless the intoxication was such as to prevent his restraining himself from committing the act in question, or to take away from him the power of forming any specific intention.

---

[156] (1838) 8 Car. & P. 546. Two years later Patteson's unwillingness to make allowances for drunkenness in a case of theft, but acceptance of its relevance to serious assault charges, provoked an angry *Times'* leader, 23 December 1840, p. 4. Also, the slightly earlier but less clear case of *Meakin* (1836) 7 Car. & P. 297. And cf. *Ferray, The Times*, 11 March 1839, p. 6 where the charge similar to that in *Cruse*, produced a less favourable more confused direction from Parke B.: 'whether the offence was committed with an intention to murder or...a frolic of intoxication'. But later: 'Drunkenness was no excuse for the commission of crime'.

[157] (1849) 4 Cox 55. However, some judges contrived to direct juries in broader, unqualified terms, such as Pollock LCB in *Quail and others, The Times*, 5 March 1862, p. 11.

Here are to be found the clear antecedents of the twentieth century distinguishing criterion of 'specific intention', whereby liability for such offences might be avoided by the *mens rea* negating effects of intoxication.

Building on Coleridge's 'specific intention' comments are the later observations of Stephen J. in *Doherty*,[158] highlighting the role of evidence of intoxication in rebutting the presumption of intention:

> The general rule as to intention is that a man intends the natural consequence of his act. As a rule the use of a knife to stab or of a pistol to shoot shows an intention to do grievous bodily harm, but this is not a necessary inference. In drawing it you should consider for one thing the question whether the prisoner is drunk or sober.

But neither here nor elsewhere is to be found a judicial account of how offences of 'specific intention' were to be identified other than by particular designation.[159] Although not usually judicially expressed in such terms (as implied by Stephen), the underlying rationale could be seen as a derivative of the rule that acts and probable consequences were, subject to rebuttal, presumed to have been intended. Clearly, the more complex and multifaceted the culpability requirements of an offence, the greater the demands on an actor's powers of perception. Consequently, evidence of befuddlement would have eased the task of dislodging the presumption of intention. Of course, such a rationalization of the conception of 'specific intention' does not necessarily lead to a rigid classification of 'specific' and 'basic' intention offences. Indeed, at least in respect of subjective fault-based offences, it would argue more towards a non-classificatory, purely evidential, case-by-case approach. The hard cases where a principled approach collided with understandable broad social concerns over not wishing to allow the law to tolerate drunken fury or misjudgement, were offences dependent upon knowledge of circumstances or foresight of consequences, such as rape and some lesser forms of wounding.

In the case of rape, the relatively early nineteenth-century decision of *Burrow* failed to address the point; here Holroyd J. spoke of the non-excusability of any crime committed by one 'when infuriated with liquor'. The defendant's lack of belief in consent, and the potential effect of intoxication upon this, were not adverted to.[160] No doubt Holroyd was greatly influenced by the fact that this offence and some woundings (where specific intent was not expressly required)

---

[158] (1887) 16 Cox 306. '[B]ut if his drunkenness prevented his forming [an intent to do grievous bodily harm] he will be guilty of manslaughter, and not murder, though such an act in a sober man would prove an intention to do grievous bodily harm'. Also *Doody* (1854) 6 Cox 463.

[159] Other than various attempt offences and wounding or causing grievous bodily harm with intent, no offence had been expressly identified as requiring 'specific intention'.

[160] *Burrow* (1823) 1 Lew. 75.

were very much forms of behaviour indulged in by the intoxicated, and where social and legal anxiety over lessening the deterrent effect of punishment were at their greatest. Certainly, the judicial view would have been that if less serious charges could be defeated by pleas of no *mens rea* as a result of intoxication, the floodgates would truly be breached. As Stephen robustly commented in *Doherty*:

> It is almost trivial for me to observe that a man is not excused from crime by reason of his drunkenness. If it were so, you might as well at once shut up the criminal courts, because drink is the occasion of a large proportion of the crime which is committed.[161]

Furthermore, exculpation would deny gratification of the strong retributive streak clearly present in punishing harm caused by intoxicated actors liberated from natural inhibitions or experiencing distorted judgment of commonplace realities. Indeed, there are resonances of constructive fault liability in the judicial handling of intoxicated offenders, where responsibility for an initial, culpable act is inflated by the vagaries of chance consequences, and where liability is placed on a risk-taking footing. In the case of intoxication, the initially culpable act is satisfied by consumption of alcohol, something regarded as an invariably hazardous activity.

It was this partly explicit rationale, combining deterrence concerns with retributive notions of prior fault, that was capable of accommodating defendants who had either become intoxicated involuntarily or whose conditions resembled those recognized by the M'Naghten Rules. Again, no doubt fearful of fraudulent claims, and anxious to curb self-induced disablement, the courts refused to accept the concept of *temporary* insanity well into the nineteenth century.[162] However, the progression of medical science was, on this occasion, also accompanied by a judicial recognition that alcoholism might qualify as a disease under the M'Naghten Rules:

> ...drunkenness is one thing, and the diseases to which drunkenness leads are different things; and if a man by drunkenness brings on a state of disease, which causes such a

---

[161] *Doherty*, 308. Similarly, Taylor, *General Principles of Medical Jurisprudence* (1873), 596. Particularly from the late 1870s, concern over the levels of alcoholism was responsible for the Inebriates Act 1879 (and subsequent Acts) under which special treatment facilities could be set up. More generally, the social and criminal problems rooted in drunkenness frequently engaged governmental and parliamentary attention throughout the nineteenth century. See e.g. *Select Committee Inquiry into Drunkenness*, PP 1834 (559), viii, 315; *House of Lords Select Committee for Inquiring into Prevalence of Habits of Intemperance Report*, PP 1877 (171), xi, 1, 11. And see 'Punishment—Inebriety' above, Ch. V.

[162] See *Rennie's Case* (1825) 1 Lew. 76 and *M'Govan* (1878) cited by Taylor, *op. cit.* 797. A contributor to the *Law Magazine* argued that liability should turn *solely* on the presence or absence of the appropriate fault requirement of the offence in issue (1841), 26, 399–400.

degree of madness, even for a time, as would have relieved him from responsibility if it had been caused in any other way, then he would not be criminally responsible…although his madness is only temporary.[163]

The limits to which an involuntariness/absence of deemed prior fault rationale could be taken in exculpating intoxicated defendants can be glimpsed in two unreported, but surprisingly liberal, decisions of the late 1880s. In *Mary R*, Chief Baron Palles observed:

If a person from any cause—say long watching, want of sleep, or deprivation of blood—was reduced to such a condition that a smaller quantity of stimulant would make him drunk than would produce such a state if he were in health, then neither law nor common sense could hold him responsible for his acts, in as much as they were not voluntary but produced by disease.[164]

Equally innovatory were Baron Pollock's comments made the following year in *Mountain*,[165] suggesting that peculiar personal susceptibility to the effects of alcohol—an 'insane predisposition'—might properly be regarded as a disease of the mind and lead to an acquittal. Clearly, the potential conceptual implications of such views for criminal responsibility and defences generally were extensive, pointing strongly in the direction of a greater subjective, more personalized conception of voluntariness. However, although of considerable historical interest, these judicial sentiments proved to be aberrational.

Unlike insanity, contemporary academic and proto-legislative views on intoxication were broadly aligned with judicial opinion. Indeed, Wright's Jamaican Code proposals were more stringent than the existing common law in that for all offences an intoxicated defendant was (with no power of rebuttal) to be 'deemed to have intended to cause the natural and probable consequence of his act'.[166] It was a stringency partly based on 'public safety' grounds: that excusing drunken actions would be contrary to this end, and that an excuse could be 'so easily feigned or fabricated'.[167] In contrast with Wright, the 1879 Code Bill

---

[163] *Davis* (1881) 14 Cox 563, Stephen J. 564. In *Baines, The Times*, 25 January 1886, Day J. seemed to go beyond this by not linking temporary insanity with a 'disease'. Possible precursors of *Davis* were the unreported decisions in *Simpson* (1845) and *Watson* (1845), both cited by Taylor, *General Principles of Medical Jurisprudence* (1873), 599. Support for this view is also voiced in (1843) 29 *LM* 408.

[164] (1887) Irish, cited in Wood Renton, *Lunacy* (1895), 913.

[165] (1888), *ibid*. Cf. the rather less sympathetic tone of Lord Coleridge CJ in *Little, The Times*, 6 May 1886, p. 7.

[166] Section 39.

[167] 'Notes', 105. The other basis for Wright's approach was an apparent misconstruing of English law which he claimed to follow in the draft provision. Wright observed that 'English authorities are not altogether consistent', but 'voluntary intoxication is generally held to be no excuse whatever, and this doctrine appears to imply that a consciousness of probable consequences is to be imputed

Commissioners sidestepped the problem by expressly omitting from their proposals any reference to the effects of drunkenness on liability:

We have thought it unadvisable to introduce any express reference to the well-known
doctrine that drunkenness is no excuse for crime, though in particular instances its
existence may show the absence of the specific intention. Reference to the matter might
suggest misunderstanding of a dangerous kind.[168]

These somewhat timid not to say unconvincing observations are doubtless indicative of the judiciary's steady concern over the 'national' problem of inebriacy.
However, they were made in advance of the judgments of Stephen J. in *Davis*
and *Doherty*.

In common with the judicial view, basing liability on the deemed fault entailed
in getting drunk figured prominently in several academic analyses of the intoxication rule. Austin, along with later commentators, stylishly characterized the
culpability as 'remote inadvertence' as to what the actor might later do: 'He
has negligently placed himself in a position from which he might have known
criminal acts were not unlikely to ensue.'[169] At the beginning of the twentieth
century, Kenny offered a slightly less transparent explanation, not expressly identifying negligence as the source of liability: 'His mens rea in allowing himself
to become intoxicated is sufficient to supply the ordinary mental elements...'.
But unlike 'ordinary mental elements' drunkenness might rebut the presumption of 'some additional mens rea'. And whilst not hazarding an explanation of
this concept, Kenny cites the examples of murder, causing grievous bodily harm
with intent, burglary, and the rather broader category of 'an intent to commit a
felony'. Kenny's account of the instances of drunkenness where 'no moral blame
attaches' included (following ancient authority) medical circumstances, colour-
fully illustrated by reference to 'treatment of snake-bites habitually adopted by
the back woodsman of the Western States of America'.[170]

---

even though it be proved to have been absent', *ibid.*, 105. *Cruse, Monkhouse* and *Stopford* (1870) 11
Cox 643 should have been sufficient to indicate otherwise to Wright.

The Criminal Law Commissioners were greatly concerned with the risk of fraud and the embold-
ening effect a defence of intoxication might have on offenders. But, unlike Wright, they acknowledged the admission of evidence of intoxication to rebut the presumption of *mens rea*; though no
such qualification was incorporated in their brief intoxication provisions drafted after *Cruse* but
before *Monkhouse*. See *Seventh Report* (1843) 20 and Art. 2 (at 31). Similarly, in the *Second Report*
(1846) and *Fourth Report* (1848).

[168] *Report*, 18.

[169] *Lectures*, 516. Cf. Paley and similarly Stephen, *HCL*, ii, 165 and Clark, *op cit.* 29. Surprisingly,
Austin denied any exception to the rule that intoxication was no defence.

[170] *Op cit.*, 60–1. Markby alone amongst commentators openly expressed doubts in respect
of the rough but practical conceptual mechanism represented by the specific and basic intent

Like their predecessors, early twentieth-century judges and commentators continued to seek a compromise between the keenly uncomfortable exculpatory outcome of an undiluted application of general principles of liability and the desire to penalize and deter the immorality of harm-causing drunkenness. The tension between the criminal law's fundamental conceptual expectations and broader social concerns to suppress the dangers of intoxication, which had fashioned the law's response to the intoxicated agent in the nineteenth century, were both amplified and augmented in the twentieth. In part, this was a consequence of the relative sharpening of general notions of fault and voluntariness. Thus in *Beard*,[171] Lord Birkenhead appeared to accept that intoxication might negate not just the presence of 'specific intent' in offences such as 'wounding with intent', but also culpability requirements of lesser crimes: 'for speaking generally…a person cannot be convicted of a crime unless the *mens* was *rea*'. This was taken by Kenny and other subsequent commentators to be a reaffirmation of the fundamental necessity of proof of the fault element for all offences: 'a man's drunkenness may preclude him, not merely from forming one of the specific intentions, but from forming any intent at all'.[172] Indeed, a party intoxicated to such a degree as to lack the necessary awareness of the nature of the action (as in simple assault) might be denying even a voluntary action.

Lord Birkenhead's dicta threatened exculpation of participants in casual assaults and drunken brawls on the basis of almost routine pleas of no *mens rea*, a matter of obvious overwhelming social and practical concern for the courts. In judicial eyes, such outcomes through the application of general principles of criminal responsibility would have been doubly unwelcome: undermining the perceived power to deter or control the incidence of alcohol-generated crimes, and offering intoxicated defendants a route to avoiding punishment for their prior fault of getting intoxicated.

However, judicial attempts at formulating a compromise between the desire to punish a drunken agent's prior irresponsibility and adherence to general concepts of criminal liability faced not only technical obstacles. There was also an underlying judicial ambivalence towards the role of prior fault, as evidenced by the approach to provocation, insanity, involuntary intoxication, and sentencing. Taking first the case of provocation, although the defendant's particular idiosyncrasies were excluded from consideration in determining the reasonableness of response, case law appeared to suggest that the increased provocability of an

---

distinctions. In essence he favoured directly punishing the endangering culpability of becoming intoxicated. *Elements of Law* (1905 edn), 362–3.

[171] [1920] AC 479, 504. Like Markby, above.

[172] *Outlines* (1929 edn), 62. Cf. *Archbold's* more restricted interpretation (1938 edn), 19.

intoxicated defendant might be properly taken into account. This more indulgent treatment of self-generated susceptibility to losing self-control extended to provocation based on a mistake of fact induced by intoxication. Recognition of an intoxicated state including 'temporary insanity' was confirmed in *Beard*. Again, neither the prior (remote) fault of heavy consumption of alcohol nor the complete absence of any obvious difference between extreme intoxication and temporary insanity inhibited the House of Lords from accepting this concession to general principles of liability.[173]

The remaining two areas of judicial ambivalence related to involuntary intoxication and the sentencing of convicted defendants intoxicated at the time of the offence. Hale's assertion that involuntary intoxication (whether innocently through medical treatment or by deception) would excuse, though frequently repeated by commentators, never received direct judicial endorsement. However, absence of prior fault was not accommodated by the general rules of liability. If the defendant as a consequence of involuntary intoxication lacked the appropriate *mens rea* he would be excused, at least in the case of a crime of 'specific intent', in the pre-*Beard* sense. If a strict view of *Beard* had been adopted, then absence of prior fault could have led to complete exculpation from any offence when intoxication had been involuntary.

Beyond the courts, by the final decades of the nineteenth century the clinical appreciation of alcoholism had, to a degree, deflected attention from moral condemnation of past voluntary consumption of alcohol towards recognition of the involuntary (determined) behaviour of alcoholics; it was an understanding which led to the Inebriates Acts 1879 to 1898, giving the courts latitude in sentencing for crimes directly or indirectly due to intoxication.[174] Yet conflicting evidence emerges of intoxication's effect on sentencing generally. In the late nineteenth century and early decades of the twentieth, Executive clemency in capital cases was advised and exercised far less frequently where the defendant had been drunk.[175] However, some judges saw intoxication as a mitigatory element in sentencing, such as in *Morton* where the Court of Criminal Appeal observed that though alcohol 'does not excuse what he did, it affects the guilty intention which he must have had, thereby justifying a reduced sentence'.[176]

Beyond the Inebriates Acts, no focused attempt was made to escape from the practical and theoretical dilemma presented by the intoxicated offender.

---

[173] Cf. the trial direction on knowledge of 'wrong' in *Meade* [1909] 1 KB 895.

[174] See 'Punishment', 'Inebriety', Ch. V above.

[175] Where there was no insanity. See C. E. Troup, *The Home Office* (1925), 67. For apparently generous Home Office commutation practices in the 1860s–1880s, see confidential *Home Office Printed Memoranda and Reports* N.A. H.O. 347/9, 688–9.

[176] (1908) 1 Cr App R 255.

Concern towards the end of the nineteenth century over apparent uncertainty about the relevance of intoxication to liability led to a reference to former Attorney-General Sir Henry James, for an authoritative opinion. Sir Henry, however, did little more than confirm a complete absence of consensus on the issue.[177] Principal medico-legal commentaries, such as Taylor's, endorsed the role of prior fault in imposing liability, while sharing a deterrence concern for the believed detrimental effect on public order and safety of too generous a treatment of intoxicated defendants.[178] A simple retreat from the theoretically unsatisfying nature of the nineteenth century basic/specific intent test was impracticable. Punishing defendants for their culpable and risky or harmful behaviour required a novel approach whereby a defendant's endangering intoxicated state *itself* was subject to adequate sanctions. For this, a ready-made model was the Legislature's response to the intoxicated motorist whereby liability sprang directly from the endangering nature of driving while under the effects of alcohol.[179]

In broad terms, the developmental path of intoxicated criminal behaviour was predestined in that an unmodified application of intoxication's *mens rea* negating powers would have left the courts with the socially alarming spectacle of appearing unable to punish many forms of objectively culpable harm-causing intoxicated behaviour. In the absence of specific legislative intervention along the lines of endangerment-based motoring offences of the twentieth century, no obvious alternative route presented itself to the criminal courts.

(3) *Duress, necessity and self-defence*

Internal mental incapacity or impairment as manifested in insanity, provocation, and intoxication was, in different degrees, the subject of judicial attention and development throughout the nineteenth century. No doubt this process was principally driven by force of common circumstances which the courts were obliged to resolve. Additionally, broader conceptual discourse probably also contributed to the law's refinement through occasional resort by enterprising judges or counsel to relatively abundant speculative literature. For similar reasons, by the opening of the nineteenth century, self-defence and intervention to prevent the commission of a crime were also already relatively well-aired defence concepts. But these evolutionary forces were for a long time substantially absent in the case of the legal effect of some forms of external forces or pressures characterizable as 'duress' and 'necessity'. Indeed, for most of the nineteenth century

---

[177] *The Times*, 4 January 1892; (1892) 1 *BMJ* 131. Sir Henry James's own vague guidelines concluded that: 'no general rule can be laid down. [Drunkeness's] existence may be considered, and may tend either in the direction of increasing or diminishing the punishment.'

[178] Taylor, *op cit.*, 1920 edn, 902–3; 1948 edn, 685–6.

[179] Criminal Justice Act 1925, s 40(1), superseded by the Road Traffic Act 1930, s 15(1).

the number of occasions on which the courts were required to consider duress pleas was severely limited; and in respect of a general necessity defence, hardly any judicial dicta appeared until the 1880s. Practically all conceptual development issued from commentators and proto-legislators. Nevertheless, duress and necessity's somewhat one-sided historical development still warrants measured examination for what it reveals of the period's general concern for, and understanding of, moral agency and criminal culpability.

While Blackstone recorded that there would be an absence of 'free will' and responsibility where acts were 'done through unavoidable force and compulsion',[180] the focus of contemporary commentators' concern was marital coercion, reflecting the particular area attracting most formal judicial attention.[181] However, the dearth of authority on other forms of duress did not inhibit Blackstone from speculating on the law's possible and desirable position. In notable contrast, as late as 1826, *Russell* was still showing little interest in the subject. Yet even allowing for the distinct difference in purpose of their respective works, this was surprising, especially as *Russell* so frequently took Blackstone as its point of reference for speculative discussion. Any judge or practitioner consulting *Russell* (1819 edition) as the period's leading work, would be offered no more than the barest recognition of a defence of *duress per minas*.[182] Not until the second edition did *Russell* get around to adding a short note incorporating[183] the proposition that 'actual force upon the person and present fear of death may, in some cases, excuse a criminal act'.

Two central questions relating to the defence at this embryonic stage merit consideration. First, what constituted *duress per minas*? Blackstone referred to 'threats and menaces, which induce a fear of death or other bodily harm'.[184] Speaking after the publication of Blackstone's *Commentaries*, Lord Mansfield[185] suggested that where a 'man is forced to commit acts of high treason, if it appears really forced, and such as human nature could not be expected to resist [then] the man is not...guilty'. Similarly, in the much later agricultural riot case of

---

[180] Blackstone, *Comms*, iv, 27.

[181] At this stage in its career as a special defence, born out of the unique position of wives, a husband's coercion was presumed, subject to contrary evidence that the wife was a free-acting agent. It was not available for offences of a 'deeper dye' or *mala in se*, *Comms*, iv, 29. *Hawkins* rested the defence on the social and legal basis of wives owing husbands 'the highest obedience', 1 PC 4n (1824). Blackstone refers to the 'matrimonial subjection of the wife to her husband', *Comms*, iv, 28. On the generally distinct basis of this special defence, see Stephen *HCL*, ii, 105–6.

[182] *Russell* (1819), 23.

[183] *McGrowther* (1746) 18 St. Tr. 391. *Russell* does not use the term 'duress' at any stage.

[184] *Comms*, iv, 30. *McGrowther* expressly excluded threats to property and required defendants to show that they escaped the effect of threats as soon as possible.

[185] *Stratton* (1779) 21 St. Tr. 1222. Though later Lord Mansfield appeared to find significant the fact that the intention of the threatener, Lord Pigot, was not to 'kill any of these men'.

Crutchley,[186] a defence of duress was regarded as available, even though the threats were almost certainly of less than death. Furthermore, whatever the level of harm, the fear induced 'ought to be just and well founded'.[187] But this and other equivocal views failed to establish whether real threats were essential; or whether it was sufficient if an imagined threat was 'well founded' in the sense of being perceived as real on objectively reasonable grounds.

The second broad question related to the theoretical basis on which duress rested. No one suggested that the defence amounted to a claim of absence of *mens rea*. Instead, as with other examples of defences involving diminution or the elimination of 'free will', two alternative duress bases can be gleaned from contemporary observations: a retributive rationale, that in cases of individuals *in extremis* there is no moral obligation to obey the law, thereby eliminating the immoral quality necessary for a criminal sanction; or a deterrence basis, whereby the threat of future punishment will be rendered inutile by the immediate threat of harm facing an actor. Lord Mansfield's 'force...such as human nature could not be expected to resist', might be possible support for either basis. Blackstone's guiding principle of liability, resting on the exercise of 'free will', appears to have led him to the moralistic conclusion that threats 'take away...the guilt of many crimes...at least before the human tribunal'.[188]

Moral pressure of a different variety was entailed in the possible defence of necessity. Whilst, unlike duress, not judicially conceded as a *general* defence, in a fragmentary sense the notion of legal necessity was recognized in one form or another.[189] Again, Blackstone offered the period's most considered account of the subject. His apparently general proposition involved the situation where 'a man has his choice of two evils set before him, and being under a necessity of choosing one, he chooses the least pernicious of the two. Here, the will cannot be said to freely exert itself', such as when someone 'by commandment of the law carrying out an arrest or dispers[ing] a riot, who in the course of such

---

[186] (1831) 5 Car. & P. 133. Patteson J. permitted cross-examination of prosecution witnesses to determine if the defendant had been 'compelled to join this mob against [his] will, and whether the mob did not compel [him] to give one blow to each threshing machine'. It was considered germane to the defence that the defendant had 'determined to run away from the mob at the first opportunity'.

[187] *Comms*, iv, 30.

[188] *Comms*, iv, 30. Cf. Blackstone's general view that punishment was justified on the basis of its deterrent value, e.g. 12.

[189] Cf. the common nuisance case of *Vantandillo* (1815) 4 M. & S. 73, where Lord Ellenborough implicitly accepted that a defence of necessity might be available. The case was taken as clear authority for a necessity defence by a commentator on the Criminal Law Commissioners' Seventh Report (1843) 30 *LM* 42. *Vantandillo* received passing endorsement by Blackburn J. in *Hicklin* (1868) LR 3 QB at 376. Also see e.g. 'Abortion', Ch. XII below.

action finds it necessary to use extreme force'. Because of the importance of preserving the peace and enforcing the law, this would 'excuse' the party from criminal liability.

Quite how restricted this concept of necessity was is difficult to gauge; Blackstone seemed to have in mind the established, uncontroversial rights of intervention to prevent the commission of offences or carry out arrests, and the linked concept of self-defence. He partly confirmed this narrow construction in his succeeding reference to 'the case of necessity which has occasioned great speculation among the writers upon general law; viz. whether a man in extreme want of food or clothing may justify stealing either, to relieve his present necessities'. Blackstone either implicitly denies such cases involved the absence of the exercise of 'free will' or sees his requirement of 'free will' as being overridden by the 'highest reason': the security of property. Property would be under a 'strange insecurity if liable to be invaded according to the wants of others; of which no man can possibly judge'. Besides, noted Blackstone, the particular problem could not materialize, for in England 'charity is reduced to a system', and it would be 'impossible that the most needy stranger should ever be reduced to the necessity of thieving'.[190]

As suggested, Blackstone's conceptualization of acts in the 'advancement of justice' as a form of necessity, by extension would include self-defence; and, indeed, in his treatment of homicide, he explicitly made such a link.[191] Turning to the case where each party is innocent, and taking up Bacon's enduring example of two shipwrecked people clinging to a plank only capable of supporting one, Blackstone agrees that he who 'preserves his own life at the expense of another man's, is excusable[192] [through] unavoidable necessity, and the principle of self-defence'. Early in the nineteenth century, *East* carried forward a similar linked conceptualization and conclusions under the title 'Homicide Ex Necessitate'.[193] However, when dealing with the plank dilemma, *East* advanced the analysis by going beyond self-defence and additionally absolving the survivor by analogy with duress where the basis of exculpation was an excusatory 'consideration of human infirmity',[194] not a justificatory balancing of harms.

---

[190] *Comms*, iv, 32 after *Hale*, 1 PC 54. Blackstone follows this disingenuous reasoning by suggesting that should any cases of true necessity ('peculiar hardship') give rise to criminal proceedings, there was always the reserve power of royal pardon.

[191] *Comms*, iv, 183–6.

[192] Blackstone appeared to attach no significance to the use of 'excusable' here, rather than 'justifiable'.

[193] 1 PC 220, 271.

[194] 1 PC 294. Also, *Russell* (1826), 784, citing *East*.

Speculative attitudes towards duress and necessity With very limited exceptions, criminal activity involving actions brought about by duress or necessity
simply did not arise, or was not prosecuted, or the appropriate plea was not
advanced by defendants. Consequently, earlier fragmentary authority remained
almost totally untouched by judges for the remainder of the nineteenth century. However, this did not inhibit a moderate growth of speculative analysis,
partly set off by the deliberations of the Criminal Law Commissioners, who in
their Fourth Report (1839) could be seen extending the concept of self-defence to
embrace 'Self-Preservation'. The ancient entitlement[195] of self-defence (of person
and property) against human assailants probably rested on notions of the assailant's forfeiture of the law's protection and a recognized basic right of resisting or
preventing criminal harm.[196] Self-defence was viewed by the Commissioners as
the most pronounced example of the 'principle of necessity where the act is essential to the defence of a man's person and property'; it was 'founded on a mixed
principle of necessity and policy'.[197] Beyond digested provisions for 'justifiable
self-defence', the Commissioners also provided that killing was 'justifiable' by
'self-preservation' where 'a man is involuntarily placed in such a situation that he
is under the necessity of killing another in order to save his own life'. Here the
Commissioners' focus was on threats from 'natural forces'. As with Blackstone,
the expressed inspiration of this 'entitlement' was Bacon's examination of the
hypothetical example of two shipwrecked survivors clinging to a floating plank
capable of supporting just one.[198]

Returning to the subject four years later, two[199] of the previous group of
Commissioners offered a significantly different analysis, with utility openly leading the way via the 'great principle' of the deterrability of free-acting agents possessing the 'power of electing to abstain from what is forbidden'.[200] Widening

---

[195] Cf. e.g. Blackstone, *Comms*, iv, 183–6. Foster, who Blackstone largely followed, notes 'Self-
defence naturally falleth under the head of homicide founded in necessity...', *Crown Cases*, 273.

[196] In relation to homicide, Foster observes 'the right of self-defence...is founded in the law of
nature, and is not nor can be superseded by any law of society', *ibid.*, 273–4. Self-defence is also considered in 'Homicide' and 'Provocation', Ch XII below. In one respect, duress could be viewed as the
bridging concept between self-defence and necessity in that, like the former, there is an immediate
unlawful threat from a human agency, but, like the latter, an innocent (or non-threatening) party
is the victim.

[197] *Fourth Report*, xxi. The defence is one of 'justification in the necessary defence of person
and property...' (xxii).

[198] Art. 39, xxxvii.

[199] Ker and Starkie.

[200] *Seventh Report* (1843), 17. Cf. Austin, who also based the defence of duress on the inutility of
the threat of punishment, where influence of a sanction would be 'gratuitous cruelty'. *Lectures*, 515.
Similarly, Bentham, *IPML*, Ch. XIII, ss 11–12. Austin expressly distinguishes the basis on which
duress rests from other defences, such as insanity, which he accounts for on the grounds of absence

the analysis to all forms of threats, the Commissioners' Digest provided for a generally applicable duress defence and one of 'self-preservation' limited to homicide. Broadly reflecting judicial authority, the 'excuse' of duress required a 'well-grounded fear of death, or of grievous bodily harm'.[201] As in the Fourth Report, the 'justification'[202] of necessity, or 'self-preservation', was restricted to homicide.

The final and (once more) changed stance of the Criminal Law Commissioners appeared three years later in their Second Report (1846).[203] Duress's scope was narrowed in that only a 'fear of death' would now excuse.[204] Acceptance of a non-deterrability rationale, however, failed to persuade the Commissioners to follow previous Reports and provide for a necessity defence. In explaining this significant change, the Commissioners deployed a mixture of moralistic[205] and pragmatic reasoning. Of the latter, the risk of abuse or excessive use greatly exercised the Commissioners because of the 'general disposition of all persons to overrate the danger to which they are exposed, and to place too low an estimate on the life of another'. Moreover, pre-empting these dangers was not practicable because it was 'impossible to precisely define [acceptable] cases'. Therefore, rather than formally provide for a 'justificatory' necessity defence, Executive clemency was favoured because there would be 'less inconvenience in leaving persons to the mercy of the Crown'.[206]

---

of awareness of 'violating his duty, and consequentially could not operate on his desires' (514). This is another instance of distinguishing volitional from cognitive impairment.

[201] Art. 6. Excluding treason and homicide.

[202] The basis of lawfulness of 'self-preservation' under the Fourth and Seventh Reports was different. In the Fourth Report, as with self-defence, there is a 'right' or 'entitlement' to 'self-preservation'. The Seventh Report's non-deterrability rationale for apparently duress and necessity cases suggests a curious use of 'justification' in relation to necessity; for if the reason for granting the defence is non-deterrability, this implies the system's preference (as in excuses) would be that the defendant had not so acted. This patently could not be the case in self-defence. In this sense the Seventh Report's approach seems to have been to relocate necessity from its self-defence base (adopted in the Fourth Report) to one of an excusatory nature, despite being termed a 'justification'.

[203] On this occasion three further Commissioners joined Ker and Starkie, the two authors of the Seventh Report. Amos had returned from India, and rejoined the Commission. Fourth Report (1848) followed the Second Report.

[204] An unspecified minority favoured extending duress to all offences, including treason and murder, on the grounds that the rationale of non-deterrability of an actor under threat of death operated for all offences. However, the majority did 'not feel justified in recommending a change of the present law' (p. 12).

[205] Implying discarding a utility rationale and returning to the 'entitlement' approach of the Fourth Report, though with different conclusions.

[206] Second Report, Art. 19n (at p. 36). In adopting this line, the Commissioners made express reference to the similar approach of the Indian Law Commissioners. Amos's role in this change of stance may have been significant. But the positions taken by the English Criminal Law Commissioners and Macaulay were distinct in that Macaulay's original Draft Code contained

Vacillation by the Criminal Law Commissioners over the acceptability of a necessity defence was hardly surprising bearing in mind the formidable combination of political, philosophical, and practical questions raised. Whilst often imbued with a broad rationalistic-cum-utilitarian ethic, the Commissioners were far from wholeheartedly committed to a simple 'greater good' calculus. Their indecision reflected fluctuating concern over the appropriate balance to be struck between individualistic 'self-defence' notions extrapolated into ideas of 'self-preservation', and the more collectivistic benefits of an avoidance of greater harm approach. But even a lukewarm embrace of utility's logic promised unappetising (moralistically and practically) calculations of the relative worths of defendants and victims. In the face of such reflections, abandoning recognition of a necessity defence and resorting to the conceptually unsatisfactory route of Executive clemency was virtually predictable.

Almost 30 years elapsed before these matters received further public consideration from legislators, judges, and theorists.[207] As part of Stephen's 1872–4 Homicide Bill's strategy of constituting an all-inclusive Homicide Code, two separate defence provisions of a necessity complexion were incorporated. The marginally entitled 'Case of Necessity' was directed at instances of self-preservation, providing that 'Homicide was not criminal' where it was carried out by the defendant to 'save his own life from imminent and extreme danger'.[208] While covering cases of self-defence, those of duress were expressly excluded, probably because of Stephen's own hostility to the defence of duress. A further defence provision aimed at a 'choice of evils', where death was caused by the defendant's life-endangering act 'done in good faith in order to avoid equal or greater danger' to any person.[209] Indications of what situations were intended to come within these provisions, together with legislative and judicial reactions to them, can be gathered from the bill's Select Committee minutes.

As key Committee witnesses, neither Blackburn J. nor Bramwell B. showed any sympathy for enacting defences which would sanction the *in extremis* examples of jettisoning passengers from boats or pushing others off floating planks. Bramwell was quite clear that he would not want to be 'turned off my

---

neither a necessity nor a duress defence. From the accompanying note to his Draft Code it is clear that he (like Bentham) regarded the rationales and substance for duress and necessity as being essentially the same and, consequently, one defence could not logically be recognized without recognition of the other ('Notes', 454–8, *Works*).

[207] Stephen's *General View* only glancingly touches on the subject. For example, speculation on necessity in relation to the use of 'malice' (83).

[208] Homicide Code cl. 17.

[209] Cl. 18. Stephen's 1872 bill version (cl. 6) required an act to prevent or avoid 'greater evil', an even clearer, utility-based, 'balancing of evils' justification.

plank'. But both these distinguished members of the bench seemed to concede that the law's full rigour would not ultimately be enforced, should such cases ever materialize.[210] In giving evidence and defending his provisions against judicial scepticism, Stephen fielded a dyed-in the-wool utilitarian justification. Not mincing words, he characterized Blackburn's denial of the moral rectitude of jettisoning some passengers to save others as 'very absurd', indicating his own support for that very principle. Furthermore, not one member of the Select Committee registered any fundamental hostility towards the broad ethic embodied in the two necessity sections. Even more surprisingly, Lord Cockburn's subsequent disapproving memorandum on the bill made no reference to these defence provisions in his specific criticisms. Tempting fate, Stephen's parting comment to the Committee characterized the issue to be of no real practical importance as such cases would 'in all probability...never occur'.

However, whether or not of practical importance, when it came to the broader codification enterprise of 1878–9, Stephen's own version of a Criminal Code incorporated generalized versions of the Homicide Bill's provisions, extending beyond homicide. While fighting shy of any such patent innovation, the Code Bill Commissioners were nevertheless unwilling to foreclose on all possibilities:

We are certainly not prepared to suggest that necessity should in every case be a justification. We are equally unprepared to suggest that necessity should in no case be a defence; we judge it better to leave such questions to be dealt with when, if ever, they arise in practice by applying the principles of law to the circumstances of the particular case.[211]

Though hardly the frontal assault on the issue favoured by Stephen then and in 1872–4, it was a small advance on the previous Criminal Law Commissioners' departing view in that the 1879 approach accepted that the matter was properly one for judicial determination rather than for Executive intervention. But exactly what governing 'principles of law' the Code Commissioners had in mind is hard to fathom. They may have been an oblique reference to the Code's catch-all provision preserving 'All rules and principles of the common law which render any circumstances a justification or excuse'.[212] Indeed, later in the columns of the *Nineteenth Century* when defending the Code generally, and in particular this provision, from Lord Cockburn's best efforts to demolish it, Stephen instanced

---

[210] *Report of Select Committee*, PP 1874 (315) ix, 471.

[211] Report, 'Note A', 44. It is noticeable that the 1879 Code provision (s 23) relating to the 'excuse' of duress is drawn very narrowly, in that the range of excluded offences extends beyond the common law's group of treason and murder to exclude 'assisting in rape', robbery, causing grievous bodily harm, and arson. Cf. the duress provision with Stephen's 1883 *Digest* statement of the law, Art. 31, which excluded no offence. In Kenny's 1904 view, it was 'impossible to say' which crimes were covered; but 'certainly not murder [nor] graver forms of treason'. *Outlines*, 73.

[212] Code Bill, s. 19.

necessity as a speculative area where the wisest course would be to wait and see, and, where appropriate, exercise the common law's residual creative powers preserved by the Code.[213]

Despite over 40 years of such official interest in the subject, it is not until 1883, with the publication of Stephen's *History of the Criminal Law*, that anything resembling a sustained, principled consideration of the defences of duress and necessity saw daylight in England. Analytically, Stephen's foundational assertion was that, apart from physical compulsion, claims of compulsion did not constitute a denial of either voluntariness or of 'intention'. A party under the direst of threats, whether from a human agency or natural causes, still chooses a course of action: 'to escape what he dislikes most he must do something he dislikes less'.[214] By detaching issues of compulsion from elemental requirements of voluntariness and *mens rea*, Stephen was free 'on the grounds of expediency' to reject a defence of duress, arguing that the whole criminal justice system was:

A system of compulsion on the widest scale. It is a collection of threats of injury to life, liberty and property if people commit crimes. Are such threats to be withdrawn as soon as they are encountered by opposing threats?... Surely it is at [this] moment when temptation to crime is strongest that the law should speak most clearly and emphatically to the contrary... [I]f impunity could be so secured a wide door would be opened to collusion, and encouragement be given to associations of malefactors...[215]

For him, mitigation of punishment was the safest and most appropriate way of meeting genuine cases of duress, where the defendant's moral culpability or blameworthiness was so diminished that full punishment was not merited. Thus, unlike earlier commentators who employed a broadly utilitarian deterrence rationale, Stephen implicitly believed in the continued effectiveness of the threat of a sanction in the face of criminal threats.

Yet, Stephen *did* favour a necessity defence, though he felt unobliged to identify why it was 'more expedient' to recognize a necessity defence than one of duress; or even whether he perceived a moral distinction between a criminal response to the threat of death from a human as opposed to a non-human source. Perhaps

---

[213] 'The Criminal Code' (1880) 7 *Nineteenth Century*, 136 at 155–6.

[214] *HCL*, ii, 102. 'A criminal walking to execution is under compulsion...but his motions are just as much voluntary as if he was going to leave his place of confinement and regain his liberty'. It was a strict viewpoint of voluntariness and *mens rea* shared by Markby. Markby, *Elements* (1905) 365–6. Similarly, Clark, *Analysis of Criminal Liability*, 36. Clark also endorsed Stephen's views on necessity (set out in the *Digest*) as 'good sense, and should be law'. Kenny asserted that compulsion cases were examples where 'unquestionably a criminal act goes unpunished for lack of the necessary mens rea', *Outlines* (1904), 77. He employed Blackstone's category term of 'where the will is overborne by compulsion' (49 and 70). See similarly (1845) 2 *LM* 110.

[215] *HCL*, ii, 107. Stephen was alone amongst principal nineteenth-century commentators in advancing this view.

he took imaginable necessity scenarios to be less open to the risk of 'collusion'. Moreover, while not expressly claiming so, possibly Stephen viewed the justificatory character or overall socially beneficial effect inherent in a necessity defence as a ground for recognition; this line of reasoning was not so obviously applicable to duress. But when it came to the challenge of formulating the defence of necessity, Stephen rather lamely proposed that cases be 'adjudicated upon by a jury afterwards'—a remarkable instance of proposed *ex post facto* law-making. Quite how this differed from the 1879 Code Commission's 'principles of law' approach is not obvious, but it is difficult to believe that Stephen really would have settled for leaving the decision entirely to a jury's normative whim.

Judicial hesitation: Dudley and Stephens The understandable 'it-will-probably-never-happen' attitude towards a necessity defence was proved spectacularly over-optimistic by the events leading up to *Dudley and Stephens*.[216] After several generations of official and judicial vacillation between claiming that individual cases would be best accommodated by Executive action or the unshackled application of 'general principles' of criminal jurisprudence, with this grisly case the moment of judicial truth had arrived. In the event, not only did the judiciary not rise to the occasion, rather, Lord Coleridge and his four brethren[217] produced a monument of ambiguity in reasoning and legal principle.

From the outset it was quite clear that no necessity-based defence would be entertained by the court, at least in these particular circumstances. Such a suggestion was 'both new and strange [and] at once dangerous, immoral and opposed to all legal principle and analogy'.[218] Moreover, after trawling through books of authority Lord Coleridge declared that if Bacon had 'meant to lay down the

---

[216] (1884) 14 QBD 273. A shipwreck caused three seaman and a youth of 17 or 18 years to be adrift in an open boat. After nearly three weeks, the last of which was spent without food or water, two of the seamen killed the youth and fed on his body. The survivors were rescued four days later. By a special verdict, a jury found the following facts: 'That if the men had not fed upon the body of the boy they would probably not have survived to be so picked up and rescued, but would within the four days have died of famine. That the boy, being in a much weaker condition, was likely to have died before them, but at the time of the act in question there was no sail in sight, or any reasonable prospect of relief. That under these circumstances there appeared to the prisoners every probability that unless they fed or very soon fed upon the boy or one of themselves they would die of starvation. That there was no appreciable chance of saving life except by killing someone for the others to eat.' *Ibid.*, 275. The case was then adjourned for final resolution and verdict by a court of five judges led by Lord Coleridge CJ. See generally A. W. B. Simpson, *Cannibalism and the Common Law* (Chicago, 1984) for a penetrating account of the case. Whilst similar occurrences involving shipwrecks were not totally unknown, *Dudley and Stephens* was the first case to go the distance through the English courts, albeit by resort to the special verdict procedure. See Blackstone *Comms,* iii, 377.

[217] Grove and Denman JJ, Pollock and Huddleston BB.

[218] *Ibid.*, 281, per Lord Coleridge CJ.

broad proposition that a man may save his life by killing, if necessary, an innocent and unoffending neighbour, it certainly is not law at the present day'.[219] But
such *relatively* unequivocal rejection of a necessity defence to a murder charge
rapidly lost its edge with Lord Coleridge's attempt to reconcile the court's collective view with the published opinions of Stephen J. (deployed by the defence)
and the Criminal Code Bill Commission's Report. Not unfairly, the Lord Chief
Justice regarded Stephen's observations in his *Digest* and *History of the Criminal
Law* as 'somewhat vague', adding that they did not in any event cover the case
before the court, an apparent admission of a possible necessity defence in other
circumstances.[220] Neither did Lord Coleridge feel that the court was 'in conflict'
with the five-year-old Code Commission Report's recognition that a necessity
defence would be appropriate in some unspecified cases.

Precedent and other authority (or the lack of it) aside, upon what legal and
ethical basis did the court reach its hazy conclusions? Attempting to identify
why the act of killing was unjustified in these circumstances, or why the defendants' behaviour in such *extremis* was not excusable, first requires skimming off
a layer of judicial rhetoric liberally distributed over the judgment's surface. Lord
Coleridge felt it relevant to observe that self-sacrifice, a Christian virtue, may be
the 'plainest and highest duty'. But its relevance is not obvious, for clearly if all
had acted upon this ethical premise all might have died to no one's benefit. This
led the Lord Chief Justice to address the utilitarian justification of causing some
harm to secure an overall benefit of avoiding greater harm. Like Bramwell and
Blackburn in their evidence to the 1874 Homicide Bill's Select Committee, Lord
Coleridge rejected utility's claim. As well as ethically objectionable, the balancing
of harms notion was unworkable: 'By what measure is the comparative value of
lives to be measured? Is it to be strength, or intellect, or what?' A simple ledger
credit balance of three human lives saved at the expense of one was dismissed as
too rough-and-ready a calculation. Moreover, the dangers of fraudulent abuse
were clear in that such a defence could be made the 'legal cloak for unbridled
passion and atrocious crime'.[221] Neither could the defendants be excused on the
basis of a just concession to human weakness in the face of overwhelming adver-
sity, because the law was:

often compelled to set up standards we cannot reach ourselves, and to lay down rules
which we could not ourselves satisfy. But, a man has no right to declare temptation to

---

[219] *Ibid.*, 286. In contrast with self-defence or intervention to prevent a crime, where the party
harmed was (or reasonably appeared to be) acting unlawfully.

[220] Lord Coleridge's authority for such a construction of Stephen's views was Stephen himself.
See *Digest* (4th edn, 1887), 24n, and below.

[221] *Ibid.*, 288.

be an excuse, though he might himself have yielded to it, nor allow compassion for the criminal to change or weaken in any manner the legal definition of the crime.

Such comments indicate recognition that the futility of the threat of punishment or its infliction would not necessarily be a sufficient basis for the law to excuse an unlawful act, even though, as in this case, the immorality of the actions was by no means universally accepted. Insofar as this view was confined to killing, it was consistent with the weight of opinion relating to duress: this denied its applicability to murder and required an actor in such a predicament to submit to self-harm and reject self-preservation at the expense of the death of another innocent party.

Taking the path trodden in some earlier public commentaries, Lord Coleridge's favoured solution was Executive clemency in any cases where the law 'appears to be too severe'. Of course, not only would this avoid openly and formally endorsing (justifying) the killing of an innocent party, it would ensure that the law retained any residual power of deterrence that might operate on the mind of a party *in extremis*. Thus, at least the façade of an unqualified sanctity of life approach might be retained, with individual justice catered for through the less visible machinery of Executive intervention.[222] But, even allowing for the formidable demands of the task in *Dudley and Stephens*, the almost complete absence of expressed principle constituted a miserable failure of judicial nerve, with the court serving up little more than an abbreviated sermon on the duty of (futile) self-sacrifice. Undoubtedly, for both necessity and duress situations, demarcating an appropriate threshold for exculpation presented a truly testing normative issue. With its intrinsic restrictions, self-defence never posed such immediately obvious and awkward questions: the nature and circumstances of the threat and the appropriate response could be both predictably and formulaically identified without deeper reflection on the notion of voluntariness, the moral acceptability of sacrificing innocent life, and the appropriate ascription of criminal responsibility. *Dudley and Stephens* produced little certain beyond confirming that on those specific facts no defence of necessity was available.[223]

Yet despite manifest jurisprudential shortcomings, the judgment's contemporary reception in both the press and legal journals was overwhelmingly favourable, with the *Law Times* eulogizing the Lord Chief Justice's judgment as:

universally recognised as having been perfect in its way…[consisting] of a lucid exposition of law and an eloquent statement of the code of morality which should govern the

---

[222] After initial Executive misgivings, the defendants' death sentences were commuted to six months' imprisonment.

[223] In *Howe* (1987) AC 417, 453, the House of Lords held that *Dudley and Stephens* settled that necessity was not a defence to murder generally.

conduct of men whose lives are in peril, which he proved is in harmony with the principles of the common law.[224]

However, this did not reflect quite everyone's opinion. Most prominent amongst dissentients was Stephen, for whom the case could be written off as of exceedingly narrow legal import: 'I can discover no principle in the judgment...it depends entirely on its peculiar facts'.[225] Consequently, his post-*Dudley and Stephens* articulation of the necessity defence remained virtually unchanged from that produced before the case. Though agreeing with the verdict, Stephen registered extensive reservations over the reasoning. Most particularly, Lord Coleridge's religio-ethical assertions much troubled Stephen (by then a religious agnostic) appearing:

to me to base a legal conclusion upon a questionable moral and theological foundation...Whatever estimate may be formed of self-sacrifice, it seems to me to be a duty of which the law can take no notice, if indeed it is a duty at all, which is not a legal question.[226]

As a matter of principle then, unlike the court in *Dudley and Stephens*, Stephen adhered to a utility-driven, necessity justification.[227]

Following *Dudley and Stephens* into the beginning of the twentieth century there was no reasonably coherent judicial examination and response to the question of necessity as a general defence to criminal responsibility. Even one particular, very real, practical question stood unresolved: the legality of (relatively) frequent therapeutic abortions where pregnancy was terminated to preserve the mother's life. Up to the late 1930s Kenny could do no more than take up Stephen's

---

[224] (1884) 1 *LT* 109. For a thorough review of press and journal coverage, see Simpson, *op cit.*, 248–51.

[225] *Digest* (1887), 25n.

[226] *Digest* (1887), 25n. This strong distaste appears in more stinging, personal terms in a letter to his long-standing confidante Lady Grant Duff: 'In the *Fortnightly Review* for March you will see an article of mine, which I do not ask you to read, but which I fancy will have been read by Lord Coleridge not without a little quiet blasphemy. He is a most curious person in the matter of religious belief. He distinctly told me not very long ago that he considered the miraculous parts of the New Testament story 'intrinsically incredible', and had done so ever since he had first thought about such matters. Yet he is continually holding himself out as the most devout, eloquent and literal of Christians. I cannot say that I specially like him anyway, but I particularly dislike him in two of his favourite characters—viz. the poor worm Coleridge and Coleridge the humble Christian'. March 1884, Stephen Papers, quoted by S. White (1986) 10 *Crim. LJ* 168, 175.

[227] Yet Stephen's preferred basis for conviction lacks any real force: that the special verdict rested on a killing where rather than *certainty* of death, the defendants 'would *probably* not have survived'. Quite what would have been the qualifying level of likelihood of death from starvation Stephen failed to reveal. His commentary on the case where he expressly distinguishes well-known hypothetical examples provides little illumination. Cf. the rather aimless article 'Homicide by Necessity' by Stephen's son Herbert (1885) 1 *LQR* 51.

speculative view that therapeutic abortion or child destruction was never made the subject of prosecution because such 'choice of evils' was lawful by virtue of a broad but unarticulated defence of necessity.[228] It was an unresolved state of affairs which well demonstrated the extreme caution with which the whole area of necessity and moral involuntariness was generally approached; with both the subject of deep judicial concern at their indeterminateness and consequential risks of abuse. In relation to duress, though recognized as a defence by a thin body of pre- and early nineteenth-century judicial authority, further development had to wait until the 1930s.[229]

(4) *Mistake of fact*[230]

The criminal law's historical response to an actor's mistake as to the circumstances or consequences of his actions well exemplifies resolution of tensions between basic principle and broader policy. After showing limited early recognition of a mistake's power to negate elemental *mens rea* requirements, the criminal law confirmed that mistakes conceptually operated in the territory of 'defences'. Some institutional support for the power of mistakes to negate *mens rea* was given by Blackstone, who, following *Hale*,[231] regarded ignorance or mistake of fact, along with insanity and duress, as an example of where there was a 'defect of will': where the 'deed and the will [are] acting separately, there is not that conjunction between them, which is necessary to form a criminal act'.[232] Categorizing mistake in this fashion possibly suggests that the substance of mistake related to an offence's definitional element. But Blackstone's employment of 'will' and his reluctance to separate matters of definitional fault requirements from general defences make his views uncertain.

Austin offered a less equivocal *mens rea* analysis of the exculpatory effect of mistake: 'Although the *proximate* ground is ignorance or error, the *ultimate* ground is the absence of unlawful intention or unlawful inadvertence.[233] Similarly, Stephen in the *History* seemed to conceptualize the issue in this fashion: 'The effect of ignorance or mistake as to particular matters of fact connected

---

[228] Starting in *Outlines* (1904), 76n. Cf. Stephen's 1878 Code Bill, cl. 168 which sought to cover both abortion and child destruction with a defence resting on the necessity of saving the mother's life. Also *HCL*, ii, 110 and *Digest* (1887), 25n and 'Abortion and Infanticide', and 'Abortion', below, Ch. XII.

[229] *Att.-General* v. *Whelan* [1934] *IR* 518. And more broadly, Smith, *Lawyers, Legislators and Theorists*, 343–50.

[230] The response to mistake or ignorance of law (insofar as it is clearly distinguishable from fact) was met by the ancient maxim *Ignorantia juris, quod quisque tenetur scire, neminem excusat* (Blackstone, *Comms*, iv, 27).

[231] Hale employed the expression 'morally involuntary', 1 PC 42.

[232] *Comms*, iv, 27.

[233] *Lectures*, 495; and *Notes*, 1095. Similarly, Clark *op cit.*, 33 and Markby, *op cit.*, 138.

with an alleged offence is a matter which varies according to the definitions of particular offences.'[234] Yet his contemporary (pre-*Tolson*) *Digest* exposition was rather less clear, no doubt in part because here Stephen was attempting to give a concise, comprehensive account of the existing state of law. As a general proposition, a defendant was 'deemed to have acted under the state of facts which he in good faith and on reasonable grounds believed to exist...'.[235] Moreover, when speculating on the effect of mistake in relation to bigamy, Stephen distinguished appropriate cases for acquittal where there was more than a 'gratuitous belief, founded on ignorance', but a belief 'founded on positive evidence', such as where a 'woman saw her husband fall overboard in the middle of the Atlantic'.[236] Quite what Stephen was seeking to demonstrate here is not easy to pin down. He may have seen his hypothetical example as properly determined by the 'general common law principle' (stated above) which had the character of a distinct defence. Alternatively, and less likely, but consistent with his observations elsewhere, by contrasting 'gratuitous' mistakes with those founded on 'positive evidence' he may have been indirectly addressing problems of proof of the genuineness of mistake, where 'reasonable' went to the evidential issue rather than a substantive requirement. Such a construction would be reconcilable with accepting mistake as a method of negating subjective *mens rea*.

Legislative initiatives in the form of Wright's Code and the 1879 Draft Code Bill offer very limited conceptual illumination. In the former, mistake of fact is treated as one of a clutch of 'General Exemptions', with infancy, insanity and intoxication. Though satisfied by a mistake 'in good faith', Wright's single illustration of the provision's operation involves the justification of the forcible prevention of an offence, which, as the example notes, required 'reasonable caution under the circumstances' to qualify as a defence.[237] Revealingly, the 1879 Code omitted incorporation of a special general provision dealing with the effect of mistakes of fact largely because of concerns over the lack of certainty of the existing 'extremely obscure and fragmentary state' of the law.[238]

Anything resembling direct judicial authority begins late in the nineteenth century with Brett J.'s unchallenged general proposition in *Prince*: 'mistake of

---

[234] *HCL* ii, 116.

[235] *Digest* (1883), Art. 34. Stephen qualified the generality of this statement by allowing (following *Prince* and *Bishop*) that the legislature may define offences so as to deny the 'excuse' of a 'reasonable' mistake made 'in good faith'.

[236] *Ibid.*, 27n.

[237] Sections 14 and 40. Wright provided no commentary on these provisions.

[238] Report, 18–19 and s 19 of the Code. In various earlier Reports of the Criminal Law Commissioners, mistake was almost invariably dealt with as an element of self-defence in the context of homicide. Here, a mistake as to the need for self-defence was required to be 'reasonable' for any homicide to be 'justifiable'. For example, *Fourth Report* (1839), Art. 34.

fact on reasonable grounds, to the extent that, if the facts were as believed, the acts of the prisoner would make him guilty of no offence at all, is an excuse, and such an excuse is implied in every criminal charge'.[239] This he deduced from the claimed general expectation of *mens rea*. The significance of whether mistake was conceptualized as pertinent to fault requirements or as a discrete defence was arguably demonstrated later in *Tolson*. Prior case law seemed to suggest that a genuine belief in the non-subsistence of a former marriage owing to the spouse's believed death was sufficient to acquit a party charged with bigamy.[240] In construing the statutory offence of bigamy, the majority of the Court in *Tolson* appeared to regard a claim of mistake as to a spouse's death as an excusatory defence which needed to have been 'reasonable' (without fault) in the circumstances. Because of the generally claimed working presumption of the requirement of knowledge as a basis of criminality,[241] doctrinally this approach would have been an easier pill to swallow than the alternative of directly characterizing bigamy as an offence (at least partly) based on negligence.[242] As Cave J. observed:

at common law an honest and reasonable belief…has always been held to be a good defence. This doctrine is embodied in the somewhat uncouth maxim 'actus non facit reum nisi mens sit rea'…Honest and reasonable mistake stands in fact on the same footing as an absence of the reasoning faculty…'.[243]

Reaching similar conclusions, Stephen noted that his view was deduced from the general doctrinal requirements of *mens rea*.[244] Neither Cave nor Stephen JJ implied at any point that reasonableness was anything other than a substantive element of the 'defence'. Indeed, Wills J. distinguished the issue of reasonableness as a necessary element of a 'defence' of mistake from reasonableness of belief as evidence bearing on the question of the credibility of belief.[245]

---

[239] (1875) 2 LR 154, 170. As Stephen J. observed in *Tolson* (1889) 23 QB 168, 190, the principle was unchallenged in *Prince*, though the question of its legislative exclusion was the source of contention.

[240] See the case law discussed by Stephen, *Digest* (1883), 27n. Cf. *HCL*, ii, 117. In *Tolson*, where Stephen was the trial judge, with the express purpose of engineering an appellate ruling, he declined to admit as relevant evidence of mistake.

[241] See *Prince* (1875) 2 LR 154.

[242] Though cf. Stephen (1889) 23 QB 168, 185–7.

[243] *Ibid.*, 181. Of course, in one sense, 'absence of the reasoning faculty' would prevent the existence of *mens rea*. As in rape, see Ch. XII, below.

[244] 'I think it may be laid as a general rule that an alleged offender is deemed to have acted under the state of facts which he in good faith and on reasonable grounds believed to exist…I am unable to suggest any real exception to this rule, nor has one ever been suggested to me' (197–8).

[245] (1889) 23 QB 168, 178.

Boosted by a scattering of other *obiter* comments,[246] *Tolson* succeeded in steering *Russell*,[247] *Archbold*,[248] and Kenny away from the recognition by some earlier commentators that a simple mistake which addressed any elemental subjective fault requirements of an offence could negate liability. In the mode of *Tolson*, Kenny asserted that as a general proposition a mistake provided a 'good defence' because it showed 'no sufficient mens rea', but that a 'defence' of mistake could only arise where, inter alia, it was a 'reasonable one'.[249] It was a conclusion he reinforced by resort to negligence-based manslaughter cases, where, by definition, an *un*reasonable standard of behaviour was the essence of liability. In common with intoxication, a mistake's relevance to criminal responsibility defied confident classification. Conceptually, both look to negating *mens rea* requirements rather than exculpating on additional, extra-elemental grounds. Yet, historically, both have been compromised by a no-fault regulator whereby initial fault (of misjudgement or risking intoxication) may be substituted for the offence's own fault requirements. Such modification pushed them both in the conceptual direction of excuse.

2. PUNISHING PREPARATORY ACTIVITIES AND ASSISTANCE: COMPLICITY AND INCHOATE LIABILITY

For self-evident reasons, the law has had a long-standing interest in penalizing behaviour which while not immediately causing harm identified as criminal, in one way or another, was culpably associated with it. At different stages in the criminal law's development, three principal strategies evolved to punish such activities. Even before medieval times, early examples of complicity liability had emerged incriminating 'accomplices' or 'accessories', whose liability ultimately depended on the criminal actions of another, identified as the perpetrator or 'principal' offender. Criminalizing assisting or encouraging a 'principal'—one who most directly or immediately caused the specified criminal harm—could be achieved by either of two ways: general rules of complicity or through incorporating such

---

[246] Especially *Bank of New South Wales* v. *Piper* [1879] AC 383, 389 and *Rose* (1884) 15 Cox 540. Cf. e.g. *Halford* (1868) 11 Cox 88.

[247] (1909 edn) vol. 1, 101 quoting Cave J., 'Honest and reasonable mistake of fact stands in fact on the same footing as an absence of the reasoning faculty...or perversion of that faculty as in lunacy'. Before *Tolson*, successive editions of *Russell* did no more than repeat Blackstone's brief proposition.

[248] *Archbold* followed a similar pattern to *Russell*. For example, 14th edn (1859), 19–20; 22nd edn (1900), 31–2; 27th edn (1927), 21 which cited Cave J.'s proposition that the 'defence' of 'honest and reasonable' mistake was 'embodied in the somewhat uncouth maxim, *actus non facit*'.

[249] *Outlines*, (1904 edn) 65–7; 1919 edn, 66–8.

actions within the definitional scope of each substantive offence. The latter technique became particularly prominent in the eighteenth century where, rather than rely on complicity's general auxiliary liability, Parliament opted for highly detailed criminal enactments, embracing diverse activities leading up to and supporting the commission of designated criminal harm. This approach was gradually overtaken by the refinement of general complicity doctrine during the nineteenth century. Either way, each party was almost always open to the same level of punishment as that of the principal offender.[250]

These two strategies for criminalizing preliminary or supportive actions were supplemented by a third with the development of inchoate liability, principally between the seventeenth and nineteenth centuries. Inchoate offences (conspiracy, incitement, and attempt) and complicity liability, whilst overlapping, in that some actions may incur responsibility for both forms of criminality, were always completely distinct: complicity was derivative or parasitic, dependent on some form of principal offence and harm; whereas, inchoate offences were autonomous or freestanding, in no way reliant on subsequent criminal outcomes. As will be suggested when examining both types of liability, this fundamental distinction carried significant implications for their respective nineteenth-century development.

Complicity

The complex rules of complicity developed in relation to felonies. In the case of misdemeanours and treason, all parties were legally regarded as principal offenders. The apparent rationale for this was that misdemeanours were anciently regarded as insufficiently serious to warrant drawing distinctions between participants; whereas for treason any form of involvement was perceived as too serious to distinguish parties: its overwhelming 'heinousness' made the 'bare intent to commit...many times actual treason'.[251] And while such rhetorical reasoning failed to convince many commentators, including Foster,[252] the great practical benefit of the law's disinclination to recognize degrees of participation in treason and misdemeanours was the avoidance of ensnarement in the web of punishment and procedural rules established for parties to felonies. Most especially, in respect of punishment, from the eighteenth century until well into the nineteenth, the judiciary's policy of strict interpretation of penal statutes resulted in non-principal offenders enjoying benefit of clergy in capital offences far longer

---

[250] Of which the Waltham Black Act 1722 (onwards) was a notable example.

[251] Blackstone, *Comms*, iv, 35; *Tracey* (1703) 6 Mod. 30.

[252] Foster, *Crown Law*, 342. See also *Hale*, 1 PC 613 and *Hawkins*, 2 PC c. 29.

than principals.[253] More seriously, at one stage, trial and conviction of all non-principals could not occur until the principal had been sentenced, 'attained or hath the benefit of his clergy'. By the mid-eighteenth century, the inconvenience of this rule, fashioned by complicity's derivative nature, had been modified whereby all 'persons present aiding and abetting are principals'.[254] Thus, trial of principals of the 'second degree', as they became designated, could proceed without the previous conviction and sentencing of the principal in the first degree. However, trials of 'accessories before the fact', participants not present, remained subject to the old procedural inconvenience until the mid-nineteenth century, after a series of inept statutory interventions.[255]

Presence was associated with influence, or at least the potential to assist or encourage.[256] But the law did not 'require a strict, actual immediate presence, such a presence as would make him an eye or ear witness of what passeth'.[257] Increasingly during the nineteenth century the constructive nature of presence became apparent, thereby further diminishing the force of any claim of it being a legitimate basis distinguishing those present from those absent at the time of the principal offence.[258] As for modes of complicity, 'aid, abet, counsel or procure' were given general statutory recognition by the Accessories and Abettors Act 1861; their meaning long recognized as not 'governed by the bare sound' but as one of legal attribution,[259] spanned secondary behaviour that was initiatory or supportive, dominant or subordinate in character.[260] Of particular significance in delimiting complicity's reach was the nineteenth-century judicial approach

---

[253] *Foster*, 355.

[254] Beginning with Bromley CJ in *Griffith* (1553) 1 Plowd. 97, 75; and *Foster*, 348.

[255] 1702, Anne 2, c. 9; 1828 7 Geo. IV c. 64, s 9; 1848 11 & 12 Vict. c. 46, s 1 enacting that an accessory might be convicted even after the principal's acquittal. Re-enacted by the Accessories and Abettors Act 1861, ss 1 and 2.

[256] '[F]or the presence of the others is a terror to him that is assaulted, so that he dare not defend himself...'. Per Bromley CJ in *Griffith* (1553).

[257] *Foster*, 349–50.

[258] *Kelly* (1847) 2 Car. & K. 379. See e.g. *Soares* (1802) Russ. & Ry. 25; *Davis* (1806) Russ. & Ry. 113; *Owen* (1825) 11 Mood. 96; *Howell* (1839) 9 Car. & P. 437. Cf. *Vanderstein* (1865) 10 Cox 177 with *Greenwood* (1825) 2 Den. 453. The *Criminal Law Commissioners, Seventh Report* (1843) define presence as 'near enough to lend any help or assistance...or to encourage [the Principal] with the expectation of help or assistance', Art. 8. Similarly, *Second Report* (1846), Art 6.

[259] *MacDaniel*, 137.

[260] Accessories *after* the fact though anciently part of complicity, were recognized by the nineteenth century as conceptually distinct. An accessory after the fact was one who assisted a felon *after* completion of the offence, with a view to shielding him from apprehension and punishment. Nineteenth-century commentators (including the *Criminal Law Commissioners, Reports*, 1839 and 1846, and the 1879 *Code Bill Commission*) identified the nature of liability as relating to the interference with, or the obstruction of, public justice.

to potential manifestations of complicity by inactivity: mere presence at the commission of a crime, and omission to exercise an entitlement to control.

THE THRESHOLD OF LIABILITY

One aspect of a person's general entitlement not to involve himself in preventing an offence which fate may cause him to witness is freedom from complicity in the offence by virtue of simple inaction. The generality of this extends even to serious offences such as murder:

[T]herefore if A. happeneth to be present at a Murder for instance, and taketh no part in it, nor endeavoreth to prevent it, nor apprehendeth the murderer, nor levyeth hue and cry against him, this strange behaviour of his though highly criminal [in a moral sense], will not of itself render him either principal or accessory.[261]

Where, as in riot or affray, an offence is substantially made up of, or dependent upon, inter-party association, the temptation to see simple presence and likely encouragement as sufficient for complicity liability is obvious; but, in *Royce*,[262] it was a move resisted by English courts. Lord Mansfield accepted that: 'aiding and assisting is a matter of fact, and ought to be expressly found by the jury; and that a verdict which only finds that the defendants were present, but finds no particular act of force committed by them is not full enough for the court to judge upon'. Actual encouragement, in one form or another, of the principal was set as the minimum requirement for complicity in any offence. Although presence following some sort of prior association would be taken as evidence of encouragement, this was not inevitable.

Against a background of the relatively rapid judicial development of unlawful assembly (see below), the position of complicity remained unmodified, as confirmed towards the end of the nineteenth century in *Coney*,[263] a prime example of a 'public performance' offence. Here the Court for Crown Cases Reserved, made up of 11 judges, was (effectively) required to settle whether simple attendance at an illegal prize fight necessarily amounted to complicity in the same. The weight of relevant earlier decisions reviewed in the judgments inclined towards the opinion that:

[S]ome active steps must be taken by word or action with intent to instigate the principal or principals. Encouragement does not of necessity amount to aiding and abetting, it may be intentional or unintentional, a man may unwittingly encourage another in fact by his presence by misinterpreted words or gestures, or by his silence or non-interference

---

[261] *Foster*, 350; *Hale*, 1 PC 439; *Borthwick* (1779) 1 Doug. 207.
[262] (1767) 4 Burr. 2073.
[263] (1882) 8 QBD 534.

or he may encourage intentionally by expressions, gestures or actions intended to signify approval. In the latter case he aids and abets.[264]

This view was taken by eight[265] members of the court in *Coney*: that presence is no more than *prima facie* evidence from which a jury *could* infer encouragement by the party present at the principal offence. Therefore, finding as a matter of fact, that a spectator's silent presence encouraged the prize fight permitted a conviction for complicity, provided that person 'intended' to encourage. However, ambiguity runs throughout the judgments as to whether more than awareness of the natural encouraging effect of attendance was sufficient. Clearly those attending an illegal fight want the event to take place. But the casual passer-by, stopping out of 'mere curiosity' to view the spectacle, would not have 'intended' encouragement in a sufficiently positive manner as to incriminate.[266] Part of the pro-conviction minority view in *Coney* rested on the claim that, as the presence of spectators was a prerequisite of performance (or continued performance), attendance in a very real sense encouraged or facilitated the unlawful fight. Not without some logic, Pollock B.[267] denied any

true analogy between a crowd of persons voluntarily collected round a fight, and those who in a public street or elsewhere are present whilst an illegal act (the sight of which in itself cannot reasonably be supposed to give pleasure to any one) is going on. In the one case it is usually the bystanders collected around who create and who are responsible for the fight as a matter of interest and amusement to themselves. In the other, unless there be some overt act by gesture or word which denotes assistance or encouragement, it would be contrary to all reason to infer that the bystanders were taking any part in the illegal act.

But even accepting this, could a measurable degree of encouragement be individually attributed to each spectator? Objections of this kind were recognized and met (in a fashion) by Lord Coleridge CJ's[268] comment that

Practical wisdom, rather than scientific exactness, seems to me to be the thing to aim at in a branch of the law which is concerned with the affairs of men generally speaking in their simplest and least complicated forms. In such a case as this the spectators really make the fight; without them, and in the absence of any one to look on and encourage, no two men, having no cause of personal quarrel, would meet together in solitude to knock one another about for an hour or two.

---

[264] *Ibid.*, Hawkins J. at 557. Presumably applause would have been regarded as an 'expression...intended to signify approval'.

[265] e.g. Lord Coleridge CJ (at 568–9).

[266] The apparent view of Stephen J., at 550. See *Young* (1838) Car. & P. 644, where much the same is suggested.

[267] (1882) 8 QBD 534, at 564; and Mathew J., at 544.

[268] *Ibid.*, at 569.

The core difference between the majority and minority in *Coney* was that the majority regarded voluntary attendance at such an event as potentially *prima facie* evidence of encouragement of the illegal fight or performance; the minority saw attendance as conclusive evidence of complicity, of 'making the fight', unless rebutting evidence could be adduced.

In respect of omission to exercise control, as in principal liability, complicity also recognized that in certain circumstances a party may be incriminated by his failure to act. Again, as with principal liability and partly for similar reasons, both the basis and scope of complicity through omission were subject to a fair measure of uncharted uncertainty. For principals, the uniform feature of liability incurred through omission was the defendant's failure to perform particular acts where the criminal law deemed such performance a duty. In complicity, the common thread linking these areas of potential liability was the secondary party's entitlement to exercise some sort of civil right to control the principal's behaviour or the use he makes of the secondary party's property. Such distinct areas of omission-based liability might include ownership or control of premises or motor vehicles, and an employer's authority over his employees. Did the recognized bases creating duties to act in principal liability have relevance in settling the legitimate range of situations for complicity by omission?

Practically no authority on such questions existed before the twentieth century. An early twentieth-century example was *Du Cros v. Lambourne*[269] where an owner-passenger was convicted of abetting dangerous driving. Although normally taken to indicate that an owner's simple failure to exercise control over a driver may be sufficient to incriminate, the Court of Criminal Appeal's judgments contain ambivalent elements.[270] Lord Alverstone CJ,[271] after referring to the finding of the defendant having driven with the owner's 'consent and approval', would not

Attempt to lay down any general rule or principle, but having regard to these findings of fact it is in my opinion impossible to say that there was in this case no evidence of aiding and abetting.

Crucially unclear was whether Lord Alverstone regarded absence of any expressed disapproval as necessarily constituting 'consent and approval'. Beyond

---

[269] [1907] 1 KB 40.

[270] Darling J. appears to have based liability purely on the owner's failure to exercise his right of control [1907] 1 KB 40 at 46.

[271] [1907] 1 KB 40 at 45–6. The third member of the court, Ridley J., agreed with Lord Alverstone's judgment. Cf. *Lomas* (1913) 9 Cr App R 220 where the CCA appeared to assume that the temporary possessor of a jemmy was legally bound to return it to its owner (P) even though believing it would be used by P for a burglary.

this ownership case, the position of an employer's failure to control an employee lacked any degree of judicial attention until well into the twentieth century.[272]

THE INDIRECT PRINCIPAL: INNOCENT AGENCY

As will be seen when considering the (so-called) doctrine of common purpose, long established distinctions between parties present at the offence's commission and those absent may have continued to shape differing *mens rea* expectations for complicity in the nineteenth century. But instead of complicity liability, a criminally engaged party, whether present or not at the commission of an offence, could be a principal offender through the doctrine of innocent agency. Though established no later than the seventeenth century,[273] more detailed specification of complicity law in the nineteenth century entailed identifying the limits to which innocent agency might operate. The Criminal Law Commissioners provided a clear summary definition of the doctrine:

> Everyone is a principal in respect of a criminal act who either does it or causes it to be done otherwise than by a guilty agent...A party shall be deemed to cause a criminal act to be done...who wilfully causes it to be done...by any innocent person (whether such innocent person act unconsciously or under compulsion...)...and whether he be present or absent...[274]

As the extensive range of case law demonstrates, nineteenth-century courts showed very little inhibition in recognizing that criminal liability could be incurred through the immediate manipulated agency of any human regarded as 'innocent', in the sense of lacking the necessary *mens rea*, legal capacity, or status. The practical attractions of innocent agency were obvious, enabling courts to sidestep the familiar dangerous territory of complicity liability where no principal offender could be convicted; without innocent agency the law in some situations faced the uncomfortable prospect of the non-convictability of culpable, manipulative actors. Consequently, a very wide range of attribution was recognized under the doctrine during the nineteenth century, including forgery, larceny, fraud offences, libel, and poisoning.[275] However, whilst accepting the doctrine's

[272] Vicarious liability also relied on the existence of an employer/employee relationship, but, unlike complicity through omission, it did not require knowledge of the likely offence. It had long been clear that there is no general criminal vicarious liability: *Huggins* (1730) Ld. Raym, 1574; *Holbrook* (1878) 4 QBD 42. Where there is such necessary knowledge, employment situations may occur where both vicarious liability and complicity through omission arise. *Howells* v. *Wynne* (1863) 15 C.B. (NS) 3; *Roberts* v. *Preston* (1860) 9 C.B. (NS) 208, contains no discursive judgment and for that reason alone is of rather limited value.

[273] Anon, 1665, Kel. J 53 and e.g. *Coombes* (1785) 1 Leach 388.

[274] *Second Report* (1846), Arts 2 and 3, p. 19 and *Seventh Report* (1843), Arts 2 and 3, pp. 29–30, 34. And *East*, 1 PC 228.

[275] See the extensive case law cited in K. Smith, *A Modern Treatise on the Law of Criminal Complicity* (Oxford, 1991), 96, and innocent agency, generally, 93–110.

broad scope, any account of its conceptual nature was decidedly limited, leaving many basic aspects of the doctrine unremarked upon let alone resolved.

In many ways the most troubling theoretical concern in innocent agency was whether there were any limits to its application, especially in respect of the type of actions that might be attributed and offences where the perpetrators needed to satisfy a prescribed description. Both questions implicitly raised the question: in what sense did the remote manipulative principal *cause* the innocent agent's actions and criminal harm? What exactly was being attributed to the principal? Where the essence of an offence was bringing about a certain consequence, such as in murder, ascribing to the manipulator the causing of such an outcome constituted no immediately unreal or artificial claim. But where an offence expressly required an offender to possess a particular or quality, the courts resisted using the doctrine to convict a manipulator who failed to satisfy such requirements, even where the innocent agent did.[276] A less technical, more linguistic inhibition potentially restricting innocent agency's reach concerned ascribing highly personal actions of an agent to the principal, such as in rape. Here the judicial dilemma might be one of deploying innocent agency by resort to a surreal use of language or acquit morally culpable parties. Quite where the line might tolerably be drawn was indicated by a limited group of cases related to poaching offences of 'entering or being' on land under the Game Act 1831. Here, the courts insisted that such offences required the offender's 'bodily presence', the agency of a gun dog being held insufficient;[277] twentieth-century judges would display a far less inhibited view of the doctrine's scope.

THE MENTAL REQUIREMENT

Of more general and crucial significance was the matter of complicity's mental culpability requirements for principals in the second degree and accessories. Most fundamentally, what degree of commitment to the principal offence was needed from a secondary party? Did complicity liability demand that a secondary party acted purposefully, with the aim of the principal offence being committed? Such a confined approach to incrimination would demand a high level of involvement of secondary parties in principal liability, excluding many cases of casual, non-committed, involvement.

Russell's early nineteenth-century account of the mental element in complicity adopts the narrow approach of institutional writers, especially Foster's authoritative *Crown Law.* For principals in the second degree, liability required action

---

[276] Cf. *Groombridge* (1836) 7 Car. & P. 582; *Butt* (1884) 15 Cox 564; *Oliphant* [1905] 2 KB 67.

[277] See the review of the nineteenth-century decisions in *Pratt* v. *Martin* [1911] 2 KB 90 where Lord Alverstone CJ, although inclined to take a contrary view, felt compelled to follow earlier authorities. For twentieth-century developments, see *Cogan* [1976] QB 217.

that 'tended to give countenance, encouragement, and protection...to ensure the success of their common enterprise'.[278] Knowledge of the nature of the assistance or aid rendered was assumed from the standard illustrations given. While, as was typical of the period, no direct, detailed requirement was identified, the strong implication was that principals in the second degree must render assistance or encouragement with the purpose of ensuring success of the principal in the first degree's criminal venture. Consequently, as already seen, mere inactive presence at the commission of an offence without prior agreement would not incriminate.[279] Association by way of assistance or encouragement with the success of the principal's criminal objective was the essence of liability also for an accessory before the fact.[280] Therefore, it would follow that no liability should attach to the ordinary sale of articles known by the seller to be intended by the purchaser for use in the commission of a crime.[281] Retreat from this requirement of a high degree of association with the principal criminal venture began in the early twentieth century for accessories.[282] However, well before this, the position of principals in the second degree (and possibly accessories) was compromised by the 'common purpose' doctrine, under which a secondary party might incur liability for any offence that was a 'probable consequence of what was ordered or advised'.[283]

A standard formulation of the doctrine of common purpose was provided by Alderson B. in the mid-nineteenth-century case of *Macklin*.[284]

It is a principle of law, that if several persons act together in pursuance of a common intent, every act done in furtherance of such intent by each of them is, in law, done by all. The act, however, must be in pursuance of the common intent.

---

[278] *Russell* (1826), i: 22.

[279] Confirmed in *Bull and Schmidt* (1845) 1 Cox 281 and *Coney* (1882) 8 QBD 534.

[280] '...procure, counsel, command or abet...showing an express liking, approbation, or assent to another's felonious design', *Russell*, 29. Later confirmed in *Bernard* (1888) 1 F & F 240, and arguably *Fretwell* (1862) Le. and Car. 16; *Taylor* (1875) LR 2 CCR 147 and Stephen, *Digest* (1883), 32. On the interpretational problems of *Fretwell*, see Smith, *A Modern Treatise*, 146.

[281] Supported by a collection of eighteenth and nineteenth-century authorities affirming the ability of suppliers of goods or services facilitating crimes to enforce contracts under which they were provided. For example *Hodgson* v. *Temple* (1813) 5 Taunt. 181 and *Pellecart* v. *Angell* (1835) 2 C.M. & R. 311.

[282] *Cook* v. *Stockwell* (1915) 84 LJKB and *Cafferata* v. *Wilson* [1936] 3 All ER 149.

[283] *Foster*, 370. Foster's comments were directed at accessories before the fact. Although clearly most relevant to circumstances where the secondary party is not present, it could also apply to principals in the second degree. Indeed, the potential for specifically uncomtemplated complicity liability was already contained in the well-established rules incriminating all parties for any offence committed by any person either in consequence of a 'general resolution against all opposers' or 'common design to execute any criminal purpose'. For example *Russell* (1826), i, 24–5; *Criminal Law Commissioners, Seventh Report* (1843), Art. 16. Here, rather than based on some form of subjective contemplation and endorsement, complicity rested on a non-specific 'blank cheque' basis.

[284] (1838) 2 Lew. CC 225.

According to Pollock CB in the later case of *Skeet*,[285] the doctrine's function and nature, at least in earlier times, was plainly a form of collective felony-murder

[arising] from the desire on the part of the old lawyers to render all parties who are jointly engaged in the commission of a felony responsible for deadly violence committed in the course of its execution. But that doctrine has been much limited in later times, and only applies in cases of felony, where there is no[286] evidence of a felonious design to carry out the unlawful purpose at all hazards, and whatever may be the consequences.

However, whatever perceived practical need may have motivated the doctrine's creation, its nature, status, and relationship to general complicity concepts and requirements remained vague well into the twentieth century.

Resort to the terminology of common purpose ('common design') occurred most frequently where the issue was the liability of an abettor for an offence additional or collateral to the primary principal offence. Most typically, during the course of a robbery an intervening third party was killed by one of a group of robbers. When determining liability for such collateral offences, the central question was whether, if at all, the basis of responsibility was different from that used in settling liability for the primary offence. More particularly, in relation to specificity of knowledge, did the *mens rea* necessary for complicity in the primary offence in any way act as a substitute for or dilute the *mens rea* that would normally be required for the complicity in the collateral offence?

As the comments of Pollock CB in *Skeet* suggest, common purpose decisions mostly concerned collateral liability for homicide, although many reported examples existed involving other offences.[287] However, it is in relation to homicide that the doctrine attracted the most frequent and careful judicial consideration. Up to the early nineteenth century, common purpose doctrine developed with increasing particularity the enquiry into what the principal in the second degree knew of (or should have known of) how the principal might act. Reported decisions suggest a three-stage development: from constructive liability for collateral offences through the qualifying guilt of complicity in the primary offence, followed by the application of an objective probable consequences test[288] and,

---

[285] (1866) 4 F & F 931.

[286] The word 'no' is obviously a slip of the judicial tongue or reporting error.

[287] e.g. theft: *Standley* (1816) Russ. & Ry. 305; *Bolster* (1909) Cr App R 81; possession of housebreaking implements: *Thompson* (1869) 11 Cox 362; possession of weapons: *Goodfellow* (1845) 1 Den. 81.

[288] For riot or affray: 'if several persons come to a house with intent to make an affray, and one be killed, while the rest are encouraged in riotous and illegal proceedings, though they are dispersed in different rooms, all will be principals in murder': Chitty, *Criminal Law* (1816), i: 256–7, citing *Hale*, 1 PC 439; *Hawkins*, 2 PC 29, section 28; *East*, 1 PC 258. See also e.g. *Griffith* (1553) 12 Plowd. 97; *Lord Mohun* (1692) Holt K.B. 479; *Wallis* (1703) 1 Salk. 334; *Edmeads* (1828) 3 Car. & P. 390; *Cooper* (1846) Q.B. 533.

later, some form of subjective requirement.[289] But no tolerably clear authoritative principle emerged from case law. Typical of the division in judicial opinion was that relating to the responsibility of an accomplice for violence of a confederate in carrying out a robbery. Some decisions held an accessory liable for any principal action performed in pursuance of the common purpose of robbery,[290] while others required positive evidence of a common design to execute the common purpose with all necessary force.[291]

Clearly influential was the individual judicial attitude taken towards constructive liability and its legitimate role in complicity. Pollock CB's observations in *Skeet* mark some attempt to limit the harshness of the felony-murder rule in complicity to circumstances where there had been agreement to use serious force. But such comments were exceptional, leaving unresolved the question of the extent of accessorial liability for acts unforeseen or beyond the confines of the common purpose. Most particularly, was there responsibility for overzealous principal actions which, although outside the common design, were carried out in its pursuance and were objectively foreseeable? The contentiousness and uncertainty surrounding the answer to this important question, and the effects on it of particular criminal jurisprudential predilections, are revealed by the treatment given to it in successive editions of *Russell*. Before and during Greaves's editorship (the 1843 and 1865 editions)[292] no reference is made in *Russell* to such an objective principle in connection with common purpose.[293] However, Samuel Prentice, Greaves's successor in the 1877 edition, inserted at the end of the common purpose section a purported summary[294] of the law:

It is submitted that the rule of law is, that where several persons engage in the pursuit of a common unlawful object, and one of them does an act which the others ought to have known was not improbable to happen in the course of pursuing such common unlawful object, all are guilty.

No supporting authority is cited for the proposition and no relevant new case law appears to have been reported between Greaves's last edition of *Russell* and Prentice's. This raises the possibility that the suggested objective probable consequence rule could have been editorial kite-flying by Prentice. Bearing in mind *Russell*'s role as the standard work of reference for Bench and Bar in English

---

[289] The exact nature of the subjective element is often far from clear; see e.g. *Collison* (1837) 4 Car. & P. 565; *Franz* (1861) 2 F. & F. 580.

[290] e.g. *Bowen* (1841) Car. & M. 149; *Harvey and Caylor* (1843) 1 Cox 21.

[291] *Price* (1858) 8 Cox 96; *Luck* (1862) 3 F. & F. 483; *Caton* (1874) 12 Cox 624.

[292] 3rd and 4th edns. *Skeet* was decided in the year following publication of the 4th edition.

[293] See Book i, Ch. 2, and Book iii, Ch. 1, in both editions.

[294] 5th edn, 164.

criminal law during the nineteenth century (and for much of the twentieth too) the significance of Prentice's modification was potentially considerable.

In one sense Prentice's addition was no more than adoption of Foster's position which applied the rule to accessories before the fact:

So whenever the principal goeth beyond the terms of the solicitation, if in the event the felony committed was a probable consequence of what was ordered or advised, the person giving such orders or advice will be an accessory to that felony.[295]

Whatever historical basis might have existed for their distinct treatment, by this time was being ignored. The complexity of the position on possible criminal liability for a 'probable consequence' was compounded by apparently distinct rules relating to 'variation' by principals. In Foster's authoritative articulation of the common law attitude:

If the principal totally and substantially varieth, if being solicited to commit a felony of one kind he wilfully and knowingly committeth a felony of another, he shall stand single in that offence, and the person soliciting will not be involved in his guilt...But if the principal in substance complieth with the temptation, varying only in circumstance of time or place, or in the manner of execution, in these cases the person soliciting to the offence will, if absent be an accessory before the fact, if present a principal.[296]

The outcome of combining the two sets of principles was that any deliberate substantial departure from the principal offence contemplated would free a secondary party unless the variant offence was a 'probable consequence' of the act of complicity. Thus, killing in the course of a robbery by striking the victim with an unconcealed club would generate 'enhanced' complicity liability; whereas killing with a gun, whose possession was unknown to the other parties, would not entail complicity.[297] Seeking to put an end to any lingering nice distinctions between accessories before the fact and principals in the second degree, the 1879 Criminal Code Bill took Prentice's approach by effectively applying the 'probable consequence' rule to all secondary parties.[298]

Judicial ambivalence and inconsistencies in respect of the operation of a probable consequence rule continued into the twentieth century for much the same reasons that had caused a similar state of affairs in relation to manifestations of constructive liability—unlawful act manslaughter and felony murder. For like these two forms of 'enhanced' criminal liability, a probable consequence rule

[295] At 370; followed in *Russell* (1826) 33 and subsequent editions.

[296] At 369. Foster's account of variation rules was adopted by all standard criminal law texts throughout the nineteenth century. No reported case law sought to elaborate Foster's statement. See Smith, *A Modern Treatise*, Ch. 7.

[297] See Stephen, *Digest* (1877), Art. 41.

[298] Sections 71–2.

in complicity was also implicitly based on a risk rationale: that the culpability attached to the voluntary engagement in one level of criminality exposed the actor to a further range of liability for unintended or even unforeseen harmful consequences. Two early twentieth-century decisions illustrate the continued absence of a clear and consistent approach in this area. First, the Court of Criminal Appeal in *Rubens*[299] appeared to apply automatically the felony murder rule to accomplices without enquiring what level of violence had been contemplated by the accomplice as part of the common purpose to rob. In doing so, the Court of Criminal Appeal chose to ignore nineteenth-century authorities, directly brought to the court's attention,[300] requiring secondary parties to 'constructive homicide' to have either agreed to fatal levels of violence or to carry out the common design 'at all hazards'.

Four years after *Rubens*, in *Pridmore*[301] the Court of Criminal Appeal ruled on the nature of common purpose where the charge was shooting with intent to murder, arising from a poaching incident in which a bailiff was shot. What is most significant is the reaction of Pickford J. (one of the court's three members) to the prosecution's suggestion, quoting Prentice's addition to *Russell*, that where a common unlawful design is pursued each party is responsible for every act of another confederate which he 'ought to have known was not improbable to happen'. Responding, Pickford J. pointed out, 'If such an act is probable in the course of night poaching there would be a common purpose in every case'. In general tenor, the court's judgment was towards requiring evidence of at least an implied understanding of the use of force to resist apprehension, but no clear indication was offered as to *how* much force must have been contemplated. No such ambiguity was found in the late 1920s' factually similar case of *Pearce*, with Avory J. for the Court of Criminal Appeal insisting on evidence of an arrangement to assault with a gun or other weapons *and* 'also to resist apprehension at all costs'.[302]

Beyond matters of mental culpability, several aspects of complicity's derivative[303] nature underwent scrutiny and a degree of refinement in the nineteenth

---

[299] (1909) 2 Cr App R 163.

[300] *Price* (1858) 8 Cox 96 and *Caton* (1874) 12 Cox 624. Also *Skeet* (1866) 4 F & F 931.

[301] (1913) 8 Cr App R 198.

[302] (1929) 21 Cr App R 79 at 81. The charge was assault of a bailiff by clubbing him with the stock of a gun. In *Short* (1932) 23 Cr App R 170, as in *Pridmore*, the conviction appealed was shooting with intent to murder. In the view of Lord Hewart CJ 'the question really is, whether there was any evidence fit to go to the jury that the appellant was a party to a common design to affect the felonious purpose, if necessary, by the use of firearms'—possibly a higher degree of culpability than may have been stipulated in *Pridmore*.

[303] A fundamental aspect of complicity's derivative nature was the arguable conceptual need for secondary party assistance or encouragement to have contributed or made a difference to the

century. This was a process driven by the criminal law's practical need to reach instigators and those rendering assistance where the party actually performing the proscribed activity was not convicted or was free of liability.[304] Part of the law's response lay in the general rules of evidence. Consequently, in *Hughes*[305] acquittal of an alleged principal offender was held not to prevent the subsequent conviction of the secondary party, even though tried by the same jury as acquitted the principal. However, as a consequence of entrenched complicity doctrine, for conviction of a secondary party at least admissible evidence of the commission of a principal offence by *someone* needed to be adduced.[306] In short, complicity liability was derived from a principal *offence* not simply the proscribed behaviour or harm.

Yet this derivative quality, according to extensive institutional authority, still permitted different levels of liability between principals in the first and second degree. As Hawkins noted in the case of a homicidal attack carried out by two or more parties, 'if there were malice in the abettor, and none in the person who struck the party, it will be murder as to the abettor, and manslaughter only as to the other'.[307] Thus, if the party who struck the fatal blow could successfully plead the partial defence of provocation they would be guilty of manslaughter, whereas any other party present would be open to conviction for murder. Yet, at the same time, the ancient distinction between secondary parties present at the 'fact' and those absent, or before the fact, meant that it was an 'uncontroverted rule' that an accessory before the fact could not be convicted of a 'higher crime' than the principal.[308] This firmly embedded distinction between principals in the second degree and accessories before the fact survived beyond the nineteenth century,

principal's actions. The need for this form of linkage between principal and secondary actions almost completely lacked pre-twentieth-century judicial or theoretical analysis. See Smith, *A Modern Treatise*, Ch. 3 and S. Kadish, 'Complicity, Cause and Blame' (1985) 73 *Cal. LR* 324.

[304] In many situations the doctrine of innocent agency was available, or the emerging inchoate offence of incitement; however, this course considerably restricted the level of punishment that might be imposed. Liability of a woman as a principal for rape under innocent agency would have been unlikely, but secondary liability was held to be possible, *Ram* (1893) 17 Cox 609 and *Lord Baltimore* (1768) 4 Burr. 2179. Similarly, for a boy under the age of legal capacity, *Eldershaw* (1828) 3 Car. & P. 396.

[305] (1860) Bell CC 242. Even if the evidence adduced at both trials were the same, a jury may form different views of its probative value.

[306] *Vaux's Case* (1591) 4 Co. Rep. 44a; *Hawkins*, 2 PC 29, s 11; and e.g. *Crisham* (1841) Car. & M. 187, and *Gregory* (1867) 10 Cox 459. Macaulay's Indian Penal Code ignored the derivative nature of common law complicity, providing that 'A person abets an offence who abets either the commission of an offence, or the commission of an act which would be an offence if committed by a person capable of committing an offence...' (s 108).

[307] 2 PC c. 29, s 7. Similarly, *Hale*, 1 PC 437–8, and *East*, 1 PC 350 II, 666. And *Lord Mohun* (1692) Holt KB 479.

[308] 2 PC c. 29, s 15. Similarly, Blackstone, *Comms*, iv, 36.

unaffected by statutory interventions aimed at ensuring that both in respect of trial procedure and punishment no distinction was recognized between second-ary parties.[309] The frequent judicial claim that the acts of one principal was the act of all present, whether in the first or second degree, clearly extended beyond a rhe-torical device to avoid the earlier trial difficulties, and represented a real assump-tion as to the greater culpability of parties present.

A final aspect of complicity quite unique[310] to criminal liability generally, was the possibility of a (potential) secondary party withdrawing from liability before the commission of the principal offence. While its recognition could be traced back to at least the sixteenth century,[311] a clutch of nineteenth-century decisions provided modern endorsement of the defence. However, such case law and insti-tutional authorities provided only the most limited guidance on the defence's rationale.[312] No indication was offered as to whether the defence's rationale was one of recognizing a party's diminished culpability or to encourage acts of withdrawal, thereby reducing the chances of a principal offence. Certainly, nine-teenth-century case law demanded no more than actions implying withdrawal.[313] Even earlier authority[314] requiring 'timely' actions received no further elaboration. A strong contrast to this state of affairs was offered by the overtly instrumentalist demands of the Criminal Law Commissioners'[315] formulation of the defence.

No person shall be deemed to be a procurer or promoter of any criminal act or omission who shall, previously to such act or omission, abandon his purpose, provided that previ-ously to such act or omission he shall countermand the criminal act or omission, and use

---

[309]   See ss 2 and 8 of the Accessories and Abettors Act 1861. Both the *Criminal Law Commissioners Seventh Report* (1843) p. 30, and Art. 14; *Second Report* (1846), Arts 2 and 11) and the 1879 *Code Bill Commission*, s 71. Macaulay's Indian Penal Code permitted the fixing of a secondary party's liability according to individual mental culpability (ss 38 and 110). Wright's Jamaican Draft Code appeared to follow the same course (ss 12(ii) and 32).

[310]   In respect of a possible defence of withdrawal the positions of complicity and inchoate liabil-ity are conceptually quite distinct. For inchoate liability, the common law never recognized a defence of withdrawal as withdrawing actions could, of necessity, only occur after liability had been incurred. For complicity, withdrawal relates to actions preceding the fixing of a secondary party's liability by commission of the principal offence.

[311]   *Saunders and Archer* (1576), 2 Plowd. 473.

[312]   Of course, if the potential secondary party was able to expunge the effects of prior actions (e.g. by recovering equipment lent to another in order to carry out an offence) then rather than a *defence*, this would constitute a denial of the *actus reus* of complicity. A true defence of with-drawal implicitly accepts that complicitous actions occurred by the secondary party. On the devel-opment of withdrawal's conceptual basis, see K. Smith, 'Withdrawal in Complicity: A Restatement of Principles' [2001] *Crim. LR* 767.

[313]   Edmeads (1828) 3 Car. & P. 389; *Young* (1838) 8 Car. & P. 644; *Phillips* (1848) 3 Cox 225. Also, Foster, 354. Saunders and Archers suggested the need for express notice; *Goodspead* (1911) 6 Cr App R 133 required something beyond failing to fulfil a promise to assist.

[314]   *Hale*, 1 PC 618; *Russell* (1826) 34.

[315]   *Seventh Report* (1843), Art. 12; *Second Report* (1846), Art. 9.

his utmost endeavour to prevent the doing of such act, or to procure the due performance of the act the omission to do which is criminal; and provided also that the party guilty of such act or omission shall know that such act or omission is so countermanded.

Rigorous requirements of this nature were clearly motivated by preventative ambitions, aimed at lowering the likelihood of the principal executing the planned offence.

Inchoate Liability: Expanding the Notion of Criminal Harm: Attempt and Conspiracy

ATTEMPT

(1) *Recognition of a general offence of attempt*

One of the criminal law's most significant nineteenth-century conceptual developments was confirmation in *Higgins*[316] of the distinct general offences of attempt and incitement.[317] For although 17 years earlier in *Scofield*[318] Lord Mansfield had recognized attempt as a form of common law liability, it is clear from the content and tone of discussion in *Higgins* that the import of *Scofield* had not been fully registered in the years following.[319] The considerable importance of *Scofield* and *Higgins* lay in their recognition that the common law should concern itself with, and assert jurisdiction over, a range of behaviour hitherto almost exclusively the subject of specific statutory enactments.

Recognition of the general concept of attempt was justified in the broadest terms in both *Scofield* and *Higgins*. In the former, Lord Mansfield asserted that:

so long as an act rests in bare intention, it is not punishable by our laws; but immediately where an act is done, the law judges, not only of the act done, but of the intent with which

---

[316] (1801) 2 *East* 5. While *Higgins* was a case where incitement was the nature of the offence involved, the judgments proceeded on the basis of taking (and confirming) the attempt case of *Scofield* as authority; no subsequent attempt decisions disputed the standing of *Higgins* as an attempt case.

[317] Incitement was an inherently simpler form of liability and, consequently, did not generate the conceptual and policy problems encountered in attempt. Moreover, in part, its criminality was already subject to penal sanctions as a form of complicity.

[318] (1784) Cald. 397. The strict technical question in *Scofield* was whether attempted misdemeanours were criminal. Reports prior to *Scofield* show early indications of a general form of attempt liability for felonies but not conceptually clearly separated from incitement and conspiracy, Hale, 1 PC 532 and 568; Blackstone, *Comms*, iv, 21. Also Curran (1931) 19 *Georgetown LJ* 197. The only previous form of criminality resembling attempts covered by the criminal law were certain forms of treason, e.g. imagining or compassing the sovereign's death. For the Star Chamber origins of all forms of inchoate liability, see T. G. Barnes [1977] *Crim. LR* 325 and note *The Case of Duels* (1615) 2 St. Tr. 1033.

[319] In relation to offences such as larceny and robbery, the practical value of a general offence of attempt was patent; see e.g. *Cherry's Case* (1781) 2 *East* 556 and *Farrel's Case* (1787) 2 East 557. In both cases acquittals followed findings of an incomplete 'carrying away'. The intervening decision in *Scofield* (1784) had no apparent impact on *Farrel's Case*.

it is done; and if it is coupled with an unlawful and malicious intent, though the act itself would otherwise have been innocent, the intent being criminal, the act becomes criminal and punishable.[320]

After hearing *Higgins* 'twice argued' by two different teams of counsel for both prosecution and defendant, 'first in Trinity term' and then in the following Michaelmas term (from which the report is derived), judgments were delivered, led by Lord Chief Justice Kenyon flanked by other members of the King's Bench. The basis of the decision in *Higgins* was both more explicit than in *Scofield* and subject to a division of opinion between the four sitting judges. Lord Kenyon saw liability for attempt and incitement as founded on behaviour that has a 'tendency, as it is said, to breach of the peace': in essence it was an endangerment-to-social-order rationale, with similar views also expressed by Grose and Le Blanc JJ. However, Lawrence J. justified liability by invoking the wider, somewhat circular, empowering doctrine whereby 'all offences of the public nature, that is, all such acts or attempts as tend to the prejudice of the community, are indictable'.[321] It was a juridical formula employed by Lawrence in *Phillips*, a subsequent attempt decision, and by Lord Hewart CJ in the controversial public mischief case of *Manley* 130 years later.[322]

Such a broad basis not only embraced the idea of action endangering or risking proscribed criminal harm, arguably it might also be taken to serve the further claim that some attempts constituted harm by virtue of disturbing social order; for example, as later confirmed in unlawful assembly, or by threatening the recognized interests of individuals, as in assault, where causing apprehension in the victim had long been considered criminal harm. Speculation of this nature is to be set against the background of extensive statutory provisions which for many years, before and after the establishing of the general concept of criminal attempt, criminalized not only actions in the nature of attempt, but also more remote activities viewed as sufficiently predictive of future criminal action to warrant punishment: more specifically, possessional and vagrancy offences.[323] Essentially, as will be seen, *Scofield* and *Higgins* established the common law's general concern with, and jurisdiction over, forms of behaviour and harms only previously the subject of specific legislative intervention. The two

---

[320] *Scofield* (1784) Cald., 402–3.

[321] (1801) 2 *East* 5. Cf. the King's Bench decision in *Sydley* (1664) 1 Keble 620, claiming such jurisdiction.

[322] (1805) 6 *East* 464 and [1933] 1 KB 529.

[323] In part repeating, as well as strengthening earlier legislation, the Vagrancy Act 1824 offences of loitering with intent (s 4) criminalized suspicious preliminary or preparatory activities seen as likely to lead to the commission of a felony. Also later, the Prevention of Crime Act 1871, s 7, criminalizing similar behaviour.

decisions marked a significant departure from the common law's entrenched consequentialist approach to criminality, whereby manifest or tangible harm acted as the 'fulcrum' of liability, an emphasis which had led most notably to constructive forms of homicide.

Extra-judicially, Bentham stood alone amongst late eighteenth to early nineteenth-century commentators in offering reflections and prescriptions on attempt liability. At a general level he recognized the benefits of the pre-emptive, interventionary ability provided by preparatory or attempt offences ('accessory offences'): 'a vigilant legislator, like a skilful general, takes care to reconnoitre all the exterior posts of the enemy, in order to interrupt his enterprises'.[324] Indeed, in his legislative guidelines, Bentham maintained that 'wherever a principal offence is created, all preparatory acts and simple attempts ought also to be pro-hibited', and so far as feasible they should be the subject of 'specific description'.[325] Of course, general attempt liability presented Bentham with the horror of uncertain law, where the precise limits of liability could not be ascertained in advance, thereby creating 'that monster of iniquity an ex post facto law'.[326] Most germanely, Bentham well appreciated the preparation/attempt distinction and the problem of proximate acts:

all attempts, all motions previous to consummation, may be considered as preparations. By attempt, we understand action, carried beyond mere preparation, but…falling short of execution of the ultimate design, in any part…[But] between preparations and attempts the distinction will (it is evident) be, in many cases, very indeterminate; and in different cases it will be widely different.[327]

Quite how the law should deal with this indeterminacy, Bentham does not tell the reader.

Notions of what constituted harm, and the criminal law's appropriate scope or reach, permeated efforts to identify the nature of the attempt's 'act' requirement: did it have an evidential function, demonstrating the actor's subjective criminal-ity, or did actions *become* criminal because of the actor's state of mind? In other words, it was a question of whether culpable *actors* or dangerous or threatening *acts* were the basis of the criminal law's intervention. As already noted, *Higgins*, along with other early attempt cases, indicate the primacy of the harmful and dangerous quality of an action. Certainly, the primitive state of policing and

---

[324] 'Principles of the Penal Code', *Theory of Legislation* (ed. C.K. Ogden, 1931).

[325] 'Penal Code', 426.

[326] *Rationale of Judicial Evidence*, Bowring, *Works*, vii: 20. Bentham wrote the work between 1802 and 1812. Edited by J. S. Mill and published in 1827.

[327] *Rationale*, 20–1. See also A. Hammond's widely distributed, *Criminal Code* (1829), ii: Pt II, 811, showing keen awareness of the proximity question.

detection of crime limited the weight of an interventionary power justification for criminalizing attempts. But whatever the judicial qualms over recognition of a general concept of attempt, the legislature had for some time accepted that particular examples of such conduct were fitting subjects for criminal sanctions. One important illustration was assault with intent to rob,[328] covering behaviour later regarded as attempted robbery. Yet even here, as was the general legislative practice, the permutations for committing the offence were specified in extensive detail in respect of the means employed ('offensive weapons or instruments'), the nature of actions ('assault, or... by menaces, or in or by any forceable or violent manner'), and the criminal objective ('demand any money, goods or chattels... with felonious intent').

This practice of highly specific definitional elements became, in part, a legislative device to counter the judicial practice of strict statutory construction of penal laws, which in turn tightened the judicial focus when construing the ambit of offences—each practice (judicial and legislative) fed on and provoked the other. Furthermore, it might be argued that such a legislative culture, as was especially entrenched in relation to eighteenth-century penal legislation, would caution the judiciary against introducing the almost open-ended expansion of the common law's reach by recognition of a general concept of criminal attempt: specific legislative enactment could be taken as marking out social and political need, and the appropriate medium of such expanded criminalization; this was true of robbery's treatment in the Malicious Injuries Act (Lord, Ellenborough's Act) 1803.[329]

Legislative developments of this nature again prompt the question: why enact these provisions soon after the establishment of common law liability for attempt? In the case of attempted murder, wounding, and robbery, why not take up this freshly established conceptual device to fill the perceived lacunae spoken of by Lord Ellenborough and met by the Act? As Lord Chief Justice of the King's Bench, and previously Attorney-General, Lord Ellenborough was uniquely

---

[328] (1734) 7 Geo. II c. 21. Punishable with seven years' transportation.

[329] This relationship of the growth of common law jurisdiction alongside legislative provision, is well illustrated by the passing of Lord Ellenborough's Act, soon after the decision in *Higgins*. The legislation was intended to extend the 'Coventry Act' of 1670, under which various forms of ambush-based woundings were made capital, non-clergyable, offences. According to Lord Ellenborough, the confined nature of the Coventry (Ambush) Act was such as to leave relatively untouched 'assaults with intent to rob, and those made with intent to murder, the latter of which, it appeared, at present, amounted only to a misdemeanour', *Parliamentary Register* (1803), ii: 471. The debate report in *Parliamentary History*, 36, 1801–3, 1246 (1820) credits Lord Ellenborough with also referring to the need to make 'attempting to fire a gun or pistol, with intent to kill, although the attempt failed by the weapon's missing fire, by flashing in the pan, or other accident, a capital felony'. At no stage did the bill meet with principled opposition. On Ellenborough's role in the parliamentary passage of this statutory clarification of the offence of abortion, J. Keown, *Abortion, Doctors and the Law* (Cambridge, 1988), Ch. 1, *passim*.

placed to have initiated amongst the judiciary a calculated expansion of the use of common law attempt liability. The existence of prior legislation in the form of the Coventry Act was one clear inhibition; the Act could be seen as raising some sort of presumption that this territory was to be governed by legislation, and not developed judicially. A second more obvious and practical reason was touched on in Lord Ellenborough's First Reading speech in the Lords: as confirmed in *Higgins*, attempt liability was only a misdemeanour, thereby attracting, in contemporary terms, a relatively light penalty,[330] and certainly excluded any capital threat. However, if that was the only serious objection to using the common law route to cover this form of liability, then a general provision arming courts with the power to punish all attempts as severely as that of the completed offence in question could have been enacted. Therefore, it appears very likely that there were other, less tangible, grounds for wishing to resort to direct specific legislation rather than choose the judicial 'legislative' route.[331]

But speculation of this nature presumes a full doctrinal embrace of attempt that neither existed in the judicial psyche, nor in that of most commentators of the day. The terminology itself, of 'felony' and 'misdemeanour', was then still redolent with significance beyond matters of sanction. *Serious* manifestations of criminality were felonies—'felonious'; whereas misdemeanours would, for some time, carry the connotation of less serious criminal infringements.[332] More substantially, the juristic and legislative cultures of the time were still very much suspicious of, if not out and out resistant to, the formulation and employment of comprehensive definitions of offences, capable of dealing with a fair range of disparate situations. The nineteenth-century treatment of murder was just one striking illustration of this accretive, case-by-case approach, voluminously carried forward by *East* and *Russell*; and, as the 1861 consolidations demonstrated, considerable definitional specificity was still a powerful legislative expectation.

A final connected potential ground for the hesitant development of attempt shows up in *East*'s treatment, or rather non-treatment, of attempt. Despite its prominence, both in terms of length of report and weighty judicial presence, no reference to *Higgins* appears in *East*.[333] The reason for its complete absence

---

[330] Punishment was a fine or imprisonment, or both, depending on the level of the offence, without forfeiture. Higgins was originally sentenced to two years' imprisonment and the pillory. Legislation in 1827 discriminated between robbery (which remained a capital felony) and assault with intent to rob, a felony subject to a minimum of seven years' transportation or up to four years in prison, 7 and 8 Geo. IV c. 29, vi.

[331] It was more than simply the presence of the abortion provision, as the enactment of other attempt provisions during the period shows.

[332] Even then there certainly existed offences of substance that were misdemeanours, such as libel and conspiracy.

[333] The Addenda of *Pleas of the Crown* contains reports of cases up to early 1803. Cf. 1 PC 411 and East's own report, n. 321 above.

is difficult to identify. Almost as baffling is the very short shrift given in *East* to *Scofield*, with absolutely no discussion of the general notion of attempt. In terms of negative influence, as the leading criminal law practitioner's treatise of the time, *East*'s omission of any clear reference to attempt doctrine was very likely to have delayed the development of a general concept of attempt for several years, probably until *Russell* first appeared in 1819 with a *relatively* full treatment of the case law.

Certainly very few reported attempt decisions appear during the first three decades of the nineteenth century. And in 1828, again, rather than resort to the general law of attempt (as augmented by special punishment provisions), in seeking to plug demonstrable gaps in Malacious Injuries Act (Lord Ellenborough's Act), the legislative path was taken[334] with the passing of Lord Lansdowne's Act.[335] Here, following the old legislative formula, to the existing list of specific activities constituting attempted murder was added attempts to poison, drown, or strangle and wounding with intention to murder. Consequently, it is hardly surprising that basic questions relating to attempt's elemental make-up received severely limited attention during this period. Identification of these requirements was, in the main, fragmentary and faltering; most centrally, just what did a defendant need to do to incur attempt liability? How close or proximate did the defendant's actions need to be to execution of the criminal objective?

(2) Proximity

Early judicial encounters with the proximity puzzle are found in a few scattered authorities, such as *Meredith*[336] and *Dugdale*.[337] In the former, Lord Abinger CB, after retrieving a memory of *Higgins*, suggested that the necessary 'step towards the commission' of the offence must be 'illegal' in itself, deducing that merely travelling to the location of an intended crime would be insufficient. In the latter case, Lord Campbell CJ and Coleridge J. were satisfied that 'procuring' or obtaining indecent prints was a sufficient 'first step towards' their illegal publication. But the full dimensions of the proximity question failed to provoke anything remotely resembling serious judicial reflection until the mid-nineteenth-century

---

[334] See *PD* 1828 (s. 2), 18: 1171–3 and (s. 2), 19: 352.

[335] There was an implicit consideration of proximity in the Offences Against the Person Act (Lord Lansdowne's Act) 1828. In the case of rape, for the full offence the law had previously required not only penetration but emission too. Because of the obvious difficulty or proof, Lord Lansdowne's Act dispensed with the latter requirement, thereby effectively moving back the stage at which attempt liability (then the offence of assault with intent to rape) became relevant. Cf. Blackstone, *Comms*, iv, 129; (1828–9) 1 *LM* 129 at 133.

[336] (1838) 8 Car. & P. 589. A charge of assault with intent to commit rape—a statutory form of attempted rape. Also see Denman LCJ in *Chapman* (1849) 1 Den. 432; 2 Car. & K. 846.

[337] (1853) 1 E. & B. 435. Earlier *Fuller* (1816) R. & R. 308 and *Heath* (1810) R. & R. 184.

case of *Eagleton*.[338] This time Lord Campbell saw the issue as of 'such importance to the administration of justice' as to require the collective adjudication of the 15 judges. *In arguendo*, Maule J. succinctly pinned down the general fundamental question before them:

What is an attempt? Must it be a proximate attempt? Does a man, intending to murder, attempt to do so if he buys a dagger and poison [or] if a man intends to commit an offence at a different place, [by] getting into a railway train, or putting on his shoes, or shaving himself in the morning, would not [it] be an attempt to do so?[339]

Delivering the court's reserved judgment, Parke B. identified the particular question as being whether Eagleton's obtaining a ledger credit for the loaves, 'a necessary step towards obtaining the money, can be deemed an attempt to do so'. Acts remotely leading towards the commission of the offence

are not to be considered as attempts to commit it, but acts immediately connected with it are: and if...any further steps on the part of the defendant had been necessary to obtain payment [then that] would not have been sufficiently proximate to the obtaining of the money. But [here] no other act on the part of the defendant [was] required. It was the last act, depending on himself, towards the payment of the money, and therefore it ought to be considered as an attempt.[340]

As, necessarily, nothing could be more proximate than the defendant's 'last act', the line adopted in *Eagleton* demanded the least degree of encroachment on an individual's freedom of action other than requiring completion of the full offence; it also indicated that the judiciary was minded to construe attempt in a clear-cut fashion. Moreover, it constituted the least dramatic shift or doctrinal derogation from the common law's consequentialist insistence on an 'overt act' causing or constituting recognized harm. Typically, despite the self-proclaimed importance of the occasion, hardly a jot of explicit conceptual analysis or policy justification was evident in the decision to confine attempts tightly to the defendant's 'last act'. Yet, surprisingly, bearing in mind the apparent emphatic tone and weight of the judgment in *Eagleton*, before the year was up a smaller 'Court of Criminal Appeal' displayed no qualms in favouring a rather less sharp-edged, more flexible approach to proximity.

In *Roberts*,[341] the defendant purchased dyes necessary for making counterfeit coin, intending to acquire the remaining essential equipment at some later

---

[338] (1855) Dears. 515. Eagleton was contracted with the parish 'guardians of the poor' to deliver loaves of a fixed specification to needy members of the parish. He delivered underweight loaves and was charged with attempting to obtain money from the guardians by false pretences.

[339] *Ibid.*

[340] *Ibid.*

[341] (1855) Dears. 539. A strong reserved cases court including Jervis CJ, Parke B., Wightman, Cresswell, and Willes JJ.

date. Predictably, counsel for Roberts sought to rebut charges of attempting to 'counterfeit foreign coin' by express resort to *Eagleton*'s newly minted proximity test: he argued that obtaining the dyes was not an act 'immediately connected' with the relevant offence, and at least the remaining essential equipment would need to be acquired before an attempt charge could succeed. Rejecting this, the court unanimously found Roberts's purchasing of dyes to have constituted an attempt because this was 'immediately connected' or 'indirectly approximating' to the offence of counterfeiting. The relative certainty of the 'last act' test, apparently constructed in *Eagleton*, had evaporated. Jervis CJ openly admitted defeat in formulating a general proximity test: 'Perhaps my learned brothers may define a line, but I will not do so'. But the Chief Justice's learned brethren could offer no more than references to acts 'sufficiently leading to' or 'sufficiently proximate' to the offence. However, the implicit test applied by at least three of their lordships bore a strong resemblance to that of 'unequivocality', an approach which was to gain considerable currency early in the next century. Jervis CJ, Parke B. and Wightman J. all found the purchase of the counterfeiting dyes unequivocally pointed to their intended unlawful use: Roberts 'could have no other object than to commit the offence'. In such circumstances the pragmatic desire to enable the law to intervene at a relatively early preparatory stage in respect of what was regarded as such a serious form of criminality, proved irresistible to the bench on this occasion.

The axiomatic distinction between lawful preparatory actions and unlawful attempts was again confronted a few years later in *Cheeseman*,[342] yet neither *Eagleton* nor *Roberts* was cited by counsel or the court. As in the latter case, here the defendant's actions were almost unequivocally linked to an intended offence. But on this occasion conviction for attempted theft was affirmed by the majority of the court, resorting to some form of interruption test: 'If the actual transaction has commenced which would have ended in the crime if not interrupted, there is clearly an attempt'.[343] Though not expressed as such, it could be that this was a variant of the equivocality model: that to extrapolate a course of action leading to the offence's commission the steps on the way must clearly be evidence of that objective. However, showing acts to be *consistent* with a later offence is less demanding than demonstrating that they could have *only* a criminal objective. Moreover, neither did an 'interruption' model indicate how far

---

[342] (1862) 31 *LJMC* 90. Cf. Pollock CB, formulation in *Taylor* (1859) 1 F. & F. 511: 'The act must be one immediately and directly tending to the execution of the principal crime'.

[343] Blackburn J., and also Willes and Mellor JJ. For examples of proximity questions being dealt with on a casual, unprincipled basis, see *Taylor* (1871) and *Vreones* (1891) 1 QB 360.

the defendant needed to proceed with his preparatory actions consistent with a criminal outcome.

Yet, at the beginning of the next century, although there had been almost a complete absence of anything resembling a principled consideration of the proximity issue, the courts had, largely through the medium of Stephen's *Digest*,[344] fastened onto an interruption test of considerable plasticity. It was a degree of plasticity also conditioned by *who* would determine at what stage in the 'series of acts' mere preparation crossed the line into attempt. Pollock CB in *Taylor* saw it as a question of law for judicial settlement. However, later comments in *Linneker*[345] seemed to suggest it be a jury matter. Obviously, any hope of a reasonably certain sense of proximity would require the issue to be one for judicial determination. But even removal of this question from the realms of jury consideration and *ad hoc* policy making, an interruption model left the law in a state of considerable uncertainty, investing extensive discretion in judicial hands. At this point all that was clear was general judicial resistance to constricting attempt by any 'last act' philosophy, relatively simple and easy to apply as it might be. This in itself was evidence of an erosion of consequentialist thinking and increased judicial recognition of the potential value of this form of inchoate liability. Though just what value or use attempt was, or could be, in a system of criminal justice, had yet to be judicially articulated.

What conceptual assistance might judges have gained from commentators and proto-legislators of this period? Macaulay's 'an act towards the commission of the offence' formulation reflected contemporary primitive judicial opinion, showing little evidence of Bentham's reflections on the subject.[346] The efforts of the Criminal Law Commissioners demonstrate that even in the late 1840s the conception of attempt still owed much to the highly act-specific culture of former times. Illustrative of the mindset is their Fourth Report's definition of attempt as 'any assault, trespass, or lying in wait, or by any act of fraud or other act whatsoever, done in part execution of a design to commit such a crime or with immediate intent to accomplish the criminal object...'.[347] Whilst it is very likely that members of the court in *Eagleton* had knowledge of the Commissioners' analysis, there is no

---

[344] 'An attempt to commit a crime is an act done with intent to commit that crime, and forming part of a series of acts which would constitute its actual commission if it were not interrupted. The point at which such a series of acts begins cannot be defined; but depends upon the circumstances of each particular case' (1883) Art. 49.

[345] [1906] 2 KB 99. Lord Alverstone at 102 and Walton J. at 104. Cf. *Button* (1900) 2 QB and *Duckworth* [1892] 2 QB 83.

[346] For Bentham and Hammond, see above. On the Indian Code, see W. Stokes, *The Anglo-Indian Codes* (Oxford, 1887), 68, and Macaulay's *Notes, op cit.*, 510. For specific act attempts see e.g. ss 307, 393–4, and 398.

[347] *Fourth Report* (1848) Art. 8 (at p. 66). Similarly, *Seventh Report* (1843) Art. 8, 90.

obvious evidence of influence. Quite what the Commissioners intended by the reference to an act 'done in part execution of a design' is less than obvious. Its apparent contrast with an act done with 'immediate intent to accomplish the criminal object' implies that some preparatory acts ought to qualify as attempt.[348]

Austin's extremely sketchy consideration of proximity notes the distinction between 'remote or merely incipient attempt' and a 'proximate attempt',[349] hinting at some form of equivocality basis: 'Overt acts [are] evidence of the party's intention'; the 'overt act' must include a 'criminal design' and serve as a 'means or steps' to the offence's commission. Stephen's *General View* hardly touches upon attempt other than to complain at the unsatisfactory nature of highly detailed legislative provisions covering various forms of attempt.[350] Twenty years on, with the benefit of mature reflection he resigns himself to accepting that the law is 'of necessity vague' and that 'no distinct line on the subject has been or as I should suppose can be drawn'.[351] Stephen's obvious limited interest in the subject even denies the reader any observations on the rationale or function of attempt liability. Such an attitude was also manifest in the period's two principal code formulations, with both the 1879 Draft Code and Wright's Jamaican Code offering no definition of the general offence of attempt.[352] However, in the case of the 1879 Code, it is clear that the Commissioners wished the reach of attempt to be kept under judicial control, expressly providing that proximity was to be a question of law.[353] For the Jamaican Code, Wright, while noting the problem of proximity was uncharacteristically, content to leave the issue at large and rely on the 'ordinary understanding of the word'.[354]

By the turn of the century, ignoring the *relative* certainty offered by *Eagleton*, three proximity positions amongst commentators were discernible: that it

[348] Yet elsewhere the Commissioners observed that in situations such as occurred in the later coining case of *Roberts*, there should be no attempt liability. *Seventh Report* (1843) Art. 8. In marked contrast with the Commissioners' treatment of most other fundamental aspects of criminal responsibility, their analysis of the general offence of attempt was noticeably perfunctory, offering no advance on Hammond's earlier enterprise. Again, this is indicative of the relative lack of the offence's development and standing, and the wide practical embrace of specific, highly detailed statutory forms of attempt. To a large degree such an approach circumvented the problem of proximity, although even here the strict approach to construing penal legislation (especially of eighteenth-century origin) had built up a complex web of ultra-refined distinctions on *exactly* what act satisfied particular statutory requirements.

[349] *Lectures*, 455 and *Notes*, 1096–8.

[350] *General View*, 124.

[351] HCL, i, 224. In the 1890 edition of the *General View* he somewhat eccentrically suggests that the necessary vagueness of attempt is beneficial in that there would be social danger if people knew precisely how far they might lawfully go in pursuit of an unlawful object (83). Greater deterrence through the law's *imprecision* was the antithesis of broad Benthamite logic.

[352] See ss. 422–424 of the 1879 Draft Code and s 30 of the Jamaican Draft Code.

[353] Section 74.

[354] *Notes*, 102.

was 'impossible to lay down a distinct test' for determining the presence of an appropriate degree of proximity;[355] the interruption model offered to practitioners in Stephen's *Digest* and in *Russell*;[356] and Salmond's equivocality test which proposed:

an attempt is an act of such a nature that it is itself evidence of the criminal intent with which it is done. A criminal attempt bears criminal intent upon its face. Res ipsa loquitur. [The] ground of the distinction between preparation and attempt is evidential merely.[357]

Not surprisingly, Salmond illustrated the application of his test by reference to *Roberts*. Indeed, Kenny, having at one stage denied the feasibility of an 'abstract' proximity test, soon after offers an unequivocal illustration of attempt: making a wax impression of a 'lock of a door in order to make a key to fit it, may constitute an attempt to commit burglary; as the only object of such a proceeding must be to open the door in question'.

This diversity of opinion, both in the courts and treatises remained essentially unchanged for over half a century.[358] A run of appellate decisions, concluding with Lord Reading's apparently solid endorsement of *Eagleton* in *Robinson*,[359] illustrated that beneath judicial uncertainty as to an appropriate proximity formula lay the familiar lack of consensus over attempt's function and legitimate reach: most particularly, just what balance to strike between a preventative/interventionist role and one where punishing an actor's subjective culpability was the principal aim.

(3) *Mens rea*

Turning to the *mens rea* of attempt, the fundamental question is why courts[360] and commentators, almost without exception, appeared to take it to be a self-evident, irresistible, truth that attempt was necessarily confined to situations where actors had direct or purposive intention to achieve the criminal objective.[361] Why was subjective recklessness or negligence, where sufficient for the relevant substantive

---

[355] Kenny, *Outlines* (1904), 80.

[356] (1909), i: 141. *Russell* hedged its bets by also including reference to an 'act directly approximating to or immediately connected with the commission of the offence'.

[357] *Jurisprudence* (1907), 346.

[358] Smith, *Lawyers, Legislators and Theorists*, Ch. 11.

[359] [1915] 2 KB 342. Cf. the different approach to proximity in *Linneker* (1906) 2 KB 99; *Laitwood* (1910) 4 Cr App R 248; *White* [1910] 2 KB 124. On the question of *who* determined sufficient proximity, the courts displayed uncertainty. Cf. *Linneker* with *Landow* (1913) 8 Cr App R 218.

[360] The judgments in *Scofield* and *Higgins* did not clearly require direct intention; use of 'intentional' throughout the nineteenth century often encompassed subjective recklessness.

[361] Neither judicial nor other nineteenth-century analyses seek to distinguish the actor's objectives from the circumstances in which they are to be achieved.

crime, not similarly sufficient for an attempt to commit such offences? What did a general requirement of intention signify in respect of the contemporary conception of attempt and its function?

The overwhelming orthodoxy either expressly or implicitly adopted throughout the century was typified by Stephen's *Digest* statement that attempt was an act 'done with intent to commit that crime'; Austin and Macaulay were apparent exceptions. At two points in Austin's brief examination of attempt, he shows an inclination to recognize something less than purposive intention as sufficient mental culpability. In one case when reviewing the meaning of 'intention' he appears to contemplate that foresight of a 'probable' result would be sufficient mental fault.[362] And in Austin's fragmentary 'Notes on Criminal Law', on several occasions he indicates that attempt requires a 'criminal design or criminal knowledge'. Of course, as seen, Austin maintained that the legal concept of 'intention' encompassed 'criminal knowledge' or subjective recklessness, and so in his own analytical terminology reference to 'criminal knowledge' was strictly superfluous—perhaps underscoring the suggested adequacy of 'knowledge'. For Macaulay, whilst his general attempt offence in the Indian Penal Code specified no particular mental state, some attempted homicide provisions expressly incorporated a fault requirement of less than purposive intention. Attempted murder, for example, stipulated an act with either 'intention or knowledge' that (effectively) death would probably follow, a provision which broadly replicated the culpability needed for the complete offence of murder.[363] As one of the offences where the harm threatened is most serious, attempted murder would have one of the strongest claims for departing from the narrow conception of fault reflected in a general intentionality requirement.

More generally, several factors might be seen as contributing to the usually narrow conception of attempt formulated over the nineteenth century. First, the tentative and relatively leisurely development of attempt would tend towards a more guarded, restricted approach to fault requirements. A similar attitude was apparent in relation to proximity, with the initial 'last act' notion. Secondly, operation of the ubiquitous presumption of intention would have reduced substantially the number of occasions on which a subjectively reckless 'attempt' might have become a live issue for adjudication. Thus, in practice *actually* reckless states of mind may in some situations have incurred attempt liability. Thirdly, the relatively narrow range of negligence-based offences (principally manslaughter)

---

[362] *Lectures*, xxiv: 480–1. 'Notes', 1096–8. The *Criminal Law Commissioners'* digested provision required an act 'done in part execution of a design to commit such crime', *Fourth Report* (1848) Art. 8.

[363] Section 307. See also s 308, 'Attempt to commit culpable homicide'.

would have severely limited the occasions upon which the question of attempt might have arisen in a negligence context. Moreover, the very essence of the situations, as in the case of manslaughter, is such that negligence which did not bring about harm would either not be manifest, or the lack of harm would have removed a substantial reason for regarding it as a proper object for prosecution and punishment. The common law's general disinclination to punish negligently caused harm, unless death resulted, would also have made punishing any non-fatal harm as attempted manslaughter (at least in appearance) rather paradoxical. Finally, with the existence of an extensive range of statutory offences criminalizing specified acts where there was 'intent' to achieve the criminal objective, it would have been natural (though not inevitable) to regard such a culpability formula as indicative of the appropriate reach of general attempt liability.

Yet, while judicial analyses of the appropriate scope for attempt liability remained relatively limited, some of those charged with formulating legislative revisions or even digested programmes of criminal law took a rather more systematic view of possible criminality in areas of behaviour immediately adjacent to attempt, differing primarily only in respect of mental culpability. Most especially, both the Criminal Law Commissioners and Wright proposed criminalization of reckless and negligent endangering activities where no consequential harm occurred. This was partly a corollary of their articulated general principle that so far as possible criminal liability should rest on an agent's mental culpability and not the chance occurrence of harm. The Commissioners suggested the enactment of two novel forms of endangerment liability where serious human harm was threatened: 'Wilfully' or 'culpably' (negligently) endangering life by any means.[364] Several decades later Wright, without supporting observations, followed with a more narrowly drawn form of negligent, life-endangering liability confined to 'Persons in charge of Dangerous Things'. Furthermore, in a fashion proposed by Bentham, Wright complemented this and his attempt provisions with a wide-ranging offence, punished as severely as attempt, covering preparatory behaviour for practically all serious offences.[365]

---

[364] See, 'Non-fatal offences against the Person', Ch. XII.

[365] Section 31. Rather than expand the mental element of inchoate liability, this offence, in effect, addressed proximity, extending back conduct which might be regarded as criminal. The offence covered preparing, supplying, possessing, controlling instruments, materials or other means for the commission of offences. No such broad provision appears in the 1879 Draft Code, which contained existing specific (ss 193–194) offences under ss 32 and 33 of the 1861 Offences Against the Persons Act dealing with intentional or negligent endangerment of railway travellers. A partly novel, wide preparatory offence of 'disabling to commit crime' was proposed in the 1879 Code, applicable to any indictable offence where violent means were employed as a preliminary to a later planned offence (ss 188–189).

The thoroughgoing symmetry of Wright's and particularly the Commissioners' reviews of the basis of liability for culpable harm-threatening and harm-causing activities extended to not only negligent *endangering* but also, logically, to negligent *causing* of non-fatal harm.[366] Together with their attempt provisions, the proposed endangerment offences represented some of the century's most calculated *general* examples of proposed penal legislation manifestly subjectivist in approach, grounding liability on an actor's fault, and running counter to the common law's broadly harm or consequentialist orientation.

(4) *Impossibility*

A final issue with implications for attempt's rationale concerned the effect on liability of impossibility, whether as to means or criminal objective. A similar absence of conceptual reflection and analysis of attempt's function, as seen with proximity, also shows up in nineteenth-century judicial encounters with the impossibility question. The basis for resistance to conceding liability where circumstances were such that a criminal objective could never be achieved was either unarticulated or simply premised on an assertion of self-evident truth. Two poisoning cases[367] from the 1850s are typical, where charges for administering poison with intent to kill were not defeated by the substances inability to kill. However, it was indicated that had the substance not been 'a poison', acquittals would have followed.

More revealing of some form of rationale for denying liability where impossibility was present were Lord Cockburn CJ's responses in *M'Pherson* and later in *Collins*.[368] In both cases application of a linear or interruption model of proximity led to the assertion that 'an attempt...can only be made out when, if no interruption had taken place, the attempt could have been carried out successfully'. This could not have been so where a pickpocket's target contained nothing to steal.[369] Of course, no inevitable logic or link existed between adoption of the interruption model of attempt and accepting an impossibility rule. But the underlying basis for punishing attempts could carry fundamental implications for both proximity and impossibility matters, in that basing attempt on a culpable

---

[366] In Wright's Code the negligent causing of 'bodily harm' was punishable with three months' imprisonment (s 98) and with a maximum of one year for 'grievous bodily harm' (s 99). Also, *Criminal Law Commissioners, Seventh Report*, Art. 42; *Second Report*, Arts 10 and 48; *Fourth Report*, Art. 38. No distinction in the maximum punishment was made for causing 'bodily harm' whether 'maliciously' or 'negligently'. See 'Non-fatal offences against the Person', Ch. XII, below.

[367] *Cluderay* (1850) 4 Cox 84; *Dale* (1852) 6 Cox 14.

[368] (1857) 7 Cox 281 and (1864) 9 Cox 498.

[369] In *M'Pherson*, Lord Cockburn had noted that 'here the attempt never could have ended in completion of the offence charged' (284). Both Willes J. and Bramwell B. took the view that a charge 'of attempting to steal such goods as were left in the house' (rather than specific goods) would have succeeded. Presumably, even then some goods would have needed to have been somewhere in the house.

or dangerously disposed *actor* rationale would tend to support conviction despite impossibility. Indeed, prosecuting counsel in *M'Pherson*, responding to Bramwell B., maintained that impossibility did not prevent the defendant being 'equally culpable', a view also taken by Pollock CB in *Gaylor*,[370] decided in the same year. The contrary might be true if punishing dangerous (harm-threatening) *acts* had been regarded as attempt's central rationale.

The position in respect of impossibility remained unchallenged for a quarter of a century until a trio of reserved cases, marked by a mixture of confusion and extreme brevity, overturned *Collins*. The first sign of a revised judicial attitude appeared in *Brown*, with Lord Coleridge CJ observing that 'in our opinion [*Collins* was] decided upon a mistaken view of the law'.[371] It was an *obiter* opinion given in the absence of counsel for either side, and, as Lord Coleridge conceded, 'it is no doubt a disadvantage that this case should not have been argued before us, but we have fully discussed the question ourselves'. Revisiting impossibility three years later in *Ring*,[372] Lord Coleridge led a strong Court for Crown Cases Reserved openly dismissing *Collins* as 'bad law', once again without offering sustaining argument or reasons. Similarly, a few years after in *Brown and others*,[373] Darling J., this time after extensive argument by prosecution and defence counsel, held that a woman taking a harmless substance believing it to be noxious to procure an abortion would be liable for an attempt. At this stage the less than satisfactory nature of the principled shift in the judicial view of impossibility lay not just in the total absence of substantiating reasoning, but also in the existence of a contemporary line of apparently opposing authority.[374]

---

[370] (1857) D. & B. 292. Confirmation of the general exculpatory effects of impossibility can be seen in *Hensleer* (1870) 11 Cox 570. On a charge of attempting to obtain money by false pretences, the Court for Crown Cases Reserved felt that the victim's knowledge of the untruth of Hensleer's claim did not prevent Hensleer's conviction for attempt. However, comments by Mellor J. and Kelly CB seemed to suggest that had the victim been without funds, then *that* reason for making the obtaining impossible would have barred conviction for attempt. In *Taylor* (1871) 25 *LT* 75, a pickpocketing case proof that the victim's pockets contained something was deemed essential to an attempt charge; and *Sheppard* (1868) 11 Cox 302, a case of throwing gunpowder with the intention of damaging property, where it was held that there could be no liability unless the gunpowder was capable of exploding.

[371] (1889) 24 QBD 357. Confusion over exactly what Lord Coleridge said is apparent from the various versions of his judgment in different reports. See Rogers (1894) 10 *LQR* 161, 168.

[372] (1892) 17 Cox 491, with Hawkins, Willes, Lawrence and Wright JJ, like *Collins* a pickpocketing case. Rather surprisingly, earlier that day the same court had indicated in relation to the statutory offence of attempting to discharge a firearm, that it was a 'serious question' whether the offence could be committed when an essential part of the gun's mechanism was missing. *Duckworth* [1892] 2 QB 83, 86–7. Cf. *Cluderay* and *Dale*, above.

[373] (1899) 63 *JP* 790.

[374] Dicta in two reserved cases of *Waite* (1892) 2 QB 600 and *Williams* (1893) 1 QB 320 suggest that a boy's presumed physical incapacity to commit certain sexual offences also prevented attempt liability. In the latter, the Court for Crown Cases Reserved was divided on the question.

To what can this judicial *volte face*, beginning with *Brown*, be attributed? What potentially influential forces or opinions might have contributed to the change? Certainly none of the three penal codes (of which most, if not all of the judiciary probably had knowledge) recognized impossibility as a bar to conviction. Macaulay's Indian Code, whilst not expressly meeting the issue, contained illustrations showing that at least in the case of empty boxes or pockets liability could follow.[375] Wright's 1877 Code expressly excluded impossibility as a bar to conviction in respect of 'means, circumstances', or by 'reason of the absence' of the criminal object. Wright justified cases where there was an absence of the criminal objective by observing that they did not differ 'in principle' from instances where the means employed were inadequate.[376] Without comment other than that the provision reversed *Collins*, the 1879 Criminal Code Bill Commissioners proposed a similar approach to Wright.[377] However, as Stephen made clear three years later, it was a change made against his own inclinations: one of 'unnecessary severity. The moral guilt is no doubt as great in the one case as in the other, but there is no danger to public, and it seems harsh to treat as an attempt one only of many kinds of acts by which a criminal intention is displayed...'.[378] This was not a view shared at the end of the century by the likes of Kenny[379] or Salmond, both of whom endorsed the approach adopted in *Ring*. Yet Salmond, in apparent self-contradiction, also briefly reflected on the theoretical implications, observing that the inability of such actions to result in harm raised at least an (implicit consequentialist) argument that punishment was unjustified.[380]

Stephen's and Salmond's scant comments of similar import, if different emphasis, show concern to ensure that the defendant's actions carried at least the real potential to cause criminal harm, even though, as Stephen concedes, the actor's mental culpability is unaffected. More widely, beyond impossibility, whilst singularly failing to reveal any underlying policy or rationale for attempt liability, contemporary commentators and proto-legislators did offer indirect insights into the general conceptualization of attempt and issues kindred to those of inchoate liability. Such insights are offered by commentators' treatments of

---

[375] Ch. XXIII, s 511. As Stokes points out, it was quite unclear whether the implication was to include all forms of impossibility. *Op cit.*, 68.

[376] 'Notes', 107. Similarly many years later as a judge in *Ring*, below.

[377] Section 74: 'Everyone who, believing that a certain state of facts exists, does or omits an act the doing or omission of which would if that state of facts existed be an attempt to commit an offence, attempts to commit that offence, although its commission in the manner proposed was, by reason of the non existence of that state of facts at the time of the act or omission, impossible', *Report* 19 and 77. See also Rogers (1894) 10 *LQR* 161, 166.

[378] *HCL*, ii, 225.

[379] *Outlines* (1904), 81.

[380] *Jurisprudence* (1907), 347.

the relationship between harm and punishment, and their views of mental culpability as a factor in determining both liability and levels of punishment. These conceptually related issues can be seen arising in relation to attempt's *mens rea* requirements and available punishments, and in the attitude towards endangering behaviour where harm fails to eventuate.

In respect of punishment, until 1861, the common law misdemeanour of attempt to murder, for example, was subject to a maximum penalty of two years' imprisonment, whilst a whole range of specific statutory attempts entailing stabbing, shooting, or poisoning were capital offences. Addressing the broad question of the appropriate punishment for attempt, the Criminal Law Commissioners noted that juries favoured punishing less severely where no harm materialized from an attempt. With offences against the person, this consequentialist attitude was translated into a substantial punishment differential between cases where bodily injury was and was not caused.[381] However, in their later Seventh Report, the Commissioners declared as a basic principle that an attempt merited the same punishment as if the offence had been completed 'for the moral guilt was...just as great'.[382] Yet this emphasis on subjective culpability was not followed through in their Digest provisions, where the maximum punishment for any attempt was three years' imprisonment. In the specific case of attempted murder, subjectivist principle yielded to consequentialist inclinations, so that an attempt which succeeded in inflicting 'bodily harm' was a capital offence, whereas a harmless attempt attracted a maximum of three years' imprisonment or a minimum of seven years' transportation.

Subsequent Reports omitted any affirmation of the principle of equality of punishment for attempt and completed offences.[383] Certainly the Commissioners were not totally free agents with an unlimited remit for principled innovation, unlike Macaulay who enjoyed a much freer hand in formulating the Indian Penal Code. Yet, here again, a results or harm-orientated approach to punishment of attempt is much in evidence, with both general and specific provisions stipulating substantially lower punishment maxima for attempts, especially where no harm occurs.[384] It is a punishment model also incorporated in the 1879 Draft

---

[381] *Second Report* (1839), 247. See e.g. Arts 74 and 75.

[382] *Report* (1843). 28.

[383] e.g. *Second Report* (1846), 37 and Art. 44 (at 45). Similarly in the *Fourth Report* (1848). Cf. Bentham's view that attempts where the defendant had done everything possible to achieve his criminal objective should be punished more severely than 'incomplete' attempts. His rationale was the encouragement of actors to retreat from pursuing their criminal design.

[384] Indian Penal Code, s 511 provided that, subject to specific provisions to the contrary, attempts were to be punished with up to half the maximum punishment for the relevant offence.

Criminal Code.[385] Wright's Jamaican Code stood apart in adhering to a principle of eligibility to equal punishment for attempt and completed offences. Additional novelty was offered by Wright's inclusion of an abandonment provision, the effect of which was to designate an attempt one of 'second degree', thereby rendering punishment open to mitigation 'according to the circumstances'.[386] Both features of Wright's Code (equal punishment eligibility and mitigation for 'retreat or repentance' rather than a harm-orientated philosophy) indicate the intended centrality of an actor's subjective culpability.

In crude terms, the almost uniform harm-orientated approach, reflected in lesser punishment levels of attempt, was consistent with attempt liability being conceived of as an interventionist, harm-preventing facility. This model relegated the defendant's dangerousness or manifest criminal proclivities to a subsidiary role. Yet the later denial of impossibility as a bar to conviction arguably points in the opposite direction, placing considerable weight on the defendant's unchanged mental culpability. As has been suggested, clear recognition of a general offence of attempt represented a significant doctrinal retreat from the common law's strong consequentialist or harm orientation. But the nature and extent of the retreat from consequentialism was not obvious: fundamentally, was the inspirational rationale objectivist in character, punishing harm-threatening activity (arguably a social harm itself), or was attempt liability a subjectivist response springing from a desire to punish manifestly dangerous, morally culpable, actors? Each of these rationales carried implications for proximity, necessary mental state, and impossibility. But, almost without exception, over a century of largely fragmentary judicial analysis provided no articulation of attempt's function(s) capable of coherently shaping these different features of liability.

CONSPIRACY

(1) An unlawful objective

Conspiracy, an agreement between two or more people to effect some unlawful purpose, shared the common law origins of attempt and incitement. However, conspiracy's credentials were well established before the nineteenth

---

[385] Sections 422–424. Specific provisions included attempted murder where an attempt attracted life imprisonment compared with death for murder (s 179), and attempted rape, seven years set against penal servitude for life for the completed offence (s 209).

[386] Section 30(ii) and see 'Notes', 103: 'Where the attempt is not defeated by causes independent of the criminal's intention, but is abandoned or rendered incomplete by his own retreat, or repentance', the penalty is greatly reduced. Without reaching any conclusion, Austin reflected briefly on the proper function, if any, of 'penitence'. 'Notes on the Criminal Law', Lectures, 1098. Because of the problem of discovering true and proper motives, Stephen regarded an abandonment defence 'dangerous to lay down…universally', HCL, ii, 226; Taylor (1859) above, was arguably implied authority against such a defence.

century.[387] Despite this, conspiracy remained a form of criminal responsibility where the judiciary and legislature felt unobliged to settle fundamental questions relating to its scope, most especially the meaning of 'unlawful'. Conspiracy liability represented a far earlier point of legal intervention than recognized by criminal attempts; indeed, an 'agreement' was essentially a mere preparatory action, an activity judicially frequently identified in contra-distinction to attempt. Thus, two broad questions arise: first, how did Victorian judges and commentators justify the criminal law's general capacity to intervene at this very early stage where two or more individuals colluded? Secondly, what activities were recognized as 'unlawful'? As will be suggested, the answer to the first question powerfully influences the answer to the second.

In respect of the justification for early intervention, a preventative explanation fails to account for criminalizing early preparatory actions constituted by an agreement involving at least two parties. Any claim that an agreement was the equivalent of a proximate act[388] would, as a matter of fact, be demonstrably false, unless the idea of equivalence related to some generalized assessment of risk of the unlawful objective being carried out; put crudely, the likelihood of criminal success was seen as rising with group activity. Just such a justification is set out by the Criminal Law Commissioners:

The general principle on which the crime of conspiracy is founded is this, that the confederacy of several persons to effect any injurious object creates such a new and additional power to cause injury as requires criminal restraint; although none would be necessary were the same thing proposed, or even attempted to be done, by any person singularly.[389]

As well as asserting an increased likelihood of a criminal outcome, the Commissioners' further justification was that collective action *in itself* increased or 'enhanced' the nature of the harm, a claim classically made later in the century by Bowen LJ in *Mogul Steamship Ltd* v. *McGregor, Gow and Co*:

Of the general proposition that certain kinds of conduct not criminal in any one individual may become criminal if done by combination among several, there can be no doubt. The distinction is based on sound reason, for a combination may make oppressive or dangerous that which if preceded only from a single person would be otherwise....[390]

---

[387] Particularly, F. B. Sayre, 'Criminal Conspiracy' (1922) 35 *HLR* 393 and R. S. Wright, *Law of Conspiracies and Agreements* (1873).

[388] Apparently Wright, 80–1, and Stephen *HCL* ii, 227.

[389] *Seventh Report* (1843), 90.

[390] (1889) 23 QB 598; affirmed [1892] AC 25. Similarly, *Quinn* v. *Leathem* [1901] AC 495, 530; and *South Wales Miners Federation* v. *Glamorgan Coal Co* [1905] AC 239, 252.

In effect, this reasoning suggests that beyond objectives criminal in their own right, some objectives become criminal by virtue of being the subject-matter of an agreement. Thus, this form of criminal conspiracy was conceptually distinguishable in that its unlawful quality was at least partly derived from the combination itself rather than solely from the independently criminal purpose. This, in turn, provided the justification for the practically open-ended concept of 'unlawful' extending beyond purely substantive crimes. Whilst providing some sort of rationale, the claim of intrinsic harmfulness of collective action could not alone determine just what might be regarded as 'unlawful'. Indeed, like the term 'malice-aforethought', 'unlawful' constituted a strong example of the highly qualified application of the fundamental principle of certainty of law.[391] For as its diverse categories demonstrated, 'unlawful' appeared to mean anything the judiciary chose to identify as such.

Both commentators and judges occasionally remarked on the potential of this power. In the *General View*, Stephen observed:

'unlawful' is taken in so wide a sense that it might include almost any form of immoral, unpatriotic, disloyal, or otherwise objectionable, conduct which involves a plan concerted between two or more persons. It is not altogether inconvenient to have a branch of the law which enables the courts, by a sort of ostracism, to punish people who make themselves dangerous or obnoxious to society at large, and the necessity for quoting precedents—the publicity of the proceedings—and the general integrity of the judges are probably suffi-cient safeguards against its abuse, but it would be idle to deny that the power is dangerous and ought to be watched with jealousy.[392]

Fitzgerald J. issued a similarly pungent judicial caution in the politically charged atmosphere of Fenian treason trials:

conspiracy is a branch of our jurisprudence to be narrowly watched, to be jealously regarded, and never to be pressed beyond its true limits.[393]

But both during (and beyond) the nineteenth century, there was little evidence suggesting that the judiciary recognized anything resembling 'true limits', for such a reserved power was commonly regarded as an essential legal long stop, capable of striking at an infinite range of novel manifestations of undesirable behaviour.

In 1769, Willes J. affirmed that 'justice, moral fitness and public convenience, when applied to a new subject, make common law without precedent'.[394] In the

---

[391] In relation to criminal law, see Jerome Hall's analysis of certainty and the principle of legality in *General Principles of Criminal Law* (Bloomington, Ind., 1960), Ch. 2.

[392] At 148–9.

[393] Quoted by Kenny, *Outlines* (1902), 291.

[394] *Millar* v. *Taylor* (1769) 4 Burr. 2303, 2312.

following century, Pollock CB endorsed these sentiments:

as regards the repressing what is a public evil and preventing what would become a public mischief...I think the common law is quite competent to pronounce anything to be illegal which is manifestly against the public good....[395]

Underpinned by such beliefs and through the mechanism of conspiracy, the courts assumed the role of *custos morum* in several directions, most especially: to defraud, to commit torts involving 'malice', to commit or induce a breach of contract, and to commit a public mischief. Of these, the courts found conspiracy to defraud a particularly useful device to punish instances of dishonest, devious, or sharp practice which they regarded as meriting a criminal sanction even though not clearly penalized by the substantive law. According to Lord Cockburn:

It is sufficient to constitute a conspiracy if two or more persons combine by fraud and false pretences to injure another. It is not necessary in order to constitute a conspiracy that the acts agreed to be done should be acts which if done would be criminal. It is enough if the acts agreed to be done, although not criminal, are wrongful, i.e. amount to a civil wrong.[396]

Cockburn's reference to tortious liability as constituting an 'unlawful' object, while true in relation to defrauding, required qualification more generally. Several nineteenth-century authorities show that even the judiciary's most punitive members[397] shied away from accepting that all torts, per se, would be 'unlawful'. Most likely, an additional element of 'malice' connoting spite or ill-will, was required to convert a tort into an 'unlawful' objective.[398] The particular example of 'public mischief' as an 'unlawful' aim, was patently the most nebulous and illusive of notions, extending beyond conspiracy into instances of substantive liability,[399] and including behaviour as diverse as judicially censured sexual immorality, fraudulently manipulating the financial markets, and deceiving government officials.[400]

---

[395] *Jefferys* v. *Boosey* (1854) 4 *HLC* 815, 936. Also e.g. *Higgins* (1801) 2 *East* 5; *Stephenson* (1884) 13 QB 331. In the early twentieth century, *Brailsford* [1905] 2 KB, 730; *Porter* (1910) 1 KB 369; and particularly the notion of the substantive offence of public mischief in *Manley* (1933) 1 KB 529, and generally in *Shaw* v. *DPP* [1962] AC 220.

[396] *Warburton* (1870) 1 CCR 274. The overwhelming majority of defrauding cases have involved the tort of deceit. On the particular judicial rationale for conspiracy to defraud, see Wright, 10–11. For the principal authorities, see Stephen's *Digest*, 253.

[397] Including Lord Ellenborough in *Turner* (1811) 13 *East* 228.

[398] e.g. *Levy* (1819) 2 Stark. 458, maliciously causing a private nuisance, and *Druitt* (1867) 10 Cox 592. See the support for the presence of 'malice' by the Criminal Law Commissioners, *Seventh Report*, 90.

[399] For the overlap with defrauding, see Lord Ellenborough in *De Berenger* (1814) 3 M. & S. 67.

[400] *Lord Grey* (1612) 9 St. Tr. 127; *De Berenger* (1814) 3 M. & S. 66; and *Brailsford* [1905] 2 KB 730.

For their part, the 1879 Code Bill Commissioners doubted the wisdom of any future exercise of this form of creative discretion, believing that it

would be received with great opposition and...place the Bench in an invidious position...If Parliament is not disposed to provide punishments for acts which are upon any ground objectionable or dangerous, the presumption is that they belong to that class of misconduct against which the moral feeling and good sense of the community are the best protections.[401]

While hardly eliminating the uncertainty and flexibility radiated by the notion of 'unlawful', the 1879 Code Commission conspiracy proposals (essentially a judicial creation) would have eliminated the term itself, substituting a defined range of criminal objectives; even then, some of the identified categories (e.g. 'to defile women' and 'to defraud') still offered substantial interpretive latitude. Following Stephen's *Digest* arrangement, the various instances of 'unlawful' purpose were removed from general conspiracy liability and placed within other categories of offences. Thus, for example, conspiracy to 'defile' (s 149) was one of 'offences against morality'; 'conspiracy to pervert...justice' (s 127) was placed within offences of 'misleading justice'; 'conspiracy to defraud' (s 284) became part of a group of 'fraud' offences. Consistent with the Code Commissioners' rejection of a reserved judicial power to create new forms of criminal liability, the Code omits 'public mischief' as a general form of substantive or conspiratorial category of liability. However, some previously recognized specific instances of public mischief were included under other forms of conspiracy.

(2) *Conspiracy's political and economic use*

Conspiracy's extensive adaptive ability to serve prosecutors in extremely diverse areas of activity was powerfully underscored by its nineteenth-century deployment in political and industrial conflict. As will be seen,[402] in state prosecutions for treason, sedition, and unlawful assembly, conspiracy charges were frequently combined with substantive allegations, thereby elongating the period of alleged criminality and drawing in a wider range of incriminating evidence against defendants. The reinforcing effects of conspiracy charges by such prosecutorial practices are readily illustrated in Chartist and Fenian trials.[403] While the prejudicial side effects of standard evidence rules operated in respect of all conspiracies, they were especially acute in politically inspired conspiracies. By virtue

---

[401] *Report*, 9–10.

[402] 'Securing the State', Ch. IX below.

[403] Courts occasionally sought to discourage combining conspiracy charges with substantive charges where the conspiracy had been carried out, e.g. Lord Cockburn in *Boulton* (1871) 12 Cox 87, 93. However, such sentiments were little in evidence in trials where political charges were at issue.

of the basic admissibility criterion of relevance to facts in issue, any evidence tending to prove the existence of an agreement and whether the defendants were parties to it could be allowed in; this included any acts or words (such as confessions) of all alleged conspirators done in pursuance of the conspiracy over the whole period of time between the claimed agreement and its execution.[404] As a consequence, the sheer aggregated weight and volume of inferences drawn from circumstantial and hearsay evidence might sink defendants.

Political conflict of a more directly economic nature arose with increasing frequency as the nineteenth century progressed and organized labour made its active presence politically irresistible. While, as Chartist agitation illustrates, wider political/industrial struggles could be a combined cause, thereby provoking more overtly political prosecutions, many industrial-labour disputes were more immediately economic and local. Statutory prohibition of combinations and societies established to improve wage rates and conditions stretched back to the sixteenth century, with such a legislative policy continuing into the early nineteenth century until the 1820s' relaxation of the laws against trade combinations.[405] Yet, uncertainty remained as to whether lawfully combining for enhancing economical leverage might be reinforced by trades unions encouraging breach of employment contracts by striking.

Between 1825 and 1871, a series of decisions[406] effectively rendered unlawful all attempts to persuade employees to strike, thereby opening up the possibility of conspiracy charges; only a bare collective agreement amongst a group of workers was regarded as protected by the 1825 legislation. After an abortive initiative in 1871, the Conspiracy and Protection of Property Act 1875 awarded protection to acts of all combinations in furtherance of a trade dispute, unless otherwise punishable if committed by an individual.[407] Although politically an almost irresistible law reform, the change was met with hostility in many quarters. Stephen

---

[404] e.g. Lord Mansfield in *Parsons* (1762) 1 Black. W. 392; Lord Kenyon in *Hammond* (1799) 2 Esp. 719; *Hunt* (1820) 1 St. Tr. (NS) 171, 437; *Mullins* (1848) 3 Cox 526; *Duffield* (1851) 5 Cox 404; *Parnell* (1851) 14 Cox 505.

[405] 1825, 6 Geo. IV c. 129. Wright, 43 *et seq*. For a detailed analysis of the nineteenth-century labour law developments including the role of conspiracy, see Vol XIII, Pt 3.

[406] Wright, 43, Stephen *HCL*, iii, 217 *et seq* and Roscoe's *Digest of Criminal Evidence* (8th edn, 1874), 423–8.

[407] 38 & 39 Vict. c. 86. Certain specific breaches of employment contracts covering gas and water supplies were not legalized. Picketing was granted statutory legitimacy by the Trade Disputes Act 1906, 6 Ed. VII c. 47, s 2. The position of agreements to induce a breach of contract not in pursuance of a trade dispute remained open; see Lord Bramwell's dictum in *Mogul SS Co* [1892] AC 25, at 48. In good measure prompted by labour disputes, wholesale statutory reform of the common law of conspiracy came under careful Home Office review in the early 1890s. Plans were dropped on the grounds of little overall anticipated benefit. See Godfrey Lushington's confidential briefing paper, 22 November 1892 *Home Office Printed Memoranda and Reports 1892*, NA HO 347/7, 267–76.

was undoubtedly far from exceptional at the time, especially amongst the judiciary, in regarding such ceding of economic and political power as repellent. With reference to seditious conspiracy, he reflected that it was a 'serious counterpoise' to the 'exorbitant influence' which 'political combinations . . . are capable of exercising'.[408] Reflecting this sort of unease, not to say outright opposition to the change represented by the 1875 legislation, over the subsequent three decades, the courts in a succession of interpretive decisions severely circumscribed the Act's legitimizing powers. It was an outcome swiftly undone by a newly elected Liberal Government with enactment of the Trades Disputes Act 1906.

[408] *HCL*, ii, 380.

VIII

Excluding Fault from Criminal Responsibility: Strict and Vicarious Liability: Quasi-criminal or Regulatory Offences?

THE criminal law's rising intrusion into most aspects of life became a feature of the superstructure of Victorian England's social and economic developments. Before the century's end, statute-based controlling mechanisms embraced, for example, the food and liquor industry, commerce, transportation, matters of public health, safety, and social welfare, along with commercialized leisure activities. As well as the standard prosecutorial authorities, enforcement of these laws lay within the remit of a specially created range of central and local agencies. But, with limited exceptions, the offences were prosecuted in, and dealt with by, ordinary criminal courts. Unsurprisingly, the judicial attitudes and expectations brought to such proceedings were, initially at least, those appropriate to all criminal trials. However, well before the close of the nineteenth century, the judiciary had, for reasons now reviewed, conceded the significant doctrinal innovation of permitting important areas of criminal liability to be incurred without proof of fault.

Early encounters with regulatory offences had prompted emphatic endorsements of the universal doctrinal requirement of fault as a prerequisite of criminal liability. Typical was Lord Kenyon's indignant reaction to the proposed fault-free construction of a bankruptcy offence in *Fowler v. Padget*:[1] it was a 'question of infinite importance [and] I would adopt any construction of the statute that the

---

[1] (1798) 7 T.R. 509. Quoted in *Prince* (1875) LR 2, 165. Eighteenth-century examples of what might be viewed as precursors of strict liability offences can be found: L. H. Leigh, *Strict and Vicarious Liability* (1982), Ch. 2 and F. B. Sayre, 'Public Welfare Offences' (1933) 33 *Col. LR* 55. By this time the common law had come to recognize that criminal liability for nuisance required no proof of fault and, like criminal libel, might be committed without knowledge or any other form of fault by a master through the acts of a servant. *Almon* (1770) 5 Burr. 2686, as an evidential presumption; *Walter* (1799) 2 Esp. 21; *Gutch* (1829) M. & M. 483. More generally on the nineteenth century, see Smith, *Lawyers, Legislators and Theorists*, Ch. 6.

words will bear, in order to avoid such monstrous consequences...'. Yet over the succeeding century a piecemeal erosion of this stance would be seen: first, through recognition of the legitimacy of strict liability; secondly, by the further step of not only jettisoning fault but also the personal nature[2] of responsibility by accepting vicarious criminal liability where statutory construction and perceived legislative policy demanded it. Full-fledged recognition of strict and vicarious liability represented acceptance of a blend of instrumentalist social and economic philosophy by a substantial section of the judiciary, with an open acknowledgement of Parliament's ability to oust the expectation of criminal fault and moral culpability.[3] Such a degree of doctrinal innovation came in fits and starts, being more readily conceded by some members of the judiciary than by others. Judicial acceptance of strict and vicarious liability marked a significant stage in the move away from the judicial mindset engendered by the eighteenth-century culture of construing penal statutes in the strictest fashion in the defendant's favour. In stark contrast with practically every other area of criminal law development during the nineteenth century, strict and vicarious liability were subject to scarcely any extrajudicial commentary or evaluation. And certainly no contemporary theoretical analysis of the general significance of these forms of liability was offered by general criminal law treatises.[4]

1. STRICT LIABILITY

Ultimately, judicial attitudes were informed by Parliament's undisputed ability to create criminal liability without moral fault; the contentious question was just how easily such a construction might be conceded in respect of any particular piece of legislation. In this shift towards greater willingness to recognise liability without proof of fault, two early interpretational approaches emerged: the practical problem of proof and perceived legislative policy. In the 1820s' case of *Marsh*, Abbott CJ confirmed a conviction for the criminal possession of game, ruling that it was 'not a sufficient defence for a carrier...to show that he did not know that the particular parcel contained game'.[5] And referring to the problem

---

[2] Complicity liability is in one sense non-personal, but solidly fault based.

[3] Even in cases of constructive liability (felony-murder and unlawful act manslaughter) responsibility at least rested on a preliminary or qualifying offence committed with the required level of fault.

[4] For the Criminal Law Commissioners, fault-free 'accidental harm' was not an appropriate subject for criminal sanctions. However, imbued with a more diluted strain of utilitarian philosophy, they were also concerned with the absence of moral fault as well as the believed inability of the threat of punishment to prevent such harm. *Seventh Report* (1843) 23 Art. 8(33) and *Second Report* (1846) Art. 6(16).

[5] (1824) 2 B. & C. 717. Also *Southern* (1821) R. & R. 444.

of proof of knowledge, Abbott continued, 'If it were necessary to aver that the defendant had actual knowledge, it would cast on the prosecutor a burden of proof which could not easily be satisfied'. The problem and practicability of proof of knowledge was to figure greatly in the expressed and implied reasoning offered by judges in subsequent decisions. But, bearing in mind the entrenched evidential rule whereby, as has been seen in relation to offences generally, actions and consequences were presumed to have been intended, it is strange that courts took this particular pragmatic path to strict liability. Indeed, in *Marsh*, Abbott's judicial brethren, Bayley and Littledale JJ, both rested their affirmation of conviction on the presumption of knowledge which was 'not rebutted by the evidence'.

Twenty years on, in construing an offence, Chief Baron Pollock leaned heavily on the perceived function of the provision before the court as being to protect public health. This objective cast on tobacco dealers a duty to 'take care', which under 'ordinary grammatical construction' resembled an absolute duty of care under the Act:

It is very true that in particular instances it may produce mischief, because an innocent man may suffer from his want of care in not examining tobacco he has received...; but public inconvenience would be much greater if in every case the officers were obliged to prove knowledge. They would be very seldom able to do so. The legislature have made a stringent provision for the purposes of protecting the revenue, and have used very plain words. If a man is in possession of an article as the defendant was in this case, and that article falls within the terms mentioned in the statute, there is no question but that the offence is proved.[6]

Judicial dispute over the tenacity with which courts should adhere to the presumption that fault was an essential ingredient of all criminal responsibility became manifest by the late 1850s. In the railways goods case of *Hearne* v. *Garton* a strong appeal court was unanimous in construing the offence of 'sending dangerous goods without notice' as requiring 'guilty knowledge'. Lord Campbell CJ took as his interpretive lodestar the maxim *actus non facit reum nisi mens sit rea*: 'Not only was there no proof of guilty knowledge...but the presumption of a guilty knowledge...if any could be raised, was rebutted by...proof [of] fraud...practised upon them...There was *neither negligence nor moral guilt of any kind* on their parts' (emphasis added).[7] But two years later some members of the court in *Sleep* were more receptive to the notion of a fault requirement being dislodged by the particular circumstances of statutory construction. Both Cockburn CJ and Pollock CB conceded that the need for a 'guilty mind' could

---

[6] *Woodrow* (1846) 15 M. & W. 404. Also *Attorney-General* v. *Lockwood* (1842) 9 M. & W. 378.

[7] (1859) 2 El. & El. 66. Similarly Wightman, Erle, and Crompton JJ. The case is also relevant to the establishment of vicarious liability. Also *Cohen* (1858) 8 Cox 41.

be 'dispensed with by statute; but the terms which should induce us to infer [this must be very strong], which was not so in respect of the offence charged'.[8]

A further interpretive device later adopted by judges turned on whether such 'regulatory' or 'welfare' offences could properly be regarded as truly criminal in complexion. If they could, at least *sub silentio*, be treated as a species apart, this would obviate any open fundamental doctrinal compromise implicit in construing penal provisions as not requiring fault.[9] And, to a degree, such a conceptual accommodation did occur, so that by the end of the century Wills J. could comfortably speak of offences 'created quite independently of the moral character of the act'.[10] But such an interpretational shift did not take place without considerable variation in emphasis and acceptance amongst the judiciary.

Of broader import, holding to the implicit segregating device of 'quasi criminal' could prevent doctrinal implications from the particular judicial construction of 'regulatory' offences from spilling over into the territory of general principles of criminal responsibility. But such a relatively painless accommodation 'regulatory' liability was interrupted by *Prince*, where the offence (abduction of a minor carrying a maximum penalty of two years' imprisonment with hard labour) was by no stretch of judicial imagination, 'quasi criminal'. Here, the evidence suggested that Prince had, on reasonable grounds, believed a girl to be over 16 years old; but was such a lack of knowledge of her under-age status fatal to a conviction? By a majority of 15 to one the Court for Crown Cases Reserved thought it was not. Strongly adhering to the universal expectation of some fault for all *actus reus* elements of an offence, Brett J. alone maintained that: 'Upon all the cases I think it is proved that there can be no conviction for crime in England in the absence of a criminal mind or *mens rea*'; thus 'whenever the facts which are present to the prisoner's mind, and which he has reasonable ground to believe, and does believe to be the facts, would if true, make his acts no criminal offence at all', an acquittal must follow. Furthermore, rather than just a matter of statutory construction of the need for *mens rea*, Brett denied liability because of the 'excuse' of a 'mistake of fact...on reasonable grounds,...such excuse [being] implied in every criminal charge and every criminal enactment in England'.[11]

---

[8] *Sleep* (1861) Le. & Ca. 44. Similarly, Cockburn LCJ in *Batting* v. *Bristol and Exeter Railway Co* (1861) 3 *LT* 665. Although it is unclear just what constituted a 'guilty mind' for Cockburn and Pollock, both seemed to require actual 'knowledge' of the essential facts. See also Martin B., Crompton and Willes JJ.

[9] e.g. references by Wills J. to 'municipal law' in *Tolson* (1889) 23 QBD 168, 172. More generally, Sayre, 'Public Welfare Offences'.

[10] *Parker* v. *Alder* (1899) 1 QB 20, 26. Similarly Lord Russell CJ, 25.

[11] (1875) *LR*, CCR 2, 169–70. On the disputed effects of mistake of fact, see 'Mistake of Fact' Ch. VII.

After agreeing that a starting-point in statutory construction was the presumption that some sort of 'guilty mind [was] an essential ingredient in a crime' two majority judgments in *Prince*, those of Blackburn J. and Bramwell B., part company. Blackburn was not prepared to give any particular meaning to the presumption. The Blackburn route to construction and conviction was clear and unselfconsciously instrumentalist: the offence formed part of a 'code for the protection of women and the guardians of young women [with] the intention of the legislature...to punish abduction, unless the girl [was of age] irrespective of whether he knew her to be too young...'.[12] Having deduced this, it was the court's function to ensure legislative policy was not thwarted: '[It] would be baffled, if it was an excuse that the person guilty of the taking thought the child above sixteen'. Of course, a mind as legally subtle as Blackburn's must have recognized that such an argument might be applied to practically any offence, and, moreover, use of other devices, such as shifting the onus of proof, could meet any legislative concerns over the need to maintain an effective method of achieving the same social objectives.

In contrast with Blackburn's relatively straight thinking and plain speaking approach, Bramwell's was suffused with strong hints of the old alchemy tied up in the *mala in se* and *mala prohibita* distinction; more redolent of Blackstone than might have been expected of Bramwell.[13] According to Bramwell, because the deliberate act of taking a girl of this age out of the parents' possession without parental consent was 'wrong in itself', 'intrinsically wrong'; the requirement of a deliberate taking gave 'full scope to the doctrine of mens rea'.[14] Obscurity of meaning and impracticability of application alone ensured that Bramwell's constructional notions enjoyed a limited career.[15] Quite what Bramwell's judgment concluded on the existence and nature of any presumption of *mens rea* or 'guilty mind' is impossible to comprehend.

[12] (1875) *LR*, CCR 2, 171. 'It seems to us that the intention of the legislature was to punish those who had connection with young girls, though with their consent, unless the girl was in fact old enough to give valid consent. The man who has connection with a child relying on her consent, does it at his peril, if she is below the statutable age' (171–2). In divining parliamentary intention, Blackburn resorted to the preamble of an earlier statute upon which the 1861 Act was substantially based.

[13] As Fifoot fairly observed of Bramwell: 'single-minded', 'refused to be bullied by precedent...the embodiment of common sense in law', *Judge and Jurist in the Reign of Victoria* (1959), 15. Less easy to accept in respect of criminal law would be Fifoot's pen portrait of Blackburn, suggesting him to be an over-scrupulous adherent to precedent: *op cit.*, 17.

[14] Bramwell's distinction could be construed as a reference to the necessary voluntariness of criminal action, *ibid.*, 175. As with Blackburn's rationale, Bramwell also took the view that the Legislature had made the taking of a girl out of parental possession carry the 'risk of her turning out to be under sixteen' (175).

[15] But cf. Wills J. in *Tolson* (1889) 13 QBD 168, 172.

The doctrinal after-wash of *Prince* was to be seen 14 years later in *Tolson*. Here, in relation to bigamy charges, a wife's *bona fide* belief of her previous husband's death was held to be a 'good defence' by a nine to five majority in the Court for Crown Cases Reserved. On this occasion the two most noteworthy judgments were those of Wills and Stephen JJ. Although, the majority view, in part at least, resembled that of Brett J. in *Prince*, Stephen also took Bramwell's judgment in *Prince* to contain 'an emphatic recognition of the doctrine of the "guilty" mind' as an element, in general, of a criminal act'. Wills regarded *Prince* as 'direct and cogent authority for saying that the intention of the legislature cannot be decided upon simple prohibitory words, without reference to other considerations.[16] Not missing the opportunity to record his distrust of the maxim requiring *mens rea*, Stephen described it as: 'too short and antithetical to be of much practical value. It is, indeed, more like the title of a treatise than a practical rule'.[17] However, taking *Prince* as of 'direct authority' for the present case, Stephen sought to show that despite other differences, Brett and Blackburn JJ and Bramwell B. each recognized the presumption of the need for fault as the basis of all offences.[18]

But just how and when such a presumption was to be departed from received no more illumination from Stephen than had been provided by Wills. Echoing Blackburn in *Prince*, Stephen also construed the relevant legislation there as meant to ensure that 'seducers and abductors...act at their peril'; however, he detected no such unqualified legislative intention in *Tolson* in relation to bigamy. Quite why this was so does not clearly emerge. Indeed, such was the variety of interpretational rationales offered up in *Prince* and *Tolson*, that Fifoot's acute reflections on these two particular decisions are very hard to resist: 'The suspicion is strong that in neither case would the interpretation have been the same had Henry Prince not been a cad and Martha Tolson not more sinned against than sinning'.[19]

---

[16] Ibid., 180. Quite what these considerations were cannot be easily identified from Will's extensive judgment; two would appear to be the reasonableness of a strict interpretation and the level of penalty attached to the offence.

[17] *Ibid.*, 186. Cf. *HCL*, ii, 117.

[18] *Ibid.*, 190. Similarly, Stephen's judgment in the CCCR case of *Bishop* (1880) 5 QBD 259 (where a reasonable mistake as to the sanity of other individuals was denied to be a defence) referred to by him in *Tolson* (191) and in *HCL*, ii, 117, where the 'nature of the evils to be avoided' led to the 'at their peril' basis of responsibility. In the *General View* (1890), Stephen included 'negligence' as a 'mental state' when discussing the presumption of *mens rea*. Comparing *Prince*, *Bishop*, and *Tolson*, he thought the 'maxim' threw no light on the appropriate statutory construction; each raised 'questions [which] must all be decided according to circumstances, which differ from case to case' (74–5). Lord Coleridge CJ also saw *Prince* as relevant and correct. Hawkins J. allied himself with the sentiments of Brett J. in *Prince*. Cf. Winfield's discussion of the tort background of this notion in 'The Myth of Absolute Liability' (1926) 42 *LQR* 37.

[19] *Op cit.*, 133. Again, as in *Prince*, it is impossible to be sure from each judgment in *Tolson* just what was the nature of the presumption of a 'guilty mind'—whether it required subjective fault or

In some respects, *Prince* might be seen as the high-water mark of nineteenth-century judicial willingness to push aside the presumption of the need for *mens rea* and construe at least an element of a fairly serious offence as requiring no fault. Certainly the reliably anodyne *Russell* was, by its standards, uncharacteristically critical of the decision, noting that the 'case was not argued for the prisoner' and that Brett J.'s judgment 'will well repay perusal'. Indeed, editorial partiality shows through in that most of Brett's judgment is reproduced, alongside a relatively short extract from Bramwell B.'s, while completely omitting reference to Blackburn J.'s observations. By the time *Russell* had reached its 1909 edition the tone was less hostile, featuring a much shorter extract of Brett's judgment, but still without reference to Blackburn's contribution.[20]

However, because of their obvious non-regulatory nature, neither *Prince* nor *Tolson* had much apparent impact on the construction of the broad run of statutory offences.[21] More typical of the judicial approach to statutory interpretation over the final two decades of the nineteenth century and beginning of the twentieth, are decisions such as *Blaker v. Tilstone*,[22] *Parker v. Alder*,[23] and *Goulder v. Rook*,[24] where three successive Lord Chief Justices,[25] with very little talk of any presumption of *mens rea*, are to be seen freely employing a combination of familiar constructional rationales: deducing and facilitating legislative policy;

---

whether objective fault would suffice. Wills J. appears to make the presumption a subjective requirement (172), Cave and Hawkins JJ seem to incline towards accepting objective fault (181, 193–4), whereas Stephen veers between denying its existence and adopting an objective fault view. Moreover, *Prince* is not easily reconcilable with *Hibbert* (1869) 1 CCR 184, where the offence of seduction of a girl under 16 years of age was held to require the defendant's knowledge that the girl was in the lawful charge of her father. Cf. J. Edwards, *Mens Rea and Statutory Offences* (1955), 60–1.

[20] 5th edn, 1877 by S. Prentice, i: 888–9; 7th edn, 1909 by W. F. Craies and L. W. Kershaw, i: 959–60.

[21] Cf. Stephen who for one took the view that they were to be adjudicated upon the same two basic principles: 'the general scope of the act, and from the nature of the evils to be avoided' (*HCL*, ii, 117).

[22] [1894] 1 QB 345. Wright, J.'s complex stand in *Sherras v. De Rutzen* [1895] 1 QB 918 against what he rightly regarded as a largely unpredictable and quixotic approach to statutory construction was itself of limited comprehensibility and ease of application.

[23] [1899] 1 QB 20. This decision is authority for the proposition that even where there is third party involvement or a *novus actus*, liability for the defendant's initial act is unaffected. See particularly Wills J. at 26, and cf. *Hearne v. Garton* (1859), 2 El. and El. 66, where the court emphatically denied that a party could be criminally liable for the acts of an intervening third party. Whilst very little judicial comment is to be found on the need for fault or blameworthiness in the form of 'voluntariness' of action or the availability of general defences, the implicit assumption appears to have been that the exclusion of fault did not extend to such fundamental features of liability. See *Marsh* (1824) 2 B. & C. 717 and Bramwell B. in *Prince*, above.

[24] (1901) 2 KB 290.

[25] Lords Coleridge, Russell, and Alverstone respectively.

circumventing the problem of proving knowledge; and the comparison of fault requirements of different provisions within the same piece of legislation.

2. DEDUCING PARLIAMENT'S WILL

As has been seen, the judicial divining of legislative intention was an early and frequently used interpretational tool. Sometimes it was a conspicuously transparent ruse or subterfuge; on other occasions courts appeared genuinely to be seeking out the legislature's will. Subsequently, it has been almost a commonplace[26] to dismiss such a speculative exercise as meaningless on the grounds that matters of criminal fault rarely engaged the legislature's attention in matters of statutory regulation.[27] This was true up to a point. However, certainly by the second half of the nineteenth century parliamentarians frequently showed themselves to be fully alive to questions of fault in regulatory laws. Such interest can be seen, for example, in operation during the parliamentary career of two important legislative measures, later to be subject to judicial construction: the Licensing Act 1872, and the Food and Drugs Act 1875.[28] Scrutiny of the legislative history of each of these bills well illustrates the misleading nature of the blanket claim of parliamentary indifference to fault questions. Most especially, the example of the Licensing Act 1872 also demonstrates that vested interests, always well represented in Parliament, were particularly sensitive to matters of criminal sanctions affecting their special constituencies.

Of the several cases entailing interpretation of the 1872 Act, two achieving particular prominence were *Sherras* v. *De Rutzen* and *Cundy* v. *Le Cocq*.[29] Part of their notoriety rests on the apparent irreconcilability of the two decisions'

[26] e.g. Edwards, *op cit.*, 246; C. Howard, *Strict Responsibility* (1963) shows no curiosity in respect of parliamentary discussion; cf. 9–10.

[27] The most concrete manifestations of parliamentary interest in matters of fault have been the enactment of specific 'reasonable care' or 'due diligence' provisions alongside the creation offences.

[28] The parliamentary passage of the Food and Drugs Act 1875 entailed a fair measure of debate on the appropriateness of fault as an element of the various offences created. For example, in relation to Cl. 3, mixing and selling of 'injurious ingredients', the bill originally included 'knowingly'; at Committee stage the government conceded the amendment to strike it out. The advocates of its removal were motivated by concerns over enforceability: PD 1875 (s. 3), 223: 1263–6. The House of Lords' Committee witnessed a similar debate over the desirability of 'knowingly', but on a division the requirement remained part of the offence: 223, 1894–5 and 225, 944. Similar moves in respect of Cls 4 and 5 (adulteration of drugs) failed: 223, 1266–7 and 1271–2. In the case of Cl. 5, 'knowingly' was later struck out and then supplemented by a special provision whereby a retailer convicted of selling adulterated food or drugs without knowledge of the adulteration might recover from the wholesaler the penalty and cost of the former's conviction: 224, 782–3. This particular offence (under s 6 of the 1875 Act) was subsequently construed in accordance with *actual* parliamentary intention in e.g. *Betts* v. *Armstead, Parker* v. *Alder,* and *Goulder* v. *Rook.* Cf. Blackburn J.'s strict approach to construing ss 2 and 3 of the earlier 1872 Adulteration of Food and Drugs Act.

[29] [1895] 1 QB 918 and (1884) 13 QBD 207.

interpretation of separate provisions of the Act. An added dimension of interest is that both cases were decided by distinguished criminal theorists and draft codifiers: Stephen and Wright JJ. In *Cundy* v. *Le Cocq* Stephen J. held that for a licensee unlawfully to sell intoxicants to a 'drunken person' contrary to s 13 of the Act did not require knowledge of the purchaser's drunken state. He reached this conclusion primarily on two grounds: from the 'general scope of the Act, which is for the repression of drunkenness', a matter of perpetual social concern;[30] and, secondly, by noting that some other offences under the Act expressly required 'knowledge', which raised the implication that where omitted from a provision the legislature had not intended knowledge to be the 'essence' of that particular offence. In adopting this view, Stephen alluded to the 'old time' when the presumption of *mens rea* held sway in construing statues, but such a presumption did not have 'so wide an application as it is sometimes considered to have...owing to the greater precision of modern statutes'.[31] Subsequently, in *Sherras* v. *De Rutzen*, Wright J. (the respondent's counsel in *Cundy*) interpreted the offence of supplying liquor to a police constable on duty as requiring knowledge that he was on duty. This time such a construction rested on the offence in question not falling within Wright's devised categories of offences where the courts were likely to recognize strict liability.[32] However, if the judges of each case had exchanged places it is hard to believe that the outcomes would not have been reversed, with Stephen still convicting and Wright still acquitting. In other words, the particular judge's attitude to the specific legislative enactment and towards the general legitimacy of fault-free liability was frequently crucial in determining outcomes.

Turning to the actuality of legislative intention as revealed in parliamentary proceedings, whilst the offence in *Sherras* v. *De Rutzen* attracted no special attention, quite the opposite was true of the relevant provision in *Cundy* v. *Le Cocq*; this particular offence greatly exercised parliamentary interest. As originally drawn, liability under the bill did not require a licensee's knowledge that the purchaser of liquor was drunk. At Committee stage, Henry Bruce, the Home Secretary, accepted an amendment whereby 'knowingly' was inserted into the offence, a move applauded by a Mr Whitbread who regarded the duties of licensees as 'very severe indeed'.[33] Two weeks later, the Home Secretary performed an

---

[30] See 'Punishment' and 'Inebriety', Ch. V, above.

[31] At 210.

[32] Principally, 'acts which are not criminal in any real sense...; public nuisance...; proceeding[s]...in criminal form [which] is really only a summary mode of enforcing a civil right' (922). See above for an evaluation of Wright's views. The adjacent provision under s 16(1), of harbouring or suffering a constable to remain on licensed premises whilst on duty, expressly required knowledge that the constable was on duty.

[33] PD 1872 (s. 3), 212: 1701–2. Bruce, for the government, observed that the bill's object was to 'secure improved order, and the great cause of disorder was knowingly permitting drunkenness' (see 'Inebriety' Ch. V, above) (1703). See also the comments of Alderman W. Lawrence on the need

apparently unselfconscious *volte face*. A proposed amendment to excise 'knowingly' was moved by a member on the grounds of the difficulty of enforcement, with the requirement of knowledge affording 'means to a low class of person of evading' conviction. This time the Home Secretary saw 'great force' in the argument endorsing the amendment, which was carried[34] despite some support in other quarters for its retention. It might be wondered whether Stephen in his non-judicial capacity had perused these particular columns of *Hansard*.

3. VICARIOUS RESPONSIBILITY

Although somewhat slower than strict liability in evolving, the judicial rationale(s) offered for vicarious liability's recognition *broadly* followed those fielded to justify strict liability. Acceptance of criminal vicarious liability entailed an even greater departure from the general tenets of criminal responsibility; under this form of liability not only could any form of personal fault be dispensed with, but also the offender's personal actions themselves. To arrive at such a modification of entrenched criminal doctrine purely through the art of statutory construction required a more substantial leap of judicial imagination than had been necessary for recognition of strict liability. Consequently, it is not surprising that vicarious liability gained a firm footing in criminal jurisprudence rather later in the day than strict responsibility. However, even in the early decades of the nineteenth century,[35] clear signs were visible of judicial willingness to contemplate extending the narrowly applied common law notion of vicarious responsibility into statutory offences. As with strict liability, the personal juristic leanings of individual members of the bench were of significance in the headway made by vicarious responsibility; this was never more so than in respect of Blackburn J., who has been rightly regarded[36] as the principal judicial facilitator of this form of criminal liability.

for vicarious responsibility to ensure the provision could not be easily circumvented (1703). Some members argued for the *removal* of 'knowingly' from Cl. 14 of the bill—keeping a disorderly house. This attempt to impose strict liability was successfully resisted by the government (1888–9).

[34] *PD* 1872 (s. 3), 213: 660–2.

[35] *Dixon* (1814) 3 M. & S. 11; *Marsh* (1824) 2 B. & C. 717: 'A master in some cases is answerable for the act of his servant, when the act is done by the servant for the benefit of the master and in the course of his employment', per Littledale J. See also *Siddon* (1830) 1 C. & J. 221. In the case of corporations, initial substantive and procedural obstacles to prosecution were overcome by the clear public need to control their activities through criminal sanctions. Vicarious and strict liability were recognized as extending to corporations as well as individuals. Development of the 'alter ego' doctrine, whereby corporations might be additionally responsible for offences requiring fault through the actions of 'directional' officers was largely a twentieth-century creation. See generally R. Welsh (1946) 62 *LQR* 345 and C. Winn (1929) 3 *CLJ* 398.

[36] T. Baty, *Vicarious Liability* (Oxford, 1916), e.g. 205. And Blackburn's role in clarifying the concept of subjective recklessness in the 1870s, 'General Principles', above Ch. VII.

While obviously not solely accountable, Blackburn undoubtedly occupied the judicial vanguard during the 1860s[37] and 1870s when in a succession of decisions he unwaveringly recognized the propriety of construing statutory offences as open to vicarious liability. A particularly clear application of the doctrine was seen in the 1873 case of *Fitzpatrick* v. *Kelly* where Blackburn, 'fresh from his Edinburgh honours of LLD',[38] held an 'unknowing' shopkeeper responsible for selling adulterated goods through a sale effected by an employee. Similarly, a year later in *Mullins* v. *Collins*, where an 'innocent' licensee was convicted for his employee's supply of alcohol to a policeman on duty, Blackburn J. observed: 'If we hold that there must be...personal knowledge in the licensed person, we should make the enactment of no effect.'[39] Difficulty of proving an employer's knowledge of the criminal actions of an employee, coupled with an anxiety not to see legislative policy circumvented, was a recurrent policy rationale expressed in judgments throughout the remainder of the nineteenth century.[40]

Yet at the century's close not only was there an absence of anything approaching an intelligible judicial articulation of the interpretive process which led to a finding of vicarious liability, even the most fundamental basis of the doctrine had not been settled: did it rest on a borrowed development of tort liability, or on principal and agent notions relating to the course and scope of employment?[41] Or was delegation of an employer's legal duty the trigger for criminal liability? Certainly, a course-of-employment approach predominates in the early period of vicarious responsibility.[42] But, particularly in the case of Blackburn's judgments, application of the delegation principle is evident, if not always expressed in such terms. By the end of the nineteenth century and into the twentieth, both bases for conviction can be observed operating side by side,[43] even though different outcomes were possible, depending on which test was applied. This was true of decisions such as *Emery* v. *Nolloth* where even though the proscribed behaviour was in the course of the barman's employment,

[37] e.g. Blackburn's judgment in *Avards* v. *Dance* (1862) 26 JP 437 (rather floridly described by Baty as an 'atrocity', *op cit.*, 206) and *Willcock* v. *Sands* (1868) 32 JP 292.

[38] (1873) LR 8 QB 337; Baty, *op cit.*, 208.

[39] (1874) LR 9 QB 292. Cf. parliamentary debates on the Licensing Act 1872, above.

[40] See e.g. Blackburn J. in *Redgate* v. *Haynes* (1876) 1 QB 89. Also *Massey* v. *Morris* (1894) 2 QB 412, and *Commissioner of Police* v. *Cartman* [1896] 1 QB 655.

[41] Cf. Edwards *op cit.*, 220. And see Salmond's discussion of the irrebuttable presumption of implied authority and of what he refers to as the 'laconic maxim, *Respondeat Superior*', *Jurisprudence* (5th edn, 1916), 375–6.

[42] e.g. *Marsh* (1824) 2 B. & C. 717.

[43] Application of the course of employment test occurred in *Budd* v. *Lucas* [1891] 1 QB 408; *Commissioner of Police* v. *Cartman*, ibid.; *Coppen* v. *Moore* [1898] 2 QB 300; and *Boyle v Smith* [1906] 1 KB 432. Examples of use of the delegation principle are *Redgate* v. *Haynes* ibid.; *Somerset* v. *Hart* (1884) 12 QB 360; Stephen J. in *Bond* v. *Evans* (1888) 21 QB 249; *Massey* v. *Morris*, ibid.

Lord Alverstone held conviction of the licensee inappropriate because of the absence of delegation of control of the premises by him.[44]

4. OVERVIEW

Several general features of the historical development of the concepts of strict and vicarious liability merit further comment. First, it is far from obvious why, when departing from the entrenched (for some judges) subjective fault version of the *mens rea* principle, courts usually vaulted over the intermediate concept of objective fault to adopt a no fault position. Indeed, initially in relation to both strict and vicarious liability, such an intermediate, negligence-based course seemed to be in the minds of some judges.[45] A particular manifestation of this was the effect on liability of express instructions by employers to employees to carry out their duties in a proper, lawful fashion. Yet, after limited judicial support for the claim that employers would be immune from conviction in such cases, the courts consistently determined that employers' instructions were irrelevant to their liability.[46]

A second general observation concerns the rationale for strict and vicarious liability that positively establishing knowledge (or even negligence) on the defendant's part would be impracticable. Here it might be questioned why did the courts not choose to have their cake and eat it by retaining some element of fault as the basis of liability but locating the onus with the defendant to disprove fault? As seen in relation to subjective and objective forms of fault, the presumption of intention was, in any case, a leading auxiliary feature of nineteenth-century substantive fault requirements. Even though occasionally judicial attempts to establish such a principle in relation to regulatory offences can be seen,[47] this approach was never enthusiastically taken up by the courts. Moreover, it was a development which became less feasible as the legislature itself more frequently incorporated 'reasonable diligence' provisions; the absence of such was then taken as further evidence of parliamentary intention to make people strictly liable for those offences not expressly benefiting from these express defences.

---

[44] [1903] 2 KB 264. Followed in *Allchorn* v. *Hopkins* (1905) 69 JP 354.

[45] e.g. in *Woodrow* (1846) *ibid.*; Pollock CB referred to the want of proper care on the part of the defendant and 'Prudent man'. Also *Dixon* (1814) *ibid.* and *Crabtree* v. *Hole* (1879) 43 JP 799.

[46] On the basis that regulations could be easily circumvented if express contrary instructions were a defence, see *Brown* v. *Foot* (1892) 66 LT 649 and *Coppen* v. *Moore* [1898] 2 QB 306. For the earlier view making employers' warnings relevant, see *Kearly* v. *Taylor* (1891) 65 LT 261. The argument was unsuccessfully pressed by Stephen acting as counsel for the respondent in *Harrison* v. *Leaper* (1862) 26 JP 373, 374. A lingering attachment to the need for some element of objective fault is also discernible in the early editions of Kenny's *Outlines*, e.g. the 1904 edition references to offenders who 'merely neglected the means of knowing' (45) and Kenny's construction of *Sherras* v. *De Rutzen* (47).

[47] e.g. *Marsh* (1824) *ibid.* and Day J. in *Sherras* v. *De Rutzen* (1895).

A third development feature of strict and vicarious liability was the distinct likelihood of the cross-fertilization of ideas from the broadly contemporaneous process in tort, where after equivocating over the relevance of fault, courts moved liability onto a largely risk basis: that those engaged in commercial enterprise did so at their own risk—a hazard to be set against the rewards of commercial endeavour. Of course, the appropriateness of such shared rationales was clearly questionable, with the objectives of tortious and criminal responsibility being distinct: compensation for economic loss compared with prevention and punishment.[48] Whilst the efficacy of deterrence or prevention was relevant to criminal offences this was not true of tort liability.[49]

Finally, just *how* fault-free liability would regulate or superintend those areas of conduct covered by legislation was not judicially articulated; such ability was assumed *sub silentio*. The judicial embracing of an openly instrumental conception of criminal responsibility in areas of behaviour not always of a welfarist or regulatory complexion, paradoxically coincided with the period when both procedurally, evidentially, and substantively, the mainstream of doctrinal development of criminal fault was beginning to flow in the opposite direction.[50] But for many it was a paradox at only a very superficial level; for no general principles of criminal jurisprudence were at stake or were properly to be deduced from strict and vicarious liability, for, at most, they were only distant cousins of 'true crimes'. It was an attitude visible and directly expressed in the 1863 edition of Stephen's *General View*:

[The offences involve] actions forbidden by the legislator...which derive their moral significance exclusively from the fact that they are forbidden by law...[T]he definition of offences of this class is a special matter little related to broad principles of any kind, especially to moral principles.[51]

---

[48] Cf. discussion of mistake of fact, above, Ch. VII.

[49] Blackburn J. also played a significant role in *Rylands* v. *Fletcher* at the Exchequer Chamber stage (1866) LR 1 Exch 265. See G. Williams and B. Hepple, *Foundations of the Law of Tort* (1984), 128–9 and see XII, Pt 4. Note also Blackburn's extensive judgment in *Mersey Docks and Harbour Board Trustees* v. *Gibbs* (1866) making public authorities vicariously liable for their employees' torts. Markby noted in the 1885 edition of *Elements of Law* the cross-fertilization of tort and crime notions, adding that 'We are perhaps approaching a considerable readjustment of the respective domains of civil and criminal law' (415).

[50] In the sense of sharpening fault requirements and terms; and beginning to distinguish more clearly subjective and objective forms of fault, see 'General Principles', Ch. VII, above.

[51] At 100. Stephen concedes no change of view after *Prince* in the work's 2nd edn (1890), 75–6. Similarly e.g. Wills J. and Lord Russell CJ in *Parker* v. *Alder* (1899) 1 QB 20.

IX

Securing the State, the Institutions of Government, and Maintaining Public Order

1. OFFENCES AGAINST THE STATE, GOVERNMENT, AND ITS INSTITUTIONS: SEDITION, TREASON, AND SECRETS

Physical manifestations of widespread public discontent with any of the state's institutions, including the monarchy, Parliament, and government, might amount to offences against both public order and the state. But while patently linked, the law's protection of the state's institutions and maintenance of public order are separable concepts and subject to particular, if overlapping, forms of legal response. Thus, many instances of offences against the state might involve neither actual nor potential disorder; at the same time, public order offences may be localized and non-politically motivated, offering no challenge to the state's existence or security. During the nineteenth and early twentieth centuries, treason, sedition, and official secrets offences constituted the principal forms of liability aimed directly at defending the state's integrity and security. However, their prominence and rates of deployment varied considerably along with nineteenth-century shifts in political and social expectations, especially relating to freedom of expression and the widening of the franchise. In broad terms, such political and social developments were reflected in the relative relegation of treason and sedition prosecutions during the first half of the century in favour of the deployment of public order offences.

Sedition

By the mid-1820s government use of sedition offences[1] to suppress or see off political agitators or especially worrisome polemicists was fast diminishing, as were the

---

[1] Since at least Star Chamber times, criminal libel comprised two classes: seditious libel, where there is a threat to state security, and private libel, originally based on the notion of the likelihood

memories of Lord Mansfield's robust and highly partisan defence of Crown and government in sedition trials more than half a century earlier.[2] Besides charges of sedition, radical societies, agitators, and pamphleteers of the 1790s onwards were also countered with the occasional suspension of *habeas corpus* and a swelling body of legislation largely aimed at particular instances of perceived (often transient) threats to political stability and security.[3] Even adverse comment on the government's handling of popular disturbances might easily attract retaliation, as Sir Francis Burdett found in 1820 when his unsparingly critical reporting of the authorities' appalling conduct at Peterloo led to his prosecution and conviction for seditious libel.[4] Defendants in such trials were generally procedurally disadvantaged from the outset. Although Fox's Libel Act 1792 relocated with juries the former judicial role of determining whether or not a publication was seditious, several procedural features still strongly favoured the prosecution: most prosecutions were commenced by the Attorney-General's *ex officio* information, thereby eliminating the twin filters of preliminary and Grand Jury hearings; consequently, at trial defendants would have no prior detailed knowledge of the prosecution's case.[5] This image and substance of politically expedient justice

of causing public disorder. Sedition had three principal manifestations: (i) seditious words; (ii) if printed, seditious libel; (iii) and an agreement to commit a seditious act was seditious conspiracy. All were common law misdemeanours originally subject to unlimited imprisonment and/or a fine. Sedition's essence was both wide and vague, inherently capable of political abuse and extending to actions likely to generate discontent with any institution or element of the state, constitution, church, or representatives of these institutions. Stephen also included promoting ill-feelings between different classes. Confirmed in *Burns* (1886) 16 Cox 354. Respectful and non-inflammatory criticism or reform proposals would not incur liability, *HCL* ii, 299.

[2] Not unusually, before appointment as Lord Chief Justice of the King's Bench, Mansfield had been Solicitor-General and subsequently Attorney-General in Whig administrations. J. Oldham, *The Mansfield Manuscripts* (Chapel Hill, 1992), i:, Ch. 1. and ii: Ch. 13 on Mansfield and seditious libel.

[3] Between 1815 and 1820 two particular examples of public agitation, Spa Fields, London in 1816 and Peterloo, Manchester in 1819, brought into action special Lords' and Commons' Committees to review intelligence on anti-government activities and threats. These 'Secret Committees' initiated an extensive range of repressive, counter-insurrectional legislation; including suspension of *habeas corpus*, the Seditious Meetings Act 1817, and the 'Six Acts' of 1819, concerning drilling, public meetings, seditious libels, search and seizure of weapons, and procedural changes relating to the trial and sedition offences. See also the related aims and ambit of the Combination Acts of 1824 and 1825, XIII, Pt 3.

[4] (1821) 1 St. Tr. (NS) 1. Burdett was chairman of the radical Hampden club, established to campaign for a wider franchise and workers' education. Between 1808 and 1821, 101 informations (ultimately 7 acquittals) were issued in sedition cases, *PP* 1821 (676), xxi, 399. Of the few reported cases after Burdett, see *Harvey and Chapman* (1823) 2 St. Tr. (N.S.) 1.

[5] Chitty, *Criminal Law*, i: 846 and J. L. Edwards, *The Law Officers of the Crown* (1964), 262–7. Lord Eldon, a consistent advocate and defender of the procedure, boasted that as Attorney-General in the 1790s he deployed the procedure more frequently than any previous or subsequent Attorney. He also successfully opposed an enquiry into *ex officio* informations in 1811, *PD* 1811 (s.1), 19: 158–60. On

was reinforced by not infrequent resort to special juries, 'packed' with members believed to be unsympathetic to the defendant's views or activities.[6]

A drastic decline in the use of sedition prosecutions corresponded with a rising recognition of the political legitimacy (or inevitability) of relatively free speech, coupled with the easing of some political tensions. Feelings of the state's vulnerability to the dangers of public disorder also slowly declined with professional policing gradually assuming an ever-reassuring and effective presence, first in London and later in the provinces. Most fundamentally, the nineteenth century saw the steady erosion of the belief that it was 'very necessary for all governments that the people should have a good opinion of it', and, therefore, that governments were entitled to suppress hostile opinion.[7] But even liberal Whig administrations occasionally felt obliged to resort to the sedition laws, although sometimes this entailed getting their collective fingers burnt in the process, as Lord Denman found when acting as Attorney-General in the unsuccessful prosecution of William Cobbett in 1831.[8]

Gradually replacing sedition (and treason) prosecutions, public order offences generally became the first line of defence for nervous governments after the Great Reform Act. Sedition charges were increasingly perceived as politically crude and maladroit; governments became more sensitive to how the practice might 'shake the stability of a ministry and destroy the popularity of an Attorney-General'.[9] However, sedition offences never became completely redundant weapons in the government's arsenal as was well demonstrated by Cobbett's 1831 trial and the charges following the Chartists disturbances of 1839–49.[10] Yet by 1843 a House of Lords Select Committee felt able to assert that although the sedition laws had

---

this period, see C. Emsley, 'An Aspect of Pitt's Terror: Prosecutions for Sedition during the 1790s' (1981) 6 *Social History* 155. For the initiatory role of magistrates, see P. Harling, 'The Law of Libel and the Limits of Repression 1790–1832' (2001) 44 *Hist. J.* 107. Brougham mounted the Whig (opposition) challenge to the procedure in (1816) 27 *Edin. Rev.* 245.

[6] On this practice, see Bentham's polemic, 'The Elements of the Act of Packing, as Applied to Special Juries, Particularly in Cases of Libel Law' (1821) Bowring, *Works*, vol. 5, 61; and T. Wooler, *The Alleged Lawful Mode of Packing Special Juries* (1817). More generally, J. Oldham, 'Special Juries in England: Nineteenth Century Usage and Reform' (1987) 8 *JLH* 149.

[7] Holt, CJ in *Tutchin* (1704) 14 St. Tr. 1095, at 1128.

[8] (1831) 2, St. Tr. (N.S.) 789. Cobbett, who conducted his own defence, was faced by the combined talents of Denman, Wightman, and Gurney, all destined for the Bench. Others, such as *Carlile* (1831) St. Tr. 2, (N.S.) 459, faired less well, incurring a sentence of two years' imprisonment. The Recorder of London's opinion expressed to the jury was as unbalanced as Lord Tenterden's in Cobbett's case was scrupulously neutral.

[9] 'Criminal Informations' (1833) 9 *LM* 361, 367. Signed 'S', the writer may have been Thomas Starkie, author of the leading defamation text, *Practical Treatise on the Law of Slander, Libel and Malicious Prosecution* (1812), and subsequent editions.

[10] For official details of the early Chartist prosecutions, see *Prisoners for Libel*, PP 1840 (600), xxxviii, 691. Peel's Second Administration (1841–6) showed a greater inclination to resort to sedition

the power to fetter seriously the 'wholesale liberty of the press', 'Mildness' in the law's use, the 'Liberality of judges and the Discrimination of Juries in modern times' had conduced to 'little practical Inconvenience' and no 'Complaint from Authors or Journalists'.[11]

Consequently, the reforms enacted subsequently by the Libel Act (Fox's Act) 1843 were almost wholly restricted to changes in the law of private libels (see below). Moreover, the rarity of nineteenth-century sedition prosecutions left a substantial clutch of unresolved aspects of liability, including, most centrally, the precise *mens rea* requirements. In relation to culpability, early nineteenth-century authority, such as *Burdett*, appears to specify no more than objective fault: simply an intention to publish. Later judgments, especially *Burns*, offer a narrower conception of sedition liability by requiring intention that public disorder was consequential to publication.[12] Inherent uncertainty and latitude are built into a jury's determination of whether or not a defendant's actions generated a real likelihood of a threat to the peace. In settling this they needed to have regard to the contemporary state of public receptivity to the defendant's actions.[13] This, allied to the power of delivering a general verdict under Fox's Act, compounded unpredictability in the outcome of sedition prosecutions, thereby drastically reducing their attractiveness to governments. This flexible, virtually untrammelled adjudicative role of the jury was unintentionally identified in Lord Kenyon's pithy rhetoric: 'The liberty of the press is dear to England. The licentiousness of the press is odious to England'.[14] Giving juries the power to make this subjective judgment was a development which, in the main, the younger Stephen endorsed: as 'ex-post facto censors', juries were 'better placed to determine the permissible level of State criticism' as representatives of those who have 'everything to dread from abuse of government power', unlike judges 'who have by their position, the strongest sympathy with authority....'.[15]

---

charges than Melbourne's or Russell's. D. Goodway, *London Chartism 1838–1848* (Cambridge, 1982) and J. Saville, *1848: The British State and the Chartist Movement* (Cambridge, 1987), *passim*.

[11] *Report, HL Session Papers; PP* 1843, (513), clix 17. This view was largely based on the evidence of John Black, editor of the *Morning Chronicle* (pp. 111–12) and Lord Brougham (p. 28); similar evidence came from the Society of Provincial Newspaper Proprietors (p. 147).

[12] Cave J., *Burns* (1886) 16 Cox 355 at 364 expressly relying on Stephen, *HCL*, ii, 339. Also *Collins* (1839) 9 Car. & P. 456 and *Aldred* (1909) 22 Cox 1. However, see Stephen's *Digest* (4th edn), Art. 94, where an objective test was stipulated.

[13] *Vincent* (1839) 9 C. & P. 91, 110; *Collins* (1839) 9 Car. & P. 456, 460. As to the extent to which the particular characteristics of an intended audience might be considered, see *Aldred* (1909) and cf. *Burns* (1886).

[14] (1799) *Cuthill* 27 St. Tr. 642, 674.

[15] *General View*, 147–8. By the 1880s Stephen regarded seditious conspiracy as a 'necessary...serious counterpoise...to the exorbitant influence which [trades unions] are capable of exercising' (*HCL*, ii, 380). On the use of conspiracy law against trades unions, see, XIII, Pt 3.

In contrast, Stephen's views of the evolution of laws governing press libels in the second half of the nineteenth century were decidedly less sanguine. As he maintained, while press comment on the 'public conduct of public men' was distinct from seditious libel, Victorian developments of this form of criminal libel had strong conceptual and political implications for the notion of press liberty more generally.[16] For this reason it is appropriate to consider non-seditious criminal libel alongside more direct forms of 'public offences'. Unlike various forms of sedition, the use of non-political criminal libel to restrict and punish publishers retained its vigour and appeal well into the twentieth century. Significant differences between seditious and non-seditious libel had become established by the end of the nineteenth century. In large part, such differences emerged as a consequence of the absence in non-seditious libel of the restraining stigma of a direct prosecutorial link with governments. And, unlike seditious libel's alleged underpinning concerns for the maintenance of public order,[17] non-seditious libel's rationale shifted towards public vindication of the prosecutor and implicitly condoned punitive vindictiveness against the defendant. But at the same time, the legitimacy of the right of a largely unshackled press to publish critical or even ferociously hostile comments on public figures was increasingly recognized. This acceptance eventually brought about the enactment of Lord Campbell's Libel Act 1843.[18]

Under the Act, in non-seditious libels, truth of a defendant's claims constituted a defence if the jury judged publication to be for the 'public benefit'.[19] It

[16] *HCL*, ii, 376. For an analysis of the use and development of civil actions, see XII, Pt 4.

[17] Brougham ridiculed this claimed basis of all criminal libels as a 'fiction of the law...for giving the court jurisdiction, merely a creature of judicial refinement', *PD* 1816 (s. 1), 34: 387.

[18] Generally supported by (1843) 30 *LM* 152 and (1833), 11 *LM* 432. Brougham made an abortive attempt at such an amendment to the law of criminal libel, including sedition, in 1816, *PD* 1816 (s.1) 34: 377, esp. 399–404. Sir Francis Burdett was the motion's seconder. Had the Bill been successful, Burdett's justified criticism of the handling of the Peterloo demonstrations would have probably resulted in his acquittal in 1820. See also Burdett's powerful speech on the prosecution of seditious activities in the first reading of the Seditious Meetings Bill, *PD* 1817 (s.1), 35: 607–16. A background of Luddite and other agitations resulted in not only the failure of Brougham's Bill but the suspension of *habeas corpus*, the enactment of the Seditious Meetings Act 1817, and the 'Six Acts' of 1819. Brougham also attacked both the system of *ex officio* informations and use of special juries (391–3). Both the Attorney-General and Solicitor-General robustly defended the status quo (393–6). Campbell himself as Attorney-General in 1840 had instigated the successful prosecution of Feargus O'Connor (editor of the radical *Northern Star*) for criminal libel, *Life of Lord Campbell* (1881), ii: 132; (1831–40) 3, *State Trials* (N.S.) 1299.

[19] Opposition to such a change came from surprising quarters: both Starkie and Ker, in what amounted to a *volte face* from their proposals in the *Criminal Law Commission Sixth Report* (1841), pp. 35 and 106 regarding a truth defence as likely to encourage the incidence of libel and deter prosecutions of it. Also, Lord Denman (p. 124). See further, *Report of the House of Lords Select Committee*, *PP* 1843 (513), cclix, p. 17. Earlier reform attempts were made in the 1830s, including 1837 when, as Whig Attorney-General, Campbell fully conceded the need for such change, denying the Bill his

was a change of law that again reinforced vague normative jury powers, making the outcome of many such prosecutions even more unpredictable and subject to the fickleness of individual juries. Expansion of the press and its steady progress towards Establishment solidarity and respectability was furthered by organized parliamentary groups representing newspaper owners seeking to cut back the scope of criminal libel and their risks of prosecution. Steady lobbying and petitioning[20] finally produced a Commons Select Committee in 1878. The resulting Newspaper Libel and Registration Act 1881 sought to keep newspaper owners out of the criminal courts in two ways: through a qualified privilege to print verbatim reports of public meetings; and by preventing prosecutions of newspaper owners or personnel without the DPP's consent.[21] Belief in some quarters that the Director was insufficiently discriminating in applying this filter led to the role being subsequently awarded by the Law of Libel Amendment Act 1888[22] to a judge in chambers.

While broadly supported beyond the realms of the press industry, these protective measures by no means enjoyed universal approval. Some, including Stephen, deplored the accelerating intrusiveness of investigative and sensationalist journalism. Criminal libel laws, without special statutory defences, were regarded as a proper means of curbing the unprincipled commercial zeal of newspaper owners. In 1883, he characterized the Newspaper Libel and Registration Act as a retrograde measure, enlarging press 'power to a height extremely dangerous to private reputations':

The section which privileges fair reports of public meetings appears to me most objectionable...It is in keeping with that indifference to personal dignity and paltry curiosity about private affairs which is one of the contemptible points of the habits of life of our day. Far from relaxing the law...I should wish to see its stringency increased.[23]

Arguing, in effect, for some form of quasi-criminal privacy law, Stephen favoured a return to the 'public good' defence of the 1843 Act. In taking this stand he

support on the basis of defective draftsmanship and a heavily congested legislative timetable, *PD* 1837 (s. 3), 38: 483. Campbell maintained that in certain circumstance *ex officio* informations were defensible (484–6).

[20] For instance, see *PD* 1868 (s. 3), 192: 604. Evidence was taken from a mix of provincial newspaper owners and a representative of the Society for Provincial Newspapers who claimed to promote the interests of half of British provincial periodicals.

[21] See the two Select Committee Reports and Evidence, *PP* 1879 (343), xi, 261 and 1880, (384), ix, 301.

[22] *PD* 1888 (s. 3), 329: 313. On the public criticism of the DPP by Lord Coleridge, the provision's promoter, see 'Prosecution', Ch. III, above. Lord Coleridge's opposition to criminal libel actions led to his ruling in *Labouchere* (1884) 12 QBD 320, favouring tight limitation of the granting of criminal informations.

[23] *HCL*, ii, 384–5. Even in his younger journalistic days, Stephen expressed concerns over excessive Press licence (1867) 15 *Cornhill Mag.* 36.

enjoyed the tacit support of others, including Mr Justice Hawkins, whose sentencing policy towards errant editors was consistently nothing less than severe.[24]

Treason and Official Secrets

In the canon of not just political crimes, but crimes in general, none has been formally regarded as more heinous than high treason, a fact graphically reflected in the severity and savagery of its punishment.[25] Stripped of technicalities, by the nineteenth century treason could be characterized as 'armed resistance, justified on [political] principle, to the established law of the land'.[26] Although undergoing significant developments during the nineteenth century, the law remained largely the product of judicial enlargement of a small collection of treason statutes, commencing with the Treason Act 1351.[27] Such constructive enlargement was never much hindered by treason's requirement of an 'overt' or 'open' deed. In 1820, Lord Tenterden regarded this as being satisfied by 'any act manifesting the criminal intention and tending towards the accomplishment of the criminal object'.[28] Within such a wide-jawed, comprehensive net might be scooped up perpetrators of all manner of very preliminary and remote activities. These included spoken endorsement of such activities, behaviour condemned by Lord Ellenborough as the 'clearest and most absolute overt acts of high treason'.[29]

---

[24] On Hawkins, see J. R. Spencer, 'The Press and Reform of Criminal Libel', *Reshaping the Criminal Law*, ed. Glazebrook (1978), 266, 278. Also, 'Criminal Libel—Skeleton in the Cupboard' [1977] *Crim. LR* 383, 391-3 for notorious examples of the injustice sometimes worked by the criminal libel laws.

[25] Until the Forfeiture Act 1870 (33 and 34 Vict. c. 23) the law permitted hanging, beheading and quartering. The last beheading occurred in 1820, Gatrell, *The Hanging Tree*, Ch. 11, *passim*.

[26] Stephen, *General View*, 36.

[27] Most importantly: (i) compassing or imagining the sovereign's death, judicially extended to conspiracy to imprison the sovereign, endanger the sovereign's life, or depose the sovereign. Confirmed in s 1 of the Treason Act 1795 and Treason Felony Act 1848 (below). (ii) Levying war against the sovereign. Any insurrectional action constituted 'war' if there was a 'national' or 'general' public dimension, e.g. Alderson B.'s charge to the Grand Jury, Liverpool (1848) 6 St. Tr. (N.S.), App. B, 1129. Unlawful assembly and riot did not require such a wide objective. (iii) Being adherent to the sovereign's enemies during war time, covering giving 'aid and comfort' to the enemy. See also the Treason Act 1702.

[28] *Thistlewood* (1820) 33 St. Tr 681, 684. Similarly, Lord Reading CJ in *Casement* [1917] 1 KB 98.

[29] *Despard* (1803) 28 St. Tr 346, 487. Treason's width was eventually narrowed somewhat in respect of adhering to the sovereign's enemies by *Ahlers* [1915] 1 KB 616, which required subjective intention to aid the enemy. For the operation of constructive intention in other forms of treason, see for instance, *Gordon* (1781) 21 St. Tr. 485 and *Tooke* (1794). More generally, see J. Barrell, *Imagining the King's Death: Figurative Treason, Fantasies of Regicide 1793–1796* (Oxford, 2000) and M. Lobban, 'Treason, Sedition and the Radical Movement in the Age of the French Revolution' (2000) 22 *Liverpool LR* 205. Treason's broad ambit was augmented by criminalizing (misprision of treason) failure to disclose information on treason to the appropriate authorities. The last reported

Yet while its potential application remained great, the usefulness and actual employment of treason charges during the nineteenth century was relatively restricted and narrow. Usually, only what were perceived of as the most threatening direct actions against the state led to the deployment of treason charges. Nothing later remotely matched the government measures and responses of 1817. Alarmed by the events of Spa Field in late 1816 and a stream of intelligence on the mounting threats of insurrection provided by the Parliamentary Committee of Secrecy, the Liverpool administration was instrumental in suspending *habeas corpus* and the detention of around 150 suspects on a range of treason charges, of which over 60 were eventually brought to trial.[30] Contrastingly, widespread Chartist activities from the late 1830s generated hardly more than a dozen full high treason charges in 1840, along with a similar number of lesser felony-treason charges in 1848.[31]

A blend of sedition and public order based offences now formed the mainstay of the state's response to sometimes severe nationwide disturbances. Such diminished charges were regarded as more appropriately characterizing the nature of the criminality: this registered a shift from denial of the legal and political legitimacy of public censure of Establishment institutions and advocacy of political alternatives, to a position where the prosecutorial focus became challenging the means by which such political attacks might be lawfully manifested. Except in the most extreme instances, inflammatory behaviour and public disorder were perceived as most appropriately prosecuted by a combined sedition-public order response. Later, with the progression of political tolerance, official confidence, and expansion of middle-class participation in radical politics, purely public order charges became the standard response. Effectively, between the 1830s and second half of the nineteenth century there occurred an almost complete legal relegation of the relevance of the objectives and motives of public agitation.

However, this general trend was not without interruption. In the 1840s the combined circumstances of Chartist and Irish Nationalist activities, set against a deeply discomforting backdrop of French and other continental revolutionary fervour, propelled Russell's administration towards enactment and deployment

case concerned the Cato Street conspiracy, *Thistlewood* (1820) 33 St. Tr 681. The offence carried a maximum of life imprisonment.

[30] Above n. 3. See the *First and Second Reports of the Committee of Secrecy PP* 1817 (387) iv, 1 and 9; and *Report of the Select Committee of the House of Lords, ibid.*, 17. Full details of those detained in 1817 on treason charges are set out in the 'Return', *PP* 1818 (89), xvi, 151. The Return reveals the extensive range of professions and trades of detainees, as well as ages (largely 20s–50s), and district of origin.

[31] *PP* 1849 (108), xliv, p. 51, a comparative table of political offences charged from 1839–48 (p. 64). The favoured charges were various combined forms of sedition and riots, which peaked in 1842 (962) and 1848 (253).

of modified treason laws. Pleading the inadequacy of sedition offences, the Home Secretary sought and gained enactment of a new species of treason modelled on high treason. But consonant with the 'salutary change' that had taken place in 'public opinion' and its greatly restricted appetite for capital punishment, rather than death, perpetrators of the proposed treason-felonies would be subject to a minimum of seven years' transportation or up to two years' imprisonment.[32] As the Home Secretary Sir George Grey implicitly conceded, the notional severity of high treason was considered an obstacle to jury convictions in Ireland and England. The 1848 Act also widened the span of treason by, for example, including incitement to treason by 'open and advised speech or by any other act', thereby ensnaring 'rabble rousers' who formerly could often only be muted by relatively mild sedition penalties. But the graver charge of high treason for the same conduct remained in place, acting as a long stop to the new treason-felonies. Use of full blooded treason charges was reserved for particularly bold and direct instances of insurrection or where a government wished to terminate, or at least remove for a considerable time, a potent and persistent anti-state leadership force; certain prominent Irish Nationalists, including the Westminster MP, William Smith O'Brien, were so regarded and dealt with accordingly.[33] Treason-felony prosecutions became virtually extinct after their deployment in the 1880s against Fenians or 'Dynamitards'.[34]

Protection from the undermining or prejudicing of state security also took on an additional new form in the late nineteenth century. Particularly, though not exclusively, in the case of military and defence intelligence, the penalizing of improper disclosure was not easily or naturally accomplished by prosecution under existing treason laws. Departmental pressure (especially from the Admiralty, War Office, and Foreign Office) for specifically engineered liability

---

[32] Sir George Grey, *PD* 1848 (s. 3), 98: 31–2. Sedition offences were considered inadequate on two grounds: the penalties were too light, and the offences were 'bailable', thereby permitting defendants to repeat offences whilst on bail (23 and 31). The Home Secretary also remarked on the Irish Nationalists being 'learned in the law' (23) or having access to such advice. Links between Chartist and Irish Nationalist were commonly assumed, e.g. *ibid.* (15–16) and the speech of the Irish Nationalist MP, William Smith O'Brien claiming such an alliance, *ibid.* (73–83).

[33] (1848) 7 St. Tr. (N.S.) 1. Trial was before a Special Commission. For others tried for high treason, the general political background, and its aftermath, see S. McConville, *Irish Political Prisoners 1848–1922* (2003), Ch. 1 'The Young Irelanders'. Treason-felony convictions were secured e.g. in *Mitchel* (1848) 6 St. Tr. (N.S.) 599 where the Attorney-General provided the court with an explanatory background to the new offences (636–9), and also *Dowling* (1848) 7 St. Tr. (N.S.) 381 (Chartist).

[34] *Gallagher* (1883) 15 Cox CC 291 and *Deasy* (1883) 15 Cox CC 334. *Gallagher*, 'The Dynamitards Case', was tried at the Old Bailey by three judges (Coleridge C.J., The Master of the Rolls, Sir Baliol Brett, and Grove J.) with the object of providing an authoritative ruling on certain features of the 1848 Act. See the observations of Sir Harry Poland who prosecuted along with the Attorney-General and R. S. Wright. E. Bowen-Rowlands, *Seventy Two years at the Bar* (1924), 190–3. Also, earlier, *Mulcahy* v. *R* (1868) LR 3 HL 306, at 320; and *Davitt* (1870) 11 Cox CC 676.

aimed at unauthorized disclosure eventually[35] resulted in the Official Secrets Act 1889. Though expressly targeted on spying and espionage, the unauthorized disclosure of lesser, non-security sensitive information, was also, with practically no dissenting voices, criminalized by the Act.[36] However, applying the full rigour of the 1889 Act proved difficult,[37] and, following two failed amending bills,[38] the government finally succeeded with the enactment of the Official Secrets Act 1911.

Despite government assurances to the contrary,[39] the new Act extended considerably beyond the reach of earlier provisions. The 1911 legislation had two broad functions: to protect the state from actions 'prejudicial to the safety or interest of the State'; and to prevent unauthorized disclosure by any state employee of any official information, whether or not secret or confidential, and whether or not related to state security. The apparent ubiquity[40] of these provisions was judicially confirmed over the course of a series of prosecutions under the Act.[41] Moreover, as the government had openly claimed, the Act shifted the burden of proof of culpability in certain cases so as to (effectively) require defendants to provide innocent accounts of their *prima facie* prejudicial activities.[42]

Thus, by the opening of the First World War, the state had furnished itself with extensive powers to prosecute at its discretion, a comprehensive range of activities stretching from those most patently damaging to state security to those of the most trivial and remotely connected nature. In spite of earlier declarations by the Lord Chancellor of his 'dislike [of] legislation passed in undue hurry',[43] the 1911 bill's passage was exceedingly swift and virtually unopposed. The perfunctory nature of the government's justification of the bill was just one manifestation of the consuming climate of rising fears over Germany's apparently inexorable strengthening of military and naval capacity. Clearly, as some[44] had maintained

---

[35] On the background to the 1889 and 1911 Acts, see D. G. Williams, *Not in the Public Interest* (1965), 15–25 and K. G. Robertson, *Public Secrets* (1982) 54–69.

[36] *Doe* (1902) *Central Criminal Court Session Papers*, vol. 136, 775.

[37] *Holden* (1892), unreported, discussed by Williams, *ibid.*, 21.

[38] The 1908 bill was sabotaged principally by a 'deputation representing the Metropolitan Press'. Reporting this meeting, Lord Loreburn LC expressed mild disappointment at the apparent misunderstanding as to the bill's scope; he looked forward to arriving at a 'common agreement' on the subject, *PD* 1908 (s. 4), 188: 673–4.

[39] *PD* 1911 (s. 5 HL), 9: 642, by Lord Haldane, Secretary of State for War. The Attorney-General, Sir Rufus Isaacs was more guarded, referring to no change 'in principle', *PD* 1911 (s. 5 HL), 29: 2252.

[40] See Debates on 1911 Act.

[41] e.g. *Crisp and Homewood* (1919) 83 *JP* 121; *Zamora* (1916) 2 AC 77, 107 confirming that for the purposes of s 1 of the Act, the needs of national security and what might prejudice it were determined by 'those who are responsible for the national security'.

[42] Lord Haldane, *PD* 1911 (s. 5 HL) 9: 642.

[43] Lord Loreburn LC, *PD* 1908 (s. 4), 190: 1478.

[44] Particularly protection of government departments by severely limiting the ability of MPs 'at once to put our finger on the blot' of maladministration, *PD* 1889 (s. 3), 339: 320–1.

during the course of earlier legislative attempts, such secrecy laws might not only truly help protect genuine state interests, but also carried the manifest potential to shield ineffective and incompetent bureaucracies and governments from public exposure and censure.

2. OFFENCES AGAINST PUBLIC ORDER: UNLAWFUL ASSEMBLY AND RIOT

In broad terms, the common law had long recognized a cluster of offences aimed at maintaining public order. Three of these misdemeanours—unlawful assembly, rout, and riot—were frequently regarded as criminalizing a continuum of increasingly undesirable and threatening activities: commencing with unlawful assembly, which became a rout 'as soon as some act has been done moving towards the execution of the joint design', and culminating in a riot when 'at least some act [is] done in part execution'. In offering this fairly orthodox conceptualization of the three offences' kinship, the Criminal Law Commissioners conceded that the demarcation point between rout and riot, between 'moving towards execution' and part execution, was 'extremely subtle'.[45] All three[46] offences eventually shared the requirement of behaviour that had a tendency to cause apprehension of public disorder. In practical terms rout became virtually extinct by the nineteenth century; riot continued to furnish the authorities with a useful weapon for deployment against manifest group violence; unlawful assembly developed during the early nineteenth century from a relatively obscure offence into a highly valuable means of suppressing or controlling menacing social and politically motivated meetings. Complementing such specific offences was the individual and collective legal duty of the magistracy and citizens to 'exert themselves in the timely repression of riotous assemblies'. As *Pinney*, and other subsequent authorities demonstrate, it was a duty most emphatically recognized until well into the nineteenth century, even after the professionalization of policing had largely assumed such responsibilities.[47]

---

[45] *Criminal Law Commission, Fifth Report* (1840) 92; Stephen, *Digest* (3rd edn, 1883), Art. 72. And e.g. Holroyd J., *Redford v. Bierley* (1822) 1 St. Tr. (N.S.) 1071, 1214; Patteson J., *Birt* (1831) 5 Car. & P. 154.

[46] The long-established misdemeanour of affray overlaps riot. Like riot and unlawful assembly, the potential apprehension of reasonably firm people was (and is) a requirement of liability; unlike riot and unlawful assembly, a minimum of two participants is required; and unlike riot, affray requires no concerted plan; thus, spontaneous fighting may constitute an affray. An affray was never deployed in a political context in the fashion common to riot and unlawful assembly. Affray fell into disuse by the mid-nineteenth century. *Hunt* (1845) 1 Cox 177 is one of the last English cases. Use of the offence was revived in the 1950s.

[47] See E. Wise, *The Law Relating to Riots and Unlawful Assemblies* (1848), 97; *Pinney* (1832) 5 C. & P. (1891) 3, St. Tr. (N.S.) 11; *Cunninghame Graham and Burns* (1888) 16 Cox 420 in relation to

Unlawful Assembly

Depending on the specific circumstances, public disorder could carry local and national dangers, both social and political. The overt political dimension and influential forces at work in the early nineteenth-century formulation of the offence of unlawful assembly are particularly marked. Although its existence was clearly recognized in eighteenth-century treatises,[48] unlike riot, the offence's use was scarcely recorded, and consequently speculatively defined in broad terms. With the major exception of politically spawned conspiracy, the common law's ambivalent attitude towards inchoate or pre-emptive forms of criminal liability[49] was probably one important conceptual factor in the relatively late full judicial formulation of unlawful assembly liability. However, the practical political need of addressing the perceived dangerous potential of large meetings had by no means escaped the attention of governments and Parliament. As already noted, by the early nineteenth century the expectation and legitimacy of public expression of social and political dissent were gaining increasingly wide acceptance. In Parliament it was a cause which Radicals and a few prominent Whigs almost routinely espoused. Rather than the substance of political dissent and challenge, the accepted legitimate role of government and the criminal law was shifting towards regulating the *form* of such public dissent. To meet these demands, alongside statutory sedition offences and proscription of politically threatening societies, came legislation restricting or prohibiting more than modestly sized, broadly political meetings. Emergency measures of substantially similar scope had been resorted to by Pitt in 1795, and Liverpool in 1817 and 1819.[50]

Such seditious meetings legislation commonly stipulated detailed limitations on political assemblies in relation to maximum size, composition, and purposes.

---

magistrates and the Metropolitan Police Commissioner. When requested, citizens were obliged to assist the police in suppressing a riot, *Brown* (1841) Car. & M. 314; *Sherlock* (1866) LR 1 CCR 20. On the use of volunteers, yeomanry, and militia in dealing with public disorder during the first half of the nineteenth century, see Radzinowicz, *History*, iv: Ch. 4.

[48] Notably, *Hawkins*, 1 PC Ch. 28, section 9; see also Blackstone, *Comms*, iv, 146.

[49] See 'Inchoate Liability', Ch. VII, above.

[50] Seditious Meetings Act 1796, 36 Geo. III, c. 8; Seditious Meetings Act 1817, 57 Geo. III, c. 19; and Seditious Meetings Act 1819, 60 Geo. III and Geo. IV, c. 86. Of fixed duration, the Acts generally required organizers of meetings of more than 50 people to give prior notice to local magistrates. Broadly, such meetings were restricted to local inhabitants. Failure to comply with an order to disperse unlawful meetings within a fixed period was a felony. The 1817 Act was mainly restricted to controlling meetings within a mile of Westminster. The last of such Acts in 1819, punished the mere attendance at an unlawful assembly with a fine or imprisonment of up to one year (s 5); failure to disperse within quarter of an hour of the meeting being declared unlawful by an authorized party carried a penalty of up to seven years' transportation (s 8); bearing or carrying flags or banners at such meetings could be punished with up to two years' imprisonment (ss 18 and 19).

Enacted as one of the 'Six Acts' in the uneasy wake of Peterloo, the temporary Seditious Meetings Act 1819 was the government's key provision in its attempt to suppress industrial and social agitation and meet what it perceived to be coordinated or conspiratorial insurrectional activities.[51] Although justifiably sceptical of national conspiracy claims, the majority of Whigs were less than resolute in their opposition to the Six Acts. But some principled disagreement did emerge on the necessity for the seditious meetings legislation, with the Opposition contending that the common law offence of unlawful assembly was adequate to prevent, or at least regulate, large political gatherings. Doubting the law's claimed lack of ambiguity, Lord Castlereagh for the government saw it as 'high time for Parliament to take care that this embarrassment should be felt no more'.[52] However, it was the trial of Henry 'Orator' Hunt and others, the following spring at York Assizes for offences arising out of Peterloo, which largely settled the matter of common law liability for unlawful assembly. Here, and soon after in *Dewhurst*, Bayley J. produced the authoritative modern affirmation of the basis of unlawful assembly liability. Modifying *Hawkins'* definition, Bayley J. ruled that an assembly might be unlawful by virtue of an unlawful object or by reason of its characteristics being such as likely to induce a public apprehension of disorder; moreover, the circumstances must be such that apprehension was likely to be caused to those of 'ordinary firmness'; and mere awareness of the unlawful purpose of the assembly would be sufficient to incriminate all those present.[53]

Through these authorities, *Hawkins'* and *Russell's* incipient riot rationale mutated into one which, as an alternative to an intrinsically criminal objective, looked to an assembly's potential to generate public disorder. Thus formulated, unlawful assembly charges might be deployed in circumstances where although no substantive unlawful objective, such as seditious claims or proposals, existed, the context and circumstances of the assembly were of a menacing nature. Unlawful assembly not only armed the authorities with a relatively clear facility for early intervention in circumstances which might easily develop into a more

---

[51] e.g. *PD* 1819 (s. 1), 41: 383–98, 1234–7.

[52] *Ibid.*, 387. Cf. Lord Eldon, *ibid.*, 40. Scarlett appeared to maintain that Peterloo and similar meetings were unlawful, *ibid.*, 41: 132–4. But cf. 167 and Canning's remarks, *ibid.*, 197. Scarlett was prosecuting counsel in both *Hunt* and *Dewhurst*.

[53] *Hunt* (1820) 1 St. Tr. (N.S.) 171; *Dewhurst* (1820) 1 St. Tr. (N.S.) 529; followed by Holroyd J. in the civil action of *Redford* v. *Birley* (1822) 1 St. Tr. (N.S.) 1071. Hunt had originally been detained on a charge of high treason, but as Home Secretary, Lord Sidmouth (on the advice of the Law Officers) conceded, this was dropped for lack of evidence. Home Office memo reproduced (1820) 1 St. Tr. (N.S.) 171, 173n. On contemporary Home Office and government attitudes as revealed in correspondence, see M. Lobban, 'From Seditious Libel to Unlawful Assembly...1770–1820' (1990) 10 *OJLS* 307, 332–8.

socially threatening or dangerous activity, it also equipped them with a politically more subtle, pre-emptive device than hitherto available:

it is far better and far more humane, far wiser and far more politic, to stop these things in
their early stages... before they proceed to outrage and violence, as a small amount of punishment, in the first instance, will probably save a great amount of crime afterwards.[54]

It might be speculated on whether, if common law unlawful assembly had been
a more prominent, solidly defined concept before Peterloo, Liverpool's administration would have resisted the urge to legislate along the lines of the Seditious
Meetings Act 1819. A cluster of reasons suggests this to be doubtful. First, as
well as far more restrictive than the later common law, the Act's notice requirements brought in a strong element of local legal control and superintendence,
which probably operated as a deterrent to many potential assemblies; secondly,
under the Act there was no need for the prosecution to establish, as in the case
of common law liability, the likely generation of apprehension of disorder; and
thirdly, the prescribed maximum penalties of imprisonment or transportation
under the 1819 Act were considerably greater than regarded as appropriate for
unlawful assembly.[55] The only serious countervailing consideration against such
temporary (five years) emergency legislation, was its immediate political association with the government of the day; in contrast, unlawful assembly charges with
their universal application lacked this immediate political resonance or taint.

Subsequent case law refinement of common law unlawful assembly occurred
periodically throughout the nineteenth century. In *O'Connell*, the offence's reach
was extended by combining it with conspiracy, thereby drawing in a conspiratorial agreement to procure unlawful assemblies.[56] Even meetings gathered for an
unlawful purpose, but voluntarily abandoned, were declared an unlawful assembly.[57] Throughout the Chartist years, the offence was freely deployed, frequently
in combination with sedition charges.[58] Alderson B. in *Vincent*, emphasized that
when assessing whether it was reasonable to conclude that a meeting generated
a fear of disorder, it had to be from the standpoint of the 'firm and rational man',
taking account of all the surrounding circumstances: 'the way in which the meetings were held, the hour of the day..., and the language used by the persons

---

[54] Alderson B.'s charge to the Grand Jury, Monmouth Assizes (1839) 9 Car. & P. 94.

[55] The power to disperse unlawful, but peaceful, meetings within 15 minutes under the threat of
felony proceedings was a strong incentive to comply. On conviction for common law offences, Hunt
e.g. was bound over to keep the peace for six months on his own recognizances of £2000: (1820) 1
St. Tr. (N.S.) 171, 488n.

[56] (1843) 5 St. Tr. (N.S.) 1 (complete volume). And Bayley J. in *Hunt* at 437–8.

[57] *Birt* (1831) 5 Car. & P. 154. This is consistent with conspiracy, the later abandonment of which
does not erase liability.

[58] e.g. *Jones* (1848) 6 St. Tr. (N.S.) 783.

assembled and by those who addressed them'.[59] Earlier unlawful assembly authorities only required the apprehension of a probable breach of peace when the meeting's objectives were not in themselves unlawful; therefore assembling as a preliminary to committing an offence by stealth would constitute unlawful assembly. But the risk of causing apprehension of a disturbance was eventually settled as an essential element of both forms of unlawful assembly in the early twentieth century by *Field* v. *The Receiver of Metropolitan Police*.[60]

Broadly, unlawful assembly had eclipsed sedition offences by the 1830s. Yet, in terms of need and use, although becoming a comparative rarity as the century wore on, whenever the authorities felt sufficiently vulnerable or outraged by the nature or scale of a disturbance, undiluted sedition charges were still pressed instead of unlawful assembly. One well-publicized example occurred after a meeting of the 'Revolutionary Social Democratic League' in Holborn in the mid-1880s fuelled by a climate of substantial economic depression. Fired up by rousing speeches, a riotous crowd of over 3000 streamed down Pall Mall, the heart of London's club land, to gather menacingly in Hyde Park. Rather than the, by then, more orthodox unlawful assembly and riot charges, the meeting's speakers were prosecuted for sedition. At trial, however, while acknowledging such behaviour to be strictly within the wide embrace of seditious liability, the general tenor of Cave J.'s jury direction strongly hinted at his scepticism as to the appropriateness of such charges. In articulating the basis of sedition liability, not only did he reject the presumption of intended consequences and specify true intention to cause disorder as the offences' fault requirement, he also repeatedly stressed the relevance to liability of the honesty of endeavour of the defendants to call to the government's attention the appalling plight of the mass unemployed. Unsurprisingly, in the light of these observations the jury acquitted all defendants.[61]

The core issue of the appropriate balance to be struck between the needs of public order and those of individual rights once again surfaced in the context of unlawful assembly in the late nineteenth century case of *Beatty* v. *Gillbanks*. Here the question was whether it constituted an unlawful assembly to do a lawful act with knowledge that it was likely to generate a breach of the peace as a

[59] *Vincent* (1839) 9 Car. & P. 91, 109, 762; Patteson J. in *Stephens* (1839) 3 St. Tr. (N.S.) 1189 and Tindal CJ in *Harris* (1842) Car. and M. 661n.

[60] [1907] 2 KB 853. Stephen thought the position unclear in 1883 but 'submitted' that the unlawful act must involve the risk of causing apprehension of disorder, *Digest* (3rd edn), Art. 70 'Illustration b'. See also Charles J. in *Graham and Burns* (1888) 16 Cox 420, 427–8.

[61] *Burns* (1886) 16 Cox 355. In *Graham and Burns* two years later the charges were unlawful assembly and riot in Trafalgar Square. The prosecution was conducted by the Attorney-General, Solicitor-General, and Treasury Counsel. Conviction attracted a six-week prison sentence.

consequence of a third party's unlawful responses. In the Divisional Court, both Field and Cave JJ declared such conduct would not amount to an unlawful assembly.[62] It was an approach more favourable to individual rights to free speech than indicated in *dicta* from judgments earlier in the century, where liability might follow from cases where the language at meetings became provocative or inflammatory by virtue of those who might choose to join the meeting.[63] However, some later authorities, particularly *Wise* v. *Dunning*,[64] arguably implicitly undermined the standing of the *Beatty* v. *Gillbanks* principle. Addressing the sensitive question three years before *Beatty* v. *Gillbanks*, the Criminal Code Commission, in the absence of authority, had adopted a compromise, proposing liability where 'such assembly needlessly and without any reasonable occasion provokes other persons to disturb the peace tumultuously'. Under this proposal, juries would be called upon to make a normative judgment on the specific entitlement to free assembly and speech, an approach consistent with that taken elsewhere to balance public and private considerations in relation to the rights of public assembly or speech,[65] including the Libel Act 1843.

Riot

Participation in public disturbances in the eighteenth and nineteenth centuries was subject to the theoretical danger and (until well into the nineteenth century) practical risk of being prosecuted for riot or even high treason. Bearing in mind the potentially vast difference in punishment between these forms of liability, the basis of distinction was crucial. According to *Hawkins*: it is riot where there is 'intent mutually to assist one another against anyone who shall oppose them in the execution of some enterprise of a *private nature* [and three or more persons] actually execute the enterprise in a violent and turbulent manner, to the terror of the people...'.[66]

The politically manipulable nature of the slippery criterion of 'private' or 'public' enterprise or objective was regularly the target of early nineteenth-century

---

[62] [1882] 9 QBD 308, 314. And see the non-committal reserved judgment in *Clarkson* (1892) 17 Cox 482. In *Beatty* v. *Gillbanks*, the Law Report only records Cave J. as concurring. However, 17 Cox at 147–8 contains a report of Cave's judgment, where he observes that had the defendants intended to oppose force with force their procession would have constituted an unlawful assembly.

[63] See Alderson B. and Tindal CJ in *Vincent* (1839) *ibid.*

[64] [1902] 1 KB 167. See the analysis in *Brownlie's Law of Public Order and National Security* (2nd edn, 1981), 124–30. Both this case and *Beatty* involved provocative religious elements. In late Victorian London, 'open air meetings' and marches were overwhelmingly of this nature. See for example 1891/2, *Home Office Printed Memoranda and Reports*, N.A. H.O. 347/7, 405.

[65] Draft Criminal Code, Part IV, and Stephen *HCL*, ii, 385n.

[66] *Hawkins*, 1 PC (ed. J. Curwood, 1795): c. 65.

critical comment. Defence counsel in Watson's treason trial spoke passionately and at considerable length against the past practice of Attorneys-General in opportunistically seeking to 'annihilate the boundaries' between riot and treason.[67] Founded on the politically expedient constructive expression of treason law, the Criminal Law Commissioners regarded the private/public distinction as 'wholly inapplicable to the present state of society' where most large assemblies were in pursuit of some 'political or supposed public grievance'. However, it was noted that through a combination of 'more enlightened views' and political expediency, what was strictly still treason was prosecuted as riot.[68] As in unlawful assembly, it was irrelevant whether or not the rioters' common purpose was 'lawful', provided the manner of the pursuit of their objectives tended to cause alarm to people of reasonable firmness.[69]

Although, in common with unlawful assembly, riot as a misdemeanour carried a theoretically unrestricted fine or imprisonment, this formal parity was modified in 1822 to reflect the generally more serious view taken of riot, with the option of hard labour added to the possible penalty for riot. However, far more significant was riot's convertibility to a (capital) felony by the provisions of the Riot Act 1714. It might be assumed that threats of a felony prosecution, with the consequential more severe punishment would weigh heavily with many rioters.[70] Indeed, the Act served as a model for provisions in the later emergency Seditious Meetings Acts where the failure of unlawful assemblies to disperse following an official declaration, generated felony liability. Of course, as a matter of practice, rather than solely the threat of such liability used to disperse very large assemblies, reliance was ultimately placed on the physical and intimidatory powers of substantial military forces, and, increasingly, large professional police contingents.

As the complexion of unlawful assemblies and riots shifted from the immediately political to one of organized industrial conflict, rather than involve itself directly in quelling or prosecuting large disturbances, central government increasingly sought to clarify the distinct responsibilities of civil and military

[67] *Watson* (1817) 32 St. Tr. 452.

[68] *Fifth Report* (1840), 90–2. Disapproval of the public/private distinction is reflected in the Commissioners' Digest formulation of riot: Art 1. *Dowling* (1848) 3 Cox 509, 514, Erle J.: where the common 'purpose is a private one, the offence is a riot; but if the purpose is public and general, it is a levying of war', and thus treason. No such distinction is recorded in Stephen's *Digest* definition of riot (3rd edn, 1883), Art. 72. But cf. Art. 53(c). No such distinction was established in relation to unlawful assembly.

[69] *Phillips* (1842) 2 Mood. C.C. 252 and *Field* v. *Metropolitan Police District Receiver* [1907] 2 KB 853 at 860.

[70] Section 1 of the 1714 Act requires a specified procedure by a justice (or other official) commanding dispersal of 12 or more rioters within one hour.

authorities, and those of local as opposed to central government.[71] It was an enterprise which enjoyed only limited success until the national scheme for mutual police force assistance, organized by the Home Office, was finally formulated by the Desborough Committee in 1920.

[71] Particularly, *Report of the Committee Appointed to inquire into the Circumstances Connected with the Disturbances at Featherstone* 1893, PP 1893–4 [C. 7234], xvii, 385; *Report of the Inter Departmental Committee on Riots* PP. 1895 [C. 7650]; and *Report of the Select Committee on Employment of Military in Cases of Disturbances*, PP 1908 (236), vii, 367.

X

Public Morality and Social Control: Prostitution, Gambling, and Obscenity

BLACKSTONE identified a particular collection of offences as seeking to promote the country's 'due regulation and domestic order'. By these offences individuals were 'bound to conform their general behaviour to the general rules of propriety, good neighbourhood, and good manners; and to be decent, industrious and inoffensive in their respective stations'.[1] Of course, as Blackstone and others were well aware, what constituted 'good manners', decency, and inoffensiveness, was highly variable, determined by time and social context. Furthermore, recognition of the shifting nature of sensibilities or social mores left unresolved the underlying question of how far the law should extend in seeking to penalize transgressions of social morality: just what might civil society censure yet not regard as the criminal law's business?

A cursory survey of the early nineteenth-century law's response to many areas of behaviour commonly regarded as socially illicit, would have generated, and did generate, much anxiety for any professional moralist, especially those of an Evangelical persuasion. Most particularly, prostitution, gambling, sales of indecent publications, and excessive consumption of alcohol[2] were, in varying degrees, all distinctive features of England's social landscape. And, while subject to a disparate body of penalties, prostitution, gambling, and sales of indecent publications were largely undisturbed as a consequence of very low levels of law enforcement. In the main, neither individuals nor local or central government agencies were sufficiently motivated to act in a sustained fashion against these forms of perceived immorality. However, for early nineteenth-century moralists, and particularly Evangelicals, often imbued with a utilitarian social philosophy, there was motivation in abundance. Their socially powerful brand of Victorian moralism spoke much of spiritual nourishment

---

[1] *Comms*, iv, 162.

[2] For the criminal law's response to inebriety and vagrancy, see M. Roberts 'Public and Private in Early Nineteenth Century London: The Vagrant Act of 1822 and its Enforcement' (1988) 13 *Social History* 273 and 'Punishment', 'Prisons, Transportation and Institutional Detention', Ch. V above.

gained through resisting earthly temptations; for individuals lacking the moral backbone to practice self-denial, the law was there to be drafted in to deny them illicit pleasures; it was a moral imperative not to permit the spiritually weak to be the authors of their own self-inflicted degeneration.

Paternalism of this highly intrusive variety frequently linked the development of social character and moral fibre with individual and national economic[3] stability, a concern voiced from time to time by official bodies throughout the century, particularly in relation to gambling and intoxication. And though far from a negligible force in seeking the enforcement and reinforcement of criminal sanctions aimed at curbing certain areas of socially censured behaviour, other religious groups, including Quakers, and secular organisations[4] were decidedly junior partners in the enterprise of ensuring law enforcement. The established lineage and active involvement of Evangelical bodies was the dominant operative force for the whole of the nineteenth century, through the initiation of prosecutions under existing law, along with persistent campaigning both within and outside Parliament. In broad terms, their collective aims were to ensure that the public face and private reality of Victorian morality bore a strong resemblance to each other.

While the sheer potency of religiously fuelled moral outrage might, through a combination of exposure and embarrassment, prod governments into legislative or, occasionally, prosecutorial action, other more pragmatic motives were also much in evidence. Most especially, fears and predictions of personal and national economic disablement were regularly offered by both campaigners and legislators as justification for the law's intervention, particularly in respect of gambling and inebriety amongst the working classes. As much as intuitively believed as empirically demonstrable, the link between vagrancy, crimes of immorality or 'social' offences and more serious forms of criminality was frequently maintained: either the corrupting consequences of indulging in immoral or social offences heightened an individual's susceptibility to a morally downward progression; or, the habits of vice-bred appetites which could for many only be fed and funded by resort to property crime.[5]

---

[3] See 'Law and Religion' and 'Law and Political Economy', XI, Pt 1. More generally, B. Hilton, *The Age of Atonement: The Influence of Evangelicalism on Social and Economic Thought 1795–1865* (Oxford, 1988), and on 'character', S. Collini, *Public Moralists, Political Thought and Intellectual Life in Britain 1850–1930* (Oxford, 1991), 91–118.

[4] W. E. Houghton, *The Victorian Frame of Mind 1830–1870* (New Haven, 1957), 366–8, and works cited.

[5] With differing emphases, see particularly the three celebrated social studies of London's poor and working classes by Chadwick, Mayhew, and Booth.

However, the process of legal intrusiveness was not entirely irreversible: some pragmatically based measures were ultimately rejected. For example, widening of the prostitution law's rationales from vagrancy and nuisance, to include protecting the health of the country's armed forces by enactment of the Contagious Diseases Acts proved an unpopular coercive step too far. Subsequent legislation curbing prostitution's exploitative dimension emerged as a more acceptable manifestation of the increasingly welfarist ethos of late nineteenth-century social politics. Though only ranking as a subsidiary justification for prostitution's suppression, an indistinct brew of notions concerning public sensibilities, decency, and moral corruptibility was at the core of the development and enforcement of the once largely moribund law of obscene publications. And while, until the nineteenth century, predominantly the preserve of the middle and upper classes, the increasing availability of commercially produced publications with explicitly sexual elements was seen as exposing to grave risk the characters of the working classes, especially young men.

More broadly, driven by a steadily developing state welfarist political philosophy,[6] the century's concluding decades marked a reinforcement of the criminal law's function in regulating social behaviour. The coherence and success of these social policies in relation to predominantly working-class sub-groups, including children,[7] juveniles, women, and inebriates, were frequently viewed as partly dependent upon the criminal law's coercive and punitive powers. In crude

---

[6] e.g. T. H. Green, *Lectures on the Principles of Political Obligations* (1895); L. T. Hobhouse, *Social Evolution and Political Theory* (1911); S. Collini, *Liberalism and Sociology: L.T. Hobhouse and Political Argument in England 1880–1914* (Cambridge, 1979). The most prominent nineteenth-century exploration of the political philosophy of suppressing immorality is J. S. Mill's essay *On Liberty* (1863). Fitzjames Stephen's *Liberty, Equality, Fraternity* (1873) provided the leading contemporary critique of *On Liberty's* central premise. But Stephen broadly sympathized with Mill's 'practical conclusions': 'the real difference between Mr Mill's doctrine and mine is this. We agree that the minority are wise and that the majority foolish, but Mr Mill denies that the wise minority are ever justified in coercing the foolish majority for their own good, whereas I affirm that under circumstances, they may be justified in doing so' (*Liberty, Equality, Fraternity*, 2nd edn by R. J. White, Cambridge, 1967), 74 and 159.

In identifying the 'circumstances' where social cohesion demanded intervention, Stephen leaned heavily on the 'public opinion' of the non-working classes. On matters of censorship and 'moral offences', Stephen personally took a relatively libertarian stance. For an analysis of the Mill-Stephen debate, and Bentham's view of crimes of immorality, Smith, *James Fitzjames Stephen*, 162–81 and *passim*. Both before and certainly after 1863, the law's direction was self-evidently against Millist anti-interventionism.

[7] The protection and welfare of children was a key area of legal development in the late nineteenth century. For example, between 1875 and 1885 the age of sexual consent was raised from 12 to 16 (Criminal Law Amendment Act 1885). A wide range of measures to ensure appropriate treatment of children and protection from neglect, cruelty and exploitation was enacted in the Prevention of Cruelty to Children Act 1904, the Children Act 1908, and the Incest Act 1908. See XIII, Pt 4.

terms, the lurking Liberal disjunction between the 'civil and social realms' was a social and political *quid pro quo*.[8] Thus, in the case of censorship, while political controls were relaxed and prosecution for seditious libel declined, so the vigour of obscene libel grew. By now the basic apparatus of enforcement was in place: central organizational professionalism and expertise at the Home Office in tandem with well-established professional policing and relatively streamlined summary court procedures. Of course, actual levels of enforcement of the expanding[9] range of so-called 'social' offences, or 'crimes of immorality', varied substantially; unlike for mainstream forms of criminality, both individual police forces and their strategically controlling authorities, whether the Home Office or local police committees, adopted frequently contrasting and shifting attitudes towards the priority to be given to the prosecution of such offences.[10]

1. PROSTITUTION

Until well into the second half of the nineteenth century, prostitution was viewed by the authorities as essentially an endemic social or 'spiritual'[11] problem; its illegal dimension was largely designated a particular strain of vagrancy. Like vagrancy and its frequent companion inebriety, prostitution carried the taint of social stigma combined with the perception of fringe or proto-criminality.[12] And broadly, in common with vagrants and inebriates, prostitution was taken not to be the law's business unless it manifested itself in forms of public offensiveness,

---

[8] On this, see I. Berlin, 'Two Concepts of Liberty', *Essays on Liberty* (Oxford, 1969) and G. Himmelfarb, *On Liberty and Liberalism* (New York, 1974), Ch. XII, 'Some Paradoxes and Anomalies'.

[9] Acts of indecency between males and incest were two notable additional forms of sexual offence created in the late Victorian/early Edwardian period. Section 11 of the Criminal Law Amendment Act 1885 criminalized indecent acts between men in public or, most significantly, private. The provision was added to the bill at committee stage with almost a complete absence of comment. F. B. Smith, 'Labouchere's Amendment to the Criminal Law Amendment Bill' (1976) 17 *Historical Studies* 165. A decade later, prosecution for the offence was the principal means of Oscar Wilde's demise. See below, 'Sexual Offences', Ch. XII. Until the Incest Act 1908, incest was not a criminal offence. Campaigning by the National Vigilance Association and the National Society for the Prevention of Cruelty to Children (along with police evidence) influenced the Home Office into supporting creation of the offence, V. Bailey and S. Blackburn, 'The Punishment of Incest Act 1908' [1979] *Crim LR* 708, and below, 'Sexual Offences' Ch. XII.

[10] On the Metropolitan Police's enforcement policies as mediated by the Home Office, see J. Pellew, *The Home Office 1848–1914* (1982) and Petrow, *Policing Morals*, below.

[11] 'Solicitation of chastity which is a spiritual offence and not…punishable at Common Law', *Peirson* (1705) 2 Raym. 1197.

[12] For the law's treatment of inebriety and vagrancy, see above, 'Prisons, Transportation and Institutional Detention', Ch. V.

becoming a persistent nuisance. The observations of the Metropolitan Police Committee in 1818 captured this attitude well:

[T]he streets are crowded every night by women of the most abandoned and profligate characters, who generally accost the passenger with some obscene and disgusting expression; who seduce those whose youth exposes them most to their artifices, and whose necessary avocations oblige them to frequent the public streets. These women, by their interference and riotous conduct, are the principal cause of the disturbances and broils that nightly disgrace the Metropolis. There seems to be a sort of system adopted among them, that gives to each class a certain division in which they prowl for their prey; secure from any interruption by the guardian of the night police, whose favour and protection they secure by sharing with them the wages of their prostitution.[13]

As a means of ensuring that the 'virtuous part of society may be in less danger of annoyance and contamination', the Committee favoured a far greater degree of vigilance and intervention by watchmen, who then bore primary responsibility for maintaining overnight peace. Such exhortations were delivered in the face of the notorious corruptibility of many watchmen, willing to tolerate soliciting in return for adequate reward. Additionally, a procedural strengthening of existing criminal law remedies was advocated by the Committee, the essence of which was adopted in the Vagrancy Act 1822. In contrast to previous legislation requiring proof of disorderly and offensive conduct, the 1822 provisions effectively cast on soliciting prostitutes the onus of 'giving a satisfactory account' of their actions.[14] But within two years this was superseded by the provisions of the Vagrancy Act 1824 whereby the prosecution once again assumed the burden of establishing 'riotous and indecent' behaviour.[15] The nuisance rationale of

---

[13] *Third Report from the Select Committee on the State of the Police of the Metropolis*, PP 1818 (423) viii, 30. For a similar focus on the 'nuisance' of prostitution, see the 1816 *Select Committee Report*, PP 1816 (510), v. 321. Led by the City of London's Lord Mayor in 1815, over 2000 citizens petitioned Parliament for more effective laws.

[14] 3 Geo. IV c. 40. On the previous difficulty in dealing with soliciting, see Sir Nathanial Conant, the Chief Bow Street Magistrate, PP 1816 (510), v. 23. Also, *Report on the Existing Laws Relating to Vagrants*, PP 1821 (543), iv, 21. On the pre-1822 law affecting prostitution and brothels, see T. Henderson, *Prostitution and Control in the Metropolis 1730–1830* (1999), *passim*. On the 1822 Act, see Roberts, 'Public and Private in Early Nineteenth Century London'. On local initiatives to remove or suppress brothels, see A. Simpson, 'The Ordeal of St. Sepulchre's: A Campaign Against Organized Prostitution in Early Nineteenth Century London' (2006) 15 *Social and Legal Studies* 363.

[15] 5 Geo. IV c. 83, ss 3–6. The principal aim of the temporary 1822 Act was clarification of an 'ill digested mess' of vagrancy laws (*PD* 1822 (s. 2), 6: 1383). Debates on the replacement 1824 Act revealed considerable concern with the dangers of prosecuting 'innocent encounters' between men and women apparently facilitated by the 1822 Act provisions (e.g. *PD* 1824 (s. 2), 10: 118). For a contemporary critique of the wide and oppressive potential of the vagrancy laws, see J. Adolphus, *Observations on the Vagrant Act...* (1824).

attempts to deal with publicly soliciting prostitutes found express articulation in the Metropolitan Police Act 1839, empowering the police to arrest prostitutes whose 'loitering' caused 'annoyance' to inhabitants or those passing.[16] However, successful enforcement of both provisions was greatly handicapped by the difficulty of establishing indecency or annoyance without the rarely available corroborative evidence demanded by the majority of magistrates until the mid 1880s.[17]

Rather than seeking direct and firm regulation (if not elimination) of prostitution because of its offensiveness, determined intervention was eventually brought about by concerns over the widespread debilitating effects on the armed forces of venereal disease. Such specific worries led to attempts to regulate prostitutes' health through the highly intrusive powers of the Contagious Diseases Acts 1864, 1866, and 1869. Applying to garrison towns and naval ports, the Acts granted magistrates the power to authorize the Metropolitan Police (and other designated officers) to detain and require suspected 'common prostitutes' to undergo clinical examination at specified hospitals, followed by treatment for any detected venereal diseases, details of which were locally registered. The alternative or complementary strategy of medically inspecting soldiers and sailors was regarded as totally impracticable and inappropriate. Aside from impracticability, the Commission perceived no moral equivalence between prostitutes who acted 'as a matter of gain' and men who indulged from a 'natural desire'.[18] Repeal of the Contagious Diseases Acts in 1886 marked the outcome of several years of campaigning by a diversity of opposition groups. On the one side the Acts were attacked for their extreme interventionary, anti-libertarian powers and for the allegedly arbitrary fashion of their enforcement by the police. But they also came under intense fire from 'purity' or anti-vice campaigners on the grounds of the Acts' tacit legitimizing of prostitution by making resort to prostitutes safer and, consequently, more enticing.[19]

---

[16] Section 54.

[17] On this enforcement problem and its partial resolution by the Metropolitan Police Commissioner and Home Office, see Petrow, *Policing Morals*, Ch. 5 *passim*, and for brothels, Ch. 6. Cf. the Town Police Clauses Act 1847 which directly criminalized 'importuning for the purposes of prostitution'. Special provisions were enacted for the protection of Britain's gilded youth, making it an offence for a 'common prostitute' to wander in a public street in Oxford (6 Geo. IV c. 97) or Cambridge (57 and 58 Vict. c. 60) and failing to give a satisfactory account of herself.

[18] *Report of the Royal Commission on the Administration of the Contagious Diseases Acts*, PP 1871 [c. 408], xix, 1, 17.

[19] See the *Report of the Select Committee on the Contagious Diseases Acts*, PP 1882 (340) ix. For the social and political background to the Acts and their repeal, see J. Walkowitz, *Prostitution and Victorian Society: Women, Class and the State* (Cambridge, 1980); F. Smith 'The Contagious Diseases Acts Reconsidered' (1990) 3 *Social History of Medicine* 197; and more broadly, P. Bartley, *Prostitution: Prevention and Reform in England 1860–1914* (2000).

As a consequence of the cumulative public pressure, instead of regulating the health of prostitutes, legislation now responded to campaigns which targeted prostitution's exploitative dimension. Most particularly, W. T. Stead's celebrated *Pall Mall Gazette* exposé of the scandal of child prostitution, rapidly led to the Criminal Law Amendment Act 1885. Its diligent enforcement was in some measure ensured by the persistent interventions of the highly influential National Vigilance Association.[20] The extensive provisions of the 1885 Act constituted a widely supported systematic effort to strike at prostitution's exploitative nature, particularly the activities of both procurers and brothel keepers. Such an exploitative rationale underpinned the further restrictions of the Vagrancy Act 1898, criminalizing pimps, souteneurs, or 'Persons trading in prostitution'.[21] However, beyond the campaigning aims of a few 'purity' groups concerned with the socially corrosive effects of immorality, there were no sustained proposals to criminalize generally simple soliciting by prostitutes.[22] At the same time, in London, just what degree of control the police should seek to exercise over street prostitution was the subject of considerable and frequent conflict between the Home Office and Metropolitan Police Commissioner.[23]

Agitation of certain political and social reform groups including the London Council for the Promotion of Public Morality, along with Metropolitan Police

[20] An important galvanizing force behind the 1885 Act was concern over the procurement of English juveniles to work in Continental brothels, *House of Lords Select Committee on the Protection of Young Girls*, PP 1881 (448), ix, 355. The Act raised the age of sexual consent from 13 to 16 (s 5) and criminalized the procuring of women for prostitution (s 2) punishable with a maximum of 2 years' imprisonment with hard labour. The Act also directly criminalized male acts of 'gross indecency' whether in public or private (s 11) punishable with a similar penalty to procuring. Brothel keepers and landlords were subject to up to three months' imprisonment with hard labour (s 13). The penalty was increased to a maximum of 1 year's imprisonment under the Criminal Law Amendment Act 1912. Countering social purity organizations seeking to eliminate prostitution were those of a civil libertarian or proto-feminist complexion, such as 'The Vigilance Association for the Defence of Personal Rights, especially in relation to Women', P. McHugh, *Prostitution and Victorian Social Reform* (1980), *passim*, and 'Law and Religion', XI, Pt 1.

[21] Section 1(1)(b) of the Act (Every male person who...in any public place persistently solicits or importunes for immoral purposes') apparently drew in homosexual prostitution including simple solicitation by male prostitutes. Procuring or attempting to procure in 'public or private' acts of 'gross indecency' was an offence under s 11 of the Criminal Law Amendment Act 1885.

[22] Petrow, *Policing Morals* Ch. 6 *passim*. In 1882 the *House of Lords Select Committee on the Protection of Young Girls* proposed that simple public soliciting be made an offence, PP 1882 (344) xiii, 823. Extending to most urban areas, the Town Police Clauses Act 1847, s 28 punished 'a common prostitute loitering and importuning...for the purposes of prostitution'. The provision's enforcement and evidence required to convict varied substantially.

[23] Particularly Home Office strenuous criticism of Sir Charles Warren's 1887 'laissez-faire' policy of policing prostitution, Police Order, 19 July 1887, and *PD* 1887 (s. 3), 318: 364. J. Pellew, *The Home Office*, 50 and 239n.

pressure, resulted in the setting up of a Royal Commission on the duties of the
Metropolitan Police in relation to drunkenness, public disorder, and soliciting. Evidence from the police and most other witnesses satisfied a sympathetic
Commission that through a judicious exercise of discretion and tacit cooperation
between the magistracy and police, the Metropolis's streets could be clear of any
serious problems relating to soliciting prostitutes. Consequently, no change in
the law was thought necessary.[24] Most especially, the proposal to criminalize the
mere accosting of women for sexual services was rejected as publicly unacceptable.[25] Of course, here and throughout the nineteenth century, upper and middle-
class patronage of prostitution was likely to have operated as a steady regulator
of just how far any criminalization might be permitted to intrude into the profession's activities.

2. GAMBLING

In common with prostitution, ambivalence characterized the state's attitude towards gambling, and most especially enforcement of legal restraints
on it. Although certain examples of gambling were subject to legal sanctions,
others, as with types of lottery, even enjoyed state sponsorship and became a
useful source of Exchequer revenue. However, the changed official perception
and early nineteenth-century demise of this latter form of gambling was indicative of shifting attitudes towards gaming more generally. The 1808 Commons'
Committee Report on the Law Relating to Lotteries voiced an uncompromisingly
hostile account of the dangers of lotteries and gaming: 'a pernicious...adventure,
where the chances are so great against the adventurer [and] where the infatuation
is...powerful, lasting, and destructive'.

Such condemnation was stoked up by fears of moral decay and dependency on
'parochial relief', anxieties later to be frequently aired when gambling as a whole
was attacked:

In the lower classes of Society the Persons engaged, whether successful or unfortunate,
are, generally speaking, either immediately or ultimately tempted to their ruin and there
is scarcely any condition of life so destitute and abandoned that its distresses have not
been aggravated by this allurement of Gaming....

---

[24] On the tactics and practices of police in relation to London prostitution, see the *Report of
the Royal Commission upon the Duties of the Metropolitan Police*, PP 1908 [Cd. 4156], l and li. Also,
R. Storch, 'Police Control of Street Prostitution in Victorian London: A Study in the Contexts of
Police Action', in D. Bayley (ed.), *Police and Society* (1977), 49.
[25] *Report*, 127.

Indeed, the Committee ascribed to this pastime what it saw as enervation of the National ethic of individualism and commercial enterprise:

whereby the mind is misled from those habits of continued industry which ensure the acquisition of comfort and independence, to delusive dreams of sudden and enormous wealth, which most generally end in abject poverty and complete ruin.[26]

Although the state's participation in lotteries was terminated in 1823,[27] ambivalence towards actually suppressing gambling continued to be manifest in respect of a large-scale failure to enforce even existing anti-gambling laws. With the presiding presence of the Duke of Wellington complemented by the Prince Regent's patronage, the establishment of Crockfords Gambling Club in 1828 marked the most public affirmation of the gaming laws' non-enforcement.[28] Crockfords and many other less salubrious gaming clubs operated in open contravention of the criminal law.[29] Their toleration and period of relative immunity from prosecution obviously rested at least partly on their socially highly placed clientele and capacity to 'buy off' police attention or intimidate legal complainants.[30] Moreover, the gambling habits of high society never carried the same spectre of widespread social instability commonly associated with gambling addiction amongst the lower classes. Yet by the 1840s even gaming houses frequented by the cream of society were firmly in the sights of the industrious, respectable, and swelling middle classes,[31] together with their parliamentary representatives.

Reflecting this increased concern with the perceived damaging consequences of gambling, 1844 brought the setting up of a Commons Committee charged with generally reviewing the scope and enforcement of the gaming laws.[32] But

[26] 1808 (323) ii, p. 12. Reference to 'disuse a spirit of speculation' was the Committee's economical way of avoiding the eternally awkward question of how gaming and the core practices of venture or speculative capitalism differed morally. Public and private lotteries were made illegal by the Lotteries Act 1823, 4 Geo. IV c. 60, which was fully operational by 1826. Gambling's link with vagrancy is expressly confirmed by the Vagrancy Act 1824, s 4 as amended by the Vagrant Law Amendment Act 1873, 36 and 37 Vict. c. 38, s 3, which penalized 'gaming in an open and public place...at some game of chance...'.

[27] D. Miers, *Regulating Commercial Gambling* (Oxford, 2004), Chs 5–7; and generally on the developments of nineteenth-century gambling law.

[28] D. Miers, 'A Social and Legal History of Gaming', *Legal Record and Historical Reality*, ed. T. Watkin (1989) 107, 115. Punishments for keeping a common gaming house were raised in 1822 by 3 Geo. IV c. 114.

[29] The clearest account was provided by Starkie for the 1844 *Select Committee on Gaming Law* (below); *Report*, App. 1, p. 224: in essence, 'All gaming houses are regarded as nuisances at common law; and those who keep them are liable...to be indicted and punished by a fine and imprisonment at discretion'. Additional local powers were given to the Metropolitan and City Police.

[30] 1844 *Select Committee Report*, vi.

[31] P. Bayley, *Leisure and Class in Victorian Britain* (1978), *passim*.

[32] PP 1844 (297), vi. '[T]o inquire into the existing Statutes against gaming of every kind, and to consider whether any and what amendments should be made in such Statutes'.

fears of extensive individual and social harm consequent upon widespread
gambling were found unpersuasive by the Committee; excepting laws relating
to gaming houses, the Committee was strongly inclined towards a liberal, individually self-regulating approach to gambling: 'the practice of wagering is still
deeply rooted in the habits of the nation'; actual enforcement of the law's 'pecuniary Penalties...would be...repugnant to the general feelings of the people'. Not
only did the Committee propose that 'wagering in general should be free and
subject to no penalty', it also recommended that wagers be legally unenforceable:
there was no 'sufficient reason why the valuable time of the courts of law should
be consumed by adjudicating [wagering] disputes...'.[33] However, the existing law
seeking suppression of gaming houses or clubs gained the Committee's most
emphatic endorsement; for here the law aimed at 'preventing Frauds, [and] common gaming-houses...which...included gaming booths on race courses, are
founded on fraud [and] maintained by fraud'. Such 'nuisances should be effectively put down'. While never directly suggesting that the various police forces
had for illicit reasons been guilty of 'much laxity and neglect' in enforcement
of the laws, the Committee expressed pointed scepticism at the several grounds
offered for inaction. Indeed, the Committee's sometimes sharp, disbelieving tone
in taking evidence from police and official witnesses, galvanized Metropolitan
Police action on the Inquiry's 'last day' against 17 'gambling houses', something
which the Committee 'learned with great satisfaction'.[34]

Embodying many of the Committee's proposals, including those relating
to police and court powers dealing with gaming houses, the Gaming Act 1845,
and subsequently the Betting Shops Act 1853, sought to control the commercial
exploitation of the expanding[35] opportunities for gambling on racing. The 1853
Act's target was betting shops and their use by the supposedly feckless working classes, increasingly attracted by the excitement of the Turf. Particular fears
engendered by working-class gambling graphically expressed by Sir Alexander
Cockburn (then Attorney-General) included the prospect of 'servants, apprentices

[33] *Ibid.*, vi. The courts had by this time for some years been disinclined to try cases where the
plaintiff was seeking to enforce a wagering contract, e.g. *Weller v. Deakins* (1827) 2 Car. & P. 618.

[34] *Ibid.*, vii. The later *Report of the House of Lords Select Committee on the Laws Respecting Gaming*
supported the view that wagering contracts should be unenforceable because of the risk of fraudulent claims. In respect of 'putting down...gaming houses', the Committee hoped that the 'Zeal and
Vigilance of the police will not be confined to Places resorted to by the Middle and Lower Classes,
but that the Law will be equally put in force against all Houses, whatever their denomination or
whatever the Class of Persons resorting to them...'. *Third Report, PP* 1844 (604), vi, vi–vii.

[35] For the background and enforcement of the 1845 Act, see Miers, *Regulating Commercial
Gambling*, Ch. 2. Expansion of the number of racecourses along with the arrival of the age of steam
bred a rapidly rising interest in racing, betting, and betting facilities. W. Vamplew, *The Turf: A Social
and Economic History of Horse Racing* (1976) and C. Chinn, *Better Betting with a Decent Feller:
Bookmaking, Betting and the British Working Class 1750–1990* (Hemel Hempstead, 1991).

and workmen...driven into robbing their masters and employers'.[36] But, rather than suppress the extent of betting on racing, the 1853 Act only succeeded in changing its form, with working-class interest turning to street betting and 'bookies' runners'.[37] In due course, this development was countered with a combination of provisions incorporated in the Betting Act 1874, the 1873 Vagrancy Amendment Act, and in local legislation.[38] Public houses supplying the working classes with what the authorities regarded as the particularly lethal, socially destructive brew of gambling and intoxicants, became prohibited under the Licensing Act 1872.

Steeply rising levels of working and middle-class betting in the second half of the nineteenth century, allied to increasing anxieties for the nation's social, moral, and economic well-being, eventually generated the formation of new (or revival of existing) campaigning groups set on severely curbing gambling, if not its complete extinction. Much in the fashion of the Temperance movement, associations such as the diversely based influential National Anti-Gambling League,[39] campaigned both to ensure existing laws were vigorously enforced and to seek enactment of more effective ones. With distinct resonances of the high-flown rhetoric of the 1808 Commons Lottery Law Committee, the anti-gambling movement of the 1890s feared for individual and national moral integrity, and economic efficiency. Allied to this, the political authors of a developing and pervasive state welfarist legislative philosophy were set on ensuring that it would not be sabotaged by the unrestricted profligate habits of the irresponsible working classes.

Eventual review of the situation, in good measure, came as a consequence of judicial intervention. Following the 1899 decision in *Powell* v. *Kempton Park*,[40] declaring bookmakers at race courses and at many other sporting venues to be legal, betting was subjected to the scrutiny of a House of Lords Select Committee. While not opposed to gambling in principle, the Committee expressed the familiar, considerable concern over the perceived excessive indulgence amongst the working classes. It was a state of affairs seen as brought about by the 'highly

---

[36] *PD* 1853 (s. 3), 129: 87.

[37] D. Itzkowitz, 'Victorian Bookmakers and their Customers' (1988) 32 *Victorian Studies* 16; M. Clapson, *A Bit of a Flutter: Popular Gambling and English Society* (Manchester, 1992); Miers, *Regulating Commercial Gambling*, Chs 9 and 10. Higher social classes could indulge their passion for racing and gambling by using credit with postal bookmakers, or through clubs, and later by telegraph or telephone.

[38] On the problems of the interpretation and enforcement of the 1853 Act, see *Royal Commission on Gambling* 1933, paras 35–40 and D. Dixon, *From Prohibition to Regulation* (Oxford, 1991), Ch. 3 *passim*.

[39] On the composition, objections, and campaigning strategies of the League established in 1890, see Dixon, *From Prohibition to Regulation*, Chs 3 and 5.

[40] [1899] AC 143, by a majority of 5 to 2.

objectionable' aggressive promotion of commercialized betting by the press and bookmakers through use of various dubious inducements and strategies, including the ensnaring of workers outside factory gates and workshops.

Embodying the Committee's principal proposals, the Street Betting Act 1906, while prohibiting betting in 'streets and public places', expressly excluded betting at race courses from the Act's scope.[41] From the outset, a small curious Commons' alliance, including Horatio Bottomley, Sir Edward Carson, and F. E. Smith, opposed the provisions as legislation specifically discriminatory against the working classes. The greatly talented compulsive fraudster Bottomley declared the bill to be: 'class legislation in its worst form. It touched the little man and left out the middle class and big man entirely'; Smith labelled the bill's provisions as 'organized hypocrisy'. Efforts to even the score and extend the restrictions to other classes by including betting by telegram were consistently evaded or resisted by the Liberal government which, at one point, implicitly conceded that the Lords would have no truck which such a measure.[42] However, through a combination of the ineffectiveness of the 1906 Act coupled with the anti-betting lobby turning its attention to the gambling proclivities of society's upper echelons, attempts to control gaming eventually underwent a strategic shift from largely criminal sanctions to one of essentially administrative regulation.[43]

3. OBSCENITY

1787 witnessed the immeasurably virtuous Evangelical philanthropist, William Wilberforce, with the aid of several bishops, achieve a royal proclamation by George III for the suppression of 'loose and licentious prints...and publications'. Wilberforce's engine of salvation, for protecting individuals and society from the self-destructive forces of immorality, was the 'Proclamation Society'. In the cause of spiritual cleansing, the Society instituted a number of prosecutions for obscene or blasphemous libels.[44] By 1802 the larger and longer lived, Evangelically

[41] *House of Lords Select Committee Report on Betting*, PP 1902 (389), v, v–viii. *Street Betting Act* 6 Edw. 7 c. 43. Following the Committee's suggestion, the Act gave powers to the owners of racecourses and other sporting venues to exclude betting by express notice, breach of which brought the offenders within the Act (s 1(4)).

[42] Bottomley, *PD* 1906 (s. 4), 162: 862 and (s. 4), 165: 112–13; Smith, (s. 4), 166: 1679; Carson, (s. 4), 162: 867; (s. 4), 165: 112–13. Home Secretary, Herbert Gladstone, (s. 4), 162: 1145–6. An amendment to cover betting by telegram was resisted by the government as 'impracticable', (s. 4), 166: 1678–84.

[43] Formerly rejected on several occasions as likely to encourage gambling, e.g. at the time of the 1853 Bill, *PD* 1853 129: 88 and by the *House of Lords Select Committee Report*, PP 1902 (389), v, vi.

[44] The indictable misdemeanour of blasphemous libel was at one stage practically any attack on the Christian religion. During the nineteenth century the offence became confined to expressions of dissent expressed in an inflammatory manner or provocative language. C. Kenny, 'The Evolution of the Law of Blasphemy' (1922) 1 *CLJ* 129; G. Nokes, *A History of the Crime of Blasphemy* (1928). For

driven Society for the Suppression of Vice had taken over the generally neglected burden of fighting most manifestations of immorality,[45] including all forms of licentiousness. With over 30 successful prosecutions for obscenity to its credit by 1817, it justifiably claimed to have revived a substantially moribund form of criminal liability.

Quite whether this neglect of the trade in obscene literature and artefacts stemmed from official tolerance or ignorance is debateable. Certainly the Society contended that 'magistrates have expressed their astonishment at the extent of the evil, of the great prevalence of which they before had no conception'.[46] Moreover, the Society could cite glowing endorsements from the Lord Chief Justice and Attorney-General for 'very properly...taking an interest in the morals and happiness of society'.[47] By 1857 the Society had been instrumental in 159 prosecutions, with only five acquittals.[48] The absence of a clear modern judicial definition of obscenity had hardly handicapped such prosecutions, with the relevant law widely conceived as being 'whatever outrages public decency, and is injurious to public morals, and done in contempt of the laws of decency...'.[49]

The relatively cumbersome and expensive nature of pursuing traders in obscene articles by prosecuting for the indictable misdemeanour of obscene libel was alleviated to a degree by the wide, catch all, embrace of the vagrancy laws. Initially, the Vagrancy Act 1824 provided for the summary punishment

the broader cultural context underlying the law's development, see J. Marsh, *Word Crimes: Blasphemy, Culture and Literature in Nineteenth Century England* (Chicago, 1998), *passim*. See also the 1879 *Criminal Code Bill Commission Report*, pp. 21–2, Draft Code, s 141; and the reference to Coleridge J.'s judgment in *Pooley* (1857). Also, *Ramsay* (1883) 15 Cox 231; *Boulter* (1908) 72 *JP* 188 and *Bowman* v. *Secular Society* [1917] AC 406. Stephen had by the 1880s outstripped his agnostic brother Leslie by resigning himself to atheism. He publicly advocated blasphemy's abolition both before and after elevation to the Bench ((1874) XXV *Contemporary Rev.* 446, 473; (1884) XXV (NS) *Fortnightly Rev.* 289). The latter article was a fierce attack on Lord Coleridge CJ's judgment in Foote's blasphemy trial ((1883) 15 Cox 231). Two years earlier Stephen confessed to having, to his enormous relief, narrowly avoided trying Charles Bradlaugh for blasphemy, for views on religion that Stephen himself held. Stephen to Lady Grant Duff, 3 August 1882, Grant Duff Papers, private collection; *Bradlaugh* (1883) 15 Cox 217. See also 'Law and Religion', Ch. XI, Pt. 1.

[45] George Pritchard, the Society's Secretary and Solicitor, identified the offences at which the Society directed its attention: '1st, the profanation of the Sabbath; 2nd, Blasphemous and licentious books, prints...; 3rd, Riotous and disorderly houses, brothels, gaming houses, lotteries...'. Evidence given to the *Commons Committee on the State of the Police of the Metropolis*, PP 1817 (233), vii, 390.

[46] *Ibid.*, pp. 479–81.

[47] *Ibid.*, p. 482. Though sometimes prosecuting the indictable misdemeanour of obscene libel at Quarter Sessions, the Society favoured the '"Kings Bench" [which while] much more expensive,...gained more publicity...tend[ing] to infuse a greater degree of dread among persons prone to such offences'.

[48] PD 1857 (s. 3), 146: 1355–6.

[49] *Starkie's Treatise on the Law of Slander and Libel* (ed. H. C. Folkard, 3rd edn, 1869), 597, based on institutional authorities.

of publicly displayed 'obscene' prints of pictures, or 'other indecent Exhibition'. Partly in response to the Society's petitioning,[50] shop window displays were also drawn into the law's scope by the Vagrancy Act 1838. But the greatest inhibition to the Society's zealous pursuit of its quarry was the inability legally to seize the often 'immense stock' of obscene materials carried by dealers; materials which might easily be passed on to others while the convicted party served out his sentence. Such powers of seizure were eventually enacted in the face of express government disapproval, if not concerted opposition, due to the determined efforts of Lord Campbell CJ.

Originally proposed by the Society for the Suppression of Vice in 1837,[51] the Obscene Publications Act 1857 equipped prosecutors of publishers or traders in obscene materials with a summary procedure for the seizure and destruction of such materials. Resembling the claimed innocence of nineteenth-century magistrates, Lord Campbell had apparently reached high judicial office unaware of the public trade in obscene publications, 'poison more deadly than prussic acid, strychnine or arsenic'. The source of this profound revelation had been a recent obscenity trial presided over by the Lord Chief Justice, the most disturbing feature of which was the ready availability of 'licentious and disgusting' periodicals 'coming out week by week, and sold to any person who asked for them':[52] in short, a potentially widespread distribution amongst the lower classes with consequential large-scale moral degeneration.

The bumpy passage of Lord Campbell's Obscene Publications Bill provides a useful barometer of contemporary political and social pressure set on limiting, if not removing, this particular form of what mid-century Victorian society publicly condemned as a moral contagion. From the outset, the government, in the person of Lord Chancellor Cranworth, politely indicated its broad satisfaction with the existing law's adequacy; any perceived problems could be met by more enthusiastic levels of enforcement.[53] However, within a month, an unconvinced Lord Chief Justice introduced a bill facilitating the seizure and destruction of obscene publications, a summary power which he compared to

---

[50] Vagrancy Act 1824, s 4; Vagrancy Act 1838, s 2. On the problem of shop window displays, see the Society's evidence given to the *Commons Select Committee on Metropolis Police Offices*, PP 1837–8 (578), xv, 134–5.

[51] *Ibid.*, 135.

[52] *PD* 1857 (s. 3), 145: 103. On the legislative background and prosecutions of Dugdale and Strange, see C. Manchester, 'Lord Campbell's Act: England's First Obscenity Statute' (1988) 9 *JLH* 223, 226–7.

[53] Lord Cranworth agreed that it was 'quite fitting that the strong arm of the law should be put in motion, and that the government should take steps for that purpose [through the Attorney-General] as he thought fit', *ibid.*, 103. Similarly, Lord Lyndhurst, 146, 333. For criticism of the 'supineness of the authorities', see (1857) 25 *JP* 467.

those given under the Betting Act 1853. The bill's second reading encountered a phalanx of irremoveable scepticism from the existing and two former Lord Chancellors: each wondered how 'obscene' would be defined; and just how might corrupting obscene publications be distinguished from enriching, meritorious acknowledged works of art and literature? The acuteness of these problems was seen to be aggravated by their being the subject of summary process. An ensuing substantial and increasingly acrimonious procedural squabble between the Lord Chief Justice and Lord Chancellor (conflicting accounts of which appear in their memoirs)[54] almost resulted in a six-month postponement of the bill's second reading. Detecting an ambush likely to kill his bill, a plainly incensed Lord Campbell heatedly accused his chief tormentor, Lord Lyndhurst, of having a 'zeal for these filthy publications'.[55] And while never fully resolving definitional difficulties, the considerably modified bill finally gained the House's approval. It is likely that the bill's successful third reading owed much to Lord Campbell's dramatic production of correspondence from the Society for the Suppression of Vice detailing impressively large quantities of obscene materials previously surrendered, along with the Society's criticisms of the existing law's inability to make substantial inroads into this ever-expanding 'abominable traffic'.[56]

Clear Commons' unease forced further concessions and amendments to the bill. But while radicals, including John Roebuck, regarded the means proposed as 'preposterous', they still 'agreed upon the desirability of stopping the abominable traffic'. Like others, Roebuck was particularly concerned by the bill's provision enabling any single magistrate to determine the question of obscenity.[57] Similarly, the legal press harboured many reservations relating to the proposed wide discretionary powers with which single magistrates and police constables were to be equipped. For some, including the *Law Times*, the most compelling objection was the potential misuse of this 'weapon in the hands of fanatics...'. For the bill's more unreserved advocates, such as *The Times*, expectations were high that the proposed powers would greatly assist in the 'purification of public morals'.[58]

[54] Campbell comments that Brougham and Lyndhurst 'violently' opposed the bill, *Life of Lord Campbell* (1881), ii: 356. Cf. T. Martin, *A Life of Lord Lyndhurst* (1883), 472–4.

[55] PD 1857 (s. 3), 146: 333, 329–38. Fulsome apologies were later made and accepted at the bill's third reading (1356–8). Such was Lord Campbell's parliamentary battering by his distinguished opponents, that he later confessed to having come close to abandoning the bill. However, he was dissuaded from this course by 'solicitations' from clergymen, many 'medical men', 'fathers of families and from young men who themselves had been inveigled into those receptacles of abomination against which his Bill was directed...', 146: 864.

[56] PD 1857 (s. 3), 146: 1355–6. Lord Lyndhurst assisted in redrafting the bill, and though not opposing a third reading, he still expressed residual reservations (1362).

[57] PD 1857 (s. 3), 147: 1475–83.

[58] (1857) 29 LT, 270; (1859) 34 LT 109; *The Times*, 14 August 1857. Also (1857) 21 JP 467 and (1857) 3 *The Jurist* 290; Manchester, 'Lord Campbell's Act', 229–31.

The final compromised outcome was an Act arming a single stipendiary magistrate or two justices of the peace with powers to authorize the police to enter premises, search and seize proscribed materials; if declared obscene, they would be destroyed unless cause could otherwise be shown. As a longstop safeguard, a right of appeal to Quarter Sessions was given.[59] In contrast to a prosecution for the misdemeanour of obscene libel, the 1857 procedure was quasi-regulatory rather than criminal insofar as confiscation not imposition of a standard form of punishment was the objective. However, while imprisonment was not a possibility, the loss of a trader's stock could be more punitive than a fine or short spell of incarceration. Additionally, as was later to be the case, the Act could be employed at an initial stage to facilitate prosecution for obscene libel.

Being the Lord Chief Justice's personal legislative crusade, it was practically inevitable that the Act's provisions would be deployed by the police with some vigour, as, indeed, they very soon were. However, within a decade through a combination of new trading practices, including extensive resort to postal sales driven by the business's highly lucrative nature, the police's use of the Act was reported as subject only to 'spasmodic contortions of vitality'.[60] Absence of an authoritative definition of 'obscene' for the purposes of both the 1857 Act and the common law misdemeanour of obscene libel, to a degree, was remedied in 1868 by Lord Cockburn's observations in *Hicklin*. Begun as a seizure procedure under the 1857 Act on the initiative of Wolverhampton Borough Watch Committee, the case eventually came for review before the Lord Chief Justice sitting in the Divisional Court, via Quarter Sessions appeal. The local bench of magistrates, including Hicklin, had declared to be obscene elements of *The Confessional Unmasked*, a virulent anti-Catholic tract containing details of 'females in confession'. The Divisional Court was required to determine the relevance of the appellant's motivation to the operation of the 1857 Act procedure if 'of the opinion that sale and distribution of the pamphlets... would be a [libel] and proper to be prosecuted as such'. Consideration of the pamphlet's obscene nature was, therefore, an essential stage en route to its final conclusion. Of the presence of this foundation requirement, *in arguendo*, Cockburn thought 'there can be no doubt', after which he proceeded to articulate the basis of his view:

the test of obscenity is this, whether the tendency of the matter charged as obscenity is to deprave and corrupt those whose minds are open to such immoral influences, and into whose hands a publication of this sort may fall.[61]

---

[59] 1857 20 & 21 Vict. c. 83, s 4. An important amendment to the original bill was aimed at protecting recognized works of art and literature.

[60] (1868) 12 *Sol. J.* 602.

[61] (1868) LR 3 QB 360, 371–4. Blackburn J. typically took considerable care in identifying the court's task in ensuring that each element of the 1857 Act was satisfied, including that there were in

Hicklin provided prosecutors of obscene libel and those employing the 1857 Act with confirmation of the low threshold needed to be crossed to establish an article's obscene quality: a mere 'tendency' or risk of corrupting any susceptible person, or 'the danger of contamination and pollution...'.

Whether emboldened by the Lord Chief Justice's observations or by the rising prurience of high Victorian mores, the post-*Hicklin* era saw obscenity proceedings move into the relatively legally untested waters of scientific publications and recognized works of literature. The vulnerability of the former had been alluded to by Lord Cockburn who acknowledged that illustrations contained in a medical treatise 'may, in a certain sense, be obscene'; their immunity from prosecution lay in the 'circumstances of their publication', whereby they were not readily seen by 'boys and girls'.[62] Advocacy of birth control practices in Charles Knowlton's *The Fruits of Philosophy—An Essay on the Population Problem,* originally published in 1832, was the first of such works to attract the active attention of those strenuously concerned with the nation's sensibilities and moral well-being. In 1877, following capitulation to charges of obscene publication by the work's publisher and seller, the book was re-published at sixpence a copy by crusading secularists and social reformers, Charles Bradlaugh and Annie Besant. Seeking to provoke a test case, Bradlaugh and Besant had given prior notice to the police of their intentions.

As anticipated, the government prosecuted for obscene libel. Much highly charged, Evangelical indignation and hyperbolic fervour was compressed into the indictment's description of Bradlaugh and Besant's sins of '...wickedly devising, contriving...to vitiate and corrupt the morals...of youth [and] other...subjects...and to incite and encourage...indecent, obscene, unnatural and immoral practices, and bring them to a state of wickedness, lewdness, and debauchery...'. The trial was presided over, after *certiorari* proceedings, by Lord Cockburn. But, as the Lord Chief Justice indicated to the Solicitor-General with unconcealed criticism,[63] the work's notoriety and boosted circulation were largely a consequence of these 'injudicious proceedings'. It was a criticism taken

---

the court's view obscene publications which could properly be the subject of an obscene libel prosecution; he had no doubt that this was so (374, 377, 378). *The Criminal Law Commissioners' Third Report* (1847), defined 'obscene libel' as 'expressing or signifying any obscene, lewd, or immoral matter or meaning, tending to deprave or corrupt the morals of Her Majesty's subjects...', PP 1847 (830), xv, l. Ch. X, Art. 1, p. 71.

[62] *Hicklin*, 367.

[63] Lord Cockburn commenced his summing up by declaring that because the criminal proceedings had enormously boosted sales of this long-established obscure work, a 'more ill advised and more injudicious prosecution never was instituted', *The Times*, 22 June 1877. No official report was produced of the trial proceedings. But see *The Times*, 18–22 June 1877. On Bradlaugh's application, the case was removed by *certiorari* from the Old Bailey to the Queen's Bench Division and heard by a special jury.

up by the *Law Times*[64] which demanded that the prosecution's instigators, if not the Government Law Officers, should be identified and bear the responsibility for this 'most effectual means of advertising a publication hitherto completely harmless'. However, though the Court of Appeal[65] (by finding their indictments technically flawed) saved Bradlaugh and Besant from serving out the six-month prison sentences handed down by Lord Cockburn on their conviction, the implications of the *Hicklin* ruling had been clearly affirmed in the trial direction of the Lord Chief Justice. Consequently, it was unsurprising that some other works of a similar nature met much the same fate at the time.[66]

For many, the potential of these decisions was profoundly disturbing. Yet running against these judgments was a body of contemporary, extra-judicial opinion which held out the possibility that the full potential of Cockburn's ruling in *Hicklin* might not enjoy unhampered application to works of acknowledged literary merit. Most particularly, the exclusion of the relevance to liability of a publisher or seller's motive came under both direct and indirect fire from several quarters. Soon after Bradlaugh's and Besant's conviction, in a Commons' intervention, the government was encouraged to legislate to restrict the operation of the 1857 Act to works 'written for the single purpose of corrupting the morals of youth, etc'. The Attorney-General indicated that 'no necessity [was seen] for any alteration in the law on this subject'.[67] An alternative approach appeared a few days later in the *Solicitors' Journal* advocating a form of justification defence if the public benefit derived from a publication exceeded the disbenefits of any exposure to the work's 'immorality or evil'.[68] Published also in the same year as Bradlaugh and Besant's case, the first edition of Stephen's *Digest of Criminal Law* also offered a 'public good defence', which the author openly conceded was

---

[64] *Bradlaugh and Besant*. The Lord Chief Justice testily observed that 'I should like to know who are the "authorities" to who the [Solicitor-General] alludes', *The Times*, 22 June 1877; (1877) 63 *LT* 131. As an observer of the trial noted, while Lord Cockburn showed emotional discomfort too, he was not defeated from doing his judicial duty when sentencing. 'I recollect, on the trial of Charles Bradlaugh and Mrs Besant, how much [Lord Cockburn] was affected, even to tears, by the impassioned appeal of the latter—but with honey in the mouth, the bee had its sting', T. E. Crispe, *Reminiscences of a KC* (1909), 70.

[65] (1878) 3 QBD 607.

[66] Including *Truelove* (1880) 5 QBD 336. However, Besant's *The Law of Population* (1879), which included advice on various birth control techniques sold over 170,000 copies within little more than a decade. The change of climate by the early twentieth century is clear from the response to Marie Stopes' *Married Love* (1918) and *Wise Parenthood* (1918), with a preface by Arnold Bennett. Both works dealt with sexual relations and the latter with birth control. And while generating initial outrage in some quarters, both books (and later works) survived enjoying enormous subsequent popularity. More generally, R. Porter and L. Hall, *The Facts of Life: The Creation of Sexual Knowledge in Britain 1650–1950* (New Haven, 1995).

[67] Mr Whalley, 26 June, *PD* 1877 (s. 3), 235: 258–9.

[68] (1877) 21 *Sol. J.* 666 at 667.

speculative. Stephen used the occasion to articulate the fundamental distinction between obscenity and immorality: that expressing highly immoral opinions in moderate language had not been and generally should not be the law's business; whereas obscenity had long been the subject of criminal sanction. The *Bradlaugh* decision was regarded by Stephen as transgressing this key distinction, giving jurors 'the powers of ex post facto censors'; powers that ought to be exercised with 'the greatest of caution'.[69]

Stephen favoured explicitly restating obscenity law on a protection of sensibilities basis—from the causing of disgust or revulsion. This he saw as a more direct and accurate basis than one seeking to relate obscenity to the dangers of moral corruption.[70] Indeed, Stephen's *Digest* definition of obscene libel omits any reference to *Hicklin*'s 'tendency to corrupt' formula. And, to emphasize a break with past practice, the nomenclature was changed to 'obscene publications'.[71] Two years later, the Criminal Code Commission version of what was claimed to be the 'existing law' also incorporated a public good defence, broadly resembling that speculatively floated in Stephen's *Digest*. Yet, the Commission's claim to represent the existing law in a 'much more definite form' was not quite so disingenuous as might at first appear for one of Stephen's fellow Code Commissioners, Lord Blackburn, was a puisne judge in *Hicklin*. Blackburn's judgment contained at least powerful hints of the existence of such a defence; and in common with Stephen, Blackburn classified liability as a form of public nuisance. However, Stephen was denied a complete conceptual victory in the 1879 Draft Code's definition of selling or publishing obscene materials for a tendency to corrupt morals was incorporated as an element of the offence.[72]

---

[69] Stephen's public good defence (Art. 172, 'submitted'): publication or exhibition of 'disgusting' or 'obscene' works was 'justified' if 'for the public good, as being necessary or advantageous to religion or morality, to the administration of justice, the pursuit of science, literature, or art, or other objects of general interest'. But justification ceased if the manner or 'circumstances' of publication 'exceed that which the public good requires…'. On offensive displays and a defence of public benefit, *Grey* (1864) 4 F. and F. 73. *Digest* Note X and Stephen J's observations on the burning of a corpse in *Price* (1884) 12 QB 247: '…many acts involving the grossest indecency and grave public mischief…are not misdemeanours. I do not think…that it can be said that every practice which startles and jars upon the religious sentiments of the majority of the population is for that reason a misdemeanour…[Criminal sanctions for such behaviour should] be admitted with the greatest reluctance, and only upon the strongest reasons'. Also, *Digest* (1st edn, 1877), 348, for comments on *Bradlaugh* (3rd edn, 1883), 116–17n.

[70] Similar to the basis of blasphemy, above n. 44.

[71] The offence is located within Stephen's compendious section on public mischief: 'Acts Injurious to the Public in General'. This change of nomenclature was noted in the Court of Appeal hearing of *Bradlaugh and Besant* by Bramwell LJ, 672. Indeed, Lord Cockburn's trial summing up in *Bradlaugh and Besant* at two points departs from the *Hicklin* formulation by suggesting 'whatever outrages decency or tends to corrupt the morals of society, is an offence…', *The Times*, 22 June 1877.

[72] Blackburn J. in *Hicklin* at 376–7. *Criminal Code Bill—The Draft Code, PP* 1878–9 [c. 2345] xx: 169, Part XIII, section 147 and *Report*, 21–2. The Code provisions indicate clear compromises: (i) s 147(a) is

Works of recognized literary merit containing elements of what were regarded as sexually explicit or other forms of immorality, appear to have remained untouched by criminal proceedings until Vizetelly's prosecution in 1888. In part, at least, this was a consequence of the book trade's self-censorship, especially that practised by the circulating libraries and national booksellers, such as Moodies and W.H. Smith.[73] But by this time the role of the most zealous defender of public morality had been assumed by the broadly based, ever active, National Vigilance Association, whose portfolio spanned the suppression of gambling, prostitution, and obscene publications. Combining Puritanism with xenophobia,[74] the association instituted obscene libel proceedings against the well-regarded bookseller Henry Vizetelly for publishing English translations of French classics, including works of Flaubert, Maupassant, and Zola. As the prosecution's principal target, Zola had attracted both high critical acclaim and much trenchant criticism in England.

Typical of the latter was a prominent and extensive attack on Zola by way of a Commons' resolution a few months before Vizetelly's prosecution. Calling for a 'vigorously enforced and, if necessary, strengthened' law against obscene publications, Samuel Smith, the 'muscular Christian' and professed ally of the National Vigilance Association, characterized Zola's works as 'only fit for swine', with Vizetelly expressly identified as the source of the polluting translations. Not only was Smith's concern for the corrupting effects on London's youth endorsed by several other members of the Commons, the Home Secretary, whilst declining to encourage the 'independent' Director of Public Prosecutions to commence proceedings, expressed hope that private individuals would not 'shrink' from 'putting the law in motion in any case of real public mischief'.[75] No doubt well

---

effectively a new offence covering ground formerly occupied by obscene libel; and (ii) obscene libel is retained undefined as a distinct separate offence. The public good defence is specified as a mixed question of law and fact, with the jury deciding if there has been 'excess beyond what the public good requires in the manner and extent or circumstances…'. The 'motives of the seller, publisher, or exhibiter' are declared 'irrelevant'.

In Stephen's original bill, the obscene publications provision (s 104, Criminal Code (Indictable Offences) Bill, *PP* 1878 (178), ii, 5) contains no reference to 'tending to corrupt morals' as later included in the Commission's Draft Code (s 147). Furthermore, again in contrast to the Draft Code, Stephen's bill includes no reference to 'obscene libel'. Additionally, Stephen's provisions leave adjudication on the evidence of a justification defence of public good exclusively to the jury. The Draft Code expressly identifies as a 'question of law' whether publication 'might be for the public good'; the jury is left to determine whether the publication still oversteps the limit, displaying 'excess'. On these alleged classificatory changes in Stephen's bill, see *Memo by Sir James Stephen Relating to the Criminal Code (Indictable Offences Bill), PP* 1878 (276) lxiii, 159, 164, cl. 101.

[73] R. D. Altick, *Victorian People and Ideas* (New York, 1973), 190–202.

[74] G. Robertson, *Obscenity* (1979), 31.

[75] *PD* 1888 (s. 3), 325: 1707–21. Smith's speech included a telling compilation of several punishingly critical literary reviews of Zola's novels.

aware of this exchange, and not inclined to shrink from performing its self-as-signed public duty, the Vigilance Association successfully set in train Vizetelly's prosecution. Objections from the jury to hearing translated extracts of Zola's *La Terre* read in open court convinced Vizetelly of the futility of persisting with a 'not guilty' plea.[76]

The example of Vizetelly's conviction emboldened occasional salutary pros-ecutions, sufficient to keep publishers and distributors alive to the possibility of the consequences of crossing the indistinct line between acceptable and non-acceptable literature.[77] Moreover, England in the early 1900s was still richly pop-ulated with societies greatly absorbed by the country's moral wellbeing. At this time, from corrosive French literature, attention moved to home produced works by the likes of H. G. Wells and, in 1915, D. H. Lawrence. And, while not lacking substantial critical opposition, authors such as Wells enjoyed weighty support amongst the established English literati, a body increasingly resistant to the leg-acy of Victorian prurience and moral censorship.[78]

During this period, the law underwent scrutiny of a joint Select Committee of Lords and Commons which favoured replacement of the disparate set of exist-ing laws governing obscene matters by a comprehensive set of quasi-regulatory[79] summary provisions. To combat what was perceived to be a 'serious and growing evil', the Committee proposed that liability should extend to offensiveness, to works that were 'objectionable or indecent'. In the opposite direction, address-ing the treatment of 'any book of literary merit or reputation or any genuine

---

[76] *The Times*, 1 November 1888. Vizetelly was fined £100, undertaking to remove Zola's works from distribution. As a consequence of publishing further works of Zola and Maupassant he was prosecuted and sentenced to three months' imprisonment in 1889.

[77] Particularly the 1898 proceedings relating to Havelock Ellis's, *Sexual Inversion*. N. St. John-Stevas, *Obscenity and the Law* (1956), 83–5. For affirmation of the importance to liability of the likely readership of obscene works, *Thomson* (1900) 64 *JP* 456. The Law of Libel Amendment Act 1888 pro-hibited the press from quoting blasphemous or obscene extracts of works read in court proceedings. The *Central Criminal Court Session Papers* (1895) vol. cxxi, 531–2 on Oscar Wilde's criminal libel action against Lord Queensberry notes 'The details of the case are unfit for publication'. Similarly, no details of the trial evidence in the two subsequent trials of Wilde for indecent acts under s 11 of the Criminal Law Amendment Act 1885 were published in the Sessions Papers. However, the 1888 Act failed to suppress reporting of salacious details from divorce court proceedings.

[78] In 1915, 1000 copies of Lawrence's *The Rainbow* were seized and destroyed under summary proceedings, *The Times*, 15 November 1915. Also e.g. E. M. Forster and, earlier, T. Hardy. See gen-erally, D. Thomas, *A Long Time Burning: The History of Literary Censorship in England* (1969) and E. J. Bristow, *Vice and Vigilance: Purity Movements in Britain since 1700* (1977), *passim*.

[79] Cf. the regulatory system of censorship established for public theatrical performances. The Theatres Act 1843, 6 & 7 Vict. c. 68 requiring the licensing of theatres and performances, gave the Lord Chamberlain complete discretion to forbid performances of the whole or part of any play for the 'Preservation of Good Manners, Decorum or the Public Peace' (s 14). With the Cinematograph Act 1909, the operation of cinemas was subject to local authority licensing which became reliant on the Voluntary Board of Censorship film classification scheme established in 1912.

work of art', the Committee endorsed inclusion of a provision exempting such works from liability; but rather than attempt what it saw as the virtually impossible undertaking of devising an exempting definition, the matter was to be left open for summary determination.[80] Trial on indictment and the use of juries in settling standards of public toleration would cease. As well as offering insights into the practices of various police forces in the law's enforcement, evidence submitted to the Committee also provided clear confirmation of the Home Office's involvement. In seeking to regulate the availability of doubtful literature, the Home Office successfully encouraged self-censorship by the 'proprietors of more than one newspaper' and '[the distributors] Messrs. Smith and Son and Wyman and Sons'.[81] While apparently[82] incorporated in a Home Office draft bill awaiting a legislative opportunity, the Committee's proposals and any reforming momentum were lost with the outbreak of the the First World War.

[80] *PP* 1908 (275), ix, 375, vii–ix. Punishment for a first offence was to be a fine of £30 or one month's imprisonment.

[81] *Evidence*, p. 22, para. 237. The Home Office, Metropolitan Police, and the Director of Public Prosecutions, all sought a wider definition of obscenity so as to include 'anything calculated to inflame the passions, or to suggest or invite immorality, or in any other way to corrupt and deprave' (p. 24, para. 263; p. 29, para. 314).

[82] Information given by the Home Secretary to the Public Morality Council in 1911. Council's Report 1911; St. John-Stevas, *Obscenity and the Law*, 88.

XI

Protecting Property from Dishonesty and Harm: Larceny and Malicious Damage

1. THE EXPANDING CONCEPT OF LARCENY

By the nineteenth century the criminal infringement of rights in property broadly divided between dishonest or, in the contemporary vernacular, 'fraudulent' dealings, and 'malicious' harming of the physical integrity of property. Of the former, developments in larceny were by far the most practically important and doctrinally significant. Except in respect of their specific forms and levels of punishment,[1] no other major property offence (including robbery, burglary, receiving, and forgery) underwent such a marked evolution as larceny. As in the previous century, larceny's later development was principally characterized by judicial and legislative responses to the constrictions flowing from theft's ancient possession-based conception. Whilst the eighteenth century had seen substantial common law and legislative inroads into the core notion of infringing possessory rights, it was during the succeeding century that the criminal law unavoidably confronted an expanded range of essentially theftuous activities. Accommodating these social and, especially, commercial changes greatly tested judicial ingenuity and the law's doctrinal integrity. So much so, that by the 1830s it had become almost commonplace to maintain, like the Criminal Law Commissioners, that the 'increased wants and enlarged experience of modern times' had encouraged courts to 'bend...ancient jurisprudence'.[2]

---

[1] All major property offences involving both dishonesty and 'malice', were subject to modifications of form as a consequence of a series of statutory consolidations. For larceny and cognate offences the process culminated in the Larceny Acts 1861 and 1916, and Forgery Acts, 1861, 1870, and 1913. The property value based distinction between (capital) 'grand' and less serious 'petty' larceny was abolished in 1827 by 7 & 8 Geo. IV, c. 29. However, until 1834 certain forms of larceny from a dwelling house remained capital. By 3 & 4 Will. 4, c. 44 (1833) these offences became punishable with not less than 7 years' transportation, with the addition of up to 4 years' imprisonment.

[2] First Report (1834), 6 and 10. Similarly e.g. Fourth Report (1839): the possession doctrine was 'wholly inadequate to the growing exigencies of a nation, the wealth and commerce of which were rapidly increasing, and which required more efficient and extensive laws for the protection of the great mass of property necessarily confided to the possession of various agents' (p. liv). This view

Amongst other things, such 'ancient jurisprudence', reformulated by renowned expositors of the common law, including Lord Mansfield, affirmed that there was 'no distinction better known than the distinction between civil and criminal law; or between criminal prosecutions and civil actions'.[3] Mansfield had expressly rested this assertion on Blackstone's classical eighteenth-century division between

> ...private wrongs, and public wrongs. The former are an infringement or privation of the private or civil rights belonging to individuals, considered as individuals; and are thereupon frequently termed civil injuries: the latter are a breach and violation of public rights and duties, which affect the whole community...; and are distinguished by the harsher appellation of crimes and misdemeanours.[4]

During the second half of the eighteenth and throughout the nineteenth century, in larceny and cognate offences, along with 'malicious' damage, both the judiciary and legislature combined to relocate many forms of actionable behaviour from the civil to criminal arena; in effect, this entailed modifications to basic conceptions of property rights. Prominent in driving this process of redesignation for misappropriation of property were shifts in perceptions of what forms of dishonesty should be regarded as within the criminal law's legitimate ambit and merit penal sanctions.[5] Coupled with this was a creeping pragmatic recognition

---

supports Jerome Hall's socio-economic account of the development of larceny law *Theft, Law and Society* (Indiana, 1952). Greater relevance is given by George Fletcher to a general doctrinal shift in the late eighteenth century away from 'manifest criminality' to subjective criminality. For larceny this gave conceptual authority for the judicial erosion of the significance of manifest acts against possession while boosting the significance of the offence's mental component, G. Fletcher, *Rethinking Criminal Law* (Boston, 1978) *passim*. However, this construction conflicts with that of contemporary commentators, including the Criminal Law Commissioners' and R. S. Wright's treatments of *animus furandi*, below. Also, as the several legislative interventions demonstrate, particularly in respect of embezzlement, the courts felt clear limits existed on how far notions of possession could be discarded.

[3] *Atcheson* v. *Everitt* (1775) 1 Cowp. 383, 391.

[4] *Comms*, iii, 2; similarly *Comms*, iv, 5, adding, for crimes 'strike at the very being of society, which cannot possibly subsist, where actions of this sort are suffered to escape with impunity'. Though apparently rejecting Blackstone's classification and distinction between compensation and punishment, utilitarianism's position contained inherent interpretive problems. On Bentham, see G. Postema, *Bentham and the Common Law Tradition* (Oxford, 1986), 175–83. For Austin's position, *Lectures on Jurisprudence* (3rd edn, Campbell, 1869), i, 'Lecture' xxvii, 'Different Kinds of Sanctions'.

[5] Blackstone well understood the difficulty of settling what violations of property rights society should regard as criminal and those merely civil, *Comms*, iv, 230. On this fundamental question, see also the *Criminal Law Commissioners, Fourth Report* (1839). Curiously, the Commissioners appear to draw a crude line demarcating the scope of dishonesty offences at that 'degree of prudence and circumspection which every man is bound to exert for his own protection'. Effectively, they appear to propose that property interests misappropriated by another as a consequence of an owner's

of the economic needs of an increasingly commerce-based society; in such a society compensation for tortious damage to individual interests became inadequate in the face of what had come to be regarded as the prejudicing of broader collective interests by the inadequate security of property rights and protection of property transactions.[6]

The Doctrinal Limitation of Possession

Decided in the late eighteenth century, *Pear's Case* is a significant illustration of the limits of judicial willingness to 'bend' ancient doctrine to accommodate perceived contemporary commercial and legal needs. Subject to a few statutory exceptions, larceny doctrine insisted on a taking of property from another's possession. Most significantly, this prevented conviction of parties who, after originally gaining possession consensually, later formed a larcenous intention (*animus furandi*) and converted such property for their own use.[7] *Pear's Case* determined that where possession was gained by a trick or other artifice, consent was negatived, thereby leaving the owner with 'constructive' possession, and facilitating the 'swindler's' conviction for larceny. The decision's innovatory nature, which Austin labelled 'feigned possession',[8] generated much conceptual heart-searching amongst the 11 members of the Bench for whom the question had been reserved, with seven eventually confirming liability on the novel grounds that deceit negatived consent to taking.[9]

gullibility did not warrant the criminal law's intervention: '…it is sufficient to leave such as are not reasonably vigilant to remedies of a civil nature' (p. li). Broadly, the apparent direction of such reasoning would have constituted an inversion of extant and subsequent criminal jurisprudence.

   [6] Clearly, the inaccessibility and ineffectiveness of civil process and remedies boosted inclinations to criminalize particular violations of property rights. On actions for Trespass, Trover, Detinue and Replevin, see XII, Pt 4.

   [7] Larceny, being an offence against possession, generated a fundamental problem in charging any sort of embezzling agent who had previously been entrusted with possession of the property. Specific abuses or areas of embezzlement by certain employees were made criminal in the eighteenth century: Bank of England clerks (1742) and Post Office clerks (1765). *Bazeley* (1799) 2 Leach 835 confirmed that servants receiving goods on behalf of their masters obtained possession and therefore could not be liable for subsequently embezzling them. The rapid legislative response, 39 Geo. III, c. 85 (1799) making such taking criminal embezzlement by any servant or clerk ('deemed to have feloniously stolen'). And see below, n. 22.

   [8] *Lectures on Jurisprudence* (ed. Campbell, 3rd edn, 1869), ii, 1078.

   [9] *Pear* was very briefly reported by Leach, (1779) 1 Leach 212, and more extensively by East 14 years later in part, from a collection of contemporary and later judicial manuscripts (2 East 685). The twelfth judge, Blackstone, was absent through illness (2 East 686). On the extent of the doctrinal shift manifest in *Pear*, see J. Beale, 'The Borderline of Larceny' (1892) 6 *HLR* 244 and J. Turner, *Russell on Crime* (12th edn), vol. 2, 921–5. *Hawkins* 1 PC (1787) ed. Leach, defines theft as a 'felonious and fraudulent taking and carrying away…' (134). In 1824, the editor J. Curwood, whilst retaining

Two far-reaching implications or uncertainties followed from the decision. First, negation of consent by deceit logically extended beyond trick-induced bailments to cases where the purpose of the transaction had been to pass ownership in goods to the fraudster. Without offering justification, the possibility of this further doctrinal leap of denying the passing of title was soon unhesitatingly excluded by judicial fiat.[10] A second uncertainty was at what stage would a trickster obtaining possession of goods incur larcenous liability? For typical examples of stealing without consent the offence would be completed by taking possession and 'carrying away' with 'fraudulent intent'. Seven years after *Pear's Case* the issue of consensual possession arose in *Semple*. Here a carriage, hired to the defendant for an indefinite period, disappeared along with the defendant for many months. At Semple's trial for the carriage's theft, it was held that absence of evidence of conversion or other disposal did not prevent Semple's conviction; for from the circumstances a 'presumption' was raised which it was 'incumbent on Semple to repel...'. Crucially, whether the 'presumption' was as to the defendant's larcenous state of mind at the time of taking possession or as to the occurrence of some later conversion of the carriage was unclear.[11]

This equivocal state of authorities left the way open for subsequent early nineteenth-century commentators to offer either of these constructions of the nature of evidence required to prove larceny in such cases. Though not specifically addressing the point, East's 1803 definition, defining larceny as a non-consensual taking with an 'intent, to convert [property] to his own use...', was adopted widely, both judicially and by other standard texts of the period, including *Russell* and, effectively, *Hawkins*.[12] Of course, as a matter of practicality, proof

---

this opaque definition in the main text, notes 'The definition [of] East...may perhaps be correct...: the wrongful or fraudulent taking and carrying away...with intent to convert them to his...own use and make them his own property without the consent of the owner (141), citing 2 East 524.

[10] *Parkes* (1794) 2 Leach 614; *East* 2 PC 671. Denying the passing of title would have prejudiced a subsequent honest third party acquiring the property from a fraudster. Cf. the unidentifiable case cited 2 Leach 475. The illogicality of this is pointed out by the Criminal Law Commissioners, *First Report*, p. 8.

[11] (1786) 2 Leach 469, 474. An illustrative citation of an unidentified decisive decision points to the former meaning. In modern times this view was adopted by J. C. Smith, *Theft* (1968), 12 and (with) B. Hogan, *Criminal Law* (1965), 353. Leach's report of *Pear* identified the question reserved as whether the owner's delivery of the horse to Pear rendered the subsequent conversion 'felonious'; and recording the ruling that such delivery did not prevent felonious conversion (254–5). East's far lengthier report of *Pear* is equivocal, though his own extended commentary on *Pear* and other authorities, including *Semple*, is capable of being construed as accepting larceny as occurring at the moment of the initial fraudulent taking (685–93).

[12] *Russell* (1819), ii: 1033 and *Hawkins* 1 PC (8th edn, 1824), 141; see n. 9 above. An early judicial adoption appears in the reserved opinion of *Hammon's Case* (1812) 2 Leach 1083, 1089.

of the intent permanently to deprive an owner of property would almost always be supplied by evidence of their subsequent disposal or conversion. But where initial possession was gained by some fraudulent artifice, as in cases like *Pear* and *Semple*, the inference of the defendant's necessary culpable state of mind would not have been difficult to draw.

Moreover, broader[13] implications for the general development of larceny and property offences were arguably deducible from such an approach to this particular issue. By creating a conceptual climate favourable to attaching greater significance to the mental elements of property offences, a diminished formalistic role might be adopted for the externals of criminality as classically demanded by the doctrine of possession. Thus, for example, in Starkie's 1824 treatment[14] of the proof of larceny, obtaining possession by fraud or force are treated as subject to similarly strong inferences of taking with larcenous intention; the implication being that in neither case would any further *action* be necessary to establish liability.[15]

Some commentators, including R. S. Wright, later suggested that there was 'reason to think that in…theft…the criminal intention was in ancient times regarded as the essential element of crime and the proof of an act done in execution of the intention was necessary and material only as evidence of the intention'.[16] Such centrality of the mental element in larceny had been explicitly affirmed by the Criminal Law Commissioners' earlier analyses of larceny. In their final draft of theft, Starkie, Ker, and Amos (like Starkie's *Treatise* before) regarded gaining possession of property by intimidation or deception as two equivalent examples of non-consensual taking; each of these actions would constitute the complete offence of theft without any further manifestation of 'fraudulent intention'. They regarded this exposition as consistent with existing law, but expressed in the 'most plain and popular terms'.[17] A similar emphasis appears 20 years on in Stephen's *General View* proposals, and later both in the 1878 Code Bill and the Code Commission Draft Criminal Code 1879.[18] But the concept's most elegant

---

[13] *Rethinking Criminal Law, passim*, and 'Attempt', Ch. VII above, and 'Offences against the Person', Ch. XII below.

[14] *Practical Treatise of the Law of Evidence* (2nd edn, 1824), ii, 828–37.

[15] *Egginton* (1801) 2 Leach 913 confirmed the need for taking possession with an intent to deprive permanently; mere abandonment was insufficient. *Phillips and Strong* (1801) *East* 2 PC 662.

[16] F. Pollock and R. Wright, *An Essay on Possession in the Common Law* (Oxford, 1888), 118. As the preface notes, the work's criminal section was exclusively of Wright's authorship. Wright based his contributions on the research carried out for his Colonial Office draft Jamaican Code 1877. See below for Wright's theft provisions.

[17] See earlier *Fourth Report* (1839), lvii and *Third Report* (1847) 'Fraudulent Appropriations' Arts 1 and 2, p. 7. The Commissioners observed that 'mere latent intent' was insufficient; offences of 'unlawful appropriation' required 'to be manifested by some plain and defined acts, manifestory of such intention'. A modified version of East's definition of theft is expressly adopted.

[18] *General View*, 125–36. Stephen proposed to combine 'all cognate offences' as theft, including 'by taking, by embezzlement, by obtaining by false pretences or by any other manner…to

realization was achieved by Wright in his Jamaican Penal Code: stealing required a party to 'dishonestly appropriate a thing of which he is not the owner'; 'appropriation' included 'any moving, taking, obtaining or delivery to deprive [another of the] benefit of ownership'.[19]

More generally, beyond the common law's shift of emphasis from larceny's *actus reus* to *mens rea* demands, by the early nineteenth century the basic requirement of taking from lawful possession had also undergone extensive statutory erosion. This was a consequence of compelling domestic and commercial necessity. On the domestic front, household servants had long been deemed by the common law to have custody[20] and not possession of their masters' property, thereby making them potentially liable for larceny of such property. But after judicial loss of nerve and readiness to go beyond the doctrinal accommodation in *Pear*, statutory intervention in 1799[21] permitted conviction of servants for theft when misappropriating property *received* on behalf of their masters from third parties, thereby further extending protection of the well-to-do from dishonest staff.

In mercantile and commercial contexts a similar process of legislative innovation followed where the judiciary felt unable to surmount possession's doctrinal constraints to criminalize a variety of dishonest breaches of bailments.[22] Such embezzlement (initially legislatively classified as larceny) covered situations where possession of property had been lawfully obtained, but where the bailee subsequently formed larcenous intent and misappropriated the property. An even more

---

appropriate...' (130). The 'test of criminality' would be 'an intent to defraud at the time of the appropriation', not the taking away; the subject-matter of theft would be the 'beneficial interest' not the right to possession (135). In different ways, both Stephen's 1878 bill and the 1879 Draft Code aimed to reformulate theft into 'taking or converting [with mens rea] to deprive the owner permanently of any interest' (*HCL* i, 163). See 1878 bill, ss 246 and 247, and Code, ss 246 and 247.

[19] Draft Jamaican Penal Code, ss 183–188, *PP* 1877 [c. 1893], lxi, 357. Larceny's requirement of taking away (asportation) and its value in proving *animus furandi* had by the early nineteenth century shrunk to a little beyond the defendant's slightest movement of the property. For example, *Walsh* (1824) 1 Mood C.C. 14; *Thompson* (1825) 1 Mood C.C. 80. Asportation had been dispensed with when the law recognized bailees could, in some cases, commit larceny. Here, some act inconsistent with the bailment terms was required to constitute criminal conversion.

[20] The distinction between custody and possession occasionally proved capricious. Cf. *Thomas* (1841) Car. & P. 741 and *Thompson* (1862) Le. & Ca. 225.

[21] Embezzlement by servants or clerks, 39 Geo. III c. 85. Enlarged by s 68 of the Larceny Act 1861. For consequential interpretive problems of this provision, see Smith and Hogan, *Criminal Law* (1965), 365–8.

[22] Legislation covering embezzlement by Bank of England clerks (1742) and Post Office clerks (1765) was extended in 1812 to bankers, merchants, brokers, and agents of 'any description', 52 Geo. III, c. 63, and again in 1857 to cover everyone receiving goods by delivery (20 & 21 Vict. c. 54) and who, after taking delivery, resolved to misappropriate the property; consolidated in the Larceny Act 1916, s 17. Without any practical purpose, fine distinctions were retained in the Larceny Act 1916 between property misappropriated after receipt from masters or employers (s 17(a) larceny) and property misappropriated when received from a third party *on behalf* of a master or employer (s 17(b) embezzlement).

substantial departure from common law doctrine between 1811 and 1857 was represented by gradually introduced criminal sanctions for the fraudulent actions of agents and fiduciaries who had not simply possession but ownership of property, held for the benefit of others.[23] Additionally, the distinct evidential problem of proving the misappropriation of money accepted on behalf of employers from clients or customers by dishonest clerks or counter assistants was eventually met by the False Accounting Act (Lopes' Act) 1875, creating the offence of false accounting.[24]

Capturing Larceny's Dishonesty Element

Relegation of the spirit (and letter) of a possession-based concept of theft, along with a raised emphasis of its *mens rea* element, in turn exposed the latter's long obscure nature. In 1819, when seeking to identify larceny's *mens rea* (*animus furandi*) Russell[25] indecisively cited three then current variations, including those of East and Hawkins. The latter required a 'felonious and fraudulent taking'; Curwood, *Hawkins'* editor of the time, described this as a 'vicious...definition', for the 'defining terms of a definition should not themselves want defining'.[26] More expansively, but hardly more transparent, East specified 'the wrongful or fraudulent taking...with felonious intent...'. In large measure, the basis of this vagueness is revealed in Hale's cautioning that the

variety of circumstances is so great and the complications thereof so manifest, that it is impossible to prescribe all the circumstances evidencing a felonious intent, but the same must be left to the due and attentive consideration of the judge and jury.[27]

Over the course of the nineteenth century both the judiciary and treatise writers sought to unravel the several strands of *animus furandi*; to put some firm substantive meat on the largely normative bones. First, Blackstone's claim that taking must be motivated by gain (*lucri causa*) though largely neutralized in 1815

---

[23] Previously, the original owner's only possible remedy lay in equity. The very limited intrusion of the criminal law in 1811 (51 Geo. III, c. 38, clerks and servants in Ireland) was broadened by s 49 of the Larceny Act 1827 (re-enacting the 1811 provisions) covering fraudulent conversion by bankers and other agents, and again by the 1857 Act, *ibid.*, covering most cases of fraudulent fiduciaries. Fraudulent conversion was consolidated in the Larceny Act 1916, s 20.

[24] 38 & 39 Vict. c. 24. In *Solomons* (1909) 2 KB 980 deliberately failing to record the correct taxi fare was held within the Act's provisions.

[25] (1819) ii, 1032–3.

[26] 1 PC (1824 edn), 141.

[27] (1682) 1 PC 509. In their *First Report*, the Criminal Law Commissioners observed the 'obscurity' of *animus furandi*, to be 'remarkable' (p. 16). Subsequent consideration by the Commissioners produced various formulations, e.g. *Fourth Report* (1839) 'with intent to despoil the owner and fraudulently appropriate' (Art. 1, p. xi); *Third Report* (1847) '...with fraudulent intent entirely to deprive him of [the property]' (Art. 1, p. 7).

by *Cabbage*, lingered on in judicial consciousness until mid-century.[28] Secondly, while implicit in early authorities,[29] *Cabbage* also provided one of the earliest articulations of the requirement of an intention to deprive owners *permanently* of property. Two potential dilutions of this rule (and consequential widening of larceny) related to cases where property was simply abandoned by the defendant in circumstances making the owner's recovery highly unlikely, and where property was retrieved in a state of greatly diminished quality or value. The former example was declared not to be larceny in the 1801 decision of *Phillips and Strong*;[30] mere indifference to the likelihood of the owner's recovery was insufficient. Expansion of larceny to cover such cases of putting at risk an owner's future recovery and enjoyment of his property was also an issue in circumstances such as the unauthorized pawning or pledging of another's goods; where a condition had to be fulfilled by the owner to regain property the defendant would be liable.[31] However, the position remained unresolved where a defendant entertained the hope of later redeeming goods. Short of the defendant's virtual certainty of his inability to redeem pledged goods, the courts appeared to regard such an endangering or prejudicing of ownership as not larceny.[32]

Very limited authority emerged on the position where there was an intention to return property in a generally depleted or badly damaged state. In the mid-century authority of *Beecham*,[33] Patteson J. directed that the return of a stolen railway ticket after use constituted theft as there had been an 'absolute taking away'. Though, theoretically unresolved for larceny, abuse of another's property would almost inevitably have constituted malicious damage (see below). However, proposals to also include such behaviour within larceny were made. In 1888, Wright complained that 'there seems to be no limit in English law to the length or extent of use or misuse which a man may mean and carry out...without being guilty of theft, so long as he intended to return the thing, except the difficulty of convincing the jury of that intention'.[34] Wright's own solution appears in his earlier Draft Jamaican Penal Code where the *mens rea* of larceny would be satisfied by less than an intention to deprive permanently if the property is (or is intended to be) 'greatly injured or depreciated' or 'pledged'.[35] But, as the Criminal

---

[28] *Cabbage* (1815) R. & R. 292; *Morfit* (1816) R. & R. 307; *Jones* (1846) 1 Den. 188, 205. On Blackstone and the history of *lucri causa*, see J. W. C. Turner (1942) 4 *Toronto LJ* 296.

[29] *Egginton* (1801) 2 Leach 913; *Phillips and Strong* (1801) *East* 2 PC 662; *Dickenson* (1820) R. & R. 420. The requirement was clearly affirmed in *Holloway* (1849) 3 Cox 241.

[30] *Ibid.*, and *Crump* (1825) 1 Car. & P. 658.

[31] *Hall* (1849) 1 Den. 381.

[32] *Phetheon* (1840) 9 Car. & P. 552; *Medland* (1851) 5 Cox C.C. 292.

[33] (1851) 5 Cox 181.

[34] Pollock and Wright, *Possession*, 225.

[35] Section 188(iii). Stephen had adopted this stance in the *General View*, 136.

Law Commissioners had earlier maintained, penalizing such temporary appropriation as dishonest would have substantially collapsed the difference between
larceny and civil trespass.[36]

Beyond requiring an intent to deprive permanently, the absence of any claim
of right was a negative element of *animus furandi*, one usually analysed in early
works as an illustrative element of 'fraudulent or wrongful' takings.[37] Indeed,
other than that meaning, 'fraudulent' took on no other significance in the nineteenth century. *Hall*[38] produced an early nineteenth-century clarification of the
purely subjective nature of a claim of legal right to property. The Larceny Act 1916
eventually articulated larceny's distinct *mens rea* components as 'fraudulently
and without claim of right made in good faith...with intent...permanently to
deprive the owner thereof...'.[39]

Beside the process of identifying larceny's standard *mens rea* elements, throughout the nineteenth century two conceptually significant examples of what was
generally (though not universally) regarded as dishonest appropriation eluded
the common law's moderately comfortable reach: keeping after the finding or
mistaken delivery of property. Larceny's fundamental rule that *animus furandi*
must coincide with the initial taking of possession governed the common law's
response to the liability of finders. In 1849, *Thurbon* confirmed the view[40] that
if a finder's initial acquisition of possession was accompanied by the reasonable
belief that the owner could not be traced, the finder would not commit larceny

---

[36] *Fourth Report* (1839), lii; *First Report* (1834), 17. Despite the Commissioners' general analytical rigour, relatively little attention is given to the *mens rea* of larceny, defined as the 'fraudulent
intent entirely to deprive him of such thing', *Fourth Report* (1847), 178–9 Arts 1 and 21. Bearing
in mind the considerable importance they ascribed to the mental element in theft, the 1879 Code
Commissioners were hardly much more discursive when considering *mens rea*, *Report*, 28. It is
defined as 'fraudulently and without colour of right...with intent to deprive the owner permanently thereof...and intending to pledge, or parting with property under condition as to its retention' which the defendant 'may be unable to perform' was sufficient; so also where the defendant
intends to deal with property in such a manner that it 'cannot be restored in its [original] condition' (s 246).

[37] e.g. *East* 2 PC 655. Curiously Stephen felt 'malicious' would be a clearer term than fraudulent to
denote the nature of *animus furandi*. *General View*, 129. His *Digest* definition refers to 'unlawfully
and without claim of right' (1883 edn), 222. By 1902, Kenny's *Outlines of Criminal Law* had jettisoned
'fraudulently'.

[38] (1828) 3 Car. & P. 409. Claim of right might be on behalf of another, *Knight* (1781) 2 East 510.

[39] Section 1.

[40] *Thurbon* (1849) 1 Den. 387. The trial judge, Parke B., had originally directed a guilty verdict.
Reed (1842) Car. & M. 306 is authority for no liability on the basis of the finder's belief in his claim
of right. *Thristle* (1849) 1 Den. 502 confirmed that even where the owner's identity was known at the
time of initial possession, a subsequent dishonest disposal was not criminal provided the finder
had originally intended to act honestly. Also *East* 2 PC 664 and *Russell* (1819), ii: 1042. Pollock and
Wright, *Possession*, 171 note that prior to late eighteenth-century case law, finders were regarded as
trespassers.

where he retained possession after subsequently becoming aware of the means of identifying the owner.[41] This at least displayed consistency with the approach developed in response to larceny by a trick where the taker's honest state of mind when originally acquiring possession was the determinant of (non) criminality; thus, for neither fraudsters nor finders could subsequent dishonesty incriminate. Though much criticized by contemporary commentators,[42] unlike larceny by fraudulent bailees, no legislative intervention occurred to criminalize the relatively small-scale problem of subsequently dishonest finders.

Greater judicial ingenuity, not to say pragmatically induced conceptual inconsistency, was apparent in a trio of decisions criminalizing the dishonest retention of property acquired as the result of a mistake. In *Riley*, the defendant's original unknowing acquisition of a sheep had been by a mistake; the Court for Crown Cases Reserved found such acquisition had constituted trespass, and because of this unlawfulness Riley's subsequent dishonest conversion made the original taking theft.[43] Thirty years on, *Middleton* formulated the principle that money mistakenly paid by a cashier to someone aware of the mistake was theft if there was dishonest intention at the moment of receipt.[44] After this, one further step was taken in *Ashwell* where an initial mistake was made by both the lender and borrower of money as to a coin's denomination. Later discovery of the coin's higher value by the borrower defendant, followed by his dishonest appropriation was held to be theft by a divided Court for Crown Cases Reserved. Lord Coleridge reasoned Ashwell 'did not take it 'til he knew what he had got; and when he knew what he had got, that same instant he stole it'.[45] Unlike the position of subsequent

---

[41] Parke B.'s apparent requirement of objective reasonableness of initial belief in the inability to find the owner was later confirmed as purely subjective in *Knight* (1871) 12 Cox 102; similarly s 1(2) of the Larceny Act 1916. See the critical comments of *Thurbon* in *Glide* (1868) LR 1 Cr. 139 and *Deaves* (1869) 1 Cox 227.

[42] e.g. (1858) 31 *LT* 65 and 32 *LT* 109. In their *First Report*, the Criminal Law Commissioners regarded claims of finding frequent enough to render clarification of the law 'important'. The *Report*'s digested view of the law is obscure, appearing to make finders 'due diligence to discover the owner' important evidence of the existence or otherwise of *animus furandi* (p. 18). Later formulae are equally unclear: *Fourth Report* (1839) lxv, Art. 21; *Third Report* (1847), 16, Art. 23. Stephen's proposed substitution of 'appropriation' for asportation would have made Thurbon liable for theft, for his later conversion with knowledge of ownership. *General View*, 135; similarly the 1879 Code Commissioners definition of theft. Like Stephen, the Commissioners saw no moral relevance of an initially innocent finding and keeping.

[43] (1853) Dears. C.C. 149. See Turner's extensive critique, 'Two Cases of Larceny', in *The Modern Approach to Criminal Law* (1945), 356, 374–89.

[44] (1873) LR 2 CCR 38; for a highly critical analysis, see Turner, *ibid.*, 356–74 and also Fletcher, *Rethinking Criminal Law*, 107–9. Cf. Pollock and Wright, *Possession*, 205–11.

[45] (1885) 16 QB 190, Lord Coleridge CJ at 225. Both Stephen's and the 1879 Code Commission's proposals would probably have produced the same outcome in *Riley*, *Middleton*, and *Ashwell*. A year after the Court for Crown Cases Reserved distinguished *Ashwell* in the similar case of *Flowers* (1886)

dishonest retention of lost property, it is likely that judges viewed the frequency and commercial consequences of retention of property gained by mistake as too pressing a problem to await eventual legislative resolution.

Larceny's Scope: Property that Could be Stolen

Larceny's deep historical roots in the violation of possessionary rights by 'taking and carrying away' carried obvious implications for the nature of property that might be subject to theft. Most specifically, three broad types of property fell outside larceny's reach: intangible property, including choses in action; anything 'savouring' of land; and wild animals. In general, the steady, pragmatic compromising of larceny's possession-based origins had only a limited effect on the range of property potentially stealable. Unlike the constructive enlargement of possession, little potential existed for doctrinal sleight of hand to expand the scope of what might be stolen. Those enlargements which did occur were largely statutory, enacted as a consequence of self-evident practical commercial need and increasingly irresistible moral logic frequently and emphatically underscored by commentators and review bodies.[46]

Unsurprisingly, such innovations affected the spread of social classes and groups differently. Much nineteenth-century legislative intervention ensured that many professional, clerical, and commercial malpractices were brought within the criminal law's scope. With shifts in the moral expectations of business practices, the nefarious activities of the middle classes—so-called 'white collar' crime, including professional and commercial dishonesty—steadily became the subject of legislation penalizing conduct such as embezzlement,

---

16 QBD 643, Lord Coleridge unconvincingly asserted that in *Ashwell* the court had not intended to question the ancient doctrine that an innocent receipt of (property) and its subsequent fraudulent appropriation 'was not theft'. *Ashwell* was rejected in the Irish appeal decision of *Hehir* (1895) 2 IR 709. On the highly problematic relationship between the reasoning in *Riley* and *Ashwell*, see Smith and Hogan, *Criminal Law* (1965), 386–8.

[46] e.g. in the case of land, title deeds were made stealable by s 30 of the Larceny Act 1861 and s 7 of the Larceny Act 1916. For stealing or damaging with intent to steal parts of buildings, fabric or fixtures, trees and other specified plants, see principally ss 31–37 of the Larceny Act 1861; s 8 of the Larceny Act 1916. Common law requirements relating to severance of land or things from land, and the necessary period of time which must have elapsed between severance and taking were noted by the Criminal Law Commissioners as 'remarkable...useless refinements [causing] considerable embarrassments', *First Report* (1834), 8, 10, 11. Similarly, *Fourth Report* (1839), lxv and *Third Report* (1837), 15, Art. 17. Stephen took the unusual line of strongly favouring making land stealable (without prior severance) by the calculated shifting of boundaries, *General View*, 132–3. See the *Criminal Law Revision Committee, 8th Report 1966*, for a review of the 'evenly balanced' arguments, 21–2. The 1879 Criminal Code Commission stopped short of proposing Stephen's radical step, limiting itself to simplifying the severance requirement, *Report*, 27 and 116, s 247.

false accounting, obtaining property by false pretences, and obtaining credit by fraud.[47] On the other hand, the working classes, in practical terms were subject to few new forms of property-based criminality. However, mainly in the case of rural populations, developments in the game and poaching laws were to have a substantial impact.

In relation to theft, wild animals had long entailed both an awkward conceptual and political dimension. Established arcane and perplexing distinctions between (stealable) domestic animals 'fit for food' or 'not of a base nature', and those of a 'base nature' (not stealable) were, mainly, eliminated by the Larceny Act 1827. Wild animals (*ferae naturae*) neither tame nor captured, were in the possession of no one and consequently not stealable. However, the long-recognized social and political borderline between larceny and poaching could be crossed where, after killing the wild animal, the poacher at least briefly abandoned possession. Such brief abandonment caused ownership and possession to vest in the land-owner, making a subsequent re-taking by the 'poacher' larceny.[48]

Early nineteenth-century changes in the poaching laws represented a prominent instance of the conflicting currents of opinion and political interest manifest during this period. Ancient hunting privileges enjoyed by the aristocracy and landed gentry came under siege on two fronts: first, by the familiar enemy, in the form of individuals and, increasingly, poaching gangs out to supply an ever more lucrative black market in game; and secondly, by the rising level of public sniping from those advocating a wider franchise embracing the middle classes, a cause eventually culminating in the Representation of the People Act (Reform Act) 1832. In this uneasy climate, game rights were vulnerable not only because they constituted a powerful symbol of an elite class, but also because protection of such rights by the poaching laws had long attracted a moral ambivalence as to whether the activity was truly criminal. Illustrative of this attitude was Wilberforce's 1817 attempt to persuade his Commons' audience that poaching laws were 'contrary to the natural feeling

---

[47] The common law's non-inclusion of certain forms of intangible personal property was largely remedied by the Embezzlement Act 1799 and s 5 of the Larceny Act 1827 which extended the law's coverage to 'chattel, money or valuable security'. The credit realities of commercial life were recognized by the creation of the offence of obtaining credit by fraud, Debtors Act 1869, 32 & 33 Vict., c. 62. On the nineteenth-century expansion of opportunities and prosecutions for white-collar crime and middle-class criminality, see G. Robb, *White Collar Crime in Modern England* (Cambridge, 1992), esp. Ch. 1; S. Sindall, 'Middle-Class Crime in Nineteenth-Century England' (1983) 4 *Criminal Justice History* 23. For the reconceptualizing of legitimate and illegitimate, lawful and unlawful, commercial and business practices, see J. Locker and B. Godfrey, 'Ontological Boundaries and Temporal Watersheds in the Development of White Collar Crime' (2006) 46 *BJ of Crim.* 976 and S. Wilson, 'Law, Morality and Regulation: Victorian Experiences of Financial Crime' (2006) 46 *BJ of Crim.* 1073.

[48] *Blade* v. *Higgs* (1861) 11 *HLC* 621.

of mankind…, which men could be never brought to think a crime…'.[49] Certainly over time the penalties had been, and remained, significantly lower than those specified for larceny. And, although, to a degree, this distinction was eroded most particularly by the heavy penalties instituted by the Ellenborough Act 1803 and the Night Poaching Act 1817,[50] most poachers never fell foul of these severe provisions.

A depressed economy combined with a flooded labour market following the post-Napoleonic wars demobilization of forces in 1815, produced a general surge in criminal activity, including poaching. But rather than the question of the punishment for poaching, the 1816 Select Committee on game laws focused on resolving the appropriate basis for game rights, eventually proposing a less anach-ronistic system by which such rights would attach to the ownership of land.[51] Not unnaturally, the resistance of landed interests to relinquishing these highly prized trappings of social superiority (often recently acquired by the industrial and commercial nouveaux riches) was fierce. Yet this was eventually overridden by increasing political isolation of the representatives of such interests, along with rising middle and professional-class appetites for game meat backed up by demands for regularization of its supply and marketing.[52] Following repeated earlier Select Committee recommendations, the eventual compromise, the Game Act 1831, both attached game rights to the ownership of land and established the long sought after licensing system for the sale of game.[53]

---

[49] *PD* 1817 (s. 1), 35: 346; and similarly Romilly, *ibid.*, 339. Also the *Report of Select Committee on Criminal Committals and Convictions*, PP 1828 (545), vi, 419.

[50] Lord Ellenborough's Act 1803, 43 Geo. III, c. 58 made a capital offence of resisting lawful arrest by even the threat of using a firearm. The Night Poaching Act 1817, 57 Geo. III, c. 90 provided a max-imum punishment of seven years' transportation for being found armed at night with any offensive weapon, including clubs, intending to take game or rabbits. Evidence to support more extensive claims of the general significance of poaching laws in partial and repressive practices against the rural poor is equivocal. For claims of the extensive hegemonic deployment and enforcement of poaching laws in the eighteenth century, see D. Hay, 'Poaching and the Game Laws on Cannock Chase' in D. Hay et al. (eds), *Albion's Fatal Tree* (1975); and also H. Hopkins' more anecdotal, *The Long Affray: The Poaching Wars in Britain 1760–1914* (1986). Note the Home Office (S. M. Phillips, Under Secretary) evidence on 'great irregularities and injustices' perpetrated by magistrates, given to the 1846 *Select Committee on Game Laws*, PP 1846 (463), ix, Part I, *Min* 6063. In part the criticism related to the irregular use of cumulative penalties. Phillips gave evidence over two lengthy sessions. By way of a general concluding observation, Phillips regarded the Game Laws as 'more severe than other laws…' (*Min.* 6671). For claims of a far less prominent and partial enforcement of poaching laws, see King, *Crime, Justice and Discretion*, 99–103, who attributes greater prominence to prosecution for the taking of wood and vegetables. Also P. Munsche, *Gentlemen and Poachers: The English Game Laws 1671–1831* (Cambridge 1981), 76–105.

[51] *PP* 1816 (504), iv, 507.

[52] *Report of the House of Commons' Select Committee*, PP 1823 (206), iv, 107; *Report of House of Lords' Select Committee*, PP 1828 (203), viii, 333. Extensive evidence of the problems of fluctuating prices and demand was provided by poulterers. Also Munsche, *Gentlemen and Poachers*, 132 and *passim*.

[53] Game Act 1831, 1 & 2 Will. IV c. 32. On the driving concern to regularize the supply of game meat to the middle classes, see e.g. the Commons' exchange in *PD* 1817 (s. 1), 35: 340 *et seq.* The

In common with punishment for many other offences at this time, the apparent ineffectiveness of the poaching laws led to a reduction of its harsher penalties and to the outlawing of two infamous anti-poaching devices, mantraps and spring guns.[54] An apparent inexorable rise in the level of violent poaching led to John Bright's public political manoeuvre of the late 1830s. Linking further modifications of the game laws to give tenant farmers game rights with repeal of the protectionist Corn Laws, Bright eventually achieved the appointment of a Select Committee on game laws in 1844. However, no proposals were included in the Commons' Report two years later[55] on Bright's key campaigning objective of concessions to tenant farmers to take game from their land. Any momentum for such change was terminated with the success of the Anti-Corn Law campaign.

Indeed, rather than further amelioration, the poaching laws became procedurally slightly harsher. With the aim of easing the process of conviction, the Poaching Prevention Act 1862 furnished emergent rural police forces with the power to stop and search suspected poachers. However, while landowners had envisaged deploying local professional police in the cause of game protection, Chief Constables showed themselves to be decidedly unenthusiastic in assuming such a role, not least because of its imagined effect on relations between the police and the rural working classes.[56] Other than Gladstone's democratic gesture of finally awarding tenant-farmers 'concurrent' rights to shoot or trap hares and rabbits, no further changes followed to the substance of game laws.[57]

---

incidental claimed benefit of rendering largely redundant gang poaching for commercial purposes never materialized, principally because of the ability of poaching gangs to undercut the wholesale price of legitimate suppliers, *Select Committee Report on Game Law*, PP 1846 (463), ix, Part II.

[54] The Night Poaching Act 1828, 9 Geo. IV, c. 6 set a sliding scale of penalties beginning with three months' imprisonment for a first offence; up to 14 years could be imposed where a gang was armed. On Cobbett's game law reform campaigning, beginning in May 1823, conducted in the *Political Register* and the movement for prohibition of the use of spring guns (enacted in 1827 by Lord Suffield's Act), see Hopkins, *The Long Affray*, 154–76. For the distinction between the generally unlawful use of spring guns and mantraps and their lawful use 'in a Dwelling House, for the Protection thereof', see the Offences Against the Person Act 1861, s 31.

[55] *Report of the Select Committee on Game Law*, PP 1846 (463), ix, Part II.

[56] Poaching Prevention Act 1862, 25 & 26 Vict. c. 114. Memo to the Home Secretary by Chief Constables, PP 1862 (201), xlv, 220–1. The Chief Constables observed that poachers 'are looked upon as village heroes for their nocturnal expeditions and assaults on keepers…'. Yet, while 'most anxious' not to be involved 'directly or indirectly' in preserving game, the Chief Constables deplored the attacks of poaching gangs. On the likelihood of prejudicing police/public relations, see also the concerns expressed in the House of Lords at the Commons' amendments giving more extensive police powers than the original Lords' Bill, PD 1862 (s. 3), 168: 1175–7.

[57] Ground Game Act 1881. The considerable penalty differential between poaching and larceny continued throughout and beyond the nineteenth century. From 1828, simple night poaching carried a maximum of three months' imprisonment for a first offender. From 1831 any day poaching carried a maximum of £2 fine which was raised to £5 by the 1852 Act. Over the same period the

2. MALICIOUS DAMAGE

The common law's criminalization of 'malicious' interference with property rights was generally far more reticent and limited than in larceny and other forms of dishonesty. Mercantile and commercial pressures in substantial measure responsible for adaptations in those areas of criminality were largely absent in relation to criminal damage. With the exception of arson, damage to real or personal property, not motivated by gain or dishonesty, was at one time regarded as exclusively a civil matter, to be pursued by a trespass action. Destruction or damage by fire of the house or outhouse of another, achieved its singular criminal status because, rather than a mere civil matter of compensation, arson, as Foster put it, smacked of 'an act of public hostility'.[58] To a large extent, eighteenth-century legislative intervention transformed this position by criminalizing the causing of malicious damage to an extensive range of real and personal property, the punishment for which was frequently capital. In *Russell*'s rather unforthcoming comment, 'different statutes [were] passed from time to time, as they appeared to be required for the protection of the community'.[59] However, more often than not, legislation was driven by publicly aired anxieties over national or regional attacks on property that carried strong class or insurrectional overtones; such activities which were not far removed from what Foster had characterized as 'public hostility'. Consolidation of a century or more of legislative accretion of these offences occurred first in 1827 as part of Peel's more general statutory tidying up, and once again in the Malicious Damage Act 1861, drafted by C. S. Greaves.

In line with the other consolidation measures of 1861, amendments to the law's substance and particular definitional forms were severely limited. As was also true of the Larceny Act, this was a consequence of a general parliamentary desire to ensure no inadvertent changes in the law occurred, coupled with the aim of specifically regulating the punishment for each particular type of malicious damage covered.[60] Beyond perpetuating eighteenth-century practices of extensive

punishment for simple larceny moved from seven years' transportation, or two years' imprisonment, to a maximum of five years' imprisonment under s 2 of the Larceny Act 1916.

[58] *Crown Law*, 192. Under the common law, burning barns containing corn or hay was a felony. Endangering houses by burning one's own house was a common law misdemeanour, Blackstone, *Comms*, iv, 221.

[59] *Russell* (1826), ii: 484. The first and most significant was the wide-ranging Waltham Black Act 1722, 9 Geo. I, c. 22 covering, inter alia, damage to real and personal property. Legislative protection of industrial targets included mines and mills, 10 Geo. II, c. 32, 1737 and 9 Geo. III, c. 29, 1769. Early nineteenth-century examples include the protection of particular weaving machines and buildings or machinery associated with mines, 52 Geo. III, c. 16, 1812 and 56 Geo. III, c. 125, 1816.

[60] See Greaves' comments, *Criminal Law Acts 1861* (2nd edn, 1862), xxxix. To ensure no unintended gaps in the law's coverage, the 1861 Act followed earlier practice by including ss 51–54.

particularity in defining various instances of malicious damage, key common definitional terms dating back prior to the 1827 consolidation were retained; most centrally, the well-worn expression 'unlawfully and maliciously' was once again deployed throughout the 1861 Act. Open to relatively wide judicial construction, neither word achieved any clear authoritative meaning until late in the century.

'Unlawfully' had long encapsulated the indistinct notion of an absence of any excuse or justification for a defendant's actions, which, realistically, might be based on some claim of right of defence of property or person. Reflecting earlier law, in relation to a claim of right, neither the 1827 or 1861 consolidation expressly[61] identified such a defence. However, following a path broadly consistent with larceny, from Lord Denman to Lord Alverstone, the judiciary directly resorted to general *mens rea* doctrine to justify recognition of a claim of right defence.[62] Despite arguable statutory and doctrinal differences between the positions of felonies, misdemeanours, and summary offences, some form of claim of right defence was unequivocally accepted by the judiciary for each category.[63] But distinctions did arise in the defence's requirements for felonies, broadly the most serious examples of malicious damage. Here, in common with larceny, the defence's demands were exclusively subjective: according to Lord Coleridge CJ '...an honest claim of right, however absurd', would acquit.[64] For misdemeanours and summary offences, an objective standard of statutory origin was construed as regulating the defence's general scope. In this specific provision[65] relating to the ouster of summary jurisdiction, the 1861 Act referred to a 'fair and reasonable supposition' of a claim of right. However, its full-blown objectivity was judicially bypassed through doctrinally doubtful resort to the reasoning applied in earlier felony authorities.[66]

The generally elusive quality of 'malice' or 'malicious' in specifying criminal responsibility was notoriously long lasting and is given particular consideration

---

[61] Except s 24 of the 1827 Act, below. The legislative history of the Act does not record why this single exception appears.

[62] For the criminal law's general and changing (from subjective to objective requirements) response to mistake and its relationship to *mens rea*, see 'General Principles' above Ch. VII.

[63] For felonies, Lord Denman CJ in *James* v. *Phelps* (1840) 11 Ad. & El. 483; for misdemeanours, Lord Russell CJ in *Clemens* [1898] 1 QB 556; and for summary offences, Lord Alverstone CJ in *Heaven* (1903) 68 *JP* 53.

[64] *Watkins* v. *Major* (1875) 44 *LJMC* 164. Also, *Day* (1844) 8 *JP* 186.

[65] Section 52, replacing a similar provision (s 24) of the Malicious Damage Act 1827.

[66] *Clemens* (1898) and *Heaven* (1903), *ibid*. Both cases incorporate an objective element in that although the belief need not be reasonable, the exercise of the right must be. This is probably an implicit reference to an owner's right to take all reasonable measures in defence of property. On the technicalities of interpretation of the ouster provisions (whereby if title to land is at issue magistrates had no jurisdiction) of the 1861 Act and s 14(1) of the Criminal Justice Administration Act 1914, see Turner, *Russell* (12th edn, 1964), ii: 1313–26.

elsewhere.[67] Yet, in relation to malicious damage, the obscurity of its meaning was shorter lived. Following earlier practice, judgments, statutes, and treatise writers favoured identifying examples of what would *not* prevent liability or was *not* essential to conviction. So, for example, it was well settled that neither 'ill-will' nor 'malice' was required against the owner of the property damaged.[68] More directly, the common law offence of arson had long been recognized in institutional works as demanding greater culpability than 'negligence or mischance':[69] a defendant needed to be at least subjectively reckless as to damaging buildings by fire. Consequently, in an apparent attempt to ensure a good standard of care and vigilance amongst servants, the legislature were forced to enact a tailor-made summary form of arson based on a lower, objective form of culpability: of 'negligently' setting fire to houses or outhouses, punishable by up to 18 months in prison.[70]

Beyond specific 'negligent' and common law arson, for malicious damage offences of statutory origin, fault requirements were less openly articulated. In his analysis of criminal damage, Greaves' 1843 and 1865 editions of *Russell* incorporated significant textual additions relating to the evidential presumption of defendants intending the natural consequences of an act. Although derived from judicial authority on a particular offence of setting fire to buildings with intent to injure or defraud, Greaves included his observations on presumptions and proof of intention to injure[71] in a general chapter on malicious damage.[72] Such an approach to proving ulterior intention was eventually expressly rejected by Blackburn J. two decades later in *Child:* a stance responsible for a series of authorities giving 'malicious' a clear meaning of at least subjective recklessness as to the consequences of an act.[73] It was a meaning consciously sought by

---

[67] See 'Concepts of Criminal Fault', Ch. VII, above.

[68] Enacted in the 1827 Act, s 25 and the 1861 Act, s 58. *Newill* (1832) 5 Car. & P. 266.

[69] e.g. Blackstone, *Comms*, iv, 222, cited in *Russell* (1826), ii: 486.

[70] Triable by two justices 1774, 14 Geo. III, c. 78, s 84.

[71] In addition to the general requirements of acting 'unlawfully and maliciously', aggravated forms of malicious damage sometimes also required an ulterior 'intent', such as 'to injure or defraud' (1861 Act, s 3). In earlier case law, such an additional requirement increased the likelihood of 'malicious' being ascribed a clear subjective meaning.

[72] (3rd edn), ii: 544–5; (4th edn), ii: 1018–19, 1030n; also i: 742. Stephen thought Greaves' interpretation of the aim of the 1861 Act correct and Blackburn's erroneous, *Digest of Criminal Law* (1877), 302. See also *Chitty* (2nd edn, 1826), iii: 1122 citing the leading general authority *Farrington* (1811) R & RCC 207. From the 1849 (8th) edn onwards, *Archbold* required that a defendant must have contemplated the consequences of his act (337–8).

[73] *Child* (1871) 1 CCR 307; also *Ward* (1872) LR 1 CCR 356; *Welch* (1875) 1 QBD 23; *Pembliton* (1874) LR 2 CCR 119; and earlier, Williams J. in *Batstone* (1864) 10 Cox 20. But cf. the equivocal mix of substantive law and questions of proof in *Faulkner* (1877) 13 Cox 550 and *Chapin* (1909) 22 Cox 10.

the Criminal Code Commissioners in their 1879 Draft Code malicious damage provisions.[74]

Finally, as well as the vital question of the mental culpability necessary for malicious damage, judicial construction of the scope of 'damage' was also of considerable significance in determining the reach of this form of criminality. Here, the judiciary displayed an inclination to extend the criminal law into distinctly marginal forms of property interference. Beyond the most obvious examples, 'damage' was very broadly construed to include any diminution in the value of property,[75] or some change of quality,[76] or even the maladjustment of machinery.[77] Such cases represented criminality's outer edge, demarcated by a combination of the civil law of trespass and criminal law's *de minimis* principle.[78]

---

[74] Section 381: 'Every one who causes any event by any act which he knew would probably cause it, being reckless whether such event happens or not, should be deemed to have caused it wilfully...'. The Commissioners sought to base their definition on the meaning given to malicious in *Child* (*Report*, 15). More generally, 'We have avoided the use of the word 'malice' throughout the Draft Code because there is a considerable difference between its popular and its legal meaning' (*Report*, 30).

[75] *Norris* (1840) 9 Car. & P. 241, slightly damaging a steam engine by running it unloaded. See 'Larceny' above for 'borrowings' causing damage to property.

[76] *Roper* v. *Knott* [1898] 1 QB 868, dilution of milk with water.

[77] *Foster* (1852) 6 Cox 25, 'dislocation or disarrangement' of a machine; *Tacey* (1821) R. & R. 452; removal of an essential part of the machine; *Fisher* (1865) LR 1 CCR 7, maladjusting a machine to render it inoperable.

[78] Compare *Gayford* v. *Chouler* (1889) 1 QB 316 with *Eley* v. *Lytle* (1885) 50 JP 308. In the specific case of arson, or fire-related offences, proof of some burning albeit 'trifling', must be established, *Parker* (1839) 9 Car. & P. 45.

XII

Offences Against the Person

BOTH the law and prosecutorial practices for the majority of offences against the person underwent substantial and significant modification during the course of the nineteenth century. This generalization holds true for the full span of criminality, extending from homicide and non-fatal assaults through to sexual offences. In respect of homicide, substantive definitional refinements were sought and partially achieved for murder and manslaughter. Inherited from the eighteenth century, a disparate ragbag of non-fatal offences against the person was subject to two radical statutory consolidation initiatives accompanied by a process of judicial reinterpretation of culpability requirements. As a consequence of both legislative intervention and common law development, the function of harm in identifying liability was diminished while that of fault attracted rising emphasis. In relation to sexual offences two distinct periods of change can be observed: marked increases in the level of prosecutions for established sexual offences in the early decades of the nineteenth century; and in the later part of the century, a widening criminalization of certain consensual sexual practices involving children, homosexuals, or people related by consanguinity.

Many developments can be ascribed to very particular causes attaching to specific offences. However, on a more general plane, broader social and political forces clearly generated a climate conducive both to substantive developments and changes in prosecution practices. In relation to the latter, legislative initiatives from the 1820s onwards significantly facilitated 'private' prosecutions, as did the subsequent spread of professional policing. Not only were the financial hazards of bringing prosecutions diminished, but the often daunting process of gathering and marshalling evidence benefited from increasing police involvement.[1] Less tangibly, a highly germane element of society's civilizing or pacifying, witnessed over the eighteenth and into the nineteenth century, was the

---

[1] See 'Prosecution', Ch. III and 'Policing', Ch. II, above. In the case of homicide, the increased frequency and greater professionalism of Coroners' inquests became an important source of preliminary evidence for further investigation of suspicious deaths. Medical Witness Act 1836, 6 & 7 Will. IV, c. 89 and I. Burney, *Bodies of Evidence: Medicine, Public Inquiry, and the Politics of the English Inquest 1830–1926* (Baltimore, 2000).

diminished tolerance of various manifestations of violence and ill-treatment: 'a shifting of the line dividing acceptable from unacceptable conduct and a strengthening of feelings of shame, guilt and repugnance about acts that had once raised no eyebrows'.[2] It was a social and political environment which, aside from pragmatic considerations, bred or underwrote the strengthening of legislation against individual violence or collective public disorder,[3] the mistreatment or exploitation of children, and cruelty to animals. Such a mood also infused the de capitalizing of most serious crimes and a growing rejection, or restriction, of other forms of corporal punishments, along with the substitution of imprisonment or other secondary punishment.[4] And not least, it was a political and social climate which led to the eventual nationwide acceptance and installation of professional policing as an essential means of achieving an increasingly ordered and orderly society. Reinforcing the criminal law's capacity to curb effectively violence and the infliction of personal harm was, self-evidently, a key component in any national advance towards a more civil, not to say, industrially and commercially effective society.

Historical developments in the law of offences against the person are considered in three distinct groupings: (1) non-fatal assaults and wounding; (2) sexual offences; (3) unlawful homicide.

1. NON-FATAL ASSAULTS AND WOUNDINGS

As two nineteenth-century would-be codifiers observed, the law governing assaults and woundings was 'singularly fragmentary and unsystematic'; moreover, until the early 1800s, the 'very grossest and worse class of offences against the person were…treated with that capricious lenity which was as characteristic of the common law as its equally capricious severity'.[5] This state of affairs was in good measure the product of eighteenth-century piecemeal penal legislative practices, and, most especially, the highly fact-specific (frequently capital) offences created by the Waltham Black Act 1722.[6] Also of considerable practical

---

[2] Beattie, *Crime and the Courts*, 138. On the general theme of the 'civilizing process', rising intolerance of violence in the late eighteenth and early nineteenth century, see N. Elias, *The Civilizing Process*, 2 vols (1978–82) and J. Carter Wood, *Violence and Crime in Nineteenth Century England: The Shadow of Our Refinement* (2004); and on the development of a civil society, P. Langford *Englishness Identified: Manners and Character 1650–1850* (Oxford, 2000). For the role of organized religion, see 'Law and Religion', XI, Pt 1.

[3] See 'Public Order', Ch. IX, above.

[4] See 'Punishment', Ch. V, above.

[5] Respectively, R. S. Wright, 'Notes' on the Jamaican Draft Penal Code 1877, 106; Stephen, *HCL*, iii, 116.

[6] 9 Geo. 1 c. 22. For a detailed analysis of the capital Act's creation and operation, see Radzinowicz, *History*, i: 49–79. The Waltham Black Act supplemented the capital provisions of the Coventry

significance was the fact that until the late eighteenth century, assaults not causing serious injury were of ambiguous status, being open to civil or criminal proceedings. This ambiguity had sanctioned judicial practices disapproved of by
several contemporary commentators, including Blackstone:[7]

> It is not uncommon, when a person is convicted of [assault or battery] for the court to
> permit the defendant to speak with the prosecutor, before any judgment is pronounced;
> and, if the prosecutor declares himself satisfied, to inflict but a trivial punishment. This
> is done, to reimburse the prosecutor his expenses, and make him some private amends,
> without the trouble and circuity of a civil action. But it surely is a dangerous practice: and,
> though it may be intrusted to the prudence and discretion of the judges in the superior
> courts of record, it ought never to be allowed in local or inferior jurisdictions, such as the
> quarter-sessions; where prosecutions for assaults are by this means too frequently com-
> menced, rather for private lucre than for the great ends of public justice.... [A]lthough a
> private citizen may dispense with satisfaction for his private injury, he cannot remove the
> necessity of public example. The right of punishing belongs not to any one individual in
> particular, but to the society in general, or the sovereign who represents that society: and
> a man may renounce his own portion of this right but he cannot give up that of others.

Migration of these assaults from being largely the subject of a civil action to one
of a criminal prosecution before magistrates or at Quarter Sessions was substantially completed by the 1820s.[8] Yet, by virtue of the frequent impracticability of bringing charges on indictment, simple common assault often remained
unprosecuted or was subject to informal compensatory arrangements. However,

---

(Ambash) Act 1670 (22 & 23 Car. 2, c. 1) which covered a variety of particular 'malicious' cuttings and
slittings by ambush, *Russell* (1826), i: 578–90. Of lesser severity, the common law offence of mayhem (a
'high misdemeanour') punished 'serious injury' inflicted 'maliciously' with a fine or imprisonment at
the court's discretion. *Ibid.*, 585–6. For contrasting interpretations of the motivation behind the Black
Act, see E. Thompson, *Whigs and Hunters: The Origins of the Black Act* (1975) and E. Cruikshanks and
H. Erskine-Hill, 'The Waltham Black Act and Jacobitism' (1985) 24 *Journal British Studies* 358.

   [7] *Comms*, iv, 356–7. On indictment, the punishment for common assault was a fine determined by
the 'heinousness of the offence', *Burn* (1797 edn), 142.

   [8] On this process of change and the increasing of punishments from fines to imprisonment,
see P. King, *Crime and Law in England 1750–1840: Remaking Justice from the Margins* (Cambridge,
2006), Ch. 7. At the end of the eighteenth century, assault was defined as any 'attempt or offer with
force and violence to do corporal hurt to another'. The earliest identification of putting the victim in fear of the application of force as being the essence of assault appears in *St. George* (1840)
9 Car. & P. 483; followed in *Ladyman* (1851) 15 *JP* 581, 1. Battery was 'any injury whatsoever, be it
never so small [including] spitting in [the] face, or any touching in anger...', *Burn* (17th edn, 1793),
i: 127–8; *Hawkins*, 1 PC, 133–4. By 1830 for assault and battery the requirement of 'malice or wantonness' [*sic*] had been added by some authors, *Burn* (25th edn, 1830), i: 219; *Russell* (1826), i: 862. Cf.
Archbold (2nd edn, 1825), 241. 'Malice' construed as foresight was at no stage confirmed as sufficient
for assault. See Turner, *Modern Approach to Criminal Law*, 351–5 for an unconvincing attempt to
demonstrate to the contrary. Both the *Criminal Law Commissioners Second Report* (1846), Art. 43
and the 1879 Draft Code, s 203, suggest the need for intention.

by extending summary jurisdiction[9] to simple common assault, with a fine or in default, up to two months' imprisonment, the Offences Against the Person Act (Lord Lansdowne's Act) 1828 made significant inroads into this enforced tolerance of relatively low level violence.

But physically abused wives was one particular category of victim where the gain from this procedural change was more notional than real. Practical legal protection eventually arrived with enactment of the 1853 'Act for the better Prevention and Punishment of Aggravated Assaults on Women and Children'. Not only did this socially highly desirable legislation increase the maximum punishment for assaults, crucially, it also enabled charges to be instigated by third parties, thereby preventing violent husbands forestalling charges by the common practice of physically or economically intimidating abused wives.[10] Also indicative of the radically altered social and political climate developing over the second half of the nineteenth century, was a whole run of abortive bills between 1856 and 1882 seeking to make flogging available for assaults on women and children. Rather than failing through any belief that flogging was excessively severe, the bills were lost principally through fears of the counter-productivity of the infliction of such punishment.[11] In reality, penal legislation alone could not adequately protect abused wives and children; this only came with powers to regulate and enforce separation and maintenance orders against husbands, especially those established under the Matrimonial Causes Act 1878 and subsequent legislation, through to the Summary Jurisdiction (Married Women) Act 1895.[12]

---

[9] Before a bench of two magistrates, 9 Geo. IV c. 31, s 27. For contemporary criticism of this change 'adding to the already exorbitant power exercised by justices of the peace...' (1830) 1 *LM* 129, 139.

[10] On the social background and general problematic nature of legally protecting wives, see A. Hammerton, *Cruelty and Companionship: Conflict in Nineteenth Century Married Life* (1992); S. d'Cruze, *Crimes of Outrage: Sex, Violence and Victorian Working Women* (1998); and XIII, Pt 4. For the effects of the diminution and final extinction of a husband's legal right to restrain and chastise his wife (classically affirmed by Blackstone, *Comms*, i, 444 and terminated in *Jackson* (1891) and relevant Matrimonial Causes legislation), see M. Doggett, *Marriage, Wife-Beating and the Law in Victorian England* (1992), *passim*. On the campaigning within the working classes to employ the law against wife-beaters, see A. Clark, *The Struggle for the Breaches: Gender and the Making of the British Working Class* (Berkeley, 1995), Ch. 5 *passim*.

[11] See particularly the 1874 Home Office consultation with the judiciary and police, the majority of whom favoured flogging powers: *Reports to the Secretary of State for the Home Department on the State of the Law Relating to Brutal Assaults* [c. 1138] *PP* 1875 (65), 29. The subsequent Offences Against the Person Act Amendment Bill was withdrawn by the government at its Second Reading in the face of broad parliamentary opposition, *PD* 1875 (s. 3), 224: 1853; Doggett, *ibid.*, 106–11.

[12] See also the specific domestic violence provisions in the Prevention of Cruelty and Protection of Children Act 1889 and the Custody of Children Act 1891. G. Behlmer, 'Summary Justice and Working Class Marriage in England, 1870–1940' (1994) 12 *LHR* 229 and XIII, Pt 4.

In respect of more serious, harm-causing assaults, Lord Ellenborough's early nineteenth-century initiative to 'generalize' the (capital) scope of a cluster of seventeenth-century statutory woundings constituted a notable move away from narrowly focused, fact-specific penal legislation. Ellenborough's 1803 Act sought to close anomalous gaps in the existing law's coverage through which several defendants had recently and notoriously squeezed.[13] Beside relative generality of substantive offences, the Act criminalized a broad range of attempts or actions preparatory to woundings. This in itself constituted an early partial legislative acceptance of the criminality of culpable acts not resulting in harm.[14] Further widening of the 1803 provisions beyond shootings, stabbings, and cuttings, came with the Offences Against the Person Act 1828—Lord Lansdowne's Act. As Home Secretary, Peel lent his support for the bill, denying any difference in 'moral turpitude' between the various possible methods employed to cause bodily harm.[15] However, the legislative approach displayed in the 1803, 1828, and 1837 Acts towards both offence definitions and the relevance of harm caused, to a degree, remained backward looking. Whilst widening the range of woundings punished to, effectively, those caused by *any* means, the Acts also retained the early fact-specific forms of offence. Thus, for example, the provisions of Lord Ellenborough's Act covering shooting, stabbing, and cutting appear in subsequent legislation, including the 1837 Act and eventually the long-standing 1861 consolidations.[16] The relevance of actual harm to attempted murder is

---

[13] 1803, 43 Geo. III c. 58. On the declared function of the Act, see *Parl. Hist.*, 1801–3, vol. 36, 1245. As enlarged by the Waltham Black Act, the Coventry (Ambush) Act 1670 (22 & 23 Car. 2, c. 1) was the principal basis of prosecution for serious assaults.

[14] See 'Attempt', Ch. VII, above. Like full offences, attempts required defendants to act 'wilfully, maliciously, and unlawfully' (s 1).

[15] *PD* 1828 (s. 2), 19: 352; and (s. 2), 18: 1171–3. And commentary (1830) 1 *LM* 129. The Offences Against the Person Act 1837, 7 Will. 4 & 1 Vict. c. 85 further widened the 1826 Act to cover attempted murder (a capital offence) by any means (s 2). However, where an attempt failed to inflict injury the punishment was decreased to a minimum of 15 years and a maximum of life transportation or three years' imprisonment (s 3). A similar level of punishment continued to be imposed for 'unlawfully and maliciously' wounding 'with intent' to 'maim' or cause other 'grievous bodily harm' or to resist arrest (s 4). The object of the attempts elements of the 1837 Act was to punish 'proximate attempts': attempts which led 'immediately to the discharge of loaded arms', a combined endangerment and culpability rationale. See Greaves's analysis of the generous crop of case law provoked by these provisions in *Russell* (3rd edn, 1843), i: 727, 723–7. Under s 4 the principal general provision for causing serious injury, 'wound' was settled to require a breaking of the 'continuity' of the 'whole skin', *Wood* (1834) 4 Car. & P. 381. Furthermore, some sort of instrument must have been used to inflict the wound; the use of bare hands was insufficient, *Harris* (1836) 7 Car. & P. 446. Unlike previous provisions, the mental element for wounding with intent to maim or cause grievous bodily harm was held to be free of any need to show the offence would have been murder had death followed, *Griffiths* (1838) 8 Car. & P. 248.

[16] Particularly ss 11, 12, 13, 14, and 15 which relate to seven different forms of attempted murder. Section 15 was a residuary provision to cover any case not specifically identified in earlier sections.

emphasized in both the 1828 and 1837 Acts, which created two classes of offence: a capital version where bodily injury was caused; a non-capital offence where the assailant failed to inflict any injury. In part, the retention and repetition of earlier enactments was a standard legislative technique, partly to make plain to Parliament the extent of any amending provisions, and partly to leave undisturbed previous authoritative interpretations thought worthy of perpetuating.[17] But, as is suggested elsewhere,[18] the relatively recent common law acceptance of a general offence of attempt, coupled with the evidential value of harm in proving mental culpability, were probably also contributory factors in the durability of such an approach.

Nevertheless, the consolidation and amending provisions of the Offences Against the Person Act 1861 represented a few steps further in jettisoning some of the living history of earlier legislation. As its draughtsman C. S. Greaves claimed, the Act established the crude beginnings of a structured grading of offences whereby the seriousness of an offence was calibrated on the twin bases of mental culpability and level of harm caused.[19] This graduated response appears in the Act's handling of the range of assaults, running from common assault without infliction of harm to intentionally wounding or causing grievous bodily harm.[20] However, not only was the overall result somewhat 'clumsy', retention of some of the formerly employed fault and harm terms almost guaranteed a continuation of much of the interpretational wrangling which had bedevilled earlier provisions.[21] In fact, the limited innovations found in the 1861 Act represented the few surviving fragments of a far more extensive failed initiative of nearly a decade earlier to restructure systematically offences against the person.

In 1852, many of the proposals and analyses of the Criminal Law Commissioners on offences against the person were incorporated in a bill prepared at the request of Lord St. Leonards LC, by Greaves and Lonsdale, the long-serving Secretary to the Criminal Law Commissioners. The bill's proposed innovation lay in its attempt to amalgamate both statute and common law. Following its

---

[17] See 'Sources and Form', Ch. VI, above.

[18] See 'Attempt', Ch. VII, above. The common law misdemeanour of attempt to commit any indictable offence (including murder) was punishable with a fine or imprisonment. The Acts of 1803, 1828, and 1837 made certain forms of attempted murder capital felonies. The Offences Against the Person Act 1861 perpetuated this specific form of attempt liability.

[19] *The Criminal Law Acts* (2nd edn, 1862), xl.

[20] Common assault was punishable with up to one year's imprisonment or six months if tried summarily; for the misdemeanour of assault occasioning actual bodily harm (s 47) and maliciously wounding or inflicting grievous bodily harm (s 20) a maximum of five years' imprisonment; for the felony of wounding or causing grievous bodily harm with intent (s 18) a maximum of life imprisonment.

[21] In relation to 'malicious', see *Ward* (1872) LR 1 CCR 356 and *Martin* (1881) 8 QBD 54.

introduction the following year by the Lord Chancellor, the bill underwent the scrutiny of an exceedingly weighty and experienced Lords' Select Committee, whose members included Lord Campbell CJ along with a clutch of past and future Lord Chancellors.[22] In the autumn of the same year, the observations of the judges were solicited on a slightly amended version of the bill. A broadly, though not entirely unanimous, hostile response to the general proposal of codification, together with detailed criticisms, effectively sank this and other similarly constructed bills.[23] Both the provisions of the failed bill and judicial responses merit at least brief review. Aside from the 1879 Draft Code Bill, the generally neglected (by historians) 1854 bill could be regarded as a high water mark for attempts to reconstruct the law in this area,[24] in that it enjoyed the specific endorsement of such a powerful and distinguished group of lawyer-politicians.

While the bill's homicide provisions drew the most fire (see below), many non-fatal offence provisions also attracted severe criticism. Most proposed changes were a mixture of the expositional and structural; a small number exhibited substantial conceptual innovation attributable to the Criminal Law Commissioners. Of the latter, general fault terms, which benefited from relatively clear articulation by the Commissioners,[25] were employed in providing a scale of non-fatal offences, with seriousness calibrated on the basis of degree of mental culpability and harm threatened or actually caused. Most notably, negligent or 'malicious' endangering of life were proposed as two distinct new forms of general offence, as was the negligent causing of grievous bodily harm or just 'bodily harm'.[26] 'Maliciously, by any means, put[ting] the Life of any...Person in Danger...' would have been punishable by up to three years' imprisonment; negligent endangerment would have carried up to one year's imprisonment. Curiously, these innovatory expansions of existing, very specific offences relating to burning ships or destroying buildings, were unsupported by explanatory justification from the Criminal Law

---

[22] Lords Lyndhurst, Brougham, Truro, and Cranworth. As Greaves relates: 'We were directed to prepare [the bill] from the Reports of the Criminal Law Commissioners...; to reconsider the clauses framed by [them] and to amend every defect which we discovered...[The Select Committee] 'sat eleven mornings on that Bill [making] sundry amendments', *The Criminal Law Acts*, x.

[23] See 'Sources and Form', Ch. VI, above for a detailed examination of this episode.

[24] House of Lords Session Papers, PP 1854 (339), xxi, 1. Beside offences against the person, the bill dealt with defences and complicity; considered above, 'General Principles', Ch. VII, above.

[25] See 'General Principles', Ch. VII above.

[26] *Second Report* (1846) s. 2, Arts 3–5, and s 7; and *Fourth Report* (1848) s. 7 esp. Arts 2, 4, 5, 6, and 38. Although 'malice' and 'maliciously' were retained in some provisions, being indirectly defined to cover intention and foresight of a probability. The 1853 bill's fault terms followed those of the Criminal Law Commissioners except 'wilful', which (unlike the Commissioners' version which included foresight of a probability) is narrowly defined as meaning intention (s 23). However, the bill incorporates a clear presumption that 'every person shall be deemed to have intended that which is the natural and probable consequence of his Act or Omission until the contrary is proved' (s 24).

Commissioners.[27] Nor, even more remarkably, did they attract comment from any of the judges.

These observations are equally apt for two proposed new general offences of 'negligently' causing either grievous bodily harm or bodily harm.[28] Along with existing assaults and woundings, these additional forms of general liability would have engineered a logical symmetry into the law's structure. Endangering offences complemented attempt liability by punishing behaviour, whilst lacking a criminal objective, nevertheless generated a risk of causing harm. Such liability might arguably be seen as seeking to punish and deter socially unacceptable, high risk behaviour, whatever the context. Similar claims could have been deployed in support of the proposed offences of negligent harm causing. Moreover, these offences would have met the apparent illogicality of punishing (as manslaughter) harm causing negligence only when death was a consequence.[29]

Overall, in this episode of would-be law reform the bulk of the higher judiciary acquitted themselves with little distinction or dignity. Judicial observations demonstrated everything, from inadequate study of the bill, pure pettiness and pedantry, to a simple lack of intelligibility.[30] Judicial objections to specific measures were almost wholly nit-picking in nature as to the draughtsmen's syntax or grammar, or claimed obscurity of meaning. In contrast, conceptual or doctrinal criticism hardly made an appearance. Greaves' and Lonsdale's restraint and painstaking, point by point, published response said more or less what Brougham expressed in an infinitely less restrained fashion in the columns of the *Edinburgh Review*.[31]

---

[27] 1853 bill, ss 111 and 112. *Second Report* (1846) Criminal Law Commissioners, p. 39, Arts 4 and 5.

[28] 1853 bill, ss 124 and 128. The former offence would have been punishable with up to two years' imprisonment, the latter, one year. *Second Report* (1846) Criminal Law Commissioners, p. 41, Art. 10; p. 45, Art. 38.

[29] Specific health and safety legislation had already and would increasingly tackle such culpable behaviour in industrial and commercial contexts. Road traffic and other means of transport also became increasingly regulated by a system of penalties.

[30] e.g. in relation to the bill's assault and battery provisions, see Parke B., and esp. Jervis CJ, *PP* 1854 (303), liii, 3 at pp. 8 and 5. *Copies of the Lord Chancellor's Letters to the Judges and of their Answers respecting the Criminal Law Bills of the Last Session.* Less than justified suspicion by Wightman J. was shown at the bill's attempt to define 'wound' and 'grievous bodily harm' (p. 19). By far the most significant positive responses came from Platt and Williams JJ. The former characterized the 'general design' for the bill as 'perfect', identifying many new sections as likely to operate 'beneficially to the public' (p. 27) including ss. 3, 19, 27, 66, 146. Williams J. endorsed (p. 29) the changes under ss 3, 19, 55, 64, 88, 110, 150, and 181.

[31] C. Greaves and J. Lonsdale, *A Letter to the Lord Chancellor containing Observations on the Answers of the Judges to the Lord Chancellor's Letters on the Criminal Law Bills of the Last Session of Parliament* (1854). Brougham (1854) 99 *Edin. Rev.* 573, esp. 576–81. See also two years later, Stephen's highly critical comments in *Saturday Review*, 18 October 1856.

A run of failed consolidation bills, lost more often through government apathy and indecision than through active opposition, eventually ended with success in the form of the Offences Against the Person Act 1861. Largely as a result of Greaves' petitioning,[32] in some areas the provisions went beyond the crude consolidation of earlier bills and admitted substantive amendments. However, as has been seen, Greaves' ambitions to jettison the long-established fact-specific style of earlier statutes were, in the main, denied. For example, intentionally wounding or causing grievous bodily harm under section 18 represented a complex attempt to blend the old specific and new generalized approach to defining offences. Yet, s 18, in combination with the lesser offences under sections 20 and sections 47,[33] constituted a distinctly simpler structure of liability for non-fatal assaults, the seriousness of which were determined by a blend of the degree of bodily harm inflicted and the assailant's level of mental culpability.

The conceptual symmetry offered by inclusion of general endangerment and negligence-based offences, advocated by the Criminal Law Commissioners and incorporated in the 1853 bill of Greaves and Lonsdale, gained the meanest toe-hold in the 1861 Act. Such liability was the essence of a completely new offence of endangering the 'life or health' of a child under two years by abandoning or exposure.[34] Desire to broaden the range of offences against the person through both general endangerment liability and non-fatal harm caused by negligence reappeared in the 1879 Draft Code. Here, limited existing provisions under the 1861 Act penalizing 'intentionally [or] wantonly endangering persons on railways' were expanded to more general forms of endangerment on railways.[35] Additionally, under the proposed 1879 revisions, the criminally negligent causing

---

[32] Greaves, *Criminal Law Acts*, Introduction, xi, xxiii–xxvi.

[33] Unlawful wounding (s 20) and assault occasioning actual bodily harm (s 47) were both originally (and subsequently) subject to the same maximum punishment. Section 20, however, demands a higher level of culpability and (arguably) harm. Section 47 is an example of constructive liability, in that the defendant's *mens rea* requirement need only relate to the assault and not the harm caused. The apparent anomaly was created by a combination of different statutory backgrounds (s 20 was derived from s 4, 14 & 15 Vict. c. 19 and s 47 from s 29, 14 & 15 Vict. c. 100) and Greaves' circumscribed consolidatory brief where, in general, overlapping but differently worded offences could not be excised. Without accompanying observations, the 1879 Draft Code Bill combines ss 20 and 47 into a single offence (s 49) which appears to retain the constructive nature of s 47.

[34] Section 27. Several earlier cases including *Cooper* (1849) 2 Car. & K. 876, and *Philpot* (1853) 1 Dears. 179 had demonstrated the common law's shortcomings. See also later child welfare legislation based on neglect or ill-treatment, culminating in the Children Act 1908, and s 26 on neglectful endangering of the life or health of apprentices or servants, based on 1851, 14 & 15 Vict. c. 100, s 29.

[35] Section 193. Under this provision intentionally endangering carried a maximum of penal servitude for life. The coverage of 'wantonly' endangering (punishable with up to two years' imprisonment) included 'any act, omission, or neglect' related to railways. In Wright's Draft Jamaican Code, s 100, liability is created for the negligent endangerment of life by persons in charge of dangerous things, such as doctors or chemists.

of non-fatal bodily harm through use of 'any carriage or vehicle' (punished by the 1861 Act), would have been extended to any criminally negligent causing of harm.[36] In England neither this conceptually significant broadening of liability, nor that relating to endangerment, attracted any serious further advocacy in the nineteenth or even twentieth century.

2. SEXUAL OFFENCES

In common with other forms of criminality, for sexual violence or abuse, both procedural and substantive obstacles inhibited not only the bringing of prosecutions but clarification of culpability requirements. A significant dimension to shifting social expectations and raised intolerance of violence evolving in the early decades of the nineteenth century concerned changing perceptions of violations of sexual integrity. However, the firm social demarcating of unacceptable sexual morality[37] and behaviour, a necessary prerequisite of its criminalization, followed an irregular and, relatively, hesitant course throughout the whole of the nineteenth century. Indeed, in relation to legal sexual agency, arguably the most substantial developments did not occur until after the mid-1870s. Nevertheless, both in terms of formal law and enforcement practices, by the early 1900s punishment of what was, or became, regarded as aberrant sexual behaviour had undergone a wide-reaching expansion; the nation's sexual proclivities, morality, and welfare had become very much the criminal law's business. In the Victorian period, criminal liability incorporating some variety of sexual deviation, violence, or exploitation, evolved or established itself in three overlapping areas: heterosexual rape; sexual or indecent assaults; and the sexual molestation or abuse of children.

Rape

Although long-established as a capital offence, until well into the nineteenth century trials for rape were prominent by virtue of their rarity.[38] Several factors contributed to what might be reasonably assumed to have been an extensive reluctance to prosecute. Beyond those reasons touching criminal prosecutions in general, such as expense and sheer organizational effort required,[39] rape trials

---

[36] Section 201. Similarly Wright's Draft Code, ss 98 and 99.

[37] See 'Public Morality and Social Control', Ch. X above, in relation to the increasing intolerance and prosecution of obscenity at this time.

[38] For the period up to 1800, see Beattie, *Crime and the Courts*, 124–32. On charging practices and the compromising of rape allegations at the pre-trial stage, see A. Clark, *Women's Silence, Men's Violence: Sexual Assault in England 1770–1845* (1987), *passim*.

[39] See 'Prosecution', Ch. III, above.

threw up their own peculiar and daunting challenges relating to both substantive and evidential demands. Their underpinning rationale appears in a scattering of institutional works: most especially, as Hale observed, while rape was a 'most detestable crime…it must be remembered that it is an accusation easy to be made, hard to be proved, but harder to be defended by the party accused', and thereby carrying the distinct risk of 'over hastily' convicting by the 'confident testimony of sometimes false and malicious witnesses'.[40] Such fear of false accusations remained a frequently explicit concern and major factor in governing the nature of the law's response to rape accusations, operating at both pre-trial and trial stages.[41]

At the opening of the nineteenth century, it was universally accepted that a conviction for rape required proof of 'carnal knowledge of a female, forcibly and against her will'. However, two centrally contentious areas caused judicial division: whether rape required emission as well as penetration; and what constituted consent. In respect of the former, judicial disagreement was finally settled by Lord Lansdowne's Act 1828.[42]

The more tenacious difficulty of resolving the question of quite what constituted true consent, in good measure, lay in its close relationship with the nature of legal evidence admissible at trial; most particularly, what limitations, if any, should there be on undermining the prosecutrix's credibility as a witness? As a starting point, the prosecutrix's reputation of 'good' or 'evil fame' was the dominant influence on the weight her evidence might be ascribed; the highly corrosive effect of evidence of ill virtue on the victim's testimony was patent. At one stage, admission of practically any evidence of the victim's character in rape cases was common practice. Beyond character, other factors cited as relevant to credibility appeared formulaically in standard legal texts from the beginning of the nineteenth century: 'greater probability' would be given to the victim's evidence if she made an early complaint, 'made search for the offender', or if he 'fled'; on the other hand, 'a strong but not conclusive presumption [arose] that her story is fictitious [if the victim] 'failed to make early complaint, or did not attempt to call for help where such cry might have been heard'.[43]

---

[40] Hale, 1 PC 635 cited by Blackstone, Comms, iv, 215. See also L. Edelstein, 'An Accusation Easily to be Made? Rape and Malicious Prosecution in Eighteenth Century England' (1998) 42 American JLH 351.

[41] Hale's cautioning observations appear in standard legal texts: for use by magistrates, including Burn's Justice of the Peace (1797), iv: 90, and all succeeding nineteenth-century editions; for Quarter Sessions and Assizes, e.g. Chitty, (1816), iii: 812.

[42] Section 18. The provision reversed the reserved judgment in Burrows (1823) R. & R. 519 which required emission. On the earlier judicial disagreement, see Chitty, (1816), iii: 810.

[43] e.g. Chitty (1816), iii, 812; Archbold (1831), 368. The common sources were Hale, 1 PC 633 and Blackstone, Comms, iv, 213.

The employment and presumptive effect of these evidential rules of thumb was probably extensive. However, along with a more general refinement of the rules governing admissibility of character evidence,[44] admission of such evidence in rape trials had become more restrictive by the 1820s. While evidence of the victim's bad reputation, 'want of chastity', or previous sexual relations with the defendant remained admissible, particular salacious details of the victim's sexual history were now ruled inadmissible.[45] Though probably lessening the destructive effect on the prosecutrix's credibility, it is hard to regard such a limited restriction as likely to have boosted substantially the number of cases brought, or to have increased conviction rates.

Rather than changes to rules of evidence, the cumulative effect of a cluster of other factors seems to offer a more promising explanation of the gradual rises in both rape charges and levels of convictions occurring by the 1830s. First, though rape remained a capital offence until 1841, with practically all offences except murder, executions for capital felonies had ceased by the mid-1830s. Consequently, any disinclination to prosecute or jury reluctance to convict caused by the capital fear was removed. Further, the steadily increasing presence of professional police forces operating in the Metropolis and beyond, together with an expanding availability of specialized medical witnesses,[46] could reasonably be expected to have expanded the range and availability of prosecution evidence. Thirdly, legislation in 1837[47] facilitated the bringing of lesser charges, alongside rape, thereby widening the possibility of at least some punishment of the defendant should the more serious charge of rape fail.[48] Finally, and possibly of greatest significance in the markedly increased rate of rape charges and convictions seen during the nineteenth century, were changing social and professional attitudes towards

[44] See 'Evidence on Character', Ch. III, above.

[45] *Hodgson* (1811) R. & R. 211 and *Clarke* (1817) 2 Stark. 241. But if on cross-examination the victim denied having sexual relations with other men, such men could be called to contradict the victim's claim, *Robins* (1843) 2 M. & Rob. 512. This patently highly prejudicial evidence of sexual relations with other men was excluded after *Holmes* (1871) 12 Cox 137 and *Cockcroft* (1870) 11 Cox 410.

[46] T. Forbes, *Surgeons at the Old Bailey: English Forensic Medicine to 1878* (1985) and S. Landsman, 'One Hundred Years of Rectitude: Medical Witnesses at the Old Bailey' (1998) 16 *Law and Hist. Rev.* 445.

[47] 1 Vict. c. 35, s 11.

[48] Charges of attempted rape (misdemeanour) were frequently brought in preference to the full offence. Besides eliminating the need to prove rape's *actus reus*, exposure of the prosecutrix's sexual history was much less likely. Contrary to the overall decline in all indictment trials from the 1830s to the end of the century, the rate of indictments for all sexual offences rose gradually, but not spectacularly, before the 1830s until the 1870s from one per 100,000 of population to two per 100,000. A dramatic doubling of the rate occurred between 1880 and 1886 (following the activities of moral purity and child welfare groups, together with the 1880 and 1885 legislation raising the ages of sexual consent, below) after which the following decades witnessed an equally steep decline below the 1870s' level.

protection of women from sexual predation. Beyond a more generalized rising intolerance of violence, a Victorian cultural re-imaging of acceptable male and female social identities and roles, arguably insinuated itself into the law's treatment and expectations of women as both criminals[49] and victims.[50]

More tangibly, returning to the substantive law, a limited reconceptualizing of the key component of the absence of the victim's consent took place in mid-century. From a central emphasis on the need for evidence of some form of force or duress used by the defendant, the courts increasingly recognized the possibility of lack of consent through other causes. As Lord Denman CJ confirmed, 'resistance' was not essential to rape. Instead of the question whether the defendant's act was 'against the victim's will', the issue became whether there was consent; it constituted a move from the prosecution needing to establish the victim's clear dissent, to a position of demonstrating no assent or consent was given.[51] Yet, residual judicial attachment to the notion of rape as an exclusively force-based offence resulted in the legal consequences of achieving apparent consent through fraud continuing to divide the judiciary throughout and beyond the century.[52]

Sexual Assaults and Sexual Molestation of Children

While sharing a good deal of rape's history of non-enforcement, sexual assault falling short of rape was also subject to its own particular development pattern. Evidential problems and the ordeal of character exposure inherent in rape prosecutions, were considerably less relevant to assaults. In essence, the extent of the law's protection from, and criminalization of, sexual violence turned on the victim's age and gender. Through a combination of reasons, in the early nineteenth century the overwhelming majority of prosecutions for sexual offences was of male defendants by female victims. For indecent assault, it appears that

---

[49] On the punishment of women, see 'Punishment', Ch, V above.

[50] For the process and functioning of this re-imaging in relation to rape, see the extensive analysis of M. Wiener, *Men of Blood* (Cambridge, 2004), Ch. 3, *passim*.

[51] Lord Denman, *Camplin* (1845) 1 Den. 89; *Fletcher* (1859) Bell 63; and *Mayers* (1872) 12 Cox 311.

[52] *Jackson* (1822) R. & R. 487; *Saunders* (1838) 8 Car. & P. 265; *Williams* (1838) 8 Car. & P. 286; *Barrow* (1868) 11 Cox 191. For the shift towards making ineffective any consent obtained by fraud as to the defendant's identity or status (by claiming to be married to the victim) or the fundamental nature of the sexual act, see *Flattery* (1877) 2 QBD 410; *Dee* (1884) 15 Cox 579; *Williams* (1923) 1 KB 340. Some confusion was generated by enacting that the use of fraud to obtain sex was a special (lesser) offence by s 3 of the Criminal Law Amendment Act 1884. Certainly, an express or implied misrepresentation as to a fact (the defendant's freedom from a sexually transmitted disease, his wealth, or freedom or marry) was held not to vitiate consent in relation to inflicting grievous bodily harm and actual bodily harm, *Clarence* (1888) 22 QBD 23. Though rape was not charged, several members of the Court for Crown Cases Reserved expressed reservations on the ancient doctrine of a wife's irrevocable consent to sexual intercourse and the exemption of husbands from 'marital rape'.

the socially constructed concept of this form of behaviour was rather narrower in relation to boy victims. The prospect of a boy's emotional trauma and moral corruption by indecent assault may have been regarded as a rather less extensive, less serious, social danger than in the case of women and girl victims.[53] As a form of assault, the concept of indecent assault made no general appearance in reported cases and treatises until the early nineteenth century, when the tenor of the offence became one of 'assault by indecent liberties with females'; even then, no concerted judicial attempt was made to define or delineate the nature of the indecency required.[54]

Additional protection of children from sexual predation materialized through a complex web of ad hoc provisions whose applicability was largely determined by the age at which the criminal law recognized effective consent might operate. In general, the wide-ranging fundamental nineteenth-century legislative changes seeking to protect children's welfare were mirrored in penal changes.[55] For girls, until 1875 the law extended a generous sexual licence, recognizing 12 years as a sufficient age for responsible sexual agency and lawful consent. Until the early 1840s, sexual intercourse with a girl under 10 years old regardless of consent was treated as capital rape. The Offences Against the Person Acts of 1828, 1851, and 1861[56] confirmed misdemeanour liability for consensual intercourse or any

[53] On the social construction of the concept of child abuse, see L. Jackson, *Child Sexual Abuse in Victorian England* (2000) and G. Behlmer, *Child Abuse and Moral Reform in England 1870–1908* (Stanford, 1982). For empirically based estimates of the rising rates of prosecutions on indictment for sexual offences against children in the Metropolis, see Jackson, *Child* (2000), 18–19. More generally, XIII, Pt 4.

[54] No doubt, many non-wounding assaults triable summarily included a sexual component which might be reflected in the punishment handed out by justices. And, obviously, prosecuting at summary level was a much more feasible proposition for victims. However, no offence identified as indecent assault appears in *Burn* until the 1825 edition which followed *Russell* (1819) citing case law appearing in that work, e.g. *Russell* (2nd edn, 1826), i 605, and the early assault cases of *Nichol* (1807) R. & R. 130 and *Rosinski* (1824) R. & Mood. 19. *Russell* (4th edn, 1865), i: 912 and cases cited. These cases involved charges of assault with a sexual element where consent had been claimed by the defence. The statutory offence of undefined indecent assault (Administration of Criminal Justice Act 1851, s 29 (as amended), below) was originally punished with a maximum of two years' imprisonment.

[55] On the general broadening of child protection in the second half of the nineteenth century see e.g. the Aggravated Assaults on Women and Children Act 1853, Prevention of Cruelty and Protection of Children Act 1889 (and 1894), and the Custody of Children Act 1891. See also 'Public Morality and Social Control', Ch. X, above.

Additionally, the established offence of abduction of girls or young women from their parents' possession indirectly sought to penalize consensual sexual exploitation of young women (e.g. Bramwell B., in *Prince* (1875) CCR 2, 154, 174). The Offences Against the Person Act 1861 punished abduction of girls under 16 years old with a maximum of two years' imprisonment (s 55). By the 1885 Act, liability was extended to cases of abduction of young women under 18 years if it could be established that the abduction was accompanied by 'intent to have carnal knowledge' (s 7).

[56] 1861 Act, ss 50, 51, and 52.

indecent activity with a girl between 10 and 12 years. A broad coalition of campaigning organizations, ranging from social purity groups to proto-feminist and
secular child welfare bodies, succeeded in raising the age of legal sexual consent
to 13 for girls in 1875, and 16 in 1885.[57] In relation to non-penetrative sexual assault,
legal consent was set at 13 for both girls and boys in 1880 by the Assault of Young
Persons Act, and at 16 by the Criminal Law Amendment Act 1922.[58]

A noteworthy increase in the criminal law's reach came with the Criminal Law
Amendment Act 1885. Its enactment was the result of a conjunction of several
factors: alarm over child prostitution, a very distinct strengthening of public and
private moral expectations in relation to sexual mores, allied to a broadening
concern for the general welfare of children and women. Together they provided
a highly receptive setting for the specific political campaigns of moral purity
and child welfare groups.[59] Beside reinforcing the law against procuring young
women for prostitution, the legislation aided conviction for charges of sexual relations with girls under 13 years by making admissible the victim's unsworn testimony.[60] The severe judicial attitudes towards deterring and punishing the sexual

[57] Offences Against the Person Act 1875, 38 & 39 Vict. c. 94, ss 3 and 4; Criminal Law Amendment
Act 1885 48 & 49 Vict. c. 69, s 5. After 1885, sexual intercourse with a girl between the ages of 13 and 16
was a misdemeanour with a maximum of two years' imprisonment (s 5). In the case of girls under 13,
the felony was subject to a maximum of penal servitude for life (s 4). For parliamentary discussion
of the relevance of moral and physical maturity in determining the age of legal consent, see *PD* 1880
(s. 3), 260: 1082; 1884 (s. 3), 289: 1213; 1885 (s. 3), 299: 717.

[58] 1880 43 & 44 Vict. c. 45; 1922 12 & 13 Geo. V c. 56. Prior to this, the position of boys was particularly obscure, being mainly governed by the use of the (originally) common law rule establishing the minimum age of criminal capacity and responsibility for rape at 14 years. This in turn was
the age employed for determining the legal effect of consent to sexual assault. Later, by s 29 of the
Administration of Justice Act 1851, 14 & 15 Vict. c. 100 'any indecent assault' of any one, or 'public and indecent Exposure of the Person', was punishable with up to two years' imprisonment. The
Aggravated Assaults Act 1853, 16 & 17 Vict c. 30, s 1 increased the maximum punishment of assault at
summary trial to six months for 'aggravated' assault of any female or boy under 14 years. While principally aimed at violent assault (*PD* 1853 (s. 3), 124: 1414 and (s. 3), 125: 669) the provision was probably
wide enough to cover other aggravating features including a sexual element. This was consolidated
in the 1861 Act, s 43. Furthermore (partly superseding s 29 of the 1851 Act) by s 62 of the 1861 Act, 'any
indecent assault upon any male' carried a maximum penalty of 10 years' penal servitude, or up to two
years' imprisonment.

[59] For parliamentary investigations, see *Reports and Evidence of Select Committees on Contagious
Diseases Acts*, esp. *PP* 1881 (351), viii, 193 and 1882 (340), ix, 1; and *Select Committees of the House of
Lords on Law relating to the Protection of Young Girls*, *PP* 1881 (448), ix, 355 and 1882 (344), xiii, 823.
On the campaigns leading up to the 1885 Act, see, Ch. X., 'Public Morality and Social Control' above.
Besides evangelical and benevolent child welfare groups (Bristow, *Vice and Vigilance*), see also the
contrasting accounts of the feminist and proto-feminist involvement in M. Jackson, *The Real Facts
of Life: Feminism and the Politics of Sexuality, 1850–1940* (1994) and L. Bland, *Banishing the Beast:
English Feminism and Sexuality Morality 1885–1914* (1995).

[60] Section 4.

seduction of impressionable 'respectable' young women from the protection of parental control is manifest in the celebrated reserved abduction case of *Prince*.[61] Here, though reasonably believing the girl to be over 16 years old, Prince's conviction for abduction was confirmed by a majority of judges, with Blackburn J. warning that any man engaging in such activity 'does it at his peril'.[62]

Beyond reinforcing punishment of the sexual exploitation or seduction of young women, the 1885 Act incorporated a highly significant provision expanding the law's ability to punish public or private indecency between males.[63] While practically any form of public indecency had long been subject to low level liability under vagrancy laws,[64] the 1885 offence reached not only the relatively neglected sexual abuse or corruption of boys, but also the actions of consenting adult males engaging in private homosexual practices. Though charges of the heavily punished crime of sodomy[65] could be deployed, the courts had generally shown themselves reluctant, especially in the latter half of the century, to convict on such charges without the most compelling evidence, even where indicted as conspiracy.[66]

---

[61] (1875) 2 CCR 154. As Brett J.'s judgment confirms, the offence of abduction also sought to protect a father's right to 'possession' of an unmarried woman.

[62] Blackburn J. (*ibid.*, 172), saw offences prohibiting under age sex and abduction as equally resting on a defendant acting at 'his peril' basis.

[63] Section 11: '...commits, or is a party to the commission of, or procures or attempts to procure the commission by any male of any act of gross indecency with another male person'. The offence was subject to a maximum of two years' imprisonment. No parliamentary opposition to the s 11 amendment occurred; its controversial nature was widely recognized only after its enactment. For the curious provenance of this provision, see F. B. Smith, 'Labouchere's Amendment to the Criminal Law Amendment Bill' (1976) 17 *Historical Studies* 165.

[64] Earlier nineteenth-century authorities denied any general misdemeanour of public '...nasty, wicked, filthy, lewd, beastly, unnatural and sodomitical practices'. *Rowed and Others* (1842) 3 QB 180; also the reserved case of *Wollaston* (1872) 12 Cox 180.

[65] Adopting the language of earlier legislation, s 61 of the Offences Against the Person Act 1861 identifies the offences as the 'abominable crime of buggery, committed either with mankind or with any animal'. The maximum sentence was penal servitude for life, or not less than 10 years. On prosecutorial practices and the surge of prosecutions in the early nineteenth century, see A. Harvey, 'Prosecution for Sodomy in England at the Beginning of the Nineteenth Century' (1978) 21 *Hist. J.* 939 and J. Weeks, 'Inverts, Perverts and Mary-Annes: male prostitution and the regulation of homosexuality in England in the nineteenth and twentieth centuries', in Weeks (ed.), *Against Nature* (1991), 10. For the possible link between the nineteenth-century increase in sodomy prosecutions and the crime of blackmail, see A. Simpson, 'Blackmail as a Crime of Sexual Indiscretion in Eighteenth Century England', in L. Knafla (ed.), *Crime, Gender and Sexuality in Criminal Prosecutions* (Westport, 2002).

[66] See the prominent Society transvestite case of *Boulton and Others* (1871) 12 Cox 87. The (failed) charges tried before Lord Cockburn CJ, included a 'general conspiracy to debauch' and several specific 'conspiracies to debauch each other'. On the context and treatment of the case, see R. Paley, 'Dragging the Law into Disrepute', in A. Lewis, P. Brand, and P. Mitchell (eds), *Law in the City* (Dublin, 2007), 283.

The social climate and campaigning fervour driving the 1885 legislation for the protection of children, were also leading forces in the enactment of the Punishment of Incest Act 1908.[67] Most particularly, the National Vigilance Association and the National Society for the Prevention of Cruelty to Children, both formative influences in the 1885 legislation,[68] went on to play sustained roles in promoting the criminalization of incest. While incestuous marriages had long been subject to ecclesiastical sanction,[69] sexual relations between persons related by consanguinity or affinity, though widely censured as grossly immoral, were immune from criminal sanction. A broad, inchoate social and official disapproving awareness of incestuous behaviour was converted into a positive case for legislation by reform groups' assiduous compilation of evidence demonstrating incest's prevalence; it was a campaign eventually actively supported, if not led, by the Home Office.[70] While in little danger of foundering, the 1908 bill, nevertheless, faced a degree of opposition. As some questioned during the 1908 bill's parliamentary passage, precisely what could justify the dramatic leap from a position where incestuous behaviour attracted no criminal sanction, to one where a perpetrator could face up to seven years' penal servitude?[71] Compelling

---

[67] 8 Edw. 7, c. 45. The proscribed categories of relationship were grandparent and grandchild, parent and child, brother and sister, half-brother and half-sister. The significance of eugenic considerations in the enactment of the 1908 Act is contentious. While not expressly figuring in earlier legislative attempts, they had made up a subordinate element of the case advanced by the supporters of the 1908 bill, PD 1908 (s. 4), 197: 1410 and (s. 4), 191: 283. However, reluctance to deploy eugenic claims more emphatically may have been a consequence of relatively extensive earlier genetic studies, which provided unequivocal support for eugenic objections to incestuous behaviour. S. Wolfram 'Eugenics and the Punishment of Incest Act 1908' [1983] Crim LR 308.

[68] See 'Public Morality and Social Control', Ch. X, above. They were also instrumental in the enactment of the Children Act 1908.

[69] Paradoxically, bigamy, another offence with clear ecclesiastical origins, was converted into a felony by seventeenth-century legislation. Eventually defined and punished under s 57 of the Offences Against the Person Act 1861, bigamy's punishment rationale rests a good deal on transgressing public as well as individual sensibilities. This dualistic character was well articulated by Lord Cockburn in Allen (1872) LR 1 CCR 367, 374: '[I]t involves an outrage on public decency and morals, and creates public scandal by the prostitution of a solemn ceremony, which the law allows to be applied only to a legitimate union, to a marriage at best but colourable and fictitious, and which may be made and too often is made, the means of the most cruel and wicked deception.'

Lord Cockburn might also have mentioned the important respects in which property ownership (and its transfer) was affected by the institution of marriage, even after the Married Women's Property Act 1884. See above for the possibility of rape where consent to sexual intercourse was obtained on the basis of a believed valid second marriage; and s 3(2) of the Criminal Law Amendment Act 1885 for the offence of procurement of sexual intercourse by false pretences. The general significance of the bigamy case of Tolson (1889) 23 QB 168 is considered in relation to 'Fault', Ch. VIII above; and see the pre-Tolson observations of the Criminal Code Commissioners, 1879 Report, on bigamy, Draft Code Bill, s 216.

[70] On this crucial relationship, see V. Bailey and S. Blackburn, 'The Punishment of Incest Act 1908: A Case Study of Law Creation' [1979] Crim LR 708.

[71] PD 1908 (s. 4), 191: 279–83.

evidence of the believed extensiveness of incest marshalled by the National Vigilance Association and National Society for the Prevention of Cruelty to Children, along with intelligence presented by Chief Constables, largely quelled such reservations.

However, some objections could not be met simply by demonstrating a believed widespread incidence of incest. In particular, concerns were voiced over the potential highly damaging effects on the parties directly involved, as well as on wider public sensibilities, of detailed public disclosure of incestuous behaviour. Such a line was most notably adopted by Lord Chancellor Halsbury, when effectively sinking the 1903 Incest Bill.[72] But remaining reservations as to the necessity or advisability of criminalizing incest were probably most effectively overcome by police and judicial assertions of the operational inadequacies of the 1885 legislation in offering effective protection of daughters from the sexual predatory behaviour of fathers.[73] In forcefully maintaining this approach, Lord Alverstone CJ, for example, both petitioned the Home Office and expressed in the House of Lords his unqualified belief in the 'urgent necessity for an amendment of the law because of the frequency of assaults by fathers on their daughters'.[74]

3. HOMICIDE

The law of homicide inherited by early nineteenth-century lawyers could match and, in most cases, surpass practically any other area of criminal law for its forbidding combination of conceptual looseness and obscurity, allied to a complex and extensive body of case law. Principally the creation of institutional works and judicial imagination, homicide law sought (and seeks), through the distinct categorization of liability as murder or manslaughter to identify and punish different manifestations of criminal fault where death was the outcome. In the first instance this was achieved by reference to the defendant's level of mental culpability and, where relevant, the particular circumstances of the defendant's behaviour. Settling with greater precision and coherence the boundaries of murder and manslaughter through *mens rea* requirements and identification of legally relevant circumstances, proved an especially demanding challenge for Victorian judges and would-be legislators. An immediate and major source of this intractability lay in the almost infinite malleability of murder's key fault

---

[72] *PD* 1903 (s. 4), 125: 822. A trial *in camera* amendment of the 1908 Bill was successfully pressed by Halsbury. Cf. the House of Lords' refusal in *Scott* v. *Scott* [1913] AC 417 to allow in camera hearings of salacious divorce evidence. For the unsuccessful earlier Incest Bills of 1896, 1903, and 1907, see Bailey and Blackburn, *ibid.*

[73] L. Tait, *An analysis of the Evidence in [70 cases] under the New Criminal Law Amendment Act* (1894).

[74] *PD* 1908 (s. 4) 197: 1409; supported by Lord Loreburn LC, *ibid.*, 1411.

term, 'malice aforethought'. As the Royal Commission on Capital Punishment (1953) aptly observed:

malice aforethought is simply a comprehensive name for a number of different mental attitudes, which have been variously defined at different stages in the development of the law, the presence of any one of which in the accused has been held by the courts to render a homicide particularly heinous and therefore to make it murder.[75]

Compounding the fundamental terminological inexactitude of 'malice afore-thought' with its clear potential for the operation of extensive judicial discretion, were broader conceptual uncertainties relating to the respective roles and differences between notions of subjective and objective fault. To such substantive questions was added the further complication of the effects of the centrally important evidential presumption of intended 'natural and probable consequences' of an act which, as will be suggested, probably retarded establishment of a cleaner, practical separation of subjective and objective forms of fault. This potent brew of imprecision and contingency, coupled with parliamentary indifference, prac-tically guaranteed a century of stumbling uncertainty in respect of many areas of murder and manslaughter. Consequently, at no time during the nineteenth century was it possible to segregate sharply murder from manslaughter; for while each had its own moderately well charted territory, an extensive degree of disputed joint occupation existed. This was particularly true where constructive and objective fault were regarded as sufficient for either murder or manslaugh-ter, as manifested in the case of felony-murder and unlawful act manslaughter. However, while for expositional reasons these offences will be analysed individu-ally, their common and abutting boundaries should not be lost sight of.

Beyond murder's and manslaughter's asserted but contested distinctive qual-ities, three significant areas of conceptual, moral, and practical dispute relating to the historical development of homicide more generally are examined: they con-cern the question of what or who qualified as human for the purpose of homicide, the requirements of legal causation, and the circumstances when an omission might serve as the basis of homicide.

Murder

'MALICE AFORETHOUGHT': MURDER'S ELUSIVE
MENTAL REQUIREMENT

In defining the broad nature of malice aforethought, the 'grand criterion by which murder is to be distinguished from any other species of homicide',[76] Russell

---

[75] Royal Commission on Capital Punishment [Cmd. 8932], p. 27.
[76] Russell (1826), i: 421.

resorted to Foster's (by then) classic characterization of the term: 'actions symptomatic of a wicked, depraved, malignant spirit,...of a heart regardless of social
duty and fatally bent upon mischief'.[77] Indeed, as Stephen rightly notes,[78] Foster's
whole treatise on homicide is an 'attempt to work out this general idea...'. Of
course, being capable of embracing a very wide range of culpable mental states,
Foster's highly moralistic description of murder's *mens rea* advanced the position
little beyond the opacity of 'malice aforethought'. Underlying these interlinked
constrictions of terminology and doctrine was, as later reform initiatives demonstrated, the perpetual combined conceptual and policy dispute over just what
range of killings the offence of murder *ought* to embrace. Yet some firm ground
did exist: causing death with intention to kill or inflict grievous bodily harm[79]
was, uncontentiously, within the scope of 'malice aforethought'. But beyond
this point, providing an account of the law involved some element of traversing
terra incognita.

First, what of cases where, rather than an intention to cause at least serious
harm, an individual acted with the foresight or knowledge that death or serious
harm might eventuate? Was such behaviour sufficiently immoral to come within
the 'grand criterion' of 'malice aforethought'? Depending on the circumstances,
it might readily be described as behaviour symptomatic of a 'heart regardless of
social duty and fatally bent upon mischief'. And, certainly, Foster's consciously
risk-taking workman fatally hurling rubble into a busy street was generally identified as guilty of murder.[80] It was a form of 'malice aforethought' taken up by all
leading nineteenth-century criminal law texts including *Russell*, *Archbold*, and
Stephen's *Digest*.[81] Adoption of this view could be justified on the basis of broad
moral equivalence between intention and acting with foresight of a probable
consequence.[82] However, judicial authority supporting this general proposition
and version of malice aforethought was almost totally absent until the Fenian
case of *Desmond, Barrett*. Here Lord Cockburn CJ instructed the jury that it
would be murder 'if a man did an act, more especially if that were an illegal
act, although its immediate purpose might not be to take life, yet if it was such
that life was reasonably endangered by it—if a man did such an act, not with the

---

[77] Foster, *Crown Law*, 'Discourse on Homicide', 256.

[78] *HCL* iii, 74.

[79] *Russell*, (1826) 455; *Errington* (1838) 2 Lew. 148, 217; *Grey* (1666) Kel. 64. Some authorities
demanded an accompanying objective risk of death. See below.

[80] At 262–3. Also *Hale*, 1 PC 472 and *East*, 1 PC, 231.

[81] *Russell* (1826) i: 461; *Archbold* (4th edn, 1831), 322; Stephen, *Digest* (1877), Art. 223. Stephen
observed in his *General View* that he had never come across any case law authority for this proposition, but that it should be retained as responding to 'public sentiment' (118).

[82] A view emphatically articulated by the Criminal Law Commissioners: e.g. *Fourth Report*
(1839), xx and xxxiv, Art. 17; and *Fourth Report* (1848) Ch. 1, section 3, Art. 3 combined with Ch. xv,
section 2, Art. 3.

purpose of taking life, but with the knowledge or belief that life was likely to be sacrificed by it'.[83]

Yet while murder had an essentially subjective fault-based complexion, a major exception[84] had long existed in the form of felony-murder. Carried into the nineteenth century by East, from Hale via Foster, the doctrine stipulated that *any* felonious intent was sufficient to qualify as 'malice aforethought' where death resulted, even if the risk of any physical harm had not been objectively foreseeable. Founded on the crude constructive fault notion that those who engaged in crime must take responsibility for whatever harm may by chance follow, felony-murder was also regarded as a valuable general deterrent against participation in criminal activities. Though commentators offered an almost united front in criticizing this form of murder liability, its judicial appeal proved singularly tenacious well beyond the first half of the nineteenth century. In the late 1830s the Criminal Law Commissioners ably set out the conceptual and moral case against felony murder:

It may be questionable whether, in point of principle, an effect wholly unexpected and unconnected with the intention and act of the party, except by accident, can properly be made the foundation of criminal responsibility; for as the objective of punishment is the prevention of crime, it ought properly to be annexed to such acts as are in themselves culpable by reason of their mischievous tendency, and the intention with which they are done, and not to such as are simply accidental and unintentional. By the law of England this doctrine is in many instances reversed, the criminal intention incident to the act intended but not perpetrated, or not in question, is supposed to be transferred to the act which was mere accidental consequence. Thus a party doing the same act in the same manner, but who by mere accident, and not through want of caution, kills another may be, according to his intention in doing that act, though such intention be wholly unconnected to the accidental result, guilty either of murder where his intention was to commit a felony, or of manslaughter where his intention was to commit a bare misdemeanour or trespass....[85]

---

[83] *The Times*, 28 April 1868. Cf. *Walters* (1848) Car, & M. 164, Coltman J. required an act which the defendant was aware 'must necessarily lead to...death'. Variations in the required level of foreseen endangerment appear in other formulations: *Archbold* and *Russell*, death 'likely' or 'probable', *ibid.*; Stephen, at least 'probable...grievous bodily harm', *ibid.* And also Stephen J. in *Serné and Goldfinch* (1887) 16 Cox 311. Cf. Stephen's 1864 analysis of judicial and jury practices which required 'wanton indifferences to life in an act likely to cause death' (1864) 69 *Fraser's Mag.* 753, 765–6.

[84] The other long-established example was death caused in the course of resisting lawful arrest by an officer of justice. In such a case conviction for murder needed no more than proof of an intention to resist arrest by force. Here liability clearly rested on the desire to enhance the general law's power to deter any level of violence against the administration of criminal justice. *Porter* (1873) 12 Cox 444, followed in *Craig and Bentley, The Times*, 10 December 1952.

[85] *Fourth Report* (1839), xxviii.

The technique of attempting to deter an initially unlawful act by 'enhancing [it] beyond its intrinsic moment' was viewed as both ineffectual and morally dubious. Why 'check it indirectly', why not punish the initial act directly and sufficiently firmly to deter? Why should the ultimate guilt of an act turn on the nature of the initial 'collateral offence'? Of course, challenges of this nature had implications beyond the Commissioners' immediate targets, such as the rationale for holding a party responsible for murder when serious harm but not death was intended. Reining back the pursuit of such a potentially awkward, highly subjectivist line of questioning, the Commissioners offered an 'expedient' modification of the existing law curtailing felony-murder to cases where the 'collateral' offence was one of 'violence to the person or habitation',[86] effectively substituting a test of negligence as to some personal harm occurring. Modifying the rule in this way promised to contribute to the deterrence of dangerous acts without the existing rule's extreme potential for ignoring enormous shortfalls between the culpability of the original act and liability for subsequent homicide.

While it was always within judicial discretion to recommend Executive mercy in such cases, it was not until the 1860s that open attempts were made by some judges to cut back felony-murder's wide latent constructive fault scope. One example was Bramwell B. in *Horsey*,[87] who sought to limit the application of the doctrine through a hybrid culpability and causal requirement of restricting liability to the 'natural and probable result' of the defendant's actions. Attempts to remove, or at least modify, the doctrine also appeared in the abortive codification initiatives of the 1870s.[88] Stephen's[89] 1872–4 Homicide Bill and original 1878 Code Bill aimed at completely excising felony-murder. Judicial uncertainty as to the doctrine's reach was embarrassingly underlined by Bramwell's and Blackburn's

[86] *Ibid.*, xxix and Art. 53. Later Reports (Seventh and Second) completely excluded the rule from their Digests. Expressly following the reasoning underpinning Macaulay's Draft Indian Code, the Commissioners roundly rejected consequentialist doctrine, adopting the utilitarian argument that felony-murder 'adds nothing to the security of life', *Second Report* (1846) 18.

[87] (1862) 3 F. & F. 287. Greaves, as editor of the 1865 edition of *Russell*, indicated his inability to swallow Bramwell's reconstruction of felony-murder (741–2). See also Wightman J. in *Greenwood* (1857) 7 Cox 404.

[88] The 1864 Royal Commission on Capital Punishment (Report, 1866) largely avoided any direct attempt to redefine the *mens rea* of murder. In its proposals for distinguishing between capital and non-capital murder, the Commissioners sought to retain capital punishment for cases of 'express malice aforethought' (intention to kill or inflict grievous bodily harm) and killing in the course of any specified felony (arson, rape, burglary, robbery, or piracy). Subsequent judicial attempts were made to widen the projected categories of capital murder, House of Lords Session Papers *PP* 1866 (61), 195 and 235; *PD* 1866 (s. 3), 183: 1545–50; and (s. 3), 184: 1163. For the Commissioner's comparative use of French and some American state laws, see *Home Office Printed Memoranda and Reports*, N.A. H.O. 347/19, 175. See also 'Punishment', Ch. V above.

[89] Stephen registered 'great objection' to the doctrine earlier in the *General View*, 119 and in his review of the 1866 Royal Commission Report on Murder in (1866) 73 *Fraser's Mag.* 232.

conflicting evidence given before the Homicide Bill's Select Committee.[90] More cautiously, much in the fashion of the earlier Criminal Law Commissioners, the 1879 Code Bill Commission proposed an abbreviated rule aimed at specified types of violent actions carried out to facilitate a serious offence; this was despite the Attorney-General's boast to the Commons that the Code would 'sweep away all constructive murders'.[91]

In the following decade,[92] through his own judicial endeavours, Stephen sought to remove some of felony-murder's 'moral ambiguity', particularly in *Serné*:[93]

I will say a word or two upon [the rule] because it is capable of being applied very harshly in certain cases, and also because though I take the law as I find it, I very much doubt whether the definition which I have given, although it is the common definition, is not somewhat too wide…To take [a] very old illustration, it was said that if a man shot a

---

[90] *Minutes*, 153 and 160, above Ch. VI. Indeed, the general uncertain and unsatisfactory state of the law of murder was the principal reason the Select Committee opposed the Homicide Bill; an alleged purely codification bill was viewed as an inappropriate vehicle for extensive substantive reforms..

[91] PD 1878 (s. 3), 239: 1947. Report, Code Bill, s 175.

[92] After the Criminal Code Bill's failure, amongst the most determined efforts to modify and clarify the law of murder were those of Sir William Harcourt, principally when Home Secretary. His original 1882 proposal would have confined capital murder to cases of 'intent' to kill, with other homicides designated non-capital murder or manslaughter. Following very wide consultation, Harcourt concluded that under his proposals many equally immoral cases would be omitted from capital punishment, and many undeserving examples would be included. Amongst judicial opinion sought on the 1882 proposals, Hawkins and Stephen JJ's are noteworthy. While favouring removal of felony-murder, both judges firmly opposed two classes of murder. Hawkins saw the three-way split between two degrees of murder and manslaughter as bound to perplex juries. Despite his severe judicial reputation, Hawkins regarded felony-murder as 'repugnant to the most ordinary feelings of humanity'. Stephen argued two degrees would 'fritter away the awful associations connected with the word "murder"'. This was similar to his reaction 20 years earlier to the 1864 Commission proposal to distinguish capital and non-capital murder (1866) *Fraser's Mag.* 232. Rather than attempt to distinguish murders meriting capital punishment by formal distinctions, Stephen favoured judicial discretion coupled with a right of appeal to the Court for Crown Cases Reserved. His identified categories of non-capital murder included infanticide, victim consent, as in mercy killings, and where the killer's mind was 'more or less affected by disease'. Particularly revealing is the confidential dialogue between Harcourt and Godfrey Lushington, then Home Office 'legal assistant under-secretary'. Harcourt's printed marginal comments on Lushington's opinion of the draft bill's ramifications expressly indicate the Home Secretary's clear willingness to permit public opinion, through jury actions, to bear directly on whether a murder was capital or not. In his 'Postscript' to Harcourt's marginal comments, Lushington declared, if enacted, the bill's flexible criteria would effectively lead to the end of capital punishment. This would be the predictable consequence of practically making juries the 'arbiters of life or death' who act 'capriciously' by yielding to 'their natural compunctions' in sending prisoners to the gallows. This was precisely the reason why Stephen wished to vest discretion in judges and strongly opposed further facilitation of jury mitigation: *Home Office Printed Memoranda and Reports* N.A. H.O. 347/8, February 1882 (Harcourt/Lushington), 177–81; (Hawkins) 160–1; (Stephen) 162–9. See also Harcourt's reflections when Chancellor of the Exchequer in PD 1886 (s. 3), 305: 780–4.

[93] (1887) 16 Cox 311, at 312–13.

fowl with intent to steal it, and accidentally killed a man, he was to be accounted guilty of murder, because the act was done in the commission of a felony. I very much doubt, however, whether that is really the law, or whether the Court for Consideration of Crown Cases Reserved would hold it to be so...I think that, instead of saying that any act done with intent to commit a felony and which causes death amounts to murder, it would be reasonable to say that any act known to be dangerous to life, unlikely in itself to cause death done for the purpose of committing a felony...should be murder.

Like Bramwell's attempt, Stephen's modification of the rule abandons its out-and-out constructive nature and reconstitutes it into one of negligence-based murder.

Other reported judicial observations on felony-murder in the late nineteenth and early twentieth centuries reveal an exceedingly diverse spread of opinion on the Bench as to the doctrine's scope. Both harsh and restricted articulations of the rule occurred,[94] with the latter resorting to a negligence-based form of liability. Yet even in this period, with the mood turning towards reining back the more discordant manifestations of the doctrine, judicial devotees of the severe strain of felony-murder were not hard to find, including Lord Alverstone CJ: 'The experience of judges shews that there are so many cases of death caused by attempts to commit felonies, that for the protection of human life, it is not desirable to relax the rule which treats such cases as murders.'[95] However, House of Lords' confirmation of the more general shift of judicial opinion towards a negligence basis came ten years or so later in *DPP* v. *Beard*, where application of the rule was limited to violent felonies.[96] While contemporary commentators tended to oppose felony-murder on the grounds of conceptual illegitimacy or plain disbelief in its power to enhance deterrence, reported judicial assertions of the rule's justification rarely appeared. Beyond Alverstone's brief reference to the 'protection of human life', obviously a deterrence account, it is likely that the indistinct retributive-penalty rationale for undertaking criminal activities still exerted a fairly compelling influence on many members of the judiciary. Such consequentialist

---

[94] For the great range of judicial treatment of felony-murder following abortion, see confidential briefing paper, *Home Office Printed Memoranda and Reports*, N.A. H.O. 347/17, 5, 17 November 1898. A no-nonsense example of the strict version of the rule came from Hawkins J. in *Culmore, The Times*, 7–9 August 1880. For a surprisingly severe Home Office stance on commutation in felony-murder cases, see the comments of Godfrey Lushington, by then Permanent Under-Secretary, N.A. H.O. 347/9, 689. Distinctly negligence-based rulings appear in the abortion cases of *Whitmarsh* (1898) 62 *JP* 711, 712; *Bottomley and Earnshaw, The Times*, 16 May 1903; Lumley (1911) 22 Cox 635.

[95] Comments made to the Liverpool grand jury, 9 March, 1909. Quoted by Kenny, *Outlines* (1929), 139. Two years later, Avory J. ignored the Lord Chief Justice's sentiment in *Lumley, ibid.*, by effectively requiring negligence as to grievous bodily harm on the part of an illegal abortionist charged with felony-murder.

[96] [1920] AC 479. Because even relatively low levels of violence sufficed the objective risk of harm might only be small.

inclinations were also very much at work in relation to felony-murder's junior sibling, constructive or unlawful act manslaughter (see below).

More generally, any account of 'malice aforethought' requires careful reflection on the significant qualifying effects of the presumption of intended consequences. Plotting the historical development of murder's nineteenth-century culpability requirements would risk serious distortion without consideration of the function and practical impact of this fundamental rule of evidence.

THE PRESUMPTION OF INTENDED CONSEQUENCES

Operation of this leading rule of evidence frequently obscured, if not totally subsumed, positive proof of the culpability requirement in any particular case; so much so that in many nineteenth-century authorities it is often quite impossible to disentangle the substantive from the evidential. Indeed, some versions of this presumptive rule strongly resemble a statement of substantive law, incapable of rebuttal. The two early nineteenth-century formulations contained in *Farrington* and *Dixon*[97] at once indicate the potential width of meaning that could attach to this presumption. *Farrington* laid down that a 'man must be supposed to intend the necessary consequences of his own act'. The slightly later formulation, also of Lord Ellenborough, in *Dixon* appeared to have a rather wider sweep—moving from a 'necessary' to a 'probable' consequence: 'When a man is charged with doing an act, of which the probable consequence may be highly injurious, the intention is an inference of law resulting from the act.' Lord Ellenborough's words were subsequently expressly endorsed in a series of decisions.[98] In the particular case of murder, *Russell* consistently noted that 'as a general rule...all homicide is presumed to be malicious, [i.e.] murder, until the contrary appears, from circumstances of alleviation, excuse, or justification: and that it is incumbent upon the prisoner to make out such circumstances to the satisfaction of the court and jury, unless they arise out of the evidence against him'.[99]

The tendency of some judges to slide from a rule of evidence into a substantive requirement can be seen in both early and later cases. In *Newill*, Gaselee J. directed that a 'person who did an act wilfully, necessarily intended that which must be the consequence of the act'. And similarly in the forgery case of *Williams v. Bayley*, Lord Westbury noted that if 'a man does an act which is attended necessarily with an inevitable consequence, he must be taken in law to have foreseen

---

[97] (1811) R. & R. 207; (1814) 3 M. & S. 11. Also see 'Law Maxims—Of Criminal Intention' (1842) 27 *LM* 370.

[98] e.g. *Hicklin* (1868) LR 3 QB 376; *Aspinall* (1876) 2 QB 65. Early editions of *Russell* simply reproduced the dicta in *Dixon* and *Farrington*. See also Stephen, *Digest* (1883 edn), Art. 94 and Kenny, *Outlines* (1929), 333.

[99] (1826), i: 422–3. Similarly, *Archbold* (1831), 310–11.

that consequence, and, in point of fact, to have deliberately intended that it should be the result of his action'.[100] Contemporary variations in the rule's formulation occur from text to text. John Pitt Taylor's highly authoritative *Treatise on the Law of Evidence* gave the presumption an irrebuttable quality: 'It is again conclusively presumed that every sane man of discretion contemplates the natural and probable consequences of his own acts.'[101] Here, as elsewhere, it was noted that the presumption of innocence was *subject* to the presumption of intended consequences.

The danger of confusing evidence with substance and allowing the former to absorb the latter was remarked upon in the Criminal Law Commissioners' Seventh Report:

It is essential…to preserve that which is a matter of legal definition quite distinct from that which is merely evidence to prove what is so defined, and especially to distinguish what *degree* of wilfulness or culpability of mind is in fact essential to criminality.

With admirable and rare clarity for the time the Report continued:

Although the state or disposition of mind which constitutes the mens rea is a matter of legal definition, the existence of the mens rea in particular instances is a matter of proof of evidence. One who does an act immediately and naturally tending to produce a particular consequence, may fairly be presumed to intend it. This, however, is but a presumption, though a strong one, but cannot be made legally equivalent to intention; if it were, it would be sufficient for the jury to find the doing of some particular act, and that some act naturally and immediately tended to a particular consequence; and difficulty would arise if the act found did not immediately and naturally tend to such consequence, and the tendency might depend upon the bearing and connection of a multitude of facts.[102]

But there was no doubting the presumption's standing. The importance assigned to the presumption is underlined by its formal recognition in contemporary draft codifying measures. In the 1874 version of Stephen's Homicide Bill, a 'natural and ordinary consequence' presumption was incorporated with quite a severe sting in its tail: for the presumption would not be rebutted 'only because it appears or is proved that at the time when the act was done the person who did it did not attend to or think of its nature or probable consequences, or that he hoped those consequences would not follow'.[103] The provision's potential ability to convict a person of murder with a relatively low level of mental culpability is obvious. In all likelihood its insertion was aimed at incriminating defendants in cases covered

---

[100] *Newill* (1836) 1 Mood 459; *Williams* v. *Bayley* (1866) LR AC 1, 221.

[101] 6th edn, 1872, i: 96 and 9th edn, 1897, i: 80. Even clear contrary evidence would not dislodge the presumption according to several authorities cited.

[102] (1843), 22. Cf. *Fourth Report* (1839), xv. Starkie, the *de facto* initial chairman of the Commissioners, was author of a pioneering evidence treatise. See 'Evidence', Ch. III, above.

[103] Clause 30. Also Select Committee evidence of Stephen, 54–5.

by the felony-murder rule which had, calculatedly, been excluded from Stephen's bill. The principal outcome of the substitution of the special presumption would have been to cut back the scope of former felony-murder cases to an objective fault basis, thereby making only inherently dangerous felonies a sufficient basis for a murder conviction. The 1879 Draft Code featured what amounted to a weaker version of this presumption.[104]

Clearly, the net effect of such a deeply entrenched presumption of intention on substantive rules of responsibility turned on how 'probable' or 'natural' consequences was applied by courts and the facility with which a defendant might rebut the presumption. As to the construing of 'probable', 'natural' or similar terms, it can be gauged from their use in cases like *Farrington* and *Wise* v. *Dunning*, that there was considerable variation in just how extensive the presumption's effect might be. But of greater significance is the question of quite *how* the presumption might be rebutted. As has been seen, until the Criminal Evidence Act 1898, defendants were debarred from giving sworn testimony, and before this defendants charged with felonies were denied even the possibility of full use of counsel until 1836. What form or type of evidence might, then, a defendant have adduced to dislodge the presumption that consequences were intended? Limited judicial guidance was offered: for example, Lord Coleridge in 1886 observed: 'If one person killed another the law of England presumed it to be murder unless the killer *showed* that it was not so' (emphasis added).[105] In the early part of the twentieth century Kenny, for one, was in little doubt:

The fact that the [defendant] had means of knowing a consequence to be likely raises a prima facie presumption that he did actually foresee it as being so. There is such a great difficulty in obtaining any evidence to rebut this presumption as to render it practically equivalent to a conclusive one. Hence it is sometimes spoken of as if it strictly were conclusive.[106]

It is hardly surprising then, even after Victoria's death, that the presumption's almost *de facto* conclusiveness was sometimes articulated as though it was indeed *legally* conclusive. Thus, for example, in the murder case of *Philpot* (1912), Lord Alverstone CJ asserted that the 'appellant who committed this act, if sane, must be held to have intended that consequence'.[107]

The impact of this manifestly powerful rule on the substantive law's development can, therefore, be assumed to have been extensive for murder in two major respects. First, distinctions between degrees of subjective fault would have considerably less practical reality. This would have been true of the distinction

---

[104] Section 174(d).
[105] *Little, The Times*, 5 May 1886, p. 7.
[106] *Outlines* (1902), 148.
[107] (1912) 7 Cr App R 140 at 143. Cf. Darling J.'s statement in *Meade* (1909) 2 Cr App R 55 at 57.

between intention to kill and to inflict grievous bodily harm. Similarly, the difference between intention and recklessness or foresight would have shrunk, if not completely collapsed.

The second direction in which the presumption was arguably influential on the development of substantive fault concepts, especially relating to homicide, concerns the subjective/objective culpability split. It could be expected that some cases where the defendant had been objectively at fault when causing harm—criminally negligent—would, as a consequence of the presumption's operation, have been uprated and taken as intentional harm. The potential for this was clearly greatest in relation to the murder/manslaughter division.[108] In other words, the factual and legally adjudicated boundary between subjective and objective fault would not have always corresponded.

The run of judgments between the Criminal Evidence Act 1898 and the benchmark decision in *Woolmington v. DPP* reveals as great a variation in treatment of the presumption as seen prior to the 1898 Act. The general question of how *mens rea* could be proved was considered by Channell J. in the early 1900s:

In all cases where it is necessary to prove anything which depends on the state of a man's mind whether it is malice, or whether it is intent, whether it is knowledge…which all depend upon what is in the man's mind,…the way in which it certainly may be and generally must be proved is by inferring it from other facts.[109]

But were such inferences or presumptions rebuttable, and if so, how? It has been seen that in the same year, Lord Alverstone made his own view apparent in the murder trial of *Philpot*. Responding to a specific jury finding that the defendant 'did not realise the consequences of his act' which killed his wife, the Lord Chief Justice insisted that it must still be held that the consequences were intended.[110] Indeed, coupled with his previously noted keen advocacy of the undiluted felony-murder rule, Lord Alverstone represented a powerful voice during this period for a firm constructive or consequentialist approach to murder's culpability requirements.

However, just as contemporary judicial attitudes towards felony-murder were fragmented, so were those on the appropriate handling of the presumption of intended consequences. For alongside those judges most forcefully represented by the Lord Chief Justice, were others either ready to concede the presumption's

---

[108] As Stephen records, in the case of homicide the presumption was specifically formulated: 'Every person who kills another is presumed to have wilfully murdered him unless the circumstances are such as to raise a contrary presumption', *Digest* (1883), Art. 230. And similarly, *Outlines* (1929), 140 at n. 4.

[109] *Lee v. Taylor and Gill* (1912) 77 JP 66, 69.

[110] (1912) 7 Cr App R 140. Also e.g. *Chapin* (1909) 22 Cox 10; *Beach* (1912) 7 Cr App R 197; *Lumley* (1911) 22 Cox 635; *Davies* (1913) 24 TLR 350.

rebuttability or even suggest that juries were not *bound* to convict in the absence of contrary evidence.[111] Just as in felony–murder, judicial ambivalence towards constructive fault's role in respect of presumed intention was eventually (to some degree) resolved by the House of Lords in *Woolmington*.[112] And, in common with the steadily contracting scope of felony murder, modification of the presumption of intended consequences was informed by the strengthening ambition of refining the link between subjective moral culpability, criminal liability, and punishment. As will be seen, such an ambition did not extend to unlawful act of manslaughter. However, extensive sentencing flexibility for manslaughter meant that judges at least enjoyed the power to match specific individual culpability and punishment.

SELF-MURDER: SUICIDE

Until the enactment of the Suicide Act 1961, suicide was the common law felony of self-murder—*felonia de se*. While in general, the law never sought to criminalize intentional,[113] non-fatal self-inflicted harm by a sane individual, suicide did attract a criminal sanction. In almost ironic tone, Blackstone explained the grounds for punishment as twofold:

...one spiritual in invading the prerogative of the Almighty, and rushing into his immediate presence uncalled for; the other temporal, against the king, who hath an interest in the preservation of all his subjects....[114]

During the course of the nineteenth century, though remaining a crime, suicide's terrestrial sanctions were gradually reduced to the point of extinction. In essence, such changes reflected the gradual ceding of (relative) civil and spiritual individual autonomy and self-determination, a development underpinned by a background of democratic concessions along with creeping intellectual secularization amongst the professional and ruling classes.[115]

---

[111] Stephen J. in *Doherty* (1887) 16 Cox 306 at 308: 'As a rule the use of a knife to stab or of a pistol to shoot shows an intention to do grievous bodily harm, but this is not a necessary inference'; *Meade* [1909] 1 KB 895, 899; *Stoddart* (1909) Cr App R 217.

[112] *Woolmington* implicitly overruled any previous authorities which asserted, *either* that the presumption of intended consequences was irrebuttable, *or*, more commonly, that unless rebutted, a jury was bound to convict. Cf. J. C. Smith, 'The Presumption of Innocence' (1987) 38 *NILQ* 223, with A. Stein, 'From Blackstone to Woolmington' (1993) 14 *JLH* 14.

[113] Technically, the *mens rea* of suicide was the same as for murder, and could, therefore, be satisfied in circumstances where the deceased had no direct intention of killing himself. Consequently e.g. the deceased might be regarded as having committed suicide if he had caused his own death in an attempt to kill another; or even where the deceased accidentally killed himself in the course of carrying out a felony, *Hale* 1 PC 413; *Hawkins* 1 PC 68. *Hopwood* (1913) 8 Cr App R 143. *Criminal Law Commissioners, Fourth Report* (1839), xliii, Art. 73.

[114] *Comms*, iv, 189.

[115] Stephen was a long-term critic of seeking to apply sanctions to successful suicides. *General View*, 122 and *HCL* iii, 107. His 1872/4 Homicide Bill provision (s 32) decriminalizing suicide attracted

Deterring would-be suicides always presented a unique problem: because a successful suicide had 'withdrawn himself from [the law's] reach' no corporeal punishment could be inflicted; any sanction was necessarily against 'what he has left behind, his reputation and fortune'. In the former case, until 1823, a would-be suicide faced the threat of 'an ignominious burial in the highway, with a stake driven through his body'.[116] Against his fortune, until 1870,[117] was levelled the more practical threat of forfeiture of goods, thereby depriving any surviving family of such means of support. However, long before the nineteenth century the law's formal sanctions were very frequently thwarted by the 'pious perjury' of jurors, humanely manipulating the requirement of a sane actor as the basis of a verdict of *felo de se*; coroners' juries were 'apt' to find 'that the very act of suicide is evidence of insanity'.[118] Indeed, the practice became so embedded in the system that even after the removal of most penalties for suicide, coroners' juries for many subsequent decades continued to exhibit considerable resistance to returning suicide verdicts.[119]

Outside coroners' courts, enormous variations were recorded across the country, both in arrest rates and charges levelled against would-be suicides. The arrival of professional policing brought a steep rise in arrests and charges of suicide, especially in London. However, only a relatively small proportion of those charged were ultimately committed by magistrates for trial on indictment. The overwhelming majority were dealt with summarily, usually with bind over orders.[120] Of those convicted at trial, only a minority received a custodial sentence; and of those, most were under a month's imprisonment.[121]

---

no Select Committee criticism. The 1879 Code Bill also took the same line, in that suicide required the act of 'another'.

[116] *Ibid.*, 190. The ending of this 'odious and disgusting ceremony [based on] custom' was without parliamentary opposition, *PD* 1823 (s. 2), 9: 550 and abolished by 4 Geo. IV c. 52, which replaced it by a requirement of burial between 9 and 12 pm without religious rites. This was modified in 1882 by 45 & 46 Vict. c. 19 which permitted some form of burial service short of the full solemnized Anglican procedure.

[117] Forfeiture for felony generally was abolished by 33 & 34 Vict. c. 23.

[118] *Comms*, iv, 189.

[119] In 1902 Kenny claimed (on the basis of published Judicial Statistics) that less than 1% of inquests on suicide cases return verdicts of *felo de se*, adding that the greater stigma for families of an undeserved finding of insanity 'gravely affected their social or matrimonial or commercial prospects', *Outlines* (1902), 113. In 1910 the Home Office proposed the abolition of the verdict *felo de se*, *PP* 1910 [Cd. 5004], xxi, 20. From the 1930s coroners' courts began adopting the use of alternative terms to 'suicide'. See Turner, *Outlines* (19th edn, 1966), 184; and XI, Pt 3.

[120] From less than 2% in 1840s' London, and around 10% elsewhere, by 1914 the percentage of committals across the country had risen to approximately 11%. O. Anderson, *Suicide in Victorian and Edwardian England* (Oxford, 1987), 282–95.

[121] Until the early 1900s when more non-custodial alternatives decreased the incidence of custody but increased the proportion of prison sentences imposed in excess of a month: Anderson, *Suicide*, 301–6.

While a *felo de se* was beyond the reach of standard punishment regimes, this was self-evidently not true of attempted suicide, nor of the associated actions of other parties. Conviction for the misdemeanour of attempted suicide could compound a failed suicide's misery.[122] But likely sympathy for failed suicides rarely extended to third parties;[123] instigating or assisting suicide, whether or not in pursuance of a suicide pact, made the survivor a secondary party to murder, thereby opening up a wide range of punishments capable of matching the perceived degree of moral culpability involved.[124]

Manslaughter

Difficulties encountered in determining the scope of murder caused by the opaque nature of the term 'malice aforethought' were amplified by the broad, indistinct negative definition of manslaughter: unlawful homicide where there is an absence of malice aforethought.[125] Manslaughter spanned a broad range of moral culpability, from acts of extreme violence to actions where no harm of any nature was intended or foreseen.[126] By the early nineteenth century, manslaughter's residual, largely undefined liability extended across two forms of culpable homicide frequently categorized as 'voluntary' and 'involuntary' manslaughter;[127] the former covered provoked killings, the latter included the deaths caused by either unlawful but non-felonious acts or by grossly negligent behaviour. At this stage, the, so to speak, least undeveloped and most prominent[128] concept of manslaughter was that governing killings where provocation had occurred.

VOLUNTARY MANSLAUGHTER

(1) *Provoked killing*

It had long been established that, rather than murder, killing with 'malice aforethought' would constitute the lesser offence of manslaughter if the defendant's

---

[122] Note the more serious felony of attempted murder under the Offences Against the Person Act 1861, s 15. *Burgess* (1862) 9 Cox 247.

[123] See the 1879 *Code Bill Commission Report*, 25, and Draft Code, s 183.

[124] Beyond instigation or assisting suicide, the killing of another under a suicide pact was made manslaughter under the Homicide Act 1957, s 4(1).

[125] e.g. from *Coke* and *Hale* through to *Foster*, *East*, and *Russell*.

[126] Before 1822, the felony of manslaughter was punishable with a maximum of one year's imprisonment. The long-recognized inadequacy of the level of punishment for the most culpable forms of manslaughter was remedied by legislation in 1822 and 1828 3 Geo. IV c. 38 and 9 Geo. IV c. 31. The Acts, initiated by the Home Office to cover the wide range of 'differing degrees of criminality' (*PD* 1822 (s. 2), 6: 1458) increased the maximum punishment to transportation for life or three years' imprisonment. With the ending of transportation, the Offences Against the Person Act 1861, modified manslaughter's punishment to a maximum of penal servitude for life or two years' imprisonment (s 5).

[127] *Hale*, 1 PC 466; Blackstone, *Comms*, iv, 191.

[128] *Foster*, 290.

actions had been provoked. Since the early eighteenth century, provocation as a partial defence to murder rested on 'excess of anger and passion', depriving defendants of their 'reasoning faculties'.[129] This rationale of the partial excuse or concession to 'human infirmity', where the defendant had experienced a sudden loss of self control, underpins all leading nineteenth-century judgments[130] and other authorities. However, variations occurred in the techniques employed for keeping the defence within what were regarded as acceptable bounds: balancing the need not to weaken the 'salutary check' of the threat of punishment against the wish to make 'necessary allowance [for] the actual subjugation of the judgment to uncontrollable passion'.[131]

Partly normative, partly doctrinal, this process of development entailed several shifts of law: an accentuated scrutiny of the defendant's state of mind when responding to provocation; a review of the recognized categories of provocative acts; and attempts to construct some form of proportionality relationship between provocation and mode of response. Together, these developments amounted to a conceptual realignment of provocation whereby the overall moral and legal acceptability of provoked action narrowed. As will be seen, in broad terms, it was a trend not manifested in other more generally applicable defences such as insanity and duress, and probably reflected an overall diminution in the social tolerance of ill-controlled human passions.

Determining provocation's initial subjective requirement of the defendant's actual loss of self-control was a question of fact for jurors. Consequently, the potential for variability in findings was especially great; sympathy for, or antipathy towards, the defendant's particular circumstances or those of the victim might easily subvert a strict application of the law. Always set against the centuries-old core requirement of acting in a fit of passion, was the likely effects of any elapse of time following the act of provocation where 'the blood might cool' and 'contrivance [and] design' might reassert control. However, throughout the nineteenth century, occasional judicial comment suggested certain provocative acts might be assumed to generate an 'impulse so violent that he could not resist it'.[132] In contrast to the requirement of actual loss of self-control, the Criminal

---

[129] *Oneby* (1727) 2 Ld. Raym. 1485, per Lord Raymond CJ, 1495–6. Blackstone identifies the defence as a concession to 'human frailty' and the effects of the 'heat of blood' before 'passion' subsides and 'reason interpose[s]', *Comms*, iv, 191. Similarly, *Foster*, 291: 'indulgeth human frailty'. For exploration of the roles of 'honour, anger and virtue' in the early development of the defence, see J. Horder, *Provocation and Responsibility* (Oxford, 1992), Chs 3 and 4.

[130] e.g. see *Ayes* (1810) R. & R. 166; *Hayward* (1833) 6 Car. & P. 157; *Eagle* (1862) 2 F. & F. 827. Also *East* 1 PC 238; *Russell* (1826) i: 434.

[131] *Criminal Law Commissioners, Fourth Report* (1839), xxxviii.

[132] Rolfe B.'s reference to a husband finding his wife in the act of adultery, *Kelly* (1848) 2 Car. & K. 815.

Law Commissioners' earlier (but not later) analyses of the provocation defence favoured a test whereby the 'ordinary power of judgment and self-control' were not totally lost but only weakened.[133]

Early nineteenth-century authorities adopted the traditional practice of fixed categories of what might be capable of legal provocation. Following this approach *Russell*, for example, ruled out a host of provocative situations, including 'affront by bare words or gestures'; on the other hand, assaults 'made with violence or circumstances of indignity upon a man's person, as by pulling him by the nose', could be sufficient; and so also would a husband catching his adulterous wife *in flagrante*.[134] Prescribing just what might be permitted to qualify as legal provocation was, in part, the residual effects of the defence's remote honour-based origins.[135] But even before the nineteenth century, the fixing of permissible categories of provocation functioned as a broader normative control mechanism, ensuring that the occasions on which provocation might be permitted to mitigate culpability was not left entirely to juries.

Judicial introduction of a general objective standard of reasonableness of response was a distinct, additional means of regulating the defence's availability.[136] In the early decades of the nineteenth century this occurred alongside adherence

---

[133] *Fourth Report* (1839), xxxvii. Especially at this time judicial dicta relate the defence of provocation with rebutting the presumption of intended consequences and malice aforethought: Coleridge J. in *Kirkham* (1837) 8 Car. & P. 115. See 'Proportionality' below. This approach to provocation, rather than simply addressing notions of voluntariness, were later described by Stephen as an 'avowed fiction' for rebutting implied malice, *HCL* i, 87. Later formulations of the defence by the Criminal Law Commissioners were radically different from their earlier views and existing law: (i) provocation was not limited to negating the formation of *mens rea*; (ii) earlier references to the standard of the 'ordinary powers of self control' were deleted; (iii) other than 'grave' no express limitation was placed on what might be permitted to cause recognized provocation. These highly personalized proposals constituted the most subjective formulation of the defence proposed during the nineteenth century, *Second Report* (1846), 25, Art. 2; *Fourth Report* (1848), 161. They were largely followed in the 1853–4 Criminal Law Amendment Code Bill. The Commissioners were much influenced by Macaulay's draft Indian Code and his reasoning. Not only did Macaulay dismiss any formal distinction between words and acts as the basis of provocation, he also doubted the value of the objective criterion of 'ordinary temper'. Agreeing, the Commissioners (including Andrew Amos returned from service as legal member of the Indian Governor-General's Council), accepted that it was 'expedient to leave consideration of (such matters) to juries, unfettered by arbitrary distinctions', *Second Report*, 25–6.

[134] (1826) i: 486–8.

[135] Cases of 'sudden combat' or 'mutual combat' though a particular instance of the provocation defence, were still retained as a distinct category well into the twentieth century by some textbooks. For example, *Russell* (8th edn, 1923), 670. For the key distinction between completely unlawful 'cold blooded' duelling and 'hot blooded' mutual combat, see 'Duelling' below.

[136] By the early 1900s, the reasonable man's behaviour and his characteristics were being laid down as a matter of law. *Alexander* (1913) 9 Cr App R 139, excluded evidence of the defendant's mental deficiency. *Smith* (1914) 11 Cr App R 36 held the defendant's pregnancy to be immaterial.

to recognized provocation categories.[137] Later, deployment of the reasonable man standard[138] not only regulated the defence's availability, but also encouraged some degree of judicial flexibility in what were regarded as legally effective forms of provocation. To the classic, long-established category of an adulterous wife being discovered by her husband in *flagrante delicto*, the courts grafted on situations where the defendant husband had learnt of the infidelity from a third party or a wife's confession.[139] However, by no means all judges favoured such a flexible course.[140] Moreover, through a combination of the notion of 'reasonableness of response' and changing social conventions or manners, some recognized categories of provocation with ancient pedigrees became doubtful. Most especially, it is difficult to imagine many Victorian judges and juries accepting examples of slight assaults accompanied by 'great indignity' (such as nose pulling) as acceptable provocation.[141]

---

[137] *Kirkham* (1837) 8 Car. & P. 115. Coleridge J.: '[B]ecause, though the law condescends to human frailty, it will not indulge human ferocity. It considers man to be a rational being, and requires that he should exercise a reasonable control over his passion'. Similarly, Coleridge J. in the judges' responses to questions on the 1853–4 Code Bills (*PP* 1854 (303), iii, based on the Criminal Law Commissioners' Reports) criticizing the absence of any reference to 'an effort…to restrain passion' (p. 14); also by Erle J. (p. 25); and Cresswell J. who thought the provisions would 'operate in favour of men of violent and ill-governed tempers…' (p. 22).

[138] *Welsh* (1869) 11 Cox 336. Keating J.: '[I]n law it is necessary that there should have been serious provocation in order to reduce the crime to manslaughter…something which might naturally cause an ordinary and reasonably minded man to lose his self control and commit such an act' (p. 339). Similarly, Blackburn J. in *Rothwell* (1871) 12 Cox 145. But leading criminal law treatises failed to reflect the conceptual significance of these cases until their confirmation by the Court of Criminal Appeal in *Lesbini* (1914) 3 KB 116. Kenny, *Outlines* (1902) makes no reference to the reasonable man test. Both *Russell* and *Archbold* incorporate the test after *Lesbini*: *Russell* (8th edn, 1923), 654; *Archbold* (25th edn, 1918), 846.

[139] *Tracey, The Times*, 16 July 1869. Hannah J: '[If] upon grounds not unreasonable, the prisoner acted on the belief that there had been improper conduct between (his wife) immediately after its discovery', *Rothwell* (1871) 12 Cox 145 Blackburn J. 'As a general rule of law, no provocation of words will reduce the crime of murder to…manslaughter but…for instance, if a husband suddenly hearing from his wife that she had committed adultery…kills his wife, it might be manslaughter' (147). In his evidence to the *Royal Commission on Capital Punishment 1864–6* (*Report PP* 1866 (3590) xxi) Bramwell B. favoured extending provocation to where a husband had been provoked by 'good information' of his wife's adultery (p. 33). More generally, he 'was uncertain whether he favoured any formal restriction on potential provocative acts or whether to leave the matter to each jury'. The Commission regarded the exclusion from the range of provocation of 'words, looks or gestures, however contemptuous and insulting' as 'most unsatisfactory', *Report*, xlix. Earlier, Stephen had advocated no 'rigid rules' but complete judicial flexibility (1864) 69 *Fraser's Mag.* 753, 766. *Rothwell* was followed by Bucknill J. in *Jones* (1908) 72 JP 215. See also *Mason* (1912) 8 Cr App R 121, 125 and *Smith* (1865) 4 F & F 1066; *Sherwood* (1844) 1 Car. & K.556.

[140] e.g. the Court of Criminal Appeal's limitations on *Rothwell* in *Palmer* [1913] 2 KB 29 and *Greening* (1913) 3 KB 846.

[141] Yet e.g. Stephen's *Digest* includes as possible provocation assaults inflicting actual bodily harm 'or great insult' (Art. 224(a)) (1877) and also Kenny *Outlines* (1902), 117.

During this period several extra-judicial attempts were undertaken to reformulate the provocation defence. In his 1872–4 Homicide Bill, besides incorporating detailed (fixed) instances of provocation recognized by the common law,
Stephen sought to facilitate an expansion of provocation's range by expressly giving judges the power to recognize provocative acts of the 'same kind' as those
cases identified.[142] In evidence to the bill's Select Committee, Blackburn J. was
in no doubt that the elastic state of the common law permitted the proper reception of deserving novel cases of provocation in a fashion not equalled by the bill's
provisions.[143] Before the same Committee, of Stephen's proposed discretionary power, Bramwell B. indicated that 'I do not like it certainly. [But] I do not
think any great harm would come from it…'.[144] In considerable contrast to the
Homicide Bill, the provocation provisions of the 1879 Code Bill, like the 1840s
Criminal Law Commissioners, sought to supersede the common law's fragmentary and idiosyncratic approach by jettisoning any limitation to specifically
recognize provocative acts. They proposed a clear-cut objective standard of any
'wrongful act or insult of such a nature as to be sufficient to deprive an ordinary
person of the power of self control'. Moreover, the jury was to be assigned the
role of determining not just whether the defendant was 'actually deprived of the
power of self control', but also whether the provocation would have had such an
effect upon an 'ordinary person'. As the Code Bill team, including Blackburn and
Stephen observed, such questions were 'pre-eminently a matter of degree for the
consideration of the jury'.[145]

---

[142] Clause 28.

[143] *Minutes of Evidence*, q. 280. In his reply, Stephen sought to demonstrate the opposite, acidly
suggesting that 'Mr Justice Blackburn appears to me not to have done the bill the honour to read
it', q. 356.

[144] *Ibid.*, q. 228. In a written memo to the Committee, Lord Cockburn CJ summed up his view of
the provocation provisions as 'ill-conceived and unhappily expressed', *Report of Select Committee*,
App. 1, p. 64.

[145] Section 176; and *Report*, 24–5. Wright's Jamaican Draft Penal Code, whilst identifying a range
of recognized provocative situations, like the 1879 Code Bill, incorporated an objectifying 'ordinary
character' requirement (ss 121–3). Indeed, the potential for juries to make unrestricted normative
assessments of defendants' immorality, manifested itself principally by either accepting judicial
directions on the non-qualifying nature of the provocation but recommending mercy; or ignoring judicial rulings and acquitting on murder charges. On the propensity of juries to recommend
'mercy upon the ground of great provocation', see Lord Cranworth LC in his evidence to the *Royal
Commission on Capital Punishment*, 8 For the judicial perception of juries' willingness to acquit
those charged with murder on provocation grounds, see Cresswell J., *PP* 1854 (303), liii, 22: 'the
very natural inclination…to escape [capital sentences] almost always induces them to believe that
the…killing was…in such a passion as suspended powers of self control'.

Assessments of the immorality of defendants provoked actions reflected in two other practical
important respects: sentencing and exercise of the prerogative of mercy. Where juries returned
manslaughter verdicts on the grounds of provocation, very wide sentencing discretion meant
that judges could refine punishments to coincide with their own views of defendants' overall

Neither these codification proposals nor most case law directly addressed a final, though indistinct feature, of the provocation defence: that of proportionality between the nature of provocation and the mode of response. While references to proportionality appear in standard treatises,[146] its relevance to provocation's scope is obscure. In the nineteenth century, two interpretations of proportionality's role were possible. The more persuasive view relates a lack of proportionality to evidence negating the defendant's claim to spontaneous action in a 'fit of passion'. Most especially, a defendant's use of a deadly weapon in response to 'slight provocation'[147] would be very unlikely to rebut the assumption that the killing had not been in a fit of passion. Indeed, in his 1874 Homicide Bill Select Committee evidence, Blackburn J. indicated a proportionality requirement in that the greater the level of the defendant's violence, the greater the nature and level of provocation needed to demonstrate loss of self-control; where there was no manifest 'intent to kill… a slighter degree of provocation would suffice'.[148]

However, not only does nineteenth-century case law offer extremely limited express support for the notion of proportionality, there are also many reported

culpability. These practices continued into the twentieth century, occasionally generating public condemnation: e.g. *The Times*, 7 October 1902, p. 10. For a detailed analysis of the enormous sentencing variations in nineteenth-century spouse provocation cases, see Wiener, *Men of Blood*, Ch. 7, *passim*. And see 'Non-fatal offences' above for discussion of shifts in nineteenth-century opinion on the criminality of violence against women. In respect of the practices of Home Secretaries and Home Office officials in dealing with commutation of capital sentences where provocation was insufficient to partially excuse murder, see Chadwick, *Bureaucratic Mercy*, Ch. 8, *passim*. As both studies confirm, the second half of the nineteenth century saw a broad trend towards less generous treatment of provoked killing.

[146] e.g. *Archbold* (4th edn, 1831), 318: 'In considering however, whether the killing upon provocation amount to murder or manslaughter, the instrument where with the homicide was affected must also be taken into consideration; for if it were affected with a deadly weapon, the provocation must be great indeed, to extenuate the offence to manslaughter; if with a weapon or other means not likely or intended to produce death, a less degree of provocation will be sufficient; in fact, the mode of resentment must bear a reasonable proportion to the provocation, to reduce the offence to manslaughter'. And *East*, 1 PC, 234 and 238–9.

[147] Particularly *Russell* (1826), i: 438–40: 'It seems, therefore, that it may be laid down that in all cases of slight provocation, if it may be reasonably collected from the weapon made use of, or from any other circumstances, that the party intended to kill, or to do some great bodily harm, such homicide would be murder' (p. 440). In their analysis of the question, the Criminal Law Commissioners appeared to oppose a fixed legal rule of proportionality (*Fourth Report*, xxvi), seeing disproportionality as important evidence countering a claim of acting in 'hot blood'. However, in its digest proposals reflecting their view of the existing law, the proposed provisions impose proportionality requirements (Arts 42 and 43). A rare judicial reference to proportionality appears in *Thomas* (1837) 7 Car. & P. 817, where the evidential role of proportionality is articulated. Stephen assigns proportionality an evidential function in his *Digest* (1877), Art. 225.

[148] *Minutes*, 36.

instances[149] where massive disproportionality existed without defeating a plea of provocation. At the very least, this suggests the absence of any absolute rule of proportionality, showing it to be just one facet of evidence which a jury should consider when determining whether a defendant actually acted in 'hot blood'. The alternative view of proportionality is to regard it as a forerunner of provocation's limiting notion of the response of the reasonable man. As one aspect of any assessment whether the defendant acted reasonably in all the circumstances, such a construction would offer some sort of explanation for proportionality's absence from the 1879 Code formulation. Additionally, it might partly account for the lack of any authoritative articulation of the rule by an English court until almost the mid-twentieth century.[150] Yet such an approach necessarily draws in the illogical conclusion that though the reasonable man may have lost self-control in the circumstances, he must still proportion his response to provocation.

(2) Duels, 'spontaneous combat' and brawls

A fundamental contrast frequently drawn in provocation cases was between killing in 'hot' and 'cold' blood: the former being the essential basis of a provocation defence, the latter typifying killing in the course of a duel: 'for wherever two persons in cold blood meet and fight on a precedent quarrel, and one of them is killed, the other is guilty of murder'.[151] Here, the law granted no concession, for, as Blackstone declared, a duel was an open and calculated act of 'high contempt of the justice of the nation... in direct contradiction to the laws both of God and man'.[152]

But while the criminal law had long identified death in the course of duelling as murder, its widely accepted social and cultural significance[153] was such as to significantly compromise all stages of the law's enforcement, from the formulation and bringing of charges, through to jury verdicts and the nature of punishment

---

[149] e.g. *Smith* (1837) 8 Car. & P. 160; *Eagle* (1862) 2 F. & F. 827; *Selten* (1871) 11 Cox 674. Evidence of the variability of both judicial and jury handling of provocation between 1864 and 1888 is collected in a confidential *Home Office Printed Memoranda*, N.A. H.O. 347/9, 678–82.

[150] *Mancini* v. *DPP* (1942) AC 1.

[151] *Russell* (1826), i: 443, following *Foster*, 295 and *Hale*, 1 PC, 453. For the criminal law's treatment of prize-fighting resulting in a pugilist's death, see 'Involuntary Manslaughter' below.

[152] Blackstone, *Comms*, iv, 145 and 199.

[153] For the broad social context and function of the notion of honour operating beyond the force of law, see R. Baldick, *The Duel, A History of Duelling* (1965); on early prosecution practices, and duelling's social function, see R. Shoemaker, 'Male Honour and the Decline of Public Violence in Eighteenth Century London' (2001) 26 *Social History* 190 and M. Peltonen, *The Duel in Early Modern England: Civility, Politeness and Honour* (Cambridge, 2003). For duelling's decline, see D. Andrew, 'The Code of Honour and its Critics: The Opposition to Duelling in England, 1700–1850' (1980) 5 *Social History* 409 and A. Simpson, 'Dandelions on the Field of Honour: Duelling, the Middle Classes and the Law in the Nineteenth Century' (1988) 9 *Criminal Justice History* 99.

meted out. Emphatic judicial denunciations of duelling and clear confirmation of its status as murder when death occurred appear through the eighteenth and well into the nineteenth century; yet convictions of duellists for murder were rare.[154] However, by the 1840s, reflecting a broad, ever declining tolerance of such practices, judges were making calculated and strenuous efforts to underscore their determination to visit the law's full severity on killings in the course of duelling. Summing up in *Cuddy*, Williams J. observed

I am bound to tell you, as a matter about which my learned brother [Rolfe B.] and myself have no doubt (nor, I believe has any other judge any doubt about it), that, where two persons go out to fight a deliberate duel, and death ensues, all persons who are present... encouraging or promoting that death, will be guilty [of murder].[155]

Yet residual equivocation towards just what level of condemnation and punishment duelling warranted clearly lingered on, as is significantly evidenced in the Criminal Law Commissioners' 1846 reflections. At this time the Commissioners proposed a change in the law for duelling, both on the grounds of principle and pragmatism, to de-capitalize such killings.

An evil ingredient in the crime of murder of great importance is wanting to the offence of duelling: death by duelling does not, like murder, spread alarm through all ranks of society, from the highest to the lowest. The grounds on which the extreme measure of capital punishment, in cases of murder, seems justifiable, are, first, to prevent the severest of personal injuries, and secondly, to prevent people from living in constant dread of being murdered. It is obvious that, in the case of duels, the danger is confined only to the higher class of society; and what is of more consequence, no one need be in dread of dying by such means, unless he chooses to enter into a voluntary compact to violate the law. As the punishment for murder is not grounded on the Jewish law, nor on our moral or religious horror at the act, but on its prejudice to society, and chiefly on the insecurity and alarm it occasions, it appears to us that there is not an adequate cause to justify the taking away of life, where death occurs in the instance of two persons voluntarily agreeing, according to certain stipulated or implied rules, to give each other an opportunity of killing his antagonist...

The reluctance of witnesses and juries to take any part in the capital conviction of a person, who has been engaged in a fair duel, especially if he may have received grievous provocation, or been the party challenged, must have been manifest to persons who have

---

[154] The conviction of two seconds for murder in *Young and Webber* (1838) 8 Car. & P. 644, is generally regarded as a turning point in the practice of prosecuting duellists and other participating parties. Yet, while in decline, reported duellings were still occurring beyond 1850. Simpson, 'Dandelions', 106–7.

[155] (1843) 1 Car. & K. 210. Indicative of contemporary attitudes, despite the strong direction and compelling evidence, the jury acquitted. Also e.g. *Barronet* (1852) 1 Dears. 52 and *Barthelemy* (1852) 1 Dears. 60.

been present at trials of this description. And there have not been wanting examples of persons of high station and character tending to diminish the public odium of the offence of duelling....[156]

Where, rather than from a prearranged, 'cold blooded' duel, killing was the consequence of a spontaneous fight, the law's response turned on the precise circumstances; depending on these, a defendant might be liable for murder, man-slaughter, or be completely exonerated. A conviction for murder would be due if the defendant had generated conflict with the objective of killing or causing another serious harm. However, where no such motivation existed, death might be 'excusable in self defence or upon chance-medley'.

Prior to the nineteenth century, the latter defence was distinguishable from simple self-defence in that for chance-medley an accused carried a degree of blame for the fatal outcome. In recognition of this, rather than being regarded as a justified killing, meriting a complete acquittal, a successful plea of chance-medley was designated an excuse, attracting the lesser penalty of forfeiture of goods. Yet even by the mid-eighteenth century, Foster was able to remark that the distinction had become more a 'matter rather of Historical Amusement than of real Importance to inquire...', as it was then standard practice either to remit forfeiture or direct an acquittal.[157] Formal termination of the obsolete distinction was effected in 1828 with the abolition of forfeiture in such cases.[158] But, while chance-medley was subsumed into the mainstream justification of self-defence, commentators long into the twentieth century felt obliged to identify the particu-lar qualifying conditions for self-defence in such circumstances: the defendant's 'retreat', and 'the necessity of killing to avoid his own death'.[159]

Killing in the course of a spontaneous or 'sudden, hot blooded' (sometimes, 'mutual combat') fight was the third category of physical conflict recognized by the criminal law. In common with chance-medley, the perpetration of an initially provocative act by the defendant was discounted in determining his ultimate

---

[156] *Second Report* (1846), 30, Art. 16n.

[157] At p. 288 and *East*, 1 PC, 279. As Foster explained: 'Homicide se Defendo upon chance-medley [a] species of self defence which is culpable and through the benignity of the law excusable' (275). *Hawkins* regarded defendants as 'too much favoured' by the defence, 1 PC, c. 29, s 17.

[158] 9 Geo. IV c. 31, s 10. For discussion of the effective end of the legal significance between 'justi-fication' and 'excuses' by the early nineteenth century, see 'Defences', Ch. VII. Forfeiture for felonies was completely abolished in 1870 by the Forfeiture Act (33 & 34 Vict. c. 23).

[159] e.g. *Archbold* (4th edn, 1831), 316–17. *Criminal Law Commissioners, Fourth Report* (1839), xxxvii, Art. 37; *Second Report* (1846), 35, Art. 13; and the Criminal Law Amendment Bill 1853/4, s lxxxviii. For the Commissioners' 1846 proposal and the 1853 Bill it was sufficient if the belief in the 'neces-sity of killing' was reasonable, though erroneous. Similarly in the 1879 Code Bill, s 56. Reference to chance-medley appeared in *Archbold* until the practice was condemned by Lord Goddard in *Semini* (1949) 1 KB 405 at 409. For self-defence generally, see Ch. VII above.

level of liability. But, unlike chance-medley, in 'mutual combat' the law reduced liability to manslaughter rather than, effectively, granting an acquittal. This difference of attitude, which acquired considerable importance after the maximum punishment for manslaughter was drastically increased in the 1820s, rested on the rationale supporting provocation in general: the notion of loss of self-control whilst in a state of 'hot blood'. Mitigation of liability from murder to manslaughter in cases of 'mutual combat upon sudden quarrels' as in provocation generally, entailed presumed absence of calculated 'malice' in both parties, where each was considered to have provoked the other. Broad parity at the commencement of fighting was a condition of manslaughter liability, for if the defendant enjoyed an initial 'undue advantage' this was taken as evidence of 'malice'.[160] But, as with all instances of provocation, liability for sudden and fatal conflict was mitigated 'as a matter of condescension to the Infirmities of Flesh and Blood'.[161] Like chance-medley and self-defence, although governed by the same principles by the early nineteenth century, 'mutual combat' and provocation were treated by criminal law texts as distinct for expositional purposes well into the twentieth century.

INVOLUNTARY MANSLAUGHTER

(1) *Unlawful act or constructive manslaughter*

Citing *Foster*, Blackstone[162] declared that causing death as a consequence of committing a 'mere trespass' would be manslaughter. Liability was enhanced by the simple unlawfulness of an initial action. *East*, likewise, initially refers to a 'bare trespass' being a sufficient basis for manslaughter,[163] yet later appears to qualify the original generality of the rule by noting that where there is no intention to cause even slight bodily harm, 'guilt' would depend on 'either that the act might

---

[160] *Mawgridge's Case* (1707) Kel. 119. *Foster*, 295; but (consistently) a later disparity resulting from the defendant acquiring a superior weapon in a state of 'hot blood' would not preclude a provocation defence. *East*, 1 PC, 243, *Anderson* (1816) 1 *Russell* 447; *Rankin* (1803) R. & R. 43.

[161] *Foster*, 296; *East*, 1 PC, 232. For a subtle exploration of links between the early mitigation of liability for *spontaneous* duels, concessions to honour notions, and absence of a 'rebellious challenge to authority' inherent in premeditated duelling, see J. Horder 'The Duel and the English Law of Homicide' (1992) 12 *OJLS* 419, esp. 427–30. However, recognition of mitigation in cases of fighting went beyond duelling to less elevated brawls; e.g. *Anderson* (1816) 1 *Russell* 447; *Kessal* (1824) 1 Car. & P. 437; *Lynch* (1832) 5 Car. & P. 324; *Smith* (1837) 8 Car. & P. 160. Moreover, commentators tended to categorize examples of sudden conflict as instances of provocation, e.g. *Foster* 296; *East*, 1 PC, 232, 241. East remarks that in cases of 'mutual combat' the 'degree or species of provocation' is not scrutinized 'so deeply into the merits as [provocation generally]' (241). It appears from East's earlier observation that 'mutual combat' was automatically accepted as 'reasonable provocation', and where the presumption of 'malice' was rebutted (232). But in all such cases, the focus of judicial investigation is whether the defendant was truly acting in 'a fit of passion' or 'hot blood'.

[162] *Comms*, iv, 192–3, citing *Foster*, 258, who followed *Hale* 1 PC, 466: 'some unlawful act'.

[163] 1 PC, 255.

probably breed danger, or that it was done with a mischievous intent'.[164] Indeed, Foster also apparently revised his own general principle; first, by excluding as qualifying unlawful acts those which were just *mala prohibita*,[165] and secondly, by reference to the unlawful act being 'done Heedlessly and Incautiously'.[166] The implications of these qualifying comments are not easily gauged, but they are most naturally construed as requiring objective fault as to some level of harm being a possible consequence of the unlawful act.

This was always *Russell*'s contention, which adopted both *Foster*'s expression 'Heedlessly and Incautiously' and *East*'s reference to risky behaviour or 'mischievous intent'.[167] But, characteristically, *Russell* made no attempt to reconcile these statements, nor the supporting case law. Clearly, if only unlawful acts that were intrinsically risky—harm threatening—could be the basis of unlawful act manslaughter, then such a limitation would constitute a form of negligence requirement. If that were so, then in what way would unlawful act manslaughter differ from manslaughter founded on lawful behaviour performed negligently (see below), a distinction asserted in standard works of authority, including *Foster*, *Blackstone*, and *East*? In common with felony-murder, nineteenth-century unlawful act manslaughter case law came to implicitly recognize culpability requirements that would, effectively, eliminate its constructive fault nature.

In the early 1830s' decision of *Fenton* the unlawful act was the tort of trespass, committed in such circumstances clearly likely to generate the risk of harm to mine workers. Directing the jury, Tindal CJ indicated that as there was an unlawful act the 'only question therefore is, whether the death...is to be fairly and reasonably considered as a consequence of such a wrongly act'.[168] Here, although Tindal CJ seemed to be addressing an exclusively causal question, the limiting potential of causal demands in at least some unlawful act manslaughter situations is clear. Applying his 'fairly and reasonably' rule of causal ascription would in

---

[164] *Ibid.*, 257.

[165] Such as certain statutory low level game offences. 'The rule I have laid down supposed death, that an Act from which Death was *Malum in se*. For if it were barely *Malum prohibitum*, as shooting at Game by a Person not qualified by Statute-Law to keep or use a Gun for that Purpose, the Case of a Person so offending will fall under the same Rule as that of a qualified Man. For the statutes prohibiting the Destruction of the Game under certain penalties *will not*, in a Question of this kind, enhance the accident beyond its intrinsic Moment' (259).

[166] *Ibid.*, 261. And see also references to the need to use 'that degree of circumspection which common prudence would have suggested' (260).

[167] See (1819), i, Book III, Ch. II, section V; (1843) i, Book III, Ch. II, section IV; and (1909), Book IX, Ch. I, section II. The latest edition, though retaining the reference to 'an act likely to breed danger' lacks the reference to 'mischievous intent'.

[168] (1831) Lew. 179. Described as an act of 'mere wantonness and sport'. In *Martin* (1827) 2 Car. & P. 211, appended to the report is a reference to Foster's requirement of an act done 'heedlessly and incautiously'.

many instances mimic the effect of a negligence requirement.[169] However, until *Franklin*, decided half a century later, the relatively extensive run of unlawful act manslaughter case reports reveals no judicial attempt to restrict this form of constructive liability to anything more than an unlawful act. This was despite the (albeit ambiguous) statements found in *Foster*, *East*, and *Russell*, which at least offered sufficient authority for a narrowing of the type of qualifying offence required, should any member of the bench have been inclined to adopt such a route.[170] Moreover, commentators across several decades were almost uniformly hostile to the broad-based version of unlawful act manslaughter, if not the whole concept. Yet not only do reports show no judicial inclination to follow such views, neither do they record any judicial interest in evaluating the function, whether critically or not, the offence's constructive fault basis.

By contrast, constructive fault greatly absorbed the interest and energies of the Criminal Law Commissioners. As has been seen in the case of felony-murder, the Commissioners were consistent critics of 'constructive' fault liability. Unlawful act manslaughter was initially given a hostile analysis in their Fourth Report because (confirming *Fenton*) liability could follow where the intention had been to commit a 'bare misdemeanour or trespass', and death resulted by mere accident in a completely unforeseeable fashion. Nevertheless, the Commissioners sought to justify some enhanced punishment beyond that due for the initial unlawful act on the basis that it was likely to deter 'crimes of violence attended with danger to the person'. Consequently, the Commissioners' digested proposals limited qualifying unlawful acts to those where there was at least the 'risk of hurt to the person of another'.[171]

Without expressly discussing unlawful act manslaughter, the Seventh Report's Digest adopted an even more restricted approach by limiting the unlawful act to 'unlawful violence or injury…or endeavour to injure'.[172] However, in a rare instance of a recorded lack of unanimity amongst the Commissioners, the subsequent Second Report (with Starkie's dissenting opinion on unlawful act manslaughter) highlights the underlying fundamental policy at stake in

---

[169] See also *Noon* (1852) 6 Cox 137.

[170] Most reported cases are in the nature of an assault and therefore carry the intrinsic risk of some harm. For example, *Martin* (1832) 5 Car. & P. 128; *Wild's Case* (1837) 2 Lew. 214; *Merton* (1862) 3 F. & F. 492; *Porter* (1873) 12 Cox 444. Non-assault cases include *Sullivan* (1836) 7 Car. & P. 641; *Plummer* (1844) 1 Car. & K. 600 and *Bruce* (1847) 2 Cox 262. Erle, J.: manslaughter if there was an 'unlawful object…although he had no intention whatever of injuring him…'. Also *McNaughton* (1881) 14 Cox 576, death in the course of an unlawful assembly would incriminate all participants with manslaughter.

[171] *Fourth Report*, (1839), xxix, Art. 67, and Art. 71. The Commissioners expressly ruled out the need for 'due caution' as to harm when a risky unlawful act is justified (xlii, n).

[172] *Seventh Report*, (1843), Digest, section 3, Art. 2 and Art. 7, 230–1.

connection with constructive criminality more generally. In the majority's view:[173]

> ...where there is a probable connection between an injury and any act or omission, such that the punishment for occasioning injury would deter persons from wilfully or negligently being guilty of like acts or omissions,... the injury may reasonably be deemed to be wilfully or negligently caused. But where there is no ground for believing that an injury was in the contemplation of the party charged with causing it, and the connection is so remote between it and the act or omission, however unlawful, which has led to it, that it cannot be imputed to negligence, and that any punishment for causing the injury cannot operate by way of example to deter others from doing or omitting what the party accused has done or omitted,... the injury should be deemed accidental and dispunishable; the party, however, remaining punishable for his illegal act, without reference to its remote and improbable consequences.

Applying such reasoning, in the Report's Digest unlawful act manslaughter was subsumed within the generality of 'Negligent homicide', thereby making unlawfulness of the initial act irrelevant to ultimate liability. The core criterion of 'Negligent homicide' was defined as 'unjustifiable' action without 'reasonable caution'[174] as to probable harm. Rather than a distinct shift in the law's reach, this represented more of a conceptual change from the position adopted by the previous Report's restriction of unlawful act manslaughter to initial acts of 'violence or injury'; for *almost*[175] inevitably in such cases there would be an objectively apparent accompanying risk of harm to the person. Nevertheless, this was a significant attempt to underscore the limits of constructive fault and place involuntary manslaughter on what was seen as a rational basis, whereby fault related not just to the initial act but to the fatal consequences as well. For the majority of Commissioners, only such a fault-based policy was consonant with the aim of punishing acts open to deterrence.

Starkie ably voiced the orthodox philosophy of constructive fault. Employing the majority's own deterrence rationale, he delivered a formidable counter-case, supporting the retention of this distinct category of manslaughter. Whilst agreeing that it was inappropriate for manslaughter to embrace killings resulting from acts 'wholly unconnected with injury to the person', Starkie asserted that it was both proper and consistent with other doctrine, to make liable for

---

[173] Amos, Ryan, Ker, and Richards, *Second Report* (1846), 17.

[174] *Second Report*, section 4, Arts 2 and 3.

[175] One arguable instance where the provision in the *Seventh Report* would cover non-negligent risk-taking would be where the defendant attempted with patently inadequate means or technique to assault or harm another. Another example would be where the victim was in a non-apparent dangerous, weakened state, where even the slightest violence would kill.

manslaughter 'a party who uses illegal violence to the person "even though injury was unforeseeable" '. For, Starkie argued:

> when [death] results from violence of the person [manslaughter liability] operates to the protection of the person in increasing the peril of offering any violence to the person, and inculcating a due sense of high regard in which human life and safety ought to be held.[176]

Though never articulated so directly and clearly, this conception of unlawful act manslaughter's function probably broadly coincided with the implicit judicial view over the course of the nineteenth century. In general, Starkie's qualified support was also the approach adopted in Stephen's 1872–4 Homicide Bill.[177] Somewhat surprisingly, the 1879 Code's manslaughter provisions totally lacked detailed definition: 'Culpable homicide not amounting to murder',[178] leaving the offence's substance quite open for common law determination. In respect of unlawful act manslaughter, an equivocal answer was provided four years later in *Franklin*.

The interest of the late Victorian case of *Franklin* lies in two areas. First, because there was more than one unlawful act, pinning down the decision's *ratio* is problematic. Here, the defendant took a 'good sized box from the refreshments stall' of Brighton's west pier and threw it into the sea, fatally injuring a swimmer. Initially the prosecution pursued a manslaughter charge on the grounds of Franklin's trespass to the refreshment stallholder's property. However, Field J., after consulting Matthew J., ruled that the case should go before the jury 'upon the broad ground of negligence and not upon the narrow ground [of trespass] because…the mere fact of a civil wrong committed [by the defendant] ought not to be used as an incident which is a necessary step in a criminal case. I have great abhorrence of constructive crime'.[179] On this question of the sufficiency of a civil wrong serving as the basis of unlawful act manslaughter, Field J. continued:

> We do not think [*Fenton*] is binding upon us in the facts of the case, and, therefore, the civil wrong…is immaterial to this charge of manslaughter. I do not think that the facts of this case bring it clearly within the principles laid down by Tindal CJ in *Fenton*. If I thought this case was in principle like that case I would, if requested, state a case for the opinion of the Court of Criminal Appeal.

---

[176] *Second Report* (1846), 'Note by the Undersigned Commissioner', 56. Starkie's approach was adopted in the 1853/4 Criminal Law Amendment Code Bill, ss lxx and lxxi. Starkie's reasoning, of course, also applied to felony-murder.

[177] Section 26, requiring 'knowledge that [an act] will or probably may cause bodily harm' less than serious harm.

[178] Section 177. Contrast Wright's Jamaica Code provisions where unlawful act manslaughter was expressly restricted to 'unlawful harm' causing 'any bodily hurt, disease or disorder, whether permanent or temporary' (ss 102 and 103).

[179] (1883) 15 Cox 163, 165.

Kenny construed these observations as requiring in unlawful act manslaughter at least torts likely to cause harm.[180] But it is curious that having made plain his dislike of *Fenton*, Field J. made no recourse to the authority found in *Foster* and *East* to limit the scope of unlawful act manslaughter.

The second noteworthy feature of *Franklin* is Field J.'s broad doctrinal criticism of unlawful act manslaughter as a manifestation of constructive crime by implicitly suggesting that the generally preferable course in involuntary manslaughter was a negligence-based prosecution. Of course, limiting unlawful act manslaughter to those acts carrying a risk of bodily harm would almost inevitably coincide in outcome with the cases where negligence as to harm existed, thereby rendering redundant the distinct category of unlawful act manslaughter. However, doubts in *Franklin* of the continued doctrinal propriety of constructive fault liability proved aberrational, for no further clear judicial qualms over the legitimacy or scope of unlawful act manslaughter were reported until the 1940s.[181] Indeed, *Fenton* was reaffirmed by the Court for Crown Cases Reserved in the 1899 case of *Senior*, where death had resulted from the misdemeanour of wilful child neglect.[182] Greater judicial willingness over a similar period to rein in the scope of felony-murder, the other significant manifestation of constructive fault, can probably be at least partly accounted for by the punishment provisions governing the two offences: felony-murder attracted a fixed capital sentence, whereas manslaughter convictions offered judges practically unlimited flexibility in calibrating punishment to the perceived moral culpability manifest in individual cases.

Finally, by way of a coda to the development of unlawful act manslaughter, the particular historical position of prize fighting warrants some specific comments. Organized prize fighting enjoyed enormous and widespread popularity as a spectator sport in the eighteenth and nineteenth centuries. As occasions for gambling, excessive public consumption of alcohol and the congregating of frequently large and unruly crowds, such events were regarded with considerable

---

[180] (1904), 120. An alternative would be that the tort of trespass to the box was not in itself an act sufficiently causally related to the death, as in *Fenton*. In some respects this would often amount to Kenny's construction, but not always. For example, if in the process of taking the box it had toppled into the sea and struck the swimmer, the causal connection would probably have been sufficient, yet the tort was not dangerous in itself. Cf. Stephen's *Digest* (1883), Art. 223 and 6th edn, 1904, Art. 244 which cited *Fenton* but not *Franklin*. *Archbold* (1910), 892, makes no clear categorical distinction between unlawful and gross negligence manslaughter. See also R. Buxton (1966) 82 *LQR* 174.

[181] Unlawful act manslaughter was limited to unlawful and dangerous acts 'likely to injure another' by *Larkin* [1943] 1 All ER 217 and *Jarmain* (1945) 2 All ER 613.

[182] (1899) 1 QB 283. Though not in the nature of an assault, the neglect carried an inherent risk to health.

disapproval along with some nervousness by the authorities.[183] Broadly, death caused by prize fighting qualified as unlawful act or constructive manslaughter.[184] But, in common with duelling, the prevailing social and cultural ambiguity towards illegal prize fights ensured that the law's enforcement at all stages was often less than unrestrained and wholehearted.

Nevertheless, for a while, the law's strict formal censure even extended to prosecuting for manslaughter all who attended prize fights where one pugilist had died as a result of injuries sustained.[185] However, later in the nineteenth century, in line with complicity law developments, *Coney* ruled mere presence at a prize fight to be insufficient to convict non-participating parties. *Coney*[186] also affirmed both the potential public disorder element of prize fighting, along with the crucial distinction between illegal prize fighting and lawful boxing. Here, the Court for Crown Cases Reserved held that the harm inflicted in the former could not be consented to, unlike that caused by lawful boxers observing 'Queensberry Rules', established by the 1870s and devised (through the wearing of gloves and limiting the duration of fights) to lessen the risks of serious harm.

Of course, legitimate but dangerous sports, including boxing, predictably occasionally produced serious injury and death without attracting criminal responsibility, unless inflicted in breach of the rules of the game.[187] Indeed, beyond the public disorder rationale, the only regulator of immunity from criminal liability for sporting injury or death was (and is) public taste or distaste.[188] In the particular case of boxing, inflicting at least moderate, incapacitating, harm

---

[183] In *East*'s words, prize-fights were unlawful because they were 'exhibited for the sake of lucre and are calculated to draw together a number of idle disorderly people, [and] such meetings have a strong tendency in their nature to a breach of the peace [and] seldom ending without bloodshed' (1 PC, 270). Such socially deleterious, criminal activity was also contrasted with lawful 'sports and exercises as tend to give strength...and skill in the use of arms, and are entered into as private recreations amongst friends'; parties killed in these circumstances would (subject to the law of negligent manslaughter) be deemed to have been killed by 'misadventure', *Foster*, 259–60. Foster thought these sports to be legal because 'bodily harm is not the motive on either side'. For the law of prize-fighting's social context, see D. Brailsford, *Bareknuckles: A Social History of Prizefighting* (Cambridge, 1988).

[184] *Ward's Case* (1789) 1 East 270. Under the 1853/4 Criminal Law Amendment Bill, killing in a contest without 'deadly weapons' was manslaughter (section LXIX), as was killing in the course of 'amicable contests' with any 'weapon, instrument or means which cannot be used without probability of causing grievous bodily harm' (section LXXIV).

[185] *Hargrave* (1831) 2 Car. & P. 234 and *Murphy* (1833) 6 Car. & P. 103.

[186] *Coney* (1882) 8 QBD 534. See also the legal effects of consent in 'General Principles', Ch. VII, above.

[187] *Young* (1866) 10 Cox 371; *Orton* (1878) 39 LT 293; *Bradshaw* (1878) 14 Cox 83. Manslaughter by gross negligence might also arise, see below.

[188] As Stephen observed in respect of the presumed legality of publicly performed dangerous acrobatics: 'To collect a large number of people to see a man put his life in jeopardy is a less coarse and boisterous proceeding than a prizefight, but is it less immoral?' (*Digest* (1883), 143n).

was always a recognized route to victory. Here the actual intentional infliction of injury, not just the risk of it, was accepted as lawful. Its lawfulness prevented (and still prevents) any consequential death leading to homicide or lesser charges.[189]

Manslaughter through negligence

At the beginning of the nineteenth century, *East* summarized the 'general principles [of] homicide from impropriety, negligence or accident' in the following terms:

The boundaries between impropriety, negligence and mere accident, are often scarcely perceptible, but as the difference between them leads to different conclusions as to the degree of offence, I shall chiefly confine myself under this head to point out the distinction; premising as a leading principle, that where a man, *doing a lawful act without intention of bodily harm to any person, and using proper caution to prevent danger,* unfortunately happens to kill another, such act amounts only to homicide by misadventure. The act must be lawful; for it to be unlawful, the case will be either murder or manslaughter,... It must not be done with intention of great bodily harm; for then the legality of the act, considered abstractedly, would be no more than a mere cloak or pretence, and consequently would avail nothing. The act must also be done in a proper manner, and with due caution to prevent danger.[190]

In attempting to expound the notion of manslaughter based on criminal negligence, by far the most troubling and revealing cases were those concerning medical treatment that had contributed to causing the patient's death. On 'administering medicine' *East* notes:

If one who is no regular physician or surgeon administer medicine, or perform an operation, which contrary to expectation kills the patient, it was formerly holden manslaughter. But Lord Hale denies this very properly: it is rather misadventure. Though this doubt should make ignorant people cautious how they tamper in these matters.[191]

As case law demonstrates, the judiciary were very conscious of the social desirability of giving no licence to conduct medical procedures often little short of butchery. Yet, at the same time, they also felt disinclined to use the criminal

---

[189] Outside lawful boxing, the inflicting of fatal disabling injury to an opponent, including rendering them unconscious was potentially murder.

[190] At 1 PC, 260–1 (emphasis added).

[191] At 1 PC, 264. Surprisingly, early editions of *Russell* omit any particular reference to medical cases and fail to record those post-*East*. On the general standard for professional conduct, *Russell* (1819) ventured two propositions: 'Due caution should be observed by all persons in the discharge of the business and duties of their respective stations, lest they should proceed by means which are criminal or improper...' (664), and 'where persons employed about... their lawful occupation from whence danger may probably arise to others, neglect the ordinary cautions, it will be manslaughter at least, on account of such negligence' (768).

law to set a standard of professional competence that might prevent the semi-skilled from continuing to bring some relief to society's poor and less well-heeled. Judgments were mediated by an awareness that a balance needing striking between notions of criminal fault and social utility. Such tensions patently inhabit Lord Ellenborough's summing up in *Williamson*,[192] where a charge of manslaughter followed the death of a woman to whom the defendant acted as 'man-midwife'. Williamson, without regular education or training, 'had been in the habit of acting as a man-midwife among the lower class[193] of people'; on this occasion he had inflicted fatal injuries which, in the view of a 'number of medical witnesses', demonstrated a 'great want of anatomical knowledge'. According to Lord Ellenborough, to substantiate a charge of manslaughter the defendant:

> must have been guilty of criminal misconduct arising from the grossest ignorance or the most criminal inattention. One or other of these is necessary to make him guilty of that criminal negligence and misconduct, which is essential to make out a case of manslaughter.

The Lord Chief Justice emphasized that he found no evidence of 'inattention', rather, the defendant had become 'shocked and confused by the dangerous situation' in which he had found himself. Left to their verdict accompanied by Lord Ellenborough's severe caution that if they found the defendant guilty 'it would tend to encompass a most important and anxious profession with such dangers as would deter reflecting men from entering into it', the jury acquitted Williamson.

Similar judicial sentiments were voiced by Hullock B. in the late 1820s' decision of *Butchell*.[194] Reaching back to invoke the high authority of 'my Lord Hale...one of the greatest Judges that ever adorned the bench of this country', Hullock ruled that 'whether the party be a regular or irregular surgeon...if a person, bona fide and honestly exercising his best skill performs an operation which causes the patient's death, he is not guilty of manslaughter'. This minimalist, non-objective standard of care principle, requiring no more than the actor doing his incompetent best—or the patient takes his surgeon as he finds him—was implicitly challenged and weakened, if not completely dislodged, by a clutch of midwifery and manslaughter decisions at the beginning of the 1830s. These

[192] (1807) 3 Car. & P. 635. *Williamson* is one of the earliest authorities stressing the need in manslaughter cases for not just negligence, but (as distinct from civil negligence) 'criminal negligence' as a basis of liability.

[193] On the practice of the wealthier classes employing physicians and the less well off making do with the formally untrained practitioners, see *Report of the Select Committee on Medical Education*, 1834.

[194] (1829) 3 Car. & P. 629.

judgments reveal a marked division of judicial opinion over the appropriate-ness of setting a patient-protecting, objective standard of competence amongst medical practitioners, whether trained or not.[195]

During this period, outside the criminal courts, concern over the dangers and harm caused by unskilled medical treatment was responsible for several unsuc-cessful legislative initiatives seeking to regulate medical practices. For example, in 1818 a bill to control who might perform surgery was introduced and spon-sored by the profession itself to prevent 'ignorant and incapable persons...from practising surgery...which has caused the health of great numbers of persons [to be] much injured and the lives of many destroyed'.[196] Despite contemporary comment suggesting that the proposed legislation was motivated solely by an attempt to secure a lucrative professional monopoly, the bill went on to a second reading where more extensive debate was provoked. Again, many speakers voiced great suspicion that the bill was intended to enrich professional physicians with-out any necessary raising of competence. Indeed, considerable scepticism was dis-played by a number of Commons' members as to whether there was widespread

---

[195] Tindal CJ in *Ferguson's Case* (1830) 1 Lew. 181, leaned towards an objective standard: whether 'in the execution of that duty which the prisoner has undertaken to perform, he is proved to have shewn such a gross want of care, or such a gross and culpable want of skill, as any person undertak-ing such a charge ought not to be guilty of'.

Reasonable competence was also required in *Long* (1834) Car. & P. 398, but these two reported judicial opinions were by no means unequivocal or at one. Garrow B. *in arguendo*, nodding in the direction of *Butchell*, set the minimum standard of competence as the same for presidents of the College of Physicians or Surgeons and for the 'humblest bonesetter of the village': 'ordinary care, skill and diligence'. Yet, just what Garrow B. had in mind appears later to reduce to no more than a person performing 'as well as he can', however badly. Parke J. took a different openly public welfar-ist line. The 'public weal is deeply interested in preventing ignorant persons from acting in medical matters, and we must be careful and most anxious to prevent people from tampering with physic, so as to trifle with the life of man'. The 'question [was] whether the experience this individual acquired does not negative the supposition of any gross ignorance or criminal inattention'. Reasonable com-petence was required: 'I call it acting wickedly when a man is grossly ignorant yet affects to cure people, or when he is grossly inattentive to their safety'.

Long was convicted and fined £250, a sizeable sum for the time. Parke J. was equivocal in his view on the relevance of the availability of trained (licensed) medical assistance. When commenting on Lord Ellenborough's judgment in *Williamson*, he noted that 'it is true...about the want of surgeons in the country, does not apply here; because, in London, all persons can obtain the assistance of the best men, however poor they are'. Cf. Bayley J. in *Simpson* when referring to the liability for rendering unprofessional medical assistance observed that the defendant had 'no right to hazard the consequence in a case where professional medical assistance may be obtained'. Express judicial concern at the consequences of the actions of unskilled practitioners produced the clearest state-ment of this period on the standard of care required to avoid criminal responsibility (Bolland B. in *Spiller* (1832) 5 Car. & P. 333): 'if any person, whether he be a regular or licensed medical man or not, professes to deal with the life or health of [another], he is bound to have competent skill to perform that task that he holds himself out to perform, and he is bound to treat his patients with care, atten-tion and assiduity'.

[196] HC, Session Paper 1818 (22) 1, 77; similarly, 1816 (531) 11, 807.

harm being caused by untutored surgeons and midwives, with Peel most prominent amongst such dissentients. As with any trade or profession, rather than regulation of the type proposed in the bill, open competition instead of legal sanction was identified by free marketeers as the effective spur to achieving high professional standards.[197]

This legislative episode indicates that judicial reticence over the first three decades of the nineteenth century to impose clear and moderately demanding professional standards in medicine was no more than a reflection of a wider feeling amongst the upper classes who, naturally, were least affected by the practices of the most unskilled practitioners. Moreover, successive failures to enact such legislation could hardly have passed unnoticed by the judiciary when pondering the issue of professional criminal negligence, and probably reinforced any existing reluctance to punish incompetence.

Beyond medicine, road traffic cases, a second common form of lawful activity sometimes resulting in manslaughter charges, also came before the courts relatively frequently. Here, borrowing freely from *Foster, East* noted that:

[if a] person driving a carriage happens to kill another: if he saw or had timely notice of the mischief likely to ensue, and yet wilfully drove on it will be murder;[198] for the presumption of malice arises from the doing of a dangerous act intentionally: there is the heart regardless of social duty. If he might have seen the danger, but did not look before him, it will be manslaughter, for want of due circumspection. But if the accident happened in such a manner that no want of due care could be imputed to the driver, it will be accidental death and he will be excused.[199]

Dealing with a death caused by collision with a cart driven at an 'unusually rapid pace', Garrow B. in *Walker*[200] ruled that it was the 'duty of every man who drives

---

[197] *PD* 1818 (s. 1), 37: 396–7, 1285–9. The influence of the medical profession on legislation during this period was patchy. Cf. the widening of the abortion law in Lord Ellenborough's Act 1803 and the role of the medical profession in relation to 'Attempt', Ch. VII, above. The Royal Society of Surgeons received its charter in 1800, and the Provincial Medical and Surgical Association (the forerunner of the British Medical Association established 1855) was formed in 1832. However, the determined elimination of untrained medical practitioners did not begin until after the Medical Act 1858. For a more general discussion on the social and professional background of these issues, see J. Donnison, *Midwives and Medical Men* (1988), 54–8 and R. Porter, *Health for Sale: Quackery in England 1660–1850* (Manchester, 1989).

[198] Indeed, until the 1830s it was very common charging practice to indict for murder in fatal road traffic accidents and convict for negligence-based manslaughter. For example, in London, *West, OBSP* 17 February 1825; *Lashbrook, OBSP,* 19 May 1825; *Curtis, OBSP,* 11 May 1826; and *Stewart, OBSP,* 15 January 1828. The marked change of practice from the late 1820s could have been related to the establishment of the Metropolitan Police and their involvement in the collection of evidence.

[199] 1 PC, 263. Repeated in *Russell* (1819), i, 671 and 769.

[200] *Walker* (1824) 1 Car. & P. 320, Garrow B. refers to the position of driving in the medical case of *Long*: 'Why is it that we convict in cases of death by driving carriages? Because the parties are

any carriage, to drive it with such care and caution as to prevent, as far as in his power, any accident or injury that may occur'. A few years later in *Knight's Case*,[201] Bayley J. appeared to insist that as a matter of law, a badly positioned driver, unable to enjoy a full view of the road, was necessarily negligent and guilty of manslaughter for the consequent death. Following this, the growing sport of racing carriages on public roads produced Patteson J.'s ruling in *Timmins*;[202] that in determining whether to convict a driver of manslaughter, a jury must be satisfied that the driving was in 'such a negligent manner that, by reason of his "gross negligence", he had lost the command of his horses'. What these relatively early illustrative decisions do not clearly establish is whether 'gross negligence' indicated the failure to achieve an objectively set standard of skill or whether, as in the earlier medical manslaughter cases, simply doing one's incompetent unskilled best was sufficient to escape liability.

Whilst even in a predominately agricultural-based society the potential for negligently caused harm was never absent, the potential for fatal injuries radically increased with the progress of industrialization, urbanization, and expansion of mechanical means of transportation.[203] In the criminal arena, the common law's response to the victims of such economic and social change was principally through the medium of the law of negligent manslaughter; Parliament's response was a vast range of situation-specific offences, both with and without express fault requirements, and both with and without (in the case of endangerment offences) the requirement of harmful consequences. Additionally, the growth of broader, welfarist, or collectivist notions of reasonable social standards of conduct coincided with developing professional standards of accountability through the establishment of clearer, more extensive enforceable regulations viewed as necessary for effective professional superintendence.

Such factors had clear relevance to the criminal law's response as to what might be perceived as harm-causing, sub-standard behaviour. By the early 1830s, although the clarificatory process of just what was the substance of negligent manslaughter had begun, several fundamental features of the basis of liability were still some way from judicial recognition, let alone resolution. The most

---

bound to have skill, care and caution'. Unlike medical parties drivers were bound to have 'skill', which suggests a person driving doing his incompetent hopeless best would be criminally liable for any fatal outcome.

[201] *Knight's Case* (1828) 1 Lew 161.

[202] *Timmins* (1830) 7 Car. & P. 499. See also the similar approach in *Williamson* (1844) 1 Cox 97, concerning manslaughter through a negligently overloaded boat. For developments of tort liability in the negligent causing of harm, XII, Pt 4.

[203] *The Times* attributed a crop of acquittals of engine drivers for manslaughter in the 1840s on justified jury reluctance to convict in the face of railway companies failing to provide safe systems of work, see *The Times*, 12 January 1842, p. 4; 22 December 1845, p. 3; and 14 October 1846, p. 5.

prominent of these were: whether negligence was properly regarded as a state of mind; whether negligence entailed personally immoral action or was simply failure to meet an externally set standard of conduct; the level or degree of objective culpability required, and how this was to be described; and whether inadvertent risk-taking could be deterred by the prospect of punishment.

During the course of the century two judicial philosophies were discernible on the nature of negligence as a form of criminal fault. One line of judgments was couched in unemotive, non-moralistic terms signifying liability based on the failure to achieve a proper, objectively defined, standard of behaviour. Thus, in *Rigmaidon*[204] involving a fatally deficient method of 'slinging' wine casks, Parke B. directed the jury on the basis of whether the mode of operation was 'reasonably sufficient'. Similarly, in a mixed group of later decisions[205] judicial language focused on 'reasonable or ordinary caution', 'reasonable care', 'proper skill...and proper knowledge', and 'proper precautions'. Contrastingly, over the same period, a substantial crop of judgments appeared containing judicial allusions to the notion of negligence as a 'moral impropriety', 'felonious', an 'evil mind', 'wicked', 'recklessly negligent', and 'blameworthy condition of mind'.[206]

This absence of uniformity in judicial directions on the nature or quality of negligence was almost as prominent in the late 1800s as in the earlier decades of the century. Thus it could hardly be said that by the end of the Victorian period the essential nature of negligence had noticeably clarified in the judicial mind. But, as has been seen, contemporary commentators were also far from always consistent in this respect.[207] Neither were judicial reflections forthcoming on the psychology and social mechanisms by which punishing negligent behaviour might act as an individual or general deterrent; or, alternatively, that the immorality of harm negligently caused warranted a retributive sanction. Such an absence of an expressed judicial rationale was particularly surprising in relation to the rapidly growing incidence of road traffic and railway accidents.

Occasional judicial references to the culpable mind, whilst no doubt reinforcing the image of negligence's criminality in a jury's eyes, at the same time may well have encouraged juries to be more reticent in finding the required level of negligence to convict. On the other hand, casting the nature of criminality in the form of failure to meet the objectively set standard of behaviour appropriate

---

[204] (1833) 1 Lew. 180.

[205] *Blewitt, The Times*, 19 June 1846, p. 5; *Barrett* (1846) 2 Car. & K. 343; *Haines* (1847) 2 Car. & K. 368; *Jones* (1870) 11 Cox 544; *McCleod* (1874) 12 Cox 534; *Salmon* (1886) 6 QBD 79; *Doherty* (1887) 16 Cox 306.

[206] *Trainer* (1864) 4 F. & F. 105; *Noakes* (1866) 4 F. & F. 920; *Handley* (1874) 13 Cox 79; *Elliott* (1889) 16 Cox 79.

[207] See 'General Principles', Ch. VII, above.

to the circumstances, although in substance equally normative, may have been an easier concept for juries to grasp. Very much part of such speculation was the degree or level of the defendant's culpability: was it high enough; was the short-fall from an appropriate standard great enough, to make the behaviour prop-erly regarded as *criminal*? Whilst the courts asserted that the level of negligence had to exceed that sufficient for civil liability,[208] a linguistic formula offering the chance of uniformity of approach by juries proved elusive. Although the term 'gross' was the single most common qualifying expression over the course of the century, its use was frequently accompanied by other terms well capable of sub-merging the impact which 'gross' might have had on the jury's collective compre-hension.[209] Beyond 'gross', as already noted, the courts sometimes in describing the level of negligence resorted to epithets such as 'criminal', 'wicked', or quite often 'culpable'.[210] Clearly, negligence was (and is) the most plastic of fault con-cepts, offering substantial flexibility for both a judge effectively to raise or lower the level of necessary culpability through the tenor of his direction, and for a jury to do so by its collective view on the appropriateness of conviction.

As seen, this normative flexibility was in play over the first three decades of the nineteenth century, when many judges in formulating the notion of crimi-nal negligence displayed a marked reluctance to punish unskilled medical prac-tice resulting in a patient's death. Here directions were almost tailored to the

---

[208] For example, *Doherty* (1887), *ibid*. Some authorities spoke of disregarding for criminal pur-poses 'every little trip or mistake' (*Finney* (1874) 12 Cox 625) or 'forgetfulness which is common to everybody or slight want of skill' *Doherty* (1887). Here Stephen J. expressed the jury's highly normative role in the plainest fashion: 'Manslaughter by negligence occurs when a person is doing anything dangerous in itself, or has charge of anything dangerous in itself, and conducts himself in regard to it in such a careless manner that the jury feel that he is guilty of culpable negligence and ought to be punished'.

[209] Cf.e.g. *Spilling* (1838) 2 M. & R. 107; *Trainer* (1864), *ibid*.; *Spencer* (1867), *ibid*.; *Elliott* (1889), *ibid*.

[210] *Lee* v. *Dangar* (1892) 2 QB 350; *Longbottom* (1848) 3 Cox 439; *Dalloz* (1908) 1 Cr App R 258; *Handley* (1874), *ibid*; *Dant* (1865) L & C; *Jones* (1870), *ibid*.; *Doherty* (1887), *ibid*. The Criminal Law Commissioners' digest stipulated: '[T]he law does not require the utmost caution that can be used, but only such a reasonable degree of caution as is appropriate to the notion of the act and the prob-ability of danger in the particular case' (*Fourth Report* (1839), Art. 68). More elaborately the *Seventh Report* (1843), Arts 6 and 7. Stephen's 1872/4 Homicide Bill refers to an act 'known to be dangerous to life' (s 29). Rather than classified as manslaughter, 'killing by negligence' (s 29) was a distinct, less grave, category of homicide. (See Stephen's defence of this claim before the Bill's Select Committee, Minutes, 116 and 168. No member of the Committee clearly dissented from the view.) See also the Criminal Law Commissioners, *Second Report* (1846); *Digest*, 31, Arts 1 and 2, 'Negligent Homicide'. Wright followed this practice but made no attempt in the Draft Jamaican Code to specify man-slaughter's required level of negligence, noting elsewhere that 'the care might bear some proportion to the risk', Notes on Part I of the Draft (p. 99). Kenny's *Outlines* treatment of gross negligence con-fusingly resorts to 'wicked' and similar epithets, and in one case to 'recklessly negligent' behaviour (1904), 26–36.

defendant's capacity, only requiring that the medical assistance was carried out to the best of that particular defendant's ability. But by the end of the 1830s, a standard objective level of 'proper skill and caution' had largely achieved dominance.[211] Yet a persisting anxiety on the part of some judges to ensure that medical practitioners would suffer a criminal sanction for only the most extreme forms of botched treatment can be seen operating in later cases where instead of an open application of the earlier 'doing-the-best-you-can' standard of performance, some of the substance of this was insinuated via the language of non-objective fault. Thus, in *Noakes*,[212] Erle CJ directed that conviction required a 'degree of complete negligence as the law meant by the word "felonious"; with Willes J. in *Spencer*[213] charging the jury that to find the 'prisoner guilty, they must trace what he did to an evil mind'. However, set against these instances were the more typical examples of medical negligence directions given as the century progressed, such as that of Denman J. in *Macleod*,[214] where the personal 'some error or judgment which anybody might have committed' was sharply contrasted with failure to achieve the external, objective standard of 'proper skill, proper care, and...proper caution'.

Overall, while some limited measure of conceptual development of criminal negligence occurred during the Victorian period, there remained an absence of anything approaching a moderately full judicial articulation of the nature and function of this form of criminal culpability. Certainly, no one hazarded an overarching doctrinal account of criminal negligence as it operated in homicide, along with its broader role in the criminal justice system. Moreover, when comparing *Russell*'s exposition of negligent manslaughter in the 1843 edition with that contained in the work's 1909 edition, it is plain that the only changes are the increases in the size and number of case-based categories[215] of negligent manslaughter, with practically no conceptual cross-referencing between them. This can only be partly attributed to the work's Topsy-like growth.[216]

---

[211] See e.g. *Spilling* (1838), *ibid*.

[212] *Noakes* was a 'medical case' in the sense of the defendant being a dispensing chemist.

[213] (1867) 10 Cox 525.

[214] (1874) 12 Cox 534. In *Markuss*, a herbalist prescribed for P a cure for a cold which killed her. Willes J., directed: 'Every person who dealt with the health of others was dealing with their lives, and every person who so dealt was bound to use reasonable care, and not to be grossly negligent...gross negligence consisted in rashness, where a person was not sufficiently skilled in dealing with dangerous medicines which should be carefully used, of the properties of which he was ignorant or how to administer a proper dose' (1864) 4 F. & F. 356.

[215] The 1909 edition of *Russell* includes the following main compartmentalized categories of negligent manslaughter: 'Business', 'Vehicles', 'Mines', 'Railways', and 'Steamships'.

[216] For *Russell*'s almost complete inability to shed redundant case law and statutory commentaries, see the decidedly tart comments on the 1896 edition of the work reviewed in (1896) 12 LQR 290.

While by the early 1900s manslaughter by gross negligence had a fairly clearly established objective fault complexion,[217] little attempt had been made to indicate the necessary extent of objectively foreseeable harm. Juries were given a substantially free hand in determining the meaning of 'gross'. This conceptual latitude had limited practical impact until the introduction of other apparently objective fault-based road traffic offences. Arrival of the motoring age, along with the increasing necessity of curbing risky driving behaviour, generated the enactment of several offences requiring various distinct levels of objective forms of culpability. Only at this stage were courts compelled to confront the combined conceptual and linguistic problem of identifying different levels of criminal negligence.[218]

Particular Problems in Homicide

HUMAN IDENTITY: EACH SIDE OF THE LINE: ABORTION AND INFANTICIDE

Institutional works identified the potential victim of murder or manslaughter as 'a reasonable creature *in rerum natura*'.[219] The most significant question raised by this definition was the extent to which homicide law protected unborn children. On practical, medical, and moral grounds, the criminal law settled the division between abortion and homicide as occurring at the stage when a child was completely delivered. Refinement of this simple obstetrical jurisprudence was tackled in a substantial cluster of nineteenth-century decisions which, in the main, required that the child had an existence independent of its mother.[220]

---

[217] Including negligent omissions resulting in death; e.g. *Instan* [1893] 1 QB 450 and *Senior* [1899] 1 QB 283. Also the Children Act 1908, s 12.

[218] Notably the Court of Criminal Appeal in *Stringer* (1933) 24 Cr App R 30, and the House of Lords in *Andrews* v. *DPP* [1937] AC 576 on the provisions of the Road Traffic Act 1930. The parliamentary debates on the similar provisions of the Motor Car Act 1903 (precursor of the RTA 1930) display a mixture of confusion and indifference over the nature and quality of 'recklessness'. The general tenor of discussion strongly suggests the term to have an objective fault meaning. No attempt was made by government or other speakers to define 'recklessness' or 'negligence'. Government spokesmen in both the House of Lords and Commons alluded to 'high authorities' who understood the significance of such terms. See *PD* 1903 (s. 4), 126: 213–14 and 1457–8. Also, (s. 4), 126: 1476; (s. 4), 125: 979, 987–9, 995–8. The debates of the 1930 Road Traffic Bill reveal a similar state of affairs. Overall, the implicit assumptions of speakers appeared to have been that the offences were to be made out solely on the basis of an objective fault criterion. See *PD* 1930 (s. 5 HC), 235: 1281–2, 1316–21; (s. 5 HC), 240: 2349–52. Cf. the offence of wanton and furious driving under s 35 of the Offences Against the Person Act 1861. This, and earlier similar offences, required the causing of 'any bodily harm'. The later offences under a series of Road Traffic Acts did not, instead basing liability solely on culpable endangerment.

[219] *Coke* 3 Inst. 47. Though referring specifically to murder, the description also extends to manslaughter.

[220] Severance of the umbilical cord was unnecessary. An independent existence entailed an independent circulation and breathing after birth, *Poulton* (1835) 5 Car. & P. 329; *Brain* (1834) 6 Car. &

Pre-natal injury from which a child died after birth, could constitute murder or manslaughter,[221] depending on the defendant's level of mental culpability.[222]

Abortion or killing a child in the course of being born was, until the nineteenth century, a common law misdemeanour.[223] Driven by a combination of factors, the offence was radically modified in 1803 by Lord Ellenborough's Act.[224] Under the 1803 Act, the law punished an attempt through poisoning to procure a miscarriage, whether or not quickening could be proved.[225] Reflecting the sharpening of medico-ethical concerns, further legislation in 1828, 1837, and 1861 both de-capitalized and widened the offence to include administering poison (or other noxious substances) or unlawful use of 'any instrument or other means' with intent to procure a miscarriage.[226] Underscoring the offence's inchoate complexion, the 1861 Act expressly required proof of pregnancy only if the defendant was the woman herself; for other defendants, the full offence could be committed even where no pregnancy existed.[227]

P. 349; *Reeves* (1839) 9 Car. & P. 25. Also case law reviewed by S. Atkinson, 'Life, Birth and Live Birth' (1904) 20 *LQR* 134.

[221] Murder: e.g. *West* (1848) 2 Cox 500; manslaughter, e.g. *Senior* (1832) 1 Mood. 346. The common law never took the further step of holding mothers responsible for pre-natal gross neglect which resulted in a child's death after birth. Liability for such behaviour would have been imposed by the 1879 Code Bill Commission (s 186) if death or permanent injury were caused. See support for this by Lord Blackburn (an 1879 Commissioner) in his evidence to the 1874 Homicide Bill Select Committee. The 1879 Code Bill would have greatly simplified conviction by dispensing with the need for evidence of 'breathing or independent circulation' (s 166).

[222] However, an apparent gap in the law's coverage existed in respect of killing a child in the course of delivery before completion of birth. Though constituting abortion and a common law 'misprision', it was not covered by later legislation from 1803 onwards. Any common law liability was described as obsolete in evidence to the 1866 Royal Commission; consequently, new legislation was required (Willes J., *Evidence*, 274–6). The 1879 Code Bill incorporated a provision of 'Killing Child at Birth' (s 212). Liability for such killings, 'Child destruction', was eventually effected by the Infant Life Preservation Act 1929.

[223] *Ibid.*, 50. The common law offence required the child to have quickened.

[224] 43 Geo. III c. 58. The most likely causes of change were: the basic need to establish clearly the offence's requirements; the medical profession's criticism of quickening as an appropriate moral determinant of the limits of criminality; and the contemporary perception of abortion as a growing social danger. Keown, *Abortion*, Chs 1 and 2.

[225] However, a punishment differential existed: death for an attempt to abort after quickening, up to 14 years' transportation without proof of quickening.

[226] Offences Against the Person Act Lord Lansdowne's Act (1828), 9 Geo. IV c. 31; the Offences Against the Person Act 1837, 1 Vict. c. 85; and the Offences Against the Person Act 1861, s 58. Striking directly at acts of complicity, s 59 of the 1861 Act created a specific supplementary offence of knowingly supplying or procuring poison, noxious thing or instrument etc. For the powerful collective and individual influence of the medical profession in bringing about this legislative change, principally for foetal protection, see Keown, *op cit.*, Chs 2 and 3, *passim*.

[227] Though distinguished from homicide, abortion, even after 1861, carried a maximum of life imprisonment. The 1879 Code Bill proposed a reduction of punishment to a maximum of seven years (s 214). And cf. 'impossible' attempts, Ch. VII above.

No provision was included in the 1861 Act for lawful therapeutic abortion. However, both before and after the 1861 provisions, the legislation spoke of 'unlawfully' carrying out the proscribed actions. This element was indecisively touched upon by Bramwell B. in *Wilhelm*,[228] and more explicitly, 40 years later by Grantham J. in *Collins*,[229] confirming the legality of terminations carried out to save the mother's life.

In contrast with relative legislative neglect and common law ambivalence towards abortion, the maternal killing of young infants attracted Parliament's early intervention; so much so, that an Act of 1623 set up a presumption that a woman who concealed the death of her illegitimate child was convictable of murder unless she could establish a stillbirth.[230] The 1623 provisions' social objectives were patent from its title: 'An Act to prevent the Destroying and Murthering of Bastard Children'. However, to a large degree the Act's laudable ambitions were thwarted by its specific means; as *East* noted: the 'very severe law, has been always construed most favourably for the unfortunate object of accusation'.[231] Repeal of the 1623 legislation by Lord Ellenborough's Act placed women charged with murdering an infant in the same evidential position as for murder generally. Supplementing this charge was the creation of a new, lesser offence of concealment of the birth of an illegitimate child, punishable with up to two years' imprisonment. However, rather than an independently chargeable offence, concealment was an alternative verdict following acquittal for murder.[232] By this manoeuvre the law fudged the whole, emotionally charged question of exactly how the infant had died, contenting itself with what was regarded as a punishment route and outcome closer to public sentiment. As well as an alternative verdict at murder trials, concealment of birth became an independently chargeable offence under the Offences Against the Person Act 1861.[233] This enabled the bringing of lesser criminal charges without the trauma of a murder trial. Beside being a more humane procedure, it was also intended to circumvent the resistance to bringing charges of murder.

---

[228] (1858) 17 *Med. Times Gazette* 658 and (1898) 2 *BMJ* 122; Keown, *op cit.*, 52.

[229] Detailed judicial consideration of the legality of therapeutic abortion did not occur until *Bourne* (1939) 1 KB 687. No provision was included in the 1879 Draft Code Bill for abortion; however, in relation to the proposed new offence of 'killing [a child at birth]' (s 212) a necessity defence to preserve the mother's life was specified. On the judicial resistance to developing a general defence of necessity, see 'Duress and Necessity', Ch. VII, above.

[230] 21 Jac. 1, c. 27.

[231] 1 PC 228, similarly Blackstone, *Comms*, iv, 198.

[232] 1803 42 Geo. III c. 58, ss 1–4. Under the Offences Against the Person Act (Lord Lansdowne's Act) 1828 the possible verdict of concealment was extended to legitimate children, and proof of whether the child died 'before, at or after birth' was made unnecessary.

[233] Proposed by the Criminal Law Commissioners, *Second Report*, 1846. On the prior judicial and jury practice of acquitting of murder despite strong evidence of guilt, see *The Times*, 17 March 1845, p. 4.

The practical, moral, and intellectual discomfort generated by the criminal law's evasion of directly dealing with the peculiar circumstances of maternal infanticide was very publicly aired in the mid-1860s before the Royal Commission on Capital Punishment. A super-abundance of dissatisfaction issued from the Commission's witnesses and minutes of evidence; the sources included practising lawyers, judges, and politicians. There was near unanimity that juries would only on relatively rare occasions convict a woman of murdering her infant: '[J]udges lay down the law and point out the strength of the evidence, as they are bound to; juries wholly disregard them, and eagerly adopt the wildest suggestions which the ingenuity of counsel can furnish'. Juries would resist convicting for murder 'whilst infanticide is punished capitally'.[234] Consequently, where the circumstances permitted, prosecuting authorities avoided charging mothers with the murder of their dead infants. And where such charges were laid more often than not, they failed. As Blackburn J. observed, 'The whole sympathies of everyone seem to me against the law which treats this crime as not different from other murders'.[235] And significantly, Blackburn was not alone in implying the law's great unpopularity with judges.[236]

In purely practical terms, the problem was not the severity of outcome; for women convicted of child murder since the late 1840s invariably were the subject of Executive commutation of their capital sentence.[237] Yet while the law was universally pilloried, extensive differences emerged between Royal Commission witnesses on quite why and how the law should be refashioned. No distinct, single rationale for not treating the killing by mothers as murder existed. Some mid-nineteenth-century opinion viewed the killing of infants as less socially disturbing than the murder of an adult; others appeared to suggest the intrinsic

---

[234] Keating J., *Report*, Appendix, p. 682. However, the reluctance of juries to convict may have been exaggerated, for as the former Home Secretary, Sir George Grey, pointed out, murder convictions for infanticide regularly occurred: 'I know that it is stated there are very few convictions for infanticide. [But] from 1850 to 1864 [except for 1857] there have been either one or more cases [annually] and in one year there were as many as seven...', *Evidence*, 1459–64. But the national incidence of infanticide not prosecuted was considered to be far in excess of those convicted. Confirmation of Grey's claim is provided by a later confidential Home Office memorandum setting out murder/ infanticide convictions from the 1850s through to the 1880s. Details reveal prison sentences actually served for infanticide were substantial: on average, around 12 years in the 1850s and 1860s, down to around six years by the 1880s: *Home Office printed Memoranda and Reports*, N.A. H.O. 347/9, 672–5.

[235] Blackburn J., *Report*, Appendix, p. 624.

[236] See also Keating J., *Reports*, Appendix, 624–5; Willes J., *Evidence*, 2092–3; Shee J. Appendix, 628–9. On the difficulty of successfully prosecuting infanticide following the verdicts of coroners courts, through Grand Jury proceedings to trial between 1839 and the 1900s, see A. Higginbotham, 'Sin of the Age: Infanticide and Illegitimacy in Victorian London', in K. Garrigan (ed.), *Victorian Scandals* (Athens, Ohio, 1992), 257.

[237] Grey, *Minutes*, 1470. The last conviction resulting in hanging was *Smith* (1849). The practice had been emphatically attacked in 1842 by *The Times*, 6 August, p. 6.

worth of a child to be less than an adult; for some a lower level of mental culpability could be ascribed to mothers because of their often severely deprived
circumstances and the desperation of their motivation for killing—avoiding the
shame and social stigma attached to an illegitimate birth.[238] Yet while not alone
in arguing for a specific offence covering child murder, Stephen was the only
Commission witness who expressly constructed a link between liability, mental
disturbance, and impairment:

[The] operation of the criminal law presupposes in the mind... a normal state of strength,
reflective power, and so on, but a woman just after childbirth is so upset, and is in such an
hysterical state altogether, that it seems to me you cannot deal with her in the same manner as if she was in a regular and proper state of health... [W]omen in that condition do
get the strongest symptoms as what amounts almost to temporary madness, and... they
often hardly know what they are about, and will do things which they have no settled or
deliberate intention whatever of doing.

Because such effects could last 'for a considerable time', Stephen argued against
any specific time limit on the defence's availability, favouring 'a little indefin-
iteness in the law [rather] than run the risk of an encounter between a law and
a public sentiment; moreover, [society] must legislate for human nature as [it]
finds it'.[239]

In the face of such diverse opinion, the Commission proposed enactment of
a new offence of 'unlawfully and maliciously to inflict grievous bodily harm or
serious injury upon a child during birth or within seven days afterwards, in case
such a child has subsequently died'.[240] Over the following decade[241] a cluster of
homicide bills incorporating both similar and different provisions, failed largely
through insufficient parliamentary time, lack of government commitment, or
principled opposition. This last ground accounted for the fate of Stephen's 1872–4
bill, by far the most significant attempt to remodel the law of homicide, including

---

[238] See *Report, Evidence*, 'Summary of Evidence', xxiii–xxvii. On the mixed wider public view of
infanticide, see G. Behlmer, 'Deadly Motherhood: Infanticide and Medical Opinion in Mid-Victorian
England' (1979) 34 *Journal History of Med.* 403; L. Rose, *Massacre of the Innocents: Infanticide in Great
Britain 1800–1939* (1986), *passim*; C. Quinn, 'Images and Impulses: Representations of Puerperal
Insanity and Infanticide in Late Victorian England', in M. Jackson (ed.), *Infanticide: Historical
Perspectives* (Aldershot, 2002), 193.

[239] *Evidence*, 2193. For the wider issue of volitional impairment as a form of insanity, see 'Insanity',
Ch. VII, above. For contemporary specialist medical knowledge on post-natal 'insanity' and previous
occasional adduction of such evidence to support insanity pleas, see Smith, *Trial By Medicine*, 150–60.
Introduction of anaesthesia and antisepsis in the final decades of the nineteenth century may have
facilitated an increase in abortions and consequential decline in infanticide. R. Sauer 'Infanticide and
Abortion in Nineteenth Century Britain' (1978) 32 *Population Studies* 81. For a contemporary assessment, see W. Ryan, *Infanticide: Its Law, Prevalence, Prevention and History* (1862).

[240] *Report*, 1.

[241] See Davies, 'Child-Killing', 271.

that relating to infanticide. Under the 1872 version, the offence remained murder, but with a discretion to sentence for a minimum of five years' penal servitude. More radically, the 1874 bill changed the infanticide to manslaughter. Conceptual innovation lay in both proposals identifying the defendant as being 'deprived of the power of self-control by any disease or state of mind or being produced by bearing the child whose death is caused'.[242] As previously seen, the Commons' Select Committee recommended that the bill should not be proceeded with on the grounds of it constituting a substantial reform of homicide law, rather than a mere codification measure.[243]

Unsurprisingly, Stephen's 1878 Draft Code incorporated a similar infanticide provision to that of the 1874 bill; but, like the 1878 Code provisions on impulsive insanity, the Code Bill Commission excised the novel infanticide offence. Whilst agreeing that the law's 'severity defeats itself, and offences which are really cases of child murder are often treated as...concealment', the Commission, without offering any real explanation, simply noted that 'on the whole we have preferred' creating offences of 'neglecting to obtain assistance in childbirth'.[244] As on previous occasions, the proposed offences sought to circumvent the anticipated resistance of juries and evidential difficulties of proving the elements of murder, by offering the possibility of conviction and punishment for a lower level of criminality.

Social and political attitudes manifested in the broad welfarist legislation, enacted increasingly from the 1880s,[245] provided the background of the Children Bill 1908. Here, Committee proceedings witnessed an attempt by Loreburn LC to add a provision giving judges complete sentencing discretion on the conviction of a woman for murder of her child under one year old. As the Lord Chancellor

---

[242] 1874 bill, s 27(3). The 1872 bill provision referred to deprivation of the mother's 'ordinary powers of self-control by the physical effects of birth'. Others separately sponsored Infanticide Law Amendment Bills of 1873 and 1874, did not involve defective self-control as the basis of mitigating liability, PP 1873 (42), ii, 163, 167; PP 1874 (200), ii, 407, 411.

[243] In his evidence to the Select Committee, Bramwell endorsed the proposed infanticide reforms as 'excellent' (Minutes, 207); Blackburn did not favour Stephen's approach, suggesting the method later taken up by the 1879 Code Commission (below, Minutes, 236).

[244] Sections 185 and 186. The former, punishable with penal servitude for life, required causing the child's death through neglect 'to provide reasonable assistance in her delivery' with intent that the child died; the latter, punishable with seven years' penal servitude required similar neglect but with intent to conceal the birth. Both offences specified death of the child 'just before, or during, or shortly after birth'. Wright's 1877 Draft Jamaican Code (s 121) overseen by Stephen, contained provisions similar to that in Stephen's 1878 Code on infanticide.

[245] The national scandal of the 'baby farming' of illegitimate children, frequently resulting in death by neglect, was exposed by the Select Committee on the Protection of Infant Life. Regulation of child carers followed with the ineffective Infant Life Preservation Act 1872. See 'Omissions' below. More generally on the social and political context of child welfare legislation, see G. Behlmer, *Friends of the Family, The English Home and Its Guardians, 1850–1940* (Stanford, 1998) and H. Hendrick, *Child Welfare, England 1872–1989* (1994).

maintained, such an amendment would avoid the judicial 'mockery' of a formal death sentence routinely commuted by Executive clemency.[246] Successful opposition led by Lord Alverstone CJ sprang from the belief that sentencing flexibility and assessment of the immorality of each case of child murder should effectively remain with the Home Secretary;[247] the law itself should emphatically underline the gravity of child killing. Characterizing such judicial humility as 'curious', Lord Loreburn acidly suggested that it would 'become the [Lord Chief Justice] better than his ermine [to accept] not only... the power of punishing but also the power of mercy'. However, in the Lords' Debates the Lord Chief Justice was manoeuvred into producing his own thin reform proposals which initially related to restoration of judicial discretion (lost in 1861) to record, rather than pass a death sentence in cases of child murder.[248] Such a measure aimed both to avoid the convicted defendant's trauma and the unreality of a sentence judicially known as practically certain to be commuted. But as a consequence of a successful and very substantial amendment moved by the former Attorney-General Lord James, the bill's substance was transformed; as modified it sought to establish a partial defence, whereby a trial judge might direct the jury that they could acquit of murder and convict of manslaughter where the defendant mother killed her infant while not fully recovered from the effects of childbirth.[249] Despite successfully navigating the Lords and reaching the Commons, the bill was lost, apparently through effluxion of parliamentary time.[250]

Modification of the infanticide laws was finally effected in the post-War era, with the Infanticide Act 1922. In large measure the work of Lord Chancellor Birkenhead,[251] the Act created an alternative verdict of infanticide to a murder

---

[246] PD 1908 (s. 4), 195: 1178. Some judges were prepared to tell a convicted defendant that the formal sentence of death would be automatically commuted. For example, G. Pollock, Mr Justice McCardie (1934), 162.

[247] PD 1909 (s. 4), 196: 458. He thought a relaxation of the law would diminish deterrence of child murder (486).

[248] Child Murder (Record of Sentence of Death) Bill, PD 1909 (s. 5 HL), 1: 963, 721.

[249] PD 1909 (s. 5 HL), 1: 957–65; (s. 5 HL), 2: 68, 144, 158.

[250] Earlier in 1909 (a month prior to Lord Alverstone's) an Infant Life Preservation Bill had been introduced in the Commons (PD 1909, (s. 5 HL), 3: 496).

[251] The previous bill, introduced with the Home Secretary's encouragement by the leading Labour MP, Arthur Henderson, would have allowed juries to convict of manslaughter rather than murder in cases where the defendant had not recovered from the effects of childbirth at the time of killing. With a single exception (PD 1922 (s. 5 HC), 155: 2485) there was no Commons' opposition. Lord Chancellor Birkenhead's intervention on the bill's second reading turned on its 'lack... in precision' (PD 1822 (s. 5 HL), 50: 440) relating both to the period after birth to which the provision applied, and to the relationship between the 'nature of the ailment' and 'deflected... will' (441). He and others were anxious that normal levels of emotional upheaval experienced at childbirth should not be a sufficient basis for limiting liability (e.g. 765). The provisions eventually constituting the Infanticide Act were moved by Lord Birkenhead at the Lords' Committee stage (758), which created an offence of infanticide rather than one of manslaughter.

charge where a 'newly born' child was intentionally killed by its mother when, as a consequence of childbirth, the 'balance of her mind was then disturbed'. Punishable as manslaughter, an infanticide conviction gave judges complete sentencing discretion. Though later requiring statutory amendment after Lord Hewart CJ's judgment in O'Donoghue[252] (which narrowed the provision's relevance to a child of less than 35 days), the Infanticide Act 1922 represented a considerable conceptual innovation in relation to the effects of volitional impairment on criminal responsibility, albeit in the narrower, self-defining context of childbirth. But the Act did not simply abandon the cognitive requirements of the M'Naghten Rules, or even any presence of volitional defect; it went further by not requiring any demonstrable causal relationship between the homicidal intent and the 'disturbed…balance of [the defendant's] mind'. In broadness of approach the defence resembled proposals later advanced in the Medico-Psychological Association's evidence to the Atkin Committee, making insanity and irresponsibility coextensive; though, unlike the 1922 Act, the Association required that the 'crime was…related to [the] mental disorder'.[253] And most significantly, the Act more or less permitted juries to mitigate responsibility for the killing of infants on grounds long employed by the Home Secretary: it facilitated a coincidence of law and public sentiment, substantially ending a state of affairs where the 'law…was really worse than a farce'.[254]

CAUSATION

In the overwhelming majority of homicides, the most immediate and legal cause of death will be indisputable. However, occasionally, more than one operative cause has patently brought about the criminal harm, thereby generating the need for rules to discriminate between purely factual and legal cause where the law specifies a particular result. Although not exclusive to homicide, because of its particular nature, historically it has been within homicide where most criminal law disputes over causation have arisen. The dearth of earlier authorities provided nineteenth-century courts with considerable scope in respect of the policies which might be adopted, formulation of specific rules, and their conceptual underpinnings. In 1836, Alfred Taylor, the medico-jurist concluded the law to be in a 'very unsettled state'.[255] However, while showing a severely limited degree of conceptual or principled articulation, in the main, judges manifested a steady

---

[252] (1927) 20 Cr App R 132. The Infanticide Act 1938 extended this period to one year. Alternative verdicts of manslaughter, guilty but insane, or concealment, remained open to juries.

[253] The Atkin Committee, set up to review several legal matters, including the insanity defence; Report [Cmnd. 2005] 1924. See Report, 29–32.

[254] Lord Parmoor, joint House of Lords sponsor of the bill, PD 1922 (s. 5 HL), 50: 438.

[255] Elements of Medical Jurisprudence (1836), 341. In his combined analysis of medical science and the legal ascription of cause, Taylor detected a broad judicial attempt to gauge causal 'moral responsibility' of defendants in manslaughter cases when determining sentence (321).

resolve to ensure that, except in the most extreme circumstances, those who culpably initiated a series of events would be held criminally responsible for any ultimate harm. Most judicial attention was directed at determining legal cause in two areas of homicide: first, where the victim's pre-existing condition, or own subsequent actions, influenced the outcome of the defendant's actions; and secondly, where intervening medical treatment given to the victim may have been a contributory, or even the sole cause of death.

Nineteenth-century case law confirmed homicide's fundamental requirement that the defendant 'hastened' or 'accelerated' death. The fact that the victim was already dying from some other pre-existing cause was immaterial if the defendant's actions 'accelerated' death.[256] More causally problematic were instances of a *novus actus*, where, *following* the defendant's infliction of harm, the victim died as a consequence of an intervening condition or third party[257] actions.[258] As the Criminal Law Commissioners observed in 1846: 'There are many nice and difficult questions as to the legal connection between an injury received and supervening death, where the original injury is, by aggravation, heightened into the cause of death…as where, by neglect or ill-treatment, the original injury turns to gangrene or produces a fever…'. Consistent with some, though not all, authority, the Commissioners argued that in these cases causal responsibility for death should remain with the 'original injury'.[259] The broad policy ground for this approach had been well articulated in *Wall* at the beginning of the nineteenth century by MacDonald LCB:

[T]here is no apology for a man if he puts another in so dangerous and hazardous situation…that some degree of unskillfulness and mistaken treatment…may possibly accelerate the fatal catastrophe. One man is not at liberty to put another in such perilous circumstances…and to make [his survival] depend upon his own prudence….[260]

---

[256] *Hale* 1 PC 428 and Lord Alverstone in *Dyson* (1908) 2 KB 454, at 457, where the victim had been suffering from meningitis before the defendant inflicted injuries. Also, e. g. *Hayward* (1908) 21 Cox 692; *Martin* (1832) 5 Car. & P. 128. *Contra*. Johnson (1827) 1 Lew. CC 164 and *Macdonald* (1844) 8 *JP* 138.

[257] The causal consequence of a 'natural' intervening event, such as tidal movements or lightning was not subject to judicial consideration. Stephen's 1872–4 Homicide Bill (s 7) appears to make causers of original harm liable for the ultimate death if they 'had reasonable ground to expect the occurrence of the intermediate events'. The 1879 Code Bill provisions did not address such a situation. For modern speculation on the existence of a 'ordinary hazard' or 'reasonable foreseeability' principle, see H. Hart and T. Honore, *Causation in the Law* (2nd edn, Oxford, 1985), 340–2.

[258] While a philosophical distinction may be drawn between causation in relation to acts and omissions, this has rarely been proposed in criminal courts or legislation. Hart and Honore, *Causation*, Ch. XIII and *passim*.

[259] *Second Report* (1846), 23, Arts 7 and 8. *Wall* (1802) 28 St. Tr. 51 and also *Holland* (1841) 2 Mood. & R. 351. According to *Hale*, 1 PC 428, the 'unruly conduct of the patient' was no ground to acquit on a homicide charge (*Rew* (1662) Kel. 26).

[260] *Wall, ibid.*, 145.

Greater dispute amongst judges and commentators was generated by situations where intervening medical treatment had demonstrably hastened death. Disagreement focused on two particular matters: whether the wound itself was potentially fatal; and the relevance of medical treatment being incorrect. Case law from the 1840s suggested that non-life endangering injuries could be causally relegated by later incompetent or negligent medical treatment, but not where competent treatment caused death.[261] This question split the Criminal Law Commissioners in 1846 soon after two relevant judgments on the matter. The majority of the Commissioners favoured regarding the effects of competent medical treatment as causally irrelevant for criminal law purposes, thereby attributing death to the original injury, whether life endangering or not. But criminal negligence, sufficient to incriminate the medical practitioner for manslaughter, would free from responsibility the party inflicting the original injury. The underlying policy was expressed in the following terms:

A person receiving an injury must be expected, by natural consequence, to avail himself of treatment for it; and although such treatment be applied with reasonable caution, and may offer the only probable means of preserving life, it may not unfrequently, in the ordinary course of events, be attended with fatal consequences. In cases of this description, the majority of your Commissioners conceive that there is such a proximate connexion between the original injury and the fatal result, as justly to render the perpetrator of the injury answerable for that result.[262]

This objective standard of 'natural consequence' or 'ordinary course of events' was not only implicit in most judgments, but also, as the Commissioners openly confirmed, the approach commonly adopted in order '*justly* to render the perpetrator...answerable...' (emphasis added). Like forms of constructive fault, here ignoring the most immediate cause of death rested on a policy of punishing eventual harm based on initial risk generation—for putting the victim in a 'hazardous situation'.

In a minority of one, Commissioner Starkie[263] favoured the more severe line of deeming an original injury of *any* severity to be the cause of death, even where medical intervention had been criminally negligent. It was a view judicially adopted later in the century where, for example, death followed the administration of chloroform during the course of an operation on a fractured jaw. Extending the reach of the endangering philosophy already embodied in case law, Mathew J. dismissed the relevance of possible medical negligence: 'For it

---

[261] *Clark and Bagg* (1842) 6 JP 508 and *Pym* (1846) 1 Cox 339. Cf. *McIntyre* (1847) 2 Cox 379.

[262] *Second Report* (1846), 23, Art. 8, n.

[263] *Ibid.*, p. 53. It is unclear whether Starkie adopted this view on practical grounds, because of the problem of 'inquiry upon the question whether the treatment had been judicious'; or whether he simply favoured a more extensive degree of causal responsibility.

would never do to have a serious injury by one man on another, and have the issue raised that death was due to want of skill on the part of medical men.'[264] Entirely consistent with the policy expressed in *Wall* at the beginning of the nineteenth century, as well as punishing the culpability of the initial endangerment, this approach sidestepped the possibly formidable problems (cogently identified by Starkie) of separating the effects of different causes and judging the competency of medical aid.

A further area of development of causal principle, though practically of far lesser consequence than medical intervention, related to the recognition of 'death occasioned by any influence on the mind'. Until the 1870s' decision in *Towers*, Hale's account had represented the law:

If any man either by working upon the fancy of another, or possibly by harsh or unkind usage, puts another into such a passion of grief or fear that the party either dies suddenly, or contracts some disease whereof he dies, though, as the circumstances of the case may be, this may be murder or manslaughter in the sight of God, yet *in foro humano* it cannot come under the judgment of felony, because no external act of violence was offered whereof the common law can take notice.[265]

Doubtless, primitive pre-nineteenth-century medical knowledge would have caused serious difficulties of proof in ascribing death to non-corporeal harm. Furthermore, fears of malicious prosecutions, especially those alleging the fatal use of witchcraft,[266] were potent reasons for adopting Hale's position. They were certainly sufficient to persuade the Criminal Law Commissioners not to propose the law's modification.[267]

---

[264] *Davis* (1883) 15 Cox 174. Supported by Field J. Each of the causation provisions of three draft codes from the 1870s was less severe. Stephen's 1872–4 Homicide Bill (s 10) excluded from causal responsibility original harm where intervening acts would constitute some form of homicide. Earlier provisions based causal ascription on an objective reasonable foresight standard. The 1879 Code Bill (s 173) differed in that causal responsibility for an injury of a 'dangerous nature' would not be erased by intervening 'improper treatment'. Neither provision attracted an explanatory comment. Wright's Jamaican Code (s 12) rather awkwardly employed a reasonable foresight test, whereby any intervening act had the ability to block responsibility for earlier actions. Uniquely, Wright also incorporated an additional filtering test aimed at eliminating unjust outcomes by giving juries the role of deciding 'whether an event is fairly and reasonably to be ascribed to a person's act as having been caused thereby' (s 12(v)).

[265] 1 PC 429; similarly *East*, 1 PC, 225. Affirmed by Byles J. in *Murton* (1862) 3 F. & F. 492.

[266] See the *Criminal Law Commissioners, Second Report* (1846) 22 n. 'd', and Stephen, *Digest* (1877), 142, n.

[267] *Second Report* (1846), 22 n. However, the Commissioners conceded 'great weight' in the reasoning urged by the Indian Law Commissioners in support of their adoption of a different course, accepting the possibility of a non-physical cause of homicide.

But by the 1870s, after his Indian interlude, Stephen was ready to characterize Hale's general position as a 'bad rule founded on ignorance now dispelled'.[268] Partly borrowing from the Indian Law Commissioners,[269] he argued:

Suppose a man were intentionally killed by being kept awake till the nervous irritation of the sleeplessness killed him, might not this be murder? Suppose a man kills a sick person intentionally by making a loud noise when sleep gives him a chance of life; or suppose knowing that a man has aneurism of the heart, his heir rushes into his room and roars in his ear, 'Your wife is dead!' intending to kill and killing him, why are not these acts murder? They are no more 'secret things belonging to God' than the operation of arsenic.

Appearing three years before the publication of these views and representing the first reported inroad into the old rule, *Towers* had confirmed the possibility of a manslaughter conviction for the death of a young child from convulsions brought on by the defendant's frightening actions. Directing the jury, Denman J. distinguished 'mere intimidation, causing a person to die from fright by working upon his fancy, [which] was not murder' from this behaviour towards a 'child of such tender years'.[270] Building on this, the 1879 Code Bill Commission proposed an extension of the law's reach to 'a child or sick person'.[271] Thirty years on, in *Hayward*, what remained of Hale's proposition was effectively excised from English law. Here, the proposal Stephen had advanced in the 1870s was more or less accepted by Ridley J., who ruled that death from 'fright alone, caused by an illegal act, such as threats of violence, would be sufficient'[272] as a causal basis for homicide.

In relation to criminal causation, *Hayward* typified the Victorian period. Overall, almost without exception, the defining characteristic of nineteenth-century developments of causal attribution in criminal cases was one of steady expansion: initial culpable behaviour endangering another which eventuated in fatal harm would, in all but the most exceptional situations, be traced back to the initial culpable actor. While rarely articulated as such, the principal regulator on causal ascription was objective foreseeability, sometimes characterized as the

---

[268] *Digest* (1877), 162 n.

[269] Reproduced in the *Criminal Law Commissioners, Second Report* (1846), 22 n.

[270] (1874) 12 Cox 530, at 533.

[271] Section 170.

[272] (1908) 21 Cox 692. The victim suffered from a 'persistent thymus gland', making her vulnerable to 'any combination of physical exertion and fright…'. This weakened state was not deemed relevant to liability. See also the less causally challenging question of death resulting from harm caused to the victim fleeing from threats. *Pitts* (1842) Car. & M. 284; *Halliday* (1889) 61 LT 701; *Curley* (1909) 2 Cr App R 96, which confirmed causal responsibility of the party generating an 'immediate sense of danger'. Both *Pitts* and *Curley* identified the requirement of a 'well grounded fear'. Cf. *Monks* (1870) CCSP vol. 72, 428 where the response to negligently produced danger had to be that of a 'firm-minded and courageous man'.

'probable' or 'natural' course of events. But even this requirement was not consistently applied, as seen in relation to the causal effects of a victim's irrational
or 'imprudent' behaviour. Though not expressly judicially identified, a normative notion of 'fair…and reasonable…' ascription, to borrow from R. S. Wright,
was an important overall operating aim. On the one side, increasingly sophisticated medical knowledge and techniques clearly offered judicial opportunities
for a more discriminating approach to causal ascription. Yet, if anything, with
the progression of the nineteenth century came a greater judicial resistance to
denying causal responsibility to an originator of criminal harm. While implicitly
incorporating objective notions of fault in some elements of causal attribution,
rather than through causation, both the judiciary and commentators looked
to the relative refinement of *mens rea* requirements or those of a defence as the
essential legal determinant of liability.

OMISSION

Criminal responsibility flowing from omission was recognized long before
Victorian times,[273] with the legal nexus between an omission and harm—generating criminal responsibility identified as a duty to act. Until the late nineteenth
century the courts, in common with the broader social and legislative climate,
were exceedingly restrictive in their willingness to confirm and enlarge the
range of such duty situations. Early nineteenth-century majority judicial opinion
accepted that an incriminating duty might arise either as a matter of common
law[274] or by virtue of a contract to maintain another individual.[275] However,

---

[273] e.g. *Huggins* (1730) 2 Ld. Raym. 1574 and the apprentice case of *Self* (1776) 1 Leach 136. For
'causing' by omission, see 'Causation' above.

[274] Blackstone, *Comms*, 1, Ch. 16, 'Parent and Child'. In respect of legitimate children, Blackstone
refers to the 'duty of parents to provide for the maintenance of their children (446); it was also
'a principle of law' enforceable by parish authorities to a statutory standard and by Quarter Sessions
procedures set out in Elizabethan legislation (448), 1601 43 Eliz. 1, c. 2; subsequently, 1718 5 Geo. 1
c. 8. Also 1848 11 & 12 Vict. c. 43 and the Poor Relief Amendment Act 1868, 31 & 32 Vict. c. 122, s 37,
'wilful' parental neglect to provide 'adequate food, clothing, medical aid or lodging' for a child in
their custody under 14 years, punishable with a maximum of six months' imprisonment. Parents of
illegitimate children also owed a similar duty, enforceable by special proceedings under this legislation (457). Like children, liability for causing harm by neglect of wives required proof of dependency.
See the equivocal case of *Patmore* (1789) *OBSP* February, 214, cited by *East*, 1 PC, 226; also *Bonnyman*
(1940–2) 28 Cr App R 131.

[275] *Friend* (1802) R. & R. 20. 'The general opinion was, that it was…a misdemeanour to refuse or
neglect to provide sufficient food, bedding etc., to any infant of tender years, unable to provide for
and take care of itself (whether such infant were child, apprentice, or servant), whom a man was
obliged by duty or contract to provide for, so as thereby to injure its health…'. . Followed in *Ridley*
(1811) 2 Camp. 649, where Lawrence J. required proof of 'tender years, and under the dominion of the
defendant'. *Smith* (1826) 2 Car. & P. 449, denied the existence of a duty to care for an 'idiot' brother
purely on the grounds of a sibling relationship.

duty alone was insufficient in that a high degree of dependency of the victim on the defendant had to be demonstrated before criminal responsibility could potentially follow; 'dependency' amounted to a victim being 'helpless', incapable of seeking aid for themselves.[276] This requirement applied to all duties, even parental ones. Thus, for example, a mother's deliberate failure to provide for a midwife to attend her 18-year-old pregnant daughter's labour was considered not to constitute a criminal omission. Quashing the mother's conviction for manslaughter, one member of the Court for Crown Cases Reserved observed that while 'No doubt, morally speaking…guilty of a shocking crime [the duty was] not…a legal one'[277] because the daughter was by then 'entirely emancipated'[278] from any parental responsibility.

Rather than springing from direct personal relationships and duties between individuals, whether common law or contractually based, enlargement of potential liability for omission originated in areas of organizational contracts of employment; here the victim might be completely unknown to the defendant. Most especially, in industrial and railway contexts, where particular company employees were immediately responsible for performing roles aimed at ensuring the safety of many others, a cluster of judgments recognized criminal responsibility for injury or death caused by an employee's omission.[279] Possible judicial scruples over the strict limits of contractual obligations arising through privacy rules blocking criminal responsibility for omissions, never seriously materialized. No doubt, in relation to industrial and national communications needs, the judiciary regarded the threat of criminal responsibility for harm generating breaches of contract as a practical operating necessity. Moreover, the whole notion of true personal dependency was patently inappropriate to harm or death

---

[276] e.g. *Smith* (1865) 1 L & C 607. In respect of a servant, 'a state of body and mind as to be helpless and unable to take care of herself, or that she was so under the dominion and restraint of her mistress as to be unable to withdraw herself from her control', Erle CJ (1543). Under 'An Act for the Better Protection of…Apprentices or Servants' (1851, 14 & 15 Vict. c. 11) it was an offence, subject to a maximum punishment of three years' imprisonment, for employers 'wilfully' to neglect to provide 'necessary food, clothing or lodging'. Though containing no dependency requirement, the Act's preamble refers to servants or apprentices being 'in care and control'. No explicit reference was made to these provisions in the Court for Crown Cases Reserved's deliberations. See also 'Causation' above.

[277] *Shepherd* (1862) 9 Cox 123, Williams J. at 127.

[278] Erle CJ, at 126. And see generally, Pt 4, below.

[279] e.g. the manslaughter conviction of a railway signalman in *Pargeter* (1848) 3 Cox 191; the manslaughter conviction of a mining company 'ground bailiff' responsible for a mine's ventilation in *Haines* (1847) 2 Car. & K. 368. In the reserved case of *Hughes* (1857) 7 Cox 301, Lord Campbell CJ, when confirming that an omission to perform a duty could found a homicide conviction of a construction worker, linked the general proposition of omission-based liability, including that of a parent. Cf. e.g. *Allen* (1835) 7 Car. & P. 153. And see workmen compensation developments in 'Law and Political Economy', XI, Pt 1 and XII, Pt 4.

caused by a sudden or single event rather than as in the typical child, apprentice, or servant examples where harm was a consequence of sustained neglect.

A conceptually more significant expansion of omission liability came about with recognition of non-contractual assumptions of responsibility. An early straw in the wind were the observations in *Marriott*, a late 1830s' case involving the killing of an aged, infirm, and dependent woman through wholesale neglect. Here Patteson J., while feeling obliged to lace his direction with contractual allusions, premised possible liability on a wider basis:

[I]t will be for you [the jury] to say, whether from the way in which the prisoner treated [the deceased] he had not by way of contract, in some way or other taken upon him performance of that duty which she, from age and infirmity, was incapable of doing. [There is] evidence on which you are called on to infer that the prisoner undertook to provide the deceased with necessaries.[280]

More than three decades on, in the manslaughter trial of *Nicholls*, where a grandmother had voluntarily taken on the care of her young illegitimate grandchild, the jury was directed that:

If a…person chooses to undertake the charge of a human creature helpless either from infancy, simplicity, lunacy, or other infirmity, he is bound to execute that charge without (at all events) *wicked* negligence; and if a person who has chosen to take charge of a helpless creature lets it die by wicked negligence, that person is guilty of manslaughter (original emphasis).[281]

Quite what would be regarded as such an undertaking remained uncertain beyond Victorian times; most especially, just what behaviour might imply an assumption of *care* of a helpless person as distinct from *control*? The 1879 Code Commission went beyond contenting itself with identifying specific instances of legal duties whose omission to discharge might generate homicide liability; it proposed both particular and general innovations which would have provided future courts with a broader, non-contractual basis for liability. Though not cited, the conceptual breadth of *Nicholls* was represented in two separate provisions. Moreover, criminal responsibility for endangering life or causing 'permanent injury' expressly supplemented the homicide liability identified in *Nicholls*.[282]

---

[280] (1838) 8 Car. & P. 425, 563. Marriott was convicted of manslaughter. The evidence of an agreement to look after the deceased comprised two elements: the defendant's assurance to third parties that the deceased was 'going home to live along with [the defendant] until affairs are settled, and I will make her happy and comfortable' (560); secondly, that the defendant had gained credit to pay off arrears of rent on a leasehold property on the understanding 'to keep [the deceased] comfortable as long as she lived' (562).

[281] Brett J. (1874) 13 Cox 75. It is arguable whether in the earlier case of *Smith* (1865) the defendant had clearly 'undertake[n] the charge' of his 'idiot' brother.

[282] Sections 159 ('Duty to Provide the Necessaries of Life') and 164 ('Duty to Avoid Omissions Dangerous to Life') had wide potential. Section 159 refers to people who are in the 'charge' of another

A decade after the Code's demise, the Court for Crown Cases Reserved judgment in *Instan* provided equivocal guidance on the key question of when a duty might be deemed to have been assumed. Here the defendant took up residence with her aunt, who maintained both of them. On the aunt becoming ill and bedridden, the defendant failed to provide sustenance and seek medical assistance. Reviewing a conviction for manslaughter, Lord Coleridge CJ spoke fulsomely of a 'legal common law duty...founded on a moral obligation'; and while there was 'no case directly in point...it would be a slur upon and a discredit to the administration of justice in this country if there were any doubt as to the present case being within it'.[283] Yet elsewhere in his judgment there were distinct resonances of implied contractual liability, with the Lord Chief Justice apparently attaching significance to the aunt having paid for both her own and the niece's maintenance.[284] Edging towards clarification, early twentieth-century authority interpreted *Instan* as implying that continued co-residence and effective control following the aunt's decline into helplessness would have been a sufficient basis for liability.[285]

'whether such charge is undertaken...under any contract or is imposed...by law...or by reason of an unlawful act'. Section 164 was even wider, speaking of 'one who undertakes to do any act the omission to do which is or may be dangerous to life'. In the specific case of the duty of the 'head of the family' (s 160) responsibility was increased so as to cover a child under 16 years if remaining a 'member of [the] household' whether the child was 'helpless or not'. See also ss 223 and 224. Stephen's 1877 *Digest* (Ch. 22) states the law in a slightly more restricted form. *Nicholls'* essence is captured in Art. 213 which resembled Code bill, s 159. Unlike the 1879 bill, liability for omissions under Wright's Jamaican Code required helplessness or dependency ('by reason of...age, or physical or mental state, or by reason of control by the accused', s 107(i)) of the victim on the defendant. For a conceptual analysis of omission liability, Stephen directs the reader to the 'subject...discussed in a striking manner by Lord Macaulay' (*Digest*, 134). Stephen's own discussion in the *History* (iii, 9–11) is limited to little beyond identification of categories of 'duties which tend to the preservation of life'. Macaulay's 1830s' notes on the Indian Penal Code declare the appropriate limits of criminal sanctions generally to be 'positive harm,...leav[ing] to public opinion, and to teachers of morality and religion, the office of furnishing men with motives for doing positive good' (105). Imposing legal duties beyond the very narrow confines of family relationships raised not only practical problems of specifying the extent and circumstances of duties, it would have constituted a marked change of social philosophy, such as to 'disturb...the whole order of society' (113). Unencumbered by English law, Macaulay was doubtless expressing the contemporary unarticulated social philosophy of the English judiciary which had recently developed an approach similar to that adopted by Macaulay.

[283] [1893] 1 QB 450, at 434. *Coney* (1882) QBD 534 had confirmed the general common law stance of mere presence at the scene of the crime not of itself incriminating a bystander; nor was there any duty to interfere to prevent the commission of an offence, or provide information to law enforcement officials.

[284] *Ibid.* Note also the tenor of the questioning of counsel by Hawkins and Cave JJ at 453.

[285] *Chattaway* (1922) 17 Cr App R 7, although the Court of Criminal Appeal rested its decision on the supposed authority of *Smith* (1865), a case where the obligation preceded the decline into helplessness. See also *Hall* (1919) 14 Cr App R 58 where Lord Reading CJ affirmed the general principle in *Nicholls*.

Charting the evolution of the common law's approach to ascribing criminal responsibility to omission is a relatively pedestrian exercise; providing an historical explanation is rather more demanding. At its most basic, judicial responses, as practically always, were open to two potential formative forces: internal or doctrinal, and the external, social-political context. In the case of omissions, the pre-nineteenth-century doctrinal and conceptual legacies were sufficiently insubstantial and vague as to offer the judiciary considerable freedom in choosing and constituting the law's developmental direction. Juridical preference for a highly restrictive approach to omission-based liability was completely consistent with widespread contemporary moral and political preferences. Taking the example of young children, arguably the most powerful moral case for a finding of a duty to care, at the opening of the nineteenth-century childhood dependency and parental duties of care were conceived of as exceedingly narrow. Part of the familiar historical story of hesitant state social interventionism and broadly untrammelled economic *laissez fairism* was the grim commercial exploitation of children as immature as four or five years, working exhausting hours in physically desperate industrial conditions. Spasmodic legislative initiatives seeking to curb some of the worst manifestations of child labour were not only badly enforced well into the second half of the nineteenth century, but left extensive areas of child labour completely unrestricted.[286] Beyond this particular area, general impressions of the contemporary moral climate and social sensibilities in relation to dependency and the extent of the law's perceived functions can be gauged from the coercive severity of the revamped Poor Law provisions of the 1830s. Deaths of destitute adults and children from starvation through failure to obtain parish relief rarely provoked criminal charges.[287]

Judicial adoption of a less restrictive approach towards the construction or recognition of duties of care for criminal law purposes would have constituted a remarkable advance on the social and political mores of at least the first half of

[286] e.g. both the Parish Apprentices Act 1802, 42 Geo. III c. 73, and the Cotton Mills Act 1819, 59 Geo. III c. 66, applied only to textile mills, placing restrictions on child labour below the age of 9 and the daily hours of work to 12. Enforcement was known to be largely ineffectual and consequently regulations were frequently flouted. B. Hutchins and A. Harrison, *A History of Factory Legislation* (1936) and N. Thomas, *The Early Factory Legislation* (1951). On the emotive subject of child chimney sweeps and the poorly enforced statutory regulations (1834–75) see P. Bartrip 'State Intervention in Mid-Nineteenth Century Britain' (1983) 23 *Journal of British Studies* 67. More generally, S. Cretney *Family Law in the Twentieth Century*, Ch. 18, 'The State, Parent and Child: Before the Welfare State' (Oxford, 2003). Also, 'Law and Political Economy', XI, Pt 1.

[287] See *The Times*' scathing attack on this lack of action against the severe practices of some 'relieving officers', suggesting manslaughter charges should always be pressed, 23 December 1846, p. 4 and 1 January 1850, p. 4. Also, M. Finer and O. McGregor 'The History of the Obligation to Maintain', *Report of the Committee on One Parent Families*, PP 1974, xvi, App. 4, and 'Law and Political Economy' Ch XI, Pt. 1 and Pts 2 and 4 below.

the nineteenth century.[288] Widening the basis of criminal liability through omission by the apparent acceptance of a non-contractual assumption of a duty to act in a scattering of post-1870s' judgments, coincided with an accelerating rate of state welfare interventions. One prominent area of concern present early in this period was the appalling and widely publicized 'baby-farming' revelations. Exposure in the 1871 Report of the Select Committee on the Protection of Infant Life, rapidly led to regulatory legislation in the following year.[289] This particular scandal exploded just two years before Brett J. spoke in *Nicholls* so directly on the duty attached to undertaking charge of 'helpless creatures'. Proliferation of both campaigning charitable organizations and broad-based welfare legislation, spanning education, poor relief, industrial safety, the protection of married women and children, housing and public health etc., were collectively indicative of strengthening contemporary acceptance of the necessity of the political and social reinforcement of many moral duties. Shifts of this order in prevailing political and social philosophy might reasonably be expected to have gained some purchase on late nineteenth-century judicial attitudes (such as Lord Coleridge's in *Instan*), indicating when moral obligations should also be regarded as legal duties.

[288] As Macaulay observed: such as to 'disturb the whole order of society'; above.
[289] The Infant Life Preservation Act 1872.

Part Two

STATUTES, SOCIAL REFORM, AND CONTROL

I

Introduction: 'Legislation the Only Remedy'[1]

VICTORIAN judges accepted that certain areas of law reform should be left to Parliament. This was particularly so in the case of innovations intended to produce radical social change. New structures and objectives for the poor law, or new systems of inspectors for factories, were the sort of changes which required legislation and this division of law-making roles was understood by the judiciary, politicians, and others. When the laws had been passed by Parliament the judges might interpret them in ways which revealed approval or hostility, but they did not challenge the idea that it was for the legislature to innovate and produce the new laws. There was no hard-and-fast explicit constitutional law or convention which drew the frontier between the legislature and the judiciary in this context; it was simply accepted that in regard to the major social reforms requiring new administrative structures it was Parliament which made new law, not the judges hearing cases presented by litigants.[2]

The making of Acts designed to produce social change required going through appropriate procedures in the House of Commons and House of Lords, but in respect of the content of legislation Parliament could decide as it saw fit. Often, the words of a clause in a bill were unpredictable to contemporaries. Even co-ordinated expressions of public concern might not lead to legislation. More petitions were presented to Parliament seeking restrictions on sport and leisure activities on Sundays than on any topic other than slavery but what was done in response to regulate sport and leisure on the 'sabbath' was often limited and inconsistent.[3] Reforms in the law on charities, and changes to the procedures of the Court of Chancery, took up large amounts of parliamentary time in the

---

[1] The reference comes from T. Sutherst, *Death and Desease Behind the Counter*, (1884), 61. The author was arguing that only legislation could prevent employers of shop assistants requiring, for instance, that the latter stood for up to 17 hours in the day.

[2] See Vol. XI, Pt 2, Ch. I, Parliament, 301. More broadly, see Vol. XI. Pt. 1, ch. 2, Government and People, pp. 32–5, and Vol. XI, Pt 1, Ch. III, Sources of Law, pp. 42–4, 53–5.

[3] B. Hilton, *A Mad, Bad and Dangerous People? England 1783–1846* (Oxford, 2006), 588. For the intricate relationship between behaviour on Sundays and other areas of legislation such as Acts

1840s but they were frequently blocked or redirected by shifting coalitions of opponents. It reached the point at which Charles Dickens could create a legal world in which he suggested the substance of change would never be achieved.[4] Again, in the 1850s and 1860s, major reforms brought to an end the role of the East India Company in the government of a population which far exceeded that of the UK yet the nature of these laws was hardly predictable to contemporaries.[5] None of the participants in any of these debates was sure of the ultimate outcomes of parliamentary work. Beyond the formalities reflecting procedural requirements, there was frequent uncertainty about what would appear in the substance of an Act. Parliament had the power to make this type of law and Parliament could be unpredictable.

This unpredictability could even be seen in highly focused programmes of reform. Catherine Seville's study of copyright law in early Victorian England reveals that it is possible in this case to talk of 'major ideas' such as utility or efficiency or humanitarianism. 'Such generalisations are in some ways helpful, yet can become parodic if attention to detail is lost.'[6] She shows that in this instance the relevant detail is voluminous and relates, say, to petitions, debates in the press, individual commitments, and (most difficult to chart) general changes in the perceptions of those with a role in political life. As it happened, in respect of the events considered by Seville there were many debates in terms of principle but in the making of the law 'political reality finally swamped the theoretical discussions'.[7]

In this respect statute law stood in contrast to the common law made by the judges. Some saw the latter as unchanging. Others could see the common law as a cautious but thoughtful response on the part of the judiciary to changing circumstances. The common law offered a form of legal development which was constrained by its own rules and professional expectations. It was not expected that it would 'run ahead' of the opinions of influential citizens, and usually it did not do so.[8]

Contrast this with statute law. Just because it was less likely to be subject to the self-imposed constraints of lawyers and judges, statute law could evolve in

restricting working time in factories, see D. A. Reid 'Playing and Praying', in M. Daunton (ed.), *The Cambridge Urban History of Britain, 1840–1950* (Cambridge, 2000), iii: 745–810.

[4] *Bleak House* (1853); and see also Charities below in Ch. III, 507–17.

[5] R. J. Moore, 'Imperial India, 1858–1914', in A. Porter (ed.), *The Oxford History of the British Empire, The Nineteenth Century* (Oxford, 1999), iii: 424–5.

[6] C. Seville, *Literary Copyright Reform in Early Victorian England, The Framing of the 1842 Copyright Act* (Cambridge, 1999), 3.

[7] *Ibid.*, 215.

[8] On the relationship between common law and statute law, see fn 2 above, and Vol. XI, Pt 1, Ch. II, Government and People, pp. 6–7, 9–10, and Vol. XI, pt 1, Ch. III, Sources of Law, pp. 41–4.

unexpected ways and could even be disruptive for established legal doctrines. Acts designed to make it easier to sell and buy land could undermine the rights which established land law might give to parties with interests in the land.[9] Legislation directed at employers might force restrictions on them in respect of their employees which the employers could have avoided under the existing law of contract.[10] Bills relating to wills could seek to limit the traditional discretions of testators.[11] The content of legislation was not only more unpredictable than the development of the common law, it could also be disruptive of the common law. It is as if, taken as a whole, legislation was not 'lawyers' law'.

Some would-be reformers had long seen this intellectual freedom for statutory reform in a positive way. It was the route to major reforms in the existing law. In particular, they sought to integrate legislative proposals into broad and radical programmes of codification.[12] Instead of promiscuous parliamentary law-making or cautious developments in the common law they looked to reason. A rational approach would systematically relate new law to principles. For Bentham in particular, the effective response to the conservatism and restraints of 'Judge and Co' lay in the careful articulation of legal principles and their application to new laws and procedures. Reflecting utilitarian thought the law would be expressed in terms which would be comprehensible to literate citizens. Self-interested legislators in pursuit of short-term personal interests would lose their grip on legal change just as much as the judges.

In practice the Victorian response to the idea of codification was both intricate and uncertain. There were lively colonial and imperial experiments, for example with Indian contract law.[13] But in England the attempts were less adventurous. Towards the end of his life Jeremy Bentham had hopes of Lord Brougham as a parliamentary champion of codification. In reality this entailed looking at projects for reform in isolation and, as Michael Lobban has pointed out, Bentham soon realized the inadequacy of a piecemeal approach 'and constantly bemoaned the absence of a ministry of justice and of a board to revise statutes, which could ensure coherence and consistency'.[14] Later, in the middle of the nineteenth century, the radical lawyer and Lord Chancellor, Lord Westbury, revealed a deep personal distrust of the common law and looked for the systematic revision

---

[9] See Vol. XII, Pt 1, Ch. III, Property: Land Transactions, Settlement's and Sales, 79, 92.

[10] See employment law, Vol. XIII, Pt 3, Ch. 1, 623–5.

[11] Wills Act 1837 (7 Will. 4 and 1 Vict. c. 26), s 7.

[12] On codification, see Vol. XI, Pt 1, Ch. III, Sources of Law, pp. 55–9; and Vol. XI, pt 1, Ch. IV, Theories of Law and Government, pp. 74–90.

[13] See Vol. XI, Pt 1, Ch. VII, Empire's Law, pp. 234–45. K. J. M. Smith, *James Fitzjames Stephen: Portrait of a Victorian Rationalist* (Cambridge, 1988), 126–32, 'A Codificatory Harvest'; D. Ibbetson, *A Historical Introduction to the Law of Obligations* (Oxford, 1999), 227.

[14] M. Lobban, 'Brougham and Law Reform', (2000) *EHR* 115 at 1214.

of statutes with a view to ultimate codification.[15] Later still, at the end of the century, there were professional draftsmen of statutes some of whom, such as Sir Courtenay Ilbert, used imperial experience to bring together substantial measures of reform.[16] But all of this fell far short of codification in the sense of there being a concern for the coherence and principled expression of the law as a whole. Once again, in England a legislative measure could, as it were, be its own thing without systematic linkage to other areas of law.

The result was a form of law-making through statute which defies easy categorization. The problems this poses for historians were described in forceful terms over 40 years ago by the historian W. L. Burn who gave sustained attention to Victorian legal issues.[17] He pointed out that if an historian attaches labels to one type of legislation or another

…one is in danger of producing a travesty of events. It is almost as though one sought to assess the proportion of dark-haired or fair-haired men pouring into Victoria Station or Liverpool Street in the London rush-hour. For some purposes the assessment might be important but it could never be as important as the fact that the stations were crowded. In mid-Victorian England people had certain matters to deal with which they deemed urgent, they had certain problems to solve. These are more important than the labels which these people attached to themselves or which posterity has attached to them. Admittedly the labels are not to be ignored but they indicate the way in which particular people sought the answers to questions rather than the answers they found.[18]

It was as if there was no guide-book for what should be subject to regulation and what should be left outside its range. More recently Richard Price has emphasized this pointing out that:

…the British state stood in a delicate relationship to action in the public sphere. Parliament established the legal basis for action in society, but the institutions of civil society derived their legitimacy from the voluntarism of private individuals acting as public citizens. To take an extreme example, no powers of taxation could be assumed without parliamentary statute, but it was possible to build a hospital or other institution having a social purpose on the initiative of voluntary association alone. Many activities fell in between these two poles.[19]

Historians have seen that the way in which the use of the law was debated could also contribute to variety in the forms of intervention. 'Victorian government did involve itself in the life of its citizens in many visible and invisible ways; but such

---

[15] Bethell, Richard, first Baron Westbury, 1800–1873, 5 *ODNB* 539.

[16] Ilbert, Sir Courtnay Peregrine, 1841–1894, 29 *ODNB* 194.

[17] *The Age of Equipoise: A Study of the Mid-Victorian Generation* (New York, 1965), esp. Ch. 4.

[18] *Ibid.*, 132.

[19] R. Price, *British Society: 1680–1880, Dynamism, Containment and Change*, (Cambridge, 1999), 193.

involvement had to be justified in strictly functional and expedient terms'.[20] Each measure was often considered in the context of its own precise debates rather than by reference to any set of general principles.

Energy, chance and issues of detail could, therefore, often dominate debates about clauses for a bill. But for the Victorians they were not the whole story. Despite all of the pressures for variety some areas of legislation revealed elements of continuity. Certain sequences of Acts were self-evidently related to each other. This could arise by reason of the nature of the law itself. For example, annual measures relating to taxation revealed continuities with occasional sudden breaks as in the introduction of Estate Duty in 1894.[21]

There was also a more pervasive link between some areas of law reform than the precise example of taxing statutes might suggest. We will see that the New Poor Law 1834 reflected numerous debates some of which had taken place over decades.[22] It passed through parliament with considerable support in both Houses and offered at least the potential for future co-ordinated links with the provision of, say, medical assistance or public health. To take another example, the reforms of the mid and late 1870s in contexts such as public health, shipping, factories, and other areas of national life were 'put through' by a Conservative government. But the measures cannot be understood without reference back to earlier reforms which crossed party boundaries and were based on the ideas of governments which had contained Peel or Gladstone. Debates in this type of context might focus on the cost of new administrative structures or the respective roles of central and local government and these issues could also be linked to a large body of pre-existing legislation. It might be said that the latter could give the debates some element of continuity. It would be impossible to predict the wording of particular statutory sections in advance of drafting and debate, but it was clear that there would be legislation of some sort on, say, public health and that this might bear a relationship to reforms in certain other areas such as housing law.

At its most general, the links between the major statutes aimed at social reforms could be found in debates about public morality. To the people who introduced them, topics such as factory conditions were compelling and of central importance and legislation, with all its defects, was an integral part of the attempt to address social 'conditions'. A unifying theme underlying major statutory reforms in public health or factory life lay in the debates on 'the condition of England' which developed with such force after Thomas Carlyle had raised

[20] J. Harris, 'Society and State in Twentieth Century Britain', in F. M. L. Thompson, (ed.), *Cambridge Social History of Britain, 1750–1950* (Cambridge, 1990), 68.

[21] Finance Act 1894, Part I.

[22] *Poor Law Amendment Act* (4 and 5 Will. IV. c. 76).

'the question'. He revealed intense concern for the destructive consequences of industrialism, the misery of the poor and the associated political threat of Chartism.[23] In part, the remedy lay in a search for controlled programmes of social reform through statute law. What was more, proposals for reform might appear to be focused on social conditions but these grim circumstances would be seen in a moral context. People should be able to live in a social setting which offered them the prospect of both survival and dignity. They could be assisted by statutory intervention but not in such a way as to compromise their accountability for their own actions. In certain respects it was a highly sophisticated form of intellectual adventure, not least in the exchanges between political economists explored by Keith Smith.[24]

The debates could range over any number of political, social, economic, and religious issues but they were united by a commitment to deep feelings and thoughts about relations between citizens. Using statute law in an attempt to bring about major changes in conditions and behaviour was a matter of earnest concern. In the final analysis it is this driving commitment to social and moral improvement which makes it necessary to consider together statutes on, say, the prevention of cholera or the improvement of education. It might be seen as a phase of law-making dominated by debates about social morality.

When these 'central' topics in statutory reform have been explored it will be possible to go further and ask if some more detailed pattern of change can be seen within the new Acts. Despite all the uncoordinated energy and variety in one clause after another, analysts from A. V. Dicey to writers of the present day have engaged in a restless search for distinctive phases of statutory change and ways of explaining types of reform. Was there, say, an age of individualism or a late drive for collectivism? It is as if the analysts of statutory reform have shared the Victorian desire to chart the interior of Africa or Australia and to allocate boundaries and names.

---

[23] See e.g. T. Carlyle, *Chartism* (1840), also revealing frustration with Parliament's failure at the time to respond effectively to 'the condition'.

[24] See Vol. XI, Pt 1, Ch. IV, Theories of Law and Government, pp. 90–123; and Vol. XI, Pt 1, Ch. VI, Law and Political Economy, pp. 158–233.

II

The Poor Law

1. THE 'OLD' POOR LAW

For centuries the poor law in England and Wales was a meeting point between social misery, government policy, and the making of rules. Sometimes the rules were expressed in statutes, sometimes in case law, and sometimes in the form of regulations produced by bodies with statutory powers. Various types of poor relief were provided in medieval times, and these were developed in the course of the sixteenth century by a series of enactments which were eventually brought within the terms of Acts passed in 1597 and 1601.[1] Under these arrangements the parish had a pivotal role. The ratepayers raised a poor rate and annually appointed unpaid overseers of the poor. The latter had numerous duties including the provision of work for the able-bodied poor and direct relief for those who were not capable of helping themselves. The overseers were accountable to the local ratepayers and their appointment and parish accounts were ratified annually by local Justices of the Peace at the Sessions.[2]

As Cornish has pointed out, the long-term importance of this lay in its structure of legal obligations.[3] The link between church and government through the parish created about 15,000 legal units. These might take the form of an open vestry including incumbent, churchwardens, and parishioners, a closed vestry or, after the passing of the Sturges Bourne Acts of 1818

---

[1] Hospitals for the Poor Act 1597 (39 Eliz. I c. 5), and an Act for the Relief of the Poor (43 Eliz. I c. 2): see, also, Statute of Charitable Uses (43 Eliz. I c. 4).

[2] There is an extensive literature on the poor law. For a focus on issues in legal history, see W. R. Cornish and G. de N. Clark, *Law and Society in England, 1750–1950* (1989), Ch. 6; F. C. Montague, 'The Law of Settlement and Removal', (1888) 4 *LQR* 40–5; L. Charlesworth, 'The Poor Law: A Modern Legal Analysis,' (1999) 2 *Journal of Social Security Law* 79–92; L. Charlesworth, 'Poor Law in the City: A Comparative Legal Analysis of the Effect of the 1834 Poor Law Amendment Act upon the Administration of Poor Relief in the Ports of Liverpool and Chester', in Andrew Lewis (ed.), *Law in the City: Proceedings of the Seventeenth British Legal History Conference 2005* (2007), 206–29; R. Cranston, *Legal Foundations of the Welfare State* (London, 1985). Legal issues are considered at numerous points in the famous Report of 1834: see *RC on the Administration and Practical Operation of the Poor Laws*, PP 1834 [44], (8323 pp.). For political, social, and other histories of the poor law see Further Reading, p. 1015 .

[3] Cornish and Clark, *Law and Society*, 418.

and 1819, a select vestry.[4] The latter were usually found in urban areas and replaced the popular assembly with elected ratepayers and were often seen as resembling a borough corporation. For any particular person in a state of destitution it was the appointed overseer who had immediate power, and the meanness and economic abuses of a significant number of the latter could make the system as a whole look less than kind to the poor. Of course, the overseers could reply that their parsimony was a reflection of the ratepayers' sustained desire to reduce the costs of the poor rate. The discretions of overseers were capable of being over-ruled by the justices who had the power to order the granting of assistance. In law no legal authority existed to question the scope or even existence of this power and justices could thus do something to control overseers.[5] In respect of other powers many poor law issues were considered at Quarter Sessions and in their tens of thousands beyond in King's Bench.[6]

As laws developed around this structure the role of 'settlement and removals' came to be of central importance. This law was expressed in statutory form in the Poor Relief Act 1662, confirming that a parish must maintain its settled poor.[7] From this it followed that 'in legal terms, poor law was largely settlement law, and settlement law provided the rights and obligations which underpinned both the right to poor relief and the duty to provide it. Hence, too, non-settled destitute people could be removed to their parish of settlement.'[8] Again, the parish remained at the heart of poor law administration.

In practice this structure created many types of legal argument and a considerable body of case law. Parishes would frequently dispute liability to pay a particular family relief with settlement being the legal issue. Settlement could be obtained under the 1662 Act in various capacities including that of 'native' or 'sojourner' or 'servant'. A wife took her husband's settlement, a legitimate child took its father's, and an illegitimate child took the parish in which it was born.[9] Under the Act, 40 days' residence was sufficient and this gave an incentive rapidly to examine recent arrivals and argue that their settlement was elsewhere. It was often a matter of brutal financial calculation. The cost of removal and the attendant risk of litigation by the parish to which an individual or

---

[4] Vestries Act (Sturges Bourne's Act) (58 Geo. III c. 69) and Poor Relief Act, (59 Geo. III c. 12). The latter is an Act of notable length and detail.

[5] See Vol. XI, Pt 2, Ch. V, Legal Government, pp. 455–7, 462.

[6] F. C. Montague, 'The Law of Settlement and Removal', (1888) 4 LQR 40–51.

[7] 13 & 4 Car. II c. 12, s 21.

[8] L. Charlesworth 'The Poor Law: A Modern Legal Analysis' (1999) 2 Journal of Social Security Law 83; and see generally M. Rose, 'Settlement, Removal and the New Poor Law', in D. Fraser (ed.), The New Poor Law in the Nineteenth Century, (1976), 25–45.

[9] For rights within the family generally, see Pt 4.

family was sent could be greater than the cost of maintaining them. When litigation did occur it sometimes produced refinements in case law which exasperated contemporaries. An Act of 1731 had tried to ensure that there was always an investigation into the truth or merits of the matter in question but subsequent elaboration of the law suggests that it was not successful in avoiding litigation over procedural points.[10] There was controversy and further statutory reform over the issue as to whether a poor person without a settlement could be removed even before he or she had applied for relief. The situation improved when the Poor Removal Act 1795 ended the rule that a poor person could be taken back to their parish of settlement simply on the ground that it appeared that they might apply for relief—in other words that they were merely 'likely to become chargeable'. The terms of the Act stated that only those who were actually chargeable, i.e. in receipt of poor relief, were subject to removal under the settlement rules.[11]

Another source of litigation came from those who were rated in order to provide the money for the relief of the poor. Liability was spread wide, including occupiers of property many of whom were often prepared to 'go to law'. To give just one example, 'The owner of a bridge resting on piles driven into the soil, one end of which is in parish A. and the other in parish B. in which parish the toll-house stands, is rateable to the poor for the occupation of land in A. pro rata, although the road over the bridge be repaired by other persons'.[12] Here too, a large body of law grew up over time.

The structure of the poor law established by the Elizabethan statutes also interlocked with the law on vagrancy and the provision of Houses of Correction.[13] Often local measures were taken to provide buildings for the totally destitute. In the course of the eighteenth century, it became more common to provide workhouses and in many cases these acquired a reputation for being ill-run and so unhealthy as to be causes of pauper deaths, particularly in respect of children. Thomas Gilbert ensured that under an Act of 1782 it was possible for parishes to come together for running a poor-house for the sick and aged, although, typically, this was left to local initiative.[14]

The poor law was further debated in the 1790s, often against a background of war and economic difficulties. In the course of everyday life a gentleman with any interest in the poor was expected to know his statutes and know how they

---

[10] Quarter Sessions Appeal Act (5 Geo. II c. 19).

[11] 35 Geo. III c. 101.

[12] *R* v. *Salisbury (Marquis)*, 8 Ad. & El. 716 *et seq.*; and see T. N. Talfourd, Serjeant-at-Law (ed.), *Dickinson's Guide* (5th edn, 1841), 693 n. (t).

[13] L. Charlesworth, 'Why is it a Crime to be Poor?' (1999) 21(2/3) *Liverpool Law Review* 149–67.

[14] Poor Relief Act (Gilbert's Act) 1782 (22 Geo. III c. 83) and see Cornish and Clark, *Law and Society*, 422.

were applied.[15] Such knowledge meshed with a broader awareness of statute law, criminal and civil, and its general impact on the poor.

2. THE NINETEENTH-CENTURY DISPUTES

By the start of the nineteenth century the established poor law was formidable in its range and contentious in its application. A recent analysis has argued that 'the English poor law of the eighteenth and early nineteenth centuries was probably the most comprehensive system of public poor relief before the coming of the welfare state'.[16] In John King's 2nd edition of Richard Burn's, *The Justice of the Peace and Parish Officer*, the poor law is placed in its full legal context and the significance of local people discharging legal duties becomes clear.[17] For example, detailed attention (with appropriate references) is given to the statutes relating to apprenticeship within a parish and the important role of local officials: 'The churchwardens and overseers, or the greater part of them, by the assent of two justices...may bind...any such children, whose parents they shall judge not able to maintain them, to be apprentices where they shall see convenient, till such man child shall come to the age of 21 (18 Geo. III c. 47), and such woman child to the age of 21 or marriage; the same to be as effectual to all purposes as if such child were of full age, and by indenture of covenant bound him or herself. (43 El. c. 2 s. 5)'.[18] Volume IV of Burns' work has 807 pages devoted to the law of the poor and the rules covered numerous aspects of the everyday life of those in poverty.

Within this intricate array of rules, what sparked intense national attention at the start of the nineteenth century was debate about the Speenhamland system. The justices of Speenhamland in Berkshire developed an additional system in 1795 under which the poor were given supplements to wages and these were increased in proportion to rises in the cost of basic necessities such as bread. It may have been effective at mitigating the worst impacts of bad harvests but, over the years, it came to be linked to numerous criticisms. It was alleged that it subsidized employers who paid particularly low wages in the knowledge that those who were rated within the parish would make up the difference in relief payments. Since the studies of Mark Blaug there have been doubts about the extent to which this system was applied in practice.[19] But there can be no doubt about its capacity to focus arguments. Giving direct supplements related to what

---

[15] For examples of informed debate, see M. E. Rose, *The English Poor Law, 1730–1930* (1971), 25–6.
[16] T. Sokoll (ed.), *Essex Pauper Letters, 1731–1837* (Oxford, 2001), 3.
[17] 1814, 5 vols.
[18] *Ibid.*, 108.
[19] 'The Poor Law Report Re-Examined', (1964) XXIV *Journal of Economic History* 229–45.

we would now call the cost of living was likely to reverberate through the entire system of relief, encouraging even more arguments about rating and settlement and, generally, about distinguishing between those who could not work and those who could work but would not do so. Others took a more theoretical approach. In his *Essay on the Principle of Population*, Thomas Malthus argued that it would be impossible to provide for all the poor and the law was in itself destructive.[20] In his view it encouraged early and inexpedient marriages and took away incentives to work. It was also cruel and an affront to those who were prepared to work and maximize their wages. At one stage Malthus was prepared to recommend the almost total abolition of the law but he modified this slightly in later years.

The competing arguments crystallized in the middle of the century's second decade. A reluctant government was driven to setting up a Parliamentary Select Committee in 1816. The old system of compulsory relief for the poor was heavily criticized. Instead, there was praise for a workhouse system along with a limit for poor law expenditure and the encouragement of parish schools, benefit clubs, and an improved system of relief administration. Within these parameters numerous views were canvassed and there were further committees, enquiries, and an extensive survey. The Speenhamland system remained a point of attention and Select Committees explored this in 1816, 1824, and 1828.[21] Many of those who looked at the issues concluded the existing system was neither efficient nor, in so far as they believed it rewarded the indolent, was it based on any defensible moral view. It distorted wage-rates and, for its critics, it was indefensible in terms of economic and social principles. It was also an area of legal contest which brought its own costs. One contemporary analysis arrived at the conclusion that the expenses of settlement litigation between 1776 and 1815 revealed a rate of increase greater than the sum expended in poor relief for those years.[22] Beneath the level of grand theoretical analysis lay the reality of local power. Within this extensive body of law, local resistance to centralized control had strong foundations in part for the simple reason that the parish had such an important role. The parish paid and it had legal duties and obligations, thus serving as the

---

[20] G. Gilbert (ed.), *Thomas Malthus, An Essay on the Principle of Population* (1806 edn), (1993). See Vol. XI, Pt 1, Ch. VI, Law and Political Economy, pp. 162–5.

[21] *SC on the State of the Poor and Charitable Donations for the Benefit of Poor Persons*, PP 1816 (22), iv; *SC on the Practice of Paying Wages of Labour out of the Poor Rates*, PP 1824 (392), vi; *SC on the Poor Laws Relating to the Employment or Relief of Able-Bodied Persons from Poor Rates*, PP 1828 (494), iv.

[22] J. R. Poynter, *Society and Pauperism: English Ideas on Poor Relief 1795–1834*, (1969), 7. For a valuable analysis of Bentham's views on the poor law, see M. Quinn, 'The Fallacy of Non-Interference: The Poor Panopticon and Equality of Opportunity', (1997) *Journal of Bentham Studies*, No. I, p. 1. In so far as Bentham influenced the debates on the 1834 reforms it was chiefly through Edwin Chadwick.

context for the daily lives of both those who had property, and who controlled the system, and others who lacked property and sometimes faced destitution. In the nineteenth century the closed vestries were the targets for local government reform through the introduction of elective vestries under the Sturges Bourne's Acts of 1818–19 and Hobhouse's Act of 1831.[23] But these changes in the direction of efficiency could further enhance local influence. Only radical reform would threaten the balance of power.

3. THE ROYAL COMMISSIONERS

In response to these debates and tensions, and also in reaction to further social unrest at the start of the 1830s, a Royal Commission on the Poor Laws began its work.[24] Seven Commissioners were appointed in 1832 and two more the next year. They were also years of argument about the reform of the franchise which reached the statute book in the 'Great Reform Bill' of 1832.[25] It was a time when major reforms could be put forward with at least the prospect of being debated. In this promising context the Royal Commission began its work with a survey. It looked at parishes with a focus on relief given to the able-bodied poor. There were replies from only about 10 per cent of the 15,000 parishes but even this information filled 15 volumes. In the preparation of its response to the survey, the Commission was dominated by Nassau Senior, a Professor of Political Economy, and Edwin Chadwick, a lawyer from Manchester and private secretary to Jeremy Bentham until the latter's death in 1832.[26]

It soon became clear that one of the main drivers of reform would be the economy. The rapid increase in the cost of the poor during recent decades was a worry to the property owners who paid for it. But the Commissioners also had a strong ideological commitment and Mark Blaug's work on their activities reveals a determination to see the problems of the poor through utilitarian spectacles.[27] Humanitarian concern was not an end in itself; ultimately, it was not even part

---

[23] Vestries Act (Sturges Bourne's Act) (58 Geo. III c. 69), Poor Relief Act (59 Geo. III c. 12), and Vestries Act (1 and 2 Will. IV c. 60). On Sturges Bourne's legislation, see Vol. XI, Pt 2, Ch. V, Local Government, pp. 445–7, 467.

[24] RC on the Administration and Practical Operation of the Poor Laws, PP 1834 [44], (8323 pp.). The Report of 1834 was signed by C. J. London, J. B. Chester, W. Sturges Bourne, Nassau Senior, Henry Bishop, Henry Gawler, W. Coulson, James Traill, and Edwin Chadwick.

[25] Representation of the People Act 1832 (2 and 3 Will. IV c. 45).

[26] M. E. Rose, The English Poor Law (Newton Abbot, 1971), 75–95. Nassau Senior is usually remembered as an economist but he was also a lawyer: Vinerian Scholar at Oxford in 1813 and a barrister of Lincoln's Inn, 1819. On Chadwick see A. Brundage, 'England's Prussian Minister': Edwin Chadwick and the Politics of Government Growth, 1832–1854 (Pennsylvania State University, 1988) and footnote 2 of the section below in Ch. IV, p. 535.

[27] 'The Poor Law Report Re-Examined' (1964) XXIV Journal of Economic History, 229–45.

of the justification of the poor law. Instead, a properly adjusted system of deterrents would ensure that any person who sought relief would only do so when all attempts at gainful work had failed. Poor law provision would be carefully pitched at a level which provided an incentive for finding any alternative work which might be available. Next to death, turning to the poor law would be any particular person's worst option. It would provide the minimum required for survival and, thereby, the maximum incentive for finding gainful employment. In the language of the day it would be 'less eligible' than the alternatives. Predictably, the contents of the survey and the conclusions of the Commissioners did not always match. For the modern historian, E. J. Evans, 'The passage of the Poor Law Amendment Act is perhaps the earliest example of the tyranny of the expert.'[28] This part of the law was being heavily influenced by metropolitan men with an interest in theory and, for them, theory had to find its expression in statute law.

The reader of the Commissioners' work is told of the 'Progress of the Law' and this focus on legal issues is sustained through large parts of the Report. For the Commissioners it was essential to improve on current arrangements and frequently this would be at the cost of local power: 'At present, the experience which guides the administration of relief is limited to the narrow bounds of a parish.... The common administration is founded on blind impulse or on impressions derived from a few individual cases; when the only safe action must be regulated by extensive inductions or general rules derived from large classes of cases, which the annual officer has no means of observing. Capacity for such duties comes by intuition even to persons of good general intelligence as little as an intuitive capacity to navigate a ship or manage a steam engine.'[29] In response to this type of problem, one witness, Dr James Mitchell, pointed to the value of his experience with the legislation for the regulation of benefit societies. Dr Mitchell was asked 'Was the appointment of a central authority or control, under the authority of the Government, to revise the regulations of the benefit societies, and enforce conformity to the will of the legislature, popular with the representatives of the working classes?' His answer was 'Yes; in order to prevent the capricious control of the various local authorities, each of whom has his own notions...'.[30] The conclusion of the Commissioners in respect of these types of

[28] E. J. Evans, *The Forging of the Modern State: Early Industrial Britain: 1783–1870* (2nd edn, 1996), 233.

[29] *RC on the Administration and Practical Operation of the Poor Laws*, PP 1834 [44], 159. There is a useful edition of the Report in S. G. and E. O. A. Checkland (eds), *The Poor Law Report of 1834* (1974), and hereafter the official Report references are supplemented by references to 'Checkland' in brackets. In the present case the reference in their edition is at p. 401.

[30] *RC on the Administration and Practical Operation of the Poor Laws*, PP 1834 [44], 164 (Checkland, 411).

argument was that 'A recommendation that the Legislature should divest the local authorities of all discretionary power in the administration of relief appears to us to follow as a necessary consequence from the mass of evidence to which we have adverted'.[31]

One logical consequence of the attack on local power was to be found in those witnesses who asked the Commissioners to ensure that the 'smallest detail [was] unalterably prescribed by the legislature'.[32] Detailed statute law would replace discretion at any level. There was logic in this, but the Commissioners rejected it as impractical and difficult to enforce even if it could be provided in very lengthy Acts. They had already made it clear that in their general view legislation did not, as it were, speak for itself:

The instances presented to us throughout the present enquiry of the defeat of former legislation by unforeseen obstacles, and often by an administration directly at variance with the plainly expressed will of the Legislature, have forced us to distrust the operation of the clearest enactments, and even to apprehend unforeseen mischiefs from them, unless an especial agency be appointed and empowered to superintend and control their execution.[33]

In response they argued that 'The course of proceeding which we recommend for adoption is in principle that which the legislature adopted for the management of the savings' banks, the friendly societies, and the annuity societies throughout the country. Having prescribed the outline and general principles on which those institutions should be conducted a special agency [which, in this instance, was constituted by one barrister only] was appointed to see that their rules and detailed regulations conformed to the intentions of the law'.[34] After these and other arguments the Commissioners came to a conclusion which they expressed rather grandly in upper case:

WE RECOMMEND, THEREFORE, THE APPOINTMENT OF A CENTRAL BOARD TO CONTROL THE ADMINISTRATION OF THE POOR LAWS, WITH SUCH ASSISTANT COMMISSIONERS AS MAY BE FOUND REQUISITE; AND THAT THE COMMISSIONERS BE EMPOWERED AND DIRECTED TO FRAME AND ENFORCE REGULATIONS FOR THE GOVERNMENT OF WORKHOUSES, AND AS TO THE NATURE AND AMOUNT OF THE RELIEF TO BE GIVEN AND THE LABOUR TO BE EXACTED IN THEM, AND THAT SUCH REGULATION SHALL, AS FAR AS MAY BE PRACTICAL, BE UNIFORM THROUGHOUT THE COUNTRY.[35]

---

[31] *Ibid.*, 165 (Checkland, 414).   [32] *Ibid.*, 165 (Checkland, 414).
[33] *Ibid.*, 157 (Checkland, 399).   [34] *Ibid.*, 167 (Checkland, 418).
[35] *Ibid.*, 167 (Checkland, 418–19).

Again and again, they put forward legal arguments, not least because law was to be the instrument of uniformity: 'Even if the Board were to frame bad regulations (and worse regulations than those now in practice they could scarcely devise), it would be a less mischievous arrangement than the present, inasmuch as the chances of opposition to a pernicious measure would be increased in proportion to the extension of the jurisdiction, and success in such opposition would be success throughout the jurisdiction. Those who are now maintainers of their own errors would be vigilant and unsparing censors of a distant authority. Under the existing system, when opposition is made to the continuance of a bad practice, and the opposition is successful, the success is limited to one parish...'.[36]

The Commissioners' approach to these wide-ranging issues of law and administration was of a piece with their policy recommendations for the everyday work of poor law officials. Instead of variety there would be uniformity under strategic central control. In almost all cases there would be 'no relief for the able-bodied or their families other than in a well-regulated workhouse'.[37] Where relief was given, the principle guiding those who gave it was not some personal concern for human suffering but 'the condition of the pauper shall in no case be so eligible as the condition of persons of the lowest class, subsisting on the fruits of their own industry'.[38] In short, the able-bodied poor and their families would have to endure a workhouse under conditions of 'less eligibility'.

4. PARLIAMENT AND THE BALANCE OF POWER

When the Poor Law Amendment Bill was debated in Parliament it reflected many of these long-standing debates. The measure was presented by Lord Althorp who argued that a rule-making central board would be the ideal proposal:

It was absolutely necessary that there should be a discretionary power vested in some quarter to carry into effect recommendations calculated he hoped, to introduce sound principles and the fruits of salutary experience into the administration of the Poor-laws. The principal subject for them to consider was, where that discretionary power should be placed. If they vested it in the local authorities, or in the local magistracy, however well intentioned they might be, deprived as they would be of those sources of general information and comparison open to a board of Commissioners, and however excellent their motives, biased as they must be by local prejudices and local feelings, it was plain that such a quarter would not be the fittest one to invest with a discretionary power for carrying the measure into effect. It was therefore his intention to propose, that his Majesty

---

[36] *Ibid.*, 169 (Checkland, 423).   [37] *Ibid.*, 146 (Checkland, 389).
[38] *Ibid.*, 127 (Checkland, 371).

should be authorised to appoint a Central Board of Commissioners, vested with such power for that purpose. It would be necessary to invest the Board with extraordinary power, to enable it to accomplish the object proposed, but that power would be subject to the constant control of the Parliament and the Executive Government.[39]

In introducing clauses designed to realize these objectives, Lord Althorp knew that government regulations and the powers they conferred on public bodies would be a major concern for his parliamentary audience. The need for change in the existing poor law was widely admitted: but the nature of the change had the potential to be contentious, particularly at those points where it gave power to un-elected officials based in London. Legal reform in response to the social problems associated with the poor law was no longer a speculative possibility. It was now threatening to produce a shift in the location of power which had the potential to be unpopular with influential provincial interests. For example the new laws required uniting adjacent parishes, usually based upon the 100 sub units of the county, into an enlarged union and the old role of the justices was to be severely weakened although they retained their oversight of parish accounts and officials. Moreover, the parish rating system remained as the source of funding for the new poor law unions. It was unclear where the balance of power would lie.[40] Althorp was not faced with grand alternatives to his proposals, but he knew he would have to tread carefully around rural and urban interests.

The proposed powers of the central authority for the administration of the Poor Law were important but fell short of what the reformers had hoped for in their Report. The fear of producing resentment at central encroachment on local powers did much to account for this. In part, it was also the consequence of avoiding the expense which would have come with highly intrusive reforms. When Lord Althorp introduced the measure he did so in his capacity as Chancellor of the Exchequer and his sustained concern for the economy was obvious. In brutal political terms, he was right in responding to earlier demands for economy; he was right in thinking that his parliamentary audience would be moved by the offer of reducing the cost of an institution which they (and many of those who voted for them) had to sustain. He also presented proposals which reduced acrimony by being strikingly unspecific in some respects about the new system which was being created. As Michael Rose has emphasized in his study of the legislation, the new Act did not require any particular method of giving

---

[39] *PD* 1834 (s. 3), 22: 881.

[40] L. Charlesworth, 'Poor Law in the City: A comparative legal analysis of the effect of the 1834 Poor Law Amendment Act upon the administration of poor law relief in the ports of Liverpool and Chester', in A. Lewis (ed.), *Law in the City: Proceedings of the Seventeenth British Legal History Conference 2005* (2007), 206–29, For judicial review in this context, see Vol XI, Pt 2, Ch. VI, Judicial Review, pp. 498–9.

relief.[41] The Commission was given the power to decide on the ending of outdoor relief and, as an alternative, the systematic use of a workhouse system if it so wished.

Generally, the Poor Law Amendment Bill 'met with remarkably little resistance'.[42] The Cabinet Committee which drafted the bill was 'composed almost entirely of ministers who had taken a close interest in the Poor Laws as landlords; the exception was Lord John Russell, and he was the Committee's least active member'.[43] For many at Westminster it was possible to see the bill as an attempt to 'police local implementation and guard against a reversion to paternalism' rather than the provision of new government agencies for economic improvement.[44]

Despite this, when it reached the statute book parts of the new legislation could look radical and threatening to parochial interests. To contemporaries they looked particularly troubling at levels above that of individual cases. For example, under s 15 it was stated that

...from and after the passing of this Act the administration of relief to the poor through-out England and Wales, according to the existing laws, or such laws as shall be in force at the time being, shall be subject to the direction and control of the said commission-ers, and for executing the powers given to them by this Act the said commissioners shall and are hereby authorized and required, from time to time as they shall see occasion, to make and issue all such rules, orders and regulations for the management of the poor, for the government of workhouses and the education of the children therein, and for the management of parish poor children...and the said commissioners may, at their discre-tion, from time to time, suspend, alter, or rescind such rules, orders, and regulations, or any of them: Provided always, that nothing in this Act contained shall be construed as enabling the said commissioners or any of them to interfere in any individual case for the purpose of ordering relief.

Using powers such as those provided by s 15, in the years following 1834 the new Commissioners were successful in bringing significant parts of the administration of the Poor Law within their range of work. In other words, they were able to make gradual and cumulative use of their discretionary powers. By the end of 1839 the greater part of relief was 'within the Act' in the very broad sense that those with local roles had at least some degree of accountability to the Commissioners. There were detailed (and sometimes subtle) alterations in the working of the nineteenth-century poor law and Charlesworth has shown how

---

[41] M. E. Rose, *The English Poor Law, 1730–1930* (Newton Abbot, 1971), 77.

[42] P. Mandler, *Aristocratic Government in the Age of Reform: Whigs and Liberals, 1830–1852* (Oxford, 1990), 138.

[43] *Ibid.*, 139.

[44] *Ibid.*, 137.

reforms in the law of settlement influenced power relationships. It was important that the poor came to lose the legal right to apply to justices for relief payments. Settlement ceased to be focused on rights and instead became an administrative subject conferring large discretions on officials.[45] Within the new law a novel national arrangement for rule-making was becoming stronger. It was elevating centralized administrative powers and undermining what were taken to be old rights secured by the established courts.

The new Commissioners had the power to appoint their own staff within statutory limits and with Treasury control over salaries. As Anderson points out the Board reported directly to Parliament annually, was dependent on an annual vote of supply, and had a five-year limitation of its powers. Also, General Orders had to be sent to the Secretary of State and could be disallowed by His Majesty in Council. The Board had to report to the Secretary of State on various matters, including its own disagreements. This somewhat convoluted system of accountability had a clear potential for failure because it was not certain who would speak on behalf of the Board in contentious parliamentary debates.[46] But for the time being the arrangement certainly gave the Board a considerable capacity for self-directed action. It was not many years before the Board had consolidated 600 unions out of a significant proportion of the existing 15,000 units based on parishes.[47]

5. A FACTORY FOR THE MAKING OF UNPOPULAR RULES

The power of the Commissioners to frame Regulations, Rules, and Orders and to compose Letters for guidance on their interpretation was striking. It seemed that there was unending potential for further refinements of existing Regulations. Under s 109 of the Act the words 'General Rule' related to rules for 'more than one Union...'. The General Rule was now a favourite of the Commissioners because it brought with it greater uniformity. In a simple literal sense, rules were becoming less local. And to contemporaries their number seemed to be ever increasing. The General Rule did have one disadvantage for the Commissioners, mentioned above, in that they had to be submitted to the Secretary of State. This did not apply to special or particular rules and it was to be expected that the Board

---

[45] L. Charlesworth 'The Poor Law: A Modern Legal Analysis,' (1999) 2 *Journal of Social Security Law* 79–92. Cornish and Clark, *Law and Society* explore the development of other discretions at pp. 58–60.

[46] On the accountability of the Commissioners, see Vol. XI, Pt 2, Ch. II Central Executive: The Legal Structure of State Institutions, pp. 348–54.

[47] For a detailed study of the geography of the reforms, see F. Driver, *Power and Pauperism: The Workhouse System, 1834–1884* (Cambridge, 1993).

might sometimes select the least accountable forms of rule-making where it was possible to do so.

In any event, the number of rules steadily increased. As early as 1842 when the Eighth Annual Report of the Commissioners appeared it was beyond dispute that a vigorous enterprise in rule-making had come into being. So in paragraph 34 the Commissioners announced that 'In our Report of last year we stated that some instances of excessive or improper punishments which had occurred in workhouses had induced us to prepare a set of regulations on that subject. These regulations we have now incorporated in the general order containing the rules and regulations for the government of workhouses, and they have thus been issued to every Union in England and Wales possessing a workhouse adapted for carrying out the provisions of the Poor Law Amendment Act.'[48] The Commissioners admitted that not everything could be legislated for in advance. But this, they argued, was what made it necessary for them to have a discretion. There had to be a lawful response to all contingencies. At times this could lead them into litigation, as when they argued that the Commissioners had the power 'to regulate the administration of relief by the Board of Guardians created by (a) local Act'.[49] At other times, as when they issued Letters, they claimed that they were doing no more than guiding officials. 'Moreover, as all general rules leave a considerable discretion to those who are to execute them, the commissioners have attempted to indicate the spirit in which the several regulations ought to be administered, and the limitations which they ought to receive in practice...'.[50]

Predictably, given the power of local interests there were also significant checks on the influence of the new Board. The Board dealt with local boards of guardians and not individuals just because disputes were a contest between local and central powers. The statute for the Commissioners ensured that their rules, orders, and regulations could be challenged on *certiorari* in the Queen's Bench but until they were set aside the instruments were valid and had to be obeyed. Challenge could be useful in drawing lines between the roles of the Board and guardians but where the Commissioners did have jurisdiction the courts made it clear from the start that *certiorari* could not be used to challenge discretionary decisions. Also, the validity of instruments prior to challenge ensured that where the Commissioners brought *mandamus* to enforce an order a union could not resist on grounds of illegality.[51] This could be of particular assistance when

[48] *Eighth Annual Report of the Poor Law Commissioners, PP* 1842 (389), xix.i, 13.

[49] *Ibid.*, para. 62, pp. 21–2 and para. 93, p. 31.

[50] Number Four Letter Accompanying General Workhouse Rules, Poor Law Commission Office, Somerset House, 5 February 1842, reprinted in *ibid.*, p. 105.

[51] These issues are further considered by Anderson in his chapter on the courts and central government: see also his chapter on judicial review.

bringing auditors and rates collectors under central control. The legal framework sometimes favoured the Commissioners whilst at the same time making it clear that they had, of course, to exercise discretions within the statute.

In the early years of the new law the Commissioners could be frustrated by numerous legal restrictions. For example, they could not order Boards of Guardians to spend more than one-tenth of their annual rate on the provision of a workhouse. In the course of decades further limits on the reforms were clear for all to see. The Commissioners were not given power to deal with unions incorporated under Gilbert's Act or under local Acts without the consent of those bodies.[52] Only in 1868 was the Poor Law Board (successor to the Commission in 1847) empowered to take control of these.[53] Even then there were still some parishes working under their own Act of Parliament.

Beyond the use of the courts and Acts of Parliament there was the everyday pressure of business. A lack of cooperation on the part of guardians could produce simple (and for the Commissioners) exasperating inaction. In many parts of England it proved to be rather more difficult to build workhouses than to unite parishes but, through numerous compromises, within five years of the new Act 350 had been constructed, mostly in the South.[54] The role of Justices was not what it had been but the Commissioners had to keep in mind the fact that it was a legal requirement that guardians were men of property and it was notorious that they had opinions of their own. Justices could appear in this new role and sometimes did so, albeit not now exercising their powers as Justices. The respective roles of those involved in the working of the poor law was frequently contested. For example, the process of amalgamating parishes could produce intricate arrangements. Each union had a common workhouse. At the same time each parish was responsible for maintaining its settled poor whether they were or were not in the workhouse and this set up a network of conflicting interests which put a check on radical reform and could make those who were rated uncooperative. In some instances it was necessary for the Board to obtain the consent in writing of a majority of guardians of any union, or of a majority of certain rate-payers and owners of property. More generally, the Commissioners wanted a system to ensure uniform approaches to accounts. In fact, initially they were only given the power to require Overseers or Guardians to appoint officers to audit accounts. There was criticism of this and eventually in 1844 the Commissioners were enabled to appoint men to serve as auditors.[55] It was only to be expected that old

[52] Poor Relief Act (Gilbert's Act) 1782 (22 Geo. III c. 83).
[53] Poor Law Amendment Act 1868, s 4.
[54] K. Laybourn, *The Evolution of British Social Policy and the Welfare State* (Keele, 1995), 27.
[55] W. C. Lubenow, *The Politics of Government Growth* (Newton Abbot, 1971), 36.

social realities were often obvious: 'The large landowners of Northamptonshire maintained their traditional hold over social policy. They had union boundaries drawn with remarkable proximity to the boundaries of their own estates, and they filled the important offices either themselves or by proxy.'[56]

Beyond this type of dispute with its focus on the respective legal entitlements of the Board and guardians there was often simple political opposition to the very existence of the law. The new Commissioners were restrained by the continuing strength of public opposition to centralizing poor law reforms. Protesters such as Cobbett had preserved a different view of the poor law and its social role. Writing of the law in the years before the reforms he stressed that '…the law so positively commands, that the poor of every parish, shall be maintained in and by every such parish. However, all law of this sort, all salutary and humane law, really seems to be drawing towards an end in this now miserable country.'[57] If anything, opinions such as these became more forceful when the Act was passed and the early warnings appeared to be confirmed. Outside of Parliament there was widespread distrust and protest, and this was shared by both the poor and those who continued to see a threat to local autonomy. In the view of *The Times*: 'To say the truth, in one word, it is AGAINST the deep-rooted and long-formed habits of this nation, the principle of all which is that the people should be made to govern themselves as much as possible, at least in their domestic concerns and relations.'[58]

Wilson has rightly pointed to the fact that criticism of particular laws interlocked with hostility to this whole area of the law in its new form. *The Times* sustained its hostility. It reprinted Oliver Twist and between 1839 and 1842 many editions of the paper revealed one scandal after another.[59] On Christmas Day in 1840 Elizabeth Wyse, an occupant of the Eton workhouse, was permitted to be with her 2½-year-old daughter and was also allowed to stay with her for one night because the child was distressed and unwell. When Elizabeth tried to attend to the child the next day she was dragged away and locked in the workhouse cage with no coat, no bedding-straw, and no chamber-pot in 20 degrees farenheit of frost. How, it was felt, could such a system be left to develop its potential?[60] In another case the scandal at the Andover workhouse shamed even

---

[56] E. J. Evans, *The Forging of the Modern State* (2nd edn, 1996), 236. Further attention to lively debates on contentious issues relating to the role of inspectors and the gentry in rural areas may be found in P. Mandler, 'The Making of the New Poor Law Redivivus' (1987) 117 *Past and Present*, 131–57 and A. Brundage, D. Eastwood, and P. Mandler 'Debate: The Making of the New Poor Law Redidivus', (1990) 120 *Past and Present*, 183–201.

[57] G. Woodcocke (ed.), *William Cobbett: Rural Rides* (1830, republished 1967), 341.

[58] *The Times*, 30 April 1834.

[59] C. Dickens, *Oliver Twist* (1839).

[60] A. N. Wilson, *The Victorians* (2002), 29.

the local Member of Parliament. In the Andover area all relief for the poor in
their own homes was stopped. Inmates working on bone-grinding resorted
to eating rotten bones and the remnants of horse flesh. Some ate candles to
survive.[61] Single women with bastard children had to wear a yellow stripe of
shame across their workhouse gown.

More generally, there was strong resistance to the whole system in the industrial parts of Yorkshire and Lancashire. In some places there were riots. At times
there was a refusal to appoint Guardians. One example after another linked cold
laws to human suffering. In part the reaction was anger in the form of the more
extreme protests of the Chartist movement. But even here it is noticeable that the
response was not usually to despair of law as an instrument of reform. Present
failings could be remedied by more law, not less. James Bronterre O'Brien petitioned Parliament in 1837 requesting that the poor of England be heard at the Bar
of the House of Commons.[62] The Charter itself appeared in 1838 and is famous
for its demand for a properly representative Parliament elected by secret ballot.
The demand for justice was also a demand for the repeal of iniquitous existing
laws and their replacement with new laws. No-one on the Board could assert
completely unrestricted executive powers, and the public knew that in the last
resort the Board had to act within laws established by Parliament or the courts.
Predictably, Chadwick, as one of the most ardent reformers, was disappointed
in many of the changes; his disappointment was sharpened by the fact that he
was not made a Commissioner and had to settle for being Secretary to the new
body. His proposal that the Commissioners be a Court of Record was dropped
and he was continually frustrated by problems of implementation and personal
feuding.[63]

6. THE PROLIFERATION OF LEGAL ISSUES

In terms of the amount of energy devoted to the creation, interpretation, and
application of laws it was, surely, an expensive and elaborate legal structure
linking the taxation of property to the powers of Commissioners, Guardians,
and Justices, and, beyond them, to the restricted entitlements of some (and only
some) of the destitute. In future decades it produced numerous reforms in central
and local government; and beneath the changing structure of government there
was always the potential for variation. Statutory alterations to the existing law

---

[61] I. Anstruther, *The Scandal of the Andover Workhouse* (Gloucester, 1973).

[62] Wilson, *The Victorians*, 41–2.

[63] For Chadwick's career, see S. E. Finer, *The Life and Times of Sir Edwin Chadwick* (1952) and
R. A. Lewis, *Edwin Chadwick and the Public Health Movement, 1832–1854* (1952). See, also fn. 30
above and below, in Ch. IV, p. 535, fn. 2.

followed one after another. To take one tiny example, at Sowerby and Soyland in the West Riding of Yorkshire certain pieces of land were 'allotted and awarded to the Overseers of the Poor of the Townships, and the proceeds directed to be applied in aid of the Poor's Rates'.[64] Major reforms and minor changes appeared at irregular intervals with the subject never being wholly absent from public debate and administration never being wholly uniform and efficient. It was as if the laws, and the rules authorized by the laws, were developing by a process of attrition.

The extent of the law-making initiated by these reforms came to be reflected in the legal literature on the subject. W. C. Glen, the editor of many annotated editions of Acts of Parliament, produced *Digests of the Poor Laws* and the second edition, published in 1873, deals with 377 statutes directly concerned with the poor law or relevant to it and makes reference to 3680 cases. There were also numerous specialist works such as Hugh Owen's *Manual for Overseers, Assistant Overseers, Collectors of Poor Rates, and Vestry Clerks as to their Powers Duties and Responsibilities*; first published in 1859 it reached a fifth edition by 1880. The Poor Law was not only about the poor, it was also about the potential for the Victorian making of law and the reaction against steps to realize this potential. In responding to rural and industrial poverty, and in reflecting the tensions between local and national interests, the rules for the new poor law were often brutal in their social impact and increasingly refined in the detail with which they were expressed.

The work on the development of rules went on despite major problems with the relationship between the Board and its successors on the one hand, and government on the other. Structural problems arose out of the ambiguities in the initial system of accountability created for the Board in 1834. As we have seen, there was a lack of clear Ministerial responsibility and this left the relationship unstable at times of political crisis. At one time in the 1840s the problem was resolved by the Home Office taking over *de facto* responsibility in parliamentary debates and public discussion. The creation of the Poor Law Board in 1847 was in part an attempt to resolve this but after years of its members trying to combine everyday administration with controversial initiatives it was replaced in 1871 by the Local Government Board. This linked the working of the poor law firmly to Ministerial accountability and, within the Local Government Board, poor law responsibilities were taken seriously, often to the chagrin of other sub-departments such as those responsible for public health. There was now a coherent system of accountability but outside the walls of the 'LGB' the new Board was not regarded as one of the more influential parts of Whitehall.

---

[64] 6 and 7 Vict. c. 10, s 62.

Changes in administrative structures did not resolve difficulty with special-ized areas of work. During the mid-Victorian years disputes over policy shifted to areas of concern such as the education of children. The commissioners of the New Poor Law had grand hopes of providing schooling independently of the workhouse. But the prospects for success were always bleak. Such proposals were expensive and socially controversial with some being alarmed at the possibility of a link between an educated poor and political radicalism. Despite this, in the 1840s there were successes at Norwood in London and in some other areas and under the Liberal government a District Schools Act of 1848 facilitated further possible reforms. But, again, there were problems in, for example, finding suit-able catchment areas (in rural places the area covered by a school could be very large) or, as ever, in persuading Guardians to find the money. With the assist-ance of a parliamentary grant there was gradual improvement in the number and the quality of teachers. There was notable progress in certificated assessment of teachers in the 1850s but even at the best of places education was intermittent because the child left the school when his or her parent found work and departed from the workhouse.[65] After Forster's Education Act of 1870 it became possible to integrate 'poor law children' into schools run by local boards of education but this was not done with any speed.[66]

The defects in educational provision were mild compared with the failings in respect of health. For many at the start of Victoria's reign there was no necessary link between personal health and government regulation. At the level of indi-vidual health what usually mattered was the capacity to pay for a doctor. For a sick person the law of contract was likely to be of decisive significance, sometimes even a matter of life and death. Usually, medical assistance had to be bought and this provided an unpromising foundation for more 'interventionist' measures for health in general and for the health of the poor in particular. Under the old poor law medical care could be provided through parishes entering into their own contracts with doctors who would then provide certain specified services to the poor.[67] As Anthony Brundage points out, the new laws of 1834 said little about this, although Justices of the Peace had the authority to order medical relief in case of sudden illness. Instead, the immensely long provisions of s 52 of the Poor Law Amendment Act allowed for certain forms of assistance which could include health care but it was not a focal point of attention in contemporary debates. In response to an influenza epidemic there were some statutory reforms such as an Act of 1840 which provided the chance of free vaccinations for the poor through

---

[65] A. Brundage, *The English Poor Laws, 1700–1930* (2002), Ch. 5.

[66] See 'Charity and Education' below in Ch. III, pp. 525, 528–9.

[67] Brundage, *The English Poor Laws*, on medical care at pp. 96–9.

the Board of Guardians.[68] But, as things stood in many parishes, the health measures under the new law were ineffectual with poorly paid doctors providing very limited assistance.

In a letter of 1842 the Commissioners pointed out that: 'One of the most important subjects considered by the Select Committee of the House of Commons, which in 1838 inquired into the operation of the Poor Law Amendment Act, was the medical relief of the poor. After examining numerous witnesses on this subject, the Committee decided to recommend no legislation by Parliament on medical relief, but having expressed their opinion that the existing arrangements might in several points be ameliorated, and having indicated several improvements, they left the introduction of these and other alterations to the discretion of the Poor Law Commissioners.'[69]

It was a notable example of Parliament delegating potential regulatory responsibilities. It was also a striking omission given the extent to which the sickness of innumerable poor people was acknowledged at the time. In the records of the early 1840s it was common to note deaths as being caused by a combination of disease, destitution, and starvation. For example, a potter aged 26 living in Burslem near Stoke-on-Trent suffered from malignant ulceration of the mouth and violent diarrhoea caused by want of food. He applied for relief but this was refused and he was offered the workhouse. He could not bring himself to leave his family. After two weeks the Poor Law authorities sent a Medical Officer and the Relieving Officer allowed food and medicine. It was too late. Such events were frequent and current arrangements could not offer an effective response.[70]

The Commissioners consulted the Boards of Guardians and found them unhelpful. They were more impressed by the ideas of doctors. The rules which resulted were largely related to the terms upon which doctors could be used to provide care for the poor and not with the direct needs for medical care, nursing, and appropriate facilities. The General Medical Order of 1842 sought an end to the contract system with the use of salaried posts. But in reality at this point the medical profession was seeking to negotiate better arrangements for its members; indeed the Commissioners were openly driven by the fact that 'much dissatisfaction continued to prevail amongst many members of the medical profession'.[71]

---

[68] 3 & 4 Vict. c. 29.

[69] Letter Accompanying General Medical Order, Poor Law Commission Office, Somerset House, 12 March 1842, reprinted in *Eighth Annual Report of the Poor Law Commissioners*, PP 1842 (389), xix.i, 138.

[70] R. G. Hodgkinson, *The Origins of the National Health Service, The Medical Services of the New Poor Law, 1834–1871* (1967), 35.

[71] Letter Accompanying General Medical Order, Poor Law Commission Office, Somerset House, 12 March 1842, reprinted in *Eighth Annual Report of the Poor Law Commissioners*, PP 1842 (389), xix.i, 138.

Predictably, then, the efforts of the Commissioners in 1842 did little to resolve the problem of health assistance for the poor. They had not even satisfied the doctors who continued to resent others (such as Guardians of the Poor) having a say in medical provision and were worried by issues of social status. They also had to contend with tensions within their own ranks.[72] As an issue it returned to Westminster and Parliamentary Select Committees produced long reports on Medical Poor Relief. In 1844, for instance, questions were asked of John Ayrton Paris, Esq. MD and his answers traced the unstable frontier between professional autonomy and possible parliamentary interference through the development of the poor law:

Chairman: You are President of the College of Physicians?—I am.

Have you been for many years physician to an hospital?—Yes, to the Westminster.

Are you acquainted with the diseases of the poor and their treatment?—Yes.

Do you think that in their cure they require the best medicines?—Undoubtedly.

Are you not of opinion that the poor of a parish, or of a district, should be attended by the same practitioners as the rich?—By competent practitioners.

That they should be attended by properly qualified practitioners?—Yes.

Do you think those practitioners should reside, if possible, in their immediate neighbourhood?—Certainly; I think that is a self-evident proposition.

Do you think the medical man should be the sole judge of the nature and the quantity, and that his orders should be strictly and immediately complied with?—Most undoubtedly.

Do you think that any person not medically educated can be a proper judge whether the poor in any infirmary have proper medicines and attendance in their respective cases of illness?—They can know nothing about it.

Can they judge of what is and what is not proper with regard to the poor who are visited at their own homes?—Certainly not.

You said that the poor should be attended. In your opinion, by competent and well-qualified practitioners; have you any knowledge of the general proceedings of the medical officers appointed under the Poor Law Act; have you turned your attention to it?—Not particularly.

Then your answers to the questions which have been put to you, are answers founded upon your general knowledge of the practice of medicine, without having turned your attention to the medical relief of the poor?—I have not turned my attention particularly to that.[73]

[72] Explored in the context of their roles in debates about the Factory Acts in R. Gray, *The Factory Question and Industrial England, 1830–1860* (Cambridge, 1996), 73–6.

[73] *SC on Medical Poor Relief*, PP 1844 (531), pp. 223–4; in part this Report built on the work in *SC on Medical Poor Relief*, First Report, PP 1844 (312) and *SC on Medical Poor Relief*, Second Report, PP 1844 (387); and see Hodgkinson, *Origins of the National Health Service*, 84.

In short, senior doctors knew there was a need for their profession to respond to the problems of the poor but had little personal interest in doing so. Beneath the lack of professional commitment three overlapping issues were involved in the uncertain development of this part of the law. Were doctors paid sums which they regarded as satisfactory? Could non doctors, and in particular Guardians of the Poor, express worthwhile views on the arrangements for medical care; in other words, was it possible that Guardians could express a more useful view than a doctor with no specialist knowledge of poor law administration? Even if these two questions could be answered what was to be done in everyday medical work; how was it to be structured—for example would it continue to be dependent on private contracts? Again, for many, money remained the central issue. The same *Select Committee* was told by Thomas Wilkinson, Esq. Justice of the Peace for Suffolk, that:

I consider that much of the evil which attends upon the present system of medical relief is caused by the inadequate payment which medical officers of unions receive for their services. This parish contains a population of 1,265; the annual allowance to the medical officer for attendance and medicines is £22 15s. The entire Walsham district has a population of 4,124; the total amount of salary to the officer being £81 13s. but in some districts the charge of the poor in sickness is committed to the surgeon who will undertake the office on the lowest terms. In a matter of so much importance to the poor man as the care of his health under bodily suffering, such a recklessly parsimonious method of proceeding can scarcely fail to have an evil influence upon his feelings and morals...Having stated to the best of my ability in what manner our system of medical relief might be improved, may I be permitted respectfully to express an opinion, founded upon observation of the working of the Act 4 and 5 William 4 [The Poor Law Amendment Act 1834], that it might conduce to the general welfare if parishes were given to understand that the object of the Legislature in passing that Act was not solely the saving of expense to the rate-payer?[74]

A modern study has revealed the extent of the problem: 'Since an escalation in poor rates had been a major cause of reform in 1834, economy became a powerful force. Instead of the previous custom of appointing a doctor in each parish, the aggregation of parishes into unions under the New Poor Law facilitated the creation of much larger medical districts. In some rural areas districts were so large as to make it insuperably difficult for even the most conscientious medical officer to operate efficiently.'[75] The author points out that there was an attempt to remedy this in the General Medical Order of 1842 which imposed a maximum size of 15,000 acres and insisted on certain medical qualifications. But enforcement

---

[74] *SC on Medical Poor Relief*, PP 1844 (531) App. 11, p. 922.
[75] A. Digby, *Making a Medical Living: Doctors and Patients in the English Market for Medicine, 1720–1911* (Cambridge, 2002), 244.

was another matter, and even in the 1860s there were districts of up to 100,000 acres. The significance is hard to grasp in retrospect, but it was substantial. As a matter of common observation, many cases of mid-nineteenth-century pauperism involved sickness. Until the end of the century the standard of medical care for those in workhouse sickbeds was often seen to be a national disgrace with much of the care being given by other pauper inmates and no assistance at night. The availability of medical assistance for those on outdoor relief was, in parts of the country, an even sadder story.[76]

This part of the Poor Law with its shifting context of medical expectations in respect of pay and simple parsimony on the part of Poor Law Guardians had numerous points of uncertainty and one of these provided an episode in legal thought. The case of *Priestley* v. *Fowler* was decided in 1837.[77] It arose out of an accident in which Charles Priestley was seriously injured when his employer's van toppled over. He was thrown from the van and after he landed on the ground about four hundredweight of meat fell on him. Amongst other injuries, his thigh was fractured and his shoulder dislocated. In accordance with the practice of the day he was taken to a nearby Inn, which happened to be the King's Head at Peterborough. There he was treated by two surgeons. His medical and lodging expenses came to about £50.

Liability for this type of bill could raise emotional issues. At the time a master's obligations towards a sick or injured servant were in transition and the change was not in favour of the servant's interests. If no support was forthcoming from the master—and in this case it was not—the servant had to turn to the poor law. Unfortunately for the servant this law was complicated. It was usually thought that the expense fell upon the parish in which the servant was being treated. Further, the major reform of 1834 appeared to confirm this in the long sentences of s 52. But for the Guardians of the parish 'caught' with the liability and what they might regard as an inflated medical bill this could feel unfair and any alternative source of support would have been most welcome. Simpson's analysis of this case is detailed and wide ranging and reveals how the action against the employer may be seen as 'a first step towards a world in which tort law became a candidate for the job of replacing older mechanisms of support'.[78] Priestley lost the case after legal argument in the full Court of Exchequer but the possibility of liability for an employer was now at large in legal debate. In other words, Priestley's action in tort may have come about by reason of the difficulties which contemporary

---

[76] Ibid., 247–9.

[77] (1837) 3 M. & W. I.

[78] A. W. B. Simpson, *Leading Cases in the Common Law* (Oxford, 1995), 100–34 at 127. See Vol. XII, Pt 4, Ch. IV, Workplace Injuries, pp. 1002–12.

Poor Law statutes presented to those dealing with the medical costs arising out of accidents. Certainly, others were exploring related problems at this time. For example, Edwin Chadwick supported the idea that factory owners should have increased strict liability in respect of employees injured by machinery.[79] It follows that the contemporary perception that the Poor Law was radically defective in this area had the potential to open a new role for tort law and, more generally, for debates on legal accountability. The Plaintiff lost the case, but the failure effectively to integrate the work of doctors into the administration of the poor law would have a long reach into legal history.

The effective use of tort law in this context was a matter for the future. Given the failings of the Poor Law's provision in respect of health it is not surprising that the central authority for the Poor Law in the form of the administration used by the Commissioners had no medical expert until 1865. In large part, the health for the poor remained not so much a matter for government and regulation as a service dependent on the extraordinary self-sacrifice of individuals. In Liverpool, the generosity of William Rathbone and the nursing work of Agnes Jones, the Florence Nightingale of the Poor Law, who died of typhus contracted in the workhouse, was of central importance. In London, Joseph Rogers was appointed medical officer to the Strand Union workhouse in 1856 and subsequently exposed scandals in his articles in *The Lancet*. There was some advance in the provision of medical assistance for the poor in the Metropolitan Poor Act 1867 which allowed for the creation in London of new infirmaries separate from workhouses. Ruth Hodgkinson's study reveals the importance of the fact that the Poor Law Medical Officers were never completely integrated into the Poor Law administration; as a result these men made some sort of progress in providing limited health for the distressed poor.[80] But the substance of reform was minimal in relation to what were seen as the demands of the problem. Often the most striking achievements were realized through groups helping themselves as with, for example, the successful efforts of the Jewish communities in London.[81]

Under the New Poor Law there was a similar reluctance to take on any responsibility for those with severe mental problems.[82] After the reforms of 1842 the powers of Guardians in respect of insane paupers were increased.[83] This, however,

---

[79] *RC into the Labour of Children in Factories*, PP 1833 (450) xx, 31. The Report reveals that it was common for employers of injured employees simply to abandon them. At the least, the commissioners wanted 'the proprietor of the machinery' which caused the accident to pay for the child's medical attendance and to provide half the wage during medical attendance: see 73.

[80] Hodgkinson, *The Origins of the National Health Service*, 682–3.

[81] *Ibid.*, 290–1.

[82] Brundage, *The English Poor Laws*, 99.

[83] Poor Law Continuation and Amendment Act 1842 (5 & 6 Vict. c. 57), s. 6.

played a part in a dismal cycle of ebb and flow from workhouses to asylums when workhouses were full or in the reverse direction when asylums were full. After numerous scandals, lunacy legislation in the 1860s brought about improvements in both workhouses and asylums. By the end of the 1860s the Poor Law Board had come to terms with the need for specialized treatment and further regulation.[84] Some of the scandals used in the reforming debates on health and mental illness revealed conditions which were squalid almost beyond belief to contemporaries, but it remained the case that such examples could encourage conservative as well as radical reactions. The financial difficulties faced by reformers were compounded in the middle of the century by the publication of accounts of the life of the poor—particularly the London unemployed—in works such as Henry Mayhew's *London Labour and the London Poor* (1851–62).[85] These could be quoted selectively to give portraits of those who would under no circumstances contemplate work and who thereby confirmed deep prejudice against the poor in general. The Victorian fascination with the possible moral accountability of those living in destitution was as strong as ever.

It remained the case that there was no consistent use of regulatory power in this type of context where professional influence could be decisive. In effect, Parliament would have to find more money before doctors would be prepared to work effectively within a system of health care for the poor. State regulation and professional power were uneasy companions, particularly where health was seen in terms of the needs of individuals rather than in the context of the general public interest. For sustained debates about statutory intervention on behalf of individuals there had to be a shift in perspective: the word 'health' had to bring to mind individual cases of suffering *and* wider social issues. It would take the major reforms of the post-Second World War Labour government to turn the issue of an individual's health into a public matter of such national significance that all health problems, private and communal, had a secure foundation in public law.

7. CONTROLLING THE MACHINERY OF THE POOR LAW

Beyond specialized areas of work there was the intricate business of everyday administration and its development over decades. Modern analysts such as Felix Driver have revealed the extent to which the links between the Board at

---

[84] Brundage, *The English Poor Laws*, 100, and, generally, P. Bartlett, *The Poor Law of Lunacy, The Administration of Pauper Lunatics in Mid-Nineteenth Century England* (Leicester, 1999).

[85] V. Neuburg (ed.), (1985).

the centre and the Guardians in the country were of great complexity in that they varied from one union to another.[86] Again and again, local influence came through.[87] This was what lay behind the most ubiquitous problem for the Board. Because it sometimes lacked local 'grip' it could not fully control the extent to which outdoor relief (as pointed out above, this was relief beyond the workhouse) continued to dominate expenditure. The expenditure on outdoor relief at this time has been calculated to have been about half of total expenditure.[88] In reality a fundamental tenet of the debates of 1834 was not being applied. People should either be outside the workhouse looking after their own interests and without support or within the workhouse and sustained at a level of deprivation which would give them every incentive to leave and 'shift' for themselves. For the most ardent reformers, outdoor relief always had the taint of indulging the idle at the cost of those who paid the poor rate.

The extent of outdoor relief became all the more of a volatile political issue after the Union Chargeability Act 1865.[89] This measure spread rateable value over an entire union and thereby incensed wealthy land owners who had previously been enjoying low contributions in slightly populated areas. The Metropolitan Poor Act 1867 produced similar tensions in London.[90] The latter Act further undermined local discretions by giving the union the status of a settlement area which enabled relieving officers rather than parish overseers to initiate removal actions. More generally, the frustrations produced by the attack on 'localism' interlocked with the views of critics who simply objected in principle to what they saw as uncoordinated and wasteful subsidies for people many of whom were, in their view, undeserving. The Society for Organising Charitable Relief and Repressing Mendicity (often known as the COS) was established in 1869 and included in its objectives the scientific investigation of individual cases with a view to distinguishing the potential worker from the workshy. A significant proportion of its membership came from 'professional' people. Charles Bosanquet, Octavia Hill, and others believed they could still recover what they took to be the pure intentions of the 1834 Act whilst ameliorating the suffering of 'genuine cases'.[91]

G. J. Goschen became President of the Poor Law Board in 1868 and in 1869 the 'Goschen Minute' was issued and it was to provide the early context for the

---

[86] See generally, F. Driver, *Power and Pauperism: the Workhouse System, 1834–1884* (Cambridge, 1993).

[87] R. Price, *British Society, 1680–1880: Dynamism, Containment and Change* (Cambridge, 1999), at e.g. 167 and 176.

[88] A. Kidd, *State, Society and the Poor in Nineteenth-Century England* (Basingstoke, 1999), 49.

[89] 28 and 29 Vict. c. 79; and see Brundage, *The English Poor Laws*, 108.

[90] 30 and 31 Vict. c. 6.

[91] For the law on charities, see pp. 507–517.

integration of poor law management into the new Local Government Board created in 1871.[92] The Circular which 'built upon' the Minute accorded closely with what the membership of COS was seeking. It revealed an intention to ensure that the completely destitute were left to the resources of the poor law whilst charities assisted those near to destitution. Most of all, Goschen and his successor at the Board, James Stansfeld, wanted to 'target' and restrict outdoor relief: 'the large increase which has within the last few years taken place in the amount of out-door relief has been regarded by the Local Government Board with much anxiety...'. In the view of the Local Government Board the problem now was not so much one of rules as implementation. Much of the increase was caused by 'defective management or administration of the law' and it followed that 'the remedy is in the hands of its local administrators, the Guardians, and may be at once applied by them'.[93] The Board made increasing use of advisory Circulars and Codes of Practice. The initiative had an impact on expenditure, not least through the appointment of 'appropriate' Guardians. In the East End Union of St George's the influence of Augustus Crowder as one of the Guardians ensured that outdoor relief all but vanished. Nationally, outdoor relief was given to 39.1 outdoor paupers per 1000 of the population in 1871 and by 1914 the figure was down to 10.5 per 1000 of the population.[94] In the years between 1871 and 1876 about 276,000, or about one in three of those on 'out-relief', were removed from the rolls. Women were particularly vulnerable with their number dropping from 166,407 in 1871 to 53,371 in 1891. In his analysis of these figures, David Englander concludes that 'The hardship and suffering concealed in these bald figures is difficult to imagine'.[95]

Later, in the mid-1880s, there was high unemployment in some of the skilled trades and even rioting in London. In response, the then President of the Local Government Board, Joseph Chamberlain, wanted municipal councils to provide for those out of work by putting on projects for employment. In his Circular of 15 March 1886 he responded to current unemployment by saying that 'What is required in the endeavour to relieve artisans and others who have hitherto avoided Poor Law assistance, and who are temporarily deprived of employment

[92] On the general role of the Local Government Board, see C. Bellamy, *Administering Central-Local Relations, 1871–1919: The Local Government Board in its Fiscal and Cultural Context* (Manchester, 1986). The 'LGB' was '... the first comprehensive client department for the local government system that emerged in British central government', p. 1. For links with modern debates, see M. Loughlin, *Legality and Locality, The Role of Law in Central-Local Government Relations* (Oxford, 1996).

[93] First Report of the Local Government Board, *PP* 1872 (516) App. A, No. 20, p. 63, 'Out-door Relief Circular from the Local Government Board to Boards of Guardians'; M. Rose, *The English Poor Law, 1780–1930* (Newton Abbot, 1971), 225–30.

[94] For the context of the 'Goschen Minute', see A. Kidd, *State, Society and the Poor in Nineteenth-Century England* (Basingstoke, 1999), 49–52.

[95] D. Englander, *Poverty and Poor Law Reform in Nineteenth Century Britain* (1998), 23.

is...work which will not involve the stigma of pauperism'.[96] To enable this to happen, Poor Law Guardians were asked (they could not be required) to work with Local Authorities. This adventurous approach to deprivation plainly broke with the methods of the 1834 Act. In the words of the Circular 'the Local Government Board have...thought it their duty to go beyond the returns of actual pauperism which are all that come under their notice in ordinary times, and they have made some investigation into the condition of the working classes generally'.[97] The new approach was supported by both Liberal and Conservative Governments and in practice it produced numerous local initiatives. Generally, it pointed towards new ways of using government to respond to poverty.[98] Further support for change came from novel studies of poverty. Andrew Mearns' *The Bitter Cry of Outcast London: An Inquiry into the Condition of the Abject Poor*, was followed by Charles Booth's major work, *The Survey into Life and Labour in London*, and Rowntree's analysis of York, *Poverty: A Study of Town Life*.[99] There was an interest in new ideas in response to deprivation.

The interest in alternative approaches was all the sharper because the Poor Law had not resolved basic problems through the Goschen initiative. Financial problems increased. There was an awareness that 'Aggregate poor relief and the amount spent per pauper had doubled between 1870–1 and 1905–6'.[100] As always, cost was a stimulus to further thought about the relief of poverty, and now there was the additional consideration that the everyday administration of the poor laws had become more difficult to control politically. Guardians could be elected from those with residential or rate paying qualifications and the system was more democratic than it had been. The result was disputes of a directly political nature as in the case of the Poplar Guardians in London under the leadership of Will Crooks and George Lansbury. Improved provision for the poor came with high rates and the latter produced protest.[101]

8. RIVALS TO THE PRINCIPLES OF 1834

By the middle of the first decade of the twentieth century the philosophy of the 1834 reforms had a significant rival. Instead of the threat of the workhouse as an instrument for controlling paupers, there was a belief that poverty should in

---

[96] Sixteenth Annual Report of the Local Government Board, *PP* 1887 [C. 5131], App. A, No. 4, p. 5.

[97] *Ibid.*

[98] Rose, *The English Poor Law,* 239, 258–60.

[99] (1883), (1886–1903), and (1901), respectively.

[100] Brundage, *The English Poor Laws*, 133.

[101] A. Offer, *Property and Politics, 1870–1914: Landownership, Law, Ideology and Urban development in England* (Cambridge, 1981), 303–8.

part at least be explained in social terms and assistance for the poverty-stricken should be targeted at their precise needs. For some years, amongst politicians in both the major parties, it was possible to find people attempting to bring together the old and new approaches with results which were sometimes mutually inconsistent. In 1904–5 the Conservative President of the Local Government Board, Walter Long, was largely responsible for the Unemployed Workman's Act 1905. The recognition of unemployment as a social evil requiring systematic legislative reform was novel. But the programmes authorized by the Act focused on using traditional combinations of poor law authorities and charitable institutions with only a limited role for local authorities.[102]

In this contentious political context the government set up the 'Royal Commission on the Poor Laws and Relief of Distress'. Created in 1905 it went on to hear evidence which in print took up 36 volumes. It was unable to reach a unanimous view on the way forward and produced Majority and Minority Reports in 1909.[103] In some contexts there was agreement. For example, all agreed that the aged and infirm should have their own form of treatment. More generally, the majority wanted a restructured poor law. This would provide 'public assistance' through an administration based on local authorities. It would unify the responses of the agencies confronting poverty and also continue with the tradition of using charities and case-work organizations. These changes could make for efficiency but they did not amount to radical change. The majority could still agree that 'The causes of distress are not only economic and industrial; in their origin and character they are largely moral'.[104]

The Minority Report was more talked-about. Produced openly by Beatrice Webb (who was a member of the Commission) and, informally, by Sidney Webb (who was not a member) it takes up two separate volumes and is formidable in its clarity.

The mere keeping of people from starving—which is essentially what the Poor Law sets out to do—may have been useful as averting social revolution: it cannot, in the twentieth century, be regarded as any adequate fulfilment of social duty. The very conception of relieving destitution starts the whole service on a demoralising tack. An Authority having for its function merely the provision of maintenance for those who are starving is necessarily limited in its dealings to the brief periods in each person's life in which

---

[102] A. M. McBriar, *An Edwardian Mixed Doubles, The Bosanquets versus the Webbs: A Study in British Social Policy, 1890–1929* (Oxford, 1987), 52–3.

[103] *RC on the Poor Laws and the Relief of Distress*, PP 1909 [Cmnd. 4499], xxxvi and [Cmnd. 4630, 4922], xxxviii.

[104] D. Fraser, *The Evolution of the Welfare State* (1973), 148, quoting the Report at [Cmd. 4499], 643–4.

he is actually destitute; and has, therefore, even if it could go beyond the demoralising dole—too bad for the good, and too good for the bad—no opportunity of influencing that person's life, both before he becomes destitute and after he has ceased to be destitute, in such a way as to stimulate personal effort....[105]

Also:

...the administration of the Poor Law has, in the course of the last generation, ceased to constitute a single service with a single technique. In place of the mere relief of destitution, with the constant aim of 'depauperisation', Parliament and public opinion—indeed the very nature of the case—have compelled the Local Government Board to advocate, and have led the Boards of Guardians to start, nurseries and schools, and hospitals and sanatoria, and farm colonies and homes for the aged, each of them involving its own expert policy, and necessitating, in the Central Authority as in the Inspectorate, its own kind of specialised knowledge.[106]

The two volumes of the Minority Report laid bare one shortcoming of the poor law after another. The general mixed workhouse was cruel and brought with it almost no prospect of improving conduct. Neither the workhouse nor outdoor relief could respond to the specialist needs of children, the infirm, the mentally incapacitated and the aged. Beyond its arguments, the language of the minority review was designed to stimulate debate: 'The very cots in which the infants lie have been previously tenanted by an incalculable succession of infants in all states of health and morbidity. It may well be that human infants, like chickens, cannot long be aggregated together, even in the most carefully devised surroundings, without being injuriously affected.'[107]

The minority view had consequences, not least in producing splits between Fabians, Socialists, members of the Labour party, and numerous others with an interest in reform. But in terms of legal change, almost nothing was to happen for the foreseeable future. At best the Local Government Board, under the direction of John Burns, issued Circulars to take away some of the most obvious failings to current arrangements. The poor law and its administrative structure was to survive into the inter-War years and to be gradually dismantled in the course of the 1930s.[108]

---

[105] S. and B. Webb (eds), *The Break-Up of the Poor Law: The Minority Report of the Poor Law Commission*, Parts I and II (1909), 518.

[106] *Ibid.*, 483.

[107] *Ibid.*, 103–4.

[108] Rose, *The English Poor Law, 1780–1930*, Ch. 5, 'The Break-up of the Poor Law, 1914–30'; L. Charlesworth, 'The Poor Law: A Modern Legal Analysis' (1999) 2 *Journal of Social Security Law*, 79–92.

9. THE FAILURE OF THE LAW

This inertia has often been explained in terms of vested interests along with the cost of reforms and the distractions of political events in the years before the First World War. There is much in this, but such explanations miss an important legal dimension. By the time of the Edwardian years, the poor law was an easy target for any contemporary critic looking at the arrangements for its rules. Historians have given this aspect of the poor law comparatively little attention but in fact it was of acute concern to the authors of the Minority Report. In the latter Report it was pointed out that the different types of Orders all had the force of law and that they existed

> ... in bewildering and literally uncounted numbers. They extend over the past seventy-five years; and they are nowhere collected or published in a complete series. The principle Orders alone are dealt with in the legal text-books which private enterprise has provided, some of which extend over 1000 pages. Many witnesses have complained to us of the impossibility under these circumstances of any Poor Law Guardian being able to find out what it was that the Local Government Board required him to do or not to do....[109]

To make matters worse, when the Orders were considered it was obvious that they were often out-of-date and that they had been replaced by unregulated administrative practice: 'The three main Orders, upon which the whole fabric depends—the General Consolidated Order of 1847 as to Indoor Relief, the Outdoor Relief Prohibitory Order of 1844, and the Outdoor Relief Regulation Order of 1852 are all of them more than half a century old. They were prepared for a state of things essentially unlike that of the present day.'[110] The result was that they had become 'diametrically at variance' with certain later developments. After about 1890 the Local Government Board had disapproved of the General Mixed Workhouse and had done much to undermine the way this part of the poor law worked, but it was still required in all its refinements under the General Consolidated Order of 1847. In respect of outdoor relief critics found the situation astonishing. Despite all the grand intentions of successive Presidents of the Board it was clear that in respect of what was 'distributed among the sick, the aged and infirm, the mentally defective, the widows, the deserted wives, the mothers of illegitimate babies, and the children of non-able-bodied fathers, there are no Orders of the Local Government Board stating whether Outdoor Relief should or should not be given to such

---

[109] S. and B. Webb (eds), *The Break-Up of the Poor Law*, 459–60.
[110] *Ibid.*, 460.

persons, or, if given, under what conditions'.[111] It followed that the existing Orders were 'to a large extent, ignored or evaded by all concerned...'.[112] Adventurous minutes by successive Presidents of the Board had increasingly inadequate linkage to rules.

To make matters even worse, there was a lack of clarity in the nature of the Orders. They failed to 'distinguish in form between peremptory laws which have to be applied judicially and inflexibly, and administrative injunctions serving as ideals and patterns which can be carried out with such modifications as local circumstances require'.[113] Failure to make this distinction had had serious consequences: 'To permit deviations from these formal Orders by private letters to particular Authorities, or by the oral sanction of an Inspector—still more to advise, by published Circular, wholesale evasions or violations of the spirit or the letter of these Orders (and this...has been the practice of the Local Government Board) is to destroy the moral authority, and prevent the enforcement of the Orders themselves.'[114]

In short, the way the Poor Law was expressed at the start of the twentieth century was near to being as important as its content. It was inaccessible even to intelligent and experienced practitioners. It was frequently observed in the breach. It is no wonder that major change did not arrive at this time. The relevant rules were so inadequate as a guide to practice that they could hardly be used as a platform for change. Beyond a radical alteration in content there would have to be changes in legal thought about the precise relationship between these prescriptive regulations and administrative variations at local levels. It was unlikely in the extreme that governments of any political hue would find the sustained energy required to produce new legal structures and modes of operation. Inertia and the survival for some years of laws which few believed in were always the most likely outcome.[115]

---

[111] *Ibid.*, 461.   [112] *Ibid.*, 462.

[113] *Ibid.*, 462.   [114] *Ibid.*, 463.

[115] For a naïve alternative view that a few reforms had had the potential to resolve the legal problems of the poor law, see H. G. Willinck (ed.), *Sir George Nicholls, A History of the English Poor Law in Connection with the State of the Country and the Condition of the People.* Sir George Nicholls was at one time a Poor Law Commissioner and Secretary to the Poor Law Board. The second volume published in 1898, covered the years 1714–1853, but, with the implicit approval of the later editorial hand, it ends on a hopeful note for the modern law at p. 436. There it is argued that issues of settlement and disputes about chargeability can be addressed and 'When this is done, there will be little occasion for further changes in our English Poor Law, which may then be readily consolidated into one comprehensive code, easy of administration, and intelligible to all.' This never happened.

10. NEW DIMENSIONS: PENSIONS AND NATIONAL INSURANCE

Given the difficulties presented by the poor law, it is no wonder that contemporary politicians and reformers looked elsewhere for realistic prospects of change. The provision of pensions and national insurance responded to ancient fears of destitution striking even those who had worked hard before old age or misfortune drove them to charity or the workhouse. Charles Booth's proofs of the incapacity for the most thrifty to provide for their old age combined with increasing public recognition that ageing was itself a cause of poverty. The Royal Commission on the Aged Poor, mentioned above, brought minor changes in the 1890s. But this sort of incremental reform did nothing to convince the authors of the Minority Report on the Poor Law in the next decade who saw the need for specialized innovation. The minority believed that in respect of pensions 'any age-limit above that of sixty-five—we might even say over sixty—will do little more than touch the fringe of the problem of Old-Age pauperism'.[116] Delays in reform were caused by friendly societies demanding that any scheme did not compete with what they offered their contributing customers. There was also, as always during these years, opposition to the simple idea of a pension. In the words of the jurist A. V. Dicey, 'Would not the stern but successful reformers of 1834 have held that old age pensions and comfortable cottage homes, provided at the cost of the tax payers, were little better than a decent but insidious form of out-door relief for the aged?'[117]

Overcoming objections such as these was no simple matter, but in the first decade of the new century the idea of financing pensions from taxation gained ground with W. H. Lever, the industrialist and philanthropist, attempting to put the change into law through a private member's bill in 1906. The attempt failed, but the Liberal government found space for a bill in 1908 and this provided 5s a week at the age of 70. At first the money was paid only to 'the deserving poor' but this requirement vanished in 1911. The money was administered through Post Offices rather than Poor Law Guardians. This was a significant administrative change. It helped to liberate an important part of British social policy from the constraints of Victorian assumptions with their focus on the Poor Law and its moral context. The law in this area now had every prospect of further development in later years.

---

[116] S. and B. Webb (eds), *The Break-Up of the Poor Law*, 346.

[117] A. V. Dicey, *Lectures on the Relation between Law and Public Opinion in England during the Nineteenth Century* (1905), 295.

The creation of pensions paid for out of general taxation contrasted with the provisions of the National Insurance Act 1911.[118] Here insurance was provided through the contributions of employers and workers. The notion of entitlement was founded on the financial sacrifice of contributors and not on some investigation into their moral worth. Of course, for it to reach the statute book there had to be an accommodation with political interests, including, again, the friendly societies and, in this case, the doctors. Analysts have frequently looked to the future and seen this as a 'foundation' for the welfare state. There is truth in it being seen in this way to the extent that contemporaries realized that something significant was being done to old ways of thinking about poverty. At the Local Government Board, John Burns was able to argue with, no doubt, considerable relief that the change was 'bigger' (his word) than either the Majority or the Minority Reports on the Poor Law.[119] It went beyond them both and thereby saved him from addressing either with great seriousness. Again the context was changing. For example National Insurance could be considered in relation to the reforms of Bismark's Germany. It was also possible for contemporaries to link these reforms to other changes in, for instance, the provision of school meals or enhanced arrangements for the unemployed. In the long term, even more radical change could be contemplated. In the words of Lloyd George, 'Gradually the obligation of the State to find labour or sustenance will be realised and honourably interpreted. Insurance will then be unnecessary'.[120]

Given that the poor laws were designed to respond to what many contemporaries regarded as the biggest problem of the society in which they lived, and also given that its rules were developed in a context fraught with political, social, moral, and economic issues, it is no surprise that the laws were continually seen as having radical failings. They could never respond to everyone's expectations. For the legal historian faced with the records of this continual criticism the laws are distinctive. The reforms of 1834 were conceived in the course of long debates about the moral accountability of individuals and the respective roles of central and local administration. After the Act had been passed the reforms provided legislation which authorized the subsequent creation of so many rules expressed in so much detail that no one person could convincingly claim to know them all. These rules were supplemented in the mid-Victorian years by policy statements and forms of practice which were often in direct conflict with the rules. For all its range, the factory of rules which was the poor law became an imperfect guide to the practice of the poor law. Laws which had sometimes

---

[118] 1 & 2 Geo. V c. 55.

[119] D. Fraser, *The Evolution of the Welfare State* (1973), 151.

[120] H. J. Bunbury (ed.), *Lloyd George's Ambulance Wagon* (1957), 116. For links with the Welfare State see R. Cranston, *Legal Foundations of the Welfare State* (London, 1985), Parts I and II.

ameliorated suffering and sometimes significantly increased it were eventually seen by contemporaries as having produced no clear route for the further use of the poor law as an instrument of social improvement. For Edwardian reformers, hopes for social change through law lay largely in ignoring the poor law and making it increasingly irrelevant through introducing alternative measures. By the start of the First World War the Poor Law had become a system of rules which was largely, but not entirely, in eclipse.

III

Charity and Education

1. CHARITY

Over the centuries, lawyers have responded to the good intentions of testators and others anxious to make charitable gifts. There have been instances where gifts have been found to be void because they fell short of legal requirements. On other occasions the legal mind has done all that can be done to enable the law to assist givers, even if the instruments the latter used have been defective and their ideas eccentric.

An important part of the law used by the Victorians had come into force at the end of the sixteenth century. In 1597 Parliament passed an Act '...to Reforme Deceits and Breaches of Trust touching Lands given to Charitable Uses' and this was re-enacted with amendments in the Charitable Uses Act 1601.[1] Amongst other innovations, the Act provided for commissions to investigate breaches of trust within the county specified in the commission. Those conducting the enquiry had substantial powers including the capacity to cure defects in conveyances. For trustees and others subject to these powers there was a right of appeal to the Chancellor. Successive Chancellors were active in developing an area of case law which, at this time, did much to ensure that the intentions of those who gave out of the kindness of their hearts and a desire to save their souls were realized in one way or another in practice. Famously, the preamble to the 1601 Act also set out at length the 'good, godly and charitable' uses over which the commission would have jurisdiction and thereby began to establish possible parameters for judges to use when assessing what could be charitable.[2]

---

[1] Respectively 39 Eliz. 1 c. 6 and 43 Eliz. 1 c. 4.

[2] 'Whereas lands tenements, rents annuities, profits, hereditaments, goods, chattels, money, and stocks of money, have been heretofore given, limited, appointed, and assigned as well by the Queen's most excellent majesty, and her most noble progenitors, as by sundry other well disposed persons: some for relief of aged, impotent, and poor people, some for maintenance of sick and maimed soldiers and mariners, schools of learning, free schools, and scholars in universities: some for repair of bridges, ports, havens, causeways, churches, seabanks and highways; some for education and preferment of orphans; some for or towards the relief, stock, or maintenance for houses of correction; some for marriages of poor maids; some for supportation, aid, and help to young tradesmen, handicraftsmen, and persons decayed; and others for relief or redemption of prisoners or captives,

Until the time of the Civil War the commissions established under this arrangement were regarded as effective. After the Restoration, for reasons which are not clear, the use of commissions fell away and was replaced with an 'Information' brought in the name of the Attorney-General at the relation of a private individual. These were sometimes inadequate and may have been less significant than notices put up in churches reminding parishioners of the existence of local trusts. In the eighteenth century it became increasingly common to encounter legal doubts as to whether judges of the previous century had gone too far in protecting the hopes of those who created charitable trusts or had been too generous in saving gifts which otherwise failed by finding alternative objects of charity.[3] The latter form of intervention by the court sometimes was taken to sophisticated lengths in the development of the doctrine of cy-près whereby Chancery would redirect the resources of the trust to another similar purpose where the precise original intention could not be realized.[4] More generally, opposition to unrestricted giving grew amongst those who saw an expanding law of charities as a threat to existing rights. In the courts the opposition was thwarted by the strength of the established case law. But in Parliament Jekyll's Mortmain Act of 1736 produced long-lasting changes, not least in declaring invalid devises of land by will upon charitable trusts. The Act reflected the interests of landowners who feared death-bed disinheritance, and, with certain exceptions, it received sustained support from a judiciary which gave its provisions a wide interpretation.[5]

As a result of these developments the law on charities became an area of legal practice in which cases and statutes could confuse a lawyer as much as a lay trustee. Trusts were, of course, being regulated by the court of Chancery and, here, the role of the poor law was important and contentious. Cornish has pointed out that: 'Chancery, indeed, began at this period to disapprove the older practice (still accepted by Eldon) of using charitable endowments to reduce the poor rate'.[6] In one case of 1805 the court found that the 'Jarvis' charity containing £100,000 for

and for aid or ease of any poor inhabitants concerning payments of fifteens, setting out of soldiers, and other taxes; which lands, tenements, rents, annuities, profits, hereditaments, goods, chattels, money, and stocks of money, nevertheless, have not been employed according to the charitable intent of the givers and founders thereof, by reason of frauds, breaches of trust, and negligence in those that should pay, deliver and employ the same'.

[3] G. Jones, *History of the Law of Charity: 1532–1827* (Cambridge, 1969), 106–7.

[4] For the early years of the application of charity funds *cy-près*, see *ibid.*, 72–91.

[5] 9 Geo. II c. 36. G. Jones, *History of the Law of Charity* (Cambridge, 1969), 113–19. Generally, on the significance of religion in nineteenth-century law, see Vol. XI, Pt 1, Ch. V, Law and Religion, pp. 132–59.

[6] W. R. Cornish and G. de N. Clark, *Law and Society in England, 1750–1950* (1989), 425; and see *Attorney General* v. *Exeter Corp* (1827) 2 Russ. 45; *Attorney General* v. *Exeter Corp* (1828) 3 Russ. 395; *Attorney General* v. *Wilkinson* (1839) 1 Beav. 390; *Attorney General* v. *Bovill* (1840) 1 Ph. 762.

the poor of only three small parishes was not open to challenge or adaptation.[7] In contrast, intervention by the court sometimes took the form of the further development of the doctrine of *cy-près*. For example, when the redemption of Christian slaves captured by Barbary pirates was no longer capable of being carried out as an object of charity the property was applied *cy-près* for the benefit of charity schools.[8]

There was a particularly important decision in *Morice* v. *Bishop of Durham* where the Master of the Rolls held a bequest void for uncertainty.[9] A testatrix bequeathed her residuary personalty for 'such objects of benevolence and liberality as (her executor) the Bishop of Durham in his own discretion, should most approve of'. In its analysis the court did not use the word charity in an everyday sense. For the judge 'its signification is derived chiefly from the Statute of Elizabeth (43 Eliz. c. 4). Those purposes are considered charitable, which that statute enumerates, or which by analogies are deemed within its spirit and intendment...'.[10] The vague terms of the gift in question could not come within these tests and the bequest was void for uncertainty. On appeal Lord Eldon upheld Grant's decision. In law charity meant 'either such charitable purposes as are expressed in the Statute or to purposes having analogy to those'.[11] It followed that a trust which merely benefited the public would not be upheld; the trust had to be charitable in the statutory sense and for the public benefit. In the words of G. Jones 'The full logic of Grant's and Eldon's pronouncements gradually led to the acceptance of the view that there could be no synonym for "charitable" and no substitute for the preamble as the source of the definition of legal charity'.[12] Unless a purpose trust fell within the preamble it was (with anomalous exceptions) void.

This line of reasoning through nineteenth-century decisions clarified a number of issues but, as Chesterman has shown, it had the consequence of divorcing the law from its initial concentration in the preamble on providing relief for the poor.[13] Poverty ceased to be a prerequisite. To stress the point, it was now possible for a purpose to be charitable if it fell within any part of the preamble or its 'equity' or 'spirit', and, additionally, a sufficiently large part of the public stood to benefit. Decisions under the Mortmain Act continued to fortify this approach in the nineteenth century, as in the case where Leach VC observed that a gift

---

[7] *Bishop of Hereford* v. *Adams* (1805) 7 Ves. Jun. 324.

[8] *Attorney General* v. *Ironmongers' Co* (1834) 2 My. and K. 576; and for its context in the law, see P. Luxton, *The Law of Charities* (Oxford, 2001), 551. On the control of private trusts in Chancery see Anderson.

[9] (1804) 9 Ves. 399.

[10] *Ibid.*, 405.

[11] (1805) 10 Ves. 522, 541.

[12] G. Jones, *History of the Law of Charity* (Cambridge, 1969), 126.

[13] M. Chesterman, *Charities, Trusts and Social Welfare* (1979), 53–62.

to a museum could be charitable without being 'in the nature of a relief'.[14] In
Attorney-General v. *Lonsdale* in 1827 there was a bequest for the establishment
of a school for educating the 'sons of gentlemen'.[15] Plainly, this had little to do
with the relief of poverty although it could be justified as charitable by a literal
reading of the preamble. Generally, nineteenth-century litigants were anxious
to argue for charitable status because in most decades it conferred various tax
exemptions.[16]

By the time of the decision in *Commissioners of Income Tax* v. *Pemsel* in 1891
it was possible for Lord Macnaghten as part of a majority in the House of Lords
to put forward the substance of this view.[17] The result is a frequently quoted and
comparatively short description of what is 'charitable'. 'Charity in its legal sense
comprises four principal divisions: trusts for the relief of poverty; trusts for the
advancement of education; trusts for the advancement of religion; and trusts for
other purposes beneficial to the community not falling under any of the preceding heads.'[18]

2. THE PUBLIC SCRUTINY OF
CHARITABLE TRUSTS

Beyond the case law there were long-standing demands for the proper everyday
regulation of the many trusts which were within the definition of charity. As early
as the middle of the eighteenth century, Parliament was passing local Acts for
the relief of the poor under which parish authorities were given specific powers
in relation to charitable trusts. For example, in Launceston Poor Relief Act 1755
Guardians of the Poor were empowered to receive and use certain property given
as charitable gifts whether to them specifically or the poor generally.[19] Thomas
Gilbert, the poor law reformer mentioned above in Ch. 2, was always alert to
the realities of poor law funding through trusts. In response to suspicions that
many trusts were badly administered he introduced a degree of accountability
through the provision of information under the Returns of Charitable Donations
Act 1786.[20] For contemporaries it was easy to see how arguments about the reform

---

[14] *Trustees of the British Museum* v. *White* (1826) 2 Sim. and St. 594: but note that it was not charitable under the general law on the full facts of the case.

[15] (1827) 1 Sim. 105.

[16] Chesterman, *Charities, Trusts and Social Welfare*, 58–62.

[17] [1891] AC 531 at 583. The dissenting judges were Lord Halsbury and Lord Bramwell who saw
an essential link between charity and poverty. See, also, G. Jones, *History of the Law of Charity*
(Cambridge, 1969), 124.

[18] [1891] AC 531 at 583.

[19] 28 Geo. II c. 38 and see R. Tompson, *The Charity Commission and the Age of Reform* (1979), 60.

[20] 26 Geo. III c. 58.

of the Poor Law could interlock with arguments about investigating and then reforming the work of charities.

The committed law-reformer, Romilly attempted a balanced approach to change in two Acts of 1812 but these proved to be largely ineffective.[21] After the failure of Romilly's Acts, attention turned away from direct statutory intervention. In 1818 Brougham and others attempted to go beyond isolated efforts at legislative reform and instead sought to set up a Commission to investigate the practical working of charities. The First Report of the Commissioners appeared in 1819. They had been required to inquire concerning charities in England for the education of the poor.[22] They considered 265 cases and wrote a Report of 643 pages. With an extended remit taking them beyond education they went on to produce a sustained series of Reports: there were another 13 by 1826. In the parliamentary session of 1826–7 they produced 'A General Index to the first fourteen Reports of the Commissioners appointed to inquire concerning charities in England and Wales', and the index took up 441 pages of references.[23] They had acquired a reputation for hard work.

The Charity Commission inquiry was, in fact, based on four commissions. Tompson points out that there were Commissions in 1818, 1819, 1831, and 1835 and by means of renewals there was, in effect, a programme of sustained enquiry until 1837. 'Throughout this period, the basic principles and constitution of the Commission were unchanged, but the composition and powers were altered from time to time, both by the successive enabling Acts and by other legislation.'[24] The Commissioners had power to enquire into estates and funds and the ways in which they had been used. They could investigate breaches of trust and abuses and whether the trusts could no longer be applied as had originally been intended. As to procedure, the Commission was heavily influenced by Chancery precedents. In respect of remedies admonition was the most common, but the Commissioners could also act as mediators; or if there was a need for a court ruling the process of certification to Chancery would be initiated.[25] Some 400 cases were sent to the Attorney-General with a view to obtaining intervention by the Court of Chancery, but in most cases the local trustees simply responded to criticism and redirected funds to appropriate purposes.

---

[21] 52 Geo. III c. 101, 102.

[22] First Report of the Commissioners appointed to Inquire concerning charities in England, for the Education of the Poor, PP 1819 (83). On the remit of the Report, see Jones, History of the Law of Charity, 167.

[23] A General Index to the First Fourteen Reports of the Commissioners Appointed to Inquire Concerning Charities in England and Wales, PP 1826–7 (281).

[24] Tompson, The Charity Commission, 122.

[25] Ibid., 122–3 and 137–8.

Tompson has also revealed the intricate context of the Commissioners' work within government. Their bi-annual reports were at first directed to the Crown and Parliament but after 1819 they went through the Home Office before reaching parliament. It is as if over time they were poised between an increasing range of officials and politicians in Whitehall and Westminster. Parliament retained the important power of funding the Commissioners by resolution of the House of Commons. Tompson is at pains to attack the established idea that 'the Charity Commission inquiry "led to" the formation of a permanent Board of commissioners'. In terms of ideas and public debate Tompson's view may underestimate the thoughts of those who read the Reports at the time or formed their own views as to the way in which contemporary charities were working. For example, the Poor Law Commissioners were not impressed with what they found. They had seen a link between their work and the role of trusts: 'Closely connected with the relief provided by the Poor Laws is the relief provided by charitable foundations. As to the administration and effect of those charities which are distributed among the classes who are also receivers of the poor-rate, much evidence is scattered throughout our Appendix, and it has forced on us the conviction that, as now administered, such charities are often wasted and often mischievous.... These charities, in the districts where they abound, may interfere with the efficacy of the measures we have recommended, and on this ground, though aware that we should not be justified in offering any specific recommendation with respect to them, we beg to suggest that they call for the attention of the Legislature.'[26] By implication, they would support a new administrative structure with permanent Commissioners.

An explicit call for such a body came from a Select Committee appointed to 'Examine Reports Presented to the House from the Commissioners appointed to inquire concerning charities in England and Wales' which reported in 1835. It contained well-known members such as Sir Robert Peel, Sir William Follett, and Daniel Whittle Harvey. It confessed that 'to examine the whole, or indeed any considerable portion of the Reports in detail, would have been a work of indefinite duration...'. By that date 26,751 charities had been looked at in England and 890 in Wales. The Committee members had read enough to recommend that:

Apart from those special cases which may call for the instant interposition of a court, Your Committee are inclined to recommend that the superintendence and, in certain cases, the administration of all property devoted to charitable uses should be intrusted to a permanent Board of three commissioners, or some other independent authority on

---

[26] S. G. and E. O. A. Checkland, (eds), *The Poor Law Report of 1834* (1974), 495–6.

whom should be imposed the duty of superintendence and control over the administration of all property devoted to charitable uses....[27]

But going beyond the terms of public debate, Tompson is right to stress that there was no immediate legislative action at the end of the Commissioners' work when 'The last payment from the Treasury to the account of the Charity Commission was made on 26th June 1841'.[28] In reality, by the start of the 1840s the practice of charities was based in part on statutes, in part on developing case law, in part on the work of trustees (which might or might not bear examination), in part on understandings between government departments, in part on the views of temporary Commissioners, and in part, at times, on a felt need to respond to public scepticism.

In this context of conflicting interests it is not surprising that change in the law for the everyday management of charities was easily thwarted. In the mid-1840s, there was, once again, talk of reform but aside from the complexity of the issues the proposals were opposed directly by the church, the universities, and other bodies which saw dangers for their various interests. The result was a series of unsuccessful bills.[29] But at the same time charitable reform remained as a public issue. It was kept in view by the fact that many of the Chancery suits brought by the Commissioners were still being heard long after the Commissioners had ceased to be paid. It was also known that Hine, at one time a Secretary for the Commissioners, had written of the episodic and therefore imperfect nature of these Chancery suits as an instrument for ensuring that charities worked as they should in everyday life across England and Wales. Like the Select Committee of 1835 he wanted a Board of Charity Commissioners which could provide administrative continuity.[30] The case for change was further strengthened by the widespread belief that Chancery itself was in need of radical reorganization. At a time when attempts at charitable reform by well-known lawyers such as Lyndhurst, Cottenham, and Truro were all being defeated the procedure of the Court of Chancery was an embarrassment. There

[27] *PP* 1835 (449) p. viii.

[28] Tompson, *The Charity Commission*, 202.

[29] These included: Charitable Trusts, A Bill Intituled an Act for Securing the Due Administration of Charitable Trusts in England and Wales, *PP* 1845 (430); (amongst other things, this Bill was designed to provide for the appointment of Commissioners); and three later Bills giving important roles to judges; Charity Trust Regulation: a Bill Intituled, An Act for Facilitating and Better Securing the Due Administration of Charitable Trusts, *PP* 1847–8 (617); Charitable Trusts, A Bill for Facilitating and Better Securing the Due Administration of Charitable Trusts, *PP* 1849 (195); Charitable Trusts, A Bill for Facilitating and Better Securing the Due Administration of Charitable Trusts, *PP* 1850 (35).

[30] Tompson, *The Charity Commission*, 205.

was an unstable mixture of opposition to reform and no satisfactory defence of the exiting arrangements.

Eventually, reform came in 1853, the same year in which Dickens published *Bleak House* with its ridicule of the ways of Chancery.[31] Under Cranworth's Charitable Trusts Act of that year there was legal and administrative innovation. In an Act which reads well, there was now to be a permanent Board of Commissioners. The Board had some significant resources and powers but there were also weaknesses reflecting the need to accommodate various interests in order for the Act to pass. Some religious bodies, for example, were given a special position. But in other respects those in search of change had reason to be pleased. There were three full-time Commissioners, one part-time Commissioner and administrative staff. In addition to powers enabling them to investigate alleged abuses, they could exercise jurisdiction concurrently with the Court of Chancery in non-contentious cases. Within significant limits they could make schemes for the use of charitable assets where purposes had not been set out in sufficient detail or where under *cy-près* the original purpose was not available. The commissioners were able to inquire, report, and certify and draft regulations relating to their work.[32] In 1855 the Secretary was made the 'Official Trustee' and could hold lands on behalf of charitable foundations.[33] After 1860 the Board could issue orders in its own right without court approval.[34] A regulatory agency with important powers had come into existence and, as with the Poor Law Commissioners, its full potential for law-making was uncertain and sufficiently threatening to cause concern.[35]

---

[31] C. Dickens, *Bleak House* (1853). An Act for the Better Administration of Charitable Trusts, 16 and 17 Vict. c. 137.

[32] An Act for the Better Administration of Charitable Trusts, 1853, 16 and 17 Vict. c. 137, s 9 stated that 'It shall be lawful for the said Board from time to time, as they in their discretion may see fit, to examine and inquire into all or any charities in England and Wales, and the nature and objects, administration, management, and results thereof, and the value, conditions management and applications of the estates, funds, property, and income belonging thereto'. For the position of the Church of England see s 46. Under s 60 the Commissioners had to make an annual report to Parliament. On the Act, see M. Chesterman, *Charities, Trusts and Social Welfare* (1979), 65–6.

[33] An Act to Amend the Charitable Trusts Acts of 1853, 1855 (18 and 19 Vict. c. 124). Under s 15 'The Secretary for the time being of the Board shall be a Corporation Sole by the name of "The Official Trustee of Charity Lands" for taking and holding charity lands and by that name...shall have perpetual succession.' Under s 6 the powers to inquire into charities were extended.

[34] An Act to Amend the Law Relating to the Administration of Endowed Charities, 1860 (23 and 24 Vict. c. 136), s 2. In some respects this power was restricted: see e.g. s 3. The Board could also play a role in selecting cases for the courts; under s 5 where any case was considered 'by reason of its contentious character or of any special questions of law or of fact which it may involve or for other reasons' the Board may send it to 'any of the judicial courts'.

[35] Tompson, *The Charity Commission*, 216.

Many of the anxieties of those who had opposed reform were to prove to be exaggerated. The Acts applied only to endowed charities where the capital was not to be given away. After 1860 the Commissioners made frequent use of *cy-près* schemes to free up trusts from purposes which had become obsolete with time. But here there were restrictions in the contemporary case law as in the requirement that *cy-près* could not be used where the purpose had become merely unwise: it had to be illegal, impossible, or impractical.[36] Restrictions on *cy-près* were an ever-present problem for the Commissioners. In 1859 Sir John Romilly clarified the doctrine as it had developed in the first half of the century. He expressed his views with some force in one of the cases arising out of a testator contemplating the 'erecting and endowing (of) almshouses for poor men and women, reduced by sickness, misfortune or infirmity' with the testator adding that if any person should 'give a site for such almshouses' then £60,000 is to be 'devoted to the several purposes of the said charity'. The question was raised as to whether the money could also go to a hospital attached to the almshouses. The answer was no. Speaking generally about *cy-près* Romilly stated that 'where a fund is given for a particular object, which entirely fails' the doctrine may be used. But that was not the case here. Looking beyond *cy-près* and the facts of the case before him he stressed that if a testator 'by his will, pointed out clearly what he intends to be done, and his directions are not contrary to the law, this court is bound to carry that contention into effect'. 'Accordingly, instances of charities of the most useless description have come before the court, but which it has considered itself bound to carry into effect.'[37] The new Commissioners had distinct limits to the exercise of their discretions within the law.

Over time, the Commissioners were assisted by some legislation on isolated topics as in the City of London Parochial Charities Act 1883 which in effect allowed Commissioners to make reasoned alterations to the terms of many 'City' charities. Enjoying the freedom to do as it wished through legislation Parliament even interfered with the exercise of discretions. For example under s 22 of the City of London Act it was required of the Commissioners that 'In making schemes for the application of charity property or endowments to educational purposes the Commission shall have as much regard to the educational interests of girls as of boys'. By 1897 the Act had been used to take an impressive range of initiatives including the establishment beyond 'the City' of two 'Polytechnic Institutes' with a third planned.[38] Considering the work of the Commissioners

---

[36] *Philpott* v. *St George's Hospital* (1859) 27 Beav. 107 at 112. M. Chesterman, *Charities, Trusts and Social Welfare* (1979), 67–75.

[37] *Philpott* v. *St George's Hospital* (1859) 27 Beav. 107 at 112–13.

[38] 44th Report of the Charity Commissioners, PP 1897 [8413], 17.

in general, Chesterman concludes that 'The commissioner's powers were at their strongest in the matter of "tidying up" the innumerable small trusts which were of little or no use'.[39]

Again, then, there was nothing simple or uniform about this process of scrutiny and control. There was an intricate history of using statute law, common law, and equity in debates about the validity and working of trusts. In his detailed study of charitable reforms, Tompson points out that 'There was no consistent policy evident in all of this activity, but there was a fairly clear pattern of increasing intervention and legislative regulation'. Beyond the law on what amounted to charity and what could be done with charitable funds he shows that this applied to charitable trusts concerned with enclosures, local improvements, and taxation as well as the poor laws. 'Within the general pattern there were two distinct modes: first, treating charitable gifts as a form of public welfare (and here the relation to legislation on poor relief was paramount); the second mode was treating charity as a form of property, and involved the various incidental adjustments which the law made affecting property...'.[40] It had taken decades for reform to become coordinated.

There were later occasions when the work of the Charity Commissioners was questioned. A Select Committee of 1894 saw a need to respond to 'the great political, social and industrial changes of the last twenty years'.[41] The Commission had developed increasingly important and, at times, controversial roles in respect of endowed schools and certain charities linked to the work of local government. It had also become larger. The work of the Committee revealed that the Commission had acquired a staff of seventy with most of the staff being clerks.[42] At the end of its work the Committee concluded that there was a need to consider a bill which would bring the Commissioners more directly under the control of Parliament and, at the same time, would give the Commissioners more power and resources to do their work. Perhaps wisely, the Committee declined to recommend precise terms for a bill or even particular reforms beyond its general statement of principle. In any event, its work was not followed by any revolutionary change.

Sensing that it was in the public 'eye' the Commission was careful to respond to political debates. So, for example, when pensions were being considered the Commissioners pointed to the extent to which their work was relevant to the provision of aid in old age.[43] Going beyond fashionable thought their take-over of limited but important judicial roles was more likely to have a long-term impact.

[39] Chesterman, *Charities, Trusts and Social Welfare*, 73.
[40] Tompson, *The Charity Commission*, 59.
[41] SC on the Charity Commissioners, *PP* 1894 (221), v.
[42] *Ibid.*, iv.
[43] 40th Report of the Charity Commissioners for England and Wales, *PP* 1893–4, [C. 6960], 20.

So in 1897 they could report that '...we have made 392 Orders during the past year, in exercise of the judicial authority first conferred upon the Board by the Charitable Trusts Act, 1860, for the appointment and removal of trustees, for the establishment of schemes for the regulation of charities, or for the vesting of their real estate....We can usually give the required relief through an easy and simple course of procedure, free from technicalities, and almost wholly free also of cost.'[44]

3. EDUCATION

At the start of the nineteenth century, education was not the business of government. It was largely left to private initiative and here benefactors frequently made use of trusts. Donors, some from the distant past, used trusts with a view to sustaining capital and income for schools into the future. They also had a way of including restrictions in the terms of the trusts, and these could prove to be controversial, particularly when trustees tried to respond to novel circumstances.

Disputes could lead to litigation and in this indirect way the Court of Chancery took on what amounted to a supervisory role in education. It interpreted the provisions of trust instruments within the framework of the law described in the section above. For example, in *Attorney General* v. *Whiteley* Lord Eldon ruled against an attempt to supplement the permitted Latin Greek and Divinity at Leeds Grammar School with modern languages, writing, and arithmetic.[45] An effort by Bentham, Romilly, and others to use a bill to defeat the impact of this decision failed. Eventually, minor modifications to trusts of this type became possible under Eardley Wilmot's Act of 1840 which gave Chancery larger powers in responding to disputes about the interpretation of educational trusts.[46]

In contrast to the restrictive approach to be found in cases such as *Attorney General* v. *Whiteley*, judges were prepared to enlarge entitlements under trusts where schools were seeking to attract boarding pupils. In his analysis of this

---

[44] 44th Report of the Charity Commissioners, 1897 [c. 8413], 8. This type of observation was expressed in similar ways through successive Reports. Generally, for studies of the social and international context of charities, see J. Innes and H. Cunningham (eds), *Charity, Philanthropy and Reform: From the 1760s to 1850*, (1998) (note esp. J. Innes, 'State, Church and Voluntarism in European Welfare, 1690–1850, pp. 15–66); M. Gorsky, *Patterns of Philanthropy: Charity and Society in Nineteenth Century Bristol* (1999); M Daunton (ed.), *Charity, Self-Interest and Welfare in the English Past* (1996); K. Waddington, *Charity and the London Hospitals: 1850–1890* (Bury St. Edmunds, 2000).

[45] (1805) 11 Ves. Jun. 241.

[46] Grammar Schools Act (3 and 4 Vict. c. 77).

attempt to increase the scope of trusts, Cornish points out that the cases revealed 'unequivocal class-preference'.[47] In a number of disputes it was declared that schools could admit borders to places which been established as day schools for local children. Eldon found that Rugby need not be confined to its role as a free school for local boys. Sir William Grant came to the same conclusion in respect of Harrow.[48] Later there were disputes over Tiverton, Kidderminster, and Bristol Grammar Schools. After the 1840s a third issue came through in the form of dissenting parents seeking to withdraw their children from (Anglican) religious instruction.[49] Ultimately, 'conscience clauses' allowing for withdrawal were often permitted so long as there was no explicit declaration as to the form of religious instruction in the foundation document. The law of trusts wove an increasingly intricate web of rules around the private provision of education and in doing so it reflected contested social and religious views.

On a different level of provision, trusts were important in supporting numerous smaller schools and these trusts often had clear terms of reference designed to ensure that they gave opportunities for education exclusively to poor children. It was believed by many contemporaries that some were being administered badly, and this is why, as we have seen above in considering charities, Brougham and others started to look at the work of trustees in general by focusing on those in charge of trusts with educational purposes. As a member of the Select Committee on the Education of the Lower Orders he supported an interim finding in March of 1818 that 'Your Committee are proceeding in the further consideration of the subject referred to them; but in the meantime they recommend the bringing in a bill for appointing Commissioners to inquire into the abuses of charities connected with the education of the poor in England and Wales; that no unnecessary delay may take place in prosecuting this investigation.'[50] Reporting in final form later in the same year the Select Committee was pleased to see some achievements in the work of charities, but, on the basis of their limited survey, they concluded that across the country the quality of education was very uneven. Often no charities were available in thinly populated rural areas and here the Committee wanted to see something like the Parish School system used in Scotland. Local people could pay for a school master but public assistance might be required for the building of school houses.[51] Most of all, the Report revealed a need for systematic work on what was happening with educational charities. In respect of many areas, no-one knew the quality of the provision.

---

[47] Cornish and Clark, *Law and Society in England,* 437.
[48] For both cases see *AG* v. *Clarendon (Earl)* (1810) 17 Ves. Jun. 491.
[49] e.g. *Re Warwick Grammar School* (1845) 1 Ph. 564.
[50] *SC on the Education of the Lower Orders, PP* 1818 (136), i.
[51] *SC on the Education of the Lower Orders,* Third Report, *PP* 1818 (426), 57.

Further information became public in the Reports of the Charity Commissioners. Again, Brougham and others were interlocking reforms to charities with the provision for education. We have seen that under the terms of their first report, which appeared in 1819, they were required 'to Inquire concerning charities in England, for the education of the poor'. The extent of their detailed work on education is striking. For example they revealed a notable number of trusts for the education of girls. At New Windsor there was a 'Ladies School' and the 'Jubilee School'. The latter was a 'school of industry for girls'. They were 'boarded and clothed and taught such employments as qualify them for situations as servants'.[52] Taken as a whole the Report was not a full analysis of charitable provision for education (amongst other things it did not look at casual contributions which might or might not be charitable) but it revealed that there was a considerable amount of educational activity. From a national viewpoint it was obviously completely uncoordinated but, again, it was clear that a lot of teaching was being done and that it was supported by charity.

There had been attempts at legislative reform for education. An Act of 1802 required masters to provide limited types of instruction for apprentices during the first four years of the apprentice's work.[53] The Act was not widely enforced.[54] More adventurously, in 1807 Samuel Whitbread sought a bill which would require each parish to provide at least two years of education. This was given a very limited form of application in 1819.[55] In 1820, in response to the work of the Select Committee and the Charity Commissioners, Brougham put forward an ambitious Parish Schools Bill which was designed to produce 'the better Education of the Poor in England and Wales'. The intention was that manufacturers would build the schools and regular income would come from a combination of rates, fees, and the redistribution of endowments. The staff were to be members of the Church of England appointed by the parish vestry; and the local clergyman could veto their appointment and dismiss them if he wished. Opposition from dissenters and Catholics was inevitable; and there were Anglicans who had difficulty in coming to terms with the notion of a national system of education. The bill failed but the debates did achieve a wider knowledge of educational provision.[56] They revealed the achievements of the National Society and the British and Foreign School Society in organizing charities for the education of children in some areas. But the debates had simultaneously pointed to the need for much greater resources and this could hardly appeal to a Parliamentary audience with current

52 *Ibid.*
53 42 Geo. III c. 73. See also below in Ch. V, p. 558.
54 See below in Ch. V, p. 559.
55 H. C. Barnard, *A History of English Education from 1760* (2nd edn, 1961), 65.
56 B. Simon, *Studies in the History of Education, 1780–1870* (1960), 151–2.

concerns about the cost of the poor law. Educational reform through parliamentary legislation was becoming an unlikely prospect. The extent to which educational issues were often seen as being linked to debates about the working of charitable trusts does much to explain why direct attempts at procuring public subsidy through legislation were so weak. For many, education remained a matter for private philanthropy.

4. 'A SUM, NOT EXCEEDING TWENTY THOUSAND POUNDS'

Parsimony and fear of religious argument thwarted further initiatives until, most radically, in 1833, John Roebuck tried to go even further than Brougham had done: 'In general terms, I would say, that I would oblige, by law, every child in Great Britain and Ireland, from, perhaps, six years of age to twelve years of age to be a regular attendant at school. If the parents be able to give, and actually do give their children elsewhere sufficient education, then they should not be compelled to send them to the national school. If, however, they should be unable or unwilling to give them such instruction, then the State should step in and supply the want,' by compelling the parent to send the child to the school of the State.'[57] This was linked to novel administrative arrangements for a national system under the control of a Cabinet Minister. The proposal was debated at length. But again the measure failed; apart from the expense involved, it raised difficult questions about the role of the churches, the raising of public money for controversial social causes and even a fear of how an educated poor might wish to exert their political influence.

In practice, the importance of Roebuck's bill lay in the response of government to what was seen as an increasingly intractable issue which required some sort of initiative even if it did not take the form of legislation. The bill may have failed but the Government voted through the first grant in aid of educational buildings. The resolution required 'That a sum, not exceeding twenty thousand pounds, be granted to His Majesty, to be issued in aid of Private Subscriptions for the Erection of School Houses, for the Education of the Children of the Poorer Classes in Great Britain...'.[58] This wording was important. The grant was in 'aid of Private Subscriptions' which meant, in practice, that it was given over to the National Society and the British and Foreign School Society and these organizations had to find local subscriptions equivalent to half of any

---

[57] *PD* 1833 (s. 3), 20: 153; H.C. Barnard, *A History of English Education from 1760*, 68.
[58] (1833) 88 *HCJ* 692–3.

particular grant.[59] It was at best a mixed achievement. For example, preference was given to large schools and this had an adverse impact on educational provision in impoverished rural areas. Even where schools were provided there was no set of minimum standards for building and, at first, there was no supervision of the teaching which took place within the buildings. Yet the grant was momentous in that it provided a mechanism for annual increases in educational provision.

As early as 1838 the limitations of what had been done were made clear to Parliament. A Select Committee on 'The Education of the Poorer Classes in Large Towns throughout England and Wales' pointed out that 'In some places schools are supported almost entirely by the bounty of one or two persons'.[60] In respect of education generally it emphasized that:

Until very recently the subject appears to have entirely escaped the attention of Government. There appear to be no returns to Parliament of any authority on this point, nor indeed are there at present adequate means of making them....And in this matter, important as it is to the welfare of all classes, there seem to exist no sources of information in any Department of Government.[61]

The clear analysis did not lead the Select Committee to recommend significant action. Sensing the religious and other difficulties involved in any radical programme it supported the continuation of the grant. There was a limited amount of administrative change in the years which followed. In 1839 Lord John Russell announced the establishment of an Education Committee of the Privy Council. It was quite unlike the Poor Law Commission. It used withdrawal of funds as its sanction and was under no more than the very limited duty of recording its principles for distributing the grant which could now be directed to more than the construction of buildings. Using its financial power, it began to insist on inspection as a prerequisite for the making of a grant. The secretary, Dr Kay, later Sir James Kay Shuttleworth, worked hard and shrewdly to establish its reputation until he retired through over-work in 1849. In 1852 the Privy Council Committee imposed conscience clauses as a precondition of grant. An organization for the provision of state education was developing and, strikingly, it was doing so largely outside the context of statute law.

Exceptions to this rule included schools provided under the poor law (about 520) and Graham's Bill of 1843 which followed the early nineteenth-century attempts to ensure that 'factory children' be given at least some form of

[59] M. Sturt, *The Education of the People* (1967), 68–92; and see B. Simon, *Studies in the History of Education, 1750–1870* (1960), Ch. 3.

[60] *PP* 1837–8 (589), iii.

[61] *Ibid.*

education. These examples kept the issue of organized provision 'alive'.[62] Again there were wrangles between Anglicans and Dissenters but the further integration of teaching into Factory regulations amounted to a type of state control. There was now a limited degree of legal compulsion in education in the sense that certain people had to provide it and certain children had to experience it. But, as before, legislative initiatives such as this were unusual. In substance the arrangement whereby national education was provided was not based on statute. Holdsworth rightly points out that the state did not begin 'actively to intervene' until 1870.[63] With hindsight, it is surely possible to see the lack of legislation as the product of a widespread belief that 'something had to be provided by way of education' and an inability on the part of successive governments to find the time and determination to take on religious and other interests which came to the fore whenever the precise provisions of bills were discussed. It was a compromise which allowed for rules produced by parts of Whitehall and ambiguities in what should make up a national scheme.[64]

Obviously, major issues remained unresolved. 1861 saw the Report of the Commissioners 'Appointed to Inquire into the State of Popular Education in England', commonly known as the 'Newcastle Commission' after the name of its Chairman, Lord Newcastle.[65] The Commission worked hard, taking a wide range of evidence. The annual grant had increased from £30,000 to £80,0000. There was a painful awareness that sometimes there were better arrangements abroad, and there was interest in Matthew Arnold's views in his role as an Assistant Commissioner with a knowledge of what was happening in Germany, France, Switzerland, and Holland.[66] In respect of the grant the Commission argued that 'This arrangement has never been recognised as ultimate or permanent, but has grown up as a sort of compromise between the admitted necessity of promoting popular education and the difficulty of devising any general system for that purpose which would be accepted by the country.'[67] Provision and standards varied markedly from one place to another. Statistics were largely a matter of guesswork: perhaps the grant system reached a million pupils; and perhaps rather more attended private schools which were often small and lacking in any permanent endowment. Despite its sense of embarrassment at England's comparative position, the Commission rejected the use of the law to secure compulsory attendance at school. Instead, moral and social pressures

[62] See below in Ch. V, pp. 585–6.

[63] Sir William Holdsworth, *A History of English Law* (1964), xiv: 226.

[64] For a study of these years, see S. J. Curtis, *History of Education in Great Britain* (7th edn, 1967), Ch. 7, 'Elementary Education in the Age of Philanthropy'.

[65] *PP* 1861 [2794–1], XXI.

[66] *Ibid.*, 7.

[67] *Ibid.*, 20.

should be used. A majority argued in support of those witnesses who wanted teachers to be paid by results. This was linked to a 'Code' of 1862 from Robert Lowe at the Education Department which gave a third of the grant for sufficient attendance and two-thirds for satisfying an Inspector's standards. This scandalized those such as Matthew Arnold who wanted education to be thought of in broader terms but in one form or another it survived for almost 40 years. For one educational historian 'Newcastle' was 'the only Royal Commission of this period which had no outcome in legislation and introduced no fundamental reform'.[68] If anything, interest in educational issues increased just as much as the belief that it would be very difficult to introduce change. It was a recipe for sustained dissatisfaction.

In 1861 the Earl of Clarendon carried out an Inquiry into the nine major 'public schools' which educated about 3000 boys.[69] This Commission supported the claim of these schools to be producing a governing elite endorsing the long-term project of limiting local entry. Its recommendations led to the Public Schools Act 1868 which enabled the schools to change their governing structure whilst leaving them largely independent of government scrutiny.[70]

Later, at the end of the 1860s, Lord Taunton chaired the Schools Inquiry Commission.[71] This looked at those schools which were not within the parliamentary grant (and had thereby been investigated by the Newcastle Commission) and not one of the nine major 'public schools' considered by 'Clarendon'. Broadly speaking, this led its investigations to three types of school: those with permanent charitable endowments; private schools which were the property of the master or mistress who conducted them; and schools owned under other arrangements such as those which were corporations. It did not pretend to look at all the schools within these categories. It could hardly do so given the numbers involved; probably the schools owned by masters and mistresses exceeded 10,000.

In the course of its wide-ranging survey it recognized that there had been some successes under existing arrangements but this involved it stepping outside its remit and referring to the parliamentary grant considered in the Newcastle Report. For example:

At Bunbury in Cheshire an old grammar school with income from endowment of about £50 a year was, before 1854, doing as little good as many small grammar schools are now. The School was quite free. The clerk of the Parish, who kept a public house, was the school-master. Upon two occasions, when the Government inspector was invited to

---

[68] Simon, *Studies in the History of Education*, 349.

[69] *RC on Certain Public Schools in England*, PP 1864 [3288], XX, XXI.

[70] Public Schools Act 1869. Under s 10 the statutes produced by the respective governing bodies were subject to the approval of Her Majesty in Council. The Act is notably specific on various matters: under s 26 there is a power for the Governors to remove a school to another site.

[71] *RC on Schools Inquiry*, PP 1867–8 [c. 3966], XXVIII.

come, and notice was given of his visit, neither master nor scholars were to be found. The School was remodelled, and made the common School of the parish. A trained and certificated master was put at the head, fees were demanded, the Privy Council Grant and inspection obtained, and the result is that for a total expenditure of £240 a year, besides a good house for the master, which was built mainly by subscription, there are 110 scholars receiving an excellent English education.[72]

Obviously the structure of national educational arrangements was becoming intricate with private endowments and public grants interlocking with each other. For the Taunton Commission the concentration on endowments and private schools led it to look in most detail at the education of the 'middle classes' and this could lead it to contentious topics. For instance, it acknowledged that in practice the views of parents were important. But it was clear to the Commissioners that '...many parents need education themselves in order to appreciate education for their children...'.[73] Elsewhere, urged on by evidence relating to their respective schools from Miss Beale and Miss Buss, the Commission looked at arrangements for girls. Matters such as this were of current interest, but the Commission's analysis could become somewhat strained in its attempt to reflect the evidence it had heard:

It must be remembered dealing practically with the question, that it is only on the whole, and balancing one quality against another, that we can speak of the equal intellectual capacity of the sexes. Many differences, such as the tendency to abstract principles in boys contrasted with the greater readiness to lay hold of facts in girls—the greater quickness to acquire in the latter with the greater retentiveness in the former—the greater eagerness of girls to learn—their acuter susceptibility to praise and blame—their lesser inductive faculty—and others are dwelt on by our witnesses.[74]

The Report may not have arrived at clarity on this issue, but it had ensured that the education of both sexes was part of public thinking for the future. Looking beyond the debates, it was predictable that the Commissioners would take a hard-headed look at the inefficiencies locked into current provision and recommend an equally hard-headed focusing of funds. They directed that endowments would be subject to radical *cy-près* analysis, parents would contribute to teaching costs, and rates would assist towards buildings. In part this was carried through in the Endowed Schools Act 1869 which, amongst other reforms, created a Commission with powers to alter endowments. The recommended changes to trusts were no longer to be the business of Chancery but were to go for agreement to the Education Department, possible appeal

---

[72] *Ibid.*, 195.   [73] *Ibid.*, 15.   [74] *Ibid.*, 553–4.

to the Privy Council, and, lastly, to be placed before Parliament.[75] Within a few years the new Commissioners had produced sufficient alarm for their function to be transferred to the existing Charity Commissioners who took a more steady approach, but even they started to redirect funds in a significant manner.

All of this work left national elementary education more or less where it had been. Over the years the work of the Taunton Commission inevitably became identified as having set up the parameters for middle-class education, and in this context its impact endured into the 1890s. But it gave little guidance on the education of the poor. By the late 1860s criticism of provision for the poor had sharpened. The extension of the franchise in 1867 produced discussion about the need to ensure that new voters were educated. Radicals in organizations such as the National Education League could point to a complete lack of education for many of the children in expanding cities such as Birmingham. Employers thought compulsory education could contribute to a more disciplined workforce. Trade Unions saw reform as a way of raising the political awareness and power of working people.[76] It was as if the Taunton Commission had left a void which had to be filled.

5. 'PARLIAMENT SHOULD GUARANTEE TO EVERY CHILD AN EDUCATION'

Major legislative reform came in W. E. Forster's famous Education Act 1870. His Elementary Education Bill received its first reading in the Commons on 17 February 1870.[77] In the course of the debates he was sensitive to incompatible views. He robustly asserted that 'In measures of constructive legislation, it seems to me that the purpose—the end aimed at—matters much; and the precise method matters comparatively little'. From the start he was sensitive to the fear of some Members of Parliament of using statute as an instrument for improving the educational standards of the poor. He knew that opposition could arise from those who were disturbed by the basic idea of poor children receiving systematic instruction. He argued that 'The question of popular education affects not only the intellectual but the moral training of a vast proportion of the population, and therefore we must not forget that in trying to do good it is possible to do

---

[75] Endowed Schools Act 1869. On the system of approvals and appeals, see ss 37 and 39. For restrictions on the role of judges, see s 52.

[76] Curtis, *History of Education in Great Britain*, 354–63.

[77] *PD* 1870 (s. 3), 199: 438.

harm'.[78] He also hoped to avoid it becoming a party issue.[79] He wanted the bill to be 'capable of development, so as to meet the necessities of the future'.[80] He spoke dramatically with reference to 11,000 day schools and 2000 night schools. He thanked those who had already provided support such as Mr Melly whose contributions on the problems of the major cities had reflected the latter's experiences as the Member for Stoke.

Throughout, Forster argued that he was not in pursuit of any particular theory of education; his commitments were, he said, realistic. Unlike the Poor Law Commissioners of the 1830s, he spoke with something like disdain for theory; ideals and practicality were the guides for innovation. 'Members will see, when they read the bill, that the practical action of it will be limited to the proved need'. The present system, he argued, did not work. 'Therefore notwithstanding the large sums of money we have voted, we find a vast number of children badly taught, or utterly untaught, because there are too few schools and too many bad schools, and because there are large numbers of parents in this country who cannot, or will not, send their children to school.' He sought rigorously to combine practicality with the 'high ideal' of the public provision of education.[81] Only in this way could he satisfy what he felt to be national requirements.

Within the bill he saw two main principles. There is to be 'Legal enactment, that there shall be efficient schools everywhere throughout the kingdom'. And there would be 'Compulsory provision of such schools if and where needed, but not unless proved to be needed.'[82] In other words the new commitment to statutory reform was based on the need for national powers of compulsion which went beyond the previous reliance on indirect financial sanctions. Statutory reform was seen as an assertion of the national interest. True, various places presented special problems. For example, 'With regard to the metropolis, the difficulties of which, from its peculiar position, defy almost all attempts at legislation, we shall be guided very much by the counsel and advice of the metropolitan Members...'.[83] But throughout he stressed the central importance of compulsory provision: 'Where we have proved the educational need we supply it by local administration—that is, by means of rates aided by money voted by Parliament, expended under local management, with central inspection and control.'[84] The countryside presented as great a challenge as the cities: 'We are behind almost every other civilized country, whether in America or on the Continent of Europe, in respect of rural municipal organisation.'[85]

[78] *Ibid.*, 438.   [79] *Ibid.*, 438.
[80] *Ibid.*, 440.   [81] *Ibid.*, 443.
[82] *Ibid.*, 444.   [83] *Ibid.*
[84] *Ibid.*, 451.   [85] *Ibid.*, 452.

The possible use of school fees was discussed at length. He knew that for many the reality was poverty. He returned again and again to the fearful destitution that existed in places like Liverpool and Manchester.[86] But, always sensitive to the concerns of his parliamentary audience, he acknowledged that religion was still very much of an issue. He pointed to debates within the Church of England as well as debates between denominations. Here, as elsewhere, he had praise for Sir James Kay-Shuttleworth and used the latter's authority to argue for the conscience clause (whereby parents could withdraw a child from certain forms of religious instruction), undenominational inspection, and compliance with conditions aimed at securing secular efficiency. Forster's final points were moral and were expressed with more feeling than eloquence: '...I am not a fanatic in this matter of education, I know well that knowledge is not virtue—that no education, much less elementary education, gives power to resist temptation—is a safeguard against calamity; but we all know that want of education—that ignorance is weakness, and that weakness in this hard struggling world generally brings misfortune—often leads to vice'.[87]

Initially, support came from numerous quarters in Parliament. Henry Fawcett argued that 'To provide, then, was not enough. Parliament should guarantee to every child an education.'[88] Sir Stafford Northcote emphasized the importance of parliamentary debate for the public. For him the argument was important because the bill would be read in the country 'and points in it will probably be better understood from explanations given in this House than from a perusal of the text'.[89] Such support revealed the extent to which a perception of national need was overriding sectional interest.

The compliant start to the debates gave way to dissent and even confusion. Educational reformers such as George Dixon, a recent Mayor of Birmingham, joined with Nonconformists in protesting at the fact that under the proposed bill religious instruction in schools could be supported by public funds and rates were to be determined by local authorities. In Dixon's view, all rate-aided schools should be unsectarian and in other schools the secular and religious instruction should be separate. Forster did not agree, stating that it was not for an Act of Parliament to exclude Bibles from schools. After three nights of debate Gladstone intervened and ensured that religious issues would be fully explored at the Committee stage. Some Members, including Disraeli, saw the bill which went to Committee as being in some respects a new measure. There was a conscience clause allowing parents to withdraw their children under certain

---

[86] *Ibid.*, 455.   [87] *Ibid.*, 466.
[88] *Ibid.*, 482.   [89] *Ibid.*, 496.

circumstances and at certain times. Further, no form of religious instruction which 'is distinctive of any particular denomination' would be taught. Rates would not be used to maintain denominational schools but they were promised an increased Treasury grant. School Boards would be elected by those on the burgess role of a borough and elsewhere by ratepayers. The result was a system which preserved the voluntary schools and enabled the use of School Boards with significant powers. The latter included the capacity to compel attendance for children between the ages of 5 and 13.[90] After prolonged and acrimonious arguments these rather elaborate compromises enabled the measure to pass through both the Commons and the Lords.

Implementing the Act was another matter. In practice, progress with School Boards was to prove slow; in rural districts it was sometimes many years before they were set up. In part this may have been the result of a fear of central overview and control. If the Board contravened the Regulations made by central government under the Act, or failed to maintain the school or keep it efficient, central government could declare it to be in default and supersede the members of the School Board by its own nominees. The arrangements for the allocations of funds had to be more intricate than had been realized in debate, and the old argument about the rate-payers of one denomination having to subsidise instruction with which they did not agree arose once more. In contrast to these difficulties, the Churches, particularly the Church of England, were strikingly successful in taking initiatives to provide extra school accommodation with remarkable sums of money being contributed by church-goers.

Curtis long ago pointed out that the 1870 Act has frequently been misunderstood:

There is a very widespread idea amongst the general public that the Act of 1870 inaugurated universal free compulsory education. Nothing is further from the truth. It is one thing to provide school places, but a very different thing to see that they are filled, and much of the interest of the next twenty-five years lay in the efforts made to secure regular attendance, to make the schools free, and to raise the average leaving age.[91]

More recently, Gillian Sutherland has remarked that Forster's Act 'at last embodied a commitment to nation-wide provision: but the form it took showed the continuing power of the denominational vested interests. The Act allowed the voluntary schools to continue unchanged, with the same committees of managers.'[92]

---

[90] For a detailed account of these political compromises, see Curtis, *History of Education in Great Britain*, 275–81.

[91] *Ibid.*, p. 282.

[92] G. Sutherland, 'Education', in F. M. L. Thompson (ed.), *The Cambridge Social History of Britain, 1750–1950*, 3 vols (Cambridge, 1990), iii: 142.

Viewed in positive terms it could be said that 'The 1870 Education Act established a locally based system of primary education. It also provided for the appointment of school attendance officers to enforce attendance and to administer the fee structure which remained a feature of primary education until 1891.'[93] Beyond these equivocal achievements, one change was likely to be of long-term significance in legal terms. The administrative rules which had been used to control various forms of provision (often through the threat of withdrawing grant allocations) were now, as it were, encased within a major piece of parliamentary legislation. Education was emphatically a legal issue.

6. NATIONAL EXPECTATIONS AND UNIVERSITY AUTONOMY

The novelty of the confident use of statute law in an educational context was reflected in parliament's approach during these years to the use of religious tests at Oxford and Cambridge.[94] Again, the need for statutory intervention came with the sense of national accountability reflected in debates about schools. In respect of religious tests this had already appeared in parliamentary debates about universities in 1865. There had been a major attempt to reform the use of certain 'religious tests' in the 1865 Tests Abolition (Oxford) Bill. At second reading there was a sustained debate with a particularly long opening speech by George Goschen whose work with the poor law has been mentioned above in the first section. Some of the reforms were quite intricate and generally did not seek to entrench on all collegiate religious requirements, particularly in respect of many fellowships. But beyond the detail much of the debate had a robust and emotional quality. 'Our position is—that our universities, historically, for all general purposes, are national institutions, and legally, lay corporations. That their exclusive connection with the Church of England is, if I may use a technical term, accidental not essential.' Many continental Catholic Universities, it was argued, apply no such tests. Further, 'To represent Oxford as a clerical seminary is to rob Oxford of its title to be a University at all.' 'Oxford aspires to give a certain tone and character to the intellect and feeling of the nation, and the establishment of her middle-class examinations, and the success which has attended them, show a growing bond of sympathy between herself and the country.' It was now being suggested by those hostile to reform that he was going to 'make a manufacturing

---

[93] R. Price, *British Society, 1680–1850* (1999), 228.

[94] For an analysis of University education at this time, see G. Sutherland, 'Education', in F. M. L. Thompson (ed.), *The Cambridge Social History of Britain, 1750–1950*, 3 vols (Cambridge, 1990), iii: 154–8.

college of Oxford'. Not so: there was no truth in 'a vague idea in the minds of Oxford men, that manufacturers are all Dissenters...'. Other obstacles to national interference in local restrictions had often been overcome elsewhere, including within Parliament itself. Referring to the admission of Jews and Dissenters to Parliament Goschen asked 'Have the Jews and Dissenters in this House swamped every other element? Are they likely to swamp it? And on what conceivable principle would they swamp the university?'[95] Generally, as so often happened in Victorian debates about the use of legislation, the justification for interference was expressed in terms of national need. Goschen argued that:

If the Universities are really thrown open, if they are freely recognised as national institutions, if they are made to feel responsible for the education of the country at large, if they recognise the duty of supplying candidates not only for the Bar and the Church, but for every department of national life, the Universities will not have been lowered in character, their tone will not have become, as some Members are not ashamed to insinuate, more vulgar, but they will have established a fresher and a surer hold, not only upon the intellect, but upon the affections and reverence of the nation.[96]

The preparedness to use statute law to interfere with religious 'tests' raised questions about the role of the Church of England.[97] Here many in Parliament felt they had to find the true role of the Church: 'Sir, the truest connection, the surest connection, between the University and the Church can never be severed by an act of this House. It must rest on the intrinsic power of the Church—on the hold of the Church over the respect and the affection of the nation.'[98] Mountstuart Grant Duff was emphatic: 'I think it will benefit the Church, because anything that can in any way contribute to making her understand that her true strength lies, not in her dogma, but in her actions upon the nation, not in the infallibility of her creed, but in the purity of her life, cannot fail to benefit her.' Others, such as Lord Robert Cecil, remained to be persuaded and eventually this particular measure failed.[99] But further attempts at change were anticipated. It was sensed that it was only a matter of time before statute law broke into another area of national life and was discussed with reference to moral and religious differences of view.

A. V. Dicey saw the significance of what had happened when the reform reached the statute book six years later. 'In 1832 a system of religious tests still closed the national universities—in the case of Oxford wholly, in the case of Cambridge all but wholly—to any person who was not an avowed member of

---

[95] *PD* 1865 (s. 3), 180: 197–9.   [96] *Ibid.*, 198.

[97] See Vol. XI, Pt 2, Ch. III, The Church and the State, pp. 385–400.

[98] *Ibid.*, 207.   [99] *Ibid.*, 211.

the Church of England.'[100] 'At last in 1871—thirty-nine years after the passing of
the Reform Act and three years after the introduction of household suffrage—
Parliament abolished the tests which kept large bodies of Englishmen away
from Oxford and Cambridge. The national universities have at length become
the universities of the nation. The length of time, the slowness of the process,
the greatness of the efforts needed for the attainment of this result—and this
during a period when liberalism was the dominant opinion of the day—gives us
some measure of the force exerted by the opposing current of opinion.'[101] Once
again, in educational matters Victorian statutory reform was achieved by attrition through the constant reassertion of what was taken to be a responsibility
to the nation.

7. SECONDARY EDUCATION

Between the robust arguments about the provision of primary education under
the 1870 Act and the intricate debates about University 'tests' lay what would
now be called secondary education. It was then conceived of ambiguously as
education beyond the elementary level. The word 'elementary' had not been
defined in the 1870 legislation. E. J. R. Eaglesham has shown that with the best of
intentions the men who debated the 1870 Act had created the potential for sustained conflict between administrators wishing to use the Act as a platform for
further reforms.[102] Beyond the uncertainty as to what was 'elementary' there was
no clear boundary between the work of the Science and Art Departments or the
Education Department or the Charity Commissioners. To make matters more
controversial, the politics of educational reform became interlocked with relations between Whitehall, county councils, local School Boards and competing
factions seeking a variety of reforms. It now proved to be of central significance
that under the 1870 Act the School Boards had been integrated into the systems
of control which had been developed for the poor law and sanitary authorities.
As a result, many contested issues went on appeal to the Local Government
Board (which might or might not consult with the Education Department) or,
on a point of law, to the Divisional Court of the Queen's Bench Division. It was
in this context that something like rate-supported nursery schools and separate

---

[100] A. V. Dicey, *Lectures on the Relation between Law and Public Opinion in England during the
Nineteenth Century* (1905), 347.

[101] *Ibid.*, 349.

[102] E. J. R. Eaglesham, *The Foundations of Twentieth Century Education in England* (1967), Ch. 1.

science schools could be struck down. Rules, law, and politics reacted one upon the other.[103]

In 1888 a Royal Commission looked at the working of the education legislation for elementary schools and such was the conflict in current fashions of thought that it produced Majority and Minority reports.[104] But it was possible to argue that 'the first and main object of the Act of 1870 has now been accomplished. Elementary education is universally available; the country is covered with a sufficient supply of efficient schools; and the attendance of scholars, though still short of the ideal standard, is satisfactory and improving'.[105] The feeling amongst some educational specialists that much had been achieved in elementary levels made it easier for the focus of debate to move elsewhere and it did so with vigour. Indeed, when in 1886, Matthew Arnold had written on *elementary* education in Germany, Switzerland, and France, he had been unable to resist going beyond his remit observing that we 'must organise our secondary instruction'.[106]

In the course of the 1880s there were calls for forms of technical training with a view to enabling a British workforce to compete with continental innovations.[107] Lord Salisbury's government responded with the Technical Instruction Act 1889.[108] But most of all, it was recognized that there was a need to assess secondary education. The 'Bryce Commission', chaired by a man with a remarkable talent for politics, diplomacy, classical studies, and the academic study of law, enquired into the numerous issues.[109] Bryce had been an Assistant Commissioner for the Taunton Commission and knew how much still remained to be done. The Commissioners were assiduous, but in this area the hard work could be dispiriting. On the first page of its recommendations it concluded that:

The ground of secondary education is, if the metaphor may be permitted, already almost all covered with buildings so substantial that the loss to be incurred in clearing it for the erection of a new and symmetrical pile cannot be contemplated. Yet these existing buildings are so ill-arranged, so ill-connected, and therefore so inconvenient, that some scheme of reconstruction seems unavoidable.[110]

---

[103] E. J. R. Eaglesham, *The Foundations of Twentieth Century Education in England* (1967), esp. Ch. 2 'Administrative Muddle'; W. R. Cornish and G. de N. Clark, *Law and Society in England, 1750–1950* (1989), 473.

[104] *RC on Inquiry into the Elementary Education Acts, England and Wales*, Final Report, PP 1888 [Cmnd. 5485] XXLIII.

[105] *Ibid.*, 232–3.

[106] *Education Department: Special Report on Certain Points Connected with Elementary Education in Germany, Switzerland and France*, PP 1886 [4752] 25.

[107] Cornish and *Law and Society in England,* 472.

[108] Even this Act had to respond to religious issues, see s 1(1)(c).

[109] *RC on Secondary Education*, 1895 [7862] XLIII, vol. i.

[110] *Ibid.*, Part IV, Recommendations, 256. Later it was rumoured that on the eve of the publication of the Report it was found that for all its length it contained no quotation from Matthew

The Commission concluded by recommending a mixture of clearly defined central controls under a Minister accountable to Parliament with an enhanced role for county councils (as distinct from school boards) in the management of secondary schools supported in part through rates. This left considerable discretion with local levels of administration. For example the curriculum of secondary schools was to be determined locally. The structure produced its own tensions but, if implemented, it at least had the potential to improve existing arrangements.

The in-fighting which then followed within the current structures was remarkable for its intensity and the successful use of the courts, including the Court of Appeal, to attack the London School Board which had what was then taken to be an unorthodox reputation. A legislative response was required to these disputes and it came in the Education Act 1902. This was famously the product of extraordinary energy on the part of a single civil servant, Robert Morant. The Act responded to 'Bryce' and effectively undermined the existing School Boards and gave a considerable responsibility to one central Board and to the County and County Borough Councils as Local Education Authorities.[111] Within this structure education could now be provided up to the age of 15 (although the minimum school leaving age remained at its 1899 level of 12) and limited provisions for scholarships were introduced.

Numerous other issues remained as contentious as they had been in previous decades. In order to get the 1902 Act through Parliament it had to be conceded that the voluntary schools of the churches would continue to be supported by the rates as well as the grant from the Board. A conscience clause allowed withdrawal from religious instruction, and the Local Education Authority had some degree of representation on the managing boards of the voluntary schools. But the fact of public funding for these schools could only lead to further disputes. This arrangement launched more years of bitter controversy with nonconformists because its practical result was to ensure that money from rates supported numerous Anglican schools.

The Board of Education now had control of most educational issues in Whitehall and it had the melancholy task of by-passing recalcitrant authorities (not least those in Wales) and litigating with discontented parties. In the well-known case of *Board of Education* v. *Rice* the Board was finally vindicated in its assertion that, subject to the procedural requirements of natural justice, it had

Arnold. This was remedied at the last moment. See H. A. L. Fisher, *James Bryce* (1927), i: 298. 'Names' were important for the status of Victorian Commissions.

[111] E. J. R. Eaglesham, *The Foundations of Twentieth-Century Education in England* (1967), Ch. 3. On the genesis of the Act within carefully contrived litigation encouraged by Sir John Gorst, the Education Vice-President, see Cornish and Clark, *Law and Society in England*, 474.

an extensive authority to settle disputes between (in this particular case) a Local Education Authority and a voluntary school's managers.[112] In effect, statute law had given the Board a very broad discretion in both the development of educational provision and its implementation.

After their election in 1905 the Liberals sought further change in respect of religious issues, but the House of Lords blocked the move and the reforming government achieved more success in securing school meals and medical testing.[113] Cornish emphasizes the important fact that reformers such as Morant steered legislative reform towards the creation of broad administrative discretions which made it more difficult to challenge educational initiatives in the courts. These discretions also had major consequences for the approach to future educational problems. For example, beyond changes in elementary education it allowed for the development of 'grammar' type schools with a strong emphasis on the humanities. 'British education was thus taking a turn crucially different from that in most European countries, where the urge to catch up in the industrial race fostered the growth of technical and other useful training.'[114] This approach with its broad administrative remit was to reach its highest point three decades later in the framing of the major Education Act 1944. The latter provided the discretionary instrument for the creation of comprehensive schools without once mentioning comprehensive schools.[115] Over the years, educational legislation has had a way of being used in a manner which is both oblique and contentious. The legislative silences have been as important as the printed words of the various Acts.

---

[112] [1911] AC 179.

[113] Cornish and Clark, *Law and Society in England*, 476 and Education (Provision of School Meals) Act 1906 and Education (Administrative Provisions) Act 1907 revealingly described as 'An Act to make provision for the better administration by the central and local authorities in England and Wales of the enactments relating to education'.

[114] Cornish and Clark, *Law and Society in England*, 477.

[115] R. Cocks, 'Ram, Rab and the Civil Servants: A Lawyer and the Making of the "Great Education Act 1944"' (2001) 21(1) *Legal Studies* 15–35.

IV
Health for the Public

1. POVERTY, HEALTH, AND THE LAW

After a typhus epidemic in the late 1830s, the Poor Law Commissioners started to look at the links between poverty and the everyday life of the poor.[1] Chadwick, frustrated at having his influence curtailed through not having been appointed a Commissioner, saw an opportunity for a personal initiative. He carried out his famous investigation into the relationship between environmental conditions, disease, and poverty and was responsible for the *Sanitary Report* of 1842. This study was uniquely forceful, but in a general way it accorded with other findings of the Commissioners and was presented to the Home Secretary and both Houses of Parliament as 'An Inquiry into the Sanitary Condition of the Labouring Population of Great Britain'.[2] New systems for sewers and water supplies would, he argued, improve health and reduce poverty. To adapt the language of the day, he was arguing that the conditions of the poor determined the 'condition of the poor'.

---

[1] Fourth Annual Report of the Poor Law Commissioners for England and Wales, *PP* 1837–8 (147), Evidence of Dr Arnott who subsequently also gave evidence to the Select Committee on Health in Large Towns considered below and at fn. 15; see also W. R. Cornish and G. de N. Clark, *Law and Society in England, 1750–1950* (1989), 159.

[2] Report to Her Majesty's Principal Secretary of State for the Home Department on an Inquiry into the Sanitary Conditions of the Labouring Population, *PP* 1842 (006); and see also Sanitary Inquiry—England, Local reports on the Sanitary Conditions of the Labouring Population of England, in Consequence of an Inquiry Directed to be Made by the Poor Law Commissioners, *PP* 1842 (007). There is a useful edition of Chadwick's Report in M. W. Flinn (ed.), *Edwin Chadwick, Report on the Sanitary Condition of the Labouring Population of Great Britain*,(Edinburgh, 1965). (In subsequent notes the page numbers are given for the official Parliamentary publication with the page numbers for Flinn's edition added in brackets). For Chadwick's work in general, see A. Brundage, *England's 'Prussian Minister', Edwin Chadwick and the Politics of Government Growth, 1832–1854* (Pennsylvania State University, 1988), esp. Chs 5–8; S. E. Finer, *The Life and Times of Sir Edwin Chadwick* (1952); R. A. Lewis, *Edwin Chadwick and the Public Health Movement, 1832–1848* (1952); C. Hamlin, *Public Health and Social Justice in the Age of Chadwick: Britain 1800–1854* (Cambridge, 1998). For Chadwick's links with the medical profession, see M. Pelling, *Cholera, Fever and English Medicine, 1825–1865* (Oxford, 1978).

The squalor of what he saw and smelled is all but impossible to recreate in retrospect. In the early-Victorian decades the urban system was facing one crisis after another. 'In provincial cities of 100,000 and above, life expectancy at birth dropped from 35 years in the 1820s to 29 in the 1830s, a marked break in the previous trend of improvement of life expectancy in towns and cities.'[3] Linked to this was the fact that systems of urban government were also in crisis. The new form of municipal corporation of 1835 gave power to local property owners who were unlikely to favour either expensive programmes of social improvement or the creation of new powers for central government.[4]

Writers on the history of public health have not given much attention to the extent to which Chadwick believed he had to address legal as well as social issues. Yet he felt obliged to show in detail that legislation was the instrument for what he wanted to achieve. Part VII of his 'Sanitary Report' is extensive and is given over to 'Recognised Principles of Legislation and (the) State of the Existing Law for the Protection of the Public Health'. He pointed out that 'Public opinion has of late required legislative interference for the regulation of some points of the internal economy of certain places of work...'.[5] In other words, parts of factory legislation set a precedent for 'interference'. More directly, in London commissioners of sewers had achieved results to the extent of their powers and, upon investigation, '...it became apparent that the limits of the jurisdiction of the commissioners of sewers, and the limits of the jurisdiction of the district surveyors around the metropolis, mark the commencement of buildings of an inferior character, built without drains, without the security from party walls, and without proper means of cleansing'.[6] The lesson was clear, people with appropriate local powers could achieve major improvements. He also pointed out that many of these challenges were addressed more systematically in certain foreign countries, particularly Germany.[7] In England the common law gave some remedies, but for centuries it had had to be supplemented by numerous incidental initiatives by Parliament as in the case of controlling the burning of lime and sea coal in London. The drainage of low areas of agricultural land was a model for the future.

---

[3] M. Daunton (ed.), *The Cambridge Urban History of Britain*, (Cambridge, 2000), iii: Introduction, p. 2. In the same collection Bill Luckin, in 'Pollution in the City' argues at p. 213 that 'nothing, except perhaps political dissidence or ingratitude on the part of the working classes, was more loathsome to the Victorian and Edwardian social elites than sewage'.

[4] For the intricate variety of political interests associated with Municipal Corporations, see Vol. XI, Pt 2, Ch. V, Local Government, pp. 425–45.

[5] Report to Her Majesty's Principal Secretary of State for the Home Department on an Inquiry into the Sanitary Conditions of the Labouring Population, PP 1842 (006), 279 (Flinn 339).

[6] *Ibid.*, 281 (Flinn 341).   [7] *Ibid.*, 288–9 (Flinn 348).

Although the larger share of the land drainage redounds to the pecuniary profit of private individuals, yet it proved so far to affect the public health beneficially, and contribute to the productive employment of the labouring classes, and to other general public advantages, that such works fairly come within the description of publicum in privato, and as such entitled to collective and legislative care.[8]

In unrelenting arguments he pressed the case for *systematic* parliamentary interference for the sake of public advantage. Birmingham then used the River Rea as its 'main sewer' but the river could not operate effectively in this role because mill owners took large quantities of water from it.[9] This sort of problem, he argued, could and should be prevented by law. What was more, there was a need for the application of various types of expertise. The doctor assists the patient and points to the disease being caused by the lack of 'proper administrative measures'. When it comes to 'the great preventatives' such as improved sewerage 'aid must be sought from the science of the civil engineer'.[10] There was also a need for trained and paid and supervised people to act as 'Public Officers for the Prevention of Disease'.

The duty of visiting loathsome abodes, amidst close atmospheres compounded of smoke and offensive odours, and everything to revolt the senses, is a duty which can only be expected to be regularly performed under much stronger motives than can commonly be imposed on honorary officers, and cannot be depended upon even from paid officers where they are not subjected to strong checks.[11]

Chadwick rounded off his long analysis by talking of the need for radical reforms and '...the urgent necessity of legislative provisions...'.[12] He pointed to 'the advantages of uniformity in legislation and in the executive machinery...'.[13] As before with the poor law, he was no friend of local organizations if their intricate powers and rights offered the sort of autonomy which could thwart national initiatives.

But a local patch-work of powers reflected a significant part of the reality with which Chadwick was faced. David Eastwood has pointed out that statute law, including private Acts of Parliament, was giving local government significant opportunities. 'In an important readjustment of private rights and public advantages, Improvement Acts, such as the Cheltenham Improvement Acts of 1806 and 1821, began to invest commissions with limited powers of compulsory purchase as well as more substantial powers to enforce minimum sanitary and building regulations in all new developments.... While it would be misleading to suggest

---

[8] *Ibid.*, 304 (Flinn 362). [9] *Ibid.*, 305–6 (Flinn 363–4).
[10] *Ibid.*, 341 (Flinn 394). [11] *Ibid.*, 342 (Flinn 397).
[12] *Ibid.*, 368 (Flinn 421). [13] *Ibid.*, 372 (Flinn 425).

that the growth of statutory bodies in Hanoverian England represented a serious erosion of property rights, their emergence did begin to subject property itself, and the exercise of property rights, to greater public regulation.'[14] Also, there was a long tradition of isolated legislative measures for public health emergencies. For example, the Privy Council had been given considerable powers by Act of Parliament to respond to the cholera epidemic of 1831.[15] More generally, the use of Commissions charged with specific tasks had become vital to local government activity.[16] The link between public health debates and local life was wryly observed in retrospect by George Eliot in *Middlemarch*, first published in 1872 but set in the 1830s:

A meeting was to be held in the Town Hall on a sanitary question which had risen into pressing importance by the occurrence of a cholera case in the town. Since the Act of Parliament, which had been hurriedly passed, authorising assessments for sanitary measures, there had been a Board for the superintendence of such measures appointed in Middlemarch, and much cleansing and preparation had been concurred in by Whigs and Tories. The question now was, whether a piece of ground outside the town should be secured as a burial-ground by means of assessment or by private subscription. The meeting was to be open, and almost everyone of importance in the town was expected to be there.[17]

Local rights in combination with uncoordinated central powers were very significant and, for Chadwick, problematical, but public expectations were changing and Chadwick's interest in radical uniformity could expect a respectful hearing. Parliamentary Select Committees expressed acute concern about social and physical conditions. In 1840 a Select Committee was 'Inquiring into Circumstances affecting the Health of the Inhabitants of Large Towns and Populous Districts, with a view to improved Statutory Regulations for their Benefit...':

Your Committee have inquired carefully into the matters submitted to them, and find that sanitary regulations in many of the principal towns of the realm are most imperfect and neglected and that hence result great evils, suffering and expense to large bodies of the community. They have proposed several remedies; viz. general Acts to facilitate regulations in building, sewerage and local improvements...It appears to your Committee, that where such evils are found to follow from the neglect or inability in these respects

---

[14] Respectively, 46 Geo. III c. 117, and 1 and 2 Geo. IV c. 116, D. Eastwood, *Government and Community in the English Provinces, 1700–1870* (Basingstoke, 1997), 124.

[15] An Act for the Prevention, as far as may be Possible, of the Disease Called the Cholera (2 and 3 Will. 4 c. 10), s 1.

[16] Anderson on Local Government.

[17] (Harmondsworth, 1994), 779.

of local authorities, that it is the duty of the legislature to take efficient steps to protect so numerous and valuable a portion of the community.[18]

The commitment to changes in the law for public health had many aspects. In discussing cotton production in Manchester and Liverpool the Committee pointed to a moral obligation: 'It seems alike a matter of duty and policy in the Legislature to take care that the industrious classes, by whose hands the great riches derived from the trade are chiefly formed, should be protected from evils (such as have been described), by the Government and the more opulent ranks, who owe so much to their unwearied exertions.'[19] The Committee saw the clearest links between housing conditions and health and pointed to '...the severe and extensive evils borne by the humbler classes from neglect of the proper statutory regulation and precautions'.[20] Amongst numerous other observations it pointed out that 15,000 people in Manchester lived in cellars.[21]

Reports such as the one on the health of urban areas produced slender practical results but they further changed the terms of public debate and do much to explain the appointment of the Royal Commission on the Health of Towns in 1844.[22] There was now sufficient interest in reform for a public Act of 1846 to permit the removal of nuisances in urban areas and the Privy Council was given still more powers in dealing with infection and disease.[23] The Act was renewed and amended in 1848 and 1849.[24] This was the start of a major phase of reform in public health law. In his detailed study of public health during these years, Christopher Hamlin has pointed out that in 1845–8 there was, in his words, broad agreement that government must be a guarantor of health.[25] But he also shows that there were intense controversies over the local unit of sanitary administration: should there be a distinct sanitary authority, or should it be part of the structure of municipal government? If the latter approach was taken what would be the standing of suburban and rural areas in relation to the large towns? The immense difficulty of reaching any sort of agreement on provision for London led to it being increasingly excluded from national proposals. If there was to be a

---

[18] Report from the Select Committee on the Health of the Inhabitants of Large Towns and Populous Districts *PP* 1840 (384), iii.

[19] *Ibid.*, xi.

[20] *Ibid.*, vi.

[21] *Ibid.*, viii, and see Ch. VI below.

[22] *RC on the State of Large Towns and Populous Districts*, First Report, *PP* 1844 (572) xvii. See, also, *Reports from Commissioners*, 14 vols, *PP* 1845 (602), vxiii. For 'Health of Towns Associations' and other current reformers, see W. M. Frazer, *A History of English Public Health: 1834–1939* (1950), Ch. 1.

[23] Nuisance Removal Act 1846, 9, 10 Vict. c. 96.

[24] Nuisance Removal Act 1848, 11, 12 Vict. c. 123; and Nuisance Removal Act 1849, 12, 13 Vict. c. 11.

[25] C. Hamlin, *Public Health and Social Justice in the Age of Chadwick* (Cambridge, 1998), 267.

General Board of Health, how was it to be held accountable? There seemed to be no end to the number of issues.

When a bill intended to create important central and local powers was presented to Parliament it brought to the fore the intensity of opposition which such proposals could arouse. Local magistrates, property owners, rate-payers, and those with a stake in municipal corporations opposed the bill: 'And to their aid came tenement landlords, factory owners, proprietors of butchers shops, and water companies for whom regulations and the expensive improvements demanded by them would mean a curbing of their freedom and the lessening of their profits.'[26] For many, social reform of any sort could look threatening. 'Interpretations of the "revolution in government" which rely on the smooth translation of outdoor pressure and "public opinion" into legislation ignore the strong ideological hostility to social reform to be found all along the high political spectrum, among middle-class Radicals, liberals in the Whig party, and Conservatives.'[27] This is significant because discordant voices revealed attitudes which would do much to shape the amendment of this area of law over the coming decades. To contemporaries, the importance of public health reform could lie as much in the opposition it engendered as in its substance. There were times when public debate was even dominated by arguments against the bill.[28]

In the Commons Colonel Sibthorp, a man representing Lincoln and well-known for opposing almost any project deemed progressive, 'had always entertained a strong objection' to the bill and set out to ridicule the measure.[29] He pointed out that London and Westminster had been left beyond the range of the bill in recognition of the need to give them special attention and to respond to powerful interest groups. The Colonel turned this into an embarrassment by mischievously suggesting that London and Westminster were the cities most in need of change if the case for change was to be accepted. 'Why, therefore, should London and Westminster, which wanted improvements, and were wallowing in filth, be excluded from a bill which professed to make pure and cleanly places which did not want such care?' In his view there was no case for change anywhere. 'Another objection which he had to the present Bill was that it created a good deal of patronage, and would be attended with a great increase of public expenditure.' 'He objected to the Bill upon its merits. Many greedy people expected places from it.' He went after the latter issue in some detail.[30]

---

[26] D. Roberts, *Victorian Origins of the British Welfare State* (Yale, 1969), 74.

[27] P. Mandler, *Aristocratic Government in the Age of Reform: Whigs and Liberals, 1830–1852* (Oxford, 1990), p. 281.

[28] C. Hamlin, *Public Health and Social Justice in the Age of Chadwick* (Cambridge, 1998), 245.

[29] *PD* 1848 (s. 3), 98: 710.

[30] *Ibid.*, 710.

'In Clause 5 of the Bill he observed that offices, clerks, etc., were to be provided for the Commissioner by the public treasurer. Now, as modesty on the part of government was a farce, he thought they might just as well have provided that champagne, turtle etc., should be supplied to the commissioners every time they sat.' 'He disapproved of the new patent water-closets, and much preferred the old system. He could not see why the pure city of Lincoln which he represented should be mixed up with the impure cities. London and Westminster required far more scrubbing, rubbing, and washing than ever Lincoln did, and therefore the Bill was partial, and, as such, he should oppose it.'[31]

Mr Urquhart (representing Stafford) was more typical in founding his opposition on a combination of legal arguments and allegations of patronage. 'He contended that we had neglected the powers of the common law, impeded the action of the municipal bodies, and the consequence had been, the spread of those causes of disease which had subsequently called public attention to this subject. Now, when they came to legislate upon the subject, they should take care that they did not create a greater nuisance than that which they endeavoured to correct. There was a most estimable class of persons—the medical practitioners—who had found in this Bill a field for the application of their science, and had become missionaries of the project. They had declared for the Bill, the whole Bill, and nothing but the Bill. But independently of their desire to promote the general good, there were other considerations which were probably calculated to operate on them, and probably to lead them astray.'[32] To make matters worse, 'Those connected with engineering, either theoretically or practically, were equally interested in it.' For him, all these offices and the new appointments which went with them were inherently objectionable. 'It had long been the pride of this country that Government had little to do in the management of our internal affairs.'[33] 'The fact was, centralisation was usurpation. It was usurpation by the Government of the powers of local bodies, and a destruction by the general Executive of local rights.' 'He resisted the Bill because it was un-English and unconstitutional—corrupt in its tendency—it was an avowel of a determination to destroy local self-government, and, if carried, its effect would be to pass a roller over England, destroying every vestige of local pre-eminence, and reducing all to one dull and level monotony.' Further, '...Any one who would take the trouble to refer to Blackstone's *Commentaries* would find that the common law provided ample means for putting down all the nuisances to which this Bill referred.'[34] 'If this Bill was passed, other Bills carrying the principle still farther would be speedily

[31] *Ibid.*, 710–11.   [32] *Ibid.*, 711–12.
[33] *Ibid.*, 713.   [34] *Ibid.*, 714.

introduced, because it would soon be found that the local bodies were not so obsequious and so subservient to the general board as they ought to be.'[35]

2. 'THE POOR MAN'S MEASURE'

In heavily modified form the bill passed through the House of Commons and in the House of Lords Lord Campbell struck a different note when he moved the Second Reading of the bill and was both moderate and thoughtful.[36] It was, he thought, '...a most important measure, and one which, though interesting to all classes of the community, might be termed, with truth, the poor man's measure'. He used statistics to show that people were healthier in Westmoreland than Lancashire: in other words he began to explore the capacity for environment to determine health. There had been forms of local progress but 'Very little, he was sorry to say, had been done for the promotion of the public health through the instrumentality of legislation and governmental assistance'.[37] He spoke with exasperation of failed attempts at reform in 1841 and his response struck the right tone for the purposes of sustaining a compromise measure and opening up the debates which would dominate many future arguments about reform.

In its final shape the Public Health Act 1848 was an obvious compromise.[38] It allowed for the setting up of a Board of Health; and it allowed local Boards of Health to be established after enquiry into local conditions. The latter could then be linked to the local machinery of enforcement with inspectors of nuisances, and surveyors, and a doctor as an officer of health. The local Boards had the power to make bye-laws and the range of their work was huge: they managed cemeteries, water supply, drainage, public parks, street cleaning, and many other activities. Hamlin argues that 'The 1848 Public Health Act was a monster, with the head of coercive medical police and the body of local self-government'.[39] The General

---

[35] *Ibid.*, 715. See also other interventions such as Mr Bankes, at col. 718 (representing 'Dorsetshire'), adopting a common way of attacking a bill by basing his opposition on the defective drafting of the measure: 'The Bill, as originally framed, was found to contain so many defects that the very men who had drawn it up were obliged to double the letters of the alphabet in order to obtain designations for the clauses which had to be improved upon. They had been fourteen months preparing the Bill, and the alphabet itself did not contain letters enough for the clauses which had to be introduced as emendations on the Bill as originally proposed.' Somewhat confusingly Bankes added the observation that he accepted the principle of the bill and wanted London to be included within its terms. Even some supporters of reform felt obliged to look unenthusiastic. Regulation could be supported, but only as the lesser of two evils.

[36] *PD* 1848 (s. 3), 99: 1402.

[37] *Ibid.*

[38] 11, 12 Vict. c. 63. And see Anderson on Local Government.

[39] C. Hamlin, *Public Health and Social Justice in the Age of Chadwick* (Cambridge, 1998), 276.

Board existed primarily to further municipal initiatives. It had the right to act in an area where the death rate rose above 23 per 1000 or it was petitioned by one-tenth of the ratepayers. Where it acted it could use the rates to support a local board of health and supervise the financing of important projects. The latter arrangement saved towns from having to use expensive private bills as much as had previously been the case. In substance the General Board could enable change rather than force it. What was more, initially it was created for only five years.

Predictably, after the enactment, the legislation was frequently called in question and attacked by interests such as existing local authorities and private water companies who saw a threat to their influence and incomes. Cornish has shown that the reasons for the Board encountering increasing national challenges were complex.[40] As always, it was difficult to integrate London into a new administrative structure, and a special London Sewer Commission provided a pretext for political attack because of its inherently disruptive work in digging up large parts of the community. Chadwick's remorseless logic was not matched by his capacity to persuade. Nor was there significant political and administrative direction from elsewhere. Of the three new Commissioners one was a Cabinet Minister but his role was ill-defined and the position was more likely to hinder than advance a political career. Behind these problems lay the sustained and unforgiving attitudes of those who had seen the new organization as a plot to subvert liberties which could be traced back to the Anglo-Saxons. As against these difficulties the reformers had certain strengths. The idea of public health was now securely part of informed debate. In 1857 Lord Stanley stressed the importance of this new way of thinking when he addressed the National Association for the Promotion of Social Science.

What do we mean by sanitary science? We mean, I apprehend, that science which deals with the preservation of health and prevention of disease in reference to the entire community, and to classes within that community, as contradistinguished from medical science in the ordinary acceptation of the term, which latter study has for its aim the restoration of health when lost, and deals with the case of each individual separately.[41]

3. SCIENTIFIC EXPERTISE

In 1858, at the end of the Board's second term, it was overwhelmed by the personal and political problems mentioned above and was discontinued. Most of its activities were given either to a part of the Home Office or, in the case of the

[40] Cornish and Clark, *Law and Society in England*, 161–6.
[41] Transactions of the National Association for the Promotion of Social Science (1857), 41. See also, A. S. Wohl, *Endangered Lives: Public Health in Victorian Britain* (1983), 1.

Medical Officership, to the Privy Council. The latter move was to prove to be of the first importance for the creation of later public health legislation. The new officer, Sir John Simon, combined Chadwick's dedication with a capacity to enlist cooperation from others. Simon was also assisted by other forms of intervention which gave the public an enhanced interest in issues relating to public health. In particular this applied to the integration of scientific expertise into the administration of regulatory controls.

Parliament was giving attention to 'noxious vapours'. A Select Committee of the House of Lords, with a full representation of landowners from the industrial north-west, heard evidence of the damage done by acids produced in the course of chemical manufacturing.[42] It was believed that the existing nuisance laws failed to respond to the magnitude of the problem and the best hope for improvement lay in statutory regulation and inspectors. But at this point there were doubts. The Committee's desire to consider the extension of the existing weak arrangements for the control of smoke caused the manufacturers some alarm and they insisted upon a focus on the processes of alkali production. This raised further difficulties because of disagreements over how the processes could be controlled. Despite this, Lord Stanley introduced a private bill designed to produce radical change and its provisions were moderated when the government intervened and took it over. The result was legislation which, amongst other things, created a new inspectorate of scientifically qualified experts but under an arrangement which was to be reviewed after five years.[43] The early legislation on public health had provided a context which could support further regulatory intervention even if the latter was expressed in hesitant terms.

At the start there were difficulties with the Treasury which did all it could to limit the salaries of inspectors.[44] Despite this, Robert Smith, the leading inspector, combined formidable activity with an attempt to gain the cooperation of

---

[42] *SC of the House of Lords on Injury from Noxious Vapours*, PP 1862 (486), xiv, 1. In considering emissions from alkali works it concluded that "the pungent vapour is perceptible, in certain states of the atmosphere, at the distance of 5 or 6 miles; and its effects within a radius of one or two miles are fearful', p. iii. For this Report, and further reading on alkali pollution, see M. Lobban on Nuisance. The case of *St Helen's Smelting Co* v. *Tipping* (1865) 11 HLC 642 became part of the debates in the mid-1860s: see A. W. Brian Simpson, *Leading Cases in the Common Law* (Oxford, 1995), Ch. 7, 'Victorian Judges and the Problem of Social Cost: Tipping v. St Helen's Smelting Company (1865)'.

[43] An Act for the More Effectual Condensation of Muriatic Acid Gas in Alkali Works, 1863 (26 and 27 Vict. c. 124): for the powers of inspectors, see ss 7–12. Under s 4 'Every Alkali Work shall be carried on in such a manner as to secure the condensation to the satisfaction of the Inspector, derived from his own Examination or from that of a Sub-Inspector, of not less than 95 *per centum* of the Muriatic Acid Gas evolved therein'.

[44] Under s 10 of the Act the Inspectors and Sub-Inspectors 'shall be paid such salary as may be determined by the Board of Trade, with the consent of the Commissioners of Her Majesty's Treasury'.

manufacturers. Smith implemented a successful process for somewhat reducing pollution which was remarkable because it did not take away commercial profits. At least in respect of emissions of hydrochloric acid, people could speak of limited but significant social and economic progress. The result was the passing of a brief Act which gave the inspectorate a permanent role.[45]

This, in turn, was a stimulus for Smith's restless mind to consider a wider remit for the inspectorate and to justify this by increasingly accurate research into damage done by different types of industry. In 1869 he called for a 'chemical climatology'. But soon afterwards the Inspectorate's activities were caught up in a major administrative reform over which it could have little control. The Local Government Board was created and, under the terms of the Public Health Act 1872, the Inspectorate became accountable to the new Board.[46] Smith now encountered John Lambert who, as the Permanent Secretary of the Board, had turned a context of hope into frustration for Simon through blocking his initiatives. In his detailed study of these reforms MacLeod shows that no practical links were established between Smith's atmospheric work and Simon's hopes for sanitary reform. But the Inspectorate now had commercial and other supporters outside government, and an Act of 1874 focused on alkalis and extended the Inspectorate's range to some new industrial processes. It also introduced a requirement which was to have a long future in the form of the need for manufacturers to use the 'best practical means' to prevent the escape of other 'noxious gasses'.[47]

Again, there were disputes about salaries but, in the course of time, and with the support of major landowners, there were also further demands for reform. A Royal Commission was established and it took expert evidence from a large number of witnesses, including Simon.[48] Despite the fashion for local systems of regulation and enforcement, it came to be accepted that there had to be a centralized administrative structure for this form of work and that the controls had to be both more intrusive and more extensive. This proved to be the start of legislative efforts which at first failed through opposition from manufacturers who saw an era of compromise giving way to a much more determined approach. Eventually, the Alkali etc. Works Regulation Act 1881 raised standards and improved the potential for enforcement.[49] The skies of British industrial areas

---

[45] An Act to Make Perpetual the Alkali Act of 1863, 1869.

[46] ss 35 and 37.

[47] An Act to Amend the Alkali Act of 1863, 1874. R. M. MacLeod, 'The Alkali Acts Administration Between 1863 and 1864: The Emergence of the Civil Scientist' (1965) 9 *Vict. St.* 81 at 97.

[48] *Ibid.*, 100; *RC on Noxious Vapours*, PP 1878 [2159] [2159-1], xliv.

[49] 44 and 45 Vict. c. 37.

provided proof of the need for much further work, but there was now no question of the Inspectorate being denied substantial power.

In setting an administrative precedent the new law was important. In the conclusion to his study of the 'Alkali Acts Administration between 1863 and 1884', R. M. Macleod rightly points to the novelty of the reform. Under the system of control an expert scientific adviser was made a civil servant and given important regulatory powers. Policy was being put into rules with associated arrangements for inspection and enforcement.[50] This was a major change. Reliance was being placed on an instrument for continuous monitoring rather than recourse on occasion to the threat of litigation using common law and injunctions. Modern textbooks on environmental law frequently refer to this change emphasizing its importance and there is no anachronism in doing so.[51] It was an adventurous attempt to make systematic use of scientific knowledge within a novel legal framework.

4. INCREMENTAL REFORM

The creation of the Alkali Inspectorate arose out of a focused legislative initiative, and it was not typical of other attempts at reform during the 1860s and 1870s. In practice the 'interventionist' role of an industrial inspectorate often stood in contrast to less active developments elsewhere. The problem for reformers in these decades lay in the need to enlarge and coordinate the range of the laws for public health. *Cooper v. Wandsworth Board of Works* was a cautionary tale for anyone who looked forward to the systematic increase in the powers of local agencies.[52] Here a sewering authority sought to take advantage of the fact that in certain circumstances it had the power under legislation to demolish a building without the builder having the right to 'put his case'. The Court of Common Pleas held that whatever the behaviour of the builder the authority must give the builder an opportunity to be heard before his property was destroyed. In substance the authority was being required to act in a judicial manner. Further friction was likely between reformers arguing for what they saw as a necessary change authorized by statute and others who looked to procedural requirements imposed by courts concerned with the rights of property owners.

Sustained pressure for reform remained, not least from speakers at the National Association for the Advancement of Social Science.[53] The Sanitary Act

---

[50] R. M. MacLeod, 'The Alkali Acts Administration Between 1863 and 1864: The Emergence of the Civil Scientist' (1965) 9 *Vict. St.* 85–112.

[51] e.g. S. Bell in *Ball and Bell on Environmental Law* (4th edn, 1997), 9.

[52] (1863) 14 C.B. (N.S.) 180. See also Ch. 5 below and Anderson on judicial review.

[53] See e.g. M. W. Flinn, *The Medical and Legal Aspects of Sanitary Reform* (by A. P. Stewart and E. Jenkins, 1886), reprinted with an introduction (Leicester, 1969).

1866 introduced a wide range of changes, some of which went beyond granting powers to local authorities and instead gave them new obligations.[54] There was an extensive duty on a local authority to inspect for nuisances and to take action against those which were found. In the view of Anthony Wohl this was the first public health Act in which compulsory clauses were dominant. For example, it was possible for the Home Secretary to take action where local powers did nothing.[55]

For some, there was now the hope that this might happen in respect of smoke. Earlier legislation such as the Smoke Abatement Act 1853 had been local and even within the areas covered initial successes in bringing prosecutions were not followed up. Now the local authorities were required to prosecute. In practice this revealed the difficulties produced by significant exemptions allowed by the law. Domestic smoke was not controlled; iron, steel, and some other industries were exempted because there was no way of avoiding smoke; the prohibition was on black smoke and it was a defence to argue that the smoke in question was dark brown; it was also possible to justify smoke by pointing to efforts to minimize emissions.[56]

Generally, in the words of Asa Briggs, there was 'ample evidence concerning the ignorance, petty jealousies and unwillingness to spend money of the mid-Victorian Local Boards of Health'.[57] Beyond local politics Sir John Simon saw that the national arrangement of the laws on sanitation was in itself a problem. In later years he looked back on this era and thought that there had been so many laws in so many Acts that they 'had become incoherent almost to the point of chaos'.

The successive bits of piece-meal legislation, uncombinable except with gaps and overlappings, and sometimes with apparent inconsistencies of intention, made a parquetry which was unsafe to walk upon. Authorities and persons who wished to give effect to the law were often finding insuperable difficulties in their way; while authorities and persons of contrary disposition found easy excuse or impunity for any amount of malfeasance or evasion.[58]

But just because public health was a fashionable topic of conversation there was always pressure for change from some quarter or another. There were numer-

[54] 29, 30 Vict. c. 90.

[55] Wohl, *Endangered Lives*, 155.

[56] An Act to Abate the Nuisance Arising from the Smoke of Furnaces in the Metropolis and from Steam Vessels above London Bridge, 1853 (16 and 17 Vict. c. 128). P. Thorsheim, *Inventing Pollution: Coal, Smoke and Culture in Britain since 1800* (Ohio, 2006), 113–14. And see Lobban 'Nuisance', 24–7.

[57] *Victorian Cities* (Harmondsworth, 1969), 20. For a study of public health in Birmingham at this time, see E. P. Hennock, *Fit and Proper Persons: Ideal and Reality in Nineteenth Century Urban Government* (1973), 111–16.

[58] Sir John Simon, *English Sanitary Institutions* (2nd edn, 1897), 323. He had been particularly frustrated at the failure to link sanitary laws with local government laws in general: see 334.

ous debates about water pollution.[59] In general terms a Royal Commission of 1869–71 sought one minister to be responsible for the laws of public health and the poor law and when this combination of roles was to be found in the new Local Government Board it soon produced the sort of tensions which had caused difficulties to the Alkali Inspectorate.[60] After its creation in 1871 the 'LGB' became increasingly important as it gained powers from the Home Secretary and the Privy Council. The concentration of powers and duties in the statutory regime for the Local Government Board made for efficiencies, but it also came with its own sources of political discord. One of the latter took the form of the possible dominance of Poor Law Officials and, after this became a reality, it eventually produced by way of reaction the resignation of Simon.[61] More generally, like the Poor Law, the regulation of public health could be seen as a compromise between competing pressures to centralize and localize. Whitehall could combine 'detailed intrusiveness and strategic weakness'.[62] Ministers and civil servants knew that there was no automatic link between their statutory powers and local action. The latter had to be negotiated.

Beyond these disputes, the creation of the Local Government Board stimulated the idea of bringing together in one Act all the law on public health so that the legal roles of the relevant organizations could be accessible and understood. When the Public Health Act 1875 was introduced, the size and range of the proposed legislation was impressive.[63] Members of Parliament were struck by the bill's 333 clauses and 28 pages of Schedules, most of which survived parliamentary debate and became law. With considerable cross-party support it was openly described as being primarily, but not solely, a consolidating Act. Old law was being put into a more intelligible and accessible form with a few additional amendments. The departure of the health legislation which had accumulated in 29 statutes in the years following the Act of 1848 was welcomed in the sense that all recognized the need for a new Act expressing the law in the simplest way possible. But some were unhappy at the extent to which the substance of the

[59] See Lobban on 'Nuisance', 19–24.

[60] *RC on Sanitation*, Second Report, *PP* 1871, [281], xxxiii, 31. The Commissioners had been sufficiently worried about the state of the law to call Henry Thring in his capacity as Parliamentary Counsel. He stated that 'Speaking generally, I consider that the statute law relating to sanitary matters is sufficient in substance, but in form very complex and exceedingly difficult to understand', *RC on Sanitation*, First Report, *PP* 1868–9 [4218], xxxii, 26.

[61] On Simon's role generally, see Cornish and Clark, *Law and Society in England* 162–4. On the Local Government Board, see C. Bellamy, *Administering Central-Local Relations, 1871–1919: The Local Government Board in its Fiscal and Cultural Context* (Manchester, 1986).

[62] J. Davis, 'Central Government and the Towns', in M. Daunton (ed.), *The Cambridge Urban History of Britain* (Cambridge, 2000), iii, 268.

[63] 38 and 39, Vict. c. 55.

old law was expressed in its new form. Lyon Playfair, a scientist and Member of Parliament with a strong reputation for being involved in the reform of public health, was insistent. Much of the law did not work. 'The law as it stands has been found in the working to be inoperative and illusory.'[64] Further, there was no prospect of the law developing in a systematic way. 'For it is a matter of great difficulty to settle law upon unsettled foundations, and the foundations on which this Bill are built are altogether unsettled. By far the largest part of it is devoted to the laws relating to the constitution of local authorities, their areas of administration, their powers, and their methods of procedure. Is this settled law? Is it not one of the most solemn promises of the present Ministry that they are to reorganise local government?'[65]

In other words, it was all the more clear after the creation of the aptly named Local Government Board in 1871, that local government law would be further entwined with public health law. This brought with it serious problems of oversight and the threat of perpetual meddling by central government. But everyone knew there were limits to what could be done from London. Sclater-Booth, President of the Local Government Board, argued that 'The Local Government Board possessed a great deal of persuasive power, and no small amount of compulsory power, (but) it was unable, and would he believed, always be unable to direct in detail the action of the local authorities'.[66] For Dr Lush (representing Salisbury) there was no reason for more intervention; he thought 'the country was not yet ripe for any large measure of compulsory sanitary legislation'.[67] Colonel Barttelot (representing West Sussex) was no friend of centralizing powers and argued with reference to one possible reform that if 'it was the intention of the Local Government Board to insist on having a central authority of medical officers, he felt certain that it would be the most unpopular thing ever attempted throughout the length and breadth of this country'.[68]

Despite the fact that the Act did more to consolidate the law than to change the law, and despite all the hesitations of contemporaries, it has a unique place in perceptions of the social reforms on the Victorian statute book. The Public Health Act 1875 was regarded as important at the time it was passed and came in the course of the next half century to occupy a central role in British debates about social improvement. As a matter of impression it became one of the most commonly mentioned of Victorian statutes. Politicians, reformers, and many others saw it as a central achievement with close links to other reforms of the decades

[64] PD 1875 (s. 3), 223: 1247.
[65] Ibid., 1246. And see Anderson on 'Local Government'.
[66] Ibid., 1257.   [67] Ibid., 1259.
[68] Ibid., col. 1262.

after 1840; it was as if they saw it vindicating what had gone before and confirming the arrival of everyday environmental regulation for the sake of health. For those who wrote and debated it was the foundation for many of the most important urban achievements. Dickens had died in 1870 and it was as if the Act of 1875 enabled Britain to move beyond his era.

The Act was a meeting point between the law and the circumstances which shaped everyday experience. Its detailed provisions came, as it were, to paint a picture of late-Victorian life. For example, Part III provided regulations for sanitation with sewerage and drainage being of obvious importance. Some other sections were designed to meet normal social needs and save lives. Under s 51 'Any urban authority may provide their district or any part thereof... with a supply of water proper and sufficient for public purposes, and for those purposes... may construct and maintain waterworks, dig wells, and do any other necessary acts...'. Under further sections the future letting of cellars as dwellings was almost eliminated.[69] Responding to the long debates about the legal control of nuisances, s 92 stated: 'It shall be the duty of every local authority to cause to be made from time to time inspection of their district, with a view to ascertain what nuisances exist calling for abatement under the powers of this Act, and to enforce the provisions of this Act in order to abate the same...'. Some sections were directed at particular problems. Section 131 stated that 'Any local authority may provide for the use of the inhabitants of their district hospitals or temporary places for the reception of the sick, and for that purpose may themselves build such hospitals...'. Further 'any urban authority may purchase or take on lease lay out plant improve and maintain lands for the purpose of being used as public walks or pleasure grounds...'.[70]

There were also general provisions creating substantial enabling powers. 'Any local authority may enter into any contracts necessary for carrying this Act into execution...'.[71] Part IX created sweeping powers for the Local Government Board and a capacity to use inquiries for any matters 'concerning the public health in any place'.[72] There was an extensive capacity to 'enforce the performance of a duty by a defaulting local authority'.[73] These sections were supported in turn by Schedules, some of which contained detailed model forms for the abatement of nuisances. In their reference to, say, ditches or drains so foul as to be a nuisance or injurious to health, they bring to mind the conditions which had led to the creation of the preceding sections. It was as if the 1875 Act had something to say about almost anything. *The Public Health Acts Annotated with*

---

[69] Sections 71 and 72.   [70] Section 164.
[71] Section 173.   [72] Sections 293–6 and 298.
[73] Section 299.

Appendices by W. G. Lumley and E. Lumley had gone through eight editions (and six editors) by 1914.

The weak point in the whole range of public health law was enforcement. Sometimes, as we have seen, this was apparent in the law itself. Just to take the example of smoke emissions mentioned above, under the new legislation of 1875 it was a defence for a manufacturer to show that he had taken steps 'as far as practicable'. Beyond the perceived failings of the law, local authorities were often accused of being too sympathetic to manufacturers. Smoke inspectors in Birmingham made 11,000 observations of chimneys in 1879 but only 369 were found to be emitting dense smoke. Where action was taken it might have little impact. Again, in Birmingham, Joshua Stubbs and Co were fined in 1887 and 1888 but were still the subject of complaints in 1889. Local people such as the Rev. Thomas Bass tried to stir up action but, in this case, they simply encountered an inactive Medical Officer of Health. The 'Manchester and Salford Noxious Vapours Abatement Association' did what it could but this did not amount to much. In 1880 London was outside the scope of some recent laws and yet *The Times* on 5 November 1880 estimated that it had 600,000 houses and six times as many fireplaces. In 1899 the London County Council fined railway companies for burning cheap smoke-laden coal and the companies concerned found it less expensive to go on paying fines rather than switch to other coal. In Sheffield the Medical Officer of Health openly stated that soot was a necessary evil if industry was to succeed.[74] The Public Health Act 1875 was a remarkable legal document but it could never come near to being the answer to all the problems with everyday health. To take another example, it did not transform the implementation of the law relating to sewerage.[75]

In addition to the public Acts there were also numerous private bills. To take just one example, the Liverpool Corporation Water Bill was concerned with an important aspect of public health which had an impact on both the North West and the West Midlands.[76] Alarmingly for the bill's promoters, there was no-one present to move the bill on behalf of the Liverpool Corporation at a vital stage of its parliamentary scrutiny. Members of Parliament from Wales and elsewhere took their opportunity and objected in strong terms. The Corporation wanted to exploit the water available in north Wales to compensate for the failings of existing sources of supply for Liverpool. In particular it wanted access to much

[74] P. Thorsheim, *Inventing Pollution: Coal, Smoke and Culture in Britain since 1800* (Ohio 2006), at, respectively, 120, 116–20, 82, 113, 82, 121, and 122.

[75] See 553–7.

[76] *PD* 1880 (s. 3), 250: 1278, Private Business Liverpool Corporation Water Bill Second Reading. On the use of private bills in this sort of context see Vol. XII, Part 1, Ch. IV, Leases, Mortgages, and Servitudes, pp. 165–6; and J. Getzler, *A History of Water Rights at Common Law* (Oxford, 2004), 350–2.

the greater part of the waters of the River Vyrnwy and the other rivers which ran into the Severn. In attempting this the city wished to go far beyond its own watershed, not least because the more accessible local supplies were impregnated with sewage from Liverpool.[77] Mr Hill was suspicious and believed that they already had almost enough for general sanitary purposes. In his view, what the Corporation really wanted was water for industrial use. 'By taking the average flow of the head waters of the Vyrnwy, and retailing it to the Liverpool manufacturers, the Corporation of Liverpool would be enabled to secure a very large revenue.' 'He was told that one sugar factory alone paid £4000 a year to the Corporation of Liverpool…'.[78] The losers in terms of water volume would be the towns in the Severn valley: Shrewsbury, Tewkesbury, Bridgnorth, Worcester, and elsewhere. But soon the arguments made it clear that, as with many private bills, the issues were complicated and political interests cut in all directions. Mr Yorke (representing 'Gloucestershire') pointed out that owners of property beside the Severn thought they would benefit from the proposals because it would reduce flooding.[79] This was true, but others pointed to the fact that reducing the level of the Severn would threaten its navigability.[80] After a variety of parliamentary obstacles had been removed, and Liverpool Members of Parliament had learned to attend in the right place at the right time, Liverpool got its Welsh water. Liverpool's politicians may have won this particular dispute but they were to lose others such as the protracted struggle over the private bills for the digging of the Manchester Ship Canal and, with it, the diversion of significant amounts of trade. Private bill legislation continued to influence the employment and health of millions of people.[81]

Beyond examples such as these, numerous reforms of the late Victorian and Edwardian years simply used the Public Health Act 1875 as a foundation for further interventions by one type of authority or another. To give only one example, the Public Health (Regulations as to Food) Bill of 1907 aroused the customary arguments about liberty, efficiency, and health.[82] Lord Belcarres was alarmed at the powers it would give to a government Minister. The latter 'would be able to go into any kitchen in the country and inspect the way in which food was being cooked'.[83] In contrast, Mr Idris, who had been for 40 years engaged in 'the manufacture of articles of food and drink', supported the extension of powers

---

[77] *Ibid.*, 1283.   [78] *Ibid.*, 1279.

[79] *Ibid.*, 1284.

[80] Sir Edmund Lechmere (representing Worcestershire) at *ibid.*, col. 1291.

[81] J. Getzler has recently revealed the full extent of private bill legislation: see J. Getzler, *A History of Water Rights at Common Law* (Oxford, 2004), 350–2.

[82] PD 1907 (s. 3), 1722.

[83] *Ibid.*, 1723–4.

of inspection and intervention. 'The sanitary inspection at present carried out was mainly directed at the protection of the people engaged in the work of the manufactories and not to the health of the people who were to consume the articles produced.' At present the public was in danger. 'The filling machines were covered with a mass of dirt and a gelatinous deposit which made them breeding grounds for micro-organisms of the worst description.'[84] Mr Bowles (Lambeth, Norwood) supported the measure but revealed the intricacy with which Public Health law had developed by showing there was a danger of a statutory section invented for one purpose being put to some entirely different use. He had taken the trouble to go back through the Acts, and he found the Public Health Act 1896 referred one back to the Public Health Act 1875. The section in the Act of 1875 which would give the government its everyday powers was s 143 and this, in fact, 'applied merely to extraordinary and exceptional cases'. It related to times when 'any part of England appeared to be threatened with or was affected by a formidable epidemic or endemic or infectious disease'.[85] Complicated legislation had a way of producing more complicated legislation, and early reforms could have unexpected consequences for the long-term development of the law.

In the same year, an Amendment Act continued the process of incremental legislative reform and took further the regulation of activities already under some form of supervision.[86] 'Public Health' came to have such a wide connotation that it could include regulations which were hardly linked to physical well-being. For example, there had long been a series of incidental controls over advertising, particularly in London, and s 91 of the new Act introduced powerful constraints over what were called sky signs with these 'signs' being given such a broad definition as to include almost any conceivable form of advertising which intruded upon the sky-line. Successive Public Health Acts were now a part of sustained national debates about everyday life.

5. PUBLIC HEALTH LAWS IN COMBINATION: LEGAL SOPHISTICATION AND THE PERSISTENCE OF STENCH

It has been pointed out above that from the time of the early debates about the introduction of legislation for public health there were related arguments about the common law. For some, it was still the case that old common law remedies were sufficiently effective to make new parliamentary laws unnecessary. For others the new laws were essential given the usual incapacity of anyone who was

---

[84] *Ibid.*, 1725.   [85] *Ibid.*, 1726.
[86] An Act to Amend the Public Health Acts, 1907: Part IX and s 91 regulate 'sky-signs'.

not rich to bring an action at common law. Beyond these fundamental questions, when legislation was passed the issue arose as to how it interlocked with
the common law. In outline it could be said, for example, that existing rights
survived save where they were expressly removed by statute. In practice the judicial analysis of any particular case could be more complicated than this suggests
because it would often require the minute analysis of private Acts of Parliament
and, given their contrasting provisions, this could not produce uniform national
approaches to the resolution of disputes.[87]

The problem was made worse by reason of tensions within the development
of the common law of nuisance at this time. The judgments in leading cases
were sometimes expressed with brevity. This arose out of a number of difficulties facing the judges. They had simultaneously to think about the role of juries
(because juries could still be used) and about the role of a judge sitting alone
(because under certain circumstances juries did not have to be used after 1854)
and about the effective use of pleadings (the rules for which were much criticized at various times and often regarded as transitional) and, not least, about
the disputed relationship between law and equity.[88] Other problems also pressed
home on the judiciary in respect of developing the tort of nuisance and made
it all the more difficult to develop a systematic approach to statutory reforms
which themselves produced mutually inconsistent standards.

The full dimension of common law disputes in this area of law is explored by
M. Lobban in the section on 'Nuisance'. One case, considered in its common law
aspect by Lobban, may serve as an example of the extent to which litigation could
be elaborate and prolonged through statute having a contentious impact on legal
argument.[89] Charles Adderley owned the Hams Hall estate near the expanding
city of Birmingham. The estate was situated in a bend in the river Tame and,
under the common law, he had the right to use the river in certain ways as it
flowed passed his land. The river became heavily polluted with the city's sewage
in the mid-1850s after the opening of a new sewer outlet. The landowner sued
the Council of the Borough of Birmingham using a relator action. The action
began in 1858 and was not settled until the 1890s. The city authorities argued
that Birmingham's sewers were lawfully constructed under the authority of the
Birmingham Improvement Act 1851 which incorporated the main clauses of the

---

[87] See R. Cocks, 'Victorian Foundations?', in R. Edmunds and J. Lowry (eds), *Environmental
Protection and the Common Law* (2004), 1–25.

[88] *Ibid.*, 12–24.

[89] See Vol. XII, Part 4 Tort, Ch. VI, Nuisance, pp. 1068–111, particularly at p. 1081. The analysis
which follows is based on L. Rosenthal, 'Economic Efficiency, Nuisance, and Sewage: New Lessons
from Attorney-General v. Council of the Borough of Birmingham, 1858–1895' (2007) 36(1) *JLS* 27–62.
See also, Cornish and Clark, *Law and Society in England,* 157 fn. 88.

Town Improvement Clauses Act 1847.[90] In short, it was statute which protected the health of Birmingham's citizens.

Accordingly, amongst the various arguments put forward by the defendants, it was stated that statutory duties had required the sewers and these duties overrode common law rights. But in the Chancery Division Page-Wood VC held that nothing in the precise terms of the relevant legislation had taken away the common law rights asserted by the plaintiff. When it was argued that 'If the drains are stopped, the entire sewage of the town will overflow. Birmingham will be converted into one vast cesspool.... The deluge of filth will cause a plague...', the Vice-Chancellor was not impressed.[91] He argued that 'The rights of the Plaintiff must be measured precisely as they have been left by the Legislature'.[92] Further, 'How the town is to be thoroughly drained without causing a nuisance is the business of the Defendants to discover'.[93] In other words the law did not respond to arguments about cost or general views of what might make for the public interest. Adderley had won this case at least in the limited sense that it was recognized that his property had suffered a nuisance.[94] At this stage, two statutes designed to produce public health had not been effective in the face of common law rights.

This inaugurated a different phase of litigation associated with the granting of injunctions and the use of writs of sequestration requiring the City to abate the nuisance. At first, the authority made various attempts to respond to the demands of the courts but, by 1864, with sewerage flow at 15 million gallons a day, it was finding the task impossible. By 1871 this had risen to 18 million and radical programmes were a necessity. Adderley was assisted by some other landowners bringing their own actions and there were now attempts by the City at further and novel improvements in the management of sewage. It began to use technical innovations involving more than 2000 acres of sewage farms along the Tame valley. Adderley and others continued to win on 'the law', but judges hearing later applications linked their findings to incidental expressions of hope that he would only stipulate reasonable requirements and would reach some agreement with the Corporation. At one stage it was possible that the parties might agree on a sale of the 'Hams' estate to the Corporation but, as it happened, they could not settle on a price and there was further litigation. The action ended in 1895 after

---

[90] 14 and 15 Vict. c. 93, and 10 and 11 Vict. c. 34, respectively. The Town Improvement Clauses Act 1847 made it easier and cheaper to prepare local Acts.

[91] 4 K. & J. (1858) 536.   [92] 4 K. & J. (1858) 539.

[93] 4 K. & J. (1858) 543.

[94] Lobban places this in the context of the general development of the law of nuisance: see fn 89 above.

some moderate but sustained improvement in the treatment of effluent and the payment to Adderley of £5000 and his costs.[95]

This was not the end of the litigation over the impact of Birmingham's sewerage in local rivers. In 1908 the authority for Tamworth, a town down-stream of Birmingham, brought a similar action and obtained an injunction. Once more the court added a rider to its decision in favour of the plaintiff. 'I think the defendants deserve gentle treatment.' The other party 'must take into consideration all the difficulties which beset the defendants in dealing with the vast problem entrusted to them...'.[96] Again there was compromise and the injunction was discharged in 1911.

Gladstone was a friend of Adderley and visited his estate in 1895. In later years this produced the comment 'The visit to Hams fills—shall I say?—a fragrant place in my recollection'.[97] The limits of the law were well-known to Victorians. In short, when it came to the enforcement of rights in the context of public health the letter of both statutes and the common law was an imperfect guide to the practical expectations of the courts. As with cases such as *Cooper* v. *Wandsworth Board of Works*, considered above, the enforcement of the law on public health through the courts could be intricate, lengthy, costly, and uncertain.[98] MacDonagh observed that it was possible for an Act designed to improve public health to combine 'ineffectuality in practice with revolution in principle'.[99] At the same time it is undeniable that in the course of the century conditions of public health did improve and that the law played some part in this.

Perhaps for the legal historian what is ultimately most striking is not the contentious issues associated with the social impact of the law, so much as the nature of the law itself. The legislative reforms were massive in their length and were made more intricate through their links with other areas of regulation relating, say, to local government or the procedures of the courts. As with the poor law, social problems had produced long and detailed clauses rather than grand declarations of principle. This could make the law difficult to follow and inaccessible to non-experts. We have seen above that Henry Thring, the distinguished

---

[95] L. Rosenthal, 'Economic Efficiency, Nuisance, and Sewage: New Lessons from Attorney-General v. Council of the Borough of Birmingham, 1858–1895' (2007) 36(1) *JLS* 41–55.

[96] *Attorney General* v. *Birmingham Tame and Rea District Drainage Board* [1908] 2 Ch. 551, 563. The action was brought under s 17 of the Public Health Act 1875.

[97] L. Rosenthal, 'Economic Efficiency, Nuisance, and Sewage: New Lessons from Attorney-General v. Council of the Borough of Birmingham, 1858–1895' (2007) 36(1) *JLS* 46.

[98] (1863) 14 C.B. (N.S.) 180.

[99] O. MacDonagh, *Early Victorian Government: 1830–1870* (1977), 157, writing with reference to the Sanitary Act 1866.

Parliamentary Counsel, thought that the sanitary laws of the 1860s were 'in form very complex and exceedingly difficult to understand'.[100] This view was surely of more general application. For Victorians, the voluminous law on public health was part of the price to be paid for trying to remove intense social deprivation. Of course, for the Victorian (and modern) reader of these Acts this degree of detail also brings with it the advantage of providing a picture of contemporary everyday life and the tensions which led to the making of the law, a point which will be further explored in the Ch. VII 'Conclusion'.[101]

---

[100] *RC on Sanitation*, First Report, *PP* 1868–9 [4218], xxxii, 26: and see fn. 60 above.

[101] See particularly at pp. 615–19 below.

V

Safety in Factories, Shops, and Ships

A focal point of law reform for nineteenth-century legislators lay in exploring the extent of the community's responsibility for controlling the rigours imposed by the workplace. The arguments swung between those who opposed any interference with the conditions of manufacturing and trade and those who saw statute law (and regulations made under statutory powers) as the only effective response to working conditions which were often degrading and dangerous. In ways which were especially vivid to participants, the debates linked, say, the dangers of a cutting machine or the condition of a ship to the broadest of social and economic issues.

1. THE POOR IN THE WORK-PLACE

The initial context for the debates was the poor law. An Act of 1802 expressed concern for the 'preservation of the health and morals of apprentices' working in mills.[1] It was not conceived of as a conscious assumption of control over industry. Its precise context was a series of scandals in the hiring of parish apprentices. The response might be seen as a form of gentlemanly benevolence on behalf of the vulnerable poor and this does much to explain why it was put through Parliament by Sir Robert Peel (father of the man who became Prime Minister) with little or no opposition. It helped that Peel was himself a mill owner and that the terms of the bill were broadly compatible with some owners' views of economic efficiency. Limiting young workers to 12 hours work a day entrenched on additional hours but the latter were unlikely to yield much profit for an employer. Requiring some form of education and separate sleeping for boys and girls pointed to moral virtues. Night work would stop and factories would be properly ventilated. In retrospect the Act looks more like an expression of mild social concern than an attempt to ensure that better working conditions were achieved. Contemporaries were not surprised when it proved to have little immediate influence.

[1] Factories Act 1802 (42 Geo. III, c. 73).

But over a period of years the reform proved to be significant for the minds of legislators. It set a precedent for regulation and, just as important, it introduced the idea of an inspectorate. True, the process of inspection was voluntary and it was under the control of Justices of the Peace who might sympathize with mill owners. As with the other provisions of this Act, the arrangements for an inspectorate proved to be ineffective in practice but the notion of inspection was now a part of parliamentary debate.[2] In 1815 Peel, speaking very much as a mill-owner, pointed out that 'the inspectors appointed under a late Act had been very remiss in the performance of their duty'.[3] Failure was a stimulus to further thought. Peel went on to chair a Select Committee charged with collecting evidence about the conditions experienced by children in factories. For example, Anthony Carlisle, a doctor who had practised for 23 years at the Westminster Hospital, was asked 'What in your opinion, would the effect of employing children from six to twelve years of age, twelve or fourteen hours a day in the winter, in a room, the temperature of which would be from 70 to 80, and afterwards their being exposed to the air?' The doctor replied, 'I should think it would be very deleterious to them'.[4]

The idea of intervening in industrial work was strengthened by the remarkable example of Robert Owen's New Lanark Mills during the first two decades of the century. Here children put to work had to be over ten and they also had the benefit of restricted working hours and some form of education. The result was economic success and a degree of admiration from a number of politicians. But legislative attempts to go beyond the terms of the 1802 Act now encountered strong opposition in Parliament from the mill-owning interest which was opposed to the creation of anything like an effective inspectorate and sought to resist additional age-limits being put into law. Debates became more organized in the sense that people were drawn to support workers or the opposing owners. For example, when Peel presented a new bill there was a national debate in pamphlets such as 'Answers to Certain Objections Made to Sir Robert Peel's Bill for Ameliorating the Conditions of Children Employed in Cotton Factories'.[5] Supporters of reform now felt despairingly that their mill-owning opponents were 'as inexhaustible almost as their funds'.[6] In response they relied on an increasing volume of evidence revealing the hardships of factory life with frequent breaches of the hours limitations in the 1802 Act. Surgeons such as William Wood of Manchester were

[2] T. K. Djang, *Factory Inspection in Great Britain* (1942), 26–30.

[3] *PD* 1815 31: 624–5.

[4] *SC on the State of the Children Employed in the Manufacturies of the UK*, 1816 (397), Evidence of Dr Carlisle.

[5] (Manchester 1819), reprinted in *The Factory Act of 1819, Six Pamphlets, 1818–1819* (New York, 1972).

[6] *Ibid.*, Preface.

alarmed at working conditions: 'I beg leave to remark, that 14 or 15 hours of labour in the day is too much for children to bear without suffering very materially in their health, particularly as it appears they are employed in an atmosphere frequently upwards of 80 degrees, and are exposed to the inclemency of the weather, oftentimes ill clad when they go and return from the Factories, which are frequently at a considerable distance from their habitations.' The result of doing the work was often 'deformities in the spine, legs, knees, and ankles' as well as 'other disorders which destroy a considerable number before they arrive at the age of maturity...'.[7] After contested debates in and out of Parliament the Cotton Mills and Factories Act, 1819 came into force. It applied solely to cotton mills and went only slightly further in the protection of workers than the existing legislation as well as doing nothing to enhance inspection.[8]

In the years which followed the focal point of attention became the maximum working hours of children. The previous reforms alerted people to the fact that there was a lack of regulation beyond cotton mills. Even in the latter it was possible to employ children as young as nine, and, as we have seen, anyone over 18 could be required to work more than 12 hours a day. The case for further reform at this point was often acknowledged by industrialists, but they were concerned at the intentions of adult workers to organize and seek universal restrictions on the working day. In some cases the arguments became entangled with views about the possibility of working children in shifts alongside adults working longer hours. Evidence revealing the suffering of children in factories became incontrovertible and in Yorkshire there were public demonstrations demanding legislative intervention. The demands for change, expressed with force and clarity by Richard Oastler, were sufficient to threaten political stability.[9] Michael Sadler attempted to push a bill through Parliament in 1831, and when this was not achieved a Select Committee began to provide more than enough justification for change. For example, it became clear that children were sometimes working from 5am to 10pm or even 11pm.[10] Sadler lost his seat and Ashley (Lord Shaftesbury) took over the role of reformer's champion. Ashley presented his own bill but his efforts were derailed by the mill-owners having the issues referred to a Royal Commission.[11]

---

[7] *Ibid.*, 59–60.

[8] Factories and Cotton Mills Act (59 Geo. III, c. 66); and see Cornish and Clark, *Law and Society in England*, 302.

[9] K. E. Carpenter (Advisory Editor), *Richard Oastler: King of Factory Children, Six Pamphlets, 1835–1861* (New York, 1972).

[10] *SC on the Bill to Regulate the Labour of Children in the Mills and Factories of the United Kingdom*, PP 1831–2 (706), 5.

[11] The terms of reference were such as to require the Commissioners to act with dispatch 'so as to enable Parliament to legislate on the subject during the present session': see *Return of the Names*

The Commission had 15 members but was under the direction of a Central Board containing three Benthamites, Thomas Tooke, Thomas Southwood Smith, and Edwin Chadwick. Evidence was gathered with some speed and their First Report set the pattern for all their findings. They recommended that no child under nine should be employed and that children under 14 should not do more than eight hours in a day.[12] Adults should be left to take care of themselves. The Commissioners noted that 'The pernicious notion of the propriety and necessity of legislative interference to restrict the hours of adult labour is mischievously sanctioned by some persons engaged in manufactures, and by gentlemen connected with them who may be served by popularity, and whose judgments may thereby be biased in favour of the doctrine'.[13] The Report also pointed out that it was essential to have officers appointed to enforce the law; and, in respect of injuries at work, they proposed that 'in the case of all accidents whatsoever from machinery occurring to children under fourteen years of age, the proprietor of the machinery shall pay for the medical attendance on the child'.

In the second Report there was substantial and varied evidence from the Commissioners with medical qualifications. When Dr Loudon visited Leicester he remarked that:

The first factory I visited was that of Mr Oldacre, which is situated in the outskirts of the town. It is a mill for the manufacturing of wool, propelled by a steam engine. The number of people employed is about 100. They usually work twelve hours a day. The smell on entering the first set of rooms was heavy and offensive. All of the people I saw in the factory, however, appeared to be in better health than they are usually in factories. They were stouter in general, and did not appear to have the care-worn countenances nor the slender shape of factory people.[14]

In contrast, when Dr Hawkins visited Manchester he provided examples of very unhealthy working conditions and also did something to explore the social context. He pointed out that in reality there was often an inadequate home to go to after work: 'Sometimes it is a cellar, which includes no cookery, no washing, no making, no mending, no decencies of life, no invitation to the fire-side'.[15] Arguments about factory legislation had a way of raising very broad social issues.

Appointed to the Factory Commission, PP 1833 (331), p. i. For contemporary debates amongst political economists over 'interference' by government at this time see Keith Smith.

[12] RC on the Employment of Children in Factories, First Report, PP 1833 (450), xx.i, 52.

[13] Ibid., 50.

[14] RC on the Employment of Children in Factories, Second Report, PP 1833 (519), xxi.i, 101.

[15] Ibid., 133. The RC on the Employment of Children in Factories, Supplementary Reports, PP 1834 (167), xix.259 xx.i, arrived after the Act had been passed and contained large amounts of statistical evidence. The Commissioners argued that it confirmed the views set out in their earlier Reports; see 16.

2. 'DEFORMING THE LIMBS OF CHILDREN' OR 'PUFFING HUMANITY'?

The parliamentary debates of the 1830s about the protection of those aged below 18 revealed a capacity to mix expressions of humanitarian concern with economic arguments and, in some cases, personal animosities. For Mr Strickland '...the real question before the House was whether or not protection should be confined to persons under thirteen years of age'. For him the answer was a definitive 'No'. He knew a case of a young man whose thigh-bone was completely bent by working 15 hours a day in a factory, and that deformity did not commence until he had attained his fifteenth year. He believed that 'no man could work for fifteen or sixteen hours a day without injury; and he must, therefore, support the proposed limitation to the eighteenth year'. In answer to the large number who opposed the reform on the ground that it would make English industry uncompetitive, he simply pointed out that 'he had too strong an opinion of the stability of the principles on which English commerce was founded, to think that its success must depend on deforming the limbs of children'.[16]

Others such as Bolling, a Tory cotton spinner, defended the mill-owners and deprecated 'puffing humanity speeches'.[17] For Mr Bolling the answer lay in the effective enforcement of the 1802 Act. Proper enforcement would have rendered Sadler's inquiries obsolete. Further, 'if the hours for work are to be reduced to eight or less, the establishment of some system of education, or a great addition to the number of constables, will be necessary. Education will certainly raise the manufacturing population in the scale of society, and prevent them going to the dram-shop or beer-house.'[18] Mr Hume had major doubts about inspectors fencing off machinery: '...the inspectors would probably not know anything of machinery, and their interference might be more injurious than beneficial. Suppose he were to offer himself for an inspector, he might be as a good an inspector as could be as to the health of the children, and their food and time of labour, but he should not be able to judge of the machinery, and he might think there was danger where there was none, and he might order fences to be put up which would stop the machinery. He thought it a good rule not to interfere in the management of a man's private concerns'.[19]

---

[16] *PD* 1833 (s. 3), 19: 898–9; for Strickland, see R. Gray, *The Factory Question and Industrial England, 1830–1860* (Cambridge, 1996), 55.

[17] *PD* 1833 (s. 3), 19: 898–9, and see 907. R. Gray, *The Factory Question* (Cambridge, 1996), 50, 183, 189.

[18] *PD* 1833 (s. 3), 19: 911.

[19] *Ibid.*, 584, 13 August 1833. On the factory inspectorate and the fencing of machinery, see P. W. J. Bartrip, 'Safety at Work: The Factory Inspectorate in the Fencing Controversy, 1833–1857' (Oxford, 1979).

In the final version of the Bill there was a clause to ensure that those under nine should never be seen inside a factory, and children under 13 were limited to a nine-hour day and 48-hour week. Those under 18 were restricted to a 12-hour day and 69-hour week. There were fines for non-compliance. The House of Commons hoped that all children would have the benefit of regular educational instruction but the Lords saw to it that the educational provisions were of no account. Perhaps the most striking provisions were for the Home Office to have a factory inspectorate of four with sub-inspectors at local level. They were given a remarkable role and some inspectors such as Leonard Horner were to achieve national reputations.[20] They were a special form of magistrate with extensive executive, judicial, and legislative powers. They could make regulations without submitting them to Parliament and hold summary proceedings. What was more, a factory occupier was made liable whether or not he knew that he was committing an offence.[21] Later, in a negative response to the wide and novel powers of inspectors, an Act of 1844 restricted them to executive roles and gave jurisdiction to conventional magistrates.[22] This did not greatly dismay the inspectors because they were given enhanced rights of entry into factories and were to be supported by a central office with clerks. They also had high hopes of new provisions for the fencing of dangerous machinery.[23] Over time the inspectorate did have an impact with improved controls over the use of children and a greater degree of intervention in respect of dangerous machinery. In later years it was possible to argue that 'the most important event in the whole history of the Factory Acts was the appointment of factory inspectors in 1833'.[24]

3. THE EXTENSION OF CONTROLS OVER WORKING CONDITIONS

The bill of 1833 served as a stimulus for future debates about the regulation of employment conditions. Far from ending the demand for reform it was often criticized as being manifestly inadequate. None of the contending parties thought it fully served their interests.[25] In particular there was dispute over further reform of the maximum permitted working hours for adults. The intensity

---

[20] *Ibid.* W. R. Cornish and G. de N. Clark, *Law and Society in England, 1750–1950* (1989), 304–5 and M. W. Thomas, *The Early Factory Legislation* (Leigh-on-Sea, 1948), Ch. 7, see Vol. XI, Pt 2, Ch. II, Central Executive: The Legal Structure of State Institutions, pp. 349, 351–2.

[21] Factories Act 1833 (3 and 4 Will. IV, c. 103), ss 17–19, 33.

[22] Factories Act 1844 (7 and 8 Vict. c. 15).

[23] P. W. J. Bartrip, 'Safety at Work' (Oxford, 1979), 18–19.

[24] R. E. Squire, *Thirty Years in the Public Service* (1927), Foreword. On strict liability see Vol. XIII, Part 1, Ch. VIII, pp. 322–3.

[25] M. W. Thomas, *The Early Factory Legislation* (Leigh-on- Sea, 1948), 74.

of debate sharpened as other areas of work became topics of national concern. The determination of reformers was strengthened by reports into conditions in mines. The First Report of the Children's Employment Commissioners presented to Parliament in 1842 painted a picture of exploitation in mines which exceeded even what had been revealed in factories.[26] Women and girls were employed underground in various areas such as South Wales, Lancashire, and Cheshire. Local Sub-Commissioners concluded that they were unfit for it and that the experience 'tends more or less to demoralise and brutalise the females employed'. Further, in responding to Victorian notions of female duties, 'their employment below ground prevents their attention to the performance of domestic duties, as diminishing their competency for the proper care and training of their children'.[27] At the same time an employer might argue that there were so many employed in the mines that 'it would be impossible to dispense with them on a sudden'.[28] There was almost as much concern about male children. In the Coalbrook Dale district of Shropshire boys as young as six were sent to work in mines.[29]

Elsewhere there was concern about a mining practice which was also associated with factories. Children in the grip of the poor law were sometimes taken from the workhouse and for all practical purposes forced into work for no return. For example, Dr Mitchell reported that 'in the coal mines of South Staffordshire the orphan whom necessity has driven into a workhouse is made to labour in the mines until the age of twenty-one, solely for the benefit of another'.[30] One observer reached the unsurprising view that such a form of labour 'is unfavourable to the acquisition of industrious habits. The young man toils for the benefit of others, and not of himself. It is also most unfavourable for the acquisition of a virtuous, moral, and religious education.'[31] In retrospect it seems to have been indistinguishable from slavery until the child reached 21—if indeed he or she did reach that age.

There was sufficient shock over what had been revealed for legislation introducing some controls over mining to be passed in 1842.[32] It sought to prevent

[26] RC on Children's Employment in Mines and Manufactories, First Report, Mines, 1842 (380) (381) (382), xv–xvii.

[27] Ibid., para. 141.

[28] Ibid., para. 142.

[29] Ibid., para. 49. Evidence on working conditions for children surfaces throughout the Report indicating, for example, that some worked in a few feet of water, and were ill-fed, ill-housed and in winter did not see the sun for months at a time: see p. 802.

[30] Ibid., para. 188.

[31] Ibid., para. 189. See also, para. 190: 'Now here is slavery in the middle of England…'. Note that these children had no holidays and worked seven days a week.

[32] Mines and Collieries Act 1842 (5 & 6 Vict. c. 122).

the employment of women underground and to regulate the work given to boys. But it soon acquired a reputation for being ineffective, particularly in respect of its inspectorate which appears to have done little to trouble mine-owners for the remainder of the decade.[33]

Other areas of work outside factories reinforced anxieties in respect of what children were experiencing when they were put into employment. Because chimney sweeping was something any householder could relate to in the course of everyday life it had a sustained history of public debates and reforms. Critics of the trade could produce precise plans of chimneys and explain exactly how a child could become stuck in a chimney and exactly how the child would die.[34] There had been an attempt to regulate the hardships of chimney sweeps in 1788 but this had failed in practice.[35] In an Act of 1834 there were new regulations in respect of the construction of chimneys and a prohibition on sending anyone up a chimney to extinguish a chimney fire. Further, no child under ten was to be apprenticed to a sweep; and no child under 14 was to be employed by a chimney sweep.[36] The failure of this measure to be properly enforced led to further legislation in 1840 which was promoted by Lord Shaftesbury as chairman of the Climbing Boys Society.[37] No-one under 20 was to be compelled to ascend a chimney and no one under 16 was to be apprenticed. But in the 1860s it was recognized that numerous abuses persisted and it was in response to one report of that decade that Charles Kingsley wrote his *Water Babies*.[38] The law was amended yet again in 1864 but this, too, sometimes proved to be ineffective.[39] After 1875 chimney sweeps who employed assistants or apprentices had to take out a police certificate and it seems that this did lead to a measure of improvement.[40]

Concern for those who worked in mines or in specialized trades such as chimney sweeping was mirrored in further developing debates about factories. A significant range of reforms were contested throughout the 1840s and 1850s. In 1847 there were enhanced restrictions on hours worked by women and children

---

[33] H. W. Arthurs, *'Without the Law': Administrative Justice and Legal Pluralism in Nineteenth-Century England* (1985), 107–13.

[34] K. H. Strange, *The Climbing Boys: A Study of Sweeps Apprentices, 1773–1875* (1982), Chs I–III.

[35] An Act for the Better Regulation of Chimney-Sweeps and their Apprentices (28 Geo. III c. 48).

[36] An Act for the Better Regulation of Chimney Sweeps and their Apprentices and for the Safer Construction of Chimneys and Flues (4 & 5 Will. IV c. 35). See also, 'Chimney Sweepers' Apprentices: An Account of the number of boys apprenticed to chimney sweepers, at the several police offices within the bills of mortality, during the last nine years', *PP* 1834 (114).

[37] An Act for the Regulation of Chimney Sweepers and Chimneys (3 & 4 Vict. c. 85).

[38] C. Kingsley, *Water Babies* (first published as a book in 1863).

[39] An Act to Amend and Extend the Act for the Regulation of Chimney Sweepers.

[40] An Act for Further Amending the Law Relating to Chimney Sweepers.

in factories.[41] This measure was to some extent subverted by systems which staggered the hours of workers. Manufacturers were supported by the courts in doing this and it took further reforms of 1850 and 1853 to regulate hours in everyday practice.[42] Across the country there were an increasing number of informal arrangements which often reflected the bargaining power of the groups involved. In London, for example, many trades had understandings as to appropriate hours for working and these hours were reduced over the course of the Victorian decades.[43]

Further reforms reached the statute book in the 1860s and regulation spread beyond textiles with, as so often, a particular concern for the experience of children. There was now some minimal degree of protection for those who worked with 'lucifer' matches and were exposed to the possibility of necrosis of the jawbone.[44] National concern was expressed about conditions in the pottery trade in North Staffordshire. Despite all the reforms of earlier years, the minimum hours of work were usually 6.30 am to 6.30 pm. Children and others working with glazes were exposed to the risk of poisoning. In the kilns some children worked in temperatures of up to 148 degrees Farenheit. The larger manufacturers such as Wedgewood and Minton, perhaps driven by a mixture of humanity and a desire to drive out cheap competition, supported reform and some measure of regulation was introduced.[45] Elsewhere, copper mills and forges were brought within Factory legislation in 1867.[46] In a reform of national importance any premises in which 50 or more were employed in a manufacturing process also came within Factory legislation, although a long list of exceptions survived parliamentary debate. This was linked to the Workshops Regulation Act 1867 which was

[41] An Act to Limit the Hours of Labour of Young Persons and Females in Factories, (10 & 11 Vict. c. 29); S. H. J. Kydd, *A History of the Factory Movement* (1857) (reprinted New York, 1966), ii: Ch. XVI.

[42] *Ryder* v. *Mills* (1850) 3 Ex. 853. An Act to Amend the Acts Relating to Labour in Factories (13 and 14 Vict. c. 54) and an Act Further to Regulate the Employment of Children in Factories (16 and 17 Vict. c. 104); and see W. R. Cornish and G. de N. Clark, *Law and Society in England* (1989), 306–7; M. W. Thomas, *The Early Factory Legislation* (Leigh-on- Sea, 1948), Ch. 18; B. L. Hutchins and A. Harrison, *A History of Factory Legislation* (1926), Ch. VI, 'The Introduction of a Normal Day'.

[43] *Ibid.*, 122 and 139; and W. R. Cornish and G. de N. Clark, *Law and Society in England* (1989), 307.

[44] Factory Acts Extension Act 1864: for the provisions relating to Lucifer matches see s 6(4) and First and Second Schedules. Another section had a broad application but lost much of its potential force through imposing a 'so far as practicable' standard: 'Every factory to which the Act applies shall be kept in a cleanly state, and be ventilated in such a manner as to render harmless so far as practicable any gases, dust or other impurities generated in the process of manufacture that may be injurious to health'. See also, T. K. Djang, *Factory Inspection* (1942), 194–5.

[45] B. L. Hutchins and A. Harrison, *A History of Factory Legislation* (1926), 151–4.

[46] An Act for the Extension of the Factory Acts.

designed to produce some sort of control over premises with less than 50 workers which did not happen to be 'caught' by laws for specialized manufacturing such as textiles.[47]

These reforms came with important changes in the way people were thinking about the dangers of work. Early debates were focused on obvious sources of physical danger as in the case of unfenced machinery. Over the decades the idea of occupational disease also became prominent and the new laws allowed for a more forceful response to the miseries caused by lead or phosphorous or arsenic or anthrax.[48] Working life was coming to be seen 'in the round', and with this came an increase in the range of an employer's responsibilities.[49]

4. BEYOND THE FACTORY GATE: 'LEGISLATION THE ONLY REMEDY'

The attempt to regulate workshops was adventurous and had the potential to improve working conditions for a large number of employees. But it brought with it major problems of enforcement and these limited the enthusiasm for further forms of intervention in industry. When an Act of 1867 was being prepared factory Inspectors had about 30,000 premises within their remit. When the Act came into force the inclusion of workshops had the potential greatly to increase the number of places for them to visit.[50] The obvious place to turn was the local authorities, and in particular to the Medical Officers of Health and other sanitary officers. Much of the reform was merely permissive. Some municipal authorities such as Chichester refused to use the Act. Stockport simply ignored it. Stafford made a success of it. With some exasperation the responsibility was transferred to the Factory Inspectorate as soon as 1871 but the Inspectorate was not resourced to take on what transpired to be 110,000 new premises subject to potential enforcement. This in its turn led back to having to use public health powers under the control of local authorities. In legal form workshops were assimilated with factories for certain purposes after 1878 but in respect of enforcement many problems remained unresolved. As late as 1901 there were attempts to monitor local scrutiny

---

[47] An Act for Regulating the Hours of Labour for Children, Young Persons, and Women Employed in Workshops, and for other Purposes Relating Thereto. It is an Act with formidable detail, as in the case of s 8 responding to problems of dust.

[48] P. W. J. Bartrip, *The Home Office and the Dangerous Trades: Regulating Occupational Disease in Victorian and Edwardian Britain* (2002).

[49] See Ch. IV for links with the developing law for public health.

[50] Factory and Workshop Act 1867.

through making the keeping of registers compulsory. It was as if workshops were on the contested frontier of regulation.[51]

It was still a fact that many in the national workforce were completely unprotected, even in respect of the hours they worked. In the 1880s a Select Committee of Enquiry into conditions in retail shops revealed that some shop assistants were working up to 85 hours in a week.[52] To make matters worse, it was clear that in certain cases assistants were working in workshops up to the maximum permitted for such places and thereafter were transferred to unregulated retail work. The evidence relating to such retail work revealed that shops frequently stayed open after 8pm on weekdays and until very late on Saturday night. 'Late' shopping was a popular Victorian pastime and assistants were the victims. There was also concern about the hours worked in warehouses. The preamble to the Act which followed referred to the fact that 'the health of many young persons employed in shops and warehouses is seriously injured by reason of the length of the period of employment'. A weekly limit of 74 hours was introduced by s 3(1) of the Act and, under s 8, it applied only to young persons who were defined as being under 18.[53]

Even this moderate reform was found to be ineffective. A few years later a Select Committee reached the unsurprising view that 'it appears to us to be undesirable that the Shop Hours Act 1886 should remain of doubtful and imperfect operation'. The Committee wanted enforcement by inspectors.[54] In 1892 the permitted hours for factories and workshops were made applicable to shops and enforcement was handed to local authorities, some of which were able to appoint inspectors.[55] The Committee had also given a lot of time to the question of whether it was desirable to reduce the permitted weekly hours of work in respect of women and not men. Faced with conflicting evidence it did not feel able to support special terms for women. Some thought that privileging women would lead to them not being employed. Others thought they would continue to be recruited because of 'the difference of wages, and the greater aptitude of women for certain departments of business'.[56] An increasing amount of medical

---

[51] For these problems with enforcement see B. L. Hutchins and A. Harrison, *A History of Factory Legislation* (1926), 226–51 and note at 226 'Quite apart from the inadequate power given to the local inspectors, the Workshops Regulation Act was a very difficult one to administer. The Act is remarkable as an evidence of the neglect of legislators to learn from past experience, for its distinguishing feature is the absence of all those safeguards against evasions of the law, which had found a place in the Factory Acts from 1833 onwards'.

[52] *SC on Shop Hours Regulation Bill*, PP 1886 (155), xii.i. For examples of long hours see paras 3137 and 3217.

[53] An Act to Limit the Hours of Labour of Children and Young Persons in Shops, 1886.

[54] *SC on the Shop Hours Bill*, PP 1892 (424).

[55] Hutchins and Harrison, *A History of Factory Legislation*, 222.

[56] *SC on the Shop Hours Bill*, PP 1892 (424), p. iii.

evidence pointed to severe health problems being caused for all assistants by having to stand for very long hours and Thomas Sutherst's book, *Death and Disease Behind the Counter*, helped to keep the issue in public debate.[57] He argued that he was 'within the mark in stating that the majority of shop-assistants in this country work from 75 to 90 hours in every week'.[58] He was clear about the problem. The usual cause of disease and even death was the demand that shop assistants 'should stand and work from 13 to 17 hours a day'.[59] After a long analysis of the failure of voluntary responses he concluded with a section entitled 'Legislation the Only Remedy'.[60] This in turn led to reflections on the need for law to strike a balance between liberty and interference.[61] But even by the start of the First World War the individual shop assistant could be forgiven for wondering if anything other than certain statutory sections had changed in the course of the preceding three decades. In reality there had always been problems with enforcement in this context.[62] As late as 1912 a consolidating Shops Act repeated existing exemptions and revealed a major way of avoiding the application of a number of important protective laws by ensuring that s 2 (which provided limits for hours of work and stipulated that no person under 18 shall be employed for longer than 74 hours a week) did 'not apply to any person wholly employed as a domestic servant'. In other words, a domestic servant working in a shop could still legally be required to work for more than 74 hours in any week.[63]

In respect of manufacturing at home the situation was considerably worse. It had been known since the 1840s that in the domestic making of hosiery there were instances of work by very young children, some aged about 3½. These 'home' conditions were often squalid, over-crowded, noisy, and disease-ridden.[64] There was a particular problem with children being over-worked at the end of the week when quotas had to be met. For decades numerous people had expressed concern but the contentious idea of intruding into domestic life and challenging poverty-stricken parents for what they were doing to their children thwarted change. Reports of abuses had an indirect impact on the move to regulate workshops on the ground that the latter were non-domestic, but legislators found this a difficult area of reform with a lack of clear boundaries between the public and the private.[65] Domestic manufacturing was closely linked to informal forms of

[57] 1884.   [58] *Ibid.*, 3.   [59] *Ibid.*

[60] *Ibid.*, 61.   [61] *Ibid.*, at e.g. 95–111.

[62] *Ibid.*, 221–2.

[63] An Act to Consolidate the Shops Regulation Acts 1892–1911, s 2.

[64] Hutchins and Harrison, *A History of Factory Legislation*, 157.

[65] Spencer Walpole, Home Secretary, *PD* 1867 (s. 3), 185: 1276–7.

'sweated' labour in small and often transient premises which fell short even of the workshop regulations.[66]

The horrors of this type of domestic work were perfectly well known but remained scarcely regulated in any way. In 1910 Sidney Webb pointed out that 'In spite of improved sanitary inspection in certain districts, and just a beginning, here and there, of supervision of the home worker, the state of the London needle-work and low-grade furniture trades in 1910 is, in fact, closely parallel to that of the Lancashire cotton trade in 1802.' Later he added 'It is, indeed, unfortunately only too true that the sweated trades literally use up the men, women and children who work at them, as omnibus companies use up their horses.'[67]

Taken together, the numerous Reports and Acts concerned with factories make up the most intricate and sustained of the nineteenth-century attempts to link arguments about commercial success to the social duties of the state towards citizens. The number of bills and the extent of associated reports and investigations put before the House of Commons was striking. A catalogue of House of Commons Parliamentary Papers for the nineteenth century reveals that in respect of factories there were 45 major bills, numerous reports of Committees, 11 reports of Commissioners, 42 Accounts and Papers, 113 reports from Factories Inspectors with their own additional Accounts and papers and so on.[68] All the major areas of enquiry have their own more specialized measures which could be looked at in detail. For instance in the case of shops there was an Act of 1899 'to Provide for Seats Being Supplied for the Use of Shop Assistants'. Under the Act there was to be a 'proportion of not less than one seat to every three female assistants'.[69]

In his study of the factory legislation between 1830 and 1860 Robert Gray points out that factory regulation 'became the site of protracted controversy, resistance and negotiation. In the process the terms of debate were themselves contested and transformed.'[70] For a working man, regulation might mean an assertion of rights; for an employer it could be an expression of benevolence or a defeat in an attempt to maintain international competitiveness; for a reformer or civil servant it could have a resonance as a form of social control directed to moral and material improvement. Given the likelihood of conflict between these views there was little prospect of the movement for reform coming to an end for as long as people engaged in organized production.

---

[66] See below in Vol. XIII, Pt 3, Ch. III, pp. 703–4.

[67] B. L. Hutchins and A. Harrison, *A History of Factory Legislation* (1926), Preface, pp. xi and xii.

[68] P. Cockton, *Subject Catalogue of the House of Commons Parliamentary Papers, 1801–1900* (1988), vol. II, 'Industry and Industrial Society'.

[69] Section 1.

[70] R. Gray, *The Factory Question* (Cambridge, 1996), 22.

In its regulatory range and detail this theme to statutory reform was remarkable, and it was all the more striking for the variety in its applications. Again and again general discussion about the duties towards workers were related to investigations into what was happening in one specific workplace after another. Moral issues were mixed with the problems of producing cotton goods or cleaning chimneys or requiring shop assistants to stand throughout the working day. The result was a very large amount of statute law intruding with imperfect effect into some, and only some, areas of employment whilst legislators had constantly before their eyes detailed information about the experience of individuals in one industry after another.

5. SAFETY ON SHIPS: THE 'PLIMSOLL-LINE'

Painted on the sides of ships, the 'Plimsoll Line' was the most visible proof of the Victorian determination to use law as an instrument for intervention in working lives. After its introduction, vessels could not legally leave harbour if their freight was of a weight that took the level of the water above the designated line.

The use of regulations to enhance safety on ships was frequently discussed during the nineteenth century and it was just as frequently opposed by shipowners. The latter saw it as an unwarranted intrusion into their affairs and a restriction on their profits precisely because it was designed to limit the amount of freight they could put aboard. As against the owners, a concern for the safety of seamen had a secure place in nineteenth-century public opinion and was reflected in expressions of concern on the part of churchmen, novelists, and painters. The latter reminded the public of maritime dangers in vivid pictures of nautical tragedies, including Grace Darling's brave act of rescue when she personally took a rowing boat out to a foundering ship in a storm.[71] Shipping, and the interests of those who worked on ships was always present in public debate, reflecting the large number of people involved: for example in 1872 ships in Britain and the British Empire employed about 329,000 sailors.[72]

In appearance at least, the safety of sailors also had a place in law, even if in the middle of the century it was not notably secure. The 'Act to Amend and Consolidate the Acts Relating to Merchant Shipping' of 1854, in conjunction with an Act of the same year repealing large parts of old legislation, was

[71] Grace Horsley Darling (1815–42): her role in the rescue of the *S.S. Forfarshire* in 1838 is now recorded in the 'Grace Darling Museum' in Bamburgh, Northumberland.
[72] *RC on the Alleged Unseaworthiness of British Registered Ships*, Preliminary Report, *PP* 1873 [853] [853-1], p. 1.

a remarkable example of draftsmanship.[73] It had 548 sections and they were presented to Parliament in a clear style which made it all the easier for the bill to be passed. Much of the Act can be read with pleasure. It was one of the early efforts of Henry Thring, a remarkable Victorian parliamentary draftsman. As a writer 'he thought in bills and clauses' and it shows.[74] The measure gave 'general superintendence' to the Board of Trade which, amongst many other powers, could appoint inspectors. Part IV of the Act was concerned with 'Safety and the Prevention of Accidents' and it was designed to ensure that there were adequate lifeboats, lights and the like. But for all its length, the Act by itself could not secure systematic enforcement and it had a notable omission in not having an effective provision for preventing the over-loading of ships carrying freight.

The unlikely catalyst for change was an obscure Member of Parliament. Samuel Plimsoll had been an Honorary Secretary for the Great Exhibition of 1851. He went on to become a coal merchant in London and developed a commitment to radical politics. Between 1868 and 1880 he was a Member for Derby. Despite representing one of the most land-locked constituencies in the country, he sustained a strong interest in mercantile shipping and developed an ever-increasing distrust of shipowners.

Nicolette Jones' detailed study of Plimsoll and his campaign for safety at sea points again and again to his capacity to link information about seafaring conditions to the Victorian imagination for hardship and disaster.[75] It was also very much a legal matter. Under an Act to Amend the Merchant Shipping Acts 1871 a sailor who had agreed to a voyage committed a criminal offence if he refused to board the ship for which he had signed even if he thought it was unseaworthy. A sailor charged with this offence had a number of potential defences but they were unlikely to be of practical use as in the instance of the right of the seaman to lodge a complaint with the Master in person—surely the height of parliamentary innocence as to the reality of working conditions.[76] In the early 1870s, 1628 sailors were sent to jail for committing this offence and, predictably, public concern increased.[77]

From 1870 Plimsoll made attempts at fundamental reform with a view to ensuring that ships were seaworthy. He wanted to see the use of a load line on every

---

[73] 17 & 18 Vict. 104 and 'An Act to Repeal Certain Acts and Parts of Acts Relating to Merchant Shipping' (17 & 18 Vict. 120). Some powers had already passed from the Admiralty to the Board of Trade under the Mercantile Marine Act 1850 (13 & 14 Vict. c. 93), s 6.

[74] Henry Thring, Baron Thring (1818–1907), *Oxford Dictionary of National Biography* (2004), vol. 54. Generally on this area of the law, see Sir William Holdsworth, *A History of English Law* (1964), XV: 101–2.

[75] N. Jones, *The Plimsoll Sensation* (2006).

[76] Section 7.

[77] Jones, *Plimsoll*, 11.

ship and produced a powerful case for saying that it would save 500 lives a year. Members of Parliament with a shipping interest such as Thomas Eustace Smith and Charles Norwood deflected the bill from the government's agenda and may have thought they had ended the possibility of reform. But the next winter was a grim one at sea, particularly in regard to the Bridlington gale of 10 February 1871. Not only was there major loss of life in the gale, in subsequent debate it was suggested that sailors died because the ships in question (colliers) were incapable of coping with the storm in part through over-loading. By 22 February Plimsoll was back in Parliament with another bill. He failed again and began to despair of progress within Westminster. He retreated to write and protest to the general public. His denunciations were unsophisticated but throughout he had a tone of massive sincerity. His honesty made an impact, and in combination with increasing numbers of public meetings and numerous articles in the press (sometimes revealing the names of sailors who had died on overloaded ships) it attracted increasing political attention.

Plimsoll's public life was gradually transformed. As his popularity increased he encountered bitter opposition from trading interests and was dogged by writs for defamation in respect of his extra-parliamentary speeches. When the issue was mentioned in Parliament he spoke in the strongest terms. At one stage it was argued that 'Plimsollism is another word for terrorism'. At a time when a possible Royal Commission on safety at sea was being debated in the Commons a ship (the *Peru*) sank after it had gone to sea despite the previous imprisonment of 15 sailors who found her unseaworthy. Feelings ran high and the support for Plimsoll became more strident. Christian groups expressed repugnance at the shipowners' lack of concern for human life. Wealthy and influential women formed a Ladies Committee chaired by the Duchess of Argyll, the senior lady in the Royal Household. Lord Shaftesbury became chairman of a 'Plimsoll Committee' and noted that he '...had placed in (his) hand a cheque for £1000. From whom did that come? From the miners of Durham alone. A number of them met, and, at the close of a short sitting, they voted that each miner in that district should give a shilling per head towards the Plimsoll Fund'.[78]

Now, in response to passionate demands, a Royal Commission was set up. Any shipping disaster was scrutinized and publicized. There was talk of trade unionism reaching ships. One particular owner, Edward Bates the Member of Parliament for Plymouth, was becoming a useful political target given his public reputation for offensive conduct. In Liverpool he was known as 'Bully-Bates'. It was as if the shipping interest could not rid itself of public scrutiny. As a result some owners suggested that the new President of the Board of Trade,

---

[78] *Ibid.*, 101, 122–3, 124.

Sir Charles Adderley, might introduce a bill offering a moderate change which would not disturb trading interests whilst responding to some demands. At the time Adderley was determined to do nothing that might appease Plimsoll: in effect he did not want to see unseaworthiness defined by Act of Parliament.[79] As was noted in Ch. IV, Adderley was happy to use the law to assert his private proprietary interests through litigation against Birmingham City Council in connection with the disposal of sewerage.[80] This personal use of the law did not lead him to support the imposition of further legal responsibilities on shipowners. When, in June 1874, he publicly refused to introduce any measure of any kind Plimsoll forced a division of the House and startled Disraeli's government by almost winning.

Soon the public debates began to interlock with the work of the Royal Commission. Created to investigate 'the alleged unseaworthiness of British registered ships' a preliminary Report of 1873 took up 631 pages and published a large body of evidence much of which challenged the need for any sort of load line. Different sorts of 'line' were considered and criticized for one reason or another.[81] The Final Report appeared on 1 July 1874 and its 988 pages reflected the strength of the interests opposed to Plimsoll and the capacity for the arguments to be linked to wider debates about accountability and seamanship.[82] Plimsoll entered into a strained exchange of correspondence with the Board of Trade over whether he had questioned the integrity of the Board's Officers.[83]

Plimsoll's protests were in vain. In their Final Report, the Commissioners came to the view that 'The proper load line in each particular case depends not only upon the principal dimensions of the ship, but also upon her form and structural strength, the nature of her cargo, the voyage and the season of the year. Discretion as to the proper loading of his ship must be left to the shipowner, or, under his directions, to the manager, on whom the responsibility rests for sending the ship to sea in a seaworthy condition, which responsibility it is inexpedient to diminish. We have, therefore, come to the conclusion, though not without regret, that we cannot prescribe any universal rule for the safe loading of all merchant ships.'[84]

---

[79] Ibid., 155.

[80] See pp. 553–557.

[81] RC on Alleged Unseaworthiness of British Registered Ships, Preliminary Report, PP 1873 [853] [853-1], p. 3.

[82] RC on the Alleged Unseaworthiness of British Registered Ships, Final Report, PP 1874 [1027], [1027-11], [1027-111].

[83] Exchange of Letters between Mr Plimsoll and the Board of Trade, it being alleged that Mr Plimsoll stated that Board of Trade Officers were corrupt, PP 1873 (372).

[84] RC on the Alleged Unseaworthiness of British Registered Ships, Final Report, PP 1874 [1027], [1027-11], [1027-111], p. vi.

This conclusion was linked to evidence which questioned Plimsoll's statements.[85] More generally there were dark comments on the decline in the quality of seamanship since the introduction of steam and the loss of opportunities for apprenticeships.[86] The hiring of good sailors was never easy: Captain Furnell acknowledged that captains from compassion and to save themselves trouble, constantly gave bad men good characters.[87] In any event, it was argued, under the Merchant Shipping Act 1873 the Board of Trade had the power to inspect and detain ships on various grounds which included overloading.[88]

More generally the Royal Commission revealed hostility to legislation itself. 'Parliament has during many years been engaged in attempting to regulate minute details connected with shipping. Shipowners reasonably complain that they have been harassed in their business by well-intended but ill-contrived legislation, and that this legislation is enforced by a Department imperfectly connected with the science of shipbuilding and with the interests of our commercial marine.' In short, it was argued, 'We believe that much legislation upon matters of detail might be advantageously dispensed with'.[89]

The problem for the shipowners was that no amount of detailed evidence could take away the public's reaction to deaths at sea. Further drownings ensured that interest soon revived after the publication of the Report. Eventually, Adderley agreed to a compromise. Plimsoll, after some heart-searching over its moderation, decided to support the bill and there was sufficient confidence in the prospects for reform for many to assume that legislative change was inevitable. All went well until 22 July 1875 when it was announced in the House of Commons that the shipping bill would have to be put over to the next session. For the moment priority would be given to changes in the laws for agricultural holdings and a number of other measures including the Judicature Bill of 1875.

In outrage and disbelief Plimsoll tried to attract attention by seeking to move the adjournment of the House to ensure that priority was given to a Merchant Shipping Bill. 'Sir, I earnestly entreat the right hon. Gentleman at the head of Her Majesty's Government not to consign some thousands of living human beings to

[85] e.g., at *ibid.*, p. 866.

[86] *Ibid.*, p. 867.

[87] *Ibid.*, p. 870.

[88] *Ibid.*, p. viii and see Merchant Shipping Act 1873, s 12. For Board of Trade activity, see *Ships Detained as Unseaworthy*, PP 1873 (178) (364). Note Plimsoll's involvement with debates about *The Parga*. Generally the language could be lively: in response to a sailor's claim that the barque *Eleanor* was 'as rotten as a pear' a surveyor found her to be 'perfectly unseaworthy'. See also, *Merchant Ships (Surveys) Return*, PP (1873) (82). For an example of a ship declared seaworthy despite complaints, see *The Coringa*, at p. 3.

[89] *Ibid.*, pp. ix, x.

an undeserved and miserable death.' Sensing that now everything was at stake he even attacked the moderate bill. It was a measure which could 'afford unlimited facilities for death-dealing volubility and hypocritical Amendments...Under the Board of Trade, since 1862, [sic] when unhappily the commercial marine of this country was committed to their care, matters have been getting worse and worse, with the aid of shipowners of murderous tendencies outside the House, and who are immediately and amply represented inside the House, and who have frustrated and talked to death every effort to procure a remedy for this state of things.' He was unrelenting. 'Every winter, hundreds and hundreds of brave men are sent to death, their wives are made widows and their children are made orphans, in order that a few speculative scoundrels, in whose hearts there is neither the love of God nor the fear of God, may make unhallowed gains...I will ask the right hon. Gentleman whether he will inform the House as to the following ships—the *Tethys*, the *Melbourne*, the *Nora Graeme*, which were all lost in 1874 with 87 lives, and the *Foundling* and *Sydney Dacres*, abandoned in the early part of this year, representing in all a tonnage of 9,000 tons; and I shall ask whether the registered owner of these ships, Edward Bates, is the Member for Plymouth, or if it is some other person of the same name. ("Order") And, Sir, I shall ask some questions about Members on this side of the House also. I am determined to unmask the villains who send to death and destruction— (Loud cries of "Order" and much excitement)'. Forceful exchanges between the Speaker and Mr Plimsoll and Disraeli followed and Disraeli spoke of the way the Member had 'conducted himself in a manner almost unparalleled'. Plimsoll was required to withdraw from the Chamber and 'as the hon Member was leaving the House he turned around and exclaimed—"Do you know that thousands are dying for this?".'[90]

Despite further resolute opposition from the shipowners Plimsoll returned to the attack on 30 July by giving notice of a question to the President of the Board of Trade.[91] He commended the Indian Government which had the simple rule that there should be freeboard of three inches for every foot of immersion.[92] But in his view in British waters the long history of shipping contained one abuse after another. 'In a ship called the *Lucy*, after 19 days privation, only two of the crew were left alive.' 'In another case the crew were left without water or provisions until reduced to the necessity of sacrificing four of their number by lot for the preservation of the rest.' 'In the *Earl of Kellie* the second mate and two men were reported to be starved to death; and in the *Caledonia*, two who were

---

[90] *PD* 1875 (s. 3), 205: 1823–6.
[91] *Ibid.*, 226: 231.   [92] *Ibid.*, 226: 233.

reported near death had their throats cut for the sake of their blood. In another, four bodies were found under the maintop all dead, with part of one of their comrades hung up, as if in a butcher's shop. In the *Anna Maria*, part of the leg of a woman was found, which had evidently served the crew for food. Probably, while he was addressing the House similar scenes of horror and suffering were occurring.'[93] In short, there was now no question of him retracting one word of what he had already said about shipowners. Plimsoll failed to save the bill from being dropped but he had created enough of a stir to ensure that there was a short temporary measure and at least apparent government commitment to a new bill in 1876.

6. '. . . ONE OF THE MOST DIFFICULT AND VEXED QUESTIONS . . .'

Disraeli was now in some difficulty. Adderley was regarded as ineffective but was difficult to move from office. The Queen was privately expressing a clear view: 'She much regrets the giving up for this year of the Shipping Bill and the state in which poor Mr Plimsoll seems to have been'.[94] In 1876 Charles Adderley presented a bill requiring the use of 'load-lines' but he did so in restricted terms. He admitted that after the failure of attempts at shipping legislation in 1869, 1870, 1871, and 1875 it was essential to achieve some result.[95] He pointed out that '. . . the wrecks since 1836 had steadily decreased in proportion to the number of voyages; and whereas for every life lost between 1832 and 1835 the tonnage was 4,600, for every life lost in the years 1870 to 1873 there were 13,000 tons employed in the foreign trade of the United Kingdom, so that the falling-off in the loss of life was the most remarkable part of these records'. But he knew that reform was necessary and he was capable of airing his frustration at the shipowners whose intransigence had done much to destroy his reputation for achieving compromise. 'The main spirit of the bill was to check reckless imperilling of life in the merchant sea-service of this country, and with this view to take steps simply as a matter of police for the public protection, but, at the same time, to refrain from harassing the whole Mercantile Marine by needless and even mischievous interference.' The bill imposed significant criminal penalties on those sending ships to sea in an unseaworthy state. The Shipowners Association was opposed to this and other increased forms of liability as 'not in the spirit of the English law' but they

---

[93] *Ibid.*, 226: 234.   [94] N. Jones, *Plimsole*, 187.
[95] *PD* 1876 (s. 3), 227: 166.

now had to contend with specific proposals in respect of loading.[96] After further debate Adderley pointed out:

The next clauses of the Bill related to the load-line, which, as the House was well aware, was one of the most difficult and vexed questions connected with the Merchant Shipping laws. The present Bill would make permanent the 5th and 6th sections of the temporary Act of 1875. The reports he had received from all parts of England with regard to the enacted load line were satisfactory, with the sole exception of Liverpool, where, at all events at first, some attempts were made to render the provisions of the Act ridiculous, if not nugatory, by fixing the load line absurdly high.[97]

The proposed financial penalty for each offence (which was put at £100) was heavy enough to cause concern but it did not thwart a general sense amongst Members of Parliament that some reform was now appropriate. In response to Plimsoll's unrelenting demands, Adderley had at last brought the load-line into existence. In matters of detail Plimsoll was far from contented with the result. But the issue of principle had been conceded.

The subsequent history of the 'Plimsoll Line' or 'Plimsoll Mark' contains intricate nautical details and its precise position on ships was not fixed for some years. But the substance of the reform was clear; ships were safer than they had been.[98] Save perhaps for Ashley's devotion to factory reforms, no other major Victorian statutory change to working conditions was so unrelentingly linked to one person. Plimsoll's persistence and eye for dramatic impact gave him moments of intense popularity and he knew how to exploit such occasions. His work also, incidentally, revealed that in opposing powerful commercial interests the immunity of parliamentary debates from actions in defamation was an essential prerequisite for success. In respect of his utterances outside Parliament, writs in defamation had caused Plimsoll one problem after another and came near to blocking reform. All these difficulties were forgotten when he died in 1898 and the 'sailor's friend' was buried near Folkstone.

There have been international conventions on the 'Load Line' since 1930, but the decades before this date produced some hazards for sailors including a retrenchment on what Victorians had achieved. In 1906 the negotiating skills of Lloyd George at the Board of Trade secured a substantial reduction in the safety value of the Plimsoll Line by introducing changes which increased freight capacity in certain contexts by 5 per cent. As John Turner has pointed out, it was an adroit political deal, and it had been 'admirably managed, except for

---

[96] Ibid., 227: 163.   [97] Ibid., 227: 174.

[98] But, of course, never completely safe: see, for instance, RC into the Spontaneous Combustion of Coal in Ships, PP (1876) [1586].

those who subsequently lost their lives in unsafe ships'.[99] The amended rule was supposed to apply only to new ships but it was soon being applied to old vessels as well. Protests mounted once again and examples of loss reached the press. For instance, the *North Briton* sank on 4 March 1912. Its freeboard had been reduced to ten inches and the sole survivor gave insufficient freeboard as the cause of sinking. The *Daily Mail* reported that 'When her condition was hopeless...the crew stayed together on the deck with their pipes in their mouths, silently, calmly and dauntlessly facing death. Without a murmur or a cry they perished in the sea. Their lives were sacrificed to 130 tons additional freight.'[100]

---

[99] J. Turner, 'Experts and Interests: David Lloyd George and the dilemmas of the expanding state, 1906–19', in R. MacLeod (ed.), *Government and Expertise* (Cambridge, 1988), 209.

[100] N. Jones, *Plimsoll*, 11. The loss of the *North Briton* was raised in Parliament: *PD* 1912, 42: 355–6, 530–1; 44: 822–3. The regulations for the safety of passengers on trans-Atlantic voyages are considered below in Ch. VII, pp. 606–10. For the development of tort law in respect of workplace accidents see Vol. XII, Part 2, Ch. IV, 'Workplace Injuries'.

VI

Building Houses and
Planning Communities

1. PRIVATE OWNERSHIP AND SOCIAL NEED

The Victorian regulation of housing took many forms, private and public. Philanthropists developed their own estates or even small towns on land which they owned. To take just one example, in 1853 Sir Titus Salt, the Bradford manufacturer, created Saltaire with its mill and the surrounding streets of neat houses for those who worked for him. Within ten years 804 dwellings had been built to a high standard which responded to his own survey of employees' housing needs. To this day, the small isolated area north of Bradford gives an echo of benevolence combined with a concern for cleanliness and economic efficiency.[1]

Taking another approach, a landowner could exercise significant control over the development of property which he did not own but in respect of which he had the benefit of a covenant. These covenants were usually created when the landowner sold off part of an estate and wished to ensure that the nature of the neighbourhood was not changed by what he regarded as inappropriate future development on the land he no longer owned. The legal issues involved famously came to a head in respect of Leicester Square, and were made visible to contemporaries in the controlled expansion of certain parts of London and the creation of fashionable communities such as Eastbourne.[2] The associated development of the law of covenants in the course of the nineteenth century is explored by Anderson. Briefly, he reveals a limited, even hostile, common law approach

---

[1] Note that taking such action presupposed that the landowner was not restricted by the terms of a private settlement which might give him limited powers over the use of the land. See J. Habakkuk, *Marriage, Debt and the Estates System: English Landownership 1650–1950* (Oxford, 1994); B. English, 'The Family Settlements of the Sykes of Sledmere, 1792–1900', in G. R. Rubin and D. Sugarman (eds), *Law Economy and Society, 1750–1914: Essays in the History of English Law* (Abingdon, 1984), 209–41; E. Spring, 'The Settlement of Land in Nineteenth Century England' (1977) 21 *Am. J. Leg. Hist.* 40. See also Vol. XII, Part 1, Ch. III, 'Property: Land Transactions: Settlements and Sales', pp. 82–3, 88, 91–4. For Saltaire, see J. Burnett, *A Social History of Housing: 1815–1970* (1980), 177–8.

[2] *Tulk* v. *Moxhay* (1848) 2 Ph. 774; D. Cannadine, *Lords and Landlords, 1774–1967* (Leicester, 1980), Part 3.

contrasting with a long-standing concern on the part of Chancery to respond to the conscience of purchasers of land. If the latter knew that previous owners had entered covenants relating to the use of the land they should, under certain circumstances, be bound by them. For example, usually it would be inequitable to allow a buyer who had purchased land at a reduced price reflecting restrictions on the nature of development simply to ignore the covenant. In the course of recognizing the enforceability of the arrangement the nineteenth-century courts also limited its scope. Covenants would not be enforceable where, as a matter of practice, Chancery could not superintend their execution. In practice (which did not fully reflect equitable doctrine) it often came to be assumed that only negative covenants preventing certain actions would be enforced. By the end of the century covenants were being put to use in the coordinated planning of new developments. This was an intricate development in legal thought which now reflected novel ideas about the possible uses of the common law and an emphasis on rules rather than equity and the intentions of the parties. The decision of Parker J. in *Elliston* v. *Reacher* in 1908 proved to be particularly influential in this regard.[3]

It was also possible for a private landowner to develop land through the use of building leases. These could be drafted in such a way as to set standards of design which would do much to preserve long-term property values. For example, Cannadine's study of the Calthorpe family and the development of its land at Edgebaston in Birmingham reveals the use of building leases for 99 years at a fixed ground rent. The lessee was required to spend a specified amount on building a house within a limited time and at the end of the lease the property would return to the lessor.[4] Building leases did much to determine the construction of nineteenth-century housing in England and Wales.

The legal context for such house building presupposed that the power to take initiatives lay with those who already had access to capital whether in land or other types of commercial investments. It left open the possibility of a drive for improvements arising out of social and political protests at squalid living conditions. Certainly, for most citizens the construction and provision of good housing was at best a hope. The majority experienced inadequate housing provided by landlords with a limited interest in philanthropy and standards of construction and, above all, a lack of concern for the long-term development of communities. Even at the end of the century about nine out of ten citizens could expect to live in leasehold rather than freehold property and for them, as Anderson shows,

---

[3] *Elliston* v. *Reacher* [1908] 2 Ch 374 (Parker J.), 665 (CA). See also Vol. XII, Part 1, Ch. IV, 'Leases, Mortages, and Servitudes', pp. 71–8.

[4] D. Cannadine, *Lords and Landlords: The Aristocracy and the Towns, 1774–1967* (Leicester, 1980), Part 2. See also, D. J. Olson, *Town Planning in London* (2nd edn, 1982). The law on leases interlocked with the development of the law on covenants: [see Anderson 'Equity: from Principles to Rules'.]

leases were a way of life.[5] As with the provision of medical services, the issue which mattered most was the capacity to make private payments—in this case in the form of rent. Almost always, the protection of a water-proof roof had to be bought.

It followed from this that the primary role of the common law in respect of housing was reactive rather than proactive. The courts heard one case after another on the law of landlord and tenant and Parliament did little to change this by interfering with new legislation. In 1838 Parliament passed an Act designed to assist landlords seeking to evict defaulting tenants.[6] In substance it enabled them to use orders from Justices of the Peace to remove a tenant, and it was expected that such a tribunal would often give primary regard to a landlord's interests. The impact of the Act was mixed: it seems that the orders were usually forthcoming when requested but that the procedure could take two months.[7] In the 1880s there was sufficient concern about the realities of eviction for another Act to move in the direction of slightly protecting tenants by limiting the right to levy distress to bailiffs holding a certificate granted by a county court judge.[8] Given this comparative lack of intervention, it is not surprising that it was only during and immediately after the First World War that anything like an effective statutory regime for the regulation of rents was introduced.[9] For the great majority it was rent which was important during the Victorian decades and rent was largely uncontrolled by law. It is worth pausing to emphasize the context provided by private law. As Anderson points out, 'for all its ubiquity the law of landlord and tenant attracted little attention'.[10] There were strong debates about the failings of landlords but little development in the existing law itself. In part this was because leases were so flexible and could be put to numerous uses within the framework of the existing law. Arguments about what a tenant could do if the house was not fit for habitation were debated and achieved a certain fame in the case of *Smith v. Marrable* in 1842.[11] But historians of housing have emphasized the difficulties

---

[5] See Vol. XII, Part 1, Ch. IV, 'Leases, Mortages, and Servitudes', III.

[6] Small Tenements Recovery Act 1838 (1 & 2 Vict. c. 71).

[7] The Act is considered in W. R. Cornish and G. de N. Clark, *Law and Society in England, 1750–1950* (1989), 135–6; M. J. Daunton, *House and Home in the Victorian City: Working Class Housing, 1850–1914* (1983), 148–54 (for the delay of two months see 148); D. Englander, *Landlord and Tenant in Urban Britain, 1838–1918* (Oxford, 1983), 12–21. At p. 12 Englander points out that 'What eviction meant is difficult to convey: words can but inadequately express the feelings experienced as homes, however humble, were tossed into the street to rot, police and vestry refusing to accept responsibility for storage or removal'.

[8] Law of Distress Amendment Act 1888, s 7.

[9] D. Englander, *Landlord and Tenant in Urban Britain, 1838–1918* (Oxford, 1983), Ch. 4 and Part 2; W. R. Cornish and G. de N. Clark, *Law and Society in England, 1750–1950* (1989), 184–7.

[10] See Vol. XII, Part 1, Ch. IV, 'Leases, Mortages, and Servitudes', III.

[11] (1842) Car. and M. 479, affirmed (1843) 11 M. and W. 6.

this flexible law produced for anyone contemplating radical reform. In the words of David Englander, 'Before the Great War the legal relation of landlord and tenant in Britain, as in Europe, was non-problematical. The operation of the laws of supply and demand bolstered by extraordinary legal privileges for securing the rent defined a juridical framework that was largely unchallenged by most housing reformers, and indeed, by most respectable tenants. The non-respectable elements—excluding Socialists—were, however, too poor to offer assent to this system, and too weak to challenge it. The aim was to survive.'[12] It was an unpromising setting for reform.

2. THE PUBLIC DIMENSION

Whatever the nature of the contemporary law, it was undeniable that the rapid expansion of towns during the nineteenth century created intense strains on the supply of adequate housing.[13] This produced some moderate attempts at legal change. In 1851, with the encouragement of the Earl of Shaftesbury, a Lodging Houses Act was passed.[14] In respect of the controlling powers of inspection which it gave to police authorities the Act produced some improvements. By 1860 many of the worst lodging houses had been closed down. But the legislation also gave local authorities the power to build or convert buildings into lodging houses. The money could come from rates or borrowing, and the rent was intended to be more than would amount to a form of poor relief and less than what was beyond the capacity of the poor to pay. Here the Act was not a success. Where it was used the provision was overwhelmed by people from elsewhere, and for the most part local authorities were vigorously opposed to it as something which stood in the way of solving housing problems through the application of negotiated arrangements between buyers and sellers. Housing might have an important role to play in debates about public welfare but it was not to be resourced out of public subsidy.[15] There was a role for charitable organizations such as the Society for Improving the Condition of the Labouring Classes, but this was obviously of limited scope and an essentially private initiative.

The resilience of this limited approach to reform was striking. The courts were prepared to scrutinize the exercise of statutory powers and could be hostile. In *Cooper* v. *Wandsworth Board of Works* the Court of Common Pleas protected the right of an obstructive property owner to be heard when faced with radical but

---

[12] D. Englander, *Landlord and Tenant*, 33.

[13] M. Daunton (ed.), *The Cambridge Urban History of Britain* (Cambridge, 2000), vol. iii: see, in particular, the Editor's Introduction.

[14] 14 and 15 Vict. .c. 34.

[15] Cornish and Clark, *Law and Society*, 180.

apparently lawful action on the part of a sewering authority.[16] More generally, reformers and experts such as the Medical Officers of Health attempted to obtain legislative change in the mid-1860s with a view to securing local powers for the demolition of unsanitary buildings and the purchase of land to build new houses. The response was a series of divisive and prolonged parliamentary struggles which produced slender results. For example, an Act of 1868 gave no power of compulsory purchase, limited support for borrowing, and provided at best a focused capacity to demolish individual houses rather than whole streets.[17]

But the Act survived and served as a stimulus to incremental reform. In 1875, the year when the major Public Health Act was passed, the Conservative government of the day responded to pressure from charities and churchmen with an Act (the 'Cross Act') which enhanced local authority powers.[18] Land could be cleared and leased to charities under restricted terms and in some circumstances there could even be local authority rebuilding. Cross achieved a number of related social reforms and his role 'in this Cabinet can only be compared with that of Neville Chamberlain in Baldwin's government'.[19] The principles which came with these reforms did something to move public debate but, predictably, very little was achieved in practice. As Geoffrey Best pointed out, by the 1870s it was clear that the market in housing was incapable of resolving the problem of housing the poor. 'It seems to have been a rule, that the bigger the city, the less commercially attractive was the provision of *good* working-class housing.'[20]

An alternative and, in the view of most reformers, potentially more promising approach to improvement lay in the use of bye-laws to regulate standards of construction. As cities grew and long terraces or enclosed courts provided a new setting for working families, there was increasing concern about, say, the capacity to construct houses built back to back without any through ventilation or proper provision for sanitation. 'Back to backs' 'had only one open face; they shared a common back wall, and stood one on each side of it'.[21] Mid-Victorian Nottingham had at least 8000 and this made up about two-thirds of its whole housing stock. A nominal ban on them in 1845 did not become fully effective until 1874.[22] Again, a cul-de-sac in the centre of a city was likely to be a good

[16] (1863) 14 C.B. (N.S.) 180. But see Vol. XI, Pt 1, Ch. VI, Judicial Review, pp. 486–522, particularly at pp. 508–9.

[17] Artizans and Labourers Dwellings Act 1868.

[18] Artizans and Labourers Dwellings Improvement Act 1875. See also, Cornish and Clark, *Law and Society*, 181.

[19] R. Blake, *Disraeli* (1978), 555.

[20] G. Best, *Mid-Victorian Britain, 1851–75* (St Albans, 1973), 45.   [21] *Ibid.*, 38.

[22] *Ibid.* See generally on Nottingham's housing at this time, S. D. Chapman, 'Working-Class Housing in Nottingham during the Industrial Revolution', in S. D. Chapman (ed.), *The History of Working-Class Housing: A Symposium* (Newton Abbot, 1971), 133–65.

source of profit for a landlord and these enclosed areas had a grim unsanitary reputation in certain places such as Leeds. A separate history can be written about those who lived in cellars. Some cities such as Leeds had few cellar dwellings whereas they were often found in Liverpool and Manchester. The conditions experienced by cellar-dwellers could be squalid beyond the belief even of contemporaries with long experience of slums.[23] The standard of old and new housing was known to be low.

In so far as people were prepared to change the existing law the appropriate response was usually seen to lie in local initiatives, but with more impact than those at Nottingham. The aim was to introduce readily enforceable regulations to establish minimum requirements for, say, light, size, and structure in new buildings. Local Acts could be used to authorize the creation of bye-laws. In Liverpool, legislation in 1842 and 1846 allowed for the creation of rules which restricted the building of enclosed courts. Henceforth the entrance would be the full width of the court and the size of the latter was to increase with the number of houses it contained. All rooms save for attics and cellars were to have a window of at least three feet by five feet and one room was to be at least 100 square feet. And so on.[24] The result was the creation of a form of 'minimal' housing with a gradual improvement in living standards in terms of sanitation, light, and space. The initiative for development within these specifications remained largely with private individuals but at least builders had to work within the framework of the regulations.

Responding to these local initiatives, the Public Health Act 1875 allowed for the creation of elaborate regulations at a national level and within a few years the Local Government Board was also producing model bye-laws. 'The development of a sanitary house, with adequate standards of construction, water supply and sewerage, was the product of the Public Health Acts and, more especially, of the building bye-laws from 1875 onwards, which brought about a major, and largely unrecognised, advance in working class housing standards.'[25] In the

---

[23] J. Burnett, *A Social History of Housing*, 58–61.

[24] Liverpool Building Act 1842 (5 and 6 Vict. c. 44) and Sanitary Act 1846 (9 and 10 Vict. c. 127). See Daunton, *House and Home*, 24 where the regulations are quoted. There is a detailed analysis in J. H. Treble, 'Liverpool Working-Class Housing, 1801–51', in S. D. Chapman (ed.), *The History of Working- Class Housing* (Newton Abbot, 1971), 165–221. Treble points out at p. 176 that 'perhaps the most distinctive form of working-man's dwelling at this period was that associated with the court system of building. That system, tracing its beginnings back to late eighteenth-century Liverpool, was based upon the principle of packing together as many houses as possible within a given area.' For an example of a general lack of action in respect of public health and housing in Leeds, see E. P. Hennock, *Fit and Proper Persons: Ideal and Reality in Nineteenth-Century Urban Government* (1973), 222–3.

[25] J. Burnett, *A Social History of Housing*, 307.

direct words of M. J. Daunton, 'The Public Health Act of 1875 was the turning point in the regulation of house-building in British cities'.[26] At least in respect of the building of new dwellings, housing could be said to be systematically regulated by the 1880s in those areas which enjoyed an active local government prepared to take full advantage of bye-laws. But, to stress the point, this did require local initiative and for the most part private capital. Even at its most assertive it related to the construction of new houses and not the removal of slums. In other words, public interference with construction was restricted in its range and had limited impact.

Contemporaries continued to criticize housing conditions, and the Royal Commission on the Housing of the Working Classes, reporting from 1884 onwards, raised contentious issues.[27] The Commission was something of a late-Victorian event. Its distinguished membership included the Prince of Wales, Sir Charles Dilke then President of the Local Government Board (1882–5), housing specialists such as Cross and Torrens, and well-known figures including Cardinal Manning and Lord Salisbury. In the course of producing reports for England and Wales, Scotland, and Ireland the members asked 24,663 questions and covered a very wide range of legal and social problems.

For the Commissioners certain themes became clear. Over the years there had been some limited improvements in housing but 'the evils of over-crowding, especially in London, were still a public scandal, and were becoming in certain localities more serious than they ever were'.[28] The evidence was detailed and extensive. In their conclusions, the Commissioners emphasized, say, that 'In Spitalfields, 35 Hanbury Street, is a house of nine rooms, and there is an average of seven persons in each room. In no room was there more than one bed.' 'At 6, King's Arms Place, Bermondsey, there were inhabiting the wash-room at the back 10 feet by 5, a father and mother, two children, and two older sons.'[29] It was clear to them that this was typical for large parts of London. Elsewhere, 'at Exeter the high death rate is considered to be mainly due to the defective sewerage system and deficient house drainage.'[30] In answer to thousands of questions, one witness after another had confirmed a picture of intense deprivation. What was more, some of the witnesses spoke from long

---

[26] Daunton, *House and Home*, 7. 'Although there had been building bye-laws based on local Acts in some towns at an earlier date, the Act of 1875 permitted sanitary authorities throughout the provinces to make bye-laws to control building standards and layout. The bye-laws specified in detail the minimum standards of construction of houses, and also laid down street widths and the amount of open space to be provided on each plot.'

[27] *RC Inquiring into the Housing of the Working Classes, PP* 1884–5 [4402] (110) xxx.

[28] *Ibid.*, p. 4.

[29] *Ibid.*, p. 8.

[30] *Ibid.*, p. 9.

experience: Lord Shaftesbury had nearly 60 years of relevant knowledge and, almost unbelievably, Edwin Chadwick was participating in the Commission's work with as much clarity and conviction as he had given to the reform of the poor law in the early 1830s.[31]

The Commissioners' response to deprivation was in part an exercise in morality with earnest debates about the accountability of the poor. 'Dirt', it was pointed out, 'is an evil almost as conducive to social misery as drinking and other self-indulgence.'[32] There was also concern about the nature of housing laws. Linked as they were to local government law, the regulations for housing were of such complexity that 'mastery of their provisions is a heavy task even for a lawyer or specialist.'[33] Even when the law was both understood and used there were acute problems with finding public money for housing. The Commissioners saw 'a most important branch of their inquiry' in their attempt to ensure more favourable terms for 'loans of public money for the purpose of providing dwellings for the working classes'.[34] They concluded that 'the general principle they would lay down is that the State should lend at the lowest rate possible without loss to the national exchequer, and that in making the necessary calculations current losses should not be brought into account'.[35] In other words, there was to be a new start. In an adventurous recommendation some of the Commissioners even argued that 'generally, with reference to all kinds of dwellings,...facilities should be given to allow capital to be repaid in rent, with a view to giving tenants facilities for becoming freeholders'.[36]

Again and again, for the Commissioners the frequent failure to use existing law was a serious problem: in places they came near to suggesting that it was their most serious problem.[37] When faced with the evidence of poor housing they roundly asserted that there was 'legislation designed to meet these evils, yet...the existing laws were not put into force, some of them having remained a dead letter from the date when they first found place in the statute book'.[38] For example, progress with housing involved demolition and there were often laws to protect the poor who were in need of re-housing after demolition work. Quite simply, this legal duty was not usually carried through. Slum clearance could

---

[31] Shaftesbury was the first witness: Chadwick's impact on the Commissioners may be found at *ibid.*, pp. 31, 33, and 34. See also, Question 13931.

[32] *Ibid.*, p. 15.

[33] *Ibid.*, p. 30. There was also concern about the cost of using a lawyer to transfer land and award compensation: far too much was 'yearly sunk in legal expenses', p. 48.

[34] *Ibid.*, p. 37.

[35] *Ibid.*, p. 40.

[36] *Ibid.*, p. 44 and see the first of the Supplementary Reports signed by ten Commissioners.

[37] *Ibid.*, p. 36.

[38] *Ibid.*, p. 4.

cause 'the severest hardship to the very poor'.[39] Clearances by railway companies caused sustained problems. 'The city engineer of Newcastle-on-Tyne, who has had experience as a railway engineer, said he had never known a single person be re-housed by a railway company after clearances in connection with railway extension. Sir Edward Watson, speaking with greater authority, stated that he did not remember any case where a railway company being under an obligation to rehouse, had fulfilled it. Miss Hill corroborated this evidence without qualification, saying that the Standing Orders which were intended to provide for the re-accommodation of the poor are practically a dead letter.' [40] Speaking more generally of demolition and the poor the Commissioners observed that "When notice is given they never seem to appreciate the fact that their houses are about to be destroyed until the workmen come to pull the roof from over their heads." Lord Shaftesbury, the Commissioners wrote, 'described how the inhabitants have been seen like people in a besieged town running to and fro, and not knowing where to turn. The evidence of the inability of the poor to protect themselves in this and in other particulars is conclusive.' [41]

The work of the Commission produced results in the form of the Housing of the Working Classes Acts of 1885 and 1890.[42] Under the Acts, local authorities in London were able to buy land where purchases were necessary for improving housing and they were also obliged to re-house at least half of those displaced by demolition. These powers could now be put to use in a political context which was more supportive of public building initiatives. In respect of the call for enforcement the county and county borough councils created by local government reforms in 1888 produced a wider franchise and this was responsive to many of the debates about poverty which were considered above in the context of the poor law.[43] There was greater incentive to act and use the law. After some useful schemes in London during the 1890s further reform in the Housing of the Working Classes Act 1900 extended the powers available to local government in London to the provinces: now local government everywhere could acquire land and build outside its district. Later, in 1909, John Burns at the Local Government Board produced an Act which abolished the requirement that the authorities sell off the buildings they had constructed and allowed the Board more scope in encouraging development.[44]

---

[39] *Ibid.*, p. 13.

[40] *Ibid.*, p 52. Miss Hill was Octavia Hill.

[41] *Ibid.*, p. 21.

[42] See E. Gauldie, *Cruel Habitations, A History of Working-Class Housing, 1780–1918* (1974), Chs 23–5.

[43] See pp. 496–502.

[44] Housing, Town Planning, etc Act 1909, ss 4, 10, and 11. Cornish and Clark, *Law and Society*, 183. The 1909 Act is considered again below in this section in the context of planning reforms.

Victorian house-building was often a complicated enterprise. As Yelling has emphasized, research is revealing that 'a chain of agencies and multitude of hands contributed to the building of Victorian cities'.[45] For example, we know that wage levels were important in explaining regional variations in building standards.[46] In addition to owners there could be developers and builders with all parties making their own estimates as to what was viable. 'New building regulations had their effects in the late-Victorian period, and may also have been a factor that encouraged the greater use of specialist developers.'[47] But in other contexts they may have had little influence.

The blunt truth was that for public authorities the years before the First World War saw more demolition than house building. John Burnett points out that 'Of all new houses built between 1890 and 1914 less than 5% were provided by local authorities, the great majority of whom were still very reluctant to enter the field of property-owning when the whole expense had to be borne from the rates'.[48] For house builders this was the era of successful privately funded middle-class suburban expansion at places such as Dulwich in London, Clifton in Bristol, and Audley Edge near Manchester. Old problems remained, not least in failing to provide new houses for the poor after substantial programmes of demolition. A. S. Wohl has shown that the London County Council estimated that in the years between 1902 and 1913 'over 45,000 rooms in central London and some 70,000 working-class rooms throughout London were destroyed to make way for various "improvements", and of these only 15,073 rooms were demolished to make way for new working-class dwellings'.[49]

Despite long, intricate, and emotional debates and lengthy additions to the statute-book, Victorian housing legislation had done little either to entrench on the powers of private landowners or to enable public authorities to produce significant amounts of new buildings. Lord Salisbury, as a member (albeit on certain points dissenting) of the Royal Commission of the 1880s, and also as Prime Minister on three occasions in the late-Victorian decades, was often broadly sympathetic to the need for housing reform and saw, for example, that certain specific initiatives were essential in central London. But he had surely crystallized the views of many in government in arguing that '...the over-crowding, so far as it

[45] J. A. Yelling, 'Land, Property and Planning', in M. Daunton (ed.), *The Cambridge Urban History of Britain* (Cambridge, 2000), iii: 474.

[46] Daunton, *House and Home*, 60–88.

[47] J. A. Yelling, 'Land, Property and Planning', in M. Daunton (ed.), *The Cambridge Urban History of Britain* (Cambridge, 2000), iii: 474.

[48] J. Burnett, *A Social History of Housing*, 181.

[49] A. S. Wohl, 'The Housing of the Working-Classes in London, 1815–1914', in S. D. Chapman (ed.), *The History of Working- Class Housing* (Newton Abbot, 1971), 13–55 at 19.

exists, in provincial towns, or in the suburban parts of London, may probably be cured by the ordinary sequence of supply upon demand'.[50] Perspectives like this ensured that the housing legislation of these years was never likely to have a major impact on social conditions.

3. PLANNING LAW

A strong middle-class concern to ensure that development took appropriate forms could encourage a different type of legislative innovation which was not concentrated on the provision of housing for the poor. Instead of being aimed at public subsidy and the control of housing this area of law would concentrate on the public control of what private builders wished to construct. 'Amenity' was a fashionable word of the day and the idea of 'planning law' designed to secure 'amenity' became a common topic of debate amongst social reformers of the 1890s. It received significant support from those who sought to provide an alternative to the existing cities with their severe housing problems rather than moderate improvements to current squalor: instead of changing existing communities the object was to create something new. There was the potential for law to play an adventurous role.

In his study of 'Britain's First Town Planning Act' Anthony Sutcliffe points to a confluence of forces producing reforms in an Act of 1909.[51] The idea of a 'Garden City' had been put forward in vivid terms by Ebenezer Howard whose Garden Cities Association was founded in 1899:

Equal, nay better, opportunities of social intercourse may be enjoyed than are enjoyed in any crowded city, while yet the beauties of nature may encompass and enfold each dweller therein;...how abundant opportunities for employment and bright prospects of advancement may be secured for all; how capital may be attracted and wealth created; how the most admirable sanitary conditions may be ensured; how beautiful homes and gardens may be seen on every hand; how the bounds of freedom may be widened, and yet all the best results of concert and cooperation gathered in by a happy people.[52]

---

[50] *RC Inquiring into the Housing of the Working Classes*, PP 1884–5 [4402] (110), xxx, 61, Lord Salisbury's Memorandum.

[51] Housing, Town Planning, etc Act 1909. A. Sutcliffe, 'Britain's First Town Planning Act: A Review of the 1909 Achievement' (1988) 59(3) *Town Planning Review* 289–303.

[52] First published as *Tomorrow: A Peaceful Path to Real Reform* (1898) and then as F. J. Osborn (ed.), *The Garden Cities of Tomorrow* (1902), Preface. See also, D. MacFadyen, *Sir Ebenezer Howard and the Town Planning Movement* (Manchester, 1970); D. Hardy, *From Garden Cities to New Towns: Campaigning for Town and Country Planning, 1899–1946* (1991). In the view of P. Hall, Ebenezer Howard's book is 'one of the most important books in the history of urban planning': see P. Hall, *Urban and Regional Planning* (3rd edn, 1992). It had links with a worldwide movement

Lively ideas about 'Garden Cities' developed alongside more restrained thoughts about 'the planned suburban extension to an existing town'.[53] In part this drew on ideas developed on the continent, particularly in Germany.[54] But it also followed the examples of private initiatives for estate development at, for example, Port Sunlight, Bournville, and Hampstead Garden Suburb. In some cases local authorities, encouraged by the London County Council, developed suburban housing strategies. More broadly, these schemes were linked to a belief in the possibility of national and regional planning with the dispersal of inner city populations and the creation of new systems for public transport. Such ideas in their turn were reinforced by widespread concern about standards of physical health which crystallized in debates about the fitness of recruits to fight in the Boer War. Given the way that most debates were concentrated on merely suburban development these sweeping concerns were unlikely to have radical outcomes in legislation, but they brought with them assumptions which made reform look more acceptable.

There are some difficulties in tracing the precise links between these ideas and the production of proposals for legislation. Sutcliffe emphasizes the role of the National Housing Reform Council (NHRC) after its creation in 1900 by active reformers such as Henry Aldridge and T. C. Horsfall. The Council was interested in numerous projects including the use of new local bye-laws as instruments of improved planning in suburban areas. This could be linked to the long-established use of bye-laws in public health reforms. But there was opposition to extending the scope of bye-laws in this way at the Local Government Board on the ground that higher spatial and structural standards would increase the cost of housing.[55]

The new Liberal administrations of 1905 and 1906 gave hope to the reformers. John S. Nettlefold, a Birmingham councillor with experience of slum clearance and a commitment to town planning, came to the fore in debates about 'town

---

of thought: see e.g. R. Fishman, *Urban Utopias in the Twentieth Century: Ebenezer Howard, Frank Lloyd Wright and Le Corbusier* (New York, 1977).

[53] A. Sutcliffe, 'Britain's First Town Planning Act: A Review of the 1909 Achievement' (1988) 59(3) *Town Planning Review* 290.

[54] A. Sutcliffe, *Towards the Planned City: Germany, Britain, the United States and France 1780–1914* (Oxford, 1981).

[55] A. Sutcliffe, 'Britain's First Town Planning Act: A Review of the 1909 Achievement' (1988) 59(3) *Town Planning Review* 290–1. On the early legislation, see S. D. Mordey, 'Major Aspects of the Development of Statutory Town Planning, 1909–1932', vols I and II, LLM Thesis, Birmingham, 1989. On the general history of urban planning and planning law, see (selected from a voluminous literature), P. McAuslan, *The Ideologies of Planning Law* (1980); M. Grant, *Urban Planning Law* (1982); W. Ashworth, *The Genesis of British Town Planning: A Study in Economic and Social History of the Nineteenth and Twentieth Centuries* (1954); G. E. Cherry, *The Evolution of British Town Planning* (1974); E. Read, *British Town and Country Planning* (1987). We still lack a full *legal* history of town planning.

extension plans' and the possible use of bye-laws in novel ways. Members of Parliament with an interest in housing were impressed with his suggestions and Nettlefold went so far as to draft his own version of a town planning bill. By the end of 1906 Henry Vivian had steered the Hampstead Garden Suburb Act through Parliament and this allowed for the local use of new bye-laws. Under his Act a body called the Hampstead Garden Suburb Trust Limited was freed from obstructive bye-laws (such as those which prevented the creation of a cul-de-sac) on the condition that no more than eight houses would be permitted for each acre. In a limited, local, context this might be called a form of planning law. For national purposes it had the advantage of fixing minds on the precise difficulties presented by the existing law. At a time when there was increasing discussion about the progress of town planning in Europe and the United States, it was possible to suggest change and attract the attention of Parliament.

Planning was also becoming in part a debate amongst lawyers and this contributed to its respectability and enhanced the possibility of legislative reform. In the early years the 'Hon Sec' of the Garden City Association was a barrister, F. W. Steere, and he was succeeded by C. M. Bailhache who later became a judge of the High Court. In 1901 the Chairman of the Council was Ralf Neville, KC and, in later years, he too became a High Court judge. 'For the Association, the elevation of Neville to the Chairmanship (and subsequently to the Presidency, until his death at the end of 1918) had its costs as well as its benefits. Under his leadership, it was not the radicalism of Howard's ideas which was to be more actively promoted, so much as the conciliatory and more moderate, reformist features.'[56]

The Local Government Board continued to resist the introduction of planning law. In part this arose because its secretary, Sir Samuel Provis, continued to think that much could be achieved within the existing framework for the restrained use of bye-laws. Little progress was made until April 1907 when planning proposals became linked to a bill for housing reforms, possibly in response to Nettlefold's draft bill which allowed for planning schemes for undeveloped land as well as public land purchases where they were necessary for the realization of any particular scheme. At this point Arthur Thring in the Parliamentary Counsel Office converted the proposals into a bill which would withstand legal scrutiny. He also, as Sutcliffe points out, had a substantive impact on the bill when he went beyond fixing the number of houses per acre and made it possible to determine the position in which houses may be built upon the land, and the

---

[56] D. Hardy, *From Garden Cities to New Towns*, refers to Steere and Bailhache at p. 19 and gives attention to the activities of Ralf Neville, see pp. 78–9.

general character of the houses to be built.[57] This produced further debate within
the Local Government Board, some of it more positive than it had been; but it
is noticeable that the idea that controls might apply to built-up areas as well as
those in the course of development was firmly resisted by both the President and
his officials.[58]

By the end of 1907 Burns was becoming more positive and more assertive. He
started to speak openly of the possibility of controls for 'town extensions'. In other
words it was now clear that the prospective regulations would not relate to either
existing urban areas or the countryside; they would focus on the control of town
expansions into undeveloped areas.[59] By January 1908 it was ready for Parliament.
Land likely to be used for building would be subject to town planning schemes
and the latter would aim for improved sanitary conditions, amenity, and convenience. Under the direction and ultimate control of the Local Government Board
the local authority would prepare the scheme and negotiate with owners.[60]

In opening the debate in Parliament Burns was almost florid in his language:
'The Bill aims in broad outlines at, and hopes to secure, the home healthy, the
house beautiful, the town pleasant, the city dignified, and the suburb salubrious.'[61]
Burns made it clear that he wanted to go beyond the old systems which had used
bye-laws to impose minimum standards. These had produced repetitive, 'model'
dwellings for all to see in long uniform lines of houses. 'I believe that model dwellings, like model men, are too often jerry-built structures... The bill seeks to diminish what have been called bye-law streets, with little law and much monotony.'[62]

He did not wish to sound entirely radical, and in particular he wanted to sanction voluntary generosity on the part of major landowners. It was not mere rhetoric when he pointed out that:

...the Local Government Board is very grateful to have one great landowner of this
country, and that is the Duke of Sutherland, for enabling them to complete the federation

---

[57] A. Sutcliffe, 'Britain's First Town Planning Act: A Review of the 1909 Achievement' (1988) 59(3)
Town Planning Review 295: for the general context, see 294–7. Arthur Thring was the son of Henry
Thring the Victorian draftsman.

[58] *Ibid.*, 295.

[59] For Burns, see K. D. Brown, *John Burns* (Royal Historical Society, 1977). Brown reveals that
Burns was not usually at his best when preparing bills (see p. 128), but the Town Planning Bill was
something of an exception (see pp. 139 and 151). See also, W. Kent, *Labour's Lost Leader* (1950) and
J. Burgess, *John Burns: The Rise and Progress of a Right Honourable* (4th edn, Glasgow, 1911). Burns
had a politically radical past behind him but had now lost some of his 'drive'.

[60] A. Sutcliffe, 'Britain's First Town Planning Act: A Review of the 1909 Achievement' (1988)
59(3) *Town Planning Review* 296–7.

[61] *PD* 1908 (s. 4), 188: 949. This bill was withdrawn in December 1908 and replaced with another
which, in respect of its planning clauses, was similar and debated within the parameters set at the
first second reading.

[62] *Ibid.*

of the Pottery towns by the useful and splendid gift of something like 800 acres of his Trentham Park Estate. By our Bill we provide facilities by means of which every other Duke can go and do likewise, and in the event of anyone being in the mood to follow his Grace's example we shall be only too pleased to accept his gift on precisely the same terms.[63]

Beyond numerous detailed amendments, the bill was in danger of being caught by shifts in political power. As McDougall has pointed out, attitudes towards land and its value were of central significance in the making of planning law. It was agreed that the creation of some sort of town planning schemes would be in the interest of the landowners: there was support for this from those, such as Lyttleton, who had been involved in the private Act relating to Hampstead Heath.[64] A proper system of plans would allow for orderly development with more predictable profits. In contrast, there was strong disagreement about the provisions concerned with compensation and betterment. Compensation provisions were intended, speaking broadly, to give back to a landowner what he lost as a result of the scheme for his area. Betterment provisions were intended, again speaking broadly, to enable a local authority to recover from a landowner any increase in the value of his land which could be attributed to the scheme. The debate was sharpened by proposals in the bill that 100 per cent of the increase of the value should be recoverable. Also, whereas the landowner could only recover compensation after the construction of buildings and roads the authority could claim betterment after approval of the scheme and before any development took place. In the course of debate the government moderated these arrangements and, as it did so, it became clear that, whatever the precise provisions, they could not work without a national system of land valuation. In the debates on the bill for 1908 the Prime Minister, Asquith, conceded this point and promised the introduction of a Land Valuation Bill.

This had political consequences. There was now a House of Commons determined to introduce new forms of land taxation and a House of Lords prepared to see limited reforms but not any systematic type of land valuation and assessment for tax. The response of the government was to support Lloyd George as Chancellor of the Exchequer in his attempt to include land valuation proposals in the budget of 1909. By this route planning legislation had become part of an attack on the landed interest and to some extent this helps to explain the strength of the counter-attacks which came to be directed at the bill.

---

[63] *Ibid.*, 956.

[64] G. McDougall, 'The State, Capital and Land: The History of Town Planning Revisited', (1979) 3(3) *International Journal of Urban and Regional Research* 361.

For example, there was significant opposition to the attempt of government to restrict the role for the courts. In the view of John Burns most disputes should be investigated and, if possible, resolved by arbitrators or inspectors. He argued that 'if town planning is to be a success...it is essential that the central body should have more control than it now has'.[65] For him the central body was the Local Government Board. His senior civil servant, Provis, was determined to block appeals on compensation issues to Quarter Sessions. 'Quarter Sessions Justices who are largely of the landowning class, do not seem very suitable persons to settle questions of compensation to landowners, and there is no precedent for there being an appeal from the Board to them. In the interests of economy it is desirable to avoid appeals with their attendant costs.'[66] In the course of producing 180 amendments the House of Lords attempted a different approach. Lord Salisbury sought to substitute the County Court for the Local Government Board as a 'tribunal of appeal' in the case of orders made by a local authority against individual owners of property.[67] This encountered opposition from the Lord Chancellor, Lord Loreburn, who recognized a residual role for the courts on points of law but wanted to go no further than this. Muir Mackenzie, the Permanent Secretary at the Lord Chancellor's Office, wrote to Provis saying 'I think you know that the Lord Chancellor feels very strongly against the amendment inserted by the opposition in the Lords giving an appeal to the County Court instead of to the Local Government Board. He thinks the judges are not well qualified for the business, and that it will interfere with their proper work.'[68]

Lord Salisbury was angered by the response when it reached him in the course of conversation. He wrote to the Lord Chancellor saying he 'was not surprised that the Local Government Board showed a desire to make itself supreme, but he confessed it gave him a shock to find that the Head of the Judicature of this country should be content to allow the Courts to be put aside in this matter, and not only that aggrieved persons should not be allowed to approach the Courts of Justice, but that the greatest pains should be taken by the Government to limit judicial reference under the procedure of the Bill'.[69] With the support of his Board and other members of the government, Burns stood firm: 'The reason we object to a court is this. A court means Lands Clauses. It means that a court or a jury is to decide, juries to view, judges or magistrates to determine. It means great delay. If you yield the court it means counsel and expert witnesses.... for these

[65] *PD* 1909 (s. 4), 196: 737.
[66] NA, HLG, 29, 100, 389.
[67] NA, HLG, 29, 96, 99.
[68] NA, HLG, 29, 96, 102.
[69] NA, HLG, 29, 96, 259–68.

reasons we cannot shift the venue from the Local Government Board inquiry, the inspector, and the arbitrator or the Board if it acts as an arbitrator....It would really destroy the vital principle of this Bill, namely, economy and dispatch, an opportunity in 99 cases out of 100 of coming to an agreement without recourse either to law or arbitration at all, through the agency of an inspector and a public enquiry.'[70]

The final result of arguments such as these was an Act which, in retrospect, looks somewhat feeble.[71] From the start of the debates it had related only to expanding suburbs rather than grand schemes of urban regeneration and now all could see that it raised difficult issues of implementation, not least in respect of compensation and betterment. But this perspective conceals the conceptual shift which came with the reform. Property rights were being subjected to the discretions of statutory bodies in a novel way. Whereas, say, Enclosure Commissioners, could reallocate rights as between current owners or, to give another example, private Acts could 'drive' a railway through an estate, it was now possible to direct the future use and development of certain areas in ways which were designed to respond to what officials took to be the long-term interests of the community. The courts would have a role but it would be one of last resort on points of law. The Conservative Opposition had seen the potential of the legislation. Now there was a structure established by law which could apply to land in the course of development across England and Wales; and under the new laws officials had the power to plan systematically for what some confidently expected to be a better future for numerous communities.

It was admitted by everyone that there was much to do. In the words of J. S. Nettlefold: 'We have been entangling ourselves with regulations as to the thickness of walls, the cubic contents of rooms, and the minimum width of roadways, without securing quality in the building material, and consequently sound houses. We also continue to allow disastrously excessive numbers of houses per acre, and we provide no playgrounds for the children or resting places for the older people, except by private charity.'[72] Now there was an opportunity to transcend these old restrictions.

In practice, between 1909 and the First World War nothing like the full potential of the idea of planning was to be realized. This had the effect of reducing the opposition to it. On 31 October 1911, *The Times* reported that 'A little impatience is being shown because the passing of the Town Planning Act has not been followed by spectacular results. It is hardly realized, perhaps, that many and long steps

[70] *PD* 1909 (s. 4), 196: 238–9.
[71] Housing and Town Planning Act 1909.
[72] J. S. Nettlefold, *Practical Housing* (1910), 5.

have to be taken by any municipal authority which desires to use the power of the Act in order to prevent vacant land from being covered with ill-planned and overcrowded streets.' Some useful proposals had been put forward: Wirral Rural District Council had two proposals, one for 5829 acres and another for 3499. Some were on a small scale as in the case of Scarborough Corporation developing a scheme for 40 acres. But by the start of War the reformers were disappointed. Looking to the future, the system created by the 1909 Act was extended and modified by the Town and Country Planning Act 1932. Radical reform arrived in the planning legislation of 1947.[73] The planning legislation of 1909 has a strong claim to having introduced novel concepts into law. But it would be hard to argue that it did much to change the appearance of England and Wales whereas much more adventurous claims could be made in respect of the 1947 Act.[74]

[73] Town and Country Planning Act 1947: on the passing of these Acts, see R. Cocks, 'Power, Policy and Co-ordination in Law Reform: A Civil Servant and Town Planning Law, 1929–1930' (2004) 25(1) *Liverpool Law Review* 1–28 and R. Cocks, 'Noel Hutton and the New Law for Development Control, 1945–47' (2001) 22(1) *JLH* 21–54.

[74] For the contemporary importance of the legislation of 1947, see Cornish and Clark, *Law and Society*, 194.

VII

Conclusion

1. A. V. DICEY AND REFORMING STATUTES

By the last quarter of the nineteenth century there was an acute awareness that something major and unsettling had happened to the English statute book. It was sensed that the volume of social legislation was ever-increasing and that in a democratic Britain with an extending franchise the possible content of future laws was cause for anxiety. Sir Henry Maine wrote with alarm about limits to the extent to which statutes should be used just as there were (to use his analogy) limits to the range of temperatures on the surface of the earth.

Neither experience nor probability affords any ground for thinking that there may be an infinity of legislative innovation, at once safe and beneficent. On the contrary, it would be a safer conjecture that the possibilities of reform are strictly limited. The possibilities of heat, it is said, reach 2000 degrees of the Centigrade thermometer; the possibilities of cold extend to about 300 degrees below its zero; but all organic life in the world is only possible through the accident that temperature in it ranges between a maximum of 120 degrees and a minimum of a few degrees below zero of the Centrigrade. For all we know, a similarly narrow limitation may hold of legislative changes in the structure of human society.[1]

Herbert Spencer was hostile but in a different way: 'What is the statute book but a series of unhappy guesses? Or history, but a narrative of their unsuccessful issues?'[2] Later, he argued that between 1872 and 1890, 3352 Acts of Parliament were amended or replaced 'the inference being that their repeal indicates their failure'.[3]

Some were more moderate. Sir Courtnay Ilbert wrote in general terms of the need for further progress in the drafting of the law, whilst also pointing to what had been achieved.[4] Sir Roland Wilson had begun to explore perspectives on the

---

[1] H.S. Maine, *Popular Government* (1885), 153; and see R. Cocks, *Sir Henry Maine: A Study in Victorian Jurisprudence* (Cambridge, 2005), 139.

[2] *Social Statics* (1868), 21.

[3] *The Man Versus the State* (1884), 61.

[4] C. P. Ilbert, *Legislative Methods and Forms* (Oxford, 1901).

links between law and debate in Parliament and the press.[5] They both hoped for a more reflective approach to legislative law-making.

Much the most sustained response came from Albert Venn Dicey in his books *Introduction to the Study of the Law of the Constitution* and *Lectures on the Relation Between Law and Public Opinion in England During the Nineteenth Century*.[6] His ideas were controversial, and since their publication Dicey's works have framed the debate about reforming statutes in the sense that even his critics have related their ideas to his thoughts. He was the major late-Victorian writer on the creation and use of legislation. In his first book, published in 1885, Dicey rejected attempts to explain the great range of modern English legal reform by reference to what had happened over many centuries. This was a break with the ways in which lawyers and historians had often written about law. Dicey could never have written as the historian Hallam did. Writing in the early years of the nineteenth century the latter had argued that:

No unbiased observer, who derives pleasure from the welfare of his species, can fail to consider the long and uninterruptedly increasing prosperity of England as the most beautiful phaenomenon in the history of mankind. Climates more propitious may impart more largely the mere enjoyments of existence; but in no other region have the benefits that political institutions can confer been diffused over so extended a population; nor have any people so well reconciled the discordant elements of wealth, order, and liberty. These advantages are surely not owing to the soil of this island, nor to the latitude in which it is placed; but to the spirit of its laws, from which, through various means, the characteristic independence and industriousness of our nation have been derived.[7]

It was no longer sufficient to refer to the spirit of the laws and in his analysis of the constitution Dicey could be sharply unhistorical. He happily referred to another historian, Freeman, as an authority on (amongst other topics) the Anglo-Saxons and argued that the latter's research could hardly be relevant to an understanding of law at the end of the nineteenth century. For lawyers '…it boots nothing to know the nature of the Landesgemeinden of Uri, or to understand, if it be understandable, the constitution of the Witenagemot. All this is for the lawyer's purpose simple antiquarianism.'[8]

---

[5] R. K. Wilson, *History of Modern English Law* (1875).

[6] Respectively, 1885 (subsequent quotations are taken from the 1902 edn which reflects Dicey's late-Victorian thoughts) and 1905. On Dicey, see R. A. Cosgrove, *The Rule of Law: Albert Venn Dicey, Victorian Jurist* (1980), esp. Ch. 8: in regard to *Law and Public Opinion* '…The book did not result from extensive research about nineteenth-century England…', 183; and R. S. Rait (ed.), *Memorials of Albert Venn Dicey, Being Chiefly Letters and Diaries* (1925), Ch. 10.

[7] H. Hallam, *View of the State of Europe During the Middle Ages* (1818), Ch. 7, Part I.

[8] *Introduction to the Study of the Law of the Constitution* (1885), 14.

Rejecting centuries of history as a way of explaining and justifying English law, Dicey sought a clear and more analytical approach to the law of his day. In respect of legislation his emphasis on parliamentary sovereignty in *Introduction to the Study of the Law of the Constitution* is striking:

The principle of Parliamentary sovereignty means neither more nor less than this, namely, that Parliament...has, under the English constitution, the right to make or unmake any law whatever; and, further, that no person or body is recognised by the law of England as having a right to override or set aside the legislation of Parliament. A law may, for our present purpose, be defined as 'any rule which will be enforced by the Courts'. The principle then of Parliamentary sovereignty may, looked at from its positive side, be thus described; any Act of Parliament, or any part of an Act of Parliament, which makes a new law, or repeals or modifies an existing law, will be obeyed by the Courts.[9]

This raised the obvious question of how such a form of sovereignty should be used and how its exercise should be understood over time. As is well known, in his study of the constitution Dicey found a large part of the answer in his notion of the rule of law. For him this was 'the supremacy throughout all our institutions of the ordinary law of the land'.[10] Further:

If the sovereignty of Parliament gives the form, the supremacy of the law of the land determines the substance of our constitution. The English constitution in short, which appears when looked at from one point of view to be a mere collection of practices or customs, turns out, when examined in its legal aspect, to be more truly than any other polity in the world, except the Constitution of the United States, based on the law of the land.[11]

At this point Dicey also makes it clear that in his view the United States Constitution rests on judge made law and in respect of England this is followed through with vigour in his analysis of the common law. His praise for the common law is intense. For him, it reflected the practical experience of lawyers doing life-times of work in the courts. Their work in turn responded to the individualistic beliefs which he thought formed the most valuable part of English public life, not least in the way these values challenged the power of state officials. The supremacy of the law

...is an idea not so much unknown...as deliberately rejected by the constitution makers of France, and of other continental countries which have followed French guidance. For the supremacy of the law of the land means in the last resort the right of the judges to control the executive government, whilst the separation des pouvoirs means, as construed by Frenchmen, the right of the government to control the judges. The authority of the Courts

---

[9] *Law of the Constitution*, 36.
[10] *Law of the Constitution*, 414.
[11] *Law of the Constitution*, 414.

of Law as understood in England can therefore hardly coexist with the system of droit administratif as it prevails in France. We may perhaps even go so far as to say that English legalism is hardly consistent with the existence of an official body which bears any true resemblance to what foreigners call 'the administration'.[12]

Manifestly, this form of analysis posed problems for anyone seeking to develop systematic ideas about the appropriate use of statute law to further the objectives of social policy. To use Dicey's words 'English legalism...' is focused on the judiciary and not on Acts of Parliament. The rule of law is identified with the judges and put in contrast to 'the administration'. It is as if all the statute law considered in the preceding pages is of secondary interest save in so far as it might in one way or another give enhanced powers to officials who could threaten the rule of law as applied by judges. Plainly, this left anyone looking for guidance on good statute law disappointed. The most that could be said was that it should not undermine the common law.

It was as if Dicey was arguing that for lawyers statute law had a merely interstitial role. At the same time this was a disturbing role because it was so extensively interstitial by the late-Victorian decades. There was, therefore, a logic in Dicey turning to statutory reforms when he subsequently gave his Harvard lectures of 1898: it was as if he had not as yet provided a convincing place for statute law within the legal system. Now, in this later book, his argument was historical but only in so far as he conceived of recent history being a distinctive phase of lawmaking. As the title suggested, his focus was on the role of what he took to be public opinion.

The close and immediate connection then, which in modern England exists between public opinion and legislation is a very peculiar and noteworthy fact, to which we cannot easily find a parallel. Nowhere have changes in popular convictions or wishes found anything like such rapid and immediate expression in alterations of the law as they have in Great Britain during the nineteenth century, and more especially during the last half thereof.[13]

His notion of what constituted public opinion could vary from one context to another but it is clear that he believed that at times it could transcend literate elites. There were occasions, as in the bills which extended the male franchise, when 'popular' could include at least half the population. In his view there were even times when women had a role, albeit indirect, as in the development of ideas about the property of married people. For Dicey the changes in popular opinion were the foundation for an explanation of Victorian law-making through

---

[12] *Law of the Constitution*, 415.

[13] *Lectures on the Relation Between Law and Public Opinion in England During the Nineteenth Century* (1905), 7.

statutes. At any given time he could identify a 'predominant current of legislative opinion'. This might originate with a particular 'thinker or school of thinkers'. It could form slowly and offer continuity across decades and it could be cumulative in the sense that one set of law reforms could be the basis of a further set of changes. Looking back, his chapter headings reveal that he saw three main currents of public opinion: the period of 'old Toryism or legislative quiescence' (1800–30); the period of 'Benthamism or Individualism' (1825–70); and the period of 'Collectivism' (1865–1900). Within each of these phases there were crosscurrents when, for exceptional reasons, 'anomalies' arose.

Dicey's scheme offered clarity and a lively commitment to the influence of ideas in public debate. But it was important that it did not lead him to modify the principles he expressed in *The Law of the Constitution* and this had the effect of placing statute in an ambivalent context. Statutes were very important but they were not the focus of legal debate amongst lawyers. To put it crudely statutes would be enforced by the courts but were best understood in terms of public opinion rather than legal ideas and traditions. There was no question of giving, say, the writing on statutory interpretation a central role in legal thought. Still less was there the possibility of recommending a programme of systematic codification. Almost always the initiative for creating major statutory reforms aimed at social change would come from outside the world of professional and judicial work. Often the reforms would not be seen in the context of evolving legal doctrines; it was as if statutes could be a law unto themselves. Whereas Dicey mentioned legal principles in the *Law of the Constitution* in his later work he emphasizes principles as being found in the purpose of a statutory measure rather than in the law itself. For example, this became clear when he wrote about the element of chance in the making of law, notably in respect of the capacity for temporary expedients to work their way into fundamental reforms over time.

People often, indeed, fancy that such random legislation, because it is called 'practical', is not based on any principle, and therefore does not affect legislative opinion. But this is a delusion. Every law must of necessity be based on some general idea, whether wise or foolish, sound or unsound, and to this principle or idea it inevitably gives more or less of prestige.[14]

This enabled Dicey to argue in regard to emergency legislation that:

It is far, indeed, from being true that laws passed to meet a particular emergency, or to satisfy a particular demand, do not affect public opinion; the assertion is at least plausible, and possibly well founded, that such laws of emergency produce, in the long run, more effect on legislative opinion than a law which openly embodies a wide principle. Laws of

[14] *Ibid.*, 44.

emergency often surreptitiously introduce or re-introduce into legislation, ideas which would not be accepted if brought before the attention of Parliament or the nation.[15]

Looking beyond emergencies Dicey argued that:

A principle carelessly introduced into an Act of Parliament intended to have a limited effect may gradually so affect legislative opinion that it comes to pervade a whole field of law. In 1833 the House of Commons made for the first time a grant of something less than £20,000 to promote the education of the people of England. The money, for want of any thought-out scheme based on any intelligible principle, was spent on a sort of subscription to two societies which, supported by voluntary contributions and representing, the one the Church of England and the other, in effect, the Dissenters, did what they could in the way of affording to the English poor elementary education, combined with religious instruction. This niggardly, haphazard subscription has proved to contain within it all the anomalies of the system which, now costing the country some £18,000,000 a year, is embodied in the Education Acts 1870–1902, with their universal, State-supported, and compulsory, yet to a great extent denominational, scheme of national education.[16]

The reader is invited to see statute law as being largely outside the control or even influence of lawyers and their professional restraints and because of this it is also seen to be open to capricious development. Perhaps the most important thing that Dicey did in respect of statute law was not to observe particular phases of change but rather to confirm a way of looking at statutes as some sort of residual category of law largely under the control of non-lawyers. The latter would use draftsmen and other lawyers but only in an instrumental way.

This is linked to the manner in which he almost treats the statutes of the nineteenth century as examination scripts in respect of which he awards good marks for those which preserved the values he associated with the common law and bad marks for those which were, in his view, too adventurous in their search for social change. This is particularly sharp in his praise for individualism and his distrust of collectivism. Here his strength of feeling could lead him into strained analysis. For example, he conceded that 'whether a poor law of any kind is consistent with the principles of thorough-going individualism is open to question'.[17] But he also argued that the New Poor Law Reforms of 1834 were individualistic in the sense that 'the object of the statute was in reality to save the property of hard-working men from destruction by putting an end to the monstrous system under which laggards who would not toil for their own support lived at the expense of their industrious neighbours, and enjoyed sometimes as much comfort as or even more comfort than fell to the lot of hard-working labourers'.[18] By talking of one (and only one) of the objects of the legislation Dicey is saved from addressing the paradox that this commitment to individualism brought with it what many contemporaries regarded as a dangerously over-centralized form of executive power. Also, the latter was designed to manipulate the lives of many individuals in pursuit of general and surely collective social goals.

Dicey's analysis of the Factory Acts was convoluted. For example he saw the reformer Michael Sadler in anachronistic terms as, amongst other things, a sort of 'Tory socialist' who 'attacked, though without any true grasp of political economy, the individualism which underlay the teaching of economists such as Ricardo. He thus introduced into the factory movement ideas which pointed towards socialism.'[19] The ultimate result is all too predictable. Writing with reference to the Factory and Workshop Act 1901 he argued that in its consolidation of previous legislation it 'is the most notable achievement of English socialism'.[20] By 1901 it was possible that there was something in this explanation but it hardly serves as an explanation for the intricate volume of Victorian Factory law; few of the reformers thought of themselves as socialists or were seen as such. But Dicey was not deterred. Elsewhere he wrote that 'The time is rapidly approaching when the state will, as regards the regulation of labour, aim at as much omnipotence and omniscience as is obtainable by any institution created by human beings'.[21]

Examples such as this could be repeated by looking at, say, the extent to which he was sometimes determined to claim Bentham for individualism rather than collectivism despite the potential for the latter's utilitarian thought to subsume individual interests within generic social goals. It is also important to note the statutes which Dicey does not discuss in any detail. His comments on the Public Health Act 1875 and the Housing of the Working Classes Acts 1890–1900 were brief in the extreme and although he mentions the preceding legislation in these areas there is no explanation of how it was that the early reforms eventually became major and very complicated Acts. Dicey simply fails to account for some of the most influential legislation of the day. Perhaps he sensed that it would be difficult to criticize collectivist law when it was designed to secure a popular objective such as improved public health.

There are other grounds on which Dicey's views of statute law could be criticized. In an unguarded moment he argued that it was quite likely that the era of intensive legislative reforms could well be drawing to a close. In this respect he was, obviously, decidedly mistaken. The reforms of the Liberal government of

---

[18] *Ibid.*   [19] *Ibid.*, 225.
[20] *Ibid.*, 237.   [21] *Ibid.*, 289.

1906 in themselves would be sufficient to prove him wrong. (At the same time it should be noted that he was not alone in being an expert on law making who failed to see what was 'around the corner'. Sir Courtnay Ilbert for all his experience with statutes failed to see the radical expansion of delegated legislation at the start of the twentieth century.)[22]

Dicey's analysis was admirably clear and had the merit of providing a platform for twentieth-century debates about the rule of law at a time when the powers of the state seemed to be ever-increasing. In respect of legal history his concepts have even been used imaginatively by opponents of his political views. The 'left-wing' work of E. P. Thompson is striking in this regard, particularly in the way he used the rule of law which he saw as the most valuable check on the potential brutality of unfettered executive discretion.[23]

But this debate about the rule of law does not reveal the complexity of the process which produced reforming statutes. It is as if Dicey never escaped the assumptions of the *Law of the Constitution* with its concentration on the common law. It is possible to criticize his strained attempts to fit one measure or another into an individualistic or collectivist mould. It is possible to criticize his associated attempt to fit law reforms into phases of change and this has been done by analysts such as Henry Parris.[24] This left large gaps in Dicey's account. It is possible to go beyond these critics and emphasize that Dicey almost ignored important statutes. In regard to the way he explained the Acts upon which he did focus his approach, this resulted in a radical lack of systematic thought about how complicated statutes directed at major social reforms came into existence. For example, their administrative context is often unexplored. More curiously, given Dicey's stress on parliamentary sovereignty, thousands of columns of *Hansard* are left untouched in preference to general debates about public opinion. For Dicey the courts were more important than either Whitehall or the details of parliamentary debates and this reduces the value of his explanation for the statutory reforms. In large part his understanding of nineteenth-century statutory change is premised on the ideas he developed in his earlier study of the constitution: the work of lawyers is of central importance and their primary task is to defend the rule of law and the major statutory reforms sometimes made this legal task problematic. Given this starting point his analysis of statutes was likely to be incomplete and controversial. Yet his books still have to be considered because of the extent to which they have influenced subsequent debates.

---

[22] Sir Courtnay Peregrine Ilbert (1841–1924) 29 *ODNB* 194.
[23] E. P. Thompson, *Whigs and Hunters, The Origin of the Black Act* (Harmondsworth, 1975), at e.g. 266.
[24] H. Parris, *Constitutional Bureaucracy* (1969), esp. Ch. IX.

2. O. MACDONAGH AND REFORMING STATUTES

A powerful alternative to Dicey's analysis came more than half a century later from MacDonagh, whose work has already been mentioned above in connection with certain areas of reform.[25] At the risk of over-simplification, it could be said that he saw five stages in the production of legislative change. The first stage revealed some scandal in the form of a gross abuse and this engendered a prohibitory Act designed to remove the evil. Secondly, when it was realized that this would not be effective, there was a subsequent piece of legislation with 'teeth' in the form of inspectors to enforce the law. Thirdly, the developing expertise of people charged with enforcement brought with it the need for organization and the creation of some central agency. Fourthly this produced its own 'view' of everyday problems and as these changed a need for further regulation was required; the deficiencies of an existing rule engendered the desire for another. In its final stage the new body of experts moved over to prevention and perhaps using scientific aids it changed some of its roles and introduced still more law.[26]

Of course there are variations in the case of any instance of reform and the strength of MacDonagh's arguments can only be understood by reference to matters of detail. In *A Pattern of Government Growth: 1800–60, The Passenger Acts and their Enforcement*, MacDonagh looked with particular care at the example of the laws which were intended to regulate conditions on ships used for emigration.[27] Early laws passed through Parliament without controversy because, amongst other things, Parliament had other major distractions and the potential for the law to develop was not sensed by possible opponents.[28] With rather more attention to the issues and the use of a Select Committee these laws were all repealed in 1825 on grounds which included the view that restraints on trade were vexatious.[29] This lasted until 1828 by which time the example of 'intolerable' realities had shown to many the need for an exception to the demands of free trade. Thereafter this exception began to develop into a large area of statutory law which also offered officials considerable discretions in seeking to implement its purposes. In MacDonagh's view, a later Act of 1842 was 'a superlative piece of social legislation'. In part this was because s 6 was expressed in unremitting detail in respect of the types and quantity of

---

[25] See Ch. IV, p. 579, fn 100.

[26] e.g. see O. MacDonagh's analysis in *A Pattern of Government Growth: 1800–60, The Passenger Acts and their Enforcement* (1961): for comments on 'phases' see Ch. 16.

[27] *Ibid.*

[28] *Ibid.*, 59.   [29] *Ibid.*, 66.

food such as biscuit which should be available for passengers.[30] Generally 'The essential merit of the Act lay...in its confident selection of the significant, in its comprehension of the relationship of the various parts to the whole, and above all in its enforceability'.[31] Unfortunately even these qualities were insufficient to ensure sustained improvements. Ways of circumventing enforcement were worked out by sea captains in the years which followed. By 1846 those in charge of maintaining standards had given up on finding one perfect statute and moved to a position in which they sought gradual improvement over time.[32] In 1848 an Act even transferred the burden of proof from the Crown to the defendant in all cases where exemption from the operation of the Acts was claimed.[33]

The Passenger Act 1855 was seen by contemporaries as a major piece of legislation. It took many months of preparation in the offices of the Commissioners for Emigration who responded to the views of numerous deputations.[34] The 1828 Act had had four sections.[35] The 1855 Act had 105 sections and took up 30 pages of the statute book.[36] The requirements imposed on shipowners were evocative in their precision. For example, the new weekly allowance of food included, say, 6 lb. of flour and breadstuffs and 1 lb. of sugar. The provision of space for passengers had at one time been described by naval officers as worse than those known to the slave trade but were now much more generous. For example, on any deck below the upper deck the allowance was 18 square feet or 25 square feet if this lower deck was less than 7 feet high or allowed less than 3 per cent of the side space to portholes. More generally in certain instances the Commissioners were given statutory authority to alter regulations by orders in council; for example this could be done with speed in the case of epidemics.[37] The press would still continue to report on gross abuses as in the case of the crew bullying passengers but basic requirements had been transformed. After mid-century there was much less legislation; the number of emigrants fell away and the major shipping

---

[30] *Ibid.*, 147–8. An Act for Regulating the Carriage of Passengers in Merchant Vessels, 1842 (5 and 6 Vict. c. 107), s 6.

[31] *Ibid.* Macdonagh, *Government Growth*, 151.

[32] *Ibid.*, 175.

[33] An Act to Make Further Provision for One Year, and the End of the Next Session of Parliament, for the Carriage of Passengers by Sea to North America, 1848 (11 and 12 Vict. c. 6). For the burden of proof, see s 18.

[34] An Act to Amend the Law Relating to the Carriage of Passengers by Sea, 1855.

[35] An Act to Regulate the Carriage of Passengers in Merchant Vessels from the United Kingdom to the Continent and Islands of North America, 1828.

[36] An Act to Amend the Law Relating to the Carriage of Passengers by Sea, 1855 (18 and 19 Vict. c. 119).

[37] *Ibid.*, ss 35, 14(3), and 59.

lines with their passenger steamships developed their own supplementary regulations which could include medical inspection. In 1872 the Merchant Shipping Act passed responsibility for legislation and emigration officers to the Board of Trade in the interests of 'economy as well as efficiency'.[38] An era of aggressive statutory reforms for passenger ships had closed.

In the course of his analysis MacDonagh points to inequalities in bargaining power, contagious diseases, malnutrition, gross overcrowding, a lack of sanitation, sexual promiscuity, incompetent management, corrupt management, drunken management, physically cruel management, decrepit ships and, in response to these and other abuses, organizational change in government and scientific advances.[39] It is a vivid portrait of an administrative agency coming to terms with one problem after another and seeking legal change as it did so.

Without the slightest spur from doctrinaires or any other a priori influence, experience and the brute facts of the situation forced those who were concerned with emigration towards centralisation, autonomy and the delegation of legislation; towards demands for discretionary powers and the direct management of certain aspects of a private trade; towards fluidity and experimentation in regulations; towards a division and a specialisation in administrative labour—in a word, towards the sort of state we recognise as modern. With surprising speed and ease an extraordinary governmental revolution was accomplished.[40]

MacDonagh argued that 'The full pattern exposed by this study (of emigration law) is no more likely to have been repeated elsewhere than one set of fingerprints to have a duplicate. But almost certainly substantial or partial counterparts are plentiful.'[41] When, in a further study, he turned to early Victorian government as a whole he moved beyond the exploration of five stages and revealed the full intricacy of the law-making process. Experts had a significant influence upon the terms of statutes in numerous cases in factory or poor law or public health reforms. For MacDonagh the emigration officers were specimens of that 'small, but immensely creative, class of nineteenth-century civil servants, the field executive'.[42] Elsewhere they were found at the Board of Works, the marine and railway departments of the Board of Trade, inspectorates for factories and mines and amongst the public health officers and sanitary engineers of the medical department of the Privy Council and the Local Government Act office

---

[38] Merchant Shipping Act 1872, Part I gave the Board of Trade 'general superintendence'. See also Macdonagh, *Government Growth*, 318–19.

[39] *Ibid.*, 7.   [40] *Ibid.*, 17.

[41] *Ibid.*, 9.   [42] *Ibid.*, 332.

of the 1860s.[43] But their influence varied from one statute or one time to another. Nor was this surprising given political tensions, individual initiatives, and all the other contingencies of legislation. They were often a source for significant legal change but their impact was not uniform. So too with scandals and the 'irreducible brute matter of the new and unprecedented social problems'. Often in respect of the latter the state was the 'only agency which could insist and enforce effectively'.[44] Sometimes experts could be used successfully by reformers and sometimes they could not but cumulatively, over time, they supported one reform after another.

The merit of MacDonagh's analysis is that it goes far beyond Dicey in linking the experience of departments and enquiries to proposals for legislation. This did not reveal the existence of 'neat' phases of change which could be explained in terms of coherent publically expressed debates about, say, collectivism or individualism. MacDonagh finds things to admire in Dicey's analysis, not least in its clarity, but he points to further shortcomings. There is no mention of a public servant unless he was also a political economist or 'thinker'. 'No reference is made to Parliamentary investigations or departmental enquiries or reports from the inspectorates. Simply, practical government does not exist for Dicey.'[45] In *Early Victorian Government, 1830–1870*, he points out that 'Collectivism was never a doctrine in nineteenth-century England, never formulated by a thinker of commanding ability, never applied deliberately and consciously to law.'[46]

MacDonagh's 'model' has considerable explanatory power. It moves beyond the sometimes forced debates about collectivism and individualism, and over recent decades it has stimulated a very large amount of research into the growth of government departments and the increasing use of experts. His analysis does more than Dicey's to explain the creation of the major statutes considered in the present analysis, not least for the simple reason that Dicey sometimes gave many of these statutes merely fleeting attention. Dicey's account fails to explain large parts of the evolution of the poor law, or the details of factory legislation, or the creation of measures for public health, or the increasing regulation of housing or the reform of measures for safety at sea. MacDonagh's concentration on precise administrative and legislative context is more revealing.

MacDonagh's work has in its turn received criticism at some points. Parris, for example, responded by arguing that MacDonagh leaves 'untouched three of Dicey's chief arguments; that there is a close connection between law and

[43] *Ibid.*, 332–3.
[44] O. Macdonagh, *Early Victorian Government, 1830–1870* (1977), 20.
[45] MacDonagh, *Government Growth*, 325.
[46] Macdonagh, *Early Victorian Government*, 11.

opinion in general; that that connection was particularly close in the case of Benthamism; and that its practical influence dates from around 1830'.[47] There is some justice in this. In seeking to correct Dicey's over-reliance on 'opinion' MacDonagh excludes its influence in creating the conditions in which it would be possible for the reforming suggestions to get a sympathetic hearing in parliament. But as Parris was the first to acknowledge, in exploring the administrative context behind law reforms MacDonagh resolved many of the difficulties in explaining how particular statutes came into draft form within one part or another of Whitehall.

The debate has been taken further by numerous other studies. The content of the statutes can be used to support those, such as Lubenow, who have stressed the importance of the reforms in the context of debates about the relationship between central and local government.[48] The same may be said of others who have linked continuities in reforming ideas across decades to the very precise political circumstances of particular years such as, say, the early 1850s. Statutes are at the heart of the elusive but important debates about how the state responded to its citizens. The context of statutory law-making is always changing and an exciting aspect of many modern studies lies in how they provide links between MacDonagh's use of detail and broader generalizations in other studies. In respect of the administration and the roles of experts there has been work on, say, the Home Office or the professional activities of engineers and some of this work on 'expertise' is of particular relevance to the making of statutes and is explored in the next section.[49]

3. EXPERTISE AND THE MAKING OF STATUTES

'The memory of the Succession Duty Bill is to me something like what Inkerman may be to a private of the Guards: you were the sergeant from whom I got my drill and whose hand and voice carried me through.' These were the words of Gladstone expressing his gratitude to Richard Bethell, barrister, Member of Parliament and later Lord Westbury.[50] They are a reminder that even the most accomplished of politicians requires legal expertise when taking a bill through parliament.

It is with this sort of need in mind that MacDonagh, Drewry, and others in looking at administrative aspects to law reform have stressed the importance

---

[47] H. Parris, *Constitutional Bureaucracy* (1969), 268.

[48] W. C. Lubenow, *The Politics of Government Growth: Early Victorian Attitudes Toward State Intervention: 1833–1848* (1971).

[49] R. MacLoed, *Government and Expertise: Specialists, Administrators and Professionals: 1860–1919* (Cambridge, 1988).

[50] J. Morley, *Life of Gladstone* (1903), i: p. 350, n.2.

of '...a professional public service, which was permanent and conducted continuous state policy...'.[51] This was linked to the decline in the role of private Members of Parliament as introducers of legislation. The politician Sir Charles Wood pointed out in 1855 that quarter of a century before that date legal changes were often put forward by independent members; whereas by the middle of the century the independent member called the attention of the government to the issue and hoped for a positive response.[52] In 1857 G. K. Rickards, Counsel to the Speaker, observed that the bills of government departments made up four-fifths of the Acts for a session.[53] In the words of MacDonagh, after about 1830 'What was required and what developed with extraordinary rapidity was a deliberate legislative policy continued from session to session....In a word legislation became both the business of the ministry, and systematic and continuous.'[54] Further, 'such a legislative policy necessitated a government instrument to execute and maintain it—commissioners, inspectorates and executive officers.' Also 'the new type of planned cabinet legislation dealing with novel and unprecedented social problems required exact knowledge before remedial action could be taken. Hence the simultaneous development of investigating instruments by Parliament.'[55] The work of experts interlocked with and supported the efforts of Select Committees and Royal Commissions. In the preparation of a measure it led logically to the parliamentary draftsman as an expert with words in a legal context.

This change took place at about the same time as discontent with the standards of drafting became a public issue. Statute Law Commissioners were established to investigate and in their First Report of 1835 they argued that 'there are numerous instances of neglect of economy in the wording of statutes' and:

The imperfections in the statute law arising from mere generality, laxity or ambiguity of expression, are too numerous and too well known to require particular specification. They are the natural result of negligent, desultory, and inartificial legislation; the statutes have been framed, not as parts of a system, but to answer particular exigencies as they occurred.[56]

---

[51] Macdonagh, *Early Victorian Government*, 197; G. Drewry, 'Lawyers and Statutory Reform in Victorian Government', in R. MacLeod (ed.), *Government and Expertise, Specialists, Administrators and Professionals, 1860–1919* (Cambridge, 1988), 27–40. See Vol. XI, Pt 2, Ch. I, Parliament, pp. 304–15, 317, 319.

[52] *Ibid.*, 33 and see C. Ilbert, *Legislative Methods and Forms* (Oxford, 1901), 2.

[53] G. Drewry, 'Lawyers and Statutory Reform', in R. MacLeod (ed.), *Government and Expertise* (Cambridge, 1988), 27–40, at 33; G. Campion, *An Introduction to the Procedure of the House of Commons* (1950), 38.

[54] Macdonagh, *Early Victorian Government*, 5–6.   [55] *Ibid.*, 6.

[56] *Statute Law Commissioners Appointed to Inquire into the Consolidation of the Statute Law*, PP 1835 (406), pp. 14 and 16. This Report concentrated on criminal law and had a distinguished membership including Thomas Starkie, Andrew Amos, and John Austin.

Amongst other numerous defects in the arrangement of statutes their titles could produce results which might baffle readers. The Commissioners pointed to the long title of 'The Statute 23d of King Geo. II, c. 26' which came to the end of a very long list of topics with the words 'and to prevent the stealing or destroying of turnips; and to amend an Act made in the second year of his Present Majesty for better regulation of Attornies and Solicitors'.[57] There was something thoroughly inelegant about the statute book.

Neither Dicey nor MacDonagh consider in any detail the experts who wrote the law. Henry Parris and, more recently, Gavin Drewery have traced the history of the men who put pen to paper. Drewery points out that there were standing counsel to departments in the eighteenth century, starting with the Board of Trade in 1718.[58] In a looser arrangement the office of Treasury Solicitor (created about 1655) was sometimes used to provide a point of reference for legal work with legal services centralized under him. As Holdsworth pointed out, in 1877 there were eight departments besides the Treasury which had legal departments of their own and, by then, the Treasury Solicitor was acting for 16 other departments.[59] By statute the position of Permanent Secretary to the Lord Chancellor was established in 1885 and it had to go to a barrister of ten years' standing and the Law Officers had a secretariat from 1893.

Within these evolving administrative frameworks Drewry has identified careers for barrister-civil servants. Sir George Harrison had important legal duties at the Treasury between 1805 and 1816 and in 1807 his brother William joined as Parliamentary Counsel to the Treasury with further assistance after 1816 from Sir Thomas Tomlins. Henry Hobhouse worked as Under Secretary at the Home Office from 1817 to 1827. Sir James Stephen was active in drafting statutes in the 1820s and 1830s as Counsel and later in other roles at the Colonial Office. From 1835 there was a standing Parliamentary Counsel at the Home Office. Under a Treasury Minute of 1842 this officer, Drinkwater Bethune, was made responsible for bills in 23 departments. In 1848 Bethune became legislative member for the Supreme Council for India and he was replaced by Walter Coulson whose work attracted praise in the 1850s.[60]

This presupposed an enlarged role for lawyers and it is easy to see how, by say the 1850s, it could come under strain. The size of Public General acts and their

---

[57] Ibid., pp. 17–18.

[58] G. Drewry, 'Lawyers and Statutory Reform', in R. MacLeod (ed.), Government and Expertise (Cambridge, 1988), 28. See also, Sir William Holdsworth, A History of English Law (7th rev. edn, 1966), xii: 10–11.

[59] Ibid., 13. For the promotion of bills by Government departments, see Vol. XI, Pt 1, Ch. II, Government and People, p. 30.

[60] G. Drewry, 'Lawyers and Statutory Reform', in R. MacLeod (ed.), Government and Expertise (Cambridge, 1988), 28–32.

frequent political sensitivity made them the subject of decision-making at a high level within departments and it was likely that the lawyer's role would be seen as being increasingly instrumental; as we have seen in various contexts, to an increasing extent the writer of bills worked to realize objectives set by others. This change found an administrative response. The scope for using lawyers in an uncoordinated way to draft occasional bills gave way to more adventurous thoughts. When Coulson died in 1860 his role was taken over by Henry Thring who was to prove to be the most distinguished draftsman of the Victorian era. But by himself he could do nothing to remedy the problems arising out of the diversity of routes by which bills could emerge from departments. Structural reform was required if uniform drafting standards were to be achieved. In 1869 Thring was made Parliamentary Counsel to the Treasury with one assistant. In 1871 this arrangement was confirmed when it was pointed out that with the benefit of Henry Jenkyns, his assistant, they had succeeded in systematizing and greatly improving the method of preparing the government bills.[61] The work-load was daunting; for example in the busy year of 1875 they had responsibility for 46 bills at various of their preparatory and parliamentary stages.

These reforms and the increasing sophistication of Parliamentary Counsel were considerable achievements. They did produce a measure of uniformity and a belief that statute law could be made more accessible to both the lay citizen and the lawyer through consistency in the use of language. But there were obvious limits to what had been achieved. The Select Committee of 1875 on Acts of Parliament set out to consider 'whether any and what means can be adopted to improve the manner and language of current legislation'.[62] Responding to past attempts at improvement the Committee canvassed numerous problems. There was a clear need for more resources and very little prospect of them being sanctioned by the Treasury. Beyond financial questions and problems of inter-departmental co-ordination there was a hinterland of unresolved intellectual issues. Statute law revision took obsolete Acts and sections from the statute book and was done with some consistency after 1868. The consolidation of statutes could achieve improvements simply through making the law more accessible. 'The importance of consolidation can hardly be overrated. The Statute Law of India has been so much simplified by it, that it has been reduced to much less than a third of its former bulk.'[63] But, for some, these were the poor relations of codification. We have seen that attempts at codification made little progress

---

[61] *Ibid.*, 37.

[62] *SC on Acts of Parliament, PP* 1875 (280), p. iii.

[63] *Ibid.*, p. v. The Select Committee had the advantage of using the work of the *RC to Inquire into the Expediency of a Digest of Law* 1870 (121). The Commissioners included Westbury, Cairns, Page-Wood, Roundell Palmer, Henry Thring, and Henry Maine. Willes J. dissented from their

despite the reputation of Bentham and the work of Brougham and Westbury. In 1853 Lord Chancellor Cranworth had hoped that a programme of consolidation might lead on to a 'Code Victoria'. In a more practical way, proposals for systematic reform through the creation of digests were taken forward in respect of the Bills of Exchange Act 1882, the Partnership Act 1890, and the Sale of Goods Act 1893.[64] But it is noticeable that the demand for this sort of improvement was not made in respect of laws aimed directly at social reform; it was, rather, the province of the specialist lawyer.

To many lawyers this moderate compromise was, no doubt, a sensible result but the idea of radical change in the nature of statute law never completely left the debates about the Victorian Acts. Thring argued for a programme of effective legislation.[65] Sir Henry Maine hoped for the reduction of case and statute law 'to continuous writing and its inclusion within aptly-framed general propositions' and went on to argue that 'the facilitation of this process is the practical end of scientific jurisprudence'.[66] But these hopes only served to reveal the extent of the challenge facing any parliamentary draftsman. He had to come to an understanding of the purpose or purposes of a suggested bill. He had to express it in terms which would make it as comprehensible as possible to Members of Parliament. He had constantly to keep in mind how judges would respond to particular words, sentences and the Act as a whole. This in turn required a regard for the canons of judicial statutory interpretation with its use of 'literal', 'golden', and other rules. Beyond this he had to have in mind relevant pre-existing case law which might, for example, attach a specific meaning to a word which would surprise a lay person. In addition to these considerations, he had to keep in mind how the final form of the bill would relate to previous legislation to which reference would be made in debates and sometimes in the interpretation of the new measure. If he had the time he could also contemplate the likely direction of future reforms and thereby anticipate later problems which others immersed in topical emotional pressures arising out of current proposals were likely to miss. Perhaps the real achievement of the parliamentary draftsmen of these years lay simply in their capacity to produce large volumes of law at comparatively short notice. Given the pressures on the draftsman it is not surprising that judicial criticism continued. For example, in 1883 Brett MR considered a section of the Bankruptcy Act 1883 and concluded in bewildered terms that 'the legislature

---

enthusiastic endorsement of a Digest. He thought a Digest would 'after all be only a makeshift for a Code': see p. 7.

[64] J. H. Baker, *An Introduction to English Legal History* (4th edn, 2002), 219–20.

[65] H. Thring, *Practical Legislation* (1902).

[66] H. S. Maine, *Village Communities in the East and West* (1889), 60.

intended this Act of Parliament to be verbose and tautologous and intended to express itself twice over'.[67]

MacDonagh points out that the recruits of this era destined for the higher ranks of the civil service 'were almost without exception lacking in scientific, mechanical, technological or commercial training or experience. Scarcely any were men who had earlier practised another profession.'[68] Lack of legal expertise at senior levels left Parliamentary Counsel with a degree of independence based on their personal experience of drafting. Of all the experts involved with law reform, it was they who could most successfully influence the choice of words for a particular clause. They did not initiate major change, but they often selected the precise words of what surely amounted to millions of sentences. Of all the experts, they were the ones most closely linked to the production of major reforming statutes, and neither Dicey nor MacDonagh gave them sufficient attention in accounting for the Victorian statute-book.

4. EXPLAINING THE REFORMING LEGISLATION

In explaining the legislation and the fashions of reforming thought we have seen that the studies of Dicey, MacDonagh, and other later analysts each have valuable elements. Dicey provided clarity, a role for 'opinion' and a capacity to provoke people with his firm and contentious allocation of labels such as 'collectivism'.[69] MacDonagh's attention to experts working within administrative structures and their capacity to influence one reform after another across decades revealed radical failings in Dicey's account.[70] At its simplest, Dicey gave little attention to how government worked. MacDonagh also provided a creative setting for further studies into the links between government growth and legislative change with the focus on the role of 'Whitehall' and new executive agencies. Responding to this, writers such as Drewry have revealed the importance of the experts who did the drafting for the Acts.[71]

All studies of Victorian legislation face a major challenge in the volume of the law. By 1870 Gladstone could point out that 'English legislation is full of

---

[67] *Hough* v. *Windus* (1884) 12 QBD 224.

[68] Macdonagh, *Early Victorian Government*, 212.

[69] A. V. Dicey, *Law of the Constitution* (1885); A. V. Dicey, *Lectures on the Relation Between Law and Public Opinion* (1905).

[70] O. MacDonagh, *A Pattern of Government Growth* (1961); O. MacDonagh, *Early Victorian Government, 1830–1870* (1977), e.g. at 58–9.

[71] G. Drewry, 'Lawyers and Statutory Reform', in R. MacLeod (ed.), *Government and Expertise* (Cambridge, 1988), 28–32. For recent studies of the context of reform, see P. Mandler (ed.), *Liberty and Authority in Victorian Britain* (Oxford, 2006).

interferences'.[72] Victorians sometimes spoke of banned activities as having become 'unparliamentary', as in Elizabeth Gaskell's description of an industrial town where 'a great oblong many-windowed factory stood up, like a hen among her chickens, puffing out black "unparliamentary" smoke'.[73] Taken as a whole, the Victorian arguments about legislative intervention had numerous themes ranging from passionate expressions of outrage at children having to work with dangerous machinery to opposition to any legislative interference for the sake of preserving what were taken to be ancient liberties. The debates have often been explained in terms of social reformers demanding humane responses to indus- trial horrors only to be countered by capitalist mill owners and other 'men of business' opposing any entrenchment on *laissez faire*. There are numerous varia- tions on this theme with some opponents of legislative intervention looking not to ancient liberties but rather to praising the end of old relationships based on status. For people such as these, hereditary roles were being replaced by free- thinking individuals who should be unhindered by law and free to contract their way through life with one form of employment after another thereby producing greater responsiveness to markets and increased personal and national wealth. It is as if behind the intricate debates about statutes some had a vision of children suffering and sought laws to prevent this, and others, wanting no interference from government, preferred to think of achievements such the Great Exhibition of 1851 with its explicit link between virtue and trade. The debates were vigorous on both sides and, in practice, as in the case of the Factories Acts and the regula- tion of public health, they often ended in compromise. Almost always, 'interfer- ence' was balanced with restraints on the powers of officials.

The lively quality of these arguments has often concealed other important themes. Many of the participants were at least as concerned with the notion of a growing sense of responsibility for shaping lives as they were with direct experi- ences of hardship or the capacity to engineer economic progress. The poor law could be given a national administration reflecting strategic priorities rather than a very diverse range of charitable intentions arising out of local initiatives. After decades of doubt, schooling could be given a state-wide structure, however imperfect and however subject to local political whim. In terms of their admis- sions policies the Universities of Oxford and Cambridge were self-consciously national institutions after the passing of the Test Acts. Local authorities had important roles in the provision of public health responding to increasing

---

[72] *PD* (s. 3), 199: 333.

[73] E. Gaskell, *North and South* (Harmondsworth, 1985) and see note at p. 532 to the Act of 1844 for the Good Government of Manchester (7 and 8 Vict. c. 40) which penalized certain emissions of smoke. For the place of her work in 'The Factory Imagined', see R. Gray, *The Factory Question and Industrial England, 1830–1860* (Cambridge, 1996), 153–9.

numbers of uniform standards (e.g. in respect of industrial emissions) and there were supervisory bodies which could act in response to centralized scientific information. In other words, reform was also about the mechanisms of control and because control was a national issue the debates in general elevated a concern for the state's accountability.

For the legal historian what presses home is the relationship between the minute attention to detail in the long statutes with their sections and schedules and the broader debates about whether individuals should be protected or left to themselves. At first it looks illogical, but it was possible for Victorian participants to think of these state-wide roles in benevolent and personal terms and see the remedy in legislation for individuals. This does much to explain the success of Samuel Plimsoll: he named the ships which sank and could bring to people's imaginations the bodies of identifiable drowned sailors. In most other cases the major reforms were the product of influence being brought to bear by numerous individuals, in and out of Parliament, each with their awareness of people who were suffering. It was a process which has a resonance with the last paragraph of George Eliot's *Middlemarch* set in the 1830s and published in parts between 1871 and 1872: '...that things are not so ill with you and me as they might have been, is half owing to the number who lived faithfully a hidden life, and rest in unvisited tombs'.

In all their detail the reforms were ultimately justified by those seeking change through reference to the individuals whose lives appeared in one report or another. This gave rise to notions of responsibility which are difficult to explain solely in terms of a fight between 'capital' and 'reform' or initiatives for centralized administration. Rather, they point to an important additional concern emphasizing responsibility attaching to government in a personal way which linked individual experience to wider social obligations developed on an instance by instance basis.

What was more, these justifications for the law came to be reflected in the nature of the law itself. The detail of the law responded more to legislators thinking of individual circumstances than general declarations of principle. There was, say, no general presumption in favour of children or employees, or for that matter in favour of employers or inspectorates. It is a characteristic of this large accumulation of rules aimed at social change that as a whole it lacked principle. A national response could also be a response allowing for numerous variations in the law in particular instances: what mattered was that there was a recognition of the need for legislative action in respect of endangered individuals. Law was created by 'the centre' but it also related to specific people in specific circumstances with the circumstances often being described in the statutes in formidable detail. Adapting the words of Spencer Walpole, an accumulation of detailed reforms gradually extended the boundaries of what might be described as a form of parental responsibility on the part of the state.[74] In the view of many Victorians the numerous Acts saved lives and secured a minimal standard of civilized living for impoverished workers and their families. Apart from individual acts of kindness what hope was there other than legal reform for poverty-stricken workers faced with unhealthy homes and dangerous work?

For contemporaries it was a mixed achievement. Even the reformers were troubled by the quality of the law. This was a recurrent concern of parliamentary debates with Members finding it difficult to follow the intricate process of reform as one Act and its associated regulations 'built' upon another Act and its regulations. It could be argued that a more serious attention to principle rather than *ad hoc* personal benevolence might have encouraged a more rigorous concern for systematic development and enforcement. Also, a higher regard for principle might have saved the law from the various exemptions secured by sectional interests. It might have reassured judges worried by the uncoordinated relationship between statute and the common law. In part, these problems were caused by difficulties in the development of the common law. At the end of the section above which deals with the creation of measures for the improvement of public health, the problems which the judiciary experienced with the common law's relationship to statutory reforms for health were considered. This revealed issues of procedure (e.g. in respect of how often juries were to be used) and challenges in evolving uniform standards when faced with hundreds of private Acts of Parliament which set different requirements for different places. As early as 1871 Professor Bryce saw this as a major issue for the whole of the common law:

Just as lines of railway have been driven through modern London without regard to the old arrangement of the thoroughfares, and have crossed and recrossed streets and squares, effacing parts of them till perhaps only a house or two is left standing, so Acts of Parliament, drawn up to meet the exigency of the moment, have paid no respect to the symmetry, such as it was, of the common law and instead of attempting to mould and reconstruct it, have laid down new positive rules which infringe upon, or almost wholly destroy, its ancient principles, by removing from their operation large and heterogeneous classes of cases. The effect of this has been to make the old principle no longer really a principle, but a positive rule in the cases not effected by the statute; and thus, as the

---

[74] *PD* (s 3) 1867, 185: 1277. In debating an extension to the laws regulating factories and workshops, and speaking with particular reference to women and children, Walpole had argued at col. 1276 that '...it is the duty of the state to protect those who are not able to protect themselves'. A little later, at col. 1277, he had stated that 'The first duty of a parent is to see that his child is physically, mentally, and morally educated, in order properly to fulfil the various duties of life. If that duty is neglected, we must come to the State, the parent of the country, to fill the place of the natural protector of the child.' At the time of speaking (1 March) Spencer Walpole was Home Secretary.

number of enactments and positive rules increases, the value of principles declines, and the confusion grows every year worse confounded.[75]

A concern for principle would certainly have made it easier for people to understand the law. It is reasonable to wonder if any Victorian read, say, the Public Health Act 1875 from start to finish; and if he or she did so it could hardly have given the reader a sense of laws based on general principles. The way in which the Act was expressed attracted criticism at the time, and the innumerable published annotations to the Act pointed to distinct areas of law rather than to some unified whole.

The problem of its intelligibility had been raised in the Select Committee on Parliamentary Statutes of 1875. A draftsman of the day was asked:

With regard to a number of Acts, the Public Health Acts, for instance, and again the Adulteration of Food and Drug Acts, and other acts of that kind, is it not necessary that they should be intelligible as far as possible to every person who is affected thereby?

To which the witness answered:

Yes; I quite agree, as far as possible; but I do not believe in the possibility of bringing the law to every man's bosom and business in that sense. I do not think it is possible to have Acts of Parliament which could be understood by everyone, even by everyone who is directly affected by them.[76]

Contemporaries usually came to terms with this problem. They could argue, and frequently did argue, that the regulatory laws responded to a national responsibility to address numerous special circumstances which were distinct and required their own attention. Legislative detail was seen as the route to saving lives, and in giving so much attention to voluminous description the large body of statutory law provided an equally precise picture of how Victorian legislators saw their world. In attempting to respond to social problems statute law mirrored poverty, stinking ditches, a lack of education, leaking ships, dangerous factories, and squalid slums. In their massive length and their 'eye' for detail these reforms were not laws for the faint-hearted.

---

[75] J. Bryce, *Studies in History and Jurisprudence* (Oxford 1901), ii: 489–90 (taken from his Inaugural Lecture delivered in 1871).

[76] *SC on Acts of Parliament*, 1875 (280) p. 41, para. 526. Lord Hervey asked the question and F. S. Reilly was the draftsman. For Thring's views on the sanitary laws of the 1860s, see Ch. IV above at footnote 100.

Part Three

LABOUR LAW

I

From Labouring to Employment: 1820–1867

As the nineteenth-century economy grew in unprecedented ways, the labour force that supplied so much of its drive altered both in structure and in form. Enterprises became larger and more complex, and as a result the great bulk of the workforce became wage labourers, engaged full or part time by a master, and having no share in the risks, costs or profits of the business. The history of labour through the period has at its core this two-sided relationship, at once inter-dependent and oppositional. Masters held command over their farms, workshops, and businesses and strove to extract whatever return they could from their servants. General accounts of the changes in labour conditions examine the attitudes and practices of work-givers and work-takers primarily from economic and social perspectives, explaining the realities of the many different labour markets and discussing the theoretical justifications offered for attitudes and policies. Legal measures form one important strand in this whole. Inevitably the explications of political economy were used to bolster the developing law.[1]

The history of labour law is much concerned with governmental institutions that set conditions for the interplay between masters and their workforce—these institutions being on the one hand legislators, and on the other, judges, magistrates, and inspectors of factories, mines, and, bit by bit, other workplaces. In order to understand the place of law in labour relationships, it is vital to keep its stage-setting character in mind. Not all aspects of its role are treated in this Part. In particular, we deal in the preceding Part with statutory administrations which sought to ensure that factory and mine operators and other types of private employer limited the hours, and later other conditions of work undertaken by women, children and—eventually in a few important cases—even adult men.[2] It was part of this drive also to impose safety conditions on enterprises. There the legal issues become entwined with defences to negligence actions at common law which were couched in broad terms in the middle quarters of the century and then reduced in scope by legislation and judicial changes of heart. Eventually in

[1] See Vol. XI, pp. 168–70, 198–205.
[2] Above, 544–70.

1897 the first, 'experimental' scheme for workmen's compensation was employed in certain industries. We treat these issues in Volume XII in dealing with the law of tort.[3]

The law affecting labour in 1820 was still as much a matter of public law as it was of private law. True, the old Tudor regulation of agricultural and craft labour—with its controls over trade apprenticeships and the authority that it gave to justices in Quarter Sessions to determine wage levels and to set manual workers to work—had in 1813 and 1814 been well-nigh abolished. But once servants had contracted to do work, the criminal law in many instances continued to punish their failure to complete it. Also still in place were the laws against trade combinations, which were used mainly to inhibit plans for collective negotiation and industrial action by workers. So far as affected masters, the movement to impose regulatory conditions on employments was a public obligation enforced through inspection and prosecution. Nor must it be forgotten that the ratepayers in each parish continued to shoulder poor law obligations which stretched to those out of work as well as those unable to work.[4]

By the 1860s, the overall dependence of British society on its labour force was coming to be recognized not just in respect of the parliamentary franchise. In relation to wage-work itself, as we shall see, legal sanctions would be withdrawn that until then had maintained the labour relationship as a 'public' status as much as a 'private' contract. Some industries then began more regularly to replace terms of work dictated by masters (acting singly or in concert) with work based on bargains between employers and trade unions representing their workforce. At the root of this lay new ways of viewing the work relationship from an economic perspective.[5] These collective agreements, often at district level, but sometimes regional and occasionally national, were treated as having no legal force in themselves. Only the embodiment of some of their terms in the individual contract that each worker had with his or her master would create obligations within the purview of courts.

At the same time, combination laws, which had sought to constrain unions from using withdrawal of labour and associated pressure to back their demands, were revised by Parliament to some degree. Even so, by the turn of the century, a phalanx of the senior judiciary would find ways of imposing civil injunctions and awards of damages through obligations in tort. These were severe enough for the rising Labour Party to demand and secure categorical legislation that reversed much of the new drive against their power. In the upshot, by 1914, labour law

---

[3] See Vol. XII, Pt. 5, Ch. IV.

[4] For the history of English labour law in this holistic sense, see esp. S. Deakin and F. Wilkinson, *The Law of the Labour Market* (Oxford, 2005), esp. Ch. 5.

[5] See Vol. XI, pp. 198–205.

is not merely confined to the private law of the individual contract of employment. In part it falls beyond the bounds of the formal legal system entirely. In no other field, however, do we observe normative practices being placed to such an extent beyond the bounds of any *legal* obligation at all. That it happened marks the labour relationship as the central area of economic and political contest in industrialized British society.

1. WORK FOR ONESELF, WORK FOR OTHERS: THE TRADITIONS

In the eighteenth century the common law had come to accept, as a first condition of personal liberty, that one person could not own another as slave or serf. Even a West Indian sugar planter could not seize 'his' Negro once he had been brought to the English shore and set free.[6] Despite this, a great part of the public labour law, in one way or another, was designed to keep labour forces working, rather than to protect them from overwork, underpayment, or sub-human exploitation. It was these special disciplinary measures that tied the manual worker by bonds of status. Sir Henry Maine's marker of a progressive society—the replacement of status by contract—was reached in Britain only when, in 1875, employers lost their right to bring defaulting workers before magistrates for punishment under the Master and Servant Acts.[7]

The movement towards contract had, however, being going on to some degree for centuries. By 1820, the British economy was moving away from predominantly agricultural activity and towards a productive world far more variegated—part urban, part mechanized, part (but still only a small part) harnessed to coal and steam as power sources, part given over to management through overseers, clerks, agents, and professionals. The business of industrialization was diffuse and gradual—at a considerable remove from any simplistic notion of an industrial *revolution*.[8] Social change likewise moved in fits, industrial cities and towns building up as production gravitated to them because of such varied stimulants as climate conditions, mining prospects, technical know-how, the

---

[6] Lord Mansfield's grudging acknowledgment of this distinction in *Somersett's case* (1771) 20 St. Tr. 1 would end fluctuating opinions on the subject among the judiciary. This presaged the anti-slavery movement, which needed the 'free-born Englishman' as a first premise: see, in the present context, R. J. Steinfeld, *The Invention of Free Labour* (Chapel Hill, 1991), Ch. 4.

[7] Below, p. 677.

[8] For the multiplicity of labour markets, see S. Pollard, 'Labour in Great Britain', in P. Mathias and M. M. Postan (eds), *Cambridge Economic History of Europe* (Cambridge, 1978), vii, i, 103; M. Berg, *The Age of Manufactures 1700–1820* (Oxford, 1985); K. D. M. Snell, *Annals of the Labouring Poor* (Cambridge, 1985).

accumulation of skilled workers, and the availability of capital.[9] For England, the early nineteenth century was an age in which those with entrepreneurial talents could show remarkable determination in seeking a fortune. But it was still a time when growth in the country's overall domestic product was far from continuous or inevitable. That would become more evident only in the middle decades of the century when the scale of industrial development had advanced further, as had the range of markets for British products and services at home and abroad.

As part of this gradualism, law affecting work relationships needed to be adaptable, either by providing generalized formulae, such as rules governing the formation and content of labour contracts, or by laying down requirements in relation to workers by sector, specific trade, or particular enterprise. Such pragmatism already had a long history. The Tudor state had deployed its directive force to impose labour regulation at a considerable level of generalization. The Statute of Artificers of 1562 had swept away much medieval law.[10] It set up a country-wide regime of control operating through the justices of the peace by giving them powers to penalize those who failed to meet its requirements. Yet even that Statute, the crucial provisions of which would remain in force until almost the end of the Napoleonic Wars, pursued policies of differentiation. A major aim had originally been to secure agricultural production so that the country would have enough food. In line with this it had subjected a splay of craft trades to restrictions that permitted only indentured apprentices to acquire the necessary skills. In agriculture, the justices of the peace had been required to set wage rates for labourers, to prevent them from leaving before the end of their year's service and to compel those without work to undertake it on the land. The wage rates were initially intended as maxima—concerned therefore with the condition where labour was in short supply and an individual farmer might otherwise offer more than the existing standard in the district.[11]

In the skilled trades covered by the Statute, an apprentice had to serve seven years, and a master in most trades could have no more than three indentured to him at any one time for each journeyman in his shop.[12] This also sought to restrict flight from the land and it reinforced the power of guilds to ration the intake into

[9] For the social and political history of industrial relations after 1820, see esp. E. H. Hunt, *British Labour History 1815–1914* (1984), Chs 1, 6, 7; A. Fox, *History and Heritage* (1985), Chs 3–6; H. A. Clegg, A. Fox, and A. F. Thompson, *History of British Trade Unions Since 1889* (Oxford, 1964), i: Ch. 1.

[10] 5 Eliz. c. 4. For its content, subsequent variation and interpretation by the courts, see Steinfeld, *Invention of Free Labor*, 15–41; Deakin and Wilkinson, *Labour Market*, 44–58.

[11] 5 Eliz. c. 4, ss 15, 18–20. An Act of 1603 (1 Jas. 1, c. 6, s 7) provided for the setting of minima in the clothing trade.

[12] Sections 31–33. An encrustation of case law had built around these provisions, in which judges increasingly expressed a dislike of their monopolistic character.

their trade in their locality.[13] The Statute was conceived primarily in respect of work done by men, though women workers were by no means unknown, both in agriculture and skilled trades. As the life of the propertied became increasingly sedate, the number of domestic servants engaged in running the household grew significantly, and a great many of these were women. They were not classed as servants under the Statute, being thought of as something even more menial. But they were servants for other legal purposes, not least the disciplinary.

The serfdom of the middle ages—a bondage that kept the villein tied to the manor of his birth—had been breaking down since the depopulation caused by the Black Death in the mid-fourteenth century. The Elizabethan Statute and laws which followed upon it were attempts to confine that process in an age when the propertied ranks held deep fears about its accumulating effects. In the same period came incarceration and other controls over rogues and vagabonds, poor law provision in each parish (which required that the overseers set able-bodied paupers to work) and the supervision of charities by the Privy Council. Thus had royal government striven to impose a severe patriarchy on the lower orders that was at odds with any romantic view of the relationships of status in a pre-capitalist era.

In the seventeenth and eighteenth centuries the Statute and various supplementary Acts had continued as a straitjacket for the working lives of much of the population and discontent with the constraints remained endemic.[14] Nonetheless, manual workers in both country and town, who formed the great bulk of the adult population, followed customary paths that allowed transitions as they advanced in age. The young worker on the land started as an in-house servant: he lived in his farmer-master's household and was provided for there, typically on an annual hiring. During the year he would have bed and board. His expectation of any wage might well be only at the end of the year, held as a guarantee of good service. The master would require much the same subservience from the servant as a father would demand of his wife and children.[15] In return, he would continue to provide for the servant even when there was no work; and likewise if the servant fell ill, though the extent of his obligation would become a matter of legal dispute.[16] In mid-life, particularly when the worker married, he would cease to be

[13] Numerous bye-laws of guilds and corporations amplified these provisions: see C. Dobson, *Masters and Journeymen* (1980), Ch. 4.

[14] For Blackstone's rough classification of servants into menials (including those providing the household with long-term labour), apprentices, short-term outwork labourers, and superior ministerials (stewards, factors, bailiffs), see *Comms*, i, 14; O. Kahn-Freund, 'Blackstone's Neglected Child: The Contract of Employment' (1978) 93 *LQR* 508.

[15] A master could correct (i.e. whip) an apprentice or servant for negligence or other misbehaviour, if done with moderation: Blackstone, *Comms*, ii, 14.

[16] See below, p. 638.

an in-house servant and would become a cottager, sometimes through provision from his former master.[17] He and his wife might produce their family's subsistence from his small tenancy and its associated rights of common. At the same time, he might continue working for one master on an annual hiring, or—as was becoming more common—under a shorter-term, open-ended arrangement with him. Alternatively he might hire his labour out to one or more tenant farmers for a daily or weekly wage as the seasons and other opportunities dictated.

While the language that epitomized these arrangements was far from uniform, the youngster living in was often referred to as a 'servant', the older outworker a 'labourer'. But if the labourer bound himself to work for one farmer he would still be classed as in service for various legal purposes.[18] If a labourer was hard-working and astute, he might begin to accumulate land and other assets of his own, and so move up to become a farmer tenanted from a large estate, or a supplier of seed, implements, or carriage. For the rest, the risks of lack of work, and of ill-health and old age, rested with the individuals and their families, with possible resort to the benevolence of their communities—to the trustees of endowed charities or to the overseers of the poor in their parishes of settlement. This pattern prevailed in traditional farming communities, especially those 'closed' villages where the vertical social hierarchy had been established for generations. 'Open' villages, by contrast, might fumble on in disarray, supplying labour to the surrounding countryside when and where they could.[19] These were patterns that could well be upset by raising rents but not wages; or by engaging in a full-scale enclosure. In the eighteenth century both these practices had grown as part of the movement for agricultural reform with its new emphasis on efficiencies in production that would bring greater returns to the farmers and their landlords.

In many trades those who made goods and materials—in villages and in towns—had acquired their skills under a formal apprenticeship for seven years, usually begun at puberty. As in agriculture the relationship was commonly a domestic one, the apprentice living in the workshop-home under the control of his master (and often, when it came to discipline, his mistress). Upon completion of this training, the young adult might well move out as a 'journeyman' or 'artificer' to a master in the craft; or, at least with time, he might work for different masters—again the categories were far from settled. He might continue to exercise his manual skills for a wage calculated by time or by finished piece, or

---

[17] The mean age for marriage was 26 for men and 24 for women, which did not vary much over time.

[18] Steinfeld, *Free Labor* (1991), 17–22; Deakin and Wilkinson, *Labour Market*, 44–6; J. Small, 'New Languages for Labour and Capital' (1987) 12 *Social Hist.* 43–72.

[19] For this difference in relation to the poor law, see e.g. A. Brundage, *The Making of the New Poor Law* (1979), 3–4.

he might become involved in distributing the products. He would be operating at his own risk and he might hope eventually to set up as a master in his own right. Whatever stage he himself reached, he would regard the right to put his son into his trade as a 'property'. In some forms of cottage industry, such as the weaving of woollen cloth, the worker might buy the raw material and own the frame on which he worked. Increasingly, it was a master who provided wool and frame, the worker receiving only a wage for his labour.[20] Patterns were forming which distinguished the entrepreneur who invested and risked capital from the artisan who worked for an agreed payment. The law of contract gave effect to the bargain, whatever it was, making it out from its actual implementation by the two sides, and more general understandings in the particular community.

The division of labour increased as skilled trades multiplied. The progression of apprentice/journeyman/master underlay the organization of local trade guilds. Guildsmen-masters became powers in their boroughs, as aldermen or justices of the peace dispensing the intricate mass of local regulations that spread over trading, food supplying, building, watering, cleansing, and protecting their towns. Among them would be those who dispensed charity, swept up vagabonds into the houses of correction, dealt with criminals, and supervised the public poor law. This was a world of alliances and mutual protections in which the associations of masters tended to be emulated by journeymen. By collective action they could accumulate funds to keep individual members and their families from having to turn to the overseers of the poor; and they could use their power of joint action to resist masters who wanted more work out of their men, or who, in times of labour shortage, were resisting demands for improved wages or the right to move to other jobs. 'Combinations' among the labourers in a trade had become a recurrent feature of eighteenth-century life in the London metropolis and other growing towns.[21]

2. THEORIES OF LABOUR

In *The Wealth of Nations*, Adam Smith had put the case for a benign natural order in which the drive to work, produce, and compete should be allowed full play free of interference by the state. His successors, Malthus and Ricardo, in their different ways, adopted a far less sanguine view of the place of labour in the

---

[20] In the late seventeenth century, an unqualified employer could not carry on a protected trade by hiring qualified journeymen: *Hobbs* v. *Young* (1689) 1 Show. KB 267; but later courts had taken a less constraining approach: see *Raynard* v. *Chase* (1756) 1 Burr. 6; *Smith* v. *Company of Armourers* (1792) 3 Peake 199.

[21] See e.g. Dobson, *Masters and Journeymen* (1980); J. Rule, *The Labouring Classes in Early Industrial England, 1750–1850* (1986), Ch. 11.

emerging capitalist economy. Malthus would warn against the state deflecting the full effects of population growth through a poor law which obliged local rate-payers to support the able-bodied through periods of unemployment or under-employment, and would support the protection of land-owners by Corn Laws that underpinned their returns on crop-farming when good seasons reduced prices—home food production must be secured for futures in which foreign supplements might be cut off by war. His analysis assumed the inevitability of growth in a population the great bulk of which provided physical labour, and which therefore could expect, because of the ever-growing number of mouths to be fed, that it would only ever be able to earn a bare subsistence wage. Ricardo pilloried the landed upper class as rent-seekers who through their ownership of land—that uniquely renewable resource—were able, save on the least product-ive land, to appropriate a rent from the tenant farmers and their labourers who did the actual farming. What then of those who laid out capital in the growing range of productive enterprise—on the one hand, those who risked fortunes in businesses that they managed, and, on the other, those who in effect lent their wealth for others to engage in the activity, assuming the risk of profit without any executive function in securing it? Ricardo's analysis of the elusive nature of value, drove him back to an extended concept of a labour theory of value, in which the capital put into a venture was treated as an earlier accumulation of labour. What then was the justification for treating the return on capital as a justified surplus?

Particularly during the years of war with revolutionary France, journeymen had pressed a few benches of justices to set wages under the Statute of Artificers. They had also sought to prosecute masters who took on new workers without a seven-year apprenticeship as the mode of entry into a growing range of trades. But soon enough they had been re-buffed.[22] By then, Adam Smith and his follow-ers had popularized the liberal case for freedom to trade.[23] Parliament had taken up the cry, repealing in quick succession the wage fixing and the apprenticing sections of the Statute of Artificers.[24] These rather dramatic shifts led historians subsequently to think that, from the latter eighteenth century, the older custom-ary stages of work had given way to naked market competition for labour. In considerable measure this must have been true. It largely explains how a great

[22] The common law courts had sustained justices in their reluctance to revive their powers under the 1562 statute or similar enactments: see *R. v. Kent (Justices)* (1811) 14 East 395; and further, I. Prothero, *Artisans and Politics in early Nineteenth Century London* (1979), 38–9.

[23] *Inquiry into the Causes of the Wealth of Nations* (1776), esp. i, Chs 1 and 4. Over a long period judges had been among those who criticized the apprenticeship constraints of the 1562 statute.

[24] 53 Geo. III c. 40 (rating of wages); 54 Geo. III c. 96 (apprenticeship). The latter, however, did not extend to the City of London and other towns with ancient customs on the matter, and the power of justices to hear complaints relating to apprenticeship was retained.

swathe of manual workers, particularly in factories and workshops, would come to endure the lifelong toil of many hours a day at bare subsistence wages that Richard Oastler would denounce as 'Yorkshire slavery'.[25] It left them exposed to reduction of work in the course of trade cycles, the dangers of accidents and disabilities from service, and a grim pauperdom if they were dismissed.

As economic change became more profound, it generated the high Victorian consciousness of class. The relation of landowners, capitalist producers, and working labour, typified in classical economic theory by their rents, profits, and wages, became the tri-partite fractions into which the society perceived itself to be divided. Loyalties coalesced within each cohort, antagonisms across the boundaries between them; and in the great tussle in the 1840s to repeal the Corn Laws each would gain a new solidity. Just as political economy would provide the main rhetoric for those confrontations, so also for the conflicts directly between the owners of businesses and their labour forces. For a time, initially in the second decade of the nineteenth century, the Lanark mill-owner, Robert Owen, attracted considerable attention as the proponent of cooperative production and distribution, as opposed to the internecine strife of unremitting competition. He illustrated his cause at his own works with their provision of housing and schooling, and their generally humane conditions; and he believed, as did other radicals such as Joseph Hume, that the superiority of his system would establish itself by such examples without the direction of the state. In the period of the 1832 Reforms he was much involved in the operation of the Grand National Consolidated Trades Union, which for a short time seemed to have the strength to build cooperative businesses engaged in production.

Often enough, the hard-headed calculations of risk, wages, production costs, and profit acquired a higher moral tone from Christian ideals of hard work and sacrifice for others. A conversion to God meant the abnegation of selfish human vice in all its manifestations. For instance, workers who stubbornly refused to go back to work on 'Saint Monday', however fervent their observance of the Lord's Day, stood condemned as strays from the path of righteousness.[26] Alongside rationalists such as Smith and Ricardo, writers such as the Anglican priest, Malthus, the Scottish free churchman, Thomas Chalmers, and the Unitarian populariser, Harriet Martineau, illuminated the spiritual dimension of economic self-sufficiency.[27] They had wide influence among the reading population for their insistence that the able-bodied must be encouraged to expend their energies on

---

[25] Initially in the *Leeds Mercury*, 29 September 1831, as a leading figure in the Short Time campaigns against employment conditions in cotton factories—for which see above (RC Vol. XIII, Part II, factory conditions).

[26] E. P. Thompson, 'Time, Work Discipline and Industrial Capitalism' (1967) 38 *P & P* 56.

[27] See Vol. XI, pp. 161–7.

work, and that depended largely on leaving them to the disciplines of the market for service. If they were sustained by charity or poor relief, then, as Malthus had warned, their concupiscence would ensure that population would increase geometrically, while at best the land for food production would expand only arithmetically. The Samaritarian instincts of Christians were thus to be repressed wherever they could not take the form of encouragements or goads to live a godly, productive life. Hence the utilitarian precept that the able-bodied should receive social aid only on conditions of 'less eligibility', which were embodied in the pauper workhouse and the separate hard-labour prison.

The leaders of economic thought, insisting on the efficiencies of free markets for entrepreneurial capitalists, saw it as essential that the supply of labour should likewise be a hive of atomistic competition. Those who provided labour, as distinct from ideas, information or financial resources, must bargain, each one of them, for what they could, both in good times and harsh. How they fared was mainly at their own risk. They must be left to plan for life, including the demands of bearing children and managing old age. The repeal of the Tudor regulations of labour accordingly raised issues at the very crossroads of political and economic organization. The debates in Parliament on the repeals of the Tudor legislation had resounded with Smithian demands of '*laissez-faire!*' for the terms of wage-work. Free competition, not public regulation, must determine who could apply for work and equally the terms offered by masters. If that meant men binding themselves to work for 14 or even 16 hours a day, so be it! By the 1830s there were factories enough for a movement to limit the length of the working day in them;[28] but in 1833 and for decades thereafter it would succeed only for women and children. Adult men were free agents and must live with the consequences.

David Ricardo, in analysing economic development as the product of free markets, treated the wages available to meet the returns to labour within the whole economy as a strictly limited proportion of gross earnings. From this it followed that if one category of workers came to earn more, others must have less. In its turn this proposition followed from Ricardo's essentially pessimistic theory that as a capitalist economy grew the profits available to investors would decline proportionately and risked the collapse of the very structure. His disciples, J. R. McCulloch and Nassau Senior, popularized the macro-theory of an 'iron law of wages'. To this Senior would add the doctrine that profits were made only in the last one or two hours of a 12-hour day—a pronouncement aimed at discouraging any renewal of the campaign for a 10-hour day for cotton factory workers.[29] Yet such assumptions would continue to found 'classical' economic

---

[28] See above, Vol. XI, pp. 358–67.
[29] N. W. Senior, *Letter on the Factory Act as it Affects the Cotton Manufacture* (1837), 12–13.

theory until at least 1869, when J. S. Mill would renounce the concept of the wages fund.[30]

Courts, as we shall see, would draw from these early justifications of an unrelenting capitalism numerous ideas about what the work terms of individuals must be. Even more importantly, the theory justified the law's criminal process against workers who refused to complete their obligations and also upon collective action by unions of men. For the latter pressure there might be many causes: to prevent outside workers from securing jobs; to keep out new machinery; to maintain demarcations between skilled trades; to object to the personality or methods of supervisors. Judges considered that to bring a master's enterprise to a slow-down or standstill was an obstruction of his freedom to use his capital to greatest business advantage and therefore was a crime of great potential significance.

By the 1860s, radical criticism against severely individualistic theories of the labour market was gathering strength. It did so alongside the growing restlessness over the exclusion of working men from the suffrage, which would lead to the Second Reform Act 1867. The franchise reforms, as we shall see, were closely paralleled by a growing acceptance that responsible trade unions should play a role in determining the conditions of the workplace. This would lead to a collectivism which some would accept as a necessary consequence of wider political maturity. Others would become increasingly alarmed by its potential for what they thought would destroy the whole libertarian-capitalistic economy. 1867 brought a crucial realignment in the history of labour relations. Accordingly, it provides the principal dividing line in this Part.

3. FREE BARGAINING AND ENFORCED OBLIGATION

Contracts for Employment

In 1820, work relationships, whether or not strictly for 'service' or 'apprenticeship', were defined primarily by terms agreed between the hirer and the labourer. So long as the Elizabethan powers of the justices to regulate the relationship had continued, this had been to some extent obscure.[31] Nonetheless, in his widely read *Principles of Moral and Political Philosophy*, Archdeacon Paley had claimed service to be 'voluntary and by contract; and the master's authority extends no

---

[30] Below, Ch. III, n. 21.
[31] See O. Kahn-Freund, 'Blackstone's Neglected Child: the Contract of Employment' (1977) 93 *LQR* 508.

further than the terms or equitable construction of the contract will justify'.[32] For the simpler sorts of job, many of the details would be derived from current behaviour—and so in that limited sense from custom. In a dispute, even where there was something by way of writing, oral evidence could be given of matters not specified—for instance, of the hours demanded of the worker.

In some cases the terms were shaped by general rules, as for instance the presumption that the period of notice required to end an annual hiring was the quarter before its completion.[33] A manufactory of some size with overseers and numerous hands might well have a detailed book of work rules, with prescriptions for hours, meal-breaks, impermissible behaviour, the assessment of wages and so forth. There was no overall requirement that service contracts in general be in writing, although the Statute of Frauds 1677 called for a written memorandum for any contract not to be performed within a year.[34] For a higher level employee, whether or not that Statute or any other applied, written terms might well be agreed.[35] In many instances they would follow a standard form, for work was a world in which increasing numbers fell into cohorts. Where there were express written rules, they would almost always govern.[36] Cases would turn on the interpretation of the language used in the given circumstances, which in court would be treated as a 'question of law'—and so for the judge, rather than the jury.

Questions about what the relationship was, and what were its terms, could arise in a civil action for breach by either the employer or the worker brought in one of the superior courts.[37] For the common law this was mainly by action on the case in *assumpsit* or *indebitatus assumpsit*, rather than by the old form of covenant. But the detailed shaping of labour obligations by judges and magistrates also followed upon other types of proceeding. Before 1875 these included, in rough order of their frequency and significance:

(a) Criminal prosecutions or dismissal proceedings before a justice for breach of contract by a servant who fell within Master and Servant Acts. These were the regular form of legal discipline right up to their replacement by civil procedures in 1875.

---

[32] 1823 edn, Bk I, Ch. 13; cf. J. A. Jaffe, 'Authority and Job Regulation' (1997) 3(1) *Hist. St. in Ind. Rlns* 1.

[33] Reinforced by 5 El. c. 4, ss 5, 6, 12.

[34] 29 Car. II c. 3, s 3. Some trades had special requirements, e.g. seamen: see 2 Geo. II c. 39, ss 1, 2.

[35] For examples, see below, p. 639.

[36] Reported cases from the superior courts tended increasingly to turn on the meaning of complex written documents, as is evident from many of the decisions cited in this Chapter, particularly those involving skilled workers.

[37] See further, below, p. 639–41.

(b) Criminal prosecutions under statutes against combinations, or against the activities of worker or employer associations, such as strikes, lockouts, and dissuasion of black-leg labour. These were much less frequent but would define the boundary beyond which collective action was to remain illegal.[38]

(c) Disputes between parishes over the removal of paupers back to their original parish of settlement, which would not be justified if the person claiming relief had served an annual hiring in a second parish and so gained a settlement there.[39]

(d) Summary prosecutions aimed at securing some protection of the servant, as in provisions against truck (wages in goods, rather than money);[40] and in factories, mines and, ultimately, workshops, against dangerous conditions or over-long hours, once they were brought under statutory regimes.[41] The inspector appointed to procure compliance with these requirements would resort to prosecution against recalcitrant owners when they saw no other way forward; but they had to accept that in many industrial districts the cases would come before magistrates whose sympathies might well favour the factory owner.

(e) Civil proceedings by an injured worker against an employer, mainly by action on the case for negligence, but subject, for instance, to the hostile 'common employment' exclusion of vicarious liability where one employee injured another.[42]

(f) Action at common law by a master against a person who enticed away his servant (but not the enticement of a person providing only particular services). The action initially bore overtones of a 'property' in the servant. At the end of the nineteenth century it would be broadened into the tort of inducing or procuring breach of any contract.[43]

Some of these proceedings applied only to manual workers, variously defined, others were of wider range. There was always some danger that differences in the type of claim, together with differences between long-term hirings and shorter-term wage contracts, would lead to inappropriate analogies in applying the law. Consider, for example, the spread of the 'butty' system in collieries, shipbuilding,

---

[38] Below, 652–66.

[39] Below, 674–5.

[40] Below, 641–3.

[41] See above, Pt. Two, Ch. V.

[42] See Vol. XII, pp. 1002–10.

[43] Above; Vol. XII, pp. 1043–6, 1054–8; and below, 693–4. Whether a person was a servant or an 'artificer' could also affect inheritance, insolvency, tax liability, ownership of money or goods received, protection against truck, and so forth.

railway construction, cotton spinning, and other trades. Under it a foreman provided his own labourers to undertake work—sometimes, as in early cotton factories, his own family making up much of the workforce. Was such a foreman
to be regarded as a servant as well as a provider of labour? The courts mostly
treated the butty-man as a servant in order to punish failure to perform work, but
they might take the opposite view, for instance, when he demanded payment in
money under the Truck Act 1831.[44]

We have only episodic knowledge of how far contentions between masters and
servants about their mutual rights and responsibilities were resolved by resort
to one of these procedures. Without some form of help, the worker was unlikely
to be able to stand up to his master. In the early nineteenth century, as trade
unions began to develop in the skilled trades, they might provide benefits that
would give some sustenance when work ceased and perhaps some aid in arguing a contention against the employer. Only slowly did unions begin to provide
legal professionals to aid their members. In the 1840s the 'Miners' Attorney-
General', W. P. Roberts, became a well-known exemplar; likewise the barrister
and Chartist, Ernest Jones. But they were ahead of their time.[45]

In exploring the legal interpretation of labour relationships in the early industrial period, the factor that above all deserves underscoring is the degree to
which masters could prescribe contractual conditions for keeping their servants
in line. In a world filled with irregularities and uncertainties, it was not only
employment contracts that had incorporated bulwarks against non-performance
or mis-performance. Among the techniques applicable to contracts in general
were imprisonment for debt, conditional bonds and other penalty clauses to pay
a set amount for failure to perform, and conditions providing that payment for
services would fall due only when they were completed.[46] In addition, criminal
statutes and bye-laws sought, for instance, to protect buyers of foodstuffs, clothing, and many other products against short measures, adulteration, and other
unscrupulous trading.[47] Nonetheless, the degree to which servants at the lower
levels were subjected to minatory obligations is striking.[48] In large measure this
power stemmed from the employer's decision on what those obligations should

[44] Erle J. was willing to give the protection of the Truck Act 1831 (1 & 2 Will. IV c. 32) to a foreman
who also engaged to take part in the labour: *Bowers* v. *Lovekin* (1856) 6 E. & B. 584; but not so the
Court of Exchequer: *Sleeman* v. *Barrett* (1863) 2 H. & C. 934; and see below, 642.

[45] See below, pp. 664, n. 67.

[46] See below, pp. 645–6.

[47] See below, 998–9.

[48] Fines for misperformance, deductible from wages, were often included in factory work rules;
and employments of highly skilled workers might be the subject of substantial money bonds against
failing to carry out the work as required.

be. When it came to work that required strength and stamina rather than craft skills, the master was often enough aided by a ready supply of other labour.

It is in the context of labour supply that the law of settlement under the Old Poor Law deserves comment.[49] Since the late seventeenth century, contests between parishes over which of them was liable to maintain a pauper who had moved from one to another often turned on whether he or she had served an annual hiring in the new parish. Only if this was so did the root obligation shift to that parish. Otherwise, it could order the pauper's removal back to the old parish of settlement. Adam Smith had attacked settlement rules for making labour-short parishes reluctant to take in new workers for fear of later downturns in demand.[50] But equally the rules could be said to provide a subsidy for the new factories and workshops from agricultural parishes with unemployment problems. The latter would escape the need for immediate support by assuming a possible liability in future—and indeed there had long been a practice of dispatching the jobless in search of work with certificates undertaking ultimately to receive them back as paupers.

For overseers and ratepayers in a parish, this stream of inter-parish disputes came to resemble any root question of taxation: lines had to be drawn between allowable avoidance and impermissible evasion.[51] The common law judges had frequently to wrestle with nice differentiations argued before them, but arrived at no general policy for deciding when to impose the obligation on the parish of origin and when on the parish of service.[52] There came to be a distinction between contracts where the master had a right to the servant's labour through day and night, perhaps with dispensations by the master for special conditions (these were treated as an annual hiring), and those where the hours, however long, were specified, as with a factory working shifts (not an annual hiring, even if the relationship continued for a year or more).[53] This at least suggests a reluctance to carry the domestic give-and-take of agricultural life into the new world

[49] For settlement as a whole, see above, 674–5. On this aspect, see S. and B. Webb, *English Poor Law History*, (1927), i: Ch. 5.

[50] *Wealth of Nations* (1776), i: Pt. 1, Ch. 10.

[51] The wishes of the paupers themselves played no part in deciding the outcome. Some may have seen better chances in a return to their original parish, many in staying where they had been employed for a year even though they had no continuing job.

[52] Quarter Sessions around the country had a constant flow of cases, thanks to the presence of barristers on the lookout to represent parishes: Webb, *English Poor Law History*, i: 347. For early eighteenth-century case law treating rather generously what could amount to a yearly hiring for the determination of a poor law settlement, see Deakin and Wilkinson, *Labour Market*, 120–1.

[53] Cf. e.g. *R* v. *Byker* (1823) 2 B. & C. 120; *R* v. *St John Devizes* (1829) 2 B. & C. 896; for the evolution of these notions, see Deakin and Wilkinson, *Labour Market*, 120–4. As might be expected, inconsistencies would build up in the case law.

of rota-driven manufacturing. The tangles of the law on settlement were felt by a wide range of the rate-paying classes to be deeply unsatisfactory. Hence with the new Poor Law regime of 1834, the law moved towards a simple test of a year's residence in the new parish.[54] That altered the thrust of old dilemmas, though the flow of settlement contests by no means dried up and the results could influence the outcome of disputes between master and servant themselves—not least over the master's entitlement to control the conduct of the servant.[55]

The Servant's Duty to do the Work

The prime obligation on the servant was to carry out the work as directed within the contract.[56] In a contract for a definite term (whether a year, a month or a week) they were to work throughout its period; in a piece-work contract they were to supply the finished articles during the term. There could be many variations in the relationship between the term, the power to give notice to end the contract, the calculation of the wages due and whether they were paid in instalments or only at the end. Inevitably there were differences over whether the worker had done what he contracted for and, especially with piecework, how the master measured or counted the results.[57] Where a servant was struck down by illness or an accident, the master might be duty-bound to continue wages during his incapacity, but it was very doubtful that he would have had to pay for medical treatment. A yearly labourer in agriculture could expect some real measure of protection against these misfortunes;[58] but by the 1850s, it was being said that even such a servant could expect aid from his employer only for short terms of sickness.[59]

The Extent of any Duty on the Master to Provide what Work he Had

The settlement cases showed clearly enough the changing nature of services. The annual hiring in agriculture was for whatever the farmer required during the

---

[54] See Deakin and Wilkinson, *Labour Market*, 118–26.

[55] Below, 644.

[56] Only at the margins could a servant hope to object to a task set for him or her—perhaps because it was novel: see P. Selznick, *Law, Society and Industrial Justice* (New Brunswick, 1980), 136.

[57] Miners, for example, were often paid by weight of ore and that opened opportunities for miscalculation. By 1860, miners' organizations were resilient enough to secure the right to have a check-weighman oversee the process on behalf of the men: Mines Regulation Act 1860, s 29.

[58] For eighteenth-century case-law on the subject, see A. W. B. Simpson, *Leading Cases in the Common Law* (Oxford, 1995), 113–17.

[59] MacDonnell, *The Law of Master and Servant* (1881).

whole of each day, while in mines and factories it came to be work governed by timetables and shifts which at maximum stretch could still call for work during most of waking hours. Higher-level employees sometimes succeeded in having their continuing contracts classed as annual hirings. In consequence the relationship would be open to termination only at the end of the year, unless the servant was guilty of serious misconduct and there would be an obligation to continue paying any periodic wage until this time.

Masters running operations with a large workforce, however, strove for the power to lay off their workers, while, particularly if they had special skills, keeping a tie with them to cope with rising demand in future. So long as they laid down the terms of agreement without real consultation they would gauge the balance to their own advantage, as did many colliery owners of Northumberland and Durham by the 1820s. They bound their men to annual hirings and paid them piece rates, but sought to avoid any legal obligation to provide work day by day when they did not have the business for it. For instance they resisted demands that, when they imposed short time, a miner would be paid a wage from the fourth day of unemployment.[60] In an *assumpsit* action, Lord Denman refused to read into miners' annual contracts a term that guaranteed them 40 days work in a year, even though they had bound themselves not to take work from elsewhere. There was no undertaking 'to keep the pit open at any time, or to find the plaintiff in employment all the year round'.[61] True, Denman might allow for a more generous approach where the express terms warranted it. Thus in two contemporaneous cases of long contracts involving the provision of know-how, he accepted that there might be a promise to pay wages at some level for any day on which there was no work.[62] These skilled-worker decisions were soon criticized and put on one side.[63] The courts came usually to decide that, while the master promised to pay for work done during the fixed period of exclusivity, he did not undertake to provide it when there was no business or when he had to close his operation down, temporarily or permanently.[64]

That position obliged the courts to reject contrary arguments on behalf of workers. The result of such a limited construction of the employer's obligation, it

[60] Even where an owner agreed to such an arrangement, he might well go in for relays of the three-days-off, one-day-on, type, see R. Fynes, *The Miners of Northumberland and Durham* (1923), 37–49.

[61] *Williamson* v. *Taylor* (1843) 13 L.J. (N.S.), 81, esp. 82.

[62] *Aspdin* v. *Austin* (1844) 5 Q.B. 669 (cement worker with special know-how); and see *Dunn* v. *Sayles* (1844) 5 Q.B. 685 (dentist's assistant).

[63] See *Emmens* v. *Elderton* (1853) 4 H.L.C. 647 (opinions of the judges sought by the HL and followed); *Whittle* v. *Frankland* (1863) 2 B. & C. 58; *Churchward* v. *R.* (1865) LR 1 QB 208.

[64] The case law appears not to have considered whether he was free to victimize a union organizer by giving others whatever work there was.

was argued for employees, was so wholly one-sided as to involve an unreasonable restraint of trade. Or it could be asserted that the promise lacked any mutuality of consideration and was for that reason not binding in law. The two arguments might in any case merge, because, as the Court of Exchequer would find in 1831, a partial restraint of trade could be regarded as binding only where there was adequate consideration for it.[65] But in 1846 the same court allowed neither objection to agreements at the Pilkington glass works which bound crown-glass workers to seven-year contracts, while paying by the piece and reserving a right of dismissal with one month's notice or wages in lieu. A seven-year tie for the master's benefit was not an invalid restraint;[66] and, said Alderson B. with dry logic, 'the power to dismiss implies that they have engaged to employ'. There was thus consideration and into its adequacy the court would not inquire.[67] A competitor who took the men on before the seven years was up accordingly committed the tort of enticement or harbouring. The case reduced the employer's obligation to an implication that he would not withhold work from the worker when he had it to give out. The distinction was used in particular to support prosecutions of miners and tin-plate men under the Master and Servant Act for walking out on term contracts, whether for a better job or to engage in strike action for better terms.[68]

So far as concerned individual contracts of employment, common law judges interpreted them with careful respect for the sanctity of contract.[69] At the same time they built into their interpretation of agreements their view of

[65] *Young* v. *Timmins* (1831) L.J. (Exch.) 68: a brass founder undertook to work exclusively for his employers during their lives; this lacked sufficient consideration because they assumed no obligation to provide work.

[66] Covenants not to engage in competitive work after leaving an employ would be treated as void if unduly broad. But that situation was regarded as quite distinct from the duty to work under a contract still in operation. See further below, 684–6.

[67] *Pilkington* v. *Scott* (1846) 15 M. & W. 657; see also *Hartley* v. *Cummings* (1846) 2 Car. & K. 434 (similar workers, similar terms, in County Durham); cf. the finding of no mutuality in the earlier *Lees* v. *Whitcomb* (1828) 5 Bing. 34 (trainee milliner not bound to stay for two years, because no reciprocal undertaking to instruct); and *Sykes* v. *Dixon* (1839) 8 L.J. (N.S.) 102 (similar finding, despite clear undertaking to give exclusive service year by year until a year's notice given). In *Pilkington* there was an obligation to pay £8 a year in lieu of housing and fuel; in *Hartley* a guarantee of some wages during non-working was given, making it clearer that the employer assumed a measure of mutual obligation.

[68] *R* v. *Welch* (1853) 2 E. & B. 356; *Re Bailey and Collier* (1854) 3 E. & B. 607, where strikers were alleging that the master had agreed to raise wages in line with those at another works and had then failed to comply.

[69] To some extent this appearance was underpinned by the need to find a formal ground for assigning an error in the declaration and other pleading; but equally there are signs enough that most judges appreciated the nub of the dispute and gave a result consistent with their view of the overall merits.

what an entrepreneurial employer could expect by way of limitation on his risks. Huberman has shown how far, in cotton spinning, local groups of employers came to avoid insisting on the toughest of dismissal terms in favour of each keeping their own workers on short-term wages through low points in the trade cycle. That, however, was the outcome of hard experience, including the debilitating effect of strike action on subsequent trade.[70] It was not because the judiciary sought to nudge employers in that direction. Adaptations of legal principle that were in any way favourable to manual workers were rare and transient. As Kahn-Freund once warned, '...to mistake the conceptual apparatus of the law for the image of society may produce a distorted view of the employment relation'.[71]

The Master's Duty to Pay or Provide

Long-term service under an annual hiring or an apprenticeship had been built upon an understanding that the servant would live within the household and any wages would be a supplementary guarantee of due diligence, whether they were paid only at the end of the term or at agreed intervals during the period.[72] The growth of out-work service for wages paid at intervals of a month, a week, or even a day went hand in hand with the assumption that the duration of the arrangement lasted formally only for each interval between payments. Either side might give notice to end the arrangement at the next payment. Any expectation that it would continue beyond that period was only a presumption that operated so far as due notice had not been given. The shift towards this open-ended, presumptively renewable, condition was already noticeable enough by mid-eighteenth century and would broaden its sweep thereafter. The decisions on poor law settlement showed the judges ready enough to accept the difference from old ways. In agriculture, it allowed seasonal demand to be met by the band of casual labourers who otherwise scraped by on other work or poor law provision. A free market for labour meant that the risk of unemployment or under-employment passed more and more to the worker. When reform of the Poor Law pressed guardians and overseers to reduce or eliminate outdoor relief for the able-bodied, it became all too apparent just how extensive that risk could be.[73]

---

[70] M. Huberman, *Escape From the Market: Negotiating Work in Lancashire* (Cambridge, 1996), Ch. 6: the upshot was spoken of as providing 'fair wages'.

[71] O. Kahn-Freund, *Labour and the Law* (1972), 116–17.

[72] S. M. Jacoby, 'The Duration of Indefinite Employment Contracts in the United States and England' (1982) 5 *Comp. Labour Law* 85, 98; P. Karsten, '"Bottomed on Justice": A Re-appraisal of the Critical Legal Studies Scholarship concerning Breaches of Labour Contacts by Quitting or Firing in Britain and the US' (1990) 34 *AJLH* 213, 218.

[73] J. Burnett, *Idle Hands: The Experience of Unemployment, 1790–1990* (1994), Chs 1, 4.

Where wages were due, there had for centuries been objections to truck— payments in kind rather than money. A run of statutes had sought to outlaw at least the most egregious of such practices because of their capacity to leave the workers short-changed.[74] Provision of bed and board for live-in servants or cottages for labourers was not thought of as truck. Even when the things were considered as a substitute for a money wage, the practice had advantages in a world where currency was not always readily available. But as regular remuneration became more frequent, so the prevention of truck by masters remained one surviving element from older regimes imposing statutory obligations on masters. Its continuance forms one small counter-trend in the whole complex of change. In consequence, there was an evident split in attitude between judges of the three courts of common law over the basic question—to which workers did the prohibition against truck apply? As elsewhere, the crux came over the foreman of a 'butty' gang—was he an 'artificer' within the language of the Act? Exchequer and Common Pleas considered him to fall outside benefit of the Act, even where he was obliged to join personally in the labour being contracted to him.[75] Queen's Bench took the opposite view,[76] but the Exchequer Chamber, composed of judges from the other two courts, overruled it.[77]

Under the Truck Act 1831, the payment of wages to all 'artificers' had to be in current coin on pain of summary prosecution.[78] The Act was promoted by Edward Littleton, a large employer in Stafford.[79] Such masters had an interest in taking up the workers' cause because they viewed truck as a tool in the hands of small competitors. Only Joseph Hume and his associates raised objection to the Act in the Commons, arguing from Ricardian theory that this was an external interference with the free labour market. As they saw it, the major economic effect of the legislation would be to prevent employers from resorting to truck provision as a means of surviving downturns in trade, whereas the practice enabled them to cut their outlay on labour without the dismissals that otherwise would be necessary. On this view, only an inflationary policy, including tax remission, would bring real economic benefit. This radical case was not heeded then, and modest additions would be made to the legislation from time to time.[80] But the ambiguities surrounding this piece of labour regulation led to only a few, irregular attempts

---

[74] See G. W. Hilton, *The Truck System: Including a History of the British Truck Acts 1465–1960* (Cambridge, 1960).

[75] *Riley* v. *Warden* (1848) 2 Ex. 45; *Sharman* v. *Saunders* (1853) 22 L.J. (N.S.) 86.

[76] *Weaver* v. *Floyd* (1852) 21 L.J. (N.S.) 151.

[77] *Ingram* v. *Barnes* (1858) 7 E. & B. 115, Erle J. (then of the QB) dissenting.

[78] 1 & 2 Will. IV c. 36.

[79] For his earlier efforts to clarify the old law, see Hilton, *Truck System*, 98–100.

[80] Not until the changed world of 1887, would the inspectors of factories and mines be given the task of supervising truck: Truck (Amendment) Act 1887, s 13(2).

at enforcement. By 1871, a Royal Commission could report that the practice was dwindling, thanks to the general rise in wages, changes in manufacturing organization, and trade union pressure.[81] The experience with truck, as with the modest measures of factory, mine, and workshop regulation, serves to underscore how little governments in early industrial Britain considered it their role to provide security for ordinary workers and their dependants. Beyond the catch-all net of the poor law and charity, the hands were left to the great mysteries of Self-Help.

Notice to Terminate

The shift towards short-term employments went on inexorably.[82] As already noted, an annual hiring in agriculture would end by notice given a quarter before the year's end; otherwise it would be assumed that a similar hiring would continue. These hirings would long survive in mining and to some extent in agriculture. There was some assumption that this rule would govern elsewhere in the absence of contrary agreement or general understanding. But it was not applied, for instance, to domestic servants. In their case, the contract could usually be brought to an end by a month's notice on either side.[83] For higher status employees such as governesses, drudge-like though their existence often was, the assumed period of notice would be three months. With skilled workers, there might be quite elaborate terms, designed to shore up the employer's interest in the technical know-how that the worker provided. Contracts with a short notice term—a month, a week, a day, an hour—came to suit factory and workshop owners who always had a weather eye for downturns in trade. But unless they were able to place longer ties on their workers, they risked losing them to higher payers when demand increased and labour became scarce. As we shall see, here was a crucial point in the collective pressures that each side could exert against the other. The legitimacy of a lock-out by masters or a strike by men turned in law on whether sufficient notice was being given to avoid a breach of each individual's contract. If there was a breach, it could be treated by the other party as serious

---

[81] *PP* 1871 [C. 326], xxxvi, 327. Some controls over similar practices were secured thereafter: against overcharging framework knitters for hiring frames (Hosiery Manufacture (Wages) Act 1874; against payment of wages in public houses, first in mining (1842) and then generally (1883); and against fining for poor workmanship as a disguised cut in wages (1896). The legislation would be modernized only by the Payment of Wages Act 1960.

[82] J. M. Feinman, 'The Development of the Employment at Will Rule' (1976) 20 *AJLH* 118.

[83] Cf. e.g. *Fawcett* v. *Cash* (1834) 5 B. & Ad. 904, where by contrast the written contract of a warehouseman clearly indicated at least a year's hiring. Judges were reluctant to alter the effect of a written contract by incorporating a custom. That would be done only where the custom was 'so universal that no workman could be supposed to have entered into…service without looking to it as part of the contract': Denman CJ QB, *R* v. *Stoke-upon-Trent* (1843) 5 Q.B. 303.

enough to give the right to end the contract forthwith. No conception developed that industrial action was merely a suspension of the relationship, which, once over, would allow the employment to be resumed. Since strikes and lock-outs could bring most serious consequences in their train, a 'right to strike' would remain beyond common law consciousness.

The Servant's Duty to Behave

Throughout the employment, servants were obliged (again by implication, if there was no express provision) not to absent themselves or misbehave—whether by stealing, embezzling, assaulting their master or his family, or causing malicious damage;[84] by failing to do the work or by carrying it out negligently; by disobeying the orders of the master or his foremen or other chargehands; by failing to show fidelity to the master's interests; by gross immorality, such as getting a maid pregnant.[85] If a farmer forbade gleaning after threshing, if a workshop owner would not allow the taking of off-cuts or leavings, there could be no right nevertheless to do so merely because these were general customs of the district.[86] The only legal questions were: had the master already bound himself to allow the practice? Was he therefore seeking unilaterally to alter a continuing contract?

Summary Termination for Breach

The question whether a servant could be dismissed before the due term would have relatively little significance for people on weekly or daily contracts. But where monthly or yearly hirings survived in agriculture or industry, early dismissal could be a disaster for the worker, just as it might create considerable difficulty for the employer. A signal of the shift towards contractual autonomy had come straight after the repeal of the Statute of Artificers. In *Spain* v. *Arnott*,[87] Lord Ellenborough tried an action by a yearly agricultural labourer against the

---

[84] As part of the 'Bloody Code', Parliament had made numerous such offences by servants subject to capital punishment, even on first conviction. Equally characteristic was the tendency to pass enactments relating specifically to workers which extended the summary jurisdiction of magistrates, in order that punishment could be dealt out swiftly by benches that knew how and where matters stood. For an instance, see the Offences Against the Person Act 1828 (9 Geo. IV c. 31, s 27).

[85] See, generally, C. M. Smith, *Treatise on the Law of Master and Servant* (1852), Ch. 8; MacDonell, *Master and Servant*, Ch. 22.

[86] For evidence about what was regarded by magistrates as a legitimate perquisite in industry, see D. Phillips, *Crime and Authority in Victorian England* (1977), 180–95.

[87] (1817) 2 Stark. 256. How such a man was able to bring a common law action remains mysterious.

master who had dismissed him on the spot. His offence had been to refuse to run an errand before eating the meal that was ready for him. The master's position was upheld. He was no longer obliged to take an insubordinate husbandsman before a justice of the peace in order to get his discharge.[88] In consequence the worker had no action for wages during the rest of his year's hiring, since they were due only at the end of the term.[89] The same unbending severity would be applied peremptorily against a domestic servant who went off to see her ailing mother, after being refused leave to be absent.[90] It was even held that immediate dismissal was justified if an order had been disobeyed, although the master did not know of the transgression at the time.[91]

Less than a half-century before, Lord Mansfield had allowed a wet-nurse, dismissed by her mistress from her annual hiring for being insolent and 'governed by passion', to claim her wages for the rest of the year—otherwise employers would be judge in their own cause.[92] Such scruples did not hold back Lord Ellenborough and his successors. Nor did it affect courts which subsequently held to the presumption that a wage was payable only on completion of a time contract, whether the period for payment was a year or some lesser period such as a month or a week.[93] The ultimate sanction of dismissal was thus given a form that could be fitted within one of the emergent principles of contract as a whole. Any significant breach of an agreement that was to be performed over time entitled the other party to treat it as terminated and to avoid any further obligation, such as, for instance, having to make a payment that was due only upon completion.[94] The ability to draw a service contract to a close thus became a unilateral power which the master could exercise in his own interest. The general rule excluding *indebitatus assumpsit* for

---

[88] Ellenborough put it dismissively: 'the relation between master and servant, and the laws by which that relation is regulated, existed long before the Statute' (p. 257).

[89] Cf. *Cutter* v. *Powell*, below, n. 95.

[90] *Turner* v. *Mason* (1845) 14 M. & W. 112. The court confounded the issue by announcing that the visit was not a necessity and pointing to the absence of any plea that the master knew the reason for it. Cf. Park J.'s slightly more accommodating view that it was not enough for a domestic to be sulky or to fail to answer the summoning bell: *Callo* v. *Brouncker* (1831) 4 Car. & P. 518, a view endorsed by Bramwell B. in *Horton* v. *McMurtry* (1862) 5 H. & N. 675. Macdonnell, *Master and Servant*, 224–6 (App. A).

[91] *Ridgway* v. *Hungerford Market* (1835) 3 Ad. & El. 171; soon qualified, however, in *Horton* v. *Fillieul* (1837) 7 Ad. & El. 557.

[92] *Temple* v. *Prescott* (1773) *Burn's Justice of the Peace* (1805 edn), iv 'Servants' 21.

[93] *Turner* v. *Robinson* (1833) 5 B. & Ad 789; *Saunders* v. *Whittle* (1876) 33 LT 816: painter paid by the week lost the wages for the week at the end of which he had an altercation with the employer over his work and walked out.

[94] So explained by McCardie J. in *Re Rubel Bronze and Vos* [1918] 1 KB 315, who chose to describe the *Spain* case without any reference to the jurisdiction of the justices and its subsequent reduction in scope. Other related issues would come to obscure the law further: for instance, how to construe a contract for a year's service, in which wages were paid weekly or monthly. See below, 683–4.

part-work on a broken contract was thought to stem from *Cutter* v. *Powell*.[95] The *Cutter* case, however, had involved a special risk contract for a ship's mate at a high final wage; and later it would be held that a seaman due a monthly wage could claim for the months completed before he was left behind because of his insubordination.[96] If there was in fact no breach, the dismissed servant could sue for past wages or for damages.[97] Masters were not subject to criminal penalties for wrongful dismissal, but only to a justice's order discharging the service, if that is what the servant wanted.[98]

Sanctions for Breach: Criminal Penalties

From the middle ages the criminal law had been used as a means of getting workers to stick to their jobs. In various forms, provisions were laid down requiring justices of the peace to deal with workers who gave up before their terms expired without giving due notice, or who took on piece-work but did not complete it within a prescribed time. One instance had been in the Statute of Artificers, which empowered the justices to incarcerate various categories of workers for a month for failing to meet duration or piece-work obligations and award a £5 fine recoverable by the master or owner of materials.[99] This was one element in the role that the justices played in overseeing labour. Either the master or the worker could bring complaints to them about failure to fulfil an agreed performance, which could lead to orders against the master, for instance, to pay the wages due or against the servant to terminate his service or to do other work. The penal sanctions, however, were available only against the servant.[100] In the eighteenth century, such provisions affecting non-completion of term or piece had a place in

---

[95] (1795) 6 T.R. 320. But in that situation also there were earlier precedents, see J. L. Barton, 'Contract and *Quantum Meruit*' [1988] *JLH* 48.

[96] *Button* v. *Thompson* (1869) LR 4 CP 330.

[97] He might proceed before a justice under Acts of 1747 and 1766 (20 Geo. II c. 19; 6 Geo. III c. 25); likewise for cruelty or other misuse. For the work actually done, there was an *indebitatus assumpsit*. It had been the view of Lord Mansfield and Lord Ellenborough that the wage could be claimed for the whole period in which the dismissal occurred: *Temple* v. *Prescott* (above, n. 92); *Gandell* v. *Pontigny* (1816) 4 Camp. 375; but that was later doubted: *Archard* v. *Hornor* (1828) 3 Car. & P. 349; *Smith* v. *Hayward* (1837) 1 Ad. & El. 544. The worker could only claim for such consequential damage as he or she might have suffered, which was not necessarily the unpaid wage.

[98] For a pro forma, see *Burn's Justice of the Peace* (20th edn), iv: 245–7.

[99] 5 Eliz. c. 4, s 4. A right to common law remedies was preserved in addition—one early recognition that the relationship was at root contractual.

[100] See 20 Geo. II c. 19 (1747); 6 Geo. III c. 25 (1766); cf. *Ashover* v. *Brampton* (1777), *Burn's Justice* (1805 edn), Servants, xxi: for the maintenance of good morals, Lord Mansfield had held that a master could on his own authority discharge a pregnant maid three weeks before end of annual hiring. The period of imprisonment rose with time to a maximum of three months. For class bias among justices, see e.g. C. A. Conley, *The Unwritten Law* (New York, 1991), 191–9.

the statutes regulating specific trades, such as tailoring, shoemaking, and wool and leather manufacture. Alongside this were more general statutes dealing with a variety of trades or with piecework.

By 1823, Parliament was prepared to piece the older jigsaw together. A bill presented by a Radical MP, Peter Moore, sought to limit the impact of the inherited law on piece-workers, but this alarmed employers and the government sided with them.[101] A new, embracing, Master and Servant Act gave a single justice of the peace power to order a defaulting worker to three months in a house of correction with hard labour.[102] The rambling definition of the types of service covered by the Act came to be treated by the courts as excluding: domestic servants,[103] and so also any partnership between complainant and defendant;[104] any higher form of clerical or management job;[105] and any case where the job was to be carried out by an independent operator in the market. It was read, however, as embracing manual workers. For this legislation there was some greater readiness to include such fringe cases as butty foremen;[106] whereas greater doubts existed over the reach of protective measures such as the Truck Acts.[107] It was accepted by this time that there was no inherent power to order the servant back to the job, any more than the master could be ordered to reinstate a person dismissed without cause;[108] and the Act did not alter the position.[109] Like its predecessors, it was

[101] For the politics of the legislation, see, R. J. Steinfeld, *Coercion, Contract*, 95–101. He notes the support for Moore from G. White and G. Henson, *A Few Remarks on the State of the Laws...for Regulating Masters and Work-People* (1823). Compare the fate of the contemporaneous move to repeal the laws against combination, below Ch. 2 [text at n. 28–40].

[102] 4 Geo. IV c. 34., repealing a good deal of earlier legislation in the process. Soon enough hard labour would mean hours on the treadmill. The question whether the justices could order a whipping lingered on, 11 such orders being made as late as 1857. For details of interpretation of the legislation and its process, see Steinfeld, *Coercion, Contract*, 125–66.

[103] *Kitchen* v. *Shaw* (1837) 6 Ad. & El. 729; Steinfeld, *Coercion, Contract*, 101–4.

[104] C. M. Smith, *Treatise on the Law of Master and Servant* (1852), 303 n. (h).

[105] This boundary line, however, would attract varying opinions in judgments.

[106] Cf. *Hardy* v. *Ryle* (1829) L.J. (M.C.) 118 and *Lancaster* v. *Greaves* (1829) 9 B. & C. 628 with *R* v. *Johnson* (1840) 7 L.J. (N.S.), 25, 26. The modern distinction between employee and independent contractor would be refined from this. In mid-nineteenth century, a major indicator was whether the undertaking was to work exclusively for the master: see e.g. *Sykes* v. *Dixon* (1839) 8 L.J. (N.S.), 102. In *Lawrence* v. *Todd* (1863) 14 C.B. (N.S.), 554, two ship-platers who undertook to complete the hull of a new ship were held to be 'artificers or handicraftsmen' within the Act, even though they were also butty foremen. They could be punished for going off beforehand—'as without some such check [the shipbuilder's] workmen might at any time frustrate all his arrangements' (Erle CJ CP, at 565).

[107] For the Truck Acts, see above, 642–3; also Steinfeld, *Coercion, Contract*, 143–5.

[108] This became the accepted position through decisions in Chancery refusing orders of specific performance: *Clark* v. *Price* (1819) 2 Wils. Ch. 163; *Baldwin* v. *Society for Diffusion of Useful Knowledge* (1838) 9 Sim. 393; accepted as common law in *Branwell* v. *Penneck* (1827) 7 B. & C. 536 and generalized as a principle that such enforcement will not be ordered of a contract for personal services of any kind. But the cases all dealt with higher level employees: Steinfeld, *Coercion, Contract*, 53–7.

[109] The amending Master and Servant Act 1867, however, would do so: s. 9.

designed to provide a short, sharp reprimand which might get manual workers back in harness, and for this the public purse paid the cost of incarceration, rather than the employer.[110] To this end the procedure was much used.[111] On the other hand, if the workers were bound to a contract for months or years, they might find the tribunal ending their service prematurely at the employer's request;[112] or, when the employer opted to keep the contract running, ordering a second term of imprisonment if they still refused to serve.[113] The employer was under no corresponding criminal liability, though he was bound to pay wages that remained outstanding. However, the Act permitted him to abate such a claim in order to bring into account contractual penalties and the like; but to do this was particularly likely to arouse the worker's irritation.[114]

Statistical information about prosecutions under this legislation began to be published from 1858. Before that, evidence has to be extracted from the notebooks of individual justices and other purely local records of proceedings. Douglas Hay has presented an impressive collection of such data. He concludes that, while the use of the 1823 Act and its predecessors varied greatly by area and even between individual magistrates, there was an overall tendency to increase its use as a disciplinary tool against servants, notably in the 30 years from 1820. In this the increasing use of incarceration in the new gaols is noteworthy, apparently running parallel with the increasing severity against them to be found in the common law rulings of the superior courts.[115] Working on the criminal law statistics from 1858, Daphne Simon drew attention to the thousands of prosecutions each year in the 1860s and early 1870s but suggested that masters who used the machinery tended to be fringe competitors struggling to gain or hold any market share.[116] Later research has brought out a more general reliance on this tough

---

[110] Imprisonment had long been a sanction for breach of other contracts, notably debt. But there the recovery action was civil in nature, with the consequence that the creditor had been expected to contribute to the debtor's upkeep in gaol. The confinement of imprisonment to debts of less than £50 by the Debtors Act 1869 was plainly aimed at working-class debtors who might have no property that could be seized by bailiffs for non-payment: see below, 683.

[111] For an instance, see C. Frank, '"He might almost as well be without trial": Trade Unions and the Master and Servant Act—the Warrington Cases 1846–47' (2002) 14(2) *Hist. St. Ind. Rel.* 3–44. See further, below (post 1867).

[112] If wages were due only on completion of the service, they would be wiped out: see above, 645–6.

[113] *R* v. *Barton-upon-Irwell* (1814) 2 M. & S. 329; followed in *Ex p Baker* (1857) 7 E. & B. 697; *Unwin* v. *Clarke* (1866) LR 1 QB 417; *Cutler* v. *Turner* (1874) LR 9 QB 502; despite a contrary decision in *Youle* v. *Mappin* (1861) 30 L.J. (N.S.) MC 234; see M. R. Freedland, *Contract of Employment* (Oxford, 1976), 273–4.

[114] 4 Geo. IV c. 34, s 3.

[115] D. Hay, 'Master and Servant in England', in W. Steinmetz (ed.), *Private Law and Social Inequality in the Industrial Age* (2000), Ch. 10.

[116] D. Simon, 'Master and Servant', in J. Saville (ed.), *Democracy and the Labour Movement* (1974), 160–200.

regimen. Steinfeld shows that by then prosecutions occurred most frequently in the largest centres of industry and trade: Lancashire, Yorkshire, Greater London, and Staffordshire. If one counts the prosecutions by head of population, the concentration was greatest in the north-west midlands from Cheshire and Derbyshire in the north to Herefordshire in the south. Not unexpectedly there was a noticeable correlation: the number of prosecutions reaches a peak at the summit of each trade cycle, hence a couple of times each decade.[117]

Some of the disputes were with individuals, for instance those who went off to a better paying employer without proper notice or those who flared up against the remorseless toil expected of them. Equally, many prosecutions were a response to strike action or go-slows or similar pressure from a well-organized union. The interlinked questions of a stake in the parliamentary franchise and a greater say in labour conditions burst forth after Palmerston's death in 1865. The admission of urban working-class householders to the vote would within a decade lead to abandonment of the summary discipline of servants.[118] From the perspective of the 1850s that prospect still looked distant even though the muscular strength of skilled trade unions, such as the Amalgamated Society of Engineers, was building up.

[117] Steinfeld, *Coercion, Contract*, esp. Ch. 4. See also D. C. Woods, 'The Operation of the Master and Servant Act in the Black Country, 1858–1875' (1982) 7 *Midland Hist.* 109–23.

[118] For repeal of the legislation in 1875, see below, 681–3.

II

The Roots of Collective Action

1. THE CONDITION OF LABOUR

The law had come to see individual service primarily in terms of contract, but as such it was a construct isolated from its context. It largely ignored the role of agreements on work terms that were negotiated collectively, just as it took no direct notice of how, in that case, the result followed from strikes, go-slows, picketing and the like on the side of workers or from lock-outs or work reductions on the side of masters (or in each case because of threats). In the eighteenth century, disruptive activities that were concerned primarily with work conditions had been frequent enough for legislation to be enacted trade by trade conferring criminal law controls over joint action by the workers. And such enactments had been made general by the Unlawful Combinations of Workmen Act 1799 and Combination of Workmen Act 1800.[1] For the most part the disruptions were local and sporadic, in nature not unlike food riots and political protests, with which sometimes they merged.[2] Desperation or indignation would bring about the crisis and some resolution would be hammered out in days, weeks, or months. In the interim the magistrates would struggle to keep order with whatever policing force they could garner. If the protesters became seriously rowdy, they were likely to commit criminal offences against people or property, and those who could be identified could face charges under the general law. So it had been, for instance, in the decade from 1811 with the 'Luddite' protests against wage reductions and cheaper methods that led to machine-breaking by handloom knitters.[3] In addition, the magistrates could require crowds to disperse under their Riot Act powers.[4] If loss of control became a serious threat, the government might send in troops, from the army or the volunteer forces, in order to

---

[1] For which, see below, n. 13.

[2] See J. Stevenson, *Popular Disturbances in England, 1700–1870* (1979), esp. Ch. 6; G. Rudé, *The Crowd in History* (rev. edn, 1992).

[3] F. O. Darvall, *Popular Disturbances in Regency England* (1934); M. I. Thomis, *The Luddites* (Totnes, 1970).

[4] Above, 349–51.

put down the trouble. Afterwards it might commission judges to conduct special trials in the hope that exemplary punishments would be meted out.[5]

The eighteenth century had witnessesd a certain growth of clubs of journeymen set up to provide mutual assistance for members unable to work and the very nature of these associations required some permanence.[6] In this there was plainly some link to the friendly societies and other provident clubs that were becoming more prominent among artisans. So far as there was a distinguishing factor from these other associations, it was likely to be that the members pledged themselves to support industrial action, and if necessary perhaps even to pay those on strike, as well as to give aid to members in need.[7] Through the nineteenth century, the trade union movement would pursue a twin trajectory: towards mutual insurance schemes that would soften the blow of being out of work; and towards the practice of withdrawing labour as a means of winning arguments against employers, a tactic which employers might also adopt by locking out their workers. Union pressure could have a variety of ends: not only to secure wages, hours, or other job conditions, but also to achieve closed shops and demarcations in the types of work undertaken by those with differing skills. Until the late 1880s, unions rarely flourished for long except among workers with skills enough to give them earnings distinctly above the subsistence level that was the lot of the unskilled.[8] It was the ability of the skilled worker to seek better conditions in times of good trade and to resist job and wage cuts in bad that excited particular hostility across the established classes and led to laws against combination—under statute, but with a sturdy bolster of common law.

2. CRIMINAL DISCIPLINE

In the inter-mixed history of crowd protest and mutual precaution which led to trade unions in the modern sense, the focus here is on the development of criminal offences relating to protest-backed demands that terms of work be improved or at least maintained, especially when the workers' conduct was well enough controlled to avoid charges of offences against person or property. For even then

---

[5] As in response to the so-called 'Swing' riots of 1830, where traditional calls by labourers on farms for seasonal charity appeared to degenerate into arson attacks and malicious damage: E. Hobsbawm and G. Rudé, *Captain Swing* (Harmondsworth, 1973).

[6] C. R. Dobson, *Masters and Journeymen* (1980); J. Rule, *The Experience of Labour in Eighteenth-Century Industry* (1981); J. Rule, *The Labouring Classes in early Industrial England 1750–1850* (Harlow, 1986), 255–84.

[7] See the documentary collections, A. Aspinall, *Early English Trade Unions* (1949).

[8] Cf. e.g. the fate of Joseph Arch's National Agricultural Labourers' Union of 1872, which gained 100,000 members at its launch but dwindled away once the market for farmworkers shrank. See E. H. Hunt, *British Labour History 1815–1914* (1981), 256–8.

the authorities and the masters—often enough in close alliance—sought to pick off the protest leaders by putting them in prison to cool off.

There were two bases for the criminal prosecution of those who organized or took part in strikes. One was by deploying the inchoate crime of conspiracy—an offence at common law that was classified as a misdemeanour and therefore triable on indictment with a jury. In a labour confrontation, what was it that groups of workers were prohibited from agreeing together to do? In 1721 the journeymen tailors of Cambridge had been convicted of conspiring to advance their wages.[9] What they had done in their cause remained obscure. The wrong was said to consist in the very act of combining, a notion that might extend to a joint agreement to do something that it would be legal for an individual to do alone.[10] John Orth has shown the tendency, in the few cases that were reported over the ensuing century, to found the crime in the initial getting together, rather than in the consequent action. He demonstrates the decisions about labour activities to be part of a more diffuse willingness to use the notion of criminal conspiracy against plotting that offended the moral sense of judges and jurors—for instance, against traders who formed a price-fixing cartel or together cornered the supply of staple commodities such as corn; or (it was said) against masters who together locked their labour force out in order to impose a cut in wages.[11] However, the trials did not occur until after the combiners had set about their collective activity. So there remained scope enough for later argument about what exactly the scope of conspiracy charges could be.[12]

The second type of prosecution charged a specific offence laid down in statute, as had been provided in the run of trade statutes that were made general by the two Combination Acts enacted in the wartime conditions of 1799 and 1800.[13] While the second of these had smoothed off various barbed edges in the first, together they still provided justices of the peace with a summary weapon with which to deal with the individuals who were planning or activating an aggressive labour

---

[9] (1721) 8 Mod. 10.

[10] For the complexities of the case, see esp. J. V. Orth, *Combination and Conspiracy: A Legal History of Trade Unionism 1721–1906* (Oxford, 1991), 28–31.

[11] Orth, *Conspiracy*, 31–40, discussing in particular, *R* v. *Eccles* (1783) 1 Leach 274 (King's Bench condemning an agreement by tailors to force a competitor or worker out of business); *R* v. *Mawbey* (1796) 6 T.R. 619 (Grose J. insisting that there might be an illegal conspiracy to do what an individual could do lawfully); *R* v. *Salter* (1804) 5 Esp. 125 (Hotham B. condemning journeymen hatters for agreeing to put pressure on a master in order to secure dismissal of one of their members who would not pay a fine to them); *R* v. *Ferguson and Edge* (1819) 2 Stark. 419 (after the repeal of apprentice restrictions in 1813, pressure to secure that a master kept his ratio of apprentices to journeymen at 1:2); but cf. *R* v. *Nield* (1805) 6 East 417. See also above, 314–20, 345–9.

[12] For the issue in mid-Victorian England, see below, 659–64.

[13] 39 Geo. III c. 81, 39 & 40 c. 106. S. and B. Webb, *History of Trades Unionism* (1894), 57–62; I. Prothero, *Artisans and Politics in Early Nineteenth Century London* (1979), Ch. 9.

dispute.[14] The Acts had drawn inspiration from the specific trade statutes,[15] and they were part of that lineage of enactments which gave local magistrates power over both piece- and time-workers who failed to complete their duties and which, as we have seen, would gain more extensive form in the Master and Servant Act 1823.[16] The Combination Acts were one response of a nervous government which suspected Jacobin sympathizers at every workbench and cloth-machine; and which was prepared to put their opponents on show trials for seditious and blasphemous libel, or sometimes even for treason. Another reaction had been to require justices to inspect local friendly societies in order to discover whether they fomented political dissidence or collected money not just for the protection of workers put out of a trade but for the conducting of strikes and other joint action by labour.[17] This twin potential of associations of journeymen—the emergent trade unions—was by then plain enough and threatening to boot.

The Combination Act 1799 had made it a summary offence, triable by a single magistrate and punishable by up to two months with hard labour in a bridewell or three months in a common gaol, for workmen to contract or combine for various ends: advancing wages, reducing or altering hours of work, decreasing the quantity of work, preventing the employment of any person whom the employer considered proper, or 'controlling or in any way affecting any person carrying on manufacture, trade or business, in the conduct or management thereof'.[18] There was an outer range of charges covering, for instance, attending trade union meetings or inducing others to join, supporting those who engaged in the illegal conduct, and managing the funds of illegal unions. The revision of 1800, instigated by a group of gentlemen radicals, had applied the same offences to combinations of masters, making them liable to fines up to £20, though not to imprisonment.[19] Some token towards workers' interests was thus offered, supposedly to redress an obvious imbalance.[20] The definitions of some illegal acts were revised so as to require the defendant to have acted 'wilfully and maliciously'. Cases had to be heard by two justices and no master in the

---

[14] An indictment for conspiracy before a superior court could be couched in terms of conduct that was unlawful under the statute in question; that left unanswered whether the extent of punishment could be greater than that laid down in the statute in issue.

[15] Legislation relating to London tailors, and then to weavers, hatmakers and many other clothing trades, Spitalfields silk weavers and papermakers was enacted, and in some cases revised, between 1720 and 1796. The growth is detailed by Orth, *Combination*, Ch. 2.

[16] See above, 646–9.

[17] Friendly Societies Act 1793, 33 Geo. III c. 54.

[18] Section 2. The proposal had originally been a bill to cover millwrights, but it was made general upon the motion of the chief scourge of the slave trade, William Wilberforce.

[19] Section 17.

[20] Prosecutions of masters were, however, virtually unknown.

trade in question could sit as a magistrate.[21] The 1800 Act not only gave a right of appeal to Quarter Sessions but it restored examination of the record by *writ of certiorari* from King's Bench.[22] It also introduced a scheme for the arbitration of labour disputes.[23] For all the modifications, the 1800 Act still gave powers which allowed swift redress against journeymen and others while they were still planning collective pressure as much as when they moved into action, and the objectives that they were not permitted to pursue encompassed the whole range of concerns that could divide masters in private enterprise from their hands.

In this form the Combination Acts were still in effect in 1820. What evidence there is of their use shows that they were resorted to strategically—for instance, against weavers in Scotland (1812) and Bolton (1817), then against spinners in Manchester (1818).[24] Dorothy George's argument that the Acts were nothing more than a generalization of earlier statutes and had little impact in practice has not attracted support from most later scholars.[25] Partly this was because many strikes of the period involved rioting or violence to others or to property, often pursued by guerrilla tactics, which could therefore be prosecuted as such; and partly, because in an era before organized police forces, it was often difficult to secure evidence that the individuals arrested were responsible for the harm that they were then accused of. The two Combination Acts were there for summary prosecution of those caught in the business of setting up labour organizations and those who conducted a relatively orderly strike.

The first major alteration of these Combination Acts came in 1824, hard on the heels of the Master and Servant Act, newly toughened in the previous year. While in that instance, the faction demanding controls over workers had won the day, in the case of combination, the radicals did at first secure a very considerable measure of liberalization. As Orth has shown, the political contredances leading to the two enactments intermingled with one another.[26] The radical, Joseph Hume,

---

[21] Sections 2, 16, 23. The problem over JPs who were local masters was particularly acute in the more remote manufactures of the Midlands and North: (see Vol. XI, Part 3, Ch. XIII. 1).

[22] Section 13.

[23] Sections 18–22. At the same period, a scheme which differed in some respects from these was introduced for cotton workers by two Acts of 1800 and 1804, see J. A. Jaffe, 'Industrial Arbitration, Equity and Authority in England, 1800–1850' (2000) *L & HR*, pp. 18, 525–58. None of these attempts to provide industrial arbitration with a framework for negotiation and enforcement would prove to have direct effect, but voluntary arrangements for arbitration would grow in frequency through the new century: see below, 667–8.

[24] S. and B. Webb, *History of Trade Unionism* (2nd edn, 1920), 80–5.

[25] In 'The Combination Acts Re-considered' (1927) *Econ. J. (Econ. Hist. Supp.)* 214 she asserted that the general legislation was a consolidation of some 50 trade statutes. The real tally for England was much smaller: Orth, *Conspiracy and Combination*, 77–8, App. II.

[26] Orth, *Conspiracy*, 68–82; and see I. Prothero, *Artisans and Politics in Early Nineteenth-Century London* (1979), Ch. 9; M. Chase, *Early English Trade Unionism: Fraternity, Skill and the Politics of Labour* (Aldershot, 2000).

closely seconded by Francis Place, steered a large Commons Committee through arguments for repeal of the laws against combination. In this they deployed the conceptual tenets of Ricardian market freedom to new ends.[27] The free market for labour must determine wages and hours; but legal prohibitions against combination amounted to a distortion of that market which provoked workers into strike action and owners into lock-outs.[28] In their eyes, if the labour market was left to itself, wages and conditions would reach their inevitable level. Collective action, whether by lock-out or strike, would have no effect. Once this was understood, disruptive action would fade away, as would the clandestine attacks on people and property that were a mark of so much brooding protest in the period.

The Committee heard a large volume of evidence, and it accepted Hume's brief list of resolutions. Thereupon Hume presented a bill for repeal of the two Combination Acts and the preceding legislation covering different trades, and it made wide-ranging exceptions to common law conspiracy. It was enacted without opposition and with notable despatch.[29] It appeared to leave summary prosecution open only in marginal cases, which were specified as injury to person or property and other threats and intimidation aimed at persons who refused to participate in the claims relating to wages, hours, and management of work.[30] It was a very different weapon from the catch-all net of the Combination Acts.

The 1824 Act was rapidly displaced by another Act in 1825 that was allied in its thrust to the Master and Servant Act 1823; and so the liberal radicals lost a second time.[31] The cause was the sudden upturn in trade which gave workers a platform for new demands. These were pursued in a succession of strikes and Lord Liverpool's government switched tack.[32] Huskisson, President of the Board of Trade, set up a new parliamentary inquiry which investigated particular trades in seven districts, as well as receiving long petitions from workers. Its report led to the new legislation, which would remain in position until the 1870s with very little alteration. It did not attempt any reversion to the position in 1800, but it sought an adjustment which recognized 'the rights of capital'.[33] Its most striking

---

[27] Above, 629–33.

[28] This radical argument was carried by the economist, J. R. McCulloch, into the 1840s when it was accepted, for instance, by J. S. Mill: see M. Curthoys, *Government, Labour and the Law in Mid-Victorian Britain* (Oxford, 2004), 26.

[29] 5 Geo. IV c. 95, ss 2, 3; for the legislation that it repealed, see Orth, *Conspiracy*, App 2. Note also the Seamen's Arbitration Act 1821, 1 & 2 Geo. IV c. 75.

[30] Sections 5, 6.

[31] See above, 653–4.

[32] A. Charlesworth et al., *Atlas of Industrial Protest in Britain 1750–1990* (New York, 1996), Ch. 6: the large cotton strike, spreading out from Blackburn, had to be put down by the army and the arrest of 26 strike leaders, including six women.

[33] Painting the issue in such primary economic colours provoked Thomas Hodgskin's reaction, *Labour Defended against the Interests of Capital* (1825).

aspect was its division of the objectives of collective labour actions into those that were acceptable and those that were not. At the same time, it placed greater constrictions on the means that were used to win the dispute.

The latter came first. The summary offences relating to collective action were re-written in encompassing terms laid down in section 3.[34] The three categories of liability may be summarized as:

(i)   forcing any workman to depart from his hiring, or to return his work before it was finished; or preventing any workman from entering into any employment;

(ii) forcing or inducing any such person to belong to any club or association or to contribute to any funds or pay any fines;

(iii) forcing any manufacturer, or person carrying on any trade or business, to make any alteration in his mode of conducting it or to limit the number of his apprentices or the number or description of his workmen.[35]

The range of these activities, particularly those falling into the ill-defined third category, was to some degree qualified. In each case the act had to be done 'by violence to the person or property of another, or by threats or intimidation, or by molesting or in any way obstructing another'—a phrase that inevitably would be fought over according to inclination and interest.

Secondly, workers and employers were given explicit exemptions from any criminal liability for certain actions. In the case of workers, they were permitted to discuss and reach agreement about their own wages and hours, as were employers concerning the wages and hours they would offer.[36] These were the acceptable objectives and were being isolated in contradistinction to anti-competitive aims, such as insistence on apprentice limitations, demarcation of skilled work, objection to new machinery, employment of non-union men, or the requirement that all hands abjure union membership. In this the 1825 Act at least continued the shift from the prohibitions on the very formation of associations under the old Combination Acts. It was noteworthy, however, that the exemption from liability related only to workers and employers who fostered their own interests over wages and hours. Masters already feared the intervention of outside organizers with plans to coordinate action in ways which local associations of men were

---

[34] The maximum penalties were made the same as under the Master and Servant Act: imprisonment for three months with or without hard labour.

[35] 6 Geo. IV c.129. The drafting neatly avoided any reference to combination among those who committed the offence, and it defined those affected by the illegal behaviour under (i) and (ii) in wide terms. Aiders, abettors, and assisters were equally liable: see R. Y. Hedges and A. Winterbottom, *The Legal History of Trade Unionism* (1930), 38–40; cf. Orth, *Conspiracy*, 86–90.

[36] 6 Geo. IV c. 129, ss 4, 5.

unlikely to achieve. Their activities related to the employment of their members, rather than themselves, and so were very likely to remain criminal.

One root issue continued to be the common law crime of conspiracy to restrain trade. The 1824 Act had largely abolished this form of offence, but in its turn that Act was repealed in 1825. There are signs enough that Members of Parliament and others were assuming that conspiracy as an indictable crime was accordingly restored, for the judges to make what they would of it in future.[37] The exemption allowing group action concerning wages and hours in the 1825 Act was permitted not only to workers but also to masters. In relation to the latter the exemption made no sense unless their acts were otherwise criminal. Since they were not liable for specified summary offences in the same way as workers, the only charges that could be lifted from their shoulders must have been at common law. In the debate Lord Eldon gave an equivocal assurance that conspiracy indictments were not contemplated by the Act, and would not be permitted; but that was a purely political undertaking.[38]

3. COMBINATION UNDER THE 1825 ACT

In 1832, a group of Lancashire miners were campaigning to have the employer's agent sack seven others at the colliery and gave notice of their intention to withdraw their labour in 14 days if he failed to act. They were charged on indictment, first, for conspiring to intimidate the agent in his trade and with preventing the targetted workmen from continuing; and, secondly, with conspiring to injure the owners and to compel them to discharge the men: *R* v. *Bykerdike*.[39] The counts were not drawn by reference to illegal acts under the 1825 statute but were framed as charges of common law conspiracy in a non-specific sense. Perhaps it was uncertain that a conspiracy charge based on section 4 conduct would allow the court to impose a longer sentence than the three months' imprisonment in the Act; perhaps the object was to ensure that evidence against each man could be used against the others; perhaps the case was a test of the separate scope of conspiracy. Patteson J. directed the jury that the 1825 Act was 'never intended to empower workmen to meet and combine for the purpose of dictating to a master whom he should employ' and that to do so was to overstep the bounds of the exemption in section 4. Such conduct amounted to a conspiracy at common law. The jury duly convicted. The sweeping tone of the judge's direction was a precursor of much that superior court judges would say about labour pressure when it surfaced in both criminal prosecutions and civil actions later in the century.

---

[37] Hedges and Winterbottom, *Trade Unionism*, 39, 42.

[38] For Eldon's position, see G. Wallas, *Life of Francis Place* (1918 edn), 239.

[39] (1832) 1 M. & Rob. 179.

This inherent potential, however, would lie dormant for two decades—a time which, particularly in the continuing depression of 1835–42, demonstrated the extreme harshness of conditions in the new industries and their towns. In the second quarter of the nineteenth century, skilled workers generated more stable unions of labour, partly devoted to the benefit functions of providing against unemployment, sickness, and retirement, and partly to negotiating terms and conditions with masters individually or through their own associations.[40]

At the same time, the propertied lived in fear of dangerous disruptions to their lives. The 'Swing riots' of arson and destruction during 1830 made claims for better treatment of farm workers in the southern countryside, urban rioting accompanied the demands for franchise reform, and at that juncture the Grand National Consolidated Trades Union won members and attracted considerable publicity but only for a short while. The GNCTU was founded by Robert Owen, the apostle of industrial collaboration, in association with John Docherty and other London activists. When its ideas reached labourers in Tolpuddle, Dorset and they were sworn secretly into a branch society, the local justices (on Melbourne's advice) had them indicted under the Illegal Oaths Act 1797.[41] Baron Williams then sought to make an example of them by sentences of seven years' transportation;[42] but—famously in the annals of trade union history—that made them martyrs and most of them had to be let home from New South Wales after a relatively short term.[43] Disgruntlement with the political settlement contained in the first Reform Act would lead on to the Chartist movement which at some stages planned and even carried out violent demands for the six democratic elements of its Charter; there would be rowdy protests against the New Poor Law and the orders of its 'Three Bashaws' of Somerset House. Anti-Corn Law demonstrations would flare up in the cyclical downturns of trade such as provoked the spiralling strikes across the Midlands and the North in 1842.[44] The spread of regular police

---

[40] A. E. Musson, *British Trade Unions, 1800–1875* (1972) stresses this consolidatory movement and takes the Webbs to task for an exaggerated account of the influence of the GNCTU: cf. S. and B. Webb, *History of Trade Unionism* (3rd edn, 1920) 119–29; see also Hunt, *Labour History*, 199–208.

[41] This Act (37 Geo. III c. 79), originally aimed at naval mutiny, was expanded in scope by the Seditious Meetings and Assemblies Act 1817, 57 Geo. III c.19, s 25 to cover the administration of any oath not required by law (with certain exceptions). By the later 1820s the authorities were increasingly concerned by the stubborn loyalty induced by oath-swearing among workers and took steps to suppress it of which the Tolpuddle prosecution was just the high point: see Orth, *Conspiracy*, 111–14; M. Lobban, 'Strikers and the Law, 1825–51' (1992), in P. Birks (ed.), *The Life of the Law* (1993), 223–4.

[42] *R v. Loveless* (1834) 1 M. & Rob. 349. Counsel for the prosecution also relied on the 1817 extension, according to this report.

[43] See R. Dickson, 'The Tolpuddle Martyrs: Guilty or Not Guilty' (1986) 7 JLH 178.

[44] Charlesworth, *Atlas of Industrial Disputes*, Ch. 7. The trial of the Chartist leader, Feargus O'Connor and 58 others, for encouraging the strikers to remain out until the political demands of the Charter were met, raised the link that there could be in confrontations over politics and

forces gave some new hope of control, and in various cases the general criminal law enabled the conviction and exemplary sentencing of strike leaders.[45] The Master and Servant Act continued to be deployed by local magistrates in cases where workers were breaking the terms of their contracts.[46]

While utilitarians—Nassau Senior being the most categorical among them—would urge Whig politicians to tighten the impact of the laws against combination in order to underpin free labour markets for what each master and man had to sell, they achieved no change in the legislation.[47] To revert to earlier practices, for instance by restricting the right of appeal to Quarter Sessions, were regarded as invasions of the rights of free Englishmen. Such reactions needed more justification than the assertion of an economic model that rang true only in a certain measure.

In 1845 prosecutors turned again to the Combination of Workmen Act 1825 and the common law. In *R v. Selsby*,[48] a mechanics' union objected to a foundry giving work to outsiders who had not served a full apprenticeship, and the workers picketed the premises in order to tell the interlopers what they thought of them. Twenty-six men, including a union organizer, were indicted for conspiracy to commit offences under the s 3 of the 1825 Act. Baron Rolfe (later Cranworth LC), adopting a tone of moderation, instructed the jury that this required proof that the defendants had made threats leaving their targets in fear of physical violence. It was not 'molestation' or 'obstruction' merely to picket in order to communicate the reasons for action in a peaceful way. The jury found the case made out only in relation to some of the defendants.

Soon enough a less temperate approach appeared. *R v. Hewitt*[49] arose out of a union objection to working with new technology—the use of steam in the production of barrels by coopers. When a member of the Philanthropic Society of Coopers went to work in a mechanized steam workshop for four days, he was fined £10 by the Society. He did not pay, so the other members at his regular mill

labour. In the end, the defendants were discharged on a technicality: see Lobban, 'Strikers and the Law', 225–8.

[45] See, e.g. J. T. Ward, *Chartisim* (1974), Ch. 5.

[46] Employers on the grand scale could also evict strikers from cottages and press local traders not to supply them, as Lord Londonderry did in breaking the strike of the Northumberland and Durham Miners Union in 1844: Webb, *Trade Unionism*, 149–51, 168 and A. J. Taylor 'The Miners' Association of Great Britain and Ireland, 1842–1848: A Study in the Problem of Integration' (1955) 22 *Economica* 52–60.

[47] For these attempts, see Curthoys, *Government, Labour*, 21–9. For the correspondence about labour unrest among the regular communications between magistrates and the Home Office, see Lobban, 'Strikers and the Law'.

[48] (1847) 5 Cox CC 495n.

[49] (1851) 5 Cox CC 162; see further, Orth, *Conspiracy*, 93–5.

demanded his discharge and then withdrew their labour in protest. For this the Society paid them 9 shillings each from the regular contributions of members for mutual benefits. The President of the Society and others were charged on indictment both with combining contrary to the 1825 Act and with conspiracy. Since their actions had disrupted work at their employer's business, this was conduct within the third head of section 3 of the 1825 Act. Even if it was not accompanied by an illegal threat, Campbell CJ QB instructed the jury that there was molestation or obstruction of the employer's business, making this 'one of the most important cases ever brought before a British jury'. When sentencing after the conviction, he pronounced that:

By law every man's labour is his own property, and he may make what bargain he pleases for his own employment; not only so—masters and men may associate together; but they must not by their association violate the law; they must not injure their neighbour, they must not do what would prejudice another man...If this were permitted, not only would the manufacturers of the land be injured, but it would lead to the most melancholy consequences to the working classes.[50]

These were years in which craft unions were growing in scope and permanence. In 1851, the Amalgamated Society of Engineers provided a 'New Model' (as the Webbs enthusiastically labelled it), which enabled skilled workers across the country to represent their interests with some sophistication.[51] Here were the foundations of an 'aristocracy of labour', remunerated more lucratively than unskilled workers.[52] They began to have hopes of improving working conditions by lobbying for new legislation. They could promote their larger goals, such as a share in the parliamentary franchise, by keeping within the terms of the law. Accordingly, in relation to industrial action, they would take prior advice, issue careful instructions and after the event also would fight charges of illegal behaviour vigorously.

This new rigour, to which Lord Campbell was reacting with such perturbation, found expression in the National Association of United Trades, fostered by the Chartist, Ernest Jones. The London-based NAUT was the first major attempt at a general union across regions and crafts since the disappearance of the GNCTU nearly 20 years before. It was directly involved in the greatest legal challenge in this period to the Combination of Workmen Act 1825. The cases of *R v. Duffield* and, four months later, *R v. Rowlands*,[53] concerned workmen employed

---

[50] (1851) 5 Cox CC at 163–4.

[51] S & B. Webb, *History of Trade Unionism* (3rd ed., 1930), Ch. 4.

[52] Just how distinct this division became has been much discussed by labour historians, see, e.g. R. Q. Gray, *The Aristocracy of Labour in Nineteenth-Century Britain* (1981).

[53] (1851) 5 Cox CC 404, 436; see M. Curthoys, *Governments, Labour*, 29–31.

by two related firms of Wolverhampton tinplate manufacturers. The firms used machinery to an extent that local competitors did not. They paid their operatives at lower piece rates than others in the town, apparently claiming that their workshops gave higher productivity. The NAUT helped to mount a campaign for wages closer to the local norm and formed a committee led by Wolverhampton men who were not from either of the works. They met the employers' refusal, at a time of flourishing trade, by convincing three groups of workers to withdraw from the works: those who had been put on exclusive time contracts requiring six months' notice on their side; those who were free to leave their existing employments with the firms; and those who were brought in by the firms from elsewhere (including some from France) but had not taken up their service. Just how they persuaded the imported men to support their action is not altogether clear, but it included, in at least some instances, making weekly payments to them; also getting them drunk and sending them off to other places.

When the strike ended, the outside leaders, from London and Wolverhampton alike, were indicted on wide-ranging counts of unlawfully combining together, most of them formulated by reference to section 3 of the 1825 Act, but a few taking the form of vaguely phrased conspiracies at common law. In the *Rowlands* case, the jury convicted on all counts left to them; and in subsequent proceedings before Queen's Bench, which attacked the drafting of the indictment, the counts as charged and therefore the verdicts were in the main upheld.[54] The NAUT, which proclaimed its intention to act only within legal limits, could derive two broad lessons from this major test. First, the judiciary were likely to take a very hostile view of industrial pressure organized not by the employees themselves (within the confines of section 4), but by outsiders on their behalf (who had no section 4 exemption at all). In sentencing the guilty defendants, Patteson J. described these people as 'volunteers' and said that, if indeed their association had large resources, it was 'of a very dangerous character, and may be used for very bad and very oppressive purposes'.[55] The principal form that a finding of illegality was

---

[54] (1851) 5 Cox CC at 466, Erle J. (also the trial judge in both cases) securing a *nolle prosequi* for two of the defendants against whom he had instructed the jury that the evidence was weak. There is much in the long reports of the trial proceedings which goes to the evidence needed to sustain allegations of conspiracy (see e.g. 432–3, 435). In *Duffield*, not guilty verdicts were returned, following the judge's warning, to the charges of having threatened men with physical violence, which turned on the evidence of one unsatisfactory witness.

[55] At p. 492. Patteson was the judge who had tried Bykerdike and his fellows almost 20 years before: see above, [text at n. 41]. Five of the six received sentences of three months' imprisonment successively on each count that was sustained, which may have amounted to nearly three years in Stafford prison. The judge made it plain that, in sentencing for conspiracy to commit an offence under the 1825 Act, the penalty was not limited to the statutory term of the 1825 Act (at pp. 494–5); cf. Rolfe B. in *Selsby* (1847) 5 Cox CC 496.

likely to take was the intimidation, molestation, or obstruction of the employers in determining what wages they would offer, and these consequences for them could arise not just from the union activators inducing workmen under term contracts to break them, but equally from causing 'the free men' (i.e. it would seem, both those who could give notice that was immediately operative and those strike-breakers who had not yet been taken on) to go off elsewhere.[56] Over the ensuing decade, conspiracy charges would be levelled in less than one case a year, but these cases served to insist that a strike action without violence could amount to an indictable crime. In the many strikes of these years, pickets and organizers were likely to be dealt with before the magistrates under the Master and Servant Acts, where the hostility towards workers' pressure remained marked.[57]

The NAUT was much reduced by its pursuit of the Wolverhampton tin-plate makers. It did, however, keep a small committee going which strove for a statutory limitation on the broad scope given to the 1825 Act offences. Starting with a bill in 1853 it would eventually succeed in securing the enactment of the Molestation of Workmen Act 1859 (as it has become known).[58] This conditioned the impact of the 1825 Act on picketing that was aimed at non-union employees and black-leg interlopers. It was no longer an offence for anyone—not just fellow-employees—to persuade others to cease or abstain from work, provided it was done 'peaceably and in a reasonable manner, without threat or intimidation, direct or indirect'. But in 1867 a large strike and lock-out in the London tailoring trade led to the union leaders being charged with a common law conspiracy to restrain trade. Before the grim eye of Bramwell B., pickets who used abusive language and gestures that would deter ordinary people—'exposing them to have their motions watched and to encounter black looks'—would still be guilty of unlawful 'coercion and compulsion'.[59] That direction to the jury stood alongside other applications of the 1825 Act in the 1860s. It was illegal, where a union member would not toe the line in a demarcation dispute, to send him to Coventry or secure his dismissal.[60] So too was a strike threat aimed at establishing a closed

---

[56] At 462.

[57] See Curthoys, *Governments, Labour*, 35–6, 39–41.

[58] 22 Vict. c. 34. For details of the support from leading legal figures in Parliament, see Orth, *Conspiracy*, 121–7; Curthoys, *Governments, Labour*, 36–8.

[59] *R* v. *Druitt* (1867) 10 Cox CC 59; Curthoys, *Governments, Labour*, 80–3. The common law charge perhaps diverted attention from the 1859 Act. Bramwell used the standard *laissez-faire* denunciations of the day, talking of the 'liberty of mind and freedom of will' of the non-strikers being picketed.

[60] *O'Neill* v. *Longman* (1863) 4 B. & S. 376; Orth, *Conspiracy*, 130–2.

shop by the removal of non-unionists.[61] Nonetheless, to have secured the 1859 Act at all showed that unions were gaining liberal friends in Parliament, Tory as well as Whig. For union leaders, the hope at least glimmered that legislative reform would become the path to improvement in their conditions of labour and life more generally. Certainly by 1860, serious debate about collective pressure in labour relations was reinvigorating the discussions.

At the same time, legal obstacles placed by the courts in the way of unions were becoming more formidable. *Hilton* v. *Eckersley*[62] concerned an agreement between cotton-mill employers in Wigan, which laid down conditions on which they would hire operatives for the next 12 months. They undertook, if necessary, to suspend or close their works, rather than concede to workers' demands. Each gave a bond of £500 against breach and the action sought to recover that amount from the largest millowner when he started to offer wages above the levels set.[63] In the Queen's Bench, Lord Campbell CJ and Crompton J. upheld a plea that the agreement was in restraint of trade and so was void in law. Both agreed that combinations of masters must be treated just as combinations of men. And, said Campbell, if the latter could sue on such a bond it 'would establish a principle upon which the fantastic and mischievous notion of a "Labour Parliament" might be realized for regulating the wages and hours of labour in every branch of trade all over the empire'[64]—the Labour Parliament being a brain-child of Ernest Jones of the NAUT.[65]

Only Erle J., whose role in *Duffield* and *Rowlands* had been even more central than Campbell's, was prepared to uphold the agreement. He maintained a more scrupulous view, which would have important echoes in the later development of the tort of conspiracy: an agreement whose purpose was to protect the common interests of a group, rather than to injure the person or group being targeted, was to be regarded as enforceable provided that their own interests were not in

---

[61] *Walsby* v. *Anley* (1861) 3 E. & E. 516 (concerning the attempt by building employers to require their workers to sign 'The Document' foreswearing union membership); *Shelbourne* v. *Liver* (1866) 13 LT (NS) 630; *Skinner* v. *Kitch* (1867) 10 Cox CC 493.

[62] (1855) 6 E. & B. 47.

[63] The practice had been treated as customary by Adam Smith, *Wealth of Nations* (1776, ed. R. H. Campbell and A. S. Skinner, Oxford, 1976), 158.

[64] (1855–6) 6 E. & B. at 65–6.

[65] In 1854 the 'Labour Parliament' had assembled in Manchester to hammer out a set of resolutions that belonged 'more to 1834 than 1854': J Saville, *Ernest Jones: Chartist* (1952), App. 4; see also M. Taylor, *Ernest Jones: Chartism, and the Romance of Politics 1818–1869* (Oxford, 2003), 174. In the *Hilton* case, Crompton J. went further and pronounced the agreement illegal in the sense of being a conspiracy chargeable on criminal indictment because it compromised the liberty of each participant to conduct his business in the manner that he chose from time to time. To this proposition Lord Campbell would not accede, and the Exchequer Chamber gave it no encouragement.

themselves illegal. When the case was taken to the Court of Exchequer Chamber, it accepted the majority view. To the rest of the judges Erle's position was quite unacceptable, since it implied that a union of workers 'could sue any workmen who might have been seduced by some designing person to sign an engagement with penalty to continue in the strike as long as a majority were for holding out'.[66] So equally, the masters' bonds had to be regarded as unenforceable.

In the years preceding, the superior courts had refused to apply the doctrine of restraint of trade to one-sided work contracts so as to exempt workers or their subsequent employers from liabilities.[67] Now they used the same doctrine with vigour in tackling the conundrum posed by the very notion of liberty to contract: contracts in which groups of people surrendered their future freedom of action over employment were to be treated as void. While the Exchequer Chamber refrained from upholding Crompton's view that the proposed conduct was criminal, the contract was one 'by which the obligors agree to carry on their trade, not freely as they ought to do, but in conformity to the will of others' and that is what made it 'contrary to public policy'.[68]

The consequences for trade union activity of this root preference for preserving freedom of future action would be brought home in the next decade. At common law a person could not be guilty of larceny or embezzlement by making off with property that he owned jointly with others. That created difficulties for fund-collecting associations of many kinds, when their treasurers defalcated. In 1855, friendly societies were given an exception to this rule, provided that they were registered with the Registrar of Friendly Societies and that they were 'established...for any purpose which is not illegal'.[69] Several trade unions that held benefit funds for members obtained registration and, so they believed, the ability to prosecute defaulting treasurers. However, in *Hornby* v. *Close*,[70] the Court of Queen's Bench, led formidably by Lord Cockburn CJ QB and Blackburn J., held the Boilermakers Society unable to rely on this provision. Their rules, requiring members to lend their support to strikes and other industrial action, rendered the union 'illegal'.[71] Whatever the position of a masters'

---

[66] Alderson B., (1856) 6 E. & B. at 76–7.

[67] See above, 636, n. 45.

[68] (1856) 6 E. & B. at 76.

[69] 18 & 19 Vict. c. 63, s 24.

[70] (1867) LR 2 QB 153; Curthoys, *Governments, Labour*, 68–73; J. McIlroy, 'Financial Malpractice in British Trade Unions: The Background to, and Consequences of, *Hornby* v. *Close*' (1998) 6 Hist. St. in Ind. Rlns.

[71] Even the Amalgamated Society of Carpenters and Joiners, which had rules carefully drawn to avoid directly restrictive obligations on members, received the same treatment: *Farrer* v. *Close* (1869) LR 4 QB 602. But there two members of the court dissented.

association might be under the criminal law, labour unions that required members to go on strike, or join in demarcation disputes or obstructive picketing or the disciplining of other members, were formed to organize conduct punishable under the 1825 Act.

This was the sense in which trade unions were to be treated as in illegal restraint of trade. As we shall see, it would be on the basis of this characterization that new legislation after 1867 would be framed in order to ameliorate their position. In the event there was sharp reaction to the severity of the *Hornby* decision. In the parliamentary session of 1868, Russell Gurney, Recorder of London, secured an Act which removed the embargo against charges of larceny and embezzlement between co-owners;[72] and the Trade Unions Funds Protection Act of the following year gave them back the ability to bring summary prosecutions against defaulting officers, relying on the Friendly Societies Act 1855. When another union treasurer was prosecuted on indictment for embezzling funds, his counsel argued that the 'illegality' of the union because of its restraint of trade rules rendered those activities in themselves *criminal* and that the defendant therefore could not be prosecuted. Cockburn CJ roughly rejected these pleas. Restraint of trade simply made the union's rules void as a matter of civil liability.[73] The hostility against the only effective forms of pressure on the workers' side, widely shared in the propertied classes and voiced firmly by most judges in the 1860s, was beginning to moderate itself in the new political atmosphere.

For the continuing legal story, it is important to set out the major arguments as they developed because they continue to provide structures in all that would follow. But they are only one element in the widespread concern over the future of the union movement at the same historical juncture. Such was the flux of attitudes that the emergence of scandal was likely to inflame sensitivities; and that is just what occurred. In the autumn of 1866, as the country was facing up to suffrage reform, a set of outrages in the building trades of Sheffield, Manchester, and elsewhere became the subject of hot debate. Reports of violence and property deprivations between different organized groups were capped out by the explosion of a building in Sheffield which proved to be behaviour that harked back

---

[72] It was immediately deployed against the treasurer of the London bricklayers union: *R* v. *Blackburn* (1868) 11 Cox CC 157.

[73] *R* v. *Stainer* (1870) 11 Cox CC 483; see Orth, *Conspiracy*, 104–6. Cockburn had sat in *Hornby*; but he had before that recognized the plight, if not the right, of working men, in seeking to improve their conditions of work: see *Walsby* v. *Anley*, above, n. 61. See also *Wood* v. *Bowron* (1866) LR 2 QB 21 in which he demanded clear evidence that, where workers stopped work without any breach of contract, their conduct was taken by the master to be a threat (in this case to secure that he reduce his number of apprentices).

to labour rivalries of a half-century before.[74] The new craft unions of engineers, carpenters and joiners, ironfounders, shoemakers, and others, needed to distance their own propriety and responsibility from such antics. In the upshot, the Royal Commission—which the government immediately set up to investigate the outrages—would expand into a full-scale investigation of the legal framework within which unions could operate both their benefit schemes and their industrial pressure activities. The Commission's Final Report in 1869, despite the differences of opinion that it displayed, accordingly provides the starting point for the final Chapter of this Part.

[74] See S. Pollard, *The Sheffield Outrages* (1971); and for the growth of unionism in the building trades, see R. Price, *Masters, Unions and Men* (Cambridge, 1980), esp. Chs 1–3.

III

Law and Organised Labour 1867–1914

1. POLITICAL CONCESSIONS AND CONSTRAINTS ON LABOUR: THE ERLE COMMISSION

At the moment of the second Reform Act, effective trade unionism was largely confined to the higher levels of manual workers, who had skills enough to command relatively good wages and to press claims both for better working conditions and for a degree of security against bad times. Union membership still fell far short of that for friendly societies in general, but the numbers would grow through the buoyant years of Gladstone's first government, declining only with the depression that became marked after 1874.[1]

A range of voluntary arrangements under which groups of workers could meet to negotiate with their employer or employers had been growing as unions spread across craft trades. As Jaffe suggests, the real roots of voluntarism in collective labour relations were being established through these experiments.[2] The mid-century decades then saw a certain growth in formal mechanisms for arbitration of labour disputes. There was increasing discussion, for example, of the work of Judge Rupert Kettle, who was appointed in 1859 to the Wolverhampton County Court. He then devoted much time to persuading the two sides of industries across the Midlands and North to set up arbitration schemes for industrial disputes, not just of grievances arising out of existing employment conditions but also of arguments over future conditions—questions of interest as distinct from questions of right.[3] To the Erle Commission he offered the reassurance that, despite the unenforceability of an arbitration award, in most cases it was accepted and acted on.[4] Equally, the leading hosiery employer in Nottingham, A. J. Mundella MP,

---

[1] Union membership in the country was not reliably recorded before the 1890s: see below, 679.

[2] Jaffe, *Striking a Bargain*, Chs 3, 4.

[3] See e.g. Lord Amulree, *Industrial Arbitration in Great Britain* (1929), Ch. 7; D. Brodie, *History of British Labour Law* (Oxford, 2003), 77–83; M. J. Klarman, 'The Judges versus the Unions: The Developments of British Labor Law 1867–1913' (1989) 75 *Virginia LR* 1487–1602.

[4] *RC on Trades Unions, 11th and Final Report, PP* 1868–9 [4123], xxxi, 1. For the 10 previous reports of evidence, *PP* 1867, xxxi; 1867–8, xxxix. Separate reports examined the outrages in Sheffield and Manchester, *PP* 1867, xxxii, 397; 1867–8, xxxix, 571.

had established a conciliation and arbitration board for the industry there and
was a prominent exponent of its advantages, for instance, at the first meeting of
the Trades Union Congress in 1868 and before the Erle Commission.[5] These practical examples bolstered the belief of radical liberals that the market for labour
should no longer be kept free for masters and men individually to make their
own choices. Instead it was accepted that collective pressures were inevitable,
particularly from workers, since they lacked the means otherwise of generating
real dialogue about employment terms.

The Law should therefore be used to foster negotiation between masters and men,
not to quash collective action by either side. Indeed the one-time Lord Chancellor,
St Leonards, promoted a Councils of Conciliation Act in 1867 itself.[6] It provided
for Councils to be licensed by the Home Secretary on the petition of masters and
workmen in a trade, and then for annual elections to the body by an electorate
specially defined. It is little wonder that industries showed no interest in such
cumbersome mechanisms, but the very fact of its enactment was symptomatic
of a belief that industrial relations could be improved only by cooperation, not
by hostile subjugation.[7] The new mood drew not only upon economic argument
of a novel kind but also from religious idealism, such as that of the Christian
Socialists, and from evolutionary philosophies—notably the social positivism of
Auguste Comte.[8]

The Royal Commission on Trades Unions was appointed by Derby's government in 1867 and reported to Gladstone's in 1869.[9] It had as its Chairman, Sir
William Erle, recently retired as Chief Justice of Common Pleas, together initially
with four senior officials and two members of each House of Parliament. After
demands from the group of craft union leaders, a leading supporter, Frederic
Harrison—Comteian positivist at Oxford—was added,[10] but no union member found a place. Harrison would work particularly with Robert Applegarth,
leader of the Amalgamated Society of Carpenters and Joiners (ASCJ), and
the other union leaders, whom the Webbs christened the Junta.[11] He and two

---

[5] Fox, *History and Heritage*, 130–1; Curthoys, *Governments, Labour*, 90–3; B. C. Roberts, *The Trades Union Congress 1868–1921* (1958), 48.

[6] See also the *SC (Commons) on Masters and Operatives (Equitable Councils of Conciliation)*, *PP* 1856, xiii, 11.

[7] There had been ineffective precursors of this Act in 1800 and 1825 (39 & 40 Geo. III c. 106; 5 Geo. IV c, 96). In 1872 an Arbitration (Masters and Workmen) Act was passed, which provided that where there was a collective agreement for arbitration, it was to be given preference over court proceedings; but only for 21 days, unless the two sides agreed an extension.

[8] See above, Vol. XI, pp. 101–6.

[9] Above, n. 4. For the Commission's recommendations and the consequences, see generally, Curthoys, *Governments, Labour*, Ch. 4; Brodie, *British Labour Law*, Ch. 1.

[10] In this radical viewpoint, he was joined by Spencer Beesly and other members of Wadham College. On these positivists, see R. Harrison, *Before the Socialists* (1965), Ch. 6.

[11] S. and B. Webb, *History of Trade Unionism* (1894, with editions to 1920), Ch. 5.

others produced a Minority Report, which would have considerable impact.[12] Nonetheless it was 'the old, old story...the wolves sitting on a commission inquiring into the benefits and promotion of the sheep interests', complained George Potter's *The Bee-Hive* on the behalf of the massed flock in the fold. Erle, by the standards of the judiciary rather more shearer than butcher,[13] nonetheless used a firm cut in the paper on trade union law that he wrote for the inquiry.[14] In it he claimed a central role for the courts as adjudicators of the line between acceptable and unacceptable behaviour in labour disputes and in the internal management of trade unions.

Ten volumes of evidence would be published and eventually the bulk of Commissioners joined him in a Majority Report that followed the prescriptions of classical political economy.[15] Strikers who engaged in any action beyond the confines fenced in by the Combination Acts should remain subject to punishment. Moreover, a union should not be rendered legal if it engaged in those unacceptable restrictive practices identified in the 1825 Act—action to limit apprenticeships, new machinery, piecework, and sub-contracting. So too for any union that had rules requiring or assisting members to take part in strikes and other industrial action. All these objectives and activities opposed the freedoms of other individuals—for instance, that of masters to conduct their trade as they wished and that of non-union labour to take jobs. As Erle chose to put it, 'the law, if wisely made and properly administered, maintains truth, kindness and health and so among other things help persons of honest industry to obey each his own will'.[16] Accordingly, only unions that did not have such objects, but were either pure benefit societies or associations which kept any ability to organize industrial action out of their rules, would be entitled to the legal protection given to friendly societies. It did not appear feasible to split unions up into separate associations for 'benefit' and 'trade' purposes; but the Majority insisted that the financial accounts for the two objectives should be kept separate. Their Report did not, however, go as far as strict opponents were seeking. Unions would not

---

[12] For the political relationships of the Junta and the establishment of an annual Trades Union Congress at Manchester in 1868, see Roberts, *Trades Union Congress*, Ch. 1; McCready, 'Britain's Labour Lobby, 1867–75' (1956) 22 *Canadian J. Economic & Political Science* 149.

[13] He had presided over the Wolverhampton trials in 1853 but dissented in *Hilton* v. *Eckersley*, see above, 660–4.

[14] Circulated to the Commission in 1868, he published it as *The Law Relating to Trade Unions* (1869). For the positions taken on the subject by Conservatives and Liberals during the 1868 election and for subsequent jockeying to influence the Erle Commission, see Curthoys, *Governments, Labour*, 93–7.

[15] Royal Commission on Trade Unions, above, n. 4.

[16] See Erle's Memorandum to the Royal Commission in its Final Report (above, n. 4), at p. lxvi.

be required to register; and their officers and members would not be subject to criminal penalties if they sought to impose restrictive industrial practices.[17]

The Minority, made up of Harrison, Thomas Hughes MP, the Christian socialist and author, and the maverick Earl of Lichfield, started from radical assumptions.[18] They espoused the new economic perceptions of labour relations: trade unions were necessary bodies in the pursuit of better conditions for the workers who made up the great bulk of the population. They deserved to be given greater legal freedom to back their causes with combined action. Through that alone could they acquire muscle to stand up to capitalist employers, who could engage with impunity in mutual wage-fixing, the blacklisting of union men and resistance to demands for closed shops. The Minority accordingly called for repeal of the combination laws, the Master and Servant Act (even in its 1867 version[19]), and removal of the restraint of trade objections to the legality of unions in civil law. As to the last of these, the view that the ruling made in *Hornby* v. *Close* should be reversed had reasonably wide support. As already noted, legislation giving permanent effect to this was enacted in the same year as the Commission's final report.[20]

2. TRADE UNION LEGISLATION IN THE WAKE OF THE ROYAL COMMISSION

The Liberal government needed time to decide how to respond to the Commission's twofold sets of recommendation and to produce draft labour laws, not least because of the continuing influence of the Junta and their collaborators.[21] By 1871 the Home Office had in place a bill that took up the Minority's call for civil status to be conferred upon 'illegal' unions; but—here siding with the Majority—it retained the criminalization of strike activity. In moves to get these counterweight proposals enacted, the government split the two portions into separate Acts, but conceded few amendments to either.

As to legalization, the Trades Union Act 1871 was built upon the premise that by the common law unions with industrial action rules were in unlawful restraint

[17] James Booth, the Commission's secretary, sent round a draft that included these recommendations. They form one measure of the full retentionist case: see Curthoys, *Governments, Labour*, 97–8.

[18] See above, n. 4, at 286–98. Some concessions were needed in order to placate Lichfield.

[19] See below, 689, n. 93.

[20] See above, 665, nn. 74–5.

[21] The flurry of proposals from all sides that followed upon the Report's publication included a pro-union bill promoted by Mundella and Hughes. It was at this point that J. S. Mill, to considerable effect, chose to abandon the Ricardian Wages Fund theory: for which see Curthoys, *Governments, Labour*, 107–12; and for the writings that preceded it by F. D. Longe et al., 76–7. See also Brodie, *British Labour Law*, Ch. 1.

of trade. Unlike friendly societies, therefore, they had no route open to them for suing or being sued in a civil court.[22] The Act prescribed how far these common law rules were to be displaced. In its final form, it made three major changes that were advocated by the Minority of the Royal Commission and accepted by the leaders of the union movement:

(i) By section 3, the Act prevented a trade union's agreements and trusts from being treated as unlawful merely because the union had purposes within the ill-defined doctrine of restraint of trade.[23] 'Merely because' indicated that other grounds of illegality remained untouched, it being left for courts to identify them.

(ii) Section 9, in reinforcing the rights of trustees over a registered union's assets, allowed them to bring or defend legal proceedings 'touching or concerning any property, right or claim to property of the union'.[24] This bore a resemblance to powers that had been conferred on other types of unincorporated association, making their position broadly equivalent to the stage reached in the development of joint trading entities in the 1830s and friendly societies themselves in 1855.[25]

(iii) By section 4, the Act provided that 'nothing in this Act' shall enable the direct enforcement by civil action of certain union rules, which in the main concerned individual members. These were: (a) restrictive agreements between union members concerning sales, business, or employment; (b) agreements between members concerning subscriptions or penalties; and (c) agreements providing for union benefits or for discharging fines. Section 4 only affected unions in illegal restraint at common law, since 'nothing in this Act' was to justify what would otherwise remain unlawful. This would lead to a line of decisions about what rules precisely gave rise to unlawfulness; and then what constituted 'direct enforcement'.[26]

Under section 4, the same exclusion of enforcement applied also to a fourth category: agreements between trade unions. The scope of this exclusion was far from clear. 'Trade union' was defined to cover combinations to regulate relations between workmen and masters, workmen and workmen, or masters and masters.[27] This definition, however, did not state who would do the

---

[22] Cf. Friendly Societies Act 1855, 18 & 19 Vict. c. 63, s 19.

[23] The parallel provision, protecting members of a union from criminal prosecution merely because its purposes were in restraint of trade (s 2), is discussed below, 675, n. 40.

[24] The phrase was construed widely in *Linaker* v. *Pilcher* (1901) 17 TLR 256.

[25] For the position of friendly societies (above, n. 13), from which s 9 derived, see above, 664–5.

[26] See below, 708–10.

[27] Section 23. As originally drafted, a trade union within the Act had to have purposes in illegal restraint of trade, but that limitation was lifted in 1876. The definition, however, continued to exclude

combining, but only what their purposes must be in order to be a union.[28] The question remained whether collective bargains between employer associations and trade unions could ever be legally enforceable.[29] More than that, it would also eventually ground high debate over whether a union was confined by the definition to that list of purposes, other purposes being treated as *ultra vires*.[30]

The clever, but convoluted, drafting was the charge of the rising civil servant, Godfrey Lushington, and it reflected considerable sympathy for the positions of Harrison, Beesley, Crompton, and their union associates. Harrison worked hard to persuade some union leaders that, for fear of antagonistic judges, legal issues involving unions and members should be placed beyond the purview of the courts.[31] As a result unions were not made corporate bodies with full rights and responsibilities as separate legal personalities; and the various pro-hibitions of section 4 were put in place. The exclusion of any direct enforce-ment of the union's own rules was easily denounced by their opponents as a subversion of the rule of law, and this at a time when unions were seeking to stamp out 'class laws' that operated against their members, such as the common employment rule in the law of negligence and the criminal prohibitions of the Master and Servant Act. Their strength of feeling against judicial interference was noteworthy, for they realized well enough that they would be accused of securing themselves a place above the law. This was not some minor deviation from the standard of full and equal legal responsibility, as was, for instance, the limited ouster of court jurisdiction in arbitration agreements, which the courts were generally prepared to accept. It was an exclusion of legal redress that many lawyers and judges, at least, would come to regard as a constitutional solecism shaking the foundations of the liberal state. In the end, no one would express that sense of betrayal more vehemently than the horrified Albert Venn Dicey.[32]

---

partnerships, sales of businesses, agreements for trade instruction, and agreements between an employer and his employees as to the employment.

[28] For amendments in 1876, designed to give trade unions that had no illegal objects the same entitlements as if they were illegal, see below, n. 33.

[29] See further below, 680.

[30] See below, 710–13.

[31] For this stage, see Curthoys, *Governments, Labour*, 118–31, who also deals with the passing intervention against the unions by the law publisher, Edward Cox; the sympathy shown them by J. D. Coleridge, Law Officer and later LCJ (see below, n. 57); and the unsuccessful attempt by the Chancellor of the Exchequer, Robert Lowe, to get rid of the Friendly Societies Registry.

[32] Notably in his attack on the rise of 'collectivism' in *Law and Public Opinion in England in the Nineteenth Century* (2nd edn, 1914), xliii–xlviii; for his views in the late 1860s, however, see Curthoys, *Governments, Labour*, 86.

The Trade Union Act 1871 began a process of securing trade union a degree of recognition in law that legislation and decision had previously denied them. But although the Act conceded immunities and protections that their leaders sought, these would not prevent an agitated judiciary from moving into attack mode when 30 years later they became highly suspicious of the post-1867 compromises. Unions were not required to register as friendly societies and a considerable number did not. Those which did ran a risk that their activities would be treated as limited by a legal requirement that they act primarily as 'trade unions'.[33] But they did gain from registration the entitlement to have trustees who would hold their property in order to exercise rights and defend responsibilities relating to it.

As for non-property obligations arising in contract or tort, it seemed that the union was not an entity that could sue or be sued as such; but the legal position, as for other unincorporated associations without special legislative powers, remained obscure. Already in 1868, Malins VC had decided, in *Springhead Colliery* v. *Riley*, that individual officers and delegates acting for a union or a branch who acted unlawfully could be the subject of an injunction from a court of equity. Members of a cotton spinners' union had withdrawn their labour against a lowering of piece rates, and their 'minders' were warning blackleg labourers not to apply as replacements—conduct which to the Vice-Chancellor involved unlawful threats and intimidation. After granting an interlocutory injunction, he heard full argument upon demurrer as to whether the injunction could be justified as necessary for the protection of 'property' in the form of the employer's goodwill.[34] Accepting that the goodwill generated by a functioning business could have that character, he concluded that the intervention 'will be one of the most beneficial jurisdictions that this Court ever exercised', it being 'to prevent these misguided and misled workmen from committing these acts of intimidation which go to the destruction of that property which is the source of their own support and comfort in life'.[35] Here was the old antagonism to union pressure

---

[33] When J. M. F. Ludlow was appointed Registrar of Friendly Societies he attempted to bring trade union registration under the general regime for those societies, a possible consequence of which might then be that they were confined to benefit activities. He did not succeed; but it was thought advisable to extend the definition of 'trade union' to include associations for regulating labour relations whether at common law they were illegal or legal: Trade Union Act (Amendment) Act 1876, s 16. In 1871, the definition (in s 23) had covered only those that were illegal: Curthoys, *Governments, Labour*, 134–6. The re-definition did not affect the exclusion in the Trade Unions Act 1871, s 4, for certain types of civil action; this continued to relate only to 'illegal' unions: see below.

[34] (1868) LR 6 Eq 551. Lord Eldon had insisted, in *Gee* v. *Pritchard* (1818) 2 Sw. 402, that the protection of property alone justified the grant of an injunction; the mere commission of crime was not enough. As we shall see, the distinction would play a prominent part in the movement, not just by Malins, but more importantly by Jessel MR, to give Chancery judges a roving jurisdiction to stamp on what they conceived to be wrongdoing: below, 864–6.

[35] (1868) LR 6 Eq 551, at 562–3.

finding new deployment. It would take another three decades to show its full power, but the union's lawyers, who included W. P. Roberts, must have appreciated something of its potential.

As to criminal sanctions against labour pressure, the Master and Servant Act and the combination laws expressed a one-sided hostility and the Minority Report of 1869 called for their repeal.[36] If labour troubles spilled into physical attacks on people or property, or threats of them, why could not the general offences laid down in the criminal law be applied to them? If the main advantage of the special laws was summary trial, why should the less serious general offences not become triable either on indictment or summarily? The prospect attracted some radical support, but it was an argument too far, flying in the face of traditions that marked the legal limits of working-class behaviour, situation by situation.[37] The main preoccupation of the reformers was therefore with curbing the full scope of the special laws.

The Criminal Law Amendment Act 1871 re-stated in broadly similar terms the wrongful types of conduct aimed at disruptive trade consequences that had been prohibited in 1825. So far as the key triggers of liability to punishment were concerned—violence, threats, intimidation, molestation, and obstruction—there were only moderate efforts at clearer definition in s 1. To be criminal, violence, threats, and intimidation had to be enough to justify a justice's order binding a person to keep the peace—not a standard notably more confined than before. As to molestation and obstruction, there was now a list of activities falling within the concepts: persistent following; hiding tools or hindering their use; and (going to the crucial question of picketing), watching or besetting a house or workplace, or, where three or more were involved, following someone in the street in a disorderly manner.[38] Even the small comfort zone of the Molestation of Workmen Act 1859 disappeared.[39]

Yet section 1 of the Criminal Law Amendment Act 1871 contained a proviso: 'No person shall be prosecuted for doing, or conspiring to do, any act beyond

---

[36]   Above, n. 18 .

[37]   See Curthoys, *Governments, Labour*, 147–52.

[38]   The union leaders were greatly concerned about these definitions as the bill moved through Parliament, gaining breadth in the process—particularly with a Lords' amendment that removed any minimum number of persons from the prohibition on 'watching and besetting': Curthoys, *Governments, Labour*, 153–60. For a clause disqualifying a magistrate who was a master or a relation of a master in the trade, see Orth, *Conspiracy*, 81, 141.

[39]   Nonetheless there were judges who accepted that this language left scope for peaceful pickets who only communicated the demands of the men on strike, and did not begin upon jeering and threatening the free labour that took on the work in their place: see e.g. the decision of the Recorder of Bolton and later the charge of Russell Gurney, Recorder of London, to the grand jury which sent the defendants to trial in *Hibbert* (below, n. 45): Curthoys, *Governments, Labour*, 146–7, 160.

those covered in Section 1, on the ground that such act restrains or tends to restrain the free course of trade.[40] Did it nonetheless remain illegal under statute to molest or obstruct a master with a view to coercing him to alter the mode of carrying on his business? If so, calling a workforce out on strike, or joining in by peaceful picketing, could still be treated as criminal. The new Act came into effect at a time of economic buoyancy, when unionization was strengthening and spreading—even for a short while into agriculture. In this atmosphere, a judicial hammer-blow was delivered. In *R* v. *Bunn*,[41] Brett J. (later Viscount Esher MR) accepted not just conspiracy charges under the statute but counts at common law which related to conduct that did not fall within the statutory definitions. Dilley had worked at one station of the largest London gas supplier, the Gas Light and Coke Co, but was sacked because he was the representative of the Amalgamated Gas Stokers Society—a new phenomenon in the industry. After secret preparations, he and other agents of the union brought the day-shift at the Beckton works out on strike, just as it was due to go on shift. Since their contracts required a week's notice, the men were in breach and also liable to prosecution under the Master and Servant Act 1867. As the judge emphasized to the jury, the GLCC did not have the technology to store much gas and had no real chance to find other workers at once, given that union stokers also came out at other plants.

The GLCC did win the struggle, partly through bringing in non-union men (a costly business) and also by linking pipelines to those of other suppliers. But the confrontation demonstrated how public expectations could be put directly in jeopardy by the severance of an essential supply; and therefore that there were dangers in assuming that union behaviour would be moderate, now that the law had been rounded off in their favour. If the withdrawal or exclusion of labour led to a serious threat to civil order or provision, the government, despite its unwillingness to intervene on either side in labour disputes, would have to consider involving the police or the army, not just to prevent fighting but to keep the service going.[42] Certainly there was an argument for special curbs on those who by striking interrupted standard supplies of this kind.

---

[40] This was supplemented by s 2 of the Trade Union Act which stated that trade union members could not be prosecuted—for conspiracy or otherwise—merely because the purposes of the union were in restraint of trade. But there could still be an illegal conspiracy if organizers and participants took part in a strike involving breach of employment contracts by virtue of the Master and Servant Act 1867.

[41] (1872) 12 Cox CC 316.

[42] There was special legislation aimed at preventing the police themselves from going on strike; but after the army was used to bring in the harvest during the agricultural labourers' strike of 1872, army regulations were amended to prevent this happening in future: Curthoys, *Governments, Labour*, 167–8.

The jury in *Bunn* convicted the strikers of combining to induce breaches of the Master and Servant Act, Brett J. taking it that the statutory immunity did not extend to such conduct. His stiff sentence was a year's imprisonment with hard labour.[43] While the jury acquitted on the non-statutory charges, Brett J.'s view remained that the counts for a conspiracy at common law had been properly drawn despite the immunity in the Criminal Law Amendment Act. For him, the precedents set in *Duffield* and *Druitt* remained the touchstones.[44] Conspiracy lay where there had been an 'improper molestation to control the will of the employers'. Two years later Cleasby B. took an equally embracing view of such charges, the case before him concerning minor, but persistent, picketing at a small employer's works. The union organizers were convicted even though the refusal to work was in response to a peremptory announcement by the employer on a Saturday that, from the following Monday, payment would shift from an hourly rate to piece-work terms.[45] These demonstrations of judicial hostility brought indignant criticism from lawyers and politicians. Among them, FitzJames Stephen used the issue to raise the flag for proper codification for the criminal law.[46] The radical lawyer, R. S. Wright, published his claim that the conspiracy cases, from the *Tailors of Cambridge* onwards, were all indictments for breach of trade statutes, not for roving offences festering in the mysterious kernel of the common law.[47] But interpretation of the law was not taken in any proceedings to the Court of Crown Cases Reserved and the Liberals dithered about an amending Act.[48]

[43] Since the maximum sentence for the summary offences was three months' imprisonment, this gave no quarter to the notion that an indictment for the misdemeanour of conspiracy was governed by the same limitation. In the event, sympathy for the men led to their release; but only after more than three months had passed.

[44] Other judges took the same position. The Cockburn Commission on Labour Laws reported a jury direction by Pollock B. in which he instructed the jury that a worker who refused to take work in order to secure the dismissal of a non-union man, was guilty of a common law conspiracy, even though the worker broke no contractual obligations. The Commission, however, did not support that position: Final Report, below, n. 49 at p. 27.

[45] *R v. Hibbert* (1875) 10 Cox CC 82. No charge was made that the strike was in breach of contract—perhaps because the master was unilaterally altering its terms. The grand jury had found a true bill, despite the advice of Russell Gurney in his capacity as Recorder of London that peaceful picketing was not unlawful. For the effect of this difference of opinion on the drafting of the 1875 amendments to the Criminal Law Amendment Act, see Curthoys, *Governments, Labour*, 226–9.

[46] Curthoys, *Governments, Labour*, 177–8.

[47] *Law of Criminal Conspiracies and Agreements* (1873). The thesis had been explored by F. D. Longe, *Inquiry into the Law of 'Strikes'* (1860). For other contributions to the debate, see Curthoys, *Governments, Labour*, 176–82.

[48] Bruce, the Home Secretary, thought that an appellate decision was needed first, for there were judges who took a more discriminating view of labour law issues. They included Hayes and Hannen JJ in *Farrer v. Close* (above, 664, n. 73), and Lush J. in *R v. Shepherd* (1869) 11 Cox CC 325, who acknowledged that there was scope of peaceful picketing.

The Conservatives took over government in 1874 and were at once faced with radical demands: the circle of change had only been sketched in the 1871 legislation and must now be drawn in full. Disraeli, with a fine eye for electoral prospects, knew that more would become necessary, though he first stalled with another Royal Commission. Chaired by Lord Cockburn CJ and ignored by leading unionists in the parliamentary Committee of the TUC,[49] it reported quickly, confirming in essence the position in the Majority Report six years before. The TUC leaders and their parliamentary supporters, mainly on the Liberal benches, kept up pressure for further legislation.[50] By 1876 they had brought the Home Secretary, Assheton Cross, to put forward two bills which, after considerable further amendment, gave the union movement much of what it wanted.

First, the Employers and Workmen Act 1875 repealed the Master and Servant legislation. The old criminal jurisdiction of the magistrates, which provided the crude sanction of imprisonment or fine for breach of employment terms by workmen, accordingly disappeared. This transformation of the employee's contractual liability into a matter of purely civil consequence was indeed evidence of the political re-orientations in the decade. As noted below, the Act had effects as part of the developing law of employment contracts.[51]

The second Act of 1875 was the Conspiracy and Protection of Property Act. The range of criminal charges that could be brought as the result of strike action was curtailed, with provisions that were designed to deprive the severe views of Brett J. in the *Bunn* case of their potency. In place of the Criminal Law Amendment Act 1871, came a declaration that any act done 'in contemplation or furtherance of a trade dispute between employers and workmen' did not give rise to an indictable conspiracy where, if the act was committed by a single person, it would not be punishable.[52] This raised a new question: what acts were not in contemplation or furtherance of a trade dispute and therefore outside this immunity? The significance of the phrase would grow with time, as further legislation used it also to confine the range of civil liability in tort.[53]

---

[49] Royal Commission on the Labour Laws, Final Report, *PP* 1875 [C. 1157], xxx, 1. The previous year it reported accounts of prosecutions for labour offences before summary courts across the country: *PP* 1874 [C. 1094], xxiv. This time there was at least a workers' representative on the Commission, Alexander Macdonald, one of the miners who had become an MP in 1874. He wrote a dissent: pp. 28–9.

[50] For the role of the Liberals in drawing Cross and Disraeli to go as far as they did, see J. Spain, 'Trade Unions, Gladstonian Liberals and the Labour Law Reforms of 1875' in E. F. Biagini and A. Reid (eds), *Currents of Radicalism* (Cambridge, 1991), 109–33.

[51] Below, 681–3.

[52] Section 3. The right to charge a conspiracy to do any act punishable with imprisonment by statute was preserved, as was the general law against public disturbances.

[53] See below, 705–6.

The new Conspiracy Act proceeded to confine the scope of summary offences during industrial action in more specific terms. These covered, first, the wilful and malicious breach of a service contract with gas or water suppliers, municipal or private, that deprived inhabitants of their supply; and similar breaches which, whatever the industry, would endanger life, cause serious bodily injury, or expose property to destruction or serious injury.[54] Thus were the dangers and inconveniences of strikes such as that of the gas-stokers in *Bunn* put into a separate category. As for industrial action in general, section 7 retained offences committed 'wrongfully and without legal authority' with a view to compelling a person to do any legal act or abstain from doing it, if this was accompanied by violence or intimidation. But the old references to obstructing and molesting disappeared and in their place came simply the list of forbidden acts of picketing that had been proscribed in 1871: persistent or disorderly following, hiding tools and the like, and watching or besetting houses or other places.[55] Even so it was in the end specified that attending at or near the place where a person carries on business in order merely to obtain or communicate information was no crime.[56]

Inevitably there remained scope for placing a wide interpretation upon words such as 'intimidation', and taking a narrow view of 'merely communicating information'. But for some two decades the courts mostly respected the new direction set by this 1875 Act. Criminal charges would not be sustained against unionists merely for threatening or bringing about a withdrawal of labour; likewise if they organized pickets and did their best to ensure that the men acted peaceably, avoiding violence and immoderate language. In two cases, *Gibson* v. *Lawson* and *Curran* v. *Treleavan*,[57] John Duke Coleridge LCJ, remembering perhaps his radical youth, came close to saying that intimidation required the threat of physical violence (as it had been defined in the different context of the Criminal Law Amendment Act 1871).[58]

Since soon enough thereafter tougher counsels would prevail on the bench,[59] the period of relative pacifism deserves some explanation. Sporadic depression, which was nonetheless biting in some industries, set in after 1874. As usual, unions

---

[54] Section 4. In 1919 this was expanded to cover electricity supply. For union activity in the police and the services, see C. Steedman, *Policing the Victorian Community* (1984), Ch. 7; G. W. Rowlands and A. Judge, *The Night the Police went on Strike* (1968), Ch. 2 and Apps 1–3.

[55] See above, 674–5.

[56] Section 7(4). Huddleston B. soon showed a certain moderation when spelling out to strikers the limits of their freedom to picket: *R* v. *Bauld* et al. (1876) 13 Cox CC 282.

[57] [1891] 2 QB 547, 553. In *R* v. *Mackenzie* [1892] 2 QB 519, a Divisional Court used the old device of finding the record of the conviction by magistrates insufficiently specific: *R* v. *Mackenzie* [1892] 2 QB 519; cf. *Ex p Wilkins and Johnson* (1895) LJ (MC) 221; *Smith* v. *Moody* [1903] 1 KB 56.

[58] Above, n. 31.

[59] Below, 692–701.

were put in defensive positions, losing members to the extent that the peak of 1874 would not again be reached until the 1890s.[60] The leaders of the largest, central- ized unions, like the Engineers and the Carpenters and Joiners, continued to build their positions at the head of efficient national organizations, which had important benefit functions. These were years of cooperation between advanced Liberals, in which the TUC's Parliamentary Committee was in constant contact with friends who included such radical employers as Thomas Brassey and Mundella. They consolidated the acceptance of their activities that had accompanied the fran- chise reform of 1867 and had led to the lifting of old curbs on their legal position by the Acts of 1871 and then, in riposte to the assertion of older attitudes by some judges, to the amendments of 1875 and 1876. Smaller unions, operating at local or sometimes regional level might be less satisfied with their status, and still resort to militant strike and picketing activities. But in uncertain economic times, their influence was difficult to build up.

3. COLLECTIVE BARGAINING AS THE AIM OF LABOUR RELATIONS

Above all, these were the decades in which collective bargaining practices became more settled and widespread, and in the industries where unions had progressed farthest, negotiation between employers' federations and unions became regular. It became a normal mechanism not just for dealing with griev- ances already in existence but for adjusting wages and other working conditions for the future to take account of trade demand, growing competition from other workers, and other economic change. The negotiations could take place within the formal ambit of voluntary arbitration of the kind pioneered by Kettle and Mundella, but often enough the arbiter brought in from outside acted more as conciliator than imposer of solutions. It was this growth in joint negotiation that Kahn-Freund would famously dub 'collective laissez-faire'.[61]

In 1825, the most that Parliament had allowed by way of acceptable collective action had been the pursuit of improved wages and hours by the workers con- cerned; and even that had been a concession too far to strict adherents of free labour theories, such as Nassau Senior.[62] The intervening experience of labour

---

[60] Overall figures were difficult to discover until in the 1890s, the Labour Department of the Board of Trade began to collect and publish them. However, in 1874, the affiliated membership of the TUC was nearly 1 million, but it would fall by almost two-thirds ten years later before beginning then to grow again: H. Clegg, A. Fox, and A. Thompson, *History of British Trade Unions Since 1889* (Oxford, 1964), 1–36, who describe the fortunes of unions in the leading industries.

[61] O. Kahn-Freund, 'Labour Law', in M. Ginsberg (ed.), *Law and Opinion in England in the Twentieth Century* (1959), 215–63.

[62] See above, 655–7.

unionization, for all its antagonisms and outbreaks of under-cover warfare, had shifted political opinion towards the lifting of legal constraints on industrial action to a degree unknown elsewhere in the world. The governing classes were having to accept that an economy built upon capitalist enterprise was possible only with the cooperation of its labour force. That backing could be secured by the broadening of the parliamentary franchise in 1867 and then 1884, some underpinning by government which was paid for by taxing the propertied classes to keep the rest of the population from hunger and sickness in bad times, and some real chance for workers to press their claims to better wages and conditions, whatever the reduction in profitability for the business.

The Trade Union Act 1871, section 4(4), had refused courts the power directly to enforce agreements between employers' and workers' confederations, so the major collective agreements between the 'sides' of an industry were immunized from litigation, and would continue only as long as both continued to adhere to the terms. While agreements between a single employer and a union were not within this exemption, there is no record of their regular enforcement by litigation. Across much of industry, therefore, it was being accepted that the results of collective negotiation, which in reality settled the determinants of employment, remained open to revision at will. The contract by which the individual worker served his or her employer provided the legal obligations between them. Wherever collective bargains were agreed their terms would be fed into individual contracts, but no umbilical cord of legality ensured this occurrence. It occurred because, to many employers, it became a better way of managing the ebb and flow of trade and available labour than through stand off and confrontation.

Unions likewise could point to gradual improvements in overall working conditions. Even where they agreed to sliding scales of wages or hours which were related to economic indicators—and for their pains might well be accused of selling out by critics among their members—they could mostly riposte that these scales tended to operate for marginal shifts but broke down when more disturbing conditions set in. In any case, only a minor part of the manual workforce benefited from such adjustable arrangements for avoiding strikes and lock-outs.[63] As before, manual labourers mostly took work where they could get it on the terms prescribed more or less specifically by the employer. Some would serve in the same job for their working lives, some provided only casual labour and might be chronically under-employed. Whatever the reality, their contracts were likely to have little enough security embedded in them. If the notice needed was a short term, it did not lengthen with years of service. There were, however, some shifts

---

[63] See, for their use in industries such as coal and iron and steel, Clegg et al., *British Trade Unions*, 18–23, 202–5.

in judicial opinion about basic implications in these contracts where there was no express provision or customary practice to the contrary. These tended to draw back from the severest positions adhered to earlier in the century.

4. EMPLOYMENT WITHOUT CRIMINAL SANCTIONS

Effects of the Employers and Workmen Act 1875

The ending of summary criminal discipline in 1875 made the nub of the work relationship a matter of contract, rather than of status. The very title of the Employers and Workmen Act displaced the old language of master and servant. It took away the summary power to punish labourers' breaches of their employment terms with short imprisonment or fine and so achieved a shift, in Durkheim's terms, from repressive to restitutive sanctions.[64] From now on, either employer or manual worker could maintain a civil action for breach of the contract by the other. The action could be brought in the county courts which already had jurisdiction up to £50 in contract.[65] Also—and here the rub of history remained—it could be before a magistrates' court, kitted out as a civil jurisdiction for the purpose, if the amount claimed did not exceed £10. Proceedings against workers in either jurisdiction echoed the old practice of bringing the recalcitrant up before the bench. The courts had power, under s 3(1), to dissolve the employment and to order a set-off, under which wages outstanding would be balanced against contractual penalties or damages for the worker's failure to turn up or complete work according to his agreement. It seems that in arriving at the level of damages to be paid by the worker, the employer was not required to prove that he had lost anything by the absence. At least in a case arising out of a strike, damages to the employer could be punitive. The Court of Appeal upheld an award of 30 shillings each against men because they had deliberately aimed at injuring the employer's business.[66]

Wilhelm Steinmetz has examined what difference the change in the basis of liability made to the business of disciplining workers and whether it gave better chances of stopping employers from dismissals on the spot or reductions in wages when they were not within the terms of the employment contract.[67] His

---

[64] See G. R. Rubin, in Rubin and D. Sugarman (eds), *Law, Economy and Society* (Abingdon, 1984), 311–12.

[65] For the growth of County Court jurisdiction in the period, see XI, Part 3, pp. 884–8.

[66] *Bowes* v. *Press* [1894] 1 QB 602, 605, the point being made by the antagonistic Lindley LJ; see Deakin and Wilkinson, *Labour Market*, 77.

[67] W. Steinmetz, 'Was there a De-juridification of Individual Employment Law in England?', in Steinmetz (ed.), *Private Law and Social Inequality in the Industrial Age* (Oxford, 2000), Ch. 11.

evidence, both from lower court statistics and from informal reports of claims, suggests that employers resorted to civil jurisdiction less readily than they used the old sting of the summary system. They could still sack workers against whom they had no evidence of fault, if they gave due notice or paid the employee in lieu; but if they were dealing with union members, there could be retaliation at the unfairness. In the wake of the Act, the balance of command in the workplace must have adjusted, but perhaps not greatly. The Act did produce some flow of plaints by workers against unjustified dismissals. But, as Steinmetz points out, these were rather sporadic, and formed a contrast to the stream of workmen's compensation cases that after 1897 would come before county courts and on appeal. That novel scheme evidenced the harsh economic consequences of work accidents for individuals who had been seriously disabled. The litigation demonstrated the willingness of unions to devote considerable resources to fighting on their behalf—the real enemy often being the employer's insurance company.[68] Pursuing an employer who failed to give proper notice for a sacking would not produce much by way of damages. And it might well prejudice the chance of getting another job, for black lists were common enough between members of trade associations. The right of the entrepreneur to choose his workers on terms set only by market conditions remained both a crucial value and a harsh reality in working lives at the dawn of the twentieth century.[69]

Among workers and their representatives, the set-off power in the Employers and Workmen Act 1875 was detested. Given its existence, employers might make their own subtractions when dismissing a worker; and he or she might be in no position to challenge the calculation.[70] A case was appealed to the House of Lords where the Law Lords treated the set-off power as a surprising qualification of their idea that free contracts consisted of independent terms for which each had to sue in order to establish entitlement. But they held that the statutory power of set-off had to prevail.[71] Doubtless it was often the worker who lost out.

Another special power, in section 3(3), allowed the court, with the employer's consent, to order a worker to complete any outstanding part of his contract

---

[68] See above, Vol. XII, pp. 1029–32.

[69] See Deakin and Wilkinson, *Labour Market*, 78–86.

[70] In *Keates* v. *Merthyr Consolidated Collieries* [1911] AC 641, the employee had made no claim in the litigation. It was the magistrates who had insisted on making the adjustment in order to dispose of all the issues that they saw between the parties. See Deakin and Wilkinson, *Labour Market*, 74–8.

[71] Five years before, in *Williams* v. *North's Navigation Collieries* [1906] AC 136, the Lords had held that the employer's own subtraction would amount to an offence under the Truck Act 1831, 1 & 2 Will. IV c. 32, as a deduction from the wage due in coin of the realm. In that litigation the set-off power given to the court by the 1875 Act was not raised as a reason for qualifying the impact of the Truck Act.

term—an order therefore of specific performance. In general, English courts refused to use specific performance in order to insist on the actual rendering of personal service that was due under a contract; but the Act did not show the same compunction. The worker had to provide security or surety for his performance and in that limited sense his consent was also needed. In reality he can have had little choice in the matter. Failure to meet any court order under the Act, including costs, would give rise to a debt which, if less than £50, could be enforced by arrest and removal to prison. This arose under the regime which applied only to these relatively small debts and which had been instituted in 1869 after decades of argument over the role of imprisonment for debt. The Debtors Act of that year, in reality if not in terms, confined such imprisonment mostly to working-class debtors. It was justified as being the only way to press people without assets to honour their obligations; but it nonetheless rankled with the labour movement as a piece of class legislation.[72]

Shifting Judicial Attitudes

With the replacement of criminal liability by civil process to such an extent, the rules of common law that over the previous half-century had added deterrent consequences to breaking an individual employment contract were also modified. Doctrines that deprived a defaulting worker of any claim to wages until he had completed the specified term, became less absolute.[73] To some extent this occurred with the continuing shift from annual contracts (long known in agriculture and mining) to agreements that required a month's, a week's or even a day's or hour's notice for termination. Long-term agreements were becoming more and more the preserve of the skilled, whether their tasks were manual, clerical, or managerial. These were employees who might come initially to be trained or to bring in know-how from outside. Their replacement could therefore be a real difficulty; and they in their turn would expect the security of a continuing contract. It was in cases involving such mid-rank employees that the higher courts first began to allow money claims or damages for such work as had been completed before dismissal; and likewise for being ready to work under a contract where the employer was obliged to continue supplying the work.[74]

The judges, for whatever reason, became readier to treat contracts for a substantial term as nonetheless giving a right to wages for each completed period

---

[72] See above, Vol. XII, pp. 837 *et seq*; P. Johnson, 'Creditors, Debtors and the Law in Victorian and Edwardian England' in Steinmetz, *Law and Social Inequality*, Ch. 19.

[73] Cf. above, 641.

[74] For the first such cases, see above, 638–41.

in which the employer customarily paid wages;[75] and they were more willing to find that the employer, expressly or impliedly, had undertaken to provide work until notice had been duly given and had expired. By the new century, the altered approach could stretch down to middlemen. In *Devonald* v. *Rosser*,[76] tinplate roll-ermen, who were paid as piece workers per ton of metal, had to face the closure of their works, but only later did their employer give the contractual notice of one month. The Court of Appeal held the men entitled to damages representing wages until expiry of the notice. Half a century before, the employer's obligation would have been read as only requiring work to be provided if there were orders enough for the product.[77]

A change of judicial heart emerged over restrictive covenants governing the period after termination of the employment, that manifested a striking difference between individual and collective agreements. Typically, by a restrictive cove-nant an employee undertook not to work for a competitor of the initial employer and not to set up a competing business if in future he left the employment of the initial employer. The term was usually inserted in the initial contract, and so was not the subject of separate payment or other compensation apart from the salary or wage. Even if limited in space or time, a covenant of this type could seriously deter the employee from leaving the job and so stood in the way of the indi-vidual's freedom to make the best of his economic abilities. Express covenants in restraint of trade had long been treated in principle as void at common law.

However, there were circumstances in which they might be justified and a long line of case law had sought to define what these were.[78] The old doctrinal dis-tinction lay between restraints that were general (in the sense of covering the whole kingdom) and those that were only partial, the latter being more read-ily acceptable. In *Nordenfelt* v. *Maxim Nordenfelt*,[79] the House of Lords replaced this increasingly awkward distinction with a test of reasonableness overall. A restrictive covenant would still be treated as *prima facie* void, so that it fell to the beneficiary of the covenant to show that it was reasonable in the interests of the parties and for the court to consider whether any public interest arose to pre-vent enforcement. In moving to this point of departure, the courts would stress repeatedly that covenants were more readily justified when they arose in the sale

---

[75] *Parkin* v. *South Hetton Coal* (1907) 98 LT 164: the claimant had been employed as a domestic servant, subject to fortnightly notice, but for each day he had been paid separately; the court found that he was therefore entitled to pay for each day worked, even though he left without due notice: *George* v. *Davis* [1911] 2 KB 445. The contrary approach, exemplified in *Walsh* v. *Walley* (1874) LR 9 QB 364, was still being maintained in *Moult* v. *Halliday* [1898] 1 QB 125.

[76] *Devonald* v. *Rosser* [1906] 2 KB 728.

[77] Above, 638–41.

[78] See above, Vol XII, 671–2, 1050–2.

[79] [1894] AC 535.

of a business than when they related to an ex-employee. The seller of a business who undertook not to compete thereby assured the purchaser that he would have the goodwill for which he paid. Lord Macnaghten stated that 'there is obviously more freedom of contract between buyer and seller than between master and servant or between an employer and a person seeking employment';[80] and this soon became the predominant view,[81] reinforced not least by judges who would most readily place legal deterrents in the way of collective action led by trade unions.[82] Lord Atkinson, for example, would characterize a restrictive undertaking by a worker as:

'oppressive' in the sense that it would, if enforced, deprive him for a lengthened period of the power of employing in any part of the United Kingdom, that mechanical and technical skill and knowledge which, his own industry, observation, and intelligence have enabled him to acquire in the very specialized manufacturing business of the [plaintiffs], thus forcing him to begin life afresh, as it were, and depriving him of the means of supporting himself and his family.[83]

The employer needed to justify the restraint, either by showing that the employee had been in contact with customers or had received information or training that went beyond the knowledge and skill that a typical employee in such a job would acquire. Even then, the prohibition in the covenant had to be for an area and a period that was reasonable in the light of what the worker had been set to do. There remained many differences over what was sufficiently reasonable to withstand an attack in court. The risk of failing could be considerable, since if a court found the terms were too wide, it would be unlikely to substitute less embracing terms; instead the whole would be struck down. This opinion made sure that employers could not use restrictive covenants to prevent the bulk of their workforce from moving to other firms as it suited them. The issue would be dealt with on an individual basis, and so the judges were willing to qualify their general adherence to sanctity of contract. In doing so, they acknowledged the lack of real bargaining power faced by many employees and concluded from this perception that the old anti-monopolistic rule against trade restraints should continue to

---

[80] [1894] AC at 566.
[81] See esp. the leading cases on employee covenants, *Mason* v. *Provident Clothing* [1913] AC 724: part-time salesman for small clothing supplier not bound by covenant not to work in the same business within 25 miles of London; *Herbert Morris* v. *Saxelby* [1916] 1 AC 688: knowledge acquired of how to organize an office not a reason for upholdng a covenant.
[82] See e.g. Farwell LJ in *Leng* v. *Andrews* [1909] 1 Ch. 763, 773, who stressed the interest of the public in allowing workers to dispose of their labour as they chose. However, not all judges fell immediately into line: see e.g. *Underwood* v. *Barker* [1899] 1 Ch. 300, where Lindley MR and Rigby LJ upheld a foreman-clerk's covenant on much the same basis as if he had been the seller of a business; but Vaughan Williams LJ, dissenting, followed the new distinction.
[83] *Herbert Morris* v. *Saxelby* [1916] AC 688 at 698–9.

have wide effect when it came to labour contracts. Their assistance expressed an attitude of 'atomistic individualism' (to use Alan Fox's phrase), which stood counter to the 'instrumental collectivism' of industrial action.[84]

More than ever, what was specifically agreed set the rules of engagement in employment and these could have both beneficial and deleterious effects for employer or worker, depending on the particular circumstances and also on economic conditions more generally. The short term of notice, which had come to apply to a great range of employments, reduced the security that had been part of the annual hiring for the core labour in agriculture and such industries as mining. But for those in unions it provided a prospect of striking without breaking their contracts. After 1875 a strike organized without belligerent picketing became a tactic that would not lead to a term of imprisonment or a fine; and unions at the same time could run their own houses without being dragged into court by litigious dissidents among members. To this extent they felt themselves to be in a much improved position, which helps to explain the very considerable growth of collective bargaining between the two sides of an industry at regional, and even national, level. At the same time, employers in many industries were finding it a long-term advantage to address the grievances among their workforce by negotiating with union representatives or officers. In the last quarter of the nineteenth century a certain culture of accommodation was emerging. It may be seen as reflecting a pacific belief that capitalists and workers were at last set on a course that would enhance higher profits and better wages in a Whiggish sort of progress. But equally it may have expressed the inevitable struggle for power and the search for tactics that would be effective in countering the other side's sallies.[85]

5. POLITICS OF EMPLOYMENT IN THE 1890s

The Rise of Non-Skilled Unionism[86]

In 1888 the Bryant and May matchgirls, stirred to action by the feminist free-thinker, Annie Besant, won a strike for better pay and some relief against their constant exposure to debilitating chemicals.[87] Early in the next year, Will Thorne

---

[84] Fox, *History and Heritage*, 192.

[85] See Fox, *History and Heritage*, 164–76.

[86] See Hunt, *Labour History*, 304–41; Fox, *History and Heritage*, 169–220; J. E. Cronin, 'Strikes, 1870–1914', in C. J. Wrigley (ed.), *A History of British Industrial Relations, 1875–1914* (Brighton, 1982), 74–98.

[87] See also P. Bartrip, '"Petticoat Pestering": The Women's Trade Union League and Lead Poisoning in the Staffordshire Potteries, 1890–1914' (1996) 2 *Hist. St. in Ind. Rlns* 3–26.

led the London gasworkers to victory in having their hours cut from 12 to eight without loss of wages. Above all, the strike of London dockworkers in 1889, led by Tillett, Mann, and Burns, won them 6d. an hour—'the Dockers' tanner'. It attracted wide support (from as far afield as Queensland) and was settled after five weeks only by the intervention of a grand Mansion House Committee (including the Bishop of London and Cardinal Manning), which brought the two sides together to sign a settlement.[88] A watershed had been reached. 'New' unions suddenly attracted massive numbers of workers, many of them tough but unskilled. The overall membership, taking old and new unions together, climbed from perhaps 750,000 in 1888 to over 2 million in 1900; and then after some stagnation would rise again from 1906 to reach 2.5 million in 1910 and more than 4 million in 1914. The successes of 1889–91 sprang from an upswing in the economy and a drop in unemployment to 2 per cent. As usual it would prove difficult to sustain the run of successes as the trade cycle descended. Old unions were not displeased, for they had viewed the novel upsurge with considerable suspicion. The new bodies could only call upon members for low contributions and so could not contemplate significant benefit funds. They could only offer joint negotiating power, backed by the ability to threaten or engage in industrial action, as a way of securing better conditions at work. Major and minor strikes ran on through the 1890s. The number of days lost between 1891 and 1898 would rise to an annual average of 12 million before dropping to 3 million between 1899 and 1907.

Through the 1890s, there came to be greater accommodation between the higher and lower levels of the labour movement. Dissatisfaction with Liberal 'friendship' spread and the prospects for an Independent Labour Party became a reality. A range of employers, some of whom had made considerable profits for themselves on the back of low-paid labour forces, saw a future in which, if they were to keep the division between capital and labour in place, it might have to be on much improved terms for the latter. One hope, of course, was that the state as a whole would share in providing those conditions by schemes of social protection that represented a spirit of community very different from the repressive poor law and its moralizing administrators. There was growing interest in Bismarck's schemes for containing the rise of unionism in the German Reich by social security measures, particularly for breadwinners unable to find enough work.[89] But parts of such plans would have to be paid for by fiscal measures; and

---

[88] In *Ayling* v. *London and India Docks Committee* (1893) 9 TLR 409, however, a Divisional Court refused to find in the settlement any indication that the strikers could claim wages for the period of the strike or any right to be taken back by their employers. There was no sympathy whatsoever for a 'right to strike'.

[89] See H. P. Hennock, *British Social Reform and German Precedents: The Case of Social Insurance* (Oxford, 1987).

so far as the taxes were on income or accumulated wealth at death, it was the propertied who provided them.

Political Alliances

Broadly speaking, those who trusted their social and intellectual superiority to carry them through in the end, with only moderate concessions being made to working-class aspirations, now gave their allegiance in increasing measure to the Conservative Party. Under Salisbury, and then Balfour, that party governed for a decade from 1895. They turned to legislative compulsion in certain significant ways affecting work. Thanks to their alliance with Joseph Chamberlain, it was the Tories who in 1897 put through the workmen's compensation scheme for work accidents.[90] In their last year in office, 1905, they sought to solve some of the difficulties and dangers of unemployment by measures that would provide labour opportunities: labour exchanges, and labour colonies in the country and chances to emigrate, all supported from special local rates and organized through distress committees in towns of 50,000 or more.[91] As it proved, both steps had only a transitional effect.

The Liberal Party offered the greater understanding and sympathy for proletarian conditions, which from the 1860s had developed among its 'Lib-Lab' radicals. Its victory at the polls in January 1906 led it to carry through the programme that set in train the twentieth-century welfare state. By that point its plans were having constantly to be measured against the positions taken by a Labour Party, now with separate representation in Parliament and closely backed by much of the trade union movement. In the nature of things, support for Labour was likely to draw away Liberal voters, rather than Conservatives. The fledgling movement of the 1890s towards Independent Labour did not grow out of adherence to any doctrine of revolutionary socialism. Instead, its aims were for the most part moderate and gradualist. It looked for political and social strength through parliamentary government, without any basic departure from the scheme of private, inheritable, property rights upon which the capitalist economy had so evidently been built.

Within these geological shifts in political affiliation lay the future of the trade union movement itself. During the 1890s some employers—notably in engineering, shipbuilding, and docks—sought to meet the growing power of unionism by forming regional associations. Allied to this were various organizations which

---

[90] Above, Vol. XII, pp. 1018–19.
[91] Unemployed Workmen Act 1905.

built up recruits ready to move into workplaces as blackleg labour.[92] William Collison, drawing together earlier efforts, established his National Free Labour Association in 1893—a body that would seek links both with the Employers' Federation (and its Parliamentary Council) and with the Earl of Wemyss' Free Labour Association. Wemyss (formerly Lord Elcho) had also founded the Liberty and Property Defence League, in order to give expression to the severely anti-statist theories of Herbert Spencer.[93] The League's roots in an obdurate individualism attracted judges such as Lord Bramwell and Lord Halsbury—the latter, as we shall see, a crucial figure in fostering common law liability in order to oppose industrial action by trade unions. It was, however, costly and difficult to maintain the 'industrial order' aspects of these moves by employers. With stagnation in the labour market increasing at the turn of the century, industrialists saw their chance to bolster collective bargaining on conditions that suited them, unions often finding themselves on the defensive.

The Devonshire Commission

The economic conditions in these years are important in explaining why voluntary agreement in settling the conditions of employment continued in preference to schemes in which legal mechanisms would oblige the two sides of an industry to accept terms imposed from outside, whether by politicians, civil servants, judges, or arbitrators. Had those conditions differed, greater enthusiasm might have been shown towards compulsion imposed by law. Certainly there was continuing discussion of legal mechanisms as they were developing in the United States (where union organization was weak) and in parts of the Empire, notably Australia (where unions were strong). When the Salisbury government reacted to the new unionism by appointing a Royal Commission on Labour in 1891, the future organization of management-labour relations became the great subject of debate. The Commission's Report, when it came after three years, registered how much had changed since the previous exercise in 1867–9. This time chaired by that grand and trusted figure, the Duke of Devonshire,[94] the Commission would assemble a large body of evidence concerning industries from the great

---

[92] Already in 1889, gasworkers in London, victorious a few months before, lost out to the South Metropolitan Gas Co, under George Livesey, now armed with a well-planned corps of replacement labour.

[93] See E. Bristow, 'The Liberty and Property Defence League and Individualism' (1975) 18 *Hist. J.* 761. As Elcho, Wemyss had associated with liberals to make the operation of the Master and Servant legislation less severe on defendants, by the amending Act of 1867. Since that time his views had become rigidly antagonistic to the collective aspirations of the working classes.

[94] As Marquess of Hartington, he had in 1886 led the Liberal Unionists (including Joseph Chamberlain) away from Gladstone into league with the Conservatives.

staples to the mean sweated trades.[95] As well as industrialists, lawyers, and politicians, it had seven prominent trade unionists among its members. Four of them
would provide a Minority Report in which modest collectivist objectives were
the foundation.

The Majority report exuded confidence in industries that had functioning
arrangements for collective bargaining. This voluntary system needed no legal
compulsion as a bulwark. The Report adopted the belief that legislation could not
provide a remedy for such evils as there were, but instead trusted 'to the gradual
amendment by natural forces now in operation which tend to substitute a state of
industrial peace for one of industrial division and conflict'.[96] At most, for disputes
about future entitlements and procedures for resolving them, the new Labour
Department of the Board of Trade should be empowered to maintain a conciliation service for cases where the two sides agreed to invoke it.[97] As to disputes
about existing rights, the Majority took some interest in the French industrial
tribunals, the *conseils de prud'hommes* instituted by Napoléon. But they would
only recommend that local authorities should have power to set up arbitral bodies where particular difficulties arose.[98] As for the use of legal disciplines in the
prevention and containment of strikes, lock-outs and other departures from normal working practice, the compromises of 1871–5 were reviewed in the light of the
current attitudes of the courts towards them. Frederick Pollock, the voice of the
law on the Commission, did no more than present an even-handed outline of the
current position.[99]

The Minority Report also took a gradualist approach, but one sharply accented
away from the voluntarist assumptions of an economy built upon private enterprise. Instead, pointing to the movement for public provision at the local level,
which had already earned the label of Municipal Socialism, this Report called
for the substitution, wherever possible, of national and municipal enterprise in
place of private capital; and 'where this substitution is not yet practicable, the
strict and detailed regulation of all industrial operations so as to secure to every
worker the conditions of efficient citizenship'.[100] This was written in the decade
when the prediction of the self-destructive mechanisms of capitalism by Karl

[95] The first Four Reports of the Commission detail the investigations and evidence of a great
range of trades, including those where unionism did not occur and conditions were often servile:
see PP 1892, xxxiv, 1 and xxxvi, 1; 1893–94, xxxii, 1 and xxxix, 1.

[96] Fifth and Final Report, PP 1894 [C. 7421], xxxv, para. 363.

[97] The elderly Mundella promoted a bill in 1893 to this effect, the Commission approved of it and
in 1896 a Conciliation Act was passed. See on the general theme, C. Howell, *Trade Unions and the
State: The Constitution of Industrial Relations in Britain, 1890–2000* (Princeton, 2005).

[98] Fifth Report (above, n. 96), paras 292–315.

[99] For his Memorandum, see below n. 114.

[100] Report, above, n. 96, p. 147.

Marx and other socialists was gaining some small currency among British intellectuals. Nonetheless the overall tone adopted by the Minority was pragmatic, the Fabian, Sidney Webb, having given much assistance in its drafting.[101] It drew on the long-established traditions of cooperative enterprise in distribution and on beliefs in the transformative effects of greater democracy; and it underscored the practical achievements of the craft unions and now the prospects for more general unionization.

The Minority did call for legal regulation of labour conditions, which implied that in place of market negotiations, government at some level would, as three centuries before, set wage and other conditions of labour. It might even revert to directing labour into agriculture or industry where it was needed—the type of regulation which the country would be obliged to adopt once war broke out on a horrifying scale in 1914. The Minority nonetheless were much concerned with particular initiatives by which the state could rein in the unrelenting demands of pure capitalism: a limitation of daily hours of work to eight for men as much as for women and young persons,[102] extension of health and safety requirements for factories and workshops and effective enforcement of the law,[103] proper housing for working people,[104] old age pensions as of right,[105] and standard union rates of pay by government departments and local authorities. The last of these built on a recognition, first by some local authorities and in 1891 by the House of Commons in its Fair Wages Resolution, that contractors used by central and local government must pay their labour forces wages that were 'accepted as current for a competent workman in his trade'.[106] Here were practical goals that would find some sympathy within both Conservative and Liberal ranks, as would become apparent over the ensuing two decades. The plan for dealing with unorganized

[101] A discussion had by then begun of the prospects for government control of wages: see S. Blackburn, ' "The Harm that the Sweater Does Lives after Him": The Webbs, the Responsible Employer and the Minimum Wage Campaign, 1880–1914' (2000) 10 *Hist. St. in Ind. Rlns* 5–42.

[102] Even in 1893, the dangers of accidents from working overlong hours led to restrictions on railways (Railway Servants (Hours of Labour) Act), and the same concern led to amendments to the Factories and Workshop Acts in 1895 and the Mines Regulation Act 1908. Here at least were breaches in the old principle that adult men must look to their own efforts in securing employment terms. In the Shops Act 1886, where there was very little union penetration, assistants of whatever age and sex had gained a 74-hour maximum week; by 1907, laundry workers could demand a 68-hour week. For railwaymen, see E. Knox, 'Blood on the Tracks: Railway Employees in Late Victorian and Edwardian Britain' (2001) 12 *Hist. St. in Ind. Rlns* 1–26.

[103] See above, 563–6.

[104] See above, 580–2.

[105] See above, 504–5.

[106] The Commons Resolution, which gave force to such respectable adages as 'A fair day's pay for a fair day's work', had been promoted by the Liberal, Sidney Buxton. See B. W. Bercusson, *Fair Wages Resolutions* (1978); Brodie, *British Labour Law*, 70–2.

'sweated' trades by creating arbitral trade boards would have to wait until 1909 for implementation. The Majority of the Devonshire Commission were, however, prepared to support it, offering as one justification that the boards might kill off the trades, leaving it for the women workers so often involved to stay at home and look after their children![107]

The Trade Boards recommended by the Commission were to be set up trade by trade, where wages were exceptionally low, and government intervention was expedient. The plan stalled until the Liberals took it up with legislation in 1909.[108] Initially there would only be four—in paper box, lace and chain production and in bespoke tailoring, but five more were added in 1913.[109] Their duty was to set minimum wages for time and piece work. Each board had equal representation of the two sides of the industry, plus a number of Board of Trade nominees as the voice of objective public interest. These independent members were to act, if necessary, as conciliators; and in the event where the two sides simply could not agree, they were to transform themselves into arbitrators in order to impose a solution. Renegade employers who failed to honour an award could be sued in a civil action or prosecuted, the Trade Board itself acting for the workers if it chose.[110] Here was government intervening under legal powers but in supplementary mode. The machinery was provided because the prospect of voluntary collective bargaining was so remote, not to thrust imposed solutions upon two well-organized sides, even when they were spoiling for a damaging fight, let alone when the battle was already on.[111]

6. JUDGES vs UNIONS

For the upper and middle classes, the onset of non-skilled unionism gave the problem of industrial disruption a new urgency, sharpening attitudes within government and at more general political levels about how to treat it. Nowhere would this be more apparent than in the views of appellate judges towards the role and place of civil obligation as a discipline governing the conduct of both

---

[107] See their Report (above, n. 49), 90–6.

[108] Trade Boards Act 1909; Brodie, *British Labour Law*, 65–9. By then it would be stimulated by investigation of a scheme operating in the Australian state of Victoria: see the Commons SC Report on Home Work, *PP* 1908 (246); K. D. Ewing, 'Australian and British Labour Law—Differences of Form and Substance' (1998) 11 *Australian J. of Labour Law* 44–68, esp. at 55–7.

[109] See further below, 715–18.

[110] Trade Boards Act 1909, s 6. The onus of proving proper payment was put on the employer.

[111] For the role of the Labour Department of the Board of Trade, and more generally for discussions of compulsory minimum wages, see e.g. C. Wrigley (ed.), *A History of British Industrial Relations* (Brighton, 1978), esp. his own Ch. 7, 'The Government and Industrial Relations', and R. Davidson, Ch. 8, 'Government Administration'; Deakin and Wilkinson, *Labour Market*, 230–4.

individuals and bodies of people acting in concert. In the courts, the period began with that great affirmation by the judges of the Smithian virtues of self-interest in the pursuit of economic growth and well-being: *Mogul Steamship* v. *McGregor, Gow.* In late 1891, the House of Lords confirmed that there was no tortious conspiracy in a shipping cartel agreeing together to bring about a secondary boycott aimed at a former member of the cartel, if the actions of those within the 'ring' involved no independent wrong and were in pursuit of their own legitimate interests, rather than being a merely malicious attack.[112] The relevance of this position to labour disputes was at once apparent, since in *Jenkinson* v. *Neild*[113] the Court of Appeal refused to find any tortious conspiracy in an employers' association giving effect to a joint blacklist of union men. Many lawyers assumed that trade union members would equally be protected against such suits.[114] There would, however, prove to be a line of judicial thought that found a crucial difference between risk-taking competitors using their legitimate muscle collectively against an outside rival and wage-labour unionists doing the equivalent against employers or non-union workers.

The case of *Temperton* v. *Russell (No.2)*,[115] decided in 1893, was the first exhibition of this dichotomy at work. The Court of Appeal upheld a verdict against officers of three unions of building workers in Hull. Together they had formed a joint action committee, which had as one main purpose to require master builders to hire only union men for their trades and therefore to press for the dismissal of non-union men. Neither the unions nor their combined Committee had the numbers to oblige one building firm, Myers & Temperton (M & T), to adopt their rules. A building supplies business (T) run by Temperton—plaintiff in the action and brother of the second partner in M & T—was therefore approached by the Committee in an attempt to get T not to supply M & T, but it proved not to have the muscle. As a second strategy, therefore, the Committee approached at least two of T's customers, B and G, to put pressure on T, by saying that they would break contracts they already had with T, and would refuse to enter further contracts, unless he in turn would put pressure for a closed shop on M & T. Thanks to having enough members working for B and G, the Committee got B and G to act against T. This complicated secondary boycott had its effect at least on T,

---

[112] [1892] AC 25, affirming the majority judgments in the CA (1889) 23 QBD 618, for which see above, Vol. XII, pp. 1049–53). The question whether, in line with *Hilton* v. *Eckersley*, the parties to the cartel had no binding agreement because it was in unreasonable restraint of trade, was not in issue.

[113] (1892) 8 TLR 549. Note also *Scottish Co-Operative Wholesaler Society* v. *Glasgow Fleshers' Trade Defence Association* (1898) 35 Scot. LR 645: unsuccessful action against a retailing cooperative for refusing to take meat from an association of butchers.

[114] Notably Pollock, in his Memorandum on Combinations to the Devonshire Royal Commission on Labour, *PP* 1894 [C. 7421] xxxv at 159.

[115] [1893] 1 QB 715.

who therefore sued for the damage to him of B and G's withdrawals of business under existing and future contracts. The special jury awarded T £250 against the union officers.

Lord Esher MR led the appeal court in much the same denunciatory fashion as, 20 years before, he had directed the jury in *Bunn*.[116] The defendants had acted 'in order to force [T] not to do what he had a perfect right to do'; and while they may not have been motivated by any personal spite or malice, still they had no right to compel T's obedience under the threat that otherwise his business would be ruined. That was 'unlawful'. An individual who intentionally induced others to break existing contracts committed a tort which, since *Lumley* v. *Gye* and then *Bowen* v. *Hall*, had been generalized from the old rule affecting only contracts of service.[117] It appeared from *Bowen* that the defendant was liable for this tort where his intention was either to injure the plaintiff or to gain at the claimant's expense. The *Temperton* decision pointed towards a proposition that inducing breach of any contract became tortious simply if the breach was intended; and a decade later the House of Lords would give it this broad scope.[118] As to B and G's refusal to bring more business to T under future contracts, any distinction was too fine for Esher, since 'there was the same kind of injury' to T. In this situation, however, the tortious liability had to be couched in terms of a conspiracy maliciously to injure another. This made crucial the act of combining, distinguishing the case from actions by a single person that would have been perfectly lawful. At the same time, the court held that those who threatened to strike formed an intention to injure their opponent that was 'malicious'.[119] The extraordinary plasticity of 'malice' in the law of torts was yet again demonstrated.

Much the same hostility underlay the injunctions granted against picketing and secondary boycotting in *Lyons* v. *Wilkins (No. 1)*.[120] A London belt-maker had resisted the demands of a leather-workers' union to accept a closed shop, which resulted in a strike by those workers who were already members. A disciplined picket—two people at a time—accosted workers still going in, giving them a card which asked them not to take the work during the dispute. There was some

---

[116] Above, n. 41. He also dissented during the CA stage of the *Mogul* case and so could not be accused of taking different lines against business and union cartels.

[117] For variations upon the meaning of malice in the earlier cases, see M. J. Klarman 'The Judges versus the Unions: The Developments of British Labor Law 1867–1913' (1989) 75 *Virginia LR* 1487–1602, at 1517–19.

[118] *South Wales Miners' Federation* v. *Glamorgan Coal* [1905] AC 239.

[119] Esher referred to the *Mogul* case only for Lord Bramwell's justification of rights against combinations that 'a man may encounter the acts of a single person, yet not be fairly matched against several'; and that prosecution of a single person would be *de minimis*, while that of several 'is sufficiently important to be treated as a crime' (729–30). Lopes and A. L. Smith LJJ had virtually nothing to say on this second head of liability.

[120] [1896] 1 Ch. 811; Klarman, 'British Labor Law', 1514–17.

minor evidence of further interference, but that was all. The union's officers also put pressure on an exclusive supplier to the firm, by bringing out members who worked for the supplier. In the interlocutory proceedings, the Court of Appeal was in no doubt that these actions must be stopped at once. Lindley LJ was unequivocal:

Trade unions have now been recognised up to a certain point as organs for good. They are the only means by which workmen can protect themselves from tyranny on the part of those who employ them; but the moment that trade unions become tyrants in their turn they are engines for evil: they have no right to prevent any man from working upon such terms as he chooses.[121]

The court therefore approved the granting of an interlocutory injunction until trial of the action in terms which forbade any criminal 'watching and besetting' as defined by the Conspiracy and Protection of Property Act 1875, s 7.[122] The terms of the injunction did exclude attending to obtain or communicate information since that was specifically permitted by section 7. The court, however, plainly considered the 'attending' of the pickets in question to go beyond that limit, since 'a great deal may be done that is absolutely illegal'.

The injunction affecting the picketing was couched to restrain criminal conduct under the Act. It was granted in response to claims that the officers had unlawfully and maliciously procured persons to break contracts with the plaintiff firm, or to decline to enter contracts with it. No clear line was therefore drawn between conduct that was criminal and conduct that was tortious. But it was clear enough that the scope of the latter was considered to embrace acts of conspiracy to injure others in their trade or employment, much on the lines sketched so broadly by Esher MR in *Temperton*. Three years later, at trial of the action, the Court of Appeal granted a permanent injunction, taking more care to define the basis for its grant. It was either that the prohibitions in the 1875 Act, s 7, by implication gave private rights of action to those injured by the forbidden conduct, or else that the picketing amounted to a civil nuisance for which the employers had a right of action because of the special likelihood of injury to them.[123] Stirling J. soon after had no difficulty in enjoining pickets from waiting at railway stations and landing stages in order to confront 'blacklegs' who were being brought in by employers' organizations.[124]

---

[121] [1896] 1 Ch. 823. It was in the course of argument that Lindley announced: 'You cannot make a strike effective without doing more than is lawful' at 820, echoing Bramwell B., *R* v. *Bailey* (1867) 16 LT (NS) 859. Much of Lindley's account of picketing law follows what Huddleston B. had said 20 years before in *R* v. *Bauld* (1876) 13 Cox CC 282, 284; above, n. 56.

[122] The injunction also ran against the secondary boycotting.

[123] *Lyons* v. *Wilkins (No. 2)* [1899] 1 Ch. 255.

[124] *Charnock* v. *Court* [1899] 2 Ch. 35; *Walters* v. *Green* [1899] 2 Ch. 696.

The higher judiciary, however, differed considerably over the extent to which civil responsibility should be imposed upon union officers and strikers, as became apparent in the litigation which reached the House of Lords in *Allen* v. *Flood*.[125] The dispute arose out of inter-union rivalry between boilermakers and shipwrights at repair yards in the London docks. Allen, as delegate of the boiler-makers' union, informed one yard-owner that their members were determined to withdraw their labour if he did not remove shipwrights who were known to have taken work at another yard in defiance of the boilermakers. All the employees were on a day's notice, so no breaches of contract would occur, either by the boilermakers or the employer of the shipwrights. The employer gave in and dismissed the shipwrights, who accordingly sued Allen and the chairman and secretary of the union. The case was argued partly on the basis that simply to inform the employer of the men's resolution was a malicious act aimed at the shipwrights, who lost their employment in consequence. At the trial, Kennedy J. ruled that there was no evidence of conspiracy, intimidation, coercion, or breach of contract and the jury returned a verdict only against Allen. The Court of Appeal, led once more by Esher MR, upheld the claim against him, insisting that the action was a 'malicious' punishment of the shipwrights for their earlier defi-ance.[126] This finding presaged a significant broadening of liability for economic torts where the defendant exhibited 'malice'—and perhaps not just in the sphere of labour disputes.[127]

Before the *Flood* case went on further appeal, however, the Lords held, in *Mayor of Bradford* v. *Pickles*,[128] that if an individual was free in law to perform an act, his intention thereby to cause economic harm to another could not render it tortious. Just as with the limitation on the tort of conspiracy in the *Mogul* case, this gave primacy in law to the great article of liberal faith—that the pursuit of self-interest was a beneficent motive force by which the 'invisible hand' secured the enhancement of a society's wealth and prosperity. Accordingly, individuals should not be inhibited by legal duties save where their conduct amounted to a wrong separately defined. In like spirit, the majority of the Appellate Committee in *Flood* overruled the Court of Appeal, accepting the argument that Allen by

[125] [1898] AC 1.

[126] *Flood* v. *Jackson* [1895] 2 QB 21, 38. Other decisions leaning in the same direction at just this juncture included *Trollope* v. *London Building Trades Federation* (1895) 72 LT 258: union liable for keeping a black list of non-union workers which it obliged owners to observe. Cf. also *Farmer* v. *Wilson* (1900) 69 LJ QB 496: picketing of a ship by union members held illegal under the Conspiracy and Protection of Property Act 1876, s 7(4), when the ship housed non-union labour, waiting to be supplied to vessels of federated shipowners.

[127] See above, Vol. XII, pp. 1058–9.

[128] [1895] AC 587. For the dispute, which concerned the unqualified right of a landowner to use water collecting under his land as he chose, see above, Vol. XII, pp. 1054–8.

himself was entitled to tell the yard owners what the union members intended. It was irrelevant that his motive could be considered tit-for-tat revenge. The decision was reached despite the determined manipulations by Halsbury LC to secure an upholding of the Court of Appeal's position. Halsbury found initially that, out of a House of seven members, only he and Lord Morris were in favour of liability.[129] Accordingly, he resorted to pre-Judicature Act practice by calling for the advice of eight of the High Court judges (gaining 6–2 in his support); but that was only advice. He then added two recently appointed Law Lords (Ashbourne and James of Hereford) to a reconstituted House which heard further argument. In the upshot that simply produced a majority of 6–3 in Allen's favour. Legal commentators of the day mostly approved the general principle thus reached after exhausting debate.[130]

Within three years, the Lords were presented with a chance to confine the scope of *Allen* by expanding the definition of tortious conspiracy. In *Quinn* v. *Leathem*,[131] the House returned to the ideas paraded in *Temperton* in a case with two striking aspects: first, it related to secondary boycotting that involved no breaches of existing contracts but only pressure not to enter future contracts; and secondly the union's pressure aimed at putting one non-union worker out of his job in a manner that could be regarded as regrettably harsh. The plaintiff, Leathem, was a Lisburn butcher who employed members of an assistant butchers' union and also non-members. The union was seeking to establish a closed shop there. Three representatives of the union sought to get the non-union men removed not just by threatening a withdrawal of their own men, but also by threatening two trade purchasers of Leathem's meat that they would suffer withdrawals of union men from their own businesses unless they put pressure on Leathem to do what they demanded. Leathem undertook to pay dues necessary for his non-union men to join the union—an offer applying in particular to Dickie, who had worked for him for ten years and who had a family of nine to support. The union would not have this buying of preference. After hearing evidence of their intransigence, the jury found the defendants to have engaged in a tortious conspiracy maliciously and wrongfully to injure Leathem.

---

[129] For Halsbury's opinion in the case, which was built upon the tortious character of 'malicious' conduct and denied any distinction between individual and joint conduct, see Klarman, 'British Labor Law', 1506, n. 96.

[130] For Pollock's changing views of the appropriateness of a basic doctrine of *prima facie* tort in respect of deliberately injurious conduct, see above, Vol. XII, p. 1059. Geldart's polite explanation was that the issues were 'not so much of law and fact as of ethics and economics': W. M. Geldart, *The Present Law of Trade Disputes and Trade Unions* (1914), 24.

[131] [1901] AC 495; see esp. J. McIlroy, 'The Belfast Butchers' in Ewing, *Right to Strike*, 31–68; Klarman, 'British Labor Law', 1505–13.

This time the Irish Court of Appeal, and then the House of Lords, unanimously found reasons for agreeing with the verdict. The House was composed of Halsbury, two members of the Majority in *Allen* (Macnaghten and Shand), who thought *Quinn* a very different case, and three newcomers, the Law Lords Lindley and Robertson, and Hawkins J., for whom Halsbury had insisted on a hereditary peerage (as Lord Brampton). It was necessary, however, to distinguish both *Allen*—the union representative acting by himself, and *Mogul*—the cartel of shippers who had acted in their own self-interest. The House achieved this by returning to the theme of *Temperton* that a conspiracy of several was inherently more threatening than the action of one individual; and then by adding that when a combination had the predominant motive of injuring an opponent in his business it acted tortiously, even though it induced no one to act in a wrongful manner, such as breaking a contract. In support of this new position, further propositions were plucked out from the tangle of labour laws. The Conspiracy and Protection of Property Act 1875, s 3, might prevent an indictment for conspiracy to undertake what an individual could lawfully do. But that, said Lord Lindley, had no relevance to the scope of civil liability. In any case the exemption in section 3 of that Act applied only to conduct in contemplation or furtherance of a trade dispute, and could not therefore protect 'officers of a trade union who create strife by calling out members of the union working for an employer with whom none of them have any dispute... even on an indictment for a conspiracy'.[132]

The leading cases on the substance of tortious liability of trade unions had all been brought against officers and members of the unions, rather than the union itself. The weakness of civil, as distinct from criminal liability, was that imprisonment was not directly available as a punishment. Even where damages were awarded against such defendants, it might be difficult to extract payment.[133] A fortnight before the judgment in *Quinn*, the House delivered its most intimidating blow against the unions. In *Taff Vale* v. *Amalgamated Society of Railway Servants*,[134] it opened up a procedural path that would require an award of damages to be met from the assets of the union itself. The Taff Vale Railway was an enterprise that had returned shareholders consistently high dividends for decades, but in the 1890s had faced increasing competition and added costs. The

---

[132] [1901] AC at 542; cf. his views in *Lyons* v. *Wilkins*, above, 694–5.

[133] According to W. J. Shaxby (*The Case against Picketing* (1897), 34–6, a tract written for Wemyss' Free Trade Association), in an unreported case, *Bailey* v. *Pye*, a jury awarded £1217 against officers of a glass bevellers' union. But in eight months only £5 had been collected.

[134] [1901] AC 426. The literature on the strike and the litigation is considerable. From a labour history perspective, see esp. F. Bealey and H. Pelling, *Labour and Politics* (1958), 55–97; J. Saville, 'The Trade Unions and Free Labour', in A. Briggs and J. Saville (eds), *Essays in Labour History* (1960), 317. For the operational background, see A. Harvey and J. Press, 'Management and the Taff Vale Strike of 1900' (2000) 42(2) *Business History* 63.

latter resulted in part from the guarantee of reasonable hours to railway workers from the Railway Servants (Hours of Work) Act 1893, promoted by Mundella. The ASRS, one of the new unions formed in the wake of the 1871 Act, had begun to assert its muscle with the rise of New Unionism in the 1890s and had been embroiled in considerable conflicts with various rail companies. The Taff Vale Railway had at first conceded a degree of recognition to the ASRS and wages scales had been agreed, but soon enough, led by its forceful general manager, Ammon Beasley, the railway's directors determined to stand out. A dispute about the basis for laying off workers led to renewed demands for recognition and collective bargaining that would improve wages and other conditions. The flash-point proved to be the dismissal of a signalman, who was said to be harshly dealt with despite the company's claim to be a good and respected employer. As the union called on the men to strike, Beasley was able to bring in a considerable corps of replacement workers from Collison's NFLA. A good deal of active picketing ensued, involving assaults, injury to property, and commandeering of trains. These led to a string of summary prosecutions.

The crucial issue of law taken to the Lords, however, related to the leading roles of the ASRS's local organizer, James Holmes, who got the strike under way, and its General Secretary, Richard Bell, who then came down from London to take charge. Following the explicit provisions of the Trade Union Act 1871, ss 8 and 9, the union had chosen to register with the Registrar of Friendly Societies and it had trustees who held and dealt with its funds. The funds were held for both 'trade' and benefit purposes and could under the rules all be devoted to fighting disputes. As the Minority Report of 1869 had argued, unions should not be compelled to keep their two funds separately if they were to have strength and efficiency; and none of the ensuing legislation had attempted to do so.[135] Many of the men whom Holmes brought out on strike did so without the requisite notice of one week being given. Union officials had accordingly induced breaches of contracts of service—the tortious foundations for which pre-dated even *Lumley v. Gye*.[136]

A settlement was negotiated after three months, very much in the railway's favour. Beasley, however, pressed forward with a civil action, initially for an interim injunction against continuance of the strike. Farwell J., with rigid hostility, accepted that the action could be laid against the union in its own name, it being registered under the 1871 Act, just as if it had been incorporated by statute

[135] To follow the Majority's proposal of an enforced separation (Report, above, 667, n 4, xxv) would be, in the liberal jargon so often pressed against them, 'an arbitrary interference with the liberty of association': Report, p. lxi. separation

[136] Above, 694.

or under the Companies Act 1862. The Court of Appeal, whatever its sympathies, held that this could not be correct, given parliament's plain decision, in the 1871 Act, to impose rights and liabilities through trustees. This after all was a procedure paralleled in the legislation on trading firms in the 1820s and 1830s before the distinct path to corporate registration was laid out in the legislation of 1844, 1856, and 1862.[137]

Although the Court of Appeal's view was widespread in legal practice, all five members of the House of Lords refused to accept it, holding that the action could be brought against the union in its registered name. Lord Halsbury's brusque announcement that he simply concurred in Farwell J.'s initial judgment could not have made his contempt for nuanced solutions plainer.[138] Lords Macnaghten and Lindley at least felt it necessary to hold, by way of theoretical answer to the Court of Appeal's position, that what was happening was in reality a form of representative action. In England this procedure had originated in the Court of Chancery, and so was appropriate to proceedings for the equitable relief of an injunction.[139] As the Lords had already insisted in another context, it was enough to show that the group being represented had 'the same interest' and that the representatives selected were, because of their functions within the group, the appropriate persons to be selected as representatives.[140] Whatever else, an action brought against a union named as such side-stepped the latter investigation.[141] Judgment against the union could lead, provided that the trustees were made parties, to an award of damages payable out of union funds. What is more, pronounced Lord Lindley, liability was to be met solely from that source, thus reshaping the representative action further, in order to defeat the argument that an order against representatives would be good against all union members to the extent of their personal assets.[142] As Klarman has pointed out, the very idea of

---

[137] Above, Vol XII, 619. Section 13 of the 1871 Act allowed the union itself to prosecute a defaulting treasurer or other member. Lord Macnaghten refused to read this as precluding the union from asserting other rights directly: [1901] AC at 438.

[138] His nominee, Brampton (Hawkins), took the same high line.

[139] Under the Judicature Act 1873, s. 24 (1), RSC 1883, o.16, rules. 1, 9, representative actions had been made available in any jurisdiction of the superior courts. In Scottish procedure, actions of this character had been allowed against unions since the 1860s: Brodie, *British Labour Law*, 35.

[140] *Duke of Bedford* v. *Ellis* [1901] AC 1, HL, correcting the view applied in *Temperton* v. *Russell (No.1)* [1893] 1 QB 435, that representation was permissible only where the group had a common proprietary interest to protect.

[141] But where, as often remained the case, the union was not registered, it became important to abide by the rules for a representative action. Neville J. had no difficulty in finding them satisfied in *Parr* v. *Lancashire and Cheshire Miners Federation* [1913] 1 Ch. 366.

[142] [1901] AC at 445; and see Haldane LC, *Vacher* v. *London Society of Compositors* [1913] AC 107 at 112. Haldane, as counsel for the ASRS in *Taff Vale*, had argued strongly against personal

choosing representatives to sue a class was thereby abnegated, since this limitation denied that any of the class could be rendered liable. He dismisses the line of argument as 'a clever, but ultimately unsuccessful, attempt to circumvent the question of parliamentary intent regarding union suability'.[143]

The question of damages was pursued. Beasley pressed the railway's case to trial, where he secured a verdict from a special jury for unlawfully molesting the blackleg labour and inducing the breaches of contract by the unionists. In 1903, the union settled damages at £23,000, plus costs of £19,000 (today, at least some £2.5 millions). No decision of the courts in our period (or perhaps any period) had a more resounding political impact, .

So far as industrial relations themselves were concerned, there were some major employers who followed the Taff Vale Railway in pursuit of unions that called strikes. In 1902, the weavers' union in Blackburn were held liable for damages of some £11,000 for unlawful picketing and libel.[144] Starting in the same year, the South Wales Miners' Federation was pursued through proceedings up to the House of Lords, with an ultimate liability of around £60,000.[145]

But, as Clegg, Fox, and Thompson stress, these were years in which all the signs of trade depression were already advancing.[146] Numbers of days lost through strikes had already begun to fall before the decision in *Taff Vale*. Strikes, such as those in the South Wales coalfields, were defensive, seeking to maintain the agreed sliding scale against demands from the colliery owners that additional cuts be made. The new liability of unions for the costs of strike action to the employer's business could scarcely be regarded as having a distinct economic impact. What mattered more was psychological and therefore political. In the years between the settling of the Taff Vale damages and the election of January 1906, by and large, employers acted in sensible self-interest. They pressed the opportunity to move towards greater guarantees of orderliness, notably through the spread of collective bargaining.

---

liability of group members: see Klarman, 'British Labor Law', 1526–8, drawing on the transcript of the hearing.

[143] Klarman, 'British Labor Law', 1521–8.

[144] Clegg et al., *British Trade Unions*, 323–4.

[145] *Glamorgan Coal* v. *South Wales Miners Federation* [1905] AC 239. Other decisions against unions included *Read* v. *Friendly Society of Operative Stonemasons* [1902] 2 KB 732 (using threat of a strike to secure the removal of an apprentice); *Giblan* v. *National Amalgamated Labourers' Union* [1903] 2 KB 600 (pressurizing an employer in order to get a union member to pay a debt to the union).

[146] Clegg et al., *British Trade Unions*, Ch. 9.

7. PUTTING PAID TO JUDICIAL ANTIPATHY[147]

Political Shifts

What the Lords' decision in *Taff Vale* did was to present both the unions and the labour movement more generally with a cause that could be put at the political masthead. In the election campaign of 1905 the Conservatives had to fight allegations that the highest judges had manipulated legal doctrine unfairly against the unions. The argument against them certainly contributed to their ouster at the polls. The Liberals were the immediate gainers. But their own position towards labour grievances was cautious enough for the movement towards separate labour representation in Parliament to continue its growth. The alliance between radical Liberals and unionists, which had stood up well enough in the first two decades after the formation of the TUC in 1868, began to show strains once unionism spread to the unskilled workforce. The formation of an Independent Labour Party in 1893 gave expression to socialist ideas deriving in part from the high theory of Marx and H. H. Hyndman and in part from the pragmatic gradualism of the Fabians. Under Keir Hardie's leadership the ILP linked with others in the TUC to form a Labour Representation Committee and it won parliamentary seats for Hardie (1900) and the railwayman, Richard Bell (1902).

In the 1906 election the LRC could field its own candidates in some cases by contributing to their election expenses and promising a salary as a member of Parliament. The labour movement gained 29 seats and the group called itself the Labour Party. Its strength was supplemented by the 14 miner MPs and a trickle of Liberals with strong sympathies for working-class concerns.[148] The Labour members were closely linked to their own unions and to the TUC;[149] and, in comparison with socialists in the movements of Continental Europe, they were notable for their practical and moderate casts of mind. It was not just the Conservative leadership that felt obliged to acknowledge a profound reshaping of British politics, but even more the Liberals, for they stood to lose a larger part of their support if a truly national spread of Labour candidates were to be presented in future elections. In less that 20 years there would be a Labour government.

---

[147] See, particularly on the politics, Geldart, *Trade Disputes*; F. Pollock, *The Law of Torts* (8th edn, 1908), 336–7; Hedges and Winterbottom, *Trade Unionism*, 144–53; E. H. Phelps Brown, *The Growth of British Industrial Relations* (1959), Ch. 5 and *The Origins of Trade Union Power* (Oxford, 1983), Chs 2, 3; J. Saville, 'The Trade Disputes Act of 1906' (1996) 1 *Hist. St. Ind. Rlns* 11; R. Kidner 'Lessons in Trade Union Law Reform: The Origins and Passage of the Trade Disputes Act 1906' (1982) 2 *Leg. St.* 34–52.

[148] See H. Pelling, *A Short History of the Labour Party* (1965), Chs 1, 2.

[149] For the TUC's campaigns of the period, see Roberts, *Trades Union Congress*, Ch. 6.

Trade Disputes Act 1906

By time of the Liberal accession to power in the winter of 1905–6 it was plain that there would have to be some adjustment of the law affecting industrial action. In opposition—represented mainly by Asquith, Haldane, and the future Lord Chancellor, Robert Reid (Loreburn)—the Liberal leadership had offered the TUC relatively minor modifications to the crime of picketing and the tort of conspiracy, to avert the excesses of *Lyons* and *Quinn*, together with a cap confining union damages to cases where officers and members had acted 'with the directly expressed sanction and authority of the rules'. This phrase, despite its rather indistinct terms, was meant to protect the leadership of a union against liability for 'wildcat' action by local activists. It was given particular point in a run of cases from 1903 onwards, which considered how far the union itself (and therefore its funds) could be liable for its officials' acts. The argument was conducted mainly in terms of a principal's liability for acts of its agents, and a Court of Appeal of generally hostile judges concluded that the union was liable in any situation where the executive committee had power to do what the agent did, without having regard to actual limitations placed on that agent's powers.[150]

The Conservatives, meanwhile, had resorted to a Royal Commission, chaired by Lord Dunedin, which reached much the same conclusions.[151] While the Commission contained no LRC nominee, it did have Sidney Webb, in some ways an astute choice from the government's perspective. The Webbs had already provided a Fabian theory of industrial relations that sought not just to build up strong, nationally based unions as counterparts to federations of capitalist employers, but to do so through a growing range of legal interventions. There would be labour legislation prescribing wages, hours, and other conditions for adult males—not merely women and children. And in the worst paid 'sweated trades', statutory boards would be established to provide for some form of compulsory labour terms. At the same time the state would ensure the complete re-structuring of public responsibility for those out of work. The programme for the dismantlement of the old poor law was advocated powerfully by Beatrice Webb in her Minority Report as a member of the Royal Commission on the Poor Laws (1905–9). When therefore it came to strikes and other industrial disputes, Sidney Webb was able to join the majority of the Dunedin Commissioners in

---

[150] *Giblan* v. *National Amalgamated Labourers Union* [1903] 2 QB 600. But the House of Lords, led by the union-friendly Loreburn LC, would then require that the action be authorized under the rules: *Denaby and Cadeby Main Collieries* v. *Yorkshire Miners Association* [1906] AC 384: see Kidner, 'Union Law Reform' 38–9.

[151] *PP* 1906 [Cd. 2825], lvi, 1.

recommending relatively minor adjustments that were close to those of the Liberal leadership.

The Trade Disputes Bill brought forward by the Liberal government early in 1906 mainly followed the Royal Commission's recommendations and so reflected a solid bloc of middling opinion. It accepted that a degree of 'communicative picketing' had to be treated as permissible in civil and criminal law; that strikes could be justified where the workers gave sufficient notice; and that in trade disputes, conspiracies should not become tortious simply because of a 'malicious' motive. At the same time, the government tried to insist that the *Taff Vale* liability of a trade union itself was justified in the name of legality; and that it should therefore be curtailed only to the extent that the union committee did not authorize conduct by officers or members (an 'absence of agency' exemption). The Labour Party MPs immediately challenged this position in a proposal of their own. The Prime Minister himself, Campbell-Bannerman, led the government's decision to concede on the issue.[152] In its final form, section 4 of the Act ruled out any action against a trade union (of workmen or masters), in respect of any tortious act alleged to have been committed by or on behalf of the union.[153] This complete embargo applied to actions in the union's own name and to representative actions in the name of members or officials. Nor could actions be brought against union trustees in respect of torts committed on behalf of unions, but the trustees' acts had to be in contemplation of or furtherance of a trade dispute.[154]

The old structure of legal understandings, however, dictated that individual activists would continue to be liable in tort, just as they could be prosecuted for crimes, to the extent that no exemption applied to them. While exemptions were now written into the new Act which were designed to afford these individual defendants greater protection, the underlying assumption was that they

---

[152] He was seeking, he said, to 'place the two rival powers of capital and labour on an equality so that any fight between them...should be at least a fair one': *PD* 1906, clv, 51–2. See Kidner, 'Union Law Reform', 46–52; Brodie, *British Labour Law*, 101–6; Saville, 'Trade Disputes Act', 31; K. D. Brown, 'Trade Unions and the Law', in C. J. Wrigley (ed.), *A History of British Industrial Relations 1875–1914* (Brighton, 1982), 127. A. J. Balfour considered it politically astute, given the election result, for his Conservatives to offer no opposition to the bill in its final form: see E. Halévy, *The Rule of Democracy 1905–1914* (1934), 96–8.

[153] But an attempt to stop an unjustified expulsion from a union by claiming that this constituted a tort would fail: the breach of the union rules lay in contract: *Parr* v. *Lancashire and Cheshire Miners' Federation*, above, n. 141.

[154] Section 4(2). This convoluted provision followed from the *Taff Vale* ruling that, under s 9 of the Trade Unions Act 1871, trustees were in principle liable to be sued for torts of the union. Section 4(2) then created an apparently limited exemption from that liability. It was read, however, as subject to the general exemption in s. 4(1) *Vacher* v. *London Society of Compositors* [1913] AC 107.

personally could be sued for activities which could not give any cause of action against their union. The new immunities for individuals were all confined to actions 'in contemplation or furtherance of a trade dispute'.[155] The expression was defined in wider terms than before. It covered, in particular, activities of union officials who were not personally embroiled in a dispute, whether the argument went to the obligations of employers to their workforce, or a clash of interests between different categories of workers.[156] Nonetheless, the phrase was a response to the considerations of motive and intent instilled in economic tort law by such decisions as *Temperton* and *Quinn*; and likewise it left scope for hostile interpretation. If the activities *were* found to be in contemplation or furtherance of a trade dispute, a person could not be liable in tort for conspiring to do something that an individual was free in law to do (section 1).[157] This was intended as a limit on the malicious conspiracy rule applied in *Quinn*. Nor could a person be liable on the ground only that the act 'induces some other person to break a contract of employment, or that it is an interference with the trade, business or employment of some other person, or with the right of some other person to dispose of his capital or his labour as he wills' (section 3). It was the once-powerful Liberal backbencher, Sir Charles Dilke, who saw to the inclusion here of the reference to breaches of employment contracts—an addition that insulated that sometimes highly effective weapon, the sudden withdrawal of labour without contractual notice.[158] But even he did not attempt to secure protection for inducing breaches of existing commercial contracts, as could occur in the secondary picketing of the *Temperton* or *Lyons* variety.[159]

While, moreover, the exemption for picketing in the Conspiracy and Protection of Property Act 1875, s 7, was now limited to actions in contemplation or furtherance of a trade dispute, it became lawful to 'attend' at *any* place, not just for obtaining or communicating information but also for 'peacefully persuading

---

[155] See ss 1–3.

[156] 'Trade dispute' was defined to mean any dispute between employers and workmen, or workmen and workmen, which is connected with the employment or non-employment, or the terms of the employment, or with the conditions of labour, of any person. Workmen henceforth covered all persons employed in trade or industry: see s 5(2).

[157] This accordingly adopted the same principle as had applied in criminal law since the Conspiracy and Protection of Property Act 1875, s 3.

[158] For Dilke's prominent role in bills to modify the law in the period before the 1906 election, as well as his crucial role in strengthening the 1906 bill, see Kidner, 'Union Law Reform', 42–6, 50–2. See also Geldart, *Trade Disputes*; K. W. Wedderburn, 'History of British Labour Law' (2004) 17(1) *Industrial LR* 127.

[159] The exemptions relating to 'interferences' here appeared to cover inducing people not to enter contracts in future, thus blocking another basis for liability under *Temperton* and *Quinn*.

any person to work or abstain from working'.[160] This did something to curb judicial hostility towards even very limited picketing, as manifested in the *Lyons* v. *Wilkins* decisions.[161] But still the question dangled: what persuasion counted as peaceful? And there were other nice issues of interpretation which could lead to difficulties. Respectable opinion continued to fear pickets as an all too effective means of coercing others out of their 'free will'.[162] After the 1926 General Strike, the law would be changed again.[163] Union protesters would then be shackled against engaging in what, a century before, Parliament had labelled 'obstructing' and 'molesting'.[164]

Before 1901, it had commonly been accepted that individuals, whether acting with or without the authority of their union committee, would themselves be liable for the tortious wrongs they committed, even when their unions were not. But for the barrier apparently raised by the unions' lack of legal personality or some equivalent, they would in many circumstances have been liable as principals for what their officers did as their agents. *Taff Vale* made the unions themselves also liable. Individual liability would then be significant mainly as a precondition for union responsibility. The bill would have confirmed that position. The Act, however, reverted to the older understanding that only the individuals could be sued, and then only if no immunity applied. Any subvention that union sources might provide in support of the individual defendant would be a matter of in-house arrangement, unless it could be characterized as an unauthorized expenditure to which a dissident member could object.[165] For decades, much of the legal community continued to find this an outrage against the rule of law. Not only were union funds sealed off from judgments against them concerning strike activity and the like, but from actions in tort of any kind.[166]

---

[160] Trade Disputes Act 1906, s 2.

[161] Above, 694–5. In the immediate wake of the 1906 election, the Court of Appeal showed some restraint, perhaps sensing things to come: *Ward, Lock* v. *Operative Printers' Assistants Society* (1906) 22 TLR 327.

[162] See e.g. *R* v. *Wall* (1907) 21 Cox CC 407; *Larkin* v. *Belfast Harbour Commissioners* (1908) 2 IR 214; *Young* v. *Peck* (1912) 29 TLR 31.

[163] For the issues in the strike that raised questions of civil liberties, see K. D. Ewing and C. A. Gearty, *The Struggle for Civil Liberties: Political Freedom and the Rule of Law in Britain, 1914–1945* (Oxford, 2000), Ch. 4.

[164] So the Trade Disputes and Trade Unions Act 1927, s 3, struck those scrupulous lawyers, R. Y. Hedges and A. Winterbottom, *Legal History of Trade Unionism* (1930), 129–33.

[165] If there was no rule that justified supporting the individual's suit, it might be open to objection. In the trial proceedings of the *Taff Vale* case, Joyce J. refused to find that the ASRS had a rule broad enough to allow support for the local representative who had originally instigated the strike and was separately sued: Klarman, 'British Labor Law', 1552.

[166] *Vacher* v. *London Society of Compositors* [1913] AC 107.

Reactions to the 1906 Formulae

The most significant challenge to the Act itself in fact came almost at once, in litigation concerning the exemptions of union officials and took up the meaning of 'in contemplation or furtherance of a trade dispute'. Was there a trade dispute if the actions of union representatives against dissident members could be characterized as personal grudge matches rather than as trade disputes? Were trade disputes only those situations where there was a general issue as to employment terms between workers and their employers or over which category of workers should be entitled to do types of work, for instance in demarcation or closed shop disputes?

In *Conway* v. *Wade*,[167] a union 'delegate', Wade, had informed a Tyneside shipbuilding firm that the union men were demanding the dismissal of Conway, a boiler-scaler. His offence was that he had refused to pay a £10 fine for breaking union rules—a dispute which stretched back intermittently over several years.[168] The firm had given in and Conway brought a county court action for £50. The jury found that Wade's actions did not arise in contemplation or in furtherance of any trade dispute and judgment was entered against him for the tort of malicious injury. The union, stung to fury, backed appeals at three levels with support from TUC affiliates. The Court of Appeal overturned the judgment, holding Wade to fall within the protection of the 1906 Act. Cozens-Hardy MR and Kennedy LJ took relatively sympathetic views of the Act's objectives,[169] while Farwell LJ, true to his record, denounced the Act as a monstrosity which the doctrine of parliamentary sovereignty nonetheless obliged him to uphold. A specially enlarged House of Lords unanimously restored the judgment against Wade, given the jury's verdict that there had been no trade dispute.[170]

What it was in Wade's conduct that amounted to a tortious wrong remained obscure. On that question, Lord Loreburn—sympathetic towards labour, but in the end somewhat equivocal—stated that a malicious motive could still be the crucial factor that made a man's action wrongful, for then the action would be

---

[167] [1909] AC 506; K. D. Ewing, 'The South Shields Case—Subverting the Trade Disputes Act 1906'; Ewing, *Right to Strike*, 71–100.

[168] The fine had been imposed when Conway was employed at a different yard and so had been a member of another branch of the union.

[169] Kennedy L. J. treated the jury's verdict as perverse, pointing out that Wade's communication to the employer was similar to the non-tortious statement at issue in *Allen* v. *Flood*. At the same time the statement showed that there was a trade dispute in existence.

[170] In peacetime, each party would retain the option to have a jury until 1933, and the property qualification for service confined jurors to the middle classes. This left the judiciary some leeway, particularly on appeal, either to accept the verdict as unimpeachable or to find that it was given under a misdirection on the law. After *Conway*, trade unionists considered that their major campaign should be for truly democratic juries: see Ewing, 'South Shields', 116–17.

characterized as 'in contemplation or furtherance, not of a trade dispute, but of his own designs, sectarian, political, or purely mischievous, as the case might be'.[171] Did this once more presage a return to 1825-like distinctions between good and bad industrial action? Was conduct to be acceptable where workers were seeking better wages and hours in economic upturns, but unacceptable when they were pressing restrictive practices to hedge against scarcity of jobs? Compounding the question of what could constitute the tort in the first place with the trade dispute issue left an esoteric conundrum. Most subsequent courts offered no real solution, although there was a distinct tendency in this period to shy away from making the outcome of a case depend on the presence of some malign motive. In the event, the courts would only return to the implications of the *Conway* case in the 1950s and 1960s, when unions had acquired the strength for drawn-out strikes and other major confrontations.

In any case there were further legal obscurities about the 1906 Act. The Dilke amendment to the tortious liability of individuals where there was a trade dispute covered two categories: the exemption applied first to those who induced breaches of employment contracts; and secondly to those who interfered with the trade, business, or employment of another, or who interfered with the right of some other person to dispose of his capital or his labour as he willed.[172] As a result the Act prevented even individual unionists from becoming liable for pursuing secondary boycotts, where either traders or their employees broke contracts or refused to enter them in future. The sweeping tort of causing economic harm because the defendants had used 'unlawful means' was no longer available in such situations. But just what those situations were would remain untested for half a century.[173]

8. GOVERNANCE WITHIN THE UNION: FURTHER LEGAL ATTACKS

The attitudes of judges towards unions also became controversial where a member contested the powers of internal management contained in the union's rules. The starting point was once again a special exemption in the 1871 Act. The legal convolutions were serpentine. Section 3 of the earlier legislation had rescued trade unions with 'illegal objects' from the consequences at common law of being in restraint of trade. By section 4, the Act then provided that the rescue operation did not extend to certain agreements entered into by this category of union. There

---

[171] [1909] AC at 512.
[172] Section 3: see above, n. 155.
[173] Notably in *Thomson DC* v. *Deakin* [1952] Ch. 646, and *Rookes* v. *Barnard* [1964] AC 1129.

could be no direct enforcement of agreements between members of the union concerning their own trade or labour, agreements for the payment of a subscription or penalty to the union, and agreements for the application of union funds to provide benefits for members.[174] Within this formula lay two uncertainties: what within a union's rules made it an unlawful restraint of trade at common law? And what amounted to direct enforcement of one of these agreements? The resultant disputes arose in (a) suits to restrain misapplication of union funds; (b) suits for restitution to membership; and (c) suits to determine the construction of a trade union's rules and therefore whether certain actions infringed them.[175]

Whether a union was in unreasonable restraint of trade was judged by interpretation of its rules, not by considering its conduct. The nicest distinctions came to be drawn, and it is difficult to suppose that the courts approached their task without having in mind that they could enforce a rule without any impediment if the union's rules did not make them in unreasonable restraint of trade.[176] Any rule which provided for fines or loss of benefits for failing to comply with a restrictive burden placed on a member was likely to render the union 'unlawful'. In *Rigby* v. *Connol*—the first major decision on section 4—where a man was fined for placing his son with a non-union shop—the rule providing for the fine was characterized in this way.[177] So equally it would be when the rule required members to go on strike, or required the authority of the union committee before going on strike, coupled with prescriptions for the conduct of the strike by it and penalties for not complying with them.[178] But, as from 1906, leading judges became highly suspicious of provisions excluding unions from legal liability, they came to hold that, if the only relevant rule prescribed a right to strike pay, that would not of itself amount to an undue restraint.[179]

What, then, of 'direct enforcement'? In *Rigby* v. *Connol*,[180] the father who had disobeyed the embargo on where he could place his son refused to pay the fine. In consequence he was expelled and sought reinstatement. But that, in Jessel MR's view, meant giving him once more his entitlement to union benefits and

---

[174] The fourth category, covering agreements between one trade union and another, has an obscure history. In the present context, it must be kept in mind that, while the definition of a 'trade union' was broadened in 1876 to cover unions that were legal as well as illegal (see above, 673, n. 33), this did not affect the application of s 4, which related only to illegal unions. See generally, C. Grunfeld, *Modern Trade Union Law* (1966), 64–92.

[175] Hedges and Winterbottom, *Trade Unionism*, 82–3.

[176] For the full range of decisions, see Hedges and Winterbottom, *Trade Unionism*, 81–4; Klarman, 'British Labor Law', 1547–52.

[177] (1880) 14 Ch D 482, CA; see further, *Cullen* v. *Elwin* (1903) 88 LT 686; (1904) 90 LT 840; *Mudd* v. *GUOC* (1910) 26 TLR 518; *Russell* v. *ASCJ* [1912] AC 421, HL.

[178] *Old* v. *Robson* (1890) 62 LT 282; *Sayer* v. *ASCJ* (1902) 19 TLR 122.

[179] *Swaine* v. *Wilson* (1890) 24 Ch D 252; *Gozney* v. *Bristol Trade Society* [1909] 1 KB 901.

[180] See above, n. 177.

so involved the direct enforcement of one of the agreements in the section 4 list. A line of cases followed this lead.[181] But almost at once a counter-trend set in. In *Wolfe* v. *Matthews*,[182] the issue was whether the officers of one union could be enjoined from merging it with another, the substantive argument being that this would prevent application of the first union's funds to the benefit of the member suing. Fry J. treated this as an action 'to prevent the payment of monies to somebody else. Either that is no enforcement of an agreement at all, or it is an indirect enforcement'. Twenty years later, after the large strike over wages in the Yorkshire collieries, interpretation of section 4 reached the House of Lords. In *Yorkshire Miners* v. *Howden*, a dissident union member (backed by an employer) challenged the union's provision of strike pay. A majority of four law lords—all Conservative—upheld his ability to bring the action, since it was not to establish a benefit to him (the *Rigby* v. *Connol* situation) but to preserve the union funds intact. The two Liberal Law Lords dissented, refusing to distinguish between this circumstance and the reinstatement sought in *Rigby*. In the upshot, no power to make the payments could be found in the rules; the union was valid and an injunction was accordingly granted, which in fact brought the strike to a close.[183]

So matters stood when the legislation on wrongs committed during strikes was revised in 1906. Within five years, a further bout of political hostilities faced the courts through two sets of proceedings brought against the ASRS by W. V. Osborne, a head porter who was secretary of a union branch in London. He was also a Liberal with no love for the emergent Labour Party. His first action challenged the financial support for Labour members in Parliament that unions were providing under their rules.[184] The action was therefore not about the 1906 Act, which had contented itself with immunities from legal liability and had not tackled the question whether unions should be given corporate status. Nor was it about the inhibition on direct enforcement of the rules of a union, provided for in section 4 of the 1871 Act, or so it appears to have been assumed.[185] Instead it went to deeper issues about the permissible objects of a trade union. Was it within the

---

[181] *Aitken* v. *ACJ Scotland* (1885) 12 CS(R) 1206; *Chamberlain's Wharf* v. *Smith* [1900] 2 Ch. 605, CA.

[182] (1881) 21 Ch D 194, preferring the Scottish solution (*M'Laren* v. *Miller* 1880 7 R. 867) to the English *Duke* v. *Littleboy* (1880) 49 LJ Ch. 194.

[183] [1905] AC 256. In favour of liability, Halsbury, Macnaghten, Lindley, Robertson; against: Davey, James of Hereford. The interpretation of the rules as not empowering strike pay was in line with earlier cases and demonstrated a tendency to side with union dissidents against majorities: see Klarman, 'British Labor Law', 1551–2.

[184] *Amalgamated Society of Railway Servants* v. *Osborne (No. 1)* [1910] AC 87, HL; see K. D. Ewing, *Trade Unions, the Labour Party and the Law* (Edinburgh, 1982), Ch. 2.

[185] In the Court of Appeal ([1909] 1 Ch. 163), counsel for the union did attempt an argument that, thanks to s 4 of the 1871 Act, the action could not lie since it would directly enforce a 'benefit' to members and was thus non-actionable; but the Court did not accept it.

powers of any body defined as a 'trade union' to adopt a rule providing for a levy on members for payments to MPs who took the Labour whip?

Osborne's objection was mainly argued on the ground of *vires* and that was the basis on which he succeeded in the view of three of the five judges in the House of Lords—Halsbury, Macnaghten, and Atkinson. The central proposition was that the 1871 Act, in rescuing unions from effects of being in unlawful restraint of trade, confined their powers to specified objects. There was an analogy to statutory companies, which were confined in their power to those stated in the statute and those that could be reasonably implied;[186] the same requirement of *vires* had been placed on companies registered under the Companies Act 1862, but there the objects could be defined in the memorandum of association as the incorporators chose.[187] In this context the *Taff Vale* treatment of unions as quasi-corporations persisted.[188]

The first place for finding a limitation on union powers was the definition of 'trade union',[189] which described them as 'combinations... for regulating the relations between workmen and masters, or between workmen and workmen, or between masters and masters, or for imposing restrictive conditions on the conduct of any trade or business'. But, as Lord James of Hereford and Lord Shaw of Dunfermline would conclude, this was language of statutory recognition, not of limitation or exhaustive definition.[190] Moreover, if it was in some way exhaustive, why did it make no reference to the benefit purposes that were major objects for which many unions were founded? In response to this last, much-pressed argument, the three members of the Lords who found for Osborne on the *ultra vires* ground searched for supplementary indications. Lord Halsbury, rather crudely, called in aid the list of contracts in section 4 that were incapable of direct enforcement. Lord Macnaghten, more plausibly, pointed to the provisions in the 1871 Act that allowed for the registration of unions as friendly societies, and therefore to the obligation to register rules in order to show that their purposes fell within the definition in the statute. Friendly societies after all had to do the same in relation to their objects.[191] Lord Atkinson held that benefit purposes were so well-known

---

[186] C. H. S. Fifoot, *Judge and Jurist in the Reign of Victoria* (1959), 57 *et seq.*

[187] Vol. XII, pp. 657–9.

[188] e.g. Lord Atkinson at p. 105. Lord Shaw took a more advanced view of them as living organisms (p. 108).

[189] For the broadening of this definition in 1876 to apply to legal as well as illegal unions, see above, 673, n. 33.

[190] At pp 98–9, 107–8.

[191] The Friendly Societies Act 1855, 18 & 19 Vict. 63, s 9, laid down the benefit purposes for which a friendly society could be registered (a list extendable by secondary legislation) and required the Registrar to certify that the rules were 'in conformity with law'. This justification, however, might leave unregistered unions in a different position.

that they were implicit in 'relations…between workmen and workmen' or were ancillary thereto.[192]

Lord James (briefly, but determinedly) and Lord Shaw (at resounding length) chose instead to decide in Osborne's favour on the 'constitutional ground' which had been forcefully adumbrated by Fletcher Moulton and Farwell LJJ in the Court of Appeal.[193] This was that where a union provided financial support for a Member of Parliament taking the Labour whip, the member's freedom of decision was so impeded as to imperil the liberal foundations of parliamentary democracy. The union's practice was accordingly on a par with bribery of MPs and other corrupt suborning and had obvious implications for the ways in which Members of all parties acquired 'interests'.[194] There were mineowners, railway directors, and friends of breweries aplenty in the Commons. So long as there were no parliamentary salaries, the consequence of this view appeared to be that only those with unearned income or professional salaries could in practice hold seats. The majority in the Lords circumspectly declined to enter on the question of constitutional acceptability.[195] It remained true, however, that the constitutional objection arose only in relation to support for Members of Parliament. The objection to lack of *vires*, as the Webbs pointed out in dismay, went to any activity for which a court could find no express or implied authority in the Trade Union Acts. They asked whether, for instance, a trade union could run education programmes or publish a newspaper.[196]

The ASRS expressed their disgruntlement at the new cap on their powers by expelling Osborne for bringing the action: he had attempted, so the union ruled, to injure the Society or break it up otherwise than as allowed by the rules. In consequence he brought a second action, this time for reinstatement.[197] If he could

---

[192] See [1909] AC at 92, 96–7, 102–3.

[193] [1909] 1 Ch. 163 at 186–8, 193–8.

[194] Lord Shaw drew on John Locke for a denunciation of the practice as ranking 'among those breaches of trust which would amount to the very dissolution of government': [1910] AC at 113. The argument that Labour MPs needed the mandate of their union for any parliamentary vote arose in the year that Conservatives in the House of Lords refused to pass Lloyd George's Finance Bill because the Liberal government had no 'mandate' from the electoral manifesto on which it won its majority: see above Vol. XI, pp. 10–11, 321–33.

[195] Of Farwell, Fletcher Moulton and Shaw, R. F. V. Heuston wrote: 'it is difficult for anyone not brought up in England to understand how three men, two of whom had been in their time members of Parliament, and thus had practical experience of the working of the party machine, should have committed themselves to statements so out of keeping with the real nature of the English constitution in the twentieth century': *Lives of the Lord Chancellors 1885–1914* (1964), 163–4; see also R. B. Stevens, *Law and Politics* (1978), 247–8.

[196] The power of a union to do the latter had been questioned, but upheld, in *Linaker* v. *Pilcher* (1901) 17 TLR 256; Cf. also *Steele* v. *South Wales Miners' Federation* [1907] 1 KB 361, accepting a political fund rule. Questioning *vires* was part of the forensic weaponry of the period.

[197] *Osborne* v. *ASRS (No. 2)* [1911] 1 Ch. 540, CA.

not succeed, then unions would have the last laugh against minority objectors. The influence of that reality can clearly be felt in the Court of Appeal's decision, which turned on two issues, the first concerning the legality of the union at common law and the second with the direct enforcement of internal rules that arose under section 4 of the Trade Union Act 1871. The Court stretched to a new extreme the case law which treated a union as illegal at common law only if it had power to order a strike, holding the rule book of a large and aggressive union to contain no sufficiently 'illegal' rule for it to be in unlawful restraint of trade at common law: in the Court's view, the union had no power to do more than provide strike pay to members who had come out of their own accord. On this basis, section 4 did not apply to the dispute at all. In the alternative, the Court held that a declaration that Osborne's expulsion was wrongful did not amount to 'direct enforcement' of a rule providing for benefits to union members. This aspect of the decision confirmed that *Rigby* v. *Connol* and *Chamberlain's Wharf* v. *Smith* had no general application to an expulsion merely because reinstatement would give a right to benefits. Rather, those decisions were confined to the particular declaration and injunction sought in each case. This was 'restrictive distinguishing' with a vengeance.

If the union was after all legal at common law, as the Court of Appeal found in *Osborne (No. 2)*, why was it held in *Osborne (No. 1)* that it 'places itself under an [act of Parliament] and by so doing obtains some statutory immunity or privilege'?[198] The ASRS had apparently been wrong-footed step by step. If the principal advantage gained under the 1871 Act was registration as a friendly society, did the *ultra vires* principle apply equally to an unregistered union? Was a union that had a political levy in its rules deprived of all the advantages of the 1871 Act, or was it just the levy rule that was void? In any case what permitted the House of Lords in *No. 1* to uphold not just a declaration that the political levy rule was void but an injunction ordering the union not to demand payment? It became plain enough that Parliament in the 1870s had not intended to confine unions to specified objects by their definition of 'trade union' or by any other provision. Egged on by Parliament's 1906 embargos on the tort liabilities uncovered by the courts in the decade after 1893, in the *Osborne* cases a phalanx of senior judges set about imposing their own fetters on the powers of the unions to place themselves above legal constraints in the management of their internal affairs.

The first *Osborne* judgment plunged some of the Labour Party MPs into financial difficulties. In 1911, the government was locked in a confrontation with the political House of Lords which, in the stifling heat before the summer recess,

---

[198] Lord Macnaghten, *Osborne v. ASRS (No. 1)* [1910] AC at 94.

would lead to the curbing of the Upper House's power by the Parliament Act.[199] Entangled in that skein was the Liberals' programme of social reform, over parts of which it had to watch the reactions of the unions closely. At the same time it found itself interceding in the hope of ending major strikes on the railways, and then in coalmining and the docks. These were the three industries with the ability and strength to bring the economy to a standstill, if they chose to act in concert. From this year on, the prospect of their 'Triple Alliance' was never far away, first in wartime and then, ominously, in peace. In this fraught atmosphere, the support of working-class MPs was an inescapable part of the agenda.

In 1911, the government introduced salaries of £400 a year for all MPs.[200] But union representatives continued to press for complete reversal of the *Osborne* rule as well. By the Trade Union Act 1913, the government conceded most of this demand.[201] First, it replaced the *Osborne (No. 1)* limitation on *vires* by the principle that powers additional to those 'statutory objects' acknowledged in the definition of 'trade union' were valid to the extent that they were conferred by the rules.[202] This allied the unions more to the position of registered companies than to statutory companies or registered building societies with limits on their powers prescribed by Parliament. However, political funds continued to be a special case, in order to allow workers like Osborne to join unions without contributing to a particular party's support. A union was permitted, after a ballot of members, to introduce a separate fund for selection of candidates, electoral expenses, MPs' salaries, and for political meetings and publicity.[203] The rules had to provide for a separate levy and each member was guaranteed the right to 'contract out' of contributing to it by simple written notice to the union.[204] The rules had to be approved by the Registrar of Friendly Societies, whether the union itself was registered or unregistered.

In justifying a move with evident political advantages for the Liberals, Haldane spoke in terms that resonated with the optimism of Joseph Hume in 1824: if trade unions were no longer confined by 'unfair' legal constraints they would

---

[199] See Vol. XI, p 323.

[200] The decision in *Osborne (No. 1)* remained unaffected by this: *Parr* v. *Lancashire and Cheshire Miners' Federation* [1913] 1 Ch. 366.

[201] See K. D. Ewing, *Trade Unions, the Labour Party and the Law: A Study of the Trade Union Act 1913* (Edinburgh, 1982), Chs 3, 4.

[202] Section 1(1). Unions could be registered or certified by the Registrar of Friendly Societies if their principal objects were within the definition of 'trade union' (which was itself somewhat simplified by s 1(2)).

[203] See the list of permitted purposes in s 3(3). Support for the Labour Party's newspaper, *The Daily Herald*, would be allowed: *Bennett* v. *NAS Housepainters* (1915) 31 TLR 203; *Carter* v. *US Boilermakers* (1915) 60 SJ 44; but cf. *Forster* v. *NU Shop Assistants* [1927] 1 Ch. 539.

[204] See ss 3, 4. Each member had to be notified how to lodge his objection. A person who contracted out could not be refused admission or be subject to any disadvantage in consequence.

become responsible and cooperative in their dealings with employers. In the event, to begin with there seems to have been a measure of 'contracting out', but it waned as the Labour Party gained parliamentary strength. After the general strike of 1926, the chief 'punishment' that the Conservative government would decide to inflict was to reverse the procedure: contributing members had for the future to 'contract in'.[205] The effect on Labour Party funding would be considerable and with the Attlee government in 1945 the reversion once more to 'contracting out' was predictable enough.[206]

9. LEGISLATIVE SUPPORT FOR BETTER CONDITIONS

In the two decades before 1914, the legislative changes promoted by the Minority of the Devonshire Commission, and supported in some degree by its Majority, were acted on bit by bit.[207] As already discussed, in 1897 the Conservatives & Unionists had imposed workmen's compensation liability on employers, and the range of industries to which this applied was made general in 1906.[208] From that year onwards, much of the Liberal government's programme of welfare measures had to do with loss of earnings arising from other causes: retirement, sickness and, above all, unemployment, whether temporary or longer lasting. Equally, in 1909 the problems set by the sweated trades were tackled by creating Trade Boards for specified industries.[209]

This was nonetheless buttressing that aimed to conserve the inherited structures of capitalism. Any fundamental attempt at redistributing the wealth of the propertied might be advocated among socialistic idealists but appeared to have no political chance. The proponents of land nationalization continued to attract attention but even Lloyd George's attempt, as part of his People's Budget, to construct a record of landholdings was side-tracked by bitter opposition from those it might eventually hurt. On the other hand, no controls came into being that would in any real sense resemble the communal grip imposed under Tudor legislation three centuries before—either by setting rates of labour or by putting the out-of-work into food or other production. National pay policies would be attempted only in the 1960s; and, while there was considerable interest among Edwardian politicians in institutions that would force the able-bodied applicants for poor relief into public works as a condition of relief, the Liberal government preferred to assist self-help, by the new, centrally run, labour exchanges and the

[205] Trade Disputes and Trade Unions Act 1927, s 4.
[206] Fox, *History and Heritage*, 335.   [207] Above, 689–92.
[208] See Ewing *Trade Unions, Labour Party*, Ch 5.   [209] Above, 692.

national insurance schemes for loss of earnings through sickness and termination of employment, whose beneficiaries had to build up entitlements through contributions from themselves and their employers while they remained in work.[210]

The prime organizational tool for labour remained the market, where demand measured itself against supply without external intervention. The assumption remained that the labouring classes would share in the risks and profits of the businesses for which they worked only to the extent that they could expect wages, conditions, and other benefits to reflect the fortunes of their employers. While from the 1840s the idea of cooperation in business ventures had shown considerable resilience, its attraction lay in the dividends payable to those involved essentially as consumers and not as employees.[211] Ventures which attempted to take up the Owenite ideal of a workforce sharing together in a partnership, particularly in a production industry, proved difficult to manage successfully, particularly through years of economic depression. For the most part, the returns for ordinary work came in a wage, without any direct mechanism for sharing a portion of profits in good years. Where unions were established, they were there to press for higher wage rates when the market demand for labour accelerated or profits were shown to have risen. Even more they were there to soften the blows of bad times or bad management, when wages would have to be cut, or workers were made redundant.

It had taken the rise of collective action by labour to move beyond a world in which competition for workers was largely a matter between competing masters. With the greatest of reluctance in some quarters, the employers in many industries had become obliged to accept negotiation with the unions as representative organs of their members. Until the late 1880s, unionism had largely been confined to skilled workers who would have some power, if they acted as a cohort, to advance their position in rising conditions and to stall too drastic a response by employers to downturns in trade out of their longer-term concerns to have a workforce available when conditions improved. By the 1890s unions embracing also the unskilled, typified by the ASRS, also acquired at least intermittent strength, foreshadowing the post-War world in which collective bargaining between national organizations of employers and employees became a central feature of labour relations in a heavily industrialized, free enterprise economy.

---

[210] Above, 505–6.

[211] It was for them primarily that the Industrial and Provident Societies Act of 1852 (15 & 16 Vict. c. 35) and succeeding legislation established a legal framework and a degree of public regulation that gave members an entitlement to a share in profits on the basis of their active contribution. The Rochdale Equitable Pioneers Club of 1844 showed how an annual dividend to its retail customers could increase membership attracted also by the promise of food and drink that had not been adulterated.

As the unions had grown and acquired a certain know-how in exerting their strength through industrial action, the propertied classes had become increasingly anxious about the effects. Their differing reactions drew them towards opposite poles. Some insisted that strikes, lock-outs, and other disruptive action be, in one or other sense, 'outlawed'. Political antagonists of this stamp collected within both the main parties. But it was the judiciary who were put in the position of deciding whether there were legal justifications for imposing sanctions on the disrupters. They did so, first, by hostile interpretations of criminal statutes and denunciatory expansions of common law conspiracy as a crime, latterly by imposing civil injunctions and damages awards for tortious conduct which some did not hesitate to broaden.

The other pole attracted those who sensed a need to reach new accommodations with the working class of the 'workshop of the world'. New theories of the entitlements of labour in a capitalist economy had led to the 1867 adjustment of the parliamentary franchise. Again, the two main political parties soon recognized the attractiveness, for the new voters, of legislative measures that freed them to engage in union activity at work, as well as other changes that offered some aid other than the tender mercies of the poor law. By socio-economic analyses of unemployment, temporary and longer-term, as well as under-employment in seasonal trades and elsewhere, they perceived that the dominant pattern of open-ended wage contracts that were terminable upon short notice offered precious little job security; and they sought to alleviate the consequences. So a wave motion set in: courts would impose penalties or liabilities on strikers and the like, but ameliorating legislation would follow soon enough, which aimed, not always successfully, to curb the courts' powers. In the course of these tidal movements, positions were reached which, to the constitutionally minded, appeared to rock the rule of law as a legal underpinning of free enterprise economy and liberal society.

The desire to protect and develop voluntary labour negotiation continued to play a leading part. In 1907, Canada would swing towards state intervention in labour disputes, by introducing a regime of compulsory arbitration. The shift would be carefully examined in Britain.[212] But neither employers nor unions in major industries could see that the results would be consistently to their own advantage, so no similar move across the board was imposed. For instance, the established trade unions had considerable suspicion of plans for labour exchanges. Already under the Conservatives' Unemployed Workmen Act 1905 there were exchanges in existence and their operations carried overtones of compulsion to

---

[212] See the Report by the Board of Trade's Chief Industrial Commissioner, G. R. Askwith, 'Industrial Disputes Investigation Act of Canada 1907', *PP* 1911–12 [Cd. 6603], xlvii, 303.

work, which in turn might lead to reprisals against those who joined in strikes.[213] Employers too had no wish to be required to notify all jobs to exchanges; nor were they ready to be required to take whoever was sent. Winston Churchill, the President of the Board of Trade, initially wanted the exchanges to be in a command position of some kind; but he and his advisers on unemployment, including the formidable William Beveridge, were obliged to give ground. In the upshot the new exchanges were treated as a voluntary resource, funded by central government to aid the workings of the labour market, but not to direct it. Even though many employers continued to fill posts by requiring application at their own works, by 1914 423 main exchanges were filling some 3,000 jobs a day and helping a quarter of the unemployed back into work.

10. CONCLUSION

At the outbreak of the First World War, the laws affecting labour were moulded to fit the special conditions of British industrial capitalism. The union organizations largely accepted that ownership and profits of industries went to investors, not to the labour force. The Edwardian decade saw a very considerable growth in collective bargaining beyond the local level towards industry agreements for regions or the whole country.[214] Even Ricardo's tough view of a 'wages fund', posited upon the theory that wages were a share of returns, not a cost that had to be budgeted from the outset, had been abandoned. Much of the working class had to be content with a mere living wage, only the managerial and the skilled doing better. Cooperation in business organization of the kind preached by Robert Owen and his followers, and then in succeeding generations by Christian socialists and others, had made little permanent advance, save in the forms of mutual protection, such as in retail distribution and various forms of small-scale capital sharing, such as building, friendly, and industrial and provident societies. Schemes for the redistribution of land had remained a matter of fringe experiment, and Marxian ideas of the means of production passing into the hands of the state were in Britain still a distant utopia. Only after the Second World War would they find echoes in Labour Party programmes of nationalization and then dictation of prices and wages to industries still in private control.

---

[213] Under the Unemployed Workmen Act 1905, larger local authorities were empowered to set up relief committees which might use farm colonies to put the unemployed to work. The measure was in line with the harshnesses of the poor law: see above, 503.

[214] One consequence was a growth of shop stewards representing members on home territory. For a time—and particularly as war broke out—they adopted an ideology more determinedly socialist than in the upper echelons of their unions; but the antagonism faded: see Webb, *Trade Unionism* (3rd edn), 488–90.

In the earlier nineteenth century there were legal as well as economic reprisals against those who failed to work the exhausting hours required or who challenged the power of their masters to command obedience. Laws such as the Master and Servant Acts and the prohibitions on combination led masters, impelled by bullish self-righteousness or a wimpish fear for their own authority, to treat these obligations as Hobbesian commands born of moral necessity and ordained by economic science. The hard men who ran factories and mines would accept no counteracting legislation that would protect anyone other than children and women. The adult male worker's ability as a free agent to take work on whatever terms were being offered was an iconic image dominating every marketplace.

Later, Victorian wage-workers would gain strategic concessions of power in industry—a development which would run in parallel to the expansion of the parliamentary franchise. As trade unions became larger and more respectable, a pragmatic strain within the propertied classes accepted that workers must have the collective power to withdraw labour and engage in similar action, since they possessed no other strength for bargaining. One was that convoluted compromise by which the legal relations of employment existed in the individual contract, but the terms fed into that contract were increasingly taken from collective agreements that lacked legal force.[215] Beside this, and in more direct transgression of rule-of-law ideals, trade unions were left to conduct their internal relationships largely without recourse to legal sanctions. Other countries would find themselves obliged to introduce more extensive legislative controls over union activity and industrial negotiation. In Britain, at the heart of Empire, the great hope remained that labour relations could be conducted voluntarily between large federations of employers on the one hand, and of workers on the other. Thus was the basic libertarian inclination adapted for a world in which labour relations had become high politics and the prospect of securing better social conditions and opportunities through existing institutions and further economic advance had sufficient appeal to counter the attractions of socialist panaceas.

There remained many—and they included politicians and supporters of both Conservative and Liberal parties—who opposed such accommodation and continued to believe that aggressive collectivism from labour would topple the whole marvellous edifice of the British economy and Empire. After 1867, the higher judiciary contained figures whose mission did not change from that in earlier decades: it was for them to retain or invent legal measures of control that were likely to be ignored by a Parliament moving towards democracy. It would prove

---

[215] See K. D. Ewing, 'The State and Industrial Relations: "Collective Laissez-Faire" Revisited' (1998) 5(1) *Hist. St. in Ind. Rlns* 1–32; S. Deakin and F. Wilkinson, 'The Evolution of Collective Laissez-Faire' (2004) 17(1) *Hist. St. in Ind. Rlns* 1.

to be part of their attitude that unions of workers must be placed under legal disciplines that did not apply to the mutual dealings of business competitors. Entrepreneurs were entitled to pursue their mutual self-interest in comparative freedom because they risked their wealth in trade and finance. Wage-workers were simply different. These judicial sallies, as we have seen, turned the courts into centrifuges of political reaction and Parliament would then set about curbing their spin-outs, first by the legislation in 1871 and 1875–6 and then that of 1906 and 1913.

Those who shared the basic attitudes of these judges saw the increase of major strikes in the years immediately before 1914, conjuring the prospect of a Triple Alliance of mining, docks, and railway unions, as an inevitable consequence of political concession rather than discipline through law. Any real demonstration of that potential would be delayed by the exigencies of war and its aftermath until the General Strike of 1926 in support of the miners.[216] The causes, the legality, and the ultimate failure of that confrontation remain in contention partly because they have to be viewed in the framework set by the pragmatic, non-revolutionary, history of British labour, including the role of law in it which has been the concern of this chapter. One continuing hope bequeathed by the politically astute was that collective *laissez faire* remained the essential promise for the future. Governments would have twice to face annihilation by warfare within less than 40 years; and yet, as peace became once more manageable, labour relations would largely revert to the old faith in collective negotiation between the two sides, unencumbered by compulsory legal machinery. Scholars writing after 1945, as much as industrial leaders and politicians of the period, would make this optimistic ideal a fulcrum of their analysis and their rhetoric. Not until the 1960s would the whole mechanism begin to shift its base back towards legal constraints, some of it judicial but much more of it under the compulsion of statutory schemes. The long survival of voluntarism in labour relations exemplified the remarkable faith in the virtues of individual liberty that had become the hallmark of British society as a whole in the long nineteenth century.

---

[216] Compulsory labour arbitration had to be introduced during the First World War. The Whitley Committee would report in 1916 in favour of a return to voluntarist consultation and discussion by setting up councils of both sides of an industry where collective negotiation was an established procedure in determining wages. These became the Wages (or Whitley) Councils, which at first blossomed but then would run into difficulties as the economic situation deteriorated: see Brodie, *British Labour Law*, 151–6; F. J. Bayliss, *British Wages Councils* (Oxford, 1962), Ch. 1; R. Davidson, *The Labour Problem in Late Victorian and Edwardian England* (1985), 85–98.

Part Four

LAW OF PERSONS: FAMILY AND OTHER RELATIONSHIPS

I

Family Law, Family Authority

1. INTRODUCTION

Civilian systems of private law begin with a discussion of the Law of Persons. Blackstone, unsurprisingly, used that title for the first book of his *Commentaries* and boxed within it an account of the constitutional structure of the country as an outgrowth of the political rights of individuals. He then treated their status as 'aliens, denizens or natives', and their holding of ranks as clergy, military, and masters of servants, before coming to the position of husbands, wives, children, and guardians; and finally to corporations as legal persons. Whether in this broad form, or in a much narrower conspectus, a law of persons has not become a primary category for common lawyers. Yet neither did nineteenth-century lawyers speak of 'family law', but rather of the law relating to husband and wife, to children, to domestic relations and so forth. Family law is a modern term suggesting a balancing of interests, rights, and responsibilities between the typical members of today's nuclear families. There is much about it now that is horizontal, involving mutual rights and obligations. Two centuries ago the lines were mainly vertical, set by the authority of the husband and father at the head down to the wife, children, and sometimes other relations. Much of this Part is concerned with the first, hesitant moves towards this 90-degree re-orientation of attitudes and law affecting the family. Hence its equivocal title. Another reason is that it deals with the law affecting the unfortunate whom Victorians labelled 'lunatics', those individuals whose mental incapacity or psychological disorder was striking enough to require special treatment in law, whether or not they had lost their family or were excluded from it by their behaviour (see Ch. VI). Since legal issues concerning families regularly overflow the boundaries of particular states, issues in English private international law concerning the major aspects of the subject are taken up here (see Ch. VII).

Interest in the history of families in Britain has grown strikingly over the last half-century. We now have a much fuller account of the family from the early modern period onwards in both demographic and structural terms. Legal history, however, is related primarily to the literature on the understanding of family relationships as a cellular element in community and state; and this in a context not only of the British Isles but of Europe and its colonizations more generally. The major study of divorce by Roderick Phillips (1988), for instance, demonstrates the value of inter-country comparisons and some of the difficulties in making them. Legal proceedings give flesh to the history of prevention and cure in families that are or may become dysfunctional. The records of courts and regulatory bodies have provided case studies for authors such as Stuart Anderson (1984), Sybil Wolfram (1985, 1987), Allen Horstman (1985), Gail Savage (1989), Lawrence Stone (1990, 1992), A. J. Hammerton (1992), and Leah Leneman (1998), who use them to show the backgrounds and the needs—selfish and unselfish, innocent, and duplicit—of the people drawn into proceedings as spouses and lovers, trustees, children, servants, detectives, charity dispensers, poor law guardians, and others.[1] But as elsewhere, the law was quite as important in its enabling role for managing successful human relationships. Here it provided groundwork for the celebration of marriages and for property arrangements and other responsibilities within the family, for the bringing up of children by providing them with education and assets, for inheritance on death and so on; and that distinct role has always to be remembered. As for systematic views of the law, an historical survey of its many aspects was provided by Graveson and Crane's centennial history of the introduction of judicial divorce.[2] That book has now been buttressed by the extensive nineteenth-century material in Stephen Cretney's fine work on the twentieth century.[3] The debt of this chapter to these books is considerable, as it is to numerous studies of family history in the period, in which the law gains its interstitial place.

2. COURTS USED FOR FAMILY DISPUTES

In the early nineteenth century the values embodied in the law affecting families were still those of a pre-industrial age. Each of the three major jurisdictions of England and Wales—the courts of common law, those of equity, and the ecclesiastical courts—had distinct roles in family matters. The *common law* (absorbing much canon learning) defined basic concepts such as legitimacy, property rights at law between spouses, the duties and responsibilities of men as husbands and

---

[1] J. S. Anderson 'Legislative Divorce: Law for the Aristocracy?', in G. R. Rubin and D. Sugarman (eds), *Law, Economy and Society* (Abingdon, 1984), 412–44; S. Wolfram, *In-Laws and Outlaws* (1987) and 'Divorce in England' (1985) 5 *OJLS* 155–86; A. Horstman, *Victorian Divorce* (1985); G. Savage, 'Divorce and the Law in England and France prior to the First World War' [1988] *J. Social Hist* 499–513; L. Stone, *The Road to Divorce 1530–1987* (Oxford, 1990) and his *Uncertain Unions and Broken Lives* (Oxford, 1992); R. Phillips, *Putting Asunder* (Cambridge, 1988); A. J. Hammerton, *Cruelty and Companionship* (1992); L. Leneman, *Alienated Affections* (Edinburgh, 1998).

[2] R. Graveson and F. R. Crane, *A Century of Family Law* (1957).

[3] S. M. Cretney, *Family Law in the Twentieth Century* (Oxford, 2003).

fathers, including their rights and duties over their wives' contracts and torts; and in such contexts it would determine whether there had been a marriage. It provided forms of action against wrongs such as breach of promise to marry, 'criminal conversation' by adulterers and seduction of daughters; and its criminal law contained various adaptations for family relationships.

Equity intervened in notable fashion by allowing a bride's father or other family to set up a marriage settlement containing a trust that reserved separate property for her. More generally property relationships within families could be placed under trusts, which made the trustees into persons to whom wrangling or estranged spouses could turn for resolution of disputes. The Court of Chancery had also assumed the Crown's function as *parens patriae* to take propertied children into wardship and appoint guardians for them when their father or his nominee failed to do so.[4] The trust would indeed prove a highly adaptable instrument in family affairs—for controlling spendthrift children, for dealing with the sick, the elderly, the mentally deficient or sick, and later for tax avoidance. What equity had already started by 1820 for the propertied would be extended down the social scale, primarily by the intervention of statute law. These shifts, to which Parliament was brought after the second Reform Act, marked in law the gradual change of attitudes towards women more generally. Even by the time of the First World War, the feminist cause was in many ways still in gestation.

The *ecclesiastical courts* could order a marriage contract to be carried out. Subsequently they had limited powers to order the separation, and in other cases the re-uniting, of spouses; but they could not award a complete divorce—that was Parliament's prerogative alone. As a major step in ending the lay jurisdictions of these courts, full divorce became a regular entitlement only in 1857, when a Divorce Court would be created which had no position within the courts of the established Church.[5] In their jurisdiction to grant probate to executors under a will and letters to administrators on an intestacy, the ecclesiastical courts secured the winding up of the affairs of a deceased person—something in which family members would have special interests. At the same juncture, this function passed to a separate Probate Court.[6]

That the ecclesiastical courts retained legal jurisdiction over matrimonial disputes and the grant of administration on death highlights the close bonds between the dictates of religious doctrine and moral scruple, on the one hand,

---

[4] For the history from the seventeenth century, see Lord Redesdale, *Wellesley* v. *Wellesley* (1828) 2 Bli. N.S. 124, at 130–2, where he rejected challenges to the existence of the jurisdiction that had been raised not infrequently in early nineteenth-century cases.

[5] Below, 781–4.

[6] See Vol. XI, 709–14 and below, Ch IV.

and the adoption and maintenance of rules of law, on the other. Those ties would remain in place long after scepticism about God's placing of man and woman full-grown on earth on the seventh day of creation began to be spread through the evolutionary theory of Darwin and his followers. Those who became prepared to admit themselves agnostics or atheists generally still subscribed to the necessity of monogamous marriage and a role for the husband as paternal dictator with dominion over wife and child. These were cultural ideals long before stamped into the Mosaic credo and little enough modified by Christian beliefs in mutual love and respect. Such instinctive beliefs, as we shall see, were buttressed at numerous points by laws that formally were becoming part of a separate cadre of authority. Religious precept was specially likely to shape whatever the law was; but the legal rules did not necessarily accord with perceptions of good and evil, or of acceptable and unacceptable behaviour, both within families and in the communities to which they belonged.

3. PRIVATE AND PUBLIC OBLIGATION

A separate aspect of law touching the family was the presence of distinct private and public elements which had effects along class lines.[7] The private law provisions, which formed the business of the main courts, mostly applied to those with property. The public law had its impact largely on the labouring population. Its basis was statutory and had been so for centuries.[8] The poor law, and the charitable trusts and gifts that were its adjunct, had particular importance when a family's source of support from work dried up—through death or disablement of the breadwinner, unemployment, birth of a child to a partnerless mother, the young without a family, and so on.[9] Where there was a family member who could be made responsible for the cost of that maintenance, the justices had power to place the burden on that person, rather than the ratepayers. Their jurisdiction applied mutually between spouses, and parents and children, extending also to grandparents.[10] In addition, the justices had long bound husbands over to keep the peace with their wives, where they had used violence or were likely to do so. The criminal law would also be extended in attempts to protect working-class wives against batterings from their husbands, or neglect through desertion. In the late nineteenth century, magistrates would be given charge over non-payment

---

[7] J. tenBroek, 'California's Dual System of Family Law: Its Origin, Development and Present Status (Part I)' (1964) 16 *Stanford LR* 257–317.

[8] Which is not to forget the rating burden borne by the propertied in maintaining the poor law.

[9] Below, 802–5.

[10] 43 Eliz. c. 2, s 7. For this and further statutory provisions, see R. Burn, *Burn's Justice of the Peace and Parish Officer* (e.g. 20th edn, 1805), iii: 974–80.

of maintenance and the disciplining of unruly children. Alongside their efforts would grow new services to cope with orphans and runaways, enforce compulsory education, insist on smallpox vaccination, and prevent sexual and other abuse of the young, all of which became part of the formation of the British welfare state.[11] By the end of our period, the elements of private and public law affecting families interweave more closely. Nonetheless, the social distinctions remained evident to a degree that has lessened considerably in the century since.

The English notion of family had long given primacy to the nuclear unit of the spouses and their children, rather than to extended groupings covering the members of all generations still living. Population historians have shown this pattern emerging early in the countries of north-west Europe, for instance, among the British and Dutch.[12] England was not a society in which there was a single custom according to which the young passed through set stages of status recognition, such as the initiation of boys into manhood by circumcision. Nor did the family dictate the choice of spouse through child betrothal, or the employment of marriage brokers,[13] or the threat of killings and other reprisals if a couple crossed the boundaries of tribe, caste, or other grouping.[14] Rites of passage there were, but they varied with social rank, education, and work prospects. The result was a legal framework that in many respects conformed to the prevailing liberalism. It offered freedom of choice, at least to those with economic power and social prestige. Where rules were established, they often enough prescribed default positions, such as the rules for making testamentary dispositions, operating alongside rules for dispositions on intestacy.

Woven into their operation, however, were limits which the law made mandatory consequences of entering a valid marriage—the division of children into legitimate and illegitimate, the rule against perpetuities restricting future interests in freehold, the determination of what constituted bigamous conduct,

---

[11] Below, 814–22.

[12] P. Laslett, *Family Life and Illicit Love in Earlier Generations* (Cambridge, 1977), Ch. 1; M. Mittrauer and R. Seider, *The European Family* (Oxford, 1981), Chs 1, 2; J. Goody, *The Development of the Family and Marriage* (1982); R. Wall (ed.), *Family Forms in Historic Europe* (Cambridge, 1982), Chs 2, 16.

[13] Equity had indeed treated agreements under which agents would be paid to arrange marriages as unenforceable, initially out of a fear of men who sought to climb socially and financially by securing an heiress as a wife. This public policy objection would only be applied at common law after the Judicature Acts: *Hermann* v. *Charlesworth* [1905] 2 KB 123, 130 (CA); C. A. Morrison, 'Contract' in Graveson and Crane, *Century*, 116–42, at 135.

[14] Kinship and marriage in non-European societies could be remarkably different—as colonization would bring home to the English. From the 1850s onwards, anthropological study provided some analysis of these differences, often with a skew towards justifying British policies over its native peoples: see e.g. Wolfram, *In-Laws and Outlaws*, 1. For the impact of these differences on English rules for conflicts of law, see below. Ch. VII.

and so forth. The dynastic sense, long in evidence among the aristocracy and landed gentry, led to this balance between rules of choice and barriers confining them. Senior figures of the family, their eyes fixed on the acquisition or repair of fortunes and estates, and on political and social position, would have much to recommend—indeed to demand—concerning the marriages of younger generations. Lawyers supplied them with marriage settlements and other complex arrangements that would reinforce ideas of male primogeniture, patriarchal control over wives and children, the return of endowed assets to the bride's family if the new line did not prosper, advancements and other benefits which would place cadet brothers in professions and sisters in marriage, and many other niceties.[15]

With industrial capitalism, considerations of family alliance led to property arrangements for the growing middle classes in simpler, more flexible forms.[16] These were mainly urban people, expecting that children would move away from parents upon marriage, dwelling more and more in respectable suburbs and giving over the running of the domestic hearth to a wife who no longer shared in her husband's work. Rather later, skilled and semi-skilled manual workers would move along a similar path which accepted these 'separate spheres' for men and women. However, with them, and even more with the unskilled, the need would remain for wives not just to bear and rear children, but also to work, however limited and ill-paid the opportunities for doing so might prove.[17] By our standards life was short, beset with constant risk and filled with the preoccupations of keeping going. English families were forming and re-forming through the hazards of existence, where today they more evidently follow the vagaries of emotional commitment.

How important it was that the essence of marriage should be the mutual affection of the spouses, rather the furtherance of financial and social position, has been a compelling focus for historians.[18] By the early twentieth century, there undoubtedly was some greater emphasis than formerly on the significance of love and companionship. But still that idea was tempered by notions of the husband entitled to obedience as the head of the family. 'The Englishman's home is his castle' was an apophthegm of long standing, as was 'Home, sweet home'.[19] In respect of the domestic relationship itself, it was the former, rather than the latter, that continued to hold sway. Deciding in 1919 that a husband's agreement

[15] See Vol. XII, 769–94.

[16] See Vol. XII, 249–52.

[17] M. Hewitt, *Wives and Mothers in Victorian Industry* (1958), Ch. 1; D. Levine, *Proletarianization and Family History* (Orlando, 1984), Ch. 1.

[18] Below, 729–30.

[19] For the many nuances in language that conjured up images of 'domesticity', see G. K. Behlmer, *Friends of the Family: The English Home and its Guardians, 1850–1940* (Stanford, 1998), 5–18.

to pay for the upkeep of his wife was not intended to create legal relations, Atkin LJ could insist that 'each house is a domain into which the King's writ does not seek to run, and to which his officers do not seek to be admitted'.[20] Such attitudes left the English with legal rules which reinforced the position of the husband and father and reduced that of the wife and children. That was so where the rules were directive and could not easily be subverted; but it applied equally where the domestic dictator had the freedom to choose his course of action without real constraint—as he had in disposing of his assets on death. The basic values enshrined in the rule of law concerned the great freedoms of men. They were contradicted over and over, when it came to wives, to children, and to a considerable extent to unmarried women and widows.

4. THE HUSBAND AS PATRIARCH

Matrimony, being a union between one man and one woman for life, was ordained a 'holy estate' by the Church of England, its teaching underpinned by its canon law. Stable family relationships in the early nineteenth century were generally founded upon marriage, which was not just an expression of religious commitment but an arrangement of prime social significance with a splay of temporal consequences. Only children born in wedlock would be legitimate, a status that could affect inheritance, just as it gave rise to a separate set of responsibilities under the Poor Law from those applying to bastards and their parents.[21] By 1820 complete divorce or annulment allowing marriage to someone else was possible in England only in exceptional cases; but if it was available, it did not depend on whether or not the couple had children.[22] A judgmental culture heaped disgrace upon those whose sexual relations went unblessed by marriage. Such attitudes bottomed the novels of Richardson, Goldsmith, Burney, Austen, and their many successors.

In the Victorian period, the values attaching to marriage were heightened. During childhood and adolescence, girls were prepared for finding husbands and accepting their own subjugate status—for once wed, the law deemed them to be *femes couvertes*. The woman who remained single, the *feme sole*, was the exception, staying within her birth family or living apart—either alone, or with a man not her husband, or in another household or community.[23] Thus it was

---

[20] *Balfour* v. *Balfour* [1919] 2 KB 571 (CA). For the reason why the issue was a novelty, see below, 765 at n. 44.

[21] See below, 776–7, 814–22.

[22] See below 777–80.

[23] Which is not to say that unmarried women and widows were few. For what they did and how they were regarded, see J. Stobart and A. Owens, *Urban Fortunes* (Aldershot, 2000).

that, on issues affecting all women, such as rights to education, professional status, and the vote, the position of married women tended to be an initial measure. The patriarchal assumptions encircling families formed by a marriage remained dominant and the constrictions press at many points in this chapter. The attitudes need to be stressed from the outset. Since the Second World War they have swivelled at such a tangent that it is difficult for the historian to recapture the old potencies. We start accordingly by emphasizing two aspects of the legal relations between spouses. The first concerns the licence left to the husband to contain his wife within the home by physical and emotional pressures and to preserve his honour by frightening off rivals for her affection and protection. The second concerns the property and obligations of married women, which, at common law, began from the common law notion that her personality in law was elided into his.

5. DOMINANCE AND DUTIFUL SUBMISSION

The unity of husband and wife was a curious abstraction. It signalled that a wife must accept subjection to her husband and show him duty, love, and tenderness. Unity, however, had numerous corollaries in the common law's purview: the wife was debarred from suing the husband (and vice versa), since one could not bring an action against oneself; and she could be party to civil proceedings by or against a third party only through him as her next friend. While the marriage continued, she lost her capacity to enter contracts in her own name, being at best able to bind her husband and his assets where she had (or was deemed to have) his authority as agent.[24] For her torts occasioned during the marriage, the husband alone was liable.[25] In criminal law, the wife gained special shelter. For all felonies save the most heinous crimes, if she participated with her husband, she was presumed to be acting under his coercion and so was excused.[26] If he returned home after committing a crime, she was not guilty as an accessory after the fact, because she was expected to harbour him as part of her marital duty. That attitude perhaps explains why, as a general rule, she could not be guilty of stealing his property[27] (but there was an exception when she was, for instance, setting up

---

[24] He was obliged to assume liability under contracts which she had entered before the marriage—an issue of sudden political moment once reform of wives' property rights began; see below, 761, at n. 22.

[25] He was also responsible for her pre-nuptial torts, but that was to become an early issue in the process of reform: see below, 738, 763–4.

[26] See, generally, D. Mendes Da Costa, 'Criminal Law', in Graveson and Crane, *Century*, 165–96, at 184–93.

[27] While the same applied to the husband, he normally owned the moveable property and the wife was more often the purloiner.

a nest with her lover).[28] Certainly a husband who killed his wife committed the felony of murder.[29] In that instance, discrimination took a different form: a wife who killed her husband was guilty of petty treason, and so punishable by burning at the stake.[30] The basic assumption was ingrained deep. When, in 1869, women householders were given the same property franchise as men to vote in municipal elections, the Court of Queen's Bench could not conceive that the new statute was intended to extend to *married* women, even when they were maintaining themselves in their own premises.[31]

The powers of the head of the family included bodily constraints, which in the case of children certainly extended to beating and to custody (as also with apprentices). A wife who lived apart could be ordered by an ecclesiastical court to return to the conjugal relationship.[32] Older books suggested not only that the husband had a legal right to chastise his wife in reasonable measure—wife-beating being very common in real life[33]—but also that he could seize her in order to bring her home and could then keep her there.[34] In *Re Cochrane*,[35] Coleridge J. concluded from older authorities that the husband had a general self-help remedy in the matter. He did not have to show any special grounds, such as that she was spreeing away with his money or consorting with 'lewd company'.[36] But

---

[28] The leading case on the exception was *R* v. *Tolfree* (1829) 1 Mood. CC 243. The logic of unity created tortuous difficulties over whether another person to whom she passed the property could be prosecuted as a receiver: see *R* v. *Streeter* [1900] 2 QB 601; liability was firmly established only by the Larceny Act 1916, s 33(1). See generally, Da Costa, 'Criminal Law', in Graveson and Crane, *Century*, 184–93.

[29] Unless provocation reduced the offence to murder or some other exception applied. For the extent of excusal where a husband killed the wife's lover, see Da Costa, 'Criminal Law', in Graveson and Crane, *Century*, 173–8.

[30] The distinction was, however, abolished by the Offences Against the Person Act 1828, 9 Geo. IV c. 3, s 2.

[31] *R* v. *Harrald* (1872) LR 7 QB 361. The same embargo was taken to apply to the electoral rights given to women when the new County and County Boroughs were set up in 1888. So deep did this prejudice run, that in 1889 the Central National Society for Women's Suffrage considered it wise to support a bill seeking the parliamentary suffrage only for unmarried women: Holcombe, *Wives and Property*, 212–13.

[32] For the jurisdiction eventually given to magistrates to order a deserting husband to pay maintenance, see below, 797–8.

[33] See, generally, M. Doggett, *Wife-Beating and the Law in Victorian England* (1992), 4–15; E. Foyster, *Marital Violence in English Family History, 1660—1857* (Cambridge, 2005). The belief that a judge (allegedly Buller J.) had said that any stick used by the husband had to be no thicker than his thumb had some currency in the late eighteenth century (Gilray packed his well-known cartoon, *Judge Thumb*, with seething derision). But the notion was mythical rather than legal.

[34] An ecclesiastical court would in any case grant him an order for restitution of conjugal rights; and until 1884 a non-compliant wife could be imprisoned: see below, 768, n. 34.

[35] (1840) 8 Dowl. 630.

[36] Cf. *R* v. *Lister* (1721) 1 Stra. 478.

in *R* v. *Leggatt*,[37] Campbell CJ refused to equate a wife with a child; and in *R* v. *Jackson*,[38] an indignant Court of Appeal held that *habeas corpus* lay to release her from being locked in at home.[39] So much for the occasional desperate strait. In the general run, the husband could decide everything crucial about their joint existence: where they would live, how their property would be used, what food, clothing, medical attention, and other basic provisions they would have in daily life, how their children would be brought up, not least in the matter of religion.[40] Duties upon him to behave reasonably, given all these circumstances, were for the pulpit rather than the bench. The husband could force sex on his wife without committing rape, though some Victorian judges would consider that he could be guilty of the lesser offences of assault with actual or grievous bodily harm, if her life or health was in consequence endangered.[41] Only within strict limits, could a husband be brought to book for terrorizing his wife, or simply for deserting her, whether for another woman or not.[42]

The subordination of wives made their sexual adventures with lovers a high insult. In the past, gentlemen had been expected to seek vengeance through a duel.[43] Adultery had also been a matrimonial offence in the ecclesiastical jurisdiction, for which the offenders could be ordered to do penance in a white sheet before their congregation; and sometimes it led to a magistrate's order to the pillory. Both these types of sanction had faded during eighteenth century. Thereafter, while Parliament was from time to time pressed to make adultery a criminal offence, legislators all too readily thought of pots and kettles.[44] Popular censure of known transgressors could still lead to ritual 'rough music'—those rowdy,

---

[37] (1852) 18 QB 781.

[38] [1891] 1 QB 671. In local communities, however, there were mass protests against this decent outcome: see Doggett, *Wife-Beating*, 134–9.

[39] Doggett, *Wife-Beating*, Ch. 1 tells the Jackson story in graphic detail.

[40] See below, 807–8.

[41] Sir Matthew Hale (*Pleas of the Crown*, I, 629) had categorically denied the possibility of rape, on the ground that the marriage carried with it an unretractable consent to sexual intercourse. But by the time of *R* v. *Clarence* (1888) 22 QBD 23, four out of 12 members of the Court of Crown Cases Reserved considered that a husband who knew of his gonorrhoea and had sex with his unsuspecting wife, thereby infecting her, was at least guilty of inflicting grievous or actual bodily harm. Wills and Field JJ, neither of them radical by temperament, cast doubt on Hale's unflinching proposition (see pp. 33, 57). From 1949 English judges would show more consistent distaste for the 'no rape' rule, and eventually the House of Lords would hold it a mistaken view: *R* v. *R* [1992] 1 AC 599.

[42] For this aspect of ecclesiastical jurisdiction, and its later substitutes, see below, 796–801.

[43] If, catching them *in flagrante*, the husband killed the lover, the provocation would reduce the crime to manslaughter; but, according to Parke B., he had to have 'ocular inspection of the act', not a mere suspicion: *R* v. *Pearson* (1835) 2 Lew. CC 216. For the complexities of vengeance in pursuit of male honour, see E. Foyster, *Manhood in Early Modern England: Honour, Sex and Marriage* (Cambridge, 1999).

[44] See further, below, 783.

drink-heated processions which shamed the culprits and sometimes led to violence.[45] The superior courts fell back on forms of private action. In the ecclesiastical courts, the petition for an order of separation (divorce *a mensa et thoro*) could be founded against a wife on the ground of her adultery, but against a husband only for his 'aggravated' adultery.[46]

At common law, the civil action on the case extended to a number of situations involving extra-marital sex.[47] In particular, a husband might sue his wife's lover for criminal conversation ('crim.con.' to lawyers and publicists).[48] Despite the name, this was an action for damages, not for punishment; and its 'conversation' went to physical rather than social intimacy. The wife was not a party to the action and so had no standing to plead her case.[49] Nor indeed had she any equivalent action against her husband's mistress. The curious history of crim. con. was gloated over in a literature, often lubricious, sometimes painful, that has been recovered by Lawrence Stone and others.[50]

At the outset of our period, cracks were opening over what the law required for a jury to make an award against the adulterer, the views of judges and jurors about the moral objectives of the law, and the behaviour that the action provoked in litigants. In the nervous period of the French Revolution, the rulers of the country had been possessed by a determination to put down immorality of all kinds, above and beyond political and anti-religious challenges to the existing English order.[51] Thanks to the damages awarded by the jury in a crim.con action, the lover of a married woman might have to live out his life in a debtors' prison. The jury was no longer instructed merely to place a value on the loss of assistance and comfort that flowed from the wife's transfer of affection to the lover. It was encouraged to reach awards that would act

---

[45] There is a colourful literature on these charivari, which could also protest against wife-beating and other transgressions of the community's sense of what was only right: see E. P. Thompson, 'Rough Music: Le Charivari Anglais' (1972) 27 *Annales* 285–312; Hammerton, *Cruelty and Companionship*. In Thomas Hardy's *Mayor of Casterbridge*, the shame of such an exposure brought Lucetta (Henchard's mistress and then Farfrae's wife) to her life's end.

[46] Below, 789–92.

[47] Two are mentioned elsewhere: the action for breach of promise to marry, used particularly by a woman made pregnant by a lover who refused then to marry her (below, 752, 805); and the action by a father for seduction of a daughter who was part of his household (below, 769, n. 10, 802).

[48] Stone, *The Road to Divorce 1530–1987*, Ch. 9; S. Staves 'Money for Honor: Damages for Criminal Conversation' (1982) 11 *Studies in Eighteenth-Century Culture* 279–97.

[49] Neither husband nor lover could give evidence, since as parties they were incompetent, until the law changed in 1851: see G. D. Nokes, 'Evidence' in Graveson and Crane, *Century*, 143–64, at 144–5. Much therefore depended on observations by the family, servants, and others.

[50] Victorian examples included F. Plowden, *Crim. Con. Biography* (1838–9) and the *Crim. Con. Gazette*.

[51] See above, 352–72.

as a general deterrent to adultery.[52] Remarkably high verdicts were recorded against adulterers from aristocratic circles.[53] In the middling social ranks the award might be less, but the amount could be equally crippling. If the husband went on implacably in search of payment, the guilty pair might escape only by living permanently abroad. What is more, he was not precluded entirely from bringing the action (as he would be for an ecclesiastical separation order) by any kind of acquiescence or connivance, nor by his own bad conduct. At most these factors might be taken into account by the jury in settling the damages.[54]

The higher the damages, the greater the attraction of crim.con. actions. Only in the 1820s do dissatisfactions begin to rear up—against greedy husbands; against trap evidence procured (or asserted) by servants or spying agents; against the inability of the wife to present her story, and so on.[55] As we shall see, the action would continue to be one step in the exceptional procedure for a parliamentary divorce, and that helped to account for why many cases went undefended, being in essence collusive.[56] In the changes to divorce laws in 1857, proving the wife's adultery by common law action ceased to be a prerequisite.[57] By then the idea of taking money to assuage a deep-set affront aroused a prim distaste, at least among members of the Upper House.[58] Nonetheless, in the divorce proceedings the right would in effect be retained in the form of a claim that a petitioning husband could make against the co-respondent lover.[59]

---

[52] There was a particular dislike of the lover who took advantage of the husband's hospitality and friendship, which showed in the attitudes of servants and other witnesses as well as in the size of damage awards: see on such witnesses, Stone, *Road to Divorce*, 211–28.

[53] In 1808 Lord Cloncurry obtained £20,000 against Sir John Piers Bt (today at least £3 million): S. Wolfram, 'Divorce in England' (1985) 5 *OJLS* 155–86, at 166–72.

[54] *Ibid.*, 265–7, 279–84.

[55] *Ibid.*, 278–90.

[56] Below, p. 778.

[57] Matrimonial Causes Act 1857, s 59.

[58] 'Many persons would rather touch a scorpion than the money which was awarded as compensation of their dishonour' pronounced Lord St Leonards: *PD* (3s), cxvii, 2031. Nonetheless in *Bell v. Bell and the Marquess of Anglesey* (1859) 1 Sw. & Tr. 565, the jury made a damages award against the aristocratic co-respondent of £10,000.

[59] The scope of the crim.con action continued to determine when these damages could be claimed. The amount had still to be assessed by a jury, and so, although damages were not supposed to be exemplary, they could appear to reflect disapproval of the co-respondent's conduct, particularly if he was of higher social status: Divorce and Matrimonial Causes Act 1857, s 33; Cretney, *Family*, 153–7. They could be awarded in acrimonious break-ups until abolished by the Law Reform (Miscellaneous Provisions) Act 1970, s 4. They never became available to the wife against the husband's mistress, as happened in the United States (for which, see L. H. Korobkin, *Criminal Conversations* (New York, 1998).

6. PROPERTY DURING A MARRIAGE AND AFTER THE DEATH OF ONE SPOUSE

Earlier Developments

Much of the law of property developed as an expression of rights and responsi-bilities within families. Family provision is of the essence in the developing law of property as a whole.[60] Here we anticipate that larger framework by drawing attention to those elements in property arrangements which depend upon the relationship of husband and wife. Patriarchal assumptions formed much of the inherited law, being categorically expressed in common law rules that gave hus-bands very considerable rights in the assets of their wives.[61] They affect both the rights to property during the joint lives of the couple, and those on the death of either. In outlining the rules in the early nineteenth century, we can, however, sense some movement away from a one-sided certainty specified in the common law towards a more even balance. Through a law of settlements involving both common law and equitable rights, families could adopt a number of different stratagems when acquiring property or bestowing it on their next generation. We still have only partial information about which social groups used these devices, how they dealt with differing types of property, and what the results were in economic and social terms. It is evident from reported case law, how-ever, that marriage settlements, together with legacies and other gifts to wives, gave rise to a stream of litigation, since the circumstances to which the law could apply were so varied. New legal forms by no means necessarily increased the protection of wives in practice. Nor can it be taken from the loss of legal guar-antees, like the widow's right to dower in the deceased husband's freehold land, that wives became increasingly subjugate to their husbands.[62] Regime change in law towards wider choices rarely produces simple consequences—and certainly not where rules become increasingly facilitative, rather than directive.

Categories of Property: General Rules of Common Law

Nonetheless, the extent of the husband's dominance through property rules can be appreciated well enough from a brief summary of the position reached in law

---

[60] See Vol. XII, Pt 1, Ch. 1.

[61] The eighteenth-century position is for exploration in Vols IX and X of this *Oxford History*.

[62] S. Staves, *Married Women's Separate Property in England, 1660–1833* (Cambridge, 1990), esp. 4–10 and Ch. 7.

and equity by 1820.[63] During the joint lives of the spouses, the rules in outline were as follows.

(1) PERSONALTY

At common law, chattels and money that the wife brought to the marriage, both before and after its celebration, became the husband's and formed part of his estate on death. The common law allowed the wife to retain strictly personal effects (clothing and jewellery—classed as 'paraphernalia'); and equity gave effect to provisions for her 'pin money' in marriage settlements.[64] Where an asset consisted of a debt or other chose in action, however, the husband had to secure payment or other satisfaction before it became his, if necessary by suing to recover it. This accordingly included earnings due for the wife's work. Even where the employer or commissioner paid the wife, this would not discharge the debt, since it was owed to the husband, unless he had given her authority to receive the money. The rule could lead to the employer having to pay a second time, even when he did not know of the marriage.[65] However, if the husband died before turning the obligation into a satisfaction for what was due, the right of action returned to the widow by way of survivorship.[66] Into the midst of these distinctions, Chancery had stepped with its doctrine of the wife's equity to a settlement, which is discussed below.[67]

(2) INTERESTS IN LAND

In the wife's freehold, copyhold, or leasehold her husband acquired the right to manage and to take the income during their joint lives. With leasehold, during his life he could also dispose of the interest as sole tenant. By contrast it was only with his wife's participation in the conveyance that he could alienate, mortgage, or lease freehold property.[68] For this high form of landholding at least, here was a form of joint interest at law in capital value, if not in income. Joint ownership

---

[63] The standard texts specifically on the subject were R. J. Donnison Roper, *Treatise on the Law of Property arising from the Relations between Husband and Wife* (2nd edn, with notes by Jacob, 1826—to which citations here are given; continued in 1849 with J. E. Bright named as author); J. F. Macqueen, *The Rights and Liabilities of Husband and Wife* (1849, here cited in its Philadelphia edn).

[64] See Roper, *Property*, ii, 131–50.

[65] *Offley* v. *Clay* (1840) 2 Man. & Gr. 172; Macqueen, *Husband and Wife*, 44–5.

[66] There was much learning about what constituted a sufficient satisfaction. Lord Lyndhurst espoused the view that it was enough in equity for the husband to assign the debt to a third party since that manifested a determination to collect it: *Honner* v. *Morton* (1828) 3 Russ. 68. But both before and after him, Chancery courts adhered to the requirement that the debt be actually collected: *Wildman* v. *Wildman* (1803) 9 Ves. 174; *Purdew* v. *Jackson* (1824) 1 Russ. 1; *Ryland* v. *Smith* (1835) 1 My. & Cr. 53; Macqueen, *Husband and Wife*, 53–68.

[67] See below, 742–44.

[68] Until 1833, this was achieved by the cumbersome and expensive device of a fine. The Fines and Recoveries Act (3 & 4 Will. IV c. 74, s 2) provided for the transaction by simple deed, though still it required a formal acknowledgment by the wife.

by husband and wife in a full sense was possible in one case alone: where a free-hold was conveyed into both their names. This tenure was 'by entireties' and it gave rise to a joint tenancy in which the survivor would eventually acquire the whole interest.[69] 'Entireties' were a form of property holding which contrasted with the equitable devices, that are noted below.[70] The latter gave the wife a *separate* right in 'her' assets. How frequently ownership in the entirety of freeholds was resorted to in the early nineteenth century is something about which little is known, though there were certainly instances reported in the case law. But with time the judges would extend it to gifts to the couple as joint donees of chattels, money, and incorporeal assets.[71] In the twentieth century, for various reasons, joint ownership of freehold and leasehold, joint stock-holdings, joint bank accounts and so forth, has become one standard basis for property-holding among spouses. It remains a matter of choice, but it has also in some cases to be recorded or evidenced in accordance with prescribed formalities, while for others any sufficient evidence of the transfer to both will do.

Treating the wife as legally conjoined to her husband had major consequences upon civil rights of action by and against her for debt, contract breach, torts, and like obligations. Since the common law insisted that the wife had no power during marriage to enter contracts in her own right, outsiders who provided for the household had in the main to deal with the husband.[72] It was he who he mostly owned the assets from which judgment could be satisfied, which was why he was obliged to assume responsibility for debts that his wife had contracted before marriage, whether he knew of them or not. That at least was a risk that was part of his assumption of control. The liability was, however, joint, for which she was personally liable as much as he.[73] After marriage he became liable for expenditures for which she had authority, express or implied, to enter on his behalf.[74] Whether the authority was to be implied was a question for the jury. It would readily be made out where the wife used a shop regularly and the husband paid

---

[69] The husband enjoyed the fruits during their joint lives and the wife had no right to acquire a separate interest, even through the discretionary jurisdiction to give effect to the 'equity to a settlement'. A gift to a husband, wife, and others gave the pair only one share, because of their legal unity. The Married Women's Property Act 1882 would end tenancy by entireties, and replace it with joint tenancy having the same characteristics as a shared interest between unmarried persons.

[70] For which see below pp. 739–44.

[71] *Ward* v. *Ward* (1880) 14 Ch D 506; *Re Bryan* (1880) 14 Ch 516.

[72] Macqueen, *Husband and Wife*, 44–6, 93–6.

[73] If both were sued, they could, for instance, be imprisoned for a debt. There was a practice of releasing the wife from prison if she did not have separate property in equity from which to satisfy the claim: see e.g. *Beynon* v. *Jones* (1846) 15 M. & W. 566; cf. *Fergusson* v. *Clayworth* (1844) 13 M. & W. 368, where the wife was shown to be living with her lover and had received substantial capital in the past. Despite the insistence on unity, even common law was prepared to admit the procedure. See further, Morrison, 'Contract' in Graveson and Crane, *Century*, 117–18.

[74] See Macqueen, *Husband and Wife*, 89–96.

the bills; it could even be proved from the fact that they were living together.[75] To bring the authority to a close, the husband had to make his decision clear to the shops or other suppliers in question. One reason for his withdrawal might well be that he was seeking to curb her profligacy; or even more, her adultery.

When, however, the husband occasioned a serious breakdown of the marital relationship—where for instance he deserted his wife, particularly for another woman—the common law had no way of insisting that she be allowed to remain in the house he provided. His right to occupation of the premises, as owner or lessee, gave him power to seek an order turning her out. Unless she had friends or relations to whom she could turn for rescue, her position could be grim. All common law would do was to insist that she might pledge his credit for necessaries wherever she might find herself; and this authority he could not withdraw.[76] Unquestionably this left many wives locked in miserable relationships with no workable key to an escape route.

For her torts against outsiders, whether committed before or during the marriage, he was also responsible for much the same reasons. She was in principle still liable for them, just as she was the person who could claim for a tort committed against her. However, the procedural barrier set up by their deemed unity meant that the husband had to be joined or to join in any action; and if the result was an award of damages in their favour, he alone would be entitled to them.[77]

As in Life, so, to a Considerable Degree, Upon the Death of One Spouse

(1) THE WIFE AS SURVIVOR

As a widow she once more became the sole owner of her freehold; and equally with leasehold, provided always that the husband had not assigned or charged it to an third party during his life. But personal property that had come to him from her passed unremittingly to his estate.

In *his* freeholds, whether or not he alienated them during the marriage, she had anciently a right of dower over one-third for her life.[78] But dower, which all too easily blighted the interests of outside purchasers, had long been replaced, in practices

---

[75] *Lane* v. *Ironmonger* (1844) 13 M. & W. 368. Juries of middling townspeople might be prepared to imply the husband's authority even when the wife was showing distinct signs of extravagance; courts might then rule that the evidence could not support a finding of implied authority: see e.g. *Firestone* v. *Butcher* (1840) 9 Car. & P. 647.

[76] Unless she herself committed adultery and he refused to forgive her, in which case there was no obligation even to supply necessaries: e.g. *Emmett* v. *Norton* (1838) 6 Car. & P. 506; Macqueen, *Husband and Wife*, 97–100.

[77] Morrison, 'Tort', in Graveson and Crane, *Century*, at 91–2.

[78] She would lose it, if she was found guilty of treason, felony, or adultery. Double standards, however, meant that an adulterous husband did not lose his equivalent curtesy in her freeholds.

affecting the landed, by a pre-nuptial jointure. Under it the husband settled specified land upon his bride for at least her life, while she surrendered any claim to dower.[79] Various special attributes of dower, notably the preference over assignees of the property, would be removed by legislation in 1833.[80] This major mechanism in the early common law for the protection of the widows of those with landed interests would only disappear completely in the land law reforms of 1925.[81]

With his other property, the earlier movement from legally guaranteed shares for wife and children to freedom of testation, backed only by the long-stop of intestacy rules, was far advanced by 1820 and would be completed by the Wills Act 1837.[82] Here was one point at which wives had undoubtedly been disadvantaged over time. Husbands had gained power to cut anyone they chose out of their wills entirely. The threat of being left without a penny was the stuff of popular melodrama, but it undoubtedly left wives with an uncertainty hanging over them, which would be resolved only when the will took effect.

(2) THE HUSBAND AS THE SURVIVOR

By 'the curtesy of England' the husband was entitled to a life interest in all his wife's freeholds after her death; but the curtesy applied only if they had a child.[83] This right was left unreformed in the 1830s, despite proposals of the Real Property Law Commissioners.[84] The husband would already have become owner of the wife's personalty, unless her marriage settlement gave her a separate estate over designated property. It is to that striking development of trust conceptions that we must turn in order to see where shifting social perceptions were making their mark in legal arrangements.[85]

Variations in Equity

(1) MARRIAGE SETTLEMENTS AND SEPARATE USES FOR WIFE

For English landed society by 1820, the common law no longer provided the whole story. Equity had long been finding ways of varying the husband's

---

[79] See Vol. XII, Pt 1, Ch. 1.

[80] 3 & 4 Will. IV c. 105, following recommendations of the Real Property Law Commissioners, First Report, *PP* 1829, x, 16–19. That Act did extend dower to estates held by the husband in equity: s 2. J. J. Park launched his career with his *Treatise on the Law of Dower* (1819) which became the standard work. In the main, the question arose only when a husband died intestate without a settlement.

[81] Copyhold gave widows and widowers similar rights of freebench, which were defined by the custom of each manor.

[82] 7 Will. IV & 1 Vict. c. 26. See generally, Vol. XII, 22–3, 58–9.

[83] The child, however, did not have to survive to majority.

[84] See their First Report, *PP* 1829, x, 16–19.

[85] See further, Vol. XII, 56–8.

autocracy so far as concerned property that the wife brought into the marriage. Of these, as we shall see, marriage settlements of assets coming from both families of the uniting couple, or from one side alone, were one way of maintaining family wealth that had become increasingly common by the early nineteenth century. Its many detailed forms were available alongside other types of family provision, such as the strict settlement of land and the executory trust for assets more generally.[86] Here we concentrate attention on special types of clause that favoured the wife as against the husband and his creditors. As a part of marriage settlements, it had become accepted practice in the eighteenth century to place some of the wife-to-be's dowry in the hands of trustees for her separate use.[87] So strongly did equity favour this traverse of the common law that it would, if necessary, treat the husband (where he was legal owner of property settled for his wife) as himself trustee of it for her separate use.[88]

A separate estate for the wife under a marriage settlement could well be subject to terms ensuring that, if the union did not produce children, the land or the fund would revert to the wife's family as a dynastic resource. If the common law's concept of unity was in reality a 'profitable guardianship' by the husband of the wife and her property,[89] then equity's device was equally a safe-keeping which allowed each family scope for shaping the property structure of a marriage in its own interests. This helps to explain why, in all the reforms to come, there was little sustained interest in England in the regimes of matrimonial property that were being revived or introduced into civilian systems as part of their codes of private law.[90] Equity nonetheless imposed its own limitations on what settlers could arrange. The creation of a separate trust for the wife stood in the way of joint ownership of assets by husband and wife together, each with an equal right to decide how they should be enjoyed. Likewise it conferred its favours only on trusts set up in contemplation of the marriage (even if the property was not made over to the trustees until afterwards). Accordingly, it was not a device that could apply to the earnings of the wife after the marriage. Unless the husband agreed to joint ownership of the salary or business returns, or to separate ownership by

---

[86] See Vol XII, 232–5.

[87] One common practice was for the bride's father to promise to settle property in the future; in which case, not only the trustees but the wife and the immediate issue of the marriage were entitled in equity to sue to secure performance of the obligation.

[88] See further below, 247–52.

[89] So it was characterized in F. Pollock and F. W. Maitland, *The History of English Law before the Time of Edward I* (2nd edn, 1898), i, 485.

[90] See O. Kahn-Freund, 'Matrimonial Property in England', in W. Friedmann (ed.), *Matrimonial Property Law* (1955), 267–314.

the wife, the stream of income remained his. The result would become a major cause of complaint, driving the first campaigns to lift the subjugation of wives in respect of their property.[91]

(2) RESTRAINT ON ANTICIPATION

A wife with her own interest in a separate estate under her marriage settlement, held for her by her own trustees, inevitably acquired a measure of independence which sat ill with continuing—indeed growing—sentiments in favour of the husband as patriarch. Much the same unease arose when the trust device was deployed as a means of providing for a wife whose husband agreed to her living apart. Yet just as equity judges proved willing to accept that device,[92] so at much the same period, they came to accept the 'restraint on anticipation' attaching to the wife's separate estate under her marriage settlement. The restraint prevented the wife, once she attained her majority, from requiring the trustees to transfer the legal interest in the property to her or her husband. If she attempted to do so, the restraint brought her interest to a close.[93] Lord Thurlow, acting as trustee for a Miss Watson, had inserted the phrase 'not by anticipation' in her marriage settlement. Early nineteenth-century draftsmen took the device up in order to prevent the husband from 'kissing or kicking' the property out of his wife. Since its effect could scarcely appeal to the husband's creditors—and might perhaps be adapted to put his own property out of their reach—there were considerable doubts about its legal effectiveness in its initial years. Yet Lord Eldon retained it, while making clear that it could not become a general device by which the husband could put his own property beyond creditors.[94] The device indeed might also be used in making a legacy or other gift to a single woman, whether a spinster or a widow; and that opened the question whether the restraint would operate from the outset for the whole of her life, or whether it would have a roving effect, imposing its restrictions on the capital only for such period or periods as she came under the coverture of one or a succession of husbands.[95]

The Lord Chancellor, Brougham, together with his Vice-Chancellor, Leach, were unwilling to hold that the restraint could have any effect upon such a gift.

[91] See below, 758–9.
[92] See below, 769–74.
[93] Roper, *Property*, Ch. 18.4.
[94] *Jackson* v. *Hobhouse* (1817) 2 Mer. 483; also *Jones* v. *Salter* (1815) 2 Russ. & My. 208 (the formidable Grant MR).
[95] *Barton* v. *Briscoe* (1822) Jac. 603; *Anderson* v. *Anderson* (1822), discussed in 'Of the validity of gifts to the separate use of unmarried women in case of Future Coverture' (1835) 13 *LM* 135, 148–53.

Equity must in that instance follow the law.[96] But then, Cottenham LC, after anxious cogitation, decided in favour of an embracing view of the restraint, so that it operated from receipt of the woman's interest until her death. To strike at it would prejudice a generation for whose protection conveyancers had followed the line of Thurlow and Eldon.[97] It was a technique essentially for families whose style of life did not conceive of energetic wives working for their economic independence.[98] In a world where young women in the propertied classes were married off by fathers or other relations on such terms as they chose to set, they gained the ability to place the wife's separate estate apart from the capital resources of the couple or either of them. To this extent her own family could retain some control over her wherewithal and perhaps therefore over her. That control came in the form of a term on which the new husband had to accept his bride. His position was therefore weaker than it would have been without the restraint on anticipation; but he did go into the arrangement with his eyes open, all as part of a negotiation about the bride-price.

(3) WIFE'S EQUITY TO A SETTLEMENT[99]

Alongside this, equity allowed another, quite distinct, concession that could be of particular value where the marriage was coming under strain. The wife's 'equity to a settlement' was an instance of that element in both equity and ecclesiastical jurisprudence by which the court assumed a power of adjustment to meet circumstances as they evolved.[100] It was also a back-stop device, which became the less important as separate estates, with or without restraints on anticipation,

---

[96] *Newton* v. *Reid* (1830) 4 Sim. 141; *Woolmeston* v. *Walker* (1831) 2 Russ. & My. 208; *Brown* v. *Pocock* (1833) 2 Russ. & My. 210, (No.2) (1831) 5 Sim. 663; *Massey* v. *Parker* (1843) 2 My. & K. 174; *Malcolm* v. *O'Callaghan* (1835) 5 L.J. (N.S.) 137; *Johnson* v. *Freeth* (1836) 5 L.J. (N.S.) 143.

[97] *Tullett* v. *Armstrong* (1840) 4 Myt. & Cr. 377 (and see his consequential decisions, *Newlands* v. *Paynter* (1840) 4 My. & Cr 408; *re Gafee* (1850) 1 Mac. & G. 541). Cottenham acknowledged that, even if the restraint could not apply, conveyancers would find alternative ways of protecting women recipients from getting their hands on the capital of the gift; but that was no reason for precluding the wider use of the restraint. His approach sat well with his view of the wife's equity to a settlement: see below, 744.

[98] In the City of London, a countervailing custom gave a wife the right to her own earnings as a sole trader. The Courts of Common Law left her to assert her position in a City court because of its greater familiarity with the custom. Nonetheless it might be pleaded as a defence to a common law action by a creditor against the husband: *Beard* v. *Webb* (1800) 2 Bos. & P. 93 (Ex Ch); see Roper, *Property*, 124–6.

[99] See Roper, *Property*, ii: Ch. 7; Macqueen, *Husband and Wife*, 70–101.

[100] Cf. awards of alimony to innocent, deserted wives by ecclesiastical courts and Chancery's willingness to order maintenance for deserted wives. It was therefore unsurprising that the Divorce Court established in 1857 would be given power to award maintenance and other ancillary relief; see below, 787–8.

were treated in equity as effective.[101] The common law allowed the husband to acquire claims for debts and other choses in action due to his wife only by asserting the right and thus bringing in their value. Where necessary, however, equity, at the behest of the wife, would order a stay of any action by him, whether or not he had yet instituted it,[102] to the extent that it was considered necessary in order to make provision for her, and through her, her children.[103] That was taken to be one important element in the donor's intention. The Court of Chancery might well refer the details of the arrangement to a Master of the Court in order to decide how much of the particular property or its income must be settled to meet her needs. The amount available, the wife's needs and that of their children, the conduct of the husband and that of the wife, all went into a moral melting pot; typically she could expect half the asset to be kept for her and the offspring.[104] If the husband was living with his mistress while refusing to make a voluntary settlement on the wife, he could expect tough treatment. If she, however, committed adultery her hands were unequivocally sullied and she could expect no help. The fact that any portion not settled in the wife's favour would pass to the husband's creditors raised the question of third-party rights that must arise when any interference is imposed in order to protect wives against the consequences of their husband's dealings. Courts of equity found it hard to arrive at a measure of consistent practice, not least if the creditors did not know of the husband's marriage when they made a loan to him or provided other contractual benefits.[105]

Differences would emerge over how far equity would extend this form of moral objection to the assertion of proprietary right. A testing instance arose where the husband needed assistance when paying off a first mortgage of freehold or leasehold. Legal title to the security would have passed to the mortgagee-lender; so in order to oblige him to re-transfer the title, the mortgagor would normally rely on his equity of redemption.[106] Resorting to the ill-focused maxim that

[101] A wife with an adequate marriage settlement would not be permitted to rely on the equity: *Aguilar* v. *Aguilar* (1820) 5 Madd. 414; *Giacometti* v. *Prodgers* (1873) LR 8 Ch App 338. If the asset was a fee simple or fee tail, the husband was in any case confined to the interest it produced from time to time: *Durham* v. *Crackles* (1868) 8 Jur. (N.S.) 1174.

[102] See *Lady Elibank* v. *Montolieu* (1801) 5 Ves. 737; *Carr* v. *Taylor* (1805) 10 Ves. 574.

[103] If the husband was in fact supporting the wife, he remained entitled to receive the income from her life interests. He could even sell them, it being presumed that he was raising money for family support: see *Tidd* v. *Lister* (1853) 3 De G. M. & G. 870; *re Duffy's Trust* (1860) 28 Beav. 386 (applied by Romilly MR only because of the force of precedent).

[104] Cranworth LC's analogy was to 'what a prudent parent would probably have done in giving a portion to a daughter': *Tidd* v. *Lister* (1853) 3 De G. M. & G. 857.

[105] See e.g. Macqueen's discussion of the Chancery decisions, *Elliott* v. *Cordell* (1820) 5 Madd. 143 and *Stanton* v. *Hall* (1831) 1 My. & Cr. 87: *Husband and Wife*, 59–61. The form tended to follow the stereotype prescribed in C. Davidson et al., *Precedents and Forms in Conveyancing* (2nd edn, 1861).

[106] For the gradual admission of a mortgagee's power of sale as a constraint on the equity of redemption, see Vol. XII, 135–6.

equity followed the law, the proponents of this view asserted that the husband's right to recover his title could not be encumbered by the wife's equity.[107] Those who considered that the wife should have her settlement, relied instead on the anti-Shylockian maxim that a person who comes to equity must do equity. Lord Cottenham LC adopted the latter approach in *Sturgis* v. *Champneys*,[108] overruling the judgment of Shadwell VC. The wife therefore took in diminution of the interest available to the husband's provisional assignee in insolvency. Wigram, who had appeared as counsel for the assignee, on then becoming a Vice-Chancellor, gave a judgment openly expressing dissent from Cottenham's ruling; but he found himself obliged to follow it.[109] Chancery, however, could only act in this way when an equitable right or power still needed to be exercised by the husband or his representatives in order to realize an asset. An odd casuistry prevailed, which perhaps made subsequent courts uncomfortable. They showed an increasing tendency to allow the wife and children three-quarters of the assets, or sometimes even the whole;[110] yet at the same time they found themselves quite often dealing with families that would never have been thought propertied or even comfortably middle class.[111] What Chancery offered was little answer to the demands of the mid-century for complete separation of married women's property, and associated private rights, from those of her husband.

7. MALE ATTITUDES TO THE OPPOSITE SEX

While the dominance of husbands remained a root attitude, a certain refinement of its earlier physical expressions bore in upon Victorian England. The wife, as already noted, was depicted, first and foremost by men, as devoting herself to the 'separate sphere' of child and household management, where previously she would probably have been much more closely involved in productive activity, such as farming or shopkeeping. She could be projected romantically as a model of purity, far above the sordid world of men; but that meant her behaviour must

---

[107] Brougham's attitude to restraints upon anticipation was based on a similar assumption.

[108] (1839) 5 My. & Cr. 97.

[109] *Hanson* v. *Keating* (1844) 4 Hare 1. Wigram maintained that his view was long established in practice, stemming originally from *Sir Edward Turner's case* (1680) 1 Vern. 1, Lords Journals, 16 November 1680. Cottenham could find no cases in the interim which went so far. He then stamped on a practice that would have subverted it: see *Whittle* v. *Henning* (1848) 2 Ph. 731. Macqueen (*Husband and Wife*, 70–2) offered a staunch apology for Cottenham.

[110] See *Taunton* v. *Morris* (1878) 8 ChD 453, (1879) 11 ChD 779. The tendency is apparent as early as *Brett* v. *Greenwell* (1838) 3 Y. & C. 230,

[111] See e.g. *Tidd* v. *Lister* (1853) 3 De G. M. & G. 857; *re Carr* (1871) LR 12 Eq 609; *Taunton* v. *Morris* (1878) 2 ChD 471; *re Briant* (1888) 39 Ch D 471; *Roberts* v. *Cooper* [1892] Ch 335.

remain impeccable. As we shall see, when it came to the grounds for separation and full divorce, wives were condemned for even a single act of adultery. Whereas with men, their adultery— however profligate, however persistent—was not of itself enough. There had to be some other 'aggravation', before the law would provide any relief.[112]

In any case, even the most virtuous woman could be characterized as mentally too limited, emotionally too wayward, to be expected to deal with activities demanding either the physical or intellectual endurance of men.[113] Of course, such attitudes were anathema to women of independent spirit, and from the 1850s they began to express their opposition with increasing force. John Stuart Mill's *The Subjection of Women* (1867) made a signal case for the feminist cause. But there is no escaping the contempt and incomprehension that greeted it within the circles of the influential. FitzJames Stephen provided a blunt riposte in the 'Equality' chapter of his assault on *Liberty, Equality, Fraternity* (1874). His case began from the limited physical capacities of women. Who could imagine a women's army—or indeed women engaging in many other activities exhibiting crucial attributes of manliness? In consequence there must be a hierarchy of authority within a family stemming from a sole head of house. Only with the acceptance of the husband and father's dominion would he be in a position to wield his authority with calm and beneficent restraint. The parallel to the nation state as law-commanding sovereign is evident. Stephen, after all, took a markedly Hobbesian view of the need for firm social organization under the precepts of utility. It would lead him to proclaim the civilizing mission of British imperialism.[114]

The husband's authoritarian position in relation to property, housing, and private obligation impinged on the very nature of legal rules and procedures in family affairs. Because in so many respects the power of decision remained his, adjudication by the courts was primarily needed to determine how the rules applied to particular circumstances. When equity intervened to give force to the terms of marriage settlements in favour of wives (through their separate estates) and children, it recognized the interests of other family and friends in settling the distribution of the available assets as the marriage became a living reality. It allowed the donor both to set out a pattern of interests and

[112] Below, 780, 783, 789–92.

[113] See e.g. J. A. and O. Banks, *Feminism and Family Planning* (1964), Chs 5, 6; J. Tosh, *A Man's Place: Masculinity and the Middle-Class Home in Victorian England* (New Haven, 1999).

[114] See K. J. M. Smith, *James FitzJames Stephen: Portrait of a Victorian Rationalist* (Cambridge, 1988), 113–22, 181–96; J. A. Colaiaco, *James Fitzjames Stephen and the Crisis in Victorian Thought* (1983), 144–53.

also to leave some decisions to the good sense of the trustees, who, at least initially, were likely to be his nominees. For the most part, the courts were not needed to decide themselves how powers within the trust deed were to be exercised, as distinct from settling what the powers amounted to; and there are distinct signs, here as elsewhere in relation to property arrangements, that judicial opinion moved from a certain readiness to give effect to what the donor appeared to intend towards closer attention to the meaning of the words used in constituting the trust.[115]

[115] In relation to the construction of wills the change was marked: see Vol. XII, Pt 1, Ch. 1, pp. 14–27.

II
Marriage

1. THE VALUES OF MARRIAGE

Whatever the role of marriage in different levels of English society over the preceding centuries, by 1820 it was overwhelmingly a religious precept, and its celebration and maintenance were matters in which the Established Church played a prominent role. Marriage was the one voluntary change of legal status that really mattered, not least because it was treated as the moment when the husband ended his old ties to his forbears and established his own patriarchy. There were consequent outpourings of advice and insistence from the gamut of experts—bishops and ladies bountiful, manual-writers, magistrates. Lawrence Stone used their tracts as one source to trace the long-term shift in views of marriage from a severe dominance concerned with property and power to the more egalitarian, companionate relationship of today. In this change, he found not so much a simple, linear progress but rather waves of action and reaction.[1] This aspect of his quest at once aroused debate among historians. Campaigns to stiffen authority and propriety within marriages tend to arise by way of reaction to laxer attitudes. For external reasons, such as a threat of French invasion or Jacobin uprising after 1790, greater social freedom would become more alarming. Nonetheless for considerable periods there might be a choppy sea of contending ideals, rather than the crashing of powerful breakers. That view certainly casts doubt on histories that pine for a return to 'Victorian values' on some assumption that they once held sway in an England bathed in righteous moralizing.[2]

Yet, as Cretney has stressed, in imposing limitations on marriage, the law's basic aim was, at most stages, preventive rather than punitive.[3] It might strive to stop marriages from taking place if, for instance, an under-age partner lacked parental consent.[4] But most of the time, if the couple nevertheless lived together as

---

[1] L. Stone, *The Family, Sex and Marriage in England 1500–1800* (1977).

[2] Exemplified by G. Himmelfarb, *The De-moralisation of Society* (1995).

[3] See S. M. Cretney, Family Law in the twentieth Century (Oxford, 2003), pp. 39–40.

[4] Promises in restraint of marriage were treated by the common law as void; but conditions subsequent to a gift by will, terminating a widow's or widower's entitlement on remarriage and passing the property instead to the children only of the first marriage, were eventually held good.

man and wife, it would not condemn them by treating the marriage as invalid—
the more so if the challenge was later mounted in order to secure freedom to
marry another or to affect the inheritance of children.

There were, nonetheless, fluxes when the balance for a time shifted towards
outright prohibition. These shifts of purpose should be seen as elements in wider
movements within and across social groupings to impose codes of proper family
conduct on inferiors and even on breakaway equals. Living in an era in which marriage has ceased to be what is expected of everyone from royalty and celebrities
to social welfare claimants, we need to ask how far early modern England really
cared about sexual relations outside marriage—everything from casual lust that
neither coupler considered even a liaison, to comfortable linkages between those
who could not marry or chose not to do so. From the mid-eighteenth century, on
the one hand, there were signs of a greater determination to make marriage a formal, recorded step; yet, on the other hand, pressure grew to deal with collapsed
marriages through a legal process of divorce or some equivalent. As Roderick
Phillips, Lawrence Stone, and others have demonstrated, a more complex set of
interactions set in, in which the lines of influence travel in two directions—up
from the public to legislators and then down again—as statutes took account
of changing public opinion and then re-moulded it. So also with lawyers and
judges, as they argued about interpretations of legislation and decided on the
scope of their own doctrines.[5]

2. CAPACITY TO MARRY AND NULLIFICATION

Marriages were open to objection if there were 'lawful impediments' but the
consequences varied, depending on the objection. A just cause arose when one
partner was already married to a living person.[6] Then the marriage was indeed
void for all purposes and there might well be a criminal prosecution of the bigamist. By comparison, if she (or sometimes he) was still under 21 and did not have
parental consent, the consequences had traditionally been less severe in legal
terms; but from the mid-eighteenth century the law was made more rigorous
against clandestine marriage.[7]

Contracts prejudicing an existing marriage (i.e. to marry a lover upon the death of the spouse, or
even upon divorce) were long considered to be contrary to good morals; but the promise to marry
after divorce would eventually be held good if entered into between decree nisi and decree absolute
(*Fender* v. *St John Mildmay* [1938] AC 1 (HL)—a decision from which two Law Lords dissented—
Russell, a Roman Catholic, and Roche, a High Church Anglican.

[5] Cf. G. Himmelfarb, *Marriage and Morals among the Victorians* (1989), Ch. 1.

[6] But not if the woman was already pregnant by another man and the petitioner-husband did not
know: *Moss* v. *Moss* [1897] P 263.

[7] Below, 751–4.

Again, if there was a minimum age for marriage (and not all authorities accepted that it existed), it was presumed by common law to be 14 for boys and 12 for girls.[8] These were ages at which the participants could normally be expected at least to understand the nature of the arrangement. In any case, on reaching adulthood, either could declare the marriage void, or both could agree to continue it, which would bind them.[9] However, whatever their age, people who were not mentally capable of consenting, or were being unduly pressed into taking part, might afterwards obtain a decree of nullity from an ecclesiastical court.[10] There were also cases of partners physically incapable of sexual intercourse where such an order could be obtained, so crucial was this 'duty' in the marital relationship.[11] But the facts had to be proved up to the hilt against the man (for instance, by showing him impotent) or the woman (for lack of a vagina), since the courts had somehow to distinguish between inability and disinclination. Accordingly, it needed a thick skin or desperation to bring such proceedings. The press or the neighbourhood could fall upon the evidence of medical investigations with prurient relish.[12]

3. FAMILIAL RELATIONSHIP: THE PROHIBITED DEGREES[13]

A separate issue over eligibility was set by the prohibited degrees of marital relationship, which stemmed originally from the Old Testament.[14] They had been stretched elastically by the medieval church in order to aid the powerful

[8] So it would remain until raised to 16 for both sexes by the Age of Marriage Act 1929 (thus coming into line with the law on sexual offences under age). Britain was in fact a society in which the young rarely married. Even in 1900 marriage of 16-year-olds was most unusual. Young pregnancies were dealt with in other ways. See Cretney, *Family*, 57–68.

[9] So Blackstone expressed it: *Comms*, i, 436.

[10] As in e.g. *Hunter* v. *Edney* (1881) 10 PD 93 (insane delusions about the relationship); *Scott* v. *Sebright* (1886) 12 PD 21 (heiress threatened with shooting or, if not, bankruptcy); but compare other instances which failed to secure a nullity decree, cited by Cretney, *Family*, 74–6.

[11] While the Church had traditionally set the procreation of children as the first object of marriage, and intercourse was taken to be a necessary step to that end, it was not until the 1870s that the penetration of ovum by sperm began to be understood scientifically: Wolfram, *In-Laws and Outlaws*, 120.

[12] See Cretney, *Family*, 76–81. Inevitably it could prove difficult to tell whether the incapacity was physical or psychological. The Gorell Royal Commission on Divorce and Matrimonial Causes, *PP* 1912 [Cd. 6478], viii, paras 353–5, argued for the introduction of various grounds of nullity, including that one of the parties failed to perform 'conjugal duties'. The Court of Appeal would not alter the law (*Napier* v. *Napier* [1915] P 184) and the proposal had to wait until A. P. Herbert's personal campaign for somewhat greater ease in ending marriage, achieved through his sponsorship of the Matrimonial Causes Act 1937, s 7.

[13] See L. Shelford, *Practical Treatise of the Law of Marriage and Divorce* (1841), Ch. 3; J. F. Macqueen, *Treatise on the Law of Marriage, Divorce and Legitimacy* (1860), Ch. 30.

[14] *Leviticus* xviii and xx defined a set of forbidden relationships, but in terms of incest rather than of marriage.

in casting off a spouse, and had then with the Reformation been modified by Canons of the Church of England.[15] The Canons still extended not only to blood relationships (parents with their issue, brothers and sisters, uncles with nieces and aunts with nephews, and so forth) but to affinities (a man with his wife's blood relations, etc).[16] The taboo against incest, which emerges in most societies, was given a broad reading.[17] There were fears of the deleterious effects of in-breeding. And there were more insstinctive revulsions: if, for example, a man and his daughter had a child, did the child know him as father or grandfather? In ecclesiastical law, marriages within the prohibited degrees were null. The common law courts, however, had refused to allow as a consequence that persons other than the couple could attack the validity of the marriage, particularly when it came to questions of inheritance arising after the death of one spouse.[18] However, in 1835, an Act associated initially with Lord Lyndhurst rendered all marriages within the Canons null and void for all purposes.[19]

The Canons had not extended to marriages between cousins german (first cousins)—propertied families, after all, might see a cousin alliance as an effective way of preserving the inheritance for the dynasty as a whole. Yet they banned the mere affinity of a man marrying his deceased wife's sister or her daughter and other equivalent relationships. After the 1835 Act, the right to enter such a marriage became a great cause within the marriage laws over which conservatives did battle with reformers—one that seemed far to outrun the occasions on which it was actually an issue. A man who had lost his wife certainly might turn to her sister as a necessary support for his household, and there might well be an inherent sexual attraction sparking the desire to marry. Other countries might raise no objection, a Royal Commission might recommend legalisation;[20] but

---

[15] Archbishop Matthew Parker's Table of Kindred and Affinities had listed 30 cases each for a man and a woman.

[16] There were always those who hoped to extend the prohibitions. In *Wing* v. *Taylor* (1861) 2 Sw. & Tr. 278, the Divorce Court refused to find that a man could not marry a daughter because previously he had had intercourse with her mother. The decision displays considerable learning, notably on the legislative feints needed to secure the second and fifth marriages of Henry VIII.

[17] Cf. W. Arens, *The Original Sin* (Oxford, 1986).

[18] After the first death only the ecclesiastical charge of incest could be brought against the survivor, leading to an award of penance. Incest did not become a criminal offence until 1908: see below, 751. If one spouse started an action against the other to annul the marriage, but never completed it, this would bar anyone else from doing so during the lifetime of both. The tactic was deployed by those who got good advice: Wolfram, *In-Laws and Outlaws*, 29; Cretney, *Family*, 34, n. 37.

[19] The Act commonly bore Lyndhurst's name; but he had intervened to save the Duke of Beaufort's marriage to his wife's half-sister, not to place obstacles in the way of marriages between affines in future: Wolfram, *In-Laws and Outlaws*, 30, n. 26; Cretney, *Family*, 43; W. M. N. Geary, *The Law of Marriage and Family Relations* (1892), 10–11.

[20] The Law of Marriage as relating to the Prohibited Degrees of Affinity, First Report, *PP* 1847–8, xxviii.

in England one reforming bill after another was rejected, mainly by the House of Lords.[21] Public opposition, particularly from the Church, was highly strung: how could an aunt move in to look after the children, if any prospect of marriage hung over her residence? What would come of the sister's relationship while the wife remained alive? How could the widower accept his sister-in-law's aid at face value?

Not until 1907 did the Liberal government finally see an Act through.[22] In the interim, those couples within the ban who had the means might wed abroad in a country that permitted the marriage. That might protect them from the social disapproval attaching to a mere liaison but not from legal consequences in England.[23] Within a year of the 1907 Act, incest finally became a serious indictable offence which both men and women might commit.[24] That may seem a curious juxtaposition. But, as disturbing evidence from the National Society for the Prevention of Cruelty to Children made plain, sexual predators with paedophilic tastes were unlikely to be restrained by strict respect for the Canons. If parental abuse of children was not only causing dreadful traumas in the victims, but also in some cases producing in-bred offspring, the only hope of a remedy lay in prohibiting sexual intercourse itself.[25]

4. PRE-CONTRACTS AND RELIGIOUS CEREMONY

The formal steps needed to celebrate a marriage had traditionally taken a loose form. Church wedding had existed for centuries, recorded in the parish registry along with births and deaths. Propertied and respectable parishioners, in town as in country, would follow the Church's forms, which would include the calling of banns in the preceding weeks. But there had come to be ways of using these rituals surreptitiously, which had led to the constraints of Lord Hardwicke's Clandestine Marriages Act 1753.[26] The historiography of marriage practices in that period has in any case become clouded by issues that continued to have nineteenth-century

[21] Wolfram, *In-Laws and Outlaws*, 30–1, notes that the matter was raised in 64 sessions, and in 18 of them a bill got as far as acceptance in the Commons. W. S. Gilbert got a neat rhyme by labelling them 'that annual blister, Marriage with Deceased Wife's Sister'.

[22] Deceased Wife's Sister's Marriage Act 1907; followed, once the female suffrage was admitted, by the Deceased Brother's Widow's Marriage Act 1921; and subsequently the Marriage (Prohibited Degrees of Relationship) Act 1931.

[23] *Brook v. Brook* (1861) 9 HL Cas. 193; below, 839.

[24] Prohibition of Incest Act 1908. The forbidden relationships for a man were grand-daughter, daughter, sister, and mother; for a woman, the equivalents.

[25] V. Bailey and S. Blackburn, 'The Punishment of Incest Act 1908: A Case Study of Law Creation' [1979] *Crim LR* 708–18; S. Wolfram 'Eugenics and the Punishment of Incest Act 1908' [1983] *Crim LR* 308–16.

[26] 26 Geo. II c. 32.

consequences and must therefore be touched upon here. They concern two root issues: whether folk-practices, such as jumping a broom or exchanging rings, followed by cohabitation, effected a marriage according to ecclesiastical or common law; and whether there were forms of mutual promises to marry that would have that consequence. As to folk practices, there have been claims that in remoter districts they retained their force;[27] but Rebecca Probert has shown convincingly that the actual evidence for this is virtually non-existent.[28]

There were certainly types of betrothal practice involving exchanges of vows to become man and wife. Ecclesiastical law had come to distinguish between *per verba de presenti* and *per verba de futuro*—promises to marry of the 'I do', rather than 'I will' variety. Still in the decades before 1753, if after using *verba de presenti* the couple then actually had sexual intercourse, the Church courts would order them to marry by formal rites. Not only did this putting to rights help to keep down the parish poor rate by making the husband primarily responsible for upkeep;[29] it also sustained the code of respectability that every marriage reinforced. Nevertheless, Hardwicke's Act had abolished this positive power to require performance, leaving the jilted party (almost always the woman) to an action for damages at common law for breach of promise to marry.[30] As Probert has also shown, there was no recognition in this period that the exchange of vows *de presenti*, followed by sex, gave rise itself to a 'common law marriage' having legal effects.[31] The expression had no currency at the time. It was in any case inconsistent both with the ecclesiastical court's order to undergo the formal ceremony and all the clumsy intrigue of getting a priest to perform a secret rite.[32] Instead she locates 'common law marriage' in a later, more esoteric need: private international law would require a rule to confer the status of marriage on those who had exchanged vows in places abroad where they could not be expected to undergo formal ceremonies.[33] And she sees a modern tendency to dress up that term with a fictional history in order to confer respectability on informal

---

[27] See e.g. J. R. Gillis, *For Better, For Worse* (Oxford, 1985), Ch. 7; followed in exaggerated terms by S. Parker, *Informal Marriage, Cohabitation and the Law, 1750–1989* (1990), Chs 2, 3. Cf. R. B. Outhwaite, *Clandestine Marriage in England, 1500–1850* (1995), 139–42; A. Macfarlane, *Marriage and Love in England: Modes of Reproduction, 1300–1840* (Oxford, 1986), 307–17.

[28] R.J. Probert, 'Common-law Marriage: Myths and Misunderstandings' (2008) 20 *C.F.L.Q.* 1–22; and see her *Marriage, Law and Practice in the Long Eighteenth Century* (Cambridge, 2009).

[29] See below, 776–7.

[30] 26 Geo. II c. 32, s 13.

[31] Instead, studies of parish records, etc. confirm the view that Church rites were followed by those who did marry: R. Probert and L. D'Arcy Brown, 'The Impact of the Clandestine Marriages Act: Three Case Studies in Conformity' (2008) 23 *Continuity and Change* 309–26.

[32] Probert, 'Common Law Marriage' (2008).

[33] Below, 838, n. 33.

partnerships that would only after 1950 begin to lose the stigma of 'living in sin'. In social terms, the problems set by what were unquestionably illegitimate births were of a much greater order. From the later eighteenth century the proportion of all children who were born bastards would rise for many decades.

The major problem at which Hardwicke's Act struck was the resort to clandestine ceremonies conducted by Established Church clergy (some of them *soi-disant*), since it was these that the law had treated as binding thereafter. For this trade, London's Fleet prison and the stews of Mayfair were notorious, but there were similar opportunities across the country.[34] Hasty couples were wont to flee their fathers or guardians. Gold-digging rakes were said to whisk guileless heiresses into marriage, leaving them to repent at penniless leisure.[35] The 1753 Act had required marriages to be in the Church's form: banns had to be published in a church for three successive weeks, and the couple had then to be married there by a priest before two witnesses and only in the morning.[36] If either partner was under 21, the consent of the father, guardian, or mother (in that order) was required. The alternative procedure of obtaining a common licence from the Bishop or his representative was also cut back since, greedily exercised, it had been the source of much of the trouble.[37] A person who knowingly conducted a ceremony which did not comply with the Act faced a criminal charge with a penalty of 14 years' transportation.[38] Above all, the marriage was wholly invalid.[39]

It was not until our period that the full force of the Clandestine Marriages Act (Hardwicke Act) regimen was curbed. Legislation of 1822–3—so contentious that it took three enactments to arrive at a final compromise—provided that a marriage lacking the prescribed formalities would no longer be regarded as invalid unless the parties had knowingly and wilfully evaded them.[40] There is evidence enough that, in the decades before this change of heart, couples continued to want some

---

[34] See esp. Outhwaite, *Clandestine Marriage*, Chs 1–3.

[35] Typical members of the Commons (often younger sons of the nobility) had shown enough sympathy for this 'fair game' to have barred earlier bills and to have objected to Hardwicke's proposal: D. Lemmings, 'Marriage and the Law in the Eighteenth Century' (1996) 39 *Hist. J.* 339, 356.

[36] 26 Geo. II c. 32, s. 3.

[37] For the long trail of complaints over curbs on this lucrative practice, see Outhwaite, *Clandestine Marriage*, 65–9, 150–7. The Archbishop of Canterbury retained his power to grant a special licence for the performance of a marriage as he directed, but that was a prospect mainly for grandees.

[38] For the most part the activities in the Fleet and similar places were cleaned up by this threat.

[39] Section 8.

[40] 3 Geo. IV c. 75; 4 Geo. IV c. 17 and 76: see esp. Outhwaite, *Clandestine Marriage*, 152–3; R. Probert, 'The Judicial Interpretation of Lord Hardwicke's Act' (2002) 23 *JLH* 129–51 at 143–6; and 'Control over Marriage in England and Wales 1753–1823: The Clandestine Marriages Act in Context' (2009) 27 *L & HR* 413–50.

form of secret or very rapid marriage.[41] Those who could reach Gretna Green or other cross-border towns had taken advantage of the easy tolerance inherent in Scots legal requirements for marriage. Others, particularly working people, had to rely on local customs and mores, or on moving away from where they were known. In the debates of 1822–3, there was concern that the Act was being used to secure nullity decrees by raking up any slight failure to comply with the elaborate requirements of Hardwicke's Act.[42] Probert has, however, shown that ecclesiastical courts had come to interpret the Act in a discriminating way.[43] By and large where the marriage had lasted in fact, the difficulty of proving that there had been no compliance with the formalities became considerable.[44] The courts were less willing to find excuses where the marriage had side-stepped parental consent, for the Act's purpose had clearly been to prevent such duplicit secrecy.

The position over clandestine marriages was not greatly changed by the shift by the legislation of 1823. Those who lied about their ages or addresses and those who forged consents from parents still entered void marriages. The banns system could make it difficult to prevent knowledge of what was about to happen from reaching the objecting parents.[45] If a father was determined to keep a daughter from a persistent lover, he could apply to make her a ward of the Court of Chancery and obtain an order that the man stay away, which it would be contempt of the Court to disobey.[46] The court might be persuaded to override the parents' wishes, but that would require unusual circumstances.[47] The law continued to strive for a balance of power in which, until 21, both the couple marrying and their parents had to agree to the wedding. Neither side could as a matter of law force the hand of the other. Of course what happened in real or fictional life was by no means settled by these rules. There would be many and varied Louisas and Wickhams, and very few could have been retrieved by the intervention of a Darcy.

---

[41] See esp. Gillis, *For Better, For Worse* (New York, 1985), Ch. 5; Stone, *Road to Divorce*, Ch. 5.

[42] Certainly there were instances of this: see Probert, 'Judicial Interpretation', 145.

[43] See also Stone, *Road to Divorce*, 132–3. The refusal to give full effect to a statute prescribing legal form was not untypical of the period, as with the best-known example, the Statute of Frauds 1677.

[44] However, not only the fact that there had been a mistake but also the suitability of the match in terms of age and social station could enter the equation.

[45] With the relative anonymity of growing towns, it was possible for some to pretend parish residence for the three weeks of bann-calling: see e.g. Stone, *Road to Divorce*, 128–32.

[46] Occasionally a young man would be made a ward and might be ordered not to marry without the court's consent: as in *Re H's Settlement* [1909] 2 Ch 260.

[47] J. D. Chambers, *Jurisdiction of the High Court of Chancery over the Persons and Property of Children* (1842) contains passing references to the ultimate duty of the court to do what was most beneficial to the child: see e.g. 20–3, 145–51.

5. THE ESTABLISHED CHURCH AND THE PUBLIC RECORD[48]

Hardwicke's Act had tightened the forms for the solemnization of marriage.[49] It had buttressed the hold of the established Church, for only Quakers and Jews had been permitted to marry according to their own rites. Neither Catholics nor protestant dissenters were allowed the same privilege. As Methodism gained its attraction for the lower classes, it maintained a certain umbilical link with the Church of England. Its adherents quite commonly used the local parish Church for their marriages. Nonetheless, as notions of freedom of religion at last spread even to acknowledging the Roman Catholic faith,[50] pressure grew for a marriage system that broke the monopoly of the official Church of the state. This pressure was evident in the debates of 1822–3, though Lord Lansdowne's contemporaneous bill to allow dissentient ceremonies was derided by Eldon and Redesdale and nothing then came of it.[51]

However, religious tolerance was spreading and it coincided with a new interest in social observation. Purposeful government demanded accurate information about the make-up of the populace. The Church was quite unable to argue that its parish registers provided any accurate record of marriages, and the ten-yearly censuses that had begun in 1801 were only a partial answer. A Registrar-General of Births, Deaths, and Marriages was created in 1836 and was given powers to operate through collaboration with the Guardians of the new Poor Law Unions around the country.[52] The guardians were to appoint district registrars who could perform marriages at their Offices without religious ceremony.[53] For these a procedure equivalent to the reading of banns was devised that would take place at the Guardians' weekly meetings.[54] If Catholics and others wanted to marry in their own churches, a registrar would have to attend and be paid for.[55]

---

[48] Macqueen, *Marriage, Divorce*, 13; Geary, *Marriage and Family Relations* (1892), 85–97, 120–1, 133–7.

[49] The original impetus for the Act had been doubt cast on a Scottish marriage of 20 years' standing through absence of adequate proof that it had taken place in any form: see L. Leneman, 'The Scottish Case that led to Lord Hardwicke's Marriage Act' (1999) 17 *LHR* 161–70.

[50] See Vol. XI, pp. 385–8.

[51] See Outhwaite, *Clandestine Marriage*, 158–9.

[52] For the local administration of the 'new' poor law in the period, see above, pp. 484–8.

[53] In the event, they mostly appointed their own clerks.

[54] See the Marriage Act 1836, 6 & 7 Will. IV c. 85. Section 7 provided a procedure for shortening the period of notification to a week. Other conditions, notably the consent of parents of those under 21, applied as for Church marriages. Registers were established for Ireland in 1845 and Scotland in 1855.

[55] The Act only permitted marriages in places of religious worship, which had to be registered.

The taint of Poor Law supervision would only be removed 20 years later.[56] Olive Anderson suggests that the new system was nonetheless very much a part of the radical reforms inspirited by the Representation of the People Act (Reform Act) 1832. It was flexible enough, as she shows, to allow localities to take up civil marriage in strikingly different degrees, in keeping with the many variations in social life that were part of Victorian England and Wales.[57]

From the outset, all marriages, including those of the Church of England, had to be formally registered. But the established Church would steadfastly resist any attempt to change its own notification system of banns or to require a registrar's presence at its ceremonies. Catholics and Non-conformists naturally resented such preferential treatment, and eventually a Royal Commission under Lord Chelmsford recommended modifications that would reduce the differences.[58] The Commission's proposals became submerged under an argument about whether a single marriage law should be introduced for the United Kingdom as a whole; and whether, in accordance with advanced liberal opinion, first there should always be a civil ceremony. The conflicts over the celebration of marriage were partly inter-denominational in this period, but partly also about the growing separation of state from religious adherence. The Scots fought resolutely against surrendering their informal marriage traditions and their rules remained different. In England and Wales it took until 1886 to secure an extension of hours as far as 3 pm, and until 1898 to remove the need for a registrar to attend weddings conducted by the non-established denominations in their own buildings.[59] Once assuaged, the law on marriage formalities would remain stable for half a century.[60]

---

[56] Marriage and Registration Acts Amendment Act 1856. The link with poor law administration would be severed completely only in 1929.

[57] O. Anderson, 'The Incidence of Civil Marriage in Victorian England and Wales' (1975) 69 *P & P* 50. By the end of the century, 70% of marriages were celebrated in the Church of England, 30% in 'nonconformist' places of worship (of which 11% were protestant, 5% Jewish and Quaker, and 4% Roman Catholic); see the SC Report, *PP* 1893–4 (368), xiii, 57. It would seem that many who did not regard themselves as members of the Established Church nonetheless used it for marriage ceremonies.

[58] The Laws of Marriage, *PP* 1867–8, xxxii, taking the view that the requirements for marriage throughout the UK badly needed standardization; but Scots resistance would continue.

[59] Marriage Act 1898; for details, see Cretney, *Family*, 17–19. The Commons SC (above, n.57) came down hard on registrars for not always turning up on time or at all; and the Registrar-General's attempt to defend them was dismissed by the Committee as seeking to protect their fees.

[60] For twentieth-century developments, see Cretney, *Family*, 20–30.

III

Wives: The Quest for Civil Independence

WE return to the Biblical conceit that fashioned Eve from the rib of Adam, and at common law implanted the wife in the legal genome of her husband. By the beginning of our period, as we have already noted, equity had ingeniously inserted a variant in favour of the families of the propertied.[1] The wife's separate estate, if held on trust, could provide for her and then the couple's progeny; and if a restraint on anticipation was also included this would prevent her from requiring the capital of that settlement to be transferred to the husband or the creditors of either spouse. But that could scarcely assist enterprising women, once they married, in running businesses or taking jobs, since a trust for separate use was essentially for the wife to be left at leisure to attend to childbirth, offspring, and the household, great or moderate. The income earned by married women, who worked as teachers, nurses, governesses, dress-makers, grocers, launderers, writers, or whatever, under common law principles belonged to their husbands.[2] With a cooperative husband, or one that the wife could dominate, she might in practice manage such activity and profit from it. Equally a watchful housewife might save out of the housekeeping supplied by her husband and, if he agreed that she should, for instance, 'inclose it in her stays', the sum would be held for her separate use. But otherwise a husband would retain his right at law to the fund and his creditors might demand an assignment of it.[3] Even if her friendly society or cooperative savings bank would only release the savings to her, he could sue for them.[4]

---

[1] Above, 739–44.

[2] Above, 736.

[3] If, however, she had the money in order to act as his agent in maintaining the household, then in that capacity she was not entitled to retain any profit from it: *Barrack* v. *McCulloch* (1856) 3 K. & J. 110.

[4] Before the Commons Select Committee on Shaw-Lefevre's bill of 1869, *PP* 1867–8 (441), vii, the influential Rochdale Equitable Pioneer Co-operative Society stated that it only allowed payments from a wife's account on her authority. The Committee thought the practice to be of doubtful legality. See also M. Finn, 'Working-Class Women and the Context for Consumer Control in Victorian County Courts' (1998) 161 *P & P* 116–54 and *The Character of Credit: Personal Debt in English Culture, 1740–1914* (Cambridge, 2003).

1. THE STRUGGLE FOR LEGISLATION

It is scarcely surprising, therefore, that in parallel with the demand for judicial divorce, came a campaign for married women to be entitled to their separate earnings and other assets, just as much as if they were held in a trust for their own use. If they were wealthy enough they might seek to set up a separate use settlement for the conduct of business affairs; but the expense of establishing the actual trust was considerable and running a business in which trustees became the legal owners of assets could well be cumbersome.[5] As with divorce, there had already been compromise enough for the law to appear engaged in social discrimination. In addition, the claim to property, by which married women would be placed on an equal footing with men and single women, had political implications, for national and local franchises turned on property qualifications as well as gender.

The political skirmishes over married women's property rights have been thoroughly explored by Holcombe, Stetson, and others.[6] One cue came from Caroline Norton, who was roused to fury in the Westminster County Court by her husband's refusal to pay for repairs to her coach.[7] When pamphleteering against her subjugate status, she played up the presence of a woman on the throne with *A Letter to the Queen on Lord Cranworth's Marriage and Divorce Bill* (1855).[8] As well as arguing the case for judicial divorce she insisted on better protection from violent and neglectful husbands and the equation of the property rights of all married women with those who had the advantage of a separate use under a settlement in equity. Among the mid-century feminists, it was Barbara Leigh-Smith (later Mrs Bodichon) who emerged as the leading organizer of the initial campaign for property rights.[9] She was able to draw on the support of liberal lawyers in the Law Amendment Society (LAS)—notably Brougham, Sir Erskine Perry, and Matthew Davenport Hill—who were also involved in the case for divorce by court decree. The claim that wives should be entitled to remain owners of their property was inherently likely to have wider impact than the demand for a regular divorce system, which would affect

---

[5] Under the separate use trust in a marriage settlement, the wife would be severely constrained against using the fund as active capital. The trustees preserved the corpus in order that it pass in remainder to her children or else back to her family.

[6] L. Holcombe, *Wives and Property* (1983); D. M. Stetson, *A Woman's Issue* (Westport Conn., 1982); and see E. S. Turner, *Roads to Ruin* (1966), Ch. 6; V. Ullrich, 'The Reform of Matrimonial Property Law in England during the Nineteenth Century' (1977) 9 *Victoria U. Wellington L. Rev.* 13–36.

[7] For details see Holcombe, *Wives and Property*, 50–7, esp. 53.

[8] See also her *English Laws for Women* (1854, privately published); below, 781–2.

[9] See her *Most Important Laws concerning Women* (1854).

only a minor segment of those locked in unsatisfactory marriages. Indeed, a marriage settlement was 'part of the regular established course of affairs to which everyone submits in his turn'.[10] But now there threatened a regime by which all property coming into the marriage would be jointly owned and so subject to joint decision-making; or else it would be divided into separate packages, with perhaps the husband still liable to meet the wife's obligations from his package.

In 1856 Perry raised the issue in a parliamentary motion and the following year promoted a property bill drawn by the LAS and bolstered by petitions to Parliament with many thousands of signatures. Its centrality became apparent from the outraged astonishment with which Tory Members of Parliament greeted it. 'If a woman has not full confidence in a man, let her refrain from marrying him', pronounced the categorical Malins QC (later a Vice-Chancellor). How could male dominance survive a reversal of principle that would allow wives, by their own choice, to emerge from the restricted perfection of their domestic circle?[11] The bill was, however, lost. Under consideration at the same time was the bill on Divorce and Matrimonial Causes, which provided that a decree of judicial separation, just as a divorce decree *a vinculo*, turned the wife into a *feme sole*, owning her property, determining the succession to it, and contracting for herself. It was this much more limited provision that became law.[12] The Divorce Act also invented a procedure before a justice of the peace or London magistrate by which a deserted wife, whether or not she was seeking a divorce or separation, could obtain a protection order for her earnings and other property that would otherwise be the husband's. If the husband then wrongly seized her assets, he could be ordered by a county court to restore the specific property *and* pay double the value to her. The choice of different courts for the two stages linked the arrangements with the contemporaneous demands for the protection of working-class wives from maltreatment and neglect by their husbands.[13]

---

[10] 'Marriage Settlements' (1863) 8 *Cornhill Mag.* 666–78; see C. Stebbings, *The Private Trustee in Victorian England* (Cambridge, 2002), 11.

[11] This line of argument was powerfully pursued by, for instance, the Attorney General, Bethell (later Westbury). See further, Holcombe, *Wives and Property*, Ch. 5; Stetson, *A Woman's Issue*, 60–4; M. K. Woodhouse, 'The Marriage and Divorce Bill of 1857' (1959) 3 *AJLH* 260–76.

[12] Divorce and Matrimonial Causes Act 1857, for which see further, below, 787. The proposal was initiated by St Leonards and insisted upon by Lyndhurst: see M. L. Shanley, ' "One Must Ride Behind": Married Women's Rights and the Divorce Act of 1857' (1982) 25 *Vict. St.* 355–76. For the somewhat wayward reporting of the debates in *Hansard* and the confusions among historians about what St Leonards was supposed to have said, see O. Anderson, 'Hansard's Hazards' (1997) 112 *EHR* 1202–15.

[13] See below, pp. 787–8.

2. PARTIAL VICTORY

For over a decade, the activists continued to press for political rights to be conferred on all women and property rights on wives. The campaign reached its climax during the 1867 debates on reform of the parliamentary franchise. J. S. Mill's brief membership of the Commons was notable for his amendment seeking the vote for women as for men. He did not succeed (and in any case a victory would have been largely symbolic, since women would still have to satisfy the same property qualifications and comparatively few would do so).[14] But two years later—just as Mill published his *Essay on the Subjection of Women*—the franchise for municipal boroughs would be extended to women with the requisite property qualification.[15]

After the Second Reform Act, bills on wives' property were promoted regularly at the instance of the Married Women's Property Committee of the National Association for the Promotion of Social Science, through parliamentary associates led by Shaw-Lefevre, Mill, and Russell Gurney. They aimed to place married women in the same legal position as their husbands, but to get the measure through in 1870 they had to accept amendments that took account of heavy opposition from the Lords.[16] Conservative opinion was having to ingest the consequences of the second Reform Act and remained opposed to any simple extension of even the private rights of married women. The resulting Married Women's Property Act was by no means without a radical streak, since it began a process of undeniable reversal. With a nod towards equity, a married woman was deemed to hold property at common law for her separate use without the establishment of any distinct trust.[17] However, this separate entitlement could arise only in relation to a limited list of assets:[18] her earnings (the great *casus belli*),[19] savings bank deposits, income from real property inherited on an

---

[14] Mill had long accepted that the legal treatment of women was unjust, and in this his relationship with Harriet Taylor played a significant part, see e.g. Stetson, *A Woman's Issue*, 25–7.

[15] See Vol. XI, 14.

[16] In the debates, grand lawyers predominated: with Romilly, Hatherley, and even Cairns (who had been Disraeli's Lord Chancellor in 1867–8) for the Liberal proposals and Penzance and Westbury (joined by the social reformer, Shaftesbury) in opposition.

[17] The main counter-proposal was indeed a bill, introduced by H. C. Raikes, which would have allowed a wife to petition a court for appointment of a trustee other than her husband in order to protect her property and earnings: see Stetson, *A Woman's Issue*, 70.

[18] Married Women's Property Act 1870, ss 1–5, 7–8.

[19] Georgiana Weldon (for whom see below, pp. 768 (n. 4), 831–2) had occasion to push this category to its limits: a house bought out of her thespian earnings was treated as her own; but she had to wait until the Act of 1882 in order to gain the power to sue in her own name for trespass to it, after an incident in which her husband's advisers had sought to take her to hospital: *Weldon* v. *Winslow* (1884) 13 QBD 784, CA; *Weldon* v. *de Bathe* (1884) 13 QBD 784, CA.

intestacy, and personal property received by her on an intestacy or (up to £200) under a will, and, if she so requested, certain investments.[20] For the rest, the old rules applied. It was the husband who was liable on contracts that she was able to make on his behalf during the marriage and for her torts during that time. One concession was granted to the husband. Given that under the common law he acquired his wife's property, he was legally liable for her debts contracted before marriage; but that was henceforth to cease.[21] Her creditors were accordingly left with recourse only against whatever separate property she might have. Their loud protests led to an amendment making the husband once more liable, but only from property that he received from the wife on marriage.[22]

3. THE VICTORIAN SETTLEMENT

These partial changes—'confused, illogical and absurd', according to Shaw-Lefevre—were not enough for the women's movement.[23] The fight continued, but in the latter 1870s Disraeli's government would not budge. Only on Gladstone's return did the campaigners secure the further shift under which the wife's property of whatever kind was deemed to be hers to acquire and dispose of 'as if she were a *feme sole* without the intervention of any trustee'. So the Married Women's Property Act 1882 provided;[24] and the Married Women's Property Committee of the Social Science Association disbanded in a glow of self-congratulation.[25] A. V. Dicey demonstrated in *Law and Public Opinion in England in the Nineteenth Century* that equity had intervened against the savage unilateralism of the common law in a way which in practical terms created a separate law for the

---

[20] Government funds, holdings in companies, and interests in friendly, building, and other societies.

[21] Married Women's Property Act 1870, s 12.

[22] Married Women's Property Act (1870) Amendment Act 1874, ss 2, 5. Under s 13 of the 1882 Act she would become primarily liable for her ante-nuptial torts to the extent of her separate estate and the husband (if he was sued as well) only for the rest of the damages awarded.

[23] One matter on which the 1870 Act took only a cautious step concerned assurance policies on a husband's life. His widow would have a considerable interest in benefiting from such a policy, but at common law her incapacity prevented her from taking out such a policy herself, and the doctrine of privity prevented her from claiming on a policy taken out by him, even where she was specifically denominated. Section 10 of the 1870 Act enabled her to do so, if the policy was expressed to be for her separate use. Section 11 of the 1882 Act would permit each spouse to take out a policy on the life of the other and to nominate the survivor and/or the children as beneficiaries with a right to sue.

[24] Section 1(1). For the Act and its consequences, see Holcombe, *Wives and Property*, Chs 9, 10; Stetson, *Woman's Issue*, Ch. 3; Grant-Bailey, *Lush on the Law of Husband and Wife* (1932), Chs 3–5; A. C. H. Barlow, 'Gifts and other Transfers Inter Vivos and the Matrimonial Home' in Graveson and Crane, *Century*, 195–204.

[25] Holcombe, *Wives and Property*, 204–5.

rich.[26] Once Parliament felt the demands of the less favoured, it took the step which Chancery judges had found no sufficient pressure to make by themselves in direct challenge to the common lawyers. But it was all too evident that most members of Parliament had no idea of the 'nice and thorny questions' that were the consequence of choosing this appeasing path.

The object of the campaign had been to remove legal distinctions between wives and other adults in their capacity to behave as individual participants in the markets of life; and so far as property ownership and dealings were concerned it did so. The property that each spouse brought into the marriage remained his or hers except when it was transferred to them jointly; or when they agreed that it should be held jointly; or when one gave or sold it to the other.[27] Thus, thanks to the legislation of 1870 and 1882, the choices open to each spouse were significantly expanded. Moreover, the High Court or a county court acquired power to make such order as they thought fit on questions of ownership and possession arising between the pair.[28] For judges to be imbued with such an apparently wide power was certainly striking.[29] So also is the fact that the common law lost its clutch of preferences favouring the husband and that abandonment bolstered the gradual shift in attitudes to gender relations. Marriage could no longer be taken to signal the submission of the wife to her husband unless carefully prepared alternatives were put in place through settlements or joint agreements. Now there was some greater scope for the partners to work out a balanced relationship on the footing of their property holdings.

However, even among the propertied, cases must have been common where most assets were brought into the marriage by the husband, through his earnings or income from assets, or from gifts or loans from his family and supporters. For that situation nothing changed, either during the continuance of the marriage

---

[26] 2nd edn, 1914, 371–98.

[27] A transfer of property from the husband to the wife could place it out of the range of his creditors. Accordingly, the case law raised nice points. If there was an informal gift, the general law required there to be delivery, or at least a symbolic handing over of part of the whole: *Cochrane* v. *Moore* (1890) 15 QBD 57 (CA). This rule was applied between husband and wife in *Lock* v. *Heath* (1892) 8 TLR 295 (gift of furniture proved from transfer of one chair). If there was a sale of household goods, it did not have to be evidenced by a registered bill of sale, because a creditor should not presume that household goods belonged to the husband, rather than the wife: *Ramsay* v. *Margrett* [1894] 2 QB 18 (CA); applied to a gift by deed in *French* v. *Getting* [1922] 1 KB 236 (CA). See Barlow 'Gifts and Other Transfers' in Graveson and Crane, *Century*, 206–8.

[28] The fear of intractable disputes had led to such a clause in Erskine Perry's 1856 proposal; and it was included in the 1870 Act (s 9), as well as the 1882 Act (s 17). For its ancestry in, for instance, the wife's equity to a settlement, see above, 742–4.

[29] During the Second World War, and after it, judges turned to s 17 as a basis for developing an equity allowing a deserted wife to stay on in the matrimonial home despite her husband's title to it: see esp. Denning LJ in *Bendall* v. *McWhirter* [1952] 2 QB 466, 475.

or on his death. Where the wealth was his, the wife remained subject to his command. It was this hierarchy of authority that Victorian men generally took to be the natural order of things and a necessary barricade against family disruption and anarchy.[30] The husband deserved his power of decision over family resources, so that he could cope in hard times and take risks in better. His power to dispose of his estate by will as he chose was to remain a significant element in that control. And if he died intestate, real property still went to his heir rather than his widow, subject only to any one-third right of dower that she might have for life, or a jointure arrangement in a settlement.[31]

Even where the wife did bring assets into the marriage, the 1882 Act did nothing to override explicit terms in settlements by which trustees held assets for her separate use; and, as section 19 prescribed, the restraint on alienation could still be used to fetter her ability to turn the assets into marketable commodities. Wealthy fathers and other settlors continued to calibrate the measure of financial independence that a wife should have from her husband. If anything, their desire to impose their own limitations probably increased in the new world where the wife now kept ownership of property that formerly would have passed to her husband.

More generally, the truce between committed liberators and reluctant equalizers that had shaped the Acts of 1870 and 1882 provided separate property for wives; but still there were obscurities affecting their status as wholly distinct individuals, particularly in respect of their obligations in tort and contract. Many of the rights and duties affecting property arose through the law of obligations and by no means all the difficulties were resolved in the legislation. Take, first of all, tort. The Acts cut into the consequences of unity in respect of the launching of actions. The wife could now sue for her separate property without joining her husband. Indeed, she could even sue her husband when he wrongly misappropriated her property, even though each remained unable to sue the other for non-property wrongs.[32] Where she was the tortfeasor, the victim of a wrong committed by her before the marriage could proceed against her separate estate. For post-nuptial torts, the husband in some sense remained liable for

---

[30] So J. F. Stephen in his confrontation with J. S. Mill: (see above, p. 745). Even Caroline Norton did not wish to alter the general position of the husband, only to secure that he did not behave as an unreasonable dictator.

[31] See above, 738–9. One modification was introduced by the Intestates' Estates Act 1890, giving the widow of a wholly intestate, issue-less, husband the first £500 of his estate. Real modification had to await the property legislation of 1925, when the Administration of Estates Act would re-write the intestacy rules so as to apply equally to realty and personalty.

[32] 1882 Act, ss 1(2), 12 and see n. 19 above. He could also be prosecuted for misappropriation. The last survival of the old regime would be the unity that prevented spouses from suing each other for non-property torts. It would not be abolished until 1962.

the wife's wrongdoing after marriage, even though he no longer acquired any of her property. If the tort arose out of her contract, her separate property was the only recourse. Beyond that, the courts differed on whether the husband was fully liable with her; whether he was secondarily liable, if she was unable to pay damages; or whether he had merely to be named as a defendant together with her as a procedural survival from earlier times. Eventually the House of Lords would hold him jointly liable with her.[33] By then many would think this a retrograde decision.[34]

As for contract, under the 1882 Act the wife gained her own capacity, but only in respect of her separate property.[35] This bred unsatisfactory results for creditors, since it was that property alone which could be seized to enforce a judgment. If she contracted a small debt for which other non-payers would be liable to imprisonment, she escaped that sanction.[36] More than that, before 1882, Chancery had allowed a wife who benefited from a separate trust a limited capacity to contract by reference to that estate.[37] This had meant that she must have had assets from that estate at the time of contracting from which to satisfy any judgment against her, even though she was not obliged then to keep the assets in readiness.[38] After 1882, the courts unimaginatively applied the same doctrine to a wife who enjoyed no corpus in the hands of trustees. The judges continued to ask: did the wife at the time of contracting have separate property to meet any liability in future?[39] This imposed a decidedly cumbersome investigation on suppliers of goods and services and on lenders; and the matter only became more obtuse as the courts struggled to define what separate property was sufficient for her to be contracting with reference to it.[40] Traders could well be reluctant to deal with the wife, an impediment for her that went to the main objection to her legal incapacity over the previous half-century. It was the business community who procured

---

[33] *Edwards* v. *Porter* [1925] AC 1, resolving opposed judicial attitudes.

[34] She would be made solely liable for her own torts, whenever committed, by the Law Reform (Miscellaneous Provisions) Act 1935, s 3.

[35] Section 1(2) put the limitation plainly.

[36] *Scott* v. *Morley* (1887) 20 QBD 120 (CA) (post-marriage debt); and see *Robinson King* v. *Lynes* [1894] 2 QB 577 (pre-marriage debt).

[37] See e.g. *Owens* v. *Dickenson* (1840) Cr. & Ph. 48; *Pike* v. *Fitzgibbon* (1881) 17 Ch D 454; *Durrant* v. *Ricketts* (1881) 8 QBD 177.

[38] *National Provincial Bank* v. *Williamson* (1876) 24 WR 10.

[39] *Re Shakespear* (1885) 30 ChD 169; *Tetley* v. *Griffith* (1887) 57 LT 673; *Palliser* v. *Gurney* (1887) 19 QBD 519; *Stogdon* v. *Lee* [1891] 1 QB 147 (CA).

[40] *Leak* v. *Driffield* (1889) 24 QBD 28 (wedding ring and bonnet not sufficient); *Braunstein* v. *Lewis* (1891) 65 LT 449 (£4 not enough to support a loan of £400); cf. *Bonner* v. *Lyon* (1890) 6 TLR 318 (extravagant purchases of jewellery and clothes sufficient).

an amending Act. The wife's holdings at the time of contracting ceased to be relevant.[41]

The former fictional unity had many consequences between the spouses. Their financial arrangements could not previously give rise to legal outcomes. Now each could keep funds in separate accounts or jointly—with the result in the latter case that both should consent to any disbursement. If a wife funded a purchase from her own resources the thing bought would be hers unless there was evidence that she had given it to the husband. If joint contributions went to buy the thing, it would be jointly owned. Each could sue the other on mutual promises, and the courts duly allowed actions, for instance, on a loan by the wife to the husband; likewise on a tenancy.[42] An agreement to separate became enforceable even when there were no trustees to give it legal bottom.[43] But a separation nullified the mutual obligation of the married to live together. What of the case where they had to be apart because of her health and his job? Then a husband's promise to pay the wife a set monthly sum was not to be regarded as enforceable. Even assuming there was consideration for the promise, the Court of Appeal would not hear of such a thing. Their innate sense of right told them that the pair could have had no intention to create legal relations.[44] A higher male morality could still prevail in an altered legal world.

In any case, there was one question on which government's interest prevailed over the new separation. For assessing income tax, income received or earned by the wife had previously formed part of the husband's income. The Inland Revenue insisted that the same regime continue after 1882. In 1894, the Liberal Chancellor of the Exchequer, Harcourt, conceded that the wife could have up to £500 assessed individually, but only where she *earned* the income in a separate occupation from her husband's. Beyond that, it was feared that an opportunity for reducing tax liability by apportionment of the joint income of businesses, or the careful allocation of bonds or shares, would lead to simple avoidance plans.[45]

Because the 1882 legislation dealt with some of the consequences of the wife retaining her property, though not all, it can appear rather less radical than

[41] Married Women's Property Act 1893; Morrison, 'Contract', in Graveson and Crane, *Century*, 124–5.

[42] *Pearce* v. *Morrison* [1904] 1 KB 80; *Butler* v. *Butler* (1885) 16 QBD at 378 (CA). The principle was not a novelty. In *Woodward* v. *Woodward* (1863) 3 De G.J. & Sm. 672, Lord Westbury had held that a wife could sue a husband to recover a loan from her separate estate.

[43] *McGregor* v. *McGregor* (1888) 21 QBD 424 (CA); *Sweet* v. *Sweet* [1895] 1 QB 12.

[44] *Balfour* v. *Balfour* [1919] 2 KB 571. The couple had, however, reached their agreement only after undertaking not to proceed on cross-summonses for assaults. The supposed amity between them appeared more than a little forced.

[45] M. Daunton, *Trusting Leviathan* (Cambridge, 2001), 218–23.

the first breach of the common law barricade in 1870. In truth, both Acts were the upshot of sharp warfare about the very core of Victorian marriage. The exchanges of shot in their making accounted for the holes.[46] It would be nearly 40 years before the campaigns for the parliamentary franchise for women would succeed, thanks above all to their extraordinary contributions to the Great War effort. But the successful campaigns after the Second Reform Act for the property rights of married women, together with the gradual growth of educational opportunities for what men patronized as the 'fair sex', and the concession of entry into the learned professions and other employments,[47] put the campaign for political rights on an altogether higher platform. Equality in matters of gender would continue to be held back by a swathe of economic and cultural factors. But in the Queen's last decades, no longer could the case for change simply be dismissed with contempt.

[46] It would take until the Law Reform (Married Women and Tortfeasors) Act 1935 for the distinction between men's and women's separate estates to be abolished: Cretney, *Family*, 102–5.

[47] Vol. XI, Pt 3, pp. 1116–17.

IV

Marital Breakdown: Separation and the Coming of Judicial Divorce

1. ECCLESIASTICAL JURISDICTION: RESTITUTION AND SEPARATION

The medieval Church's dignification of marriage as a sacrament had stamped it as indissoluble; but Rome had proved inventive in enlarging the degrees of prohibition on marriages between those already related by blood or marriage, particularly so that powerful kings and nobles could rid themselves of inconvenient wives. This disingenuity had led Martin Luther to one of his most searing indictments of the faith under the Popes. In the course of it, he insisted that marriage was nothing more than a contract. The Reformation left Calvinistic Scotland with a provision for divorce by order of a court. Scots law did not belittle wives to the extent of empowering their husbands to divorce them as and when they chose. Nor did it give the pair the power simply to agree upon an end to the relationship. For the court to intervene, one party had to commit an essential breach of the tie—either adultery or desertion for four years. The grant of a divorce did terminate the marriage, freeing the wronged party to marry another, and the wrongdoer also to marry anyone save (so it seems) the adulterer cited in the proceedings. The divorce itself was *a vinculo matrimonii*—from the very bond. By the mid-nineteenth century, the Edinburgh Commissary Court was making some 20 divorce orders a year, nearly half of them in favour of women.[1]

After some uncertainty, the seventeenth-century Church of England, deeming marriage to be a holy estate, had decided that its ecclesiastical courts could not grant any such order.[2] Indeed those courts would try to insist that a partner who had left home should return; this was the object of proceedings before them for

---

[1] See L. Leneman, *Alienated Affections* (1998), Ch. 1. The Chelmsford Commission, Report, *PP* 1867–8, xxxiii, noted that there were various legal obscurities about the details of Scots law on the subject.

[2] A recent study of the consequences is J. Bailey, *Marriage and Marriage Breakdown in England, 1660–1800* (Cambridge, 2003).

restitution of conjugal rights.[3] Citations seeking restitution seem to have been instituted only occasionally, even after a statutory reform in 1813 empowered these courts to order a non-compliant spouse to be imprisoned.[4] Apart from that, the church courts could only decree a divorce *a mensa et thoro*—from board and bed. This forerunner of modern judicial separation did not leave either the innocent or the guilty party free to marry others. It merely ended their obligation to live together. By the 1840s, such 'divorces' were being granted in some 50 cases each year, mainly in the Consistory Courts of London and York, and so touching only a minute proportion of all marriages in England and Wales.[5]

The divorce *a mensa* was confined to cases of matrimonial wrongdoing, more narrowly defined than in Scotland. Desertion was not itself a ground, since the remedy for that was to order restitution of conjugal rights, obliging the straying partner to return home. The decree required proof of cruelty, adultery, or unnatural sexual activity.[6] Cruelty was an allegation mostly made by wives; and in the late eighteenth century, that doughty civilian, Sir William Scott (Stowell), had issued a check against too readily finding cruelty in what would today be regarded as psychological oppression.[7]

The Court would be likely to order a guilty husband to provide alimony for the separated wife and that could be the direct value to the wife in seeking the decree. By the nineteenth century, an innocent wife-petitioner could expect to receive a third, perhaps even a half of his income, the amount varying in particular with the property that she had brought him in the marriage.[8] The Court of Chancery might equally press a husband to provide for a deserted wife out of

---

[3] Ecclesiastical courts had power to deal with a converse case: an order for jactitation of marriage forbade a person from claiming falsely to be married to another, but could be brought only by the person wrongly accused: *Campbell* v. *Corley* (1862) 31 L.J. P.M. & A. 60. Though not abolished until 1970, this process was virtually obsolete by the nineteenth century.

[4] The old sanction of penance and ultimately excommunication had lost any real force by this period. In 1883 the pertinacious litigant, Georgiana Weldon, would secure a committal of her estranged husband for failure to comply with an order for restitution. It was not enough that he took a house and supplied servants for her to live in separately, in addition to £500 a month. He was a man with some social cachet and Parliament rapidly lifted the sanction: see *Weldon* v. *Weldon* (1883) 9 PD 52; Matrimonial Causes Act 1884, s. 5; and for the Weldons, see e.g. Cretney, *Family*, 144–5; B. Thompson, *A Monkey among Crocodiles* (2000).

[5] The courts in provincial dioceses had very little matrimonial business: see S. Waddams, 'English Matrimonial Law on the Eve of Reform (1828–57)' (2000) 21 *JLH* 59–81. In the archdiocese of Canterbury, appeal lay to the Court of Arches; until 1833 a second appeal lay to the Court of Delegates and even very occasionally beyond on what amounted to a petition to the Crown. After 1833 the Judicial Committee replaced the Delegates: see Vol XI, 547–50.

[6] *Mogg* v. *Mogg* (1824) 2 Add. 292, where a conviction of a husband for sexual assault on an apprentice was treated as sufficiently serious to support the libel.

[7] See below, 790–1.

[8] See L. Stone, *The Road to Divorce, 1530–1987* (Oxford, 1990), 210.

the capital or income that she brought into the marriage settlement.[9] A guilty wife-respondent could expect nothing to support her. As to seeing her children, which was a Chancery question, there would be no chance if the husband objected. So she might well contest his petition for a divorce *a mensa*. That led into contradictions of evidence from partisan friends and relatives and from observant servants and informers.[10]

As we shall see, a decree of divorce *a mensa* had become one preliminary step in the exceptional business of obtaining a full divorce by Act of Parliament.[11] Whether or not that was the purpose of the ecclesiastical proceedings, the spouse seeking the order was supposed to show a truly righteous sense of injury. There must be nothing by way of connivance towards the adultery, or condonation of it afterwards, or collusion in getting up the proceedings; and the claimant must have committed no adultery—otherwise the suit would be barred by this 'recrimination'.[12] The ecclesiastical courts did not share the common law's view that marital unity prevented one partner from suing the other. The proceedings began with the claimant's formal 'libel' and then, if the respondent contested it, a recorded exchange of allegations between the parties. Evidence was procured through sworn declarations and recorded answers to the court's examiners and then formal interrogatories in writing put by the opposing party.[13] Without oral cross-examination the courts tended to obtain only a slanted view of the truth— and even more so when the husband and wife each wanted to end their relationship and the defendant therefore offered no contest.[14]

2. SEPARATION BY AGREEMENT

When one spouse had no wish for separation, the only hope was to seek an order from a Church court: as with the husband who lived for the violent subjugation of his wife or who sought to evade any responsibility for having deserted her. Beyond that, a decree of divorce *a mensa* was sometimes sought in order to give ground rules for the business of living apart. But if the pair were able to agree

---

[9] See Macqueen, *Husband and Wife* (2nd ed., 1872) III.

[10] Stone, *Road to Divorce*, 211–30 provides a rich account of such deponents, their opportunities and their self-interests.

[11] Below, text at nn. 123–32.

[12] See Stone, *Road to Divorce*, 206–10.

[13] Ecclesiastical Courts Commission, *PP* 1831–2, xxiv, 18–19; Stone, *Road to Divorce*, 183–98. The examination of witnesses *viva voce* would be introduced shortly before the Church court jurisdiction ended: 17 & 18 Vict. c. 47; R. B. Outhwaite, *The Rise and Fall of the English Ecclesiastical Courts 1530–1860* (Cambridge, 2006), 157–8.

[14] See Royal Commission on Divorce, *PP* 1852–3 [1604], XL, paras 44–9. The different stages of the procedure were criticized as involving 'three bodies which distrust one another'.

terms, that suggested a simpler way out; and from at least the late seventeenth century, contracts to separate had become increasingly frequent among the upper and middling ranks. Standard precedents had become well known in the 1730s and had typically provided a number of clauses which set out to alter the various obligations that arose under the general rules of common law, equity, and ecclesiastical law. Here was practice responding to the demands of the unhappily married in a world where full divorce remained virtually unattainable and where the Church courts limited even separations to cases of the innocent pitted against the guilty.[15] But could the different jurisdictions allow general marital obligations to be varied by agreement, or would that undermine religious imperatives that had been built into law?

In each of the jurisdictions, the issue proved to be a difficult testing ground. Conflicts arose between liberal temporizers and stern moralists that reduced the law to a quagmire. An accommodating view had begun to prevail in the courts of common law in the later eighteenth century, which tended to treat agreements to separate as effective, whatever the moral position of each party. But that had changed considerably as part of the geyser-spurt against moral laxity after 1789, led in the courts by Kenyon, Eldon, Stowell, and others. The basic undertaking in a separation agreement was that each party was to be freed from the duty to live together and in a simple case this might be the extent of the contract. Even so, issues could arise over the position of the wife in relation to creditors—since once living separately she might well have to arrange all the incidents of practical life for herself. In the eye of the common law the doctrine of unity between husband and wife might have prevented her being considered a separate legal person. Under Lord Mansfield, however, King's Bench had leant in favour of allowing a wife separated by agreement some capacity to enter contracts on her own behalf, just as she could when protected by an ecclesiastical divorce *a mensa*. Yet, by 1801, the Court of King's Bench had reversed that pragmatic attitude.[16] The theory of unity was applied implacably to stop traders from suing her when she had obtained goods, money, or services on credit.[17] This

---

[15] For the early developments from seventeenth-century precedents, see S. Staves, *Married Women's Separate Property in England, 1660–1833* (Cambridge MA, 1990), Ch. 6.

[16] *Marshall* v. *Rutton* (1800) 8 Term. Rep. 545, reversing *Ringsted* v. *Lady Lanesborough* (1783) 3 Doug. KB 197; *Barwell* v. *Brooks* (1784) 3 Doug. KB 373; *Corbett* v. *Poelnitz* (1785) 1 Term. Rep. 5. Subsequently, Lord Ellenborough CJKB would insist that the amount of separate maintenance being provided by the husband be sufficient according to the degree and circumstances of the husband; otherwise he would remain liable if she pledged his credit for necessaries: *Hodgkinson* v. *Fletcher* (1814) 4 Camp. 70; cf. *Nurse* v. *Craig* (1806) 2 Bos. & P. N.R. 148.

[17] On a different tack, the existence of a separation agreement did not prevent the husband from suing his wife's lover for crim. con., the agreement at most operating to reduce the damages: Lord Brougham, *Warrender* v. *Warrender* (1835) 2 Cl. & Fin. 488, at 527.

made it crucial to follow the scheme using trustees, which had been evolving in eighteenth-century practice. Under it, trustees for the wife were put in funds, whether by the husband or her family or both, to see to her maintenance. The husband remained liable for her debts, but the trustees undertook to indemnify him. This undertaking was taken as undeniable consideration for his promises.

Under the trust there could well be further arrangements concerning the property brought into the marriage by the wife or on her behalf, depending in part on how far these provided her with pin money or gave her a separate estate in equity. There might be provision for custody and access to the children, though public policy might deny it any legal force against the husband. The position reached by 1820 is accordingly best viewed by considering separately the objectives of the typical deed of separation.[18]

First of all, the husband would undertake to maintain the wife in her separate condition, either by providing a capital sum or a periodic allowance. So far as the promise was carried out, the courts would not require its undoing. But if it was still executory, common law could not countenance an action by her for damages, because of their notional unity. In Chancery, Lord Loughborough had refused to accept that the equitable order of specific performance could instead give effect to an obligation to *her*.[19] This reinforced the need for trustees to hold and administer property that would provide for the wife's maintenance, since they could sue for specific performance of promises to transfer the property to them and the court would then supervise them as it would other trustees. In this special role the trustees could be seen as a 'domestic forum' put in position to arbitrate between the spouses, when disagreements arose over the agreed terms.[20] Lord Eldon had made clear that he would have liked to go a considerable distance in attacking 'these fluctuating contracts', but in the end he considered the precedents in favour of upholding them to be too settled to allow for complete reversal.[21]

Nonetheless he raised a number of difficulties and one at least would long be accepted. Where a warring couple were brought to agree a reconciliation, it might well be provided that a trust for separation on specified terms would come into operation if later the wife once more had cause to leave—a matter which the 'family tribunal' could be well placed to decide. Eldon regarded such an

---

[18] See Roper, *Property*, ii, 273–368; Shelford, *Practical Treatise of the Law of Marriage and Divorce* (1841), 361–4; Macqueen, *Husband and Wife*, 106–24.

[19] *Legard* v. *Johnson* (1797) 3 Ves. 352, overruling Buller J. in *Fletcher* v. *Fletcher* (1788) 2 Cox Eq. Cas. 99 and Pepper Arden MR (Alvaney) in *Guth* v. *Guth* (1792) 3 Bro. C.C. 614.

[20] *St John* v. *St John* (1805) 11 Ves. 526; *Bateman* v. *Ross (Countess)* (1813) 1 Dow. 235.

[21] However, he refused to order trustees to make payments to the wife out of her separate estate: see Roper, *Property*, ii: 291–2, 296.

arrangement *in futuro* as an incentive to separate. It was a direct undermining of marriage and not to be tolerated.[22] Soon afterwards, the common law courts agreed, reversing their earlier position.[23] Eldon also questioned whether articles of separation were valid if neither party had engaged in conduct that would have justified a divorce *a mensa*—adultery by the wife, adultery or cruelty by the husband.

A separation agreement was highly likely to contain undertakings not to commence proceedings in an ecclesiastical court for a judicial remedy. Was it to be accepted that private agreement could render the courts otiose in these circumstances? The ecclesiastical courts would brook no undermining of their authority. They would disregard an undertaking not to apply to them for restitution of conjugal rights or a divorce *a mensa*. Sir William Scott (Lord Stowell) took high offence at the 'dereliction of these mutual offices which the parties are not at liberty to desert... —obligations which both of them have contracted in the sight of God and man, to live together "till death them do part"'.[24] His brother Eldon, sitting in Chancery, saw great difficulty over lack of consideration in the agreement to separate struck by the Earl and Countess of Westmeath. In it his undertaking to pay her an annuity was backed only by her agreement not to sue for ecclesiastical court relief, omitting the usual consideration of the trustees' undertaking to indemnify him for paying her debts.[25] Not until 1848, in *Wilson* v. *Wilson*, would the House of Lords accept that the ouster of ecclesiastical court jurisdiction would suffice for an order that the husband carry out his obligations to the trust. In so holding, the cause of the separation was treated as an irrelevance.[26] The judges were, after a half-century, coming once more to accept the benefits of voluntary arrangements. By putting the issue in terms of consideration, the shift over public policy could be accounted for by an abstract formula.[27] The startling aspect of the conclusion was that here the consideration consisted in the very promise to which the Church courts would give no quarter. At a stroke, not only did the Lords show the groundswell of opinion favouring readier relief

---

[22] *St John* v. *St John* (1805) 11 Ves. 526; *Hindley* v.*Westmeath* (1827) 6 B. & C. 200; *Westmeath* v. *Salisbury* (1830) 5 Bli. N.S. 339. For the full awfulness of the Westmeaths' embattled relationship, see L. Stone, *Uncertain Unions and Broken Lives* (Oxford, 1992), 510–612.

[23] *Durant* v. *Titley* (1819) 7 Price 577, reversing *Rodney (Lord)* v. *Chambers* (1802) 2 East 283.

[24] *Mortimer* v. *Mortimer* (1820) 2 Hag. Con. 310 at 318.

[25] *Westmeath* v. *Westmeath* (1830) 1 Dow. & Cl. 519.

[26] *Wilson* v. *Wilson* (1848) 1 HL Cas. 538 (decided by Cottenham LC alone, though Brougham and Lyndhurst had heard part of the argument). Another Lords' decision, *Hamilton* v. *Wright* (1842) 9 Cl. & Fin. 111, pointed in the same direction; see Macqueen, *Husband and Wife*, 332–3.

[27] There would be a whole line of obtuse decisions about what exactly constituted valuable consideration in this context, see e.g. S.N. Grant-Bailey, *Lush on Husband and Wife* (4th edn, 1933), 459–61.

against marital breakdown, but equally their willingness to cut the ground from under the ecclesiastical jurisdiction over matrimonial disputes.[28]

The Divorce Court set up in 1857 took over the old ecclesiastical powers to grant separation orders and the restitution of conjugal rights, as well as the new divorces *a vinculo*.[29] With this shift of focus, all courts could adopt a relatively flexible approach to the enforceability of the various terms in separation agreements. There was a growing tendency to judge them by principles governing contracts in general, as Lord Westbury and Jessel MR made plain in leading judgments.[30] Those principles still left some scope for treating separation agreements as not binding, in whole or in part. Indeed, they would be quite readily undone if they had been reached upon a shared mistake of fact or unfair pressure, particularly by husbands imposing on their wives.[31] Certain terms might also be deemed void as contrary to public policy. Where the wife had accepted an agreed level of maintenance, that term would be taken to wipe the husband's slate clear of previous matrimonial offences, since the agreement amounted to condonation of them. But if he then committed adultery or maltreated her, the wife might petition for a separation order or a divorce *a vinculo*, and thus by-pass the earlier terms concerning maintenance in order to secure a higher award from the Divorce Court, or different arrangements concerning the children. Over this delicate issue, the case law long remained unclear.[32] Only in 1929 would the House of Lords settle that a divorced wife was not bound by the earlier terms, even if they were expressed to continue when there was a subsequent matrimonial wrong.[33]

All in all, the case law in this realm developed with 'more fluctuation and obscurity than in any other' relating to husband and wife.[34] Its thrusts and feints occurred because individual judges differed in their instincts over how far the

---

[28] In a later stage of *Wilson* v. *Wilson* (1854) 5 HL Cas. 40, Brougham expressed strong doubts about the 1848 decision. But Cranworth LC and St Leonards were not prepared to escape from it; and so it stood.

[29] Below, 784–9.

[30] *Hunt* v. *Hunt* (1861) 4 De G.F. & J. 221; *Besant* v. *Wood* (1882) 12 Ch D 605, 620.

[31] See e.g. *Crabb* v. *Crabb* (1868) LR 1 P&D 601; cf. *Procter* v. *Robinson* (1866) 14 WR 381.

[32] In *Gandy* v. *Gandy* (1882) 7 PD 168, the Court of Appeal held that the maintenance term in a separation agreement must continue to govern, despite a later separation order based on a subsequent adultery. But the same court soon strove to confine that decision to its particular circumstances: *Bishop* v. *Bishop* [1893] P 138.

[33] *Hyman* v. *Hyman* [1929] AC 601. It was considered contrary to public policy to enter an agreement to keep down the level of maintenance, because this would increase the chance of the wife becoming a charge on the poor law. How far separation orders could alter earlier agreements would remain a difficult question: see J. L. Barton, 'The Enforcement of Financial Provisions' in Graveson and Crane, *Century*, 352–73, at 367–9.

[34] See e.g. Grant-Bailey, *Husband and Wife*, 429 and the ensuing chapter.

Christian view of marriage as an indissoluble union could be qualified by voluntary arrangements where the relationship had broken down. The judges had to deal with the perplexities of policy, while listening to histories of deep personal unhappiness. Often enough each spouse would tell a very different story about why the arrangement to separate had unravelled. Little wonder that so much remained unpredictable.

3. INFORMAL ARRANGEMENTS TO SEPARATE: DIVORCE BY LOCAL CUSTOM AND BY WIFE SALES

Formal agreements to separate involving trustees were for the propertied classes—people who might well have arranged property settlements on the occasion of the marriage. Some historians believe in the informal survival of social customs in remote regions, such as returning rings, jumping back over brooms, or leaving buildings by separate doors. The legal consequences remained obscure, but in essence these appeared to be endings of marriages by consent, whether the main cause was cruelty or friction, lack of children, or a movement on to a new partner or to other employment.[35] The practices might fly in the face of the Church's basic teaching; but, compared with simple desertion, they had an orderliness that might appeal when each spouse continued to live in the same community. By the nineteenth century such ceremonies were a folk survival, mostly confined to remote country areas, though creeping to some degree into industrial towns.[36]

More intriguing, for all that it occurred only occasionally, was the practice of wife sale.[37] In its most public form this subjected the wife to a crude property transaction, the husband leading her into a market by a halter so that she could be knocked down to another man for a price. This at least notified the community—and particularly its tradespeople—that the purchaser was assuming responsibility for her. Rather less publicity would occur if the transaction took place in an inn, with the innkeeper or potman acting as witness and perhaps

[35] See Gillis, *For Better, For Worse*, 196–200; reports of such things may well have been swollen by hearsay.

[36] See further, S. P. Menefee, *Wives for Sale* (Oxford, 1981), 20–3; Gillis, *For Better, For Worse*, 211–19; R. Phillips, *Putting Asunder* (Cambridge, 1988), 294–6; E. P. Thompson, *Customs in Common* (1991), Ch. 7; and for an early study, C. S. Kenny 'Wife-Selling in England' (1929) 45 *LQR* 494–7, at 496.

[37] The practice, in its various manifestations, was investigated extensively by Menefee, *Wives for Sale*, providing a useful source book, despite being patronized for its diffuse ethnographicity by Thompson, *Customs in Common*, 406–7 and Phillips, *Putting Asunder*, 289.

putting his mark to a sale 'paper'.[38] Even in the mid-eighteenth century, wife sales were regarded as a travesty which challenged respectable feelings about marriage and family. Lord Mansfield had listed them among the offences against public morals that could be tried as a common law misdemeanour.[39] By the 1830s, magistrates were attacking the scandal by instigating prosecutions for this offence. Thanks to their sense of outrage, wife sales became the stuff of folk tales and press stories. It is hard to say how frequently these sales occurred, but even in times of social disturbance, such as the French wars, they were only sporadic.[40]

Where a contemporary report does survive, the most interesting question about it is whether the transferred wife was, for whatever reason, a consenting party, or whether she was being dealt with against her will. A first clue is that in most cases the transaction was organized in advance, the buyer being on hand for the final ritual. Not untypically, part of the 'price' was for liquor with which to send the new couple on their way. The bartered wife could be eager to join her new partner and the whole affair a cheerful celebration. Another indication is that the wife would sign or mark the 'paper' as well as the two men and a witness. Indeed, an attorney might be involved with a document that was ready prepared.

E. P. Thompson finds indications that, if the wife was not satisfied with what had happened, she could reject the purchaser and go back to her husband.[41] Taking his evidence as a whole, the custom was mostly a cheap, unofficial, means of making a new liaison for the wife that would be accepted at least by those of the same social class.[42] Since the sale did not affect the official marital status of the participants, it might raise awkward questions. In law it was the first husband who still had to maintain the woman, and that might be important if she received poor relief and the officers wanted recourse against him.[43] If the first marriage was valid and the woman formally married the purchaser she would commit bigamy. There were, however, very few indications of such objections

---

[38] The paper might indeed be stamped, in order to give it authenticity.

[39] *R v. Delaval* (1763) 2 Burr. 1434.

[40] For figures of known, reasonably authenticated cases, see Menefee, *Wives for Sale*, Ch. 3, App.; Thompson, *Customs in Common*, 408–16.

[41] So it was with Henchard's disposal of his wife, Susan, at the Weydon Priors (Weyhill) Fair in Thomas Hardy's *The Mayor of Casterbridge*. Hardy probably worked from general tales, rather than from contemporary events: see C. Winfield, 'Factual Sources of Two Episodes in *The Mayor of Casterbridge*' (1970) 25 *Nineteenth Century Fiction* 224–31.

[42] Thompson, *Customs in Common*, 456–8 describes the hostile reception that his lectures on the subject provoked from pro-feminist audiences in the 1970s who were intent on denouncing the degrading nature of the rite of passage.

[43] Thompson, *Customs in Common*, 435–8, suggests that the authorities of the poor law would use their position and understanding of the legal position to reduce their own liabilities as far as possible.

being raised. If anything, it was the sale ceremony itself that became the target of the magistrates for its offensiveness to their ideas of public propriety.[44]

Wife sale seemed therefore to operate roughly as a separation agreement would work for the propertied, both being intended to relieve the husband of his rights and duties towards the 're-married' wife. While separation agreements were regarded by the judiciary and others with varying degrees of suspicion, they did not attract the wholesale condemnation voiced over wife sales— particularly of the halter-and-auction type.[45] The difference probably stemmed from the rowdy cock-a-snook that the latter offered to the Church and the civic authorities, especially when taken together with the symbolic degradation of the wife-chattel. At all events, authenticated reports of wife sales after the mid-nineteenth century are rare.[46] The custom was not one that would blossom into any distinctive procedure in modern law; whereas private, lawyerly, separation deeds, long organized through trustees,[47] were allowed to provide a voluntary alternative to court processes for separation and full divorce.

4. THE POOR LAW AND DESERTION

The deserted wife who had no means to maintain herself or her children could look only to charity or to the poor law authorities. The latter, as noted above, could seek to cover their expenditure by having the justices order the husband to pay maintenance.[48] But that hope must often have been thwarted: he might have disappeared or might lack any resources.[49] The overseers would be ready to suspect collusion of some sort with the husband (whatever their relationship). They might therefore refuse outdoor relief to the wife and require her instead to enter the workhouse, with all its marks of 'less eligibility'. If she committed adultery, relief would terminate, and if she deserted, it would be suspended.[50]

---

[44] The husband would face the same danger if he re-married. The formalities first required by Hardwicke's Act could give protection to some: cf. Stone, *Road to Divorce*, 144.

[45] In *Walton* v. *Walton* (1859) 28 L.J. P. & M. 97, the court refused to give effect to a separation agreement that amounted to 'an assignment of Mrs W. to her new lover'. But her marriage to Mr W. had produced 12 children and she was going to a man who had 15.

[46] See generally, Menefee, *Wives for Sale*, 140–68.

[47] For their preservation within the regime of the Married Women's Property Act 1882, see above, p. 763.

[48] See above, 726. Only from 1819 could this power be exercised summarily. In default, the husband could be subject to a fine of 20s per month. Not until 1886 was the wife given her own power to bring proceedings before magistrates: see below, 797–8.

[49] The justices could imprison a defaulter for a month under the Vagrancy Act 1824, 5 Geo. IV c. 83, s 3; but such orders were quite likely to produce no positive results: see O. R. McGregor and M. Finer, *Report of the Committee on One-Parent Families*, PP 1974 [Cmnd. 5629], App. 5.

[50] *R* v. *Flintan* (1830) 1 B. & Ad. 227.

Harsh as this might be, the deserted wife was in somewhat better condition than the mother of illegitimate children. As will be seen, the poor law authorities had an interest in making putative fathers provide, but that meant establishing their parentage. The Old Poor Law had made it easy for the mother to accuse and hard for the man to rebut her claim. The Poor Law Commission were stirred by stories of false finger-pointing (particularly at those with means), peculation by officers and accumulation by mothers of maintenance orders against different fathers.[51] In accordance with their general determination to instil less eligibility, the Commission advocated a much sterner line. The 1834 Act accordingly placed prime responsibility for maintaining the child on the mother. It required her accusation of paternity to be taken before Quarter Sessions, where corroboration of her evidence had to be produced.[52] Inevitably, this was in turn said to undermine the old community pressures on a man to marry his pregnant sweetheart; and step by step, the law would be once more reversed, in particular by the Bastardy Laws Amendment Act 1872.[53]

5. FULL DIVORCE BY PRIVATE ACT OF PARLIAMENT

After 1689, the landed and the entrepreneurial in English society had used the private bill procedure of the legislature to circumvent the operation of the general law in many situations affecting private rights and obligations. These had come to include Acts granting individual couples a divorce *a vinculo*, completely severing the bonds and allowing even the guilty party to re-marry. In the first half of the eighteenth century there had been only 20 instances, mostly involving the aristocracy. They were enough to establish the essential constraints upon this exceptional process, which came to involve investigative procedures in three tiers. The one allegation that would justify a divorce Act was adultery, and at first it was always the husband who made the allegation against his straying wife.

The case had to be made out in ecclesiastical proceedings for divorce *a mensa et thoro*; but the evidentiary weaknesses of that process had early led to an insistence in most cases that the husband also secure a common law verdict against the lover for 'crim. con.' with his wife.[54] Only after both these steps would

---

[51] Report, *PP* 1834, xxvii, 92–9, 195–8. See further below, 803–5.

[52] Poor Law Amendment Act 1834, 3 & 4 Will. IV, c. 76, ss 71–3.

[53] Sections 3, 4, giving justices in petty sessions power to award up to 5s per week. By the end of the nineteenth century there were some 6000 maintenance orders each year against putative fathers, compared with 4000 against husbands.

[54] For the growth of this action on the case, see above, 733. Various excuses came to be admitted, so that in 1841–57 almost a third of the petitioners did not sue at common

the House of Lords, which supervised private bill petitions, consider one for divorce. The House insisted that the allegation of adultery be proved all over again. Likewise, answers had to be provided to any question of condonation, connivance, collusion, or adultery by the petitioner.[55] As a way of showing that the whole arrangement was not a put-up job, the adulterer had actually to have paid the damages awarded against him by the jury in the crim. con. action. There was nothing to prevent the husband paying them back afterwards, but there was always the risk that he might renege. The Lords' proceedings were oral as well as documentary, and in particular they came to include an examination of the petitioner.[56] The papers were afterwards sent to the Commons and back, but procedure there was more perfunctory. The moral climate in the Lords would swerve to some extent, depending a good deal on the personal attitudes of those who tended to sit in what became increasingly a judicial procedure. The censorious Lord Auckland, having failed to make adultery a criminal offence, had the Standing Orders for divorce petition altered in 1810 so as to include a prohibition on the adulterous wife marrying her lover; but it seems not always to have been included.[57]

From 1750, the number of divorce statutes had begun to grow a little. It was in these years that the relatively open Scots divorce came to be more regularly used.[58] In both countries, despite the legal differences, religious and communal attitudes had previously acted as a veto. In England in the 1790s the average was four parliamentary divorces a year, a level that would not be reached again until the 1840s. By then, attitudes were responding to the greater mobility of the population as part of industrial development, and the shift of wives either into a wider range of employments or else into the domesticity of the middle-class hearth. But why should full divorce be kept for those who could squeeze through

law: S. Anderson, 'Legislative Divorce: Law for the Aristocracy?', in G. R. Rubin and D. Sugarman (eds), *Law, Economy and Society,1750–1914* (Abingdon, 1984), 412, at 436–7. A crim. con. verdict was not relevant where the wife petitioned for divorce, since English law gave no right to wife against mistress. Stone, *Road to Divorce*, Ch. 9, examines the action in detail.

[55] These were not legal bars to the crim. con. claim; nor was separation under an agreement with trustees until they approved it: *Chambers* v. *Caulfield* (1805) 6 East 244. A claimant might secure damages from the common law jury, only to find the ecclesiastical court refusing him a divorce *a mensa* because of his own immorality or condonation: for an instance in 1809, see Wolfram, *In-Laws and Outlaws*, 82; Stone, *Road to Divorce*, 279–84. His cruelty to his wife, however, was not a bar: *Chambers* v. *Chambers* (1810) 1 Hag. Con. 440.

[56] This had been instituted by the relatively accommodating Loughborough LC under a Standing Order of 1798. For the sterner cast of Thurlow LC before him, and Eldon and Brougham, as successors, see Anderson, 'Legislative Divorce', 424–7, Stone, *Road to Divorce*, 328–35.

[57] See Phillips, *Putting Asunder*, 414.

[58] See above, p. 767.

the needle-eye of the parliamentary procedures? Gradually some would accept that a proportion of marriages would fall apart; it was then better to bring these to an end than to attempt to bind the couple together or to leave them in sin with changed partners. There remained counter-arguments aplenty. The very occasional passing of divorce Acts was denounced as a threat to the sanctity of marriage—that bolster of respectability, thrift, and individual endeavour.[59]

The small number of cases has allowed detailed study of the individuals involved and their social background. In the early eighteenth century, the tiny band of petitioners had almost exclusively been from the aristocracy. But as the rate increased thereafter, more came from the middling ranks—merchants, bankers, military men, lawyers, doctors, clergy, and other professional men; and in some cases they had entered secret marriages with distinctly lower-class women. In the nineteenth century, husband petitioners stretched further down, as far as clerks, a schoolmaster, a tobacconist.[60] The costs resulting from the various steps were usually considerable, and would have been a great strain on people with small resources.

The petitioner's bill would be lessened or wiped out if the damages awarded him by the jury in the crim.con. action were significant.[61] However, there might well be collusion in getting the whole case together so that one or both of the spouses could regularize new relationships. These essentially undefended proceedings were likely to be cheaper than those where the wife or her alleged lover fought back. Certainly, cost and the sheer need for persistence explained why Parliamentary divorces stayed at a low and fairly steady level.[62] Another was that three Lord Chancellors—Thurlow, Eldon, and Brougham—took a firm line in the Lords. They would examine from their bench, searching out admissions of collusion and the like, which could cost the collaborators dear.[63]

No wife petitioned against her husband until 1801 and altogether up to 1857 only seven carried their petition to a vote in the Lords, four of whom succeeded. The imbalance of the sexes was skewed at a very acute angle—unlike in Scotland, where four-year desertion was one ground for divorce and a third or more of the petitioners were women.[64] In England, where the parliamentary procedure allowed adultery as the sole ground, the scale was further weighted by

---

[59] See Stone, *Road to Divorce*, 319–21, 335–9.

[60] Anderson, 'Legislative Divorce', 416–36; Wolfram, 'Divorce in England', 162–6. Of them all, only one of them (a clerk) was allowed to proceed *in forma pauperis*: Anderson, 435.

[61] For awards of damages, see above, 733–4.

[62] In our period, the numbers per decade of British male petitioners were: 1821–30: 32 (81% success rate); 1831–40: 30 (86%); 1841–50: 41 (95%): Anderson, 'Legislative Divorce', 415–16.

[63] Anderson, 'Legislative Divorce', teases out the evidence for this at 424–32.

[64] For the position after 1857 in England: see below, 733–4.

confirmation of the rule that a petitioning wife must show that the husband was also guilty of 'aggravation' in the form of bigamy or incest—for instance where he had had intercourse with the wife's sister. Cruelty was enough for the divorce *a mensa*; but it was not an aggravation of a husband's adultery that could lead to a divorce *a vinculo* by Parliament.[65] This was the Lords' expression of the 'double standard' which accepted that, while men needed outlets for their sexual drive, a wife's adultery, whether casual or persistent, was a blatant affront to his esteem; and moreover it could also lead to the birth of a child that was not the husband's but which he might find himself obliged to accept as legitimate.[66] That horrid risk had been much played up in the eighteenth century, but gradually lost its force. Not enough, however, for its eradication when the major reform took place in 1857, though the difference then became somewhat less severe. A deep-set belief remained that the husband remained the pinnacle of authority, making his wife's adultery a most dreadful betrayal. Equality in the grounds for divorce would have to wait until after the shifts of perception brought about during the First World War.[67]

Many explanations can be hazarded for the eventual shift to full divorce by court process that was introduced in 1857 by the Matrimonial Causes Act. There were immediate factors. First, the change was one element in the whole business of ending the temporal jurisdiction of the ecclesiastical courts and the absorption of their judges, practitioners, and officials into the superior lay courts.[68] Alongside the new Court of Probate rose the Divorce Court, with rights of audience given to barristers as well the remaining advocates of Doctors Commons, and with preparatory work going to solicitors as well as proctors. Secondly, Palmerston, the Whig Prime Minister, seemed anxious to find a good debating project that would demonstrate his authority over his own party as well as in Parliament more generally.[69] For him this was social reform that could divert attention from the issue of the right of women to vote in parliamentary and local elections. He had just won a considerable victory at the polls and was determined that it should not signal a new dose of franchise reform.

---

[65] Stone, *Road to Divorce*, 360–2.

[66] See K. V. Thomas, 'The Double Standard' (1959) 20 *J. Hist. Ideas* 195—216; R. J. Probert 'The Double Standard of Morality in the Divorce and Matrimonial Causes Act 1857' (1999) 28 *Anglo-Am. LR* 73–86.

[67] See below, 800–01.

[68] See Outhwaite, *Ecclesiastical Courts*, Chs 13–15; and see Vol. XI, pp. 704–14.

[69] Certainly he went to formidable lengths to get a version of his bill adopted, requiring both Houses to sit for long hours through a particularly sultry summer: see M. K. Woodhouse, 'The Marriage and Divorce Bill of 1857' (1959) 3 *AJLH* 260–75; Stone, *Road to Divorce*, 378–82.

6. CAMPAIGN FOR A DIVORCE COURT

These, however, were matters of the moment. Of themselves they were unlikely to have carried the day. The expectations of marriage, lying deep in the idea of the family at every social level, were gradually rising. Christian dogma insisted upon marriage as the great kernel of faith-inspired love, an institution for instilling adoration of the Godhead from an early age. The Church of England accordingly adhered to the doctrine of indissoluble marriage.[70] But while the self-righteous and the censorious might insist that even mistaken, unhappy marriages could not be undone, more sympathetic attitudes continued to stir. A bankrupt union of spouses should sometimes be capable of an orderly discharge, but it would have to be under the supervision of a court. It was not enough to leave couples to split apart and re-marry through desertion or mutual agreement. The remedy should be confined to those cases where one spouse was proven guilty, and the other not shown to be other than a disapproving innocent.

It is less easy to explain why, given the long availability of judicial divorce in Scotland and its spread to other Protestant countries, the step did not come earlier. Jeremy Bentham, for instance, had been an advocate of fully consensual divorce, but subject to time delays for reflection and a bar on the re-marriage of a guilty party.[71] Certainly some measure of reform had surfaced among the projects of the First Reform Act period. In 1830, the second Lord Ellenborough secured a parliamentary divorce despite a scandal over his evident connivance and collusion.[72] Dr Joseph Phillimore, a leading civilian, had thereupon promoted a general bill for a judicial procedure in place of murky manipulations in the legislative chambers.[73] Brougham had sought the same type of step in his plans for a Judicial Committee of the Privy Council, but this had to be dropped from the 1833 Act which set the Committee up.[74] He kept his campaign going, promoting a bill in 1844 that was examined by a Lords' Committee. He spoke strongly in favour during his second speech on law reform (in 1848) and used his chairmanship of Lords' divorce hearings to rail against the barriers raised by the parliamentary divorce bill procedure.[75]

---

[70] See e.g. A. Horstman, *Victorian Divorce* (1985), Ch. 3.

[71] *Principles of the Civil Code*, which in English was published in the Bowring edition of his *Works*, I, 352–5; a rather less radical view, emphasizing the needs of the poor, was taken by Sir Samuel Romilly, *Memoirs*, iii: 372. For earlier writings, M. Sokol, 'Jeremy Bentham on Love and Marriage' (2009) *JLH* 1–21.

[72] See the debates on his Bill: PD (3s), xxiii 439; xxiv 1279.

[73] It was a period when the judge of the London Consistory Court, Dr Lushington, waxed eloquent against the 'double standard' imposed against women in relation to parliamentary divorces: see S. M. Waddams, *Law, Politics and the Church of England* (Cambridge, 1992), 173–5.

[74] See Vol. XI, 553.

[75] The Society for Promotion of the Amendment of the Law, which he sired, was a vocal source of support. Caroline Norton chimed in with two pamphlets, *English Laws for Women in*

The growing mood was captured by Maule J. in his sarcastic description to a bigamist of the intricate procedures he should have followed in order to rid himself of his first wife by parliamentary divorce:[76]

[He] might perhaps object to this that he had not the money to pay the expenses, which would amount to about £500 or £600—perhaps he had not so many pence—but this did not exempt him from paying the penalty of committing a felony.

The notion of huge expenditure which confined parliamentary divorce only to the extremely well-off was often exaggerated by reformers, since it related to the comparatively few instances where there was real opposition and expensive counsel were involved.[77]

Moreover, thanks to crim.com. damages, the husband might come off more or less harmless, the adulterer footing the bill for the tri-partite process. In cases where husband and adulterer worked in league for the former to marry his mistress while the latter took over the wife, the procedures were simply manipulated. Carefully screened evidence made out the claim but hid the connivance, collusion, or recrimination—a manipulation equally offensive to traditionalists and reformers like Brougham. A Royal Commission—chaired by Lord Campbell CJQB and well-stocked with Whig temporizers—repeated the claims that were being made about the huge expense and social exclusiveness of parliamentary divorce.[78] The Commission's proposals were cautious enough: the grounds for divorce would not change. Instead, a three-man court (one judge each from common law, chancery, and church) would be empowered to grant men judicial divorce for adultery, but only after careful testing according to common law procedure. Save where there was exceptional aggravation, women petitioners would be left to the mercies of the parliamentary divorce procedure.[79]

Yet Lord Redesdale, the Tory voice on the Commission, warned that even the proposed process would set up a demand for 'cheap law... [which] must

the Nineteenth Century (1854) and A Letter to Queen Victoria on Lord Chancelllor Cranworth's Marriage and Divorce Bill (1855): see above, 758. For her questionable influence, see Probert, 'Double Standard of Morality'.

[76] R v. Hall, The Times, 3 April 1845, reporting that Hall was nonetheless sentenced to four months' imprisonment for deceiving the second 'wife'. Versions, such as that relayed by O. R. McGregor, Divorce in England (1957), 15–17, have the judge freeing Hall at once. Lord Campbell would quote a version to the Lords in 1857: Parl. Debs (3rd edn), 142, 1935. The tenor of Maule's remarks were echoed from the bench over the next decade and found their way into popular novels, such as Dickens' Hard Times (1854). For hypocrisy over illicit sexual relations exhibited by writers and their circles, see e.g. Horstman, Victorian Divorce, 113–16.

[77] See Anderson, 'Legislative Divorce', 436–44.

[78] For the reformers of the period, see A. Horstman, Victorian Divorce, Ch. 4.

[79] PP 1852–3 [1604], xl, 12–22.

ultimately lead to extreme facility in obtaining such divorces'.[80] His vision of a social pestilence infecting the lower orders found a ready enough response in mid-Victorian England, linked as it was to Christian beliefs in the sanctity of marriage. But the campaign for simplified judicial divorce would have sufficient force to succeed. The Lord Chancellor, Cranworth, presented a bill in 1854 which in somewhat modified form he would introduce again in 1856. It had support from such formidable judicial peers as Brougham, Lyndhurst, St Leonards, and Campbell, all of them convinced that the lay jurisdictions of the Church courts must pass elsewhere as part of the overall reform of the superior courts.

In the 1857 Session, Palmerston, fresh from his election victory over the curious coalition that had fought the Crimean War, drove the bill forward; but he had to keep his party in formation at Westminster long into the summer in order to secure final enactment.[81] Christian opposition was led in the House of Lords by 'Soapy Sam' Wilberforce, Bishop of Oxford, and in the Commons by Gladstone, who led the Conservative opposition to the bill.[82] A vociferous group of the clergy pronounced it to be against their conscience to marry divorced persons; and indeed the Act had to secure them their freedom to refuse.[83] Gladstone also decided to argue that no just law could retain any element of the 'double standard' by which Parliament had disfavoured wives. On this front he did not succeed, even though other leading figures took the same position.[84] Instead, there was much pushing and pulling of amendments in order to arrive at a list of 'aggravations' that a petitioning wife would have to show in addition to her husband's adultery.[85] In the end these were limited by adding wilful desertion for two years, cruelty and unnatural sexual practices to the previous grounds of bigamy and incest that Parliament had eventually allowed for divorce by private Act. Beyond this the cynical opinion prevailed that men must be allowed the licence of 'accidental', and indeed deliberate, adultery.

[80] *Ibid.*, 26.

[81] See esp. M. K. Woodhouse, 'The Marriage and Divorce Bill of 1857' (1959) 3 *AJLH* 260–76; Stone, *Road to Divorce*, 371–82.

[82] For Church of England opposition, see Horstman, *Victorian Divorce*, Ch 3.

[83] Divorce and Matrimonial Causes Act 1857, 20 & 21 Vict. c. 85, ss 57, 58. They were obliged to allow other clergy to use their churches in order to perform re-marriages and against that there remained considerable grumbling. For the voices of the Church in the debates, see Woodhouse, 'The Marriage and Divorce Bill of 1857', 266–9; and for the theological background, see Horstman, *Victorian Divorce*, 53–7.

[84] Indeed he was echoing sterling Tories of an earlier generation, notably Eldon and Stowell: see Stone, *Road to Divorce*, 375, 379; Probert, 'Double Standard of Morality'.

[85] In the Commons there was much hostility between Gladstone and Bethell, the Attorney-General (later Westbury), over an amendment which would allow a wife to divorce for her husband's adultery in the 'conjugal residence'. The quarrel was mysteriously patched up: see Woodhouse, 'Marriage and Divorce Bill', 271–3.

The Church led a campaign to disqualify any defendant from marrying after the divorce because of their adultery. But in that case a divorced husband would be left free to ignore any promise made to his lover. The amendment was accordingly lost.[86] There was even a Lords' amendment seeking to criminalize adultery, but neither House was remotely likely to expose either sex to that minatory prospect. Instead, largely at the behest of the Commons, some vestige of a male lover's liability to pay crim. con. damages was kept as part of divorce proceedings.[87]

Was it the inhibition on full divorce that most needed reform? For many unhappy wives, the prospect of dissolving their marriage would remain an unattainable dream. How could they expect to escape from a threatening or neglectful relationship in circumstances where their economic prospects after separation would be precarious? What they needed were curbs on two aspects of marital patriarchy: on the husband's entitlement to property and earnings that his wife brought into the marriage, and on the husband's authoritarian powers of physical control. Both were matters on which there had already been some shifts in the law, but they had provided only the most limited protections.[88] A good deal was heard about both questions by the time that the divorce bills were being put to Parliament. But these issues challenged traditional ideas of the essentials of marriage and, in the 1850s, the prospect of any substantial remedy for either was still too novel to make much political headway. Divorce reform would precede them because, at least in its cautious 1857 form, it would still have only a penumbral effect. As Sybil Wolfram rightly insists, full divorce by court process did not flow from the emancipation of women. Rather, it was one of the first signs that some greater measure of equality might be accorded to wives within the family. Other aid to wives would come only later, as it would to women in general in matters of education, work, and politics.[89]

7. JUDICIAL DIVORCE *A VINCULO* IN ACTION

The Procedures and their Results

In many respects the 1857 Act carried the prior law on matrimonial relief through into the new era.[90] The Divorce Court acquired the ecclesiastical jurisdiction to

---

[86] As was a separate amendment from Wilberforce that the guilty party be denied the right to marry the co-respondent: see Woodhouse, 'Bill of 1857', at 265–6.

[87] 1857 Act, ss 33, 59; above, 734.

[88] For Erskine Perry's contemporaneous bill as an influence upon these provisions, see above, 759.

[89] Wolfram, 'Divorce in England', 179–81.

[90] See s 22. The causes other than full divorce are described, for instance, in G. Browne, *Treatise on the Principles and Practice of the Court of Divorce and Matrimonial Causes* (1864), 7–28.

grant divorces *a mensa* (re-christened judicial separation), decrees nullifying the marriage, and restitution of conjugal rights on the old terms,[91] and it replaced the parliamentary process for divorce *a vinculo* on the ground of adultery (for husband against wife) and on the ground of adultery plus further aggravation (for wife against husband). In the latter case, as already mentioned, the forms of aggravation were expanded to include cruelty and two years' desertion—both of them all too common—as well as rape, bigamy, and unnatural offences.[92] This constituted the one major expansion in substantive law.[93] The claim made by the government that the changes were essentially procedural was otherwise justified.[94]

The new Divorce Court was a superior jurisdiction which gained its own Judge Ordinary.[95] Initially he was to sit with two other superior judges, but that wasted precious judicial time. Soon enough Parliament was persuaded to let him get through the business alone.[96] The Court sat only in London and thus added deliberately to the expense and inconvenience of parties from the provinces and their witnesses.[97] Their disadvantages, however, benefited the band of London practitioners who built practices around the new court.[98] It would be decades before campaigners could secure a divorce jurisdiction at provincial assizes; and a century before undefended causes could be brought in the county courts.[99] There was a power to award costs against the co-respondent adulterer—a deterrent of a kind against the biblical sin.[100]

---

[91] Section 2. See below, 787–8.

[92] Sections 27, 57. When, after the Weldon fracas (above, n. 4), the Matrimonial Causes Act 1884 abolished imprisonment for refusal to comply with an order for restitution of conjugal rights, it substituted the power to grant judicial separation with an order for maintenance of wife and children or settlement of property. This slightly increased the number of such orders. But the Act did not reduce the period of desertion needed (together with proof of adultery) for a full divorce.

[93] Another was the clarification of the types of recrimination which might lead the court to refuse to grant the divorce: see below, 793–4.

[94] Stone, *Road to Divorce*, 378–87.

[95] 1857 Act, ss 8, 9. The judge likewise sat in the new Probate Court.

[96] Divorce Court Act 1859. Appeal lay within three months to the Full Court and ultimately to the House of Lords in divorce cases: 1857 Act, ss 50, 51. The Full Court was constituted by the Chiefs and senior puisnes of the three courts of common law: 1857 Act, s 8.

[97] A motive that the government eventually admitted: see Woodhouse, 'Marriage and Divorce Bill', 273–4.

[98] Textbook guidance appeared almost at once from the indefatigable J. F. Macqueen, *A Practical Treatise on the Law of Marriage, Divorce and Legitimacy* (1858, 1860); then came Browne, *Court of Divorce*, which evolved into the standard text, *Latey on Divorce*.

[99] Jurisdiction for High Court judges to grant divorces at assizes did not come until the explosion of petitions after 1918: see the Administration of Justice Act 1920, following up a recommendation of the Gorell Royal Commission on Divorce, Report, *PP* 1912–13 [Cd. 6478] viii, para. 77. For these developments and the subsequent history, see Cretney, *Family*, Ch. 8.

[100] 1857 Act, s 35.

Despite these various inhibitions, at last a court existed that dealt regularly with a stream of divorce petitions. The procedure, moreover, followed that of common law courts and gave a right to cross-examine both the parties and their witnesses.[101] The flow would rise steadily.[102] The petition would succeed in some three-quarters of all petitions actually filed. Even so, by 1914 it amounted only to 0.5 in 10,000 persons.[103] About half of the petitioners seem to have been from the echelons of the gentry and the professional and managerial classes, a quarter from the lower-middle class, and a quarter working-class—most of them skilled. Among all but the raffish, a divorce was regarded as a degrading fate. Even the most pathetic of innocent petitioners could expect exclusion from respectable society. Indeed, until the 1950s, divorced persons were not admitted to the Royal Enclosure at Ascot, which doubtless caused perturbations even among the racing set.[104] For leading politicians to be involved as co-respondents (whether directly accused or not) was likely to be a shrivelling blight on their career. Two who were found out were Sir Charles Dilke, Gladstone's likely heir in the Liberal Party, and Charles Stewart Parnell, from whom Gladstone felt obliged to split despite their affinities over Irish home rule.[105] Precisely because divorce was now more open to contemplation, the branding of the divorced became a preoccupation of sterling institutions, such as the Mothers' Union of the Church of England. The re-establishment of the Roman Catholic hierarchy in 1851 and the increasing number of its adherents in England thereafter provided a vigilant source of oppo-

---

[101] Sections 46–54. The Court had power to order the trial of facts by a jury (ss 36–40) but it was not greatly used. The Court was given power to examine a petitioner, which was plainly directed at connivance in uncontested cases: s 44.

[102] For statistical measures for the various types of matrimonial jurisdiction, see above, Vol XI, 43–5; Ct); Wolfram, 'Divorce in England', 182–6; Horstman, *Victorian Divorce*, 156; G. L. Savage, 'Divorce and the Law in England and France prior to the First World War' [1988] *J. Social Hist.* 499–513, at 506; Stone, *Road to Divorce*, 385–6.

[103] By 1923, this proportion would be 1.48; by 1937, 2.6, and by 1950, 11.7.

[104] Wolfram, 'Divorce in England', 178, n. 98. It likewise created a difficulty in appointing a barrister to be a judge. Re-marriage in the Church of England was allowed only in 1985. See also P. T. Cominos, 'Late Victorian Sexual Respectability and the Social System' (1963) 8 *Int. Rev. Soc. Hist.* 18–48, 216–50.

[105] For Dilke's disastrous pressure on the Queen's Proctor to secure the re-opening of the Crawford divorce, in which he had already been found not to be a co-respondent, see R. Jenkins, *Dilke: A Victorian Tragedy* (1958), Chs 11–17. He reckoned without the belligerent antagonism of the Proctor, Sir Augustus Stevenson. For Parnell and the O'Shea divorce suit, see P. Bew, *C. S. Parnell* (1991), 108–12. The Prince of Wales (ultimately Edward VII)—well-known for his liaisons—appeared as a witness in the *Mordaunt* case of 1870 (for seven minutes, without cross-examination). Sir Charles Mordaunt did not name him as a co-respondent, there being others. Lady Mordaunt became mentally unhinged, and the proceedings were long held up, a majority of the Lords eventually deciding that a divorce could be granted against a woman incapable of understanding the proceedings: *Mordaunt v. Moncrieffe* (1874) LR 2 Sc & Div 374.

sition to the very idea.[106] At the end of the century, when divorce reform bodies took up the cause of easier access to the courts, they had to face the formidable ranks of a Marriage Defence League.[107]

After 1857 a considerable number of petitioners were wives. They would gain between 38 and 46 per cent of the divorces granted in the years to 1914. This represents a remarkable difference from attitudes in the Lords when the occasional wife had struggled through to petition for a parliamentary divorce, only be met with derisive laughter.[108] Now a wife secured freedom to re-marry, if only she could surmount the added burden imposed by the double standard. As a *feme sole*, she gained rights to all property coming to her including her own future earnings.[109] In addition, as a petitioner without stain upon her, a wife could expect the court to order a deed of settlement, securing her a capital sum or an annual payment, with interim payments of alimony where that was appropriate.[110] The overall objective came to be that she and the children should be put in the same financial position as before the break-up.[111] But the assumption was that the parties divorcing would have an established income, at least in part from the marriage settlement: hence the reference to the sum being 'secured'— the husband was not a debtor.[112] In line with the former practice of ecclesiastical courts, the wife could probably expect an arrangement giving her one-third of

[106] Phillips, in his comparative study, *Putting Asunder*, identifies the opposition to divorce of the Roman Catholic Church as the major brake upon reform movements in Western society: see pp. 1–5, 15–30.

[107] Its President, the Duke of Northumberland, poured scorn on a bill to equalize the position of wives in divorce: 'To get rid of Christianity between tea and dinner on an afternoon in the spring is no light matter': PD (5s) 1920, xxxix, 860. Reflecting on the chief core of antagonism to divorce, the London magistrate, Cecil Chapman, wrote: 'Anglo-Catholics have never become reconciled to the abolition of ecclesiastical jurisdiction in family matters by the Divorce Act of 1857. They range themselves on the side of Roman Catholics in holding that marriage which is consecrated in a church is a sacrament, and therefore indissoluble except for the reason which, in the opinion of many learned divines, was admitted by our Lord himself': *From the Bench* (1932), 121.

[108] That had been the treatment meted out to Mrs Dawson even as recently as 1848 when she tried to show that her husband's adultery had been sufficiently aggravated: Horstman, *Victorian Divorce*, 42–3; Stone, *Road to Divorce*, 360–2.

[109] See above 759. Intriguingly, those obtaining only a decree of judicial separation were also categorized as *femes soles* and would keep the property thus gained even if the wife rejoined the husband and coverture took over once more: see 1857 Act, s 25; similarly for contracting and suing: s 26. Here indeed was a signpost on the road to separate property.

[110] 1857 Act, ss 32, 24.

[111] See e.g. *March* v. *March and Palumbo* (1867) LR 1 P&D 440; *Hodgson Roberts* v. *Hodgson Roberts* [1906] P 142. At first—a mark of the adjustment of attitudes required—Cresswell J. doubted whether an innocent wife who nonetheless chose to seek divorce for her husband's aggravated adultery was entitled to more than a pittance. His successor, Wilde (Penzance), made the transition: cf. *Fisher* v. *Fisher* (1861) 2 Sw. & Tr. 410; *Sidney* v. *Sidney* (1865) 4 Sw. & Tr. 178.

[112] The business of deciding on this maintenance was originally to be referred to conveyancing counsel of Chancery, but it soon came to be dealt with by the Registrar of the Divorce Court.

joint income; but that standard was not allowed to become more than a starting point. If, for instance, her family had contributed substantially to the husband's wealth she might get more; or she might have restored to her the property that had passed to the husband under their marriage settlement. Fifty years would pass before the Court gained power simply to order the husband to pay her periodic maintenance.[113]

She might be awarded custody or at least access to the children, thus for the first time giving over part of Chancery's supervision of children to a matrimonial court.[114] Wife petitioners would face severe financial hurdles in many cases—set by the costs of the action or by the uncertainties of a separate life where the husband was not in a position to provide a corpus from which to secure maintenance. Whatever their predicaments, those who succeeded were merely a portion of the Victorian wives who faced the grimness of life with an adulterer or abuser, or the bleakness of desertion.

Nonetheless their condition was more hopeful than the wife found guilty as a respondent. For two decades, she could expect nothing by way of maintenance. The discreet custom in parliamentary divorce had been for a 'lady's friend' to ensure that the wife, for all her guilt, would not be left unprovided. Now the ethos was quite against any such intercession. Eventually, Jessel MR objected that the legislation was not meant to turn the wife out into the streets to starve.[115] This, it seemed, led to awards to her of very small amounts. It was extremely unlikely that she would be allowed access to her children, let alone custody. Cresswell J. said soon enough that this embargo was needed as 'a salutary effect on the interest of public morality'.[116]

The 1857 Act made new practice for lawyers and for detectives and others whose business was the production of evidence of the matrimonial offences on which the divorce jurisdiction depended. The substantive grounds were solely those laid down in the statute. But the precise scope of the Court's jurisdiction

---

See J. Barton, 'The Enforcement of Financial Provisions', in Graveson and Crane, *Century*, 352–73; Cretney, *Family*, 396–414.

Section 32 required the Court to take account of her fortune (if any). By the end of the century, the Court of Appeal was restricting the amount, in the case of the seriously rich, to a ceiling of £3,000 per year: *Kettlewell* v. *Kettlewell* [1898] P 138. On an order *pendente lite*, she might expect one-fifth of the joint income.

[113] Matrimonial Causes Act 1907, s 1. By that time, magistrates' courts were regularly making such awards to deserted wives: see below, 797–8.

[114] See below, 797.

[115] *Robinson* v. *Robinson* (1883) 8 PD 94. His sympathy did not prevent him from observing that a washerwoman 'can very well go back to washing again', unlike the wife of 'a gentleman of large means who obtains the special privilege by Act of Parliament'.

[116] *Sedden* v. *Sedden and Doyle* (1862) 2 Sw. & Tr. 640; cf. Lord Cairns' rather more sympathetic view in *Symington* v. *Symington* (1875) LR 2 Sc & Div 415.

was often a matter of interpretation, and on some questions, its discretion.[117] Accordingly its decisions were poured over for their effect on similar cases.

The Substantive Grounds for Divorce[118]

Whether it was husband or wife who petitioned, in every case there had to be proof of adultery (or against men its almost unmentionable equivalents, sodomy or bestiality[119]). Just as before in a contested case, where the adultery was not admitted, it was most often proved by evidence of inclination and opportunity. However, where a couple were alleged to have been spotted *in flagrante*, the defence was limited to asserting that the witness was lying or imagining. As part of general reforms in civil procedure both husband and wife had become competent to give evidence. In divorce cases this exposed them to cross-examination by the other side and to questioning from the bench in a way that previously had been found only in the House of Lords under the parliamentary divorce procedure.[120] However, they were not to be *compelled* to answer questions about, for instance, communications between them during the marriage. And there was a special distaste against a partner having to testify about his or her own sexual activity. Eventually the Lords would rule that, as a matter of public decency, such evidence was wholly inadmissible;[121] and at much the same time a campaign would finally succeed in having the press reporting of evidence in divorce proceedings suppressed.[122]

---

[117] As in the society case, *Mordaunt* v. *Moncrieffe*, above, n. 105.

[118] They were set out in the 1857 Act, s 22.

[119] Unnatural offences were originally omitted from the list because, said Lord St Leonards, the Act 'would be in the hands of the purest women in England' *PD* 1857, cxlvii, 2029.

[120] They were, however, protected from answering questions that would tend to incriminate them as to adultery: see Divorce and Matrimonial Causes Act 1857, s 43; Evidence (Further Amendment) Act 1869, s 3; G. D. Nokes, 'Evidence' in Graveson and Crane, *Century*, 143–64 at 149–53, putting the rule in the context of other evidential privileges; and for competence and compellability as a witness at all, see Vol. XI, Pt 3, pp. 608–10.

[121] Previously the witness had not been obliged to answer the question. Now the question could not be put: *Russell* v. *Russell* [1924] AC 687—the rule was abolished by the Law Reform (Miscellaneous Provisions) Act 1949, s 7.

[122] Judicial Proceedings (Regulation of Reports) Act 1926. In *Scott* v. *Scott* [1913] AC 417, the House of Lords, overruling the courts below, took the view that the PDA Division had no power to order that a nullity of marriage suit should be held in camera to protect public sensibilities about medical tests on an impotent man. There was a stronger interest in the openness of court proceedings. Both Queen Victoria and her grandson, George V, had protested vigorously against lurid tales from matrimonial proceedings; but change only followed the latter's intervention: see Horstman, *Victorian Divorce*, 86; S. M. Cretney, *Law, Law Reform and the Family* (Oxford, 1998), Ch. 4.

A wife-petitioner who could prove her husband's adultery, but not two years' desertion, was mostly obliged by the double standard to show cruelty.[123] What could constitute cruelty was one of the standards inherited from the ecclesiastical courts. There were cases where a physical attack or recurrent battering settled the issue all too plainly—where indeed the authorities would bring criminal charges for grievous harm or even attempted murder.[124] Hammerton's account of the allegations of physical violence set out in the early divorce cases makes for uncomfortable reading, not least because the stories recur today in a world where it has become more acceptable for women to overcome their own sense of shameful failure and speak out. He shows how servants, landlords, and lodgers could become embroiled in husbands' attacks on their wives and could indeed then be the target of violence themselves. As to social status he concludes:

Contrary to popular belief, upper-class men were as likely, amongst those appearing in court, to strike their wives with pokers and similar weapons, throw them downstairs, threaten murder, beat them during pregnancy, enforce sexual intercourse after childbirth, and indulge in marital rape or enforced sodomy, as were those lower in the social scale.[125]

Divorce, however, was a civil procedure dependent upon blame. It was often difficult to decide which partner, pitted in emotional warfare, was more likely to be telling the truth; and likewise hard to assess whether the claimed injuries seriously endangered the health of the wife in accordance with the old test of cruelty laid down for divorce *a mensa* by Sir William Scott (Stowell):[126]

What merely wounds the mental feelings is in few cases to be admitted where they are not accompanied with bodily injury, either actual or menaced. Mere austerity of temper, petulance of manners, rudeness of language, a want of civil attention and accommodation, even occasional sallies of passion, if they do not threaten bodily harm, do not amount to legal cruelty.

Commenting on cases where both parties were in some degree at fault, he had continued:

---

[123] Hammerton, *Cruelty and Companionship*, 105–6, shows that by 1882, cruelty was cited in 80% of wives' petitions. From case papers, he also extracts tales of vigorous retaliation by wives— pulling whiskers, up-ending chamber-pots, using any weapon to hand (107–14). If that stock joke, the hen-pecked husband, dared to sue for divorce, he had to prove the termagent wife's adultery, but only that.

[124] On the whole question, see esp. M. Wiener, *Men of Blood* (Cambridge, 2004), Ch. 6.

[125] Hammerton, *Cruelty and Companionship*, 82–101.

[126] For the extent to which cruelty was relevant to ecclesiastical relief, see above, n. 6.

...the suffering party must bear in some degree the consequences of an injudicious connection; must subdue by decent resistance or by prudent conciliation; and if this cannot be done, both must suffer in silence.[127]

Wife complainants ran against jarring beliefs about the proprieties of marriage. Despite the growing notion of separate spheres, the husband's position as master of the family went scarcely questioned at any social level. Somehow, therefore, judges had to allow him power to dictate the course of family affairs. His very authority could be regarded as a manly virtue by a masterful personage such as FitzJames Stephen, not least because it might condition a wife to abstain from any challenge.[128] Stephen and many contemporaries pictured the husband as acting firmly but with wise restraint. They saw the greater physical strength of men as leading inevitably—indeed 'naturally'—to a stronger decisiveness and ability to coerce, which needed recognition in the law of marital relations. Courts, however, had to wrestle with cases where husbands harangued their wives and children with long hours of accusation, obliquy, and demands for repentance, while imposing conditions, such as sending away servants, relations, and friends, insisting on separate bedrooms and even taking household management out of the wife's hands—a particularly degrading punishment. In such cases wives might be driven to retaliate, thereby creating situations in which there was some evidence against them, of which their husbands might make the most.[129]

The first two divorce judges, Cresswell and Wilde (Penzance), began to accept that there was cruelty in borderline cases where the husband deployed domineering strictures and abuse on such a scale that the burden on the wife appeared intolerable.[130] By 1870, in *Kelly* v. *Kelly*, the standard was lowered to the extent of treating behaviour of this kind as cruelty when the wife's health was placed in permanent jeopardy.[131] If, like Mrs Kelly, she had suffered a mental breakdown, her case would be made out. Penzance spoke sternly of the husband's patriarchal authority as extending only 'to all things reasonable'. At last some contrast was introduced between abrasively authoritarian denunciation of the wife and

---

[127] *Evans* v. *Evans* (1790) 1 Hag. Con. 35.

[128] Stephen's main outburst (see above, 745) was against J. S. Mill's *The Subjection of Women* (1869), with its radical case for truly companionate treatment of wives.

[129] Hammerton, *Cruelty and Companionship*, 118–33.

[130] The development is detailed by J. M. Biggs, *The Concept of Matrimonial Cruelty* (1962), 9–14. Cresswell's reactions were apparent at once in the difficult case of *Curtis* v. *Curtis* (1858) 1 Sw. & Tr. 192; and see *Suggate* v. *Suggate* (1859) 1 Sw. & Tr. 489; *Milner* v. *Milner* (1861) 4 Sw. & Tr. (Supp.) 240. Penzance began with *Swatman* v. *Swatman* (1865) 4 Sw. & Tr. 135.

[131] *Kelly* v. *Kelly* (1869) LR 2 P&D 31, 75, which gives details of Mrs Kelly's abasement in face of the Revd Mr Kelly's awful wrath over a period of 20 years. See also Hammerton, *Cruelty and Companionship*, 94–101.

other decisions that judges had no wish to remove from the husband's sphere: where the family should live, where and in what religion the children should be schooled, how he should spend his money or pursue his own amusements.[132] This was still an ideal of marriage far removed from today's world in which, when discord arises, the pair will be treated at root much as a business partnership—to be wound up, as necessary, on terms that start with a presumption of equality, and only then introduce variations through a rough weighting against unacceptable conduct.

The Bars to Divorce

Any scheme for ending marital obligations on the basis of fault is likely to be manipulated by those who simply want their freedom, where there may be no provable fault on either side or where both are guilty. The long experience of matrimonial jurisdiction in the ecclesiastical courts, as well as the shorter experience of parliamentary divorce, had shown that clearly enough. Yet ecclesiastical doctrine had barred divorces *a mensa* where there was connivance at adultery, condonation of adultery or cruelty, or collusion over maintaining the proceedings, whether or not it involved the manufacture of false evidence; and it had generally treated the adultery of the petitioner, or other misconduct by him or her, also as foregoing any relief. The 1857 legislation continued these objections.[133]

The much increased flow of cases before the new Court produced shoals of decisions about the meaning of these concepts. A husband's connivance—turning a blind eye to obvious signs of intimacy, perhaps with a lodger or regular friend of the family—meant that he had not exacted 'a due purity' from his wife, a moral failing on his part which would debar a subsequent divorce. Beyond that in any case the discretionary grounds of refusal included unreasonable delay in bringing the proceedings and wilful neglect of the wife, which had led her into the arms of a lover out of financial need or loneliness.[134]

It was not connivance, however, on discovering the adultery, to let it continue in order to get evidence for a divorce petition. Much the same distinction pervaded the related notion of condonation. Once the wife's adultery had become known to the husband and he had taken her back into the relationship—notably

---

[132] Such examples were deployed, for instance, by Dr Lushington in *Chesnutt* v. *Chesnutt* (1854) 1 Spinks 196, in order to adhere to Stowell's strict standard (but see Waddams, *Law, Politics*, 178–9, for variations in his approach to cruelty). It was in 1870 that the husband's entitlements over property brought into the marriage by the wife were curtailed in ways not touched by equity: see above, 760–1.

[133] Sections 29–31. See Browne, *Divorce*, 31–47.

[134] As to the latter, see e.g. *Baylis* v. *Baylis* (1867) LR 1 P&D 395.

by resuming sexual intercourse with her—he could not change his mind and petition for divorce.[135] Wives might also be 'guilty' of connivance or condonation of their husband's adultery, but at least their subordinate position would be taken into account. They could not be expected to make their husbands toe the matrimonial line; nor would they be taken to have accepted his straying just because they were obliged by their dependence on him to continue the matrimonial relationship.[136]

Collusion in organizing the divorce proceedings—the third absolute bar—could take many forms. The judges soon made plain that the bar applied beyond deliberate faking of evidence about the matrimonial wrong or the suppression of evidence about connivance, collusion, or the petitioner's own adultery (all of which could amount to the crime of perjury, or at least be a contempt of court). It also covered advance arrangements between the pair to provide evidence (for instance of adultery), or to deal with their property, pay maintenance, or bring up their children. Since it was common for otherwise respectable people to want to do such things, legal practitioners evolved protocols which defined what could safely happen by way of implicit negotiation before proceedings commenced. Where for instance the husband was minded to give his wife a divorce by providing 'hotel evidence' of his apparent adultery, there was a certain form. He would send her solicitor the bill for the night spent with the woman hired for the job, the solicitor would then have inquiries made among desk-staff and chambermaids for those who could swear that the couple occupied a single room and were seen in bed together in the morning.[137]

Collusion was particularly linked with the separate bar to divorce constituted by 'recrimination'—conduct of the petitioner (most often adultery) which sullied his or her own hands.[138] If there was proof of this bar neither party could normally expect a divorce from the other and they might be condemned to their marriage tie, however nominal it had become. If each had found another partner, they were obliged to live on in sin, their new children being bastards.

---

[135] He could not 'connive at the adultery of his wife on Monday, and yet be at liberty to complain of a repetition of the adultery on Tuesday': Lord Westbury, *Gipps* v. *Gipps* (1864) HL Cas. 1, at 14. The wife had to reveal all the sins to be forgiven: see e.g. *Dempster* v. *Dempster* (1861) Sw. & Tr. 438. The husband would not prejudice his position merely by saying that he forgave her: *Keats* v. *Keats and Montezuma* (1859) 1 Sw. & Tr. 334.

[136] See the *Keats* case, above, n. 135, at 337.

[137] Hotel evidence would become more prominent once the 'double standard' went in 1923, and a wife could divorce simply upon proof of the husband's adultery; see Cretney, *Family*, 176–7, 228–33. The one witness before the Gorell Commission to discuss the issue—the Scottish judge, Lord Salvesen—was quite clear that such conduct should remain a bar to the divorce. He proposed only that essentially beneficial contacts between the husband and wife, such as over arrangements for the children, should be permitted: see *PP* 1912–13 [Cd. 6478], xviii, qq. 6684–9.

[138] See Browne, *Divorce*, 47–53.

The whole object of the divorce law was to ensure that such an outcome should act as an awful deterrent against infidelity. The law itself offered only one possible accommodation: if the petitioner put the full truth of his or her own lapse before the court, it did have a discretion after all to order the divorce. But the judges soon announced that this discretion would be exercised only in exceptional cases.[139] Within a decade they had spelled these out as: 'accidental adultery', where there was no reason to believe that the other spouse was still alive;[140] 'unwilling adultery', where, for example, a husband forced his petitioner wife out to be a prostitute;[141] and 'condoned adultery', where the respondent had fully forgiven it.[142] Doing the proper thing by throwing oneself on the court's mercy rarely had the desired effect. It would need the hugely unsettling effects of two World Wars to bring about much change in judicial attitudes on the matter.[143] In the interim, the petitioner's solicitor might have a very delicate line to tread in consulting his client about personal relationships, since he would owe the court a duty not to see it misled.

The Queen's Proctor

Before the changes of 1857, many of the petitions in the church courts and in Parliament were commonly thought to be collusive, where they went undefended. The same suspicions surged up as soon as the new Court opened its doors. An unconstrained press fell upon the untoward goings-on underlying, as they claimed, case after case. 'Unless some remedy were applied the Court would become in a short time a sort of Encumbered Estates Court for the transfer of women.'[144]

Such was the strength of feeling that a functionary was put in to prevent the simple mockery of the constricted moral basis of the new divorce law. Upon a proposal that originated from Lord Cranworth, an Act of 1860 provided that a divorce once granted went through a period of suspense before becoming effective: first there was a *decree nisi* and only after three months would it become

---

[139] An attitude quite unchanged in the Edwardian era: see Gorell Barnes J., *Evans* v. *Evans and Elford* [1906] P 125, 127.

[140] As instanced in *Joseph* v. *Joseph and Wenzell* (1865) 34 L.J. P.M.& A. 96.

[141] As in the grim case of *Coleman* v. *Coleman* (1866) LR 1 P&D 81.

[142] But judges differed on how far to allow this excuse. It became entangled in arguments about whether the petitioner's wrong (such as the husband's casual adultery) caused the respondent in turn to stray: see e.g. *Clarke* v. *Clarke* (1865) 34 L.J.P. M .& A. 94; *McCord* v. *McCord* (1875) LR 3 P&D 237.

[143] The House of Lords would make the decisive shift only in 1943: *Blunt* v. *Blunt* [1943] AC 517; Cretney, *Family*, 269–71.

[144] Sir G. Bowyer, *PD* (3s) 1860. clx, 1746.

absolute (from 1866, the period became six months).[145] The intermediate period was there to allow an investigation into undefended petitions to see whether they had been arranged collusively or had failed to reveal recriminatory conduct on the petitioner's part. The detection was to be organized by an official, the Queen's Proctor, acting where he or the Court had their own grounds for suspicion or where anyone else made allegations.[146] In an essentially private law procedure, it was exceptional to find the judicial process being supported by a distinct investigative arm. In the nature of things the state would bear much of the cost. Snooping informers would find a new outlet for their propensities and they would be sure to draw hostile reactions. Such, however, was the antagonism towards a ready divorce law that the Proctor's role was created. It can also be related to the inquisitorial tradition of the non-common law courts in England, feeble though their evidence-garnering functions had been.[147]

The Proctor's office examined the papers for every undefended *decree nisi*, dealt with information from outsiders, sent inquiry agents out when there were suspicious circumstances and informed the Attorney-General where evidence of collusion or recrimination resulted. The Attorney might then intervene, causing the judge to refuse the decree absolute.[148] Costs of the whole proceedings would then, in all likelihood, be awarded against the petitioner, and the couple would remain married. The husband who arranged that his wife's lover would pay for his divorce proceedings against her would fail, the adulterous pair would be left to live in adultery, and the husband would be unable to marry again. The wife who sought to escape from the domination of a cruel and adulterous husband would be left under his yoke, if it turned out that she had had sex with someone else.[149] The Earl of Desart, formerly the King's Proctor, who would give evidence

---

[145] Divorce Court Act 1860, s 7. For details of the 1859–60 campaigns to adjust the new divorce regime, see G. L. Savage, 'The Divorce Court and the Queen's/King's Proctor: Legal Patriarchy and the Sanctity of Marriage in England, 1861–1937' [1989] *Historical Papers (Quebec)* 210–27.

[146] The Court could also appoint counsel to argue such issues as collusion or condonation before it when they arose at the trial (1860 Act, s 5). The power was frequently used: Cretney, *Family*, 179.

[147] So Cretney suggests, pointing to the explicit requirement in the 1857 Act, ss 22, 29, that the Court itself investigate condonation, collusion, and recrimination: *Family*, 177–8.

[148] While the Proctor had to make out his case, the standard of proof was less strict than over the allegations that the petitioner had also committed adultery, because there was no danger of collusion: *Hulse* v. *Hulse (No. 2)* (1872) LR 2 P & D 357. The Attorney's policy became to intervene only in clear cases, so mostly he succeeded. By the 1900s, he would do so in only some 5–10% of the cases investigated by the Proctor (which ran between 306 and 631 per annum). See the evidence of Alverstone LCJ (formerly Att.-Gen.), to the Gorell Commission, PP 1912–13 [Cd. 6478–82], xviii, Evidence, vol. 2, qq. 8269–8310; and that of the Proctor mentioned below. This is confirmed by the evidence from a systematic sampling of the Proctor's interventions in unreported divorce cases undertaken by G. Savage, 'Queen's Proctor', 222–3.

[149] *Drummond* v. *Drummond* (1861) 2 Sw. & Tr. 269.

before the Gorell Royal Commission on Divorce of 1910–12, felt that his intervention 'over and over again…has done more harm than good'.[150]

Our story of the law of marriage termination will close with a short account of
the Gorell Commission on Divorce (1909–12), whose collecting of evidence and
the opinions of its majority in many ways summarized the views and expectations of the forward-looking among the middling-classes. Before we come to this,
however, we must observe the movements in late Victorian England to modify
other aspects of divorce law, carrying forward parts of the history touched
upon elsewhere: the property and private rights of married women; the public
protection of families in danger, including spouses and children exposed to brutality; and the respective rights of parents over children.[151] These were all matters
which would have greater impact on the future of separation and divorce law
than in the past.

8. VIOLENCE AND DESERTION AMONG ORDINARY PEOPLE

Both cruelty and desertion put marriages in serious jeopardy and their occurrence had long been widespread, but the 1857 Act left many wives without real
hope of turning to the courts for orders of divorce or judicial separation as relief
from their predicaments. The restrictions on access were too formidable. The
deserted wife, together with the mother of an illegitimate child, might have only
the public poor law to keep her from complete destitution, though, as has been
seen, some authorities exercised their powers to chase after husbands and fathers
for support.[152] Those wives who suffered violence from their husbands might
turn to the justices for an order to keep the peace under recognizances to pay
set sums if they did not.[153] In 1853, the justices were also given added jurisdiction
to decide criminal charges for assault with power to sentence the attacker for up

---

[150] PP 1912–13 [Cd. 6479], xix, qq. 15,867–75. For individual cases where the consequences seem
spectacularly harsh, see Savage, 'Queen's Proctor', 223–4 (Williams: wife unable to divorce a husband who had left her with five children, because she was found then to have lived with another
man, who was later killed in a mining accident. Wilson: husband not entitled to divorce: the wife's
adulteries found to have been because he put her to prostitution—his connivance and condonation left her tied to him); and Cretney, Family, 180 (deserted wife had decree nisi rescinded after
false accusation of adultery with her employer, the subsequent enforcement of costs leaving her
destitute).

[151] See above, pp. 761–6; below, pp. 814–19.

[152] See above, pp. 776–7.

[153] There is also some evidence that, as time went on, communities became less tolerant of wife
batterers and might expose them to rough music or their own beatings. Whether or not this induced
moderation towards the wife would in the nature of things be questionable.

to six months in prison—a power that was regularly used to deal with domestic violence.[154]

The plight of wives who were maltreated physically was kept in the public eye during the campaign for divorce jurisdiction and afterwards by the revelations in Divorce Court hearings. But further help, particularly for working-class wives, continued to have a prominent place on the agenda for legal reform. The judges tended to advocate whipping as the best remedy— brute force to be met in kind, whatever the consequences for the wives. In the 1870s, particularly thanks to the advocacy of Frances Power Cobbe in her pamphlet, *The Truth about Wife Torture*, a new approach was tried. In 1878, on a parliamentary by-wind, magistrates were given power to order that a wife who had been subjected to aggravated assault by her husband be entitled to live apart from him, he becoming liable to pay her weekly maintenance, and she entitled to custody of children under 10 (later raised to 16).[155] The essentially criminal behaviour at the root of the new jurisdiction made it natural to place it with the justices rather than in the expanding county courts. In any case there was heavy resistance to allowing county courts to adjudicate upon matrimonial disputes, for they might come to include cheap and ready divorce and that was not to be accepted. The 1878 procedures were soon expanded. In 1886, a power to award maintenance was also given against a deserting husband, up to a maximum of £2 a week.[156] By 1895, there could be an order for separation, limited payments, and custody of children on various grounds: conviction for aggravated assault, desertion, persistent cruelty (causing the wife already to leave home), or wilful neglect to maintain.[157] Some of the marks of moral obliquy that affected divorce applied here also. No wife would secure a separation order from magistrates if she herself was guilty of adultery, unless her husband had condoned it.[158]

Even in the most deserving cases the magistrates could only order separation; the marriage remained. In courts around the country thousands of these orders were obtained: here was a new form of mass justice for the working classes. In 1893 applications ran at 3,482, in 1900 the number had become 9,553, and in 1910–13 the

---

[154] Aggravated Assaults Act 1853, 16 & 17 Vict. c. 30, expanding a power in the Offences Against the Person Act 1828, 9 Geo. IV c. 31, s 27.

[155] Lord Penzance, conservative by temperament but long-experienced in adjudicating matrimonial conflict, added the power to a bill on the costs of the Queen's Proctor: this became the Matrimonial Causes Act 1878, s 4. See Foyster, *Marital Violence*, 250–5.

[156] Only in 1920 would it become possible to add 10s a week for each child under 16.

[157] Summary Jurisdiction (Married Women) Act 1895. In 1902, the Licensing Act, s 5, provided for separation orders when either husband or wife was an habitual drunkard. Further grounds would follow in the Summary Jurisdiction (Separation and Maintenance) Act 1925.

[158] 1878 Act, s 4; 1895 Act, ss 6, 7.

annual average was 10,765. Around 70 per cent succeeded. The spread of work varied across the large number of magistrates' courts. Some poor law unions were reluctant to pursue neglectful husbands themselves in the hope of recouping the costs of giving out-relief or workhouse accommodation to their families. Instead, they could insist that the wife first obtain a separation order from the magistrates. Where they did so, they were out to catch scrounging couples whose desertions were simply a blind. They hoped that the proceedings would uncover the deception.

The work of these courts is of particular interest in any assessment of the social significance of legal processes and the ways in which they developed as part of a growing culture of aid from the pillars of the community to the classes who served them. The magistracy acquired its jurisdiction over marital breakdown in the period when the London Police Courts were beginning to take on the 'missionaries' whose investigative and support services would blossom into the work of professional probation officers.[159] They were to be found in these courts in the 1870s representing the temperance societies of the various religious denominations—hence their name—and from that their work with families, children, and criminals grew. It was the period when other social work activities also developed, the almoners attached to hospitals and aid workers who undertook to sort the deserving from the undeserving both for indigent charities and the public poor law.

The magistrates began from situations where orders to separate spouses and make financial and other provision most evidently needed to be imposed; but their work—and that of a missionary, where there was one—soon enough brought them to explore how far particular families might be kept together and how some measure of truce between husband and wife could be sustained for the future. To a degree they doubtless adopted the role of mediator, seeking to get each partner to see the other's point of view and reach a reconcilement for themselves. Behlmer's telling survey of the records of London's South-Western Police Court shows a court largely staffed by stipendiary magistrates who would acquire well-tested attitudes to the flow of matrimonial cases before it, sometimes with a certain cynicism or lack of sympathy creeping in and at other moments offering tactical advice to women who were standing up for themselves against long years of degrading or neglectful treatment.[160] Many of them started from strongly judgmental assumptions, with the language of religious condemnation ready at hand. Often enough their advice to the couple could consist of pointing out that they could not afford to live apart; and that in any

---

[159] See below, p. 820.
[160] G. K. Behlmer, *Friends of the Family* (Stanford, 1998), 195–213.

case having a maintenance order was one thing, but getting regular payments all too often quite another.[161]

The legal system thus acquired a new discrimination between classes. The propertied could proceed in the High Court for full divorce, the working population in practice had to be content with a separation ordered by magistrates. Gorell Barnes J., one of the judges most experienced in the dreary business of dealing with matrimonial disputes, was prepared to speak out. Shortly after becoming President of the Probate, Divorce and Admiralty Division, he gave judgment in *Dodd* v. *Dodd*,[162] in terms that amounted to an unequivocal condemnation. A woman had for nine years lived apart from her leech of a husband under a magistrate's order but had continued to support him financially through this period. She had just discovered his adultery. Barnes felt obliged to hold that she could not then obtain a full divorce from him for the adultery aggravated by the desertion. The separation order permitted him to live apart and so could not constitute desertion. She had to be left in her limbo, but Barnes roundly condemned the curious inhumanity of such an outcome. Indeed, he denounced the divorce law administered in his court as 'full of inconsistencies, anomalies, and inequalities, almost amounting to absurdities'.[163]

The impetus that these developments gave to divorce reform was noteworthy. By 1909, the government conceded a Royal Commission on Divorce and Matrimonial Causes of which Gorell Barnes (ennobled as Lord Gorell), was made the chairman.[164] The Commission worked with great application for three years before producing Majority and Minority Reports. McGregor characterized the former as being 'of remarkable clarity and intellectual distinction'.[165] Much of the evidence to it came from lawyers and others directly engaged in litigating or advising on matrimonial disputes.[166] In addition, comparisons with

---

[161] Behlmer finds instances of women who used separation orders as goads to get husbands back into line for at least a while; but they were the good managers who might well be looked upon as harridans.

[162] [1906] P 189. Previously, other members of his Division had striven to reach the opposite conclusion: Cretney, *Family*, 208–9.

[163] [1906] P at 207.

[164] The peerage was conferred so that he could sit on House of Lords' appeals. He used the chance to speak in the legislative chamber on the need for divorce reform, notably by arguing that cases between low income spouses be heard in the county courts—a recommendation that was made by a Lord Chancellor's Committee on County Court Procedure, which he chaired: Report, *PP* 1909 (71), lxxii, 22–6. He spoke to it at length in the Lords (*PD* (5s) 473–85), but was followed by the Archbishop of Canterbury (Davidson) in high traditional voice.

[165] O. R. McGregor, *Divorce in England* (1957), 26.

[166] Significant support for Gorell's position came from the experienced London magistrate, A. C. Plowden, approaching both marriage and divorce with a lay pragmatism, while making plain that a battered wife who took her husband to a summary court for assault would be likely to face

jurisdictions elsewhere in the Empire and beyond showed how highly conservative English attitudes remained. This helped the Majority towards essentially practical recommendations, without stranding themselves on the rocks of any one religious position and advocating 'an unfettered consideration of what is best for the interest of the state, society, and morality, and for that of the parties to suits and their families'.[167]

The Majority made three basic recommendations. First, there must be gender equality in divorce law.[168] Secondly, the grounds for divorce should extend beyond adultery to cruelty, desertion for three years, insanity, incurable drunkenness, and imprisonment under a commuted death sentence.[169] Thirdly, there should be a granting procedure sufficiently open and cheap to allow equal access to full divorce across the population.[170] Only with changes on all these fronts would it be possible for many in the population to escape the deep frustrations of a magistrate's order of separation, despite the marriage being preserved. The Minority, comprising the Archbishop of York, Cosmo Gordon Lang, the conservative law don, Sir William Anson Bt, and the Dean of Arches, Sir Lewis Dibdin, were willing to notice the inequalities of sex and social position. But since they were intent on insisting that the 1857 settlement must be regarded as final, they found it harder to offer practical prescriptions that would reduce the anomalies.

By 1912, Asquith's Liberal government, beset with major distractions, had no stomach for the major parliamentary battle presaged by the Majority's proposals. The First World War would produce a much increased demand for divorce, including aid with its costs. This would be met only by opening the procedures in limited ways to a wider public; indeed, after some false starts, in 1923 the aggravations that a petitioning wife had to show against her adulterous husband were removed. Not until 1937, with the campaigning of A. P. Herbert, would the list of matrimonial wrongs justifying divorce be extended on Gorell Commission

---

dreadful retribution when he had served his prison sentence: Evidence, *PP* 1912–13 [Cd. 6479], xix, qq. 19.021–6.

[167] Report, *PP* 1912–13 [Cd. 6478], xviii, 48–50. The recommendations would follow upon the eight principal questions investigated by the Commission.

[168] Report, Part XIV.

[169] Report, Part XV. For proposals to widen the categories for annulment, see Part XVI. These comprised cases where a petitioner entered the marriage without knowing of the other party's habitual drunkenness, venereal disease, or pregnancy. Refusal to perform 'conjugal duties' once married would also become a ground for nullification.

[170] Gorell's own influence was to be felt in the proposals to provide divorce jurisdiction across the Assize circuits, rather than only in London, for those with an annual income up to £300 and assets up to £200; and to bring within the High Court the granting of separation orders by a simple process. The magistrates' courts would be used only in cases requiring immediate action, as where a wife's safety was at issue: see the Report, Parts XI–XIII.

lines.[171] But even with a second cycle of increased demand in the wake of the Second World War, it would not be until 1969 that divorce law would cease to be based purely on accusation of misconduct made by the spouse-victim. That could happen only with a seismic shift in social attitudes towards heterosexual partnership. In the end the Christian insistence on marriage as a lifelong union would give way; and the legal system would have to cope with family breakdowns on a quite unprecedented scale; but this was an end scarcely to be foreseen in 1914.

[171] For this period, see Cretney, *Family*, 214–73.

V

Children

1. THE WEDLOCK-BORN AND THE BASTARD

As has often been suggested, before industrialization children were perceived primarily as potential adults. Their survival at birth and in infancy was still a matter of chance. The upbringing of most was devoted to realizing their economic potential, which by today's standards, held severely limited prospects in the vast bulk of cases.[1] A mark of this in the common law was the father's right of action where his daughter's seducer took her off from home.[2] Formally at least, since it was one variety of the *actio per quod servitium amisit*, it aimed to compensate him for the loss of her economic contribution to the household; but with daughters, as distinct from servants, juries could award exemplary damages as a mark of the insult to family honour and respectability.[3] In the early nineteenth century, the idea that children might have emotional and educational needs that deserved attention and sympathy was only beginning to spread down the social ranking. The primary new institution of production—the factory—was indeed subject to legal control, first in respect of child labour and soon afterwards that of women.[4] A small measure of education, instituted in factories from 1844 (after some false starts), would grow into a national policy for children in general by 1870. In a stepwise progression, elementary education would be made compulsory for younger children, being provided free through Churches or Local School

---

[1] See generally, P. Ariès, *Centuries of Childhood* (New York, 1962); Stone, *The Family, Sex and Marriage in England* (1977), Ch. 9; J. Walvin, *A Child's World* (1981), esp. Ch. 11.

[2] That action also lay simply for the enticement or harbouring of a spouse or a child. Like suits for breach of promise, these would survive until abolition by the Law Reform (Miscellaneous Provisions) Act 1970; Cretney, *Family Law*, 157.

[3] Morrison, 'Tort' in Graveson and Crane, *Century*, 112–14; Stone, *Road to Divorce*, 83–5. There was an old non-clergyable felony of forcible abduction and marriage—'vulgarly called stealing an heiress', according to Blackstone, *Comms*, iv, 208. Only in 1885 would 'carnal knowledge' of girls under 16 be made an indictable criminal offence, whether or not they consented (it became a felony, if the girl was under 13): see generally, Criminal Law Amendment Act 1885 ss 4–10. The Act grew out of W. T. Stead's campaign, in his *Pall Mall Gazette*, against the evils of procuring and brothel-keeping, white slavery and indecency between men (but not between women—as well, perhaps, for the wife of Archbishop Benson).

[4] Above, Pt 2, Ch. V.

Boards. Parents would be placed under public duties to see that their children went to school and brigades of truancy officers would move into position.[5]

The common law insisted on a division between legitimate and illegitimate offspring. It remained a root distinction throughout the Victorian period and beyond.[6] It is of course hard to recapture its meaning today, when bastardy no longer carries a stigma, long-term relationships of parents outside marriage and single parentage are quite regular phenomena, whether planned in advance or not. Whatever the supervisions and admonitions of parents, sexual intercourse might become a part of courting and could well lead to marriage when the girl became pregnant. There is evidence that the average age of marriage came down in good economic times; and then also the rate of illegitimate births and of marriages to a woman already carrying a child rose, so that together these cases might exceed more than half of all births. So far as can be shown from patchy records, the rate tended to be higher in the countryside than the towns.[7]

Social studies of bastardy at the beginning of the nineteenth century suggest that it involved complex and sometimes equivocal attitudes. One factor was this. In England, the Old Poor Law imposed a public duty on the mother, if she could, and the father, if he could be identified, to pay the parish at least a bare amount for maintenance of their destitute children. Since having the child might put an end to any prospect of the mother continuing to work, the better hope was to put the man accused of fathering the infant *en ventre* under pressure either to marry the mother before its birth, or else to throw him into prison until he came up with some security for paying maintenance.[8] Before the 1834 revision, the investigative Royal Commission, notoriously, read the evidence before it as supporting their moral and economic case for a reversal of policy. They objected that overseers and justices had been too ready to pay maintenance grants, while failing to get fathers to contribute for their children. Instead, heavy social pressure to get married produced dysfunctional families. At the same time moral laxity meant that more children were being born at an early stage of the parents' working lives,

[5] Above, Pt. 2. Ch. III. 5.

[6] See e.g. A. H.Simpson, *Treatise on the Law and Practice relating to Infants* (1875) 126–8; W. P. Eversley, *Law of Domestic Relations* (1885) Pt II, Ch. 1. The demographic and social history, including comparisons between regions, was fostered by P. Laslett et al. (eds), *Bastardy and its Comparative History* (1980).

[7] For historical demonstrations of these trends, see A. Levene, T. W. Nutt, and S. Williams (eds), *Illegitimacy in Britain, 1720–1920* (Basingstoke, 2005). The essays by J. Black and Nutt address issues of paternity.

[8] See, generally, U. R. Q. Henriques, 'Bastardy and the New Poor Law' (1967) 37 *P & P* 103–29; also S. and B. Webb, *English Poor Law History*, Pt I, 308–13; Pt II(I), 96–8, 177–8. For the Report of the Royal Commission on the Poor Laws on the subject, above, 776–7.

thus contributing to the great Malthusian fear of the effects of over-population. Their Report objected that those accused of paternity had in effect to disprove the mother's claim. Some who wanted the mother to assume the primary responsibility for upkeep argued that her conduct was the more blameworthy because she risked producing a child that ultimately the community might have to pay for. The Commission indeed argued that a putative father should not have to contribute at all to the child's maintenance. Rather, it was the mother who should do so; and if she failed then her parents should take on the burden for their failure to inculcate in her the right values.

Once the government introduced its Poor Law Bill, so rigid an apportionment of blame was denounced by High Tories, led by Henry Philpotts, Bishop of Exeter. A compromise was then hammered out: the father would continue to share responsibility with the mother. But she would have to proceed before Quarter Sessions (rather than Petty Sessions) in order to establish paternity if it was in dispute, and that step alone would lead to an affiliation order that he pay maintenance.[9] It was a legislative experiment that did not work, evoking immediate protest, both from those who administered the New Poor Law at local levels as well as recipients, actual and potential. Despite resistance from the central Poor Law Commission, a Commons Select Committee favoured returning the paternity jurisdiction primarily to justices, with certain safeguards. In 1844 Parliament did accede to this. It was for the mother, if she was able, to bring the summary proceedings against the accused father. Poor law officers were forbidden to bring or intervene in the proceedings themselves.[10] Only after nearly 30 years would they get back that power.[11]

So long as there were no scientific theories or tests for determining who were a child's parents, the question of legitimacy was settled by rough-and-ready rules.[12] Children born in wedlock (i.e. to a wife during the lifetime

---

[9] 4 & 5 Will. IV c, ss 1–7. It became an offence, inter alia, improperly to promote the marriage of parents of a bastard child: s 8.

[10] 7 & 8 Vict. c. 100, s 1. Earlier that year, the Commissioners inquiring into the Rebecca riots in Wales (*PP* 1844, xvi, 77, Report, 30–1) reported the widespread opinion that there had been a considerable increase in illegitimate births since it had become less easy to ensure that the couple married.

[11] The Poor Law Act 1868 gave the guardians power to seek an attachment order upon any moneys being paid by the father to the mother for the child. The Bastardy Laws Amendment Act 1872 gave the mother or the guardians power to have two justices determine whether the person summoned was the father, and gave them power once more to seek orders for maintenance from father or mother. For these swivels in policy, see Henriques, 'Bastardy', 119–20.

[12] The discovery of blood grouping in 1900 was the first step towards accurate determination of parentage: Cretney, *Family*, 536–7.

of her husband or within nine months of his death) were presumed legitim-ate.[13] So strong was this presumption that the superior courts would require proof to the contrary to be beyond reasonable doubt.[14] In the *Aylesford Peerage* case, the House of Lords did refuse to accept the legitimacy of Lady Aylesford's son, born five years after she took off to live with Lord Blandford. In Lord Bramwell's opinion, it was hard to 'conceive of anything so nauseous' as that Lord Aylesford would have had intercourse with her after their long, offensive separation.[15] More usually, the courts' reluctance to bastardize such a child seems to have overridden their doubts.[16] The ability to obtain a declaration of legitimacy was introduced in 1858 by statute; if the court made the declaration, it would have binding effect on all who were made parties to the proceed-ings and their successors, as the peculiar story of the Ampthill Russells would eventually demonstrate.[17]

Where a man made a woman pregnant out of wedlock and they were free to marry, there were strong social pressures to do so, backed in some cases by the common law's action for breach of promise of marriage.[18] But in the com-mon law, medieval notions of bastardy had not been modified (as they had, in Scotland and elsewhere);[19] if the parents' marriage occurred after the child had been born it would remain illegitimate.[20] Manorial customs might determine otherwise, but these survived into the nineteenth century only in occasional places.[21] When eventually by the Legitimacy Act 1926, the concept of legitim-ation by subsequent marriage was introduced into English law, it would still retain a special element of moral disapproval. If the child resulted from forni-cation by two unmarried people, their later marriage would make it legitimate; but that would remain impossible when at the child's birth one of the parents was married to someone else.[22]

---

[13] If she re-married at once on the husband's death, and a child was then born which either husband could have fathered, the child could elect one as his or her parent on reaching adulthood.

[14] e.g. *Gordon* v. *Gordon* [1903] P 141.

[15] (1885) 11 App Cas 1, 18.

[16] In affiliation proceedings before magistrates after 1872, there was a readier tendency to find corroboration of the mother's accusation of paternity from the general circumstances: Cretney, *Family*, 530–3.

[17] It is regaled in the *Ampthill Peerage Case* [1977] AC 547.

[18] See Stone, *Road to Divorce*, 85–95 for this predominant use of the action.

[19] *Legitimatio per subsequens matrimonium* had roots in later Roman law and so was found in many parts of Europe.

[20] For consequences in private international law, see below, 837.

[21] Gillis, *For Better, For Worse*, 19.

[22] Cretney, *Family*, 550–1. The introduction of legal adoption in the following year would provide an alternative route to respectability which even more would use: O. R. McGregor et al., *Separated Spouses* (1970), 175.

2. CAPACITY IN CIVIL LAW

When it came to the legal capacities of children themselves, there was no equivalent to the measures which underpinned the subjugation of wife to husband in matters of property and obligation.[23] An 'infant' for these purposes only attained majority at the upper-class age of 21.[24] Nonetheless before coming of age children could legally own money and other property, whether it came to them by gift, on sale, or as earnings.[25] Fathers did not assume any vicarious liability either for the contracts or the torts of their offspring.[26] So far as the children themselves were concerned, the chief constraint upon them concerned their contractual capacity, which was limited by the common law, with a certain reinforcement by equity, and from 1874 a considerable buttressing by statute.[27] The common law had as its default position a rule that infants could repudiate a contract up to majority and a reasonable period thereafter. That was the position, for instance, with the grant of a lease or the purchase of shares in joint ventures. Even then, if it was found that the transaction was not for the infant's benefit, it could not be sued upon. Equity refused to order specific performance against an infant, or indeed against the other party;[28] but there were indications that it would require an infant who told lies to return property or money received before repudiating the agreement. Equity also intervened if the other party obtained the agreement by undue influence, which was presumed to arise between parent and child unless there was evidence of independent advice sufficient to undo its effect.[29]

Two major exceptions applied to the general position at common law. Minors under 21 were bound by apprenticeships and service contracts, provided that the terms were beneficial to them.[30] So economic reality dictated, since, for much of the population, adult work began well before the age of 21. Likewise they were bound by contracts for the supply of necessaries to themselves and their families. Juries of townspeople were apt to find things provided on tick to young bucks were necessaries; but the judges took it upon themselves to rule that some items

---

[23] The discussion of children's obligations appears to ignore the question of their legitimacy, though those who were worth suing were likely to have been part of a family.

[24] The age of majority would be reduced to 18 only in 1970, when those under age became 'minors'.

[25] In a common law action they would have to sue or be sued by their next friend: Simpson, *Infants*, 437–51, 452–63.

[26] See e.g. *Bebee* v. *Sales* (1916) 32 TLR 413.

[27] Infants Relief Act 1874.

[28] *Flight* v. *Bolland* (1828) 4 Russ. 298.

[29] See e.g. *Wright* v. *Vanderplank* (1855) 2 K. & J. 1.

[30] See e.g. *De Francesco* v. *Barnum* (1890) 44 ChD 430; *Clements* v. *LNWR* [1894] 2 QB 482,CA.

in question could not fall into that category.[31] Parliament lent its support with a similar counter-move intended to keep infants within their allowance from their fathers. The Infants Relief Act 1874 rendered contracts with minors 'absolutely void' if for the supply of 'non-necessary' goods or loans for 'non-necessaries'.[32] Traders were thus encouraged to deal with the young only on down payment, and moneylenders were well-advised to stick to pawnbroking or other transactions covered by a security. The courts in due course endorsed this piece of protective discipline, holding that a loan could not be recovered even from a minor who lied about his age. Where the Act abnegated the contract, there could be no proprietary, tortious, or quasi-contractual liability that could be used to circumvent its policy.[33] As for liability in tort beyond this constraint, the minor could be sued, if it was worth doing so.[34]

3. LEGITIMATE CHILDREN: THE GOVERNANCE OF THE FATHER

Within a married family, common law and equity together provided structures for wealth-holding as between parents and their children (of whatever age) which went to the very foundations of real and personal property. With freehold property the fee tail and the life estate were conceived in inter-generational terms. The law of inheritance and the transactional arrangements underlying strict settlements, marriage settlements, and other family trusts balanced the power and the responsibility of the current beneficiaries against those of their successors. Patriarchal ties between the father of such a family and his offspring gave rise, in many legal respects, to a strict autocracy. The parents might choose to treat children during their minority with a mixture of indulgence and silliness, as with the contributions of Mr and Mrs Bennett to the upbringing of their five precocious daughters. But if it came to insistence, the power was with the father.

Blackstone had noted some responsibility upon a father to maintain, protect, and educate his legitimate children, but had characterized any broad

[31] A stir was caused by *Foster* v. *Redgrave* (1868) LR 4 Ex 35, n. 8 (Oxford jury wrongly found waistcoats to be necessary, when the undergraduate already had an ample wardrobe); and *Ryder* v. *Wombwell* (1868) LR 4 Ex 32 (jewelled presents for a marquess could not be necessaries).

[32] Also for accounts stated upon such transactions: s 1. The Act allowed the enforcement of a promise for new consideration, if given after majority (s 2); but for bets and loans even this was disallowed by the Betting and Loans (Infants) Act 1892. The Acts were not repealed and the common law position restored until the Minors' Contracts Act 1987.

[33] *Leslie* v. *Shiell* [1914] 3 KB 607 (CA), applying the general rule at common law (for which see e.g. *Burnard* v. *Haggis* (1863) 14 C.B.N.S. 45) and criticizing *Stocks* v. *Wilson* [1913] 2 KB 235. See Morrison, 'Tort', in Graveson and Crane, *Century*, 109, 139–42.

[34] Morrison, 'Tort', 109.

interpretation of it as a moral, rather than a legal, duty.[35] When a struggle arose
between the father and mother, the father's rights over them were pronounced
'sacred'. Whatever his duties towards them might be, they were not capable of
being surrendered by agreement with his wife.[36] So it would remain for much of
the nineteenth century. A father could accordingly recover his children from the
mother or someone else with whom they were living. A common law court would
require, by writ of *habeas corpus*, that anyone held under restraint be brought
before it.[37] In the case of children old enough to decide for themselves and who
wished to go free, the court would grant that freedom and warn relations who
might interfere not to do so. But those still too young to decide would be given
into proper custody, which would belong to the father, unless he had disqualified
himself by his misconduct.

The father's writ, moreover, would survive his death. If he appointed a
guardian of the children by his will that person would exercise power in his
place, and could overrule the wishes of the mother, if she were not appointed a
guardian. Only if there were no testamentary guardian and none appointed by
Chancery, would she stand in the husband's place. Like the father, the guardian
would decide where the children were to live, how they would be educated and
helped into office, business, or employment, in what faith they would receive
religious instruction, what they would wear, what medical treatment they would
receive, and so on and on.[38]

Chancery had a further power, acting on behalf of the Crown as *parens
patriae*, to make children wards of court, and more generally to consider their
needs upon petition, whether the issue was their custody, the right of a parent
to access, the appointment or supervision of guardians, arrangements for their
education, religion, or launching in life.[39] The Court might examine the child
personally in order to find out what its preferences were.[40] While the father
remained alive it was he alone, in any normal case, who could get the court to

<hr>

[35] *Comms*, i, Ch. 16. Unlike a wife, a child could not, it seems, even pledge the father's credit for
necessaries, save with express authority: *Mortimer* v. *Wright* (1840) 6 M. & W. 482; later the mother
could do so for herself and any children: *Bazeley* v. *Forder* (1868) LR 3 QB 559.

[36] e.g. *Hope* v *Hope* (1857) 8 De G.M. & G. 731, 743–6.

[37] Chancery could also hear *habeas corpus* applications, rather than deploying its protective
powers.

[38] See generally, J. D. Chambers, *Jurisdiction of the High Court of Chancery over the Persons and
Property of Children (1842)*, Ch. 5, sections 1–4; Simpson, *Infants*, 235–7, 305–20, 323–4.

[39] The scope of this jurisdiction was regularly challenged by counsel, but Thurlow and Eldon
pronounced that only the House of Lords could impose restrictions upon it. It was finally confirmed
in *Wellesley* v. *Wellesley* (see below, n. 45).

[40] King LC had done so long before: *Ex p Hopkins* (1732) 3 P. Wms 151. Whether it was a wise step
still caused some anxiety in the late nineteenth century, but was supported by Kay LJ in *R* v.. *Gyngall*
[1893] 2 QB 232; and Fitzgibbon LJ in *Re O'Hara* [1900] 2 IR 232, 240.

enforce his interests over them—for instance, by ordering the mother or some other keeper to give them over to him. In any case, as Lord Eldon insisted, Chancery granted its shield only to children with substantial property—a limitation that would be cut away gradually once he ceased to sit;[41] but even after that, the great bulk of the population could scarcely conceive of proceeding in Chancery over their family quarrels.

The parallel jurisdictions of common law and equity over the custody of children is a particularly interesting example of their relationship before the Judicature Acts and beyond. There had been various signs that equity in particular would not accede the husband's demands when all the circumstances suggested that he had been or would become neglectful—for instance where he was bankrupt, or was proposing to take the children down into social and educational positions that would demean them, given their expected wealth and status.[42] Charles Dickens' portrayal of the supervision of the Jarndyce wards by his Lord Chancellor gives the flavour of the reported case law.[43] During the Napoleonic Wars, both King's Bench and Chancery had insisted upon a husband prevailing over his wife as the pair tussled over the custody of a very young baby. It mattered not that the husband was French and somewhat revolutionary in his leanings, while the wife was English. His *habeas corpus* claim succeeded. That would have been the outcome also in Chancery had Eldon not conducted one of his thorough investigations into the circumstances and found reason to give custody to neither.[44] The father was not entitled to custody because he could well try to take the child to France and the court would not stand for such a removal from its jurisdiction. The mother had disgraced herself by running away with the child to her family.

Eldon would continue to find against the father in cases of neglect, moral depravity, injury to status or threat to remove from the jurisdiction. For instance, the Hon. William Wellesley—son of Lord Maryborough and nephew of Marquess Wellesley and the Duke of Wellington—had taken his heiress wife and young children off to Naples and then Florence and Paris, where he inculcated them in his seamy life under the regime of his unscrupulous mistress, Mrs Bligh. Among

---

[41] *Wellesley* v. *Beaufort* (1827) 2 Russ. 1, 21; cf. *Re Spence* (1847) 2 Ph. 247; *Re Race* (1857) 1 Hem. & M. 420. See P. H. Pettit, 'Parental Control and Guardianship', in Graveson and Crane, *Century*, 56–87, at 62, 68; J. Seymour, '*Parens Patriae* and Wardship Powers' (1994) 14 *OJLS* 159–88.

[42] *Creuze (or Cruise)* v. *Hunter* (1790) 2 Cox Eq. Cas. 242; *Powell* v. *Cleaver* (1792) 2 Bro. C.C. 42; *Ex p Warner* (1792) 4 Bro. C.C. 101.

[43] *Bleak House* would not appear until 1853, but the figure is perhaps based on Eldon, who ended his reign in 1828.

[44] *R* v. *De Manneville* (1804) 5 East 221; *De Manneville* v. *De Manneville* (1804) 10 Ves. 52. In the end Eldon referred the difficult business of finding a suitable placement to a Master, expressing the hope that adequate access to the child would be afforded to both parents.

his many peculiarities, he encouraged his son to swear because, he said, it was greatly preferable to lying. At the time of Wellesley's petition for their custody, their mother died of a wasting disease, and the children were inheriting interests under her marriage settlement, which was producing income of £40,000 a year (at least £2.5 million today).[45] Wearily Eldon sent the case to a Master to seek out a guardian who would take charge of them, if any could be found. Maryborough certainly made his own reluctance plain. Likewise, the poet Shelley was deprived by Lord Eldon of access to his children because his pronounced atheism was 'such as the law calls upon me to consider as immoral and vicious'.[46]

In general, Eldon would give no account to the mere fact that the spouses adhered to different religions. It was for the father to decide which persuasion was to be impressed upon the children and no court would attempt to interfere with his decision. As with custody, he was entitled to change his mind, whatever he might have promised his wife or her family at the time of his marriage. For all this, Eldon, quite typically, preserved some discretion to override the husband's claims when 'the parent is capriciously interfering with what is clearly for [the children's] benefit'.[47] From this stemmed a tradition that in Chancery the child's welfare was the ultimate concern, and the court would act objectively as would a wise parent.[48]

Rather more unyielding was the position in King's Bench. In *habeas corpus* proceedings, *R* v. *Greenhill,* a mother, who had left home because the husband had a mistress, was ordered to surrender up three girls to her husband, the eldest not yet six; and no provision could be made for access. His conduct would have barred his claim only if he had installed the mistress at home with the children, instead of keeping her in a different establishment.[49] Sergeant Talfourd (who

---

[45] *Wellesley* v. *Beaufort* (1827) 2 Russ. 1, where Eldon set out the proof of his sins over pages; and for the appeal to the Lords (*sub. nom. Wellesley* v. *Wellesley*) (1828) 2 Bli. N.S. 124. The Lords were much perturbed by his attempt to remove the children by force with a view to taking them abroad and so out of the reach of English courts. That danger was already well known, as in the *de Manneville* case (see above, n. 44). It remains a grave concern today.

[46] *Shelley* v. *Westwood* (1817) Jac. 266; for unchanged attitudes after 60 years, see *Re Besant* (1878) 11 ChD 508 . As W. S. Gilbert's Lord Chancellor proclaimed in *Iolanthe*: 'And I, my Lords, embody the Law'.

[47] *Lyons* v. *Blenkin* (1821) Jac. 245, at 256. The father having left the children for a long period with an aunt and grandmother was not allowed to take them away because he did not like the man that the aunt was to marry. Lesser figures, such as Hart VC would prove more rule-oriented. In *Ball* v. *Ball* (1827) 2 Sim. 35, he ordered a blameless mother, living apart from her husband, to surrender up the children to him; and could find no precedent for even allowing her access to them, although he 'knew of no act more harsh or cruel than depriving the mother of proper intercourse with her child' (p. 36).

[48] Chambers, *Chancery over Infants*, 20–3, 145–51.

[49] (1836) 4 Ad. & El. 624. Eventually she absconded abroad with the daughters: see J. Wroath, *Until They are Seven* (Winchester, 1998), Pt 1.

appeared for the unsuccessful mother) campaigned in Parliament for at least some relaxation. In this he was sustained by a pamphlet from Pearce Stevenson, the pseudonym of the author, Caroline Norton.[50] By his Custody of Infants Act 1839, Chancery could permit the mother access to her children when living separately from the husband or it could award custody of a child under seven to the mother, but only to the extent that it was 'convenient and just'. Mothers guilty of adultery were excluded from this concession.[51] Even a wife who preferred living in association with some other man without consummation would not succeed in court; likewise one whose extravagance showed her incapable of managing her household.[52]

If little else, the 1839 Act did prove to be a precursor of change. Over the decades that would see other shifts towards a more balanced view of interests within the nuclear family, concerns for the child began to find greater space. A separate incentive would come from the 1857 legislation giving the Divorce Court a matrimonial jurisdiction which extended to outright divorce. Section 35 allowed both interim and final orders to be made concerning the children—a power for which there had been no precedent in the ecclesiastical courts.[53] The orders could embrace whatever was 'just and proper' concerning custody, maintenance, and education; and if necessary the Divorce Court could refer the case to Chancery for its protection of the child.

It did not follow that there should be the same broad discretion when a couple were separating voluntarily, even where guilt lay all on one side. But still the balance came gradually to be re-thought in the years after 1867. A second Custody of Infants Act, in 1873, allowed the Court, where it was proper, to award the mother custody of a legitimate child, not merely during nurture, but up to the age of 16; or alternatively she might be allowed access.[54] The Act also sought to ensure that normally a husband who had surrendered custody to the mother in a separation agreement would be kept to his promise.[55] But, as the aetheistic Annie Besant found to her dismay, her clergyman-husband could change his

---

[50] *Plain Letter to the Lord Chancellor* (1837). At this juncture in her public conflicts with her husband, Mrs Norton, confidante of the Prime Minister, Melbourne, was locked in battle over access to her children: see also above, 781; and A. Acland, *Caroline Norton* (1948), 84–91; Wroath, *Until They are Seven* (1998), Pt 2.

[51] 2 & 3 Vict. c. 54, ss 1, 2.

[52] *Shillito* v. *Collett* (1860) 8 WR 683; *Re Winscom* (1865) 2 Hem. & M. 540.

[53] The relief applied to judicial separation, nullity of marriage and divorce proceedings and was extended in 1878 to magistrates' separation orders (for children up to 10); and in 1884 to cover restitution of conjugal rights.

[54] Section 1. The former exclusion of the adulterous wife was removed from the legislation, but with what effect it is hard to say.

[55] Section 2.

mind, if he could then persuade a court that it was for their daughter's benefit that she should be separated from her mother.[56] Mrs Besant was in the midst of her campaign with Bradlaugh to promote contraception as a saving grace for women. For re-publishing Knowlton's *The Fruits of Philosophy*, a jury had convicted them of conspiring to deprave public morals, Hardinge Giffard AG (later Lord Halsbury), for the prosecution, having described it as a 'dirty, filthy book'.[57] In the custody suit, James LJ fulminated against the book, despite its being 50 years old, as 'so repugnant, so abhorrent to the feelings of the great majority of decent English-men and English-women, and would be regarded by them with such disgust...as violations of moral decency and womanly propriety that the future of the daughter would be incalculably prejudiced' if left in her mother's charge.[58]

In its protective jurisdiction over children, Chancery's standard was thought by many lawyers to be more balanced than the common law's attitudes in *habeas corpus* proceedings. The Judicature Act 1873 accordingly specified that, since all divisions of the new High Court could exercise both jurisdictions, they were to apply principles of equity, rather than of common law to questions of the custody and education of infants.[59] But the standard of the wise parent was much more likely to be emphasized when the case was not a custody quarrel between a husband and wife over the fate of their children, but was, for instance, a contest between a mother and a foster-carer, or between more distant relations.[60] Between spouses, it was not an objective standard that prevailed, but the decision of the husband. His 'sacred right' had been given pride of place in two court decisions which confirmed the right of a martinet Anglican to wrest his children away from their Catholic mother and place them with a firmly Protestant governess.[61]

This explains why the opponents of paternal dominance continued to seek legislative change. To some extent they succeeded. In 1886, the guardianship laws were revised to give the widowed mother equal place with any guardian

---

[56] *Re Besant* (1878) 11 Ch D 508.

[57] See S. Chandrasekar, *'A Dirty, Filthy Book'* (Berkeley, 1981).

[58] (1878) 11 Ch D 521.

[59] Section 25(10).

[60] *R v. Gyngall* [1893] 2 QB 232 (CA), became the leading decision: a widowed mother's preference for a Catholic home to take in her children did not prevail over the Protestant home provided by family friends, because the court doubted her capacity to provide for them. See also *Re O'Hara* [1900] 2 IR 232 (Ir CA).

[61] *Re Agar-Ellis (No. 1)* (1878) 10 Ch D 49 (CA); *Re Agar-Ellis (No. 2)* (1883) 24 Ch D 317 (CA). In the second case he kept his control over one daughter, who was already 17 and plainly wished to be able to see her mother. The decision would be described by Lord Upjohn decades later as 'dreadful': see *J* v. *C* [1969] 1 All ER 788 at 829.

appointed by a deceased husband's will.[62] Moreover, the Act permitted a mother to seek custody of her child or access to it which the court could order having regard to the infant's welfare, the conduct of the parents and the wishes of each of them. The Custody of Children Act 1891 would cut into the father's right to demand that his children be restored to him when he had neglected or deserted them, or had left them to others (including the guardians of the poor) to bring up. The High Court was not to require delivery of the children to either parent unless satisfied that they were fit, 'having regard to the welfare of the child'. The main fear was of the parent who let a child go until it was able to earn and then demanded it back.[63] Even after women had won their parliamentary franchise in 1918, the National Union of Societies for Equal Citizenship would have to fight a tenacious five-year battle to secure legislation stating that in custody cases the child's welfare should be the first and paramount consideration *and* that the father's powers should not be regarded as superior to the mother's.[64] Officials and politicians fought to insist that, as a matter of law, there must be one voice in a family to decide whether a child could go away from home, or undergo an operation, or whatever the issue might be. They had in the end to give way. But still some judges would insist on giving place to other considerations, such as the wishes of a parent in the matter of religion.[65]

In any case, these stepwise changes were to private law, and required an application to the High Court. Only people who could meet the financial risks, provide their own legal representation, and show the sheer nerve needed to face the ordeal, could expect to gain much benefit. The lot of the illegitimate, in particular, was likely to be very different. In a pre-contraceptive world, bastard offspring proliferated at every social level. Kings, princes, and aristocrats had their morganatic wives and mistresses, many kept more or less in the open. The Duke of Clarence, ultimately William IV, lived at Hampton with the comedy actress, Dora Jordan, and had ten children by her.[66] If there was wealth around, illegitimate children might find themselves reasonably well placed. But the law of inheritance—and of property more generally—had a good measure of disapproval embedded in it. Bastards had long been treated as *filii nullius*,

---

[62] Guardianship of Infants Act 1886, s 2. The mother was given a provisional power to appoint a testamentary guardian, but it only took effect if a court found the father to be unfitted as sole guardian: s 3(2). They were eventually placed on an equal footing by the Guardianship of Infants Act 1925, s 4.

[63] Even when the court would not restore custody, it was obliged (in all but extreme cases) to respect the legitimate father's legal right to determine the faith in which a child should be brought up: s 5. A similar provision was inserted in other legislation of the period.

[64] Guardianship of Infants Act 1925, s 1.

[65] Notably in *Re Carroll (No. 2)* [1931] 1 KB 317 (CA).

[66] C. Tomalin, *Mrs Jordan's Profession* (1994).

incapable of being 'heirs' in the descent of freehold estates or 'children' under rules of intestacy. If settlements, trusts, and similar documents used such general terminology, it was likely to be read in the same vein. Only if they were specifically named could they be at all sure of receiving their designated share. Should questions of their custody and the like arise under general law, it was likely that the wishes of the mother would be respected, though she was not allowed to enjoy the categorical rights of that a father had over legitimate children.

4. ENDANGERED CHILDREN: PLIGHTS AND RESCUES

In the lower classes, special dangers lay in wait for children born outside marriage. For instance, a mother could well face dismissal from domestic service or other employment if the truth came out; or shame could jeopardize her marriage prospects; or keeping the child could force her into pauperdom or prostitution.[67] She might herself kill the child,[68] she might leave it out in the desperate hope that others would rescue it as a foundling, or she might give it over to a baby-farmer for some pittance in the name of what was called 'adoption'. By the 1860s such practices, long known, began to touch the consciences of the respectable in new ways. Baby-farmers who caused their charges to die from opiates, hunger, neglect or deliberate poisoning, were prosecuted. In big towns it was guessed that 70–90 per cent of farmed babies soon met their deaths.[69]

When in 1870 Margaret Waters was convicted and hanged for the murder of farmed children in Brixton,[70] an anxious Parliamentary Committee recommended regulation through a scheme of local inspection. The Infant Life Preservation Act 1872 only required that a baby farmer register with their local

---

[67] For changing attitudes in administration of the poor law, see above, pp. 499–501.

[68] Infanticide by the mother tended to attract the sympathy of coroners, trial judges, and their juries. Even those who were prosecuted and convicted of murder, would, like George Eliot's Hetty Sorrel (in *Adam Bede*), have their execution commuted to transportation or penal servitude. So a Royal Commission on Capital Punishment, after reviewing the splay of opinion on the subject, opted for the introduction of a lesser offence of infanticide if the mother killed or harmed the child within seven days of the birth: Report, *PP* 1866, xxi, 50. Attempts to secure an enactment of this kind recurred in the 1870s, but it would not be achieved until the Infanticide Act 1922. See generally, J. McDonagh, *Child Murder and British Culture, 1720–1900* (Cambridge, 2003).

[69] There was no way of estimating what really happened, because of the many chances of concealment.

[70] Preceded five years before by a Charlotte Winsor, who worked the Devon countryside. For the scandals that caused public uproar, albeit for shortish periods, see G. K. Behlmer, *Child Abuse and Moral Reform in England, 1870–1908* (Stanford, 1982), 20–38; and his *Friends of the Family: The English Home and its Guardians, 1850–1940* (Stanford, 1998), 274–84.

authority and receive a licence— a control easily enough evaded.[71] It would not be until 1897 that the authorities were put under a duty to inspect or to ensure that a voluntary worker visited.[72] Eventually the Children Act 1908, Part I, somewhat strengthened this legislation, making it applicable to those who received children up to the age of seven. Other measures may have done a little more. Medical campaigners secured increased penalties for parents who failed to register births.[73] It was made difficult to insure the lives of farmed children.[74] When in the gardens of baby farms a series of infant bodies were unearthed, the courts allowed the similar fact evidence of all the exhumations to be introduced in order to show that the cause of death of one of the farmers' charges was murderous neglect, not mishap.[75]

A widespread movement to rescue not just babies but all children in danger began to gather force from the 1850s onwards.[76] From a legal perspective, it had three main manifestations, all of them depending considerably on the goodwill of private people, acting in charitable organizations or as individuals prepared to take on the responsibilities of respectable fostering.

First there were children who passed through the channels of the criminal law proper (charges being dealt with increasingly by magistrates sitting in summary jurisdiction[77]), or were condemned by courts as vagrants.[78] From the 1850s judges and magistrates obtained statutory powers to place those who had committed criminal acts into the charge of reformatory schools, rather than exposing them to prison life.[79] Those who got by somehow as homeless vagabonds could be sent to industrial schools—best regarded as a new, juvenile form of the old Bridewells—which became places for training them up in manual trades or for domestic service.[80] Enthusiasts, led initially by Mary Carpenter, established and

---

[71] Behlmer, *Child Abuse*, 38–40; M. L. Arnot, 'Infant Death, Child Care and the State' (1994) 9 *Continuity and Change* 271–311. A few local authorities—notably the London County Council—would use their public health powers to monitor those it licensed and to watch newspaper advertisements for 'adoption services'.

[72] Infant Life Protection Act 1897.

[73] Registration of Births and Deaths Act 1874.

[74] Friendly Societies Act 1875, s 28.

[75] *Makin v. Att.-Gen. for New South Wales* [1894] AC 57, JC.

[76] See Behlmer, *Child Abuse*, Ch. 2; H. Hendrick, *Child Welfare, England 1872–1989* (1996), Ch. 2.

[77] It was with child defendants that less serious indictable offences first became triable summarily, if the defendant did not request trial by jury: see above, Pt. One, Ch. III. 3.

[78] For children under the criminal law, its procedures and its regimes of punishment, see D. Mendes Da Costa, 'Criminal Law' in Graveson and Crane, *Century*, 194–6.

[79] For the treatment of convicted children, see above, 170–3.

[80] Over time there would be more industrial schools than reformatories. One origin of the reformatory lay in the 'ragged schools' set up to do something for the ragamuffins of the towns: see C. Seymour, *Ragged Schools, Ragged Children* (1995).

ran many of the new schools.[81] The churches became heavily involved.[82] The two categories of school in practice came to offer much the same drab conditions for the reform of their inmates. Because they were the end point in the process of state discipline, they were the subject of a stream of legislation,[83] which would eventually be consolidated and revised in the Children Act 1908, Part IV. The schools had to be certified and fell under the remit of a Home Office inspectorate. They were not the only initiatives of this period that were part of a drive to treat young offenders and vagrants as capable of being turned out with a new character. The probation service opened the prospect of them doing so while remaining in the community under outside supervision, and separate institutions for young adults were set up on the model of the experiment at Borstal.[84] A growing anxiety bred among the respectable classes the belief that if they did not strive to reform their misfits the whole social edifice would come under threat. Salvationist theories propounded the urgent need to herd wild youngsters off into institutions for whatever remained of their formative years; otherwise they would fall prey to the corruptions of prisons or the cruelty and neglect that was said increasingly to characterize the lowest families.

Secondly, there were institutions and societies which took in and otherwise aided children, on what, compared with the schools just mentioned, was a voluntary basis. Orphanages and other children's homes built up through the forceful work of Dr Thomas Barnardo, Dr Thomas Bowman Stevenson, the Church of England Waifs and Strays Society, the Roman Catholic Crusade of Rescue, and numerous other charitable endeavours, many with a denominational foundation. They likewise aimed to provide training enough for the children to be sent out for useful employment. They often set their institutions in the healthy countryside, away from the urban stews where the children, left to themselves and whatever family connections might still exist, would sink into lives of crime

---

[81] See her *Reformatory Schools for the Children of the Perishing and Dangerous Classes* (1851) and *Juvenile Delinquents, Their Condition and Treatment* (1853).

[82] The movement gained strength from outbreaks of scandal, such as W. T. Stead's revelations about girls sucked into prostitution and shipped abroad as 'white slaves', and his dramatic demonstration of how to buy a girl for the purpose—for which he was prosecuted.

[83] Reformatories were originally created by legislation in 1854, industrial schools by Acts of 1857 and 1861.

[84] The traditional form of a short, sharp shock had been a whipping order; and in a country where this was how parents controlled their children, and teachers their pupils, army officers their ranks, and ships' captains their crews, that power would continue, the objectors being 'the crankiest people in the world' as the tough Edward Troup of the Home Office would disdain them: H.O. 144/998/124607/16. Within the reformatories and other institutions, corporal punishment was administered with precious little control over those in charge, though there were some who argued that magistrates should have limits placed on their powers to order a birching: see L. Radzinowicz and R. Hood, *A History of English Criminal Law* (1986) v, 711–19.

and prostitution.[85] Their resources were almost always restricted and they looked to build up fostering arrangements with respectable families, a course which, when successful, could overcome the emotional deprivations of an institution. The arrangements by which children passed into a charitable institution and stayed there must frequently have seemed to them close enough to compulsion, for what other choice could there be in many cases? If their placement was by a parent or other family member, it fulfilled the duty to see that the child was maintained. What the rights and obligations of the placer would afterwards be would be set out primarily in the institution's terms for accepting the child.

In the 1880s, the London (later the National) Society for the Prevention of Cruelty to Children added to all the discussion and lobbying for improvements by their investigations into conditions of slum life.[86] The Society's inspectors found evidence of widespread hunger, bare clothing, and lack of schooling among the children, coupled with vicious cruelty, bigamous liaisons, incest, and paedophilia—all of which heightened the case for action against the scandals. The Society had strong parliamentary connections and promoted its 'Children's Charter' through successive enactments. These Acts armed the NSPCC and other societies with weapons for their campaigns. Much of their aim was already set in the Prevention of Cruelty to, and Protection of, Children Act 1889.[87] Section 1 laid down a range of criminal offences of wilfully assaulting, ill-treating, neglecting, or abandoning children in a manner likely to cause unnecessary suffering or injury to their physical or mental health.[88] Section 3 made it an offence to set children to beg or perform or do other similar things. Where such crimes occurred the police were given powers to arrest the adults involved without a warrant. Moreover NSPCC and similar inspectors could secure search warrants with powers to force entry in order to seek out children at risk. The warrants would be executed together with a senior police officer. The children could be seized and taken to a place of safety, after which magistrates might order that they be committed to a relative or other 'fit person' (often a children's home) until they were 16.[89] These somewhat draconian powers were Parliament's answer to

---

[85] A severance even more complete could be to send children off to colonies in the Empire where labour was needed and life chances were seen in rosy terms. Only a small proportion of children in care were dealt with in this way.

[86] See e.g. Behlmer, *Friends of the Family*, 104–16.

[87] See the additions and consolidations in a similar Act of 1894 and then the Children Act 1908, Pt II. Cretney, *Family*, 631–5.

[88] This and later Acts were careful to preserve the right of parents, teachers, and others to administer punishment, but gave no indication of where the line was to be drawn: see e.g. the 1889 Act, s 37.

[89] See ss 4–6.

the calamitous conditions presented in the revelations. Little attention was at this stage given to the possibility of voluntary homes being mismanaged, since the Home Office only had a power to visit, and actual inspections would be conducted by NSPCC officers or the like.[90]

Thirdly, the guardians of the poor, in their 640 Unions, had to deal with the pauper children who came under their care, again on the formal basis that those who were in their workhouses or were being maintained on outdoor relief had submitted themselves 'voluntarily'. Long before the Elizabethan poor law had been restructured in 1834 with greater determination than ever to make its regimes a port of final call for the destitute, pauper children had imposed a particular strain on the parish authorities. They were used as a source of cheap labour from young ages in the mines and the early factories, in agriculture and for brutes like Crabbe's fisherman, Peter Grimes. The 'new' Union workhouses were supposed to separate children from both fathers and mothers. But that meant the considerable expense of running children's homes. Like their predecessors, the poor law guardians continued to seek work for their charges where there were opportunities.[91] They also had a strong interest in placing children in private homes, either for paid fostering or else for an 'adoption' where the receiving family would agree to take over all responsibility for the child.[92] Adoption in the modern sense was still unknown in Britain. There was no legal procedure which would transfer parentage of a child to an adopting couple so as to end both the duties and the rights of the natural parent or parents. That concept would be introduced only in conjunction with the 1925 changes in the law of guardianship already mentioned.[93]

Various arrangements did exist in Victorian England for placing children permanently in new families. From well-intentioned adopters—typically childless couples with respectable homes to offer—there was always some demand, and it was met partly through the help of medical practitioners, the clergy or their wives.[94] As between natural parent and 'adopters' of this kind, to give the arrangement legal force the most that could be attempted was a contract—typically obliging the birth-mother to surrender her parental rights for good.[95]

---

[90] Children Act 1908, s 25. A formal system of inspection would have to wait until the Children and Young Persons Act 1932, Pt III.

[91] See above, 476, 564–5.

[92] The older usage of 'adoption' found its way into statute: see e.g. the Poor Law Act 1899, s 3.

[93] Adoption Act 1926, for which see Behlmer, *Friends of the Family*, 299–308; Cretney, *Family*, Ch. 17.

[94] There were channels by which the daughters of the respectable could give birth to their illegitimate children in strict privacy, immediate 'adoption' being one part of the arrangement.

[95] If the child was legitimate, the father was the person who, first and foremost, had to sign away rights.

Both sides might stay convinced that the agreement settled the position. But if the mother sought *habeas corpus* to get her child back, the contract would have no binding force. Public policy was held to render the natural bond inviolate, often enough to the great distress of the 'adopters' when the claim was made.[96] One reason for the parent's demand could be that the child had reached earning age. Equally, as the denominational charities grew in strength, it was they who might push the natural mother to 'reclaim' the child. This could well be to secure it in an institution run by the mother's denomination. Dr Barnardo was given to resisting claims from Catholics with his hands held high.[97]

The poor law authorities did gain rather more direct powers of control than under the law applicable to the voluntary societies. By the Poor Law Act 1889, the guardians could pass a resolution giving themselves all parental rights and duties over a child that had been deserted or subjected to a criminal offence for which the parent was imprisoned. Ten years later the list of grounds for intervention was considerably expanded.[98] If the guardians placed such a child with 'adopters' or foster-parents, the natural parent could no longer, as a matter of law, simply take the child back.[99] The guardians had to re-consider the situation. Ultimately the case could be referred to the magistrates, who on a complaint by the parent, had power to cancel the guardians' resolution.

5. JURISDICTION OVER CHILDREN

Amid all this activity, the question of who should have power to place children in care came to rank high; and rightly so, for where there was a parent or other relative who was losing the child, the scar could be considerable. Chancery's long-running jurisdiction over children who were made wards of court set a precedent for intervention, but was only open in reality to those with a respectable propertied background.[100] As the magistrates and the guardians came to

---

[96] The Custody of Children Act 1891 did give power to refuse to return the children when the parent was unfit to have custody. The Church of England Waifs and Strays Society sought to have all relatives sign a formal 'Adoption Agreement' under which they were said to be liable for financial reimbursement if they reclaimed the child. The Society was well aware that it would have no effect in law: Behlmer, *Friends of the Family*, 298. Section 4 of that Act and other legislation of the period preserved the parent's right to determine the religion of the child, even where not awarded custody.

[97] The courts would take very different views of his exploits: *R v. Barnardo* (1889) 23 QBD 305; *R v. Barnardo* [1891] 1 QB 194; *Barnardo v. McHugh* [1891] AC 388; *Barnardo v. Ford* [1892] AC 326. He had earlier confessed proudly to having engaged in the philanthropic abduction of 47 stray children.

[98] Poor Law Act 1889, s 1; Poor Law Act 1899, s 1.

[99] It became an offence to do so: 1899 Act, s 2.

[100] An attempt had been instituted half a century before, by the Infant Felons Act 1840 (3 & 4 Vict. c. 90), to use Chancery itself as the means of securing a 'fit person' order; but it seems that the process was not used.

acquire their various powers over the fate of children in danger, they had to face objections about how they exercised their powers—of which their refusal to comply with the father's or mother's demand for return of the child was just one aspect. To act properly they often needed information about family background and previous record and they might fail to obtain it.

While the children's homes and the guardians might have their own investigating officers, the courts—and particularly the magistrates' courts—had no such in-built machinery. From the 1870s the religious denominations had been sending voluntary workers—'missionaries'—to some summary courts, notably the Police Courts of the Metropolis. Stipendiaries and justices had consulted them; and soon enough their reports were being sought and relied upon—in many instances concerning juvenile offenders. Out of this beginning the formal probation service would build up.[101] Sentencing to probation, with its intrusive home visiting by officers, would become a standard measure for dealing with relatively minor offenders and vagrants. The magistracy, as previously noted, was also acquiring power to order maintenance to be paid by deserting husbands to their families. In this the guardians might also be involved indirectly, since they might make poor relief for a wife and children dependent on her obtaining a maintenance order against the husband and trying to have it enforced.[102] Investigation was melding into decision-making and then into consequential action. The process could seem both intrusive and alienating to those on the receiving end, appearing sometimes to blame the whole family.[103] An all-purpose function was returning to the magistracy regarding children which had strong echoes of their eighteenth-century powers and practices.

With this was associated one legal issue of structural significance. The NSPCC and its associates urged that a distinct juvenile court should be created within the system of magistrates' courts, with its own premises or room and a stipendiary or justices nominated for the work. This would demonstrate that criminal defendants and others before the court were being dealt with in their own best interests, rather than as part of some impersonal, invariate treadmill of deterrence. It would keep them away from the contaminating and alienating potential of contact with adult criminals. The Children Act 1908 took up this cry, in a terse section requiring their setting up within every court of summary jurisdiction and permitting wholly separate juvenile courts within the net of London Police Courts. Thus began the Juvenile Court system on a wave of good intention, but,

[101] It was created by the Probation of Offenders Act 1907.
[102] See above, pp. 798.
[103] The strength of such reactions is well explored by Behlmer, *Friends of the Family*, Ch. 5.

as Behlmer argues, with much less precision about the objectives justifying the separate structure.[104]

Even in the years before the First World War, while the new courts were getting under way, there were public arguments over what they were really for. These would intensify in the post-War years. Among leading advocates of the new scheme, William Clark Hall, stipendiary at the Old Street Court on the fringes of the City of London, crusaded for his own vision of their future. Even in handling youngsters accused of serious offences, the approach of the judge should be to win their respectful confidence and so become an inspiration guiding them on the path to an honest, industrious life. Accordingly, retribution for the crime and deterrence through the threat of punishment should give place to a paternal concern for the miscreant's future. In searching for answers, reliance should be placed not on the law's requirements so much as expertise from the new mental sciences—psychiatry, psychoanalysis, and psychology. Much would also depend on building a corps of probation officers and youth workers, who would bear the month-by-month brunt of trying to keep youngsters out of trouble and in training for a decent life. This could be achieved in part through activities at 'settlements' and school requirements, but, in many cases, it involved the intrusive business of home visits and therefore knowledge of the family as a whole, which caused considerable resentment. Clark Hall's own sources of inspiration were Americans such as the publicity-conscious Ben Lindsey of Denver.[105] His own background gave him the missionary zeal of Christian Socialism and involvement in university and church settlements in the slums of cities. Clarke Hall exuded an earnest personal charisma—in his court, his writings, and his many public offices.[106] He was indeed typical of many church and charity leaders of his era.[107] He opened his court to show visitors from around the world what could be achieved. He would rank among the paragons of forceful virtue who shaped the early years of modern social work in Britain.

In the post-War period, Clark Hall's novel ideas would in some measure be reinforced. For instance, with adult women at last being admitted into the parliamentary franchise, and also to serve on juries and the justices' bench, in London the juvenile bench consisted of a police magistrate and two JPs from a

---

[104] Behlmer, *Friends of the Family*, Ch. 5 is a mine of information about the whole movement.

[105] The first children's court in the Empire (Adelaide, 1890) aroused no interest 'at home', where attention was on the rapid developments in parts of the United States.

[106] His books included: *Law Relating to Children* (1894); *The Queen's Reign for Children* (1897); and *The State and the Child* (1917).

[107] He was closely linked to his father-in-law, Benjamin Waugh—implacable secretary of the NSPCC.

special list, one of them a woman.[108] But the plan would run into bitter criticism in the course of its enactment, not least from stipendiaries, who saw it as an attack on their independence of judgment and long experience. Among such reactionary forces were civil servants such as Sir Edwin Troup of the Home Office, who railed against listening to 'foolish persons who have dabbled a little in the obscene publications of Freud and his School'.[109] One significant consequence would be the retention of a retributive element in the disposal of juvenile offenders. The comparative seriousness of the offence would still rank in deciding the length of separation from family, school, and a free life.

There is a danger of assuming that the development of legal structures to deal with refractory and neglected children of itself led to their success in practice. With juveniles, the chance of achieving some transformation in their personalities and lives seemed inherently strong; and the conditions from which they were being rescued could be inhumanly bleak. In the resilient efforts for child rescue in pre-1914 England, much must be accounted good. It disfigures the story to present it, in Foucaultian fashion, as an unrelenting exercise in social control through legal and administrative powers, on a scale quite unknown. Inevitably—as we see from today's scandals as much as from investigations of the past—in welfare work there are always those in charge whose motives are far from the altruistic benevolence which inspires the best work. There will always be those who relish control over those with less intelligence and knowledge, or who are driven by sexual or sadistic urges, or who show the lazy insolence of neglect. A history must not ignore their occurrence or the account will be unduly triumphalist. In the end, however, those who weigh the evidence have somehow to balance the instances of malfunction against the comparative benefits of the system. The view of the social historian, James Walvin, is that 'the British child in 1949 was incomparably better cared for than its great-grandparents had been. And in this the law had played a major and formative role.'[110] Since the law's impact has primarily been in dealing with the unfortunates of the ordinary population that judgment is encouraging.

[108] Sex Disqualification (Removal) Act 1919, s 1; Juvenile Courts (Metropolis) Act 1920.
[109] Speech text, 1923, quoted by Behlmer, *Friends of the Family*, 259–60.
[110] J. Walvin, *A Child's World*, 168–9.

VI
Insanity and Mental Deficiency

1. INTRODUCTION

Across every generation, those who do not exhibit the mental capacities that pass for rationality all too readily activate 'the leaven of the dark ages'.[1] Whatever the nature of their mental incapacity, their distressing condition can at best arouse tender care, mostly thanks to the compassion of their close family. At worst it brings out a fearful or aggressive antagonism that may have dreadful consequences for the sufferer. In historical terms, the problems were unlikely to be relieved by human intervention, at least until the evolution of modern psychiatric understanding and drug therapy. If the condition was episodic, explanations for the periods of respite were very difficult to identify; likewise predictions about their recurrence. So Britain learned in the sad instance of George III. In earlier times the mad were all too readily spurned as being possessed by the devil, religion prescribing rituals of exorcism to bring about a rescue. By the eighteenth century, doctors had largely replaced priests, bringing their regimens of incarceration, physical restraint (straitjackets, leg and neck irons, chains and so forth), bleeding, constricted diet or starvation, induced vomiting, herbal nostrums, beatings, and solitary confinement. Such treatments tended to be carried out in physical conditions that varied from the spartan to the zoo-like, and could well be accompanied by gross abuses from the keepers.[2]

Those without the ability to understand the meanings or the expectations of ordinary life were very different from children in need. Childhood remained in the memory of adults as a shared experience. The young who became social problems presented a special chance for improvement of character and capacities and that hope underlay all the earnest Victorian pressure for education, home-finding, and institutional reformation that were reviewed at the end of the

---

[1] The phrase was Sir Andrew Halliday's; for whom see below, n. 32.

[2] See, in general, K. Jones, *Asylums and After: A Revised History of the Mental Health Services from the Early Eighteenth Century to the 1990s* (1993); A. T. Scull, *The Most Solitary of Afflictions: Madness and Society in Britain 1700–1900* (New Haven, 1993); R. Porter, *Madmen: A Social History of Madhouses, Mad-doctors and Lunatics* (Stroud, 2004); P. Bartlett, 'Legal Madness in the Nineteenth Century' (2001) 14 *Social History of Medicine*, 107—31.

previous Chapter.[3] For those that the Victorians labelled 'mad', 'insane', 'lunatic', 'demented', 'senile', 'idiotic', 'imbecile', or 'of unsound mind', what could be done except to keep them in physical conditions where they would not harm themselves or others? That at least might save them from the worst indignities of hunger, incarceration, and exposure to the public,[4] that had been all too often their fate in the early modern period. The hard fact remained that it was very difficult to relate their various conditions to strategies for improving their mental health.

2. LEGAL OBLIGATIONS AND THE MENTALLY DISTURBED OR DEFICIENT

The public preoccupation with people lacking mental capacity revolved around their treatment in institutions, whether those institutions were themselves private or public.[5] Before tackling those questions, however, we must say something of the common law's approach to their disability in relation to the workings of its general rules. Sir William Markby was one who remarked on the paucity of direct precedents as 'a matter on which one is surprised to find our law books nearly silent'.[6] With one exception, this seems right. The exception concerned the insanity of a testator at the time of executing a will. Allegations that the person was not capable of understanding what he or she was doing had to be made out by those attacking the validity of the instrument. They might succeed by showing such 'disorder of the mind [as] shall poison his affections, pervert his sense of right, or prevent the exercise of his natural faculties'.[7] The issue went most often to the ecclesiastical courts under their jurisdiction to grant probate of the will; then after 1857 to the Probate Court.[8]

So far as concerned the insane person's own rights, there was little need to alter the operation of general rules. As a victim of crime, he or she did not need to be the prosecutor, for others could act in that capacity. The main difficulty could be evidential—because, for instance, the victim could not give a coherent,

---

[3] Above, Ch. V. 4.

[4] One way of raising funds for keeping them was to exhibit them to the public in order to be ridiculed and baited, as happened with the Georgian inmates of London's Bethlem Hospital: see also below, n. 28.

[5] For the effect of insanity on criminal liability, see above, 234–57.

[6] *Elements of Law* (1885), 131. One of the difficulties of definition was that mental defect was somewhat differently defined for each legal category—crime, contract, testament, property transfer, and so on: see H. M. R. Pope, *Treatise on the Law and Practice of Lunacy* (2nd edn,1890), 21–2.

[7] Cockburn CJ, *Banks* v. *Goodfellow* (1870) LR 5 QB 549. For case law on this subject and on the avoidance of conveyances and other grants *inter vivos*: see *The Digest* (3rd re-issue, 2007) xxxiv, 121–34.

[8] See Vol. XI, pp. 610–13, 733–42.

or a credible, account of what had happened. If the incapacitated person suffered from the commission of a tort or breach of contract, then an action on his or her behalf could be instituted by a committee appointed by Chancery to attend to matters of property, or else by a next friend.[9] The mental state of the plaintiff played no role in the primary definition of many torts, although it could affect the operation of defences, such as contributory negligence or voluntary assumption of risk, which might well be excused by insanity.[10] Likewise, it was apparently rare for a lunatic who, despite having no understanding of the nature of the wrong or its effect on his actions, to seek redress for breach of the contract into which he appeared to enter. One case, however, where the lunatic, or someone relying on his conduct, might seek to assert rights was the contract of marriage; and there the special nature of the voluntary union for life led to it being treated as void *ab initio*, whichever party subsequently objected.[11]

Questions of the insane person's liability were more often in point. So far as criminal law was concerned, the test of whether the insane had the *mens rea* necessary to be found guilty was made to turn on whether they could appreciate the nature and consequences of their act through being able to tell right from wrong.[12] In tort, insanity might abrogate any liability that turned either on deliberate or negligent conduct; but the matter was less clear, for instance, when an insane innkeeper lost a guest's goods, since his liability was strict.[13] Then the issue might be whether the concept of 'inevitable accident' could give rise to an excuse.[14]

As to contractual liability, nice issues could arise. Roman law and civilian systems followed the simple formula, which could be comfortably accommodated within notions of will theory. A person accused of contractual breach would not be liable for it if he or she was not able to consent to the obligation when otherwise it would have arisen.[15] English judges, however, turned to a different approach, which in its way showed a decided reluctance to accept all

---

[9] *Beall* v. *Smith* (1873) LR 9 Ch App 85.

[10] So argued, with ingenuity and good sense, by W. G. H. Cook, *Insanity and Mental Deficiency in Relation to Legal Responsibility* (1921), 53–60.

[11] See e.g. *Hancock* v. *Peaty* (1866) LR 1 P&D 335; *Durham* v. *Durham* (1885) 10 PD 80; Pope, *Law of Lunacy*, 270–5; Cook, *Insanity*, Ch. 4.

[12] J. P. Eigen's *Witnessing Insanity: Madness and Mad-doctors in the English Court* (New Haven, 1995) investigates the history of medical evidence concerning the insanity of the accused in criminal trials in the period 1760–1843.

[13] As had been held in *Cross* v. *Andrews* (1598) Cro. Eliz. 622.

[14] Cook, *Insanity*, 20–34, argued strongly for this solution.

[15] Cook, *Insanity*, 61–74, provides considerable evidence for this. It was a separate question whether to impose some form of quasi-contractual obligation to pay for benefits actually received. Thus the Sale of Goods Act 1893, s 3, imposed an obligation to pay a reasonable price for goods supplied,

the implications of that theory.[16] In this view, everything turned on the understanding of the party alleging the contract: if that person knew that the other party was 'so insane as not to be capable of understanding what he was about', then, but then alone, there would be no binding obligation.[17]

This could be regarded as an extreme example of instrumentalism, in which commercial appearances would override any sympathy for the insane person, save where the plaintiff could not honestly maintain his position. But, as early contributions to the *Law Quarterly Review* argued, the common law rule was capable of more subtle and practical justification, which reflected the distinctions that medical experts might draw when giving evidence about types of mental disturbance.[18] This rule would prevent contractual liability from arising in the most evident cases, where the insane person was shown to have no real understanding of the world around him whatsoever. The tendency of the simple civilian rule may indeed have been to confine the excuse to such cases.[19] But what was to happen where the person had a mind distorted by strange obsessions or other unreal beliefs only on certain subjects, or was a person whose lunacy waxed and waned, perhaps with the phases of the moon? In those intermediate, tricky cases, the English rule put the burden of showing sufficient peculiarity in the conduct of the person claiming insanity to put the other party on notice of his or her lack of mental capacity. The rule would after all not operate in isolation. In many circumstances, there could be a question of undue influence by the other contracting party, or some other unfair taking of advantage amounting to what was called 'equitable fraud'; if shown, the transaction could be avoided if the parties could be restored to their original position.[20] There were a host of relationships relating to property transactions in which the effect of the insanity of one of the parties might lead to avoidance of the normal legal consequences of the dealings that had apparently occurred, provided that *restitutio in integrum* remained possible.[21]

provided that (as with infants) they constituted necessaries for the person concerned at the time: see also *re Rhodes* (1890) 44 Ch D 107. See also below, n. 20.

[16] See Pope, *Law of Lunacy*, 252–64.

[17] See esp. *Brown* v. *Randall* (1827) M. & M. 105; Patteson J., *Molton* v. *Camroux* (1849) 4 Ex. 17; Esher MR, *Imperial Loan* v. *Stone* [1891] 1 QB 601; *Daily Telegraph* v. *McLaughlin* [1904] AC 776, JC; *The Digest* (above, n. 7), 109–21; Cook, *Insanity*, 74–90.

[18] H. Goudy, 'Contracts by Lunatics' (1901) 17 *LQR* 147; R. Wilson, 'Lunacy in relation to Contract, Tort and Crime' (1902) 18 *LQR* 21. Wilson, however, noted in this context the growing dissatisfaction of psychiatric doctors with the reluctance of judges to accept that a person who in one sense knew that what he was doing was wrong, nonetheless was overpowered by mental impulses to do it.

[19] So Wilson suggests: *ibid.*, 21–2.

[20] See Vol. XII, 414–15.

[21] See e.g. Pope, *Law of Lunacy*, Pt II.

3. DETENTION AND RELEASE

The law affecting those mentally incapacitated nonetheless became bulky during our period and much of its flesh had to do with administering the regimes under which they would be kept. Lawyers, medical personnel, managers of institutions, and others needed instruction on their legal powers and responsibilities, as is evidenced by the considerable growth in legal texts on the subject.[22] Of all the issues, the most basic was institutional restraint, since it involved such a gross infraction of personal freedom. With the obviously deranged, it was not difficult to conclude that any refusal by them to be locked away would have to be overridden; but in less evident cases, the question of involuntary detention could be very difficult. By the eighteenth century, procedures of a sort had emerged for certifying the individual as deranged enough to need admission to a madhouse or asylum.[23] The individual or a person acting for him or her could afterwards proceed upon a writ of *habeas corpus* to secure release. Relatives pursuing their own interests, whether to free themselves from their burden or to get their clutches on property, might thus be found to have put away a person who then fought successfully to demonstrate sanity and secure release.[24] Such scenarios would continue to play upon the susceptibilities of the public, giving rise to scandals that might trigger reviews of the whole practice of incarceration.

Private Madhouses

As with other aspects of family life that had become dysfunctional, in our period statutory schemes would increasingly seek to regulate both private and public institutions for those of unsound mind. When individuals were placed in an institution, where they were sent depended largely on their social position. If they were born or brought up among the propertied, they might find themselves kept somewhere within their family. Otherwise they might be put into private asylums or homes for the demented—business activities that grew profitable under the

---

[22] In addition to Pope, already mentioned, note J. S. Stock, *Practical Treatise on the Law of* Non Compotes Mentis (1838); L. Shelford, *Practical Treatise on the Law Concerning Lunatics, Idiots, and Persons of Unsound Mind* (2nd ed., 1849); C. P. Phillips, *Law Concerning Lunatics, Idiots and Persons of Unsound Mind* (1858); W. Wood, *Insanity and the Lunacy Law* (1878); D. P. Fry, *Law Relating to Lunacy and Mental Deficiency* (1914).

[23] See below, 828.

[24] One well-remembered case had led to the release of a Mrs D'Vebre from the Chelsea madhouse in which her husband had placed her: *R* v. *Turlington* (1761) 2 Burr. 1115. Lord Mansfield found in her 'not the least appearance of insanity'. He refused to return her to her husband because of 'the danger apprehended by her from him'. Later the pair agreed to separate.

conditions of urban living.[25] In either case, the physical needs of such people and their supervision might be supported by funding from the family or elsewhere. The process of commitment could be initiated by petition to the Lord Chancellor who would then order a medical opinion on the basis of which he might entrust the person to the care of a 'committee'. The Chancellor did not, however, have power, as he had over children, to make them his ward, thus undertaking or supervising the management of their property.[26] At most, he could assure himself that financial arrangements necessary to support the commitment were in place. In any case, many commitments to private madhouses were arranged without any reference to Chancery but simply by contract between the family and its proprietor, based upon the certificate of a doctor or apothecary. This could be in the crudest form until statutes began to prescribe formalities, requiring examination by a medical man appointed by two justices.[27]

Private institutions could be run in bestial fashion, even by the standards of their own day. An initial Madhouses Act of 1774 had provided for the inspection of these homes in London and its surrounds by investigative Commissioners, who were to be members of the Royal College of Physicians.[28] As scandalous as the worst madhouses appeared to be, the only sanction provided against recalcitrant operators was a posting of the Commissioners' findings at the College. This was a world of nascent professionalism, where good money could be had from the travails of 'mad-doctoring'. Viewing control over madhouses by Oliver MacDonagh's schema of administrative reform,[29] what clearer instance could there be that horror at a situation would achieve very little. Indeed, instituting a public scheme of inspection might well amount to no more than conscience-scratching. In 1828, the powers given to the Royal College for the Metropolis were replaced by setting up a body of Commissioners appointed by the Home Secretary.[30] Among their duties, they were to issue licences to madhouse operators, inspect the asylums four times a year, recommend refusal or revocation of a licence, and release individuals who were confined without justification. For the

---

[25] For early texts, see A. Highmore, *Treatise on the Law of Idiocy and Lunacy* (1807); G. D. Collinson, *Treatise on the Law Concerning Idiots, Lunatics, and Other Persons* non compos mentis (1812).

[26] See James LJ, *Beall* v. *Smith* (1873) LR 9 Ch App 85, 92—a case in which a Chancery committee was found to have exceeded its powers; and see Pope, *Law of Lunacy*, 24.

[27] Pauper asylums would be given a standard *pro forma* in 1819: see 59 & 60 Geo. III c. 127.

[28] 14 Geo. III c.49. Despite its notoriety, Bethlem (or Bedlam) Hospital in London, which allowed visitors to be entertained by looking at the wild, chained creatures within, managed to keep officials from inspecting it regularly until 1853.

[29] For which see above, 606–9.

[30] Madhouses Act 1828, 7 Geo. IV c. 34. After 1845, the Commissioners were re-christened Masters in Lunacy.

provinces, regular visitations by groups of two justices and a medical officer were instigated and given similar powers.

Poor Law Asylums

People from the lower orders with difficulties of comprehension or lack of behavioural control might also be kept at home, often imposing grave strains on the emotional and financial resources of their family. If not, they would fall to be dealt with under the public poor law or some charitable alternative to it. During the eighteenth century, the overseers of the poor had rarely provided any separate institutional arrangement for lunatics or the mentally deficient. Pauper lunatics were all too frequently bundled in among those others who were dealt with as vagrants and subjected to incarceration in bridewells (houses of correction); or they might be placed in county or borough gaols, the horrors of which were coming under growing criticism.[31] This fate might equally befall people of means, who had lost their financial resources, perhaps by virtue of their mental condition. In 1807, a Commons Select Committee, with leading Evangelicals such as Wilberforce and Whitbread prominent among its membership, had set about establishing how many lunatics and idiots were held as paupers in poor law institutions. They received grossly underscored answers from many of those in charge, but nonetheless they were moved by what they uncovered.[32] This new stirring of concern then resulted in the County Asylums Act 1808, which gave the justices of the peace in Quarter Sessions power to establish such asylums and then to appoint a committee for their inspection. The overseers of the poor had to notify them of the admission of lunatics.[33] The institutions were to provide separate accommodation for men and women, and for convalescents and incurables. They were to be healthy and airy and the arrangements might provide for medical assistance. As with the private madhouses of London, the voluntary nature of the enactment achieved little. Yet the justices would not be placed under any systematic obligation for another 20 years.

By this stage, however, there were political, medical, and other influential reformers anxious to keep the condition of lunatics regularly on the public agenda,

---

[31] KS. Criminal Lunatics Act 1800. The power to deal with lunatics as vagrants came from the Vagrancy Acts of 1714 and 1744, 13 Anne c. 26 and 14 Geo. II c. 5. The insane who committed criminal acts could be detained at the monarch's pleasure under the Criminal Lunatics Act 1800, 39 & 40 Geo, III c. 94; see above, p. 235.

[32] The evidence was collected by the leading physician, Sir Andrew Halliday. He would remain much interested in lunacy reform and would publish an influential account of early findings and reforms in his *General View of the Present State of Lunatics and Lunatic Asylums* (1828). See also Jones, *Asylums*, Ch. 3; Scull, *Museums of Madness*, Ch. 2; W. L. Parry-Jones, *The Trade in Lunacy* (1972).

[33] 48 Geo. III c. 96.

whether they were held in public or private institutions. Select Committees of 1815 and 1816 gathered horrible instances of what could happen.[34] At the time some attention was being conferred on the regime established by William Tuke and his son, Daniel, at the Quaker Retreat at York.[35] This gained some international renown for its practice of 'moral' treatment in place of physical clamping, those in charge of the inmates working to give patients as much freedom as their condition allowed to realize their capacities as human beings. The prevailing tone of generosity and positive encouragement arose naturally from the general culture of the Society of Friends; and only Quakers could be admitted to the Retreat as patients. The regimen required much more commitment to the welfare of inmates, and therefore to expenditure on the institutional accoutrements and staffing. It was never to be an easy model to get others to emulate, but slowly basic conditions for decent treatment began to be required. In part this would follow from the thoroughly Benthamic requirement of proper records of admission, steps taken in the daily routine, and discharge, all of which could then be inspected by those appointed to visit.

The administrative history of mental institutions was accordingly shaped by a persistent drive to raise the standards of care within them. The battle was maintained by a core of Evangelically-minded enthusiasts who would fight long battles against, on the one hand, the madhouse-keepers, most of them doctors of some sort with a likely eye on profits; and on the other, overseers of the poor (and then the guardians), keen to cap the growing demands on the poor rate. A new inquiry in 1827 produced legislation that did something to put inspection by outsiders in place simply to empower managers who might be willing to improve conditions.[36] The results were an extended patchworking of what had gone before.

As already mentioned, the Madhouse Act replaced the old powers given to members of the College of Physicians to inspect private houses in the London Metropolis, with a statutory body of Commissioners—five of them physicians and ten who were not, only the former being paid.[37] The young Lord Ashley (later Shaftesbury) was among the first lay Commissioners and he became the leading advocate of improvement in mental establishments until his death almost 60 years later.

---

[34] See the reports of SCs on Madhouses, PP 1814 (296), iv, 801; 1816 (227, 398, 451), vi, 249 et seq. The reformers, however, did not achieve any immediate action.

[35] In 1813, Daniel Tuke published his Description of the Retreat, an Institution near York for Insane Persons of the Society of Friends; see A. Digby, Madness, Morality and Medicine (Cambridge, 1985). See further, below, 833–4.

[36] SC Report on Pauper Lunatics in Middlesex and Lunatic Asylums, PP 1826–7 (557), vi, 75.

[37] For the position under the New Poor Law, see above, 495–6.

The County Asylums Act 1828 placed the pauper institutions for the mentally ill and deficient under similar systems of admission, inspection, and release, by giving over responsibility to the same set of Commissioners for the Metropolis and placing justices nominated by their Quarter Sessions to carry out equivalent functions in the provinces. Under the two 1828 Acts, those who inspected were responsible for making regular reports to the Home Secretary. So it was that county asylums were set up, unnecessary restraints were cut down, measures of work and exercise were introduced to occupy patients who could manage them, and diet was improved, to a level somewhat above that for ordinary paupers in deterrent workhouses. From that turning point, every 15–20 years there would be new pressure to review what was going on in mental institutions.[38] More of the asylums came to be provided by the justices, until eventually they passed into the responsibility of the new County and County Borough Councils, created in 1888. As the century passed, the number of private madhouses declined.[39]

The ultimate outcome was the Lunacy Act 1890, an unwieldy consolidation of 342 sections, which returned to the old fear that strange and eccentric people would be swept into institutional care for the rest of their lives mainly on the say-so of those who, for whatever reason, did not want the responsibility of caring for them personally, and of medical men who might have an interest in them as patients or as financial sources. The public had a keen appetite for press reports about such conduct and often enough there were people obsessed with the dangers, whether from their own experience or not. In 1845 an Alleged Lunatics Friend Society was set up. Decades later, the redoubtable Mrs Georgiana Weldon lit the skies with her burning story. She had separated from her husband, Harry (much later Sir Henry), and was living in her own house,[40] when, in 1878, he sought to have her placed in a private asylum as a lunatic. But while the forcing party, made up of distinguished medical figures, was seeking to get in her front door, she had the aid of the Secretary of the Alleged Lunatics Friend Society in escaping from the back, disguised as a nun. Once she became entitled to sue in her own name,[41] she moved into splatter-gun mode with writs, and appearances in person, alleging torts, such as trespass, false imprisonment and defamation. Her targets were Harry, his collaborators in this great outrage, and editors who

[38] SC Reports on the Regulation of Care and Treatment of Lunatics in England, *PP* 1845 (373, 408, 694), xv, 183, 408, 289; leading to the Lunacy Act 1845, 8 & 9 Vict. c. 100, s 90; Operation of Acts for the Care of Lunatics and their Property, *PP* (1859), iii, 75.

[39] Inspection of single lunatics kept for profit would be instituted by the Lunacy Act 1845, 8 & 9 Vict. c. 100, s 90; but the Commissioners gained power to visit those kept at home or elsewhere without payment only in 1890 by the Lunacy Act, ss 198–200.

[40] For her rights to the house, because it was bought with her earnings, see above, 760, n. 19.

[41] By the Married Women's Property Act 1882, s 1.

took up the story.[42] In consequence, parliamentary and public agitation on the subject would remain to the fore.

Selborne, Herschell, and Halsbury, Lord Chancellors of the period, were of one mind on the question of involuntary admission: there must be a magistrates' court order, rather than merely certification by doctors and supervision by the Lunacy Commission. It was also argued that lunacy orders should have time limits after which they would need to be renewed in court. Shaftesbury would feel so keenly the injustice of these criticisms that he resigned from chairmanship of the Commission. Eventually, the guarantee of the individual's liberty by interventionist court proceedings became law and was then incorporated into the statutory consolidation, the Lunacy Act 1890.[43] Doctors whose interests lay in psychiatric practice considered that they were being placed under rigid surveillance. They were hampered in seeking flexible and imaginative solutions for the many difficult cases that it was their lot to handle, often over long periods. There was a comparison to be made with the invariate regimes for the punishment of criminals, once the prisons were nationalized in 1877.[44] The object of lunatic asylums was not to suffuse the lesson of deterrence through the community as a whole, but rather to safeguard both the patients themselves and to prevent them from harming others. It was at this very period that discussion grew about how to deal with habitual criminals whose recidivism could be checked only so long as they remained locked up.

It was a period in which new lines of scientific inquiry were opening up, not least under the dark cloak of eugenic theory. Both mental illnesses and innate deficiencies were coming to be investigated as inherited conditions. The lack of sexual control among many with mental problems had long been evident, and as births proliferated within their family groups, they could be shown to produce high proportions of mental inadequates. The varied aetiology of different types of mental illness and inability became better identified. Serious attention was then given to the question whether innate feeblemindedness deserved not only its own regimes but even its own institutions.[45] A Royal Commission chaired by the Earl of Radnor recorded a great volume of evidence on the subject. It recommended

---

[42] She even hired the Royal Opera House as a venue to promote her cause: see Cretney, *Family*, 144–5; and she pursued Harry for restitution of conjugal rights: see above, Ch. IV, n. 4.

[43] To drive the point in, central supervision of the Lunacy Commissioners and the local authorities was passed to the Lord Chancellor's Department. But when the Commissioners' functions were generalized by the Mental Defectives Act 1913 and they became a Board of Control, direction would be transferred to the Home Office.

[44] See above, 164–8.

[45] In Britain, the work of Francis Galton did much to influence eugenic ideas about hereditary traits; see e.g. Jones, *Asylums*, 121–2.

that local authorities should be obliged to set up separate 'colonies' for the mentally deficient[46] (a description also used in the Unemployed Workmen's Act 1905 in providing for farm colonies for those out of work).[47] They would be educational in character, without regular medical supervision. The prevalent fear was that 'simple' girls put into them would be as susceptible to sexual advances as happened when they were left in the outside world. The Commission, however, baulked at the idea of sterilization. So segregation by gender had to be an underlying rule in the establishments and the Mental Deficiency Act 1913 provided a new statutory frame.[48]

In the event the removal of the mentally deficient from the poor law asylums proved slow and far from encouraging. Those in charge of custodial institutions for both the insane and the mentally inadequate continued to face intractable problems of day-by-day, year-by-year management. The quality of staff they could hope to secure only became worse as war set in. The sheer numbers being received into the asylums had been increasing for decades with little enough respite. Some of the institutions held more than 2000 inmates. Families seemed to lose whatever willingness they had shown in earlier generations to cope by themselves. Many medical men and asylum administrators complained bitterly about the straitjacket of legal conditions surrounding the admission and care of mental patients. They felt that their professional training and experience equipped them to know what best to do. But the libertarian strain in the make-up of Victorian society in Britain insisted that compulsory admission to a mental institution be supervised by outsiders in the community who were based within the legal system: hence the supervisory role of the magistracy.

It would be another half-century before pharmaceutical treatment began to allow an exodus out of incarceration and back to life in freedom. The idea of care in the community came to be welcomed by many across the political spectrum. In Britain it was the Conservative Minister of Health, Enoch Powell, who in 1961 would carry through the necessary legislation. From a range of perspectives, the very idea of being able to distinguish between the mad and the sane was by then being questioned. History would be put to the task. Using a technique of worst-case story-telling, Michel Foucault would condemn even the humane efforts of

[46] *PP* 1908 [Cd. 4202], xxxix, 159. For the very considerable evidence, see Cds 4203–15.

[47] See above, p. 718.

[48] In 1886, an Idiots Act had given local authorities the power to set up separate institutions for idiots and imbeciles. Where they chose this route, the institutions became subject to licence and inspection by the Lunacy Commissioners. Since the Act was promoted by Shaftesbury and the Charity Organisation Society, it gave some answer to the contemporary criticism of the Lunacy Commissioners aroused by the *Weldon* case.

the Quakers at the York Retreat for their attempts to build upon the capacities of their patients where possible. He denounced them for using the upright, orderly bourgeois family as a fearsome model.[49] In this Part we have, of course, seen enough of the rigid paternalism of Victorian home-life to realize how life-enhancing it has since been to adopt a more egalitarian set of relationships within families, not least in terms of the law. But to shovel the task of treating the mentally disabled into that mould of criticism, without trying to understand the scale and difficulty of dealing with such intractable people, is to risk ridicule.

[49] *Folie et Déraison* (Paris, 1961), translated by R. Howard as *Madness and Civilisation* (New York, 1965), 242–51. For this example and more generally, see e.g. Jones, *Asylums*, 30–1, 170–5.

VII
Foreign Elements in Family Disputes

In dealing with the emergence of English private international law,[1] discussion of the principles applying to family relationships was postponed until this Chapter. To a particular degree the conflicts of law in resolving family disputes reflect differences of social structure, religion, attitudes to paternal power, and legal tradition. Assumptions and beliefs about family relations vary so much from country to country that they soon generate mutual misunderstanding. Rarely can family law rules simply be transposed from one system to another.[2] When differences between family laws arise in litigation, legal systems are likely to be protective of their home position and suspicious of foreign laws that take a different line. Even within the UK, religious differences after the Reformation had given Scotland a laxer set of requirements for the celebration of marriage and a more complete form of judicial divorce than England, on top of which there were important differences over the legitimacy of children. The difficulties would increase where the measure of mutual trust between different countries was uncertain. The Victorian consensus remained, as with public international law, that conflicts rules could be formulated only within the compass of Europe's legal systems, when taken together with the Americas and other countries sharing its cultures through colonization and trade.

The pragmatic, utilitarian thrust of English private international law, as it emerged during the nineteenth century—captured in the label 'comity'—meant an absence of commitment either to territory or to person as the presumptive organizing idea of the whole field. Comity embodied notions of mutual respect between legal systems. This at least suggested a certain preference for applying the same law to the solution of a legal issue, and for recognizing the decisions of foreign courts, particularly where they were following a parallel course to that on which an English court would take jurisdiction over a dispute with a foreign element and were applying the law that an English court would also apply. Nonetheless the combinations of foreign and local elements could weave patterns

[1] See above, Vol. XI, Part 1, Ch IX.
[2] See O. Kahn-Freund, 'Uses and Abuses of Comparative Law' (1974) 37 *MLR* 1–27.

too various to provide ready-made solutions. Nowhere was that more evident than in respect of family matters. In this sphere one can observe some growing readiness to accord some place to foreign laws and the decisions of foreign courts. But the basis on which those courts took jurisdiction was still a matter of caution and suspicion; and English courts were ready to insist that the principles embedded in foreign laws should be subject always to basic policies of English law.

1. DOMICIL

The notion of a personal law borne by each individual from country to country inevitably took some hold in relation to families and in this sphere it forms a prominent part of English doctrine, as it does in other countries. The concept that came most immediately to express this connection was domicil. As we have seen, Victorian writers and judges on private international law devoted great effort to defining their view of the concept, for reasons that were partly ideological and partly jurisdictional.[3] At root domicil differed from nationality because it was a personal attribute, not a concession from the state concerned.[4] The modern characteristics of domicil became settled only as the nineteenth century ran on. Eventually it was accepted that a person always had a domicil, but at a given time only one—and that for all purposes. The common law ascribed domicil at birth, legitimate children acquiring their father's, and the illegitimate their mother's.[5] After reaching majority, most adults other than married women could change their domicil voluntarily.[6]

The courts, however, proved reluctant to say that army officers, administrators, and traders in the colonies or elsewhere had sloughed off their English domicil of origin without the clearest proof that they intended to remain permanently in their territory of service, even after their attachment ended.[7] By the new century, the House of Lords was ready to insist on clear proof of a 'final and deliberate intention' to abandon a domicil of origin through choice

---

[3] See Vol. XI, Pt 1, Ch. 9, where the necessity for such a concept within a federation of jurisdictions was emphasized.

[4] In mid-century some judges appeared to be considering a shift from domicil to nationality as the basis for personal law rules—see notably *Whicker* v. *Hume* (1858) 7 H.L. Cas. 124; *Moorhouse* v. *Lord* (1863) 10 H.L. Cas. 272; not, however, for long; e.g. *Shaw* v. *Gould* (1868) LR 3 H.L. 86; *Udny* v. *Udny* (1869) LR 1 Sc & Div 457.

[5] For details of a growing body of law, see e.g. Dicey, *Conflict of Laws* (1st edn, 1896), Ch. 2; J. Westlake, *Private International Law* (5th edn, 1912), Chs 2, 14 (and cf. 1st edn, 1858), Ch. 3.

[6] See Vol. XI, pp. 285–8.

[7] For a time in the nineteenth century, as part of the searchings for differentiations between situations, a category of Anglo-Indian domicil was in vogue for at least some of such people who served on the sub-continent: see Westlake, *Private International Law* (1st edn, 1858), 337–49.

of another country.[8] Therein lay much of the distinction from mere residence. From nationality, domicil was distinguished by an ability to change it even on arrival in the new territory, rather than waiting upon official processes; but the evidence of intention to acquire the new domicil had to be unequivocal. The good liberal's vigilance had to be as eternal in private affairs as in public life.

One category of people did not share in that freedom. When women married they were deemed, under the patriarchal notion of legal unity, to take their husband's domicil for the duration of the marriage. That fitted the Victorians' perception of family obligation structured around the husband's power of decision.[9] It made for simplicity, for instance, over questions of succession when a marriage of different nationals lasted until the death of one of them and the other claimed an inheritance. Given that most civilian systems adhered to regimes of matrimonial property, which in many circumstances secured portions of the deceased's estate to the surviving spouse and children, there could be very considerable differences from the common law regime of free disposition by will.

Equally there could well be differences on an intestacy. The distended case of *Birtwhistle* v. *Vardill*[10] concerned a Scots domiciliary who had been legitimated under Scots law by the subsequent marriage of his parents—an unknown prospect in English law.[11] In the end he was held unable to succeed to a freehold estate in England as 'heir', because the matter was one purely for English law. The majority of the House of Lords, led by counsel, opinions from the judges and their own learning through intricate histories of medieval practice, preferred the ancient runes of English feudality to the modernist morality of a personal law. The implication of the decision could well be that, wherever the land was situate, and whatever the point at issue, the *lex situs* alone determined the outcome in English litigation and a foreign judgment would be recognized only if it applied that law.

It would take nearly 70 years for the fire-power of the decision to be deflected, turning it into a particular rule of English law for a dispute over title to English land. Unswerving preference for the *lex situs* began then to wane. De Nicols, the Frenchman who made the Café Royal in Piccadilly Circus the resort of society, both grand and louche, died after changing his domicil from French to English. His wife claimed entitlements not just to his movables but even to his English freeholds. They had married in France under a matrimonial regime

---

[8] *Winans* v. *A.G.* [1904] AC 287.

[9] As to which, see above, pp. 729–30.

[10] Finally disposed of after many years: see (1826) 5 B. & C. 438; (1830) 2 Cl. & Fin. 571; (1835) 2 Cl. & Fin. 582; (1840) 7 Cl. & Fin. 895. Brougham failed in his vociferous campaigns to secure the opposite result.

[11] See above, p. 805.

which guaranteed her a share in all his property on his death. This was held to settle the question in the wife's favour, the subsequent change of domicil having no effect. So the House of Lords found in relation to the movable property, and Kekewich J. applied the same broad principle to the freeholds.[12]

2. MARRIAGE AND DIVORCE

The long-term tendency to uphold marriage but to impede divorce found note-worthy expression in conflicts rules. There was one preliminary question: what constituted a marriage at all in the eyes of common lawyers? Lord Penzance adhered to Christian doctrine for the answer: it was the single, life-long union of a man and a woman until the parting of death. A polygamous union, actual or potential, could not be regarded in an English court as a marriage, whether it was in the Mormon faith of Utah, or a Muslim community in Turkey, or whatever.[13] A partner in polygamy was therefore untouched by any of the legal consequences of marriage, from bigamy to inheritance.

When it came to the formalities of a marriage in the Christian sense, it had long been accepted in European legal systems generally that compliance was required with the law where the ceremony occurred, but not that of, for instance, the domicil of each party.[14] This provided simplicity and certainty and there-fore sat well with the desire to uphold marriages where that was what the couple intended.[15] English couples, one of whom was under age, might travel to be mar-ried by the blacksmith at Gretna Green or elsewhere in Scotland in order to avoid the requirement of parental consent under Lord Hardwicke's Act; their marriage would be upheld under English law. Where, on the other hand, a couple married in England in order to avoid having to comply with a severer requirement of parental consent in the domicil of one or both parties, English courts were more reluctant to override the objection.[16] Those who married by exchange of vows in far-off places where no Christian ceremony could be had, and then lived together,

---

[12] [1900] AC 21 (HL); [1900] 2 Ch 410. Kekewich J.'s judgment in favour of the wife in the movables action had been overruled by the CA, but restored by the HL; which gave him a certain authority as the judge hearing the immovables action.

[13] *Hyde* v. *Hyde* (1866) LR 1 P & D 130; and see e.g. *R* v. *Naguib* [1917] 1 KB 359 (Egyptian who mar-ried two women in English ceremonies committed bigamy during the second, even though he had previously been married by Moslem law in Egypt). Special arrangements for the British to be mar-ried in their embassies and consulates abroad, or by an appointed marriage officer, were allowed at common law and then under the Foreign Marriage Act 1892.

[14] J. Westlake, *Private International Law* (5h edn, 1912), 61–8.

[15] In England this had been settled early: *Scrimshire* v. *Scrimshire* (1752) 2 Hag. Con. 395.

[16] See *Simonin* v. *Mallac* (1860) 2 Sw. & Tr. 67, following a number of decisions of the Court of Delegates in the eighteenth century. A distinction was drawn, however, between cases where the foreign bar to the marriage was absolute; and those where lack of consent could have been overcome

were treated by the ecclesiastical courts as properly wed.[17] It was the need for such a rule that seems to have led to a later belief in the effectiveness of 'common law marriage' at home.[18]

The 1835 Act which annulled marriages prohibited by the Church of England's Canons applied no matter whether either of the parties had an English domicil.[19] In *Brook* v. *Brook*,[20] an English gentleman had taken his deceased wife's sister to Denmark in order to marry her there, as was allowed by Danish law. The couple then had three children; but after their own deaths, the House of Lords ruled the children illegitimate and so unable to inherit. Some judges would seek to avoid the undoubted severity of this rule. If the parties could have taken steps to avert the objection to their capacity to marry, their position might well be adjudged only by referring to the law of the country of celebration.[21]

The subjugacy of the wife's domicil could bear hard when the relationship splintered while both remained alive, leaving the wife in need of maintenance and perhaps a formal separation; or else (in those Protestant countries which allowed it) termination through divorce, together with orders for maintenance and arrangements for the children. So long as England had no regular system of complete divorce, the main conflicts issue was whether a foreign divorce would be recognized by English courts. The House of Lords, deciding *Lolley's case* in 1812, had accepted a resolution from the common law judges that the matter was one of substantive law and that no foreign divorce from an 'English marriage' would be recognized if it was on a ground that was not permitted for dissolution *a vinculo* in England.[22] Since this could only be a reference to parliamentary divorce, it showed how that procedure was coming to be considered essentially judicial.

The *Lolley* decision demonstrated how inchoate this branch of English law remained. What account was to be taken of the law of a place of celebration other than England, of changes in the husband's domicil at the different stages of the marriage, of the law of the place where a wife was abandoned by a straying husband, or any other possibility?[23] For much of the century, judgments would twist and turn as the courts learned how very different the laws concerning termination

by following a set procedure. In the latter case, the marriage was likely to be treated by the English court as valid.

[17] *Dalrymple* v. *Dalrymple* (1811) 2 Hag. Con. 54 (Sir William Scott).

[18] See above, 752.

[19] See above, 750.

[20] (1861) 9 HL Cas. 193.

[21] *Simonin* v. *Mallac* (1860) 2 Sw. & Tr. 67.

[22] (1812) Russ. & Ry. 237.

[23] Clarity was not aided by Brougham LC, who in *McCarthy* v. *Decaix* (1831) 2 Russ. & M. 614, quixotically announced himself bound by *Lolley* to hold that the dissolution of an 'English

of marriages were in Western countries.[24] In the 1880s, it emerged that a foreign divorce would be recognized in an English court only if granted in a court of the matrimonial domicil— in other words, the domicil of the husband at the time of the proceedings. It mattered no longer that the grounds for it did not exist in English or any other relevant law; and there was no rule specially protecting 'English marriages'.[25] Awkward questions would remain: while it was clear that residence abroad could not lead to a foreign divorce decree that English courts would recognize, what about jurisdiction assumed on the basis of the nationality of one or other party? What of the deserted wife, who sought relief in a foreign country where the husband had been domiciled, when he changed domicil as part of his move away from her?

These issues were not made easier to resolve by the introduction, in 1857, of an English proceeding in the Divorce Court. The legislation said nothing about the matter directly. The ecclesiastical courts had at most granted decrees *a mensa et thoro* which kept the marriage alive, but without the obligation to cohabit. Given the patchwork of ecclesiastical jurisdictions around the country, it seemed that a court would act if the claimant had the relevant local residence. Could that approach be carried over to the realm of divorce *a vinculo*? A Frenchman married an English wife in Gibraltar and then went alone to French consular duties in Newcastle-upon-Tyne. His wife, left to herself, committed adultery. A majority of the Court of Appeal held him entitled to an English divorce for her adultery, because previously he could have proceeded *a mensa* in the Bishop of Durham's Court, that being the jurisdiction of his residence.[26]

This would be a less severe rule than that applying to the recognition of foreign divorces. In dissent, Brett LJ considered that neither judicial separation nor full divorce petitions could be heard on the basis of residence in England. The contract of marriage affected status as ordained by law, not merely by the volition of the parties. Parliament could therefore not have intended the new court to intervene on so insubstantial a connection as residence. His view that domicil alone, in the strict English sense, entitled an English court to hear a

---

marriage' in a foreign court could never be recognized in England. At the same time he proceeded to denounce the outcome.

[24] Major differences are brought out in Phillips' *Putting Asunder* in a discussion of the prospects for a 'migratory divorce' through well-advised forum shopping, pp. 473–8.

[25] For this approach, Hannen P. was influential: see *Briggs* v. *Briggs* (1880) 5 PD 163; and upholding his judgment at first instance, *Harvey* v. *Farnie* (1882) 8 AC 43 (HL). For the intervening case law, see Westlake, *Private International Law* (5th edn), 101–3.

[26] *Niboyet* v. *Niboyet* (1878) 4 PD 1; doubted in *Le Mesurier* v. *Le Mesurier* [1895] AC at 536–7.

divorce petition was upheld in the Privy Council in *Le Mesurier* v. *Le Mesurier*.[27] Deciding the issue nominally in relation to the Roman-Dutch law of Ceylon,[28] the Scottish Law Lord, Watson, led a strongly conservative Judicial Committee through those English precedents which favoured the 'domicil only' approach; and he provided a penitential account of how Scottish courts had moved back from the idea that residence, or a lesser 'matrimonial domicil', could be sufficient.[29] Thus he brought the rule back into line with that for the recognition of foreign divorces.

The rule helped people to know where they stood. What, after all, could be worse than a marriage that was regarded as terminated in one country and continuing in another? But the decision glossed over the inevitable uncertainties of domicil. It took little account of the many European systems that called for a grant of nationality to establish a change of personal law. And it could have harsh consequences for the deserted wife who wanted a divorce decree of an English court from a husband who was then living abroad. Her one prospect was to bring proceedings in the courts of whatever country was his domicil, and that could be very difficult if she herself had returned to England. However, an English court would recognize a divorce granted by a court abroad which was not in the husband's domicil, when the courts of his domicil would themselves recognize the divorce.[30] Unless she had financial support from elsewhere, she was likely to face a grim future—penniless and in social terms a pariah. In the governing English perspective, divorce remained far too tense a subject for foreign precepts to play a part, even in cases where one party was in some sense foreign.

Britain played virtually no role in the early efforts of the Institut de Droit International and the Hague Conferences to establish Conventions on marriage, divorce, and guardianship of minors.[31] These were adopted by 12 European states in 1902 and were followed in 1905 by others on the relations of spouses, succession and wills, and guardianship of adults. Had that on divorce been

---

[27] [1895] AC 517.

[28] He cited Huber, Rodenburg, and von Bar to show that his approach was accepted in international law: see [1895] AC at 537–8.

[29] 'Matrimonial domicil'—a loose term—had been adopted as a variant on residence in *Jack* v. *Jack* 24 D 467 (1862).

[30] *Armitage* v. *AG* [1906] P 135—a good example of Gorell Barnes J.'s readiness to adopt a flexible approach. See also his decision in *Armytage* v. *Armytage* [1898] P 178, that an English court would grant an order of judicial separation on the basis of the petitioner's residence in England, no change of personal status being involved. He thus saved a wife from having to return under the husband's tutelage, where further physical attacks were to be expected.

[31] For this movement, see Vol. XI, p. 297.

adopted, jurisdiction could have been taken on the basis of nationality or domi-cil in the sense of non-temporary residence. The ground for divorce would have to exist in the law of nationality or nationalities of the partners and in the law of the forum, unless the latter excluded its own application. There would be a number of special rules to cope with deserted wives and the like. For Westlake, the failure to adhere to the Divorce Convention of 6 June 1902 showed how remarkably the English principles on the subject fell short of 'receiving univer-sal assent'.[32] The Gorell Commission argued for jurisdiction based on residence in parts of the British Empire; jurisdiction based on the wife's own domicil, when her husband's desertion entailed a change of his domicil; and for rec-ognition of foreign nullity awards, when a foreign court had taken jurisdic-tion under its own laws.[33] But nothing came even of these limited proposals. The eruption of full-scale war, with its great increase in matrimonial upsets, made no difference. The late Victorian constraints were set firm for most of the twentieth century.

3. FAMILY GOVERNANCE: CHILDREN

The English had strong legal ideas about the position of the husband and father as head of his family, which justified his use of a degree of physical coercion and gave him power of decision over a considerable range of family affairs. While during the later nineteenth century there were substantial changes in the law of matrimonial property and divorce, much remained of the old paternal domin-ance. The principles reflected common moral attitudes and, indeed, had about them the character of public policies shaped to fit the expectations of the domes-tic populace. A foreign element could enter family relationships, if an English court was asked to treat a father with foreign domicil or residence according to the law of that place; or a child's guardian or lunatic's custodian was appointed by a foreign court and sought to have the law of that place determine what he could or could not do in relation to his charge; or differences between laws arose as to the age of majority, or the legal disabilities that affected minors at particu-lar ages.[34]

By the time that Dicey wrote, a small corpus of decisions had set precedents on such questions. The judges were categorical: any order made by them would have effect on the conduct of the parties on English territory; English law alone

---

[32] Westlake, *Private International Law*, 104–5.

[33] PP 1912–13 [Cd. 6478], paras. 331–44, 348–9.

[34] Scotland provided a proximate example, since the law there treated those aged 13–14 as pupils and those aged 14–21 as minors. Of various consequences that followed, a minor was able to acquire a domicil of choice: see e.g. Macpherson, *Infants*, Ch. 43.

was to determine the outcome.[35] No legal consequences could formally attach in England to a foreign appointment of a guardian; the courts did, however, retain a discretion to reach an outcome that followed the position in the relevant foreign law.[36] Any idea, however, that in these close personal relationships individuals would be able to assert their foreign personal law as the norm governing their conduct in England was not open to contemplation. They had chosen to come and must abide by the legal consequences.

[35] Dicey, *Conflict*, Rules 127, 128, 130, 135–6.
[36] Dicey, *Conflict*, Rule 130.

Part Five

PERSONALITY RIGHTS AND INTELLECTUAL PROPERTY

I

Personal Reputation, Privacy, and Intellectual Creativity

IN 1890 there appeared in the young Harvard Law Review an article by Samuel Warren and Louis Brandeis which was to become one of most enduring pieces of scholarly enthusiasm in the common law tradition.[1] The writers advocated the recognition through case law of a 'right to privacy', which they posited as wholly appropriate to the state of development which advanced society had reached. They traced the gradual evolution of legal rights against gross infractions of life, liberty, and physical property to a condition in which 'the right to life has come to mean the right to enjoy life,—the right to be left alone; the right to liberty secures the exercise of extensive privileges; and the term "property" has grown to comprise every form of possession—intangible, as well as tangible'. Steps in this development included the law of libel and slander, actions for seduction of a wife or a daughter and 'the wide realm of intangible property, in the products and processes of the mind, as works of literature and art, goodwill, trade secrets and trademarks'.

This development of the law was inevitable. The intense intellectual and emotional life, and the heightening of sensations which came with the advance of civilisation, made it clear to men that only a part of the pain, pleasure, and profit of life lay in physical things. Thoughts, emotions, and sensations demanded legal recognition, and the beautiful capacity for growth which characterizes the common law enabled the judges to afford the requisite protection, without the interposition of the legislature.[2]

Their progressivist tone was optimistic, but it was matched by the vigour with which they then attacked the great new evil in their sights—the gossip-mongering of the popular press. Their denunciation had a powerful rhetorical flow and a grand culmination:

Easy of comprehension, appealing to that weak side of human nature which is never wholly cast down by the misfortunes and frailties of our neighbors, no one can be surprised that

---

[1] 'The Right to Privacy' (1890) 4 *Harvard LR* 193–220.
[2] *Ibid.*, 195.

it usurps the place of interest in brains capable of other things. Triviality destroys at once robustness of thought and delicacy of feeling. No enthusiasm can flourish, no generous impulse can survive under its blighting influence.[3]

Their ensuing discussion of the legal evolution to the last decade of the nineteenth century is transatlantic—a mark of the continuous cross-referencing between the two great common law jurisdictions that lasted throughout our period. Much of the authority on which the authors relied was English, and in both countries similar cases raised novel concerns before the courts.

For all their enthusiasm, the idea of a right of privacy would for decades remain rather shadowy in America, while in England the refusal to pass from established instances to a grand category of legal obligation bearing that label was categorical. Given the nature of these Volumes, we cannot go far into developments in the United States. Nor can we follow the story in England to its sudden denouement in response to the absorption of the European Convention on Human Rights into the English common law tradition, since that has had to wait until the present century. Our task is to trace the evolution of various legal ingredients from which Warren and Brandeis sought to concoct their privacy recipe. In the forefront were the laws of defamation, copyright, confidence, goodwill, and trade marks.[4] All of these were compounded of rules that were by 1914 a good deal better baked than they had been a century before. That very development served to emphasize the discrete character of each area of protection, with its own basic objectives and principles marking its outer limits.

All these fields, as Warren and Brandeis claimed, were concerned with information relating to individuals, the rights all placing limits on the way that others might use the information (or mis-information) despite the fact that it encroached on the general freedoms that are the pride of any society with a rooted belief in the virtues of liberty. The very intangibility of the subject-matter makes it inherently difficult to establish principles by which to define what is protectable under these rights. Because information is by nature capable of being passed on as often as wished—an obvious characteristic much adumbrated in economic theory—contentions about the proper, or the efficient, range of these rights remain ripe for public debate in each generation. It was easy enough to understand the general moral case for juristic restraints. The difficulty was in arriving at hard distinctions over what should and should not be within the range of legal regulation. That is why judges, lawyers, and jurists play such a part in the historical record that we have.

---

[3] *Ibid.*, 196.

[4] At the time all were protected by rights that had a substantial basis in common law, equity or both. Patents for inventions had a statutory basis, though more so in the United States than in England.

Before proceeding to detail about the development of each right, we need to notice the degree to which they did, or did not, attract the attributes which English law tended to ascribe to rights of property. For present purposes there are three primary aspects of labelling a right 'property'. First, it leads to the characterization of the right as exclusive, the analogy being to ownership of tangible assets; the right thus extends against third parties with whom the proprietor had no contractual or trust-based relationship. Secondly, the right becomes capable of transfer to a new proprietor who thereby gains the power to sue those in breach of it. And thirdly, the right can be enforced not merely by monetary compensation for the effects of a breach, but also in equity by the grant of an injunction, which in appropriate circumstances can include interlocutory restraint until trial of the issue.

As our period opens, Lord Eldon would insist that injunctions lay only for the protection of property, a proposition that would remain foundational until at least the era of the Judicature Acts.[5] This association between 'property' and equitable remedies recurs at a number of points through the material that is treated in this Part.

The first distinctive forms of what is today called intellectual property—patents for inventions and copyright in books—were by 1820 assumed to have the basic characteristics of property just mentioned.[6] Later types of statutory copyright, together with 'copyright in designs' (to use the Victorian label), would attract broadly similar treatment by accretion.[7] But the protection of trade marks and similar signs, first through the tort of passing off and later through a registration scheme, were not so easily aligned to property in any complete sense.[8] As for the relief available against the copying of unpublished books and against breaches of confidence, the issue remained unresolved until the very end of our period, leaving the relief available from courts as a form of innominate equity.[9] One root of this equity drew upon analogies to the property right in published books conferred by the copyright Statute of Anne. But equally it seemed to be conditioned, when it same to some breaches of confidence, by the requirement that the defendant be shown to have assumed an obligation to keep the information in question secret. That assumption of duty could be seen

---

[5] Eldon's key decision was *Gee* v. *Pritchard* (1818) 2 Swanst. 402; see below, 864–6. It would be given an expansive impetus by the Court of Appeal in Chancery, as the very basis of liability in *Emperor of Austria* v. *Day* (1861) 3 De G. F. & J. 217. The injunction restrained the printing in England of a new currency for a Hungary which was to be freed from its Austrian overlord by revolutionaries under Louis Kossuth. The Court held the Emperor to have a proprietary interest in the existing currency of his dominions. The question of what else might be sufficiently property-like to gain injunctive relief would prove to have a variety of ramifications: see above, 673–4 and the references in this Part in n. 14 below.

[6] Below, Chs II, III.   [7] Below, Chs II, IV.

[8] Below, Ch. VI.   [9] Below, Ch. V.

as an analogous obligation to that which equity had imposed on trustees, professional advisers, agents, and other fiduciaries to act only for their beneficiary's benefit, not for their own. If that was so, then any proprietary considerations were in a sense secondary. Yet they might determine how far an indirect recipient of secret information—one who had no contractual relationship with the initial discloser—must also respect the confidence. They might also determine whether the discloser held an asset that could be transferred to others as an entitlement on which those others could sue in their own interest. Obligation and property, as so often with 'restitutionary' claims, tend to form correlative aspects of a single claim to relief.[10] By contrast, the action against defamation of personal reputation by regaling untruths lay only at the instance of the injured party, and its non-proprietary character clearly influenced the limitations that were imposed on remedies.[11] An enlightened ideal to which eighteenth-century jurists had been ready to give their allegiance was the idea of free expression, most evidently embodied in the freedom of the press, not just from governmental censorship but also from private claims. Where the issue was defamation of an individual, there would come to be categories—of privilege and fair comment—where one person could make untrue allegations about another with impunity, at least where he acted honestly rather than maliciously. The public interest in receiving some kinds of information might override copyright in the material published, and, in modern times, might even limit the right to expect that confidences will be maintained.[12]

As to this Blackstone had delivered a famous encomium on the precise nature of freedom of speech, which consisted 'in laying no *previous* restraints upon publications, and not in freedom from censure for criminal matter when published'. After publication, the libeller could be brought to account, where necessary for 'the preservation of peace and good order, of government and religion, the only solid foundations of civil liberty'. What was intolerable was to 'subject the press to the restrictive power of a licenser,...i.e. to subject all freedom of

[10] See Vol. XII, Pt 2, Ch. VII, pp. 572–3, where it is pointed out that the extent of remedies available to the plaintiff might turn on a different comparison between the proprietary and the personal which arises where the defendant holds traceable assets that represent the specific benefit received by him.

[11] Moral ideas against defamation could well be expressed in terms of property. As Iago in his cunning put it:

'Who steals my purse steals trash...
But he that filches from me my good name
Robs me of that which not enriches him,
And makes me poor indeed.'

In 1923, Spencer Bower included in his *Code of the Law of Actionable Defamation 1909* (2nd edn, 1923) provisions that treated reputation as property (240 *et seq.*); but the idea did not catch on.

[12] See below, p. 989.

sentiment to the prejudice of one man, and make him the arbitrary and infallible judge of all controverted points in learning, religion and government'.[13] Press freedom had therefore to be balanced by a 'seasonable exertion of the laws'. This limitation had to do with the availability of remedies; and the question of enforcement becomes a recurrent theme throughout this Part.[14] A balance of competing social interests had to be struck, very largely by the courts, and an awareness of the acute difficulties of doing so explains some of their reluctance to embrace broadly protective concepts, such as the 'right of privacy' so vaunted by Warren and Brandeis.

Concern over remedies is part of the desire to ensure that legally defined wrongs should be prevented from occurring, or, to the extent they have already occurred, should be made good by a monetary or other *ex post facto* remedy. As our discussion of 'quasi-contractual' and parallel equitable actions has amply demonstrated, this was a large realm where traditional concepts of contract and property did part of the work. But there were penumbral cases, which some judges sought to classify in large moral terms drawn together in a notion of 'unjustified enrichment'; but which others were afraid that they would have to give heightened support to those who regretted what they had done or left undone in their business or personal affairs through stupidity, lack of watchfulness, or sentimental weakness.

The major elements within the jumble of 'restitutionary' case law which recur in this Part, are two. First, what is the nature of that innominate equity which apparently emerges from the chrysalis of 'common law copyright' to become a cause of action against breaches of confidence? Is it the basis of an embracing right of protection for the individual personality, not only against calumny (the province of the defamation tort) but also against invasions of privacy? Is it equally the means of shoring up the technical and commercial value in types of information that comes to be a law of trade secrets? Secondly, does something emerge from torts that protect aspects of trading goodwill (such as arise from trade marks, business names, and deceit in the market-place) which can be categorized as a general law against unfair competition? Is this form of wrong ubiquitous enough that it can protect one competitor not only against conduct that misleads customers, but also against the misappropriation of business ideas wherever they have a value in exchange—and not merely when the ideas amount to patentable inventions, copyright works, or novel designs? This second area

---

[13] *Comms*, iv, 150–3. He was considering the criminal charges of seditious or blasphemous libel, but his view applied equally to defamation.

[14] See, in particular, below, 864–6; (in relation to defamation) Ch. II, pp. 884, 898–900, 906; (in relation to copyright) pp. 985, 988–9 (in relation to trade and other confidential information); pp. 995–8 (in relation to passing OH).

of classificatory interest will also occur at a number of points, but principally when discussing the breach of confidence equity in an economic context,[15] and then as a long-stop to the wicket-keeping of the discrete forms of intellectual property.[16]

1. DEFAMATION OF CHARACTER

The Legal Inheritance

From the early sixteenth century, a tort of defamation was known through forms of action on the case at common law against written libels and spoken slanders.[17] In three centuries of picaresque development these forms evolved as one legal means for resolving major clashes of personality.[18] The civil action stood alongside both criminal and ecclesiastical proceedings and its predominance over them was finally settled only in the course of the nineteenth century.[19]

As to criminal charges, where political or religious attacks involved accusations or calls to action that threatened government, local leadership, or the church, the technique of prosecuting for the misdemeanour of seditious, blasphemous, or defamatory libel was increasingly used in the eighteenth century. The enthusiasm of the courts for such proceedings had been marked in such characteristics of the law as that truth was no defence and that guilt was to be measured by the effect of the statements on others, not by the malicious intent of the accused.[20] One of the great stands in favour of liberty of speech, however, had been against those judges who ruled that it was for them, and not juries,

---

[15] Below, 988–9.

[16] Below, 1013–14.

[17] For the beginnings, see Baker, Vol. VI of this *Oxford History*, 781–99.

[18] The high-born and the militaristic were gradually weaned of their code of honour which demanded that insults be repaid with the challenge of a duel. The Duke of Wellington, when Prime Minister, fought one of the last celebrated duels with pistols. Peppery or unbalanced Victorians favoured administering a good thrashing: see for example the alleged slander in *Doyley* v. *Roberts* (1837) 3 Bing. (N.S.) 835: for defrauding his creditors, the plaintiff was said to have been 'horsewhipped off the course at Doncaster'. See generally, M, Peltonen, *The Duel in Early Modern England* (Cambridge, 2003); D. Andrew, 'The Code of Honour and its Critics: The Opposition to Duelling in England 1700–1850'(1980) 5 *Social History* 409–34; S. Banks, 'Killing with Courtesy: The English Duelist, 1785–1845' (2008) 47 *J. British Studies* 528–58.

[19] Scotland was slower than England in admitting civil process against personal defamation. When it did so, the question of compensation could be considered alongside penal provisions aimed at public protection. The superiority of this approach was argued vigorously by the Scots advocate, Sir Algernon Borthwick, in his pamphlet, *Observations upon the Modes of Prosecuting for Libel according to the Law of England* (1830), 1–4. For Borthwick, see below, n. 93.

[20] For the effect of the latter rule upon the formulation of civil liability, see below, pp. 861–3.

to determine whether a document was seditious, blasphemous, or otherwise libellous. In this endeavour, Fox's Libel Act of 1792 had proved decisive.[21] With the political shifts of the second quarter of the nineteenth century, criminal prosecutions for seditious and blasphemous libels became less frequent and those for defamatory libel were also increasingly rare, though they were occasionally pursued when the statement was asserted to be likely to cause a breach of the peace. Lord Campbell was among those who thought this allegation in the indictment a mere matter of form.[22] In the 1880s, however, as a response against the investigative journalism of Henry Labouchere and others, the number of prosecutions began to increase. Evidently alarmed, Lord Coleridge CJ insisted on evidence that violence had been an impending danger.[23] In 1843 other criticisms of this form of criminal liability had been put before a Lords' Committee and at once Campbell, as the Committee's chairman, had promoted an Act mainly concerned to impose limits on its apparent reach.[24] As we shall see, some of the Act's provisions also related to civil actions.[25]

As to ecclesiastical offences, by the nineteenth century the jurisdiction was a rump which would eventually be severed as a first step in removing lay jurisdiction from the Church's courts in 1855–7.[26] As the Royal Commission into that whole issue had found 25 years before, the claims could only be made for accusations that did not amount to common law defamation. In effect this restricted the scope of a once powerful jurisdiction mostly to spoken aspersions

[21] 32 Geo. III c. 60. From time to time, the Act's recognition of the central task of the jury would be carried over into nineteenth-century judgments on liability for defamation in tort: e.g. Lord Blackburn, *Capital and Counties Bank* v. *Henty* (1882) 8 App Cas at 772.

[22] See his summary to the House of Lords Committee on Libel, *PP* 1843 (513), v, 259, and G. W. Cooke, *Law of Defamation* (1844), App.

[23] His targets were the Director of Public Prosecutions for allowing the proceedings and Hawkins J. for his partisanship favouring figures of the turf: see J. R. Spencer, 'The Press and the Reform of Criminal Libel' in P. Glazebrook (ed.), *Reshaping the Criminal Law* (1978) 266; and his 'Criminal Libel in Action' [1979] *Crim LR* 60. Coleridge had the power to approve proceedings against newspaper proprietors shifted from the DPP to a judge in chambers: Law of Libel Amendment Act 1888, s 8: see *Fraser on Libel and Slander* (8th edn, 1936), 209–11, quoting Lord Alverstone's Grand Jury charge, 22 June 1906.

[24] Libel Act 1843, 6 & 7 Vict. c. 96. While the civil action was restricted to statements that could not be justified as true, criminal libel could arise even for truthful words. Campbell's Act provided a severer penalty for publishing a false accusation maliciously and introduced a defence of public benefit against libels that were true (see ss 4–6). In summarizing the work of his Lords' Committee, Campbell argued for liability that extended even to statements that were true, if e.g. the reference was to events of long ago, personal defects, or family circumstances, in which the public has no interest. The argument led nowhere, but it did anticipate much of the cause that Warren and Brandeis would espouse 50 years later (above, 847–8).

[25] Below, n. 32.

[26] See 18 & 19 Vict. c. 41; R. B. Outhwaite, *The Rise and Fall of the English Ecclesiastical Courts, 1500–1860* (Cambridge, 2006), 158–9.

on the sexual conduct of women; and, even though defamers could not defend themselves by showing the truth of what they said, and their victims had only to provide an affidavit which was not the subject of cross-examination, a sprink-ling of cases could be traced in the 30 years from 1815.[27] Even though the spiritual punishments of penance and excommunication had been strengthened in 1813 by imprisonment for failure to comply with the order, this brought little change.[28] Certainly the 1832 Commission considered that such cases would be better transferred to the summary jurisdiction of magistrates. In the event, that would not happen. Nor would the county courts acquire the power to hear civil defamation suits. Rescuing one's honour by court process would effectively be reserved to those who could face and finance an action in the superior civil jurisdictions. Many who had to cope with harrassers or poison-pen obsessives had little chance of legal recourse that would suppress the source of a nagging distress.

By 1820, the plaintiff who brought civil proceedings for defamation accused the defendant of maliciously 'publishing' an untrue statement about the plaintiff so as to bring him or her into 'hatred, ridicule or contempt'.[29] What was being protected was a reputation as a civil right, standing on 'the same footing with [the plaintiff's] right to the enjoyment of life, liberty, health, property and all the comforts and advantages which appertain to a state of civil society'.[30] It was long settled that, at trial, it was for the defendant to justify the statement as true, not for the plaintiff to show that it was untrue.[31] To be actionable, it sufficed that the 'publication', in written or oral form, had been made to a single person other than the plaintiff.[32] The effect of the statement fell to be judged by the standard of right-thinking members of the community. Where the defendant accused the plaintiff directly of criminal or other dastardly acts

---

[27] *PP* 1831–2, xxiv, 63 and App.; extensively explored in S. M. Waddams, *Sexual Slander in Nineteenth Century England* (Toronto, 2000).

[28] See 53 Geo. III c. 127.

[29] The older rule, which attempted to confine the action by requiring ambiguous words to be interpreted in their best, non-defamatory, light, had disappeared in the early eighteenth century. The concept of protecting reputation or good name had fully emerged by *Thorley* v. *Kerry* (1812) 4 Taunt. 355. See L. McNamara, *Reputation and Defamation* (Oxford, 2007), 91–103.

[30] Thus did Starkie (*Slander and Libel*, pp. viii, xxii) put it in enlightened terms—which feed through to Warren and Brandeis' article (above, n. 1).

[31] 'As much must be justified as meets the sting of the charge', said Burrough J. in *Edwards* v. *Bell* (1824) 1 Bing. 403; the application of that principle gave rise to much case law: *Fraser on Libel and Slander*, 97–101.

[32] Lord Campbell and his Committee (above, n. 22) wanted to tighten the requirement of publication, but the law was not changed. Campbell's recommendations on civil liability were, however, enacted in the colony of New South Wales, notorious for its braggardly public life: see P. Mitchell, 'The Foundations of Australian Defamation Law' (2006) 28 *Sydney LR* 477–504.

or opinions, the matter could be dealt with straightforwardly. But since there were often inferences that might be drawn from apparently innocent or equivocal things said about the plaintiff, it was quite possible for honest citizens to have differing opinions. Courts did not take evidence from witnesses claiming to be such people. The reference to the opinion of right-thinkers was no more than code by which judges left most issues of defamation for which there was some evidence, as well as questions of defences and damages, for the verdict of the empanelled jurors.[33] The prime risk that each party took in pursuing or defending a defamation action concerned their ability to convince whoever their particular jurors turned out to be. In the twentieth century, when jury trial as of right would be withdrawn from most civil litigation, it was retained for a limited number of torts, including in particular actions for libel and slander, and appellate judges would for decades prove reluctant to condemn very large awards of damages for plaintiffs as unreasonable.[34]

As already noted, the tort would remain distinctively personal, giving rise to a claim to damages primarily for the hurt to feelings, and only additionally for loss (for instance of a job or business opportunity).[35] The cause of action did not share the characteristic of transferability that was readily enough allowed to the various forms of intellectual property.[36] Moreover, Lord Eldon's bar against interlocutory relief in equity was made to turn on this lack of proprietary character; but it is hard to overlook the fact that judges used it as a tool in making their choices between the competing interests of free speech and privacy without saying much directly about what they were doing. We return to the consequences at a later stage.[37]

Information is by nature infinitely shareable and so an appropriate subject for property rights only in special cases. Nonetheless, good name, as distinct from other personal information, had long inspired high moral allegiance. Defamation—the lowering of reputation through false accusation—accordingly stood apart from other demands that legal protection be accorded against

---

[33] By the 1840s, Fox's Libel Act 1792 (see above, n. 21) was taken as support for the principle that the jury decided what was defamatory in a *civil* libel action: see e.g. *Parmiter* v. *Coupland* (1840) 6 M. & W. 105; Mitchell, *Making of Defamation*, 37–9.

[34] See below, 864–6.

[35] Only after long uncertainty would it be accepted that an injunction could be available after trial (and sometimes before) in order to prevent continuance, repetition, or threat of publication: see below, text at nn. 72–80. While the personal quality of the action remained of essence, a certain pragmatism allowed incorporated bodies and even unincorporated associations to sue where their 'property' was injured by the disparagement: see *Metropolitan Saloon Omnibus Co* v. *Hawkins* (1859) 4 H. & N. 87; and for subsequent case law: Mitchell, *Making of Defamation*, 43–51.

[36] When, eventually, tortious claims were permitted to accrue to the estate of a person injured, this would not extend to defamation suits: Torts (Miscellaneous Provisions) Act 1934, s 1.

[37] See below, p. 864, n. 73.

intrusions into private life, such as those denounced by Warren and Brandeis. As the judges sought to refine its principles, there are many signs that they shared the distaste of those authors for the excesses of an increasingly popular press.[38] Their antagonism became more noticeable as the market for newspapers spread down the social scale in the late nineteenth century. But the basic attitude was no novelty. It followed upon the century-long movement for suppression of vice among the lower social strata, which included the distribution of much that was disrespectful, scurrilous, or pornographic.[39]

In the course of the nineteenth century there was a constant flow of case law seeking to spell out the legal tests of what a judge could put to the jury in deciding aspects of defamation claims and the defences to them. A balancing between judicial boundary-setting and jury decision-making is at work in much of what occurs in this elaboration of doctrine.[40] It is a course typical of common law development in the period. One strand in it in relation to personal reputation was that jurors were no longer expected to bring their own knowledge of the litigants to bear on their decision. There was also the fact that, until 1851, the parties were not competent to give evidence themselves.[41] When they did gain the right to go into the witness box, juries could have much stronger impressions of the individuals, a change which may well have influenced judges to exert greater control over verdicts. The result, as Paul Mitchell has demonstrated in depth, was that, while refusing to allow the legal commodification of reputation as property, the courts gradually insisted that untrue statements affecting a person's reputation were actionable, whatever the state of mind of the primary libeller, unless he or she could show a set of circumstances falling within specified categories of absolute or qualified privilege, or fair comment.

The individual's right to maintain his reputation against unjustifiable calumny had attracted political speculation and legal support from classical times. Thomas Starkie, when a young barrister, had written a treatise on the *Law of Slander and Libel; and incidentally of Malicious Prosecutions* (1813). After becoming Downing Professor in Cambridge, this swelled into a second edition in 1830. A long Preliminary Discourse addressed in philosophical terms the difficulties

---

[38] See P. Mitchell, 'Nineteenth-Century Defamation: Was it a Law of the Press?' (2008) 13 *Media and Arts LR* 293–302.. There would be a marked contrast with the decorous decency of broadcasting in Britain, during the decades in which the British Broadcasting Corporation alone held possession of the airwaves.

[39] For the offences, see above, Pt 1, pp. 363–73.

[40] Another control mechanism was to be found in the requirements for pleading. For an instance, see *Ayre* v. *Craven* (1834) 2 Ad. & El. 1; below, n. 52.

[41] See Vol. XI, Pt 1, pp. 608–10.

of turning the basic moral injunction against calumny into legal principles that took proper account of the expediencies of real life. This was then related, with some repetition, to a description of the case law, starting with the requirements for criminal charges and then for civil action.[42] This substantial work drew quite heavily on Algernon Borthwick's perceptive treatise on the Scots law, but the two authors did not always agree.[43] *Starkie* was for long the English lawyer's repository on the subject.[44]

2. LIBEL AS AGAINST SLANDER

The distinct torts of libel (for written words or other expressions that had a degree of permanence) and slander (for speech) had taken their place within the action on the case after the abolition of Star Chamber and the restoration of Charles II. By our period, no longer was there much trace of the notion that slanders had to be particularly scandalous.[45] The main difference went to the question of injury: slanders were actionable only upon proof of special damage, while with written libels this was unnecessary. The division, however, was more than a question about quantification and it was retained at the beginning of the nineteenth century by Sir James Mansfield CJCP, even though he could find nothing sufficient in arguments that the wider liability for libel deserved to be kept separate from that for slander.[46] He did not accept that written statements were, because of their permanence, inherently more likely to cause injury to the person named than those that were spoken. There could be highly damaging speech and relatively moderate writing. Bayley J., who brought much learning to the whole subject in the 1820s and 1830s, would take a contrary view. Writing, he said, 'is premeditated, and shews design; it is more permanent and calculated to do a much greater

---

[42] This marked an advance on F. L. Holt's *Law of Libel* (1816), which concentrated primarily on political libels open to prosecution.

[43] See below, 878.

[44] Cooke (*Defamation*) in 1844 and J. C. H. Flood (*Libel and Slander*) in 1880 each claimed to be providing practical guides, there being no existing equal to Starkie. Then, in 1881, came W. B. Odgers' *Digest of the Law of Libel and Slander*, a heavy compendium not given to reflective digression. At the same period the role of newspapers in provoking libel and other litigation led to books on the subject from that angle, notably H. Fraser's *Law of Libel in Relation to the Press* (1889), which grew into a leading text (7 edns to 1936); and J. R. Fisher and J. A. Strahan's *The Law of the Press* (1891).

[45] Mitchell, *Making of Defamation*, Ch. 1; Veeder, 'The History and Theory of the Law of Defamation' (1904) 4 *Columbia LR* 546.

[46] *Thorley* v. *Kerry* (1812) 4 Taunt. 355, 365. Starkie waivered in his view on whether slander should remain more restricted in scope, ending (before Campbell's Committee) by supporting continuance of the distinction.

injury than slander merely spoken'.[47] And so the essential distinction would not be eradicated in English law.[48]

The distinction was in any case more complicated, since in certain categories of slander the requirement of special damage did not apply: where the false allegation was that the plaintiff had committed an indictable offence;[49] or that he or she was carrying an 'obnoxious' disease (such as leprosy or venereal infection); or that the statement would injure him or her in a profession or trade. The last category raised constant questions, as judges struggled to define what statements would fall within it. Bayley J. insisted that there must be a 'natural tendency' for the statement to reflect on the work being done; a probable consequence was not enough. However, he asserted that a 'want of general requisite, as honesty, capacity, fidelity, &c' would suffice—a puzzling phrase in this context.[50] The lines between the two types of slander could produce curious distinctions. Lord Campbell considered it 'absurd that a woman of rank and character may not maintain an action for words imputing to her a want of chastity, spoken in the most public and offensive manner and that a man cannot maintain an action for words at a county meeting denouncing him as a liar, a coward, and a scoundrel' without proving special damage;[51] whereas a doctor of whom it was said that he was in an adulterous relationship would not need to do so, if he pleaded and proved the innuendo that he was thereby breaching the trust of a patient.[52]

3. THE COMMUNICATION AND 'MALICE'

As they came to refine the law during the nineteenth century, common law courts could have required proof that the defamation consisted of deliberate (or at most reckless) untruths directed at the complainant.

---

[47] *Clement* v. *Chivis* (1829) 9 B. & C. 172. Inevitably, nice questions could arise over whether it was the libel that caused the harm, not least when a wife sought to clear off allegations of infidelity: see *Lynch* v. *Knight* (1861) 9 H.L.C. 577. There were signs of a reluctance to delve into the motives of the person by whom the slander was stated: see e.g. *Knight* v. *Gibbs* (1834) 1 Ad. & El. 43.

[48] Most writers favoured abolishing the distinction, which did not exist in Scots law: Mitchell, *Making of Defamation*, 10–14, also exploring the American position.

[49] Courts were willing to take a broad view of these categories. Still, there were other questions, such as whether harm would be caused. In *Fowler* v. *Dowdney* (1838) 2 Rob. & M. 119, Denman LCJ found that to say of a man that he was a returned convict was an allegation of indictable crime that had lost its sting because the sentence must have been served.

[50] *Lumley* v. *Allday* (1831) 1 C. & J. 301. See Mitchell, *Making of Defamation*, 14–24 for details of the case law; and for decisions tending to broaden the boundaries of libel—covering for instance waxworks and effigies for burning: 24–30.

[51] Above, n. 22; and see his speech in *Roberts* v. *Roberts* (1864) 5 B. & S. 384, HL. The special damage had to be averred and shown to be the natural and reasonable consequence of the slander. Eventually, the Slander of Women Act 1891 removed the need to show special damage in the case of a woman accused of unchastity.

[52] *Ayre* v. *Craven* (1834) 2 Ad. & El. 1; cf. *Jones* v. *Littler* (1841) 7 M. & W. 423.

A separate tort already existed in the action on the case for, initially, slander of title to land, then for slander of goods, and eventually for any injurious falsehood concerning trade. But injurious or malicious falsehood lay only on proof of 'malice' in its sense of personal spite against the plaintiff or some other 'by or sinister purpose'; and in addition it was necessary to show special damage. This tort, like the lesser slanders, related to false statements about another's property or business which did not involve a lowering of personal esteem and reputation but nevertheless had a damaging effect on economic interests. The circumstances in which it was the only recourse open to an individual trader or firm were by no means clear. Statements implying that a bank would not honour its obligations, or that a person had committed an act of bankruptcy, were readily treated as defamatory (unless shown to be true) because they were taken to cast moral aspersions on business competence. Some courts were willing to direct that statements about the plaintiff's trading might cast personal aspersions on him.[53] Injurious falsehood, with its major limitations of scope, was kept in place because judges had a firmly held view that statements about a trader's products or services, particularly if they involved a direct, disparaging comparison with those of another, were part of the hurly-burly of competition. The 'mere puffs' that made up so much advertising, were beyond the reach of civil action. Only in egregious cases of lying about the plaintiff's merchandise in ways that caused him identifiable economic harm did liability arise. Any wider liability, so it was feared, would provoke a flood of litigation concerning the comparative qualities of products or services.[54]

At least by 1900 it was accordingly an economic tort of narrow scope, reined in much the same way as the tort of deceit.[55] Defamation, by contrast, was taken to raise dangers to the individual persona that needed broader protection from the courts. The distinctions between, on the one hand, written libels and the types of specially injurious slanders; and, on the other hand, other slanders and injurious falsehoods concerning the plaintiff's trade (whether written or oral), resulted in

[53] e.g. *Ingram* v. *Lawson* (1840) 6 Bing. N.C. 212; *Jenner* v. *A'Beckett* (1871) LR 7 QB 11.

[54] *Evans* v. *Harlow* (1844) 5 Q.B. 624—advertisement stating that the plaintiff sold defective siphons: action for defamation disallowed. In the 1870s, some tendency to broaden the scope of injurious falsehood was for a time apparent: see e.g. *Western Counties Manure* v. *Lawes* (1874) LR 9 Ex 218, CA—if the untrue statement was about the quality of the goods, and there was special damage the action would lie without proof of malice. But this was halted in the 1890s: see e.g. *Ratcliffe* v. *Evans* [1892] 2 QB 524, CA; *White* v. *Mellin* [1895] AC 154, HL; *Empire Typesetting* v. *Linotype* (1898) 81 LT 331, HL; *Hubbuck* v. *Wilkinson* [1899] 1 QB 86; *Lyne* v. *Nicholls* [1906] 23 TLR 86, CA. The issue seems to be connected with the range of interim relief in equity, but without any clear upshot, see below, 864–5.

[55] On the range of economic torts, see Vol. XII, Pt 4, Ch. IV.

a conceptual maze implanted by earlier common law history, which no one had the interest to tear apart and start again.[56]

So far as concerned defamation, the basic direction to a jury was given a new form by King's Bench in *Bromage* v. *Prosser*.[57] The evidence in the case suggested that the defendant had been asked by another person about the stability of the plaintiffs' bank; in response the defendant said that he had been told that it had stopped payment and that he was going off to find out. On discovering that he was wrong, he contacted his questioner in order to clarify the truth. It was standard form in a defamation pleading to allege that the defendant had acted maliciously. Defence counsel argued that it was for the judge to rule whether there was malice, not for the jury to find. Bayley J., speaking for the Court, offered a doctrinal palimpsest on the allegation of malice in a defamation writ:

Malice in its common acceptation means ill will against a person, but in its legal sense it means a wrongful act, done intentionally, without just cause or excuse.[58]

In libel or slander, he continued, only malice in law needed to be alleged, and it meant no more than that the defendant must be presumed to have intended the consequences of his publication of the defamation. This refined presumption became a foundation of the tort. It instructed judges what evidence sufficed for the issue of defamation to be left to the jury, and then how the jurors should be instructed. In the case in hand the slander was evident and the doubts concerned whether the defendant had acted in circumstances that soon afterwards would be characterized as qualified privilege.[59] Given that uncertainty, the jury should have been asked whether the defendant's answer had been given *bona fide* in response to the request for advice, and only then whether the response was shown to be malicious in fact, the plaintiff bearing the burden of proof on this issue. On the prime question whether there was any defamation at all, Bayley J. implied that the defendant's own state of mind played no decisive role. Instead, if the statement at issue was found to have been made about the plaintiff, the objective standard of its effect on right-thinking persons would determine whether it was defamatory of him or her. If the jury found it so, it would be wrongful unless a countervailing ground for excusal was made out by the defendant. Accordingly,

---

[56] The maze was indeed thicker: injurious falsehood came to require proof of actual malice as well as special damage, the lesser slanders needed proof of special damage alone.

[57] (1825) 4 B. & C. 247, 255.

[58] He accordingly disapproved Park J.'s general direction to the jury that they should consider whether the defendant had shown that he acted *bona fide* and without malice (for which see (1824) 1 Car. & P. 475, 476: the direction had resulted in a verdict for the defendant).

[59] See below, pp. 868–70.

given the evidence in the case, a new trial was ordered.[60] This rendered irrelevant such excuses as that the defendant did not realize that his statement would have a defamatory effect, or that he spoke only in jest.

Whether the presumption of intending the consequences of one's acts was ever open to rebuttal, except through an established defence such as qualified privilege or fair comment, would take more than 80 years to receive any judicial answer. But Starkie had a firm moral view of the matter. Adhering in unqualified terms to the 'neighbour principle' of fault liability and the legal standing given to it in *Buller's Nisi Prius*, he insisted that a defamer must be liable to damages, whether his publication was wilful, or through negligence or folly. For him such conduct constituted a 'wilful invasion of the natural and absolute right of another man—an act for which, in point of natural justice, he is responsible, and from which, malice, in its legal sense, is necessarily to be inferred'.[61]

For decades thereafter the question was scarcely even addressed.[62] A significant chance eventually came in *Capital & Counties Bank* v. *Henty*,[63] a case in which the defamatory meaning could arise at most only by innuendo from the document published. The defendant, D, a brewing firm, did business through occupants who ran public houses for it in Sussex and Hampshire. Cheques payable both by these occupants and their own customers, which were drawn on various banks, were handed to D's collector in payment for supplies. Cheques drawn on branches of the plaintiff bank had been sent by D's collectors to its Chichester branch; but a new manager there refused to continue the practice unless the cheques were presented by a known collector who had D's express authority to do so. D threatened to instruct its tenants not to take cheques of the P Bank. The manager said that he was indifferent whether they did so or not. D carried out its threat which allegedly caused a run on the Bank. After failure of the jury to reach a verdict, three appellate courts considered whether there had been evidence enough to put two questions to a second jury: whether D's statement was capable of bearing the inference that it did not trust the solvency of the P bank; and if so, whether the statement had been made in privileged circumstances, concerning which nonetheless there was evidence of D's 'malice in fact', arising from its row with the manager.

---

[60] The root proposition was at once treated as having a general effect, not one tied to the question of who decided the issue of 'malice': see e.g. *Fisher* v. *Clement* (1830) 10 B. & C. 211; *Ward* v. *Weeks* (1830) 7 Bing. 211; Mitchell, *Making of Defamation*, 103–4.

[61] Starkie, *Slander and Libel*, 225–6.

[62] However, in *Harrison* v. *Smith* (1869) 20 LT 713, the defendant wrote an article about a swindler, General Plantaganet Harrison. His defence was that he had made the extraordinary name up and did not mean to refer to the plaintiff, who actually bore the name. Lush J. directed the jury that, if they found this true, there could be no defamation.

[63] (1882) 8 App Cas 741. Mitchell, *Making of Defamation*, 104–14.

Majorities in both the Court of Appeal and the House of Lords were against ordering a re-trial of these issues, one element in their doubts being whether the statement was any real cause of the widescale withdrawal of business from the bank. At considerable length, the Lords examined whether the statement could be found libellous. Was the impact of D's letter on its customers the only factor? Or must it be shown either that D intended to defame the bank or that it should have appreciated that recipients would read the defamatory inference into it? Most members of the Lords were not prepared to say that D would escape liability unless it could be shown to have written with intention to defame.[64] But as to D's failure to appreciate the defamatory implication in the letter, Lord Blackburn was clearest: D would be responsible if he 'did what he knew or ought to have known was calculated to injure [P]'. He appeared to adopt the position that Starkie had pronounced a half-century before: liability was still dependent on showing a degree of fault measured by the standard of a reasonable man.

Starkie, however, had treated the right not to be defamed as of the highest order in the catalogue of natural and absolute rights and had not made clear why this did not lead to strict, rather than fault, liability. One way of reading Bayley J.'s conception of the law was indeed that the defendant's state of mind only became relevant to the question of libel or no libel, where one of the established defences—of the various privileges or of fair comment—were open. It was exactly this strategy that was propounded in the text by W. B. Odgers, which appeared before the appeal reached the House of Lords.[65]

The Lords would return to the issue a quarter-century later, in a second, much criticised, decision, *Hulton* v. *Jones*,[66] which went to the question of whether the libel was directed at the plaintiff. *The Sunday Chronicle* ran a piece on the ambiance of the Grand Prix in Dieppe, mentioning the appearance there of one Artemus Jones, churchwarden of Peckham, with a lady apparently not his wife. An established barrister, of the same unusual name as this 'fictional' character, brought libel proceedings, alleging that his acquaintances took the reference to mean him. He had previously been a journalist on the paper but the writer and

[64] Lords Blackburn, Penzance (the dissentient) and Bramwell. Lord Selborne, agreeing with Cotton LJ in the Court of Appeal, thought that D would only be liable if gratuitously it had spread its statement by public notices. This approach seemed to bundle the questions of the defamatory nature of the communication and the privilege of the occasion into one.

[65] Blake Odgers, whose *Digest of the Law of Libel and Slander* first appeared in 1881, was firmly of the view that fault was in no sense an ingredient of defamation (p. 261):see Mitchell, *Making of Defamation*, 108–9. Romer J. appeared to be an adherent of this persuasion: *Viztelly* v. *Mudie's Select Library* [1900] 2 KB 403.

[66] [1910] AC 20. P. Mitchell, 'Artemus Jones and the Press Club' (1999) 20 *JLH* 64 explores the allegation that the writer actually knew the plaintiff. The plaintiff's widow gave that as her opinion to the Porter Committee on Defamation in 1948.

the current editor denied any knowledge of the relationship and the case had to proceed in an atmosphere of unresolved suspicion.[67] His case was put on the footing that it was no answer to the claim that the sketch was written about someone non-existent. Whether the statement at issue did defame the plaintiff was to be determined solely by reference to its impact on those who read it. Jones won a verdict for £1750. Both the Court of Appeal (in substantial judgments) and the House of Lords (perfunctorily) upheld this outcome, apparently opting for strict liability.[68] Under the doctrinal construct of *Bromage* v. *Prosser*, the presumption that the defendant intended the consequences of his statement was now treated as irrebuttable, even where there was evidence to the contrary and liability arose only from inference in all the circumstances.

About this there was an unsureness of touch which echoed the outcome of *Capital and Counties Bank*. Thus in the Court of Appeal, Farwell LJ offered both the opinion that liability in all defamation arises from the impact of the statement on right-thinking members of the public; and that, when a description is given by which the plaintiff is recognized by his associates, the publisher is responsible both for intentional harm and for a description 'made recklessly, careless whether it hold up the plaintiff to contempt and ridicule or not'[69] (a less severe standard than Lord Blackburn's). This Janus-like juxtaposition gained in impact, in that two members of the House of Lords, Lords Atkinson and Gorell, associated themselves expressly with Farwell LJ's judgment.[70] The reaction of the judges bore the hallmarks of a decision designed to impede defences based on personal states of mind that might well be hard to disprove.

The case was taken to establish in English law that the defendant's state of mind was not relevant to the question, 'libel or no libel', but only to those defences where either intention, recklessness or at least negligence remained in issue: i.e. to qualified privilege, fair comment, and the liability of distributors.[71] In the very period in which most tortious liability, other than that concerned with injury to 'property', had come to be limited at least by the concept of fault, it betrayed a determination to foist liability onto the media of the day, in much the same spirit as Warren and Brandeis; but the liability was limited by the whole history of the cause of action to false accusations affecting personal reputation.

---

[67] See P. Mitchell, 'Malice in Defamation' (1998) 114 *LQR* 639.

[68] For the perfunctory attitude shown by Loreburn LC in some of the appeals before him, including this one, see R. F. V. Heuston, *Lives of the Lord Chancellors, 1885–1940* (1964), 181.

[69] [1909] 2 KB 444, 480–1.

[70] For the great puzzlement among later commentators, see Mitchell, *Making of Defamation*, 111, n. 79. Much of the harshness of the decision would eventually be softened by the Defamation Act 1952, s 4.

[71] See below, pp. 866–72.

The English front line in the sands of liability was thus drawn relatively narrowly, but to overstep it risked an award of damages that could shake even the notably profitable endeavours of the popular press. The power of juries to adjust the outcome of a libel action to give expression to their sense of moral outrage against the defendant or their contempt for the plaintiff was certainly very considerable.[72] It balanced the refusal to give an interlocutory injunction to stop impending publication of a libel or slander. Blackstone had seen this as the essence of press freedom in a liberal society and Lord Eldon had 'juridicized' the position by insisting that libel was not a matter of property, which alone attracted this equitable form of relief.[73] Until the era of the Judicature Acts, therefore, it went unquestioned. But then the question of 'prior restraint' became caught up in issues over how far equitable notions of justice and fairness could be employed to broaden the scope of civil rights of action and how far equitable remedies could serve as a catalyst to this end, perhaps by labelling injuries as being to 'property' to an extent that Lord Eldon would not have countenanced. Malins VC, an early promulgator of this notion, used a defamation claim as one of his first opportunities to develop such a power.[74] His re-direction of doctrine in this and other causes would excite harsh criticism.[75] Nonetheless, it continued to attract attention, not least because it was taken up by the powerful Jessel MR after the Judicature Acts drew the old jurisdictions together into a single administrative structure. The Judicature Act 1873, s 25(8) provided that the new superior courts could grant

---

[72] While judges retained a power to order a new trial if they thought the level of damages awarded by the jury was wholly unreasonable, they were reluctant to intervene in this way. As circulation figures of the popular press reached ever higher, awards for the injury to feelings also rose. But since it would be accepted that for deliberate injury, the damages could be exemplary as well as compensatory, it was rare for the size of a verdict to be successfully challenged: see Mitchell, *Making of Defamation*, 53–62, for the case law which for much of the twentieth century continued the same approach. Eventually, under regular criticism from the press, attitudes would change sufficiently that the Court of Appeal became entitled to substitute a lesser figure for a verdict that it regarded as extreme: Courts and Legal Services Act 1990, s 8(1).

[73] *Gee* v. *Pritchard* (1819) 2 Swanst. 402, 413, on the rather inadequate ground that '[t]he publication of libel is a crime; and I have no jurisdiction to prevent the commission of crimes'. His Blackstonian position would be echoed by Langdale MR in *Clark* v. *Freeman* (1848) 11 Beav. 112, 119 (refusal to give relief to a doctor named as commending a medicine without his permission). But Langdale decided that there was a basis for intervention in *Routh* v. *Webster* (1847) 10 Beav. 561 (injunction to restrain the naming of an individual as a trustee of a company when he was not); and Campbell LC in *Emperor of Austria* v. *Day* (1861) 3 De G. F. & J. 217, 238–9 also took an extensive view of the type of injury that could be treated as going to 'property'—for which see above, n. 5.

[74] *Dixon* v. *Holden* (1869) LR 7 Eq 488. Re-classification as property was the basis of this judgment, just as it had been of Malins' injunction against strikers in *Springhead Spinning* v. *Riley* (1868) LR 6 Eq. 551, 561 (above, 673–4).

[75] First and foremost by Lord Cairns (once Malins' pupil) in *Prudential Assurance* v. *Knott* (1875) LR 10 Ch App 142, 146–7.

interlocutory injunctions, where 'just and convenient... unconditionally or upon such terms or conditions as the Court shall think just'. This he and others were apparently prepared to treat as sidestepping the question whether a defendant was under any ultimate liability in law or equity—a highly interventionist way of reading a provision relating only to an interim procedural measure.[76] Even more extraordinary, however, was the revivification of the 1854 provisions which first gave common law courts the power to grant injunctions, interlocutory as well as final, to restrain committal of 'any breach of contract or other injury...'.[77] In relation to defamation, it was argued and by some judges accepted, that this had, 30 years before, given common law courts a right to restrain the wrong without regard to the exclusion by equity of that wrong from the category of 'property'. If this could be rationally or historically justified, it meant, as Mitchell says, that after 1854 'all the attempts to have defamation recognised as a type of property... had been completely pointless'. But, as he demonstrates convincingly, such a view was not countenanced in preparatory material or publications at the time. The argument is much more a product of the new world of Judicature, when the two great jurisdictions, common law and equity, were considering their muscle power for the future. Chancery had long held to its superior moral position as adjuster of general rules of law order to achieve justice in particular cases. A contest appeared to be at work over their continuing ability to act according to their own dictates of conscience—a role which, at common law, was largely left to the 'equity' of the jury.

So far as the cases on interim injunctions were concerned, several of the reported decisions on injury to reputation were pleaded as the separate, malice-based tort of trade libel (injurious falsehood).[78] One line of argument for which Lindley LJ and others appeared to express sympathy was that the protection of free speech was a less compelling reason for injunctive relief when the libellous statement concerned the plaintiff's business, rather than his personal integrity.[79] Whether this was one signal that the restrictions upon the trade libel tort (malice, special damage) called for reassessment is difficult to gauge. Certainly by the

---

[76] When Jessel went so far as to hold, on the basis of the Judicature Act provision, that an injunction would issue against a local authority to prevent it from disqualifying the plaintiff as an alderman (*Aslatt* v. *Corporation of Southampton* (1880) 16 Ch D 143; preceded by *Beddow* v. *Beddow* (1878) 9 Ch D 89), his justification was called into question by Brett and Cotton LJJ (see *North London Rly* v. *Great Northern Rly* (1883) 11 QBD 30 at 37, 39–40).

[77] Common Law Procedure Act 1854, ss 79 and 82, which were then treated as a foundation of the Judicature Act 1873, s 25(8).

[78] See above, pp. 859–60.

[79] *Saxby* v. *Easterbrook* (1878) 3 CPD 339. (Allegation that the invention patented by the plaintiff had been obtained from the defendant (a competitor). The decision, however, was concerned with final relief after the jury's finding of libel, not with an interlocutory motion.)

1890s, the higher courts stood out against any such development.[80] In the end, so far as concerns defamation itself, the refusal of a pre-trial injunction was moderated to a limited extent. The court hearing a motion for the court's intervention would consider whether the intended statement was so evidently injurious in law that a jury's verdict to the contrary would be upset;[81] and whether, on the other hand, the defendant proposed to deny liability by justification, privilege, fair comment, or any other public interest.[82]

4. SECONDARY LIABILITY

The relevance of the defendant's state of mind had an impact on issues of consequential liability. The act of 'publication' which completed the tort was performed by the writer, artist, or speaker of the defamatory statement; and, as with copyright, that first step could equally be taken by the person who organized its circulation, such as the publisher.[83] But as books and newspapers passed down distribution chains, the same problem arose as in the criminal law affecting merchandise marks and the like: should only those who knew of the wrong be held to account? Or were they liable until they proved their innocence and provided the plaintiff with the name of the actual perpetrator? Was the same approach to apply as to the instance of a person who, having received defamatory information from another, proceeded to repeat it? The latter situation had been dealt with as one of the elucidations of doctrine in the *Bromage* v. *Prosser* years. Both Common Pleas and King's Bench refused to accept that the repeater was in any different case from the originator: the excusals in the name of public policy, such as inaccurate statements in response to requests for a 'character', could not extend to any defamers whose sole excuse was that they were not the originators of the false accusation.[84]

---

[80] See above, n. 54.

[81] So stated as a rule by Esher MR in the trade libel case of *William Coulson* v. *James Coulson* (1887) 3 TLR 846, but treated by some judges later as a more general guide to determining whether a *prima facie* case had been made out.

[82] *Bonnard* v. *Perryman* [1891] 2 Ch 269, CA; *Monson* v. *Tussauds* [1891] 2 QB 671, CA. How far the court needed to be satisfied from the defendant's affidavits that he would succeed in his defence at trial remained ill-defined. Mitchell's view is that some judgments had, at the interlocutory stage, placed the burden of establishing untruth on the plaintiff, rather than the defendant, as would happen at the trial (see Mitchell, *Making of Defamation*, 90–7, esp. 95); but many pronouncements about this procedural stage emphasize its discretionary quality.

[83] In the book trade, the line between the publisher and the secondary distributor was increasingly clear; but the difference would prove more difficult when it came to electronic technology, starting with broadcasting: Mitchell, *Making of Defamation*, 132–6.

[84] *de Crespigny* v.*Wellesley* (1829) 5 Bing. 392 (libel); *McPherson* v. *Daniels* (1829) B. & C. 263 (slander). As well as allowing an apology to be put in evidence in mitigation of damages, Campbell's Libel

As for distributors, the issue was a recurrent one and a considerable practical difficulty. There were more or less scatological newspapers that regularly contained attacks of one kind or another on the reputation of those in the public eye; and there were many other publications where damaging attacks cropped up unexpectedly. It would be tempting to say that booksellers and others should check material of the first kind, but could scarcely do so for the second. In the 1830s judges appear to have been leaving it to juries to decide whether to let a distributor off if he showed that he did not know of the libel.[85]

Only in 1883 did the Court of Appeal address the issue with less willingness to allow juries to trust the defendant's protestations of innocence. In *Emmens* v. *Pottle*,[86] it placed distributors under a duty to take reasonable steps to ensure that defamation did not occur in the material, Bowen LJ, referring in particular to newspapers that 'are likely to contain a libel'. The jury's findings that they had done all that was reasonable to avoid liability sufficed to excuse them. Mitchell regards it as ironical that, until *Hulton* v. *Jones*, this should place secondary defamers under wider liability than those initially responsible.[87] But *Emmens* was decided in the immediate aftermath of the *Capital & Counties Bank* case, which left uncertainties over the liability of primary wrongdoers. It was one indication of the marginalizing of the defendant's fault, that in *Vizetelly* v. *Mudie's Select Library* Romer LJ, after commenting on the harshness of some aspects of the law of libel, would nonetheless state the rule as: 'a man who publishes a libel is liable to an action although he is really innocent in the matter, and guilty of no negligence'.[88] The Court of Appeal then treated distributors as *not having published* the libel, if they could show they put the material out without negligence. The case was against the country's best-known circulating library, whose manager admitted to a policy of not checking for libel because it was cheaper to risk the occasional action. In those circumstances the library lost. Booksellers and newsagents were ready to protest at the burden upon them, but in 1891 they failed to persuade Parliament that they should be granted a defence of simple ignorance of the libel.[89]

Act 1843 gave innocent newspapers the right, on making an apology in a given way, to pay money into court as amends and so avoid liability: 6 & 7 Vict. c. 96, ss 1, 2.

[85] *Chubb* v. *Flanagan* (1834) 6 Car. & P. 431; *Day* v. *Bream* (1837) 2 M. & Rob. 54.

[86] (1883) 16 QBD 354.

[87] *Making of Defamation*, 133.

[88] [1900] 2 KB 170, 187–9.

[89] The Law of Libel Amendment Act 1888 accordingly did not incorporate their proposal: Mitchell, *Making of Defamation*, 131. Had the law been so changed, it would have reverted to a position taken in earlier cases such as *Day* v. *Bream* (1837) 2 M. & Rob. 54; cf. *Fisher* v. *Clement* (1830) 10 B. & C. 472.

5. LIMITS TO LIABILITY

Qualified Privilege[90]

As writings about defamation recognized soon enough, *Bromage* v. *Prosser* set in train a reshaping of rules for defining what issues should be left to defamation juries and what directions they should be given in consequence. In part these sought to avoid the ambiguities inherent in the pleading of malice by directing attention to two major categories of excuse which the defendant might raise: qualified privilege and fair comment. Malice, in its lay (and sometimes legal) sense of ill-will directed against the plaintiff, would destroy the privilege otherwise allowed for communications falling within these categories. The burden of proving malice in this context lay firmly with the plaintiff; whereas, if the defendant sought to justify the truth of the statement, the burden was his. The balance thus struck might seem curious, since truth was a matter that the plaintiff would know more about, while the motive for privilege and comment concerned the defendant's actions; but so it was.

The archetypal case for a qualified privilege arose from a request for a reference concerning a former servant or supplier of services. Securing a 'character' was of great importance to servants, apprentices, and others in the labour force.[91] The eighteenth-century view appears to have turned on the distinction between malice in law and in fact. So long as the defendant's response to such a request was an honest assessment, it was not an actionable wrong, however inaccurate and injurious to the person concerned. The request in *Bromage* for information about whether the plaintiffs' bank had stopped payment showed that there were other situations in which the question of privilege could be left to the jury. The great difficulty lay in arriving at a general definition of privileged 'occasions'. The circumstances could not be put in terms of a pre-existing legal duty to speak or write, since that did not fit many kinds of communication that masters, mistresses, or business people made to one another in managing their affairs. Plainly the judges felt unable to impose liabilities on such people when they offered critical statements that turned out to be unjustified but were nonetheless an honest response. The way forward was set by Parke B. in *Toogood* v. *Spyring*. The statement would be excused if it is made by a person

in the discharge of some public or private duty, whether legal or moral, or in the conduct of his own affairs, in matters where his interest is concerned. If *fairly* warranted by any

---

[90] See generally, Mitchell, *Making of Defamation*, Ch. 7.

[91] See J. J. Hecht, *The Domestic Servant in Eighteenth-Century England* (1980), 160; P. Langford, *Public Life and the Propertied Englishman 1689–1798* (Oxford, 1991), 505. There was no legal right to demand one.

reasonable occasion or exigency, and honestly made, such communications are protected for the common convenience and welfare of society; and the law has not restricted the right to make them within any narrow limits.[92]

Mitchell traces the new emphasis on moral duties in given circumstances to natural law ideals of the eighteenth century, and more immediately to the writings of Borthwick and Starkie,[93] the latter's formulation being directly copied by Parke B.[94] It seems clear that these authors were speaking of actual duties and interests. They were not content that a defendant might shelter behind an assertion that he believed he had a responsibility to write or speak.

The judges worked with propertied, male jurors, who could be expected to share broadly similar views of when it was 'right' to offer criticisms of other people, even if the statements proved to be wrong. Nonetheless the question of what was privileged they kept for themselves as an issue of law, leaving juries to decide whether the plaintiff had showed malice in fact overriding the privilege. Identifying when such duties or interests arose would prove to be a preoccupation on which judges begged to differ. Was it enough that the person making the statement believed that the occasion was privileged, even though a judge might later rule that it was not?[95] If this was so, was the essential issue still the question whether the plaintiff could show 'malice in fact'?[96] In any case, whose standards determined whether there was sufficient duty or interest? The duty might be purely moral, the interest might be that of the defendant or that of the person seeking information.[97] What role was played by the 'common convenience and welfare of society' in deciding what could be permitted? Could the answer be found only in the conscience and experience of the judge?[98] Should the talk of duties and interests be abandoned in favour of the older, more transparent, notion of 'such occasion as would make it right for a person to speak'?[99]

---

[92] (1834) 1 C. M. & R. 181, 193; much quoted: e.g. *Harrison* v. *Bush* (1856) 5 E. & B. 344; *Huntley* v. *Ward* (1859) 6 C.B. (N.S.) 514.

[93] A. Borthwick, *Treatise on the Law of Libel and Slander* (Edinburgh, 1826), 236; which led to the treatment of the subject by Starkie, *Slander and Libel* (2nd edn, 1830), lxxv–lxxvii, 315–20.

[94] Mitchell, *Making of Defamation*, 152–5.

[95] The issue was addressed in cases where a report about conduct was made to a person who had no authority to deal with it, e.g. *Blagg* v. *Sturt* (1846) 10 Q.B. 899; and see *Waller* v. *Loch*, below, n. 100.

[96] An adherent of this approach was Erle CJ, who refused to confine privilege to circumstances of duty and interest: *Coxhead* v. *Richards* (1846) 2 C.B. 569, 607–8; later, once it had become clearer that fair comment was a separate defence, he fell into speaking of duties and interests: *Whiteley* v. *Adams* (1863) 15 C.B. (N.S.) 392, 414. Cf. also the differences of view in *Bennett* v. *Deacon* (1846) 2 C.B. 628; *Blackman* v. *Pugh* (1846) 2 C.B. 611; Mitchell, *Making of Defamation*, 155–63. It at least became clear that the defendant had only to prove privileged circumstances, not to establish his own *bona fides*: *Jenoure* v. *Delmege* [1891] AC 73, JC.

[97] See e.g. Blackburn J., *Cowles* v. *Potts* (1865) 15 C.B. (N.S.) 392.

[98] See e.g. Lindley LJ, *Stuart* v. *Bell* [1891] 2 QB 341, 350.

[99] This proved to be Blackburn J.'s touchstone in *Davies* v. *Snead* (1870) LR 5 QB 608.

A good example of the perplexities was provided by *Waller* v. *Loch*,[100] which arose from activities of the Charity Organisation Society (COS). The COS, highly influential in the emergence of social work as a profession, existed to investigate whether paupers were morally deserving of beneficent support, or were set upon work-shy sponging, fit only for the 'less eligibility' of the public poor law. A lady involved in an effort by others to raise a subscription for an indigent gentlewoman, Mrs Waller, sought advice about her from Loch, the Society's forceful secretary, and received a critical reply. Since she lost her hopes, Mrs Waller sued Loch for libel; but the Court of Appeal found that the communication was privileged and that there was no evidence of malice. Clearly the judges approved of the Society's mission and actions. They therefore accepted Loch's belief that his advice was being sought by an intending subscriber to the scheme and so gave rise to the privilege, even if this belief was not justified. Jessel MR and Cotton LJ found it sufficient that Loch thought himself to be acting 'in discharge of a duty, legal moral or social—a legal duty or a duty of imperfect obligation'.[101] Jessel and Brett LJ referred also to the ineffable criterion of what was 'right in the interests of society'.[102] Opinion then turned against this broad view of privilege, perhaps the most dramatic incident being the *volte face* of Brett (as Esher MR) in favour of the duty being actual, rather than imagined.[103] Eventually this more limited position would prevail,[104] but not before the division of views had been through a second round of contention.[105] It is hard to escape the impression that the confusion of opinions on the subject operated to allow judges indirectly to express their own moral judgment on the defendant's actions, sometimes upsetting the jury's verdict. Once it became clearer that there must be actual duties or interests, rather than those merely supposed, the scope for judicial intervention was reduced.

Fair Comment

The uncertainty in defamation law stemming from the distinction between malice in fact and in law infused the development of a defence of fair comment. From the end of the eighteenth century the courts began to talk of a core idea

---

[100] (1881) 7 QBD 619.

[101] At pp. 621, 622, applying *Harrison* v. *Bush* (1855) 41 L.T. (N.S.) 588; and see also Erle CJ, *Whiteley* v. *Adams*, above, n. 96.

[102] Referring to Blackburn J.'s view in *Davies* v. *Snead*, above, n. 99.

[103] *Pullman* v. *Hill* [1891] 1 QB 524, 528; *Hebditch* v. *MacIlwaine* [1894] 2 QB 54, 60–2.

[104] *Adam* v. *Ward* [1917] AC 309.

[105] In *London Association for the Protection of Trade* v. *Greenlands* [1916] 2 AC 615, Lords Atkinson and Parker favoured the approach in the *Loch* case; but the former had some hard things to say about Blackburn J.'s position in *Davies*, and Lord Loreburn sought to impose a duty to check the truth of the communication.

that, for the free discussion of public affairs, people should be entitled to express critical opinions about others provided that they respected certain limits.[106] This disturbing period of the wars with France saw prosecutions for seditious and blasphemous libel being brought amid high controversy in attempts to suppress radical thought. As to derogatory vilification of public figures, from royalty downwards, there was a constant flow of squibs and cartoons for the reading public. Nonetheless the voices of retrenchment on the bench were prominent in insisting on the values of free public comment. 'Liberty of criticism must be allowed, or we shall have neither purity of taste nor of morals', intoned Lord Ellenborough.[107] How then to arrive at limitations that would prevent juries from going too far when they took a dislike to a plaintiff? Some courts considered that, for the defence to apply, the plaintiff had first to make literary or artistic works public, or to do some other public act, and the criticism had then to go to what had been done, and not to personal defects in the plaintiff's character.[108] The criticism had also to be honestly made, and it was not to stray into excessive vilification, or reckless disregard for the truth.[109] Once qualified privilege acquired its distinct role as an excuse for making a defamatory statement, unless it was shown to be malicious in fact, there were indications that fair comment fell into the same category. In rather strained fashion, it might be said that the public's interest in learning comments on public acts fell within Parke B.'s idea of privilege as a duty or interest to communicate or to receive. As with other privileged circumstances, it would then be for the plaintiff to prove actual malice in denial that the comment was 'fair'.

In *Campbell* v. *Spottiswoode*,[110] however, the Court of Queen's Bench set fair comment on its own feet, free of any association with qualified privilege. Instead, the court treated it as an aspect of 'libel or no libel', which implied that if there was a linkage it was to justification by showing the truth of the statement. The plaintiff had published articles in his newspaper espousing the cause of converting the Chinese to Christianity; the defendant, in his own paper, had

---

[106] Mitchell, *Making of Defamation*, 169–71.

[107] *Tabart* v. *Tipper* (1808) 1 Camp. 350. How otherwise could Locke have published his refutation of Filmer's paean on the divine right of kings?: *Carr* v. *Hood* (1808) 1 Camp. 355, 357. Lord Kenyon had been his precursor: *Dibdin* v. *Swan* (1793) 1 Esp. 28. The same sentiments were as common in the 1860s: see e.g. *Turnbull* v. *Bird* (1861) 2 F. & F. 508; *Hedley* v. *Barlow* (1865) 4 F. & F. 224.

[108] e.g. *Dunne* v. *Anderson* (1825) 3 Bing. 88 (petition to Parliament criticized). Here there is a link in thought to the development of fair comment for the purposes of criticism or review as a defence to infringement of copyright, which turned on the importance of free speech: see below, 926–7.

[109] See e.g. *Thompson* v. *Shackell* (1827) M. & M. 187; *Cooper* v. *Lawson* (1838) 8 Ad. & El. 746; *Gathercole* v. *Miall* (1846) 15 M. & W. 319; Mitchell, *Making of Defamation*, 174–86.

[110] (1863) 3 B. & S. 769, at 778, 781, 782–3.

alleged that the plaintiff had no fine motive for doing this but was seeking to increase his circulation. The jury had found for the plaintiff, with the proviso that the defendant had believed his imputations well-founded. In holding that this was not enough of itself to make out fair comment, the Court was searching to express the notion that there must be some basis in the circumstances which led to the comment being 'fair', over and above the defendant's motive for the libel.

There followed a period in which the judges explored the ramifications of this re-positioning. They continued to be against defendants having the freedom to make comments that were either 'malicious in fact', or in some sense went beyond the bounds set by the plaintiff's own public actions, whether as an author or a public figure, or whatever else.[111] Accordingly, there remained a basic difference between fair comment and justification, the defence which established for all purposes that there could be 'no libel' by what was true. Nonetheless, judges and textbook writers began to treat the two as complementary: justification related to statements of fact, fair comment to statements of opinion. The difference was taken to depend on whether or not the statement was verifiable. The dichotomy would have a long life in judgments and textbooks, but it was inherently difficult to apply. What, for example, of a statement that a doctor was a 'quack'?[112] Was that excusable only where (say) the man had no medical qualification? If that is what 'quack' meant, was the only issue justification? If it contained an added layer of comment, to be fair did it first have to refer to the lack of qualification? The perplexities were incapable of resolution by adopting a general principle.[113] At a trial, the court would have to decide what was justifiable truth and what was comment. As part, then, of determining 'fairness', a major factor was likely to be the lack of any demonstration of malice; and that meant malice in fact in the same sense as for qualified privilege.

Public Interests

The jurisdiction over defamation that triumphed in Victorian England was the personal action in the superior courts. But there were various public interests that tempered its scope. Of these fair comment was the most general; but the 'duties' and 'interests' that admitted qualified privilege were also recognition

---

[111] One curb was to require that the comment should itself include sufficient reference to the plaintiff's acts or publications to provide a basis for a fair comment: *O'Brien* v. *Marquess of Salisbury* (1889) 54 JP 215.

[112] *Dakhyl* v. *Labouchere* [1908] 2 KB 325n (HL).

[113] See Mitchell, *Making of Defamation*, 186–91, who continues the history through the succeeding century.

that social intercourse in many and varied circumstances demanded freedom of expression, however inaccurately disparaging of reputation it might be, provided that it was honest. Accordingly, difficulties in the general tests of justification, fair comment, and qualified privilege would be side-stepped in cases where there was a distinct 'public interest' in the freedom to publish statements about others, however defamatory.

First there were the 'absolute privileges', concerning which the plaintiff was not permitted to demonstrate that the defendant's malice in fact overstepped the mark. The categories, worked out one by one in case law and occasional legislation, concerned statements in Parliament, in judicial proceedings, and in communications between senior figures in government and the armed services. Secondly, by their side there developed special types of qualified privilege to cover reports of parliamentary and other governmental proceedings, of court and tribunal proceedings, and possibly of other public affairs, such as meetings. In all these situations, statements to the disadvantage of individuals could be particularly damaging to them, whether they were celebrated personages or ordinary people caught up for a moment in the glare of publicity. Accordingly, the reasons for denying them the chance to clear their name by bringing a defamation action needed to be strong, however much they varied with the types of institution concerned. Particularly in relation to the conduct, and then the reporting, of court and tribunal proceedings, a considerable body of case law developed through our period. This has been perceptively analysed by Mitchell who shows how difficult the courts found it to define the outer limits of what had to be tolerated.[114]

Take, first, the making of defamatory statements in the proceedings of the Commons or the Lords. Parliamentary speech had long been recognized as beyond the jurisdiction of the courts to adjudge, a position that was affirmed by Art. 9 of the Bill of Rights 1689. In the nineteenth century it went without contest. The reporting of debates in Parliament was more contentious. The well-known case of *Stockdale* v. *Hansard*[115] concerned the reports of Commons proceedings authorized by that House. Queen's Bench refused to accept that these were as exempt from libel actions as the Commons proceedings themselves. The legislature at once intervened to confer an absolute privilege on official reports and like material.[116] As to unofficial reports of parliamentary proceedings, the attempts in the eighteenth century to stamp upon them as being breaches of

---

[114] See Mitchell, *Making of Defamation*, Chs 9–10, esp. at 204–31 (judicial proceedings), 233–55 (reports thereof).

[115] (1839) 9 Ad. & El. 1.

[116] Parliamentary Papers Act 1840, 3 & 4 Vict. c. 9, s 1.

Standing Orders had given way by our period to an acceptance that they were unstoppable and that, indeed, reporters needed places to gather their accounts of what occurred in the chambers. This retraction made the reporting of defamatory remarks a distinct issue. With all the deliberation due to a question that was raised in the aftermath of the Second Reform Act, the Court of Queen's Bench, led by Cockburn CJ, treated them as subject to qualified privilege, the limitations being that they must be fair, rather than garbled or partial, and published without malice.[117]

Secondly, in proceedings before courts and tribunals, defamation was continual, for they were places where accusations of personal failings occurred all the time, some true, some false. So far as trials were concerned, the proceedings were mostly in public, for trials behind closed doors conjured visions of Star Chamber. In myriad circumstances, objections might be taken to the defamatory content of pleadings and indictments, of what witnesses said, of what documents provided by way of evidence, of how lawyers representing parties (and indeed the parties themselves) put their case, of how judges, justices, and jurors expressed themselves. While the judges of the superior courts had, from the late eighteenth century onwards, held themselves immune from action if they made defamatory remarks, at lower levels, the question tended to become intermixed with more general responsibilities not to exceed proper jurisdiction. Only when magistrates and county court judges were accorded general exemptions from suit for assuming power to conduct proceedings beyond their remit, did the Court of Exchequer finally decide that those with magisterial authority in all courts should be treated as immune from libel or slander actions. This was said to be necessary, in the interests of the public, in order to ensure that judges of all kinds remained free and independent in the conduct of the business before them; or, on a somewhat different tack, that they could not be expected to excuse themselves to a jury.[118]

When it came to counsel and witnesses, the earlier law had not excused defamations made maliciously and the same approach was being applied around 1820.[119] But as with judges 50 years later, a complete immunity was said to be required in the interests of freedom to speak in court (and it was

[117] *Wason* v. *Walter* (1868) LR 4 QB 73.

[118] *Scott* v. *Stansfield* (1868) 3 Ex. 220. This, however, came after judgments from Lord Denman CJ and then Lord Cockburn CJ had sought to retain liability in the course of duty where there was express malice and lack of reasonable and probable cause: *Kendeillon* v. *Maltby* (1842) Car. & M. 402; *Thomas* v. *Churton* (1862) 2 B. & S. 475. Even after this, Lord Coleridge CJ reverted to the restricted line: *Seaman* v. *Netherclift* (1876) 1 CPD 540; but was corrected by the Court of Appeal: *Anderson* v. *Gorrie* [1894] 1 QB 668; Mitchell, *Making of Defamation*, 204–11.

[119] *Hodgson* v. *Scarlett* (1818) 1 B. & Ald. 232; *Lewis* v. *Walter* (1821) 4 B. & Ald. 605.

an immunity from other proceedings as well, such as negligence). This had to prevail, it was held, despite the occasional malicious person taking advantage of the courtroom.[120] In all these situations there were points about exactly what fell within the immunity.[121] While the preference for complete immunity became the Victorian orthodoxy, one justification offered for it was the existence of other sanctions for abuses of court process—the power of courts to punish contempts, prosecutions for perjury, and actions for malicious prosecution. As Mitchell points out, the choice that was really being made was about the type of proceeding by which defamatory declarations could be policed.[122]

Reports of court proceedings containing defamatory matter were repetitions of what had happened in a public forum and therefore raised the issue whether, if the reporting was accurate, it must be excused because of a public interest in knowing what happened. The issue was much litigated in the uneasy 1820s. Richard Carlile, irrepressible publisher in every radical cause, not least the campaign for press freedom, had put the report of a trial in his *Republican*, which the Queen's Bench found to be blasphemous and indecent. The court held that no report of proceedings could contain anything defamatory, seditious, or morally offensive.[123] In Common Pleas, however, Tindal CJ and Park J. took the view that there was a privilege to publish a court report, even though it contained defamatory matter, provided that it was a fair account—which in the case before them was not made out.[124] The emphasis on fairness meant that there was no question of an absolute privilege.

In 1888 the Law of Libel Amendment Act—responding to the demand for clarification from the press lobby—explicitly provided that a contemporaneous newspaper report of court proceedings heard in public was privileged if it was fair and accurate. Since the privilege was not stated to be absolute,[125] this was

---

[120] *Dawkins* v. *Lord Rokeby* (1875) LR 7 HL 744, 752.

[121] These included questions of which bodies precisely were covered by the immunity; and likewise of wholly extraneous statements: see Mitchell, *Making of Defamation*, 219–31.

[122] *Ibid.*, 216–19.

[123] *R* v. *Carlile* (1819) 3 B. & Ald. 167, building particularly on *Curry* v. *Walter* (1796) 1 B. & P. 525 and *R* v. *Fisher* (1811) 2 Camp. 563; see also *Lewis* v. *Clement* (1820) 3 B. & Ald. 702, 710. Abbott CJ would depart from this stern view of the issue where the publisher of *The Times* was the defendant (*Lewis* v. *Walter* (1821) 4 B. & Ald. 605, 612); but his fellow judges stuck to their line: *see Flint* v. *Pike* (1825) 4 B. & C. 473. For a contemporary account, see Starkie, *Slander and Libel*, Ch. 10; and see generally, Mitchell, *Making of Defamation*, 233–55. The foundational case of *Curry* put the issue in terms of pleading, holding that under the general issue the defendant could raise the answer that a press report was nothing more than an accurate account of what was said in court; followed in *Hoare* v. *Silverlock* (1850) 9 C.B. 525.

[124] *Saunders* v. *Mills* (1829) 3 B. & Ad. 167; *Roberts* v. *Brown* (1834) 10 Bing. 519.

[125] The original bill proposed doing so: Mitchell, *Making of Defamation*, 245. It has been inserted in the modern law, just as some of the other limitations in the Act have been removed.

arguably no more than a restatement of the common law position, with a limitation to contemporaneous reports (as a warning against rehashing old scores that had gone to court). At least it clarified the nature of the proceedings to which the privilege could apply, on which there had been a good deal of case law over time. The hearing had to have been in public.[126] No matter, then, that it was only *ex parte*, or that it was a preliminary hearing before magistrates of a criminal charge on indictment.[127] It still had to be fair, and arguments continued over how far this meant a verbatim account of all that was said by witnesses, counsel, judge, and jury that related to the alleged slander. Eventually, the regular practice of the press of abbreviating lengthy exchanges, for instance by only reporting the judgment, came to be treated as sufficing for the privilege. But this was only as a consequence of the convoluted proceedings in *Macdougall* v. *Knight*,[128] in which the Court of Appeal favoured the generous approach, the House of Lords in dicta then expressed doubts about so categorical a stance, and finally in a second action between the parties, the Court of Appeal restated its position. This was scarcely precedent making on any secure basis.

Altogether the history of defamation in the nineteenth century shows the circumlocutions that are inherent in the creation of settled rules out of reasons for judgment. The vagaries can be traced in other less central issues, where analogies would be drawn upon piecemeal where they fitted the result that the judge was after. For instance, it was not until 1895 that the Court of Appeal established that communications between at least high-ranking officers in government should have an absolute privilege.[129] The case before them concerned a defamatory statement in a memorandum from the Secretary for India to his Under-Secretary that was made in order to enable the latter to answer a parliamentary question. But how far this extended would remain shrouded.

As to reports of public meetings, the possibility of conferring a qualified privilege alarmed Lord Campbell CJ in 1857.[130] Two decades later, there were signs that some concession would be made, but the judgments of the Divisional Court and the Court of Appeal in *Purcell* v. *Sowler* showed how difficult it was to lay down limitations on the scope of the privilege.[131] Leading press proprietors

---

[126] See the influential decision in *Wason* v. *Walter*, above, n. 117.

[127] One reason earlier given for not excusing reports of these proceedings was that the defamation might prejudice a forthcoming trial (see *Duncan* v. *Thwaites* (1824) 3 B. & C. 556; *Lewis* v. *Levy* (1858) 27 LJ QB 282), which meant that the privilege could apply when the charges were dismissed (a view finally accepted by the Court of Appeal in *Kimber* v. *Press Association* [1893] 1 QB 65).

[128] (1886) 17 QBD 636, CA; (1889) 14 App Cas 194, HL; (1890) 25 QBD 1, CA.

[129] *Chatterton* v. *Secretary of State for India* [1895] 2 QB 189.

[130] *Davison* v. *Duncan* (1857) 7 E. & B. 229.

[131] (1877) 2 CPD 218, CA.

secured a Commons Select Committee to investigate the issue in 1879 and 1880.[132] The upshot was the Newspaper Libel and Registration Act 1881, s 2. A report of a public meeting in a newspaper was accorded privilege on four conditions: it had to be fair and accurate; the publication must be without malice; it must have been in the public interest to publish the matter; and the opportunity to publish a reasonable letter of explanation or contradiction must have been accorded.[133] Press interests remained dissatisfied and argued for more precise definition in their favour. The Law of Libel Amendment Act 1888, s 4, allowed a second chance. The provision now included an elaborate listing of public meetings; and for good measure also encompassed lawful meetings that were 'for the furtherance or discussion of any matter of public concern'. However, the 'public benefit' condition was now cast in a tighter net. The defence did not extend to 'any matter not of public concern and the publication of which is not to the public benefit'. These were eventually characterized as matters of law for the judge to decide.[134] In the sphere of public meetings, they raised the troubling distinction between what the public liked being told and what it deserved to know. At this early stage in the spread of popular newspapers, the difference was already becoming a frequent puzzle for editors and courts in balancing press freedom against undue intervention in private lives. It was not a problem that would recede with greater experience.

The Continuum

Defamation as a private wrong came of age in the nineteenth century. It was defined very largely by common law, but by the end there were signs that legislation would be used to mark off its extent, particularly when the fourth estate pressed its demands for limitations. Deep-seated indignation against calumny—the bearing of false witness against neighbours—was an age-old human emotion, but it was no longer to be avenged by physical violence. Nor was criminal process to be much used, perhaps because the disturbances that might follow from exciting mobs against individuals by accusations of wrong conduct were becoming less frequent and threatening. Instead, the legal process through which counterattack was to be channelled was mainly to be the civil action for defamation, the sanction, for libel and some types of slander, being an award of damages taken at large, rather than being conditioned on proof of specific economic loss.

---

[132] SC on the Law of Libel, *PP* 1880, x, 301. For the politics of the 1881 Act and its successor in 1888, see Mitchell, *Making of Defamation*, 261–9.

[133] For the aims of press interests in securing this protection, see Mitchell, 'Law of the Press?'.

[134] *Adam* v. *Ward* [1917] AC at 332, 351.

In his *Preliminary Discourse* published in 1830,[135] Thomas Starkie made many claims for the expediency of this approach, though then he thought the survival of the distinctions between libel and slander to be anachronistic. He certainly regarded a law that only required recantation and apology as weak. He found in damages a tool that allowed the extent of publication and therefore of the injury done to be brought into account. He approved of the 'publish and be damned' attitude which underlay the refusal to grant injunctive relief by way of prior restraint, which was strictly applied in his day. He saw in the development of categories of privilege an instrument by which to fashion exceptions where the ordinary business of the world demanded that statements besmirching reputation be excused. But it was right that the judges should determine the circumstances that gave rise to each privilege. Where it was qualified rather than absolute, it would then be for the jury to decide, if there was evidence in support, that the defendant had acted with malice and so remained liable. Beyond the range of such defences, Starkie gave voice to the theory that the liability was based ultimately on fault, rather than on an invariate presumption that the person publishing the libel must be taken to have intended the consequences of his act.

For Starkie, the one absolute was that to be actionable the statement must have been false. He steadfastly opposed the idea of a legal weapon that could be used to discourage the making of statements about people that were true of them, however galling or nerve-wracking it might be to have them known. To the contrary, Borthwick had argued the virtues of Scots law in its tendency to make truth only one factor to be weighed in the balance of liability. Starkie fired back, insisting that even a defendant motivated by spite should be under no liability for true statements. Rather, communities must always be entitled to know the truth about their members, however disreputable it might be. It was, he observed, 'the most dishonest and worthless members of society [who]...use the greatest exertions to preserve a fair exterior'. It was a bullish attitude that was already stamped into English law where it would remain unquestioned. Warren and Brandeis might urge the recognition of a common law right to the protection of personal privacy, but the English would show no inclination to allow the tort of defamation to provide its starting point.

[135] See above, pp. 836–7.

II

Copyright[1]

1. PRINT AND ITS PURVEYORS: DEMANDS FOR A 'COPY' RIGHT

In the early seventeenth century patents for inventions took a first step towards the modern form of a right open to the world based upon legal principles and enduring for a specified period (the 14 years allowed by the Statute of Monopolies 1624, s 6).[2] The modern idea of copyright comes a century later (with the Statute of Anne, 1710) and is to some extent modelled on the invention patent. But patents remained a relative rarity until the mid-nineteenth century, for reasons that we will in due course explore. Copyright, on the other hand, became a crucial anchor of book production and marketing in the course of the eighteenth century and so in an economic sense became the prime form of intellectual property (to use a modern categorization). For that reason we deal with it first.

The emergence of laws restricting the publishing of books, pamphlets, and the like had followed upon the introduction of printing into England in the late fifteenth century. For the next two centuries, monarchs and their political and religious counsellors had striven to eliminate the threatening prospects of the new medium. The Crown took to granting patents to print both specified books (such as translations of the Bible) and types of books (such as religious, legal, and medical books, together with those annual necessities known as almanacs).[3] In 1557 a licensing system was organized through the offices of the Stationers' Company, stationers being the 'booksellers' (i.e. the forerunners of modern publishers) who organized publication and distribution and so had their own commercial interests in the matter. Under this separate scheme, powers were

---

[1] Statutory and other sources are available on *Primary Sources in Copyright* (where comparisons may be made with material from France, Germany, and the US): www.copyrighthistory.com. Where this is so, it is indicated in footnotes by '*Primary Sources*'. Each file is accompanied by a scholarly commentary ('Comm'). In the case of the UK these are by Ronan Deazley.

[2] See below, 932.

[3] The Statute of Monopolies 1624 (21 Jac. 1, c. 3) contained an exemption allowing such privileges to continue: see s 10. For the almanacs monopoly granted by James I to the Stationers Company itself and its fate, see C. Blagden, 'Thomas Carnan and the Almanack Monopoly' (1961) 14 *St. in Bibliography* 24.

conferred to prosecute those who had no licence to publish, and these related both to prohibited books and imitated books. The royal patents, which were a useful source of income to the Crown, continued to have significant effect into the eighteenth century, whereas the licensing system had weakened after the Restoration, and spluttered to a final halt in 1695, once the succession crisis had given new strength to the crusade for free speech.

By then the book trade, made up mainly of booksellers and printers, was well established, with growing prospects for considerable profits. By its internal rules the Stationers' Company had built up a mutual non-aggression pact: each member would purchase and hold the right of 'copy' in his books; the others would not bring out their own editions of the same work. This arrangement could in principle be made to last in perpetuity, though the right to copy might be acquired only for a limited time; and—property-like—it could be divided into shares, giving rise to a market within the Company under which 'copies' were transferred or split up among investing members. Liaisons among the various participants led to deals over distribution that earned the linkages the name of congers.[4]

As publishing spread in harness with growing literacy, however, piratical editions of books had become more common. But the Stationers' arrangements were internal and the old remedies against outsiders that were part of the licensing system had been lost. The Company had led the lobbying for new protection against these outsiders. In 1710 they secured the first enactment of the copyright type that would endure in the civilized world—the Statute of Anne.

The Statute had given special penal remedies for infringing the right of 'copy' in published books. However, evidence is now emerging that in the later seventeenth century, Chancery had regularly issued interim injunctions against book pirates, thus providing copyright owners with a civil cause of action which survived from then on. Its basis would eventually be established as a common law right for damages, which equity supported by injunction.[5] It acknowledged that the right arose in authors and their successors in title; and it limited the duration of the right which it conferred to a term of 14 years, with an extension, if the author was then still alive, for another 14.[6] By proclaiming that writers of books

---

[4] 8 Anne c. 19, s 1. The penal provisions went, first, to forfeiture of unauthorized copies for their destruction; and, secondly, to a penalty of a penny per infringing page, to be divided equally between the Crown and the proprietor of the Copy-right. By 1820, the penny had increased to threepence.

[5] See H T Gómez-Arostegui, 'What History Teaches Us about Copyright Injunctions and the Inadequate-Remedy-at-Law Requirement' (2008) 81 Southern California LR 1197–1280. The injunction appears to have been the form of relief that booksellers wanted. There is little sign that they proceeded for the 1710 statutory penalties instead.

[6] Sections 1, 11. The second term was capable of being understood as imposing a reversion of the copyright from any publisher back to the author. But later it was held that an assignment of both periods to a publisher at the outset overrode any reversion to the author or his representatives: see

gained this right subject only to registration with the Stationers' Company, the Statute advanced the perception that here was a private entitlement, not a privilege dependent on authorization from the Crown.[7] The right was one that could be assigned or licensed to others and as such it was therefore property in a legal sense, rather than a 'propriety' among the Stationers. All of which was highly important in setting basic patterns of thought—first and foremost, that it was the carrying out of authorship that justified the market-place exclusivity against imitators, even though in reality it was the authors' assignees—the booksellers—who were the key beneficiaries. To some extent it represented compromise, since the objects named in its preamble were not only the 'very great prejudice and detriment' to authors and proprietors from pirates, but also 'the encouragement of learned men to compose and write useful books'. The right was not merely that of an entrepreneur to prevent unfair competition affecting the bookseller's market position at any particular time. Its proprietary character sustained whatever marketplace popularity the book had to extract monopoly profits. But against that prospect, there was also cumbrous machinery against unduly high prices being charged for books;[8] and the Stationers' Company was subject to penalties if it wrongly refused to register a title.[9] Otherwise the Statute left much obscure.

2. THE LEGAL SOURCES OF COPYRIGHT

The eighteenth-century history of book copyright brought volatile debate and action. We are concerned with the consequences from 1820, and to bring the story to that date, it is crucial to emphasize two points. First, the existence at so early a stage of a statutory regime, however incomplete, meant that expansions of the subject-matter or the scope of the right would mostly require further legislation.[10]

Carnan v. *Bowles* (1785) 2 Bro. C.C. 80; for this and for the impact of the amending Act of 1814, 54 Geo. III c. 156, s 8, see R. Godson, Practical Treatise on the Law of Patents for Inventions, and Copyright (London, 1823).

   [7] When it suited judges, however, they might revert to the idea of privilege as an answer to arguments based on universal natural right: see, for instance, Bayley J., *Clementi* v. *Walker* (1824) 2 B. & C. 861, 867–8, below, n. 145. Compare the rather slower re-conception of patents for inventions: below, 937–8.

   [8] Lord Brougham would call it 'absurd', but it was a demonstration nonetheless of the legislature's intent in 1710 only to benefit British authors, printers, and publishers: *Jefferys* v. *Boosey* (1854) 4 H.L.C. at 971–2. The price-setting regime was not used and was abandoned in 1739.

   [9] 8 Anne c. 19, ss 2, 3.

   [10] Thus in 1735, William Hogarth had been the leading advocate of an Act giving protection to engravings and the like: 8 Geo. II c. 13. In 1767, the term of this right was extended from 14 to 28 years from first publication: 7 Geo. III c. 38; D Hunter, 'Copyright Protection for Engravings and Maps in Eighteenth Century Britain' (1987) 9 *The Library* (6th edn), 128. Acts of 1798 and 1814 had given a 14-year term of protection to statues: 38 Geo. III c. 71; 54 Geo. III c. 56. See also the first step

Nonetheless, the judges proved willing enough to recognize the basic justice of the cause promoted by booksellers in the name of their authors. Alongside the summary process laid down in the Statute they accepted that an action on the case would lie for damages at common law.[11] In addition, by equitable process, injunctions would lie against pirates, which in plain cases could take the form of interlocutory relief. The very fact that the two systems between them were prepared to do so, showed a readiness to foster 'literary property' that became embedded from at least the early eighteenth century. It is both an undervaluation and an exaggeration to claim, as Mark Rose and others have done, that it was only in the last third of the century that the judges had transformed the publishers' protection of 1710 into an authors' right.[12] The judges' view of the matter led them necessarily to examine the precise scope of the right to attack unauthorized copying. One fundamental aspect of this was whether the Statute's summary process co-existed beside a more embracing right at common law, founded upon a requisite of natural justice. If this was so, how far did the latter embrace circumstances that were not within the range of the Statute? Exercises in historical jurisprudence of this kind would recur whenever copyright policies were in debate, until the whole law was placed within a single statutory frame by the 'Imperial' Copyright Act 1911.

Secondly—being the great issue that followed upon that jurisprudential question—the limited duration expressed in the Statute was far from certain in effect.[13] Did its term apply only to the penal remedies, or did it also bring to an end any common law copyright that there might be? From this had grown high controversy—the 'Battle of the Booksellers'—between, on the one hand, the London Stationers and their 'congers' and, on the other, provincial challengers

---

in 1787 towards protecting industrial designs—in this instance on linen and the like: 27 Geo. III c. 38. A publisher of music, the youngest son of J. S. Bach, persuaded King's Bench to treat his compositions as a 'book or other writing' within the Statute of Anne: *Bach* v. *Longman* (1777) 2 Cowp. 623. For the impact of these developments by 1820, see Godson, *Patents and Copyright*, Chs 5, 6; I. Espinasse, *Treatise on the Law of Actions on Statutes* (1824); R. Maugham, *Treatise on the Laws of Literary Property* (1828), 65–76.

[11] For cases dealing with the issue after *Donaldson*, see R. Deazley, *Rethinking Copyright* (Cheltenham, 2006), 26—37.

[12] See e.g. M. Rose, *Authors and Owners* (Cambridge, 1993) and 'The Author as Proprietor' in B. Sherman and A. Strowel, *Of Authors and Origins* (Oxford, 1994), 23; J. Feather, 'The Book Trade in Politics' (1980) 8 *Publishing Hist.* 19; cf. L. R. Patterson, *Copyright in Historical Perspective* (Nashville, 1968).

[13] For the now extensive literature on the controversy, see R. Deazley, *On the Origin of the Right to Copy* (Oxford, 2004); I. J. Alexander, *The Metaphysics of the Law: Drawing the Boundaries of Copyright Law 1710–1911*, (Ph. D. Thesis, Cambridge University 2007), Part A. On the Scots side of the argument, note esp. R. S. Tompson, 'Scottish Judges and the Birth of British Copyright' [1992] *Juridical Rev.* 18.

whom they kept out of their ranks. First, Chancery judges, and eventually King's Bench, had been prepared to hold that common law copyright was, as a form of property, perpetual in nature and therefore survived the expiry of the remedies enacted in the Statute of Anne.[14] But the Scottish courts had refused to acknowledge such a right in Scots law.[15] Since it was Edinburgh booksellers who most pugnaciously challenged the London coterie, the opposed positions in law were of high significance.

In *Donaldson* v. *Becket* (1774) the great question had gone to the House of Lords. By way of preparation, the common law judges were summoned to answer five questions posed on behalf of the House, and the 11 answers received—an important record of reasoned opinion—showed a fairly even range of views for and against a perpetual right in published books. In a jury-like vote, the Lords overruled the King's Bench position: once the term in the Statute of Anne had expired no other copyright in a published work would continue.[16] A resolution had been reached against perpetuity that most of the world would follow, as states began to introduce laws on authors' rights.[17] Suddenly in 1774 unauthorized booksellers had acquired the freedom to publish older books that still had a market. Within the Stationers' Company sales of 'copy' and mutual arrangements for the distribution of books continued on the assumption that among members no time limit applied to exclusive rights; but soon enough there were challenges from outside; and in numerous instances they led to the appearance of markedly cheaper editions of books with a long life in the market.[18]

---

[14] See esp. *Millar* v. *Taylor* (1768) 4 Burr. 2303, where Lord Mansfield gave the lead, supported by learned disquisitions from Willes and Aston JJ, but over the categorical dissent of Yates J. Blackstone, it may be noted, was a firm supporter of Mansfield's position: *Comms*, ii, 405–7.

[15] 11 of the 12 judges of the Court of Session refused to find it a place in the law of nature or nations or of Scots common law: *Hinton* v. *Donaldson* (1773), reproduced in S. Parks (ed.), *The Literary Property Debate: Six Tracts, 1764–1774* (New York, 1975), item C. A perpetual monopoly, said Lord Kames, 'would raise a fund sufficient to purchase a great kingdom. The works alone of Shakespeare, or of Milton, would be a vast estate' (p. 19).

[16] (1774) 2 Bro. P.C. 129, *Primary Sources* UK . Lay peers engaged in the hearing decided the appeal by vote. In the immediate aftermath, the London booksellers failed to secure a reversal of the decision by statute: Deazley, *Origin*, Ch. 9.

[17] By 1828, France would have a copyright of the author's life plus 20 years: see generally, J. Ginsburg, 'A Tale of Two Copyrights', in Sherman and Strowel, *Authors and Origins*, 131. While some German states did much the same, others opted for perpetuity—an approach that would survive until 1842. For both countries, see W. Patry, *Copyright* (2007), i: paras 1.3, 1.4.

[18] For a range of examples, see R. D. Altick, *The English Common Reader* (Chicago, 1957); J. Raven, *Judging New Wealth: Popular Publishing and the Responses to Commerce in England 1750–1800* (Oxford, 1992); I. Rivers (ed.), *Books and their Readers in Eighteenth Century England* (2001); W. St Clair, *The Reading Nation in the Romantic Period* (Cambridge, 2004); J. Raven, *The Business of Books* (New Haven, 2007).

3. JUSTIFICATIONS AND THE EVOLVING LAW

Donaldson v. *Becket* had established that copyright was a form of property relating to published books that was peculiarly circumscribed by the limitations on its term as set by the Statute of Anne. The Lords' vote left unsettled how far countervailing interests—of rival booksellers and printers, and of the purchasing public—would also deserve to be recognized where they related to other issues.[19] While those who had argued for perpetual copyright claimed it as an essential entitlement of those who engaged in authorship, their opponents could not proceed in such categorical terms. Since the Statute dealt only with published works, it was soon assumed that a 'common law' right in English law must attach to any manuscript as yet unpublished for as long as it remained so. Indeed, in the case law of 1769–74 no English judge had denied that position. Arguments there might be about whether any legal right could extend beyond the author's decision to permit publication and the consequent presentation of the book to the public, but before that moment there had to be an individual right to prevent others abusing so intimate a relationship as that between the creator and his work. This could be important, for instance, in respect of the text of plays, which might well not be published even after successful runs of performances.[20]

This 'common law' copyright, quite apart from the Statute, was, it seems, acknowledged as a right that might found a common law action in the strict sense; but in practice its enforcement was through injunctions. In courts of equity the relation between that remedy and the substantive basis for granting it was allowed to remain imprecise enough for Lord Chancellors and others to give rein to their considerable sense of moral propriety.[21] As this jurisdiction expanded to cover obligations of confidence and trust, within or beyond the bounds of enforceable contracts, it would be seized upon by authors such as Warren and Brandeis as a likely catalyst for developments of legal doctrine that responded to modern susceptibilities. A remarkable pragmatism thus prevailed. Copyright in published books was the subject of a statute, but was in turn limited by a court's interpretation of the effect of that enactment; rights in material that was fixed but not published, or was not fixed at all, turned on a right of action recognized in equity,

---

[19] There is now a considerable literature on what answers were given to the Lords' questions by various judges who provided advice in *Donaldson* v. *Becket*; on the subsequent understanding of that advice and the decision in the case; and on what could and should have been treated as having some value as a precedent: see esp. H. Abrams, 'The Historical Foundation of American Copyright Law: Exploding the Myth of Common Law Copyright' (1983) 29 *Wayne LR* 1119–91; R. Deazley, *Right to Copy*, Chs 8, 9; and *Rethinking Copyright*, 15–24, 56–64.

[20] *Macklin* v. *Richardson* (1770) Amb. 694; *Primary Sources* (UK Comm. to Dramatic and Literary Copyright Act 1833 para. 3); but for later doubts about the decision, see below, n. 75.

[21] See below, pp. 898–900.

which was indeterminate in duration, applied without consideration of national allegiance of the person claiming to be injured, and had a scope that turned on the individual judge's sense of moral impropriety that was largely undefined even by decisions in equity.

The eventual recognition of any common law right is a response to evolutionary pressures which may themselves leave only a clouded mark on the record. In the case of copyright, there continued to be much historical argument about whether a common law right against copying a text had emerged before enactment of the Statute of Anne. If it had, its independent characteristics were arguably the stronger. The difficulty, however, was in showing that a general property had been acknowledged by 1710, which could afterwards be treated as distinct from the rights conferred under printers' privileges and the compacts within the Stationers' Company. Much was posited on the basis of what King's Bench might have done, if only it had had the chance. This style of 'must-have-been' speculation was, for instance, still being pursued by the formidable Thomas Scrutton in his prize essay on the subject.[22] It was a polemical deployment of history to a degree that invited debunking—and among Scrutton's contemporaries this was provided by the ebullient Augustine Birrell.[23] It may, however, have had a substance in Chancery practice that neither side appreciated.

Today suppositional history mostly takes less fact-specific forms. But it remains present in arguments that copyright laws were largely developed in a coupling with the romantic ideal of the Author. This passionate article of faith treated authors as figures of original genius with powers of perception and expression ranging far beyond those of pedestrian mortals, and in Britain at least its adherents saw it embodied most numinously in the poets of the 'Age of Revolution'.[24] In Britain what mattered more, in terms of the legal development of copyright, had been what the courts were prepared to do more than half a century before, because it was then that they had found a right of property implicit in the Statute of Anne. Given the precocious development of literary property in England, the current of influence ran, if anything, from legal rule and business practice to later hero-worship of the Author, rather than the reverse.[25] In the nineteenth century

---

[22] First and most extensively published as *The Laws of Copyright* (1883), Ch. 1 (three later editions to 1904 curtailed this discussion).

[23] *Seven Lectures on the Law and History of Copyright in Books* (1899), Ch. 1. See W. R. Cornish, 'The Copyright History of What-Must-Have-Been', in G. Roussel et al. (eds), *Mélanges Victor Nabhan* (Montreal, 2004), 61.

[24] The Romanticists' glorification of originality was soon enough challenged in Britain by authors and critics of more sceptical mien: see esp. R. MacFarlane, *Original Copy* (Oxford, 2007); also C. Pettit, *Patent Invention* (Oxford, 2004).

[25] In *Authorship and Copyright* (1992), David Saunders makes a convincing case for a complex interweaving of ideological positions and trade practices in eighteenth-century developments. See

each conception would bolster the other in sustaining copyright as something far more than just an initial protection of the investment needed to secure the creation of literary and other artistic material.[26]

In *Donaldson* it had not been necessary to decide the intermediate case—whether the common law right retained a co-valent status with rights under the Statute of Anne. The basis for civil remedies against infringement during that all-important period appeared to arise apart from the Statute, which suggested that the common law retained a role after publication. That, however, was treated in the nineteenth century as too nice an understanding and common law copyright was mostly taken to run only until publication. The Statute became the sole instrument having effect thereafter and interpretation of its language was accordingly the one source open to the judges so far as concerned material that they construed to be a 'book'. As we shall see, they took the Statute to cover printed publications of a wide range, which in terms of content stretched from the sublime to the mundane, the elaborate to the trivial; and they treated what would constitute infringement on a scale that broadened with their estimate of the quality and quantity of what was taken from the original. For work that could not fall within that capacious conception, there remained the ill-defined concept of 'common law' copyright or the securing of new legislation.[27]

4. THE VICTORIAN DEBATES: OF DURATION AND OTHER BASIC CONCEPTS

In the nineteenth century, the legal inheritance was never far from serious contention. There would be heated debates over Talfourd's bills of 1837–42, leading eventually to the Copyright Amendment Act 1842, which for 60 years would define the scope of copyright in published 'books'. Likewise they arose when extensions of the law to new forms of work were sought, the most notable of these in Victorian Britain being the introduction of a statutory copyright over drawings, paintings, and photographs by the Fine Arts Copyright Act 1862. The Royal Commission on Copyright of 1876–8 devoted considerable attention to the divisions between enthusiasts for authorial property and their economist detractors; and in that era philosophic differences became part of the international debate over copyright in the global trade in books, music, and reproductions of art. The

---

also his 'Dropping the Subject: An Argument for a Positive History of Authorship and the Law of Copyright', in B. Sherman and A. Strowel (eds), *Of Authors and Origins* (1994), 93–110.

[26] See further below, pp. 887–9.

[27] For an instance of small subjects tackled by legislation, see the creation of lecturers' right in 1835, below, 899.

ideological confrontations continued to be much about limiting the duration of copyright. But equally they ran over into such questions as: the types of work to be protected; the determination of 'authorship' and thus the initial entitlement to the right; the categories of activity which others could not carry out without the proprietor's permission; the degree to which the right was truly exclusive property, rather that just an obligation to pay compensation; and the 'moral' protection that might inure to an author even after disposal of the manuscript or the entitlement to exploit it. It is these issues that will provide the main discussion in this section.

We are dealing with a complex picture, its foreground occupied by an enactment of a strikingly early date for what is essentially a private right, even though it is, from 1710 onwards, regulated by legislation dealing with formal and essential conditions. The nineteenth-century course of statute law continued to draw in new subject-matter as technology advanced to provide new media of expression—and even more, new apparatus for multiple copying. The result, as with so many other fields of regulation, was a growing jigsaw of instances in legislation, not necessarily cut to fit with one another. The interpretive skills of judges were accordingly taxed and complaints about aligning different elements in the image overall came to fill much of the debates.

The notion of a right that derives from an author's creation, but advantages the publishers who risk capital for returns on their publications, has an inherent ambiguity that becomes the more incongruous as the term of the right extends. Duration does not matter to ephemeral works, whatever their initial popularity, if that dissipates quickly. It is material when the work has an enduring value to the public, whether that is for its aesthetic worth, its factual or theoretical content, or because of some non-literary association, arising for instance from the author's or the subject's private or public life. A substantial duration meets the claims for works that were initially ignored and later recovered and for those good for periodic revival or for re-vamping, as where a novel is serialized in a magazine or translated into a foreign language.

In 1814, the term for copyright in published books laid down in the Statute of Anne had for the first time been extended. The regular term for all books became 28 years; if the author was then still alive the copyright in work ran until his or her death.[28] This was a concession designed to deflect intensive lobbying against the official deposit requirement in the Statute of Anne,[29] under which publishers of

---

[28] 54 Geo. III c. 156, s 5, *Primary Sources*. The extension did not apply to books previously published: *Brooke* v. *Clarke* (1818) 1 B. & Ald. 396.

[29] 8 Anne c. 19, s 5. The scheme had had a precursor under the Licensing Acts but it had disappeared in 1695.

new editions were obliged to place copies with the Royal Library, six Universities in England and Scotland, Sion College, and the Faculty of Advocates in Edinburgh.[30] Largely ignored in the eighteenth century, calls for revival of this system in the name of public learning had provoked vociferous objections by the booksellers. They argued for instance that it was on the most costly books with limited print runs that the impact of this 'tax' was most keenly felt. While they made little impression on Parliament, the system was in some measure revised.[31] at the same time, the extension of copyright term was offered as a not inconsiderable sop.[32]

In 1837, Thomas Talfourd—at the time, Serjeant, playwright, and Member of Parliament—took up the cause of the copyright of writers. The six years of intense debate that ensued have been perceptively recreated by Catherine Seville.[33] Talfourd was able to draw several great literary figures, including Carlyle, Thomas Arnold, Southey, and (chief among them) the elderly Wordsworth, to lend support to the cause.[34] Talfourd sought a copyright term of the author's life and 60 years thereafter and so put his claim on the inherent right of the creator of a work to a period of market exclusivity in considerable measure equivalent to the real and personal assets that a man of property might leave as his estate.[35] Much was made of the plights into which even great authors could fall, such as Walter Scott's position after the failure of the Bannatyne printing business and his extraordinary burst of writing to meet his obligations as guarantor. Some publishers and booksellers were likewise in favour of the sweeping extension of term; but by no means all, since by this time those who traded in cheap reprints

[30] In the wake of the Union with Ireland in 1800, UK copyright was extended to that country, and two libraries in Dublin—Trinity College and the King's Inns—also became entitled to deposit copies: 41 Geo. III c. 107, s 6.

[31] 54 Geo. III c. 156, ss 3, 4.

[32] The Libraries Deposit Act 1837, 6 & 7 Will IV, c. 110, and then the Copyright Act 1842, ss 6–10 would reduce the number of recipient libraries to five: three in England and one each in Scotland and Ireland. See R. Partridge, *History of the Legal Deposit of Books* (1938); I. R. Willison, *Legal Deposit: A Provisional Perspective* (1999) 45 *Publishing House* 66; J. Feather, *Publishing, Piracy and Politics* (1994), Ch. 4; Alexander, *Boundaries of Copyright*, Ch. 5.2.

[33] C. A. Seville, *Literary Copyright Reform in Early Victorian England* (Cambridge, 1999).

[34] Deazley, *Rethinking Copyright*, 37–42, emphasizes a rather thin line of legal literature that supported innate rights of authors expressed through a notion of 'common law copyright'. Of this Espinasse's and Maugham's *Treatises* had been examples in the 1820s. They were succeeded by J. J. Lowndes, *Historical Sketch of the Law of Copyright* (1840, *Primary Sources*), dedicated to Talfourd. The substantial *Treatise on the Law of Copyright* (London and Boston, MA, 1847) by the American, G. T. Curtis, would take the same line. The influence of this last work in Britain was preserved through the extensive borrowings from it by W. A. Copinger, *Law of Copyright* (1870, 15 edns to date). See *Primary Sources* (UK Comm.) which labels Copinger a plagiarist.

[35] John Locke, whose justification of property by a labour theory of value was often enough taken as the foundation of authors' copyright, had argued for such a period of protection a century and a half before: see W. Patry, *Copyright* (New York, 2007), 1–15, n. 28.

and remaindered copies were a significant force.[36] Moreover, in regard to existing copyrights, Talfourd at first sought to protect authors from their publishers, by providing that after 28 years his elongated term would revert to the author. To gain more support among the publishers, he was obliged to modify this transitional provision considerably.[37]

The printers had little to gain from the extension and so joined the opponents, who in Parliament were led by Benthamite radicals, including Joseph Hume and the founder of *The Lancet*, Thomas Wakley. Their argument was couched in the language of political economy: at a moment when the flag of free trade was hoist so high, they attacked copyright as monopolistic and therefore acceptable only to the extent that it benefited the public from an increased supply of worthwhile literature. In 1841, Thomas Babington Macaulay gave consummate expression to their antagonism on the floor of the Commons, famously characterizing copyright as 'a tax on readers for the purpose of giving a bounty to writers' and insisting that the longer the term the less justifiable it was, not least because it gave the rightholders a power of censorship.[38] Talfourd laboured on, demanding for authors some restoration of the right of which the Lords had deprived them in *Donaldson*.[39] But the Act finally achieved in 1842 gave considerably less than he sought. All authors acquired a 42-year term from publication; and if they were still alive at its end, the right continued until seven years after their death.[40] Depending on one's point of view, the compromise could be regarded as a victory, or as a token concession, to the conception of a property right that survived death. The term of copyright in published literature, drama and music would remain unchanged until its long extension in 1911 to cover the author's life plus 50 years.[41]

5. NEW SUBJECT-MATTER

Types of Visual Art

Copyright relating to the visual arts became increasingly complicated, as it was made to cover a growing number of artistic forms. The eighteenth-century

---

[36] The most forceful voice of this sector of the trade was Thomas Tegg; for whom see Seville, *Literary Copyright Reform*, 123 *et seq.*

[37] The eventual outcome was the Copyright Act 1842, s 4.

[38] The tax, he insisted, was 'on one of the most innocent and most salutary of human pleasures; and never let us forget, that a tax on innocent pleasures is a premium on vicious pleasures'. He did, however, sympathize with the need of the ordinary professional author to have a moderate measure of copyright: see generally, Seville, *Literary Copyright Reform*, 60–7.

[39] In the final success, the parliamentary reins were taken over by Lord Mahon.

[40] 5 & 6 Vict. c. 45, s 3, *Primary Sources.*

[41] Or, if the work was not published before the author's death, 50 years from publication.

legislation, already noted, survived but related only to the early means of reproducing artistic works—first by engraving, lithography, and the like and, secondly, by reproducing sculptures from moulds.[42] Where the initial artwork was a painting or drawing, it gained no copyright. There would be those who considered that the whole value, moral as well as economic, lay in the uniqueness of the work, so that, even where it was by some technique copied, there should be no copyright preventing any secondary access of this kind for the public.[43] However, it became increasingly common for leading artists to charge engravers very considerable fees for access to their work so that versions of it could be made and reproduced.[44] The only copyright under statute was then in the engraving, which could be used against those who in turn pirated it, but the person having the right to do so was the engraver, not the original artist; and under the Engraving Acts the copyright in the engraving arose upon its 'first publication'.[45] With the introduction of photography in the 1830s, not only was there a technique for capturing subjects and scenes that had commercial value in the multiple copies that could be made from the first plate, but it allowed copies of two-dimensional paintings and drawings to be reproduced more rapidly and cheaply.

In an Irish decision, *Turner* v. *Robinson*[46]—a case that bridged the older techniques and the newer—Henry Wallis' plangent painting, 'The Death of Chatterton', was lent by its owner, Augustus Egg, to an engraver to whom he granted exclusive rights to make a print of the picture. Once the engraving was done, the engraver showed it to potential subscribers and the defendant took the opportunity to view it. Afterwards he arranged models in the same attitudes, photographed them and sold copies.[47] The engraver obtained an injunction for infraction of what was conceded to be his common law right, because, as the Court

[42] See above, p. 881, n. 10. For the detailed interpretation of these Acts, see e.g. Copinger, *Copyright*, Chs 12, 13; Scrutton, *Copyright* (4th edn), 170–9, 201–4.

[43] Immanuel Kant had argued in this vein (see 'On the Wrongfulness of Unauthorised Publication' in M. J. Gregor (trans.), *Practical Philosophy* (Cambridge, 1996), 34–5) and FitzJames Stephen would take a similar position before the Royal Commission of 1876–8 (*PP* 1878 [C. 2036], xxiv, 163); but it was not a view that attracted sustained support in Britain.

[44] For successful paintings, the right to engrave them could sell for a considerable sum, but the returns to the engraver could still provide him with a substantial profit: see the instances assembled by L. Bently, 'Art and the Making of Modern Copyright Law', in D. McClean and K. Schubert (eds), *Dear Images: Art, Copyright and Culture* (2002), 331; and more generally, B. Sherman and L. Bently, *Making of Intellectual Property*, 126–8.

[45] With sculptures, the right under 54 Geo. III c. 56 arose from their 'first putting forth and publishing'.

[46] (1860) 10 Ir. Ch. 121, 510, CA; and see *Mayall* v. *Higbey* (1862) 6 L.T. (N.S.). 362. No point was taken that either the reconstruction of the scene or the use of photography carried the defendant's activity beyond the ill-defined limits of the common law right.

[47] Wallis' model was the young George Meredith; the engraver's was a different young man.

of Appeal found, there had been no activity that could amount to publication. That, however, dealt with only one situation: neither the original painter nor the current owner of the painting would have had an equivalent right. At the time of the Great Exhibition, when the Society of Arts had become a great supporter of the positive reform of the patent system, it appointed an influential Committee in the hope of bringing both clarity and greater protection to art publishing.[48] After a decade of proposals, the Fine Arts Copyright Act 1862 gave copyright, not from publication but from creation, in *new and original* paintings, drawings and photographs themselves.[49] After considerable argument in Parliament, however, it was necessary to register a memorandum of the painting at Stationers' Hall; until this was done, no damages would be available for wrongful acts.[50] The right then endured until seven years after the artist's death.[51]

The preamble to the Act scarcely assisted clarity by pronouncing that previously no copyright in these types of work had existed. Scrutton, as part of his campaign for the survival of common law copyright wherever it was not eliminated by statute, argued that this general right, by analogy to the copyright in books, applied to paintings and drawings until they were published. He was then forced to the rather uncomfortable position that under the 1862 Act there were overlapping statutory and common law rights between creation and publication—a period which in many instances could be lengthy. But even he did not claim that common law copyright could run beyond the period allowed by the 1862 statute.[52] And it was taken thereafter that to qualify for copyright a form of art needed to be specified in a statutory definition.[53] Accordingly, as movements blossomed for well-designed versions of household objects, they had to wait until the definition of 'artistic works' was expanded to encompass 'works

---

[48] See the Report of that Committee in 1858. D. R. Blaine bolstered the cause with his *On the Laws of Artistic Copyright and their Defects* (1853); and then in *Suggestions on the Copyright (Works of Art) Bill* (1861).

[49] The 'new and original' requirement, already found in the Sculpture Copyright Act 1814, s 1, was qualified by a provision allowing any person (including the original author) to repaint, re-draw, or re-photograph a scene or object from scratch, even where the initial copyright had become vested in another person: s 2. A related problem concerned the effect on the copyright of the first disposition of such a work. If it passed by gift, the copyright was presumed to end, unless expressly reserved by the creator the copyright; but on a sale, it was presumed to pass to the new owner of the physical object, unless it was reserved: s 1.

[50] In *Ex p Beal* (1868) LR 3 QB 387, Blackburn J. held that a short descriptive title of a painting would suffice for the memorandum. He refused to apply to copyright the need for a full description of the subject-matter which courts had insisted on as necessary to justify patents for inventions.

[51] Fine Arts Copyright Act 1862, s 1, *Primary Sources* (with Comm. covering numerous aspects of the development).

[52] T. E. Scrutton, *Copyright* (4th edn), 169–70, 186.

[53] The 1862 Act did not adopt the more radical proposal in the previous year's bill for a single statute covering all artistic works.

of artistic craftsmanship' in the Imperial Copyright Act of 1911. By the time that happened, the law had lagged seriously behind shifts in aesthetic appreciation. The intervening decades had seen the great swell of the arts and crafts movement from its beginnings among the Pre-Raphaelites, and British designers had contributed significantly to the art nouveau of the century's end, and the further refinements that would follow from it, for instance, in art deco.

One aspect of the 1862 Act that caused little concern was the admission of photography to the ranks of protected works. Parliament had admitted it to the new canon, despite some argument that the technology was an apparently impersonal, mechanico-chemical operation. In consequence, it might extend to 'snapshots' capturing images and events, as distinct from pre-arranged set-pieces intended as 'art'. Other countries would question the appropriateness of admitting photographic copyright so casually; not so the British.[54] This important expansion served to underscore that most of copyright law was founded upon statute. Once Parliament had been persuaded to intervene, the policy was, as so often elsewhere, taken to be set.

This broad pragmatism had its consequences. The 1850s had seen increasing concern over misrepresentations relating to the authorship of drawings, paintings, and photographs, which chimed in with broader protests over the source of products in general.[55] In this there was some seed for offering protection to authors and artists for their association with their own works and the preservation of the works against unacceptable alteration. From the late nineteenth century, such ideas would blossom in France, Germany, and elsewhere into the concept of authors' moral rights. In the 1862 Act, however, all that grew was the power to object to cheating activities which might deceive the purchasing public. These included: selling art under the name of an artist who was not the creator (a wrong close to passing-off in general), selling copies as having been made by the original artists, and selling an original or copies of it as being unaltered when that was untrue.[56]

Until this Act it was highly doubtful that British law fulfilled the expectation of reciprocal protection for drawings and paintings in bi-lateral copyright treaties negotiated under the International Copyright Act 1844. In the bills of 1861 and 1862 it was proposed to take a step in the direction of universal protection

---

[54] Later, in the 1911 Act, s 21, the duration of the right in photographs would be specially limited to 50 years from making the original negative, the owner of that negative being deemed to be the initial copyright owner.

[55] For which see below, pp. 993–5.

[56] Section 7. Following earlier Acts, for all wrongs the legislation provided penalties and for delivery up. But it preserved common law actions for damages and equitable relief and arrangements for customs seizures.

without any consideration of the nationality or residence of the artist, or the place of creation.[57] Soon enough, however, the 1862 bill was amended so as to follow the model set up for literary, dramatic, and musical works. Accordingly the new copyrights were confined to British subjects and those resident in British dominions, other foreigners could enjoy the new rights in Britain only under the terms of the relevant Treaty. To that extent at least the government had been moved to make its international position respectable.

6. AUTHORSHIP AND ENTITLEMENT

The statutory copyright in published books had been built in 1710 upon the creative act of an 'author'. However much in real life this only foreshadowed the value that the associated bookseller would extract from the right as assignee or licensee, it settled a root understanding out of which the very idea of a property in literature could be sustained. For there to be a book, there had to be a writing and, to benefit from the Statute, there had to be publication. The subject-matter thus defined itself, providing a corpus from which could emerge the doctrinal refinement that copyright protected the expression of ideas, but not the ideas as such.[58] Registration with the Stationers' Company only fulfilled the secondary function of determining proprietorship and its changes.[59]

Not that entitlement was always a straightforward issue. For one thing, joint authorship had to be defined, given its own duration, and subjected to conditions operating between the individuals concerned. Then there came to be a separate notion of successive copyrights: where the work was made not by some joint design but by one person first fashioning it and another then altering or improving it, each author would be treated as having a separate copyright, with a duration measured partly by reference to his or her life.[60] From another angle there were coming to be difficulties over the relations between

[57] The Society of Arts Report (1857–8) J. Soc. Arts J. 6, 294 urged this step as a solution: see Fine Arts Copyright Act 1862 in *Primary Sources* (Comm., 11).

[58] See also below, pp. 901–3. An early exploration of this issue arose over the performing right in plays and music, where proprietors of theatres got their writers or composers to provide material for which they outlined their requirements. Doing so was not enough for them to claim to be authors: *Shepherd* v. *Conquest* (1856) 17 C.B. 437; *Eaton* v. *Lake* (1888) 20 QBD 378. It is uncertain in this period, whether it was a general rule, as distinct from a contractual presumption, that a person acquired copyright in anything which he employed another to write. Copinger called this a 'well-known rule' but refers to case-law on joint authorship, which was in any case far from clear on the meaning of 'employment': *Copyright*, 44.

[59] See generally, e.g. Copinger, *Copyright*, Ch. 3; Scrutton, *Copyright*, 129–35.

[60] See *Levy* v. *Rutley* (1871) LR 6 CP 523. The ingenuity of literary creators could create conundrums within the emergent forms of copyright—as for instance with the agglomerate *Centos* at the heart of P. K. Saint-Amour's sparkling *The Copywrights* (Ithaca, 2003).

authors and their employers or commissioners—a topic to which we come at a later stage.[61]

Registration presented its own perplexities. For 'book' copyright, the 1842 Act would limit registration by providing that it was necessary only before issuing a writ for infringement. The Fine Arts Copyright Act 1862 took a different line, partly because the right existed from creation, rather than publication.[62] Registration with the Stationers' Company had to take place before the alleged act of infringement was committed.[63] Adding to peculiarities, that Act was far from clear who was to be registered as the author—yet that determined duration.[64] The author's copyright could be lost altogether unless the work was produced on commission or there was a written agreement, signed before first sale of the work, which determined who was to have the copyright.[65] There would be uncertainties about what types of 'copying' this right covered.[66]

As to the personal status of the 'author' of a work of fine art, the Act provided that a British subject qualified wherever he executed the work; but arguably he might lose his entitlement if he then published the work first in a foreign country.[67] In any case, it would be held that the Act could be infringed only by activities in the UK.[68] The law on the protection of artistic works of one kind or another was accordingly a prime contribution to the Royal Commission's condemnation of the whole field as obscure. The Report describes it as '…wholly destitute of any sort of arrangement, incomplete, often in many parts so ill-expressed that no one who does not give it such study can expect to understand it'.[69]

Before that a second battle over justifications for the very system would take place before the Royal Commission on Copyright, instigated by Disraeli.[70] The Commission, chaired by the Postmaster-General, Lord John Manners, was

---

[61] See below, 923–4.

[62] As to which, see *Tuck* v. *Priester* (1887) 19 QBD 629, 639, CA.

[63] See below, 928, n. 223.

[64] Over photographs taken by a commercial business, the Court of Appeal held that it was not the firm which should be registered; and Esher MR suggested that it was not the actual photographer either, but the employee supervising the session: *Nottage* v. *Jackson* (1883) 11 QBD 627; and see e.g. *Wooderson* v. *Tuck* (1887) 4 TLR 57. Scrutton labelled the result 'ridiculous': *Copyright*, 189.

[65] Section 1.

[66] See Scrutton, *Copyright*, 196–7.

[67] See Scrutton, *Copyright*, 181–2.

[68] *Graves* v. *Gorrie* [1903] AC 496, JC. In a colony, therefore, there had to be local legislation. But there were considerable obscurities about the impact of the International Copyright Act 1886, s 9, giving rights to Berne Convention claimants, which included the Dominions as well as Britain.

[69] *PP* 1878 [C. 2036], xxiv, 163; *Primary Sources* (UK Comm.).

[70] Five years before, while leading the Opposition, Disraeli had scored a notable success with his novel, *Lothair*. Reviewers were apt to put the novel down as a flippant, wooden exercise in the worship of dukes, but demand remained high, even if the author exaggerated it.

composed of leading authors and publishers, politicians, barristers (including FitzJames Stephen who wrote a rather opinionated code of the law for the Commissioners' benefit), and civil servants (including Sir Louis Mallet of the India Office and T. H. Farrer, Permanent Secretary to the Board of Trade). The great debate before the Commission was between proponents of the rights of authors couched as an inherent entitlement to literary property and so to an exclusive right; and antagonists who sought to downgrade the right to a claim against copiers for a royalty on their sale price—a claim, moreover, that would be the author's, not the publisher's.

The believers in literary property could found their case on the Lockeian theory that true value derived from labour, including the labour of 'occupancy',[71] which in this case comprised the 'skill, labour and judgment' that went into literary, musical, or artistic creativity. Authors and their publishers were entitled to set and maintain prices free of competition from those who merely re-printed their works. The disbelievers argued that this very monopoly could not be justified because it turned on an artificial legal intervention in the normal processes of competition, which created a scarcity where otherwise there would be plenty, information of any kind being open to infinite sharing. In their view, the effect was to buttress the price of books at levels which brought their publishers monopoly profits. The commercial activities of publishers did not differ from those of other investors risking their capital. The specific royalty system being proposed provided the author with a risk-linked return while leaving the publisher to the operations of the market.

The roots of the argument lay in Ricardian perceptions of the benefits of opening markets to competition so earnestly pursued by the Manchester School. In the Commission's Report the case was put in uncompromising terms in the general dissent written by Sir Louis Mallett; and before that in the evidence of several witnesses who canvassed both the theory and the details of its administration. That arch-purveyor of free-trade economics, Robert Macfie, had presented a paper to the Commission arguing for an exclusive right lasting only a year, followed by competition with outsiders who would be obliged to pay the author a 4 per cent royalty on their sales, actual or estimated.[72] In his oral evidence, he suggested, rather more moderately, that the first publisher should have exclusivity until he covered his costs, followed by free competition. A government office would have authority to receive and check the publisher's costs and returns in order to decide when the copyright term had come to an end. Macfie was willing to stomach this bureaucratic control, though his opponents would pour scorn on

---

[71] So did Blackstone regard the matter: *Comms*, ii, 405.

[72] For Macfie's antagonism against the patent system, see below, pp. 958–9.

its regulatory or socialistic tendency.[73] Farrer, Permanent Secretary of the Board of Trade, another critic, endorsed the principle of an entitlement to reprint without permission upon payment of a set royalty, but suggested its introduction into Britain only in stages. He had been much involved in the confrontations between the publishers and governments of Britain and Canada. The compromise outcome, of which he did not approve, had just been embodied in both Dominion and Imperial legislation of 1875.[74]

7. INFRINGING ACTS

Permanent Form and Publication of the Protected Work

The very idea of a book as the subject of copyright meant that lectures, speeches, sermons, or performances by actors or musicians, for which there was no prior text or notation, gained no protection. The need for a fixation in writing or some relatively permanent form came before the steps of registration and publication that also acted as preconditions for protection under the Statute of Anne and its 1842 successor. There were intermediate cases as well: companies of actors often kept their plays to themselves, rather than allowing their publication, so as to reap rewards from their uniqueness. If they worked from a written script, and rivals after watching performances published versions of the text, their approximation could perhaps be actionable as a matter of common law copyright; but that, after *Donaldson*, had been doubted.[75] In any case the rivals' performances from their stenography or memory did not amount to the re-publishing of books and so did not infringe the Statute of Anne. After some lively argument before a Select Committee, the author and controversialist Edward Lytton Bulwer secured a Dramatic Copyright Act in 1833,[76] which gave the blessing of a considerable statutory penalty not just to a performing right over plays, but also to the copying of an *unpublished* script, as well as one that was published.[77] In this way

---

[73] See also R. A. Macfie, *Copyright and Patents for Inventions*, 2 vols (Edinburgh, 1879, 1883).

[74] See below, pp. 910–11 For this constitutionally significant imbroglio, see C. A. Seville, *The Internationalisation of Copyright Law* (Cambridge, 2006), Ch. 4, esp. 103–9.

[75] In 1770, when Lord Mansfield's views were ascendant, such an activity had been enjoined (*Macklin v. Richardson* (1770) Amb. 694, *Primary Sources*); but later decisions raised doubts: *Coleman v. Wathen* (1793) 5 TR 245; *Murray v. Elliston* (1822) 5 B. & Ald. 657. *Primary Sources* (UK Comm.), 4, 5.

[76] 3 & 4 Will. IV c. 15; *Primary Sources* UK Comm. It was preceded in 1830 by a bill promoted by the playwright and actor, George Lamb. See generally, McFarlane, *Copyright: The Development and Exercise of the Performing Right* (Eastbourne, 1980), Ch. 3; Alexander, *Boundaries of Copyright*, Ch. 8.1.

[77] Bulwer started by proposing a penalty of £50, but had to reduce it to a minimum of 40s per use. For his role in copyright affairs, see C. A. Seville, 'Edward Bulwer Lytton Dreams of

the 1710 formula was reshaped to fit the demands of a different art form as its playwrights faced the competition of an increasingly commercial world. The 1842 Act would extend this performing right equally to music, while for unauthorized publication in sheet form the rights remained those under the common law in the unpublished composition and those under Statute of Anne after authorized publication.[78] The differing structures contributed significantly to the difficulties in understanding the growing body of copyright law.

But with music, obtaining payments for the licensing of individual compositions was perplexing for both owners and users.[79] So far as concerned pirated copies, publishers continued to claim grave losses from the 'theft' of their copyrights and in 1902 were able to obtain a Musical (Summary Proceedings) Copyright Act. This gave them the right to have a constable seize pirated copies, particularly those being hawked in the streets, and bring them before magistrates for destruction. This enactment was also in its way reactive, for publishers already had their vigilantes out to seize hawkers' material, claiming that it infringed their rights.[80] Arguably, they in any case had a power of recaption, since it had been provided in the Copyright Act 1842, s 23, that pirated copies in a physical sense belonged to the copyright owner. Four years later, they finally had the production and distribution of unauthorized sheet music turned into a summary criminal offence. Nonetheless they did not succeed in having the burden of proof that a copy was not a copyright infringement placed on the defendant.[81]

Writings Recorded but Not Published

Here, however, we must return also to the mysteries of 'common law copyright' and the equitable action for breach of trust or confidence which would become its modern derivative—notably after the Imperial Copyright Act 1911 restricted copyright to the rights that it defined. In the nineteenth century 'common law copyright' was a fluid idea with a capacity to fill at least some holes left open by

---

Copyright: "It might make me a Rich Man"', in F. O'Gorman (ed.), *Victorian Literature and Finance* (Oxford, 2007), 55–72. For a business venture in collecting penalties for unauthorized musical performances which would bring public vilification and curbing by statute, see below, 920–1.

[78] 5 & 6 Vict. c. 45, s 20.

[79] The position was complicated in any case by the fact that copyrights in the words and music of a song were distinct according to British law. Once the term was measured by the author's life, the copyright of lyricist and composer would endure for different periods; and they might well have different owners. Other copyright laws would adopt the opposite approach where there was collaboration.

[80] W. Boosey, *Fifty Years in Music* (1931), Ch. 13.

[81] For the practices and the politics, see I. Alexander, 'Criminalising Copyright' [2006] *CLJ* 625.

the various copyright statutes. Lord Eldon was notably ready to play with the concept, both in order to institute a censorship of the politically dangerous or morally corrupting, and to allow intervention by injunction against misuses of material that had not been given to the world.

As to the exclusion of the censurable, Eldon plainly regarded it as his duty to refuse any interlocutory injunction, whether the right being pursued was under the Statute or the common law.[82] Beginning with 'Peter Pindar's' lampoons of George III, he refused relief until a jury at common law found the work to be morally unobjectionable. So also with the youthful Southey's poem, *Wat Tyler*, Byron's *Cain* and *Don Juan* and Lawrence's *Lectures on Physiology, Zoology and the Natural History of Man*.[83] When the issue reached the King's Bench, Abbott CJ led with a stern pronouncement that *Memoirs of a Courtesan* (Harriette Wilson) were so improper that there was no property in the work that could be protected.[84] As these judges appreciated, their weapon was a boomerang, since it left others free to put out cheap versions of the disgraced text, and the judgment against liability might of itself provide some publicity. In succeeding generations there was little interest in sustaining public morality by this curious means.[85] If the text was blasphemous, or seditious or pornographic, they could in any case be the subject of a prosecution.

When it came to worthwhile material, Eldon was ready to enjoin those who got hold of the protected text in the course of a communication which did not amount to publication and by inference conferred a liberty to read but not a licence to publish. He decided so in the case of *Gee v. Pritchard*,[86] where he insisted that for an injunction to be granted, there must be property to be protected. A letter sent by a mother to an adopted son became his property so far as concerned the physical object, but the writer retained a sufficient property in it to prevent publication, when clearly he must all along have known that she opposed it. So too with the famous lectures on surgery given at Guy's Hospital by Dr Abernethy. His students, so Eldon held, were entitled to take notes for their own study, but the presumption was that they were not free to publish them. He enjoined *The Lancet*, owned by Thomas Wakley, against continuing to do so.[87] Both cases suggested the breadth of the cause in equity. In *Gee* the

---

[82] He was not alone. See e.g. Maugham, *Literary Property*, 93–7.

[83] *Walcot* v. *Walker* (1802) 7 Ves. 1; *Southey* v. *Sherwood* (1817) 2 Stark. 107; *Murray* v. *Benbow* (1822) Jac. 474n; *Lawrence* v. *Smith* (1822) Jac. 471.

[84] (1826) 5 B. & C. 173. For a full account, see I. Alexander, 'The Lord Chancellor, the Poets and the Courtesan', in A. Lewis et al. (eds), *Law in the City* (Dublin, 2007), 230–48.

[85] Ponderously, Younger J. would refuse to recognize copyright in Elinor Glyn's once notorious *Three Weeks*: *Glyn* v. *Weston Feature Film* [1915] 1 Ch 261; but that was the end of it.

[86] (1818) 2 Swans. 202.

[87] *Abernethy* v. *Hutchinson* (1825) 1 H. & Tw. 28.

property in the letter had passed to the defendant, but the mother's 'property' against publishing it arose simply from the defendant's understanding of her wish for privacy. In *Abernethy*, the lectures were delivered orally, but were based on a manuscript at least partly written by the surgeon, which he intended to publish later. The conditions on which the students were admitted to the lectures provided the implication that publication was not permitted. A copyright-like basis for equitable relief was thus emerging which, as we shall observe later, would gradually become a wide-ranging form of protection for 'confidential information'.[88]

The publishing practice in *Abernethy* continued to be an irritant. A decade later, Lord Brougham saw through a Lectures Copyright Act which gave an 'author or lecturer' the right to a penalty of a penny a sheet against unauthorized publication of the content of a lecture.[89] It was accordingly an extension of the Statute of Anne and it lasted in operation until 1911. But it was unclear what it added, if anything, to the common law copyright. It gave no right against unauthorized recitals of the content, and it remained uncertain whether a 'lecturer' included a person who never committed his text to paper, as distinct from one who did so before or after delivering it. In any case, lectures in various types of public institution were left to the common law right.[90]

Lord Eldon's lead was one that other judges were willing enough to follow. *Prince Albert* v. *Strange*,[91] which would become a classic authority, concerned etchings by Queen Victoria which she had had privately reproduced from the plates for the delectation of a strictly limited circle in her court. When some of the copies found their way into a would-be publisher's hands, Cottenham LC enjoined the proposed use not just of the engravings themselves but even publication of their titles. The defendant engaged in grovelling protestations of loyalty, but claimed that he came by his copies without impropriety. He did not, however, offer any explanation of how this might be, and the Lord Chancellor assumed that the etchings came to him as a result of 'a breach of trust, confidence or contract'.[92] There was no difference from the acts of a confidential clerk

---

[88] Below, Ch. V.

[89] Lectures Copyright Act 1835, 5 & 6 Will. IV c. 65.

[90] So lectures on moral philosophy to fee-paying students of Glasgow University were subject to the line drawn by Lord Eldon in *Abernethy*. If the public could attend free, their content was released to the public for whatever purpose they chose; however, since there was a fee, the public dedication was only conditional and did not allow publication by another without licence: *Caird* v. *Sime* (1887) 12 AC 326, HL; see also *Nicols* v. *Pitman* (1884) 26 Ch D 374; Scrutton, *Copyright*, 68–72.

[91] (1849) 1 Mac. & G. 25. At first instance, Knight Bruce VC placed heavy stress on the property enjoyed by the Queen in her unpublished works: (1849) 2 De G. & Sm. 652, 694–5.

[92] The intriguing prospect that they had been obtained via one of HM's recipients was something 'not to be supposed', according to Cottenham: (1849) 1 Mac. & G. at 44–5.

in seeking to publish the substance and effect of his employer's accounts.[93] Nor would there be, if a physician published an account of what he saw and heard while attending George III in his madness.[94]

The last example was particularly pertinent to the case for a right of privacy made by Warren and Brandeis, since it was not dependent upon there being a wrongly taken 'text', whether a letter or a photograph or whatever, that fell within 'common law copyright' as a form of 'property'. The whole point made in their article was that the implication of trust or contract was 'nothing more nor less than a judicial declaration that public morality, private justice, and general convenience demand the recognition of such a rule, and that the publication under similar circumstances would be considered an intolerable abuse'.[95] In their view, the law should expand its principle so as to cover not only circumstances where implications of contract or trust could be made from pre-existing relationships; it must also cover those situations where there was no such basis, as where photographs of a stranger were taken surreptitiously.[96]

In Britain it would take another century to reach that position; and then only through the necessity of adapting the common law to the standards of the European Convention on Human Rights.[97] Until that juncture, as the House of Lords would insist, no distinct right of privacy exceeded the bounds of contract, breach of confidence, and the innominate tort of intentionally and unjustifiably inflicting recognized psychological harm.[98] For most of that period, liability over confidential information was thought to arise only where there was a prior relationship between the parties, such as employment or commercial services.[99] While that requirement would gradually be relaxed, neither courts nor Parliament, left to themselves, were prepared to decide that a free press must be placed under more persistent vigilance. The print media, needless to emphasize, would remain a vociferous defender of their own interests.

---

[93] Hence Wigram VC's injunction in *Tipping* v. *Clarke* (1843) 2 Hare 309.

[94] An example given by Eldon in an unreported case of 1820 (*Wyatt* v. *Wilson*), according to Cottenham: above, n. 91, at 45–6.

[95] (1890)4 *Harvard LR* 193, 210 Their phraseology echoed the natural law sentiments of Willes J. (*Millar* v. *Taylor* (1769) 4 Burr. 2303, 2312) with which they prefaced their article.

[96] A particular stepping stone in their argument was provided by North J.'s judgment in *Pollard* v. *Photographic Co* (1888) 40 Ch D 345, holding that a photographer who took a portrait on commission had impliedly undertaken not to exhibit it or sell copies of it. If so, why not equally where there is no relationship between photographer and subject?

[97] See e.g. *Campbell* v. *MGN* [2004] 2 AC 457.

[98] *Wainwright* v. *Home Office* [2004] 2 AC 406.

[99] Once the Copyright Act 1911, s 31, gave statutory copyright to unpublished as well as published works, it thereby abrogated 'common law copyright'.

Substantial Taking

The real nub of copyright lies in the rules defining infringement, since they determine what others may not take without permission from the right-holder. Because, in the terms to the Statute of Anne, the right was in the claimant's 'book'—or as it was expressed in the preamble, the 'book or other writing'—it was assumed that the wrong would consist in copying that book, and not in arriving at the same content by independent means, such as taking from the same source or separately collecting data.[100] The exclusive right was thus over the detailed content of the work and applied most straightforwardly to exact reproduction of the words, numerals, or signs of which it was composed. An equity judge, faced with a bill for an injunction, would take the two 'books' off to read, in order to determine how far there was such copying.[101] He would then decide either to dispose of the case for good himself, or, if in doubt, would reserve the issue for trial by a common law jury. The right was in its nature much more limited than those printing privileges granted by the Crown which covered whole categories—for instance of law books, or almanacs—a practice which had continued to some degree into the eighteenth century.[102] It could prove difficult sometimes to decide what the 'book' was—particularly when it was a compilation of contributions, such as a newspaper, encyclopedia, or a collection of factual information.

How far had there to be complete and exact copying? The Statute gave no real indication, yet the matter was a constant concern at a stage of the book trade's development when many publications were evidently derived in part from earlier books. As our period begins, Godson could write that

one man may compose a work, for instance in the Latin language, another abridge it, a third translate it, and a fourth write annotations upon it; and every one of them will acquire a copyright in the product of his own ingenuity and labour.[103]

Clear enough, then, that these persons were each to be treated as an author with copyright in their own intellectual labour and had power to object to outsiders publishing their work without permission. But what of their relations one with

---

[100] The Statute, s 1, made it wrongful to 'print, reprint, or import, or cause to be printed, reprinted, or imported, any such book...'.

[101] Lord Hardwicke LC had offered this ability as justification for resort to the jurisdiction in equity: *Gyles v. Wilcox* (1741) 2 Atk. 141, 144—a case in which he had a Master of the court labour through the two books.

[102] A mix between the two was to be found in the patents conferred on leading composers to protect the publishing of all their works: see D. Hunter, above, n. 10. For the constrictions on the market in law books, see T. A. Baloch, 'Law Booksellers and Printers as Agents of Unchange' [2007] *CLJ* 389–421.

[103] *Patents and Copyright*, 238.

another? Must those in the chain obtain the licence of the others in order to put out the end product of them all?[104]

Hardwicke LC had distinguished taking part of a book, which remained infringement, from abridging a work, which was left open to others.[105] In this, 'abridgments' were like translations. They helped in the diffusion of knowledge by making more readable and cheaper versions of a book available in a way that did not offer direct competition with the initial text itself. On a related front, Lord Mansfield had been ready to welcome the production of 'new work' when, as with map-making, it incorporated corrections in an older version.[106] But the distinction from merely colourable shortening, or publication of only a part, or the introduction of new material, if any of these could be given real meaning, imported moral and literary attitudes that were difficult to evaluate. What, for example, did it mean to say that a permissible abridgement had to be 'fair and real'? How far did there have to be invention, learning and judgment by the person who altered the original?[107]

By mid-nineteenth century, the freedom to make an abridgement without the permission of the original author was beginning to lose ground,[108] as was the notion, of even broader implication, that a 'new work' must be tolerated even where it was wrought out of materials that included extracts from an earlier book.[109] Instead came a greater determination to recognize the author's property in his composition, whatever use was being made of it. Strikingly, judges tended to refer to the protection needed by the author, even where it was entirely the publisher's interest in exploitation that was in issue. For much of the nineteenth century, only a few top authors were able to bargain for a share in royalties, or for separate rights in each edition. The great majority assigned or licensed their right for a lump sum or for nothing. Emphasizing the author's property would

---

[104] Yates J., the dissentient in *Millar* v. *Taylor* (above, p. 883 n. 14), had questioned 'whether those who should compile notes on a publication, and should insert the text, should be liable to an action for it' (at p. 2394).

[105] R. Burrell and A. Coleman suggest that the distinction had the effect of expanding the scope of copyright beyond strict reprinting of the whole text to include part-taking: *Copyright Exceptions: The Digital Impact* (Cambridge, 2005), 255; cf. Alexander, *Boundaries of Copyright*, 54–62.

[106] *Sayre* v. *Moore* (1785) 1 East 361n; *Carnan* v. *Bowles* (1786) 2 Bro. C.C. 80. See also Lord Ellenborough in *Cary* v. *Kearsley* (1802) 4 Esp. 168, 170 on the dangers of putting manacles on science.

[107] For tendencies in the case law before the 1842 Act, see Alexander, *Boundaries of Copyright*, Ch. 7; and for subsequent developments, Ch. 10.

[108] See e.g. *Dickens* v. *Lee* (1844) 8 Jur. 183; *Tinsley* v. *Lacy* (1863) 1 H. & M. 747, 754; but the Royal Commission on Copyright treated it as current, while recommending its abolition: *PP* [1878] [C. 2031], xxiv, para. 68.

[109] See *Wood* v. *Boosey* (1867) LR 3 QB 223, 228–9. The Royal Commission (above, n. 108) also criticized this rule, but North J. recognized it in *Walter* v. *Steinkopff* [1892] 3 Ch 489, 495.

lead eventually to rights over the work even where it was deployed in a different medium—as where a novel was made into a play, or an opera into a selection for piano, a picture into a photograph or sculpture, or an engraving into a drawing.[110] Authors were confined neither by their intentions in creating the work, nor by the ways in which they afterwards exploited it. Here was much of the difference between property in the intangible and a mere right to exclude unfair competition as it occurred in the market from time to time.

A doctrinal concept expressing the essence of what constituted infringement gained ground over a course that spanned Victoria's reign and it would have an important aggregative effect. The defendant was not permitted to copy a 'materially valuable part', or a 'vital part, coming up to an unfair use',[111] or an amount 'showing an *animus furandi*'.[112] In the end it was required that a 'substantial part' of the plaintiff's book or other material must have been taken, a bland expression which left each court with considerable scope to make its own moral assessment of the circumstances. Stress might be laid on the type of work, on the degree of marketplace competition between the works, on what the defendant might have done to avoid copying, on the degree to which what was taken was crucial to the plaintiff's intellectual labour, the use to which the defendant had put it; but not one of these factors could be taken necessarily to predominate.

Take for instance, *D'Almaine* v. *Boosey*,[113] where the English publisher of Auber's opera, *Lestocq*, who had paid the composer £80 for the British copyright, successfully sued another music seller for putting out dance music mainly arranged from its airs. As Abinger CB chose to put it, while *Viner's Abridgment* and *Comyn's Digest* could be classed as new works because of their usefulness in the law, in musical arrangements different principles applied: 'The original air required the aid of 'genius for its construction, but a mere mechanic in music can make the adaptation or accompaniment'. That was only one view of the skill of musical composition, but it showed what considerable scope there

---

[110] Artistic works posed increasing difficulties on such issues, and solutions were not aided by the existence of different statutory regimes for engravings and prints, sculptures and (from 1862) paintings, drawings, and photographs. Examples included: (1) a Berlin wool pattern taken from a print (of a different artist's painting: held not a copy: *Dicks* v. *Brooks* (1880) 15 Ch D 22; (2) a *tableau vivant* (though stationary) at a music hall which embodied a photograph: held capable of being a copy if sufficiently exact: see the line of cases culminating in *Hanfstaegl* v. *Baines* [1895] AC 20, HL: for the chronology, see Scrutton, *Copyright* (4th edn), 183–4, note (n).

[111] See e.g. *Bramwell* v. *Halcomb* (1836) 3 My. & Cr. 737; *Bohn* v. *Bogue* (1847) 10 Jur. 420; *Murray* v. *Bogue* (1852) Drewry 353; accepted by the HL in *Chatterton* v. *Cave* (1878) 3 App Cas 483.

[112] Eldon LC, *Mawman* v. *Tegg* (1826) 2 Russ. 385, 401. To make what was not fair turn upon the defendant's intent to misappropriate bore some resemblance to the limit to fair comment as a defence against defamation, with its stress on malice in fact: see Mitchell, *Making of Defamation*, 172–3.

[113] (1835) 1 Y. & C. Ex. 288.

was for adapting the approach to different types of work. There were in consequence a stream of attempts to spell out the governing principle. Later, Page Wood VC (Hatherley) would draw attention to a dictum of the great American jurist, Story J., who stated that the need was to 'look to the nature and objects of the selection made, the quantity and value of the materials used, and the degree in which the use may prejudice the sale, or diminish the profits, or supersede the objects of the original work'.[114]

The earlier limitation which allowed takings for abridgement or for a new work would continue to make occasional appearances even in twentieth-century case law. For the most part, however, they became particular instances to be judged according to the general rubric of substantial taking. At the same time, that concept was being qualified by more specific categories of 'fair use' or 'fair dealing'. To these we come later.[115] The overall trajectory was towards protecting the copyright holder wherever there was any significant extraction for reproduction (and in some cases for performance) from the book or other subject-matter in issue. Particularly with compilations of data, there was to be no borrowing in place of collecting the information independently. In a leading case on street directories, it was said that even a single line should not be taken if the aim was to save labour and trouble.[116] Hand in hand went the idea that a work could attract copyright in the first place with only a very modest measure of labour, skill, and judgment above the mere copying of a pre-existing source. Certainly that mental activity could consist in the amassing of factual information, often of a pedestrian nature.[117] By way of counterbalance, the courts moved towards the notion that where the author's contribution was only just enough to secure copyright at all, the range of infringement would be closely confined. The simple depiction of a hand pointing to the voting square on British ballot papers was treated as gaining artistic copyright but it was a copyright infringed only when it was precisely copied in every detail.[118] The interlock between these two concepts left judges

---

[114] *Folsom* v. *Marsh* (1841) 9 F. Cas. 342, 344; *Scott* v. *Stanford* (1867) LR 3 Eq 718. *Folsom* was introduced to the British in Palmer Phillips' *Law of Copyright in Works of Literature and Art and in the Application of Designs* (1863), 125–6; and see Scrutton, *Copyright*, 146–7.

[115] See below, pp. 926–7.

[116] *Kelly* v. *Morris* (1866) LR 1 Eq 697, 702; cf. *Pike* v. *Nicholas* (1870) LR 5 Ch App 251; *Morris* v. *Wright* (1870) LR 5 Ch App 279. See also *Harper* v. *Biggs* (1907) [1905–10] MacGillivray CC 168— wrongful to take 10 pages out of several numbers of a magazine; *Cate* v. *Devon* (1889) 40 Ch D 500, 507.

[117] As was evident from the 'map' cases and then the 'compilation' cases (above, n. 106, 116) Accordingly, Peterson J.'s 'rough practical test' that 'What is worth copying is *prima facie* worth protecting' (*University of London Press* v. *University Tutorial Press* [1916] 2 Ch 601, 610) would gain currency, not least for its ability to twist the tails of authors' rights advocates.

[118] *Kenrick* v. *Lawrence* (1890) 25 QBD 99. The crux of the drawing, said Wills J. contemptuously, would be to allow 'the remaining ignorance, male and female, in the three kingdoms [to] be swept into the electoral fold'.

with some considerable power to direct the outcome of fringe cases according to their overall impression of the controversy.

Exceptions

The property characterization had numerous consequences. Thus the infringer who did the actual copying, or who authorized a printer to do so as the first step towards publishing, was liable irrespective of whether he knew that he was infringing. The one distinction in the Statute of Anne was that those who then distributed illegal copies were liable to its remedies only when they acted knowingly.[119] Equally, it was accepted that copyright was infringed whether or not the rightholder was seeking to exploit the material himself. Competitive losses were a question only in the assessment of damages.[120] The basic scope of copyright infringement expanded somewhat jerkily through the nineteenth century. By way of counterbalance, certain categories of defence began to emerge, but it could be unclear whether they were just ways of showing whether the taking was substantial enough to count as infringement or whether they had a dimension of their own.[121]

The first of these was a right to use extracts from a copyright book in order to comment upon or otherwise review it. Lord Eldon had followed Lord Ellenborough in recognizing this limitation, while warning that the extracts quoted must not be so considerable as to amount to a piratical annexation of the work itself.[122] A key to the difference accordingly lay in whether the defendant's book gave much the same information as the plaintiff's, thus damaging the market for the latter.[123]

---

[119] 8 Anne c. 10, s 1. Contrast on this question, the difficulties of defining the liability of distributors in defamation: above, 866–7.

[120] As the authoritative Parker J. stated in *Weatherby* v. *International Horse Agency* [1910] 2 Ch 297, 305; for the same view of invention patents, see *Meters* v. *Metropolitan Gas* (1911) 42 RPC 157; *Watson Laidlaw* v. *Potts Cassels & Williamson* (1914) 31 RPC 104, HL.

[121] For the evolution of these exceptions, see D. Bradshaw, '"Fair dealing" as a Defence to Copyright Infringement in UK law' (1995) *Denning LJ* 67; Burrell, 'Reining in Copyright Law: Is Fair Use the Answer?' [2001] *IPQ* 361–90; Alexander . *Boundaries of Copyright*, Chs 10–12.

[122] See esp., *Roworth* v. *Wilkes* (1807) 1 Camp. 94; *Wilkins* v. *Aikin* (1810) 14 Ves. Jun. 422; *Mawman* v. *Tegg* (1826) 2 Russ. 385.

[123] A somewhat similar exercise in narrow line-drawing arose over translations. The act of translating gave rise to a distinct work of authorship by the translator: *Wyatt* v. *Barnard* (1814) 3 Ves. & B. 77. But the author of the work translated had no right to prevent the translation. French law knew no such limitation and a compromise was therefore fashioned in the Anglo-French Treaty of 1851, which was given effect in the International Copyright Act 1852, 15 & 16 Vict. c. 12, ss 2–5: in order to apply the principle of national treatment in a way that gave a measure of reciprocity, the original author gained a five-year right against unauthorized translation of his work if it was not first published in Britain; but the work had to be registered at Stationers' Hall and

A different defence—that there was a right of fair use in the reporting of news—would not receive much emphasis in Britain until the development of a press aiming at high circulation to a popular market.[124] By that stage, tit-for-tat borrowing between newspapers was common practice and accepted as inevitable; but attitudes among proprietors were changing. If the particular wording of a press report was taken without permission, they could seek to have this treated as an *unfair* misappropriation of 'expression'. The judges were suspicious that this deployment of copyright might monopolize the very information constituting the news. But drawing any distinction between 'news' and particular expressions of it could be elusive. North J. would use the idea that copyright only protected expression, rather than its content, so as to confine any copyright to precise formulations, such as telegrams or articles of literary or scientific interest.[125] That outcome sought to delimit the range of what one newspaper could object to as an attack on its investment by a rival. The courts were prepared to allow some scope for the freedom of the press and the cognate interest of the public that no one outlet should be able to monopolize scoops of the day.

In other circumstances there might be no commercial rivalry over the deployment of a published work. Then the question whether private uses should be free posed a different issue. Mid-century dicta made clear that the copyright in artworks could scarcely extend to a single copy in pen and ink, especially if drawn by a lady for her own amusement.[126] But as a general rule this idea of a private sphere failed to take wing. Whether it was raised as an interpretation of what the relevant statute restricted, or as a defence to its scope, it was open to the counter-argument that the right was an exclusive property, at least as a presumption that gave the proprietor a claim to prevent or be compensated for a use, whether or not it was competitive.[127]

---

an authorized translation published, both within short time spans. This provision applied only to translations in a strict sense, and not to adaptations. For an example of the latter, see *Wood* v. *Chart* (1870) LR 10 Eq. 193.

[124] See its emergence through *Walter* v. *Howe* (1881) 17 Ch D 708, CA; and *Cate* v. *Devon Newspaper* (1889) 40 Ch D 500; Scrutton, *Copyright*, 167. However, a forerunner had been included in the 1852 Act which expanded the powers of the International Copyright Act 1844 in order to allow implementation of the Anglo-French Copyright Treaty of 1851 and other similar agreements: re-publication or translation of news of the day with acknowledgment of source was permitted by way of exception. In the case of 'political discussion' this operated without any power being given to the author explicitly to assert his right after all.

[125] *Walter* v. *Steinkopff* [1893] 3 Ch 489.

[126] *Gambart* v. *Ball* (1863) 14 C.B. (N.S.) 318; *Dicks* v. *Brooks* (1880) 15 Ch D 36.

[127] The issue also arose over what performances of plays or music were 'in public'. The Court of Appeal was prepared to treat an in-house performance for hospital staff as if it were domestic and so required no licence of the 'play right': *Dicks* v. *Brooks* (1880) 14 Ch D 22; but a half-century later, right holders would succeed in securing royalties for Women's Institute plays and for 'Music while

8. THE OVERALL DIRECTION OF VICTORIAN COPYRIGHT LAW

The idea that authorship of 'books' would result in 'literary property', so that on registration and publication the author or his assigns (meaning in practice the bookseller-publisher) had remedies against unauthorized copiers was a striking eighteenth-century novelty. It received one strategic check against treating the right as perpetual, but otherwise the property characterization was sketched out and applied, mainly by the courts, in ways that acknowledged the implications of 'property-ness' somewhat earlier than occurred even with patents for inventions. In the grand debates of the 1760s and 1770s, even judges and authors of the Mansfield school had accepted the need to limit infringement to unlicensed copying—making it plain, for instance, that a person who imitated an informational work, like a map or a directory, by collecting the information again for his own publication produced no infringement: all that had been taken in such a case, to use later language, was the idea for the book, not the written expression in which copyright alone resided.[128] In a variety of interstitial ways, over the next century, the judges, with some crucial help from the legislature, filled out the capacious body of the copyright idea so as to make it a useful basis for the often harrowing, often aggressive, business of taking publishing risks.

As to why authors should generate this property, Georgian and to some degree later writers would use the language of natural or absolute rights, the exercise of intellectual skill being honoured as a specially intimate and valuable achievement of the individual persona. As the tone of English law moved towards a general positivism, however, this natural law subjectivism lost its effect. In a sense that is hard to identify precisely, copyright was treated simply as a commercial exclusivity, which it was up to the rightholder to turn into a value in exchange, guarding it by litigation as necessary, and using it as a basis for assignments and licences of which the details were worked out by negotiation and dealt with legally as any other contract about property. Occasional cases would arise where justice seemed to demand legal protection outside the range of the Statute of Anne and other enactments—because, for instance, a manuscript had not been published, or a lecture or other performance was extemporized, or an art work was destroyed, or wrongly attributed. Some form of civil liability might

---

you Work' in factories: *Jennings* v. *Stephens* [1936] Ch 469; *Turner* v. *Performing Right Society* [1943] Ch 167.

[128] Thus in *Sayre* v. *Moore* (1785) 1 East 361n, Lord Mansfield, in discussing the nature of copyright in a map, had confined copyright to 'piracy of the words and the sentiments; but it does not prohibit writing on the same subject'. The distinction was then developed by Lord Thurlow (*Carnan* v. *Bowles* (1786) 2 Bro. C.C. 80)) and Lord Kenyon (*Trusler* v. *Murray* (1789) 1 East 362n.

provide relief, and these would include the rather indeterminate entitlement to an injunction, perhaps by implication of a contract, perhaps because of 'fraud' in some indefinite, essentially tautologous, sense. Otherwise they might have to be dealt with by a relatively specific enactment, as happened for example with lectures.

9. FOREIGN RELATIONS

Foreign Elements

The views of polite British society about the inherent values of literary, musical, and artistic creations might reflect a John Bullish preference for native work, but the growth of interchanges between the country and the European continent, North America, and an Empire of increasing sophistication raised two unavoidable questions for publishing trades. On what basis could British authors and their publishers claim protection under the copyright laws of other countries? And on what basis might a 'foreign' author be entitled to copyright in the UK? Those who admired authorship as an inspirational attainment of human potential were likely to answer such questions in universalist terms. A country's copyright law should be open to authors irrespective of their denizenship. After all, the law of moveable property rarely made political allegiance a condition of entitlement, any more than with a personal right of action, such as defamation or deceit. Or it might even be held that, if the law of a country gave its own authors copyright, they would be entitled—as part of their personal law—to have that right applied and enforced in other countries, whatever their own copyright laws might or might not provide.[129]

In Britain, neither of these solutions was at all likely to succeed.[130] Certainly the territorial basis of copyright as a state-supported entitlement limited to activities within its geographical territory was taken for granted.[131] That became clear once the United States (1790), France (1791, 1794, and 1806), and then a range of other European states followed the British lead towards copyright protection. Long before, the Statute of Anne had suggested a pragmatic approach, since it had excluded from its scope the importation of books printed abroad in

---

[129] For personal law theories of private international law, see Vol. XI, Pt 1, pp. 284–5.

[130] The furthest that the idea of personal attachment would be carried in English law, was to hold that the right of a British subject to copyright in Britain extended to a person such as Edward Gibbon, who lived in Lausanne for many years but retained his English domicil: *Jefferys* v. *Boosey* (1854) 17 H.L.C. 814,

[131] See e.g. the clear exposition by Pollock CB in *Chappell* v. *Purday (No. 2)* (1845) 14 M. & W. 303, 316–17.

Greek, Latin, or any other foreign language.[132] But that provision did not touch the entitlement of foreigners to British copyright. As other countries came to introduce copyright laws, it could hardly be expected that they should offer English authors and publishers the benefit of their laws, without considering what English law offered their own authors in return. They were highly unlikely to allow proceedings before their courts concerning acts done on their territory contravening an English author's copyright as defined in English law. From the 1830s, the need for solutions became more pressing, not least because the United States in many circumstances refused protection to the works of English authors, an issue taken up by Charles Dickens during his visit there in 1842.[133] By then it was apparent that only by agreements between states could there be a mutual recognition of authors' rights for the citizens or residents in those states. Such basis for collaboration began in bi-lateral experiments, Britain entering agreements with Prussia and its associated German states from 1846, then with France in 1851, and a few other European countries thereafter.[134]

It was soon enough accepted that each participant state would offer rights under its own law to persons from the other state or states according to a principle of equal treatment with their own citizens. Too many differences existed between national laws, not least as to the term of copyright, for agreements to reach common solutions to be an achievable goal. Inevitably, however, there was likely to be no transnational agreement at all if the degree of reciprocity was not in rough measure equal. As we shall see, the local printing requisite in the United States would long prove a form of protection too far for collaboration with Britain.

The mid-century diplomacy over copyright led the Foreign Office and the Board of Trade to feel discomfort over the subject-specific enactments on copyright in Britain. Their engagement would contribute to the idea of a revised and integrated domestic law.[135] However, the eventual achievement of a unified copyright regime in 1911 would come only after long arguments with 'anti-monopolists', the appearance of both producer and author groups in lobbying on the home front, the development of new 'copying' technology

---

[132] 8 Anne c. 19, s 7; and see the Importation of Books Act 1739, 12 Geo. II c. 36.

[133] For his visit and the lobbying for mutual arrangements between the two countries which followed in the 1840s, see J. J. Barnes, *Authors, Publishers and Politicians* (1974), 126–34, Ch. 10; Seville, *Internationalisation*, 165–84.

[134] The Crown's power to negotiate these agreements and then to bring them into force by Order-in-Council was granted by the International Copyright Act 1844 (7 & 8 Vict. c. 12, *Primary Sources*). This had been preceded by an Act of 1838 (1 & 2 Vict. 59, *Primary Sources*, with Comm.), which, not untypically for its time, failed to produce any agreements, probably because of the comparative limitations in British law: Barnes, *Authors*, 116–17.

[135] Sherman and Bently, *Making of Intellectual Property*, 119–25, place much emphasis on this factor.

such as sound recording and film, the intervention of trade and labour groups whose interests were opposed to copyright, difficulties with Canada and other emerging Dominions, the hesitant British collaboration in drafting the Berne International Convention of 1886 and the reluctance of successive governments to make choices among the bewildering alternatives thrown up by all the arguing.

The 'British Dominions'

Take, first, the position regarding the colonies, over which copyright proved to be a subject in which old mercantilist assumptions were only slowly eradicated. Those assumptions meant that copyright was an entitlement that flowed from the home country outwards without any compensatory return. How could legislation be otherwise understood when its system called for new titles to be registered with the Stationers' Company in London and there was a requirement for copies to be deposited for a number of British libraries? Even when the Copyright Act 1842 reduced the number of those libraries to six (to the disadvantage primarily of the Scots and the Irish) and restricted registration to a requirement to be fulfilled before launching litigation, there was no change aiding colonial authors who published in their own territory. On the contrary, the copyright arising under that Act for books first published in Britain would thenceforth be infringed by importing or selling unauthorized reprints in any British colony or possession.[136] But a Canadian author could have that copyright only by securing first publication in Britain. As colonies gained a degree of legislative independence, they might fill the local hole by enacting a copyright law for their own territory on whatever terms they might set as to qualification, but the Colonial Office's instinct was to treat such legislation as requiring Imperial approval, even when it was more permissive over patent and trade mark enactments.

The major tensions arose with Canada, where American publishers were ready to furnish much cheaper versions of books than the British publishers who held copyright in them under the 1842 Act.[137] The price differential could indeed be enormous. An attempt was instituted to deal with the problem by requiring

---

[136] 5 & 6 Vict. c. 47, s 2, rather grandly described them as 'British dominions'.

[137] The Canadian saga is admirably told by C. A. Seville, *The Internationalisation of Copyright Law* (Cambridge, 2006), Ch. 4; to be read with R. Burrell, 'Copyright Reform in the Early Twentieth Century: The View from Australia' [2006] *JLH* 239–65; L. Bently, 'Copyright and the Victorian Internet: Telegraphic Property Laws in Colonial Australia (2004) 38(1) *Loyola LA LR* 71–176.

importers to pay a tariff as the price of entry;[138] but the levy was rarely collected and distributed to claimants. In 1867 Canada became the first colony to acquire Dominion status, and its Federal Parliament would soon become frustrated by Westminster's refusal to improve the lot of Canadian authors and publishers. Approval was required even after the grant of Dominion status to Canada in 1867, when the Governor-General reserved an enactment for consideration at Westminster.[139] From this came clashes over the power of the Dominion to enact its own local copyright without securing assent from Westminster—perhaps the longest running saga of its kind.

While matters improved somewhat when the UK acceded to the Berne Copyright Convention, difficulties would remain over the issue of colonial autonomy. A quarter-century later, one indication of changed attitudes towards the leading dominions was the Imperial Copyright Conference. This was held in 1910, as the British government worked towards implementing the Berlin Act of the Berne Convention, signed in 1908.[140] The all-but-independent Dominions in the Empire (by then Canada, Australia, New Zealand, and the South African Union) won substantial concessions preserving their ultimate power to decide whether to participate in the proposed system of Imperial copyright.[141] At the same time, two basic matters were accepted. The Berlin amendments to the Berne Convention should be ratified by the British government for the Empire as a whole; and the proposed British Act would serve as a standard text for the mutual recognition of copyrights across the Empire on the basis of first publication in one of the Crown's territories or, failing that, citizenship or residence in some part of the whole panoply.[142]

Foreign Authors and Britain; British Authors Abroad

With the growth of copyright systems in Continental countries and in the United States, the status of foreign authors to share in the entitlement received differing answers. France, with its universalist tendency, called only for first publication in the country and took no account of nationality. To the contrary, Spain and Portugal, Sweden and Finland, and crucially the United States, excluded the works of foreign nationals. The German states in the main opted for German

---

[138] Under the Foreign Reprints Act 1847, 10 & 11 Vict. c. 95, *Primary Sources*; Seville, *Internationalisation*, 26.

[139] British North America Act 1867, ss 55–7.

[140] See below, 924–8.

[141] L. Bently, 'Copyright, Translations and Relations between Britain and India in the Nineteenth and Early Twentieth Centuries' (2007) 82(3) *Chicago-Kent LR* 1181–240.

[142] See the Memorandum of Proceedings, *PP* 1910 [Cd. 5272], LXV, 799.

nationality or first publication there by a German publisher—thus taking a middle way that would have considerable influence.[143]

As for Britain, it was accepted, first of all, that an author from another country who both resided in England and first published there was within the Statute of Anne.[144] Situations where the British elements were slighter came before courts in increasing number after the peace in Europe, and the terms and the intent of the Statute became the fighting ground. Back came the root issue left dangling after *Donaldson*—did the Statute provide the only form of copyright from the moment of publication until expiry, or could a common law right be relied upon in addition during that period? Would the benefit to the British public from publication within the UK justify either type of claim, and if so was this confined to first publication anywhere? In *Clementi* v. *Walker*, Bayley J. expressed a strong view of the public policy apparently at work in the Statute:

> The British Legislature must be supposed to have legislated with a view to British interests and the advancement of British learning. By confining the privilege to British printing, British capital, workmen and materials would be employed, and the work would be within the reach of the British public. By extending the privilege to foreign printing, the employment of British capital, workmen and materials might be suspended, and the work might never find its way to the British public.[145]

This strain of nationalistic utilitarianism would recur frequently in the ensuing judgments and confrontations about policy. It set a train of reasoning, but it by no means indicated the precise terminus. A decade later, in the Court of Exchequer, Abinger CB took the view that British copyright extended to the work of a French composer where the assignee of his copyright (the English publisher, Boosey) provided its first publication in England, rather than elsewhere; the assignee could therefore sue a British rival who obtained his own copy from a later publisher in France.[146] In contrast there was no copyright in Britain where the first publication occurred abroad.[147] With that position the Courts of Queen's Bench and Common Pleas came to agree.[148] But the

---

[143] Ricketson and Ginsburg, *Berne Convention*, paras. 1.25–1.28.

[144] The question had not even been raised in *Bach* v. *Longman*, above, n. 10.

[145] (1824) 2 B. & C. 861, 867–8. The application of the analysis resulted in judgment for the defendant but this appeared to depend on the particular dealings over British rights engaged in by the composer.

[146] *D'Almaine* v. *Boosey* (1835) 1 Y. & C. 288; see above, n.113.

[147] *Chappell* v. *Purday* (1841) 45 Y. & C. 485; *Chappell* v. *Purday (No. 2)* (1845) 14 M. & W. 303 (both concerned with dealings in rights from Auber's best-known opera, *Fra Diavolo*). For the upsurge of case law in the period, see esp. Seville, *Internationalisation*, 174–8; Deazley, *Rethinking Copyright*, 42–55; Alexander, *Boundaries of Copyright*, Ch. 9.1.

[148] *Cocks* v. *Purday* (1848) 5 C.B. 860, 6 C.B. 69; *Boosey* v. *Davidson* (1849) 13 Q.B. 257.

generation of Exchequer judges after Abinger drew back from such a concession to foreign authors.[149]

The whole question was finally taken to the House of Lords in *Jefferys* v. *Boosey*, the published music at issue consisting of arias from Bellini's *La Sonnambula*.[150] The composer had assigned the copyright in the opera to a fellow Italian, Ricordi, that great expert in the control of rights in operas.[151] Ricordi had arranged for first publication in Britain and he had assigned his right to Boosey, an English national. At the trial, Rolfe B. (soon to be Cranworth LC) instructed the jury that there could be no British copyright in the circumstances; but the Court of Exchequer Chamber, made up of judges from the other common law courts, held that first publication in Britain was sufficient to give rise to British copyright. It was precisely at this moment that an effort in the United States to secure a mutual recognition treaty with Britain gained the support of Secretary of State, Daniel Webster. But the decision of Exchequer Chamber offered British protection to American authors without the need of a convention and the prospect faded before it was ever put to Congress for endorsement.[152]

Given all the disputation between the judges on the question, the *Sonnambula* ruling was appealed by writ of error to the House of Lords by publishers who wanted to remove any relatively easy procedure allowing foreign authors and their publishers to secure British copyright. Cranworth, by then Lord Chancellor, summoned all the common law judges—including his fellow Barons from Exchequer—to advise their Lordships. Six out of the ten judges who gave advice favoured recognition of the copyright by virtue of first publication in the UK;[153] the others stood by the Exchequer line. The three members of the Lords who gave judgment took the latter position. Cranworth himself was not minded to change his opinion at trial; Brougham had supported the opposition to Talfourd's extensions of copyright; and St Leonards followed his conservative presumption against extending the scope of rights. For them, copyright—in the sense of the exclusive right to prevent copying of books already published—was entirely the creature of statute; and neither the 1842 Act nor any other enactment gave

---

[149] The leading voice was that of Pollock C.B.: *Chappell* v. *Purday* (No. 2) (1845) 14 M. & W. 303; *Boosey* v. *Purday* (1849) 4 Exch. 145.

[150] (1854) 4 H.L.C. 815.

[151] Casa Ricordi, founded in 1808, became the largest music publishing house in Europe. As copyright assignee of most major Italian opera composers, it charged large sums for performances of their works. By only hiring out material such as orchestral parts, it developed a form of exclusivity that was in effect indeterminate.

[152] See esp. Barnes, *Authors*, Chs 8–12; Seville, *Internationalisation*, 180–4.

[153] See above, n. 150.

any sufficient indication that its protection extended beyond the case where the first publication was in Britain *and* the work's author was a British subject or a resident in some sense.[154]

Their speeches reiterated the divergent precedents and rehearsed the source-of-law arguments, but had little to say about the economic impact of their decision or the politics of securing mutual accords between states. Yet what they were deciding appeared to make it easy for interlopers unconnected with foreign authors to print and sell rival versions of popular literature and music. And they were in effect laying down a default solution that would operate between Britain and those countries with which it had no convention. The decision might therefore increase pressure from authors and their publishers to push ahead with negotiations. Although Lord St Leonards specifically mentioned the lack of a copyright treaty with America, he was quick to say that the issue could have no influence on his decision.[155] This may have involved a certain disingenuousness. At the same time, it must have been evident that any result would have politically inflaming consequences for the various groups of publishers and their authors who had interests in trans-national publishing; and it was a perplexing exercise to calculate the consequences for each of them.[156] It made juridical sense to reach judgments that made much of policy choices that could be imputed to the Parliament of 1710 rather than to contemporary preferences.

The decision left unsettled what degree of permanence was needed to show residence by the author. One theory was that even temporary presence of a few days in a British possession at the time of first publication in Britain would suffice, because during that period the author would owe allegiance to the British sovereign. This view was affirmed by the House of Lords in *Routledge v. Lowe*.[157] A popular American author, Maria Cummins, was held to have gained residence by a short stay. Her residence moreover was elsewhere in the Empire—in Canada. So American authors of crowd-pulling books had only to make a short trip northwards in order to gain a British copyright effective throughout the Empire, if the book was during that sojourn also first published in Britain.[158] The decision was hardly likely to benefit busy writers and composers of short pieces, who could scarcely make repeated visits.

---

[154] The earlier notion that assignment of the British copyright to a British publisher could rescue the claim of a foreign author, disappeared. The assignment was after all no guarantee that the assignee would not secure his own supply by importing copies printed elsewhere.

[155] (1854) 4 H.L.C. at 989–90; likewise Lord Brougham, in less specific terms: at 962.

[156] For their tactics, see S. Nowell-Smith, *International Copyright Laws and the Publisher in the Reign of Queen Victoria* (Oxford, 1968), Ch. 1; Barnes, *Authors*, Chs 9–12; Seville, *Internationalisation*, 180–9.

[157] (1868) LR 3 HL 100.

[158] If first publication took place in any other country (including Canada) there would be no British copyright in the Empire.

In any case, the limited concession contained in this judgment was not enough to satisfy two of the five judges involved, Lord Cairns LC and Lord Westbury. In their view, no residence requirement at all should have been adopted in *Jefferys* v. *Boosey*. As with *Donaldson* v. *Becket*, an opinion that ran against the wisdom of a majority of the judges would leave open some prospect of modification in subsequent case law and it was in that direction that Cairns and Westbury were pointing. In the event the uncertainty would in some measure be resolved in the course of international negotiation. The Berne Convention of 1886 would provide its Union of countries with the assurance of mutual recognition either on the basis of first publication, or, failing that, on the basis of residence. The United States stayed outside Berne, but came to a separate accommodation with other countries under its Chace Act 1891.[159] To fall within its terms so that British authors might gain copyright there, the British government had to assure the United States that American authors need only show first publication in Britain. This was achieved by having the Law Officers rely on the dicta of Cairns and Westbury in *Routledge* v. *Lowe*. This act of political faith, if not exactly of good faith, proved enough for an American government that by then was embarrassed by the defiant isolationism of its copyright law during the previous 40 years.[160]

The Berne Convention: International Protection of Literary and Artistic Works

In 1878 *l'Association littéraire internationale* was formed in France under the Presidency of Victor Hugo, in order to promote the cause of authors and within a few years to press for a Union of countries devoted to the recognition of authors' rights as a matter of high principle.[161] By 1883 this plan had progressed to a draft treaty epitomized in its initial declaration:

The right of the author in his work constitutes, not a concession by the law, but one of the forms of property which the legislature must protect.

This property was declared to be perpetual.[162] It should be recognized by a common code for authors' rights among civilized nations.[163] As with the movement

---

[159] For the history in general, see Seville, *Internationalisation*, Ch. 5.

[160] Seville, *Internationalisation*, 245–7.

[161] Soon rechristened *l'Association littéraire et artistique internationale* (ALAI), in which form it continues today, using English as its second language.

[162] See Ricketson and Ginsburg, *International Copyright*, para. 2.07. Drawing on the French acknowledgment of universality by its Decree of 1852, the same fervour had been expressed two decades before in the Resolutions of the *Congrès de la propriété littéraire et artistique* in Brussels which had called for recognition of the property of authors in the legislation of all civilized peoples—the responsibilities to be accepted by countries towards one another even in the absence of reciprocity.

[163] Just such an objective was raised by Germany at the Berne Diplomatic Conference of 1884: Ricketson and Ginsburg, *International Copyright*, para. 2.24.

for an international treaty on industrial property which had been launched in earnest in 1873 and came to fruition ten years later,[164] the initial meetings were led largely by academic figures, together with professionals and entrepreneurs from the industries most interested; grand gestures were only to be expected.

When it came to governments, however, most countries considered such a high-minded stance to be unrealistic, given that one focus had always to be on persuading additional states to join in any international alliance that might be forged. The *Association* pressed on towards a more sustainable objective and found an ally in the Swiss government. It proved willing to set up Conferences in 1884 and 1885, leading to the formation of a Copyright Union with its own Bureau, under the Berne Convention for the Protection of Literary and Artistic Works of 1886.[165] The British, innately suspicious of visions of the Author as originating genius, were drawn into the negotiations after showing considerable reluctance, and they extracted a range of concessions by virtue of their large commercial interests in the field.[166]

The Berne Union was initially an alliance of only 11 states, predominantly European. However, France, Belgium, Germany, Italy, and Spain brought in their colonial possessions, and the UK did likewise even in relation to those parts of the Empire that were partly or predominantly self-governed (territories which therefore included India). Outside the circle were Austria-Hungary, Russia, Portugal, and the Scandanavian countries. Japan had sent observers and would join after 13 years; the United States also had its observers, but that country would refuse to participate until very different circumstances brought a change of heart in 1989.[167]

The Union was founded upon the principle of national treatment for the copyright works of authors between its member states.[168] Its technique reflected the practicalities of publishing. Once the author could show that his work had a country of origin in one of those states, it was entitled in all others to the

---

[164] For subsequent expansions of the Convention, see below, 917–18.

[165] For the original version of the Convention, see e.g. Scrutton, *Copyright*, 296–310; and for the consequent British International Copyright Act 1886, giving the government powers to apply copyright legislation to the works of authors of other Convention countries: *Primary Sources* (UK Comm).

[166] Ricketson and Ginsburg, *International Copyright*, paras 2.19–2.50; L. Bently and B. Sherman, 'Great Britain and the Signing of the Berne Convention in 1886' (2001) 48 *J US Copyright Soc.* 311. The principal British representative at the negotiations, J. H. G. Bergne, wrote a lucid account of the outcome: 'The International Copyright Union' (1887) 3 *LQR* 14–31. See also W. Briggs, *Law of International Copyright* (1906).

[167] By that time the computer industry had become avid for international protection of software by copyright. In 1952, UNESCO had promoted the Universal Copyright Convention whose lesser requirements enabled international relations to be established between the United States and other countries.

[168] Berne Convention 1886, Arts 2, 3.

copyright protection that they each afforded to their own authors. The connecting factor that gave the author's work a 'country of origin' was primarily the place of first publication;[169] only where the work was unpublished, was it the country to which the author belonged. To this, there were two qualifications: conditions and formalities required in the country of *origin* had to be carried out (but nothing more); and the term of protection required by the Convention could not exceed that in the country of origin. The Convention covered a great variety of works in the realm of literature, science, and art—writings, dramatic pieces, musical compositions and the fine arts.[170] No general right to prevent reproduction was expressed,[171] but a right of public performance was required for dramatic and musical works.[172] A minimum period for the duration of the right would have to wait until the Berlin Revision of 1908.[173] Minimum standards did appear on particular issues such as articles in newspapers and periodicals; and the entitlement to take extracts for educational or scientific purposes was specifically left to national legislation.[174] British membership of the Union made it necessary to push a bill through Parliament bringing the existing law into line with Convention requirements.[175]

A first attempt to clarify and extend the Berne Convention was pressed at a Conference in Paris in 1896, but resulted only in modest changes. The diplomacy required was laborious, given that the states involved already had national laws in place which they were not ready to change. Paris at least settled that the one way forward was by agreeing Acts and Declarations at each revision, which the Union countries and new members would have to ratify separately. The legal effect would become highly intricate. At least this would not prove to be a field in which states would take formal steps to secure recognition of the obligations of others by proceedings at an international level.[176]

---

[169] Even the initial version started down the road of defining what was to count as 'simultaneous publication' and it determined that, of the countries involved, whichever gave the shorter term of protection would be treated as the country of origin. From this Americans would gain access to Convention rights by simultaneously publishing through the back door of Canada—for long a distinct blotch on the Convention's record.

[170] Art. 4.

[171] Appropriately enough, the right to translate was contentious: it was limited to ten years from first publication by Art 5. The translation itself gained copyright as a literary work: Art. 6.

[172] Art. 9. Note also Art. 10 on protection against adaptations, arrangements of music, and other indirect appropriations of works.

[173] But the Convention did apply to existing works, which made its impact immediate: Art. 14

[174] See Arts 7, 8.

[175] Copyright (International Conventions) Act 1886, modifying the earlier International Copyright Acts to comply with the new Convention.

[176] See Ricketson and Ginsburg, *International Copyright*, paras 3.01–3.07. Only in countries which followed a doctrine of direct applicability of international obligations would the legal scope of the Convention be a direct issue in national litigation. In the UK, parliamentary sovereignty precluded such a doctrine.

The second revision in Berlin (in 1908) saw advances closer to the core of the subject,[177] the most basic of which was the general concept that the rights of authors in Union countries other than their own were independent of those in their country of origin.[178] Beyond this, members were not permitted to require registration or other formality as a precondition of protection, and the agreement in principle that authors of virtually all types of literary and artistic work should enjoy copyright for at least their lives plus 50 years *post mortem*.[179] To the list of protected material was added architectural, choreographic, and dumb-show works and also—recognizing a rapidly developing new medium—certain cinematographic works.[180] However, that other great arrival, the phonograph industry, did not secure any international guarantee of copyright in its productions. The extension of copyright to cover uses of the material that involved a modification of content or change of medium or nature was carried further, making it a more complete 'property'.[181] Including a copyright work in a film or a phonogram became acts requiring licence.[182] But in the latter case, Union states were permitted to introduce compulsory licensing arrangements, designed to prevent a single enterprise from holding the exclusive right to record particular pieces of literature, drama, or music.[183] In all this, the cause of authors as the subjects of innate rights in their creations was advanced at crucial points and Britain and her colonies would accept the new dispositions within three years. That is a culminative event in a history which ends with 1914. Before we come to it, however, we need to return to aspects of the domestic scene in the 30 years which followed upon the Report of the Royal Commission of 1876–7.

British Copyright Law After the Royal Commission

In Britain the act of authorship as the fount of a copyright had been recognized first by the Statute of Anne, and the adherents of 'literary property' over time used that acknowledgment to bolster arguments for wider and deeper rights. When their demands became too exigent the courts might be provoked into reaction,

---

[177] Ricketson and Ginsburg, *Berne Convention*, paras 3.08–3.21.

[178] Berlin Act, Art. 19, an abnegation of the idea that copyright was a right so personal that it would be carried around the world. For the one major exception, see n.179.

[179] Berlin Act, Arts 4, 7. Most members adopted life-plus-50 at once, though the provision would not become mandatory until the Brussels Revision in 1948. To the extent that duration in the country of origin was less than in the country of protection, the 'principle of the lesser term' applied.

[180] Art. 14. See P. Kamina, *Film Copyright in the European Union* (2002), section 1.2(1).

[181] There were further provisions relating to translations, newspaper articles, abridgements, musical arrangements, plays turned into novels and vice versa.

[182] Arts 13, 14.

[183] Art. 13(1).

as with the great confrontations of *Donaldson* and *Jefferys*. Equally, Parliament or an official investigation might turn a sceptical eye on claims for extension of protection—such as those voiced by Macaulay and his sympathisers in 1841–2. That hostility grew from an instinct that the exclusive right was causing monopolistic behaviour beyond the bounds of any reasonableness.

Throughout the nineteenth century those who bought books in Britain and its Empire complained of their cost, not least in comparison with prices in the United States and in France and Germany. In part these were the result of taxes on paper and the like,[184] and in part of restrictive practices in distribution, as booksellers in a modern sense separated from publishers. A cartel of London booksellers and publishers had struck a deal in 1829 which required retailers to re-sell at minimum prices if they were to continue receiving wholesale supplies.[185] By 1852, enough of the arrangement continued in operation to provoke considerable indignation, led in the Commons by Gladstone, then Chancellor of the Exchequer. The members of the club found themselves obliged to accept an arbitration presided over by Lord Campbell CJ. Turning to the common law's condemnation of monopoly, that body pronounced the practices 'unreasonable and inexpedient', and the participants felt that they must abandon them.[186] The rebuff was in one sense unsurprising, since it occurred at the height of the commitment to free trade. The scheme came to grief despite the root entitlement of the publisher to copyright exclusivity, because it was not confined to the distribution of single works but affected a sizeable portion of the whole market in books.[187] The issue was accordingly one in which the line between individual property and anti-competitive agglomeration was straightforward to draw.

The notion that copyright of itself led to high prices for books was never far away, as for instance before the Royal Commission of 1876–8. In the upshot the majority report would give the guardians of literary property a victory for the cause of literature and the other arts, since the continuation of copyright as an exclusive legal entitlement was endorsed. In this at least the interests of creators

---

[184] The tax of 1.25 per cent on paper was halved in 1836 but not abolished until 1861. For newspapers, the anti-radical stamp duty of 4*d* was reduced to 1*d* in 1836 and removed in 1855: Raven, *The Business of Books*, 346–7.

[185] For a diatribe against their cartel by one who suffered, see W. Pickering, *Booksellers' Monopoly* (1832).

[186] See J. J. Barnes, *Free Trade in Books* (Oxford, 1964), Ch. 12; Seville, *Internationalisation*, 260–4; Alexander, *Boundaries of Copyright*, Ch. 9.2.

[187] It would take until the 1890s for a somewhat more circumspect practice of price maintenance in the retail book trade to emerge in the form of the 'Net Book Agreement'. The NBA would justify itself on the ground that it was needed to keep small bookshops in business, when faced with the competition in popular lines from large stores. It would survive, despite the increasing suspicion of competition law authorities, until 1995: Barnes, *Free Trade*, Ch. 15.

and producers were essentially at one. But one price of success was an increasing awareness that, in their internal relationships with publishers, creators needed greater recognition and independence. One element therefore in the late nineteenth-century evolution of copyright is the emergence of clubs of creators, notably the Society of Authors (1884), alongside often older cartels of producers. Indeed, in 1872 a Copyright Association was set up to assert the common interests of producers as well as authors, hoping in part to weld the two sides together against schism.

Creators would remain obliged to join with producers, and sometimes distributors, in battles against consumers over the price of their products or against unauthorized competitors who saw prospects for exploiting their works without paying.[188] One impetus would accordingly be towards the establishment of collecting societies where they were the practical method of producing a cash return. A collective organization of some sophistication had been formed as early as 1832. The Dramatic Authors Society was there to obtain fees for plays in theatres under Bulwer's Dramatic Copyright Act when he secured it in the following year.[189] Its Secretary gave extensive evidence of its activities 40 years later to the Royal Commission.[190]

The need for joint action was arguably greater in respect of the performing right in songs and other short pieces of music. In the 1870s Thomas Wall acted with success as the agent for owners of copyrighted songs. He spotted that the Statutes giving copyright in public performances contained stiff penalties for breach. Threatening court proceedings, he was able to extract high fees from music hall proprietors and the like.[191] They in turn squealed that they were being unfairly trapped. Wall's practices were eventually curbed by two pieces of legislation, demonstrating that effective copyright could not survive without public support.[192] So had Macaulay insisted against Talfourd's campaign for longer copyright in books.[193] In the years leading to the Berne Convention, collecting

---

[188] Thus the Copyright Association played a prominent role in putting the authors' case against the royalty licence for which the Canadian government was pressing: Seville, *Internationalisation*, esp. 97–109.

[189] See above, n. 76.

[190] These are examined by McFarlane, *Performing Right*, Ch. 4. When the Society came to an end is not known.

[191] The Court of Appeal found itself reluctantly obliged to uphold the 40s minimum penalty for each performance of a musical work, as laid down in 5 & 6 Will. IV c. 65 and 5 & 6 Vict. c. 45, s 20: *Wall v. Martin and Taylor* (1880) 11 QBD 102. Despite the provision for double costs in the Acts, the Court refused to award any. See McFarlane, *Performing Right*, Ch. 5.

[192] See the Copyright (Musical Compositions) Acts 1882 and 1888. The first required a reservation of rights on the sheet music, the second reduced the penalty and gave a defence to innocent infringers.

[193] *PD* (53) 1841, lxi, 1396–7.

societies emerged in some numbers in France, Germany, and elsewhere. The Wall episode, however, in all likeihood put off the formation of less egregious collecting societies for composers, librettists, and their publishers in Britain. The Performing Right Society would not be established until the brink of war in 1914. And for many years afterwards it would be forced into battle in order to gain acceptance of its legal demands.[194]

These various trade practices provide some answer to the question why substantial reform of the statute law would remain in suspense until 1911. The Royal Commission had on the whole favoured continuing and enhancing the copyright concept as a key to the promotion of the various cultural industries in Britain; and it had found the complications and uncertainties of the law lamentable. Bills to give effect to its recommendations were presented in its immediate wake, the most significant being that of its Chairman, Lord John Manners, Postmaster-General. But as with later efforts to secure either general legislation or amendments on particular issues, there was no decisive will to push through changes.[195] Governments and their civil servants, remembering the intensity of debates during the Royal Commission, showed even less enthusiasm for grasping the nettles of domestic reform than they had for the negotiations towards an international convention on authors' rights. In an era of general reduction in the volume of legislation, the Board of Trade was much involved in forming a Patent Office and accordingly put its efforts into the legal frameworks for patents, trade marks and registered designs.[196] The informal sphere of copyright tended to be left to backbench initiative, and discarded bills found their way year after year to the parliamentary scrapheap. The emergence of collective lobbies for producers, authors, and users of copyright material could lead all too readily to dissension between them. And on the government side, the continuing disputation with Canada posed its own curb on reform.[197]

---

[194] See McFarlane, *Performing Right*; A. T. Peacock and R. B. Weir, *The Composer in the Marketplace* (1975), 69–87.

[195] One specific issue that resisted clarification by statute was how far the copyright in a book such as a novel was infringed by dramatizing it (and vice versa). Cases in the 1860s took it that printing the new version was wrongful but that there was no performing right deriving from the literary work. See esp. *Reade* v. *Conquest (Nos 1 and 2)* (1861) 9 C.B. (N.S.) 755, 11 C.B. (N.S.) 479; *Reade* v. *Lacy* (1861) 1 J. & H. 524; *Tinsley* v. *Lacy* (1861) 1 H. & M. 747. The increasingly casuistic differences were subject to scathing attack by, e.g., Scrutton (*Copyright* (4th edn, 83, 86); but nothing would change until 1911. See also Seville, *Internationalisation*, 265–70; Alexander, *Boundaries of Copyright*, Ch. 10.3.

[196] See below, pp. 956, 981, 1003.

[197] For the leading personalities who argued for reforms, despite the lack of progress, see esp. Seville, *Internationalisation*, 275–89; Alexander, *Boundaries of Copyright*, Ch. 11.4.

The Moral Claims of Authors

In the last third of the nineteenth century those in France, Germany, and other Continental countries who advocated authors' rights as a principle of natural law (or a fundamental human right, as it might be described today), were coming to derive from it the tenet that authors enjoy a *droit moral*, a *Persönlichkeitsrecht*, in their creations. This would encompass the right to authorize the first publication of their work, to require that they be named on it when it was exploited, to object to alterations to it and perhaps also the right to require that it be withdrawn from circulation, to prevent the original being moved to a different situation and to object to its destruction. This moral right did not exist to enhance economic potential—that was the proprietary aspect of authors' rights. To the contrary, it was to have a peculiarly personal association. So it would be inalienable, even though it might, under due safeguards, be capable of being waived.[198] The economic rights might pass to others through assignments and licences, but the author would always retain his moral right, even when that would limit what an assignee wished to do, thus leaving him to seek whatever waiver the law would allow him in the particular circumstances. It could be a powerful constraint on market freedom, affecting both those through whom an author chose to exploit his work and third parties against whom the author, having transferred away his economic rights, might have no other basis for legal action.

To leave authors to negotiate contractual terms that would secure their own protection for publishing, naming, non-alteration and so forth was an approach far less secure. The movement was motivated in part by a belief that all creators but those who were already famous had to take what contracts they could get and were likely therefore to have to accept terms that gave too much to entrepreneurs. Market forces might produce literary agents, music publishers, and art dealers, whose commission was to promote the creator's interests. But to those who conceived authors' rights as founded in natural law, these commercial solutions were deemed to provide only sporadic answers, of greatest help to those already on the road to high returns for their talents. Legal reinforcement was therefore needed not only for the purely 'moral' but also for the economic, and might result in the exclusion of lump sum payments in place of royalties, the inalienability of the economic rights (as distinct from the grant of use rights) and the compulsory arbitration of standard rates for services where they were traditionally low-paid. There were no obvious end-marks to such potential developments, and moral rights became the focus of much pontifical disputation. Thus at root, proponents of the dualism dominant in French theory insisted that moral

---

[198] On the author's death, the rights would fall to be exercised by a nominated inheritor.

right must be perpetual; whereas the monism that eventually predominated in German theory treated economic and personality rights as branches of the same tree and therefore each limited to the same duration.

This high-toned debate calls only for the briefest mention here because it had so little impact in Anglo-American legal circles.[199] The English courts continued to talk the language of property and civil obligation. The latter in the main meant contract—either express, or implied where that seemed commercially necessary; with, in addition, torts, such as defamation, deceit, or inducing breach of contract;[200] and the innominate equity that in the nineteenth century would incorporate common law copyright and in the twentieth would be seen as providing remedies against breaches of confidence. To the judges, copyright was essentially about commercial gain. The right to exploit went to the publisher or other entrepreneur by assignment or exclusive licence from the author. So it was up to the latter to bargain for what he or she could get, rather than to rely on any legal guard-rail to keep the market fair.

Even among its European proponents, it could not be said that, before the First World War, the moral right had anything much by way of agreed content.[201] The Rome revision of the Berne Convention in 1928 would see the acceptance of a clause, drafted by Italy, which recognized a 'paternity right' and an 'integrity right'.[202] But there would have to be a number of concessions particularly to accommodate common law objections to characteristics that overrode contractual freedom. Thus Britain would insist that it did not have to be through its copyright law that the Convention obligations to protect moral rights were met. It could therefore continue to regard its own law of contract, tort, and property as sufficiently fulfilling what was required of it. The phlegmatic pragmatism in this dominant British attitude ran deeper than just an acceptance of sovereign

---

[199] See the exhaustive treatment of its evolution by S. Strömholm, *Le Droit Moral de l'auteur en droit allemand, français et scandinave* (Stockholm, 1966–71), Pt I; and E. Adeney, *The Moral Rights of Authors and Performers* (Oxford, 2006), Pt I. As already noted, the penalty rights given by the Fine Arts Copyright Act 1862, , s 7, were in the nature of consumer protection measures: see above, 892.

[200] Instance the finding of a jury that it was defamatory to serialize a story in a newspaper by leaving out detail and adding 'curtains' at the opening and closing of each episode. This was taken to have a derogatory effect on the author's reputation: *Humphreys* v. *Thompson* [1905–10] Macgillivray's CC 148.

[201] See Strömholm, *Droit moral*, Ch. 5. In part the nineteenth-century developments had paralleled the division, already introduced in Britain by the terms of the Statute of Anne, between material that had been published and that which remained only in manuscript. The author's personal control over the latter was expressed as a right of divulgation, and had evident similarities to the common law copyright that came to be moulded out of the decision in *Donaldson*. The classic German decision in 1846 protecting the university lectures of the philosopher, F. W. J. von Schelling, dealt with facts very similar to those leading to injunctions in *Abernethy*, *Nichols* and *Caird* (see above, 898–9).

[202] See Ricketson and Ginsburg, *International Copyright*, i, para. 3.28.

command as the sole source of English law. The arts, it was assumed, were best treated as a marketplace for commodities and labour. Creators must compete individually or collectively, subject to the limited economic advantages conferred by copyright or the general laws of civil and criminal obligation.

The essence of this attitude was also expressed over the law's determination of initial entitlement to copyright in works that were created to order. The 1842 Act first introduced a distinction, which touched the case of employees who wrote contributions to encyclopedias, periodicals, and the like. The employer who organized production of the serial or composite work gained title to the copyright for that purpose, unless there was a contractual arrangement to the contrary. These were types of publication where the material had a first, often ephemeral, objective, but the material might well have secondary uses, and this special arrangement operated for the bulk of those engaged in writing the material. The underlying preference for the capitalist organizer was a mark of its time and one that would only grow. By the Copyright Act 1911, it was presumed that for works produced in the course of apprenticeship or employment, copyright belonged initially to the employer; the presumption could only be displaced by an express or implied contract to the contrary.[203] On the other hand, work produced by independent authors under commissions remained their copyright until they assigned it.[204] To those who believed that the status of the author must prevail over such pragmatic commercial differentiation, this development was of course anathema and became one of the crucial dividing factors in international discussion of the subject. At much the same time, it was imported with increasing readiness into the relation between employed inventors and their employers, this being a period in which inventors also worked increasingly within the structure of employment. But the argument from the special condition of the creator was always more potent over aesthetic work than in respect of technological development.

10. IMPLEMENTATION OF THE BERLIN ACT AND THE ESTABLISHMENT OF IMPERIAL COPYRIGHT

With a reforming Liberal government in place at home from 1906, the Board of Trade was able to promote a more embracing and logical enactment on copyright than lay in the scattered shells of nineteenth-century legislation.[205] A first

[203] Section 5. A new version of the divided rights presumption of 1842 would apply to employed journalists.

[204] To this the Fine Arts Copyright Act 1862 had already admitted exceptions which were continued in the case of engravings, photographs, and portraits. A legal assignment had to comply with written formalities, but in equity a contract to assign for valuable consideration would be treated as enforceable against the author.

[205] Already in 1905, the Conservatives had put a major revision of trade mark law into place and the Liberals had followed with a Patents and Designs Act 1907.

objective was to give effect to the obligations under the Berlin Act of Berne. A Committee, set up by the Board of Trade and chaired by Lord Gorell, was established to consider these. Its membership included distinguished representatives of the various types of 'author', as well as of literary, musical, and art publishing and the new types of media— sound recording and film. The main witnesses were from the copyright-dependent industries, though some of them were both rightholders themselves and at the same time users of copyright material of others. Neither businesses nor consumers who would be obliged, directly or indirectly, to pay rightholders had much chance to put counter-arguments.

The Gorell Committee's Report accepted the Berlin requirements. It also went beyond its formal remit in order to reinforce the government's determination to revise British law itself.[206] The generally favourable backing by representatives at the ensuing conference with the main dominions on 'Imperial Copyright' overcame a potential source of difficulty.[207] Given the preceding history with Canada, so much of which was a consequence of the isolationist attitudes of the United States, this outcome said much for the skilful chairmanship provided by Sidney Buxton, who had succeeded Winston Churchill as President of the Board of Trade.

In the nineteenth century, the broad notion of copyright was applied in statutes that idiosyncratically divided the literary from the musical and dramatic (though that only in part), and again from the artistic. While it was evident that the technologies of copying, and the commercial practices associated with each, called for some legal differences, the resulting law had lacked any straightforward coherence—a shifting sand which often enough became a quagmire once the courts got to work on points of statutory interpretation. The Imperial Copyright Act certainly supplied a new level of transparency, since copyright pertaining to literary, dramatic, musical, and artistic works, whether published or not, was put on essentially the same basis.[208] Copyright now arose on creation of the work, whatever its category, without preliminary formalities. It lasted in general for the author's life and 50 years thereafter, no matter at what stage in the author's career the works were created.[209] 'Common law copyright' ceased to have any presence within this scheme and the equitable obligation to respect trust and confidence gained its own principles, whether the information involved

---

[206] See *PP* 1910 [Cd. 4946], xxi, 241; Seville, *Internationalisation*, 289–95; Alexander, *Boundaries of Copyright*, Ch. 12.2.

[207] Above, 911.

[208] Copyright Act 1911, s 1(1). Section 31 provided that all copyright was in future statutory, thus abrogating the concept of common law copyright.

[209] Section 3.

was technical, commercial, or personal.[210] All works except the artistic,[211] if they were first published only after the author's death, would continue in copyright for 50 years from that publication—an outcome which carried forward the assumptions of the previous history.[212]

Necessary differences between the types of work were dealt with largely at a secondary level. Copyright was divided into primary rights, which were against reproduction (including publishing) and public performance, and were actionable whether or not the defendant acted knowingly;[213] and secondary rights, which lay against those who dealt knowingly with illegal copies or allowed unauthorized performances in places of public entertainment.[214] Acts of infringement fell to be judged by the general criterion of substantial taking.[215] Copyright covered those uses of the material that competed directly with the work in its original form. At the same time it extended also to other applications, first by a general formula requiring authorization for any 'reproduction in a material form';[216] and, secondly, by specific provisions. The latter gave protection to adaptations of material in given ways: reproducing or performing a work in translation; converting a dramatic work into non-dramatic form, and vice versa;[217] and making 'contrivances' such as records for mechanical performance. These were all practices over which there had been long argument during the preceding decades. Their inclusion set the seal upon copyright as 'property', rather than just a means of preventing loss through unfair competition. In that important respect, the expansion of rights was at one with natural right approaches of European neighbours.

Purists in these Continental traditions regarded the author's entitlement as a subjective right that was accordingly capable of qualification only in extreme cases. They looked upon the introduction of exceptions and limitations to the right with heavy suspicion.[218] From that perspective, the 1911 Act contained ele-

---

[210] Section 32.

[211] For artistic works the 50 years post mortem applied irrespective of publication: s. 17.

[212] Section 7.

[213] Persons who authorized the commission of any of these acts were also liable as primary infringers: see s 1(2)—a provision which extended vicarious liability beyond the acts of employees to those who commissioned publications and performances.

[214] Section 1(2), 2(2), 2(3).

[215] Section 1(2), codifying the common law rule discussed above, 898–900.

[216] Section 1(2). There was no performing right for artistic works in the 1911 Act. Coleridge J., however, decided that where a *Punch* cartoon was staged as a 'living picture' that constituted a 'reproduction': *Bradbury Agnew* v. *Day* (1916) 34 TLR 349.

[217] The latter included converting an artistic work into a dramatic work, which gave statutory force to the outcome of the *Hanfstaegl* cases concerning *tableaux vivants*: above, n. 903, n. 110.

[218] The Berlin revision of Berne, however, continued the Convention's exception for news of the day, and added one for articles in newspapers (but not periodicals): Ricketson and Ginsburg,

ments of betrayal. The legislature set out a specific list of situations where, if the dealing was fair, unauthorized copying was excused. As already noted, the judges had shown some willingness to allow two types of exception defined by purpose: the use of quotations in the course of criticism or review; and the use of material to report newsworthy events. In addition, there were a few indications that copying for purely private purposes was exempt. The government's stated intent was simply to clarify the effect of this judge-made law. The provisions that were finally accepted left to the courts some scope to balance the conflicting interests of rightholders and users since they had to decide what of the various types of dealing was 'fair'; the older phrase, 'fair use', which by then had a vigorous role to play in American doctrine, was not used.[219] In the bill there was a general provision exempting private use; but leading music publishers campaigned against an escape clause that they thought might allow amateur choirs and church congregations to make multiple copies from a single purchase. Instead, only fair dealing for purposes of private study or research were admitted.[220]

The rules concerning initial and transferred ownership, and those on transactions in the property, became for the most part standard.[221] The greatly extended term was moderated in the author's favour in one respect. For the last half of the 50 years *post mortem auctoris*, there was a reversionary right in the author's favour.[222] For the same final period, the monopoly potential of popular works was curbed by allowing competitors to produce rival copies on payment of a royalty of 10 per cent of their sale prices. The first of these modifications expressed some sympathy for the commercial ineptitude that was assumed to be part of the creative temperament; and the second echoed faintly the case against a monopoly right that had been ventured 30 years before by witnesses to the Royal Commission. But they were minor adjustments to a property scheme that had been extending its reach, bit by bit, through the nineteenth century.

The Statute of Anne had required registration of any published book in the Register of the Stationers' Company, as a step in acquiring copyright. Accordingly, the trade association of book publishers—the very entrepreneurs who would gain primarily from the right itself—were the one professional group who exercised

---

International Copyright, i, para. 3.15.

[219] Under modern conditions there is great concern about establishing such a balance and, in consequence, the history of the concept has been much investigated: see e.g. in addition to the literature listed in n. 121 above, R. Burrell, 'Reining in Copyright Law: Is Fair Use the Answer?' [2001] *IPQ* 361–88; M. De Zwart, 'An Historical Analysis of the Birth of Fair Dealing and Fair Use: Lessons for a Digital Age' [2007] *IPQ* 60–91.

[220] Section 2(1)(i).

[221] Section 5.

[222] Section 5(2). Some foreshadowing of this was perhaps intended by the Statute of Anne, s 11. Now tighter language was used, but in the end it too would lead to litigious difficulties.

any formal authority over conferment of the right, and registration had continued on for books and fine art in emaciated form after the 1842 and 1862 Acts.[223] The Berne Convention, marking some adherence to natural right theory, had by 1908 insisted that copyright should be acquired by the act of creating the work without any condition of registration.[224] The 1911 Act accordingly removed any such formality from the enjoyment of copyright in the 'literary and artistic works' within the Convention. Copyright was accordingly aligned to forms of tangible personal property. It was left to the courts to determine, if necessary, what material fell within the general provisions of the statute. The preponderance of industrial property rights, by contrast, by this time made an application to the Patent Office a precondition of entitlement.[225] This bred a cadre of civil servants within the Office as well as specialist professionals who engaged with them in the application process. And so in organizational terms, for much of the twentieth century copyright and industrial property would be considered separate spheres.

The one truly radical step in the Imperial Copyright Act came from the persistent demands of the new phonographic industry.[226] In *Walter v. Lane*,[227] the House of Lords, led by Halsbury LC, had been willing to accord an author's copyright (under the 1842 Act) to reporters from *The Times* who used stenography to take down speeches on the hustings by the Liberal politician, Earl Rosebery. Rosebery himself disclaimed any proprietary interest in them. Treating the recording of another's speech as an authorial activity was accordingly used as a pretext; it gave protection against the person who independently sought to publish a book of the speeches without paying *The Times* any licence fee in recompense for the costs of getting the speeches down on paper. The Court of Appeal had rejected such special pleading. Likewise, Lord Robertson, who dissented in the Lords, asked pertinently what was the difference between stenography and recording mechanically on a wax cylinder, an activity which he thought it absurd to treat as authorship.

The use of copyright as one weapon against commercial 'reaping without sowing' was a temptation which would cause courts much later to revive *Walter v. Lane* as a precedent in a changed world.[228] But its greater interest in its own time

---

[223] The 1842 Act had required registration only as a means of proving title in litigation (see s. 23); for artistic works, however, the requirement was much more draconian: see above, n. 63.

[224] Berlin Revision 1908, Art. 4; Ricketson and Ginsburg, *International Copyright*, para. 3.12.

[225] See below, Chs 3, 7.

[226] The industry's prominence before the Gorell Committee was all too apparent: see above, n. 208.

[227] [1900] AC 539. Adherence to the decision has continued to the present, despite the introduction in the 1911 Act of the requirement that, to be copyright, a work must be original. The tendency has been to apply it only where there is quite substantial originality: N. P. Gravells, 'Authorship and Originality: The Persistent Influence of *Walter v Lane*' [2007] IPQ 267–93.

[228] e.g. *Sawkins* v. *Hyperion Records* [2005] RPC 808, CA; cf. *Roberton* v. *Lewis* (1960) [1976] RPC 189.

lay in the favour that the 1911 Act conferred on sound recording—a commercial activity that would soon become a general medium for giving permanence to oral presentations. This first 'neighbouring' or 'related' right to copyright was separately conferred, not on any figure who exercised intellectual judgment, but upon the enterprise which arranged the recording. It gave protection against the copying of that recording and was thus narrower than a right to object to any recording of a play or piece of music while it remained in copyright. A sense of proportion confined its term to 50 years from the initial registration of the performance.

Nonetheless, the step set in motion the prospect of entrepreneurial rights that were independent of the rights of authors and which might be used in commercial negotiations as arguments for adjusting the proportionate shares due to the participants involved in creating, producing, marketing, distributing, and protecting literary, artistic, entertainment, and informational material. The step was a counterbalance, given that a right over recording was being conferred by the Act on authors and composers, thus reversing earlier case law;[229] and a fixed statutory licence was being introduced to prevent recording companies from obtaining exclusive property in these rights—in particular that to record copyright music.[230] The direct support of entrepreneurs that was being offered would become all too apparent in the future. The equivalent 'creator' for such a right would have been the actual performer, who might after all bring to the process of recording the element of aesthetic skill and choice that would provide some analogy to the 'labour, skill, and judgment' of authors in the copyright sense. Some countries would accordingly make a performer's right the first neighbouring right to acknowledge. In Britain, however, having themselves succeeded in 1911, the record producers would fight vociferously to resist any distinct civil right of action being conferred on performers, who might then use it as a key to improved earnings. Since musicians would become well-organized in trade union terms (while most authors were not), giving them their own intellectual property was a cause to be resisted. The most that would happen for many decades would be the introduction of criminal provisions against 'bootlegging'—the unauthorized recording of performances.[231]

---

[229] *Boosey* v. *Whight* [1900] 1 Ch 122 ; *Newmark* v. *National Phonograph* (1907) 23 TLR 439; *Monckton* v. *Gramophone Co* (1912) 28 TLR 205, (composer's copyright not infringed by making a pianola roll, nor a phonograph). The record manufacturers claimed that these restrictive interpretations of the 1842 Act had allowed the investment necessary to launch the British industry: the publishers, on the other hand, predicted their own ruin: see Alexander, *Boundaries of Copyright*, Ch.12.2(c)).

[230] For which see the Copyright Act 1911, ss 1(2)(d), 19(2)–(8).

[231] Beginning with the Dramatic and Musical Performers' Protection Act 1925.

If the nineteenth century was the age of piecemeal, ill-related rights for authors, which led the industries concerned to demand more complete generalization of their rights, the twentieth century would become the age of neighbouring rights—for sound and film producers, for performers, for broadcasting organizations, and even—in face of photocopying and now digital reproduction and display—with rights for publishers.

Once neighbouring rights, given in most cases directly to investors, became legally recognized, the potential for conflict between the various interests (including those of authors) became much greater than in the nineteenth-century evolution of the 'classical' copyrights. In international terms the movement posed a fundamental threat to the core strategy of many who believed that authors' rights formed the legal core of their national and international culture. The French, in particular, with their dualist conception of authors' moral rights, would stand out against the introduction of neighbouring rights into their own law until 1985. For the British, copyright was little more than an instrument of necessary commercial protection. The essential approach of both the legislature and the courts would remain that authors needed no special status beyond the various rights to exclusive exploitation; and so other investors in aesthetic, entertainment, and informational productions could be accorded similar types of property for appropriate terms.

III

Industrial Property: Patents for Inventions

'Industrial Property' became a collective term for the types of intellectual property which turned, at least partly, on registration. From 1883, registration was a function of branches of the Patent Office, which then replaced earlier administrative arrangements.[1] The generic term thus included patents for inventions, industrial designs, and registered trade marks. The registration procedure might amount to little more than a deposit (as with designs), or it might occur only after an official examination that went to the substance of the proposed subject-matter; but whichever procedure prevailed the development brought with it new roles for civil servants and for professional advisers to applicants. Chief among the latter were the patent agents who as a profession achieved the dignity of a royal charter of incorporation in 1882.[2] Registration was thus a main reason why the forms of industrial property were grouped together, and distinguished from copyright, which at this time was the special prerogative of only a few commercial trades. Industrial property, by contrast, grew to apply to 'industry' in a much broader sense.

The British system of patents for inventions, conferring exclusive rights over the exploitation of new technologies, has the longest historical continuum of the various types of intellectual property in existence today. From its outset in Tudor and Stuart England, its main role has been in structuring industrial policy. Patents had a capacity to foster new technology in the economy by appealing to the risk-taking instincts of experimenters and their financiers. At the same time they held the potential of turning a single enterprise into the dominant monopolist in a whole field of production by providing a period of exclusive protection on the market for a crucial invention.

In taking up its history in the first great period of industrial achievement we find these two root elements of the system at work. Over the half-century before

---

[1] See below, 938, 956.

[2] See K. Boehm and A. Silberston, *The British Patent System: Administration* (Cambridge, 1967), esp. Chs 1–3; H. I. Dutton, *The Patent System and Inventive Activity during the Industrial Revolution* (Manchester, 1984), Ch. 5; D .Van Zyl Smit, ' "Professional" Patent Agents and the Development of the English Patent System' (1985) 13 *I J Soc. & Law* 79–105.

1820 the courts had striven to tame the monopolistic instincts of inventors and their associates who held patents on major advances. In this they saw the need to excise various weaknesses in the law of earlier times, such as it was. Their direct power to apply legal tests of what amounted to patentable inventions came in litigation after the patent was granted. As will become apparent, they had less control over administrative steps that led to the granting of patents in the first place.[3] It was the granting process that would need overhaul by Parliament before the judges' changes in the legal basis of entitlement could reach anything near satisfactory operation. It is necessary therefore to plot the development of the British patent system from 1820 by setting the legal against the administrative. That is an intricate course, affording one explanation of why this Part treats the subject after dealing with copyright.[4] While copyright grew out of the precedent set by patents, by 1820 it had had a century of development as a tool for regulating commerce in published books, music, and engravings. Patents for inventions, by contrast, had evolved more gradually, making it over-emphatic to think of a 'pre-modern' system that contrasted with the 'modern' system of the mid-nineteenth century. Patenting was not a parallel of copyright, let alone the poor law.[5]

1. ORIGIN AND ESSENCE OF A PATENT SYSTEM

Patents for inventions had received legislative recognition in the Statute of Monopolies 1624.[6] Parliament's will, set forth in that enactment, had been to curb James I's penchant for granting letters patent containing trading monopolies as rewards to favourites.[7] Yet, section 6 had allowed an exception for 'the sole working and making of any manner of new manufacture within this realm, to the true and first inventor...'. During the preceding reign of Elizabeth, the number of such patents on novel technology had already increased. So the Crown was being allowed to retain the right to grant patents over these methods, provided that the period was no more than 14 years. This would allow for the training of two

---

[3] However, the monarch's Attorney-General and Solicitor-General, and also the Lord Chancellor, played significant roles in the granting process: see below, 964.

[4] See above, pp. 881–2.

[5] Cf. Sherman and Bently, *Making of Intellectual Property*, Pt II.

[6] 21 Jac. c. 3. For the early modern evolution, see E. W. Hulme, 'On the History of Patent Law in the Seventeenth and Eighteenth Centuries' (1902) 18 *LQR* 280–8; W. Hamilton, 'Origin and Early History of the Patents' (1936) 18 *JPOS* 19–34; A. A. Gomme, *Patents for Invention* (1946); H. G. Fox, *Monopolies and Patents* (Toronto, 1947); C. McLeod, *Inventing the Industrial Revolution: The English Patent System 1600–1800* (Cambridge, 1988); E. C. Waterscheid, 'The Early Evolution of the United States Patent System: Antecedents' (1994) 76 *JPTOS* 697–714. For a comparative investigation, see T. G. Essenden, *Essay on the Law of Patents for New Inventions* (Boston MA, 1812).

[7] It would take until 1689 to eliminate the practice entirely.

complete cycles of apprentices.[8] Though limited in scope to their novel 'manner of manufacture', these invention patents had a similarity to the broad printing patents of the same era, which were one precursor of copyright.[9] Both created legal monopolies effective against the world, not only against imitators.[10] Competitors were liable whether or not they imitated the patentee's goods or processes. And since inventions concern the useful properties of natural phenomena, the chances of different inventors making the same discovery were by no means a fluke. In *Dollond's case* it had become accepted that if two persons made the same invention, and the second in time obtained a patent for it, his grant was good, provided that the first had neither publicized nor made use of it in manufacture.[11]

In the nineteenth century, when industrial competition became a prime motor of economic change, there were often rivals searching for the solution to a technical problem, spurred by the race to get there first. The grant of a patent to one of them might well render the efforts of others a waste and a disincentive, particularly when no other way might remain for competitive activity and the patentee might prevent them from using his invention altogether or demand a high licence fee. This basic characteristic of the patent system invited controversy, as did even more fundamental questions: did technological advance really provide economic benefits on an irresistible scale? Were these advantages enough to justify a scheme for rewarding invention from subsequent market returns, quite apart from the encouragements that governments might provide through research grants and rewards for success?

In the early centuries of patenting it was by no means assumed that wealth and well-being would flow from the establishment of new technologies, let alone from offering inventors legally protected exclusivity in markets.[12] Inventors and their backers might urge that innovation would bring new employment. But equally it might put traditional workers out of their livelihoods. This could well follow from mechanization of a previously labour-intensive form of production—very much a concern in the early nineteenth century, as groups

---

[8] For this explanation, see Boehm, *British Patent*, 17.

[9] By the Statute of Monopolies, patents for printing were among miscellaneous exceptions permitted by s 10.

[10] By the 1624 Act, s 2, moreover, determining the validity and scope of a granted patent passed from Star Chamber to common law and Chancery.

[11] *Dollond's case* (1764), referred to esp. by Buller J. in *Boulton* v. *Bull* (1795) 2 H. B. 487 and see Hayward's PC, i, 165; *Forsyth* v. *Riviere* (1819) Hayward's PC, i: 785. Equally there could not be two patents for the same invention; so the first in time would alone be valid: see e.g. *Ex p Dyer* (1812) Holroyd 59; W M. Hindmarch, *Treatise on the Law relating to Patent Privileges for the Sole Use of Inventions* (1843), Ch. 3.4. For the system of caveats which sought to mediate between rival claimants, see below, pp. 963–4.

[12] MacLeod, *Inventing*, Ch. 2.

such as the handloom weavers mouldered on into extinction. From another perspective, among the small numbers who obtained patents, there were those who did so in order to improve their position as government suppliers (not least of armaments and other weaponry), or in order to overcome many types of rule and practice that regulated trades, or to seek an imprimatur for what they made or provided. Gaining a patent could therefore involve arguments over whether the Crown should confer the right in a given case.

2. TERMS OF THE ROYAL GRANT

The Letters Patent set out the legal attributes of an invention patent and did so for the most part more fully than the Statute of Monopolies, section 6. Having specified positively that the grantee and his transferees were to have the right to 'make, use, exercise and vend' the subject invention in England and Wales for 14 years from grant under the monarch's hand, it proceeded to abjure all others from making, using, or putting the invention in practice.[13] The negative quality of the grant was made plain in a provision specifying that the patent did not override a patent granted for any other distinct 'invention or work whatsoever which hath heretofore been invented or found out by any other'. Following the wording of section 6, the grant specified that it was rendered void if it was contrary to law, prejudicial or 'inconvenient'; if it was not new 'as to the public use and exercise thereof' in the realm; or if it was not invented or found out by the patentee.[14] The grant also made references to assignment and licensing of the right, thus assuming that, once granted, it constituted property, however much its conferment remained a matter of privilege.[15]

The original aim of the special exception for invention patents had been to stimulate industrial growth at a time when the English economy was still backward in comparison with France and the Low Countries. The promotion of the 'useful arts' was recognized as a public good that justified the temporary

[13] With time, separate invention patents would be granted for Scotland and then for Ireland—a tripartite nuisance which survived until the procedural cleansing in the Patent Law Amendment Act 1852 (below, p. 955).

[14] Section 6 specified as 'inconvenience', anything 'mischievous to the state, by raising prices of commodities at home or hurt of trade'. This attempt to set a curb on the potentially monopolistic effect of the very grant had little consequence for centuries, even though today it raises difficult issues over the objectives of competition law and the patent system. Another prohibition on potential monopoly in the grant constricted the sharing of interests to no more than five persons, grouping executors and the like as a single person. This was a survival from Bubble Act prohibitions on share speculation: R. Godson, *Practical Treatise on the Law of Patents for Invention, and Copyright*, (1823), 161–2; MacLeod, *Inventing*, 55–7. It was abandoned in 1852.

[15] Blackstone had characterized it as a form of personal property limited in duration: *Comms*, ii, Ch. 27. For the amount of trade in inventions, see Dutton, *Patent and Inventive Activity*, Ch. 6.

monopoly of invention patents even before the Statute of Monopolies. The Crown's prerogative of grant was accordingly acknowledged by the common law before that enactment.[16] One mark of this was the readiness to treat as 'inventors' not only those who worked out technical advances for themselves but also those who had travelled to secure knowledge of novel products and processes in operation in other countries, whether by hook or by crook. As Lord Holt noted, section 6 of the Statute referred to 'methods of new manufacture *within this realm*'.[17] There were other indicators that the system was as much about the economic exploitation of ideas as it was about the initial technical discovery. Certainly the 'true and first' inventor had to apply for the grant. But from an early stage he could allow his name to be joined with others. Those supplying capital for the stages of practical innovation could accordingly be named in the grant.

As there might be a surreptitiousness about securing ideas from foreigners, there was reason enough not to require that the invention covered by the patent be made public by the grant. Mercantilist inclinations to covet whatever was of value abroad only added to the nationalistic spirit of gain that underpinned the early use of invention patents. As the muscles of British industry gained tone, interest lay not just in patents for 'finding out' foreign technologies; at the same time there were attempts to bar the export of English ideas. As early as 1696, the export of knitting frames was forbidden,[18] and in 1719 it became an offence to entice skilled workers in metal trades to foreign manufactures.[19] Prohibitions of one or other kind were applied to other trades through the eighteenth century,[20] and a consolidation of Customs Regulations in 1833 showed how far the coverage had spread.[21] Ten years later, with the triumph of free trade over protection, Peel abandoned the very concept.[22] Only with this step would successive governments become readier to accept the value of a patent system which linked publishing the invention to the award of an exclusive right to exploit it. Even then, as we shall see, the consequence that a technical idea could be patented in

---

[16] See *Darcy* v. *Allin* (1602) Noy. 182; *Clothmakers of Ipswich* (1615) Godbolt 252, 254.

[17] *Edgeberry* v. *Stephens* (1697) 2 Salk. 477. The standard form of the royal grant referred at some points to those who 'invented or found out'. Cf. the construction of the Statute of Anne in favour of first publication in Britain: above. The importer as inventor would live on in the law until 1977, partly because it could be useful for a patent agent or other nominee to make the petition—for instance on behalf of a foreign inventor or a British inventor who had already patented his concept abroad.

[18] 7 & 8 Will. III c. 20, s 3.

[19] Sedition of Artifices Act 1718, 5 Geo. I c. 127.

[20] For instance, in 1774 (14 Geo. III c. 71) exports of 'utensils' used in cotton and other fabric trade became the subject of penalties.

[21] Customs Regulation Act 1833 3 & 4 Will.. c.52. The regime accordingly operated through the highly complex net of customs inspection of shipping.

[22] 6 & 7 Vict. c. 84, s 24.

Britain, but still taken away for free use in another country where there was no patent, was a bothersome reality that would only be hesitantly resolved by international convention.[23]

For a whole mesh of reasons, invention patents were long a rarity. The number of grants before 1750 had been tiny and thereafter the figure rose only in moderate steps. By the 1820s, the average per year had become 146. In the 1830s it was 245 and by the 1840s, 458.[24] Only with the first major reforms of the administrative system in 1852, would there be any exponential growth in applications and grants.[25]

3. JUSTIFYING THE PATENT SYSTEM

Secrecy vs Publicity

Patents accordingly worked against the natural instinct of inventors that they should keep new technology secret as long as the circumstances allowed—the chance of doing so varying with the extent to which the invention would necessarily be revealed in the course of marketing a product or process. Therein lay an inevitable divergence of objectives. Striving to prevent foreigners from obtaining British technologies was scarcely compatible with a scheme that insisted on their publication. One way in which leading inventors and manufacturers had sought to resolve the dilemma was to argue for the power to keep the specification of a patent secret during the term of protection—an advantage to them whether their rivals were at home or abroad.[26] Bills to this effect had occasionally been presented but had made no headway.[27] From 1794, *The Repertory of Arts and Manufactures*, which appeared several times a year, transcribed and published the specifications enrolled for invention patents.[28] That may help to explain why there was little political concern over the purpose and usefulness of the patent system. In 1829, a Select Committee of the Commons would spend a session exploring the subject and receiving criticism from many quarters about its inadequacies.[29] But it would

---

[23] See below, 961–3.

[24] For detailed figures, see Boehm, *British Patent Administration*, 22–3.

[25] See below, 956.

[26] For the part in this of James Watt and Richard Arkwright, see below, 944 n. 61.

[27] Four bills between 1793 and 1820 were noted in the Report of the 1829 SC, below, n. 29, App. A, 415; and see Dutton, *Patent and Inventive Activity*, 41–2. For secrecy in which government had an interest, see below, n. 60.

[28] A rival *London Journal of Arts and Sciences* began in 1820; and, when taken on by the engineer, William Newton in 1828, it turned its voice against the debilitating system in operation. See below, n. 94.

[29] *PP* 1829 (332), III, 415.

need the ensuing two decades, tough but in the end remarkably successful in economic terms, for there to be any convincing movement for reform.

In the meantime, the courts insisted that, if an inventor chose to patent, he must publish and take the consequences. As already noted, technical know-how could instead be kept as a trade secret, but that could be of practical value only where the eventual product did not reveal its workings or its method of production to purchasers. The tactic could be advanced by contractual covenants binding operatives not to disclose the information and not to leave their posts for other masters or businesses. Instances of such stipulations in Victorian industry led courts to refuse to uphold them when they seemed unreasonably wide.[30] Beyond this again was the question whether there was also an obligation to respect technical information held in circumstances of confidence outside direct contractual restraints—an equitable duty growing from a property-like root, rather in the manner of 'common law copyright' and 'common law trade marks'.[31]

Privilege or Entitlement

The patent system would never lose its dependence on formal grant to the degree that occurred with the registration of published works for copyright under the Statute of Anne.[32] Letters Patent remained an act under the royal prerogative; and, said Godson in 1823, the grant emanated from the monarch *as the Patron of Arts and Sciences* at the humble request of his subject...as a gracious favour'.[33] By then, for the most part the grant no longer turned on an overt assessment, as a matter of policy or privilege, that the particular application for protection was stronger than the advantages of allowing others to copy or adapt an invention without inhibition.[34] Even so, something of the old condescension would survive. In eighteenth-century practice it was still possible to petition for a further patent on an invention when the first expired, but a special case had to be made.[35] In

---

[30] See above, pp. 684–6.

[31] See the discussion below, 984–7.

[32] See A. Mossoff, 'Rethinking the Development of Patents' (2001) 52 *Hastings LJ* 1255. For formal registration with the Stationers' Company as the sole precondition of copyright in published books, see above, p. 881

[33] Godson, *Patents and Copyright*, 43. For the humble petitioning and gracious condescension that went into the Crown's grant, see the precedents provided at pp. 369–74. The same characteristic still remains in e.g. Frost, *Patent Law* (4th edn, 1912), ii: 1.

[34] For the gradual reduction of policy factors, such as potential injury to excise and other royal revenue, see MacLeod, *Inventing*, Ch. 2.

[35] In some cases, a petition to Parliament did procure the vote of a reward for an invention already successful: below, pp. 941–2.

1835, Parliament, stirred by Brougham, would allow the term of an existing patent to be extended by up to seven years, but only upon a petition to the Crown, the merits of which would be left to be decided by the Privy Council.[36]

Professional Persuaders

In 1820, industrialization in a broad sense was beginning to be perceived as a key to quite novel growth of the economy. Inventing was ceasing to be the pastime of those well enough off to indulge their natural curiosity and was being taken up by those who made a business of it. These professionals had a more evident interest in turning promising ideas to commercial account and therefore looked more regularly to the protection against free adoption by rivals that flowed from a patent. A market in inventions themselves grew and patents supplied some security to the business of assigning and licensing technologies.[37] Such developments only confirmed the proprietary basis of the right. As the numbers of grants increased, a new class of professionals arose to see through the process of securing the grant and then dealing with it. Some of these early patent agents began their careers in the government posts involved in the pre-grant procedures. Their seizing of the commercial chance undoubtedly helped the number of applications to grow.[38] On the legal side, in each generation there would be a few barristers, some with scientific or technical knowledge, who formed the beginnings of a patent bar in London. But only very occasionally would they find their way onto the bench.[39]

Classical Economists

The justifications relied upon for having the system at all needed to be regularly rehearsed. As we have seen, the natural rights of individuals to property in their labour, which played such a part in the enlightened thought of the eighteenth century, had found expression in England when it came to the great debate over the nature and extent of copyright in published books. John Locke's ideas of property in one's very self and therefore in every type of human labour, including

---

[36] 5 & 6 Wm. IV, c. 83, s 4 (as to which see also 2 & 3 Vict. c. 67 and 7 & 8 Vict. c. 69). Brougham also favoured giving extensions to copyright in books by deploying a similar discretion.

[37] For the economic history in detail, see Dutton, *Patent and Inventive Activity*, Chs 6, 7.

[38] Dutton, *Patent and Inventive Activity*, 86–96; D. Van Zyl Smit, 'Patent Agents'; and his thesis, *The Social Creation of a Legal Reality: A Study of the Emergence and Acceptance of the British Patent System as a Legal Instrument for the Control of New Technology* (Edinburgh University PhD, 1981), Ch.4.4.

[39] They would include Richard Webster (later Lord Alverstone LCJ), W. R. Grove, and Fletcher Moulton (later Lord Moulton).

the intellectual, provided a philosophical position that was long remembered.[40] Given that invention patents provided one model on which to found copyright in authorship, it was to be expected that inventors would be treated as having an inherent claim to a property in the successful outcome of their intellectual skill. There were English commentators who supported the idea of a patent system for its just recognition of this most valuable human capability. Even the economist, J. R. McCulloch, could write, in Lockeian vein, that if 'anything can be called a man's exclusive property, it is surely that which owes its birth entirely to combinations formed in his own mind, and which, but for his ingenuity, would not have existed'.[41]

The tendency of such thinking was to bolster arguments for systems that were free of preliminary hurdles to obtaining grant, open to all the world, and subject to no overriding because of 'mischievous' consequences. Equally the right once granted should not be subject to qualification through compulsory licences or local working requirements. Patents should instead give unfettered exclusivity for long periods with low fees. But the fact that a patent was available only to the first inventor to secure a grant, made it inherently difficult to take natural entitlement as the sole basis of the system in operation. As Duncan has shown, the rhetoric of natural rights would play a focal role in justifying invention patents as of right in revolutionary France.[42] In Britain, so far as the debate was one of basic principle at all, the public policy of encouraging technical advance for its economic advantages was almost always in the forefront. Had innate individual entitlement played a greater role in British thought, the inventors who tried to insist that they had a right to keep their invention to themselves as an adjunct of the patent grant might perhaps have gained a foothold for their demand. As it was, the judges insisted that patents could be given only to those who in return made their inventions public within four months of the grant to them. The public, and in particular the industry as a whole, were entitled to no less by way of advantage.

Justifying invention patents in terms of benefits to society ran along two tracks, which led to rather different termini. The first, increasingly prominent for a half-century from the 1770s, saw the grant as a bargain between inventor and state which carried overtones of that other great theme of enlightened political theory—the idea of social contract. Its thrust was to place real weight on

---

[40] For their relation to patenting, see P. Drahos, *A Philosophy of Intellectual Property* (1996), Ch. 3.

[41] See Dutton, *Patents and Inventive Activity*, 18. For the inventor as hero, see C. MacLeod and A. Nutolari, *The Ingenious Crowd: A Critical Prosopography of British Inventors* (2005).

[42] For a short period, the inventor's right was treated as perpetual: see L. J. Duncan, *From Privileges to the Paris Convention: The Role of Theoretical Debate in the Evolution of National and International Patent Protection* (Monash University PhD Thesis, 1997), Chs 1, 2.

the 'consideration' that the inventor must supply in return for the right conceded to him. He was obliged therefore to describe his invention sufficiently for other workmen in the field to understand it and to deploy it themselves once the patent expired, and to indicate what it was that he claimed to be the invention. The second justification posited the patent as an incentive to work out the technological novelty and to introduce it into practice in the country.[43]

The first theory had as a consequence that the patent should be granted only when the idea had been developed far enough for the industry to be informed of a workable result. The second theory allowed an applicant to have a patent once he could show some realistic prospect of ultimate success. Each approach concentrated on particular practical goals. When finally in mid-Victorian Britain patenting became the subject of sustained criticism it went almost wholly to issues of whether the system attained its objectives within a framework of liberal economics. Root-and-branch critics questioned whether it did produce early information about new technology that would not otherwise be so readily available; equally they might deny that the incentive to work up inventions was so exigent that it justified an exclusive right to develop the idea and then turn it to commercial advantage. Neither issue was at all easy to resolve in empirical terms, so the theories operated by dogmatic assertion, supported by stories of what had happened to well-known inventors and their best-remembered inventions.

For the early generations of political economists, patents, as temporary blocks upon free access to markets, posed a theoretical conundrum. Nonetheless Adam Smith had accepted the system in principle. By his reckoning the system provided a reward to inventors that had sufficiently beneficial consequences for the economy and the welfare of citizens generally.[44] Both he and Jeremy Bentham argued the essential appropriateness of the reward coming from market exclusivity. With striking clarity Bentham asserted that the infinitely shareable character of information meant that an inventor who had no means of preventing others from taking up the invention without contributing towards the cost of making it would be discouraged from what was often lengthy and arduous experimentation. Patents were therefore a necessity for the increase of wealth. Enhanced reputation, the possibilities of secrecy, and grants from the state were simply inadequate as means of compensating an inventor for what he gave the public.[45] J. S. Mill would later use largely utilitarian ideas in reaching the same

---

[43] For the idea that an inventor gained a deserved reward from a patent, and so fell outside the general anathema of the common law against monopoly, see *Mitchel* v. *Reynolds* (1711) P. Wms 181, 188.

[44] A. Smith, *Wealth of Nations* ('Glasgow edn', Oxford 1976, 1979), ii, 754.

[45] Bentham spelled out this strictly utilitarian justification for patents in his *Manual of Political Economy* (1795), for which see W. Stark's edition of his *Economic Writings* (1952), i, 219, 260–5;

conclusion. Yet, echoing McCulloch, he pronounced it 'a gross immorality in the law to set everybody free to use a person's work without his consent, and without giving him an equivalent'.[46] It was not enough that inventors, driven by their inquisitiveness, found their reward in recognition by their peers and the general public. Equally these writers gave little weight to the claim that most who succeeded with inventions did very little by their own originality of thought, when compared with the extent of knowledge learned from their predecessors. From the 1820s there had been a thin stream of criticism also from radicals who questioned the very assumptions of capitalistic production, seeking to argue that working-class inventors deserved a far larger share in returns from the exploitation of their ideas. Chief among them were Thomas Hodgskin and J. C. Robertson, his collaborator on the *Mechanics Magazine*. But in the era of rampant entrepreneurial assertion, they made little impression, save within their own groups.[47]

Among the classical economists, however, little enough attention was paid to the patent system, so long as its impact on industrialization was, by and large, only tangential. On the political front, in the absence of a patent system, what alternative could suffice to provide any ready incentive to invention? It was a question which a mid-century generation of objectors would find it difficult to answer convincingly. From the early eighteenth century, Parliament had on occasion voted lump sum awards to inventors and entrepreneurs as a reward for their success after the event. Samuel Crompton, for instance, was accorded £5000 (perhaps £400,000 today) for his cotton-spinning mule, while Edward Jenner gained £30,000 for his smallpox vaccine.[48] In these instances, the public conscience was pricked into recognizing the proven desert of the individual inventor.[49] Equally there were institutions, notably the Royal Society and the Society for the Encouragement of Arts, Manufactures, and Commerce, which made similar awards.[50] The latter, a London body with provincial emulators, tended to object to the very principle of the patent system, with its prospect

---

and returned to it in his *Rationale of Reward* (1825), 319–20. It was treated as foundational in, e.g., J. Coryton, *Treatise on the Law of Letters Patent* (1855), 36–7.

[46] *Principles of Political Economy* (1848) Bk V, x, 4. Of abolitionists, he wrote that they 'would enthrone free stealing under the prostituted name of free trade, and make the men of brains…the needy retainers and dependants of the men of money-bags'.

[47] See Van Zyl Smit, *Creation of Legal Reality*, 111–20.

[48] Mantoux, *The Industrial Revolution in the Eighteenth Century* (1961), 227–8.

[49] The grants to 1813 were tabulated in the SC on Patent Law, *PP* 1829 (332), III, 415, App. A. For SC Reports on petitions, see Dutton, *Patents and Inventive Activity*, 212–13; Duncan, *Privileges to Paris*, 113–16.

[50] See H. T. Wood, *History of the Royal Society of Arts*. Cf. the Royal Literary Fund, established in 1790 as a charity for the relief of authors in distress.

of exclusive market access as a stimulus to research and development yet to be undertaken, rather than to reward established success. Those who would attack patents in the Victorian years mostly believed that some stimulus was necessary to encourage technical research. The weakness of their position was mainly that they had no panacea for attaining real success other than a government reward scheme. Patent enthusiasts mostly dismissed that proposal as manifestly insufficient.

4. THE LONG COURSE TO A PATENT GRANT

Until the mid-nineteenth century, a supplicant had first to seek approval for his initial petition and later for the bill formed from it. Both stages needed the authority of the Attorney- or Solicitor-General. The bill then required the imprimatur of the Home Secretary, the Clerk to the Signet, the Lord Keeper and, finally, the Lord Chancellor, and in the whole process the monarch's own signature had to be solicited twice. In this maze, consideration of the merits of the supposed invention became submerged beneath formalities that called for the payment of fees and 'tips'.[51] If a rival mounted a challenge to the bill, however, the Law Officer, or occasionally the Lord Chancellor, would hear both parties and decide which had the better claim. To that degree there was a pre-grant examination of the petition. It was, moreover, aided by the ability of the outsider to lodge a caveat with either Law Officer in order to be notified of petitions on specified subjects. In 1844 there were 229 caveats and only 140 patents granted.[52] Some patentees appearing before the 1829 Select Committee complained bitterly about the practice, because rivals could get wind of the application and themselves anticipate it before its grant by publication or public use. Under the different procedure of the 1852 Act, however, caveats and opposition continued. The procedures were relatively cheap and effective in sapping the claim to protection before it became established. As rivalry over technical advances intensified in a range of industries, keeping watch over the patenting activities of others became a necessary form of self-protection.

---

[51] For the evolution of the practices, see A. A. Gomme, *Patents of Invention* (1946), 13–16; Godson, *Patents and Copyright*, Ch. 6; W. Carpmael, *The Law of Patents for Inventions Familiarly Explained for the Use of Inventors and Patentees* (1832) ; Hindmarch, *Patent Privileges*, Ch. 12. Charles Dickens, who took great interest in the practical potential of the system, delivered a timely exposure of the old system in *The Poor Man's Tale of a Patent* (1850); and created the figure of Daniel Doyce, struggling against the Circumlocution Office in *Little Dorrit* (1854–5): J. Phillips, *Charles Dickens and 'A Poor Man's Tale of a Patent'* (Oxford, 1984).

[52] Dutton, *Patents and Inventive Activity*, 183–4.

In the early eighteenth century patentees had been required to enrol a specification describing the invention with the Court of Chancery and this had been standard practice from 1734. Historians have debated whether it was a move initiated by patentees in the hope of bolstering their entitlement, or whether it was required in order to give proper warning to the patentees' competitors of what the patent forbade them to do.[53] Probably both motives played some part. Whatever the real impetus it was a step of profound importance to the system as a whole, because, as we shall see, the leading judges of both common law and equity would use the contents of the specification as the major instrument in determining whether a sufficient case for protection had been made out, giving prime attention to the theory of social exchange as the basis for the grant. They would insist that the specification be precise enough to show workers in the relevant industry the real discovery and the best way of carrying it out known to the grantee. Likewise there must be nothing deliberately misleading, nor might things be included (such as a list of alternative substances or mechanical devices), if it was then shown that some at least did not work.[54] In this undoubtedly they became aware of the dangers inherent in providing leaders of new industries with monopoly powers. There were warnings enough: in 1785, for instance, Lancashire cotton traders had put up considerable resistance to Arkwright's patents on his water frame for cotton spinning.[55] The strictness with which the judges insisted on public accountability would be a striking example of their power to weld an ill-defined earlier scheme into an operating system that fitted the changing economic conditions of their time.[56]

5. DEVELOPING THE SUBSTANTIVE LAW

'True and First Inventors' and their Obligations

In 1753, the Privy Council had given over its power to determine whether patents were valid. The courts in consequence were left as the sole forum in which

---

[53] The practice of requiring a specification to be enrolled within a given time as a condition of individual grants had been growing from the latter seventeenth century, and particularly from *Naismith's Patent* (1711): see D. Brennan, 'The Evolution of English Patent Claims as Property Definers' [2005] *IPQ* 361–99, 362–6, reviewing previous literature.

[54] It was particularly tempting to leave out subsidiary details that made the invention work really well. Hence the requirement that the inventor describe the best-known method of performing the invention.

[55] R. S. Wadsworth and A. P. Fitton, *The Strutts and the Arkwrights, 1785–1830* (Manchester, 1958), 82–6.

[56] The controversies had begun to stir a literature: see J. Collier, *Essay on the Law of Patents for New Inventions* (1803); W. Hands, *Law and Practice of Letters Patent for Invention* (1806).

both the validity of the grant and breach of it by others would be determined. As with copyright, at common law infringement was pursued by an action on the case for damages, tried with a jury. For an injunction, a bill in equity had to be pursued.[57] To secure the revocation of a patent, proceedings had to be brought by the Crown or any subject upon a writ of *scire facias*.[58] The invalidity of a patent could also be raised as a plea to an allegation of infringement and a verdict for the defendant on the issue would in law bind only the parties to the action.[59] With this patents moved closer to being property rights governed by rules, rather than a conferment by the Crown based on some assessment of advantages and disadvantages.[60]

It was in the half-century before 1820 that the courts had imposed quite new obligations on patentees to describe what their inventions were. They went about this reshaping with a will. It became a common belief among inventors and industrial investors that the bench was unrelievedly hostile to patents and that attempting to enforce them was a costly and unpredictable errand that only a fool would undertake. These objectors, however, were figures like James Watt, who wanted an inventor to be able to withhold any exact description of their inventions until their patents had expired.[61] Asked by the 1829 Select Committee if he knew of granted patents that had been lost on some technical point, Marc

---

[57] Chancery practice by 1820 allowed the court to order an immediate injunction *ex parte*, which might then be sustained or vacated upon the defendant's answer to the bill. The Court could at that juncture make the injunction permanent (in very plain cases) or interlocutory until the issue could be tried at common law, it being possible for Chancery to direct a 'feigned' issue there (for an instance of which see the enduring saga of *Kay* v. *Marshall*, esp. (1841) 8 Cl. & F. 96). Alternatively, the injunction might be refused, but the defendant ordered to keep an account until the trial: see Lord Eldon's judgment in *Hill* v. *Thompson* (1817) 3 Mer. 622; Godson, *Patents and Copyright*, 183–9; Hindmarch, *Patents*, Ch. 10.2.

[58] For the procedure, which started in the common law office of Chancery, and had become available as of right to the objector (see Hindmarch, *Patents*, Ch. 10.5). It was subject to the provision of substantial security.

[59] Dutton, *Patent and Inventive Activity*, 70–2; MacLeod, *Inventing*, 60–4.

[60] In a state frequently at war the Crown was deeply concerned with novel military hardware and therefore had interests in engaging the best talents, using promising inventions as soon as possible, keeping the knowledge from potential enemies and paying for the weapons only what it thought it could get away with. In Victorian England, this would lead to a crucial decision that the Crown was not itself bound by its own grants (*Feather* v. *Regina* (1865) 6 B & S 657); and to a scheme for keeping such patents secret in the interests of foreign policy. The modern law would be given its essential form in the Patents, Designs and Trade Marks Act 1883, s 27. In essence, the Crown was made liable for infringement but was given a form of statutory licence for 'Crown use'. For the convoluted story, see T. H. O'Dell, *Inventions and Official Secrecy* (Oxford, 1992).

[61] As early as 1785, Watt, probably with the collaboration of Arkwright, had drawn up Heads of a bill to amend patent law, which in the 1790s he sent to influential people. One main object was to secure that the specification could only be seen by outsiders with the Lord Chancellor's authority in the course of actual litigation: see E. Roll, *An Experiment in Industrial Organisation* (1968), 145–7.

Isambard Brunel responded that 'it is generally known that there are such cases, and a great hardship it is, when, for a trifling flaw, a patent is set aside'.[62] It is hard to see in the judges' attitude a naked contempt for the patent system. Rather, they insisted that patents were dependent on the 'consideration' of a sufficient description and publication of its content. In a handful of judgments, they laid legal foundations that have survived through to modern times, the growing case law of the Victorian era in many respects filling in an outline that was settled by the early years of our period.

The 'true and first inventor' could be the person who conceived the invention or imported it from a foreign source, and it made no difference, as already noted, that another person had made the same invention earlier, if the latter 'kept it to his closet'.[63] Much had come to follow from this. From Lord Mansfield's time onwards, the judges had insisted upon the patentee's responsibility to identify and describe the protected invention through the medium of the enrolled specification. Their thinking can be encapsulated around three ideas that gave content to the concept of 'invention': manner of manufacture, novelty, and inventive subject-matter.

'Manner of Manufacture'

The subject-matter had to fall within general notions of practicality denoted by the expression 'manner of manufacture'. Patents were not to be had for a 'mere abstract principle', since 'the elements of every science are common property— data—upon which every man may exercise his ingenuity'.[64] This, the forerunner of the distinction between discovery and invention, had an evident role in preventing the monopoly of a patent grant from too readily enclosing a very wide ambit. 'Manufacture' indicated practical production and plainly included machines, finished articles, or compounds of ingredients—including medicines (provided always that the things were themselves new).[65] From this came the notion that there must be a 'vendible product' which constituted the invention or resulted from it. With time there would be concerns over whether this breadth of approach did not go too far. From mid-century, the German chemical industry began to show its considerable strength and took with a will to obtaining patents

[62] *PP* 1829 (332), iii, 415, 453.

[63] See *Dollond's case*, above, n. 11. Lord Campbell doubted whether a person who had secretly used an invention could later have a patent for it. That would allow him to pick the most advantageous time for the monopoly, but the public would not receive knowledge of the invention as soon as possible: *Heath* v. *Smith* 278. The question was left unresolved for decades thereafter: see Frost, *Patents*, i: 129–31.

[64] *Hill* v. *Thompson* (1818) 8 Taunt. 375; *R* v. *Wheeler* (1819) 2 B. & Ald. 345; *Neilson* v. *Harford* (1841) Web. PC 295.

[65] Godson, *Patents and Copyright*, 97.

for artificial substances such as dyestuffs. When they obtained a British patent ahead of local rivals, they created considerable discomfort—an attitude which would boil over during the First World War. As a result, limitations were placed on food and medicine patents, restricting any claim to a substance as prepared or produced by a specified method.[66]

Patents could also be granted on new processes for making old things, and for making them from new materials, for these were *manners* of manufacture.[67] But a process could be regarded as merely one variety of a method. How far other methods could fall within the Statute was, and would remain, open to debate. What of Dr Hartley's patent for a method of placing iron plates in the walls of a building at places so as to produce a negative result—reduction in the fire risk? Among the judges who had discussed the example, only Eyre CJ had thought it patentable. He, however, was prepared to accept even a mere 'principle' as within the Statute; and in that he was alone.[68] On the other hand, James Watt had described his steam boiler as embodying principles for increasing the efficiency of the machine by preserving the temperature of the steam, where previous boilers had caused the steam to cool. The Common Pleas was initially divided on whether the patent was valid; but then the King's Bench held that the specification could be construed as a variation in construction of the boiler itself and so as a novel, improved 'manufacture'.[69] Those who sought to exclude mere 'methods' from the system were expressing a concern over protecting simple, minor improvements; but this way of doing so drew no manageable distinction. By 1841, Tindal CJ would state plainly that there could be a patent not only for a new article made by a combination of steps, but also for 'a better article, or a cheaper article to the public than that produced before by the old method'.[70] From that point the same concern took a new doctrinal direction.[71]

---

[66] See generally, L. F. Haber, *The Chemical Industry during the Nineteenth Century* (Oxford, 1969); and below, pp. 976–7.

[67] Sir Edward Coke in *Bircot's* case (3 Inst. 4) had ruled that there could be no patent on an improvement, indicating that Tudor and Stuart grants were considered justifiable when they introduced completely new industries. Lord Mansfield, however, considered this to be inappropriately severe, given that most technological improvement by his time took the form of enhanced versions of existing things: *Morris* v. *Bramsom* (1770) cited in Bull. N.P. 76; and see *Boulton and Watt* v. *Bull* (1795) 2 H. Bl. 463.

[68] A related restriction would follow: a person could not have a patent for demonstrating the scientific theory that explained what was already known to work in practice: see e.g. *Neilson* v. *Harford* (1841) 1 Web. PC 295; Jessel MR, *Otto* v. *Linford* (1881) 46 LT (NS) 35 at 42.

[69] See the great cases of *Boulton and Watt* v. *Bull* (1795) 2 H. Bl. 463 and *Hornblower* v. *Boulton* (1799) 8 T.R. 98.

[70] *Crane* v. *Price* (1842) 4 M. & G. 580, 603–4, referring for support to *Wheeler* and *Hill* (in Chancery), above, n. 64; and to several other instances.

[71] See below, pp. 248–9.

'New Manufacture'

The invention had to be new, which, in the later eighteenth-century case law, had come to mean that neither the patentee nor any other person had made it available to the public before grant. The old idea of novelty had focused on the first practising of the invention in the realm, whether it came from local experiment or a 'finding out' from abroad.[72] But the later emphasis on the specification as providing the patentee's 'consideration' for the grant had come to mean that an anticipation of the invention could occur by publishing it in the realm, by working it there under conditions that outsiders could observe or by selling a product from which the invention could be worked out by reverse engineering or chemical analysis.

It was, however, necessary to show an earlier description or use that was successful, and was not merely an experiment abandoned by the way. One of the many objections raised against Richard Arkwright's patent on his water-frame had been that his reference to a roller in a particular position was not novel but had been suggested to him by others in Britain who already knew of it and had used it. As Buller J. had then emphasized, it was no answer to show that many in the trade remained ignorant of the idea.[73] The law was already set on a course that would treat any complete description or use of the invention as an invalidating anticipation, if it was not kept confidential.[74] The test was not one that had to do with the way in which the inventor reached his conclusion—whether by flash of inspiration or by long and careful labour or by fortuitous accident.[75] What mattered was the result when measured against what had gone before. In the search for a test that was simple and objective, the judges treated novelty as a notional concept, lending an air of artifice to the question of which, among rivals, should have a valid patent. This may well have expressed a general distrust of grants too easily procured. At the same time it gave objectors a test of novelty that could be satisfied by relatively straightforward proof.

'Inventive Subject-matter'

In a period when patent specifications, from whatever cause, tended to be imprecise, ambiguous or misleading, there were instances enough in which

---

[72] See above, pp. 935, n. 17.

[73] *King* v. *Arkwright* (1785) 1 Webst. PC 64.

[74] See generally, Hindmarch, *Patent Privileges*, Ch. 5.2.

[75] Lord Mansfield's direction in the *Liardet* v. *Johnson* trials of 1778, though not directly reported, was remembered for this proposition (see *Boulton* v. *Bull* (1795) 2 H. Bl. at 486); see also E. W. Hulme's reconstruction in 'History of Patent Law' (above, n. 6), and Tindal CJ, *Crane* v. *Price* (1842) 4 M. & G. 580, 605.

additions or variations of existing machinery were proposed and the question was whether these were in some sense immaterial, or a mere equivalent.[76] In *Brunton* v. *Hawkes*, for instance, one question was whether, given that an anchor with one fluke was already known, there could be a patent for a double-fluked anchor. The King's Bench thought in the circumstances that there could not be.[77] In raising this issue the courts were clearly enough pursuing ideas that in Britain would later form the general criterion of inventive step: an addition or alteration to the 'prior art' must not be obvious to the ordinary skilled worker in the field.[78]

In *Crane* v. *Price*, the patent was for a highly advantageous development on Neilson's hot-blast furnace for smelting iron, namely its use with anthracite rather than bituminous coal, and it was upheld. Finding out how to use the furnace with anthracite was by no means straightforward. Various competitors had tried without success before the patentee, Crane, produced his result.[79] His disclosure permitted better quality ore to be produced more cheaply. Neilson had already claimed the use of any fuel in his furnace, so the upholding of Crane's patent turned upon his disclosure of a way of using the particular fuel. This formed an early example of what would in the twentieth century be characterized as a selection patent.[80] Authority was accordingly given to the all-important pyramidal conception of patent rights: improvement patents could be gained within the territory of base patents, provided that they in turn described an additional invention and the advantages that it gave. As long as each patent in the pyramid lasted, other patentees would have to seek a licence if they performed

---

[76] Given that today 'equivalence' is so controversial in determining the scope of a patent, its earlier use in relation to novelty deserves remark: see, e.g. Frost, *Patents*, i, 115–16.

[77] (1820) 4 B. & Ald. 550.

[78] In the United States, the concept was more clearly distinguished from novelty at an earlier stage, notably in *Hotchkiss* v. *Greenwood* 52 US 248 (1850).

[79] See above, n. 75. Commercial success after long-felt want, and absence of any earlier claimants to the patentee's type of solution would become common indicators of inventiveness (see e.g. T. Terrell, *Law of Patents* (1884), 605–6). It was one object of Harold Fox's value-burdened history, *Monopolies and Patents*, Pt II, to denounce this emergence of inventive step as a vehicle for uncomprehending judges to apply unreal standards against patents for what were widely recognized as commercially valuable inventions. The issue recurs periodically, but the criticism has gained little following in modern times. Victorian judges were ready enough to acknowledge the value of great inventions, such as Neilson's hot-blast furnace using anthracite and Otto's crucial contribution to the internal combustion engine: see *Neilson* v. *Harford* (1841) 1 Web. PC 295; *Otto* v. *Linford* (1881) 46 LT (NS) 35.

[80] The eventual importance of 'selection' would lie in providing a way of patenting pharmaceutical inventions that had been picked out, for their superiority, from an already known class of substances: see *IG Farbenindustrie's Patents* (1930) 47 RPC 289 (building upon the mechanical invention case, *Clyde Nail* v. *Russell* (1916) 33 RPC 291, HL). The later claim could thus be for a substance or composition—a highly significant technique in this technical field, given that 'method of treatment' claims for medical procedures would be debarred in law; see below, p. 968.

that invention; but this fact did not deprive them of a patent for their own inventive improvement.

6. SPECIFICATIONS AND THEIR DRAFTING

Until 1883, it was for the petitioner and his agent to settle what went into a specification without any official intervention occurring before grant. The document
might well refer to inventive elements that were indeed novel but disguise them
amid a jumble of other assertions about the machine, article, substance, or process. The judges, having the opportunity to look at the patent and its specification
only after grant and filing, struggled to arrive at principles for directing juries
and deciding other cases themselves. The difficulties of describing new technologies in words and diagrams made the business elusive.[81] The issue of what was in
reality new became entwined with a requirement that the specification should
identify what was said to be new. Again take *Brunton* v. *Hawkes*: the patentee
stated as his invention an anchor and a mooring chain of specified kinds. The
Court of Queen's Bench were of opinion that the anchor had no novelty, but that
the chain was an invention. However, the judges concluded that a patent that was
bad in part was wholly void. Bayley J. pronounced that the consideration inducing the king to make the grant was entire, 'and if it fails in part, it fails *in toto*'.[82]
The concept was particularly difficult to apply where, as so often, the novelty
really lay in part of a whole machine, such as a new movement introduced into a
watch.[83] The courts therefore insisted that the patentee distinguish what was new
from the rest of a known machine or article.[84] 'Every old part which is essential
material in producing the intended effect will be considered as claimed, if it be
not designated as old,' wrote Godson.[85] The judges were determined that patentees should not gain a monopoly over more than their invention covered, though
they would be permitted to generalize from the particular embodiment of their
concept that they chose to describe.[86]

---

[81] The nineteenth century would see considerable improvement in the art of technical drawing.

[82] (1820) 4 B. & Ald. 550.

[83] See Buller J., *Boulton and Watt* v. *Bull* (1795) 2 H. Bl. 489.

[84] *Macfarlane* v. *Price* (1816) 1 Stark.199; *Harmer* v. *Playne* (1807–9) 11 East 101; 1 Davies PC 311; it
was such a disclaimer that permitted the plaintiff to patent his improvement claim in *Crane* v. *Price*,
above, n. 81.

[85] Godson, *Patents and Copyright*, 133–4, and see 111–18, 131–2.

[86] The importance of this was compounded by the absence of any distinct test of what constituted infringement. Treating what would be an anticipatory publication before grant as amounting
to infringement after grant was an idea only of the 1860s: see *Seed* v. *Higgins* (1860) 8 H.L.C. 550, HL;
Plimpton v. *Spiller* (1876) LR 6 Ch 412, CA; *Dudgeon* v. *Thomson* (1877) 3 App Cas 34, HL; Brennan,
'Claims as Property Definers' 380–4.

By the 1820s there was much about the re-defined law which exposed a patentee to dangers—hence the emergence of patent agents who processed petitions
for grants.[87] The courts insisted that the invention be described in detail enough
for the ordinary worker in the field to be able to carry out the invention. The
specification 'must be minute without perplexity, and luminous without being
overwrought. When it descends to particulars, the elements that are known to all
should not be noticed; nor yet, in its fulness, should any thing be included that is
not necessary to render it intelligible.'[88] Undue vagueness or ambiguity would not
be countenanced, especially if the specification in reality only stated the technical problem, without disclosing any solution. The patentee must not knowingly
include anything that would mislead, nor could it describe something that did
not work: in this sense there had to be utility. The specification must indeed give
the best method of performing the invention known to the petitioner, in order
that he should not after all keep for himself the real path to success.[89]

There were difficulties in obliging the patentee to state what it was he claimed
as his invention, even though that was coming to be seen as necessary to decide
upon its novelty and subject-matter and to define what it covered. One objectionable practice was to include a splay of improvements in a single patent, thereby
saving time and fees. These might be interacting parts of a whole machine or
product; in which case it was the combination that constituted the invention
and the patent would properly extend to the whole entity. Such cases, however,
were to be contrasted with separate improvements to different parts of the thing,
where the judges insisted that the novelty should be claimed as lying in the particular pieces alone; if it was said to lie in the product or machine as a whole, the
patent would be struck down. In addition, at the beginning of our period, the
courts were insisting that there must be no essential variance between the title
given in the patent grant and the contents of the specification. They feared that
otherwise the title could be a decoy to distract searchers from realizing what was
really being covered.[90] To the succeeding generation, this would seem too severe
a requirement.[91] The warning seems largely to have done its work. To inventors

---

[87] See above, p. 938.

[88] Godson, *Patents and Copyright*, 125. See also Hindmarch, *Patents*, 161–88; Terrell, *Patents*, 64–89.

[89] Lord Mansfield began this insistence in *Liardet* v. *Johnson*—as recalled in *Boulton and Watt* v. *Bull* (1795) 2 H. Bl. 463; and see Buller J., *King* v. *Arkwright* (1785) 1 Webst. PC 64, 70; *Bovill* v. *Moore* (1816) 1 Hayward's PC 618; *Morgan* v. *Seward* (1836) 1 Webst. PC 170, 174.

[90] The matter was stressed in both *Hill* v. *Thomson* and *R* v. *Wheeler* (above, n. 64) as well as other cases around 1820: see Brennan, 'Claims as Property Definers' 376–80.

[91] e.g. Parke B., *Neilson* v. *Harford* (1841) 8 M. & W. 806, 826–7; Tindal CJ, *Cook* v. *Pearce* (1844) 8 QB 1064, 1065; Hindmarch, *Patent Privileges*, 46; but see Terrell, *Patents*, 58, seeking to keep alive an objection that the specification showed a major variance between title and content.

and their agents the judges insisted that a patent was not simply an entitlement to sole exploitation of whatever they said was their invention. Because the right was capable in some circumstances of producing an exceptional commercial return, a sufficient case for it had to be made out from the start. There could well be hard feelings from those who were indeed serious inventors, but the judges remained firm in their basic attitude.

7. APPLICATION AND GRANT: ADMINISTRATIVE REFORM

Those who interested themselves in the patent system had considered the prospects for reforming it in the decades before 1820.[92] At that juncture, Parliament considered two bills of quite substantial scope, including the prospect of a board of experts to examine bills petitioning for patents; but neither got beyond second reading. The question of reform continued to smoulder in a small way.[93] By 1829 there was enough interest in patents, and alternatives to them, for the Commons to establish a Select Committee at the behest of Thomas Lennard, who became its chairman.[94] But there was little drive towards reforming the system in a way that would open it up to more numerous applicants and at the same time improve the lot of the serious inventor. The Committee took evidence from 19 witnesses much concerned with advancing technologies: in the main, inventors, manufacturers, and those concerned as professionals or officials in the patenting business. It was not re-appointed in the following year and left only the record of evidence given to it.[95]

The witnesses, concentrating on practicalities, poured forth a stream of complaint about the excessive to-ing and fro-ing in making a petition and then pursuing the bill.[96] Beside this, there were structural concerns, which included complaints about the severity of the courts' attitudes over sufficient, non-misleading specifications, which had been Watt's great burthen; so also the

---

[92] See above, pp. 944–5.

[93] For these first stirrings, see Dutton, *Patent and Inventive Activity*, 34–43; Duncan, *Privileges to Paris*, 120–3.

[94] Lennard was a Whig grandee with a strong reformist bent. William Newton (for whom see above, p. 936) was a persistent critic during this period, who published (and perhaps wrote) the tirades of 'Vindicator' (set out in J. Phillips, *Charles Dickens and 'The Poor Man's Tale of a Patent'* (Oxford, 1984), 38–53).

[95] For a description of the main arguments and their relation to justifications of the system, see Duncan, *Privileges to Paris*, Ch. 2B. She stresses the virtual absence of witnesses representing lobby groups.

[96] There were differences of opinion, however, over whether the process should be made cheaper.

hazard set by the fact that any publication or public use of the invention before grant would render the patent void for lack of novelty.[97] Smart-footed rivals or patentees themselves could cause this to happen. The caveat system, which allowed outsiders to watch out for petitions, could be used as a form of lucrative obstruction. The caveat might well be placed by a potential opponent whom the petitioner would find it cheaper to pay off than to fight.

So far as there was any discussion of the basis of the system, most witnesses accepted the bargain-for-information theory of which the judges had made so much, whatever their objection to the stringency with which it was being applied. There were also advocates of the incentive-reward position. The engineer-cum-patent agent, John Farey, and the American machine-maker, Dyer, argued the need for experimenters to have security while they sought to refine their inventive idea, in order to get their return from later putting it into practical operation. Thus the idea of patents as 'licences to prospect' was by no means a modern novelty.[98] The proposed solution was a scheme by which novelty fell to be judged at the date of initial petitioning, coupled with a power to present a provisional specification that could be followed by a second, more complete specification. It would take until 1852 before legislation could be secured to effect such reasonable alterations to a system that had been born so long before and had been strait-laced through its adolescence.

In the political upheavals of the years immediately following the Select Committee, there were somewhat inept attempts to get new legislation, which came to nought.[99] Lord Brougham was eventually induced to lend his weight to the cause of patent reform. In 1835, an Act known by his name was passed, taking up one issue that had been discussed to some extent in the Committee—the ability to increase the term of a patent in the light of any factor considered relevant.[100] Brougham's particular interest in procuring this power of extension (for up to seven years) was to give it to the Judicial Committee of the Privy Council which he had done much to create and for which he had personal ambitions.[101]

---

[97] Another problem was the absence of any method of securing a patent of addition to an existing grant, which could extend coverage to improvements without needing to show novelty or inventive subject-matter. This would eventually be rectified in 1907 by the Patents and Designs Act, s 19.

[98] Cf. E. Kitch, 'The Nature and Function of the Patent System' (1977) 20 J. L. & Econ. 265–90.

[99] See Dutton, *Patent and Inventive Activity*, 46–8, noting the bill of 1833 which sought to give any person who received knowledge of an invention the right to apply for a patent and would have redefined the range of the system to cover even principles and discoveries, and the severe criticisms of it by the *Mechanics Magazine*.

[100] This left the Judicial Committee with a very considerable measure of discretion.

[101] 5 & 6 Wm. IV c. 83. Dutton, *Patent and Inventive Activity*, 48–51; and see Vol. XI, Pt 3, pp. 548–50.

His Act also introduced an amendment procedure, allowing either the grant or the specification to be re-written, provided that it did not extend the exclusive right originally granted.[102] A disclaimer under the Act—a qualification that reduced the scope of the protected invention—might in particular avoid the nullifying effect of prior art that had come to light only after grant. This step would herald a gradual transformation of wider—indeed of basic—importance in the drafting of specifications. Over time it would remove the necessity of stating what was disclaimed; instead positive claims would provide the measure of what the invention was said to be; and in their turn, these claims would mark what constituted infringement of the patent.[103]

8. A NEW OPENNESS

From the mid-1840s the patent system came to altogether novel prominence in public debate. The shift is an element in the surging confidence in British industrial entrepreneurship which swept to the high water of the Great Exhibition of 1851. Urged by Sir Henry Cole, Prince Albert advocated that his adopted country should be the first to hold an *international* display of manufacturing achievements, even ahead of France. In Paxton's Crystal Palace, British attainments in industry after industry emerged triumphant and other peoples looked enviously at 'the workshop of the world'. Since her successes seemed to have evolved rather by happenstance and dogged labour than through any long-term planning, the half-century became a moment in which to ask whether the country's industrial precocity could be sustained and how its riches could be deployed to create a polity in which expectations were somewhat more readily shared. Suddenly in the late 1840s, patent law reform associations appeared, chambers of commerce took up the subject, as did the bodies that were beginning to represent the interests of professionals—notably the various engineers, the lawyers, the patent agents.[104] Many different views of the system were adumbrated and a great variety of practical changes were proposed. In the general euphoria, most favoured easier access to patent grants and greater use of inventions. Only a minority remained sceptical or argued for abandonment of the very idea.

When during its Revolution France had debated the introduction of a patent system, fine oratory had proclaimed the natural, ineluctable entitlement of an

---

[102] It took more than a quarter-century, however, for the House of Lords to settle that a disclaimer was permissible whenever the scope of the right became more limited as a result of the amendment: *Seed* v. *Higgins* (1860) 8 H.L.C. 550.

[103] See further below, pp. 964–5.

[104] See above, p. 938.

inventor to property in his idea.[105] In England, with its shadowy system already in place, such fervent idealism had rarely been voiced.[106] But now, the Society of Arts, with its impressive Council of the influential, surrendered its old distaste for patenting and adopted a grand moral tone. It announced that rights in inventive labour, 'being intellectual, are entitled, if possible, to a higher kind of recognition than other kinds of human labour'.[107] It therefore rejected the possibility of an examination by a patent office before any application could be approved for grant. The Society thus represented one pole of opinion before a Select Committee of 1851, this time of the Lords, which investigated the subject. Its object was to consider the reforming ideas expressed in two bills introduced in the spring of that year.[108] A majority of the witnesses before the Committee shared the Society of Arts' favourable opinion—for the most part, emphasizing the role of patents as incentives to technological innovation. Less was now heard of the role of the system in informing the public of inventive developments. A stream of radical opinion argued that patents would encourage capitalists to foster the ideas of ordinary workers and turn them into successful products and processes, thus forming a bridge across classes.[109] The patent question thus acquired a wider political urgency and it would remain a strong cause amongst mechanical workers over the crucial quarter-century that followed.

Among the witnesses there were notable doubters. They included Lord Romilly MR, Sir William Reid, Executive Chairman of the Great Exhibition Committee, the renowned inventors and industrialists, Isambard Kingdom Brunel and William Cubitt; and not least, the sugar-refiner-cum-free-trade economist, Robert Macfie, whose later attacks on copyright have been noted.[110] In calling for abolition, they aimed fire at the morass of patents, some good but more bad, which could build up and block the advance of a new technology—telegraphy being a prominent example at the time.[111] The Committee itself was in some doubt, not least because Earl Granville, in charge of the subject as Vice-President of the Board of Trade, remained an abolitionist. Among the

[105] See Duncan, *Privileges to Paris*, Ch. 1.

[106] For an early instance, however, see W. Kenrick, *Address to the Artists and Manufacturers of Great Britain* (1774).

[107] Society of Arts, *First Report on the Rights of Inventors* (1850).

[108] For its Report and Evidence, PP 1851 (486), XVIII, 233; Dutton, *Patent and Inventive Activity*, Chs 3, 8; Duncan, *Privileges to Paris*, Ch. 2D, 2E; V. M. Batzel, 'Legal Monopoly in Liberal England' (1980) 22 *Business Hist.* 189.

[109] See Van Zyl Smit, *Emergence and Acceptance*, Ch. 5.5; Duncan, *Privileges to Paris*, 156–8, 164–75.

[110] See above, pp. 894–6. See also C. MacLeod, 'Negotiating the Rewards of Invention: The Shop-Floor Inventor in Victorian Britain' (1999) 41/2 *Business Hist.* 17.

[111] G. Hubbard, *Cooke and Wheatstone and the Invention of the Electric Telegraph* (1965).

press, only *The Economist* was categorically for abolition; *The Times* and others preferred to advocate reform. The case against patents was quite as strongly supported as it would ever be again; but at this juncture the attack was against the old, inefficient, gummed-up inheritance.[112]

A Patents (Amendment) Act was passed in 1852, but it was a piece of experimental, temporizing legislation, largely concerned with procedure.[113] A single patent for the UK replaced those granted separately for England, Scotland, and Ireland.[114] Commissioners of Patents took over supervision of the granting process, the Attorney- and Solicitor-General becoming those in practical charge. As before they earned considerable fees from the process of certifying applications but, save where there was opposition from a third party, they conducted no investigations into the substantive content of the patent specification.[115] The official fee for the grant was much reduced by spreading the amount due over the 14 years.[116] The major complaints about the dangers of anticipation by publishing or using in advance were addressed, first by allowing an application to be provisional, accompanied only by a specification in outline, provided that within six months it was followed by an application with a specification giving a complete description of the nature of the invention and the manner in which it was to be performed.[117] The term of the patent was given a retrospective effect, since its duration was now measured from the date of application.[118] The date of application was also to be treated as the 'priority date'—the point in time when the novelty of the patented invention was to be assessed. Taken together these improvements struck a more manageable balance between the insistence

---

[112] However, one leading patent agent, William Carpmael, feared the consequences of making patents too cheaply and readily available—for the encouragement that it would give to the merely manipulative: *PP* 1851 (486), xviii 233, qq. 31–8.

[113] 15 & 16 Vict. c. 83. The Act was put through by Aberdeen's government, but it was little changed from the Tory bill presented in 1851 after the Committee's Report. The two bills that had led to the Committee's appointment had gone a good way further.

[114] Section 18. The patent did not extend to any colony. Specifications were now filed in Chancery, and were printed and published. A register of proprietors was introduced: s 27.

[115] The Commissioners' Clerk who administered the Patents Office, Leonard Edmunds, showed such incompetence over accounting that a scandal erupted, giving the first impetus towards Westbury's resignation as Lord Chancellor in 1865.

[116] Official fees and stamps had previously been in the region of £100 for each part of the UK (and there was a run of gratuities). Now they were reduced to £25 for the application and £30 for the first three years from grant; renewal fees became payable at the fourth and seventh years bringing the total to some £180 for those patents worth maintaining so long: see MacLeod, *Inventing*, 76. For the fees that most inventors also paid to their patent agents, see Van Zyl Smit, 'Professional Patent Agents and the Development of the English Patent System' (1985) 13 *IJ Sociology of Law* 79–105.

[117] 15 & 16 Vict. c. 83, ss 8, 9.

[118] *Ibid.*

on public information and the need for an experimenter to apply for protection once the research identified a real lead.

The average annual grants in the 1840s had been 458. From 1853–59 the average would be 3010 applications, leading to 1965 grants; for 1860–9, 3487 and 2160; for 1870–9, 4495 and 2971. In 1883, the initial fees were reduced to £1 (application) and £3 (grant).[119] Once more there is a striking increase in applications: for 1884–9 there were 17,174 applications per year and 7778 grants; for 1890–9, the averages were 25,851 and 12,284; for 1900–9, 28,396 and 14,791; and for 1910–14, 28,947 and 16,176.[120] In 1883, the long resistance to the *ex officio* examination of each application was overcome (in the wake, as we shall see, of design and trade mark registrations).[121] It proved to be the prelude to the official examination of every application for lack of novelty, instituted in 1905.[122] The expansion of business for patent agents that all this brought was marked by the formation of an Institute of Patent Agents in 1882, which gained powers of professional control by 1888 and a Royal Charter by 1891.[123]

At these different stages the proportion of applications not reaching grant remained considerable. The reasons were undoubtedly complex, as they remain today. Some, in the excitement of their own results, went on in ignorance of prior art until it came to light. The old system had in any case provided no complete publication of granted patents and that could well prevent applicants from knowing what stood in their paths.[124] Others again would withdraw because further developments of the inventive idea showed that they needed to start again from scratch. Patenting was a business that remained fraught with hazard.

9. ABOLITION OR INTERNATIONAL SOLIDARITY?

Nonetheless some inventive ideas of real significance were gaining patents where previously they had been released for competitors to adopt or were not followed through because the risk of imitation detracted from potential profits.

---

[119] See further, the 1883 Act, Sch. 2.

[120] Extracted from more detailed figures in Boehm, *British Patent System*, 32–7. For comparisons with other intellectual property registrations, see below, 1006, n. 100.

[121] Patents, Trade Marks and Designs Act 1883. In the preceding years there had been a succession of bills seeking adaptations that would make the system more accessible, particularly to individual inventors. Selborne LC (Roundell Palmer), when presenting the 1883 government bill in the Lords, recalled his earlier adherence to the anti-patent movement and admitted its failure. The Act allowed the UK to ratify the Paris Industrial Property Convention of the same year: for which see below, 961–3. See Van Zyl Smit, *Emergence and Acceptance*, 232–9.

[122] See below, n. 160.

[123] See Patents, Designs and Trade Marks Act 1888; Van Zyl Smit, 'Professional Patent Agents'.

[124] In the five years after 1852, the Commissioners' assistant for specifications, Bennet Woodcroft, would fill this gap by publishing over 14,000 patents from the years 1617–1852, with indices and other documents.

At the same time, because the system was so much concerned with attracting venture capital into commercial experimentation, retooling, and advertising, its allure drew in others—most obviously those whose alleged inventions were simply old ideas. As the system had not been amended to introduce any case-by-case examination of an application to consider the patentability of its subject-matter, particularly against whatever 'prior art' was known, it was all too easy to obtain a grant and raise it against an unsuspecting manufacturer or seller. Since patent litigation among competitors was a costly and tedious business, those attacked by patentees were often enough persuaded to settle rather than fight.[125] A right enforceable against all the world can be an invitation to hold rivals to ransom. Once patents became relatively cheap fears spread that this type of behaviour would all too readily result.

Certainly a crescendo of argument would take place during which the case for abolition or major limitation found vociferous proponents. Here, even more than over copyright before the Royal Commission of 1876–8,[126] the economics of free competition were said to demand an end to patent monopolies over inventions. If any intervention was needed to supplement the natural advantage of being first with the chance of exploitation, there must be a reversion to such policies as rewards for success that were provided *ex post facto*. As a movement in economic opinion it provided a particular test of the constructs of competition and monopoly and their adjustment by state intervention. In some countries that were still well behind Britain in the drive to industrialize, the abolitionist cause made considerable headway, not least in smaller economies where governments saw a future in copying and improving technologies adopted by big foreign industries.[127] The Netherlands did indeed abandon its patent system in 1869, being much influenced by Switzerland's continuing refusal to introduce one.[128] At this period, a formidable opponent was Otto von Bismarck. Yet after achieving the unification of the German Reich he would insist on a unitary patent system to build up its industrial might.[129] In this resolve, he was reacting to the great depression of 1873 and the movement towards national protection of markets that was its consequence. But also the growing strength and independence of the German chemical and electrical industries was giving a new sense of confidence. With this came the desire for a patent system from which national enterprises would become major beneficiaries.

[125] By the 1860s, the British dyestuffs industry was embroiled in major actions, Haber, *Chemical Industry*, 82–4.

[126] See above, pp. 894–6.

[127] In France, however, the conviction that an inventor had a natural right to property in his invention remained dominant: Duncan, *Privileges to Paris*, Ch. 4A.

[128] E. Schiff, *Industrialization without National Patents* (1971); Duncan, *Privileges to Paris*, Ch. 4B.

[129] Duncan, *Privileges to Paris*, Ch. 4C.

The considerable ferment surrounding the patent idea raises historical difficulties. For economic historians the very debate is of great interest. In their well-known account of the abolitionist movement, Machlup and Penrose concentrate on the arguments themselves and conclude that for a time abolition posed a very considerable threat. They argue that it was headed off only when powerful industrial interests organized the counter case, securing legislative improvements at the national level and pushing for an international solution to the conflicts concerning the protection of foreigners, which would be resolved in the Paris Industrial Property Convention of 1883.[130] Louise Duncan has shown, however, that in Britain the balance of political opinion throughout favoured buttressing the system:

[T]here was very little likelihood that the patent abolitionists would succeed in achieving their aim. This was because most abolitionists remained part of limited occupational groups, such as lawyers, economic philosophers and a few members of Parliament. Most inventors, engineers, manufacturers and workmen continued to support the patent system. Although the patent abolitionists tried to attract the support of scientific and cultural organisations, they failed miserably. This was largely because abolitionists did not offer any practical alternative to the patent system.[131]

Much of the running in favour of abolition was made by Macfie, working with the economist, the Rev. J. E. Thorold Rogers, and such figures as the politician, Lord Stanley, the armaments inventor, Sir William Armstrong and the Attorney-General, Sir Roundell Palmer (Selborne). *The Times*, it is true, switched its support in their favour, and *The Economist* remained staunch.[132] But Macfie's persistent efforts to bring round the National Association for the Promotion of the Social Sciences and the failure of the abolition motion that he put to the Commons in 1869 suggest that there was firm and persistent opposition to his great idea. If, however, patents were to survive, abolitionists were as willing as upholders to insist that inventions deserved to be protected across countries. If not, in a free trade environment, imitators could take their production facilities

---

[130] F. Machlup and E. Penrose, 'The Patent Controversy in the Nineteenth Century' (1950) 10 *J. Econ. Hist.* 1; V. M. Batzel, 'Legal Monopoly in Liberal England: The Patent Controversy in the Mid-Nineteenth Century' (1980) 22 *Business Hist.* 189. For contemporary literature, see W. Hawes 'On the Economical Effects of the Patent Laws' (1863–4) 16 *LM & LR* 61; and 'Patent Law Amendment' (1863–4) 16 *LM & LR* 355; and the contributions to R. A. Macfie (ed.), *Recent Discussion on the Abolition of Patents for Inventions in the United Kingdom, France, Germany and the Netherlands* (1869).

[131] Duncan, *Privileges to Paris*, 190–1.

[132] In its first editorial on the subject, *The Times* distinguished patents from copyright as full monopolies affecting independent inventors: 15 August 1864. See Duncan, *Privileges to Paris*, 230–7.

to countries lacking protection and reap benefits where they did not contribute to initial costs.[133]

The Commons Select Committees that reviewed the controversies in the 1871 and 1872 Sessions heard from many witnesses in favour of retention rather than renunciation.[134] They included famous inventors, such as Nasmyth, Bessemer, and William Siemens, as well as leaders of the patenting professions, who between them insisted on the need for market exclusivity, if research were to be carried on and new production lines set up.[135] The 1872 Report adopted their stance and stressed the importance of the British government pursuing international agreements for mutual protection. There was already some bilateral treaty-making in hand, and in some instances it covered designs and trade marks as well.[136] In the case of copyright, such bilateral arrangements as there were in these decades concentrated on publishing and tended to last for some years.[137] But when it came to industrial property rights, they were typically tacked on to general commercial treaties and were liable to be short-lived.[138]

While British governments and other experts would have a flaccid record over fully international accords concerning copyright,[139] they were rather more prominent in the patent sphere. The movement took wing at the Vienna International Patent Congress, which grew from the Universal Exhibition in that city in 1873 and from American refusals to exhibit at it because of the one-year 'home working' requirement of the Austro-Hungarian patent law.[140] The Congress, attended by large numbers of Germans, Austrians, and Americans,

---

[133] Thus Macfie, being a Liverpool sugar refiner, found no difficulty in arguing for the extension of British patent rights to the West Indies (and other colonies) in order to curb the introduction of British refining machinery there by his competitors: Duncan, *Privileges to Paris*, 220–1.

[134] *PP* 1871 (368), x, 603; 1872 (193), xi, 395.

[135] For an analysis of the witnesses' positions and the Report, see Duncan, *Privileges to Paris*, Ch. 3, Pt C; Van Zyl Smit, *Emergence and Acceptance*, 226–36.

[136] Duncan, *Privileges to Paris*, App. 3, lists the more important commercial treaties entered into by the UK and its principal trade rivals, together with sources for the information.

[137] Above, 908–10.

[138] See S. P. Ladas, *International Protection of Industrial Property* (Cambridge MA, 1930), Ch. 3.

[139] Above, 916.

[140] The event occurred in the same year as the first meeting of the future International Law Association in Brussels (see Vol. XI, 277). At that event, the great American codifier, David Dudley Field, presented his Draft Outlines for a general code of international law, public and private. In the book concerning the law of nations under peace, the rights of authors, inventors, and designers were to be declared sacred and maintained in all countries. Thomas Webster, Rolin Jacquemans, and Passy, all leaders in the practice of industrial property, were prominent figures in the general discussions: Duncan, *Privileges to Paris*, 374–81; T. Webster, 'Reform and Codification of the Law of Nations' (1874) 3 *LM & LR* 1015; see also I. G. J. Davis and J. Harrison, 'Prelude to the United Kingdom's Accession to the Paris Convention, March 17 1884' [1984] *Industrial Property* 395.

and nationals of 15 other states, heard some statements against the very system.[141] It did indeed concede that compulsory licences should be provided for in national laws when the public interest so required, this being considered a judicious move to aid the cause of unifying the German patent law in the divisive atmosphere of that country. But the basic resolutions were all strongly in favour of patent systems. The root assertion that 'the protection of inventions should be guaranteed by the laws of all civilized nations' echoed the French belief in a natural right of property. There followed a set of references to ideas of reward to inventors as incentives to industrial development and to the general economic benefits of publicizing novel ideas as opposed to holding them back as secrets.

The path towards mutual recognition of rights under an international union of countries was then blazed by three further Conferences, all held in Paris. The first of these, in 1878, was still non-governmental and allowed a large participation, especially of the French. There were long expositions on the theoretical nature of patent rights and the speeches demonstrated, if nothing else, how varied might be the implications of categorizing them as 'property', as distinct from an entitlement bargained by social contract for the public benefit. Resolution 1 went so far as to pronounce that the civil law could regulate this property, but did not create it. So it was easy to declare that foreign inventors should be treated in the same manner as nationals under local patent laws; and to criticise the extensive powers to gain compulsory licences that had become part of the German and Austrian systems under the influence of economist antagonists.[142]

A striking, if somewhat diffuse, universalism thus prevailed. Enthusiasts took it to signal a movement towards international agreement on the legal scope and administrative structure for patent laws throughout the 'civilised world'. Rights in designs and models, and in trade marks and commercial names, were also to be embraced. The Conference established a Permanent Committee in France to find formulae that would express a comprehensive set of industrial property laws at the international level.[143] A Draft Treaty was indeed prepared; but then matters passed into the hands of government representatives for the Paris Conferences of 1880 and 1883. What realistically could be agreed between states had now to be worked out by diplomatic initiative, and it proved to be far less than the grand expectations of the Vienna and first Paris Conferences. The French government insisted on paring down treaty proposals to what seemed attainable, given the considerable differences on specific provisions in the national laws of

---

[141] Macfie, for one, was present.

[142] See Duncan, *Privileges to Paris*, Ch. 6.

[143] The leading role of France was evident: 14 of the 34 members were French including the Président, Bozérian; 12 other countries had between 1 and 3 members. Drafting the proposed Treaty, however, was done mainly by the Swiss, Bodenheimer.

the countries most likely to join in an accord.[144] Even then the German government was too nervous to participate in discussions that might require it to amend the 1877 statute creating the *Reichspatent*. In that country the arguments of the patent abolitionists had cut deeper than in Britain, even though they did not decapitate the Medusa.

10. THE PARIS INDUSTRIAL PROPERTY CONVENTION OF 1883

The Diplomatic Conference of 1880 settled most of what would find a place in the 1883 Paris Convention, which, following the precedents for postal services and telegraphic services, established a Union of States for the protection of industrial property.[145] It did not fulfil the ambition of the 1878 Resolution to secure recognition of a higher, innate entitlement to that protection or therefore to make the rights in each contracting state open to all persons regardless of their origin. Accordingly, only those persons (individual and corporate) who were nationals or domiciliaries of a contracting state were to be the subject of the mutual benefits that the Convention procured.

Of these there were two. First, the Convention adopted the principle of national treatment, already a staple of bilateral treaties in this field, and the foundation of contemporaneous work towards the Berne Copyright Convention.[146] Secondly, it created a new scheme of international priority. An applicant was enabled to take the date of application in the home territory as the priority date for applications concerning the same invention, design, or mark in other contracting states, provided that applications there were filed within a specified period—for patents this was settled in the end at six months, and for the other rights at three months.[147] Before this, applications to protect an invention in different states needed to take place on the same day, for fear that otherwise publication of the earlier might anticipate the later, or might lead to rivals getting the national patent in different countries. Between contracting

---

[144] The French diplomat, Charles Jagerschmidt, proved to be a skilful draftsman of the text, for which see Duncan, *Privileges to Paris*, App. 8.

[145] The Union had a permanent bureaucracy; and once the Berne Copyright Convention was signed in 1886 with an equivalent structure, the two Bureaux internationaux were given homes in Berne by the Swiss government: see Ladas, *International Protection*, 116–30. In 1967 they would move to Geneva to form the World Intellectual Property Organization under United Nations auspices.

[146] Article 2. Arriving at a definition that eliminated misapprehensions among the government delegates in Paris in 1880, however, was not straightforward: Ladas, *International Protection*, 80–1; Duncan, *Privileges to Paris*, 528–33.

[147] Article 4. The legislation to implement was introduced by the UK in the Patents, Designs and Trade Marks Act 1883, s 103. The periods were subsequently extended to 12 months and six months respectively by the Brussels text of 1900.

states the Convention offered an escape from a procedure that, even with the spread of telecommunications across borders, was inordinately cumbersome. But, as patenting across borders increased, industrialists and patent agents pushed their governments towards membership of the Paris Union in order to have the advantage of this attractive solution. It was much more accommodating than the alternative pursued at the 1878 Conference of allowing contemporaneous applications to be lodged on the same day through national consulates.[148] After considerable argument, the Convention prevented a contracting state from revoking a patent where the patentee had imported the invention from abroad. Nonetheless, particularly because of fears among smaller countries that they might be swamped by foreign manufactures, states were entitled to adopt compulsory licensing measures when the patentee had failed to work the invention within their territories.[149] More general issues concerning compulsory licensing of patents would continue to plague the future of the Convention.

There were no guarantees of minimum entitlements, even as to the term of the grant; and an attempt to recommend that the term of the country of origin should not reduce a longer term elsewhere was abandoned at the 1880 Conference. Most striking of all, there was no requirement that a contracting state should actually have a patent system at all.[150] The conditions laid down in the Convention merely applied where there was one.[151] The grand proposals of 1873 and 1878 for uniformity at a high level would remain a shrouded Valhalla for more than a century. In the meantime, patents which came more and more to support giant multi-national businesses would fall under the suspicious gaze of new attackers—notably countries that were beginning down the trail to industrialization. They would be brought to accept greater mutuality in patent matters only as part of the 1994 revision of the General Agreement on Tariffs and Trade, which offered as its *quid pro quo* a loosening of restrictions on their access to world markets for agricultural and other products.[152]

---

[148] Precious time would have been lost, if translations of specifications into the relevant languages had first to be made. See Ladas, *International Protection*, 74–8; Duncan, *Privileges to Paris*, 537–44.

[149] Article 5.

[150] This was equally true of other types of 'industrial property', a term which would not be defined in the Convention until the Hague Revision of 1925. The first major expansion required protection against unfair competition, a first version of Article 10*bis* being inserted by the Brussels Revision of 1900. See further, below, 1012.

[151] Thus the 11 initial signatories included The Netherlands and Switzerland, neither of them having a patent system. Important states which joined only over the ensuing 30 years included those two countries, the United States, Germany, Austria-Hungary, and Russia. As with the Berne Convention, countries would subscribe to different versions of the Convention, making the precise relationships between Contracting States an elaborate patchwork: see above, 917.

[152] The Agreement on Trade-Related Intellectual Property Rights (TRIPs) would form a controversial counter-balance in the structure of the new World Trade Organization agreed at Marrakesh in 1994.

The Convention signed in Paris in 1883, modest through it undoubtedly was, did something to normalize the idea of patent systems in those 'civilized states' that had some measure of industrial development. Regular revision conferences would serve to strengthen the web of international acceptance.[153] Less developed nations could hope, as the English had hoped three centuries before, to gain some technologies by sending trainees abroad, bringing in defecting foreigners, paying for industrial spying, engaging in reverse engineering of products, and so on. But it would be increasingly apparent that many techniques were too complex to be procured in any way other than dealing with those who had already developed them in a more advanced economy. To gain transfer of such technology, those who provided it would look for legal guarantees of their private rights over inventions and other industrial property. In such countries a patent system therefore became a necessity, alongside government support for industrial development, in order to entice in foreign know-how. The concept therefore had some attraction, even when its early consequence would be that scarce national resources would be siphoned off to foreign rightholders. It is little surprise that patent systems gained solid acceptance in the era of when the international trade competition of colonizing white nations became ever more fractious.

11. THE NATIONAL SYSTEM FROM 1883

As we have already seen the British patent system lost its extravagances over securing a grant in 1852 and it became much cheaper for applicants after 1883.[154] Fears grew in consequence of what would today be labelled 'anti-commons effects'. Patents were easily secured on inventions that were already known and thus in reality void, if competitors were prepared to seek revocation or set up a defence in an infringement action. Official examiners had in the past been proposed to undertake a search of prior literature at the application stage and to eliminate those which did not meet substantive criteria for validity. In the United States the first patent law of 1790 had introduced a pre-grant examination for novelty, though the initial result had been that the Patent Office was overwhelmed by the business. In the early reform movements in Britain some had urged the virtues of such a system. But in 1852 Parliament had resisted establishing a substantive inquisition into the justification for a patent before it was granted. Instead, at that juncture the only pre-grant policing continued to come from individuals who

---

[153] The main Convention was revised in Rome (1886), Brussels (1897 and 1900), and Washington (1911); then again at The Hague (1925), London (1934), Lisbon (1958), and Stockholm (1967), before the stalemate between developed and developing states prevented further development at Nairobi (1981). The Convention, however, has an almost global reach as a limb of the TRIPs Agreement of 1994.

[154] See above, p. 956.

raised oppositions and could secure some help for keeping abreast of their rivals' plans by lodging caveats.[155]

In place of the 1852 Commissioners, the 1883 Act set up the modern Patent Office, run by a Comptroller-General and responsible to the Board of Trade.[156] Examiners in the new Office henceforth considered in every case whether the necessary formalities had been complied with, and also whether the description of the invention was fair and the title sufficient.[157] But it would not be until 1905 that there would be an official search of existing literature—primarily the contents of prior British applications (once published) and patents, excluding those published more than 50 years before the application.[158] The application was then examined against any prior art produced by the search to see whether it had already disclosed the invention claimed in the application. If an objection occurred, a grant would be allowed only after amendment to exclude the anticipation, if that proved possible.[159] This was an expensive form of regulation, since it required professionally trained searchers and examiners to investigate every file, not just to adjudicate on the few that were opposed by outside parties on evidence which they produced.[160]

12. PATENTEE AND COMPETITORS: THE BALANCING CRITERIA

The Specification and its Interpretation

By the 1870s the courts were working away at the criterion of sufficiency of description on which, a century before, they had begun to insist in earnest. They had long held that a patentee must not only describe his product, mechanism, or process but must identify what it was in that description that was properly the invention. In the diffuse specifications of the early industrial period, it will

---

[155] See above, p. 942. For the practice, see Hindmarch, *Patents*, 519–20, 526, 530–2.

[156] Patents, Designs and Trade Marks Act, 1883, ss 82–102. The Law Officers retained a role as an appellate tribunal from decisions of the Patent Office.

[157] Patents, Designs and Trade Marks Act 1883, s 6. The 50-year exclusion was one preliminary way of dealing with the problem of old ideas that had been re-discovered and deserved patenting: see e.g. R. D. Frost, *Law of Patents* (4th edn, 1912), i: 116–17.

[158] The step was recommended by the Fry Departmental Committee on aspects of Patents and Designs Law (*PP* 1901 [Cd. 506], xxiii); and enacted in the Patents Act 1902.

[159] From 1883, the Comptroller had to resolve conflicts between two or more applications claiming the same invention, even where the first application had not been published by the date of the second—the objection of 'prior claiming'.

[160] Opposition had been cut back by the 1883 Act, s 11; 1907 Act, s 11. It was no longer available for objections of non-utility, lack of novelty, or lack of subject-matter; these would have to wait for revocation proceedings after grant: see e.g. Frost, *Patents* (4th edn), ii: 35–71.

be recalled, this meant *disclaiming* rights both in old precursors and in vague or speculative material or suggestions which were not fair generalizations from what had been revealed in detail.[161] Patent draftsmen responded by inserting clauses in the description which had this essentially negative effect. The significance became particularly apparent when, upon a defect in the original specification being discovered, an attempt was made to re-write it. The power to secure amendments to the specification accompanying the initial grant, if they reduced the scope of the protected invention, was a particular procedure for disclaimer. This had an impact on specification drafting in general. Where a set of improvements were being proposed to (say) a machine, distinct claims might be made to the whole entity when it contained each improvement. Sometimes, again, the claims would seek to satisfy the letter rather than the spirit, by setting forth as the invention simply what had already been described and drawn in detail (which came to be called an 'omnibus' claim). As the amount of litigation over the meaning and scope of specifications grew, judicial pronouncements on what sufficed, and the reaction of draftsmen to these standards, acquired a new refinement.

In the Act of 1883, a requirement was included that a complete specification must end with a distinct statement of the invention claimed. In the long term this would have a crucial effect in balancing the scope of the right attaching to each patent as well as providing others with notification of what they might not do. When, however, one commentator maintained that failure to comply would render the patent void,[162] leading practitioners insisted that the requisite was 'merely directory', there being no greater obligation to provide claims than there had been under the former practice.[163] Asked whether a patent with only an 'omnibus claim' was now invalid, the House of Lords in *Vickers* v. *Siddell* adopted the latter view, treating the claim requirement as relevant solely during the pre-grant application.[164]

Curiously, however, that decision did not detract from the same court continuing a movement of thought which soon came to treat whatever claims there

---

[161] See above, p. 949.

[162] J. E. Crawford Munro, *Patents, Designs and Trade Marks Act 1883* (1884), 8.

[163] See (1885) 1 *LQR* 125; ; Terrell, *Law of Patents*, 88–9; Frost, *Patents*, i, 244.

[164] *Vickers* v. *Siddell* (1890) 15 App Cas 496; 7 RPC 292. One technical argument in favour of the 'merely directory' view, was that the 1883 Act, s 26(3) provided as grounds for revocation or defence only those that formerly could have been rendered void by *scire facias*. The House proceeded to ignore earlier case law, which had held that failure to identify the scope of the claim in relation to the description in the specification did justify a *scire facias*: see D. Brennan, 'Claims as Property Definers', 384–7. A patent that failed to describe the improvement to a mechanical sewing machine was castigated by Lord Westbury in *Foxwell* v. *Bostock* (1864) De G. J. & S. 298; Lord Cairns took a more benign view of the circumstances in *Harrison* v. *Anderston Foundry* (1876) 1 App Cas 574, HL. The 1883 Act did introduce a new rule that each patent must concern only one invention, but it expressly made this an objection that could be raised only before the Patent Office: s 33.

were in the granted patent as determining the scope of the right. Five years later, in *Nobel's Explosives* v. *Anderson*,[165] the House held that a claim to an explosive compounded of nitroglycerine and soluble nitrocellulose did not extend to the defendant's alternative formulation in which the nitrocellulose was insoluble. Placing such weight upon interpretation of the language of the claims was no new technique in this context. It had been growing over the century since the judges had begun to insist that the new must be distinguished from the old in the specification itself, notably by a distinct statement of what was disclaimed. By 1908, Fletcher Moulton LJ, who as a scientist-barrister had been a leader of the patent bar, would assert that 'Claims are universally used and indeed are obligatory'. The meaning placed on the claims would determine what the patentee asserted to be new and inventive and equally what would amount to infringement.[166]

The obligation to avoid appreciable ambiguities now attached primarily to the claims, although if obscurities arose in the description they too could lead to the patent being held void.[167] The implication underlying claims had been reversed. There was no need any longer to state what was disclaimed as old.[168] The adage, 'What is not disclaimed is claimed', had become, 'What is not claimed is disclaimed'.[169] If the *Vickers* view had prevailed, so that an 'omnibus' claim was taken to satisfy the formal requirement of the law, each court might have come to decide for itself what the scope of the patent was after reading the whole specification and hearing expert evidence about what the artefact, substance, or process achieved. As long as juries had determined the question of infringement, their verdicts would, as like as not, have been reached by that imprecise calculus. But for half a century equity judges had been trying patent cases by themselves in accordance with Chancery traditions.[170] The 'contract' with the state called

---

[165] (1895) 11 RPC 128.

[166] *British United Shoe Machinery* v. *Fussell* (1908) 25 RPC 631, 650–1, CA. As claims became limiting statements in their own right, an 'omnibus claim' would remain a typical long-stop, though it is one that has today been much restricted in the practice of the European Patent Office.

[167] Thus the House of Lords held a patent for colouring film bad where claims referred to the useable colours as 'tri-red' and 'tri-green' without further precision: *Natural Colour Kinematograph* v. *Bioschemes* (1915) 32 RPC 256.

[168] *British United Shoe Machinery* v. *Fussell* (1908) 25 RPC 631, 653–6.

[169] For the former, see Godson, *Patents and Copyright*, 133–4.

[170] For this gradual, but significant shift, which advanced with the power given to equity courts (by Lord Cairns' Act 1858, 21 & 22 Vict. c. 27) to award damages in lieu of or in addition to an injunction, see above, 864–6. Frost, *Patents*, i: 486–7 indicates that jury trials in patent actions had become rare by the time of the Judicature Acts. In *Patent Marine Inventions* v. *Chadburn* (1873) LR 16 Eq. 447, Lord Selborne, sitting in Chancery, refused to order a jury trial, because the questions of law and fact tended to be intertwined, so that much depended on the interpretation of documents (which was for the judge); and in general because of the complexity and difficulty of patent actions. They were excluded, save exceptionally, by the Patents and Designs Act 1907, s 31(1).

for the formal expression of scope by means of distinct claims in order to fore-warn the rest of the industry concerned.[171] German and other Continental laws by contrast tended to leave the ultimate decision about the scope of the monopoly to the judgment of courts, rather than to the verbal expression of claims.[172] It has taken decades of argument to move the Contracting States of the European Patent Convention 1973 towards any common understanding of what is meant by the provision in its Art. 69 that claims determine the scope of the patent right.[173] Whatever the precise outcome of that argument, it has at least become clear that a modern patent system must leave it open not just to patent office examiners but also to judges after grant to hold invalid claims that stretch beyond any fair generalization of the invention from what has been disclosed by the patentee in the specification. That is an ultimate issue for any patenting regime. It is one that English judges had tackled with a will from the late eighteenth century onwards. When combined with the technique of pre-grant examination, the basic prin-ciples governing validity and infringement were by 1914 providing a fine-mesh filter for British patents, operated by courts, and at earlier stages by Patent Office examiners. Patented inventions had undoubtedly been commodified, but the 'property' in them was confined by a set of basic constraints that were applied through a specialized bureaucracy. To these constraints we must return.

Novelty and Inventive Step

By granting letters patent Tudor and Stuart monarchs created rights good against the world at large and that basic conception was rarely questioned in all that followed. Because patents even bound those who later made the same invention themselves or obtained it from a different source, there was a set of related con-sequences. First, there could not be two patents for precisely the same invention. The earlier of two grants was alone valid and was distinct from the requirement of novelty; but until claiming practice became standard and it became possible to compare two discrete claims, the objection was rarely relied upon.[174]

Secondly, the requisites of novelty and inventive subject-matter or inventive step assisted in determining not just which of two applicants had a superior claim

---

[171] Eventually, it would be laid down by statute that to be valid claims must sufficiently and clearly define the scope of the monopoly: Patents and Designs Act 1932, s 25(2)(i).

[172] This may well have developed from their greater use of court experts in deciding the issue.

[173] Article 69 has its own Protocol on Interpretation which attempts to define a central position between extremes. By the EPC 2000 amendments to the European Patent Convention, this has been given a supposedly pro-patent adjustment by requiring account to be taken of 'equivalents' to a thing called for in a claim. But to what stretch may the search for equivalents be extended?

[174] See Frost, *Patents*, i: 295, 412–13.

but also whether anyone had an entitlement to the claimed invention. Once the 1852 Act had settled that the date for judging whether there had been 'prior art' (i.e. the publication or non-secret use of the invention) was the date of application, the testing of novelty and subject-matter gained greater precision and fairness.[175] Novelty might lie in a whole entity. If the invention was a machine consisting of known parts which interacted to give a new function, there could either be a claim to the machine itself or to the process that it enabled.[176] Such a machine would remain new, despite the incorporation of the known parts. The right would cover not only the functions that were being described for it but any future use as well. Likewise with a substance or compound that had not been made before or which had no previously known use: a claim could be made to the thing itself which extended to all uses—as occurred, for instance, when known dyestuffs were shown to have novel medicinal properties. Showing that a substance had a first practical use thus sufficed to secure a monopoly potentially much wider than the knowledge gained by the public from the revelation of that use. But the wide effect allowed to such a claim became a dogma in the lore of patents. It was simply not asked whether it satisfied the legal requirement for the patentee to supply full consideration for the grant to him. The question is one that has had to wait until very recently, when it has become a touchline in the patenting of biotechnological material.

Patent claims covering improvements and variations of something already known had to be curtailed in scope to take account of the fact that the entity itself was not any longer novel.[177] It was here that method and process patents proved significant.[178] Rules of considerable subtlety had to be devised to keep the patent system sufficiently open to those engaged in the subsequent development of a technology. In relation to medicines, the issue would be complicated by an emergent prohibition on patents for methods of medical treatment.[179] This expressed a

---

[175] See above, p. 955.

[176] See above, pp. 945–6.

[177] Certainly there could be no patent merely for demonstrating as a matter of theory how an existing practice worked; while there could be a patent even where theoretical explanation was not correct: e.g. *Patterson* v. *Gas Light & Coke Co* (1878) 3 App Cas 239, HL; *Badische Analin* v. *Usines de Rhone* (1898) 15 RPC 368.

[178] Hence the importance of *Crane* v. *Price* (1842), which finally accepted that such patents had 'subject-matter'; above, pp. 948–9.

[179] By the time that the issue of whether a patent could be granted, e.g. for a new surgical or diagnostic procedure, it was accepted that recipes for new substances and mixtures which had beneficial medicinal effects were 'manners of new manufacture'. When in wartime an application was made for a new method of removing shrapnel from the body, the Solicitor-General, Sir Stanley Buckmaster, disallowed it because it was in a distinct sense just a method claim: *C & W's Application* (1916) 33 RPC 235. He was guided by an ill-defined sense of general policy. Circumspectly he refused to link his decision to a conviction among doctors that such patenting should be discouraged. The

deep-seated feeling that surgery, therapy, and diagnostic testing were procedures too precious to human life and health to be rationed once they became known; and at the same time, it was assumed that the ethical commitment of doctors to their patients meant that they needed no commercial incentive to develop new forms of treatment. It would then be left to the twentieth century to draw lines which nevertheless allowed considerable scope for patents upon novel pharmaceuticals, a sphere in which the patent system would come to have ineluctable prominence.

Lack of novelty in a strict sense could arise through an earlier publication or use in a manner that afforded at least a notional opportunity for others to understand the invention in a practical sense.[180] The courts pushed towards a distinction that was artificial but straightforward to apply: to defeat the patent it was held enough to show a single instance of a person in the UK who had the opportunity to learn the invention and was therefore free to deploy as he wished, without being under any obligation of confidence relating to the knowledge.[181] The earlier publication or use did have to describe an activity that would lead virtually always to performance of the very invention.[182] In this respect there could be complications of proof. As this body of law developed, it added significantly to the critical artillery first positioned by the judges of the late eighteenth century. Many inventors, often to their consternation, would find their chance of a patent blocked at the Patent Office door or, when it came to a real fight, their grant would be overthrown in subsequent litigation. Where the invention proved commercially successful, the self-interest of competitors lay in searching persistently for any piece of 'prior art' that would stand as an anticipation.

For much of the nineteenth century, the cognate idea of lack of inventive subject-matter was treated without much distinction either as showing lack of 'newness', or as a separate objection.[183] The root question became: was the supposed invention, though new, nonetheless obvious to the man skilled in the art,

approach would become standard Patent Office practice and eventually would be written into the European Patent Convention 1973, Art. 52.

[180] See e.g. Tindal CJ, *Cornish v. Keene* (1835) 1 Web. PC 501, 508–9: incomplete experiments are not enough. The relative nature of the test for novelty, confining it to what was known or used in the UK, followed from the Statute of Monopolies: see above, 932, n. 6. The case law soon proliferated: see e.g. Frost, *Patents*, i: Ch. 4. 'Absolute' novelty, measured against a global state of the art, would become a requirement in British law only with the European Patent Convention 1973, Art. 52 and the Patents Act 1977, s 2.

[181] e.g. *Carpenter* v. *Smith* (1841) 2 Web. PC 530; *Heath* v. *Smith* (1854) 2 Web. PC 278; *Humpherson* v. *Syer* (1887) 4 RPC 407, CA.

[182] Lord Westbury, *Hill* v. *Evans* (1862) 31 LJ Ch 457, 463; and Jessel MR, *Plimpton* v. *Malcolmson* (1876) 3 Ch D 531, 556, provided the leading judgments.

[183] Thus in 1912 Frost, *Patents*, i: Chs 3 and 4, continued to treat inventive step as an aspect of 'Subject-Matter', apart from and before 'Novelty'. Terrell, *Patents*, appearing first in 1884, drew no

given his supposed state of knowledge at the application or other priority date? In an oft-quoted instance, a sausage machine was held unpatentable because it merely brought together a known meat-cutter and a known forcing screw, without any additional usefulness being apparent.[184]

In 1883, the Patent Office gained power to examine whether the specifications accompanying applications sufficiently described the invention. That did little to address the persistent claim that too many grants were made for inventions that in fact were anticipated by prior knowledge. The seriousness of the problem was acknowledged by the Fry Committee.[185] In consequence a limited search and examination of the novelty of the claimed invention became part of the Patent Office's treatment of applications, at which point the distinction between novelty and obviousness needed clearer definition. Regarding the latter, the courts would strive to characterize who was to rank as the ordinary, non-inventive person, whose supposed powers of deduction would determine what was obvious; and what 'common general knowledge' and specific literature he would have known about in tackling the problem. The outcome would often turn on such considerations as whether the course of research was at the time pointing elsewhere for solutions, whether the invention answered a long-felt need, and whether the thing had been a commercial success. Each case involved an evaluation of the particular circumstances. The courts certainly allowed a patent to stand where the invention lay mainly in 'apprehending the desideratum', rather than in working out the technique for achieving it. In a well-known instance, a claim was upheld for applying the technique of 'shogging', used in net-making machines, in order to obviate waste in lace-making machines, because it was not obvious that this was the technique to apply.[186] On the other hand, many claims would fail which simply applied a known material or manufacturing technique to an analogous use, for which it had not previously been tried.[187]

While judges and others would sometimes discuss whether the supposed invention produced an improvement in the technology, technical progress did not become a separate criterion for patentability, as it did in Germany and other countries.[188] At most, showing that the technology was 'better' might help to

---

clear distinction. The objection that 'the invention is obvious and does not involve any inventive step' only gained statutory force in the Patents and Designs Amendment Act 1932, s 93.

[184] *Williams* v. *Nye* (1891) 7 RPC 37, CA.

[185] Report by the DC on Aspects of the Law of Patents and Designs (chaired by Fry LJ, with Alverstone and Fletcher Moulton among its most knowledgeable members): *PP* 1901 [Cd. 501], xxiii, 599.

[186] *Hickton's Patent Syndicate* v. *Patents and Machine Improvements* (1909) 26 RPC 539.

[187] For the detailed case law by 1911, see Frost, *Patents*, i: 58–70.

[188] See H. Ullrich, *Standards of Patentability for European Inventions* (1977), Ch. 1 Pt II.

settle that there was an inventive step. The patentee might for instance argue that no one else had previously taken the crucial last step, and so it must have been inventive to do so. The attacker's response might well be that any fool would think the idea obvious, but would not carry it out because it would not produce any advantage over the known art. Some judges pronounced that only a scintilla of invention had to be shown, but there was a tendency nonetheless to set a reasonably high standard of 'non-obviousness'. The great bulk of patented inventions dealt with some improvement on a known idea or some variation in how that idea could be applied—perhaps using new materials or extending the idea to new purposes. In hard-fought cases, where the commercial prospects of the technology appeared considerable, the business of proving inventive step provided the most persistent and expensive joker in the litigation pack. In the first modern history of the common-law patent systems, Harold Fox devoted the second half of his *Monopolies and Patents* to a sustained attack on what he saw as the rootless development of the 'inventive subject-matter' doctrine, heaping blame primarily on mid-Victorian judges in England, the United States, and Canada.[189] He characterized it as allowing the courts to treat a patent as invalid even though business rivals took time and trouble to incorporate it in their own products or methods of production. The judgment of the latter

ought not to be swept aside as it so often is by a judge, exercising a legally and not a scientifically or industrially trained mind, by the operation of a sophisticated and hypothetical doctrine composed of a group of negative rules that are used in place of a positive definition...Now we have nothing but a number of 'personal views' of what constitutes invention, the number seemingly limited only by the number of judges.[190]

This was history in the service of polemic, and an instance that in subsequent decades would fail to convince. The subject-matter test of inventive step is regarded as an essential ingredient of modern patent law in most national systems and now also at the international level.[191] In the later Victorian years, the drafting of specifications in Britain became a matter for trained professionals who were able to work within the inherited criteria of sufficient description and claiming. Since the

---

[189] He launched this attack on the precedents by quoting Tindal CJ's remark in *Price v. Crane* (1841) 1 Webst. PC at 410 that 'if the monopoly be new and useful to the public, it is not material whether it be the result of long experiments and profound research, or whether by some sudden and lucky thought, or mere accidental discovery'. Since there need be no intellectual 'invention' at all, it had been taken that it was for the court to decide whether there was subject-matter or not—for Fox, the essential false step.

[190] H. G. Fox, *Monopolies and Patents* (Toronto, 1947), 289; and see generally, Pt II, 'Invention and Patent Law'.

[191] See the Agreement on Trade-related Aspects of Intellectual Property Rights (World Trade Organization, 1994), Art. 27(1).

courts continued to feel that patents should not be granted for relative trivia, they turned increasingly to the external standard of 'non-obviousness' as the major criterion for expressing their view of the essential desert of the claimed invention.

13. EXPLOITATIONS OF PATENTED TECHNOLOGY

In this sketch of legal developments, the varied uses that inventors and investors made of patents have been touched on from time to time. Business and technology histories now fill out the picture much more fully.[192] The grantees of a patent, who still under the legislation of 1907 had to include the 'true and first inventor', were able to transfer their interests to each other or to third parties as they might agree. So long as there were joint proprietors of the legal right, the extent to which they could each work the invention was governed by rules which in practice favoured investors rather than 'real' inventors.[193] Beyond that, agreements about proprietary interests could have effect in equity even before the steps necessary to transfer the legal entitlement had been carried out. Leaving the course of exploitation primarily to contractual agreement allowed great flexibility to the parties to express what the parties intended their relationship to be. At the same time, the courts could play a supplemental role by implying licences or, if necessary, assignments and other terms in ways that would fill out conditions to give the relationship a 'necessary' business basis, even where it had not been expressly agreed. They showed no inclination to comb out clauses that restricted future choices open to the parties by treating them as void for being in restraint of trade. Thus Jessel MR upheld a clause in the sale of a patent which required the original patentee to assign further patents that he might acquire for the same technology in fine liberal terms:

if there is one thing which more than another public policy requires it is that men of full age and competent understanding shall have the utmost liberty of contracting, and that their contracts when entered into freely and voluntarily shall be held sacred and shall be enforced by Courts of justice.[194]

In Victorian England this had not led to any general presumption that it was the master, rather than the technical or managerial inventor-servant, who was entitled to the beneficial interest over any invention that resulted from the work done

---

[192] See e.g. J. Jewkes, D. Sawers, and R. Stillerman, *The Sources of Invention* (1958); A. D. Chandler, *The Visible Hand* (Cambridge MA, 1977), and his *Shaping the Industrial Century* (Cambridge MA, 2005); J. Z. Fullmer, 'Technology, Chemistry and the Law in early Nineteenth Century England' (1980) 21 *Technology & Culture* 1.

[193] See e.g. Frost, *Patents*, i: 156–60.

[194] *Printing and Numerical* v. *Sampsen* (1875) LR 19 Ch 462, 465.

for the employment, unless a contract had it otherwise.[195] The beginnings of a shift in that direction could be seen in *Worthington Pumping* v. *Moore*,[196] where the inventor of a major improvement to the plaintiff company's pumps had patented it and was asserting it against the company. But from his position as general manager of the company's operations outside America, Byrne J. implied a duty of good faith between an employer and an employee in such a key position, under which he must not put personal advancement ahead of the employer's business. From that starting-point, a whole range of cases would arise which dealt with different types of employees engaged in technical development and senior management would come to be decided in ways that showed increasing favour towards the capitalist enterprise and against the individual employed within it. The shift well-nigh obliterated any scope for treating patents as the natural entitlement of inventors. But that experience would belong in the main to the period after 1914.

Treating patents as property gave their proprietors very considerable civil remedies against infringers. The embracing terms of the patent itself imposed obligations on all who might 'make, use, exercise and vend' the invention, meaning that restrictions might be placed on distribution and actual deployment of the invention throughout its useful commercial life within the term of the grant. It was dangerous to do anything other than seek a licence, whenever it was reasonably clear that the patent was valid and the rival's product or process fell within one or more claim. Those who held valuable patents therefore followed various tactics in deploying them. They could refuse to license anyone else to produce the patented product or deploy the patented process or method. On the other hand, they could grant bare licences to others who already had their own production facilities and wanted only to use the invention as part of them. Sometimes the leaders of an advanced technology would engage in a cross-licensing of distinct but related inventions. This pooling of patents was by no means unknown as the basis of production cartels. Often it was international in character, as with such instances as dyestuffs, telegraphy, and telephony; and later wireless broadcasting, pharmaceuticals, and chemicals of many other kinds.[197]

Again, the licensing of patent rights (often enough coupled with know-how, design rights, and trade marks) could ground the provision of a whole

---

[195] A dictum in *Bloxham* v. *Elsee* (1827) 6 B. & C. 169, repeated by counsel in *Allen* v. *Rawson* (1845) 1 C.B. 551, suggested that an employer could apply to patent an invention made by a servant who had been specifically employed to investigate the problem. But the suggestion seems to have been treated only as a possible exception for unusual cases.

[196] (1903) 20 RPC 41. See also J. Phillips and M.J. Hoolahan, *Employees' Inventions in the United Kingdom* (1982) 7–12.

[197] For this international movement, see H. Kronstein, 'The Dynamics of German Cartels and Patents I' (1942) 9 *U. Chicago LR* 643–71; and his *The Law of International Cartels* (1972), Ch. 15.

technology to a licensee who was starting more or less from scratch. The result could be a contract with complex obligations on both licensor and licensee to protect the other, as improvements and other developments flowed from working the machinery or production line.[198] By and large the parties were left to settle the terms of their own bargain, even when the result was to impose exclusive rights and other restrictions on one or other party. That satisfied the predilections of judges in favour of the upholding of contracts. Likewise it had long been accepted that the purchaser of a patent bought the risk of its validity. If it was successfully challenged subsequently, he was not entitled to recover the price.[199]

In consequence there emerged a form of protection in international trade that coalesced out of two basic doctrines. One was the power given in the letters patent to control uses and further sales of the patentee's own products; the other was the territorial character of the right, which was taken to confine the grant to activities in the geographical boundaries of the granting nation. Where there were price differentials across national boundaries the patentee (or an exclusive licensee) might well want to prevent importation from the cheaper market into the more expensive, relying on the separate grant of a patent in the latter. To deploy these characteristics of patent exclusivity was justifiable if it was accepted that patents were needed to foster invention, for chances of realizing monopoly profits could well be increased by preventing parallel importation. In Britain, with its commitment to the virtues of international free trade, however, this use of patents to add to the patentee's own exploitation of the invention gave rise to considerable unease. As a first position, it was accepted that if a patentee sold a product containing the patented invention, he must be taken to confer on purchasers, direct or indirect, the entitlement to use or re-sell as they chose.[200] Did that implied licence extend to sales in another country where the patentee held an equivalent patent? In *Betts* v. *Willmott*,[201] Lord Hatherley took a temporizing position which, typically for its time, used the presence or absence of notice to others as the decisive factor. Products which the holder of a French patent marketed in France could not then be imported into England by purchasers who had explicit notice that they should not do so without licence under the

---

[198] Thus the precedent set out by Frost, *Patents*, ii: 445, required the licensor to give all technical assistance to enable the licensee to use the invention to greatest advantage; but it bound the licensee not to challenge the validity of the patent.

[199] *Taylor v. Hare* (1805) 1 Bos. & P. 260.

[200] As a general principle, this was a necessary implication from first sale: see *Thomas* v. *Hunt* (1864) 17 C.B. (N.S.) 183. The derogation from the grant of the licence would otherwise have defeated its very object.

[201] (1870) LR 6 Ch 239.

manufacturer's equivalent patent for Britain. But if the importer did not know of this restriction, the implication from the first sale of the 'legitimate product' in France was that it could thereafter be taken and re-sold in Britain, even though the patentee had an equivalent patent there.[202]

By the turn of the century, the same doctrinal understanding allowed restrictive conditions to be attached to the sale of a patentee's own products purely within the domestic market.[203] Thus minimum retail prices to consumers could be set by the manufacturer, and the territories of exclusive dealers could be sealed off. With adequate notice, such restrictions would pass down the line through the wholesaler to the retailer, without meeting the difficulty over the lack of contractual privity that arose with unpatented goods.[204]

This would leave open the question whether the same rule applied to goods that were the subject of copyright or registered design rights: after acquiring the British rightholder's goods cheaply abroad, could a person import them into Britain where they were subject to equivalent intellectual property rights?[205] Of greater practical significance, producers would seek to apply the same legal technique to trade marks on the products, even though the policy justifying trade mark protection was quite different. If the marking had originally been made by the British mark-owner or a foreign associate, what confusion of the public could be said to occur? That issue must be reserved for later consideration.[206]

There were, however, certain ultimate points at which Parliament chose to override particular licence terms that unduly hindered competition. So at least it was persuaded by Lloyd George, who in 1907 was cutting his ministerial teeth as President of the Board of Trade. He had in his sights the alleged 'abuses of monopoly' under which the United Shoe Manufacturing Company of Boston

---

[202] Where, however, the goods were initially made and marketed by an exclusive licensee for a particular country, the Court of Appeal reached the opposite result. The licensee for one country had no power to sub-license the sale or use of his products in another country, when he had no licence for that second territory: *SA de Manufacture des Glaces* v. *Tilghman* (1883) 25 Ch D 1. The Court indicated an antipathy to the solution in *Betts* v. *Wilmott*, which it confined to cases where the patentee was the first marketer.

[203] *Incandescent Gas Light* v. *Cantelo* (1895) 12 RPC 262. Several cases explored what was sufficient notice to withdraw the implied licence conferred in *Betts*: see esp. *Badische Analin* v. *Isler* (1906) 23 RPC 633, CA. It was not open to a manufacturing licensee to confer a right on others (such as that of landlord to distrain for rent) merely by implication from the licensee's entitlement to use or re-sell the goods in question: *McGruther* v. *Pitcher* (1904) 2 Ch 306. The Privy Council confirmed the approach in *National Phonographic* v. *Menck* [1911] AC 336.

[204] See in general above, XII, Pt 2, pp. 389–95.

[205] For copyright, the question would long remain unanswered.

[206] Below, 1010–11.

licensed use of its patented machinery to British shoemakers.[207] One prohibition concerned the obligation of the licensee of a patented invention also to take unpatented starting materials or services from the patentee, whether this obligation was expressed in positive or negative terms. Another constraint concerned terms which extended obligations under the licence—for instance to pay royalties—even after expiry of all the patents initially licensed.[208]

What if the patentee did not secure actual manufacture in Britain using the protected invention? Should it matter whether the motive for failing to do so was to engage in importation from abroad or to prevent the new technology from being exploited anywhere because less efficient types of product brought greater returns? These were concerns, particularly affecting struggles between the British and German chemical industries over organic and artificial dyestuffs which led to the introduction of compulsory licensing provisions in patent law in 1883 and then to some strengthening in 1907.[209] The licence would be on terms set by the Comptroller-General or the court. If the patentee resisted, it could take a long time to determine that the statutory conditions were satisfied and to have the terms of the licence settled. Very few compulsory licences would ever be granted in Britain under these general powers.[210] The provisions would be retained in the Patents Acts of 1949 and 1977 in the belief that they would induce patentees to adopt some measure of reasonableness in their voluntary

---

[207] '...for the first time they saw in their nakedness the methods of the American trusts': Lloyd George *PD* (s. 4), 1908, cviii, 674. See W.R. Cornish, 'Legal Control over Cartels and Monopolization 1880–1914', in N. Horn and J. Kocka, *Law and the Formation of the Big Enterprises in the Nineteenth and Early Twentieth Centuries* (Göttingen, 1979), 280, 299. Litigation had already revealed the long period for which United Shoe tied their licensees to use only their machines: see T. A. Freyer, *Regulating Big Business: Antitrust in Great Britain and America 1880–1990* (Cambridge, 1992), 129–30; *BUSM* v. *Somervell* (1907) 95 LT 711; and see (from Canada) *USMC* v. *Brunet* [1909] AC 781.

[208] Patents and Designs Act 1907, ss 38, 39. For unlawful tying, not only was the term null and void, but an action for infringement of the patent in question would be barred so long as the contract remained in existence (s 38(4))—a savage consequence, which later courts would struggle to avoid. These and their later variants would survive until the Competition Act 1998, s 70.

[209] Patents and Designs Act 1907, s 27, interpreted restrictively, however, esp. by Parker J. in *Hatschek's Patent* (1909) 26 RPC 228. For the initial history, see O. Brand, 'The Dawn of Compulsory Patent Licensing' [2007] 2 *IPQ* 16–35. For Ivan Levinstein, the main British protagonist for wider compulsory licensing powers: see L. F. Haber, *Chemical Industry*, 198–204.

[210] Very different would be hostile reaction against the profiteering of war-time suppliers of food and drugs. On the recommendation of a Committee chaired by Lord Parker (as he had become), patents in those fields were to be the subject of compulsory licences virtually as of right: Patents Amendment Act 1919, s 38A(2), which was hotly debated in the Lords before enactment: see *PD* (5s, Lords) 1919, xxxvi, 222–39. The Committee's unpublished Report can be found in draft at BT 209/485. The pharmaceutical industry would succeed in having this qualification removed in 1977 only after a sustained fight between the Swiss firm, Hoffmann-La Roche and the Department of Health. This provoked a reference to the Monopolies Commission over the pricing of two leading tranquillisers: HC Paper 197, 1973.

licensing practices. Ultimately patentees could be prevented from extracting the last pounds of monopoly flesh from their exclusive rights, but only in unusual and extreme cases, which were inherently unlikely to be those where successful exploitation was bringing very substantial rewards.[211] Small the step may have been, but it was something that returned the patent system to its seventeenth-century origins. The original thrust had been to stimulate industrial innovation for the productive advance of the country as a whole. Patents were an economic tool to stir the energies of those with the intellectual acumen or financial adventurousness to engage in the hazardous business of exploiting new technologies. By being in the van of capitalistic enterprise throughout Victoria's reign, Britain had learned the immense economic returns of her own position; but latterly also, the difficulties of sustaining those advantages as the United States, Germany, and other countries challenged them. Legislators were readier than before to see that patents could be used 'abusively' and that there was a national interest in curbing the excesses.

---

[211] Patents and Designs Act 1907, s 24.

IV

Industrial Property: Designs for Products

1. THE DESIGNS REGISTER: APPEARANCE AND FUNCTION

Once the basic notions of 'intellectual property' had taken hold, it became less problematic to secure extension to further instances where imitation of originators appeared to be undercutting their expectations from intellectual and financial investments. One significant case concerned industrial designs—features introduced into mass-produced articles either to add to their visual appeal through decoration or shape, or to improve their technical functioning, or both. Parliament had first been moved to intervene in 1787, the case being promoted by London calico printers who feared the design imitations of the new cotton manufacturers of Lancashire.[1] Starting from the copyrights of authors and engravers, the legislation had conferred on those who invented, designed, and printed 'new and original' calico designs the right to stop others from printing or marketing their designs. But protection was only for two months (increased to three months in 1794), mainly because manufacturers would change their patterns each season. Pieces had to be marked with the proprietor's name, but no registration was needed.[2] It was a small beginning for what, over the course of a century, would become a popular type of protection.[3] In 1806, Imperial France, drawing on pre-revolutionary precedents, had decreed a regime for the protection of designs, which started with the city of Lyons and became general.[4] It also became the model to which other countries would turn. In time the British would come to associate the self-interest of commerce with the improving role of good taste in polite living. Without attention to design, it was feared that the flood of British manufactures would go to waste beside the productions of more refined nations. This was

---

[1] Designing and Printing of Linens Act, 27 Geo. III c. 38, renewed by 29 Geo. III c. 19 (1789), and 34 Geo. III c. 23 (1794).

[2] Extended to three months by the 1794 Act.

[3] See below, p. 1006.

[4] See Ladas, *International Protection*, 367–8.

taken up in the invasive spirit of intervention bred by the First Reform Act.[5] Not only did the Benthamite President of the Board of Trade, Poulett Thomson, lead an endeavour to establish schools of design and to promote national art institutions, he also strove to introduce an incentive of the patent or copyright type into industry itself, administered by a central bureaucracy.[6] In 1839 a Designs Register was set up for manufactures in general, in which, essentially by deposit, a registrant could secure protection for one year or three years, depending on the type of article. The new scheme drew upon the utilitarian hope that the law could be shaped to its purpose by a process of differential classification. Thus three years was given only to metal products.

The new Registrar ordered that the design itself should be kept undisclosed until the registration expired, thus protecting designers from copying before they released their own versions of the design on the market.[7] This contrasted with the insistence of judges that specifications of patents should be enrolled in Chancery and open thereafter to inspection by all-comers.[8] It was one reason why manufacturers of many products at once took to registering designs for elements in their products that were technical, rather than eye-catching. Placing a plain record of subject-matter on a public roll established an assertion of 'property' that had a value beyond that simply of suppressing piratical imitators. For ideas that would have only a brief commercial life, it was a boon to be able to do so cheaply and rapidly, while giving nothing away in advance.

However, the fact that the registration system was for 'copyright in designs' indicated that its progenitors had been thinking of 'eye appeal', rather than of 'function'; the aim was to encourage the production of good-looking artefacts of all kinds, not just fabrics.[9] So at once the new scheme was under review. For a nick in time, design protection acquired a political cachet that could rank alongside

---

[5] Sherman and Bently, *Making of Intellectual Property*, Ch. 6.

[6] He promoted the case through a Commons Select Committee on Arts and their Connection with Manufactures (*PP* 1835 (598), v, 375; 1836 (568), ix, 1. In its brief Report, the Committee stressed the importance of having a cheap and ready tribunal to deal with infringers: p. vii.

[7] Reluctantly, Poulett Thomson allowed the three-month, wholly informal, right in printing on cloth to continue, expanding it to cover animal-based fabrics as well as those that were vegetable-based: Fabric Designs Act 1839, 2 Vict. c. 13. But the calico printers soon had a change of heart about its usefulness and fabric designs were brought into the registration system in 1842, even though the period for their protection was kept at 12 months. The variations in attitude can be seen in the voluminous evidence to the Commons Select Committee on Copyright of Designs, *PP* 1840 (442), vi, 1 (see Sherman and Bently, *Making of Intellectual Property*, 67–85). The Committee itself did no more than support expansion of protection on the lines of a bill before them.

[8] See above, p. 943.

[9] Designs Registration Act 1839, 2 Vict. c. 17. One echo of the Statute of Anne was that wrongdoers were subjected to a penalty; but as with that forebear, Chancery was prepared to grant injunctions as well: see the evidence of G. Brace to the 1840 Select Committee (above, n. 7), qq. 8 *et seq.*

the movement towards the Copyright Act 1842.[10] In that same year, an amendment to the Designs Act 1839 attempted to confine the registration of designs applicable to the ornamenting of any article of manufacture or substance.[11] But the Registrar was not made the arbiter of what could be placed on the register, so little would change.[12] In the next year, swinging towards the demands of manufacturers, a further Act explicitly admitted useful designs to the register.[13] Britain thereby gained an early form of 'utility model' protection—exclusive rights could be secured in the shape or configuration of an article that improved its function.[14] These registrations were not, however, partitioned from designs that were decorative or ornamental, and the difficulties inherent in dividing the two categories were in large measure averted.[15]

The utility design could thus provide a short-term exclusivity for technical ideas without entering the labyrinth of the unreformed patent system. Indeed, the 1843 Act should be seen as both a response to defects of that patent system and as an element in explaining why patent reform would remain unmet in that decade.[16] The 'copyright in design' would remain only a partial answer, since it could not touch inventions or other ideas that consisted in processes and methods, nor in products that had no form or that could take a multitude of shapes and configurations. Nonetheless this limited type of 'petty patent' would provide one protective path across the no-man's-land between patents and the various copyrights.[17] In its early years, according to the critical author, Thomas Turner, the leading patent professionals—or as he termed them, the 'licensed gamekeepers of the manor of useful art'—insisted that the design protection extended only to imitations of the precise shape of configuration registered.[18] Even at that time Turner

[10] Above, Ch.2, pp. 888–9. As leader of the movement, Emerson Tennent took over when Poulett Thomson became Governor-General of the Canadas.

[11] Ornamental Designs Act 1842, 5 & 6 Vict. c. 100.

[12] The office of Registrar would in 1875 be absorbed by the Commissioners of Patents, and then in 1883 would become part of the Patent Office.

[13] Utility Designs Act, 6 & 7 Vict. c. 65; see L. Bently and B. Sherman, 'The United Kingdom's Forgotten Utility Model: The Utility Designs Act 1843' (1997) 1 *IPQ* 265–78.

[14] Later, Germany would introduce such a *Gebrauchsmuster* (utility model), which was distinct from a *Geschmacksmuster* ('good-taste' model).

[15] There was, however, a distinction between the low fees for fabric and other decorative designs and the fees for utility designs under the 1843 Act, which were some 10 times higher, when combined with a £5 stamp. The distinction, which lasted until 1883, was handled at the administrative level.

[16] See above, pp. 952–3.

[17] Neither the legislature nor the courts would see difficulty in allowing cumulative protection of patent and utility design for an invention, so far as it was expressed by a novel shape or configuration: see e.g. *Hecla Foundry* v. *Walker* (1889) 6 RPC 554, HL; *re Bayer's Design* (1907) 24 RPC 65, HL; cf. below, pp. 982–3.

[18] T. Turner, *On Copyright in Design in Arts and Manufactures* (1849); and *Law of Patents and Registration of Invention and Design in Manufacture* (1851). Among the patent protectors he named Carpmael, Webster, and Newton.

claimed that the protection did not extend to a design which involved a mode or principle of construction, or anything which was in substance a mere mechanical device.[19] This proved to be a forerunner of the distinction introduced in 1949 disallowing the registration of a design dictated solely by the function of the article to which it was applied.[20] That likewise has proved to be a distinction replete with ambiguity and one of the twin catalysts of the present, wildly unsatisfactory, law covering both registered and unregistered designs in the UK.[21]

Design registration was utilized in the latter nineteenth century to a degree that is no longer appreciated. The system was reformed in the Patents, Trade Marks and Designs Act 1883 and amended in certain details by the Patents and Designs Act 1907. It would reach a zenith of over 43,000 applications—virtually all allowed—in both 1911 and 1912.[22] Since the 1883 Act kept official fees low and increased the possible period of protection to 15 years (through extensions at the fifth and tenth years),[23] a substantial number of producers thought registrations were a benefit worth acquiring, where it was the decoration, shape, or configuration of their product that was likely to be imitated.

Once registration was introduced in the 1840s industrial design protection gradually drew closer to the patent system. Thus it came to be assumed that the right in a design was infringed not only by copying but even by independent creation.[24] Most disputes, however, involved a claim that the defendant had deliberately copied from the plaintiff; and the issue was in any case deflected until 1883 by a restriction permitting damages to be claimed for the period after the registrant had notified the alleged infringer of the registration.[25] Eventually,

---

[19] This limitation was later accepted by the courts: see *Walter v. Falkirk* (1887) 4 RPC 390; *Moody v. Tree* (1892) 9 RPC 333.

[20] Registered Designs Act 1949, s 1.

[21] For the modern law, see *Russell-Clarke and Howe on Industrial Designs* (7th edn, 2005); *Copinger and Skone James on Copyright* (15th edn, 2005), Pt IV. To add to the complexity, there are now two European Community Design Rights in addition to the British rights.

[22] Between 1923 and 1938, the annual average would be some 21,609. By the 1950s it fluctuated between 8000 and 11,000 each year. For comparisons with other intellectual property, see below, 1006.

[23] The 1883 Act set the period of registration at five years. In 1907 this would be extended to allow two further periods of registration, each of five years: Patents and Designs Act 1907, s 53. The period during which the registration would be kept from public inspection was set at two years from application: s 56.

[24] Edmunds and Bentwich, *Law of Copyright in Designs*, (2nd. ed., 1908), 21–4.

[25] Much the same position was reached over passing off, where an injunction for the future was available whether or not the defendant knew that he was acting wrongfully; but an action for damages at common law could only relate to commercial activity after the defendant was informed of the plaintiff's prior right: see below, p. 997. Similar constraints were introduced by statute for other forms of intellectual property: see Patents, Trade Marks and Designs Act 1883, s 59 (designs); Patents and Designs Act 1907, s 27; Copyright Act 1911, s 8—and for secondary infringement, see s 11.

the right was treated as effective even against an independent designer who per-chance applied the same design or used one that was an 'obvious imitation' in the eye of the beholder.[26] As another dimension of this idea, the registration was valid only if it was novel and the Patent Office undertook a search of prior regis-trations once it received an application—a form of control that preceded the nov-elty search in the procedure for obtaining a patent. The Office could then refuse an application where an earlier registration that was closely similar was found in respect the same articles.[27]

2. CUMULATION OF INTELLECTUAL PROPERTIES

The tendency of most modern law is to allow rights of civil action to develop independently, even if more than one emerges as applicable to a given fact situation. The result is a cumulation of rights. Design rights, however, can lie in an awkward relationship to other types of intellectual property. The result has been complex shifts both over defining their scope and over the need to prevent them from existing in overlap. In Victorian times, when copyright in designs had a sturdy breadth and independence, this question of cumulation or non-cumulation was not of much significance. As already noted, designs could be for technical improvements, whether or not they embodied patentable inventions.[28] So far as trade marks and get-up were concerned, their charac-terization as distinctive insignia of the origin of goods made overlaps between liability based on registration and passing-off unproblematic. When it was pos-sible to establish that a shape element in a product itself had come to be treated by the public as distinctive in this sense, then a passing off action could be made out, even if the shape element was not the basis of a registered design; but that was a fringe case.[29]

With copyright protection, however, the issue would eventually prove more intransigent. In 1842, the only subject-matter of copyright that was inherently likely also to qualify as a registrable design was sculpture and sculptures were

---

[26] Patents, Trade Marks and Designs Act 1883, s 57; Patents and Designs Act 1907, s 93. Beyond these cases, there was liability for 'fraudulent imitation' where the defendant intended it, as equally there was for articles that were sold knowing of the invasion of the design right; Edmunds and Bentwich, *Copyright in Designs*, 147–52.

[27] The Herschell Committee on Trade Marks and Designs (*PP 1888* [C. 5350], lxvi, 495) rejected the case for abandoning this pre-registration examination. They considered it necessary in the inter-ests of others in the industry concerned.

[28] The separate functions were clearly stated in *Werner Motors* v. *Gamages* (1904) 21 RPC 137, 261.

[29] The best-known example of such a claim succeeding was *Edge* v. *Niccolls* [1911] AC 693. For 'cumulation' with trade mark and passing off rights, see below, 1006, n. 116.

specifically excluded from the designs system.[30] Two-dimensional artistic works were considered to give rights only in two-dimensional reproductions, so there too, allowing a cumulation of rights was not a significant question.[31] But the generalization of copyright categories in the Copyright Act 1911 altered matters, since the definition of what could constitute infringement thereafter included 'reproduction in a material form'. It was at once appreciated that this could render it wrongful to turn a two-dimensional work into a three-dimensional object and vice versa. If so, using a production drawing from which to make a physical article could give copyright over industrial production of that article for the designer's life and 50 years thereafter (the new 1911 term for artistic works). The government therefore decided, given this potential overlap, to go down the path of 'non-cumulation' of rights. The approaches followed by other countries on the matter varied greatly. If British copyright was available generally, it was likely that under the Berne Convention product designers from other countries would claim to enjoy far greater protection in Britain than the British would be offered in their countries.[32] As a result, while artistic copyright could indeed apply to industrial production of a design, this was not so where the designs were registrable and were 'used or intended to be used as models or patterns to be multiplied by an industrial process'.[33] Here was the second cause of the quagmire into which industrial designs law has been sucked today.[34]

---

[30] But they were admitted to registration in 1850 and removed again in 1883: see for this and other minor legislation on design protection, L. Edmunds, *Copyright in Designs* (1895), Ch. 1.

[31] In 1842 these were only etchings, lithographs, and the like. Drawings, paintings, and photographs, given artistic copyright in 1862, were subject to the same limitation: see above, 891–2.

[32] Adding to these international differences was the question of how far other countries acknowledged copyright in objets d'art. In the 1911 Act they were being given protection as 'works of artistic craftsmanship', but no guarantee of this would enter the Berne Convention until the Brussels Revision of 1948: see Ricketson and Ginsburg, *International Copyright*, paras 8.59–8.69. Despite the divergences between countries, the Paris Industrial Property Convention had applied the principle of national treatment to industrial designs: see Ladas, *International Protection*, Chs 15–19.

[33] Copyright Act 1911, s 22. Little direction was given to its interpretation until *King Features Syndicate* v. *Kleeman* [1941] AC 417, HL ('Popeye' dolls).

[34] See the works referred to in n. 21 above.

V

Trade Secrets and Other Confidences

1. THE INNOMINATE EQUITY AGAINST BREACH OF CONFIDENCE

Secrecy could provide its own basis of protection against imitating industrial goods and, even more, the method by which they were produced; and against making use of any information which was obtained under the same cloak.[1] As we have noted in the context of copyright, in our period Chancery became ready to enjoin a person who had received information in confidence against disclosing it or using it in ways that conflicted with the obligation that they had undertaken.[2] Lord Eldon ordered a servant who had copied out his master's recipes for veterinary medicines just before leaving his post not to disclose or use them in competition.[3] In the nineteenth century, most reported decisions concerned business relationships. They were likely to involve either technical information about how things were made, what recipe or prescription was followed, or about commercial strategies and activities—in marketing, selling, financing, and the like. These trade secrets were not a general category which the law enclosed with a full-blown right of property against the world, as happened with patentable inventions. Indeed, the right against breaches of confidence was by its very nature confined to cases which did not have to do with the appearance of products that could be protected by a patent, copyright, or a registered design, since once those items were available for purchase, there would be nothing left secret,

---

[1] In the early nineteenth century, cases seeking injunctions over medicinal or gastronomic secret recipes, began to be reported. Lord Eldon expressed doubts about granting relief where proof of misuse would be inherently difficult: see *Newbery* v. *Jarvis* (1817) 2 Mer. 446; *Williams* v. *Williams* (1819) 3 Mer. 57. The commercial value of the secrets could be considerable: see e.g. *Canham* v. *Jones* (1813) 2 V. & B. 218 ('Velno's Vegetable Syrup', which had sold for £6,000).

[2] The point at which this liability attached was accordingly much the same as that reached for passing-off by mid-nineteenth century. Since, however, its development lay wholly in equity, rather than in a difference between common law and equity, there was in formal terms a distinction: cf. below, 994–6.

[3] *Yovatt* v. *Winyard* (1820) 1 Jac. & W. 394; and see *Tipping* v. *Clarke* (1843) 2 Hare 363: clerk in counting house; *Morison* v. *Moat* (1851) 9 Hare 383: son of business partner was wrongly told the recipe for 'Morison's Universal Medicine'; *Escourt* v. *Escourt Hop Essence* (1875) LR 10 Ch App 276.

with the exception of production know-how that did not leave its trace on the article made.

The emergent right drew its moral force from the undertaking to keep the information secret. It came to be treated as arising on a principle of equity, rather than of common law. The equitable remedy of injunction was the most appropriate form of protection in the general run of cases; and beneath that the claim for relief turned on the transposition of a commonplace moral precept into a normative proposition—something that was in the nature of equity to bring about. How precisely to categorize the equitable action against breach of confidence was, however, more difficult. The cases arose out of some assumption by the person to whom the information was revealed to respect the confidence thereby shown; and in many situations that could give rise to contractual obligation.[4] If the information was then passed to an indirect recipient, issues of privity of contract would compete for predominance over obligations required of fiduciaries and the liability of tortfeasors for inducing or procuring breaches of contract. When there was a breach of contract or other legal property right, an injunction in equity to restrain misuse of confidential information would be an auxiliary remedy to damages at common law. What then of situations where there was no breach of contract or tort? The foundational Chancery judgments of mid-century—*Prince Albert* v. *Strange*[5] and *Morison* v. *Moat*,[6]—treated the duty to respect confidence or trust as an 'equity'. The duty appeared to have some characteristics of equitable property— enough at least to bring it within the jurisdiction to grant injunctions.[7] Moreover, Turner VC, in a well-known dictum, considered that an injunction could extend not only to persons who received confidential information directly from the person who imposed the confidence but also to those who had it by an indirect channel, unless they were purchasers for value without notice of the obligation affecting it.[8]

How far such proprietary overtones provided a definitional framework for the right would be left for speculation to this day. To protect the *bona fide* purchaser to some extent constrained the ability of a person who imparted a secret to turn his information into 'property' simply by making an obligation of confidence the basis on which the information would be provided. There were reasons enough to hesitate before applying the property label too readily. In respect of technical information, for instance, was it compatible to have both a patent system, giving protection against the world to inventions

---

[4] An early instance of the significance of contract is *Smith* v. *Dickenson* (1804) 3 B. & P. 630.

[5] (1849) 1 Mac. & G. 46., above, pp. 899–900.

[6] (1851) 9 Hare 241.

[7] For which, see above, pp. 849–52.

[8] *Morison* v. *Moat* (above, n. 6), pp. 263–4.

on condition of their revelation to the public, while offering the possessors of such ideas legal support for keeping the information tied up within a tight circle of collaborators? English judges mostly accepted that the undertaking to respect confidence made the two situations different enough,[9] but the question could not be regarded as beyond speculation.[10] To a large degree, the scope of confidence protection was qualified by a general assumption: if the means of ascertaining the secret was put in the hands of the public it thereupon lost its 'confidential' nature because the secret could be independently unearthed, if necessary by reverse analysis or reverse engineering.

The action in equity against breach of confidence had a moral ubiquity well illustrated by *Prince Albert* v. *Strange*, with its intrusion into the private life of the sovereign herself. In the second half of the twentieth century its potential for protecting both governmental and personal information would begin to be explored. But its technique would have little meaning against secret-breakers who would scarcely be touched by civil remedies. Occasional scandals in Victorian England showed how the spread of secret government information could heap difficulties on ministries such as the Foreign, Colonial, War, and Home Offices. Secrets might appear in the press betraying the lack of scruple of the government machine; commercial information might be revealed that would affect the terms on which the armed forces could procure weapons;[11] hidden knowledge grounded the whole business of espionage, which would quicken with the war-mongering of the Edwardian years.[12]

Already in 1889, the government turned to the criminal law as the best hope for deterrence. It was able to procure an Official Secrets Act that penalized the passing, procuring, and receiving of such information. Under it, occasional prosecutions were pursued, but often it proved difficult to offer evidence enough to nail the defendants. A serious question of civil liberties was thus aroused: how to frame an enactment that would lead to convictions on evidence of suspicion, while still guarding against wrongful conviction? It took more than 20 years for further legislation to succeed.[13] The Official Secrets Act 1911 shifted the burden of proof significantly in favour of government prosecutors: defendants who had been found observing or recording sensitive information about military

---

[9] Of this Turner VC had no doubt: *Morison* v. *Moat* (1851) 9 Hare 241 at 258–9.

[10] The same position would eventually be reached in US law, but not before the issue had been prominently contested: see the eventual resolution by the Supreme Court in *Kewanee Oil* v. *Bicron* 416 US 470 (1974).

[11] Sir Richard Webster, A-G and a leading counsel in patent cases, spoke from personal knowledge of an instance, for the need in the 1889 Act to cover it: *PD* 1889(35), cccxxxiii.

[12] For the *causes célèbres* of the period, see D. Williams, *Not in the Public Interest* (1965), 15–19.

[13] See Williams, *Public Interest*, 19–22.

installations and the like had to prove that their actions were for an innocent purpose. Those who failed would face a finding of felony carrying a maximum penalty of 14 years' imprisonment.[14]

In the pre-War years, several prosecutions for spying were brought against Germans or those who passed military secrets to them. The public took their every detail to heart.[15] The cases helped to prepare opinion for the drastic constraints which the Defence of the Realm Regulations would clamp on the home population once hostilities were declared. Government secrets, however, were a special case. Private information, gleaned by the industrial spy or the newshound, could be protected only by a civil action brought by the person to whom a confidential obligation was shown to have been broken. And so the matter would remain in the UK, even though other countries decided that punishment was needed for the deliberate act of breaking trade or other secrets. The press were of course all too ready to cry censorship at any attempt to sequester its freedoms to report whatever satisfied its readership. Behind such political engagement lay an unease that those with power and a taste for repression through litigation would all too easily be able to keep their activities from public opprobrium with legal powers to prevent the revelation of truth, alongside the power to prevent defamation by the spreading of untruth.

2. CONTRACT EXPRESS OR IMPLIED

The liability for breach of confidence arose out of an undertaking, which could mean that in many instances contractual obligation explained the entitlement to sue. Even in the heartland of Chancery, Jessel MR would adopt the view that the equity against breach of confidence was properly grounded in contract, express or implied.[16] To treat the *consensus ad idem* reached by discloser and initial recipient as the core of the right was a preference very much of its day and one that would attract common law minds once the two jurisdictions were combined.[17] At the same time, spelling out a contract allowed the scope of liability to be adapted to the particular circumstances. Undoubtedly there were situations where the contract needed to be agreed, if the defendant was not to be left free to use the information as he wished; and there were also circumstances where assumptions about honest business behaviour provided a ready key to liability.

[14] Sections 1, 2.

[15] Williams, *Public Interest*, 28–32.

[16] *Reuters Telegram* v. *Byron* (1874) 43 LJ Ch 661.

[17] See e.g.,*Vokes* v. *Heather* (1945) 62 RPC 135; but soon after giving this decision, Greene MR, saw the upshot as too narrow—as he would make plain in the leading modern authority of *Saltman* v. *Campbell* (1948) 65 RPC 203.

Deploying the language of implied terms gave the courts plenty of scope to balance the arguments of each side according to their sense of essential justice. But confidential information, so inherently capable of being spread around, could easily be passed to people who were not in any direct relationship to its original holder. And at common law stretching obligations so as to bind third parties ran against the grain of contractual privity. Where the information was passed from recipient to recipient and so reached the defendant indirectly, transmitted down a line of disclosers, it needed the additional bolstering of property, trust, or some requirement of honest or proper behaviour arising in equity. In the post-Judicature Act world, breach of confidence became one of the equitable concepts within which common lawyers would seek to confine liability.[18] Only after 1945 would it become accepted that there were situations in which even an implied contractual obligation of confidence would supply no adequate explanation of the liability that the courts wished to impose. Could, for instance, the entitlement given to courts of equity to award damages in lieu of, or in addition to, an injunction be relied upon where the right in issue arose solely in equity rather than at common law?[19] To equity purists, to allow this to happen would provide an instance of the fusion heresy catalysed by the Judicature Act 1873. As late as 1957, the Court of Appeal would be exercised about whether they could award damages where not even an implied contract could be shown to have been broken.[20]

Most judges would prove reluctant to treat such information as any discreet form of property, even in equity. Cases in which they were tempted to do so tended to be those where the defendant came by the information by a channel that could not be identified. Of this *Prince Albert* v. *Strange* was a prominent example.[21] Another concerned a sports publication which was shown to be copying its cricket results from a limited subscription service, but it could not be said by what route.[22] In the modern law a *sui generis* obligation of good faith arising from the moral obligation to keep secrets would become the usual

[18] So unconfined were the subjects on which people might seek to impose confidential obligations, that legal textwriters would add the topic simply as 'related matter'. Thus it turns up in late nineteenth-century texts on patents and even on trade marks, such as L. B. Sebastian, *Law of Trade Marks and their Registration* (1878), 257 and D. M. Kerly, *Law of Trade-marks, Trade Name and Merchandise Marks* (1894), Ch. 19. In general surveys, it found a place in discussions of remedies (notably the injunction) to prevent 'irreparable injury': see e.g. J. Story, *Commentaries on Equity Jurisprudence* (2nd English edn, 1892), 608–20.

[19] This procedural power was given originally by Lord Cairns' Act 1858.

[20] *Nichrotherm Electrical* v. *Percy* [1957] RPC 207.

[21] At first instance, Knight Bruce VC referred to the breach of trust and property involved, and then Lord Cottenham spoke of the 'right and property' that an author or composer had in an unpublished work: see (1849) 1 Mac. & G. at 42, 42–3.

[22] *Exchange Telegraph* v. *Howard* (1906) 22 TLR 375.

explanation of the right.[23] This opaque rationalization was enough to support an entitlement to an injunction, whether or not a contract was being breached. Even indirect recipients of the information *bona fide* and for value would be enjoined against disclosing or using the information from the time that they were alerted to the fact that it had originally been acquired under conditions of confidence. Later, when the doctrine began to be used to protect the privacy of individuals from intrusion by the press and others into their lives, the need to show that the defendant acquired the information down a chain in which an obligation of confidence had been assumed at some stage would be airbrushed away. But that would occur only when the demand for privacy was roused by the excesses of 'investigative' journalists, prone to scandal-mongering on a scale that dwarfed the alarums of pre-1914 society. In Britain it would take many decades of shifting experience for the *cri de coeur* from Warren and Brandeis to resonate.

---

[23] See generally, e.g. F. Gurry, *Breach of Confidence* (Oxford, 1984), Ch. 3.

VI

Industrial Property: Trade Marks and Unfair Competition

1. PUBLIC AND PRIVATE CONTROL OF MARKETING PRACTICES

In the commerce of the early modern world, raw deception lurked around many corners and laws chased out after it. Well-established traders looked to rights from membership of guilds, possession of franchises, rights in markets and so forth, which could reduce the consequences of fraud for them, as well as shore up their own position as producers and sellers. Myriad regulations operated, many of them at the local level: rules which sought to define the quality or quantity of what was sold—prescriptions on weights and measures, on the content of everything from precious metals to foodstuffs and against adulteration of things that had a recognized 'purity'. Here was a pre-modern agglomeration of laws involving criminal, administrative, or communal processes; and enforced typically by penalties. These regulations existed to protect buyers, and even more the competitors whose trade might be damaged as a result. Officials might prosecute those in breach. Buyers who were deceived might also seek to have these public obligations enforced and rivals could activate the processes.

In the nineteenth century, distribution chains lengthened, and with them grew the labelling, packaging, and advertising of products and services. Accordingly these activities also called for control. Rival traders would suffer when a dubious salesman engaged in deceitful marketing. A public remedy was appropriate when it was hard to say which of the competitors lost business as the result of the fraud.[1] But one of the surer guides to quality for the public lay in the particular marks or names or get-up that reputable providers used to distinguish their products and businesses from those of others. If a trade rival misled purchasers

---

[1] The adulteration of food provides a rich history, which lies at the fringe of the present chapter. It embraces not just fraudulent practices but also the manipulation of the legislative process by groups of traders seeking the exclusion of others who have sought to introduce alternative products (margarine in place of butter being a well-known instance): see F. A. Filby, *History of Food Adulteration and Analysis* (1934); I. Paulus, *The Search for Pure Food* (1974).

by imitating such a 'badge of origin' and the victims objected to the poor quality of what they got by mistake, they would in many cases have an action on the case either in contract or, if fraud could be made out, for the deceit. But it was the trader who first used the mark who was likely to suffer sustained injury from its imitation.

2. THE COMMON LAW ACTION AGAINST 'PASSING, PALMING, OR PUTTING OFF'

In the pre-industrial period there had been virtually no printed reports either of common law courts awarding damages, or courts of equity granting injunctions, to traders who suffered this type of injury.[2] But already relief by civil process had begun, which formed the nucleus of the modern law of trade marks.[3] Lord Mansfield had made notes of cases before him in which plaintiffs gained damages for imitations of packaging, false attribution of artistic prints, and misuse of marks.[4] During Lord Eldon's reign in Chancery, he granted injunctions against 'that sort of fraud which has been attempted by setting up the same trade in the same place, under the same sign or name, the party giving himself out to be the same person'.[5] His approach to jurisdiction was by analogy to actions for infringement of patents and copyright.[6] The cause of action accordingly arose at

---

[2] Marking practices were well-enough known from the medieval period onwards and were policed through one or other form of trade or local regulation. In a few fields—gold and silver wares, cutlery and cloth—special systems evolved and to some extent continued their own arrangements into modern times. These will not be pursued here. But see generally, F. I. Schechter, *Historical Foundations of the Law relating to Trade-Marks* (1925) Chs 2–5; L. Bently, 'The Making of Modern Trade Mark Law: the Construction of the Legal Concept of Trade Mark (1860–1880)', in L. Bently et al. (eds), *Trade Marks and Brands* (2008), Ch. 1 at 5–6.

[3] See Schechter, *Historical Foundations*, Ch. 6. For the critique of the modern law that was the end-point of his history, see below, 1010–12.

[4] J. Adams, 'Intellectual Property Cases in Lord Mansfield's Court Notebooks' (1987) 8 *JLH* 18, 22–4; and see *Singleton* v. *Bolton* (1783) 2 Doug. 293. Victorian courts were given to finding an historical justification for the common law action in Popham's report of *Southern* v. *How*, despite the lack of substantiation in other reports: (1618) Poph. 143; cf. Cro. Jac. 468; 2 Roll. Rep. 26; J. Bridg. 125. They had then to explain Lord Hardwicke's refusal of an interim injunction in *Blanchard* v. *Hill* (1742) 2 Atk. 484. One way of doing so stressed that the plaintiff's claim had been based on a title to use a mark on playing cards granted by the Playing Card Makers Company; and the Lord Chancellor had disparaged the company as an illegal monopoly: see N. Dawson, 'English Trade Mark Law in the Eighteenth Century' (2003) 24 *JLH* 111.

[5] *Hogg* v. *Kirby* (1803) 8 Ves. 215 (title of a magazine); *Crutwell* v. *Lye* (1810) 17 Ves. 335 (business name of carrier); *Day* v. *Day* (device mark): 1816, referred to in *Eden on Injunctions* (1821), 314.

[6] The similarities would be a recurrent theme, as passing-off liability became established; see e.g. Lord Cranworth, *Leather Cloth* v. *American Leather* (1865) 11 HLC 523, 533–4. The signal difference was that the right to protect a mark would always be seen as lasting as long as used in order to sustain a reputation (and later, with trade mark registration, as long as the mark remained on the Register).

common law, with equity acting in its auxiliary role.[7] Eldon would grant relief disposing of the whole cause in very clear cases.[8] Otherwise he would either give interlocutory relief until the allegation of passing off could be established by the verdict of a jury in a trial at common law; or he would provide no relief until the plaintiff had obtained his verdict, with the possibility that he might direct a 'feigned issue' to be tried at common law.[9]

Describing this movement in the courts of law and equity in terms of the different relief that they could provide evokes comparisons with the jurisdiction over personal defamation. As we have seen, in defamation a strong strain of liberal independence ensured that libel and slander claims could not trigger injunctive relief in equity.[10] By contrast, liability for passing off moved quite swiftly to become in some sense a means of protecting a proprietary element in the value of a business, thereby making equitable procedure a means for suppressing the considerable growth in misappropriation of trade marks. The division of jurisdiction would, however, shed some of its significance once, in the 1850s, each of the courts would be given the other's remedial powers; and then, by Rolt's Act of 1862, Chancery courts were required to determine issues of common law without referring them for trial to a common law jury, unless it was 'more convenient' to have them decided at Assizes.[11] Even more significant in the case of passing off, was the introduction of parallel protection through the registration scheme for some trade marks for goods under legislation of 1875.[12]

The more intriguing parallel, in any case, came over the question whether liability turned on the defendant's deliberate intent or recklessness. As we have seen, with defamation the courts for decades avoided settling this theoretical issue, only opting finally for strict liability in 1911.[13] In passing off, equity was already moving in that direction by the mid-nineteenth century, but only by a transition in which the root justification for what the courts were doing took second place to pragmatic choices over how far the cause of action should be allowed to go.[14] Amid this uncertainty, situations that were in a sense intermediate between

---

[7] Accordingly, in *Lord Byron* v. *Johnston* (1816) 2 Mer. 29, the reprobate poet secured an injunction to stop poems not by him from being published under his name.

[8] Two decades later, Cottenham LC would regard it as unacceptable for him to direct that no common law proceedings should take place: *Motley* v. *Downman* (1837) 3 My. & Cr. 1. By the 1840s, the great advantage of interlocutory relief, if only it could be obtained, was tempered in one important way: the plaintiff would be required in return to give an undertaking to meet the defendant's damages if it turned out at trial that the plaintiff had no claim.

[9] See above, pp. 944, n. 57.

[10] See above, pp. 849–51.

[11] Chancery Regulation Act 1862, 25 & 26 Vict. c. 42, ss 1, 2.

[12] See below, pp. 1001–4.

[13] See above, pp. 862–3.

[14] For the position in respect of patents, copyright and designs, see above, 981, n. 17.

defamation and passing off—those that were treated as 'trade libel', or 'injurious falsehood'—were restrained within the confines of malice and specific damage that ring-fenced business torts in general.[15] Not so for the opposite poles of passing off and defamation: both concerned conduct that was treated as legally unacceptable in the absence of defined justification. The structure of thought could seem cumbersome, even arbitrary, in its refusal to adopt such large concepts as rights to privacy and against unfair competition. But that is how England's superior judges built on traditions that were by instinct pitted against unnecessary regulation and compounded out of hard experience both at the bar and on the bench.

Reported decisions at common law concerning passing off begin after 1820 when issues arose about the scope of the action that was emerging by analogy to deceit. In *Sykes* v. *Sykes*[16] the defendants had imitated the plaintiff's name-mark, 'Sykes' Patent', on their shot belts and powder flasks, and were pronounced liable even though the retailers supplied were not misled into thinking they came from the plaintiff. It was enough that the retailers were supplied with the means of misleading their own customers—supplying the 'instruments of fraud' as the activity was later called.[17] The danger that the plaintiff might lose trade from the misuse of his badge in the marketplace gave him his own action and the King's Bench gave no sign that it was deciding anything new. In *Blofeld* v. *Payne*,[18] the defendant had obtained some of the 'envelopes' in which the plaintiff sold his hones, in order to pass off his own hones as the plaintiff's. Again, the King's Bench took an expansive view: the action lay even in the absence of any proof that the purchasers would get a product of lesser quality or that the plaintiff had suffered specific damage. The jury were therefore entitled to award damages upon the likelihood that trade loss would have followed.[19]

A decade later Lord Cottenham granted an injunction in favour of Millington, owner of the great Crowley Ironworks of County Durham, against Fox, who stamped his steel with 'Crowley' and associated marks. Fox pleaded both that he knew nothing of the plaintiff and his business, and that the stamps had a generic meaning, indicating the quality of the steel, not its origin; but in any case

---

[15] See above, pp. 859–60.

[16] (1824) 3 B. & C. 541.

[17] Later this principle would be extended to foreign trading where the customers who would be misled were in colonial or other jurisdictions abroad: see, notably, *Johnston* v. *Orr-Ewing* (1882) 7 App Cas 219, HL.

[18] He did not have to show that any purchaser had been deceived; the mere likelihood was enough: *Blofeld* v. *Payne* (1833) 4 B. & Ad. 410.

[19] In the case the damages had been assessed at a farthing, the jury finding no difference in quality. Coupled with equity's ability to grant an injunction *quia timet* to stop a threatened injury, this would make clear how determined both courts were to put down passing off.

he undertook not to use them in future. The Lord Chancellor heard the appeal mainly to consider whether the plaintiff should have his costs after the defendant had conceded defeat. But he was prepared to maintain the injunction (thus accepting that the stamps indicated origin, not quality as such); and he did so even though no intention to deceive had been shown.[20] The circumstances of the case scarcely suggested a major shift in the developing law. Five years later, dealing with another stamping of iron case in which the defendant had won a verdict on a plea that the stamps had become a generic indicator of quality, Tindal CJ insisted that in the common law conception it was necessary to show that the defendant intended to pass off his goods as the plaintiff's.[21] This kept it in line with its progenitor, the tort of deceit, where proof of fraud was a requisite.[22]

Had an essential difference emerged between the wrong at common law and in equity—the former protecting against a fraudulent act, the latter enforcing an equitable property in the mark? Or was equity merely using its auxiliary jurisdiction in a creative spirit that supplemented the common law decisions? An injunction, after all, looked only to the future. At just this time, Lord Langdale MR would state a proposition that would be regularly relied upon in both jurisdictions, before and after they were amalgamated in 1876: '[A man] may not be allowed to use names, marks, letters or other *indicia*, by which he may induce purchasers to believe that the goods which he is selling are the manufacture of another person';[23] and he denied that the claim could be based on property in the mark or name.[24] In the 1850s, Page Wood VC (later Hatherley LC) would take the same position that the basis of the action was fraud, not property; and it was he who heard a great many of the rising tally of passing-off cases.[25]

What the distinction in the approaches of the two systems amounted to would long retain a certain mystery, contributing thereby to the somewhat fluid nature of the wrong. Whilst common law and equity remained separate jurisdictions,

---

[20] But he was not allowed his costs!

[21] *Crawshay* v. *Thompson* (1842) 4 Man. & Gr. 356.

[22] This places the emerging wrong in a context where equally equity had larger ideas of liability than at common law: see the growth of the doctrine of innocent misrepresentation and its ultimate limitation: see above, Vol. XII, Pt 2, pp. 417–32.

[23] *Perry* v. *Truefitt* (1842) 6 Beav. 66; often relied on thereafter: see e.g. Lord Kingsdown, *Leather Cloth* v. *American Leather* (1865) 11 H.L.C. 523, 538; Lord Herschell, *Reddaway* v. *Banham* [1896] AC 199, 209. In the headnote of *Perry*, the term 'passing off' was used, though 'palming off' and 'putting off' were at the time employed as synonyms: Wadlow, *The Law of Passing Off* (3d edn, 2004), 17.

[24] This led him to refuse a leading doctor an injunction, when his name had been used to endorse a medicine without any consent, because essentially he was not a pill-maker: *Clark* v. *Freeman* (1842) 11 Beav. 112. Later judges tended to criticize the decision as unduly narrow in not recognizing a person's 'property' in his own name: see e.g. Cairns LJ, *Maxwell* v. *Hogg* (1867) LR 2 Ch App 307, 310.

[25] For his role alongside others on the bench, and for the sudden burst of lawbooks and other literature on the subject, see Bently, 'Trade Marks as Property', 12–15.

the question whether fraud had to be proved was answered in procedural terms: equity would give interlocutory relief when the case was plain; but if it was not, the issue would be referred to a jury and the defendant's intent to injure the plaintiff would be used as the practical test of whether he had a sufficient right.[26] Passing off was to be an unusual tort, in that prohibitory relief was becoming available against future wrongful acts, even where no damages, or account of profits or equitable compensation was allowed for past innocent conduct.[27] The action accordingly presented a trade risk to an 'innocent' who did not know of the earlier use of a sign as a mark, or believed it to be a generic description—and in the local worlds of so much Victorian trade, this was a not infrequent hazard. Equity obliged him to keep eyes and ears open, however much he might be investing honestly in presenting and promoting his own business through the mark.[28] In any case, a different characteristic of the action might keep it within bounds. This was the need to show that the defendant's conduct gave him a benefit at the expense of the plaintiff. Later in the century, the Court of Appeal insisted that it did not suffice just to show that the plaintiff was benefiting from its conduct. The plaintiffs, proprietors of the well-known morning newspaper, *The Morning Post*, failed to stop the defendant from changing the name of its evening paper to *The Evening Post*. While the court suspected that the change had been made because the public would take it that the two were from the same stable, the fact that the two papers would appear at different times of the day meant that the plaintiffs had not suffered any identifiable loss.[29] There had, in other words, to be at least a likelihood of damage to the plaintiff's goodwill. It was not therefore open to a court to find passing off just on the basis that purchasers were likely to assume some association in trade between plaintiff and defendant. It would, for instance, be difficult to prevent one trader from 'diluting' a mark by applying it to products or services of a different kind from the plaintiff's.[30]

As elsewhere, Lord Eldon's tying of injunctions to the protection of property played a role in the development.[31] Indeed the analogy to 'property' was the easier to make than with patents or copyright, in that no specific duration of the right

---

[26] See *Croft* v. *Day* (1843) 7 Beav. 84. 87; *Farina* v. *Silverlock* (1856) 6 De G. M. & G. 214, 217—22.

[27] See Lord Westbury, *Edelsten* v. *Edelsten* (1863) 1 De G. J. & S. 185, 199. The same essential distinction would later be inserted into the statute law of patents, copyright, and designs: see above, p. 981, n. 35.

[28] Even in the twentieth century it was not unusual for counsel to argue for enlarging (or constraining) equity by seeking to show that Chancery had (or had not) been the first to intervene—a curious use of history in search of legal policy.

[29] *Borthwick* v. *Evening Post* (1888) 37 Ch D 449.

[30] See further below, pp. 1009–10.

[31] Injunctions only protected property, in Lord Eldon's view: see above, 849, n. 5. Re-emphasis of this view in *Emperor of Austria* v. *Day* (1861) 3 De G. F. & J. 149 would prove timely.

needed to be set. Since objections to wrongful marking prevented no one from trading in commodities or services under other signs, and since the misleading of customers would go on so long as the user with the reputation continued in business, there was no reason why any specified time limit should be placed on the right. A final injunction would accordingly carry no time limit, though it would be drafted so as to limit its scope to the prevention of whatever passing off had been proved.[32]

In the 1860s there was a drive to give added meaning to the idea that the right to the mark was a form of property. Lockeian theory had after all conceived property as arising through 'occupancy'; and in the case of a trade mark that might be said to occur from the use of it, at least in circumstances where it had no other meaning. A businessman would naturally prefer a secure right that was effective from his first adoption of a mark, and this could be crucial where rivals, for whatever reason, were after the same mark. One way of establishing surer priority would be through a register—an idea which, as we shall see, some chambers of commerce and other industrial groups were pursuing vigorously in the mid-century decades.[33] A particular virtue of registration would be as an aid in fighting the misuse of well-known British trade marks abroad. Other countries were developing protection on that basis and were wary of reciprocal trade agreements for which the British could only show a right built upon judicial precedent.[34]

In 1862, however, Palmerston's government preferred to strengthen the criminal laws against misuse of merchandise marks without introducing registration as a preliminary step in respect of trade marks.[35] Almost at once thereafter, Westbury LC heard a string of cases in which he insisted that equity's injunctive relief was based on property in the mark and that the proof of passing-off activity was only evidence going to establish that property.[36] In his eagerness to stress the superiority of this conception, he not only disapproved of the rejection of any property justification for passing off;[37] he also made the dubious claim that the common law's advances in *Sykes* and *Blofeld* had been achievements of equity.[38]

---

[32] See below, p. 1003, n. 79.

[33] See below, p. 999.

[34] See below, n. 55.

[35] See below, pp. 1000–1001, for a perceptive assessment of passing-off doctrine, see E. Lloyd, *Law of Trade Marks* (1862).

[36] *Edelsten* v. *Edelsten.* (1863) 1 De G. J. & S. 185, 199–200; *Leather Cloth* v. *American Leather Cloth* (1863) 4 De G. J. & S. 137 (LC), (1865) 11 HLC 523 (Lords Cranworth and Kingsdown accepting Westbury's characterization); *Hall* v. *Barrows* (1864) 4 De G. J. & S. 150; *McAndrew* v. *Bassett* (1864) 4 De G. J. & S. 965. Westbury (LC, 1861–5) had (as Bethell) previously been Palmerston's AG, as well as a formidable leader of the Chancery bar.

[37] *Leather Cloth* (above, n. 36) at 140.

[38] *See Edelsten* (above, n. 36) at 199–200. Later judges were inclined also to insist that at law the two marks had to be the same, not merely deceptively similar—but this too seems to have been a gloss put by equity on earlier common law judgments.

The first reason for Westbury's resort to a property characterization was to justify injunctive relief even against an innocent defendant, thus erecting *Millington* v. *Fox* into a primary authority. It was a strategic departure from the slowly emergent business torts at common law and may rank as equity's largest border raid of modern times.[39] Otherwise Westbury derived only moderate consequences from his property characterization. He used it to tackle some of the more intractable difficulties in defining a plaintiff's entitlement. When the mark had been used by a succession of business owners, it could be tricky for the current user to show that the reputation with the public had become his;[40] and he would fail where the mark 'belonged' to a third party.[41] Westbury was clear that a trade mark could be transferred only as part of the goodwill of a business; property in the mark implied no ability to assign it separately—a view that might be thought to undermine the very characterization as property.[42] He insisted that ownership of the mark went only to its use on the owner's type of goods, rather than on some other type of article;[43] and that it could be lost if he used it himself to mislead customers about, for instance, geographical origin or physical qualities;[44] likewise if it had become a generic word for the type of product, since then the ability of the mark to distinguish trade origin was lost.[45] These were limitations that led to a continuing insistence that passing off was remediable only where plaintiffs could show damage, or the likelihood of it, to themselves.[46]

He did not, in his four years as Lord Chancellor, seek to move the law towards a position in which the mere adoption of a mark was enough to found a passing-off claim. Rather he avoided specifying the point in time at which it could be

[39] Equally, criminal liabilities under the Merchandise Marks Act 1862 required proof of *mens rea*. Only in the 1887 Act would the onus of proof shift to the defendant in certain instances.

[40] *Edelsten*; *Hall* (above, n. 36); and for an earlier example, *Motley* v. *Downman* (1837) 3 M. & Cr. 1.

[41] *Leather Cloth* (above, n. 36).

[42] *Hall* (above, n. 36): sale to the survivor of a partnership permitted provided that it included value of mark as part of goodwill. If members of a family business went off into separate enterprises, were they each entitled to the reputation accorded to the mark before the split? Page Wood VC held that each had a right to prevent a third party from adopting the mark: *Dent* v. *Turpin* (1861) 30 LJ Ch 495; *Southorn* v. *Reynolds* (1865) 12 LT (NS) 75; cf. Vaughan Williams LJ, *Jamieson* v. *Jamieson* (1898) 15 RPC 193, CA.

[43] *McAndrew* (above, n. 36); as to this important limitation, see below, 1009–10.

[44] Not infrequently, a plaintiff was attacked for claiming that his product remained patented when that was no longer true. Absence of clean hands was one prominent reason for refusing the plaintiff relief in *Leather Cloth* (above, n. 36).

[45] *Wotherspoon* v. *Currie* (1872) LR 5 HL 508 ('Glenfield' starch). For the case law immediately before the introduction of registration and the Judicature Acts, see H. Ludlow and H. Jenkyns, *Law of Trade-Marks and Trade-Names* (1873); and with equal emphasis after 1875 in F. M. Adams, *Treatise on the Law of Trade Marks* (2nd edn, 1876); cf. Sebastian, *Trade Marks*, Chs 2, 7–8.

[46] See *Borthwick* v. *Evening Post*, above n. 29.

said that a trader had become the proprietor of the mark. The claimant, he said, did not have to show a general reputation with the public at large. It was enough that articles bearing the mark had gone into the market and there obtained acceptance and reputation, 'whereby the [mark] gets currency as an indication of superior quality, or of some other indication which renders the article so [marked] acceptable to the public'.[47] Where there was reason to doubt whether the alleged insignia was understood as an indication of origin, but the defendant was shown to be intent on passing off, the mark was presumed to be distinctive of the plaintiff.[48] Thus on the question of proof, fraud could still have a decisive role.[49] Evidently enough, in the decade when the concept of a governmental register of trade marks was still resisted, Westbury seemed intent on formulating a passing-off action that could calm the concerns of leading traders over the imitation of brands. How much further he might have sought to go cannot be known; he resigned from office in 1865 for his part in two separate scandals.[50] At this period, talk of a 'common law trade mark' seems to have gained a certain currency, though with what consequences it was difficult to say. As with 'common law copyright', or for that matter, 'common law marriage', it was a form of terminology that arose with attempts to persuade judges to evolve rules by precedent. In this case, it is hard to see what meaning distinct from the right of action against passing off it ever acquired.

3. A REGISTER OF TRADE MARKS

The campaign to create an official register for trade marks proved to be a form of regulation over business that went too far for politicians in early 1860s. True it was that by then trade mark 'piracy' had spread across many British industries, not only in the home market but in the colonies and elsewhere. By the 1850s, there was much use of group names from Britain by foreign producers in international trade: 'Sheffield' for cutlery, 'Manchester' for cotton goods, 'Lancashire' for iron, and so on. Prussians, Russians, Austrians, and many others were ready to use these shared labels, as much as the brands of individual makers, in markets around the world. But to impose any control beyond Britain required recognition by other states; and it was becoming apparent that the only basis for this could be reciprocal legal protection in each country. Once the French set up

---

[47] *McAndrew* (above, n. 36), at 386.

[48] *McAndrew*, at 386–7.

[49] As Lindley LJ would later put it, 'Why should we be astute to say [the defendant] cannot succeed in doing that which he is straining every nerve to do?': *Slazenger* v. *Feltham* (1889) 6 RPC at 538, 539.

[50] See above, p. 955, n. 115.

a registry for marks in 1857, the lack of any equivalent in Britain made mutual recognition difficult to seek without considerable strengthening of the law at home.[51]

A Commons Select Committee of 1862 received voluminous evidence about the problems—from the cutlery industry around Sheffield, cloth manufacturers in Lancashire, threadmakers in Glasgow, and a whole splay of others around the country.[52] Plenty of graphic examples of fraudulent labelling and advertising were placed before the Committee. Indignation ran high. Most of these witnesses had as their first objective a strengthening of the criminal law, particularly in respect of the 'forging' of trade marks for goods, but also for other false labelling; and above all the complainants wanted summary process so that they could put down blatant imitation cheaply and quickly.[53] The Committee's first task was to review the bill that became the Merchandise Marks Act of that year. At the same time it had before it a bill, promoted by the Sheffield Chamber of Commerce, involving the registration of trade marks at the Designs Registry.[54]

This second bill sought to use registration as a means of fostering civil law sanctions. One attraction of doing so would be to provide an equivalent platform to that in countries such as France. As already mentioned, this could improve the chances of negotiating mutual protection agreements for marks in trans-national trade; and indeed the 1860s saw a growth of such provisions as part of bi-lateral trade agreements.[55] However, it adopted the strategy of treating a registered mark as personal property, 'transmissible according to the ordinary rules of law affecting personal property'. As Bently has shown in detail, to allow a mark to be attached to the business of whoever became its registered proprietor from time to time provoked great concern among witnesses to the Committee. For them, the essence of marking was the association that would arise with a

---

[51] For details of this growing realization, the reform pressures that followed, and the burst of legal literature, see L. Bently, 'The Making of Modern Trade Mark Law: The Construction of the Legal Concept of a Trade Mark (1860–1880)', in L. Bently et al. *Trade Marks and Brands* (Cambridge, 2008), 6–16.

[52] For the prominent part played by chambers of commerce, see A. R. Ilersic and P. F. B. Liddle, *Parliament of Commerce* (1960), Ch. 9; G. R. Searle, *Entrepreneurial Politics in Mid-Victorian Britain* (New York, 1993), Ch. 5.

[53] One reason why attacks on fraudulent marking received such prominence was that if an objection was to be taken to, for instance, adulteration of a product, this was likely to involve scientific evidence, and could lead to conflicts such as those between public analysts and government chemists. For some of the difficulties, see Paulus, *Search for Pure Food* , esp. Ch. 2.

[54] *PP* 1862 (17), V, 275, building upon a shorter bill of the previous session, on which Westbury (then Bethell AG) would have been consulted: *PP* 1861 (54), 535.

[55] Clause 23 would have given the Board of Trade power to negotiate such bi-lateral agreements. In the event provisions concerning trade marks continued to be attached to general trade agreements.

particular source of the goods, and the public could easily be deceived by such changes of ownership.[56]

The government's bill, drawn for them by leading patents counsel, W. M. Hindmarch, abjured any register.[57] Hindmarch strongly opposed a system that would provide rights over marks in advance of their actual use in trade.[58] His fear was of undue monopoly; so his opinion held something of the same suspicion that strict free-trade liberals were directing against patents and copyright in just this period.[59] Common law and equity gave no protection of marks before use and, not surprisingly perhaps, Hindmarch proclaimed the effectiveness of those jurisdictions, while admiring their awareness of the need to impose controls over the scope of the markholders' rights.[60] So criminal process provided the path towards greater control. The Merchandise Marks Act first created the misdemeanour of 'forging or counterfeiting a trade mark', thus adding to the borrowings of 'theft' and 'piracy' to describe industrial property infringements. Only after this did it proceed to outlaw other forms of deceptive trading, such as making deliberately false statements about the qualities of goods to be sold. The special identification of trade mark forgery in this law not only underscored the particular objection to such a form of false trading, it also settled on a definition of 'trade mark' which characterized it in terms of its ability to distinguish goods by their origin. So the offence applied to any 'name, signature, word, letter, device, emblem, figure, sign, seal, stamp, diagram, label, ticket or mark of any other description lawfully used by any person to denote any chattel, to be the manufacture, workmanship, production or merchandise of such person'.[61] As Bently shows, this was much more embracing in scope than some of the notions

---

[56] L. Bently, 'From Communication to Thing: Historical Aspects of the Conceptualisation of Trade Marks as Property', in G. Dinwoodie and M. D. Janis, *Trade Mark Law and Theory* (2008),16–19.

[57] *PP* 1862 (187), III, 197. Sir William Atherton, Westbury's successor as AG, was one of its sponsors.

[58] See his evidence to the Select Committee, above, n, 54, qq. 2752 *et seq.*

[59] See above, 894–5, 954–60.

[60] The Merchandise Marks Act 1862 (25 & 26 Vict. c. 88) would contain his s 11, which expressly preserved the rights of action at law and in equity. It added that the privilege against self-incrimination would not apply in such proceedings on condition that the evidence could not then be used in a prosecution. This would only survive until the 1887 Act, but it would be resurrected a century later in the Supreme Court Act 1981, s 72.

[61] Broad as it was, it was by no means clear that it stretched to cover shared interests in geographical names of the 'Sheffield for cutlery' type, or other words or signs that suggested other qualities than the place of manufacture. These, however, were important in a world which had yet to conceive the idea of certification marks or rights in geographical denominations of origin. There was accordingly a distinct tendency to allow passing-off relief where the misrepresentation was about locality, rather than individual source: see Bently, 'Modern Trade Mark', 29–32, for texts and judgments which suggested this.

being promoted at the time, which might have limited protection (particularly protection through a register) to personal names, or elaborated devices, or numbers or stamps identifying particular ranges of product.[62] At the same time, as he points out, at this early stage of marketing as a distinct business strategy, marks often used the name of the owner of the business and thereby established a personal association of a kind not totally distinct from the claim of an author to copyright or an inventor to a patent.[63] It is perhaps that perception which enabled Warren and Brandeis to include trade mark rights among the legal developments pointing towards the protection of individual privacy.[64]

The idea of a register that provided rights equivalent to public use from the moment of registration did not, however, die. In 1869, the government presented an extensive bill providing for such a system and containing much that would in the event only gradually filter into British law in its twentieth-century form.[65] Thus it allowed for the registration of all 'trade marks' with only limited exceptions. Marks would be admitted save where there were earlier registrations or uses of the same or deceptively similar marks. The bill set out conditions that would allow more than one person to register the same mark, where genuine trading established a basis for doing so. It had elaborate arrangements for the problems of transfer that had taxed Westbury and other Chancery judges. It preserved rights of action in law and equity.[66] But Gladstone's government did not see it into law.

The change came about only in 1875, introduced by Cairns LC for the succeeding Conservative regime.[67] This Registration of Trade Marks Act was more reticent than the 1869 bill, leaving much of the development of detail to the new Registrar, and tribunals above him.[68] Although the drafting avoided stressing the matter, registration was assumed to give some form of ownership, the registrant being a 'registered proprietor'.[69] For new marks, registration was permitted for particular forms of business names and signatures and for 'a distinctive device, mark, heading, label or ticket'. Only if they were already old, were special and distinctive words or numerals registrable.[70] The Act explicitly stated that

---

[62] Bently, 'Modern Trade Mark', 20–7.

[63] For examples, see *ibid.*

[64] See above, p. 848, n.4.

[65] *PP* 1869 (287), vii.

[66] See cls 14–21, 50.

[67] An outstanding leader of the Chancery bar, Cairns was prominent in many of the passing-off cases of the 1850s and 1860s.

[68] Appeals lay to the Commissioners of Patents.

[69] Bently, 'Trade Marks as Property'.

[70] Section 10. '…a fancy word…or words not in common use' were admitted by the Patents, Designs and Trade Marks Act 1883, s 64, but the phrase provoked many disputes: see e.g. the

registration 'shall be deemed to be equivalent to public use'.[71] However, proceedings for infringement of any mark that could be registered were disallowed until registration had occurred.[72] No reservation of the jurisdiction in passing off was included in the Act, in contrast with earlier legislative drafts.[73] In 1872, the Board of Trade published papers on the registration systems of France, Italy, the German states, and elsewhere;[74] and the patterns revealed by this exercise had some influence on these and other provisions of the 1875 Act and its successor in 1883.[75]

The perception of Kerly, 20 years later, was that

[the sections] seem to have been undoubtedly intended to limit and define the classes of symbols which could be applied as trade-marks, to restrict the latitude of choice of trade-marks which existed before 1875, and to make registration a condition precedent to all litigation in respect of subsequently acquired trade-marks corresponding to the trade-mark... before the Acts; but the intention was not clearly expressed.[76]

Quite simply, the courts at first assumed, and then expressly held, that nothing in the Registration Acts took away or altered the passing-off right previously established.[77] If the provision in the Trade Marks Act requiring registration before suit had any effect at all, it was to scotch attempts to sue upon unregistered or 'common law' marks for which the plaintiff had no sufficient trading reputation from which to demonstrate passing off.[78] In *Faulder* v. *Rushton*, the defendant had succeeded in having the plaintiff's mark ('Silverpan' for jams) removed from

---

Departmental Committee Report (below n. 95), paras 25–7. For the wider definition introduced in 1905, see below, 1005.

[71] Section 2.

[72] Section 1, revised at once (by the Trade Marks Registration Amendment Act 1876, s 1) to apply to common law as well as equitable proceedings for infringement. Much concerned initially with getting old marks onto the register, this Act also provided for a certificate of refusal of registration of such marks, so that they could at once be the subject of proceedings in court concerning the refusal: s 2.

[73] Cf. e.g. the proposal of 1869, above, 1001.

[74] *PP* 1872 [C.896], liv, 585. There would later be quite regular investigations of the law and practice elsewhere, starting with *PP* 1878–9 [C. 2284, 2420], lxiii, 469, 613; but cf. the Commons SC on the Trade Marks Bill, *PP* 1875 (365), xiv, 541, 574.

[75] See, however, the Merchandise Marks Act 1862, s 11; above, n. 60.

[76] Kerly, *The Law of Trade-Marks,Trade-Name, and Merchandise Marks* (1894) 382, and also 265–70; see also Bently, 'Modern Trade Mark', 33–7.

[77] The first cases to make this assumption included Lord Blackburn's disquisition in *Singer* v. *Loog* (1882) 8 App Cas 15, HL; *Mitchell* v. *Henry* (1880) 15 Ch D 649, CA; *Goodfellow* v. *Prince* (1887) 35 Ch D 9, CA; *Jay* v. *Ladler* (1888) 40 Ch D 649. One consequence was that a mark with a considerable reputation only in a foreign country could not be sued upon in England until it had gained registration or sufficient recognition there: Kerly, *Trade-Marks, Trade-Name*, 454; *Collins* v. *Reeves* (1858) 26 LJ Ch 56. This can scarcely have contributed to bi-lateral negotiations for mutual protection.

[78] Cf. Wadlow, *Passing Off*, 29. See *Great Tower Street Tea* v. *Langford* (1887) 5 RPC 66 (Stirling J.); *Curtis* v. *Harvey & Pape* (1887) 5 RPC 146 (North J.). One explanation is that the new Act abolished

the register. In subsequent proceedings for passing off, in which the plaintiff succeeded, Cozens Hardy MR pointed out that, were the mark still registered, the
plaintiff would have had an infringement action without proof of likelihood of
damage. He would also have obtained an order not to use the mark on goods for
which it was registered, as distinct from passing-off relief in the form of an order
not to use the mark so as to mislead customers as to trade source.[79] Infringement
of the mark and relief against passing off were accordingly separate and, where
appropriate, cumulative causes of action.[80] And so the Trade Marks Act 1905
would explicitly provide, burying any further scope for argument.[81]

The 1875 Act required registrations to be for goods or classes of goods (a form
of pigeon-holing that would in time gain international agreement[82]). A mark
could not be registered for the same goods or 'goods of the same description' as
another mark already on the register;[83] but only if the latter was the same or similar enough to be 'calculated to deceive'.[84] Infringement of the registered mark was
confined to its use on goods within the registration; but it would occur where
there was the same degree of similarity between the marks.[85]

In the early years, the Registry had to get through the pile of applications covering some 45,000 'old' marks. In some cases it was faced with genuine claims
from unrelated traders for the same or similar marks for the same or similar
goods. That the marks had been separately used without demur until registration
suggests how local so much trade was. The Registrar evolved a rule of thumb:
up to three such applicants could have concurrent registrations; but over that
number the mark would be considered common to the trade and registrable by
none of them.[86]

any notion that there had previously been an action for infringement of a 'common law trade mark'.
Evidence that there had been such an action in some way distinct from passing off seems elusive.

[79] This qualified form of injunction against passing off had been introduced in *Seixo* v. *Provezende*
(1866) LR 1 Ch App 192, CA.

[80] (1903) 20 RPC 477, CA.

[81] Section 54.

[82] In the Nice Agreement on Classification of Marks 1957.

[83] The reference to 'goods of the same description' was introduced in the 1883 Act, s 72(2), giving
rise to such decisions as *Re Australian Wine Importers' Trade Mark* (1889) 6 RPC 311, CA. The 1875
Act, s 6, had instead referred to 'marks in the same class'.

[84] The phrase 'calculated to deceive' had been used in passing off decisions, much as in defamation law, in the sense of 'fit' or 'adapted' to mislead. It referred only to the effect of an action and not
to the intention of the defendant: see e.g. *Rodgers* v. *Nowill* (1847) 5 CB 109. In the Registration Acts
it was taken in the same sense.

[85] See Kerly, *Trade-Marks, Trade-Name*, 305–8, 318–21. A statutory definition of infringement of a
registered mark occurred only in the Trade Marks Act 1905, s 39.

[86] The rule was given statutory form in the 1883 Act, s 74(3), but not repeated in 1905. The effect
was that the concurrent proprietors could each sue to restrain third parties from using their mark;
but they could not sue each other, save on evidence showing passing off: Kerly, *Trade Marks, Trade-
Name*, 325–8.

In limiting transfer of a mark to situations where the goodwill of the business was being assigned or transmitted, it was also provided that the registration should be 'determinable with such goodwill'.[87] This anticipated the power to have a mark removed for non-use. A mechanism would be provided in the 1905 revision of the statute law, which allowed an interested person to petition for the removal or limitation of a registered mark on the ground that it had not been registered with a *bona fide* intent to use it on the goods prescribed or had not been used as a mark for them during the previous five years.[88] This was a fairly lenient curb on the stockpiling of trade marks.[89] Even so, it made the important point that, in British law, even the registered right conferred no absolute property on the registered proprietor.[90] Likewise with transactions that purported to transfer a mark independently of the goodwill in a business with which the proprietor was connected. If that occurred, with the result that it was then unclear which of two separate businesses was the source of the marked products, the registration would be declared void.[91]

The Act of 1875 was drafted to give the privilege of registration only to those marks which were at the time commonly taken to be indications of the origin of the goods concerned, and which therefore did not bear other meanings, such as words suggesting that the products had specific or general qualities, or that they came from a particular place, or bore a personal name that others might want to use as their own.[92] The Registry, it seems, was scrupulous in rejecting marks of the latter kind. They could, after all, be protected from encroachment where claimants could show passing off because the mark had become distinctive of their own products. As we have just seen, the courts refused to allow passing off to be conditioned by any investigation into whether the mark could, and therefore should, have been registered.[93]

---

[87] Section 2.

[88] Trade Marks Act 1905, s 37; non-use could be excused if there were exceptional circumstances in the trade. The registration had to be renewed at 14-year intervals—a useful source of income for the Patent Office: see ss 28–31.

[89] Under later legislation in the United States and Canada, for instance, some use would have to be positively proved at each renewal of the registration.

[90] It would take decades more for the French and German registration systems, gummed up in some industries by stock-piled registrations of what were regarded as the 'best' marks, to introduce controls over unused marks: G. Schricker, 'Loss of Trademark Rights by Nonuse: A Study of German and Comparative Law' (1971) 2 *IIC*, ii, 173–205.

[91] *Bowden Brake* v. *Bowden Wire* (1913) 30 RPC 561, HL.

[92] There were other difficult cases, such as letters of the alphabet, numerals, colours, and pictures of the product itself: see e.g. *Re James' Trade Mark* (1886) 33 Ch D 392, CA; and see Kerly, *Trade-marks, Trade-Name*, Ch. 8.

[93] See e.g. *Faulder* v. *Rushton*, above, n. 80.

After a quarter-century's experience of registration, many businesses—and particularly those with well-established market shares—were pressing to be allowed greater scope for registration of their marks. Since official examination and opposition had acquired a status that could scarcely be questioned, it was to a modulation of these official controls that the campaigners turned. At the turn of the century, bills to strengthen trade mark registration were for a few years as frequent as those seeking the re-framing of copyright.[94] In the case of trade marks, an important measure of success was achieved in 1905, when a Commons Committee once more heard numerous trade witnesses on their travails in combating trade mark piracy.[95] Fletcher Moulton QC drafted the bill then under consideration, sat on the Committee, was the first witness before it, and was thus its driving force.[96] In dealing with the scope of the register, the resultant Act introduced a general distinction between marks that were straightforwardly distinctive of a trader and those that were not. The former could be registered even before any trading with them; the latter needed sufficient evidence of use in the market to show that in practice they had become distinctive of origin.[97] Given this new scheme of grading, it was possible to generalize the basic definition of a mark registrable without proof of use: it was to include marks consisting simply of an invented word or indeed of other words, provided that they did not have direct reference to character or quality of the goods, or were a geographical name or a surname.

Whatever the hesitations, in considerable measure patents, industrial designs, and trade marks had become subject to a process of registration, a function which from 1883 was performed by the Patent Office. Only copyright, influenced both by feelings of admiration for the very act of authorship and by the limitation of the right to the act of copying, would move away from even a subsidiary requirement of deposit. For the industrial property rights, registration or grant had the effect of turning the right into a discrete business asset accruing to the person currently registered as proprietor. Placing an invention, design, or trade mark on the official government register fulfilled two basic functions: the public listing

---

[94] Cf. above, p. 921.

[95] *PP* 1905 (231), XIII, 257.

[96] In the 1883 Act, which introduced the arrangements of the Paris Convention on Industrial Property into British municipal law, patents, designs, and trade marks had been drawn together. The Committee accordingly considered whether this conjunction should be continued, but decided that revision processes were complicated enough without handling them all at once.

[97] In 1919, the distinction would be refined by introducing a Part B category of marks that were not yet completely distinctive. But how far these marks gave less protection would remain obscure, and the category had to be abandoned in 1994, as trade mark law became 'Europeanized'.

was an industry-wide source of information about claims already maintained;[98] and increasingly it served, by way of prior examination, to eliminate applications that did not satisfy the substantive legal conditions for the right.

The latter objective had scarcely any effect, so far as designs were concerned. It became a regular discipline over patent applications only in 1883 with the examination for sufficiency of description, and was further heightened by the limited examination for novelty from 1905. For registered marks, however, from the outset there was a preliminary examination which determined whether a mark fell within the limited statutory definition of 'trade mark', and whether there were marks already on the register for the same goods or those of the same description. Professional agents to handle the business of applying for industrial property registrations continued to expand.[99] In particular the growth of the patent agents as a profession was matched by that of officers in the Patent Office: profession faced profession in a world which tended therefore to exclude the applicant in person, and anyway they became corporate rather than individual.

These varying conditions for registration affected demand for the different types of industrial property. Certainly in the years before 1914, more designs were being registered than patents and certainly more than trade marks.[100] Design applications almost always succeeded, whereas a considerable proportion of patent applications fell by the wayside—a proportion, however, that was not greatly affected by the increasing range of examination.[101] Most surprising of all, the proportion of trade mark applications that succeeded was also low, and did not greatly increase when the 1905 Act admitted a wider range of marks to the system.[102] So with trade mark registration there was an administrative hurdle to mount that made registration less popular than many in industry hoped.[103] But the common law at least allowed passing off proceedings based on reputations arising from use in commerce. If deliberate piracy could be shown, mark

[98]   In respect of trade marks, the original registration became incontestable after five years. No such rule applied to patents or designs.

[99]   See above, p. 956, and generally, Sherman and Bently, *Making*, Chs 8–10.

[100]   In 1912, a typical year: designs registered: 42,077 (cf. the lower numbers for patents and trade marks in the next two notes): see the Annual Report of the Comptroller-General of Patents, *PP* 1913 (48) XXXV, 61. For subsequent decline, largely to do with the inter-war downturn of the fabric industry, see L. Bently, 'Requiem for Registration; Reflections on the History of the United Kingdom Registered Designs System', in A. Firth (ed.), *The Prehistory and Development of Intellectual Property Systems* (1997).

[101]   For 1912, there were 30,089 patent applications and 15,814 grants. Because of the time needed for searching and examining, the grants would have come from earlier applications.

[102]   For 1912, 10,014 applications and 4912 registrations (again often of earlier applications).

[103]   Initially the administration was slow and cumbersome, as a Board of Trade Committee (chaired by Lord Herschell) found: *PP* 1888 [Cd. 5350] LXIV.

imitators could be prosecuted for forging trade marks under the Merchandise Marks Acts, just as they could for other lies about their products to be found in their labelling and elsewhere.[104]

4. TRADE MARKS IN INTERNATIONAL TRADE

As we have already noted, the concern of British manufacturers over imitation of their marks and get-up was reaching a first climax in the 1850s and continued to rankle when in 1862 the government refused to back the introduction of a register. Part of the difficulty over securing mutual protection treaties with other countries was that such arrangements as had been introduced in the various national systems varied very considerably in detail. At first base there were differences over what should count as a 'trade mark' and others then arose over intention to use or actual use, definitions of infringement, and provisions on remedies.[105]

By the 1870s, when ideas for an international convention began to supersede bilateral agreements in relation to patents, lawyers, professors, and patent attorneys played a prominent part in raising the level of debate about an international future, meeting first at the Vienna Conference of 1873.[106] The possibility of covering industrial designs and trade marks as well as invention patents in international arrangements covering all 'industrial property' became a major theme in the second non-official meeting (that of 1878 in Paris).[107] At that stage, however, it was unclear whether the main movement was for international agreement on the substance of the rights or only for mutual recognition of entitlement under each country's own national laws. When the issues passed into inter-governmental hands—in Paris in 1880—the political objectives were in the main confined to the second type of arrangement. Nothing more was realistically achievable. Although in one draft a recommendation was made for an elaborate definition of a trade mark, it did not survive in later versions. In the final text, trade marks, along with patents and industrial designs, became subject to the principle of national treatment; and an application in any Convention country provided a three-month period of priority over rival applications on other participant states.[108]

---

[104] In 1887, a new Merchandise Marks Act replaced that of 1862. Parliament gave in to pressure to make offences relating to misuse of a trade mark or a false trade description the subject of strict liability in certain circumstances. The vendor or possessor of offending goods, who acted innocently, having taken reasonable precautions not to break the Act, would not be guilty of an offence; but only if he proved it: s 2(2).

[105] As was amply demonstrated in the Board of Trade returns, above, n. 74.

[106] See above, pp. 959–60.

[107] See above, p. 960.

[108] Arts 2, 4. The priority period was extended to six months at the Brussels conference in 1900.

5. PASSING OFF AS AN ADJUNCT OF TRADE MARK REGISTRATION

Once the British register was established for trade marks, judges were less keen than Lord Westbury had been, to insist on a proprietary basis for passing off.[109] Typically they would say that the action conferred 'some of the rights which are incident to property';[110] or that at most any property lay in the business or the goodwill, rather than just in the mark itself. In this they appear to have sensed the circularity that arises from arguing that economic value justifies the legal right, when it is the conferment of the legal right that gives rise to the economic value.[111] In the case which put an end to such conceptual passage-work, *Spalding* v. *Gamage*, Lord Parker contrasted this 'attribute of goodwill' with the 'real right of property' existing in a registered trade mark. Nonetheless the decision in the case allowed a passing-off claim where the defendant had misrepresented one football made by the plaintiff as being another of theirs that was of better quality.[112]

With such a measure of flexibility, there proved to be much left for passing off to do.[113] A succession of cases were pressed as far as the House of Lords, and these were notable for dealing with situations where there was difficulty in proving the plaintiff's trading reputation. A brewer of 'Stone Ales' in the small town of Stone secured an injunction against a rival who adopted the word and tried to add distinguishing information.[114] As to this Lord Macnaghten produced his long-ringing deprecation: 'Thirsty folk want beer, not explanations'. The makers of 'Maizena', 'Flaked Oatmeal' and 'Cellular Clothing' failed in their efforts to show that these were more than descriptions of the goods themselves;[115] but, in what became a classic authority, the House held that even 'Camel Hair Belting' for exactly that commodity could become distinctive if sufficient evidence was produced that the trade or customers treated it as distinguishing the plaintiff's goods from those of competitors. Emphasizing a related element, 'Yorkshire Relish' was held to indicate that it came from a particular trade source, even though the

---

[109] Lord Blackburn led the way: *Singer* v. *Wilson* (1877) 3 App Cas 376, 400.

[110] e.g. Lord Herschell, *Reddaway* v. *Banham* [1896] AC 199, 209–10.

[111] Famously made the basis for Felix Cohen's attack on Schechter's argument for the existence of a 'dilution' right from the impact of modern branding: 'Transcendental Nonsense and the Functional Approach' (1935) 35 *Columbia LR* 809; for which see S. Wilf, 'The Making of the Post-War Paradigm in American Intellectual Property Law' (2008) 31 *Columbia J. Law & Arts* 139, Pt II.

[112] [1915] RPC 273, 284–5 ('Orb's' passed off as 'New Orb's').

[113] See e.g. Kerly, *Trade Marks, Trade Name*, Ch. 16.

[114] *Montgomery* v. *Thompson* [1891] AC 217, 225, HL.

[115] *National Starch* v. *Munn's Patent Maizena* [1894] AC 275, JC; *Parsons* v. *Gillespie* [1898] AC 239, JC; *Cellular Clothing* v. *Moxton & Murray* [1899] AC 326.

public could not name the actual producer.[116] These names, so hotly litigated, were brands that had particular value to the traders who built them up. Where the public thought of them as a guarantee of the qualities they were after and at the same time had some notion associating that with the source from which they came, the mark could gain a hold on purchasers that the courts would protect from annexation by others.[117]

With such popular marks, owners were likely to find others using them on quite different goods or services—the problem that would later be labelled 'trade mark dilution'. Mark owners could tackle the imitators, if they acted in time, by expanding their registrations to cover goods in which they did not trade; but that would come to be at risk of removal for five years' non-use;[118] and anyway it was a cumbersome and expensive tactic. Occasionally, judges would admit passing-off claims in such cases, finding sufficient likelihood of damage, for instance, in the danger that the mark owner would be mistakenly sued for, for instance, breach of contract over the thing supplied.[119] But in large measure they would continue through the twentieth century to regard the damage requirement for passing off as a barrier to actions claiming 'merchandising rights' across whole ranges of other goods. They showed considerable determination to prevent passing off in some 'non-classic' form from being treated as a property entitling the owner to demand an injunction or a licence fee no matter what the trade use. Equally—at least by mid-twentieth century, when merchandising practices became important offshoots of advertising—the courts were reluctant to allow 'celebrities' to have any equivalent right to the use of their personal names, the names of characters that they portrayed, their images, or their voices for such purposes.[120] One

---

[116] *Powell* v. *Birmingham Vinegar* [1897] AC 710, HL (a case where the registered mark had been removed from the register). *Payton* v. *Snelling Lampard* [1901] AC 308 would accept that the deception about reputation could arise from packaging or other get-up of the goods as well as from distinct trade marks—a concept carried dangerously close to protecting the shape of the product itself in *Edge* v. *Nicholls* [1911] AC 693. But other decisions showed a reluctance to accord competitors a right of action against misdescriptions of the quality of goods or services: *Native Guano* v. *Sewage Manure* (1889) 8 RPC 125, HL; *Magnolia Metal* v. *Tandem Smelting* [1900] 17 RPC 477, HL.

[117] One instance of this arose with the name given to a patented novelty. The patentee would alone be able to use the name until expiry of his grant, thanks to the patent. Thereafter attempts to insist that the name had come to identify this one source would be treated by courts with very considerable suspicion: *Linoleum Manufacturing* v. *Nairn* (1878) 7 Ch D 834; *Magnolia Metal* v. *Atlas Metal* (1897) 14 RPC 389; *British Vacuum Cleaner* v. *New Vacuum Cleaner* [1907] 2 Ch 312. For the subsequent history of the passing-off action, see e.g. H. Carty, 'The Development of Passing Off in the Twentieth Century', in N. Dawson and A. Firth (eds), *Trade Marks Retrospective* (2000), 31–55.

[118] See above, p. 1004.

[119] Before 1914, the striking example was Byrne J.'s injunction against the use of 'Kodak', by then a well-known mark for cameras, in the promotion of bicycles: *Walter* v. *Ashton* [1902] 2 Ch 282.

[120] Notably in *McCulloch* v. *May* [1947] 2 All ER 845; *Sim* v. *Heinz* [1959] 1 All ER 547.

reason for abjuring any 'right of privacy' was that in practice it would mostly be used as a commercial 'right of publicity'.

In 1925, the American scholar, Frank Schechter, analysed the development of passing off and trade mark registration with considerable skill. He claimed that there was no principled basis for what both British and American courts did and produced a sceptical historical foundation for a celebrated campaign. For him the law embodied an inherent conservatism which had not kept pace with modern marketing techniques. In his perception, trade marks had gained an independent, often glamorous attractiveness, which could well provide greater cachet with the buying public than the actual products themselves. Accordingly, the law should have abandoned its attachment to the 'origin' theory for protecting marks and recognized other functions that marks fulfilled in business practice. Of these, Schechter pressed particularly for rights to stop 'dilution' of trade marks onto goods quite distinct from those on which the original user of the marks had placed them. It was a cause that would intermittently attract legislatures on both sides of the Atlantic, but in common law countries it tended to be deprived of value by courts suspicious of inflated claims to trading privilege.[121]

Had it gained real acceptance, it could have led to a revival of a 'property' theory that would have very considerable range—giving legal protection to such ill-defined notions as 'quality functions', 'merchandising functions', 'investment functions', and 'advertising functions', as and when businessmen demanded them. A conceptual separation of rights to a mark in different national territories might have been held to follow, even where the mark belonged in all the countries to a transnational business, or to one or other subsidiary in a corporate group, or through a web established between a licensor and licensees who were granted production or distribution rights in their own, exclusive territories. The result would then have been that a trade mark could be used to prevent 'parallel importers' from transhipping the legitimate goods of the mark-owner from one country in which they were initially sold cheap to another in which they commanded higher prices. While in the 'second industrial revolution', the issue had to some extent arisen over patents and copyright,[122] British advocates seem not to have considered it a viable line of argument when it came to trade mark protection until the inter-war years. Even then it was cold-shouldered. If the mark was initially applied by the English mark-owner, then it was either regarded as unlikely to deceive English consumers, even though the initial sale

---

[121] In Britain, the 1938 Act would allow 'defensive' registration of well-known marks composed of invented words; but the courts took a very limited view of what could be included; see e.g. *Ferodo's Application* (1945) 62 RPC 111.

[122] See above, pp. 974–5.

to the chain of distributors took place abroad and a sub-purchaser imported the product into England.[123] Alternatively, if there was such deception it came about because the plaintiff had chosen to use the same mark in different national markets.

Common law judges certainly remained hesitant to adopt any embracing generalization of marketplace wrongdoing, such as 'unfair competition' or 'unlawful trading' as a basis for tortious liability. It was by employing such a roving concept that Continental European systems, such as Germany and its followers, would come to show readier favour towards claims brought by those first established in a market against new entrants who sought some association with them, or disassociation from them, in their attempts to advance their own position. 'Dilution' of a popular trade or association mark by transporting it to a different field of activity was but one example of what might be caught; comparative advertising is another example.[124] Passing off, it is true, provided a core example of unfair competition; and in the twentieth century English judges would extend it to allied cases which did not fit the classical model—but only with circumspection. They had a strong sense of the danger of applying a broader brush. Fry LJ famously pronounced that 'To distinguish between fair and unfair competition, between what is reasonable and unreasonable, passes the power of the courts'.[125] While he was referring to pre-market activity that today is tackled through anti-trust laws, his distaste applied also to situations arising in the marketplace itself—and there his warning remains as resonant today as it was in late Victorian England.[126] The British showed no inclination to allow one trader a civil action to put down a false assertion by a rival, unless it went to the trader's own reputation. As a Victorian example, to stamp 'Prize Medal' on jars of pickles without warrant, might found a criminal prosecution for misleading buyers, but not a passing-off action or any equivalent that would give competitors a civil cause of action.[127]

---

[123] See esp. *Champagne Heidsieck* v. *Buxton* [1930] 1 Ch 330: the proper scope of the right of passing off was confined by Clauson J. to conduct by the defendant that was likely to confuse customers as to the origin of goods (relying on *Farina* v. *Silverlock* (1856) 6 De G. M. & G. 214); and a registered mark was treated as having no broader effect.

[124] The constraints placed on the tort of injurious falsehood put paid to regular objections to comparative advertising; only extreme cases would succeed (see above, Ch. 1, p. 859). The Trade Marks Act 1938 would attempt automatic protection where a Part A registered mark was involved in the comparison. But the hostility of some judges would render the extension in s 4(1) virtually of no effect.

[125] *Mogul Steamship* v. *McGregor Gow* (1889) 23 Ch D 598, 625–6, CA.

[126] For the controversies arising over harmonization of unfair competition law in the European Union, alongside the rise of the European Community Trade Mark, see e.g. W. R. Cornish and D. Llewelyn, *Intellectual Property* (6th edn, 2007), Pt V.

[127] *Batty* v. *Hill* (1863) 1 H. & M. 369. The courts would long refuse to hold that the Merchandise Marks Acts and modern successors impliedly gave a competitor any action for the damage flowing

As Wadlow has demonstrated,[128] British governments strove to secure that, under the Paris Industrial Property Convention, Article 10*bis*, contracting states were bound to provide 'effective protection' against unfair competition to traders from other contracting countries.[129] It was not enough to guarantee these traders equal treatment under whatever measures for repression of unfair competition they gave their own nationals.[130] In revisions of the Convention after 1918, the British would insist that examples of what might constitute unfair competition be included in the text of this Article. At the same time they procured the power to continue the structural balance achieved by statute and case law in the 1860s and 1870s. Participant states were left to satisfy the Convention obligation by criminal prohibitions, or civil actions, or both, to the extent that they chose in national law. A contracting state could therefore restrict civil relief to those types of unfair competition that particularly affected individual competitors. Misleading advertising, labelling, and packaging that could affect a trade in general could thus remain a matter of public law, subject to criminal sanctions only—as was the case in the British Merchandise Marks Acts 1862 and 1887, forerunners of modern consumer protection laws.[131] Likewise, national laws would determine what could be protected by registration of trade marks and what by a right stemming from actual trade reputation. The range of options thus secured left considerable latitude to states of the Paris Union to decide for themselves how they would tackle differing types of 'unfair competition'. One consequence would be that any harmonization of 'unfair competition law' within the EU would be very hard to achieve.

Belief in the superiority of national ways of doing things had other effects. In 1891, a number of Paris Convention countries made use of the Convention's Bureau (BIRPI) to establish the Madrid Agreement for International Registration

---

from misleading claims about quality; cf. the same attitude to the enactments on rights in performances: above, p. 929.

[128] *Passing Off*, 52–103.

[129] It was a British proposal that added this element to Art. 10*bis* at the Washington Revision of the Paris Convention in 1911.

[130] The original version of Art. 10*bis* secured this in the Brussels revision of 1900: the proposal came from France.

[131] At the 1891 Madrid Meeting which established international trade mark registration, a second Agreement for the Repression of False or Deceptive Indications of Source on Goods was reached. This could cover everything from names of countries to small regions or even individual productions but participating states were left free to define what their national laws covered. It served therefore only as a precursor for international conventions on denominations of origin. The British had been active in promoting Art. 10 of the Paris Convention itself, which to a limited degree applied its import prevention regime (Art. 9) to false indications of geographical origins. However, the country showed no interest in the 1891 Arrangement. For the movement towards this Arrangement, see Ladas, *International Protection*, Ch. 30.

of Marks. Once a firm had registered a mark in its home state, it could apply for registration with BIRPI for other participant countries. Each of the latter had one year in which to give reasons why it should first be processed through its ordinary application procedure. If that did not happen, the mark would be treated as registered in the particular state. For those who used their marks without alteration in trans-national trade, the arrangement had much to be said for it. But it did not suit the British, who considered that it favoured countries using a deposit or limited examination system which led to early home registrations. The fee structure under the Agreement likewise favoured such countries, providing no distinction for countries such as the UK, where an *ex officio* examination for conflicting registrations was part of the cautious approach to giving heightened protection through registration.[132] In its modern version, the main Convention would accordingly acquire provisions which allowed objections to be taken to the registration of well-known marks in other EU countries, and which limited the objections that could be taken to registration of a mark in EU countries beyond its country of origin.[133]

6. ENVOI

We have drawn to a close the three Volumes of this *History* that cover the period 1820–1914 by surveying a set of private rights that touch the intangible, either in relation to personal reputation or to the commercial value flowing from exclusive rights of exploitation, or both. All the rights could be fitted within the sub-partitioned pigeon-hole that was coming to be called Tort; and there they needed to be, since in essence they constituted interventions restricting freedom of action by persons who had no voluntary relationship with the claimant. Tort could restrict defamation claims to the person whose reputation was injured, while allowing copyright, patents, trade marks, and the like to be conceived for the most part as property or 'property-like' and thus a transferable asset.

However, the very fact that the subject-matter was not defined by reference to a physical object raised manifold questions about the scope of liability that could be answered only by rather imprecise criteria—lowering of reputation in the view of right-minded people for defamation, substantial taking of 'expression' for copyright infringement, inventive step over the prior art for a valid patent, using a mark or get-up that was liable to cause confusion, and so on. In varying

---

[132] It would take another century to reach a Protocol that allowed countries such as the UK to participate in the procedures of the Madrid Arrangement. For its origins, see Ladas, *International Protection*, Ch. 28.

[133] See the Paris Industrial Property Convention, Lisbon revision, 1957, Arts 6*bis*, 6*quinquies*.

degrees this led to statutory interventions, which were commonly formulated only after considerable contests between potential claimants and defendants, some of whom—publishers, the press, leading industrialists—had powerful political voices. Even where these enactments were complete enough to constitute a codification—as could well be claimed for Imperial Copyright in 1911—they still bore the basic impress of judicial decisions which first delineated the nature and scope of the different types of action.

It was the judges who decided that the patent system should operate upon a principle of *quid pro quo*—protection in return for sufficient description; they who settled that patents, copyright, and marks should be treated as property so as to entitle their holders to damages at common law, but more importantly to injunctions in equity; they who confined defamation to demeaning statements that could not be shown to be true and had no legal excuse, but nonetheless they accepted that defendants were liable even where they did not know of the plaintiff's existence. Starting in the half-century before 1820, precedents were built up by constant litigation in all these fields, consolidating the wrongs from the early period of industrialization. The judges took strong lines in much of what they did in order to offer effective protection to those who fell within the law's limits. At the same time, they undoubtedly sensed that by expanding any of these rights they were reducing the scope of basic freedoms which in the common law represented the default mode: freedom of expression which included liberty to criticize others, and freedom to engage in competitive enterprise and therefore to copy or build upon what others were doing. These were political liberties that upright, purposeful, judgmental Victorians held in deep respect and they tied in with beliefs that, however much they would have to be curtailed in the interests of general social welfare, the country would grow richer and happier if individuals were left as far as possible to develop their own interests by their own initiatives.

Further Reading

Part One: Criminal Law

Establishment of English policing

Bailey, V. (ed.), *Policing and Punishment in 19th Century Britain* (1981).

Brogden, M., *The Police: Autonomy and Consent* (1982).

Conley, C., *The Unwritten Law: Criminal Justice in Victorian Kent* (Oxford, 1991).

Critchley, T., *A History of Police in England and Wales* (1978).

Emsley, C., *The English Police* (1996).

Emsley, C., *Crime and Society in England 1750–1900* (2004).

Harris, A., *Policing in the City, Crime and Legal Authority in London 1780–1840* (Columbus, Ohio, 2004).

King, P., *Crime, Justice and Discretion in England 1740–1820* (Oxford, 2000).

King, P., *Crime and Law in England 1750: Remaking Justice from the Margins* (Cambridge, 2006).

Palmer, S., *Police and Protest in England and Ireland* (Cambridge, 1988).

Porter, B., *The Origins of the Vigilant State: The London Metropolitan Police Special Branch before the First World War* (1987).

Radzinowicz, L., *A History of the Criminal Law*, Vol. 3: *The Reform of the Police* (1956).

Reiner, R., *Chief Constables* (1992).

Reynolds, E., *Before the Bobbies: The Night Watch and Police Reform in Metropolitan London 1720–1830* (1998).

Shpayer-Makov, H., *The Making of a Policeman* (2002).

Steedman, C., *Policing and the Victorian Community: The Formation of English Provincial Police Forces 1856–80* (1983).

Thurmond Smith, P., *Policing Victorian London* (1985).

Vincent, D., *The Culture of Secrecy: Britain 1832–1998* (Oxford, 1998).

The criminal trial

Allen, C., *The Law of Evidence in Victorian England* (Cambridge, 1997).

Beattie, J., *Crime and the Courts in England 1660–1800* (Oxford, 1986).

Beattie, J., 'Scales of Justice: Defence Counsel and English Criminal Trials in the Eighteenth and Nineteenth Centuries' (1991) 9 *Law and Hist. Rev.* 221.

Bentley, D., *English Criminal Justice in the Nineteenth Century* (1998).

Cairns, D., *Advocacy and the Making of the Adversarial Criminal Trial* (Oxford, 1998).

Cornish, W., 'Defects in Prosecuting—Professional Views in 1845', in P. R. Glazebrook (ed.), *Reshaping the Criminal Law* (1978), 305–16.

Davis, J., 'A Poor Man's System of Justice: The London Police Courts in the Second Half of the Nineteenth Century' (1984), *Hist. J.,* 319.

Devlin, P., *The Criminal Prosecution in England* (1960).

Duman, D., *The English and Colonial Bars in the Nineteenth Century* (1983).

Eastwood, D., *Governing Rural England, Tradition and Transformation in Local Government 1780–1849* (Oxford, 1993).

Feeley, M., 'Legal Complexity and the Transformation of the Criminal Process' (1997) 31 *Israel Law Rev.* 183–222.

Gallanis, T. P., 'The Rise of Modern Evidence Law' (1999) 84 *Iowa Law Rev.* 499–560.

Gatrell, V., 'The Decline of Theft and Violence in Victorian and Edwardian England', in V. Gatrell, B. Lenman, and G. Parker (eds), *Crime and the Law: The Social History of Crime in Western Europe since 1500* (1980), 274.

Hay, D. and Snyder, F. (eds), *Policing and Prosecution in Britain 1750–1850* (Oxford, 1989).

Herrup, C., *The Common Peace* (Cambridge, 1987).

King, *Crime, Justice and Discretion: 740–1820* (Oxford, 2000).

Kurland, P. B. and Waters, D. M., 'Public Prosecutions in England, 1854–1879' (1959) 9 *Duke L.J.* 493.

Landsman, S., 'The Rise of the Contentious Spirit: Adversary Procedure in Eighteenth Century England' (1990) 75 *Cornell Law Rev.* 498–605.

Langbein, J., *The Origins of Adversary Criminal Trial* (Oxford, 2003).

May, A., *The Bar and the Old Bailey 1750–1850* (Chapel Hill, 2003).

Pue, W., 'The Criminal Twilight Zone: Pre-Trial Procedures in the 1840s' (1983) 21 *Alberta Law Rev.* 335–63.

Shapiro, B. J., *Beyond Reasonable Doubt and Probable Cause: Historical Perspectives on the Anglo-American Law of Evidence* (Berkeley, 1991).

Smith, B., 'The Presumption of Guilt and the English Law of Theft, 1750–1850' (2005) 23 *LHR* 133–71.

Smith, K., *James Fitzjames Stephen: Portrait of a Victorian Rationalist* (Cambridge, 1988).

Twining, W. L., *Theories of Evidence: Bentham and Wigmore* (1985).

Twining, W. L., *Rethinking Evidence* (Oxford, 1990).

Sentencing and review

Chadwick, R., *Bureaucratic Mercy: The Home Office and the Treatment of Capital Cases in Victorian England* (New York, 1992).

Devereaux, S., 'The Criminal Branch of the Home Office 1782–1830', in S. Devereaux and P. Griffiths (eds), *Penal Practice and Culture 1500–1900 Punishing the English* (2004).

Emsley, *Crime and Society in England 1750–1900* (above).

Thomas, D. A., *The Penal Equation: Derivations of the Penalty Structure of English Criminal Law* (Cambridge, 1978).

Thomas, D. A., *Constraints on Judgment* (Cambridge, 1979).

Types of punishment

Beattie, *Crime and the Courts in England 1660–1800* (Above).

Bochel, D., *Probation and Aftercare: Its Development in England and Wales* (Edinburgh, 1976).

Chadwick, *Bureaucratic Mercy* (above).

Davis, J., 'The London Garrotting Panic of 1862: A Moral Panic and the Creation of a Criminal Class in Mid-Victorian England', in V. Gatrell, V. Lenman, and G. Parker (eds), *Crime and the Law* (1980) 190–213.

DeLacey, M., *Prison Reform in Lancashire 1700–1850* (Manchester, 1986).

Forsythe, W. J., *Penal Discipline, Reformatory Projects and the English Prison Commission 1895–1939* (Exeter, 1991).

Garland, D., *Punishment and Welfare: A History of Penal Strategies* (Aldershot, 1985).

Garland, D., *Punishment and Modern Society* (Oxford, 1990).

Gatrell, V., *The Hanging Tree* (Oxford, 1994).

Handler, P., 'The Limits of Discretion: Forgery and the Jury at the Old Bailey, 1818–21', in J. Cairns and G. McLeod (eds), *The Dearest Birth Right of the People of England* (Oxford, 2002), 155–72.

Harrison, B., *Drink and the Victorians* (1971).

Hay, D., 'Property, Authority and the Criminal Law', in Hay *et al.* (eds), *Albion's Fatal Tree* (1975), 17–63.

Hilton, B., 'The Gallows and Mr Peel', in T. Blanning and D. Cannadine (eds), *History and Biography: Essays in Honour of Derek Beales* (Cambridge, 1996), 88.

Hughes, R., *The Fatal Shore: A History of Transportation of Convicts to Australia 1787–1868* (1987).

Ignatieff, M., *A Just Measure of Pain* (1978).

Jones, K., *Asylums and After: A Revised History of the Mental Health Services* (1993).

McConville, S., *A History of English Prison Administration* (1981).

McConville, S., *English Local Prisons 1860–1900* (1995).

Radzinowicz, L., *A History of English Criminal Law*, Vol. 1: *The Movement for Reform* (1948).

Radzinowicz, L. and Hood, R., *A History of the Criminal Law*, Vol. 5: *The Emergence of Penal Policy* (1986).

Shaw, A. G., *Convicts and the Colonies* (1966).

Shiman, L., *Crusade against Drink in Victorian England* (1988).

Smith, *James Fitzjames Stephen* (Above).

Smith, K., *Lawyers, Legislators and Theorists* (Oxford, 1998).

Smith, K., 'Anthony Hammond: "Mr Surface Peel's Persistent Codifier"' (1999) 20 *JLH* 24.

Stack, J. A., *Social Policy and Juvenile Delinquency, 1815–1875* (1974).

Thompson, E. P., *Whigs and Hunters: The Origins of the Black Act* (1975).

Whiteley, C., *Brief Life* (1942).

Wiener, M., *Reconstructing the Criminal* (Cambridge, 1990).

Zedner, L., *Women, Crime and Custody in Victorian England* (Oxford, 1990).

Sources and form of the criminal law

Devlin, P., *The Judge* (Oxford, 1979).

Hedley, S., 'Words, Words, Words; Making Sense of Legal Judgments 1874–1940', in C. Stebbings (ed.), *Law Reporting in Britain* (1995), 169–86.

Kadish, S., 'Codifiers of the Criminal Law' (1978) 78 *Col. Law Rev.* 1098.

Lobban, M., *The Common Law and English Jurisprudence* (Oxford, 1991).

Manchester, A. H., 'Simplifying the Sources of Law: An Essay in Law Reform' (1973) *Anglo-Am. Law. Rev.* 395.

Simpson, A. W. B., 'The Rise and Fall of the Legal Treatise: Legal Principles and the Forms of Legal Literature' (1981) 48 *Univ. of Chicago Law Rev.* 632.

Smith, *Lawyers, Legislators and Theorists* (above).

Smith, K., 'Macaulay's Utilitarian Penal Code: An Illustration of the Accidental Function of Time, Place and Personalities in Law Making', in W. M. Gordon and T. D. Fergus (eds), *Legal History and the Making of Law* (1991), 145–64.

Smith, K. and White, S., 'An Episode in Criminal Law Reform through Private Initiative', in P. Birks (ed.), *The Life of the Law* (1993), 235–56.

General principles of criminal law

Chadwick, *Bureaucratic Mercy* (Above).

Eigen, J., *Witnessing Insanity: Madness and the Mad—Doctors in the English Court* (New Haven, 1995).

Friedland, M. L., 'R. S. Wright's Model Criminal Code: A Forgotten Chapter in the History of the Criminal Law' (1981) 1 *OJLS* 207.

Hall, J., *General Principles of Criminal Law* (Bloomington, 1960).

Horder, J., 'Two Histories and Four Hidden Principles of Mens Rea' (1997) 113 *LQR* 95.

Kadish, S., 'Complicity, Cause and Blame' (1985) 75 *Cal. Law Rev.* 324.

Sayre, F. B., 'Criminal Conspiracy' (1922) 35 *HLR* 393.

Sayre, F. B., 'Criminal Attempts' (1928) 41 *HLR* 822.

Simpson, A. W. B., *Cannibalism and the Common Law* (Chicago, 1984).

Smith, *Lawyers, Legislators and Theorists* (above).

Smith, K., *A Modern Treatise on the Law of Criminal Complicity* (Oxford, 1991).

Smith, R., *Trial by Medicine: Insanity and Responsibility in Victorian Trials* (Edinburgh, 1981).

Walker, N., *Crime and Insanity in England* (Edinburgh, 1968).

Excluding fault from criminal responsibility

Edwards, J., *Mens Rea and Statutory Offences* (1955).

Fifoot, C., *Judge and Jurist in the Reign of Victoria* (1959).

Leigh, L. H., *Strict and Vicarious Liability* (1982).

Sayre, F. B., 'Public Welfare Offences' (1933) 33 *Col. Law Rev.* 55.

Winfield, P., 'The Myth of Absolute Liability' (1926) 42 *LQR* 37.

State security and public order

Edwards, J. L., *The Law Officers of the Crown* (1964).

Emsley, C., 'An Aspect of Pitt's Terror: Prosecutions for Sedition during the 1790s' (1981) 6 *Social History* 155.

Goodway, D., *London Chartism 1838–1848* (Cambridge, 1982).

Harling, P., 'The Law of Libel and the Limits of Repression 1790–1832' (2001) 44 *Hist. J.* 107.

Lobban, M., 'From Seditious Libel to Unlawful Assembly... 1770–1820' (1990) 10 *OJLS* 307.

Lobban, M., 'Treason, Sedition and the Radical Movement in the Age of the French Revolution' (2000) 22 *Liverpool Law Rev.* 205.

Oldham, J., 'Special Juries in England: Nineteenth Century Usage and Reform' (1987) 8 *JLH* 149.

Oldham, J., *The Mansfield Manuscripts* (Chapel Hill, 1992).

Spencer, J. R., 'Criminal Libel—Skeleton in the Cupboard' (1977) *Crim. Law Rev.* 383, 391–3.

Spencer, J. R., 'The Press and Reform of Criminal Libel', in P. R. Glazebrook (ed.), *Reshaping the Criminal Law* (1978) 266–86.

Public morality and social control

Bailey, V. and Blackburn, S., 'The Punishment of Incest Act 1908' (1979) *Crim. Law Rev.* 708.

Bartley, P., *Prostitution: Prevention and Reform in England 1860–1914* (2000).

Berlin, I., 'Two Concepts of Liberty', in *Essays on Liberty* (Oxford, 1969).

Bristow, E. J., *Vice and Vigilance: Purity Movements in Britain since 1700* (1977).

Collini, S., *Liberalism and Sociology: L. T. Hobhouse and Political Argument in England 1880–1914* (Cambridge, 1979).

Collini, S., *Public Moralists, Political Thought and Intellectual Life in Britain 1850–1930* (Oxford, 1991).

Dixon, D., *From Prohibition to Regulation* (Oxford, 1991).

Henderson, T., *Prostitution and Control in the Metropolis 1730–1830* (1999).

Hilton, B., *The Age of Atonement: The Influence of Evangelicalism on Social and Economic Thought 1795–1865* (Oxford, 1988).

Himmelfarb, G., *On Liberty and Liberalism* (New York, 1974).

Houghton, W. E., *The Victorian Frame of Mind 1830–1870* (New Haven, 1957).

Marsh, J., *Word Crimes: Blasphemy, Culture and Literature in Nineteenth Century England* (Chicago, 1998).

Miers, D., *Regulating Commercial Gambling* (Oxford, 2004).

Porter, R. and Hall, L., *The Facts of Life: The Creation of Sexual Knowledge in Britain 1650–1950* (New Haven, 1995).

Robertson, G., *Obscenity* (1979).

St John-Stevas, N., *Obscenity and the Law* (1956).

Thomas, D., *A Long Time Burning: The History of Literary Censorship in England* (1969).

Walkowitz, J., *Prostitution and Victorian Society: Women, Class and the State* (Cambridge, 1980).

Property offences

Fletcher, G., *Rethinking Criminal Law* (Boston, 1978).

Hall, J., *Theft, Law and Society* (Indiana, 1952).

Hopkins, H., *The Long Affray: The Poaching Wars in Britain 1760–1914* (1986).

Munsche, P., *Gentlemen and Poachers: The English Game Laws 1671–1831* (Cambridge, 1981).

Robb, G., *White Collar Crime in Modern England* (Cambridge, 1992).

Smith, J. C., *Theft* (1968).

Smith, J. C. and Hogan, B., *Criminal Law* (1965).

Turner, J. W., 'Two Cases of Larceny', in *The Modern Approach to Criminal Law* (1945), 356.

Wilson, S., 'Law, Morality and Regulation: Victorian Experiences of Financial Crime' (2006) 46 *B.J. of Crim.* 1073.

Offences against the person

Anderson, O., *Suicide in Victorian and Edwardian England* (Oxford, 1987).

Behlmer, G., *Friends of the Family, The English Home and Its Guardians, 1850–1940* (Stanford, 1998).

Burney, I., *Bodies of Evidence: Medicine, Public Inquiry, and the Politics of the English Inquest 1830–1926* (Baltimore, 2000).

Carter Wood, J., *Violence and Crime in Nineteenth Century England: The Shadow of Our Refinement* (2004).

Clark, A., *Women's Silence, Men's Violence: Sexual Assault in England 1770–1845* (1987).

d'Cruze, S., *Crimes of Outrage: Sex, Violence and Victorian Working Women* (1998).

Doggett, M., *Marriage, Wife-Beating and the Law in Victorian England* (1992).

Donnison, J., *Midwives and Medical Men* (1988).

Forbes, T., *Surgeons at the Old Bailey: English Forensic Medicine to 1878* (1985).

Hammerton, A., *Cruelty and Companionship: Conflict in Nineteenth Century Married Life* (1992).

Jackson, L., *Child Sexual Abuse in Victorian England* (2000).

King, *Crime and Law in England 1750* (Above).

Landsman, S., 'One Hundred Years of Rectitude: Medical Witnesses at the Old Bailey' (1998) 16 *LHR* 445.

Langford, P., *Englishness Identified: Manners and Character 1650–1850* (Oxford, 2000).

Porter, R., *Health for Sale: Quackery in England 1660–1850* (Manchester, 1989).

Rose, L., *Massacre of the Innocents: Infanticide in Great Britain 1800–1939* (1986).

Smith, J. C., 'The Presumption of Innocence' (1987) 38 *NILQ* 223.

Stein, A., 'From Blackstone to Woolmington' (1993) 14 *JLH* 14.

Thompson, E. P., *Whigs and Hunters: The Origins of the Black Act* (1975).

Wiener, M., *Men of Blood* (Cambridge, 2004).

Part Two: Statutes, Social Reform, and Control

Poor Law

Anstruther, I., *The Scandal of the Andover Workhouse* (Gloucester, 1973).

Bartlett, P., *The Poor Law of Lunacy, The Administration of Pauper Lunatics in Mid-Nineteenth Century England* (1999).

Bellamy, C., *Administering Central-Local Relations, 1871–1919, The Local Government Board in its Fiscal and Cultural Context* (Manchester, 1986).

Brundage, A., *The English Poor Laws, 1700–1930* (2002).

Brundage, A., Eastwood D., and Mandler P., 'Debate: The Making of the New Poor Law Redivivus', (1990) *P & P* 183–201.

Blaugh, M., 'The Poor Law Report Re-examined', (1964) *JEH*, xxiv, 229–45.

Bunbury, H. J. (ed.), *Lloyd George's Ambulance Wagon* (1957).

Cranston, R., *Legal Foundations of the Welfare State* (London, 1985).

Charlesworth, L., 'Poor Law in the City: A Comparative Legal Analysis of the Effect of the 1834 Poor Law Amendment Act upon the Administration of Poor Relief in the Ports of Liverpool and Chester', in A. Lewis (ed.), *Law in the City: Proceedings of the Seventeenth British Legal History Conference 2005* (2007), 206–29.

Charlesworth, L., 'The Poor Law: A Modern Legal Analysis,' (1999) *Journal of Social Security Law*, ii, 79–92.

Checkland, S. G. and Checkland, E. O. A. (eds), *The Poor Law Report of 1834* (Harmondsworth, 1974).

Cornish, W. R. and de N. Clark, G., *Law and Society in England, 1750–1950* (1989), Ch.6.

Driver, F., *Power and Pauperism: The Workhouse System, 1834–1884* (Cambridge, 1993).

Englander, D., *Poverty and Poor Law Reform in Nineteenth Century Britain: 1834–1914* (1998).

Fraser, D. (ed.), *The New Poor Law in the Nineteenth Century* (1976).

Kidd, A., *State, Society and the Poor in Nineteenth-Century England* (Basingstoke, 1999).

Lees, L. H., *The Solidarities of Strangers: The English Poor Laws and the People, 1700–1948* (Cambridge, 1997).

Mandler, P., 'The Making of the New Poor Law Redivivus', (1987) *P & P* 117 at 131–57.

McBriar, A. M., *An Edwardian Mixed Doubles, The Bosanquets versus the Webbs: A Study in British Social Policy, 1890–1929* (Oxford, 1987).

Montague, F. C., 'The Law of Settlement and Removal', (1888) *LQR* xiii, 40–5.

Poynter, J. R., *Society and Pauperism. English Ideas on Poor Relief 1795–1834* (1969).

Quinn, M., 'The Fallacy of Non-Interference: The Poor Panopticon and Equality of Opportunity', (1997) *Journal of Bentham Studies*, 1, 1.

Rose, M. E., The English Poor Law, 1780–1930 (1971).

Webb, S. and Webb. B. (eds), *The Break-Up of the Poor Law: The Minority Report of the Poor Law Commission*, Parts I and II (1909).

Webb, S. and Webb. B., Part I, *English Poor Law History*; Part II, *The Old Poor Law: The Last Hundred Years* (1929).

Charities

Alvey, N., *From Chantry to Oxfam: A Short History of Charity and Charity Legislation* (1995).

Chesterman, M., *Charities, Trusts and Social Welfare* (1979), 53–62.

Cornish, W. R. and de N. Clark, G., *Law and Society in England, 1750–1950* (1989), 413–17, 422–5.

Jones, G., *History of the Law of Charity: 1532–1827* (Cambridge, 1969).

Simon, B., *Studies in the History of Education, 1750–1870* (1960), 95–6, 329–36.

Tompson, R., *The Charity Commission and the Age of Reform* (London and Henley, 1979).

Education

Barnard, H. C., *A History of English Education from 1760* (2nd edn, 1961).

Cornish, W. R., and de N. Clark, G., *Law and Society in England, 1750–1950* (1989), Ch. 6.

Curtis, S. J., *History of Education in Great Britain* (7th edn, 1967).

Eaglesham, E. J. R., *The Foundations of Twentieth Century Education in England* (1967).

Simon, B., *Studies in the History of Education, 1750–1870* (1960).

Sturt, M., *The Education of the People* (1967).

Sutherland, G. (Gen. ed.), *Education: Commentaries on British Parliamentary Papers* (Dubin, 1977).

Sutherland, G., 'Education', in F. M. L. Thompson (ed.), *The Cambridge Social History of Britain, 1750–1950*, 3 vols (Cambridge, 1990), Vol. III.

Health

Brundage, A., *England's 'Prussian Minister': Edwin Chadwick and the Politics of Government Growth, 1832–1854* (Pennsylvania, 1988).

Cocks, R., 'Victorian Foundations?', in R. Edmunds and J. Lowry (eds), *Environmental Protection and the Common Law* (2004), 1–25.

Cornish W. R. and de N. Clark, G., *Law and Society in England, 1750–1950* (1989), 154–66.

Daunton, M. (ed.), *The Cambridge Urban History of Britain: 1840–1950* (Cambridge, 2000), Vol. III.

Digby, A., *Making a Medical Living: Doctors and Patients in the English Market for Medicine, 1720–1911* (Cambridge, 1994 and 2002).

Finer, S. E., *The Life and Times of Sir Edwin Chadwick* (1952).

Flinn, M. W., 'Medical Services under the New Poor Law', in D. Fraser (ed.), *The New Poor Law in the Nineteenth Century* (1976), 45–66.

Hamlin, C., *Public Health and Social Justice in the Age of Chadwick: Britain 1800–1854* (Cambridge, 1998).

Hodgkinson, R. G., *The Origins of the National Health Service: The Medical Services of the New Poor Law, 1834–1871* (1967).

Lewis, R. A., *Edwin Chadwick and the Public Health Movement, 1832–1848* (1952).

MacDonagh, O., *Early Victorian Government: 1830–1870* (1977), Ch. 8.

Rosenthal, L., 'Economic Efficiency, Nuisance, and Sewage: New Lessons from Attorney-General v. Council of the Borough of Birmingham, 1858–1895', (2007) *JLS* 36(1), 27–62.

Wohl, A. S., *Endangered Lives: Public Health in Victorian Britain* (1983).

Safety in factories, shops, and ships

Bartrip, P. W. J., *Safety at Work: The Factory Inspectorate in the Fencing Controversy, 1833–1857* (Oxford, 1979).

Bartrip, P. W. J., 'British Government Inspection, 1832–1875: Some Observations', (1982) *Hist. J*, 605–26.

Bartrip, P. W. J. and Burman, S. B., *The Wounded Soldiers of Industry: Industrial Compensation Policy, 1833–1897* (Oxford, 1983).

Bartrip, P. W. J., *The Home Office and the Dangerous Trades: Regulating Occupational Disease in Victorian and Edwardian Britain* (2002).

Carpenter, K. E. (ed.), *The Factory Act of 1833: Eight Pamphlets, 1833–34* (1972).

Cornish, W. R. and de N. Clark, G., *Law and Society in England, 1750–1950* (1989), 301–9.

Djang, T. K., *Factory Inspection in Great Britain* (1942).

Gray, R., *The Factory Question and Industrial England, 1830–1860* (Cambridge, 1996).

Hutchins, B. L. and Harrison, A., *A History of Factory Legislation* (1926).

Jones, N., *The Plimsoll Sensation* (2006).

Kydd, S. H. J., *A History of the Factory Movement* (1857), reprinted in New York (1966), Vols I and II.

Thomas, M. W., *The Early Factory Legislation* (Leigh-on-Sea, 1948).

Turner, J., 'Experts and Interests: David Lloyd George and the Dilemmas of the Expanding State, 1906–19', in R. MacLeod (ed.), *Government and Expertise* (Cambridge, 2002).

Housing

Anderson, S., *Lawyers and the Making of English Land Law* (Oxford, 1992).

Best, G., *Mid-Victorian Britain, 1851–75* (St Albans, 1973).

Burnett, J., *A Social History of Housing: 1815–1970* (1980).

Cannadine, D., *Lords and Landlords* (1980).

Cornish W. R. and de N. Clark, G., *Law and Society in England, 1750–1950* (1989), 179–94.

Daunton, M. (ed.), *The Cambridge Urban History of Britain* (Cambridge, 2000), Vol. III.

Daunton, M., *House and Home in the Victorian City* (1983).

Englander, D., *Landlord and Tenant in Urban Britain, 1838–1918* (1983).

Gauldie, E., *Cruel Habitations, A History of Working-Class Housing, 1780–1918* (1974).

Nettlefold, J. S., *Practical Housing* (1910), Popular Edition (first published by the Garden City Press in 1908).

Planning

Ashworth, W., *The Genesis of British Town Planning: a Study in Economic and Social History of the Nineteenth and Twentieth Centuries* (1954).

Brown, K. D., *John Burns* (1977).

Cherry, G. E., *The Evolution of British Town Planning* (1974).

Fishman, R., *Urban Utopias in the Twentieth Century: Ebenezer Howard, Frank Lloyd Wright and Le Corbusier* (New York, 1977).

Hall, P., *Urban and Regional Planning* (3rd edn, 1992).

Hardy, D., *From Garden Cities to New Towns: Campaigning for Town and Country Planning, 1899–1946* (1991).

MacFadyen, D., *Sir Ebenezer Howard and the Town Planning Movement* (Manchester, 1970).

McAuslan, P., *The Ideologies of Planning Law* (1980).

McDougall, G., 'The State, Capital and Land: the History of Town Planning Revisited', (1979) *International Journal of Urban and Regional Research* 3(3), 361.

Read, E., *British Town and Country Planning* (1987).

Sutcliffe, A., 'Britain's First Town Planning Act: A Review of the 1909 Achievement' (1988) *Town Planning Review*, 59(3), 289–303.

Sutcliffe, A., *Towards the Planned City: Germany, Britain, the United States and France, 1780–1914* (Oxford, 1981).

Major studies in Victorian statutory reform

Clifford, F., *A History of Private Bill Legislation* (1885, 1887).

Cornish W. R., and de N. Clark, G., *Law and Society in England, 1750–1950* (1989).

Dicey, A. V., Introduction to the Study of the Law of the Constitution (1885).

Dicey, A. V., *Lectures on the Relation Between Law and Public Opinion in England During the Nineteenth Century* (1905).

MacDonagh, O., *A Pattern of Government Growth: 1800–60, The Passenger Acts and their Enforcement* (1961).

MacDonagh, O., *Early Victorian Government, 1830–1870* (1977).

For literature on the Parliamentary process of statutory reform see Vol XI, p. 1231.

Part Three: Labour Law

Briggs, A. and Saville, J. (eds), *Essays in Labour History* (1960)

Brodie, D., *A History of British Labour Law, 1867–1945* (Oxford, 2003).

Brown, K. D. (ed.), *Essays in Anti-Labour History: Responses to the Rise of Labour in Britain* (1974).

Clegg, H., Fox, A., and Thompson A. F., *A History of British Trade Unions since 1889: Vol. 1 1889–1910* (Oxford, 1964).

Curthoys, M., *Governments, Labour, and the Law in Mid-Victorian England: The Trade Union Legislation of the 1870s* (Oxford, 2004).

Davidson, R., *The Labour Problem in Late Victorian England* (1985).

Deakin, S. and Wilkinson, F., *The Law of the Labour Market: Industrialization, Employment, and Legal Evolution* (Oxford, 2005).

Ewing, K. D., *Trade Unions, the Labour Party and the Law: A Study of the Trade Union Act 1913* (Edinburgh, 1982).

Ewing, K. D. (ed.), *The Right to Strike: from the Trade Disputes Act 1906 to a Trade Union Freedom Bill 2006* (Liverpool, 2006).

Fox, A., *History and Heritage: Social Origins of the British Industrial Relations System* (1985).

Hedges, R. Y. and Winterbottom, R. S., *The Legal History of Trade Unionism* (1930).

Hobsbawm, E., *Labouring Men* (1964).

Hobsbawm, E., *Worlds of Labour* (1984).

Howell, C., *Trade Unions and the State: The Construction of Industrial Relations Institutions in Britain, 1890–2000* (Princeton, 2005).

Hunt, E. H., *British Labour History 1815–1914* (1981).

Jaffe, J. A., *Striking a Bargain: Work and Industrial Relations in England, 1815–1865* (Manchester, 2000).

Kahn-Freund, Sir O., 'Labour Law', in M. Ginsberg (ed.), *Law and Opinion in Twentieth Century England* (1959), 215–63.

Kahn-Freund, Sir O., *Labour and the Law* (3rd edn, by P. Davies and M. Freedland, 1983).

Kidner, R., 'Lessons in Trade Union Law Reform: The Origins and Passage of the Trade Disputes Act 1906' (1982) 2 *Leg. St.* 34–53.

Klarman, M. J., 'The Judges v the Unions: The Development of British Labour Law, 1867–1913' (1989) 75 *Virginia Law Rev.* 1487–1602

Lobban, M., 'Strikers and the Law, 1825–51', in P. Birks (ed.), *The Life of the Law* (1993).

Musson, A. E., *British Trade Unions 1800–1875* (1972).

Orth, J. V., *Combination and Conspiracy: A Legal History of Trade Unionism, 1721–1906* (Oxford, 1991).

Pelling, H. M., *A History of British Trade Unionism* (1976).

Price, R., *Masters, Unions and Men: Work Control and the Rise of Labour, 1830–1914* (Cambridge, 1984).

Roberts, B. C., *The Trades Union Congress, 1868–1921* (1958).

Steinfeld, R. J., *The Invention of Free Labor: The Employment Relation in English and American Law and Culture* (Chapel Hill, 1991).

Steinfeld, R. J., *Coercion, Contract and Free Labour in the Nineteenth Century* (Cambridge, 2001).

Thompson, E. P., *The Making of the English Working Class* (rev. edn, 1980).

Wedderburn, K. W. (Lord), *The Worker and the Law* (3rd edn, 1986).

Wrigley, C. (ed.), *A History of British Industrial Relations* (1982).

Part Four: Law of Persons: Family and Other Relationships

General

Cretney, S. M., *Family Law in the Twentieth Century* (Oxford, 2003).

Graveson, R. and Crane, F. R. (eds), *A Century of Family Law* (1957).

Macfarlane, A., *Marriage and Love in England: Modes of Reproduction, 1300–1840* (Oxford, 1986).

Outhwaite, R. B., *The Rise and Fall of the English Ecclesiastical Courts, 1530–1860* (Cambridge, 2006).

Shanley, M. L., *Feminism, Marriage, and the Law in Victorian England, 1850–1895* (Princeton, 1989).

Stetson, D. M., *A Woman's Issue* (Westport Conn., 1982).

Stone, L., *The Family, Sex and Marriage in England 1500–1800* (1977).

Trumbach, R., *The Rise of the Egalitarian Family* (New York, 1978).

Waddams, S. M., 'English Matrimonial Law on the Eve of Reform (1828–1857' (2000) 21 *JLH* 59–81.

Marriage

Anderson, O., 'The Incidence of Civil Marriage in Victorian England and Wales' (1975) 69 *P & P* 50.

Gillis, J. R., *For Better, For Worse* (Oxford, 1985).

Outhwaite, R. B., *Clandestine Marriage in England 1500–1850* (1995).

Perkin, J., *Women and Marriage in Nineteenth-century England* (1989).

Probert, R. J., 'The Judicial Interpretation of Lord Hardwicke's Act' (2002) 23 *JLH* 121–51

Wolfram, S., *In-laws and Outlaws: Kinship and Marriage in England* (1987).

Property of wives

Holcombe, L., *Wives and Property* (Oxford, 1983).

Kahn-Freund, Sir O., 'Matrimonial Property in England', in W. Friedmann (ed.), *Matrimonial Property Law* (1955), 267–314.

Shanley, M., *Feminism, Marriage and the Law in Victorian England 1850–95* (1989).

Staves, S., *Married Women's Separate Property in England, 1660–1833* (Cambridge, 1990).

Marital breakdown

Anderson, J. S., 'Legislative Divorce: Law for the Aristocracy?', in G. R. Rubin and D. Sugarman (eds), *Law, Economy and Society* (Abingdon, 1984), 412–44.

Biggs, J. M., *The Concept of Matrimonial Cruelty* (1962).

Doggett, M. E., *Marriage, Wife-Beating and the Law in Victorian England* (1992).

Foyster, E., *Marital Violence* (Cambridge, 2005).

Gibson, C. S., *Dissolving Wedlock* (1994).

Hammerton, A. J., *Cruelty and Companionship* (1992).

Horstman, A., *Victorian Divorce* (1985).

McGregor, O. R., *Divorce in England* (1957).

Menefee, S. P., *Wives for Sale* (Oxford, 1981).

Phillips, R., *Putting Asunder* (Cambridge, 1988).

Probert R. J., 'The Double Standard of Morality in the Divorce and Matrimonial Causes Act 1857' (1999) 28 *Anglo-Am. Law Rev.* 73–86.

Stone, L., *The Road to Divorce 1530–1987* (Oxford, 1990).

Thompson, E. P., *Customs in Common* (1991), Ch. 7 'Wives for Sale' (402–66); Ch. 8 'Rough Music' (467–538).

Waddams, S. M., *Law, Politics and the Church of England: The Career of Stephen Lushington* (Cambridge, 1992).

Wolfram, S., 'Divorce in England' (1985) 5 *OJLS* 155–86.

Wolfram, S., *In-Laws and Outlaws; Kinship and Marriage in England* (1987).

Woodhouse, M. K., 'The Marriage and Divorce Bill of 1857' (1959) 3 *AJLH* 260–76.

Children

Behlmer, G. K., *Child Abuse and Moral Reform in England, 1870–1908* (Stanford, 1982).

Behlmer, G. K., *Friends of the Family* (Stanford, 1998).

Gillis, J. R., 'The Evolution of Juvenile Delinquency in England, 1890–1914' (1975) 67 *P & P* 96.

Heywood, J. S., *Children in Care* (3rd edn, 1978).

Parsloe, P., *Juvenile Justice in Britain and the United States* (1978).

Pinchbeck, I. and Hewitt, M., *Children in English Society* (1969–73).

Walvin, J., *A Child's World* (Harmondsworth, 1982).

Insanity and mental defectiveness

Bartrip, P. L. W. J. *The Poor Law of Lunacy: The Administration of Pauper Lunatics* (1999).

Bartrip, P. L. W. J. 'Legal Madness in the Nineteenth Century' (2001) 14 *Social Hist. Medicine* 107–31.

Jones, K., *Lunacy, Law, and Conscience, 1744–1845* (1955).

Jones, K., *Asylums and After* (1993).

Porter, R., *Madmen: A Social History of Madhouses, Mad-doctors and Lunatics* (Stroud, 2004).

Scull A. T., *The Most Solitary of Afflictions: Madness and Society in Britain: 1700–1900* (New Haven, 1993).

Smith L. D., 'Cure, Comfort and Safe Custody': Public Asylums in early Nineteenth Century London (1999).

Part Five: Personality Rights and Intellectual Property

General

Sherman, B. and Bently, L., *The Making of Modern Intellectual Property Law: The British Experience 1760–1911* (Cambridge, 1999).

Drahos, P., *A Philosophy of Intellectual Property* (Burlington VT, 1996).

Ladas, S. P., *International Protection of Industrial Property* (Cambridge MA, 1930).

Defamation and rights of personality

Beverley-Smith, H., *The Commercial Appropriation of Personality* (Cambridge, 2002).

Beverley-Smith, H., Ohly A., and Lucas-Schloetter. A., *Privacy, Property and Personality: Civil Law Perspectives on Commercial Appropriation* (Cambridge, 2005).

McNamara, L., *Reputation and Defamation* (Oxford, 2007).

Mitchell, P., 'Malice in Defamation Law' (1998) 114 *LQR* 639–58.

Mitchell, P., *The Making of the Modern Law of Defamation* (Oxford, 2005).

Mitchell, P., 'The Foundations of Australian Defamation Law' (2006) *Sydney Law Rev.* 477–504.

Mitchell, P., 'Nineteenth-Century Defamation: Was it a Law of the Press?' (2008) *Media & Arts Law Rev.* 293–302.

Veeder, V. V., 'The History and Theory of the Law of Defamation' (1904) 4 *Columbia Law Rev.* 33–56.

Waddams, S. M., *Sexual Slander in Nineteenth Centuiry England* (Toronto, 2000).

Copyright

'Primary Sources in Copyright' (with Commentaries), *www.copyrighthistory.com*

Adeney, E., *The Moral Rights of Authors and Performers* (Oxford, 2006).

Alexander, I. J., 'The Metaphysics of the Law': Drawing the Boundaries of Copyright Law 1710–1911 (Cambridge University Ph.D., 2007).

Altick, R. D., *The English Common Reader* (Chicago, 1957).

Burrell, R. and Coleman, A., *Copyright Exceptions: The Digital Impact* (Cambridge, 2005).

Collins, A. S., *The Profession of Letters* (1928).

Deazley, R., *On the Origins of the Right to Copy* (Oxford, 2004).

Deazley, R., *Re-Thinking Copyright: History, Theory, Language* (Cheltenham, 2006).

Feather, J., *A History of British Publishing* (1988).

Feather, J., *Publishing, Piracy and Politics: An Historical Study of Copyright in Britain* (1994).

Gómez-Arostegui, H. T., 'What History Teaches Us about Copyright Injunctions and the Inadequate Remedy-at-Law Requirement' (2008) 81 *Southern California Law Rev.* 1197–280.

Kaplan, B., *An Unhurried View of Copyright* (New York, 1967).

McClean, D. and Schubert, K. (eds), *Dear Images: Art, Copyright and Culture* (2002).

McFarlane, G., *Copyright: The Development and Exercise of the Performing Right* (Eastbourne, 1980).

Macfarlane, R., *Original Copy: Plagiarism and Originality in Nineteenth Century Literature* (Oxford, 2007).

Myers, R. and Harris, M. (eds), *Development of the English Book Trade, 1700–1899* (Oxford, 1981).

Patry, W., *Copyright* (New York, 2007), Vol. I.

Peacock, A. T. and Weir, R. T., *The Composer in the Market Place* (Cambridge, 1975).

Raven, J., *The Business of Books: Booksellers and the English Book Trade* (New Haven, 2007).

Ricketson, S. and Ginsburg, J., *International Copyright and Neighbouring Rights* (Oxford, 2005).

Rose, M., *Authors and Owners: The Invention of Copyright* (Cambridge MA, 1993).

Saint-Amour, P. K., *The Copywrights: Intellectual Property and the Literary Imagination* (Ithaca, NY, 2003).

St Clair, W., *The Reading Nation in the Romantic Period* (Cambridge, 2004).

Saunders, D., *Authorship and Copyright* (1992).

Sherman, B. and Strowel, A. (eds), *Of Authors and Origins* (Oxford, 1994).

Scherer, F. M., *Quarter Notes and Banknotes* (Princeton, 2004).

Seville, C. A., *Literary Copyright Reform in Early Victorian England: The Framing of the 1842 Copyright Act* (Cambridge, 1999).

Seville, C. A., *The Internationalisation of Copyright Law: Books, Buccaneers and the Black Flag in the Nineteenth Century* (Cambridge, 2006).

Industrial property: patents, registered designs, confidential information

Batzel, V. M., 'Legal Monopoly in Liberal England: The Patent Controversy in the Mid-Nineteenth Century' (1980) 22 *Business Hist.* 189–201.

Boehm, K. and Silberston, A., *The British Patent System: Administration* (Cambridge, 1967).

Brennan, D., 'The Evolution of English Patent Claims as Property Definers' [2005] *IPQ* 361–99.

Coulter, M., *Property in Ideas: The Patent Question in Mid-Victorian Britain* (Kirksville, MI, 1991).

Duncan, L. J., *From Privileges to the Paris Convention: The Role of Theoretical Debate in the Evolution of National and International Patent Protection* (Monash University Ph.D., 1997).

Dutton, H. I., *The Patent System and Inventive Activity during the Industrial Revolution* (Manchester, 1984).

Gurry, F., *Breach of Confidence* (Oxford, 1984).

MacLeod C., *Inventing the Industrial Revolution: The English Patent System 1600–1800* (Cambridge, 1988).

Pettitt, C., *Patent Inventions: Intellectual Property and the Victorian Novel* (Oxford, 2004).

Van Zyl Smit, D., *The Social Creation of a Legal Reality: A Study of the Emergence and Acceptance of the British Patent System as a Legal Instrument for the Control of New Technology* (Edinburgh University Ph.D., 1981).

Van Zyl Smit, D. '"Professional" Patent Agents and the Development of the English Patent System' (1985) 13 *Int. J. Society & Law* 79–105.

Trade marks and unfair competition

Bently, L., 'From Communication to Thing: Historical Aspects of the Conceptualisation of Trade Marks as Property', in G. Dinwoodie and M. D. Janis (eds), *Trademark Law and Theory* (Cheltenham, 2008), Ch. 1.

Bently, L., 'The Making of Modern Trade Mark Law: The Construction of the Legal Concept of a Trade Mark (1860–1880)', in L. Bently, J. Davis, and J. G. Ginsburg (eds), *Trade Marks and Brands* (Cambridge, 2008), Ch. 1.

Schechter, F. I., *Historical Foundations of the Law relating to Trade Marks* (New York, 1925).

Wadlow, C., *The Law of Passing-Off* (3rd edn, 2004).

INDEX OF NAMES

This is the composite index for vols XI–XIII, inclusive. It relates mainly to persons who were active in the period 1820–1914. Double surnames are given under the first of the names. Peers with titles differing from their family name are given under the family name, with a cross-reference from the title.

* indicates a person who served as a superior court judge in Britain and/or as a judicial member of the House of Lords. The same indication is given to persons of equivalent status in other jurisdictions.
** indicates a person who served as a county court judge.
*** indicates a person who served as a Stipendiary Magistrate or Recorder, or in other judicial office not mentioned above.
† indicates a firm of solicitors or a legal family.

Abbott, C. (Lord Tenterden) * XI 531, 583, 704, 959, 967, 975, 991, 1026, 1043, 1074 1104, 1160 XII 99, 115, 169, 364, 447, 496, 498, 527, 534, 573, 586, 589, 617, 713, 748, 753, 759, 773, 915, 916, 1036, 1096, 1118, 1136 XIII 322, 323, 340
Abdy, J.T. *† XI 998, 1003, 1188n
Abercromby, J. XI 673
Abinger, (Lord) *see* Scarlett, J.
Acton, Sir E. XI 1001
Adams, W. XI 715
Adderley, C.B. (Lord Norton) XII 1081 XIII 554–6, 574–5, 577, 578
Addington, H. (Viscount Sidmouth) XI 15, 1006
Addison, C.G. XII 302, 313, 337, 374, 389, 398, 505, 508, 880, 893, 934
Adolphus, J. XI 642, 971n, 991, 1050
Albemarle, Lord XI 911
Albert, Prince Consort XI 302, 534 XIII 640, 953, 986
Alcock, W. XI 1132
Alderson, Sir E.H.* XI 507, 570, 622, 965, 984, 988, 1213 XII 99, 143, 446, 533, 536, 541, 544, 640, 900, 911, 925–6, 942, 954, 998–9, 1003, 1037, 1133 XIII 290, 340, 347
Alexander, Sir W. * XI 531, 676, 959, 972, 982
Allcock, H. XI 1155
Allen, G. Bough. XI 766, 1025
Alley, P. XI 642
Althorp, (Viscount) *see* Spencer, H.
Alvanley, (Lord) *see* Arden, R. P. *
Alverstone, Lord *see* Webster, R. *
Ames, J.B. XII 310, 313, 382–3, 387–8, 396–8
Amos, A. ** XI 610, 998, 1176, 1179, 1185 XIII 194–5, 198, 204–5, 221, 246, 378
Amos, S. XIII 214
Amphlett, Sir R.P. * XII 938
Ancaster, Duke of *see* Bertie, B.
Anderton, J. XI 1149

Andrew, F. XI 1150
Andrew's † XI 1131
Andrews, T. XI 642, 1050, 1105
Andrews, W.D. * XII 995
Anson, T.G. (Earl of Lichfield) XIII 670
Anson, Sir W.R. Bt * XI 1187, 1205 XII 308, 310–11, 313, 351, 355, 365, 376, 380–2, 387, 390, 395–6, 433, 469, 505, 517, 520, 569 XIII 800
Applegarth, R. XIII 668–9
Arabin, W. ** XI 644, 867
Archbold, J.F. XI 493–4 XIII 182
Arden, R.P. (Lord Alvanley) * XI 667 XII 21, 519
Arkwright, R. XIII 944, 947
Armitage, W.H. XI 1129
Armstrong, J.W.S. XI 1019, 1054
Armstrong, Sir W. XIII 958
Arnold, M. XI 727–8 XIII 522–3, 532
Arnould, Sir J. XII 699
Ashbourne, E.G. (Lord) * XI 539, 540
Ashburton, Lord *see* Baring, W.B.
Ashley, C. XII 356, 397
Ashley-Cooper, A. (7th Earl of Shaftesbury) XI 141, 149, 152, 153, 164, 174, 210, 352, 356–7, 460 XIII 560, 565, 573, 583, 587–588, 830
Ashley-Cooper, C. (6th Earl of Shaftesbury) XI 330–1
Ashton, A.J. XI 1024, 1029
Ashurst, Morris, Crisp † XI 1122, 1130, 1131, 1140, 1141
Ashurst (or Ashhurst), Sir W.H.* XI 92, 146, XII 133, 491, 532
Asquith, H.H. (Earl of Oxford and Asquith) XI 146, 208, 224, 225, 312, 912n, 964, 974, 1019, 1066 XIII 594, 703, 800
Atherton, Sir W. XI 975, 1063, 1066
Atiyah, P.S. XII 297–8, 315

Atkin, J.R. (Lord) * XI 965, 979 XII 944
  XIII 729
Atkinson † XI 998
Atkinson, J. (Lord) * XI 539, 995
  XII 982, 988, 1028 XIII 685, 711, 870
Atkinson, Lord * XI 539 XIII 863
Atlay, J.B. XI 1091
Attenborough, R. XII 849
Austin, C. XI 1052, 1053, 1062, 1069
Austin, J. XI 8, 21, 72, 84–90, 94, 98, 120,
  124, 126, 131, 258–60, 1179, 1180, 1186, 1203
  XII 242, 306, 568, 925–6, XIII 183, 192,
  194–196, 220, 221, 222, 223, 225, 228, 232,
  241, 270, 279, 308, 376
Avory, Sir H.E. * XI 645n, 970, 987
Avory, H.K. XI 642, 643, 645
Ayrton, A. XI 776, 783, 784n
Ayrton, W.S. *** XII 812

Bacon, F. (Viscount St Alban) XII 928, 950
  XIII 191, 206, 257, 270, 275
Bacon, F.H. ** XI 898, 1000
Bacon, Sir J. * XI 857, 965, 981, 988 XII 147–8,
  345, 443–4
Bacon, M. XII 1125
Badger † XI 1122
Bagehot, W. XI 18, 20, 316–17, 319, 321,
  354, 359, 535
Baggallay, Sir R.* XI 741, 800, 1067, 1069, 1072,
  1073 XII 119, 583
Bagshawe, W.H.G. ** XI 997 XII 842
Bailhache, Sir C.J. * XI 990
Baker, Sir R.*** XI 1001
Baker, W. * XI 942, 944
Balfour, A.J. (Earl) XI 28, 313, 912, 1074
  XIII 688
Balguy, J. XI 1029
Ball, W.V. XI 1019, 1023, 1044
Ball, W.W.R. XI 1019, 1024
Ballantine, W. XI 641, 970, 1007, 1010, 1056,
  1057, 1058, 1094
Bankes, Sir J.E. * XI 832, 984
Banks, W. XI 1131
Barber, C.C. ** XI 997
Barber, W. ** XI 1001, 1036
Barber, W.H. XI 1120, 1123, 1149, 1166
Baring, W.B. (Lord Ashburton) XI 579
Barker, C.M. XI 1120
Barker, E. XI 102
Barnardo, Dr T. XIII 816, 819
Barrington, C. XI 1194
Barrow, W. XI 1122
Barry, Sir C. XI 782
Barry, E.M. XI 783, 1084
Barton, T. XI 1128, 1136n, 1145
Bass, M.A. (Lord Burton) XI 905
Bateson, W.G. XI 1142

Bathurst, H. (3rd Earl) XI 910n
Bathurst, H.A. XI 701n, 731
Baxter Norton Rose see Norton Rose
Baxter, D. XI 1118, 1141
Baxter, R. XI 1121, 1138, 1139
Bayley, F. ** XI 993, 1003, 1004
Bayley, Sir J. * XI 184, 512 XII 331, 498, 540, 574,
  585, 586, 587, 708, 731, 751, 767, 906–8, 1038
  XIII 857, 881, 912, 949
Baylis, T.H. ** XI 871
Beaconsfield, Earl see Disraeli, B.
Beadon, W.F. *** XI 709
Beale & Co. † XI 1122, 1154, 1155
Beale, C.G. XI 1153
Beale, J.H. XII 382
Beales, E. ** XI 993
Beasley, A. XIII 699, 701
Beaven, M.R. XI 1218
Beawes, W. XII 756
Beccaria, C. XI 80 XIII 141
Beck, A. XIII 132, 134–5
Beckett-Denison, E.
  (Lord Grimthorpe) XI 567, 1054
Bedwell, F.A. ** XII 840
Bell, J. XI 661, 669
Bell, R. XIII 699, 702
Bellenden Ker, C.H. XII 23, 49, 51–2, 60–1, 63,
  78, 181, 193, 620–1, 626 XIII, 194, 196, 197, 198,
  204, 338, 378
Bellot, H.H. XII 868
Benbow. J. XI 1145
Benjamin, J.P. XI 967, 1060 XII 308, 345, 433,
  466, 484–5, 510–11, 759
Bennet, W.H. XI 960
Bentham, J. XI 8, 46, 56–7, 72–84, 91, 94,
  101, 134, 172, 219, 258–9, 599, 604, 611, 616
  XII 50–1 XIII 25, 102, 141, 188, 189, 190, 192,
  193, 197, 200, 218, 220, 230–232, 299, 309, 336,
  469, 478, 517, 604, 614, 940
Beresford † XI 998
Beresford, C.H.W. ** XI 1000, 1002
Bernard, M. XI 261, 277, 1188n
Bertie, B. (Duke of Ancaster) XI 907
Besant, A. XIII 368–70, 686–7, 811–12
Bessemer, Sir H. XIII 959
Best, W.D. (Lord Wynford) * XI 370, 532n,
  533n, 584, 702, 969, 977, 982, 1054 XII 38, 481,
  527–8, 577, 712, 742, 749, 770–1, 895, 910, 914,
  1120
Best, W.M. XI 607, 1036, 1237
Bethell, R. (Lord Westbury) * XI 154, 341, 534,
  535, 543, 554, 560, 565, 659, 660, 710, 711–12,
  746n, 753n, 755, 760, 763, 782, 783, 785, 911n,
  978, 982, 987, 991, 996, 997, 1039, 1043, 1050,
  1062, 1066, 1067, 1069, 1102n, 1104, 1106, 1181,
  1182, 1183, 1186, 1215, 1216n, 1217, 1221n
  XII 8, 89, 194, 198, 211, 368, 422–3, 528, 650–1,

818–20, 822, 837, 1070, 1073, 1075, 1100
  XIII 205, 206, 207, 416, 773, 783, 793, 915,
  965, 969, 995–8, 1001, 1008
Bethune, J.D. XI 890
Beven, T. XII 948–9, 955–6, 982–3, 995
Beveridge, Sir W. XI 208, 217, 218 XIII 718
Bexley, Lord see Vansittart, N. *
Bickersteth, H. (Lord Langdale) * XI 396, 532n,
  533n, 560, 647, 654, 657, 658, 659n, 660, 664n,
  678, 687, 968, 990, 991, 1041, 1051, 1100, 1106,
  1166 XII 24, 35, 236, 248, 261, 275, 437, 762
  XIII 994
Bigham, J.C. (Lord Mersey) * XI 539, 725, 748,
  753n, 813, 823, 970, 984
Birkenhead, Earl see Smith, F.E.
Birnie, Sir R. *** XI 1005
Biron, Sir C. *** XI 1009, 1011, 1046, 1061
Birrell, A. XIII 885
Bismarck, O. (von) XI 265, 269
  XIII 687–8, 957
Blackburn, C. (Lord) * XI 33, 372–3, 375–7, 383,
  520, 537, 539, 544, 746, 768, 778, 886, 965, 966,
  967, 969, 981, 983, 988, 990, 997, 1213 XII 34,
  45, 99–100, 302, 304, 308, 339, 341–3, 386–7,
  424, 449–50, 452, 465–6, 483, 488, 493, 503,
  514–15, 517, 519–20, 539, 658, 708, 749, 764,
  776, 898, 921, 930–1, 938–40, 962, 966, 972,
  1073, 1083, 1104, 1120, 1123, 1125, 1139–40,
  1143–4, 1147, 1150 XIII 64, 103, 208, 210, 227,
  248, 272–3, 325–327, 330, 331, 370, 390, 407,
  413, 426, 427, 449, 862–3, 869–70, 891, 1002
Blackburne, F. * XII 929
Blackstone, Sir W. * XI 7–9, 24, 60, 75–6,
  84, 88, 180, 238–9, 257, 262, 325, 530, 581,
  584, 927, 1025, 1099 XII 98, 316, 887, 917
  XIII 14, 23, 116, 181, 182, 188, 217, 218, 219, 220,
  229, 230–233, 236, 237, 241, 257, 267–70, 279,
  352, 375, 380, 394, 420, 428, 431, 541,
  627, 807–8, 934
Blair, J.K. ** XI 1015
Blenkinsop, J. XI 1128
Blennerhasset, R.P. XI 1059
Blofield, T. C. XI 1048, 1091, 1095
Blomfield, C.J. XI 395–6
Bolland, Sir W.P. * XI 492, 984 XII 1134
Bompas, C.C. XII 919
Bompas, H.M. ** XI 969
Bond, N. *** XI 1006
Bonner, G.A. XI 831
Boodle, E. XI 1117
Boodle, Hatfield & Co. † XI 1122, 1145, 1149
Boodle, J. XI 1146
Booth, C. XIII 499, 504
Booth's † XI 1025, 1118
Boothby, B. * XI 242
Borthwick, Sir A. XIII 852, 857, 869, 878
Bosanquet, Sir F.A. ** XI 644

Bosanquet, Sir J.B. * XI 122 560, 570, 635, 659,
  1104 XII 362, 364–5, 918
Bosanquet, Sir S.R.C. XI 1093, 1136
Botterell and Roche † XI 1142
Bottomley, H. XI 817
Boulter, C. XI 1141
Bousfield, W. XI 1025
Bouverie, P. XI 708, 1111
Bovill, Sir W. * XI 377, 760, 769, 795, 973, 977,
  990, 1041, 1063 XII 581, 954–5, 971, 979
Bowen Rowlands, E. XI 1025
Bowen, C.S.C. (Lord) * XI 301, 341, 516, 537,
  803, 809, 818, 961, 965, 968, 977, 979n, 1025
  XII 354–5, 366, 490–1, 580, 582, 604, 695,
  1008, 1014, 1050–52, 1058, 1062, 1145
  XIII 315, 867
Bowker, A.E. XI 1031, 1032, 1033
Bowring, Sir J., Bt XI 84
Bowyer, Sir G. XI 536, 1079, 1083 XIII 794
Bradlaugh, C. XI 387–8, 503, 610, 613 XIII 364,
  368–370, 812
Bradley, I. XI 947, 952
Bradshaw, T.J.C. ** XI 994
Brampton, Lord see Hawkins, H.
Bramwell, G.W.W. (Lord)* XI 202, 230, 232,
  539, 544, 602, 759, 803, 815, 961, 965, 967, 979
  988 XII 44, 299, 341–2, 344, 353, 410, 429–31,
  455, 464, 489, 513, 517, 525, 546, 548, 592–3,
  625–6, 920, 922, 964, 968, 974, 1007, 1012,
  1052, 1073, 1098–99, 1103–4, 1142–43, 1147,
  1149 XIII 5,107, 208, 244, 247, 248, 252, 272,
  310, 311, 325–327, 413, 426, 448, 510, 662, 689,
  694, 805
Brandeis, L. XIII 847–8, 851, 854, 856, 863, 869,
  878, 900, 989
Brassey, T. (Earl of Brassey) XIII 679
Bray, Sir R.M. * XI 790, 830 XII 873
Brereton, C.D. XI 927
Brett, W.B. (Viscount Esher) * XI 39, 400, 407,
  517 547, 718, 722, 769, 802, 803, 809, 817, 819,
  977, 979, 981, 987, 988, 989, 991, 1031, 1034,
  1221 XII 342, 348–9, 376, 483, 494, 505–6, 516,
  548, 660, 671, 687, 700, 724–5, 763, 890, 893,
  937, 939–41, 945–6, 948–9, 951–2, 957, 970,
  974, 981, 988, 990, 1013–15, 1033, 1046, 1049,
  1051–8, 1061–2, 1086, 1089, 1119 XIII 280, 324,
  326, 327, 407, 463, 675–7, 694, 866, 870
Bridgeman, B.J. XI 887, 891, 893
Brierley, E. *** XI 1016
Bright, J. XI 112, 167 XIII 153, 207, 387
Broderip, W. *** XI 1006, 1012
Brodie, P.B. XII 60, 73
Brougham, H.P. (Lord Brougham and
  Vaux) * XI 57, 84, 134, 182, 231, 394, 432, 529,
  532, 533, 534, 547–8, 549, 550, 553, 557, 558,
  560, 563, 575, 576, 579, 582, 598, 602, 606,
  608, 609, 612, 614, 628, 629, 631, 638, 640,

678, 680, 695, 702, 704, 720, 751, 773, 774,
855, 858–60, 862–3, 864, 876, 904, 909, 927,
963, 967, 975, 982, 991, 998, 1007, 1035, 1065,
1056, 1059, 1098, 1111, 1144, 1176, 1180 XII 28,
39, 71–2, 145–6, 159–60, 248, 288, 405–6, 415,
749, 795–7, 805–8, 810, 813–14, 836 XIII 23,
25, 74, 102, 131, 148, 193, 194, 197, 201, 205, 211,
338, 399, 469, 511, 518–519, 614, 741–2, 758, 773,
778–81, 783, 837, 839–40, 899, 913, 938, 952
Brougham, J. *** XI 50, 797
Browne, J.H.B. XI 829, 971, 994, 1054
Brownlow, Earl *see* Cust, J.
Brownlow, Lord XI 907, 908
Bruce, Sir G. * XI 722, 724, 820, 973 XII 1130
Brundrett, J. XI 1056
Brunel, I.K. XIII 954
Brunel, M.I. XIII 944–5
Bryan, Sir T. * XII 342
Bryce, J. (Lord) XI 263, 312, 317, 912, 1186, 1188,
1201 XIII 532, 618–19
Buchan, J. (Lord Tweedsmuir) XI 1035
Buckland, W.W. XI 1205
Buckle, H.T. XI 103, 106
Buckley, H.B. (Lord Wrenbury) * XI 1039
XII 156, 661, 667, 1101
Buckmaster, S.O. (Lord) * XI 504, 1047
XIII 968–9
Bucknill, Sir T. * XI 724, 1093
Buer, H. XII 859–60
Bullen, E.U. XI 1053, 1061 XII 595
Buller, Sir F. * XII 525–6, 592, 904 XIII 731,
861, 933
Bulwer, E. Lytton (or Bulwer
Lytton) XIII 896–7
Burdett, Sir F. XI 653 XIII 335, 338
Burge, W. XI 281
Burke, E. XI 631 XIII 25
Burn, R. XIII 476
Burnet, T. * XII 789
Burns, J. XI 510–11 XIII 501, 505, 588,
593–95, 687
Burrough, Sir J. * XI 972, 984 XII 337
Burrow, Sir J. XI 1212, 1213
Burton, Lord *see* Bass, M.A.
Burton, E.F. XI 1133
Burton, F. XI 632
Busfield, J.A. XI 903
Bute, Marquis of XI 634, 635
Butler, C. XI 1051
Butt, Sir C.P. * XI 722, 724, 747, 748, 982
Buxton, S. XIII 691
Buxton, Sir T.F. XI 135–8, 141, 145, 149
XIII 143, 159
Byles, Sir J.B. * XI 372, 621, 1027, 1179
XII 379, 731, 738, 747, 859, 1008,
1098 XIII 245
Byrne, Sir E.W. * XI 983 XIII 973

Caillard, C.F.D. ** XI 995
Cairns, H.C.M. (Earl) * XI 398 536, 542,
545, 562,565, 566, 567, 760, 761, 762, 763,
778, 780 785, 794, 800, 805, 822, 874, 879–80,
965, 966, 967, 970, 973, 975, 983, 986, 989,
994, 1039, 1049, 1063, 1068, 1190, 1192, 1195,
1196 XII 29, 91–3, 107, 197, 200, 208, 211,
340, 424, 466, 603, 648, 650–1, 757, 776,
938, 940, 1004, 1144, 1146 XIII 68, 210,
788, 915, 965, 1001
Camden (Earl) *see* Pratt, C.
Campbell, J. (Lord) * XI 184, 339–40, 370,
372, 375, 408, 496, 518, 533, 534, 559, 560,
578, 589, 597, 598, 616, 660, 712, 759, 760,
774, 780, 804, 959, 962, 965, 966, 967, 969,
975, 981, 988, 991, 1020, 1024, 1025, 1030,
1031, 1034, 1057, 1063, 1065, 1068, 1071, 1077,
1091, 1096, 1099, 1109, 1215 XII 39, 51, 54,
59–61, 73, 100, 150, 185–6, 352, 417, 419–21,
448, 500–3, 543, 545, 600, 702, 706, 710,
713, 740, 802, 933, 950, 961, 986, 996–7,
1007, 1036, 1045, 1127–8 XIII 90, 97, 104,
109, 130, 131, 201–202, 211, 302, 323, 338,
365, 398, 542, 662–3, 731–2, 781, 783, 853–4,
858, 864, 876
Campbell, J.F. (1st Earl Cawdor) XI 631, 635
Campbell, R. XII 926
Campbell-Bannerman, Sir H. XI 29, 208, 324,
XIII 704
Canning, G. XI 164, 961, 1063, 1067
Carew, J.M. XI 891
Carlyle, T. XI 83, 91, 94, 134, 155, 188, 193, 200
XIII 158, 471
Carpenter, M. XIII 815–16
Carsdale, J.S. XI 1132
Carson, E.H. (Viscount) * XI 725, 961, 977,
1020, 1032, 1060, 1062, 1102, 1105 XIII 363
Carter, S. XI 1037
Cartmell, H. XI 1121, 1153
Cartmell, Harrison and Ingram † XI 1163
Cassels, Sir J.D. * XI 1036
Cave, G. (Viscount) * XI 913
Cave, Sir L.W. * XI 516, 826, 881, 981
XII 873, 875, 893
Cawdor, Lord *see* Campbell, J.F.
Cecil, R. XI 1091
Chadwick, D. XII 640
Chadwick, E. XI 74, 84–5, 91, 173, 176, 195, 334,
348, 354, 356, 446, 462, 477–8, 917n XII 1001
XIII 25–27, 29, 38, 46, 478, 488, 495, 535–8,
543, 561, 587
Chaffers, A. XI 817
Chalmers, Sir M.D.** XII 307, 308, 326, 483,
485, 679, 688, 731–2, 742–3 XIII 215, 216
Chalmers, Sir McKenzie. D. XI 617, 766n, 893,
894, 897, 905, 995, 1001
Chalmers, T. XI 163–5, XIII 631

Chamberlain, J. XI 28, 151, 193, 196, 206, 210, 217, 223, 225, 317, 553 XII 824, 841, 848, 1018–19 XIII 498, 688

Chambers, A.M. XII 785–6

Chambers, Sir T. ** XI 644

Chambre, A. * XII 526, 587, 709

Chan, T. XI 1197

Channell, Sir A.N.* XI 790, 823n, 830, 832n XII 519, 867–8 XIII 98, 253, 419

Channell, Sir W.F. * XI 1036 XII 919, 935, 1006

Chapman, C. *** XI 1008, 1009 XIII 787

Charles, Sir A. * XI 791

Charlesworth, Wood and Brown † XI 1148

Charley, Sir W.T. ** XI 536, 644, 1036

Chelmsford, (Lord) see Thesiger, F.

Cherry, Sir B.L. XII 203, 224, 226, 228–30

Chetwynd-Talbot, C. (Earl Talbot) XI 909

Chitty, J. XI 586, 1176, 1177

Chitty, J. (the elder) XII 316, 731, 745 XIII 58, 72, 74, 92, 112

Chitty, J. (the younger) XII 301, 303, 313, 317, 336, 364, 378, 389, 396, 398, 508, 541

Chitty, Sir J.W. * XI 436, 790, 816, 843, 990 XII 93, 293, 646, 725, 1110

Chitty, T.W. XI 789, 790, 818, 823, 1025, 1049

Christian, E.B.V. XI 1110

Christie, J.H. XII 61, 63, 72, 77, 181, 193

Churchill, Sir W. XI 128, 137, 170, 173, 194, 208, 213, 217, 225, 403 XII 680 XIII 718

Clabon, J.M. XI 1099, 1208

Clark H. XI 1037

Clark Hall, W. XIII 821–2

Clarke † XI 1094

Clarke, Sir E.G. XI 608, 753, 962, 976, 1020, 1030, 1043, 1066, 1070, 1167

Clauson, A.C.* (Lord) XIII 1011

Cleasby, Sir A. * XI 973 XII 944 XIII 676

Clerk, J.F. XII 952–3, 1125

Clifford Turner † XI 1141

Clive, G. ** XI 1008

Cluer, A.R. ** XI 1008

Coase, R.H. XII 885

Cobbe, F.P. XIII 797

Cobbett, W. XIII 336, 487

Cobden, R. XI 112, 165, 167, 197

Cock, A.J. XI 991

Cockburn, Sir A.J.E. * XI 58, 261, 273–5, 383, 408–9, 411, 416, 501, 746, 760, 761, 762, 767n, 768, 769, 788, 799, 805, 966, 978, 979, 987, 991, 1067, 1077, 1082, 1093, 1105 XII 341–2, 489–90, 504, 510, 547, 593, 603, 687, 695, 766, 898, 931, 951–2, 954, 961, 964, 993, 1006, 1099 XIII 64, 65, 66, 134, 208, 211–213, 239, 241, 243, 248, 249, 273, 310, 317, 323, 361, 367–369, 408, 411, 426, 665, 676–7, 824, 874

Cohen, A. XI 970, 1020, 1101

Coke, Sir E. * XI 1099 XII 386, 401 XIII 218, 237

Cole, A.W.M. XI 1020

Cole, F.T. XI 1042

Colebrooke, H. XII 301

Coleridge, B.S.J. (Lord) * XII 969

Coleridge, J.D. (Lord) * XI 204, 516, 598–9, 604–5, 746, 763, 764, 768, 769, 770, 779, 788–9, 795, 799, 803, 809, 817, 823, 826, 827, 828, 830, 832, 901, 964, 967, 976, 977, 978, 979, 981, 985, 987, 989, 1041, 1044, 1060, 1064, 1066, 1068, 1070, 1073, 1091 XII 528, 939, 965, 994, 1016, 1046 XIII 70, 125, 126, 186, 210, 213, 275, 276, 278, 286, 311, 364, 383, 384, 389, 418, 461, 463, 672, 678, 853. 874

Coleridge, Sir J.T. * XI 390, 393, 493, 495, 500, 559, 622, 782, 964, 965, 1033, 1061 XII 371, 461, 527, 766, 987–8, 1045 XIII 731

Coleridge, S.T. XI 91–6, 117

Collier, J.F. ** XI 994 XII 866

Collier, J.P. XI 1026, 1055

Collier, R.P. (Lord Monkswell) * XI 561, 710, 712, 777, 976, 1054 XII 837

Collini, S. XI 122

Collins, A. XII 859

Collins, R.H. (Lord) * XI 538, 546 XII 519, 705, 989

Collison, W. XIII 689, 699

Colonsay, Lord see McNeill, D.

Colquhoun, P. XI 141, 144, 1006 XIII 25–7

Coltman, Sir T. * XI 965 XII 920

Colvile, Sir John (Colvile) * XI 557, 559, 560, 561, 982

Comte, A. XI 96, 101–3, 105–6, 154, 192, 257 XIII 668

Comyns, J. XII 302, 1096, 1098–9

Cook, E.R. XI 1167

Cook, J. XI 1046

Cook, T. XII 327

Cook, W.G.H. XIII 824–5

Cooke, W.H. ** XI 880

Cookson, W.S. XI 1207

Cooper, C.P. XI 529, 685

Copley, J.S. (Lord Lyndhurst) * XI 370, 432, 507, 531, 532, 533, 534, 535, 553, 558, 579, 598, 656, 657, 658, 671, 674, 677, 688, 702, 706, 749, 859–60, 862–4, 874, 959, 964, 969, 972, 979, 984, 987, 988, 1008, 1030, 1055, 1056, 1057, 1065, 1074 XII 39, 60, 159, 181, 252, 368, 436, 454, 708, 767, 805–6, 918 XIII 74, 76, 201, 202, 240, 366, 513, 750, 783

Cottenham, (Earl) see Pepys, C.C.

Cotton, Sir H. * XI 370, 432, 507, 803 XII 393, 425, 428–30, 570, 1087 XIII 513, 750, 783, 870

Couch, Sir R. * XI 561 XII 561, 562

Courtenay, W. (Earl of Devon) XI 532, 558, 675, 677, 685
Coventry, M. ** XI 997
Coward Chance † XI 1118, 1125, 1129, 1131, 1140, 1141
Coward, L. XI 1086
Cowper, H. XI 1213
Cox, E.W. XI 1019, 1024, 1030, 1033, 1057, 1058, 1206–10, 1216 XIII 672
Cox, H. ** XI 21, 994, 1002
Cox, S.C. XI 675
Cozens-Hardy, H.H. (Lord) * XI 984 XII 176, 1025, 1029, 1031–32 XIII 707, 1003
Crackanthorpe, M.H. 1193
Cranworth (Lord) see Rolfe, B.
Cresswell, Sir C. * XI 408 622, 625, 636, 640, 735, 746, 1213 XII 337, 459, 704, 1141 XIII 788, 791
Cripps, C.A. (Lord Parmoor) * XI 511
Crisp, Sir F. XI 1130, 1141
Crispe, T.E. XI 1039, 1040, 1103
Crompton, Sir C. * XI 871, 1213 XII 6, 352, 390, 496, 501, 512, 541, 545, 1005, 1044, 1052, 1073 XIII 663
Crooks, W. XIII 499
Cross, F. XI 676
Cross, J. XI 1059
Cross, R.A. (Lord) XI 764, 779, 826, 1014 XIII 584, 586, 677
Cross, Sjt XI 1059
Crosse, E.W. XI 700
Crouch, Sir R. XII 995
Crowder, Sir R.B. * XI 1093 XII 1098
Crump, F.O. XI 1089
Cubitt, W. XIII 954
Cuffe, H.J.A. (Earl of Desart) XI 753, 807 XIII 975–6
Cullen, A. XII 786
Cust, J. (Earl Brownlow) XI 907, 908

Dalhousie (Marquess) see Ramsay, J.A.B.
Dallas, Sir R. * XI 371, 408, 988 XII 497, 574, 914, 1096
Dampier, Sir H. * XI 797n
Dance, H. XII 800
Danckwerts, W.O. XI 829, 971, 1050
Daniel, W.T.S. ** XI 1003, 1004, 1064, 1211, 1216–18 XII 842
Darling, Sir C.J. (Lord) * XI 806, 832, 966, 974, 987, 1047 XII 518, 1061 XIII 254, 311
Darwin, C. XI 114 XIII 726
Dasent, G.W. XI 697, 698
Dauncey, P. XI 1093, 1105
Davey, H. (Lord) * XI 537, 539, 544, 838, 991, 1038 XII 155, 214, 216, 641, 647, 653, 1078 XIII 710
Davidson, C. XII 11, 72–3, 81, 86, 89–91, 101–3, 105, 137, 140, 150, 209

Dawes, H. XI 893
Day, J. XI 1056
Day, Sir J.C.F.S. * XI 592, 826, 962, 967, 979, 989 XII 351
de Grey, J.A *** XI 1009, 1010
de Grey, W. (Lord Walsingham) * XI 757
de Rutzen, Sir A. *** XI 1015
Deacon, C. XI 1148
Deane, Sir B. * XI 725, 748, 754
Deane, Sir J.P. XI 698, 722, 1064
Deloitte, W.W. XI 1138
Denman, A. * XI 795
Denman, G. *** XI 1008
Denman, G.L. *** XI 612 XII 1124
Denman, T. (2nd Baron) * XI 339–40, 390, 513, 532, 537, 609, 612, 614, 622n, 624, 781, 804n, 805n, 859n, 942, 963, 981, 985, 986, 988, 1024, 1035, 1037n, 1044, 1046, 1059, 1074, 1075, 1094 XII 28, 112, 350, 364–5, 375, 377, 402, 413, 459, 492, 498–9, 574, 577, 593, 706, 749, 762, 915, 922, 1126, 1135 XIII 60, 74, 93, 97, 115, 119, 131, 140, 146, 148, 238, 336, 404, 639, 643, 874
Denning, A.T. (Lord) * XI 547 XII 444
Derby, Lord see Smith-Stanley E.
Desart, Earl see Cuffe H.J.A.*
Devon, Earl see Courtenay, W.
Devonshire, Duke of see Cavendish, S.C. *
Dibdin, Sir L.*** XIII 800
Dicey, A.V. XI 10, 18, 22, 72, 74, 90, 112, 115, 130, 227, 281–3, 512, 527, 1046, 1097, 1187, 1201, 1205 XII 47–8 XIII 472,504, 530, 598–604, 606, 609, 612, 615, 672, 761–2
Dickens, C. XI 142, 232, 646, 695, 1007, 1109, 1146 XIII 468, 514, 550, 809, 909, 942
Dickens, Sir H.F. ** XI 970, 987, 1039
Dickinson, T.E. XI 629
Digby, Sir K.E. ** XI 1198
Dilke, Sir C.W. XI 912 XIII 586, 705, 708, 786
Dinsdale, F.T. ** XI 999
Disraeli, B. (Earl of Beaconfield) XI 18, 25, 27, 202, 209, 221, 460, 535, 536, 963, 1091, 1149 XIII 576, 677, 761, 894
Disturnal, W.J. XI 815, 922
Dixon, G. XIII 527
Dodd, C. ** XII 839
Dodgson, H.H. XI 767, 1027
Dodson, Sir G. ** XI 1041, 1042, 1044
Dodson, Sir J. * XI 965, 698, 709, 711, 733
Doherty, J. XIII 658
Domat, J. XII 537
Douglas, S. (Lord Glenbervie) XI 1213
Drew, J. XI 1141
Du Cane, Sir E. XIII 12, 125, 164–9, 175, 179
Dube, B. XI 1020
Duer, J. XII 699–700
Duignan, W. XI 1111
Dumont, E. XI 75, 80, 85
Duncan, J. XI 1199

Duncombe, Sir T.S. XI 707, 1008, 1010, 1011
Dundas, Sir D. XI 976
Dunedin (Viscount) *see* Murray, A.G.
Duval, L. XI 1051 XII 69, 74
Duxbury, N. XI 129–30
Dwarris, Sir F.W.L. XI 41, 47, 53–4, 629
Dyke and Stokes † XI 699

East, Sir E.H.* XI 557 XIII 181, 230–231, 269,
   301, 302, 377, 380, 412, 431, 437, 438, 441, 448
Eddis, A.S. ** XI 1196
Eden, R. XII 794 XIII 778
Eden, R.H. (Lord Henley) XI 676
Eden, W. (Lord Auckland) XIII 139, 188, 219, 778
Edge, J.B. ** XI 940
Edlin, Sir P. ** XI 921, 922
Edmunds, L. XIII 955
Edmunds, L.H. XI 1093
Edward VII, Prince of Wales, King* XII 518
   XIII 786
Edwards, H. XI 1127
Eldon (Earl of) *see* Scott, J.
Ellenborough (1st & 2nd Lords) *see* Law, E.
Ellis-Davis, J. XI 1092
Ellison Nares † XI 1125
Ellison, C.E. ** XI 1015
Ellison, T. XI 992
Elmhirst, C. XI 1154
Elmsley, W. ** XI 1001
Elphinstone, Sir H. Bart XI 707, 1205 XII 220,
   222, 224
Elton, C. XI 1082
Emden, A.C.R. ** XI 1000, 1003
Émérigon, B.M. XII 677
Erichsen, J.E. XII 993
Erle, T.W. XI 600, 1132
Erle, Sir W. * XI 390, 408, 498, 518, 746, 972,
   981, 982, 984, 990, 1057, 1216 XII 306, 355–6,
   379, 474, 484, 502, 512, 702, 720, 922–3, 970–1,
   974, 986, 1000, 1044, 1051, 1057, 1097, 1129
   XIII 95, 445, 459, 636, 663–4, 667, 669, 869
Erskine, Sir T. * XI 560
Erskine, T. (Lord) * XI 146, 642, 683, 1048, 1105
   XII 441
Esher, Viscount *see* Brett, W.B.
Espinasse, I. XI 960, 1212, 1213
Evans XI 1136
Evans, J. XI 570
Evans, Sir S.T. * XI 725, 738–9, 748, 965, 1065
Evans, Sir W.D. XII 301, 360, 567
Ewart, W. XI 1216
Eyre, Sir J. * XII 753, 910 XIII 946

Fairfield XI 1160
Falconer, T.F. ** XI 993, 1001
Fane, R.G.C. *** XI 678 XII 806, 812
Farr, Dr W. XI 945
Farrer & Co. † XI 1123, 1131, 1135, 1140, 1145

Farrer, J.W. XI 535, 676, 678, 679, 680
Farrer, T.H. XIII 895–6
Farrow, T. XII 862–5
Farwell, Sir G. * XI 503–6, 518, 1036
   XII 983 XIII 707, 712, 863
Fawcett, H. XIII 527
Fawcett, W.M. XI 1210
Field, D.D. XI 589, 758 XII 306–7 XIII 249, 959
Field, E.W. XI 658, 677, 686, 687, 782, 783, 1121,
   1124, 1167, 1208
Field, W.V. (Lord) * XI 509, 516, 539, 809,
   981, 989 XII 991, 1017, 1052, 1056, 1085, 1138–39
   XIII 435–6
Finlason, W.F. XI 643
Finlay, R.B. (Lord) * XI 261, 976, 1191
Fisher, R.A. ** XI 900, 994
Fitzgerald, J.D. (Lord) XI 537
Fitzmaurice, H.P. (Marquess of
   Lansdowne) XI 549, 550, 558
Fitzroy, H. XI 876
Fletcher Moulton, H. (Lord Moulton) XI 511,
   535, 808, 966, 978, 991, 1084, XII 975, 1148,
   XIII 712, 966, 1005
Follett, Sir C.F. XI 1111, 1147
Follett, Sir W. XI 861, 975, 1043, 1060, 1061,
   1093, 1100 XIII 512
Foote, J.A. XI 969, 1091, 109
Forbes, J. XI 969
Ford, C. XI 1156
Forster, J. XI 647, 654, 682
Forster, W.E. XI 597 XIII 490, 525–9
Fortescue Brickdale, Sir C. XII 202, 219,
   222, 224–5
Foss, E. 960
Foster, Sir M.* XIII 220, 283, 289, 290, 293, 388,
   411, 412, 430, 432
Foucault, M. XIII 152, 177–9, 833–4
Foulkes, W.D.I. XI 960
Fourier, C. XI 113
Fowler, H. (Viscount Wolverhampton) XI 764,
   766, 889, 1001, 1152
Fox C.J. XIII 853
Fox, R.V. (Lord Holland) XI 532
Fox, W. XII 302
Francis, C. XI 1123
Francis, C.K. XI 1009
Fray, R. XI 803
Free, E.D. XI 695
Freeman, E.A. XI 21–2
French, D.O.C.** XI 898–9
Frere Cholmeley † XI 1130
Frere, G. XI 1155
Freshfields † XI 1040, 1121, 1122, 1131, 1136,
   1149, 1169
Freshfield, J.W. XI 1117, 1155
Fry, Sir E. * XI 261, 803 XII 100, 162, 394, 425,
   428–9, 467, 550, 559, 870, 1138 XIII 710, 1011
Fulton, Sir F. ** XI 1038

Gale, C.J. XII 880

Gandhi, M.T. XI 1020

Garrold, T.W. XI 1133

Garrow, Sir W.* XI 642, 963, 975, 984, 1066
XII 914, 1134

Gascoyne-Cecil, R.A.T. (Marquess of
Salisbury) XI 28, 302, 317–18, 321, 345, 465
XIII 532, 586, 589–90, 595, 688–92

Gaselee, Sir S. * XI 621

Gatty, G. XI 686

Geldart, J.W. XI 1176, 1194

Gem, T.H. XI 1154

Gent, J. ** XII 848

Geoghegan, G. XI 642

George III (King) XI 17, 26 XIII 823

George IV (King) XI 17, 302

George V (King) * XI 754 XIII 789

George, Prince, Duke of Cambridge XI 406,
411, 417, 420

Gibbs, Sir V. * XI 370, 983, 988, 989, 991, 1026,
1074, 1110 XII 455, 511, 532, 587, 977

Gibson and Weldon † XI 1200

Gibson, E. (Lord Ashbourne) * XIII 697

Giffard, Sir G.M. * XI 660 XII 1074

Giffard, H.S. (Earl of Halsbury) * XI 516–18,
540, 543, 544, 561, 613, 765, 786–9, 794, 809,
814, 817, 823, 826, 843, 871, 880–4, 891, 912,
963, 964, 970, 973–4, 976, 977,979, 980, 981,
989, 990, 993, 994, 995, 997, 1040, 1047, 1049,
1065, 1070, 1074, 1089, 1100, 1102, 1167, 1191,
1193 XII 33, 37, 43, 214–17, 529, 665, 754, 864,
1055–7, 1062, 1078, 1108, 1129 XIII 689,
697–8, 700, 710–11, 812, 832, 928

Giffard, J.W. de L. ** XI 993

Gifford, R. (Lord) XI 531, 549, 1041
XIII 126, 135, 409

Gilbert, Sir J. XI 607

Gilbert, T. XIII 475, 486, 510

Gilbert, W.S. XIII 751

Giles, D. XI 1040

Gill, C.F. XI 1025, 1075

Gladstone, H.J. (Viscount) XIII 12, 135,
167–169, 170–173, 179

Gladstone, W.E. XI 6, 25, 112, 154, 182, 183, 188,
201, 202, 208, 221–223, 304, 309, 313–14, 317,
320, 335–464, 536, 560, 561, 713, 763, 764, 783,
912, 963, 976, 980, 983, 986, 1070, 1166
XII 620 XIII 211, 387, 471, 556, 610, 615,
667, 761, 783, 786, 1001

Glasse, W.B. XI 991

Glen, W.C. XIII 489

Glenbervie, Lord see Douglas, S.

Gloag, R. XII 326

Glyn, T.C. XII 795

Goddard, R. (Lord) * XI 1032

Goldsmid, F. XI 1020

Goodhart, A.L. XI 1220

Gordon, E.S. (Lord) * XI 537, 539, 544

Gordon, I. XII 469, 862–3

Gordon, W.E. XII 313

Gorell Barnes, J. (Lord Gorell) XI 539, 718, 714,
738, 748, 828, 967, 989, 1028, 1038, 1042, 1043
XIII 799–801, 863, 925–6

Gorst, Sir J.E. XI 977, 1066

Goschen, G. XI 113–14 XIII 497–499, 529–530

Goulburn, E. *** XI 628, 629, 635, 705 XII 811,
1132

Graham Murray, A. (Viscount
Dunedin) * XIII 509, 518 XII 529, 988, 1028

Graham, George J. XI 582

Graham, Sir H.J.L. XI 542

Graham, Sir J. XII 807, 836

Graham, Sir J.R. XI 346, 354, 678, 680, 705,
706, 713, 863, 922, 942, 1014

Graham, Sir J.R. * XI 346, 354, 559, 620, 988

Graham-Campbell, Sir R. *** XI 1010

Grant, A. XII 642, 661

Grant, J. 961

Grant, Sir W.* XI 548, 981, 985, 988, 989
XII 22, 24, 41, 135–6, 257, 391, 417, 439

Grantham, Sir W. * XI 795, 826, 831, 963, 974,
978n, 981

Granville, (Earl) see Leveson-Gower, G.G.

Gray † XI 1148

Gray and Dodsworth † XI 133, 1145

Gray, W. XI 1118, 1120

Greaves, C.S. XIII 64, 66, 123, 130, 132, 184, 202,
204, 211, 292, 388, 390, 396, 397, 399, 400

Green, G.J. XII 112–13

Green, T.H. XII 299

Greenhow, W.T. XII 841–2

Gregorie, D.W.*** XI 1010

Gregory Rowcliffe † XI 1123, 1128, 1131–2, 1145, 1149

Gregory, G.B. XI 1117, 1165

Greville, C.C.F. XI 550, 562

Grey, C. (Earl) XI 659, 860

Grey, Sir G. XI 534, 707, 1015

Griffits, J.O. XI 1061

Grimthorpe, Lord see Beckett, E.

Grose, Sir N. * XIII 652

Grosvenor, R. (Earl) XI 635

Grove, Sir W.R. * XI 767, 973 XII 680

Guichard, W.M. XI 1122

Gully, W.C. XI 1096

Gunning and Francis † XI 1132

Gurdon, W. ** XI 999, 1000

Gurney, Sir J. XI 971n

Gurney, R. *** XI 310–11, 644 XIII 665, 674, 760

Gutteridge, H.C. XII 609

Hadfield, G. XII 188, 285

Haggard, J. XI 696

Haldane, R.B. (Viscount Haldane) * XI 403,
543, 546, 547, 552, 553, 561, 566, 567, 787, 789,

796, 825, 827, 831, 840, 884, 967, 970, 974, 985, 1036, 1038, 1040, 1043, 1060, 1066, 1102, 1193, 1211 XII 157–8, 220, 228–9, 607–8 XIII 254, 510, 703, 714–15
Hale, Sir M.* XIII 181, 229, 258, 265, 279, 402, 412, 456, 457
Hall, H.C. XI 1161
Hall, Sir B. XI 479 81, 708
Hall, Sir C. * XI 837, 969 XII 7, 237, 261
Hall, E. XI 260
Hall, E.M. XI 645, 970, 1031, 1033, 1039, 1102
Hall, R. XI 1183
Hall, T. XI 1008, 1010
Hallam, H. XI 21 XIII 599
Halliday, Sir A. XIII 823, 829
Halsbury, Earl of see Giffard, H.S.
Hamilton, H.* XI 1033
Hamilton, J.A. (Lord Sumner) * XI 511, 539, 967, 979, 984 XII 609, 983, 989
Hamilton-Gordon, G. (Earl of Aberdeen) XI 391
Hammond, A. XIII 191, 299
Hanbury, H.G. XII 609–10
Hancock, W.N. XII 855–6
Hand, L. XI 615
Hannen, J. (Lord) * XI 261, 517, 537, 723–4, 731, 746–7, 752, 965, 973, 979, 984, 989, 1166 XII 963 XIII 676
Hanworth (Viscount) see Pollock, Sir. E.M.
Harcourt, Sir W.G.G.V.V. XI 113, 261, 977, 1014, 1034, 1067, 1070, 1071, 1072 XII 378 XIII 765
Hardcastle, H. XI 55
Harding, Sir J.D. XI 709, 697, 698
Hardman, Sir W. XI 922
Hardwicke, (Lord) see Yorke, P.
Hardy, T. XIII 775
Hargrave, J.F. XI 75
Harington † XI 998
Harington, Sir R. ** XI 999, 1000, 1008, 1010
Harmsworth, A. XI 1035
Harriott, J. XI 1006
Harris, G. XI 996, 1037, 1121
Harrison* XI 942
Harrison, F. XI 106, 127, 131, 1019, 1020, 1025, 1034 XIII 210, 668, 670
Harrison, W. XI 1053
Harrison, W.E. XI 969
Hart, Sir A. * XI 962, 983, 1020
Hart, H.L.A. XI 131
Harvey, D.W. XI 648, 1081 XIII 512
Harvey, E. XI 1126
Hasse, J.C. XII 927
Hastie, A.H. XI 1156
Hastings, Sir P. XI 1024, 1034, 1035
Hatherley, Lord see Page Wood, W.
Hawke, Sir J.* XI 965

Hawkes, B. XI 1129
Hawkes, H. XI 1153
Hawkins, H. (Lord Brampton) * XI 375, 517, 539, 613, 641, 829, 969, 979, 988, 989, 991, 1032, 1047, 1062, 1100 XII 354, 1053, 1056–57, 1062–63 XIII 99, 340, 414, 698
Hawkins, J. XI 1053
Hawkins, V. XI 1036
Hayes, W. XIII 676
Hayward, S. XI 1077, 1203
Hazlitt, W. XI 166
Headlam, F.J. *** XI 1016
Headlam, T.E. XI 413
Heald, G.S. XI 661, 669, 988, 1024
Healy, T. XI 1020
Hearn, W.E. XI 21
Heath, D.D. ** XI 997, 998 XII 842–3
Heath, Sir J. * XII 526–8, 579, 590
Hegel, G.W.F. XI 117–18, 122–3
Hemming, G.W. XI 823, 1218
Hemyng, B. XI 1035
Henley, J.W. XI 678
Henley, Lord see Eden, R.H.
Henry, Sir T. XII 856
Herbert Smith † XI 1141
Herbert, A.P. XIII 749, 801
Herbert, G. (Earl of Powis) XI 912
Herbert, Smith XI 1141
Herbert, W. XI 697
Herford, E. XI 934, 944n 947, 948n
Herschell, F. (Lord) * XI 318–19, 503, 517, 542, 543, 546, 789, 791, 793–4, 847, 871, 912, 935, 967, 999, 1001, 1060, 1074, 1096 XII 217, 252, 430–1, 683, 841, 1057–58, 1062 XIII 69, 127, 832, 1006
Hewart, G. (Viscount) * XI 218, 1044, 1061 XIII 254–5, 298, 453
Hey, R. XI 697
Heywood, G.J. XI 894
Heywood, S. ** XI 634
Higgin, W.H. * XI 829
Higgins, M. J. XI 865
Hill, A.S. XI 1093
Hill, M.D. XI 629n, 644, 970, 1094 XIII 758
Hill, O. XIII 497, 588
Hilliard, F. XII 880
Hill-Kelly, S.A. ** XI 1003
Hilton, B. XII 779–80
Hindmarch, W.M. XIII 1000
Hobbes, T. XI 88, 90, 101, 119 XII 372
Hobhouse, A. (Lord) 540, 544n, 501, 505
Hobhouse, L.T. XI 113, 122, 209 XIII 478
Hobson, J. XI 206
Hodgskin, T. XIII 941
Hogarth, W. XIII 881
Hogg, A.S. ** XI 1015
Hogg, J.E. XII 190, 223–4

Holker, Sir J.* XI 973, 1029, 1068, 1069, 1096, 1106 XII 776
Hollams, Sir J. XI 609, 761, 764, 766, 779, 802, 1049, 1133, 1140, 1142, 1147, 1155
Holland, H. (Lord) XI 532
Holland, Sir H.T. XI 1072
Holland, Sir T.E. XI 123, 125–6, 260, 277, 1205 XII 310–12 XIII 183
Holme, B. XI 1155, 1156
Holmes, J. XIII 699
Holmes, O.W. * XI 130 XII 311–13, 372, 394–5, 548, 880, 890–1, 893, 941–3, 1112, 1145 XIII 214
Holroyd, Sir G.S. * XI 1024 XII 740, 907 XIII 260
Holt, Sir J. * XI 1212 XII 731, 916, 1048, 1141 XIII 935
Hone, W. XI 857
Honyman, Sir G.E. * XI 981 XII 341
Hooley, E.T. XII 644
Hope-Scott, J.R. XI 1053
Hopkins, A. *** XI 1011
Horne, Sir W. XI 975, 1063, 1069
Horner, L. XIII 563
Horridge, Sir T.G. * XI 974 XII 989–90
Horton, T.W. XI 1122
Hosack, J. *** XI 1011
Hotham, Sir B. * XII 752
Houghton, B. XI 1033
Howard, E. XIII 590
Howard, J. XI 137–8
Howarth, A.L. XI 1133
Howarth, J. XI 1119
Howell, J. XII 811
Howley, Archbishop W. * XI 702, 708
Hoyle, W.F. XI 1162
Hubbard, J.G. XII 776
Huber, U. XI 281
Huddleston, Sir J.W. * XI 770, 973, 981, 988, 1049
Hughes, D. XI 1161
Hughes, G.B. ** XI 997
Hughes, Sir T. XI 156, 190 XIII 670
Hullock, Sir J. * XI 621, 972
Hume, D. XI 81, 117
Hume, J. XI 147, 330–1, 333 5, 448, 464, 576, 695, 696, 702, 721, 916, 986 XII 800–1 XIII 631, 642, 654–5, 714, 889
Hume-Williams (Sir), E. XI 1045
Humphreys, J. XI 57, 1023 XII 49–53 XIII 190
Hunt, H. (cor) XI 944
Hurlstone, E.T. XI 1218
Huskisson, W. XI 164, 170 XIII 655–6
Hutton, A.E.H. *** XI 1010
Hutton, C. ** XI 880, 994, 1001, 1003
Hyde, Sir N.* XII 1096
Hyndman, H.H. XI 27, 113 XIII 702

Ilbert, Sir C.P. XI 53, 313–14, 766 XIII 470, 598, 605

Inderwick, F.A. XI 748, 970
Inderwick, W.A. XI 733
Ingham, T.H. ** XI 999, 1004
Inglis, Sir R. XI 707
Isaacs, R.D. (Marquess of Reading) * XI 504, 967, 975, 1032, 1062, 1065, 1067, 1071, 1073 XIII 253, 307

Jackson, G. XI 685
Jager, H. XI 1028
James II, King XI 9
James, C. XI 843
James, E. XI 1059, 1077, 1082–83
James, H. (Lord James of Hereford) * XI 540, 565, 803, 913, 962, 976, 1043, 1088, 1067, 1068, 1089 XII 204, 840, 861, 1057, 1062 XIII 266, 452, 697, 710–12
James, Sir W.M. * XI 761n, 764, 803, 967, 988, 991 XII 28, 30, 36, 38, 40–4, 46, 126, 170, 261, 276, 344, 428, 648, 650, 757, 1078, 1101
Janson, F. XI 1208
Jarman, T. XII 14, 22, 25–6, 83, 112, 242, 273
Jeaffreson, J.C. XI 1025, 1034, 1043
Jebb, J. XIII 11, 160–5, 179
Jekyll, J. XI 677
Jelf, Sir A.R. * XI 965, 991
Jenkins, G.T. XI 736, 796, 797
Jenkinson, C. (Earl of Liverpool) XI 30 XIII 655
Jenkinson, R.B. (Earl of Liverpool) XI 653
Jenks, E. XI 1198, 1200
Jenner † XI 695, 708, 737
Jenner, Sir H. * XI 696, 702
Jenner-Fust, H. XI 698n
Jervis, Sir J. * XI 494 XII 474, 815 XIII 304
Jessel, Sir G. * XI 765, 770, 795, 803, 838, 962, 965, 967, 988, 990, 991, 1020, 1060, 1062, 1067, 1069, 1073, 1188, 119 XII 15, 26, 34, 38, 41–2, 45, 139, 171–2, 176, 205, 260–1, 267, 273, 276, 280, 392, 425, 427–8, 528, 570, 582, 603–5, 607 664–5, 694, 874, 965, 1077, 1089–90, 1101–3 XIII 673, 773, 787, 864–5, 870, 969, 972, 987
Jeune, F.H. (Lord St Helier) * XI 420, 724, 738, 747–8
Johnson, G. XI 1201
Johnston, Sir A. * XI 557
Johnston, W. XI 1146
Jones, A. XI 810, 869
Jones, C. XI 1011
Jones, Sir D.B. ** XI 995
Jones, E. XI 26 XIII 636
Jones, H.C. XI 649, 765
Jones, H.R.M. *** XI 996
Jones, Sir J. XI 631
Jones, Sir W. XII 913–14, 916, 926–7
Jones, W. XII 800
Joplin, T. XI 1140
Jordan, D. XIII 813

Jordan, T.H. ** XI 1002
Joyce, Sir M.I. * XI 831, 977, 1052

Kames, Lord see Home, H.
Kant, I. XI 91, 96, 108, 117–18, 121 XIII 890
Karslake, Sir J.B. XI 975, 994, 1004, 1068, 1071
Kay, Sir E.E.* XI 791, 801, 845, 847, 989, 1160 XII 34, 40, 42, 46, 147, 404, 406, 646
Kaye, C. XI 1121
Kay-Shuttleworth, (Kay) Sir J. XI 178, 229 XIII 521
Keane, D.D. XI 1094
Keating, Sir H.S. * XI 559, 575 XII 305, 379, 772, 854, 966
Keble, J. XI 1213
Keep, A.P.P. XII 893
Keighley, Arnold and Sismey † XI 1163
Keir-Hardie, J. XI 28
Kekewich, Sir A. * XI 843, 973, 988, 1052, 1061 XII 283, 1053, 1077, 1101–2, 1108, 1146 XIII 838
Kellner, Sir G. XI 841
Kelly and Keene † XI 1139, 1148, 1149
Kelly, Sir F.E. * XI 567, 711, 760, 763, 803, 959, 966, 967, 977, 978, 987, 1092, 1100, 1198 XII 343–4, 504, 720, 944, 960, 964–5, 1148–49
Kemp, T.R. XI 1062
Kemp, W.R. XI 797
Kenealy, E.V. XI 1059, 1083
Kennedy, C.R. XI 643, 1049, 1094, 1099, 1101, 1102, 1192
Kennedy, T. XI 1179
Kennedy, Sir W.R. * XI 970, 1129 XIII 696, 707
Kenneth Brown Baker † XI 1131, 1135
Kenny, C.S. XI 1194 XIII 183, 223–225, 230, 233, 252, 263–264, 278, 282, 307, 312, 418, 436
Kenyon, L. (Lord) * XI 506, 1110, 1213 XII 20–1, 27, 45, 118, 412, 413, 457, 459, 594, 782, 910 XIII 235, 298, 321, 337, 770, 871
Kerly, D.M. XIII 1002
Kerr, R.M. ** XI 644, 868, 900, 1049
Kershaw, L.W. XI 807
Kettle, Sir R.A. ** XI 310, 886 XIII 667, 679
Kimberley (Lord) see Wodehouse, John
Kindersley, Sir R. * XI 514, 559, 660, 846 XII 42, 106, 147, 234, 420–1, 554–5, 1107
King, Lord XI 532
King, P.J. XI 842
Kingsdown, Lord see Pemberton-Leigh, E.T.
Kingsley, C. XI 188, 189 XIII 565
Kinnear, A. (Lord) * XI 539
Kirkwood, J. XII 862, 864
Knight Bruce, Sir J.L. * XI 396, 560, 566, 658, 660, 679, 990, 991, 1030 XII 39, 105, 138, 257–9, 420, 556, 558, 1097
Knolys, N. ** XI 643
Koe, J.H. ** XI 995
Kynnersley, T.C.S.*** XI 1015

Labouchere, H. (Lord Taunton) XIII 523–5, 532
Lace, A. XI 1208
Lailey, B. XI 1169
Laing, A. *** XI 1006–7
Lake, Sir B. XI 1163–64
Lamarck, J.-B. XI 104–5
Lamb, Sir J.B. XII 788
Lamb, W. (Viscount Melbourne) XI 24, 925
Lambert, J. XIII 545
Lane, R. *** XI 1011
Lang, Archbishop W.C.G. (Lord) XIII 800
Langdale (Lord) see Bickersteth, H.
Langdell, C.C. XI 73 XII 308, 310–11, 313, 346–8, 365, 380–1, 386, 398
Langhorne, J.B. XI 733
Lankester, Dr E. XI 938, 943, 944, 947–8
Lansbury, G. XIII 499
Lansdowne (Marquess of) see Fitzmaurice, H.P.
Last, J.T. XI 1155
Law, C.E. ** XI 643, 1007
Law, E. (Lord Ellenborough) * XI 512, 606, 618, 620, 625, 630, 858, 942, 964, 942, 964, 988, 989, 990, 1027, 1041, 1059, 1067 XII 118, 177, 304, 315, 330, 384, 480, 487, 492, 495–6, 511, 579, 587, 604–5, 617, 712, 751, 908, 910, 912, 1122, 1131 XIII 89, 91, 140, 141, 300–1, 340, 416, 439, 440, 644–6, 770, 902, 904
Lawford, E.C.B. XI 795, 831
Lawrance, Sir J.C. * XI 795, 828, 831, 974, 989
Lawrence, E. XII 819
Lawrence, N.T. XI 91, 208–9
Lawrence, Sir S. * XII 491, 684–5, 688
Lawrence, Rev. T.J. XI 260
Layard, Sir A.H. XI 783
Layton, J.H. XI 1169
Le Blanc, Sir S. * XII 579–80
Leach, Sir J. * XI 436, 531, 549, 648, 654, 656, 669, 671, 672, 685–6, 963, 969, 981, 982, 983,988, 990, 991, 1065 XII 46, 247, 454, 553 XIII 509, 741–2
Leahy, D. ** XI 992
Leake, S.M. XII 307, 338–9, 345, 398, 434, 441, 466–7, 471, 504, 519, 568–9, 595
Lee, G. XI 971
Lee, J. XI 698
Lee, W. XI 1061
Leese, W.H. XI 1169
Lefroy, T.E.P. ** XI 880, 1002, 1160
Lefroy, T.L. * XII 934
Leigh Pemberton, H. XI 792
Leigh, Sir E.C. XI 1054
Leigh-Smith, B. (Mrs Bodichon) XIII 758
Lennard, T. XIII 951
Lens, J. XI 1065
Leonard, P.M. ** XI 1003
Leopold II, Belgian King XI, 267, 269
Letts † XI 1122, 1130

Letts, M. XI 1121, 1122
Lever, W.H. XIII 504
Leveson-Gower, G.G. (Earl Granville) XIII 955
Lewes, G.H. XI 103
Lewin, T. XII 238–9, 242
Lewis and Lewis † XI 737, 1134
Lewis, Sir G.C. XI 753, 942, 1118, 1130, 1154, 1158n, 1164
Lewis, W.D. XI 1183
Leycester, H. ** XI 634
Liddell, A.G.C. XI 787, 1037, 1040, 1944
Lightwood, J.M. XI 1210
Lindley, N. (Lord) * XI 539, 544, 790, 803, 979, 1024, 1025, 1043, 1058, 1195, 1205, 1211, 1215, 1220 XII 148, 154–5, 175, 292–3, 346, 355, 408, 429, 560, 597, 605, 644, 666, 668, 963, 975, 981, 1062, 1066, 1086–87 XIII 685, 695, 698, 700, 710, 865, 869
Lindley, W.B. XII 641
Lindsell, W.H.B. XII 952–3, 1125
Lindsey, B. XIII 821
Linklater and Paine † XI 1122, 1127, 1131, 1149
Littledale, Sir J. * XI 383, 583, 596, 621, 653, 968, 972 XII 592, 594, 896
Littleton, E. XIII 642
Liverpool, Lord see Jenkinson, R.B.
Lloyd George, D. (Lord) XI 29, 206, 208, 211, 213, 216, 225–6, 470, 504, 1070, 1116, 1152 XIII 505, 578, 715, 975–6
Lloyd, H. ** XI 994, 1062
Lloyd, S. XII 822
Locke, J. XI 81–2, 88, 117, 119, 1189 XII 887 XIII 938
Lockwood, Sir F. XI 977, 1067
Lofthouse, S.H.S. XI 1089
Long, G. XI 1183
Long, W. XIII 500
Lopes, H.C. (Lord Ludlow) * XI 539, 752, 802 XIII 694
Loreburn (Earl) see Reid, R.T.
Lorimer, J. XI 123–4, 262, 277
Loughborough, Lord see Wedderburn, A.
Loughborough, T. XI 1123
Lowe, A.L. XI 895
Lowe, J. XI 654, 661, 669, 681
Lowe, R. (Lord Sherbrooke) XI 112, 195, 197, 204, 222, 1073 XII 197, 462, 625–8 XIII 102, 523
Lowndes, M.D. XI 1148, 1208
Ludlow, J.M.F. XI 112, 190, 204 XII 299, 627 XIII 523, 673
Ludlow, Lord see Lopes, H.C.
Lush, Sir R. * XI 803, 809, 970, 991, 1027 XII 359, 393, 899, 951, 962, 989, 1138 XIII 103, 676
Lushington, Sir G. XI 27, 229, 1014 XIII 134, 319, 441, 672

Lushington, Sir S. * XI 135, 139, 147, 534, 560, 565, 653, 654, 695, 696, 698, 703, 704, 709, 715, 716, 719, 720–2, 726, 727–9, 960 XII 759, 1049 XIII 62, 792
Lushington, V. ** XI 994
Lyell, Sir C. XI 946, 948
Lyndhurst (Lord) see Copley, J.S.

MacAskie, S.C. XI 1033
Macaulay, T.B. (Lord) XI 20, 174 XII 306 XIII 184, 225, 241, 271, 308, 312, 313, 461, 889, 920
MacDonagh, O. XIII 606–610, 612, 615
MacDonald, A. XIII 677
Macdonald, Sir A. * XII 117, 1075–76 XIII 454
MacDonell, Sir J. XI 556, 718, 737, 744, 793, 810
Macfie, R.A. XIII 895–6, 954, 958
Mackenzie, M.M. XII 828
Mackinnon, Sir F.D.* XI 1031
Mackintosh, Sir J. XI 135, 137, 138, 164, 261, 1048 XIII 118, 122, 143–5
MacKonochie, A. XI 555
MacKonochie, J. ** XI 995
Macnaghten, E. (Lord) * XI 518, 537, 547, 561, 967, 979, 983 XII 152, 155, 778, 982–3, 1024, 1055, 1062, 1092 XIII 510, 685, 698, 700, 710–11, 713, 1008
Macpherson, W. XII 433
Maenan, Lord see Taylor W.F.K.
Maine, Sir H.J.S. XI 58, 63, 73, 100, 106–12, 114–15, 123, 126, 129, 263, 1034, 1183–84, 1186, 1188 XII 298, 394, 568 XIII 598, 614, 625
Maitland, F.W. XI 124, 130, 772, 1203 XIII 214
Malcolm, J.C. XI 940
Malins, Sir R. * XI 711, 763, 991, 1051, 1107 XII 33–4, 36–7, 39–42, 44, 170, 176, 259, 261, 267, 276, 285, 558, 560, 603, 994, 1076, 1107 XIII 673, 759, 864
Mallett, Sir L. XIII 895
Malthus, Rev. T. XI 162–4, 169, 192, 231 XIII 477–478, 629–31
Mancini, P.S. XI 262, 285–6
Manisty, Sir H. * XI 769, 966, 979
Mann, T. XIII 687
Manners, Lord J. XIII 894, 921
Manners-Sutton, T. (Lord Manners) * XI 695, 962
Manning, Cardinal XI 157 XIII 687
Manning, J. ** XI 995, 1056
Mansfield, Sir J. * XI 57, 408 XII 579, 702, 910 XIII 857
Mansfield, J.S. *** XI 1015, 1160
Mansfield (Lord) see Murray, Sir W.
Manson, E. XI 960
Markby, Sir W. XI 1205 XIII 183, 233, 252, 824
Markham, H.P. XI 923
Marriott, G. XI 694

Marshall † XI 892, 1015

Marshall, A. XI 191, 192, 193, 198, 201, 211, 224

Marshall, T. XII 847

Marten, Sir A.G. ** XI 994

Martin, F.W. XI 1154n

Martin, Sir S.* XI 393, 622n, 759n, 990, 991
XII 379–80, 385, 455, 512, 543, 545–7, 570, 575,
625, 654, 920, 922, 1006, 1073, 1086, 1117, 1121,
1136, 1142–43

Martineau † XI 1154

Martineau, A. ** XI 891, 996n

Martineau, H. XIII 631

Marx, K.H. XI 27 XIII 702

Mary II, Queen XI 6

Mathew, Sir J.C. XI 588, 809n, 820, 828, 962,
969, 1038, 1049, 1195 XII 205, 752, 866

Mathews, J.B. XI 1061

Mattinson, M. XI 1086

Maude, D. *** XI 1012, 1015

Maugham, R. XI 75, 114, 1149, 1157, 1160, 1206

Maule, Sir W.H. * XI 968, 981, 984n, 991, 1087,
1213 XII 600, 959, 972, 1141 XIII 124, 303, 782

Maurice, F.D. XI 93–4, 189, 190

Maxwell, P.B. XI 55

May, J.F. XII 856

May, Sir E. XI 21, 308, 320

Mayer, S. XI 1219n

Mayne, J.D. XI 566 XII 536–7

McCall, R.A. XI 1062

McCardie, Sir H.A. * XI 987, 1030, 1044, 1060
XII 470, 1065 XIII 645

McCulloch, J.R. XI 169, 171, 174, 195, 228, 231
XIII 632, 939

McFea, F.B. XI 892

McGovney, D.O. XII 357

McIntyre, A. ** XI 995

McKeand, C. XI 1029

Mead, F. *** XI 1008, 1009

Mearns, A. XI 113 XIII 499

Melbourne, Lord see Lamb, W.

Mellish, Sir G. * XI 966, 983, 990 XII 344–5,
450, 593, 653, 950, 1148

Mellor † XI 998

Mellor, Sir J. * XI 171, 188, 228 XII 483, 694,
951, 1100

Melville, R. ** XI 993

Merivale, J.H. XI 654

Mersey, Lord see Bigham, J.C.

Mews, J. XI 1218

Meyrick, Sir S. XI 698n

Middleton † XI 737n

Middleton, C.J. XI 748

Mill, J. XI 171, 188, 228, 582

Mill, J.S. XI 21, 73, 74, 85, 90–103, 117, 123,
172, 192, 197, 198, 200, 201, 203, 221, 222, 225,
228, 231 XII 298, 950 XIII 153, 183, 354, 633,
745, 760, 940–1

Miller, J. XI 565n

Milward & Co. † XI 1163

Milward, R.H. XI 1142

Mingay, J. XI 1631

Mirehouse, J. ** XI 643

Mitchell, J. XIII 479

Mitford, J.F. (Lord Redesdale) * XI 368,
531, 536, 649, 653, 654, 661, 685, 857, 962
XII 28, 31–2, 35, 38, 145, 792, 798
XIII 755, 782

Moffat, G. XII 819

Moffatt, G. XI 777, 779, 867

Moncrieff XI 697n, 911n

Monkswell (Lord) see Collier, R.P.

Montagu, B. XII 786–8, 795–6

Montesquieu, C.S. (Baron de) XI 4–5

Moore-Bayley, J. XI 1142

Morant, R. XIII 533

Mordaunt, Sir C. XIII 786

More, P. XIII 649

Morgan, Sir G.O. XII 203–4, 207

Morris, J. XI 1140

Morris, M. (Lord Killanin) * XI 539, 543,
544 XIII 697

Morris, L. XI 881

Morrison, C. XI 1117

Morrison, J. XI 1140

Morton, Sir C.H. XI 790, 1172

Motteram, J. ** XII 860

Mould, J. XI 1121

Mowatt, Sir F. XI 846

Moysey, A. XI 632

Muir-Mackenzie, K.A. (Lord) XI 542, 736, 738,
741, 766, 786, 878, 789, 791, 795–6, 799, 810,
827, 828n, 837, 840, 842–3, 847, 880, 884, 887,
895, 964, 1003, 1059, 1061, 1065 XIII 595

Muir-Mackenzie, M. XI 766

Muir, Sir R.D. ** XI 642, 970

Mundella, A.J. XI 309–11 XIII 667–8, 670,
679, 690, 699

Murphy, J.P. XI 969

Murray, A.G. (Viscount Dunedin of Stenton) *
XII 529, 988, 1028

Murray, W. (Earl of Mansfield) * XI 167,
257, 262 268, 274; 280, 291–2, 369, 408,
599, 601, 615, 629, 757, 1063, 1075, 1076, 1215
XII 359, 361–2, 364, 366, 374, 395, 525,
566–7, 576–7, 583, 593, 609–10, 686, 731,
733, 744, 749–50 XIII 184, 267, 268, 285,
297, 335, 375, 625, 645, 646, 770, 775, 883,
896, 902, 907, 947, 950

Muscott, Rev. E. XI 708

Musgrave, A. XI 754

Nalder, G. XI 1142

Napier, Sir J. * XI 559, 962. 982

Nasmyth (or Naesmith), Sir J. XIII 959

Neate, C. XI 1050
Neild, J. XII 798
Nelson, H. XI 1139
Nelson, S. * XII 537
Nettlefold, J.S. XIII 591–2, 596
Neville, Sir R. * XI 982
Newcastle, Duke of see Pelham-Clinton
   H.P.H. XI 909
Newman XI 1032
Newton, R.M. XI 1008
Nicholl † XI 696
Nicholl, Sir J. * XI 695, 703, 706, 720
Nichol, J. (JR) XI 881
Nicholls, G. XIII 503
Nichols, W. ** XI 996, 1025
Nicholson, Sir R. XI 923
Nicol, H. XI 889, 890, 895, 897, 995, 1003
Niebuhr, B.G. XI 106
Nikolai II, Tsar XI 271
North, Sir F. * XI 908, 985 XIII 900, 902, 906
Northcote, Sir S. XII 184 XIII 527
Norton Rose † XI 1118, 1121, 1122, 1125, 1126,
   1139, 1141
Norton, Sir C. XI 1141 XIII 758
Norton, G. XI 1010
Norton, H.E. XI 1118
Norton, H.T. XI 1141, 1154, 1155
Norwood, C.M. XI 768, 879–80, 881, 1101

O'Brien, B. XI 26 XIII 488
O'Connell, D. XI 533, 589
O'Connor, F. XI 26, 589
O'Hagan, T. (Lord) * XI 539
O'Malley, P.F. XI 1092, 1094
Oastler, R. XI 12, 268 XIII 560, 631
Odgers, W.B. XIII 862
Oppenheim, L. XI 260
Orme, E. XI 1116
Osborne, W.V. XIII 710–15
Owen † XI 737
Owen, D. XII 688
Owen, H. XIII 489
Owen, R. XI 26, 165, 175 XIII 658, 718
Owen, S.H. XI 735
Owen, W.S. ** XI 898, 1003 XII 865

Page Wood, W. (Lord Hatherley) * XI 341, 441,
   660, 679, 761, 762, 764, 770, 777, 817, 874, 880,
   966, 967, 970, 976, 979, 989, 993–4, 1067, 1189
   XII 24, 249, 258–9, 285, 391–2, 426, 439–40, 466,
   551, 555, 557, 560, 603, 606, 665, 939, 966, 1076,
   1084–7, 1089, 1098, 1109–11 XIII 904, 974, 994
Paine, T. [radical] XI 26, 84
Paine, Sir J. XI 1118, 1129, 1142, 1166
Paine, W. XII 313
Paley, Archdeacon W. XI 87, 135 XIII 23, 108,
   138, 139, 141, 191

Paley, W. [legal author] XI 486, 492
Palles, C. * XII 995, 1061
Palmer, F. XI 753n
Palmer, R. (Earl Selborne) * XI 498, 511, 535,
   536, 545, 565, 566, 659, 760, 761, 763, 764, 768,
   770, 773, 778, 780, 785, 794, 798, 799, 800,
   803, 841, 870, 880, 889, 970, 973, 981, 985, 991,
   999, 1024. 1031, 1040, 1041, 1049, 1051, 1060,
   1063, 1066, 1072, 11079, 1089, 1100, 1111, 1148,
   1188–90, 1194, 1217 XII 40, 45, 199, 208, 387,
   403, 1102 XIII 125, 832, 958, 966
Palmer, W. (cor) XI 942, 951
Palmerston, Viscount see Temple, H.J.
Pardessus, J.-M. XII 304
Paris Smith and Randall † XI 1130
Park, Sir J.A. * XI 874, 972, 1020, 1212 XII 458,
   573, 770 XIII 875
Park, J.J. XI 21 XII 698, 1180, 1203
Parke, J. (Lord Wensleydale) * XI 54, 375, 493,
   534, 560, 570, 588, 592, 595, 614, 622, 636,
   642, 643, 727, 967, 975, 979, 984, 988, 1026,
   1067 XII 27, 32, 116–7, 129, 162, 350, 363, 371,
   384, 401–2, 412–13, 459, 474, 481, 484, 496,
   499, 526–8, 575, 584–6, 599–600, 625, 697,
   704, 727, 769, 772, 924, 929–30, 933, 990,
   1039, 1047, 1123, 1129, 1131, 1133, 1135 XIII 95,
   303–304, 440, 868–9
Parker, Sir J. * XI 983
Parker, Archbishop M. XIII 749–50
Parker, R.J. (Lord) * XI 539, 969, 977n, 984
   XII 158, 176, 277, 556, 1092–3
Parker, T. (Lord Macclesfield) * XII 552
Parkes, J. XI 683, 855, 1203
Parkyns, M. XII 823
Parnell, C.S. XIII 786
Parry, Sir E.A. ** XI 899, 906, 995, 1040, 1042,
   1052 XII 843–4, 846, 848
Parry, J.H. XI 1050, 1057
Parsons, T. XII 356
Pashley, R. XI 486, 495–6
Paterson, W. ** XI 995
Patteson, Sir J. * XI 390, 499, 570, 964, 965,
   981, 984 XII 125, 371, 374, 900, 917, 921, 931
   XIII 259, 268, 381, 442, 460, 657, 661–2
Payne, E.T. XI 1117
Peacock, Sir B. * XI 380–1, 566
Peake, T. XI 1212
Pearson, Sir J. * XI 845, 965, 983 XII 583, 1086
Pechell, Sir G.C. XI 929
Peed, W. XI 1163
Peek, Sir H. XI 1161
Peel, Sir L. * XI 557
Peel, Sir R. XI 18, 24, 25, 137, 141, 164, 175, 182,
   188, 220, 222–3, 302, 304, 335, 351, 389, 461,
   492, 598, 599, 627, 652–3, 656, 705, 706–8, 713,
   856, 858, 859, 862, 925, 928, 971, 975, 1005,
   1006, 1007, 1056, 1074 XII 50–1, 803

XIII 27–36, 49, 145–7, 188, 191, 192, 198, 201, 204, 396, 471, 512
Peel, Sir R. Sen. XI 165 XIII 558–9
Pelham-Clinton, H.P.H. (Duke of Newcastle-under-Lyne) XI 909
Pember, E.H. XI 1054
Pemberton, C. XI 1148
Pemberton-Leigh, T. (Lord Kingsdown) * XI 535, 558,559, 560, 566, 727, 966, 975, 991, 1034, 1065
Penzance (Lord) see Wilde, J.P.B.
Pepys, C.C. (Earl of Cottenham) * XI 340, 370, 435, 533, 534, 558, 578, 657, 658, 659, 665, 671, 672, 679, 686, 689, 861–2, 864, 961, 981, 987, 988, 991, 992, 995, 1025, 1058, 1065 XII 30, 106, 130, 138–9, 159, 170–3, 197, 235, 242, 248, 252, 255, 257, 337, 368–9, 391–2, 406, 537, 559, 653, 803, 805 XIII 149, 513, 742, 744, 899–900, 993–4
Percy, A.I. (Duke of Northumberland) XIII 787
Perry, Sir T.E. XIII 758–9
Petersdorff, C.E. ** XI 995, 1057, 1179
Peterson, Sir M.D. * XIII 904
Petty-, Fitzmaurice, H. (Marquess of Lansdowne) XIII 755
Philbrick, F.A.** XI 1019
Phillimore † XI 695, 711
Phillimore, J.G. XI 589, 1176 XIII 780
Phillimore, Sir R.J. * XI 261–2, 275, 698, 709, 711, 722, 731, 989 XII 934
Phillimore, Sir W.G. * XI 725, 827, 970, 980
Phillips, C. XI 642
Philpotts, Bishop H. XI 553 XIII 804
Phipson, S.L. XI 605
Pickersgill, E.H. XI 905 XII 841, 843–4
Pickford, W. (Lord Sterndale)* XI 970
Pigott, Sir G. * XII 937, 1007
Pitt, W, the Younger XI 1113 XII 689
Place, F. XIII 654–5
Pleydell-Bouverie, J. (Earl of Radnor) XIII 832–3
Plimsoll, S. XIII 571–9, 617
Plowden, A.C. *** XI 1008, 1010, 1030, 1037, 1045 XIII 799, 800
Plumer, Sir T. * XI 549, 672, 963, 977, 983 XII 24, 146, 440
Plunket, W.C. (Baron) XI 532, 961
Pockett, H.T. XII 862–3
Poland, Sir H.B. XI 642, 962, 970, 1074 XIII 81, 82, 135, 137, 211, 342
Pollock, Sir C.E. * XI 981 XII 936, 1138
Pollock, E. XI 823
Pollock, Sir F. XI 73, 123–4, 126–30, 263, 275; 512,545, 804, 1045, 1193, 1205, 1211,1219, 1221 XII 307, 308–13, 322, 339, 345, 347–8, 351, 353–4, 355, 357, 360, 365–6, 371–2, 370, 374, 380–3, 386–7, 390, 394–9, 430–1, 433–4, 449, 452, 467, 469, 471, 548, 609, 731, 888, 890–4, 941–4, 947, 949, 954, 955–7, 1033, 1047–52, 1055–6, 1059, 1060, 1066, 1112–13, 1125, 1145, XIII 214, 693

Pollock, Sir F. Sen. XIII 95, 109, 286, 291–2, 305, 311, 317, 323, 332, 913
Pollock, J. ** XI 993, 995
Pollock, Sir J.F. XI 534, 570, 591n, 622n, 906, 967, 968, 975n, 979, 989, 991, 1048, 1077, 1096, 1212 XII 160, 371, 456, 461, 465, 482, 487, 509, 543–4, 546, 567, 575, 597, 882, 895, 932, 935, 973, 978, 1006, 1073, 1100, 1135, 1137 XIII 95, 109, 286, 291–2, 305, 311, 317, 323, 333, 913
Pollock, Sir W.F. XI 624, 797, 1046
Polson, A. XI 1023
Ponsonby, G. XI 631
Pope, S. XI 1054
Posner, R. XII 885
Pothier, R.J. XII 301–4, 336, 343, 345–6, 433, 450, 452, 466–7, 469–70, 513–14, 537–8, 541, 543, 587, 677, 742, 770–1, 896, 987
Potter, G. XIII 669
Poulett Thomson, C. (Lord Sydenham) XIII 979–80
Powell, J.J. XII 89n, 135, 338, 360
Powis, Earl of see Herbert, G.
Praed, W.M. ** XI 992
Pratt, C. (Earl Camden) * XII 383, 385, 1125
Prendergast, M. ** XI 644
Prentice, S. ** XI 997
Preston, R. XI 1051, 1185
Price, R. XII 676
Prinsep, C.R. XI 697
Pritchard, W.T. XI 700, 701, 748
Prothero XI 1136
Provis, Sir S. XIII 592, 595
Pugh, C. XI 680
Puller, C. XII 362, 364–5
Pulling, A. XI 643, 1058, 1210, 1217
Purcell, E. des A. XI 1019, 1042, 1062
Pye, H. XI 1006, 1094

Quain, Sir J.R. * XI 701, 764, 769, 777

Raine, J. 635
Ram, J. XI 41, 47, 49, 60
Ramsay J.A.B. (Marquess of Dalhousie) XI 335, 355
Ramshay, W. ** XI 992, 1002
Rathbone, W. XIII 495
Read, J. *** XI 1008
Reading, Lord see Isaacs, R.D.
Redesdale, Lord see Mitford, J.F.
Rees, J.T. XI 824
Reeve, H. XI 557, 563, 564, 565, 567
Reid, R.T. (Earl Loreburn) * XI 511, 540, 561, 567, 769, 795, 813, 825n, 829n, 830n, 831, 832n, 833–4, 891, 905, 912–13, 967, 970, 974, 994, 1060, 1167 XII 228, 522, 1024, 1026–7, 1065 XIII 703, 707–8, 863
Reid, T. XI 105, 129
Reid, Sir W. XIII 953

Rentoul, G. XI 1102
Rentoul, J.A. XI 868–9, 1039
Rhodes, F.P. XI 1142
Ricardo, D. XI 27, 134, 160–2, 165, 171, 219, 228, 231 XIII 629–31, 718
Richards, Sir R. * XI 963, 983, 1061 XII 35, 97, 134, 436, 553
Richardson, Sir J. * XI 972, 979, 985
Richbell, Capt. XI 1006
Richmond, Duke of see Lennox, C.
Rickards, G.K. XIII 611
Ridley, Sir E. * XI 823, 973–4, 989 XII 867
Rigby, Sir J. XI 981 XIII 685
Ripon (Earl of) see Robinson, F.
Ritchie, J. XI 113–14, 117, 122 XII 313
Roberts, Sir H.W. ** XI 1000
Roberts, W.P. XI 1153 XIII 636, 674
Robertson, J. (Lord) * XI 539
Robertson, J.C. XIII 941
Robertson, J.P.B. (Lord)* XIII 928, 698, 710
Robinson, B.C. XI 1025, 1057, 1058
Robinson, Sir C. * XI 697, 705, 719, 720
Robinson, C.F. XI 623
Robinson, F. (Earl of Ripon) XI 565
Robinson, G. XI 754
Robinson, H.C. XI 1019, 1044, 1094
Robson, W.S. (Lord) * XI 539, 972, 979, 983, 1019, 1065 XII 841
Roche, Wilson † XI 1142
Roe, Sir F.A. *** XI 1005, 1010
Roebuck, J.A. XI 993, 1077 XIII 520
Rogers, Rev. J.E.T. XIII 958
Rolfe, R.M. (Lord Cranworth) XI 534, 535, 558, 598, 659, 660, 680, 710, 711–12, 738, 752, 783, 876–7, 976, 979, 984, 1001, 1065, 1066, 1067, 1216 XII 28, 32, 39, 87–8, 90, 150, 152, 162, 257–9, 276, 289, 368–9, 391, 410, 420–1, 423, 448, 585, 854, 896, 1003–4, 1075–6 XIII 202–205, 244, 365, 514, 516, 659, 783, 794, 913
Rolle, H. * XII 509
Rollit † XI 1163
Rollit, Sir A. XI 832, 884, 1118 XII 827, 831
Rolt, Sir J. * XI 699, 701, 1063, 1106 XII 340 XIII 992
Romer, Sir R. * XI 436, 804, 979 XII 642, 666–7, 1064–5 XIII 867
Romilly, J. (Lord) * XI 85, 660, 679, 680, 762, 839, 876, 977, 1041, 1051, 1083 XII 8, 38, 86, 131, 140, 147, 176, 182, 259–60, 285, 306, 340, 406, 418, 426–7, 435, 438, 440, 442–4, 549–50, 554–5, 557–8, 651, 663, 665, 1074, 1085, 1101 XIII 515, 743, 954
Romilly, Sir S. XI 135, 136, 138, 152, 164, 665, 875, 1041 XII 182, 407, 788, 792 XIII 23, 25, 118, 122, 139–41, 144, 155, 159, 188, 191, 511, 517
Roscoe, E.S. * XI 730, 731

Roscoe, H. XI 871
Roscoe, W. XI 1116
Rose, Sir P. XI 1141, 1142, 1152
Rose-Innes, Sir P.** XI 969
Rosslyn, Earl see Wedderburn, A.
Rothery, H.C. XI 717, 721, 726, 727, 729, 730–1
Rousseau, J.-J. XI 107
Rowlatt, Sir S. * XI 832n
Rubinstein, J.S. XI 1156
Ruggles-Brise, Sir E.J. XIII 12, 169, 173
Runnington, C. XI 581 XII 799
Russell † XI 998
Russell, C. (Lord Russell of Killowen) * XI 537, 613, 790, 871, 966, 967, 976, 983, 988, 1020, 1044, 1060, 1062, 1096, 1191
Russell, Charles & Co. † XI 747
Russell, F.X.J. (Lord Russell of Killowen) * XI 261 XIII 106
Russell, G.L. ** XI 1004 XII 840
Russell, J. (Earl) XI 25, 221, 353–4, 387, 390, 397, 669, 685, 721, 814, 832, 861, 909, 964, 974, 1007 XII 803, 836 XIII 38, 39, 55, 143, 145, 148–150, 153, 157, 159–60, 196, 200, 483, 521
Russell, J. (Lord John) ** XI 998, 1002 XII 843–4
Russell, W.O. XI 635n, 1054
Russell, Sir W.A.* XIII 181
Ryan, Sir E. * XI 557, 559, 560, 1188
Ryland, A. XI 1142, 1148, 1153, 1208
Rylands † XI 1153

Sadler, M. XIII 560, 604
Saint-Simon, C.H. XI 113
Salisbury, Marquess of see Gascoyne-Cecil, R.A.T.
Salmond, Sir J. XI 123, 125, 127 XII 893–4, 943, 953, 955–6, 1066–67, 1112–13, 1125–26
Salter, Sir A.C. * XI 1028, 1032
Sandbach, J.B. XI 1036, 1043
Sandford, Sir D.K. XI 697
Sargent, Sir C.H.* XI 977
Saunders, C.T. XI 1156
Saunders, T.W. XI 1011
Savigny, F.C. von XI 124, 284, 1181 XII 308–10, 339, 346, 353, 371–2, 390, 399, 433, 449, 453, 467, 471 XIII 190, 233, 307, 312
Saward, J.T. XI 1082
Scaccia, S. XII 769
Scarlett, J. (Lord Abinger) * XI 576, 583, 596, 598, 613, 614, 657, 781, 972, 977, 991, 1026, 1030, 1033, 1043, 1048, 1059, 1061, 1071, 1096, 1160, 1167 XII 116, 375, 412–13, 459, 477, 536, 578–9, 584, 589, 593, 744, 769, 908, 910, 925, 1002–3, 1045 XIII 76, 302, 346, 903, 912
Schechter, F. XIII 1010–11
Schofield, P. XI 81
Schuster, C. (Lord) XI 563, 787, 789, 964, 965, 1010
Sclater-Booth, G, (Lord Basing) XIII 549

Scott, J. (Earl of Eldon) * XI 146, 153, 154, 182, 230, 368, 434, 436, 528, 529, 531, 533n, 557, 646, 647, 648, 649, 652, 653, 654, 655, 656, 662, 672, 673, 676, 683, 685–6, 874, 909, 939, 963, 964, 972, 974, 975, 979, 984, 986, 988, 991, 1033, 1045, 1050, 1051n, 1058, 1059, 1065, 1103, 1068, 1074 XII 13, 24–5, 31, 35, 38, 116, 126, 134–6, 138, 145, 239, 249, 253, 255, 262, 332, 360, 373, 416–17, 558, 560, 599, 617–18, 684–5, 787, 792, 1075 XIII 140, 508–9, 517, 518, 657, 673, 741–2, 755, 770–2, 778–9, 808–10, 848–9, 853, 864, 898–9, 903

Scott, Sir L.F. * XI 1033

Scott, W. (Lord Stowell) * XI 93, 262, 533, 695, 697, 715–16, 719, 720–1, 728, 960 XIII 768, 770, 772, 790, 888, 900, 903–4, 984, 991–2, 995

Scott, W.H.J. XI 683

Scriven, W. XI 754

Scrutton, Sir T.E. * XI 818, 828, 979, 987, 989, 1031 XII 956, 1093 XIII 256, 921

Seddon, J.A. XII 844

Sedgwick, T. XII 305, 536–8, 541

Selborne, (Lord) see Palmer, R.

Selden, J. XI 46, 107

Selfe, Sir W.L. ** XI 895, 994

Sellon, B.J. *** XI 1054

Selwyn, Sir C.J. * XI 680, 782, 983 XII 666

Senior, N.W. XI 165, 171, 173, 228 XII 225 XIII 478, 632, 659, 679

Sewell, S.J. XII 874

Seymour, W.D. XI 1020, 1050, 1078, 1083

Shadwell, Sir L.* XI 655, 656, 658, 659, 672, 983, 991, 1051 XII 42, 131, 175, 255, 273, 281, 283, 406, 553, 558–9, 691–2

Shaen, W. XI 1171

Shand, A.B. (Lord) * XI 436, 539, 561 XIII 698

Shand, Judge Sir C.L.** XI 997

Sharpe, J. XI 1092

Sharpe, S. XI 664n, 1203

Shaw, T. (Lord) * XI 539

Shaw, T. (Lord Shaw of Dunfermline) * XII 681 XIII 711–12

Shaw-Lefevre G.J. (Baron Eversley) XII 204 XIII 757, 760–1

Shearman, Sir M.* XI 382, 812

Shedden, Miss XI 817

Shee, Sir W.* XI 600, 962, 1057

Shelton, T. XI 645

Shepherd, Sir S. XI 975, 1054, 1071

Sheppard, W. XII 401, 508

Sibthorp, Colonel C.D.W. XI 707

Sibthorp, Colonel de L.W. XIII 540–541

Sidebottom, C.J. *** XI 1015

Sidgwick, H. XI 113, 115–17

Sidmouth (Lord) see Addington, H.

Siemens, W. XIII 959

Silvester, Sir J. ** XI 643

Simmons † XI 1153

Simmons, L. XII 863, 864

Simon, J.A. (Viscount) XI 1040, 1066, 1067, 1071, 1072

Simón, Sir J. XII 324

Simpson, A.W.B. XII 1140

Simpson, H.B. XII 843

Sinclair, F. XI 1121, 1155

Singh, R. XI 110

Slade, Wadeson and Appach † XI 700

Slaughter and May † XI 1121, 1130, 1141, 1150

Slaughter, W. XI 1141

Smith, A. XI 27, 159, 161, 192, 219 XII 324 XIII 629–31, 637, 940

Smith, Sir A.L. * XI 803, 804, 972, 989, 1075 XI 205, 468–9, 1108 XIII 694

Smith, B. XI 1119

Smith, F.E. (Earl of Birkenhead) * XI 261, 968, 1023, 1028, 1038, 1062, 1071, 1086, 1094 XIII 264, 363, 452

Smith, H. XII 893, 927, 947–8

Smith, J. (IG in Bankruptcy) XII 637, 668, 826, 831–2

Smith, J. (MP) XII 786, 794

Smith, J.W. ** XI 649, 880, 900, 1003, 1133 XII 305

Smith, L. ** XI 868–9 XII 866, 1030

Smith, Sir M.E. * XI 561 XII 962

Smith, N.H. XI 1121

Smith, R. XIII 544, 545

Smith, R.P. XI 653

Smith, Revd S. XI 132, 186

Smith, T. XI 1132

Smith, T.S. XI 83–4

Smith-Stanley, E. (Lord Derby) XI 535, 709

Smyly, W.C. ** XII 847

Snell, F.W. XI 1142

Soane, Sir J. XI 780

Southwood-Smith, Sir T. XI 176, 229

Spankie, T. XI 1034, 1056, 1104

Spence, E.F. XI 1032, 1102, 1121, 1129

Spence, G. XI 677, 685, 1025, 1061, 1183

Spencer, H. XI 103–06, 113–15, 122 XIII 598, 689

Spilsbury, Sir B. XI 949

Spinks, F.L. XI 711, 756, 1058

Spinoza, B. XI 123

Spofforth, M. XI 1152

Spurrier, J.W. XI 1185

St Leonards (Lord) see Sugden, E.B.

Stanley, A.H. XI 1142

Stanley, E.J. (Lord) XI 14, 27 XIII 958

Stansfeld, J. ** XI 1147 XIII 498

Starkie, T. ** XI 1148 XII 928 XIII 84, 108, 194, 195, 198, 199, 200–201, 338, 378, 433–435, 455, 854, 857, 861, 869, 878

Stead, W.T. XI 113 XIII 802

Stephen † XI 998
Stephen, Sir G. XI 1111, 1116, 1120, 1135, 1154
Stephen, H.J. XI 75, 570, 578, 581, 586, 587 XIII 103, 104
Stephen, J. XI 675, 1034
Stephen, Sir J. XI 238, 550 XIII 612
Stephen, Sir J.F. * XI 58, 100–02, 123, 154, 604–5, 644, 769, 780, 980, 989, 994, 1034, 1076, 1185 XII 25–6, 307, 370, 731 XIII 64, 89, 96, 102, 103, 109–11, 115, 125, 132, 151, 163, 181, 182, 183, 186, 206–9, 210–11, 213–16, 221–3, 227, 231–2, 233, 234, 246, 248, 249, 252, 257, 260, 261, 263, 272–5, 276, 278, 280, 281, 306–8, 312, 316, 319, 326, 329, 333, 337–9, 348, 364, 370, 378, 411, 414, 418, 420, 426, 444, 450, 457, 461, 745, 791, 890, 895
Stephen, Sir L. XIII 364
Stephenson, Sir A. *** XIII 786
Stevenson, Dr A. XIII 816
Stevenson, T. XI 49
Stewart, Sir C. XI 843
Stewart, J. XI 1176 XII 60, 71, 73, 75, 77
Stirling, Sir J. * XI 514, 977 XII 430, 605, 1092
Stokes XI 731
Stonor, Sir H.J. ** XI 1001, 1004
Story, J. * XI 281, 1180 XII 305, 359, 374, 435–6, 699, 731, 737, 756, 896, 987 XIII 904
Story, W.W. XII 336
Stowell (Lord) see Scott, W.
Strahan, J.A. XI 1028
Stratford, F.P. XI 676, 1160
Street, G.E. XI 36
Stringer, F. XI 795
Stuart, Sir J. * XI 660 XII 39, 41, 139, 148–9, 205, 235–6, 262, 276, 404, 422, 865
Stuart-Wortley, Sir J.A. (Lord Wharncliffe) XI 533, 976
Sturges, H.M. ** XI 1002
Sturges-Bourne, W. XIII 473
Sugden, E.B. (Lord St Leonards) * XI 534, 538, 559, 612, 646, 657, 658, 659, 660, 674, 678, 680, 709, 746, 782, 878, 965, 967, 991, 993, 1036, 1051, 1058, 1062 XII 29, 33, 51, 70, 73, 76, 89–90, 100, 107, 124–5, 138, 150, 152, 181, 183–6, 188, 235, 255, 258, 276, 285, 288–90, 302, 441, 559–61, 796 XIII 202–203, 397,668, 759, 783, 913
Sumner, Archbishop J.B. XI 708
Sumner, Lord see Hamilton, J.A.
Sutherst, T. XIII 569
Sutton, Sir H. * XI 973, 977, 978
Swabey, H.B. XI 702, 728–9
Swan, R. XI 701, 706
Swanston, C.T. XI 1083
Swift, Sir R.P.W. * XI 987, 1062
Swinnerton, W. XI 874
Sykes, G. XI 1025

Tait, Archbishop A.C. XI 394, 397, 400, 554–5
Talbot, Earl see Chetwynd-Talbot, C.*
Talfourd, Sir T.N. * XII 918 XIII 810–11, 886, 888
Tassell † XI 892
Tassell, A.J. XI 1015
Tauton, Sir W.E. * XI 635
Taylor and Humbert † XI 1118, 1121
Taylor Roscoe † XI 1125
Taylor, A.S. XI 949
Taylor, J. XI 1120, 1130, 1136, 1146, 1154 XII 1022
Taylor, J.P. ** XI 609, 877, 892, 1000
Taylor, M.A. XI 637, 646, 653, 850 XII 1094
Taylor, R.S. XI 1118
Taylor, W.F.K. (Lord Maenan) ** XI 872
Temple, C.** 993
Temple, H.J. (Viscount Palmerston) XI 25, 534, 712, 1066, 1072 XII 1094 XIII 649, 780, 783
Tennent, E. XIII 980
Tennyson, A (Lord) XI 1186
Tenterden (Lord) see Abbott, C.
Terrell, T.H. ** XI 999
Thackeray, W.M. XI 865, 1027, 1034
Thayer, J.B. XI 607
Theobald, H.S. XI 766n, 1036, 1061
Thesiger, A. * XI 965 XII 308, 344, 605
Thesiger, F. (Lord Chelmsford) * XI 535, 560, 649, 671, 741, 763, 963, 965, 966, 974, 982, 991, 1062, 1101 XII 407, 420–1, 540, 561, 608, 966, 1004, 1077, 1085, 1103 XIII 756
Thomas, L. XI 1062, 1101
Thomson, Sir A. XI 676
Thomson, H.B. XI 1021, 1043, 1049, 1061, 1149
Thorne, W. XIII 687
Thring, A. XIII 592
Thring, Sir H. XI 53, 410, 420 XIII 548, 556–557, 572, 613–14
Thurlow, E. (Lord) * XI 1160 XII 130, 133, 247, 438, 441 XIII 741–2, 778–9, 808
Tickell, J.H. XI 645
Tidd, W. XI 570, 1025
Tillett, B. XIII 687
Tindal, Sir N.C. * XI 514, 587, 595, 614, 625, 643, 716, 974, 982, 1056, 1057 XII 330, 481, 526, 533, 566, 577, 600, 685, 706, 801, 882, 907, 918, 920–1, 977, 1040, 1097, 1132 XIII 62, 239, 432, 440, 975, 969, 971
Tindal-Atkinson, H. ** XII 838–9
Todd, A. XI 21
Tolhurst, A. XI 1119, 1121
Tolhursts † XI 1130
Topping, J. XI 988
Torrens, Sir R.R. XII 215 XIII 586
Toulmin-Smith, J. XI 934, 949
Townsend, J.F. XI 795
Trafford, L. ** XI 1004
Traill, J. *** XI 1008

Trelawny, Sir J. XI 612
Trevelyan, C. XI 1083
Tristram, T.H. * XI 697, 713n, 714, 765
Trollope, A. XI 1112, 1130
Troup, Sir F. XI 1074 XIII 816
Troutbeck, Dr J. XI 946–7, 951
Truro (Lord) see Wilde, T.
Tuke, W. & D. XI 152 XIII 830
Turner, Clifford † XI 1121, 1141, 1150
Turner, F. XII 851, 854
Turner, Sir G.J. * XI 518, 560, 659, 665, 679,
    1213 XII 16, 86, 275, 407, 419, 421–4, 552,
    757 XIII 985
Turner, T.C. XI 1124
Turquand, W. XII 648
Tweedsmuir, Lord see Buchan, J.
Twiss, Sir T. XI 261–2, 277, 697, 698, 722, 817,
    1185
Tyrell, T. XI 1130, 1140

Underhill, Sir A. XI 1038, 1040, 1155
    XII 226, 230, 240
Underhill, J.E. XI 1115

Vane, C.W. (Marquess of
    Londonderry) XIII 659
Vangerow, K.A. von XII 353
Vansittart, N. (Lord Bexley) XI 909
Vattel, E. de XI 257, 262, 276
Vaughan, Sir J. * XI 620, 963n, 984
Vaughan Williams † XI 998
Vaughan Williams, Sir R. * XI 804, 979
    XII 516, 518–19, 668, 1139 XIII 685
Vechter, Van Veeden XI 1061
Venables, G.S. XI 1061
Verey, H.W. XI 822
Vesey, F. XI 684 XII 332, 414–15
Victoria, Queen XI 302, 389, 753 XIII 789
Villiers, G.W.F. (Earl of Clarendon) XIII 523
Vinogradoff, Sir P.G. XI 70, 129, 1205
Vizard, W. XI 654, 685, 1117, 1170
Vizards † XI 130
Vulliamy, L. XI 1176

W. Banks & Co. † XI 1126
Wade, W.H. XI 1118
Wakley, Dr T. XI 937–8, 942–3, 944, 947, 953,
    954, 1007 XIII 889, 898
Walker, C.H. XI 1160
Walker, W. XI 1024
Wall, T. XIII 920
Walpole, Sir R. (Earl of Orford) XIII 617, 618
Walters, R. XI 1024
Walton, Sir J. * XI 976, 1084
Walton, W.H. XI 765
Wansborough, H. XI 1118, 1154
Wansboroughs † XI 1119, 1129

Warr, A.F. XI 1142
Warren, C. XI 972, 1053
Warren, S. XI 1033, 1044, 1109, 1180
    XIII 847–8, 851, 854, 861, 869, 878, 900, 948
Warton, C.N. [judic T, MP] XI 769
Waterlow, Sir S. XI 775
Watson, W. (Lord)* XI 539,
    543, 552, 561
Watson, W. (Lord Watson, then
    Thankerton) * XI 539, 543, 552 XII 669,
    671–2, 771, 980,
    1062 XIII 841
Watson, W. (Lord Thankerton)* XI 503
    XII 1083
Watt, J. XIII 944, 946
Webb, S. and B. (Lord and Lady Passfield)
    XI 212, 429 XIII 500, 501, 502, 570,703, 712
Webster, D. XIII 915
Webster, R.E. (Viscount Alverstone)* XI 271,
    275, 504, 518, 539, 613, 699, 722, 752, 753, 806,
    807, 809, 824, 825, 827, 829, 830, 831, 976,
    977, 978, 980, 987, 1025, 1038, 1041, 1047,
    1049, 1060, 1070, 1073, 1106 XIII 82, 99,
    115, 128, 135–136, 253, 287, 409, 415, 418, 419,
    452, 795, 938
Webster, T. XIII 959
Wedderburn, A. (Lord Loughborough, Earl of
    Rosslyn) * XI 408, 1123 XII 133 XIII 771, 778
Weldon, G. XI 817 XIII 760, 768, 785, 831–2
Welford, R.G. ** XI 997
Wellesley, A. (Duke of Wellington) XI 15, 302,
    315, 320, 418, 862, 908
Wellington, 1st Duke of XI 862, 908
Wemyss-Charteris-Douglas, F. (Lord Elcho,
    Earl of Wemyss) XIII 689
Wensleydale (Lord) see Parke, J.
West, H.W. XI 1047
Westbury, (Lord) see Bethell, R.
Westlake, Sir J. XI 260, 276–7, 282
Wetherell, Sir C. XI 971, 976, 1030, 1062
Wharncliffe, Lord see Stuceet Worthey, J.A.
Wharton, F. XII 925, 927, 929
Wheaton, H. XI 260
Wheeler † XI 998
Whewell, W. XI 93–4, 117
Whitbread, G. ** XI 994
Whitbread, S. XIII 519
White, W.A.A.*** XI 1010
Whitehead R. XI 1122
Whitehurst, C.H. XI 1180
Wickens, Sir J. * XI 837, 969, 991, 1188
Wightman, Sir W. * XI 416, 570, 592, 965,
    981 XII 590, 933, 1044, 1073, 1129
    XIII 194, 245, 304
Wigmore, J.H. XI 605–6
Wigram, Sir J. * XI 657, 658, 664 XII 33, 255,
    257, 557, 652 XIII 744, 900

Wilberforce, Bishop S. XIII 783

Wilberforce, W. XI 134, 135–7, 140, 147, 148, 152, 168 XIII 155, 363, 385

Wilde, J.P.B. (Lord Penzance) * XI 398, 738–9, 744, 746–8, 770, 775, 777n, 781, 965 XII 45, 940 XIII 135, 791

Wilde, Sapte † XI 1130, 1145

Wilde, T. (Lord Truro) * XI 609, 659, 680, 795, 966, 974, 1056, 1062, 1064, 1099, 1122, 1168 XII 36, 379–80, 528, 545, 559, 930 XIII 513

Wilkins, C. XI 970

Wilkinson, T. XIII 493

Will, J.S. ** XI 994

Willes, Sir J.S. * XI 33, 407, 592, 759, 965, 967, 969, 977, 987, 991 XII 305–6, 338, 353, 537, 539, 547, 572, 585, 597, 660, 680, 686, 687, 705, 710, 720, 923, 933, 944, 966, 978, 987, 1098, 1100, 1124 XIII 310, 316, 445, 883, 900

Willes, W.H. XI 1099

William III, King XI 6, 302

William IV, King XIII 813 XI 17–18

Williams, E.E. XII 670

Williams, Sir E.V. * XI 635 XII 145, 355, 371, 445, 488, 511, 921, 933, 978, 1099, 1126

Williams, J. [John] XII 305, 596, 1060, 1126

Williams, J. [Joshua] XII 74, 149, 225–6, 233

Williams, M. XI 645n, 1011n

Williams, P. XI 1169

Williams, Sir J. * XI 559, 652, 654, 681, 981, 1025, 1052 XII 496

Williams, T.C. XI 1205 XII 47, 220, 224, 226, 228–9, 231

Williamson, E.W. XI 1156

Willis, W. ** XI 995

Williston, S. XII 310, 313, 356, 372, 381–3, 398, 505–7

Willoughby, Sir C. XI 921

Wills, Sir A. * XI 517, 521, 970, 988, 989 XII 1058 XIII 82, 281, 324

Wilson, A. XI 765

Wilson, G. XI 971, 1059

Wilson, R. XII 190, 194, 199

Winfield, Sir P.H. XI 421–2 XII 610, 944

Wing, J.W. ** XI 995

Winter and Kaye † XI 1121

Winter, J. XI 654

Winterbotham, W.H. XI 792, 843

Withers, Sir J. XI 1118

Witt, J.G. XI 971, 1019, 1041, 1099, 1169

Wodehouse, J. (Lord Kimberley) XII 858

Wolstenholme, E.P. XII 91, 195–6, 208, 212, 223, 236

Wolverhampton, Lord see Fowler, H.

Wontner, T. XI 644

Wood, Sir G. XI 981, 1025

Wood, G.W. XI 910

Wood, W. * * XII 846

Woodfall, R. ** XI 993

Woodroffe, J.T. XI 1059

Wooler, T. XI 1080

Woolley, C. XII 670

Wordsworth W. XIII 888

Worlledge, J. ** XI 1000

Wragges † XI 1122

Wrenbury (Lord) see Buckley, H.

Wright, R.A. (Lord Wright of Durley) * XII 399

Wright, Sir R.S.* XI 820, 989 XII 408, 1078, 1147 XIII 184, 210, 213, 223, 253, 262, 280, 306, 309, 310, 312–314, 327, 329, 378, 379, 381, 456, 458, 676

Wright, W. XII 644, 661–2

Wyatt, Sir R. XI 923

Wyman, G. XI 1133

Wynford (Lord) see Best, W.D.

Wynne, W. XI 1155

Wyse, T. XI 1180, 1181

Yardley, E. *** XI 1010

Yates, Sir J.* XIII 902

Yeatman, J.P. XI 817, 1094

Yerburgh, R.A. XII 862–3, 865

Yorke, P. (Earl Hardwicke) * XII 25, 403, 552–3, 555

Young, A. ** XI 997

Young, W.B. XI 1121, 1149, 1163

Younger, R. (Lord Blanesburgh) * XIII 898

INDEX OF SUBJECTS

This Index is for the contents of Vols XI–XIII of the series.

abortion
  see homicide; offences against the person
accidents,
  see regulation of working conditions, tort
    (personal injuries), workmen's
    compensation, workplace injuries
accomplice,
  see complicity
account
  action of XII 563
  in equity XII, 564–5, 601–3, 645–6, 663, 692
accounts, solicitors' XI 1143, 1162–5, 1199
accountants XI 1135, 1137–8, 1143, 1144,
    1159, 1164
accumulations, rule against XII 21, 215, 250
accused
  see adversarialism; criminal procedure
Acts of Union,
  see United Kingdom
administration orders XI 836–7, 845,
    886–7, 903
administration suits (Chancery) XI 651–2,
    836–7
administration of estates,
  see succession
administrative law,
  see judicial review, public law
administrative tribunals,
  see judicial review
Admiralty, Court of
  admiralty actions in county and local
    courts XI 828, 868, 878
  appeals XI 553, 556, 720, 723
  clerks XI 730–1
  fees XI 716, 719, 728
  judges XI 719–25, 733
    assessors XI 727, 732
    remuneration XI 719–21
  jurisdiction and business XI 714–15, 717, 718
    criminal XI 718–19
    enlargement of XI 715–17
    levels of business XI 717–19
  lawyers
    civilians XI 696, 698
    proctors XI 699, 712–13
  registrar XI 727–8, 731
  rules and procedure XI 721, 725–7, 729–31
    actions *in personam* XI 725–6

actions *in rem* XI 715, 716, 717–18, 725–6
  Admiralty Court Act 1840 XII 687
  arrest of ships XI 726
  juries XI 717
  pleadings XI 726, 730
  practice books XI 727
  short cause rules XI 725
  1883 revision XI 731–2
  Select Committee 1833 XI 705, 715–16, 719, 720
  see also PDA, County Courts, City of
    London
Admiralty (department of state) XI 334,
    379, 381
adultery,
  see Divorce Court, marital breakdown
adversarialism XIII, 58–121
  Director of Public Prosecutions XI 310,
    XIII 7, 64–70
  summary jurisdiction, rise of
  trial: defence XIII 71–85
    Criminal Evidence Act 1898 XIII 8, 10,
      78, 80–81, 89, 90, 92, 102–107 250, 265,
      418, 419
    Defendant's Counsel Act 1836 XIII 7, 61,
      74, 76, 77, 94, 101
    participation of lawyers XIII 7, 8, 9,
      13, 71–76
    Poor Prisoners' Defence Act 1903 XIII 8,
      80, 81–83, 106
  trial: prosecution XIII 58–70
    ameliorating disincentives to
      prosecute XIII 59–61
    citizens' right to prosecute,not the state's
      function XIII 6, 7, 18, 58–63
    police prosecutors XIII 7, 21, 56, 57,
      63–67, 68, 70
    prosecution associations XIII 62–63
  see also summary jurisdiction
advertising XII 327–8, 352–5
advocates (civilian) XI 527, 696–8, 733
  in Admiralty XI 696–8
  number and entry XI 696
  social and educational background XI 697–8
  work, earnings and prospects XI 697–8
  see also Doctors' Commons
affray,
  see public order, protecting
    the state

agency firms,
  see also solicitors
agents XI 1135, 1159 XII 305–6, 324–5, 454, 456,
    595, 657
  account for profits XII 602–5, 645–6, 662–3
  agent contracting for non-existent
      principals XII 462, 469
  apparent authority of XII 761
  bills of exchange, and XII 743
  company directors as, XII 421–3, 657–60,
      662–4, 738–9
  company promoters as, XII 392, 420, 645–6
  del credere XII 324, 448
  factors, XII 324, 742, 761, 790, 1122–4
  Factors Act 1889 XII 762, 871–2, 1124
  fiduciary aspects XII 404–5, 663
  frauds and misrepresentations
      of agents XII 412–13, 419–21, 423,
      659–60
  general and particular XII 657
  principal's liability for XII 419–21, 423,
      659–60, 699–701, 894–9
  purchases from principal XII 662–3
  warranty of authority XII 463
Agriculture, Board of XI 359, 365
amalgamation of the legal professions,
  see also fusion
ambassador,
  see international law
animals,
  see tort
annuities XII 591
  commercial
    for life XII 142–4, 153
    judicial control XII 143–4, 147
    registration XII 143–4, 185
  settlements, in XII 10
  see also mortgages, settlement of property
      generally
appeals XI 767, 810, 811
  Admiralty XI 553, 556, 720, 723
  Chancery XI 658, 672–3
  Common Law Courts XI 601–2
  Coroners XI 804
  County Court XI 900–1
  Divorce XI 750, 756
  Ecclesiastical Courts XI 458, 553–5
  JCPC XI 394–8, 400
  King's Bench Division XI 809–10, 830
  petty sessions XI 491, 495–7
  quarter sessions, by case stated XI 491–2,
      495
  see also JCPC, Lords, House of (appellate)
      courts of appeal, petty sessions,
      quarter sessions
appointment,
  see powers of appointment (proprietary)

apprentices,
  see employer and employee
arbitration XI 310, 718, 774–5, 810,
    829, 882
  see also tribunals of commerce, labour
      relations
army, XI 342–3, 401–22
  administration XI 404–6
  civil disorder, and XI 402–4
  command XI 401–4
    Commander-in-Chief XI 402, 405–6, 409,
      411, 414, 418, 420
  common law courts and XI 407–10,
      414–16
  discipline XI 407–10, 414–16
  Judge-Advocate General XI 404, 409,
      412–14, 416–21
  Ordnance, Board of XI 404–5
  Parliamentary control XI 402, 404–6
    disciplinary regulation XI 409–12
  prerogative powers XI 342–3, 401–3, 405–6
  Secretary at War, War Office XI, 402,
      404–5, 409
  sovereign, and XI 401–3, 410
  see also military law
articled clerks XI 1122–24, 1178
  see also solicitors
assault and wounding XIII, 61,
    392, 393–401
  assault XIII 61, 117, 394–395, 397, 399
    civil or criminal XIII 394
    Offences Against The Person Acts 1828
      and 1861 XIII 395–397, 400
    women and children, legislation
      protecting XIII 395
  wounding XIII 61, 396–401
    change from specific to non-specific
      harm XIII 396, 398
    Criminal Law Commissioners XIII
      397–400
    endangering offences XIII 398–399
    consolidation of offences XIII 392, 397
    Lord Ellenborough's Act, 1803 XIII 396,
      400
    Lord Lansdowne's Act, 1828 XIII 396, 397
    Offences against the Person Act, 1861
      XIII 397, 400–401
assessors
  in Admiralty XI 727, 732
  in JCPC XI 557–8
assignment
  insurance policies XII 688–9, 691–3
  of choses in action XII 691–3, 733, 757
  of liabilities XII 595
  of intellectual property XIII 847, 972, 997,
      1001–2
  of negotiable instruments XII 733, 757

assizes XI 526, 636–40, 735, 750,
        776–80, 825–7
    bar and XI 1037, 1048
    business on XI 825–7, 879
    Clerks of Assize XI 628, 795, 1094, 1147
    Commissioners XI 969
    Fourth Assize XI 768, 778, 779, 826
    grouping XI 779, 789, 826, 827
Association of British Chambers of
        Commerce XI 773, 775
Association of Provincial Law Societies XI 1171
assumpsit, action of XII 314–20, 326, 396, 447,
        454, 498, 524–5, 527, 530, 563–6, 569, 587
    indebitatus assumpsit, XII 314–15, 319, 495–6
        530–34, 575
    see also contract
asylums
    see insanity, lunacy, and mental deficiency
attempt to commit crime XIII, 15, 282, 297–314
    fault requirement XIII 307–310
        intention XIII 307–309
        wider notions: Austin and
            Macaulay XIII 308
    origins and conceptual recognition XIII
        297–302
        statutory attempts XIII 300–302
    proximity and the law's reach XIII 302–307,
        310–314
        acts immediately connected XIII 304
        impossible attempts XIII 310–313
        'interruption' test XIII 304, 305, 307
        'last act' test XIII 303, 304
        'overt' acts XIII 306
        unequivocal acts XIII 304, 307
    punishment XIII 313–314
attorney,
    see solicitors
Attorney-General see Law Officers
audience
    County Courts XI 897–8, 1098–99
    courts of request XI 853
    Law Society and XI 1166, 1169
    Petty Sessions XI 929
    Probate court XI 733
    quarter sessions XI 1037
Australia,
    see British colonies and empire
average,
    see marine insurance

bail XI 570, 571, 575–9
    see also criminal procedure
bailiffs XI 889, 896, 902–3
bailment XII 305–6, 1116–18
    bailees XII 514
        duty of care XII 913–16, 1118
        hire-purchasers as XII 871,

insurance by XII 695
pawnbrokers as XII 852
gratuitous XII 374, 927
ballot
    see elections
Bank of England XII 275, 728–31
banking XII 728–31, 764–78
    Bank Charter Act 1844 XII 729, 764
    bank notes XII 728–9
        duties to customers XII 766–9
        incorporation of XII 619, 728–9
        limited liability of XII 629–30, 633
        winding up of XII 630
    Institute of Bankers XII 307
bankruptcy XI 138, 1143, 1144–45, 1147,
        1161, 1166 XII 68, 121, 182, 265, 326,
        578–9, 779–97, 804–33
    acts of bankruptcy XII 781–6, 793, 804,
        813–15, 817, 831
        fraudulent conveyances XII 782–3,
            813–14
    Bankruptcy Act 1825 XII 793–4
    Bankruptcy Act 1861 XII 818, 820,
        821, 837,
    Bankruptcy Act 1869 XII 647
    Bankruptcy Act 1883 XII 561, 824–6, 825–8,
        830,
    Bankruptcy Act 1890 XII 827, 832, 864
    Bankruptcy Consolidation Act 1849
        XII 808–9, 816
    Bankruptcy and Deeds of Arrangement
        Act 1913 XII 829, 832
    commissioners XII 781, 786–8, 792, 795,
        806, 809, 812
    composition agreements XII 384–5,
        783–4, 793–4, 809–10, 820–2, 824–6,
        828, 830–3
        Deeds of Arrangement Act 1887 XII 831
    creditors' assignees XII 788–9, 822
    DC (1906–8) XII 828–9, 832–3, 847, 874
    discharge of XII 823, 825–9
        certificate of conformity XII 781, 791–2,
            794, 805–6, 810–13, 818
        examination of XII 824–5, 827–8
    fraudulent XII 798–9, 801–2, 804–8, 810, 813,
        818–20, 823–4, 826, 828–30
    London Bankruptcy Commission XI 791
    official assignees XII 796, 809, 817, 822
    official receiver XII 824–6
    'poor man's' XII 840–1, 844–8
    reputed ownership, doctrine XII 692,
        789–90, 817, 860–1, 873–4
    reform of courts XII 795–6, 817, 820
    RC (1839–40) XII 804–5
    RC (1854) XII 813, 815, 820, 822
    SC (1864) XII 821–1
    see also insolvency

bar
  Admiralty XI 717, 722, 724–5
  Birmingham XI 1030, 1054
  Central Criminal Court XI 641–5, 970,
    1030, 1038, 1042–43
  Chancery XI 757, 760, 763, 1050–52
  common law XI 1047–50
  divorce XI 747–9
  JCPC XI 548, 566
  local bars XI 1028, 1040, 1092
  Liverpool XI 1028
  Manchester XI 1028
  Parliamentary XI 1052–54
  relations with solicitors XI 1040–41, 1111
  see also barristers, etiquette
Bar Committee XI 809, 1017, 1038–39, 1210
Bar Council XI 801, 831, 1039, 1065,1089,
    1090, 1092, 1168
bar examinations XI 1019–20, 1036, 1181,
    1183, 1184, 1195–97
bar mess,
  see circuits
barristers
  chambers XI 1027–30
  clerks XI 1031–33
  colonial posts XI 1044, 1046–47
  composition XI 1020
    Irish XI 1020, 1022, 1054
    Scottish XI 1020, 1054, 1059
    Welsh XI 1020
  'devilling' XI 1038–39
  earnings XI 1043–44, 1050
  'huggery' XI 1040
  numbers XI 1017–20
  public offices XI 1044–47, 1147, 1166
  pupillage XI 1023–5, 1038, 1176–77
  quarter sessions XI 1036–8
  role of juniors XI 1049
  social background and education
    XI 1020–23 1175–201
  'soup' and 'dockers' XI 1041–43
    expense XI 1033–34
    journalism and literature XI 1034–36
  transfers between professions
    XI 1168–69
  see also bar, Inns of Court
bastardy,
  see children
beggars,
  see vagrancy
benefit of clergy,
  see punishment
bills of exchange XII 68, 121, 182, 265, 303, 305,
    307, 325, 729–54, 766
  acceptance XII 733–7
  accommodation bills XII 732, 736,
    746, 752–3

Bills of Exchange Act 1882 XII 731, 739, 741,
    743, 747, 749, 751, 753–4, 773, 777, 864
  consideration XII 743–8
  joint stock companies' use of XII 738
  deposited with bank XII 767–8
  dishonour XII 337, 735–7
  fictitious payees XII 752–4
  foreign XII 729, 734, 736, 740
  forged XII 749–52
  indorsement XII 732–3, 740–3
  inland XII 729–30, 734, 736, 740
  negligence, and XII 748–9
  payable to bearer XII 732, 739–40
  payable to order XII 740
  Regulation of Acceptances Act 1821 XII 734
  see also cheques
bills of lading XII 324, 758–64, 790
  Bills of Lading Act 1855 XII 760
  indorsement of XII 759–61
bills of sale XII 121, 152, 154, 156, 783, 789,
    813–16, 859–62, 874–6
  Bills of Sale Act 1854 XII 816
  Bills of Sale Act 1878 XII 859–60
  Bills of Sale Act 1882 XII 861
  see also mortgages
Birmingham
  Assize at XI 637, 639
  Birmingham Law Society XII 105, 108, 227
  court of requests XI 853, 855
  local bar XI 1030, 1054
  solicitors in XI 1110, 1114, 1115, 1119,
    1142, 1149, 1154
birth,
  see registration of births, deaths and
    marriages
blasphemy,
  see obscenity
bonds XII 314, 393, 524–5
  conditional XII 497, 524–5
Board of Education,
  see education
Board of Trade, XI 335, 343, 352–3, 355,
    357, 359,1142, 1145–46, 1166 XII 619,
    626, 630, 683, 824–6, 830–3, 968,
    997, 1021
Boroughs XI 425–45, 453, 458, 465–6
  borough fund XI 435–6, 440–2
  county XI 337, 426, 465–7, 471
  magistrates XI 423, 431
  metropolitan XI 485
  see also municipal corporations, Recorders
borough courts XI 850–1, 861, 866
breach of confidence
  emergence of innominate
    equity XIII 984–7
    character of right XIII 985–6, 988–9
    indirect recipient XIII 985

relation of the equity to forms of intellectual
    property
  to copyright XIII 898–900, 984–5
  to patents XIII 985
  influence of contractual terms XIII 987–9
protectable subject-matter
  commercial and technical secrets XIII
    984–5
  government secrets XIII 986–7
  private personal information XIII 987
remedies for breach
  injunction XIII 985
  monetary compensation XIII 988
  see also copyright, intellectual property,
    fiduciary duties
breach of promise,
  see marriage
Bristol Tolzey Court XI 850, 870, 871
  local bar XI 1029–30
British colonies and empire XI 234–54
  acquisition of colonies XI 238–44
    by conquest XI 238–9
    by settlement XI 239–40
  British Commonwealth XI 235–6, 247
  common law transposed to colonies
    adaptation to circumstances XI 240–1,
      247–8
    labour contracts XI 250
    land rights XI 248–9
    personal law XI 241
  constitutional relations XI 238–47
    colonial administrations XI 241–2
    colonial judiciaries XI 242,
      243–7, 550–3
    colonial legislatures XI 242–3
    dominion status XI 245
  empire and international law XI 276–7
  English reactions to colonial legal
    developments
    copyright XIII 910–11
    compulsory labourl arbitration XIII 717
    juvenile courts XIII 821
    labour exchanges XIII 717–18
    land registration XII 215–6,
      218–22
    trade boards XIII 692
    women's electoral rights XI 243
  India
    appeals from XI 549, 556, 560–1
    bar students from XI 1020, 1087
    court systems XI 240–1
    dominion status Australia, Canada, New
      Zealand, South Africa XI 235–6
    Change and registration to land titles
      registration XII 215–6,
      218, 224
    SSH imperialism XI 237

East India Company XI 240–1
India Office XI 238
sovereignty in international
  law XI 264–5
Indian Law Commission XII 306–7,
  369, 386, 485
Indian Contract Act XII 307–9, 345
Privy Council XI 237–8
JCPC XI 245–7, 550–3
Proposal for an Imperial Court of Appeal
  XI 247, 552, 557, 562
sources of law in colonies
  British statutes XI 240
  binding precedent XI 51
  Colonial Laws Validity Act 1865 XI 242
theories of colonization
  liberal approaches XI 236–7
  imperialism XI 237
  see also international law, private
    international law
British subjects,
  see private international law
building,
  see housing
burglary,
  see larceny
burial,
  see public health
Byelaws XI 427, 429, 443–4
  judicial review of XI 518–21
  see also housing, public health

Canada,
  see British colonies and empire
canon law,
  see Church of England, Ecclesiastical Courts
capital punishment,
  see punishment
cartels XII 670–3
carriers XII 904–16, 926, 958–69
  Carriers Act 1830, 458, 473, 543, 915
  liability for goods XII 458, 474, 909–16, 1118
    use of exemption clauses XII 473–5, 543,
      911–16, 967–9
    shippers' duties to disclose dangers XII
      986–7,
  railways XII 959–67, 985
  road XII 904–11
case law,
  see sources of law
Central Criminal Court XI 640–5, 1074
  'soup' and 'dockers' XI 1941–3
  Admiralty sessions XI 719
  bar XI 970, 1030, 1038, 1042–43
    bar mess XI 642
  clerks XI 642, 645
  courtrooms XI 784

Central Criminal Court (*cont.*)
  judges XI 640–1, 643, 829
  solicitors XI 1135–6
  'soup' and 'dockers' XI 1041–43
  trials XI 644–5
central government, departments
    of XI 305
  finance of XI 380–4
  judicial review of XI 382–4, 487,
      502–4, 511–12
  legal forms of XI 345–6, 361–6
  liabilities of XI 378–84
  ministers XI 345, 365–6
    accountability XI 347–8, 354,
      421, 505
  see also Admiralty, Board of Trade,
      Colonial Office, Excise Commissioners,
      Home Office, India Office,
      Lord Chancellor's Office, Public
      Works and Buildings Commissioners,
      Secretaries of State, Sewers
      Commissioners, Treasury,
      War Office
Central Office Committee XI 765,
    792–3
certificated conveyancers XI 1027
certiorari, writ of,
  see judicial review
Chancery XI 647, 656, 689
  Chancery Division XI 835
  county courts XI 878, 886
Chancery Bar XI 1030, 1038, 1050–2, 1061
    1099–100
  refreshers XI 1107
  retainers XI 1106
Chancery, Court of (1852–1876) XI 559, 710, 713,
    715, 716, 718 XII 321–2, 414, 434–5,
    564–5, 624
  Accountant-General XI 688–9
  bankruptcy appeals XII 787–8,
    795, 812
  business XI 648, 680, 689–91 XII 7, 85,
    87–8, 235–7, 323
    types XI 649–52
  clerical organization
    chief clerks XI 1147
    expanded role XI 679–81
    reforms XI 686–9
    six clerks and sworn clerks XI 678,
      684–5
    taxing masters XI 841–2, 1147
  enforcement of judgments XI 673–4
  equity jurisprudence in XII 171–2
  evidence XI 610, 667–71, 689, 758,
    affidavit XI 670
    examination and interrogatories
      XI 668–70

feigned issue XIII 944
  oral evidence XI 670–1
fees
  changes in 1852 XI 688
  fees increases XI 686–7
  sinecures XI 682–3
fusion of jurisdictions XII 321–2, 770–3
  preference for equity, in Judicature Act
      1873 XII 161, 178, 425
injunctions,
  interlocutory XIII 864–6, 898–900, 944
  no prior restraint of defamation
      XIII 864–6
  to enjoin infringements of intellectual
      property XIII 898–900, 944, 996–8,
      1003
  to prevent breach of personal service
      contracts XII 559–61
  to prevent breaches of charterparties
      XII 561–2
  to prevent nuisances XII 1071–8, 1081–2,
      1089–91, 1101–11
judges XI 655–60
  Lord Justices of Appeal XI 660, 986
  shortage of XI 655–6
  Vice-Chancellors XI 658, 672–3, 985–6
procedure and practice
  appearance XI 662, 666–7, 837
  motions for decree XI 666, 672–3
  orders XI 649, 664
  pleadings XI 661–4, 666
reforms of 1850s XII 194, 271
  Cairns' Act XII 540, 551–2, 1108
  originating summons XI 665–6
  Rolt's Act XII 1107–8
  special case XI 665
  summary procedure XI 665, 672
specific performance XII 161, 173–4, 253–4,
      312, 321, 548–59
  building works XII 556–8
  denied where fraud, surprise or
      mistake XII 373, 414, 439–41
  personal services XII 558–9
  sale of goods XII 552–6
  sale of land XII 103–4, 438, 550–2
  sale of shares XII 553–4
trials
  appeals XI 658, 672–3, 677
  delays XI 671–2
  re-hearing XI 672–3
  under Lord Eldon XI 646–52
  see also contract, injunctions, Lord
      Chancellor, Master of the Rolls,
      Vice-Chancellor
Chancery, Court of Appeals in XI 541
  creation XI 659–60
  judges XI 673

Chancery Division (1876–1900) XI 834–47
  business XI 834–7 XII 236–7
  DC on staff (1886) 840, 841–2, 844–6
  delays XI 845
  judges XI 764, 770, 837–9
    delegation to masters XI 839
    in chambers XI 846–7
    on circuit XI 837
    pairing XI 811, 830, 838–9
    masters (chief clerks) XI 839–40
    costs and expenses XI 845, 847
    DC on staff (1886) XI 840–2, 844–6
    practice and procedure XI 844–7
    registrars XI 681–2, 842–3
    DC on staff XI 843–4, 847
    suitors' fund XI 687, 782
Chancery procedure XI 844–7
  costs and expenses XI 845, 847
  originating summons XI 844–5
  pleadings XI 844
  witness actions and evidence XI 845
Chancery reforms
  RC on Chancery (1824) XI 652–5, 664,
    674–5, 677, 682, 684, 1103 XII 795
  RC on Chancery (1850) XI 664, 666,
    669–71, 682, 690, 709, 710
charities XII 4, 241
Charity Organisation Society XI 115, 221
  development of charities law
    and Poor Law XIII 508–510
    Chancery XIII 507–510, 513
    cy-près XIII 508, XIII 508–9, 515
    Jekyll's Mortmain Act 1736 XIII 508–509
    interpretations of 'charity' XIII 508–510
    public, non-proprietary character XII 241
    secret trusts for XII 4
  Elizabethan reforms
    Acts of 1597 and 1601 XIII 507–708
    charitable purposes XIII 507–510
    County Commissions of
      Inquiry XIII 507–508
    information XIII 508
  scrutiny and management of charities
    Commissions of Inquiry, 1819–1837
      XI 431–3, XIII 511–513
    Cranworth's Charitable Trusts Act
      1853 XIII 514
    failed bills of 1845, 1847, 1849,
      1850 XIII 513
    permanent Charity Commissioners and
      staff, 1853, 1855, 1860 XI 360,
      431–3, XIII 514–7
    Poor Law Commissioners and
      charities XIII 512
    Select Committees of 1835, 1894
      XIII 512–513, 516
    staff of Charity Commissioners XIII 514, 516

  permanent Charity Commissioners in 1853
  see also companies, municipal corporations
charterparties XII 324, 489–90, 495–6, 503,
    511–12, 561
chartism XI 13, 15, 73, 84 XIII 347, 488
  see also political economy, public order
cheques XII 730–1, 764–78
  Bills of Exchange (Crossed Cheques)
    Act 1906 XII 778
  Crossed Cheques Act 1856 XII 774
  Crossed Cheques Act 1858 XII 775, 777
  Crossed Cheques Act 1876 XII 772, 777
  crossing cheques XII 773–8
  forged XII 769–73, 775
  Stamp Act 1853 XII 772, 777
  see also bills of exchange
children
  adoption XIII 818–9
  capacity in civil law XIII 806–7
  custody
    father's 'sacred' right over legitimate
      children 807–10 XIII 812
    mother's entitlement against
      father XIII 810–13
    right between parent and third parties:
      guardianship XIII 813–4
  endangered children Prevention of
      Cruelty Act 1889 XI 310
    baby-farming, regulation of XIII 814–15
    Children Act 1908 XIII 815–16
    discipline XIII 816
    homelessness XIII 815–17
    homicide XIII 814–5
    industrial schools XIII 815—16
    Juvenile Courts XIII 821–22
    magistrates XIII
    'missionaries' and the probation
      service XIII 820
    orphanages and similar institutions
      XIII 815–8
    poor law support XIII 818–19
    Prevention of Cruelty:
      Act of 1889 XIII 817–18
    reformatories and punishment XIII 815
    seduction of daughter, action for
      XIII 725, 802
  guardianship and wardship XII 12–13, 244
    Act of 1886 XIII 812—3
    Chancery jurisdiction XIII 808–13
    power of appointment XIII 808, 813
  illegitimacy
    affiliation proceedings against
      father XIII 803–5
    effect of birth in wedlock XIII 804–5
    incidence of XIII 803–4
    legitimation by subsequent
      marriage XIII 805

children (*cont.*)
    poor law relating to XIII 803
    right and responsibility of mother XIII 803–4
    occupier's liability for XII 980–4
    see also education, guardianship, private
        international law, punishment
chimney sweeps,
    see regulation of working conditions
choses in action XII 615, 743–4
    assignment of XII 691–3, 733, 757, 789
Christian Socialism XI 93
church rates XI 693–4, 713
Church of England XI 310 XII 113, 169
    appointments XI 389–90
    church discipline XI 394–400
    Church Estates Commissioners XI 355, 357
    church legislation (canons) XI 391
    convocations XI 390–2, 396–7
    Ecclesiastical Commissioners XI 388–9
    education, and XI 362–3, 386
    Parliament and XI 388–9, 391–2
    public funding XI 312, 319, 386, 449
    secular courts, and XI 390, 392–400,
        507–8, 510, 516
    see also Ecclesiastical Courts, religion
church rates,
    see Church of England (public funding),
        Ecclesiastical Courts
circuits XI 636–40, 776–80, 826–7, 1030–31,
    1040 , 1090–6
    changing XI 810
    decline of XI 1091
    etiquette XI 1091, 1104–5
    Home XI 637, 777, 1030 , 1095
    judges' liability XI 724, 837
    Midland XI 639, 1030, 109
    Norfolk XI 639, 640, 779, 1030, 1094–95,
        1103, 1105
    North-eastern XI 1096
    Northern XI 639–40, 1031, 1095–96,
        1103–6
    Oxford XI 639, 1030, 1035, 1093, 1105
    South-eastern XI 779, 1094–95
    Welsh XI 635–6
    Western XI 639, 1030, 1091, 1093, 1096, 1105
    see also Assizes
City of London
    Corporation of XI 425, 472–4,
        477–80, 484–5
    policing in XI 28, 34–5, 474, 476
    see also local government, London,
        municipal corporations
    courts
    Civil Judicial Statistics XI 810, 826
    SC on civil service expenditure (1873)
        XI 786, 792, 794, 839, 888
    see also London

civil service
    RC on, 6th report XI 739, 741–2, 787, 794,
        797, 813, 842, 843
    see also Crown, local government, London,
        municipal corporations
clergy
    as magistrates XI 730–1
    disciplinary procedures XI 705–6,
        710, 714
clerks
    Admiralty XI 730–1
    Chancery XI 678, 684–5
    Common Law Courts XI 627–30
    County Court XI 893–4
    District Probate Registries XI 739–40
    House of Lords XI 542
    of Assize XI 628, 795, 1094, 1147
    of the Peace XI 920–4, 1148
    Principal Probate Registry XI 735–8
    Supreme Court of Judicature
        XI 791–7
    see also courts of law
Code Civil (France) XII 301, 304, 541
codification XI 74, 78–9, 82–3, 86, XII 306–8,
    679, 731–2
    Society for the Reform and Codification
        of the Law of Nations XII 715
    see also criminal law sources,
        international law
collectivism XI 118–23
    see also labour relations, political economy,
        trade unions
Colonial Office XI 552 , 1046, 1072
colonies, British,
    see British colonies and empire
combination laws,
    see industrial disputes, political economy,
        trade unions
commercial law,
    Mercantile Law Commission XII 556
    see also agents and agency, banking, bills
        of exchange, bills of lading, companies,
        debtors and creditors, insurance, sale
        of goods
Commercial list (Court) XI 814,
    820, 828–9
Commissioners, local XI 423, 428, 437–8, 442,
    450, 453, 475, 479
    election of XI 428
    liability of XI 369, 435–6
    contract XI 371, 376
    torts XI 369, 374–6
Commissioners of Assize, as route to bench
    by coroners XI 854–5
    by justices XI 930
committee on education,
    see education, Privy Council

commons,
  see inclosure
Commons, House of XI 303–15
  accountability to XI 347–8, 354–60, 362
  finance, control of XI 304, 313, 358, 360,
    379–84, 405, 481
  functions of XI 304–6
  government, relation with XI 305–6, 311,
    313–16, 324, 337–8
  redress of grievances XI 307–8, 313
  House of Lords, relation with XI 307–8,
    314, 316, 318–24
  Members of Parliament
    local legislation and XI 327–8, 332, 443
    private members' bills XI 305, 309–12,
      319, 392
  petitions to XI 306
  political parties in XI 302
  procedure in XI 304–9, 311–15
    closure of debate XI 306, 308–9, 313–15
    local and private bills XI 325, 327–38
  speaker of XI 309, 322, 324, 387–8
  see also elections, legislation,
    Lords, House of Parliament
companies XII 613–73
  accounts XII 621–3, 628, 641, 653–57
  auditors XII 621, 628
  Bills of Exchange given by XII 737–9
  Bubble Act XII 617–18
  cartels XII 670–3, 1050–2
  Davey Committee XII 638, 641, 656, 667–70
  debentures XII 636–8
  dividends, paid from capital XII 654–6, 664
  directors XII 621, 623, 738
    as agents XII 420–3, 657–60, 662–4
    breach of fiduciary duties XII 604, 662–5
    criminal liability of XII 661–2
    liability for misconduct XII 422, 426–30,
      654–5
    liability for negligence XII 666–7
    liability for *ultra vires* acts XII 663–4
  floating charges XII 157–8, 636–8
  formation of XII 620, 638–47
  Gladstone Committee XII 620–2
  incorporation XII 613, 620–3, 628
  investors, protection of XII 618, 623–5,
    648–9
    rescission of share purchases XII 418,
      420–6, 648–9
  limited liability XII 298, 620–1, 625–30, 633
  Loreburn Committee XII 638, 657, 667
  management of XII 652–67
    rule in *Foss* v. *Harbottle* XII 652–3
  private XII 633, 667–70
  promoters
    fiduciary duties of XII 603, 643–6
    flotation of companies XII 638–9, 643–6

rescission of contracts with XII 643,
  645–6
prospectuses XII 641–2, 644, 670
shareholders
  disputes over company membership XII
    339–40, 343–4, 648–9
  liability of XII 622–3, 649–50
shares XII 120, 287
  founders' shares XII 635
  preference XII 634–6
  scrip XII 623–4, 638
  underwriting of issue XII 646–7
Trading Companies Act, 1834 XII 619
ultra vires doctrine XII 392, 421, 606–10,
  657–61
  payment of dividends from capital XII
    654–5
unincorporated XII 616–21
winding up XII 628–30, 647–52
company legislation
  Companies Act 1862 XII 630, 647,
    652, 656, 659
  Companies Act 1867 XII 640
    s 38 XII 428, 640–2, 643
  Companies (Memorandum of Association)
    Act 1890 XII 659
  Companies Act 1900 XII 638, 641, 647,
    656, 670
  Companies Act 1907 XII 657, 667, 670
  Companies Clauses Consolidation
    Act 1845 XII 622, 636, 662
  Companies (Winding Up)
    Act 1890 XII 651–2
  Directors' Liability Act 1890 XII 644, 651
  Joint Stock Companies Act 1844 XII 621–2,
    625, 627–8, 738
  Joint Stock Companies
    Act 1856 XII 627–8, 738
  Limited Liability Act 1855 XII 627, 780
  Winding Up Act 1844 XII 624, 630
  Winding Up Act 1848 XII 624–5, 630
Compensation for loss of office
  Ecclesiastical Court officers XI 733
  Patent Office XI 858
  six clerks XI 686–7
  see also tort, workmen's compensation acts,
    workplace injuries
complicity XIII, 15, 282, 283–297
  acts and agency XIII 284–289
    assisting XIII 284
    encouraging XIII 286
    innocent agent XIII 288–289
    mere presence XIII 285
    omitting to exercise control XIII 287
    principal or non-principal XIII 284
    withdrawal from complicity XIII 296–7
  mental culpability XIII 289–296

complicity (*cont.*)
    broad or narrow concept of
      involvement XIII 289–290
    common purpose or design XIII 290–295
    constructive fault XIII 293–4
    purpose, knowledge or foresight XIII
      289–290
confidence and confidentiality,
    see breach of confidence, companies,
      fiduciary duties
conflict of laws,
    see private international law
Conservative Party
    House of Lords, and XI 321–25
    Housing and Town Planning Act 1909,
      and XI 510–11
    property law, and XII 119, 197, 199, 204,
      206, 208–9, 211, 213–17, 224, 228
    see also political affiliations
consideration,
    see contract
consolidation of statutes,
    see criminal law sources
Conspiracy, criminal and tortious XIII, 15,
    282–314,
    rationale of criminal liability XIII 314–16
    tort of XII 1048, 1050–3, 1060–7,
    unlawful objective XIII 315–20
      Conspiracy and Protection of Property
        Act 1875 XIII 319, 320
      economic pressure XIII 318–20
      judges as custodians of morality XIII 318–20
      political conflict XIII 318–20
    see also industrial disputes, trade unions
constables
    see police
construction,
    see statute, will, contract, patent
consumers XII 326–8, 352, 355, 473, 522,
    834–76, 881, 924, 988–90
    railway tickets XII 327–8, 967–71
contingent remainders,
    see estates in land
contract
    accord and satisfaction XII 383–4, 492,
      740, 994, 998
    breach
      anticipatory XII 494–508
      marine insurance policies XII 702–3
      termination for XII 487–90
      waiver of XII 491, 494
    caveat emptor XII 98, 400, 409, 414, 451,
      479–81, 483–4, 641
    conditions XII 305, 485, 488–91
      dependent and independent XII 485–7
    consideration XII 301, 310, 313, 315–17,
      358–90, 394, 486–7
      adequacy of XII 360, 372–4

Ames's views on XII 382–3, 387–8, 396–8
Anson's views on XII 365, 376, 380–2, 387,
    390, 395–6
Bills of Exchange XII 743–8,
causa and 394
forbearance to sue XII , 375–6
gratuitous promises XII 333–4, 358
Langdell's theory of XII 380–1
meritorious consideration XII 233–5,
    265, 361, 388
moral consideration XII 361–6, 567
motive and XII 370–1
part-payment of debts, and XII 383–7,
past consideration XII 362, 364–6
performance of existing duties
    XII 376–83, 386
Pollock's views on XII 360, 365–6, 371–2,
    374, 380–3, 386–7, 394–9
promise as consideration XII 396–7
sufficiency of XII 372, 374–5
theories of XII 380–1, 394–9
total failure of XII 436, 448, 450, 588–95
treatment in equity XII 233–5,
    265, 359, 372
contractual intention XII 309–10, 355,
    369–72, 399
intention to create legal relations
    XII 309–10, 371–2
deed XII 253–4, 360
duress XII 148, 322, 400–2,
    duress of goods XII 401–2, 576
    duress to the person XII 400–1
executed and executory XII 315–16, 319, 331, 592
freedom of contract XII 120, 147–8
frustration XII 508–21
    in sale of goods XII 509–11
    leases XII 509, 513
    notion of implied condition XII 514–15
    of commercial purpose XII 516–19
    Pollock's views on XII 522
good faith XII 148, 312, 409, 415, 418
    insurance contracts XII 697–701
guarantee XII 306, 349, 355
illegal XII 508, 591–5
    wagers XII 594–5
implied in fact XII 531–3, 600, 986, 963, 1013
implied in law XII 568–9, 580
indemnities XII 425–7
Indian Contract Act 1872 XII 307–9, 345
Indian Law Commission XII 306–7, 369, 386
infants XII 363 XIII 807
intention to create legal relations XIII 765
Is it
    implied XII 117, 409, 473, 475, 480–5, 510
Lord Tenterden's Act 1828 XII 331, 363, 1040
offer and acceptance XII 301, 303, 309–57
    acceptance by conduct XII 342, 473–4
    Anson's view on XII 351, 355

auctions XII 333
communication of acceptance XII 336–45
Langdell's view on XII 347–8
'mirror-image' rule XII 334–5
'objective' view of contract formation
XII 310, 332–3, 338–9, 451
Pollock's view on XII 339, 345, 347–8, 351,
353–4, 355, 357
postal rule XII 335–7, 343–5
revocation of offer XII 345–6, 355–7
'subjective' view of contract
formation XII 336–7, 343, 346
theories of XII 347–8
unilateral contracts XII 348–57, 757
parol evidence rule XII 411, 446, 699
pleading and procedure XII 313–22
privity of contract XII 360, 388–94, 969
Pollock's views on XII 390
rectification XII 435, 437–9,
442–3, 446
rescission
for fraud XII 411, 415–16
for mistake XII 436–7, 441, 590
for non-fraudulent misrepresentation
XII 418–25, 431–2, 649
for undue influence XII 408
in sale of goods XII 478, 589
loss of right to XII 408, 411, 460
on terms XII 416, 645
restraint of trade XII 371, 527, 671–2,
1050–2
retail price agreements XII 672–3
Roman law influence XII 306, 309, 434, 449,
450, 505, 514–15, 518, 566
seamen's contracts XII 377–8, 532
termination XII 494–521
terms
exemption clauses XII 473–5, 870,
911–16, 967–9
incorporation of XII 474–5, 968
standard terms XII 327, 473, 476–7
waiver of performance XII 491–4
theories of contract XII 94, 98
bargain theory XII 360, 371–2,
387, 395–6
reliance theory XII 311–12,
366–70
will theory XII 297, 301–3, 306, 308–13, 315,
346, 360, 370, 433, 452
variation XII 492
void and voidable XII 400, 408, 434,
436–7, 444, 448–9, 452–4, 458–60,
462, 465, 468–72
warranty
express XII 479–80
see also damages, employer and
employee, forms of action, fraud,
misrepresentation, mistake,

sale of goods, specific performance,
statute of frauds
contributory negligence,
see negligence
conversion XII 121, 401–2, 464–6, 1115–22
damages in XII 900
hire traders and XII 871
pawnbrokers and XII 853–4, 871
conveyances
covenants for title, in XII 101–2, 209
deed, by XII 60–1, 90
lease and release, by XII 49, 60
recitals in XII 64
short forms of XII 72, 77, 203
statutory XII 71–2, 90, 209, 211
stamp duty on XII 57, 59–61, 72
see also conveyancing, sale of land
conveyancing XII 48, 86, 107, 140,
186, 202–3
attendant terms XII 62, 65–8,
72–3, 77
barristers, and XII 52, 66, 75, 96–7, 101, 196,
202, 220, 222–5, 227, 230
conditions of sale, and XII 76–7,
96, 102–9
costs of XII 67, 77, 98, 211–2
fee scales XII 207, 211–12
judgment debts, and XII 61, 184–90
land and succession taxes, and XII 183–4
landed estates courts, and XII 197–8
real property commissioners,
and XII 56–8
registers of charges, and
annuities XII 143, 185
Crown debts XII 143, 185
consolidated XII 213
judgments XII 185–90
land improvement loans XII 185–7
land registry, and XII 187, 213, 219
lites pendentes XII 185
local authority charges XII 227
official searches XII 210–11
searching XII 187, 210–11
simplifying XII 176, 208–13
solicitors, and XII 65–6, 68, 70–1,
187–9, 208, 211
see also conveyances, registration of deeds,
sale of land
copyhold XII 53, 55–6, 59, 82, 230
copyright
artistic copyright
Fine Arts Copyright Act 1862
XIII 890–2
lithography, etc. XIII 889–90
photography XIII 890–2
sculpture XIII 890
tableau vivant XIII 903
work of artistic craftsmanship XIII 891–2

copyright (*cont.*)
   author
      author's reversionary right XIII 927
      British author abroad XIII 892–3
      contracts of service XIII 893–4, 923–4
      entitlement XIII 893
      joint authorship XIII 893, 901–2
      moral rights XIII 892, 907–8, 922–4
      romantic conception of XIII 885–6
   copying:
      abridgment XIII 902, 904
      adaptation XIII 902–3
      substantial taking XIII 901–5, 926
   dramatic copyright
      collecting societies XIII 920
      'play-right' XIII 920
   exceptions and limitations
      fair criticism and review XIII 905, 926–7
      fair reporting of news XIII 906, 926–7
      fair private study and research XIII 927
      industrial designs XIII 982–3
      mechanical right: statutory
         licence XIII 919
   Imperial Copyright 1911 XIII 882, 925
   international relations XIII 894, 911–18
      Berne Convention for Literary and
         Artistic Works (1886, 1896, 1908)
         XIII 915–18
      bilateral agreements XIII 908–10
      British and colonial copyright XIII 896,
         910–11, 915–16, 925–6
   library deposits XIII 887–8
   licences to publishers, performers and
      other users
      pricing practices and price fixing
         XIII 919, 927
   literary copyright
      'book' XIII 893
      fixation and registration XIII 896,
      lecturer's copyright XIII 899
      political and moral objections XIII 898
   musical copyright
      collecting societies XIII 921
      rights in performances XIII 920–21
   nature and scope
      Act of 1842 XIII 889–90
      attacks on economic grounds XIII 888–9,
         895–6
      justifications XIII 895
      Royal Commission 1876–1878 XIII 894–6
   originality XIII 904–5
   origins of copyright
      common law copyright XIII 882, 897–9
      licensing system (1557) and printing
         patents for books XIII 879–80
      Statute of Anne (1710) XIII 880–3
   performers' neighbouring right XIII 929
   reproduction of work in material
      form XIII 926
   sound recording producers' neighbouring
      right XIII 928–9
   territorial scope
      'British Dominions' XIII 910–11
      foreign author's claim to British
         rights XIII 911–15
      rights of British authors elsewhere XIII 914–15
   term of copyright XIII 882–3
      effect of Statute of Anne on the claim for
         indeterminacy XIII 882–6
      extensions of statutory terms: 1814, 1842
         1862, 1911 XIII 887–9, 925–6
corn laws, repeal of XI 24–5 XII 229, 779
   see also political economy
coroners XI 934–55
   Coroners Society XI 942, 946, 950
   deputies XI 943–4
   elections and appointments XI 938–9
   juries XI 952–4
   justices and XI 940–3
   miscellaneous duties XI 955
   qualifications XI 936–7
   remuneration XI 940–3
   tenure and removal XI 939–40
   types and distribution XI 934–5
coroners' inquests XI 934, 935, 944–55
   committals XI 954–5
   DC on XI 945, 947, 952
   evidence XI 951–4
   growth in and expense XI 941
   notification of deaths XI 946–7
   reporting XI 951
   scope of duty XI 944–5
   venue XI 949
   view of the body and post-mortems XI 947–9
coroner's jury XI 952–4
costs
   Chancery 46–7, 682–3
   Chancery Division XI 845–7
   Common Law Courts XI 626–30
   Court of Requests XI 863
   County Courts XI 877–81, 888–9
   Great Sessions XI 635
   House of Lords XI 530, 543
   JCPC XI 567–8
   King's Bench Division XI 813–21
   old local court's XI 849, 851
   Security for costs 673, 751–6, 754
   Supreme Court of Judicature XI 765
Council of Legal Education
   composition of XII 306
counties XI 454–71
   County Councils XI 374, 424, 465, 467, 471
      elections to XI 465
      powers of XI 459, 465

justices, rule by XI 454–64
  asylums XI 460–1
  highways XI 447, 457, 461–2
  liquor licensing XI 461–3
  petty sessions, in XI 461–4
  policing XI 458–9
  prisons XI 457, 459–60
  see also justices, parishes,
    quarter sessions
County Councils XII 220
County Courts XI 527, 622, 1029, 1048, 1049,
    1092, 1103, XII 123, 327, 522, 803, 807–8,
    819–20, 826, 832
  County Courts RC (1854) XI 867,
    876–8, 888, 897
  DC (1906) XI 755, 883
  divorce XI 755, 883
  enforcement of judgments
    execution against goods XI 902–3
    imprisonment for debt XI 903–6
  equity XI 834, 878, 880, 886
  judges XI 632, 890, 992–1004,
    1147
    characteristics XI 995–8
    conduct and lifestyle XI 880,
      899–901
    deputies XI 891, 1046
    promotion and transfer XI 1001–2
    remuneration XI 883, 998–9
    retirement and pensions XI 1002–4
  Judicature Commission XI 777, 779,
    879, 888
  jurisdiction and business XI 876–87
    admiralty XI 717, 878
    bankruptcy XI 886
    costs sanction XI 877, 880–1
    equity XI 834, 878,880, 886
    probate XI 733, 741, 878
    remitted actions XI 811, 880–1, 886
    torts XI 877, 879, 885–6
  old county courts XI 848–50, 857–8
  organization XI 887–901
    bailiffs XI 889, 896, 902–3
    districts XI 890–1
    finances and fees XI 888–9
    Home Office XI 887
    Lord Chancellor's office XI 887
    Treasury, County Courts
      Department XI 87
  procedure and practice XI 894–902
    appeals XI 900–1
    audience XI 897, 977–8,
      1048, 1133–35
    evidence XI 609–10, 898
    instalments and 'banking
      system' XI 901–2
    judgment in default XI 574, 896–7

juries XI 596, 899
  pleadings XI 589, 896
  register of judgments XI 902
  Rule Committee XI 894–5
  service of process XI 896
  venue XI 897
registrars XI 879–81, 891–6, 1147
  association of XI 892, 895
  clerks XI 893–4
  pluralism XI 891–2
  remuneration XI 892–3
  workmen's compensation XI 881
  SC (1878) X 879–80
  see also local courts
Court for Crown Cases Reserved,
  see criminal appeals
Court of Appeal XI 526, 541, 764, 765,
    798–804, 830
  costs XI 802, 815
  membership XI 799–800
  organization XI 800–3
  practice XI 801–2
  see also Divisional Courts
Court of Arches,
  see Ecclesiastical Courts
Courts of Common Law, reform of
  Common Law RC (1828), and judges
    of local courts XI 569–72, 576–9,
    582, 584–6, 587, 598, 603, 619–21,
    622, 631–6, 638, 1026, 1056, 1081
    XII 317–19, 801–2
  Common Law RC (1850) XI 571, 574, 580,
    586–7, 589–90, 597, 600, 604, 611, 612,
    614–15, 618 XII 319
Court of Common Pleas XI 525, 569, 570, 601,
    764, 1107
  Chief Justice XI 763, 974–5, 985
  jurisdiction XI 619
  serjeants' monopoly XI 1055–57
  unpopularity XI 620–1, 622
  see also serjeants
Court of Criminal Appeal,
  see Criminal appeals
Court of Delegates,
  see Ecclesiastical Courts of
Court of Exchequer
  see Exchequer, Court
courts, borough XI 850–1
  after 1846 XI 865–75
  Derby Court of Record XI 872
  Hull XI 870–1
  Judicature Commission XI 866–7,
    870
  Newcastle XI 866, 871
  Norwich Guildhall XI 871
  Rules and default judgment
    XI 870–1

courts, borough (*cont.*)
  see also Bristol Tolzey Court, Liverpool
    Court of Passage
courts, local XI 847–73, 1134
  Common Law Commissioners
    (5th report) XI 860–1
  county courts (old) XI 848–50, 864–5
  Hundred Courts and Courts
    Baron XI 850
  Palace Court XI 865–6
  Oxford Vice-Chancellor's XI 870–1
  reform of XI 857–65
  varieties of XI 847–51
Courts of Requests XII 803, 836
  see also Requests, Courts of
Courts of Review XII 795–6
Courts Martial,
  see military law
covenant, action of XII 314, 316, 495, 599
'crammers' XI 1191, 1196, 1199–200
creditors,
  see debtors and creditors,
    judgment debt
criminal appeals XI 86, 645, 805–8, 830,
    1076–77 XIII 127–37
  Court of Criminal Appeal
    and House of Lords XI 808
    bases for appeal XIII 127–9, 135–7
    effects on KB Division XI 830
    membership XI 805–6
    number and sources of
      appeals XI 806–7, 808
    rules and procedure XI 805, 807–8
  reform initiatives XIII 128–31, 133
    Beck Committee 1905 and the politics
      of reform XIII 134–37
    royal prerogative–executive review
      XIII 131–4
criminal conversation, action for,
  see marital breakdown
criminal defences XIII, 14–15, 229–82
  duress and necessity XIII 266–79
    absence of free will XIII 267–69
    Cockburn's, Lord, critique XIII 273
    Criminal Code Commission 1879 XIII 273–5
    Criminal Law Commissioners' Reports
      variation in proposals XIII 270–2
    Dudley and Stephens, 1884 XIII 275–8
    Homicide Bill 1872–4 XIII 272–3
    homicide *ex necessitate* XIII 269
    in extremis, absence of moral
      obligation XIII 272–3, 276–7
  general principles XIII 229–34
    Criminal Law Commissioners' Reports
      XIII 232
    deterability of action, relevance XIII 232,
      234

    excuse and justification decline in
      distinction XIII 230–1
    fault or *mens rea*, relevance of
      XIII 231, 233
    notion of 'will', or moral choice
      XIII 229–30, 233
    objective fault, role of XIII 234
    variation of views XIII 232–3
  insanity XIII 234–257
    automatism XIII 234, 256–257
    Criminal Code Bill, 1879 XIII 249–51
    Criminal Law Commissioners XIII 241–2,
      243n, 246n,
    Criminal Lunatics Act, 1800 XIII 235,
      236, 237
    'deficiency in will' XIII 236–8,
      241, 248
    executive review XIII 236n, 249, 250,
      251–2, 254–6
    fluidity of judicial opinion XIII 237–9,
      252–6
    Hadfield 1800 XIII 234–7
    Homicide Bill, 1874 XIII 247–9
    'irresistible impulse', judicial resistance
      to XIII 242–9, 250–1
    M'Naghten rules XIII 239–42
    volitional or cognitive
      impairment XIII 243–56
  intoxication XIII 257–66
    alcoholism XIII 258, 261, 265
    Criminal Code Commissioners,
      1879 XIII 262
    draft Jamaican Penal Code
      XIII 262
    fault in getting intoxicated XIII 257, 261,
      263, 264
    Inebriates Act 1879, 1898 XIII 261, 265
    intoxication as an aggravating
      factor XIII 257
    mens rea negated by intoxication XIII 257,
      260, 261, 263–266, 264, 266
    'specific intention' offences and
      intoxication XIII 259–60
    temporary phrenzy XIII 257
  mistake XIII 279–82
    'defence' or denial of *mens
      rea* XIII 279
    Draft Criminal Code Bill, 1879
      XIII 280
    draft Jamaican Penal Code XIII 280
    mens rea, power to negate XIII 279–82
    Prince, 1875 XIII 280
    reasonableness of mistake, relevance
      XIII 281–2
    Tolson, 1889 XIII 281–2
  self-defence XIII 232, 233, 258, 266,
    269–72, 276–7

links to homicide by Foster, Blackstone
and East XIII 270, 280, 430–1
criminal evidence XIII, 83–13
burden of proof XIII 107–13
character evidence XIII 86, 88–90
competency of defendants XIII 100–7
confessions XIII 94–100
corroboration XIII 86–88
hearsay XIII 86
self-incrimination XIII 94–107
similar facts XIII 90–92
standard of proof XIII 107–13
criminal fault XIII, 13–14, 217–29
general *mens rea* and fault concepts
XIII 219–24
conceptual variations of
commentators XIII 219–23
Criminal Law Commissioners
XIII 220–22
objective fault XIII 219–21, 223
presumption of intention XIII 225, 229
subjective fault XIII 219–22, 223
language and terminology of fault
XIII 224–29
commentators XIII 224, 225, 228
Criminal Law Commissioners XIII 224,
225, 226
intention XIII 225, 226
judicial equivocation XIII 226–7, 228
malice XIII 224, 227
moral equivalence of different states of
mind XIII 228
negligence XIII 226, 228
recklessness XIII 225, 228
strict liability XIII 321–30, 332–3
judicial hesitation the pragmatic
disposing of fault XIII 322–4,
327, 332–3
notions of quasi-criminality
confounded XIII 324–7
statutory interpretation and Parliament's
will XIII 328–30
vicarious liability XIII 330–3
conceptual ambiguities XIII 330–2
thwarting legislative policy
XIII 331, 333
see also homicide, evidence
Criminal Law Commission (1833) XI 86
criminal law sources XIII, 180–216
codification and consolidation
XIII 187–216
Bacon XIII 188, 191, 200, 206
Bentham XIII 188, 189, 190, 192, 193, 198,
200
'Code Victoria' and the Statute Law
Commission XIII 203–5
Criminal Code Bill 1879 XIII 209–16

Criminal Law Commissioners
Reports XIII 193–8
draft Jamaican Penal Code, 1877
XIII 184, 213
Homicide Bill XIII 1872–4 207–9
judicial consultation and rejection
XIII 199–203
Indian Penal Code, 1836/8 XIII 184,
198, 207
Peelite gradualism XIII 191–3
judgments
style and substance XIII 181, 184–7
treatises XIII 181–4
Archbold XIII 182, 185, 186, 209
Blackstone XIII 181, 182
East XIII 181
Kenny XIII 183
Russell XIII 181–2, 185, 186
Stephen XIII 181, 183
criminal procedure XIII, 92–94,
115–21
pre-trial examination XIII 92–94
interrogatory examination under Marian
Statutes 1554–5 XIII 92
judicial inquiry under Jervis' Acts,
1848 XIII 93–94, 97
summary trial XIII 115–17
expansion of range during nineteenth
century XIII 115–16
increased powers of punishment
XIII 116–17
rapid rise in trial numbers XIII 117
trial by jury XIII 117–21
criticism of juries as lenient, partial or
quixotic XIII 118–20
influence on substantive law–homicide,
defences XIII 117–18, 120–1
Crown XI 427, 473, 481
Crown servants XI 343, 345–6,
361–5, 406–7
contracts of XI 367,
371, 376–7
mandamus to XI 382–4, 487
rates immunity XI 367, 371–4
tortious liability XI 367,
370, 376–7
immunities of XI 366–84
petition of right, to XI 370, 377
see also sovereign
Crown Counsel XI 1029–38,1049, 1052,
1055, 1058–62
benchers XI 1078–9
civilians as XI 698
earnings XI 1061–2
numbers XI 1058–9
Crown, debts to XII 57, 183,
185–6, 188

Custom,
 see sources of law
Custos Rotulorum and magistrates XI 908,
 912–13, 922, 927–8

damages XI 690, 718, 729
 contractual
  anticipatory breach of contract
   XII 505–6
  expectation XII 99–100, 501, 534–9
  in equity XII 322, 540
  land sales XII 98–100, 539–40
  loaned stock XII 535–6
  lost profits XII 537–8
  mitigation of XII 534–6
  penalties and liquidated damages
   XII 523–9
  Pollock's views on XII 548
  quantum meruit XII 530–4
  remoteness XII 305, 541–8
  tort XII 899–902, 905, 934–5, 954–6,
   990–1000, 1041–2, 1107–8
  misrepresentation, 426–30
 writs of inquiry XII 524
debtor and creditor XII 834–76
 imprisonment for debt XII 185
  County Courts XI 880, 903–6
  Courts of Requests XI 885–6
  Debtors Act 1869 XII 819–20,
   827–9, 837
  local courts XI 863–4
  on final process XI 579 XII 797–803,
   805–8, 813, 818–20, 835–44
  on mesne process XI 571, 575–9
   XII 400–01, 797–803
  SC (1873) XII 840, 844
  SC (1893) XII 841
  SC (1909) XII 841–3, 848
  see also enforcement of judgment,
   insolvency
debt, action of XII 314, 320, 565
 on bond XII 314, 316, 523–5
 on simple contract XII 314, 320, 530
deceit XII 320, 322, 411–14, 428–30, 462, 540,
 924, 947, 1040 XIII 991–2
 see also fraud, misrepresentation
declaratory judgment,
 see judicial review
defamation
 civil jurisdiction in higher courts XI 408–9,
  580, 703, 885–6
 criminal libel XIII 852–3
 ecclesiastical offences and jurisdiction
  XIII 853–4
 fair comment XIII 870–2
 in Ecclesiastical Courts XI 693
 in High Court XI 812

 libel and slander XIII 852–8
  personal liability, not proprietary
   XIII 855
  relation to injurious falsehood
   XIII 858–60, 865–6
  relation to blasphemy, sedition
   XIII 852–3
  treatises of Borthwick, Starkie and later
   authors XIII 856–7
 justification XIII 872
 'malice' XI 408 XII 1038, 1058–9,
  malice in law and in fact XIII 858–66,
   868–72
 press:
  freedom of information and
   publication XIII 862–3,
   875–7, 989
  treatises on press law XIII 857
 privilege, absolute and
 other public interests XIII 872–7
  court proceedings and reports XIII
  communications between officers of
   government XIII 876
  parliamentary proceedings and
   reports XIII 873–4
  public meetings: reports XIII 876–7
 privilege, qualified XIII 868–70
 publication XIII 866–7
  distributors XIII 867
 relation to protection of personal
  privacy XIII 878
 remedies
  allowing publication of explanation
   XIII 877
  damages XIII 864
  injunction, interlocutory XIII 864–6
  self-help: duelling, etc. XIII 852
  special damage XIII 857–9
Delegates, High Court of XI 548, 550, 622, 695,
 696, 702, 720
 see also Ecclesiastical Courts
democracy XI 303–3, 321, 467
 see also parliament, franchise
deodand XII 996–7, 1001
detinue, action of XII 577, 1116–18
'devilling'
devise,
 see land, wills
Director of Public Prosecutions
  XI 1073–74, 1076
 and perjury,
 see adversarialism
discovery,
 see interlocutory proceedings
dissenting judgments
 in House of Lords XI 543–4
 in JCPC XI 398, 566

dissenters XI 385–7, 392, 435, 449
  XII 55
  and magistracy XI 515
  see also political economy,
    religion
distress XII 401–2
  hire traders and XII 872–3
  see also landlord and tenant
District Councils XI 453–4,
    467, 470–1, XII 164
District Probate Registries
  XI 738–42
  clerks XI 739–40
  jurisdiction and business XI 740–2
  registrars XI 738–40, 1147
Divisional Courts XI 724, 765, 799–800,
    801, 830
  see also King's Bench Division
Divorce Court XI 526, 724, 742–56
    XIII 784–96
  ancillary relief XI 742,
    750–1, 755–6
  bar XI 747–9
  business and litigants XI 743–4
  campaign for XIII 781–4
  cost XI 744, 754–5
    in forma pauperis XI 754–5
    poor persons' procedure XI 755
  interlocutories XI 750–1
    appeals XI 553, 750, 756
    jury trials XI 750
  judges XI 733, 745–8
  jury trials XI 750
  practice and procedure
    collusion XI 750–3
    evidence XI 751–3
    rules XI 749
    service and pleadings XI 749
  publicity XI 753–4
  registrars XI 748–9, 756
  see also marital breakdown,
    Queen's Proctor
dock warrants XII 324, 753–4
Doctors' Commons XI 527, 694–5, 701,
    713, 736, 1176
  see also advocates,
    ecclesiastical courts, proctors
domicil,
  see private international law
dower XII 9, 56–8, 129
  see also married women's property
duress,
  see contract, criminal defences

easements and profits XII 159–71
  acquiescence, and XII 161–2, 177
  air XII 168

contracts, in equity XII 161
deeds, at law XII 160–1
  non-derogation XII 165, 167–8
equity, and XII 161
implied XII 167–8
in gross XII 163
licences, and XII 160–2, 165, 167
light XII 168–70 1071–9
lists of permissible XII 162
mining and quarrying XII 166–7, 200,
    1127–34, 1136, 1141–2
  subsidence XII 166–7, 1129–40
negative XII 171
nuisance, permitting XII 163, 167, 1083–6,
    1089–92
prescription XII 58, 160, 163, 168–71
  Prescription Act 1832 XII 169–70, 1073,
    1076–8
Real Property Commission,
    and XII 58, 168
profits XII 159, 177
statutory alternatives XII 163–6,
    177–8
title registration, and XII 222, 226
water and watercourses XII 159, 162–6,
    1082–88
  see also nuisance, restrictive
    covenants
Ecclesiastical Commissioners
    England,
  see Church of England
Ecclesiastical Courts XI 692–714, 756
  appeals XI 548, 553–5
  church discipline XI 394–400
  Court of Arches XI 692, 705, 709
  diocesan registries XI 708–9, 712
  evidence XI 693–4
    after 1857 XI 714
  fees XI 714
  High Court of Delegates XI 548, 552,
    692, 702
  judges XI 694, 704
  jurisdiction over laity XI 693–4, 713
  London Consistory Court XI 695,
    709–10, 719
  Prerogative Court of Canterbury XI 692,
    733, 734, 737
  procedure XI 693–4, 703, 710–11
  RC of 1829 XI 702–14
    first report XI 702
    probate proposals XI 703–4
  reform XI 704–13
    bar and XI 706–7
    country solicitors XI 707, 711–13
    Law Society XI 707
  registrars XI 694
  reports of cases XI 47–8

Ecclesiastical Courts (*cont.*)
  review of, by secular courts XI 390,
    392–4, 398–400, 516
  types and distribution XI 692–3
  see also defamation, marital breakdown,
    probate, tithes
ecclesiastical law,
  see Church of England, Ecclesiastical
    Courts
education
  charities and education XI 433
    British and Foreign School
      Society XIII 519
    Chancery and educational trusts
      XIII 517–18
    Charity Commissioners and
      education XIII 519
    conscience clauses in educational
      trusts XIII 518
    Eardley Wilmot's Act, 1840 XIII 517
    National Society for the Education
      of the Poor XIII 519
    parish school system XIII 518
    Select Committee on Education of the
      Lower Orders, 1818 XIII 518
  indirect control by government
    apprentices and education XIII 521–2
    Bill of, 1833, XIII 520
    conscience clauses XIII 521
    Education Committee of the Privy
      Council, 1839 XIII 521
    foreign examples of direct control
      XIII 522–3
    grant in aid of public subscriptions,
      1833 XIII 520–1
    National Education League XIII 525
    poor children XIII 525
    religious issues XIII 520, 522
    Royal Commissions, 1861, 1861, 1867,
      XIII 522–5
    school inspectors XI 362–3
    Select Committee, 1838 XIII 521
    trusts and endowed school reforms
      XIII 524–5
  mandatory elementary education XI 363
    Forster's Act of 1870 XI 452
      XIII 525–9
    Birmingham's elementary
      education XIII 525
    Board of Education XI 360, 366
    Charity Commission XIII 531
    conscience clauses XIII 527
    financial issues XIII 526
    moral issues XIII 525, 527
    religious issues XIII 527, 528
    rural problems XIII 526
    school attendance officers XIII 529

    school boards XI 452 XIII 528
    social deprivation XIII 525, 527
    Stoke-on-Trent's elementary
      education XIII 526
    unsystematic implementation XIII 528
    voluntary schools XIII 528
  secondary education XI 469–70
    Act of 1902 XI 409, 469
      XIII 533
    Board of Education XIII 531, 533
    conscience clauses XIII 533
    county councils XIII 533
    education department XIII 531
    litigation XI 503–4 XIII 531, 532
    Local Government Board XIII 531
    medical testing XIII 534
    religious issues XIII 533
    Royal Commission, 1888 XIII 532
    Royal Commission, 1895 XIII 532–3
    school boards XIII 533
    school meals XIII 534
    technical education XI 469
      XIII 532, 534
    voluntary schools XIII 534
  universities
    Church of England and XIII 529,
      530, 531
    dissenters and XIII 530
    national accountability of the
      universities XIII 529–31
    religious tests XIII 529–30
    Tests Abolition (Oxford) Bill, 1865
      XIII 529
    Universities Tests Act, 1871 XIII 531
  see also charities, legal education
elections
  ballot, secret XI 13, 14, 303
  judges, and XI 387–8, 429, 431,
    452, 764
embezzlement,
  see larceny
empire, British,
  see British colonies and empire
employer and employee,
  descriptions of relationships XIII 625–9,
    633–6
    apprenticeship XIII 628–9, 633
    butty foremen XIII 642
    journeymen XIII 628
    master and servant XIII 628
  duties of employee
    good behaviour XIII 644–6
    long-term ties XIII 638–40
    sickness XIII 638
    work under time contracts XIII 638,
      644–6
    work at piece rates XIII 638

duties of employer
 duty to provide work XIII 641–3
 payment of wages XIII 628
 sickness and other benefits 638
 Truck Acts 1831–96 XIII 642–3
 notice to terminate XIII 643–4
 public and private law elements
  XIII 633–48
 freedom of contract:
  interpretation XIII 633–5
  poor law settlement XIII 637–8
  Statute of Artificers 1562 and its
   repeal XIII 626
  Statute of Frauds 1677 XIII 634
 sanctions for breach XIII 644–9
  Employers and Workmen Act 1875
   XIII 677, 681–3
  Master and Servant Acts 1823 and
   1867 XII 299, 1043 XIII 646–9, 670,
   674, 677
  summary dismissal XIII 644–6
 types of employment XIII 625–9
  agricultural XIII 627–8
  domestic XIII 627
  pre-industrial and industrial XIII 628–9
  slavery and serfdom XIII 625, 627
 wrongful dismissal XII 496–7, 501
 see also industrial disputes, labour
  relations, regulation of working
  conditions, workplace accidents
  trade unions
employers' associations
 definition as 'trade unions' XIII 671–2
 'illegal' restraint of trade XIII 663–4
 role in collective bargaining XIII 688–9
 see also industrial disputes, labour relations,
  regulation of working conditions,
  trade unions, workplace accidents
employers' liability
 Employers Liability Act XI 112, 121 XII 677
 Employers Liability Insurance
  Corporation XII 1018, 1020–1
 see also workmen's compensation,
  workplace accidents
enclosure XI 326, 333–4, 356
 Enclosure Commissioners XI 335,
  356–9 XII 86–7, 90, 187
 judicial review of XI 358–9
entail,
 see estates in land
equity XI 689–90, 757–60
 common law judges, and XI 760
 County Courts XI 834, 878, 880, 886
 Courts of Requests XI 856
 evidence XI 606–7, 667–71, 689
 preference for in Judicature
  Act 1873 XI 770–2

see also breach of confidence, Chancery,
 fiduciary duties, 'fusion', injunctions,
 specific performance, trusts
equity draftsmen and conveyancers XI 1024,
 1027, 1043, 1051, 1052
 see also conveyancers
error
 see appeals
estates in land XIII 186, 223
 abolition of XII 225, 230
 contingent remainders XII 19–20, 22, 31–2,
  49, 53, 62–4, 215
 fee simple XII 190–4, 196, 198, 246
 fee tail (entail) XII 14, 16, 29, 31, 45, 79–80,
  93, 214–15, 217, 246
 life estate XII 19, 29, 80, 83, 90, 92, 112, 142,
  196, 215
 life tenant XII 54–5, 85, 92–3, 233–4
 reduction of XII 196, 229
 remainders and reversions XII 10, 16, 18–19,
  38, 103, 148, 191, 258
 see also land
estoppel XII 129–30, 338, 451, 456, 750–1,
 754, 770
 by negligence XII 929–30
 by representation XII 366, 371, 416
 promissory XII 367
etiquette of the bar XI 1049,
 1096–107
 direct access to clients XI 1097–99
 refreshers XI 1107
 remuneration XI 1099–1103
 retainers XI 1104–96
 two-counsel rule XI 1103–7
evangelicalism,
 see religion, political economy
evidence, civil XI 604–18, 1054
 development of rules XI 606–8
  best evidence rule XI 607–8
 in Admiralty XI 726–7, 729
 in County Courts XI 609–10,
  898
 in Divorce 750–3
 in Ecclesiastical Courts XI 694, 703,
  710, 711
 in equity XI 606–7, 667–71, 689
 in inquests XI 951, 954
 in probate XI 733–4
 documentary XI 617–18
 examinations XI 613–15, 642
 expert witness XI 615–16, 621
 oaths XI 610–13
 reported cases XI 606
 testimony of parties XII 321, 433
 theories and treatises XI 604–5
  in Chancery division XI 845
  interest and infamy XI 608–9

evidence, civil (*cont.*)
    parties XI 609–11 XII 321, 433
      XII 321, 433
    see also perjury
evolution, theories of XI 102–12
Exchequer, Court of XI 526, 569, 570, 573, 592, 601
  abolition XI 764
  abolition of equity side XI 621, 656, 657–8
  and County Courts XI 900
  attorneys' monopoly XI 620–1
  Chief Baron XI 763, 985
  jurisdiction on plea side XI 619
  tithes
  unpopularity and recovery XI 620–2
Exchequer Chamber, Court of XI 569, 602, 802
Excise, Commissioners of XI 343–5
executors XII 7, 22–3, 54, 130, 180, 189, 194, 214,
    216–17, 278, 290, 293
  restitutionary actions against XII 575–6
  trustees, as XII 242–3
  see also wills, probate

factors,
  see agents
factories XI 347–52
  factory inspectors XI 347–52
  see also employer and employee, regulation
    of working conditions
factors,
  see agents and agency
family
  family law XIII 723–30
    common law XIII 724–5
    equity XIII 725
    ecclesiastical XIII 725–6
    public and private XIII 726–30
  family lore
    doubts XIII 725–6
    lineage and companionship XIII 728–9
    male attitudes XIII 744–6
  family types
    extended and nuclear XIII 727
    propertied and plebian XIII 728
    see also children, husband and wife, insanity,
      lunacy and mental deficiency, marital
      breakdown, marriage, married womens'
      property, private international law
fee simple,
  see estates in land
fee tail,
  see estates in land
fees in courts of law
  Admiralty XI 716, 719, 728
  Chancery XI 682–3, 687–8
  Chancery Division
  Common Law Courts XI 625–7, 629–30
  County Courts XI 888–9

Ecclesiastical Courts XI 695–6, 699
  King's Bench Division XI 815
  parliamentary inquiries XI 708–9
  probate XI 733, 739, 741
felony,
  see criminal law
fiduciary duties
  breach of XII 404, 564–5, 601–5
  company directors XII 604, 662–3
  company promoters XII 643–5
  undue influence and XII 402–9
  see also breach of confidence
fine (pecuniary), assessment by judge,
  see punishment
fines and recoveries XII 49, 58, 103
fire,
  see insurance
Fleet Prison,
  see marriage
Foreign Office XI 698, 1064, 1072
forestalling *see*
forgery,
  see capital punishment
forms of action XI 569–70, 587 XII 310,
    314–15, 317, 319–20, 565, 569, 582, 880,
    887–8, 923, 1127, 1141, 1149
  see also superior courts
franchise, electoral, XI 449, 453, 464–5, 473,
    475, 479
  district councils XI 467
  local board elections, in XI 438,
    444, 450–1
  local commission elections, in XI 439
  municipal corporations XI 429–30,
    439, 444
  Parliamentary XI 303, 429
    Reform Act 1832 XI 12–13
    Reform Act 1867 XI 13–14, 73, 100,
      112, 121
    Reforms of 1884, 1885 XI 14–15
    Reforms of 1918, 1928 XI 15
    relation to population growth
      XI 12–15
    women electors XI 15
  women, and XI 303, 430, 439
  see also elections
fraud XII 100–1, 117, 301, 321, 326, 409–32,
    434–5, 453, 457–60, 899, 924,
    929–31, 978
  at common law
    'legal' and 'moral fraud' XII 412–14,
      417–19, 429–31
    false pretences, obtaining goods by
      XII 457
    fraudulent purchases XIII 457–69
  in equity
    rescission for XII 414–15

'long-firm' frauds XII 463–9
see also deceit, larceny
freedom of contract, theory of XI 100, 112, 116,
121 XII 297–9, 385, 400, 473, 528, 625,
672, 839, 855–7, 859, 865–7, 870, 1009,
1055
friendly societies XII 1010–11
registration of trade unions as XIII 664–5,
670–1, 673
'fusion' XI 689–90, 782 XII 321–22,
doctrinal XI 770–2
of courts XI 653, 757
of legal profession XI 1167

gambling
Gaming Act 1845 XII 594–5,
632–3, 680,
see also offences against public
morality
game laws XI 23–4, 111–12
see also larceny
'General school of law', proposals for
XI 1188–92
Grand Jury XIII 113–15
abolition XIII 114–15
alleged value XIII 115
functions XIII 113
Gray's Inn XI 1079, 1080, 1083, 1084–6, 1130,
1188, 1191, 1218
guardianship and wardship,
see children

highways and bridges XI 447,
450, 465, 467
justices XI 447, 461–2, 916
London, in XI 476–7
roads board XI 470
hire and hire purchase XII 121, 123,
835, 869–76
County Courts XI 903
Hire Traders Protection Association
XII 870–4
Home Office XI 352, 357–60, 402, 443, 458–60,
788, 806, 827–88, 935, 949, 950, 1008,
1009, 1014, 1045, 1074, 1106 XIII 23–5, 33,
38, 42, 49, 50, 51, 52, 56, 65–6, 69, 70, 126,
131, 146–7, 156, 166–7, 170, 175, 235, 251,
347, 371–373, 395, 408–9, 414–15,
421, 427, 452–3
County Courts XI 887, 891
Home Secretary XI 357–8, 443, 788, 806,
1045, 1074, 1106
factories inspectors XI 351–352
Inclosure Commissioners, and XI 358
magistracy XI 911, 1010, XIII 70
stipendiary magistrates XIII 23–28
mines inspectorate XI 352–353

Poor Law Commission, and
XI 353–4
recorders XIII, 70
sentencing XIII, 126, 131–4, 146–7,
170, 175, 251, 452
see also police (London)
homicide XIII 17, 392, 409–63
general issues in homicide XIII 392,
409–10, 446–63
causation XIII 453–8
human identity: abortion and
infanticide XIII 453–8
omissions XIII 458–3
manslaughter (involuntary)
objective fault requirement
XIII 433–436
prize-fighting, 'Queensberry rules'
XIII 436–8
Starkie and the Criminal Law
Commissioners XIII 433–5
'unlawful act', meaning of XIII 431–6
negligence XIII 438–46
East XIII 438
fault: judicial variations XIII 439,
443–6
industrial accidents XIII 442–3
medical negligence; attempted
regulation XIII 439–41
road traffic accidents XIII 441–2
manslaughter (voluntary)
provocation XIII 422–31
Criminal Law Commissioners'
Reports XIII 423–4
defendant's mental state XIII 423–5
duels, brawls and 'spontaneous
combat' XIII 428–31
fixed categories of provocative
acts XIII 424
flexibility and the Homicide Bill,
1872–4 XIII 426–8
proportionality and reasonableness of
response XIII 424–5
murder XIII 410–20
Criminal Code Bill, 1879
XIII 414, 418
Criminal Law Commissioners' Reports
XIII 411, 412–13, 414, 417
felony-murder XIII 412,
414–16, 416–20
'heart regardless of social duty'
XIII 411
Homicide Bill, 1872–4 XIII 413, 417
malice aforethought: 'the grand
criterion' XIII 410–20
presumption of intended
consequences XIII 416–20
suicide XIII 420–2

hospitals,
  see poor law
House of Lords, (legislative and appellate),
  see Lords, House of,
House of Commons,
  see Commons, House of
houses of correction,
  see punishment
house tax,
  see revenue
housing
  private development
    building leases XII 54, 82–3,88–9, 112,
      142, 172 XIII 581
    covenants XII 171–7 XIII 580–1
    freehold land XIII 580–1
    Saltaire XIII 580
    settled land XIII 580
  private renting XII 116–17
    eviction of tenants XII 124–7
      XIII 582
    law of landlord and tenant XIII 581–3
    powers of JPs XII 122, 124 XIII 582
    powers of the County Court XIII 582
    scrutiny by the courts XI 498,
      508–12, 519–21
  public regulation and housing
      quality XI 477
    Act of 1868 XIII 584
    Act of 1875 XIII 584
    Court scrutiny XI 498, 508–12,
      519–21 XIII 583–4
    lodging houses XII 122 XIII 583
    powers to build sewers and 'public
      works' XIII 583–4
    Society for Improving the Condition of
      the Labouring Classes XIII 583
    'back-to-backs' XIII 584
    byelaws XIII 584
    cellars and courts XIII 585
    cul-de-sacs XIII 584–5
    light XIII 585
    local and private acts XI 516 XIII 585
    Local Government Board XI 510–11,
      XIII 585
    Public Health Act, 1875 XIII 585–6
    sanitation XIII 585
    space and dimensions XIII 585–6
  Royal Commission on Housing, 1884
    complexity of the law XIII 587
    demolition without rebuilding
      for the poor XIII 587–9
    failure to enforce existing laws
      XIII 587–588
    failure to finance housing XIII 587
    overcrowding XIII 586
    poverty and bad housing XIII 586–8

response in legislation of 1885, 1890
    and 1900 XIII 588–9
hundred courts XI 850, 866
husband and wife
  common law theory of unity XIII 729–31
    feme couverte, feme sole XIII 729–30, 759
  criminal responsibility of wife XIII 730–1
  husband as patriarch XIII 729–30, 744–6
  husband's authority in the home
    action for criminal conduct XIII 732–4,
      777–8, 784
    dutiful submission of wife XIII 730–4
    marital violence and restraint XIII 730–2
  political rights of wife XIII 731
  'separate spheres' XIII 728, 744–5, 791
  see also marital breakdown, marriage,
      marriage settlements, married women's
      property, private international law

illegitimacy,
  see children
'Imperial court of appeal' XI 552, 557, 562
  see also British colonies and empire
imprisonment for debt,
  see also County courts, Courts of
      Requests, debtor and creditor
in forma pauperis XI 790
  Chancery division XI 845
  Divorce Court XI 754–5
  House of Lords XI 542–3
  King's Bench Division XI 816
inclosure
  see enclosure
Inclosure Commissioners XI 335, 356–9
    XII 86–7, 90, 187
  judicial review of XI 358–9
incorporeal things,
  see debt, easements and profits,
      intellectual property
income tax,
  see political economy (revenue)
indebitatus assumpsit,
  see assumpsit
independent contractor XII 896–7, 945, 963, 973
India,
  secretary of state in council XI 380–1
  see also British colonies and empire
indictment,
  see trial by jury
individualism XI 99–100, 105–6, 113–17
industrial designs
  evolution of right
    18th-century Acts XIII 978
    reforms, 1835–1850 XIII 978–81
    infringement of right XIII 981–2
    registration XIII 979–82
    secrecy XIII 979, 981

term XIII 978–81
validity XIII 979–81
industrial disputes
anti-union organizations XIII 661–2
National Free Labour Association
XIII 689
crimes by combination of workers
18th-century instances XIII 650–2
Cockburn Commission (1874–5) 675
Combination Acts 1799, 1800
XIII 668–70
Combination Acts 1824, 1825 XIII 654–7,
659–62
Common law conspiracy XIII 652,
657, 659–62
Conspiracy and Protection of Property
Act 1875 XIII 677–9
Criminal Law Amendment Act 1871
XIII 674–6
Erle Commission (1867–9)
XIII 668–70
illegal oaths: Tolpuddle XIII 658
'molestation', 'obstruction' during
picketing XIII 656–7,
659–62, 663
offences against person or property
in a labour context XIII 650–1,
658, 667
strikes in essential industries
XIII 675–6, 678
tortious liability
closed shop employment XIII 693–5,
697–8
conspiracy XIII 692–3, 697–8,
705, 707–8
damages XIII 698–701, 704, 706
demarcation disputes XIII 696–7
Dunedin Commission (1904–6)
XIII 703–4
inducing breach of contract XIII 693–4,
697–8, 704, 708
injunctions XIII 673–4, 695, 699
'malicious' interference with trade
XIII 694, 696–7, 708
secondary boycotts XIII 693–4,
697–8
Trade Disputes Act 1906, exemptions
under XIII 705–8
union officers as defendants
XIII 692–8, 704–6
unions as defendants: *Taff Vale* case
XIII 698–701, 703–4
wrongful picketing XIII 694–5,
705–8
see also employers' associations,
labour relations, political economy,
tort, trade unions

infant,
see children
infanticide,
see homicide
informations, criminal XI 1074–75
see also criminal procedure
inheritance,
see succession, settlements
(of property generally), wills
injunction,
see Chancery
Inner Temple XI 1019, 1080, 1081, 1082, 1087,
1180, 1188, 1191
Inns of Chancery XI 1087–1130,
1191
Inns of Court XI 1019, 1041, 1078–87, 1175,
1217, 1218
admission and call XI 1079–81
women XI 1080
and proposal for legal education XI 1175,
1182–90, 1192–97
benchers XI 1078–79
Bar council XI 1090
chambers and libraries
XI 1084–87
conduct and disciplinary
XI 1081–83
Inns of Court RC (1854) XI 1079–80, 1088,
1167, 1184–86
insanity, lunacy and mental deficiency XI 840,
916–18 XII 244 XIII 823–34
as a social phenomenon XIII 823–4,
832–3
attitudes to treatment XIII 823
medical understanding XIII 823,
832–3
civil rights and liabilities XIII, 824–6
entitlement to sue XIII 824–5
civil liability XIII 825–6
confinement, private institutions
XIII 827–9
Chancery Committee XIII 828
living conditions XIII 828–9
madhouse inspection by Physicians
XIII 829–30
quaker house of retreat, York XIII 830,
833–4
confinement, public institutions XI 356–7,
460–1 XIII 829–34
asylums under the Poor
Law XIII 829–32
inspection by commissioners
XI 356–7 XIII 828–32
inspection from 1828 XI 356–7
involuntary admission XIII 831–2
movements for reform and legislative
changes XIII 828–32

insanity, lunacy and mental deficiency (*cont.*)
   system of separation for mentally
     deficient XIII 829, 832–3
   criminal liability XIII 829
   testamentary capacity XIII 823
   see also criminal defences
insolvency XI 878, 1144–45, 1166 XII 797–805,
   807–8, 817–33
   Debtors' Arrangement Act 1844 XII 807
   Insolvent Debtors Act, 1842 XII 807
   Insolvent Debtors Court XII 798–804,
     807, 817
   see also bankruptcy
inspectorates XI 347, 356–7, 362–3
   accountability of XI 347–8, 351–4
   judicial review of XI 349
   liability XI 352
   see also education, factories; public health,
     regulation of working conditions
instalments, debt repayment by XI 911–12
   see also debtor and creditor
insurance XII 304, 674–727
   accident XII 677, 991, 1011–12,
     1018–22, 1024
   Average Clause Act 1828 XII 721
   duties to disclose XII 697–9, 705–11
   Employers Liability Insurance Companies
     Act 1907 XII 1021
   fire XII 675, 693–6, 703–4, 706–7,
     719–26
     'average' policies XII 721–2
     Fire Prevention (Metropolis) Act 1774
     XII 694
   Gambling Act 1774 XII 676, 679,
     691, 694
   insurable interest XII 679–80,
     684–96
   law of insurance companies XII 629–30
     winding up XII 650–1
   life assurance XII 449, 676–7, 689–93,
     703–11, 726–7
     assignment of policies XII 691–3
     Life Insurance Companies Act,
       1870 XII 630
     Life Assurance Companies (Payment into
       Court) Act 1896 XII 693
     premiums XII 703–6, 711
     suicides XII 692, 726–7
   marine insurance XII 674, 679–89,
     696–703, 711–19
     abandonment XII 716–17
     assignment of policies XII 688–9
     'C.F.I.' policies XII 683
     general average XII 714–16
     'lost or not lost' policies XII 700
     Marine Insurance Act 1906 XII 679,
       681–2, 688, 700, 703, 717

     Marine Insurance (Gambling Policies)
       Act 1909 XII 681
     particular average XII 716–19
     payment of premiums XII 697
     policy XII 711–14, 716–19
     'P.P.I.' policies XII 678–81, 683
     professional average adjusters
       XII 678, 715
     time policies XII 701–2
     valued policies XII 681–4, 717
     York Antwerp rules XII 715
   Policies of Assurance Act, 1867 XII 692
   principle of indemnity XII 678, 682–4,
     686, 689–90, 693–5, 725
   reinsurance XII 675, 679, 704–5
   rules as to causation of loss XII 712–14,
     719–20
   subrogation XII 694, 723–6
     emergence of general concept
       XIII 849–51
     proprietary characteristics XIII 849
       assignability of right XIII 849
       injunctive relief XIII 850–1
       exclusive right XIII 849, 905–6
   see also breach of confidence, copyright,
     industrial designs,
     patents, trade marks
intent,
   see criminal fault
international law
   arbitration of inter-state disputes
     adjudicative institutions XI 271, 276–7
     agreements to arbitrate XI 270–1
   English law, and
     implementation of treaties XI 275
     international custom as part of common
       law XI 272–6
   humanitarian law
     anti-slavery and sweated labour
       XI 268–9
     conditions of war: Red Cross XI 269
   institutions fostering legal developments
     Institut de droit international XI 277
     Society for the Reform and
       Codification of International Law
       XI 277 XII 715
   labour law and conditions
     International Labour Organisation
       XI 269
   regulation of economic activity XI 270
   sources of
     custom XI 257–258
     international institutions XI 266–7,
       269–71
     treaties XI 270–1, 275
   states, as subjects of XI 264–7
     equality of treatment XI 265–6

identification of XI 266
internal independence XI 266–7
sovereignty XI 264–5
theories of international law
  Austin's positive morality XI 258–60
  Austin's critics among British writers
    XI 260–5
  English pragmatism XI 257–8, 263
  influence of Christian beliefs XI 255–6,
    262–3
  natural law and law of nations XI 256,
    262–3
  positivism XI 257–9
  social contracts of states XI 256–7
  see also British colonies and empire,
    private international law, public
    international law
invention,
  see patents for invention
interlocutory matters XI 530, 623, 717,
    734, 750–1, 767, 812, 814, 820–1,
    1048, 1049, 1051
  see also Chancery (injunction), discovery,
    interrogatories
interpleader XI 759, 903
Ireland XII 145, 197–8, 851, 1053
  appeals from XI 530, 537
  bar students XI 1185
  Irish Land Act XI 112
  judges from XI 967
  legal education XI 1180
  solicitors XI 1115

jactitation of marriage, see marital
    breakdown
  political rights XI 387
Judge-Advocate General,
  see army, military law
judges
  Admiralty XI 719–25, 733
  age XI 964–6, 980
  and Judicature Acts XI 767–8,
    779–80
  and juries XI 595–6
  behaviour and judicial style XI 64–71, 987–9
  Central Criminal Court XI 643–4
  Chancery XI 655–60, 673, 759,
    770, 782, 783
  clerks XI 628, 893–4
  common law XI 763, 830–3
  divorce XI 745–8
  education XI 967–8
  eligibility XI 961–2
  House of Lords XI 531, 533–5,
    536, 538–40
  independence XI 32–5
    behaviour and style XI 64–71

connections with politics XI 32–5
  infirmities XI 981–2
  JCPC XI 557–62
  length of service and retirement XI 832,
    978–83
  Lords of Appeal in Ordinary
  on circuit XI 837
  opinions for House of Lords XI 530, 543
  origins and background XI 966–7
  politics and appointments XI 971–4
  promotions and transfers XI 982–5
  responsibility for appointments XI 823,
    962–4
  religion XI 962, 971
  salaries and pensions XI 978,
    981–2, 985
  superior courts XI 586, 587,
    959–91
Judges, Council of XI 788–9, 810, 819, 821,
    826, 831, 842, 845
judgment by default XI 527, 765,
    810, 811
  County Courts XI 574, 896–7
  Local Courts XI 871
  Superior Courts XI 572–5, 579
judgment debts XII 386, 838, 813, 841–2
  conveyancing, and XII 61, 184–90
  Crown, to XII 57, 183–6
  enforcement against land XII 61,
    184–90
  equitable execution XII 189
  receivers, and XII 189
  security, as XII 144–5
  writs of execution,
  see also deb, mortgages
Judicature Acts 1873–5 XI 758–84, 1049
    XII 320, 393, 425, 439, 636, 693
  preference for equity, in Judicature Act
    1873 XII 161, 178, 425
Judicature Commission (1867) XI 717, 723,
    740, 748, 768–9, 773–80, 934–5,
    1049, 1133, 1147
  appeals XI 535–537, 560–1
  appraisals of XI 761–2
  county courts XI 777, 779,
    879, 888
  local courts XI 866–7, 870
  officers XI 628, 795
  Probate, Divorce and Admiralty XI 535–7,
    560–1
  provincial justice XI 879
  quarter sessions and XI 827
  structure XI 637–9
  terms and membership XI 760–1
  tribunals of commerce XI 773–6, 880
  Wales XI 635–6
  see also circuits, judges

Judicial Committee of the Privy Council
       (JCPC) XI 526, 547–68, 1066
   and House of Lords XI 538, 539, 541
   business XI 549
       Colonial appeals XI 562–3
       Indian appeals XI 549, 556, 560,
           562, 565
       levels XI 555
       religious disputes XI 391, 394–8, 400,
           553–5, 565
   costs and expenses XI 567–8
   creation XI 547–50
   judgments XI 566–7
       dissents XI 398, 566
       reports of cases XI 549
   jurisdiction XI 550–5
       proposal for Empire Court
   membership XI 556, 557–62, 565
       assessors XI 557–8
       Lord President XI 557–8
   registrar and clerical organization
       XI 562–3
   rules and practice XI 551–2, 563–5, 567
judicial discretion,
   see criminal evidence, punishment
judicial precedent,
   see sources of law
judicial review XI 349–51, 358–9, 407,
       414–16, 418, 427, 435–6, 440,
       456, 486–522
   bias, for XI 489, 515–16
   byelaws, of XI 427, 518–21
   case stated, relation to XI 491–2, 496–8
       tribunals, appeal from XI 497, 509–10
   certiorari XI 416, 488–504
       central departments, to XI 502–4,
           511–12
       licensing decisions, to XI 501–2, 513,
           516–17
       statutory XI 349, 436, 498–9
   Courts Martial, of XI 416
   declaration XI 504–6
   delegated legislation, of XI 503, 521
   discretionary decisions, of XI 350, 394,
       400, 512–18
   error on record, for XI 489–91
       Jervis's Acts XI 494–5
   jurisdictional error, for XI 350, 399–400,
       416, 488–9, 493–6, 505–6
   justices
       orders, of XI 489–90
       summary convictions, by XI 489–90,
           492–5
   liability, relation to XI 488–91, 493–4, 506
   literature about XI 486–7
   mandamus XI 339, 349–50, 376–8, 382–4,
       390, 486, 488, 494, 501, 505

procedural error, for XI 506–12
prohibition XI 350, 399, 486, 502
provisional orders, of XI 359–60, 502
       Enclosure Commissioners XI 358–9
   see also public law
judicial separation,
   see marital breakdown
juries XI 527, 593, 595–599, 703,
       757, 766, 1050
   Chancery XI 671, 690
   coroners XI 952–4
   County Court XI 596, 899
   DC (1912) XI 813, 823–5
   in contract cases XII 316–18, 320, 530–2
   in tort cases XII 899–901, 936–40
   King's Bench Division XI 769, 810, 823–5
   majority verdicts XI 598–9
   payment XI 825
   Probate, Divorce and Admiralty XI 717,
       734, 750
   qualifications XI 597–8, 824
   special juries XI 595, 598,
       599–600, 824–5
   summons XI 593–4, 824
   Wales XI 633
   see also grand jury
Justices of the Peace XI, 423, 455–7,
       467, 487, 497–8, 500, 908–33,
       1209 XII 122
   borough XI 424, 431, 910–14
       politics and XI 912–13
   county XI 454–64
       appointment XI 454, 911–13
       clergy XI 908–9
       composition XI 454–5, 908–10
       numbers XI 454, 908, 913
       solicitors XI 1147–48
   in petty sessions XI 924–6
   in quarter sessions XI 914–24
   in special sessions XI 931
   Justices, RC (1909) XI 913
   liability of XI 369, 371, 373, 489–91, 493–5
   see also liquor licensing, petty sessions,
       quarter sessions
juvenile offenders,
   see punishment

King,
   see Attorney-General, crown,
       sovereign
King's Bench, Court of XI 526, 527, 569, 570,
       577, 585, 601, 924, 927, 950
   Chief Justice of XI 620, 703. 975, 985
   jurisdiction and business XI 619, 621–2
   see also superior courts
King's/Queen's Bench Division XI 527, 810–33
   costs XI 813–21

County Courts XI 813, 819, 833
delays in XI 788, 807, 810–13, 823,
    826–7, 832–3
Fees
    Treasury and XI 815
Judges
    divisional court XI 768, 830
    shortage of XI 829–31
    pre-trial process XI 818–21
    interlocutory XI 812
    pleadings XI 818–19
    summons for directions XI 819–20, 828
    quantity and types of business XI 810–12
    trials XI 821–5, 828–33
    see also Court of Criminal Appeal
King's College, London,
    see London University
King's counsel,
    see Crown counsel

Labour Party
    Independent Labour Party XI 28
    Labour Representation Committee XI 28
    Parliamentary Labour Party XI 28–30
    see also political parties
labour relations
    collective bargaining XIII 679–81
    'collective laissez-faire' XIII 679
    compulsory arbitration XIII 717–18
    voluntary arbitration XIII 667–8
    Devonshire Commission (1891–4)
        XIII 689–92
    government, role of XIII 690–2
    Majority Report XIII 690–1
    Minority Report XIII 691–2
    sweated trades and trade boards
        XIII 690, 692
    employers' associations XIII 688–9
    government, role of XIII 690–2, 715–18
    Board of Trade: Labour Division
        XIII 690, 717
    Statute of Artificers 1562 and its
        repeal XIII 626–9
    labour exchanges XIII 717–18
    Liberty and Property Defence League
        XI 113 XII 299, XIII, 689
    National Free Labour Association XIII 699
    political economy of labour XI 167–71,
        192–6, 198–205 XIII 629–33,
        667–8, 715–17
    unskilled workers XIII 687–88
    see also employer and employee,
        industrial disputes, political economy,
        trade unions
laissez-faire economy,
    see political economy
Lancaster, Duchy of

coroners XI 936
County Court XI 912
magistracy in XI 912
    see also palatinate courts
land
    creditors' remedies against XII 57,
        180–90
    deceased debtor XII 54, 180–3
    living debtor XII 184–90
    devises XII 7–8, 180–3
    interpretation XII 19–22, 25–6, 28–9,
        31–3, 38–9, 43–6
    executory trusts of XII 14–18
    partition XII 86–7
    real property, law of XII 47, 49,
        53, 61, 225
    assimilation with personalty XII 54, 56,
        77, 179–201, 207, 214, 225–31
    codes and digests XII 49–54,
        225, 230
    simplification XII 195–6, 204, 224–31
    taxation of XII 183–4, 228
    trusts of XII 4, 80, 82, 92, 94, 106,
        110, 192–4, 201, 203, 232–5, 243–4,
        256, 263–6, 268
    see also: estates in land, perpetuities, sale
        of land, settlements, strict settlement,
        succession, tenure
Land Registry XII 187, 198–9, 213, 219
    finances of XII 205, 219
    land brokers at XII 218, 220
    Middlesex Deeds Registry, and
        XII 205, 219
    officials at XII 219, 228
    posts in XI 1147
    Registrar XII 203, 219, 226
    rule-making XII 214, 217, 222
    solicitors, and XII 220, 225–8
    workload of XII 198, 205
    see also registration of title, sale of land,
        vendor and purchaser
landlord and tenant
    distress XII 120–4, 401–2, 596, 598–9,
        872–3, 875, 1115
    remedies for unlawful XII 121
    statutory limitation XII 122–3
    eviction XII 124–7
    fixtures XII 117–8
    forfeiture XII 114, 124–7
    relief against XII 124–6, 209
    notice XII 113, 119
    obligations, implied XII 116
    fitness for habitation XII 116–17
    penal rents XII 115, 119
    tenant right XII 118–19
    waste XII 114, 116
    see also leases

larceny
  Larceny Act, 1827 XII 463–4
  Larceny Act, 1861 XII 463, 467–8, 661, 827
  see also property offences
Law Amendment Society XI 84, 597, 609,
      782, 789, 1098, 1165, 1167, 1206, 1181,
      1183, 1217
  Attorney-General
    'devil' XI 1071
    head of the bar XI 1064–5
  clerks law officers' department XI 1071–2
  County Courts, and
  court business
    appeals XI 1076–7
    nolle prosequi XI 1075–76
    privileges XI 1075
    prosecutions XI 1073–5
  judicial appointments of XI 974–8
  opinions XI 1064, 1072–3
  patent grants XIII 955
  pleadings, and
  private practice of XI 1068–70
  public interest XI 1077–8
  real property law, and XII 58, 60, 71, 75, 194
  remuneration XI 1068–69, 1070–1, 1073
  role in government and parliament
      XI 1065–9 XII 221
  Solicitor-General XI 1063
  tribunals of commerce, and
  judicial office, and XI 1038, 1055, 1063–78
  see also Attorney-General,
      Solicitor-General
law reform XI 22–32, 72, 80, 83–4 XII 49–64,
      220–1, 276, 290, 306, 308 XII 317–207,
      569–70, 619–27, 779–80, 793–7, 800–8,
      810, 813, 817–33
law reports XI 1211–22
  Admiralty XI 721
  authorized reporters XI 1212–13
  Chancery courts XI 1212
  Ecclesiastical Courts XI 694
  House of Lords XI 1212
  Incorporated Council of Law Reporting
      XI 1208, 1215–20
    Digest XI 1218
    English Reports XI 1221
    Law Reports XI 1218–22
    Revised Reports XI 1221
    Weekly Notes XI 1218, 1219
  JCPC XI 549
  journal reports XI 1214
  Law Amendment Society XI 1216, 1218
  law reporting DC 1222
  Nisi Prius XI 606, 1212
  nominate reports XI 1214
  Weekly Reporter XI 1214, 1220
  see also Incorporated Council for Law
      Reporting

law societies XI 1113, 1137, 1144, 1160,
      1167–73, 1188 XII 70, 96, 108, 207, 211–12,
      220, 291
Law Society XI 809, 820, 831, 840, 845, 847,
      1088, 1089, 1109, 1126, 1129, 1133, 1135,
      1142–43, 1144–45, 1155–67, 1206, 1217
      XII 141, 208, 212–13, 276
  and site of new courts XI 782
  audience XI 1166, 1169
  Chancery XI 669–70
  conduct and discipline XI 1160–65
  constitution and organization
      XI 1157–58
  conveyancing, and XII 107, 196, 208,
      211–12, 227
  Council XI 1158–59, 1164
  County Courts XI 880–1, 882, 889
  Ecclesiastical Courts XI 707
  exchanges between the professions XI 1168–69
  'fusion' with the bar XI 1167
  law stationers XI 1159
  legal education, general XI 1179, 1180, 1182,
      1187, 1191, 1194, 1198
  membership XI 1158–59
  notaries XI 1173
  title registration, and XII 196, 222, 226
  trusts law, and XII 213, 276, 291, 293
  see also solicitors
law writers XI 1125–26
leases XII 54, 71, 97, 104, 107, 185, 234 XIII 581–3
  agricultural XII 88, 111–15, 119
  building and repairing XII 54, 82–3,
      88–9, 112, 142, 172
  church and XII 113
  covenants in XII 112–17, 124–32, 172, 174
    equity and XII 115, 127, 130–2, 173
    mortgagees and XII 128–31
    real property commissioners
        and XII 110–11
    running of XII 127–32, 177
    usual XII 174
  drafting of XII 110
    short forms XII 71–2
  houses, of XII 116–17
  lives, for XII 111–13, 196
  private statutes, under XII 54, 112–13
  settlements, under XII 54, 81–4,
      87–90, 112–13
  title registration, and XII·220
  universities and XII 113
  yearly tenancies XII 113, 118–19
  years, for XII 111–12
  see also housing, landlord
      and tenant
Leeds
  Assizes XI 639, 781, 826, 828,
legacies XII 7, 25, 181, 242–3,
      246, 249, 258

legal departments Royal Commission on the
(1874) XI 737, 740, 786, 791, 792, 794,
841, 893
Legal Education Association XI 1188–91
Committee on (1846) Inns of Court and
examinations
changes to
exemptions from
inception of compulsory standards
overseas students in
proposals for law university
changes to
compulsory
exemption from
proposed general school of law
legal offices committee XI 731, 791
legal periodicals XI 1201–11
by individual title 1201–9
influence XI 1210–11
legal and XI 72, 123–31
analytical jurisprudence XI 78,
88–90, 125
formalism XI 72
natural law XI 75–7
positivism XI 76–7, 85, 109–11, 126
see also international law, political theory
legislation (delegated)
and the church XI 392
judicial review of XI 503, 521
legislation (local and private) XI 325–41, 374,
428, 437, 440–4, 449–50, 474 XII 85,
163–5, 177–8
see also Victorian legislation and social
reform
Clauses Acts 1845 XI 330, 336–7, 428, 441, 450
XII 85, 163, 622, 629, 636, 654
extent of XI 325–7, 337, 442
government control of XI 332–8
interpretation of XI 338–41 XII 165–6
parliamentary agents, and XI 329,
331–2, 334
parliamentary process XI 327–38, 443
House of Lords, in XI 329–32
local inquiries XI 334–5
provisional order legislation XI 334, 336–7
legislation (personal)
divorce XI 334, 336–7
estate XI 326 XII 54, 83–4, 87, 112–13
parliamentary process XI 326
legislation (public general)
see Victorian legislation and social reform
discriminatory XI 23
game laws, abolition of XI 23–4
government responsibility for XI 304–9,
311, 319
House of Lords, and XI 316–24
Parliament Act 1911 XI 322–4

parliamentary process XI 305–15 XII 207
closure of debate XI 306,
308–9, 313–15
select committees XI 333
private members' legislation XI 304–5,
309–12, 319
see also rule of law
Letters of Credit XII 754 8
Liberal Party
and local government XI 452–3,
467, 469–70
and the House of Lords XI 320–4
and the state XI 360
land law, and XII 119, 123, 198–9, 204–5,
208–9, 214, 217, 225, 228
see also political affiliations
liberalism XI 97–102, 112
Liberty and Property Defence League
XI 113 XII 299
'new' liberal theories XI 117–23
licensing,
see liquor licensing
lien XII 69, 121, 123n, 685, 695,
760, 762, 767
life assurance,
see insurance
life estate,
see estates in land
life tenant,
see estates in land, strict settlement
light, easement of,
see easements and profits, nuisance
limitation of actions XII 56, 58, 102, 362, 427,
604, 766–7, 1128–29
Lincoln's Inn XI 1021–22, 1034, 1052, 1079,
1080–81, 1083–84, 1086–87
courts of equity XI 781, 782, 1086
legal education XI 1176, 1196
liquor licensing XI 467
justices' sessions XI 461–3, 917–18, 931
judicial review of XI 501–2, 515–17
litigants in person XI 816–18
Liverpool XII 122
as Assize town XI 639, 778, 826
Chamber of Commerce XI 775
Court of Passage XI 717, 850, 871–2
Law Society XI 1171, 1172
new courts XI 781
solicitors XI 1119, 1133, 1142, 1143,
XII 96, 108
stipendiary magistrates
XI 1013, 1015
see also Bristol Tolzey Court,
courts, borough London, Liverpool
Court of Passage
local boards of health,
see public health

local courts, judges of
Common Law RC (1828) XI 317–18,
801–2
see also borough courts, Bristol
Tolzey Gourt, County Courts,
courts of requests, Liverpool Court
of Passage,
local government
borrowing XI 443–4, 458
XII 284, 286–7
byelaws XI 427–9, 443–4, 518–21
central departments, and XI 443–5
local legislation XI 337–8, 443
funding of XI 337–8, 443
legal forms of XI 423–5
Local Government Board XI 338,
353, 365, 438, 443–4, 453–4,
487, 497
Local Government Act Office
XI 443–4
spending by
Borough Fund Act 1872 XII 164
structure of XI 423–5
see also boroughs, City of London,
counties, district councils,
franchise, local boards, municipal
corporations, parish, quarter
sessions, solicitors in
Local Government Board,
see local government
London XII 68, 70, 82, 89, 110, 134, 187, 324–5,
467, 475–6, 807–8, 823, 849, 855, 858,
1071, 1072, 1076, 1095
see also poor law and public health
banking XI 728, 730, 773
bankruptcy commissions
XII 786–7, 795
central departments, and XI 476–81
district boards XI 480–2
local commissioners, in XI 474–5, 479
London County Council XI 484–5
metropolitan boroughs XI 485
Metropolitan Board of Works
XI 480–4
parish vestries, in XI 449, 474–5,
478–84
elections to XI 479
reform of XI 479–80
powers of XI 480, 483
policing in XI 476
poor law in XI 475–6
public health in XI 477–80, 482–3
roads in XI 476–7, 481
solicitors in XII 96, 205
see also City of London
London Corresponding Society XI 84

London County Council and
coroners XI 945, 949
London, courts in City of
Lord Mayor's court XI 575–9,
867–9
small debts court XI 866, 867–9
solicitors in XI 1119–20, 1140–42,
1150, 1151, 1173
London Stock Exchange XII 631–4,
638–40
London University XI 1179, 1185,
1188, 1189
'Albert charter' XI 1192
'Gresham University' XI 1192–93,
1196
King's College XI 1179–80, 1185,
1192, 1194
University College XI 1192, 1194
long vacation XI 621–2, 788,
831–2
Lord Chancellor XI 745, 788, 792, 794, 800
XII 220–1
and coroners XI 939–40, 951
and magistracy XI 911–15
bankruptcy jurisdiction XII 781,
786–9, 795–6
in Chancery XI 648–9, 656, 659,
660, 672, 676
in House of Lords XI 317,
529–30, 540
in JCPC XI 558
income XI 986
officers XI 785
President of Supreme Court of Judicature
XI 533, 653, 656, 659
proposed changes to role XI 533,
653, 656, 659
Lord Chancellor's Office XI 964,
1167 XII 220, 230
creation of XI 786–7
county courts XI 842, 887, 889, 891
local courts XI 870–2
permanent secretary
XI 786–7, 964
Lord Chief Justice XI 794,
798, 805,
Lord Lieutenant,
see custos rotulorum
Lords, House of, (appellate) XI 302–3,
315–24, 526, 528–47, 569, 712, 756
799, 1076 XII 221
appeals committee XI 529
costs of appeals XI 529–30, 543
interlocutory appeals XI 530
judgments XI 542, 544
judges' opinions XI 530, 543

jurisdiction XI 541
jurisprudence XI 544–7
  judicial review XI 546–7
  precedents XI 545–6
  statutory review XI 546
lay peers XI 532–3, 538
Lords of Appeal in Ordinary
    XI 538–40, 561
membership of the judicial lords XI 531,
    533–5, 536, 538–40, 972
number and outcome of appeals XI 534,
    535, 541
peers
  attendance by XI 315–16
  bills of XI 317
security and recognizances
    XI 529–30, 542
sources of appeal XI 528, 530, 541
standing orders XI 528–9
see also Judges, Superior Courts of
    Common Law
Lords, House of (legislative)
functions of XI 316–19 XII 220
House of Commons, relations with
    XI 307–8, 314, 308–24
political parties in XI 320–1
powers of XI 316, 319–20
  Parliament Act, 1911 XI 322–4
procedure and organization XI 315–16,
    318–19, 542
  local and private bills XI 329–31
  personal bills XI 326
  public general bills XI 326–7

magistrates,
  see appeals, criminal procedure, judicial
    review, justices of the peace, quarter
    sessions
malice,
  see criminal fault, defamation,
    mens rea,
malicious damage,
  see property offences
managing clerks XI 1124, 1127–29
Manchester,
  Assizes XI 637, 639, 778, 826
  county courts in XI 1002
  Law Society XI 1109, 1201
    XII 227
  new courts XI 781
  solicitors in XII 108
  stipendiaries XI 1012
  stipendiary magistrates
  see also Salford Hundred Court
mandamus,
  see judicial review

manslaughter,
  see homicide
marine insurance,
  see insurance
marital breakdown
  criminal conversation
    action for XIII 725, 733–4
    damages for XIII 733–4
    liabilities of co-respondent under 1857
      Act XIII 734, 785
    step in Parliamentary divorce
      XIII 777–8
  'divorce', informal
    local custom XIII 774
    sale of wives XIII 774
  divorce a mensa et thoro
      (judicial separation)
    alimony XIII 768–9
    bars XIII 769
    Ecclesiastical Court jurisdiction
      XIII 767–8
    evidence XIII 769
    Grounds XIII 768
    provision from marriage settlement
      XIII 768–9
    step towards parliamentary divorce
      XIII 769, 777
  Divorce a vinculo, judicial XIII 781–96
    1857 Act jurisdiction XIII 780–5
    adultery and the double standard
      XIII 789–92
    bars XIII 792–4
    children: custody and access
      XIII 788
    cruelty XIII 790–2
    desertion XIII 785
    Divorce Court evidence and
      procedure XIII 786, 789
    Gorell Commission (1909–12)
      XIII 799–801
    maintenance XIII 787–8
    publicity of proceedings XIII 789
    Queen's/King's Proctor XIII 794–6
    Reform of Divorce Law XIII 780–4
    social status of parties XIII 786
    women petitioners XIII 787–8
  divorce, parliamentary
      XIII 777–80
    grounds and bars XIII 777–8,
      780
    hearing in House of Lords
      XIII 778–9
    sex and class of petitioners
      XIII 778–9
    three stages XIII 778–9
  magistrates' orders

marital breakdown (*cont.*)
    Acts of 1878–95 XIII 796–8
    against husband's violence XIII 796–7
    class differences and reform of
        matrimonial causes law XIII 797–801
    custody of children XIII 797
    Gorell Barnes' criticisms XIII 799
    number of cases XIII 797–8
    relation to poor relief XIII 798
    Poor Law XIII 726
    desertion by husband XIII 776–7
    restitution of conjugal rights XIII 767–8
    separation agreements
        denial of desertion XIII 772–3
        future separation XIII 771–2
        legality at common law XIII 770–2
        treatment as other contracts
          XIII 772–3
        trust as basis XIII 771
        wife's power to pledge credit XIII 770
    see also children, Divorce Court, husband
        and wife, marriage settlements, married
        women's property, poor law, private
        international law
maritime law,
    see bills of lading, charterparties
marriage
    as social institution XIII 747–8
    breach of promise action XII 498,
        504, 512–13
    capacity to marry XIII 748–9
        bigamy XIII 748
        mental inability to understand XIII 749
        minimum age XIII 749
        physical and psychological inhibitions on
          intercourse XIII 749
        relation to sexual offences XIII 749
    ceremony of marriage
        clandestine marriages: lack of parental
          consent XIII 753–4
        established Church procedures XIII 753
        informal exchange of vows XIII 752–3
        later Victorian reforms XIII 756
        Lord Hardwicke's Act 1753 XIII 751–5
        Marriage Act and Births, Deaths and
          Marriages Act 1836 XIII 755–6
        marriage by rites of other faiths and
          secular marriages XIII 755–6
        parish records XIII 755
        registrar-general XIII 756
    divesting event XII 7
    marriage law
        effect on inheritance XIII 738–9
        parental consent XIII 747–8
        preventive and punitive elements XIII 747–8
    promise to marry
        breach of promise action XIII 752

Canons of Church of England XIII 749–50
    dum casta clause XIII 747–8
    incest XIII 751
    Lord Lyndhurst's Act 1835 XIII 750
    marriage with deceased wife's sister,
        deceased husband's brother XIII 750–1
    prohibited degrees of relationship: blood
        or affinity
    while married to another XIII 747–8
    see also children, husband and wife, marital
        breakdown, marriage settlements,
        married women's property, private
        international law
marriage settlements XII 9, 66, 232–5, 257, 264,
    283, 323–4, 330, 436–7, 443
    articles for XII 13–15
    Judges' execution of
    covenants in XII 260–1, 265–6
    marriage consideration XII 254, 260, 264–5,
        368–70
    usual form of XII 11, 14, 132, 262–3, 283
    volunteers under XII 264–6
    see also children, marital breakdown,
        marriage, married women's
        property, trusts
married women's property, other rights and
    obligations
    contract
        authority to pledge
        husband's credit XIII 730, 737–8
        Reforms of 1870 Act XIII 760–1
        Reforms of 1882 Act XIII 763–5
    campaigns for law reform XIII 757–66
        for Act of 1870 XIII 760–1
        or Act of 1882 XIII 761–6
        relation to divorce reform XIII 759
    property brought into marriage by wife
        XII 264–5
    debts and choses in action XIII 736
    interest in land XIII 736–8
    paraphernalia XIII 736
    personalty XIII 736
    reforms in 1870 XII 8 XIII 760–1
    reforms in 1882 XII 8 XIII 762
    rights on death of partner XII 215
    separate use XII 8, 159, 178, 247–52
    rights on death of other spouse
        husband as survivor XIII 739
        wife as survivor XIII 738–9
    taxation of income XIII 765
    variations in equity
        restraint on anticipation XIII 741–2
        trust for separate use by wife XIII 739–41
        wife's equity to a settlement XIII 742–4
    tort
        action by husband XIII 763
        ante-nuptial liability of wife XIII 763

liability of husband XIII 761, 763–4
 see also dower, marital breakdown, marriage
  settlements private international law,
  settlement (of property generally)
master and servant,
 see employer and employee
Master of the Rolls,
 appointment XI 632, 794, 800, 976
 appellate judge XI 837
 in Chancery XI 656, 657, 660
 in JCPC XI 548–9
masters XI 790, 793, 796
 in Chancery XI 656, 674–81
  abolition and restoration XI 687–81
  Chancery Commission (1850)
   proposals XI 677
  duties and delays XI 674–6
  orders of 1850 XI 678
 in common law courts and SCJ XI 624,
  765, 818
 see also Chancery (chief clerks)
match manufacturing,
 see regulation of working conditions
matrimonial proceedings,
 see marital breakdown
mens rea,
 see criminal fault
mental deficiency,
 see insanity, lunacy
mercantile law,
 see commercial law
merchandise marks,
 see trade marks
merger,
 see companies
Metropolitan and Provincial Law
  Association XI 679, 1159, 1161, 1171, 1188,
  1198, 1207, 1210 XII 141
Metropolitan Law Society XI 1156
Metropolitan Stipendiary Magistrates
  XI 1012–14
 appointment and terms XI 1006–8, 1009–10
 Chief Magistrate XI 1005, 1007, 1008
 organization XI 1004–6
 profile XI 1010–12
 promotion and transfer XI 1008–9
 see also children
Middle Temple XI 1079, 1083, 1084, 1085, 1087,
  1181
Middlesex
 County Court XI 849
 sessions XI 641
military law XI 409–12, 416–20
 courts martial XI 412–22
  Judge-Advocate General XI 412–14, 416–21
  procedure XI 412–15, 418–19, 422
 judicial review and XI 414–16

parliamentary control XI 404, 409
 sources of XI 409–12
 see also army
mines and mining,
 see regulation of working conditions
ministers,
 see central government departments,
  secretaries of state
ministry of justice, proposals for XI 794
misdemeanour,
 see criminal procedure
misrepresentation XII 400, 409–32, 924
 change of circumstances XII 410
 damages for XII 426–31
 fraudulent XII 412–14
 in equity
  indemnity XII 425–7
  making representations good XII 338,
   367–9, 416–19, 425, 428
 in insurance law XII 698–9, 706–7
 negligent misrepresentations XII 418–20,
  942, 944, 947, 949
 rescission for XII 419–25, 649
 Pollock's views on XII 370, 430–1
mistake in contract law XII 301, 303, 307, 309,
  313, 319, 321, 433–72, 588
 common mistake XII 437, 448
 common law XII 445–52, 445–70
 cross-purpose XII 446
 in equity XII 434–45
  rectification XII 435, 437–9, 442–3, 446
  rescission for mistake XII 436–8,
   441–5, 590
 of identity XII 434–5, 452–70, 1119
  in equity XII 452–4
 of law XII 441–2, 587–8,
 of quality XII 440–1, 445, 449–52
 of rights XII 442
 of subject-matter XII 435, 448
 Pollock's views on XII 433–4, 449, 452, 467,
  469, 471–2
 unilateral mistake XII 439–43,
  447, 451–2
mistaken payments, recovery for XII 583–8
 bills of exchange XII 751–2
 change of position XII 586
monarchy,
 see Crown, sovereign
money had and received, action for,
 see restitution
moneylenders XII 835, 841, 858–69, 874–5
 Money Lenders Act 1900 XII 867–9
 select committee (1897) XII 865–6
 summary diligence procedure, use of
  XII 864, 866
monopolies,
 see cartels

moral philosophy
　altruism XI 99–100, 105
　idealism XI 117–23
　intuitionism,XI 73, 91–3, 105
　utilitarianism XI 73, 79–83, 87–8, 94,
　　96–8, 101, 115–16
　see also political economy, religion
mortgages XII 47, 81, 85, 92, 94–5, 132–58
　annuities, and XII 142–4, 147, 153, 156
　assimilation, and
　chattels, of XII 152
　collateral advantages XII 142, 145–8, 153
　contracts, as XII 139–41, 147–50
　conveyancing XII 65–7, 132–3, 137–40
　　Real Property Commissioners XII 134
　debentures XII 155–8
　deeds registration XII 65, 69, 71, 133, 206–7
　devolution of XII 137
　equity of redemption
　　clogs and fetters on XII 135, 138, 150–9
　forms of XII 153
　　by charge XII 200–1, 203, 207, 222–3, 229
　　by deposit of deeds XII 69, 71, 133–5,
　　　206, 222
　　by term of years XII 136
　　by transfer XII 136, 196, 229
　　by trust for sale XII 135–6
　　with power of sale XII 135–41, 151, 158, 194
　foreclosure XII 61, 135–6, 141
　further advances XII 133, 149–50, 207
　investment in XII 132, 283, 285
　　powers of
　judgment debts XII 61, 144–5
　leases, of XII 128–31, 142
　mortgagees,
　　in possession XII 145–6
　　sale by XII 137–40, 149
　　oppression by XII 138–40, 145–9
　powers in XII 137–41, 208–9
　priorities of XII 149–50
　　consolidation XII 133, 209
　　tacking XII 133, 136, 149–50, 206, 208
　sale XII 61, 106
　　purchaser protection XII 139–41
　substance of XII 152–4
　title registration, and XII 142, 222–3
　usury laws, and XII 142–6, 152
　see also annuities, bills of sale, judgment
　　debts, pawnbroking
mortmain,
　see charity
municipal corporations XI 367–8, 374, 386–7,
　423–4
　audit of XI 444
　borough charities, and XI 431–3, 441
　borrowing by XI 434, 443–5
　byelaws XI 427, 429, 443

judicial review of XI 518–19
charter XI 427
　acquiring XI 425–6, 439–40
contracts of XI 376
councils of XI 429–31
　elections to XI 387, 429–30
county boroughs XI 425
distribution of XI 425–6
local boards, as XI 438
powers of XI 427–9, 437–45
　judicial review XI 435–6, 499
property of XI 427, 433–7
rates XI 368–9, 427, 439–42
reform XI 425, 429–37, 472, 509
see also borough, City of London, local
　governments
murder,
　see homicide
Mutual Law Association XI 1099

natural justice,
　see judicial review
negligence XII 888–91, 894, 903–57, 1014, 1118,
　1127, 1131–32, 1134, 1136
　causation of harm XII 922, 928–34, 937–8,
　　950–3
　cheques, drawing of XII 770–1, 929–30
　common carriers XII 911–16
　contributory negligence XII 908, 931–2,
　　938–40, 953, 973, 1005, 1014–15
　damages in XII 934–6, 990–1000
　duty of care XII 922–8, 944–50, 982–3,
　　985, 987–90
　　breach of duty XII 936–7, 954–7
　estoppel by XII 929–30, 947
　faulty vehicles XII 910, 961–4
　fire, keeping of XII 916–20
　foreseeability XII 890, 935, 946, 950–7,
　　966, 988
　'gross' XII 913–16
　misrepresentation XII 418–32
　Pollock's views on XII 941–4, 947, 949, 954,
　　955–7
　professional XII 882–3, 916
　railways XII 919–21, 958–67, 985
　'reasonable man' standard XII 917–18,
　　925–7, 942, 944
　res ipsa loquitur XII 960, 976, 980
　road accidents, 904–911, 970–1, 973–6
　Salmond's views on XII 943, 953,
　　955, 990
　see also negligence
negotiable instruments,
　see bills of exchange, bills of lading, cheques,
　　promissory notes
neutrality,
　see public international law

New York, law code XI 589, 758
New Zealand,
  see British colonies and empire
notaries XI 1150, 1173–74
  proctors as XI 699
notice XII 67, 97, 128, 171, 174–6, 210
  charges registration, and XII 181–6, 189
  deeds registration, and XII 69, 205–7
  mortgages, and XII 133, 139–41, 206–7
  restrictive covenants, and XII 171, 174–6
  trusts, and XII 181–2, 201
nuisance XII 163, 895, 1068–1111, 1127, 1130,
    1141–42, 1145–46, 1149–50
  common law actions XII 1069
  injunctions against XII 1105–11
  interference with light XII 169–70, 1071–79
  noise XII 1102–3
  Nuisances Removal Act 1855 XII 1094
  public nuisances XII 972–6, 985, 1069, 1082
    indictment XII 1069
  'reasonable user' XII 1079
  remedies XII 1105–11
  smoke pollution XII 1085–86, 1093–101,
    1104
    Smoke Nuisance Abatement (Metropolis)
      Act 1853 XII 1094
  strict liability in XII 1069
  water pollution XII 1080–93
    percolating underground water XII 1083,
      1086–87
    prescriptive rights to pollute XII 1083–85,
      1090, 1092
    Rivers Pollution Commission 1867 XII 1084
    Rivers Pollution Prevention Act 1876
      XII 1080, 1088, 1090–92
    statutory regulation XII 1088–93
nullity of marriage,
  see Divorce Court, marital breakdown

obscenity,
  see offences against public morality
offences against public morality XIII 16, 352,
    373
  gambling XIII 352, 353, 359–63
    class legislation XIII 361–3
    lotteries XIII 359–60
    rationale: dangers of social decay and
      dependency XIII 359–61
  obscenity XIII 352, 355, 363–73
    Bradlaugh and Besant XIII 364, 368–70
    blasphemy XIII 363–364, 370n
    Campbell, Lord XIII 365–6
    Home Office XIII 373
    literature: meritorious, educational or
      obscene XIII 367–73
    National Vigilance Association
      XIII 371–2
  Obscene Publications Act 1857 XIII 365,
    366
  Proclamation Society XIII 363
  Society for the Suppression of Vice
    XIII 364, 365
  Vizetelly, H. 371–2
  prostitution XIII 352, 354, 355–9
    child prostitution XIII 358
    Contagious Diseases Acts 1864–1886
      XIII 357
    fringe criminality XIII 355
    rationales: nuisance, indecency, disorder,
      exploitation XIII 356–7, 359
    vagrancy's sister XIII 355–6
  see also law and religion
official referees XI 821–3
official secrets,
  see protecting the state
official solicitor XI 792–3
'officialism' XI 1144, 1166, 1210, 1216
officials
  immunity from rates XI 367–9, 371–4
  liability XI 367, 369–71, 374–84
  see also Crown
Old Bailey,
  see Central Criminal Court
Ordnance, Board of,
  see army
Overend, Gurney & Co XII 426, 640,
    661, 666, 729–30

Palatinate Courts
  Duchy of Lancaster
    Chancery XI 833–5
    common pleas XI 872–3
  Durham
    Chancery XI 875
    common law XI 872
  for Chester *see* Great Sessions of Wales
pandectists XI 85 XII 306, 309, 311
panopticon,
  see punishment
parent and child,
  see children
parishes, XI 445–54
  churchwardens XI 445
    liability XI 371
  councils XI 425, 468
  lighting and watching XI 447–9
  officers of XI 423, 456
    justices, and XI 455–6
  rates XI 456
  unions of XI 424, 446–7, 461–2
    liability XI 371
  vestry XI 445–51, 455
  see also local government, London, public
    health, (local boards of health)

Parliament
  accountability to XI 346–8, 354–63, 421, 505
  army, and XI 404–6, 409–12
  church, and XI 388–9, 391–2
  parliamentary agents XI 329–32, 334
  sovereignty of XI 4–11, 301, 404, 428
  see also Commons, House of, legislation,
      Lords, House of (legislative)
Parliamentary bar XI 1053–54
parties, political XI 302, 308, 313
  see also political parties
partnership XII 153, 306, 613–16
  en commandite XII 626–7
  liability of partners for each other's acts
      XII 665
  Pollock's digest XII 731
  use of Bills of Exchange by XII 737
  see also companies
patents for invention XII 590–1
  classification as 'industrial
      property' XIII 931
  Crown use XIII
  evolution of system
    alteration of system 1852–1914 XI 359
    assignment and licence XIII 972–7
    before 1820 XIII 932–4
    employed inventor XIII 972–3
    'inventor' from abroad XIII 932–3
    reform 1829–1852 XIII 951–6
  grant of patent
    amendment XIII 953
    comptroller of patents XIII 964
    Lord Chancellor and Law Officers
        XIII 932, 964
    official search and examination for
        novelty XIII 963–4, 970
    old procedures (to 1852) XIII 942–3, 950–1
    patent grant as source of right XIII 934–7
    provisional application
        and priority XIII 955
    procedural reforms (1852–) XIII 953–6
  infringement of patent
    proceedings in Chancery XI 835 XIII 966–7
    claims and their interpretation
        XIII 949–50, 964–7
    scope of right XIII 973
  international relations XIII 959–63
    bi-lateral agreements XIII 959
  justifying patents
    economic perspectives in favour
        XIII 938–42
    economic perspectives against
        XIII 954–55, 956–9
    entitlement as of right XIII 937–8
    public access XIII 936–7
  licensing
    commercial licensing practices XIII 973–6

  duration XIII 976
  enforceability of licence terms XIII 972
  parallel importing XIII 974–5
  resale price maintenance XIII 975
  tying arrangements XIII 976
  'manner of new manufacture'
    objective tests of validity XIII 945–9
  movement to procure international
      convention XIII 959–61
  international priority XIII 961–2
  international relations XIII 959–63
  Paris Industrial Property Convention
      (1883) XIII 961–3
  revocation, licence of right and
      compulsory licence 960, 962, 976–7
  patent agents XIII 938, 956
  term of patent XIII 934
    extension XIII 952–3
  validity
    disclosure in specification XIII 943–5,
        949–50
    fair basis; best method disclosure in
        specification XIII 943, 950
    inventive step, obviousness XIII 947–9,
        967–72
    novelty XIII 947, 967–9
    patentable subject-matter XIII 945–6
    utility XIII 950–1
passing off, action against,
    see trade marks
pawnbrokers XI 463 XII 401, 836,
        849–58, 871 XII 146, 401, 836,
        849–58, 871
  calculation of interest XII 851, 855–6
  Pawnbroking Act 1872 XII 853,
        855, 857
  Pawnbrokers' Reform
      Association XII 856
  pawnbroking (1870) XII 855–7
penalties XII 115, 523–9
perjury XI 616–17, 899
perpetuities XII 9, 48, 55
  modern rule against XII 19–22, 62–4,
        247, 249
  'old' rule against XII 18–20
  cy-près XII 20–1, 25–6
personality right
    see breach of confidence, defamation,
        right of privacy
petition of right,
    see Crown
petty sessions XI 461–4, 491, 924–30
  appeals XI 491, 495–7
  expansion of XI 924–5, 928
  Jervis's Acts XI 495–6, 925, 919–30
  powers of XI 447, 449, 458
philosophic radicals XI 83–4, 90–1

planning law
 debates about urban planning
  Bournville XIII 591
  byelaws XIII 591–593
  foreign examples XIII 591–592
  Garden Cities Association XIII 590, 592
  Hampstead garden suburb XIII 591–2
  Local Government Board XIII 591
  London County Council XIII 591
  National Housing Reform Council XIII 591
  Port Sunlight XIII 591
  strength of middle-class support XIII 590
  town extension plans XIII 593
 parliamentary debates
  linked to budget proposals and national
   land valuation XIII 594
  minimal role for the courts, opposed by
   conservatives XI 510–11 XIII 595–6
  planning law given restricted scope
   under control of Local Government
   Board XIII 595–6
 proposals for legislation
  'amenity' and suburbs XIII 590, 593
  betterment tax on landowners
   XIII 594, 596
  compensation for land owners XIII 594, 596
  courts, limited role of XIII 595
  land 'in the course of development' XIII 593
  Local Government Board XIII 592–3,
   595
  local government inspectors XIII 596
 weakness in implementation
  limited use of powers under the Act
   before WWI XIII 596–7
pleadings XI 526, 818–19
 Admiralty XI 726–30
 Chancery XI 661–4, 666
 Chancery Division XI 844
 Common Law Courts XI 580–91 XII 313–15,
  317, 319, 905–6
  equitable pleas XII 321–2, 446–8
  general issue XII 316–18
  Hilary Rules, 1834 XII 318, 320
  joinder of parties XII 315
  special pleading XII 314, 317–18, 320
 County Courts XI
 divorce XI 749
 Great Sessions of Wales XI 633
 Judicature Acts XI 765–6
 old county courts XI 849
 probate XI 734
 see also superior courts of common law
pledges XII 761–3, 791
 see also debtor and creditor, pawnbroking
police XIII 5–6, 18, 21–57
 and coroners XI 944, 946–7
 and quarter sessions XI 917

London XI 474, 476 XIII 21–35, 44–52
 accountability: to home secretary,
  metropolitan police commissioner
  inspectorate XIII 44, 47–48, 49–50, 51–2
 City of London police XIII 30, 34–5
 development of professional policing
  XIII 32–35
 Metropolitan Police Acts 1829 and
  1839 XIII 27–35
 parliamentary investigations XIII 22–4,
  27–8, 29, 30, 32
 pre-1829 system XIII 22–7
 reform proposals XIII 25–7
policing, general acceptance of XI 15–16,
 XIII 44–9, 56–7
provincial urban policing XI 458, 465
 XIII 36, 40–4, 50–2
 accountability: chief constables and watch
  committees XI 458 XIII 44, 50, 51–2
 Municipal Corporations Act 1835, County
  and Borough Police Act 1856 XI 430,
  437 XIII 40–1, 43–4
 public disorder: deployment of the
  military; emergency legislation
  XI 402–4 XIII 41
rural policing XIII 36, 37–40, 44, 50, 51–2
 accountability: chief constables, quarter
  sessions and county police committees
  inspectorate XI 458 XIII 44, 50, 51–52
 County Police Act 1839
 County and Borough Police Act 1856
  XI 448 XIII 37, 39
 Lighting and Watching Act 1833
  XI 448–51, XI 448–9 XIII 38
 Parish Constables Acts 1842 and 1850
  XI 448–9 XIII 40
 public disorder and local
  inadequacies XIII 36, 37
 quarter sessions adoption policies
  XIII 37, 39
 Report of the Royal Commission on Rural
  Policing 1839 XIII 38, 39
specific roles of policing: in prevention and
 detection of crime XIII 23, 52–6
 Bow Street and Police Offices XIII 23, 24,
  34–5
 censure and distaste for police
  surveillance XIII 52–3
 criminal investigation department XIII 53–5
 Special Branch XIII 55–6
political affiliations XI 26–32
 changing relation of MPs to party XI 30–2,
  301–15
 labour
  early working-class consciousness XI 26–7
  Chartist movement 26–7
  later political formations XI 28–30

political affiliations (*cont.*)
  tories/conservatives
    administrative agencies, and XI 356
    municipal corporations, and XI 429, 431
    'Old Torydom' XI 24
    public health, and XI 437
    reduction and repeal of corn laws,
      and XI 24–5
    Reform Act 1867 XI 27–8
    social allegiance XI 28
  whigs/liberals
    administrative agencies, and XI 355–6, 362
    Anti-Corn Law League, and XI 24–5
    army, and XI 401, 404
    changing appeal XI 27–32 XIII 688–9
    municipal corporations, and XI 429, 432
    public health, and XI 437–8
    Reform Acts 1832, 1884–5 XI 13–15, 24, 27–8
  see also Conservative Party, judges, labour
      relations, Labour Party, Liberal Party,
      socialism, trade unions
political economy XI 158–233
  laissez faire, industry and legislation
      XI 158–67, 172–86, 192–8,
      205–9, 227–33
    Cobden and free trade XI 165, 167, 197
    corn laws and Peel XI 168 XII 229, 779
    companies, liability and structures
      XI 179–86, 196–8
    employment conditions XI 168–70, 192
    Factories Acts XI 168–70, 192
    industrial accidents and compensation
      XI 194–6
    judiciary XI 171
    minimum wages XI 193–4
    monopolies and restrictive practices
      XI 184–6
    patents XI 232
    railways XI 183–4, 233
    water and sanitation XI 232
  religion and political economy XI 163–5,
      188–90
    Anglican Christian Socialist League XI 190
    Chalmers, T. XI 163–5
    Christian Socialists XI 189–90
    Christian business ethics XI 190–1
    Christian Social Union XI 189–90
    evangelicalism XI 188–9
    Kingsley, C. XI 189–90
    Maurice, F. D. XI 189–90
    Sumner, (Bishop) XI 164
  'science' of political economy XI 159–75,
      188–203
    Carlyle, T., *Past and Present* XI 188, 192, 200
    Chalmers, T. XI 163–5
    McCulloch, J., *Principles of Political
      Economy* XI 169, 171, 174

    Malthus, T., *Essay on Population
      Growth* XI 162–4, 169
    Marshall, A., *Principles of Economics*
      XI 191, 192, 198n, 201
    Mill, J. S., *Principles of Political Economy*
      XI 172, 192, 197, 198n, 200–1, 203
    rent theory XI 160, 161
    Ricardo, D., *Principles of Political
      Economy* XI 160, 162, 171
    Senior, N., *Outline of the Science of
      Political Economy* XI 165, 171–3
    Smith, A., *Wealth of Nations* XI 159–61
    utilitarianism XI 172–5, 227–28
    wage fund theory XI 162, 169, 171, 199
  social welfare legislation and political
      economy XI 171–9, 205–26
    Beveridge, W. XI 217, 218
    Chadwick, E. XI 174, 176–7
    Chamberlain, J. XI 206, 211, 217, 223
    Fabianism XI 212, 213, 217, 218
    Hobson, J. A. XI 205, 206, 209n
    Hobhouse, L. T. XI 205, 209
    housing XI 176, 178, 207, 209–11, 225
    Kay-Shuttleworth, J. XI 178
    Lloyd George, D. XI 206, 208, 211, 213, 216
    McCulloch, J. XI 171, 172
    Mill, J. S. XI 171, 208, 212
    municipal or civic welfarism XI 211
    New Liberalism XI 191, 205–6, 209,
      213, 216
    old age pensions XI 206, 208, 209,
      211–12, 216
    Owen, R. XI 165, 175
    Poor Laws XI 162, 172–4, 177, 228
    population control XI 162–3
    public health XI 176–8, 209–211,
      214–15, 218
    Southwood-Smith, T. XI 176, 229
    Spencer, H, and social democracy XI 188,
      205
    unemployment benefit XI 207, 211–13,
      216–18
  taxation XI 186–188, 218–26
    Commissioners, General and Special XI 226
    death duties XI 224–5
    'differentiation' of tax source XI 223–4
    direct and indirect XI 187, 219, 221
    Gladstone, W. XI 221–4
    graduation of tax rates XI 187, 221, 223–5
    income tax, a 'war tax' XI 187, 218, 221–4
    judiciary, role of XI 226
    land, taxation of XI 187, 219, 224–6, 232
    Lloyd George, D. XI 225–6
    Lowe, R. XI 222
    Mill, J. S. XI 219, 221, 222–3, 225
    Peel and income tax XI 221–3
    social redistribution XI 218, 223–5

trade unions and collective action
XI 168–70, 198–205
combination acts XI 168–70
'iron law of wages' XI 199–200
judicial hostility XI 198–205
legislative intervention and regulation
XI 201–4
McCulloch, J. XI 199
Malthus, T. XI 169
Ricardo, D. 169
'Wage fund', J.S. Mill and the
XI 199–200
see also company law, contract, labour
relations, law and religion
political theory XI 20–22, 73, 303–3, 321, 467
see also legal,
rule of law
poor law
Elizabethan poor law
able-bodied poor XIII 479, 481
Act for the Relief of the Poor, 1601
XIII 473
administration of the poor law XI 445,
455–7 XIII 473–6
apprentices XIII 476
cost of the poor law XIII 474, 475,
477, 478
guardians of the poor XIII 475
Hobhouse's Act, 1831 XIII 478
Hospitals for the Poor Act, 1597 XIII 473
incapable poor XIII 479, 481
Justices of the Peace XIII 473, 474
King's Bench XIII 474
litigation XIII 474–5
local power XIII 473–6, 477–9
outdoor relief XIII 479
overseers XIII 474
parishes and the poor law XIII 445–7,
473, 474
political and philosophical debate
XIII 476–84
poor rate XI 456
Poor Relief Act, 1662 XIII 474
Poor Relief Act, 1782 XIII 475
Poor Removal Act, 1795 XIII 475
Quarter Sessions Appeals Act, 1731
XIII 475
ratepayers XIII 473–5
removals XIII 474
SCs, 1816, 1824, 1828 XIII 477
settlement XIII 474
Speenhamland system XI 457
XIII 476–477
Sturges Bourne's Acts 1818, 1819
XIII 473–4, 478
vagrancy XIII 475
vestries XIII 475, 478

New Poor Law 1834
administration of XI 446–7
XIII 481–503
Andover workhouse XIII 487–8
'Chamberlain Minute', 1886 XIII 498, 499
Chartism XIII 488
children XIII 490
circulars XIII 498
cost XIII 482, 493
doctors XIII 490–6
Education Act, 1870 XIII 490
Eton workhouse XIII 489
general orders XIII 484–8, 496, 502–3
General Medical Order, 1842 XIII 491,
493, 494
'Goschen' Minute, 1869 XIII 497–8
guardians XIII 485, 488, 491, 493,
495, 497–9
Home Office XIII 489
Justices of the Peace XIII 486, 488, 490
legislation as the instrument of
reform XIII 478–81
'letters' XIII 484
Local Government Board, 1871 XIII 489,
498, 502
local power XIII 481–503
medical officers XIII 495
medical provision: mental health
XIII 490–5
medical provision: physical health
XIII 490–5
Metropolitan Poor Act, 1867
XIII 495, 497
orders XIII 484–9, 496, 502
outdoor relief XIII 483, 486, 497–8
overseers XIII 486, 489
political and philosophical debate
XIII 476–84, 496–9, 500–3
Poor Law Amendment Act, 1834
XIII 481–8
Poor Law Board, 1847 XIII 486, 489, 496
Poor Law literature XIII 489
Poplar Guardians XIII 499
principle of less eligibility XIII 479
Queen's Bench XIII 485–6
Regulations XIII 484–8, 496, 502–3
Royal Commissions, 1832–4
XIII 478–81
schools XIII 490
social causes of poverty XIII 497–500
Society for the Organising Charitable
relief and repressing mendicity
XIII 497
tort law and the poor law XIII 494–5
Unemployed Workmen Act, 1905 XIII 500
unemployment XIII 498–9
Union Chargeability Act, 1865 XIII 497

poor law (*cont.*)
 unions of parishes XI 424, 446–7
  XIII 482, 486
 workhouses XIII 483, 485, 486, 490, 502
 reform of the new poor law 1834
  national insurance XIII 505–6
  pensions XIII 504–6
  RC, 1892 XIII 500–3
  social causes of poverty XIII 498–506
  unemployment XIII 498–9
Poor Law Board XI 354, 365, 487
Poor Law Commissioners (1834) XI 353–4
 accountability of XIII 484, 486, 489, 496,
  498, 502
 annual reports of XIII 485
 challenges to their the rules, etc. XIII 485
 discretions of XIII 482–4
 judicial review of 349–50, 498–500, 513
 powers to appoint staff XIII 484
 powers to issue rules XIII 482–9, 496, 502–3
 pressure of business XIII 486
 The Poor Law Board, 1847 and the Local
  Government Board, 1871 XIII 484, 489,
  496, 498, 502
 weakness in local control XIII 485–6
Poor Law, justices and XI 916 XIII 473, 474,
  482, 486
poor man's lawyer schemes XI 816
poor persons' procedure XI 755, 816
 see also bankruptcy
Post Office XII 226, 336–7
 liability XI 379–81
 post office savings bank XII 1011
potteries,
 see regulation of working conditions
powers (proprietary) XII 80–1, 262,
  266–7, 271
 appointment, of XII 8, 30, 243,
  262–3
 literature on XII 89
 theory of XII 89–92
precedent
 in Admiralty XI 721
 in Court of Criminal Appeal
  XI 808
 in House of Lords XI 545–6
 see also judicial precedent
pre-determination,
 see judicial review
prerogative XI 302, 307, 345–6,
  361, 427
 army, and XI 342–3, 401–3,
  405, 41–12
prerogative of mercy,
 see criminal appeals
prescription,
 see easements and profits

press,
 see defamation
pressure groups XI 311–12
Prime Minister XI 302, 345,
  389, 402
Principal Probate Registry XI 76,
  81–2, 108–9
 clerks XI 735–8
 registrars XI 735–6
 working hours XI 738
prisons
 and justices XI 916–18
 and quarter sessions XI 457,
  459–60
 see also punishment
privacy, right of
 failure in England to adopt
  XIII 848
 opposition by press XIII 850–1
 Warren and Brandeis XIII 847–8, 851, 863,
  900, 989
 see also breach of confidence
private bills and acts,
 see also legislation, local and private
private international law
 between jurisdictions of a state XI 279–80,
  285
 contract XI 291–3
 domicil XI 285–8
  contrast with nationality
   XI 285–7
  dependency XI 285–6
  of choice XI 286
  of colonists XIII 836–7
  of origin XI 285
  succession disputes XIII 837–8
 foreign judgments XI 289–90
  enforcement XI 289–90
  recognition XI 290
 international movements to harmonize
   XI 296–7
 jurisdiction
  general basis XI 288–9
  procedure and substance XI 288–9
  RSC, Order 11 XI 289
 personal law
  children: guardianship XIII 842–3
  marital breakdown XIII 839–42
  marriage XIII 838–9
  matrimonial property and
   inheritance XIII 837–8
 property XI 293–5
  land XI 293
  personalty XI 293–5
 renvoi XI 287–8
 theories of
  classification under 'statutes' XI 280

comity XI 281–4
  predominance of personal law
    XI 284–5
  predominance of territorial
    allegiance XI 281
  torts XI 295–6
Privy Council XI 361, 439–40
  committee on education XI 343, 361–4
  see also judicial committee (JCPC)
Prize Court XI 696, 712, 714–15, 720, 721,
    725, 732
  appeals to JCPC XI 53, 556
prize law XII 685
probate XII 5, 8, 10, 57, 67, 191
  bona notabilia XI 703, 705, 707
  County Courts XI 733, 741, 878
  Ecclesiastical Courts RC XI 703–4
  reform of ecclesiastical courts'
    jurisdiction XI 710–14
Probate Court,
  appointment of judge XI 733
  evidence XI 733
  fees XI 733
  Judicature Commission XI 735
  jurisdiction and business XI 733–5
  jury trial XI 734–5
  rules and practice XI 733–4
probate registries
  Principal Probate Registry XI 76, 81–2,
    108–9
    clerks XI 735–8
    registrars XI 735–6
    working hours XI 738
Probate, Divorce and Admiralty Division
    (PDA) XI 723, 724, 756, 793
  President XI 723, 794
  divisional court XI 724, 756
  see also Admiralty court, Probate court,
    Divorce court
procedure,
  see civil procedure, criminal
    procedure
proctors
  country
    as solicitors XI 699–701
    numbers and entry XI 700–1
  in Doctors' Commons
    earnings and compensation XI 700–1
    numbers and entry XI 699
    work XI 699–700
  see also doctors' commons
prohibitions XI 715, 716, 718
  see also judicial review
promissory notes XII 144–5, 728–9,
    732–3, 862
  see also bills of exchange
property offences XIII, 17–18, 374–91

larceny XIII 374–87
  animus furandi XIII 380
  conceptual development: domestic and
    commercial pressure XIII 374–6,
    379–80
  criminal or civil role XIII 375
  dishonesty XIII 380–4
  Pear's case and consent to possession
    XIII 376–80
  poaching XIII 385–7
  property: what could be stolen
    XIII 384–5
  'white collar' crime legislation
    XIII 384–85
malicious damage XIII 388–91
  criminal or civil wrong XIII 388
  damage, wide meaning of XIII 391
  fault or mens rea element: malice's
    elusive nature XIII 389–91
  Foster's 'act of public hostility'
    XIII 388
  Malicious Damage Act 1861 XIII 388,
    389, 390
prosecution,
  see adversarialism; criminal
    procedure
prostitution,
  see offences against public morality
provincial law societies association
    XI 1171
  see also MPLA, metropolitan
    and provincial
provocation,
  see criminal defences
public finance,
  see commons (house of), local government,
    rates and rating, revenue
public health XI 424, 437–8, 498
  demand for public health reform
    Alkali Acts XIII 544–6
    Birmingham, conditions in XIII 537,
      551, 554–6
    cholera XIII 538
    commissions XIII 536, 538
    foreign laws on public health XIII 536
    legislation the 'instrument of reform'
      XIII 536, 537
    life expectancy XIII 536, 542
    Lincoln, conditions in XIII 541
    Liverpool, conditions in
      XIII 539, 551–2
    local demands XIII 537–8
    London, conditions in XIII 536, 539
    Manchester, conditions in XIII 539, 552
    National Association for the Promotion of
      Social Science XIII 543, 546
    nuisances XIII 539, 550, 554–5

public health (*cont.*)
    Poor Law Commissioners and public
        health XIII 535
    Royal Commissions XI 452–3 XIII 539,
        545, 548
    Sanitary Report, 1842 XIII 535–6
    scientific expertise XIII 537, 543–6
    select committee XIII 538–9, 544
    smoke XIII 544, 547, 551
    typhus XIII 535
opposition to public health laws
    ancient rights infringed XIII 540–3
    common law sufficient XIII 541
    local autonomy XIII 537–8, 540–1,
        543, 549, 552
    London's self-government XIII 540, 543
    municipal corporations XIII 536,
        540, 543
    rate payers XIII 540
public health controls
    Alkali Act 1863 XII 1095
    Boards of Health XIII 542
    byelaws XI 443 XIII 542
    common law XIII 546, 553–6
    General Board of Health XI 334, 336,
        357, 365, 444, 450–1, 478–9 XII 74
        XIII 542, 543
    Home Office XIII 543, 547–8
    inspectorates XI 352–3, 356 XIII 544–6
    judicial reponse to legislation XIII 546,
        553–7
    local boards of health XI 336–7, 372, 376,
        424, 438, 442–4, 450–1, 453, 498
        XIII 542–3, 547
    Local Government Board, 1871 XIII 545,
        548–50
    medical officers XI 474 XIII 544, 549, 551
    Privy Council XIII 544
    Public Health Act 1875 XII 1088, 1090,
        1095
    Sale of Food and Drugs Act 1875 XII 881
    Sanitary Act 1866 XII 1095
quality of the law
    complexity of the law XIII 547, 548,
        548 n60, 553, 555–6
    drafting difficulties XIII 556–7
    legal expertise, need for XIII 547,
        548 fn 60
    omissions in the law XIII 547
    private acts XIII 551–2, 554, 556
    Public Health Act XIII 548–53
    town improvement clauses XIII 555
    volume of the law XIII 547–8
use of the law
    courts and injunctions XI 497–8,
        514–15 XIII 554–6
    defences for polluters XIII 547, 551

    failures of enforcement XIII 545, 547–51,
        553–7
    Alkali Act 1863 XII 1095
    Board of Health XII 74
    Public Health Act 1875 XII 1088, 1090, 1095
    Sale of Food and Drugs Act 1875 XII 881
    Sanitary Act 1866 XII 1095
    see also nuisance
public international law,
    see international law
public law
    immunity from rates XI 368–9, 371–4
    liability in tort and contract XI 369–71,
        374–84
    public trust XI 367–8, 434–6, 440–2
    see also judicial review
public order,
    see affray, Chartism, riot, securing the state,
        unlawful assembly
public trustee office XI 1147, 1164
public works and buildings, commissioners
    of XI 365, 378–9, 382, 480
punishment XIII, 10–12, 138–79
    capital punishment XIII 138–54
        abolitionists' cause XIII 150–4
        Capital Punishment RC, 1865 XIII 133,
            151–3, 163, 164, 166, 175
        Criminal Law 1824 XIII 145
        Criminal Law Commissioners XIII 141,
            149, 153, 163
        deterrence and Paley's uncertainty
            principle XIII 138, 139, 140, 141, 144,
            145–6, 147, 149, 151, 153
        discretionary commutation XIII 138, 141
        eighteenth century capital statutes XIII 138
        Mackintosh's Select Committee of
            Inquiry, 1819 XIII 142, 143–4, 149
        Peel's Capital Statutes Consolidation
            XIII 145–8
        public petitions XIII 142–3, 144
        Romilly's initiatives XIII 139, 140, 145
        Russell's reforms of the 1830s
            XIII 148–50
    corporal punishment: flogging, whipping,
        stocks and pillory XIII 124, 139, 144,
        152, 154, 161, 164, 171, 393
    fines XIII 154n
    prisons and detention XIII 154–79
        Du Cane, Edmund, and national
            uniformity XIII 164–8, 169, 179
        Gladstone Committee Report, 1895,
            reform proposals XIII 167–71, 173,
            174, 179
        Habitual Criminals Act, 1869 and
            Prevention of Crimes Act 1871 and
            1879 XIII 164, 170, 172, 176
        inebriety XIII 173–5, 176

Jebb and the directorate of prisons
    XIII 160–4, 165, 166, 179
juveniles XIII 158, 170–3
localism versus national institutions
    XIII 155, 159
Millbank XIII 146, 155, 156, 157, 158, 178
Parkhurst XIII 158, 171
Pentonville XIII 158, 159, 160, 177, 178
Prison Act 1898: discriminatory
    approaches. XIII 168–9
Prison Inspectorate and Home Office
    XIII 156, 157
prison objectives: redemption or
    deterrence XIII 155, 157, 158, 159, 161,
    163, 164, 168, 169, 174, 179
recidivism XIII 157, 158, 163, 168, 169–70,
    172, 173
silent and separate systems XIII 156–8,
    160, 164, 169
Transportation and Penal Servitude RC
    1863 XIII 163
vagrancy and the 'feeble-minded' XIII 174–7
transportation XIII 138, 146, 154–162
    declining rate of transportation XIII 159
    doubts over efficacy XIII 154
    hybrid schemes: public works projects and
        'ticket of leave' XIII 161–2
    Molesworth SC XIII 159
pupillage XI 1023–25, 1038, 1176–77

quarter sessions XI 424, 455–61, 779
    administrative structure XI 457–8
        appeal from XI 804
        case stated XI 491–2, 495
    and coroners XI 940–3
    appeal to XI 455–6, 491, 495
    asylums, and XI 458, 460–1
    borough XI 918–21
        and Assizes XI 827
        audience XI 1136
        business XI 915–19
        chairman XI 920–2
        cost XI 916–17
        organization and procedure XI 919–24
    judicial review of XI 455–6, 491, 512–15
    policing, and XI 448, 457–9
    prisons, and XI 457–60
    powers of XI 447, 457–61
    see also police, criminal procedure
quasi-contract,
    see restitution
Queen,
    see Crown, Sovereign
Queen's Advocate,
    see law officers
Queen's Bench Division,
    see King's Bench Division

Queen's College, Birmingham
    XI 1185, 1192
Queen's Proctor XI 745, 752–3
    XIII 794–5
    see also Divorce Court, marital
        breakdown

railway companies XI 335–6, 340 1, 500
    XII 76, 84, 90, 235, 287
    see also solicitors
railways XI 352 XII 327, 402, 870, 879, 897,
    1010–11, 1103
    accident litigation XII 958–69, 992
        attempts to limit liability XII 474–5,
            967–9
        liability for fires XII 920–1
        liability for stations XII 979–80
    Commissioners XI 335, 355, 357
    investment in XII 631
    private legislation for XI 329,
        331–2, 335–6
    Railway and Canal Traffic Act, 1854
        XII 474, 967
    railway mania XII 328
    see also political economy
rape,
    see sexual offences
rates and rating XI, 376–7, 427–8, 435–7,
    439–42, 456, 481–2, 513–24
    public interest immunity XI 368–9,
        371–4
real property,
    see land
Real Property Commission XI 705 XII 3, 5–6,
    9, 22, 48, 50–78, 96, 102, 110–11, 134, 171,
    178, 185, 193, 196, 206–7
    see also land
receiving stolen goods,
    see larceny
recklessness, criminal,
    see criminal fault
Recorders XI 921, 996, 1009, 1011, 1045
refreshers XI 815, 1107
registrars, solicitors as
    Admiralty XI 723, 727–9, 731
    Chancery XI 681–2
    Chancery Division XI 791, 842–3
    County Court XI 879–81, 891–4
    Court of Criminal Appeal XI 806
    Divorce XI 748, 756
    Ecclesiastical Courts XI 694, 703
    Probate XI 735–6, 738–9
registration of births, deaths and
    marriage XII 55, 59
    see also marriage
registration of charges,
    see conveyancing

registration of deeds XII 49, 64–71, 73–8,
       134, 192, 196, 203–8
   bills for XII 70–1, 73–4
   caveats, and XII 206, 210, 226
   conveyancing costs, and XII 64, 75,
       77–8, 196
   forgery, and XII 203
   indexing XII 69–70, 74
   land registry, and XII 205
   Middlesex, in XII 69, 204–6
     reform of
   notice, and XII 69, 205–7
   Real Property Commissioners, and
       XII 52–3, 57, 64–71, 134, 206
   Select Committee on (1852–3) XII 192
   Select Committee on (1878–9) XII 203–4,
       207, 215, 226
   solicitors, and XII 70, 74–5
   Yorkshire, in XII 206–7
   see also conveyancing
registration of title XII 69, 106–7, 194–202,
       214–25
   absolute title XII 194, 215, 222, 226
   boundaries, and XII 199, 214, 217
   centralization, and XII 200, 216, 228
   compulsory XII 199, 203, 216–28
   consols, analogy with XII 190–7,
       200, 203
   costs of XII 222, 226
   fee simple ownership, and XII 192–7
   insurance fund XII 214, 216
   land taxes, and XII 228
   landed estates courts, and XII 197–8
   leases, and XII 200
   London, in XII 204, 218
   mortgages, and XII 200–1, 222–3, 226
   obstacles to XII 93, 195
   possessory title XII 194, 211, 222
   real representatives, and XII 193, 199, 201,
       214, 216–18
   RC (1857) XII 192, 194, 196–9, 216
   RC (1870) XII 106, 198–9
   RC (1909–11) XII 201, 218, 223, 225, 226–8
   servitudes, and XII 222, 226
   simplification of title, and XII 195–6, 204,
       224–5, 229–31
   solicitors and XII 199, 202, 215–20, 222,
       225–7
   strict settlement, and XII 93
     Westbury's Act 1862 XII 194, 198–9
   theories of XII 192–5, 198, 200,
       202–3, 223–4
   Torrens system XII 215–6, 218, 224
   see also land registry
regulation of working conditions
   enforcement issues
     cost XIII 576

   problems of enforcement and
       inspectorates' roles XIII 544–51,
       553–97, 559, 562, 567–8
   sweated labour XIII 569–70
factories, early reforms
   Act of 1802 (Factories) XIII 558–9
   Act of 1819 (Factories) XIII 559–60
   Act of 1833 (Factories) XIII 560–3
   apprentices in mills XIII 558
   conditions of work for children
       XIII 558–60, 562–4, 566
   conditions of work for men
       XIII 561, 562
   conditions of work for women
       XIII 560–561
   hours of work for children XIII 558–3,
       565–6
   hours of work for men XIII 560–2
   hours of work for women XIII 561,
       565–6
   inspectors of factories XIII 559,
       561, 563
   Parliamentary debates XIII 558–60,
       562
   political protests XIII 560
   RC, 1833 XIII 560–61
   SC, 1816 XIII 559
   SC, 1831 XIII 560
   volume of investigations into factory
       work XIII 570
increased scope of regulations
   Act of 1840 (chimney sweeps) XIII 565
   Act of 1842 (mines) XIII 564–5
   Act of 1859 (amending factories Acts:
       hours of labour) XIII 566
   Act of 1864 (factories acts extension:
       Lucifer matches, etc.) XIII 566
   Act of 1867 (factories acts extension:
       forges, etc.) XIII 566
   Act of 1867 (factories and workshops)
       XIII 566–7
   Act of 1886 (hours for shop-workers)
       XIII 568
   Act of 1901 (factories and workshops)
       XIII 604
   chimney sweeps XIII 565
   match manufacturing XIII 566
   mines XIII 564–5
   parliamentary investigations XIII 570
   pottery XIII 566
   RC, 1842 XIII 564
   SC, 1886 XIII 568
   SC, 1892 XIII 568, 570
   shops XIII 568–70
   sweated labour XIII 569–70
ships
   Act of 1854 (shipping) XIII 571–2

Act of 1871 (shipping) XIII 572
Act of 1873 (shipping) XIII 575
Act of 1876 (shipping) XI XIII 575–9
Board of Trade XIII 572–3, 575–6, 578
enforcement issues XIII 572, 578–9
Parliamentary debates XIII 573–8
passenger safety XII 233 4
'plimsoll line' XIII 571–9
public support for reform XIII 571–7
RC 1873–1874 XII 682 XIII 571, 573–5
ship-owners' opposition to reform
XIII 573–9
see also labour relations, public health,
trade unions, workplace accidents
Requests, Courts of XI 527, 851–7, 860, 1133,
1166 XII 803, 836
abolition of XI 865
assessors (judges) XI 853–5, 993, 864
Bath XI 852, 854, 856
Bristol Court of Requests XI 854
committals XI 855–6
expansion and distribution XI 851–2, 857,
864–5
jurisdiction and business XI 851–2, 854
religion, and law XI 132–57
Christian morality and law enforcement XI
140–5
anti-sabbatarian National Sunday League
and Dickens XI 142
moral laxity and criminal
prosecutions XI 141–3
National Vigilance Society and Vice
Society XI 140–1, 143
Proclamation Society and the Society for
the Suppression of Vice XI 139–41
sabbatarianism and the Lord's Day
Observance Society XI 140–2
temperance 143–5
evangelical activism XI 132–9
Buxton, T. F. XI 135–8
evangelicalism and utilitarianism
XI 133–5, 137
Holford, G. XI 137–8
prison reform XI 134–5
Quakers and prison reform XI 136–8
Russell, W. XI 138
Wilberforce, W. XI 135–7
religion, law and politics XI 145–9, 154–7,
387–8
Christian chartist churches XI 149
Christian socialism XI 149, 156–7
Lushington, S. XI 147
More, H. XI 148
political economy XI 147–8
prosecuting blasphemous and obscene
libels, *Essays and Reviews* XI 146–7,
154–5

Wilberforce, W. XI 146–8
social reform XI 149–57
Booth, W. XI 156
divorce laws XI 154
education XI 150–2
lunacy XI 152
poverty XI 156–7
Shaftesbury, Lord XI 149–50
remainders XII 10, 16, 19–23, 32,
38, 45, 49, 62–4, 80, 92, 103, 183,
233, 243, 245
see also estates in land
rent,
see landlord and tenant
rentcharges XII 9, 142–3, 172, 200
replevin, action of XII 121, 124, 1115
restitution
account XII 564–5, 601–3, 645–6, 663, 692
action for money had and received
XII 401–2, 562–3, 566–7, 570–95
action for money paid XII 563, 595–601
failure of consideration XII 588–95
common counts, use of XII 578–80
mistaken payments XII 583–8
bills of exchange XII 751–2
change of position XII 586
quantum meruit XII 530–4
theories about XII 565–70,
601, 608–10
Anson's views XII 569
'quasi-contract' XII 566–70, 607–10
tracing XII 570, 604, 608
waiver of tort XII 562, 573–83
restitution of conjugal rights,
see marital breakdown
restrictive covenants XII 159, 171–8
Brougham, and XII 171
building schemes, in XII 173, 175–6
Cottenham, and XII 171–5
early uses of XII 172
in gross XII 176–7
Jessel MR, and XII 176–7
notice XII 171, 174–6
tenants, and XII 174–5
positive obligations, and XII 173–4
property interest, as XII 176–8
see also easements
retainers XI 1104–6
revenue see also XI 468–70, 504
custom and excise duties XI 468–9
succession and estate duties XI 468–9
see also political economy
reversions XII 103, 148, 191, 258
see also estates in land
revising barristers XI 1045–6, 1052
riot,
see public order; securing the state

riparian rights,
  see easements and profits, nuisance
robbery,
  see larceny
Roman Catholics, XI 385–6, 388
  see also judges, religion
Roman law XII 306, 309, 434, 449, 450, 505,
    514–15, 518, 566, 1047–8
Royal British Bank, failure of XI 109
Royal Courts of Justice
  'battle of the sites' XI 781–3
  features of XI 784, 792
  financing XI 782, 815
rule against perpetuities,
  see perpetuities
rule committees,
  see Supreme Court, County Courts,
    Court of Criminal Appeal
rule of law XI 6–22, 32–5
  beneficiaries of 11–16
  individual liberty, and 6–7
  constitutional conventions, and
    money bills 10
    annual Parliamentary session 22
    Parliament Acts 1911, 1949 10–11
    royal assent to bills 8
    Standing Orders of Commons, Lords 10
  control over executive discretion
    cabinet government and ministerial
      responsibility 16–22
  growth of democratic rights 12–15, 302–3,
    321, 467
  guarantee of property
  impact of social unrest 15–16
  independence of judiciary 32–35
  parliamentary supremacy, and 6–10
  rights 7–8
  social contract theory, and 8–9, 76, 81–2,
    108–9
  see also *political theory*
Rules of the Supreme Court
  see also civil procedure

sale of goods XII 304, 306, 330, 409, 415,
    475–85, 509–10
  arbitration and XII 476–7
  by description XII 477
  damages in XII 534–9,
  duties of disclosure XII 409–10, 479
  express warranties XII 479–80
  fraudulent purchasers XII 457–69
  implied warranties XII 986
    of quality XII 409, 473, 475, 480–4
    of title XII 484–5, 510
  liens XII 762
  market overt, sales in XII 457, 459
  nemo dat quod non habet, rule XII 760

passing of property in XII 478, 509–10, 761
property, passing of XII 476–7
quality obligations XII 475–85
rescission in XII 478, 589
Sale of Goods Act 1893
  s 11 XII 490, 494
  s 14 XII 483–4
  s 24 XII 468
  s 25 XII 762
  s 31 XII 488
  s 51 XII 535
  s 52 XII 556
  by sample XII 476, 483
  specific performance of XII 554–6
  stoppage in transitu XII 760, 762, 790–1
sale of land XII 94–109
  auction, by XII 95–6, 107
  buyer's remedies XII 98–102
  conditions of sale XII 47, 76, 96, 102–9
    common forms XII 96, 102–6
    criticisms of XII 103
    deeds registration, and XII 76–7
    enforcement of XII 103–4
    law societies and XII 105, 107–8
    statutory XII 107
    uses of XII 96, 102
  contract for XII 94–108
    exchange of XII 108
    interpretation of XII 101, 104
    open XII 97, 107–9
  conveyancing counsel XII 96–7
  leasehold, of XII 97, 104
  particulars of sale XII 95
  private treaty, by XII 96, 107–8
  process of XII 95, 107–9, 168
    costs of XII 98, 105–8
    solicitors and XII 95–6, 107–8
  title registration, and XII 106–7
  see also conveyancing, vendor
    and purchaser
Salford Hundred Court XI 866, 871–2
Salvage XII 721–2
  see also insurance
Scotland
  appeals from XI 529–30, 534, 537, 541
  bar students from XI 1020, 1054, 1059
  judges from XI 967
  solicitors XI 1115
secretaries of state XI 342–3, 346, 352–3, 361,
    364–5, 404, 406, 409, 420
seduction of daughters,
  see children
set-off XII 455
securing the state XIII, 16, 334–351
  public order: riot XIII 344, 349–351
    distinguished from affray and
      treason XIII 344, 349

offences against the state:
sedition XIII 334–340
  Burdett, F., and Peterloo 1819 XIII 335
  Chartism XIII 336
  Cobbett, W. XIII 336
  Lord Campbell's Libel Act, 1843 XIII 337,
    338, 852–3
  Press Restrictions and Newspaper Libel
    and Registration Act, 1881 XIII 338,
    339–40
  sedition prosecution, decline in XIII 336
treason and official secrets XIII 340–4
  Official Secrets Acts 1889 and 1911
    XIII 342–4, 986–7
  treason, and treason/felonies XIII 340–2
unlawful assembly XIII 344, 345–9
  Beatty v Gillbanks, 1882 XIII 348–9
  Chartism XIII 347
  growth in use of offence XIII 346–8
  political and social dissent
    distinguished XIII 345
  'Six Acts' XIII 335, 346
  Wise v Dunning, 1902 XIII 349
sedition,
  see securing the state
sentencing and criminal appeals XIII 122–37
  Court Of Criminal Appeal XIII 127–8,
    135–7
  Criminal Law Commissioners XIII 122–3
  executive review XIII 130–5
  informal tariffs XIII 126–8
  judicial discretion and disparities XIII 124–7
  see also punishment
separation agreements,
  see marital breakdown
serjeants-at-law XI 527, 621, 1054–58
  King's serjeants XI 1055
  King's ancient serjeant XI 1055
Serjeants Inn, sale of XI 1054, 1057–58,
    1079, 1088, 1218
servant,
  see employer and employee, Crown
set-off
  in wages claim XIII 682
settlement (of property generally) XII 3, 5, 67,
    77, 110, 232–5
  common forms of XII 10–12, 234–5
  executory XII 13–18, 83
  land, of XII 12, 112–14, 116, 192, 196, 203,
    263–6
  married women's equity to XII 12–13, 18
    XIII 743–4
  personalty, of XII 11, 13–18, 21, 25–6, 39, 41,
    43–4, 220–4
  testamentary XII 233–4
    creditors and
    usual power XII 54

  see also marriage settlements, strict
    settlements, trusts, wills
settlement of pauper,
  see Poor Law
sewers
  Commissioners
    London, in XI 474, 477–83
sexual offences XIII 17, 392, 401–9
  bigamy XIII 408
  rape XIII 401–4
    consent, problems of meaning XIII 402,
      404
    evidence of victim's reputation
      XIII 402–3
    Lord Lansdowne's Act, 1828 XIII 402
    need for early complaint XIII 402
  sexual assault XIII 404–5
  sexual molestation of children
    XIII 405–9
    ages of consent for girls and boys
      XIII 405–6
    Assault of Young Persons' Act,
      1880 XIII 406
    Criminal Law Amendment Act,
      1885 XIII 406–7
    Prince XIII 407
    Punishment of Incest Act, 1908
      XIII 408–9
    sodomy XIII 407
    see also children
shares and shareholders,
  see companies
Sheffield Court of Requests XI 854
  Law Society XI 1133, 1142
sheriffs XI 575–9
sheriffs' court (City of London)
  see City of London
ships and shipping,
  see charterparties, regulation of working
    conditions
shorthand writers XI 807
sinecure offices XI 626–7, 694, 727
six clerks,
  see Chancery
slander,
  see defamation
social Darwinism XI 114
Social Democratic Federation XI 113
Social Science, National Association for
    the Promotion of XI 96, 102–3, 105
    XII 817, 822
  see also political economy and
    legal theory
socialism XI 27–30, 113
  Fabian Society XI 113
  Social Democratic Foundation XI 27, 113
  see also Labour Party and political economy

société en commandite,
 see partnership
Society for the Abolition of Ecclesiastical
  Courts XI 708
Society of Gentlemen Practisers XI 1113,
  1155–56
Solicitor-General,
 see law officers
solicitors XI 1108–73
 agency firms XI 860, 1041
 and Chancery XI 685
 and Ecclesiastical Courts XI 701
 and Superior Courts XI 584, 628–30
 articled clerks XI 1122–24, 1178
 as coroners XI 937–9
 as proctors XI 699–701
 'Attorney-advocates' XI 977–8, 1099, 1134
 Central Criminal Court XI 643
 Chancery division XI 847
 clerks XI 820, 1110
 conveyancing, and XII 53, 65–6, 68, 70, 74–5,
  95–6, 105, 107–8, 187–89, 199, 203, 207
 costs XI 847, 814, 820–1, 1133, 1137, 1138–39,
  1144, 1146, 1156
 county courts XI 898
 Courts of Requests XI 853
 defalcations XI 1112, 1160, 1161–65
 earnings XI 1149–51
 education, school and university XI 1178,
  1182, 1189–90
  articles 178
  examinations 1114–15, 1198–2000
  in provinces 1199–201
  lectures 1179–81, 1182, 1187, 1191, 1193, 1194n
 educational background XI 1117–19
 judges' criticisms XI 1110, 1160
 Liverpool XII 96, 108
 London XII 96, 205
 Manchester XII 108
 managing clerks XI 1124, 1127–29
 offices XI 1127–31
 partnerships XI 1120–22
 politics XI 1151–53
 public offices, solicitors in XI 1147–49
 relations with the bar XI 1111
 scale charges XI 1110, 1133, 1137, 1166, 1172
 size and composition of the profession
  XI 1113–15
 social status XI 1108–12, 1146–47, 1154–55
 society XI 1154–55
 title registration, and XII 215–20,
  222, 225–8
 trustees, as XII 235, 237, 269, 288
 Wales XI 633
 women XI 1115–16, 1127, 1170
 work
  business XI 1137–43

  conveyancing XI 1132, 1136–37, 1166, 1172
  crime XI 1135–36
  estate management XI 1131–32, 1145–46
  family and trusts XI 1145–47
  financial services XI 1140–42
  insolvency and bankruptcy XI 1138,
   1144–45, 1166
  litigation XI 1131–36
  petty and quarter sessions XI 1136
  tax XI 1143
 see also articled clerks, Law Society, law
  societies, legal education legal
  professions, managing clerks, political
  economy (taxation), registration of title,
  women
sources of law XI 41–71
 Acts of Parliament and delegated
  legislation XI 42–4
  doctrine of parliamentary
   supremacy XI 42
  public, local and private Acts XI 42–4
 characteristics in general XI 41–2
 codification of legal principles XI 55–9
  Bentham's writings on XI 56–7
  civilian examples XI 56
  English attempts XI 57–9
  Indian XI 57–8
 custom XI 40, 61–4, 77, 86, 126–7
  customs of trade XI 63
  evolution of common law XI 61–2
  variation of common law XI 62–3
 interpretation of legislation XI 53–5
  literal rule XI 54–5
  maxims of interpretation XI 54
  mischief rule XI 53–4
  Parke's Golden Rule XI 54
  writings on XI 53–5
 judicial precedent XI 44–8
  Admiralty XI 721
  binding on lower court XI 48–9
  binding on same court XI 48–9
  Court of Criminal Appeal XI 808
  distinguishing XI 52–3
  House of Lords XI 48–9, 545–6
  ratio decidendi and *obiter dictum* XI 52
  reporting of cases XI 44–5, 47–8
  stare decisis, doctrine of XI 48–53
 language of judgment XI 64–71
  'commonsense' XI 70–1
  formation and realism XI 64–5, 69–70
  nature of appellate process XI 65–6
  'public opinion' XI 67–9
 legal literature XI 60–1
 see also British colonies and empire,
  South Africa
Sovereign, XI 302, 345, 361, 389
 army, and XI 342, 401–2, 406, 414

immunities of XI 370
see also crown, prerogative
sovereignty
see Parliament
special pleaders XI 527, 586, 587, 696, 1023–24,
    1025–26, 1055
special sessions XI 931
see also liquor licensing
specific performance *see* chancery
Speenhamland
see Poor Law
state, theories of XI 81–3, 86, 117–23
    Coleridge's XI 92
    Green's XI 119–21
    Mill's XI 97–100
    Spencer's XI 105–6
    Stephen's XI 101–2
Statute of Frauds XII 329, 333, 337–8,
    368–70, 389, 447, 476, 492–3,
    533, 565
    s 4 XII 329–30
    s 17 XII 329–31
    part-performance rule XII 329
statutes,
see construction, legislation,
    sources of law
statutory duty, breach of,
see also tort
stipendiary magistrate (provincial) XI 928,
    1012–15
see also metropolitan stipendiary
    magistrates
Stock Exchange
    speculative booms on XII 617, 623,
        631, 728
see London Stock Exchange
stoppage in transitu,
see sale of goods
strict liability,
see criminal fault
strict settlements XII 11, 16, 48,
    79–94, 233
    borrowing under XII 81, 85, 185
    Enclosure Commissioners, and XII 86–7
    exchange and partition XII 86–7, 92
    estate acts XII 83–4, 112
    leasing under XII 81–4, 88–9, 112,
        114, 116
    life tenant XII 53–4, 82–3, 85, 92
    owner, as XII 85
    mortgages, and XII 81–2, 92
    politics of XII 92–3, 208–9, 214–5
    powers in XII 81–4, 112–13
    sale XII 82, 87–8, 92
    reform of XII 87–94, 112, 196,
        199, 208–9
    Settled Estates Acts 1856 XII 87–90, 193

Chancery approvals XII 87–8, 193
Settled Land Acts 1882 XII 91–4, 112, 208–9,
    214–15, 287
title registration, and XII 93, 193, 198–9,
    204, 226
trustees in XII 67, 82, 92, 233
usual forms XII 80, 112
see also marriage settlements, settlement
    (of property generally)
strikes and lockouts,
see industrial disputes
subrogation XII 694, 723–6
succession XII 5–46, 67, 180, 182
    heir XII 5–6, 8, 23, 54, 65, 137, 180–2, 193, 214,
        216, 264, 272–4, 277
    intestate XII 214, 217
        personalty XII 5
        realty XII 5–6, 207, 214
    partible inheritance XII 10, 214, 233
    primogeniture XII 11–12, 48, 54, 93, 214,
        217, 233
    real property commissioners, and XII 5–6, 54
    real representatives XII 23, 54, 192–3, 199,
        210, 207, 214, 216–18
    taxation on XII 183–4, 217
see also husband and wife, wills
succession and estate duties XII 183–4, 217
suffragettes XI 73
suicide,
see homicide
suitors' fund (Chancery) XI 687–9
    accountant-general's office XI 687–9
    reforms XI 688–9
    funding new law courts XI 742
summary jurisdiction
    expansion of XI 926, 928–30
see also judicial review, justices of the peace
summons for directions XI 812, 819–20, 828
Superior Courts of Common Law, jurisdiction
    and business
    appeals
        bills of exceptions XI 601
        motion for new trial XI 601
        writ of error XI 601
    clerical organization XI 627–30
    coercive measures XI 572–4
    Common Law Procedure RC and Hilary
        Rules 1834 XI 36, 585–9, XII 318, 320
    Common Law Procedure RC and Act of 1854
        XI 36–7, 580–600 XII 185–7, 321, 556
    cost of initiating process
        criticisms XI 626–9
        solicitors' costs XI 628–30
    fees XI 625–7, 629–30
        inquiries and reforms XI 627–30
        sinecures XI 626–7
    finances XI 815

superior courts of common law, jurisdiction and business (*cont.*)
  harmonization of fees and rules XI 621
  hours and vacations XI 621–2
  impact of County Courts XI 623
  imprisonment upon mesne process XI 575–9
  joinder of parties XII 315
  judgment in default XI 572–5, 579
  masters XI 624
  payment into court XI 579–80
  pleadings XI 580–1, 594 XII 313–15, 317, 319, 905–6
    critics XI 581–4
    functions XI 580–1
    general issue XI 584–5, 587, 588, 590 XII 316–18
    multiple pleas XI 584, 587
    special pleadings XI 581–9 XII 314, 317–18, 320
    variances XII 314, 317–18
  practice and procedure
    forms of action XI 569–70, 587
    joinder of parties XI 571–2
    service and appearance XI 570–2
  problems XI 765–70
  trials XI 591–5, 624–5
    arbitration XI 593
    judgment and execution XI 603–4
    special case XI 592
    venue XI 591–2
  see also juries, Common Pleas, Exchequer, King's Bench, pleadings
Supreme Court of Judicature XI 526, 786–97, 837
  Central Office XI 793, 1125
  committee on the central office XI 765, 792–3
  committee on clerical offices XI 791, 839, 841
  Chancery Registrars XI 791, 842–3
  clerks XI 791–7
  masters
    Chancery division XI 839–40
    King's Bench Division XI 765–6, 793
  patronage XI 793–4
  pay office XI 689, 791
  probate clerks XI 735–8
  taxing office XI 791, 794
  'White Book'(*Supreme Court Practice*) XI 790
  women in XI 793
  see also courts of appeal, King's Bench Division, Chancery Division

Supreme Court Rule Committee XI 608, 732, 789–91, 816, 842, 870
sureties XII 599–600

tallymen XI 879, 901
taxation,
  see political economy
tenant,
  see landlord and tenant
tenure and tenures XII 56, 186, 230
  abolition of XII 53, 55, 225
  borough english XII 55
  copyhold XII 53, 55–6, 59, 82, 230
    Commissioners XII 59, 86
  gavelkind XII 55
  Real Property Commissioners, and XII 55
term of years,
  see leases
theft,
  see larceny
tithes XI 693, 694
title (to land) XII 37, 56, 66, 75, 86, 96–100, 102–4, 106, 108, 199, 203, 229
  abstracts XII 97, 109
  covenants for XII 101, 209
Tories,
  see political affiliations
torts XI 812, 877, 879
  actio personalis moritur cum persona XII 576, 582, 996
  action on the case XII 888, 905–9, 970
  animals, liability for XII 917, 922, 1126
  assault XII 1034–6
    consent to XII 1035–6
  breach of statutory duty XII 1007–8
  conspiracy XII 1048, 1050–3, 1060–7
  damages XII 544, 899–902
  defective products XII 881, 988–90
  economic torts XII 1033, 1039–67
    procuring breach of contract XII 1043–7, 1057, 1059, 1064–5
    seduction XII 579–80, 1041–4
  false imprisonment XII 1034
  inevitable accident, defence of XII 889, 903, 909, 916, 970–1, 1148–49
  liability of public officials XI 352, 367, 369–84
  litigation rates XII 883–4
  Lord Campbell's Act 1844 XII 883, 997–1001
  malice XI 408 XII 1033–9, 1044–59
    Pollock's views on XII 1033, 1047–52, 1055–56, 1059, 1066
    Salmond's views on XII 1066–67
  malicious prosecution XII 1036–38
  non-delegable duties XII 898–9, 1005

occupiers' liability XII 976–84
  children XII 980–4
  railway companies' XII 979–80
personal injuries
  boiler explosions XII 984–6
  damages for XII 990–1000
  dangerous goods XII 985–90
  nervous shock XII 991–6, 1025
  railway accidents XII 936–40, 958–69, 985
  road accidents XII 904–11, 970–6
  workplace injuries
'prima facie' torts XII 1047, 1050–51, 1054–59, 1066
property torts XII 1112–50,
  Pollock's views on XII 1112–13, 1125–26
Rylands v. *Fletcher*, rule in XII 1093, 1140–50
sic utere tuo ut alienum non laedas
  XII 895–7, 918–19, 926, 1097, 1126, 1129, 1142–43
slander of title XII 1039 XIII 858–60, 865
strict liability XII 894, 896, 943
  Pollock's views on XII 1112, 1145
  Salmond's views on XII 1112–13
theories of XII 880, 885–94, 941–4
  Holmes's XII 891, 941–2
  Pollock's XII 890–4, 942–3
  Salmond's XII 893–4
trespass,
see also conversion, defamation, malice,
  negligence, nuisances, trespass,
  workmen's compensation,
  workplace injuries
tracing,
see restitution
trade marks and names
  passing off and related wrongs XIII 991–8, 1008–13
  action against injurious falsehood XIII 858–60, 865–6
  action to protect goodwill: purpose and scope XIII 991–8
  comparative advertising XIII 1011
  defendant's state of mind XIII 993–5
  dilution by use on other goods or services XIII 1009–11
  merchandise marks, consumer protection XIII 990–1, 999–1001, 1011
  parallel importing XIII 1010–11
  proprietary character XIII 996–8, 1008
  relation to registration of trade mark XIII 1002–3
  remedies XIII 991–4, 1002–3
  unfair competition XIII 1012
  registration of marks XIII 998–1007
  Acts of 1875 and 1905 XIII , 1001–5
  bilateral arrangements between states XIII 998–9

campaigns for XIII 998–1001, 1005
'common law trade mark' XIII 1002–3
infringement, action for XIII 1003
marks with seniority; concurrent use XIII 1003
Paris Industrial Property Convention (1883) XIII 1012–13
proprietary character XIII 1001, 1004
purpose of protection XIII 1001–2, 1004
registration procedures XIII 1003–7
non-registrable marks and signs XIII 1001, 1005
see also defamation, industrial designs
trade secrets,
  see breach of confidence
trade unions
  conspiracy XII 1050–4, 1060–67
  Conspiracy and Protection of Property Act 1875 XII 1060, 1062–63
  definition of XIII 671–2 711
  development of
    skilled trades XIII 636, 651–2
    unskilled workers and 'new unionism' XIII 686–8
  'illegality' of union or its actions
    Erle Commission's views XIII 668–70
    MPs' mandate from union: *Osborne (No 1)* XIII 710–12
    prosecution of defaulting officer XIII 663–5
    Trade Union Act 1871, ss 1–3 XIII 670–2, 709–12
    Trade Union Act 1913 XIII 714–15
    ultra vires acts XIII 711–12
    union support for industrial action XIII 709–10, 712–13
  membership: rights and responsibilities
    expulsion and fines XIII 707–9, 712–13
    direct enforcement under Trade Union Act 1871 s.4 XIII 709–10, 712–13
    Osborne (No 2) XIII 712–13
    unenforceability under Trade Union Act 1871 s.4
  political relationships
    Conservative Party 677, 688, 703–4
    Liberal Party 714–16
    ILP, LRC, Labour Party 687–8, 714–15
  Trade Disputes Act, 1906 XII 1064 XIII 702–8
  Trades Union Congress XI 28, 310–11 XIII 669, 679, 702
  see also employer and employee, industrial disputes, labour relations, political economy, political parties

transport,
   see carriers, railways
transportation,
   see punishment
treason,
   see securing the state
Treasury XI 345, 348, 404, 469, 476, 509–10,
      628, 867, 739, 741, 733, 786, 792, 793, 794,
      822, 880, 882, 889, 893 , 1069–70,
   land registry, and XII 205, 219
   local authority borrowing, and XI 434–5,
      443–4, 481
   public expenditure, control of XI 348, 379,
      382–4
Treasury solicitor XI 1074
treaties, legal
   'civilian' XII 300–01, 305, 336, 433, 450–2,
      466, 541, 677
   contract law XII 300–13, 340, 346,
      433, 452, 466,
   insurance XII 677–8,
   negotiable instruments XII 731
   tort XII 880
   see also international law, private
      international law
trespass
   to goods XII 1114–17
   to land XII 121, 972–3, 980–4, 1125–6, 1141–43
   Salmond's views on XI 1125–26
   vi et armis XII 888, 903, 905–8, 970
tribunals of commerce XI 880, 1049, 1166
   Judicature Commission XI 761, 773–6
   see also arbitration
trustees XI 836–7 XII 235–8, 268–94
   apportionment and conversion XII 245,
      278–9
   Chancery as XII 235–7
      investment by XII 236, 279–82, 284
   charitable XI 368, 371, 375, 432
   corporate XII 235, 237, 290
   court advice to XII 290, 293
   death of XII 271–4
   delegation by XII 269–70, 288–94
   executors as XII 242, 278
   fraud by XII 288
      Fraudulent Trustees Act 1857 XII 288, 661
   investment by XII 132, 232–4, 268–9, 278–87
      Chancery practice XII 279–84
      clauses regulating XII 234, 279, 282–4, 287
      legislation on XII 284–7
      standards for XII 279–80
   liability XI 435–6 XII 207, 288–94
      defences against XII 289–91
      reduction of
      restitutionary remedies against XII 564–5,
         601–2
      standards for XII 238, 289–94

   powers of XII 82, 87n, 90–2, 106, 137, 213
   precatory, duties of XII 244–6
   public trustee XII 235, 237, 290–1, 293
   receipts XII 181–2, 201
   retirement and replacement XII 90, 201, 210,
      269–78
      discretions, transmission of XII 201, 269,
         273–5
      property, transmission of XII 270–5
   solicitors as XII 235, 237, 269, 288, 290–1
   see also trusts, settlements (of property
      generally), strict settlements
trusts
   charitable XII 241
   common forms of XII 232–5
   constitution of XII 253–62
   constructive XII 240, 565, 601
   debts, for payment of XII 240–1
   discretionary XII 250–1
   Eldon, and XII 239, 249, 253, 255,
      258–60, 262, 267
   enforcement of
      by volunteers XII 255–8, 263–8
   executory XII 13–18, 22–6, 283
   inter vivos XII 242–4
   land, of XII 4, 80, 82, 92, 94, 106, 110, 192–4,
      201, 203, 232–5, 243–4, 256, 263–6, 268
   literature on XII 238–40
   marriage settlements, in XII 254, 257, 260–1
   married women, for XII 246–8
   powers of appointment, and XII 262–3,
      271, 273
   precatory XII 5, 35–7, 244–6
   property relation, as XII 239–44, 246–52
   protective XII 249–52
   purposes, for XII 241
   revocability of XII 262–8
      by creditors XII 256, 258, 267
   sale, for XII 135–6, 143, 180–1, 194, 233–4, 243
   secret XII 4
   termination of XII 242–4, 252–3
   testamentary XII 10–11, 231, 233–4, 242–4,
      252, 257
   see also education (charities), settlement
      (of property generally), trustees

undue influence XII 148, 321–2,
      400, 402–9
   expectant heirs XII 148, 403
   money lenders XII 865–6
   presumption of XII 403–8
United Kingdom,
   see British colonies and empire
United States XII 170, 251–2
universities XI 385–6, 1176, 1185, 1188, 1197,
      1201 XII 113
   see also education, London University

unjust enrichment,
see restitution
unlawful assembly,
see securing the state
usury XII 535, 626, 729, 876, 851, 855, 859, 865
see also annuities, mortgages
utilitarianism,
see political economy, religion

vacations XI 622, 788, 809, 831–2
vagrancy,
see offences against public morality,
punishment
vendor and purchaser
damages XII 539–40
misrepresentations XII 414–16
rescission XII 436–8, 441,
specific performance XII 373, 438–41, 550–1
see also sale of land
venue XI 591–2, 776, 825, 897
vicarious liability, XII 894–99, 964–7, 1003–4,
1012–13
see also criminal fault, torts
Vice-Chancellors, appointment of XI 658, 660,
672–3, 985–6
Vice-Chancellor of England, appointment
of XI 647, 659, 672
Victorian legislation and social reform
analysts, Victorian XIII 606–615
analysts, modern XI 73 XIII 598, 599,
600–605, 615
debates about legal change
ancient liberties XIII 540,
541, 543, 616
collectivism XIII 602, 603, 605, 609
'condition of England' XIII 471–2
emergencies XIII 602–603
experts and reform XIII 604, 605–615
humanitarianism XIII 616
individualism XIII 603, 605, 609
laissez-faire beliefs XIII 606, 616
legislative programmes XIII 611
Parliamentary Sovereignty XIII 468,
469, 600
repeal as a 'proof of failure' XIII 598
'spirit of the laws' XIII 599
the state as a 'parent' XIII 616–18
statutory reform in phases XIII 600–605
statutory reform and 'public opinion'
XIII 601–2, 609, 610
unpredictability XIII 467–72
utilitarianism XIII 469–72, 602, 610
French laws
contrasted with British laws XIII 600–1
investigations and law-making
inspectors' reports
Royal Commissions XIII 609, 611, 617

Select Committees XIII 606, 609, 611,
613, 617
private acts and reform XIII 489, 537–8, 543,
544, 551–2, 552 fn 81, 553–7, 585, 585 fn
24, 618
public acts and reform
codification XIII 602, 613, 614,
469, 470
common law and statutes XIII 494–5,
469, 470, 485–6, 507–510, 517–8, 531–4,
541, 542, 546, 547, 553–7, 566, 580, 580
fn1, 581, 582, 583, 595–6
consolidation XIII 613, 614
equity and statutes XIII 507–10, 517–18,
553–7, 580–1
Parliamentary Counsel XIII 556–557,
571–2, 592–3, 610–15
quality and quantity of the law XIII 557,
611–13, 618
unpredictability XIII 469–72
United States of America's laws
compared with British laws XIII 592

wager of law XII 1116
wages,
see employer and employee
waiver of rights,
see contract, restitution
Wales
barristers from XI 1020
Chester, Chief Justice XI 632, 969
County Courts XI 891
Great Sessions XI 631–6
abolition XI 635–6
attorneys XI 633
business and fees XI 634
criticism and inquiries XI 631–2
judges XI 632
juries XI 633
pleadings XI 633
judges from XI 967, 995
justices in XI 913
circuits XI 827
War Office XI 379, 402, 405–6
see also army
warrants of attorney XII 401, 523, 866
warranty XII 432, 473, 478–9
implied XII 409, 473, 475, 480–5
insurance XII 698, 701–03, 706, 708–10
see also contract
water,
see easements and profits,
nuisance
Westminster Hall
courts in XI 780–1
Whigs,
see political affiliations

whipping
    see punishment
wills XI 651–2, 695, 694, 703–4 XII 3, 68, 227
    common uses XII 4, 10–11, 39, 242
    conveyance, as XII 23
    debts, directions to pay, in XII 180–2
    formalities XII 3–4, 56
    interpretation of XII 19, 22–46, 278–9, 282–4
        class gifts XII 22, 30, 39–41, 44–5
        executory trusts XII 13–18, 20, 24–6
        'general intention' XII 21, 26–3, 45, 262
        Malins VC, and XII 33–4, 37, 39–42, 44
        'ordinary meaning' XII 31–46, 261
        precatory words XII 35–7, 45
        purpose of XII 33, 44–6
        rules of construction XII 27–8, 37–46
        standards for XII 26–46
        'technical words' XII 31–2
    land, of XII 6–7, 16, 18–24, 29, 31–2
    numbers of XII 9–10
    real property commissioners, and XII 22–3
    testamentary freedom XII 6–9, 48
        restraints on marriage XII 7–8
    Wills Act 1837 XII 3, 19, 22–3, 58–9
    see also executors, probate, settlement
        (of property generally), succession
winding up XI 679, 689, 834
    see also companies
women XI 314, 1115–16, 1127, 1170
        XII 8, 37, 57, 266–7
    as litigants in person XI 816–17

franchise, and XI 303, 312, 430, 439
    in divorce courts XI 742–4
    professions, and XI 310
    see also franchise, husband and wife,
        marital breakdown, married
        women's property
workmen's compensation XII 1018–32
    accident, definition of XII 1023–6
    appeals XI 542
    compensation XII 1019, 1029–32
    County Courts and XI 881–2, 887, 895
    course of employment, definition of
        XII 1026–9
workplace injuries XII 1001–32
    common employment rule XII 894–5, 985,
        1003–5, 1012–13, 1015, 1018
    contributory negligence XII 1005,
        1014–15
    Employers Liability Act 1880 XII 677,
        1012–18, 1022
    volenti non fit injuria XII 1006–9, 1012,
        1014–15, 1018
    see also regulation of workplace conditions,
        workmen's compensation
wounding,
    see assaults and woundings
writing,
    see conveyancing, copyright,
        Statute of Frauds, wills
writs,
    see civil procedure